HUMAN RIGHTS LAW IN THE UK

FIRST EDITION

A retitled new edition of Civil Liberties: Legal Principles of Individual Freedom

by

EDWIN SHORTS, M.A.
Barrister–at–Law

and

CLAIRE de THAN, LL.M.
Senior Lecturer in Law, University of Westminster

LONDON
SWEET & MAXWELL
2001

Published in 2001 by
Sweet & Maxwell Limited
100 Avenue Road
Swiss Cottage
London NW3 3PF
(http://www.sweetandmaxwell.co.uk)

Typeset by LBJ Typesetting of Kingsclere
Printed in Great Britain by M.P.G. Books Ltd, Bodmin, Cornwall.

A CIP catalogue record
for this book is available
from the British Library

ISBN 0 421 75460 5

This book is dedicated to

Mrs Sabine Shorts

PREFACE

These are exciting and challenging times for students, academics and practitioners of law. The field of human rights and civil liberties is undergoing a period of change and expansion, without any concrete indication so far as to the end result. Every person involved in law in the United Kingdom has a new factor to take into account, whether he studies, teaches, practises or creates laws, and regardless of his field of inquiry. Whether a new "human rights culture" will be created by this continuing process is not yet predictable. The Human Rights Act 1998 may have set in motion a period of radical change, or it may merely give the appearance of change and allow pre-existing laws to be upheld and given "human rights validation". The first year since incorporation of the European Convention on Human Rights has seen a huge number of human rights challenges to domestic statutes and case law, and also moves towards the creation of new rights. How many of the challenges will be successful in the long term remains unseen. But, at the least, we are in the middle of a dynamic time of rethinking and re-evaluation of domestic law, which is in itself a notable achievement.

The purpose of this book is to provide the reader with a practical and comprehensive analysis of the principles of human rights in England and Wales, although reference is made where possible to Scotland. The emphasis is primarily upon the examination and interpretation of the law and relevant theory associated to each topic, as opposed to the sociological debate which surrounds civil liberties and human rights. We have tried to convey to the reader, in a pragmatic yet innovative way, the approach we take when researching or teaching this particular subject. Our style is designed to allow the reader to grasp the fundamental principles of the law clearly and thus uses clear, comprehensible language, but does not sacrifice depth of critical analysis or scope of inquiry. Since no subject may be understood in isolation, at the start of each chapter there is an introduction which explains the history and development of the relevant legal rules, and introduces issues, debates and themes for that chapter. Further, because of the vast (and rapidly expanding) volume of relevant legislation, there are detailed analyses of specific sections and key terms of statutes in order to assist the reader in overcoming problems of interpretation. Since case law has a great significance in this field, we have provided detailed reference to relevant cases, and those considered to be of key importance are set out in detail with facts, decision and criticism, in order to assist the reader greatly in understanding and evaluation. Of course, there is no substitute for reading full judgments, and we recommend that those readers who are undergraduate students should develop this enjoyable and productive habit. At the end of each chapter there is also a brief summary and bibliography for further research.

Although the sheer volume of cases which have been generated by the Human Rights Act 1998 precludes the inclusion of them all, we have incorporated not only those which have a legal impact or significance but also, where possible, those which are challenging or thought-provoking. The reader will notice a large number of both domestic and ECHR decisions from 2000 and 2001. There are also many new statutes which have been examined, including the Terrorism Act 2000, the Data Protection Act 1998, the Public Interest Disclosure Act 1998, the Immigration and Asylum Act 1999, the Regulation of Investigatory Powers Act 2000 and, of course, the Human Rights Act 1998. Future legal developments are suggested and debated throughout. Due to the nature of the subject, it is impossible to include all domestic human rights: to maintain the depth and detail of analysis we have sadly had to exclude some topics which we would have covered. Thus, for example, Prisoners' Rights and Mental Health have had to be omitted. Nevertheless we have endeavoured to ensure that the vast majority of issue on the topics included are covered, although we do believe that each of the human rights examined in this book deserves an entire work in its own right.

The authors have enjoyed the process of writing this book (and others) together, and would like to acknowledge that it is truly a joint effort, although some chapters were written individually. Both of us wish to thank all those at Sweet and Maxwell who have made this book possible.

Edwin Shorts would like to thank the library staff of Lincoln's Inn for their professional assistance. He is particularly endebted to Martina Frey for all her patience and support, and for undertaking the arduous task of typing, proofreading and carrying out research on his contribution.

Claire de Than would like to thank her long-suffering family and friends for their support. She dedicates her contribution to Lucille de Than. She would like to thank Peter Burbidge for his help with data protection and surveillance issues, and the staff and students of the University of Westminster for providing the inspiration over the past year.

Claire and Edwin would both like to express their profound gratitude and appreciation to the following persons for their contribution to this book:

Dr Jonathan L. Black-Branch, of Oxford Brookes University, for writing Chapter 1, "The Evolution and Development of Human Rights".

Mr Bruce Tattersall, Barrister, for writing Chapter 11, "Immigration, Extradition and Deportation".

Bruce Tattersall would like to thank the staff of Middle Temple library, all his students at the University of Westminster and SOAS for their inspiration, and particularly Maggie, without whom it would not have been possible.

In conclusion, we hope that the reader finds this new and comprehensive approach to human rights both beneficial and enlightening. The law stated is as it stands at May 2001, although some later material has been added where it was possible to do so, without (we hope) too much aggravation to our publishers.

CONTENTS

CHAPTER 1: THE PHILOSOPHICAL, POLITICAL AND LEGAL EVOLUTION OF HUMAN RIGHTS: INTERNATIONAL AND CONSTITUTIONAL PROTECTIONS

All references are to paragraph numbers

CHAPTER 2: THE EUROPEAN CONVENTION ON HUMAN RIGHTS, THE HUMAN RIGHTS ACT 1998 AND A NEW ERA OF DOMESTIC HUMAN RIGHTS?

CHAPTER 3: POLICE POWERS AND INDIVIDUAL FREEDOM

CHAPTER 5: OFFICIAL SECRECY AND FREEDOM OF INFORMATION

CHAPTER 6: OBSCENITY, INDECENCY AND CENSORSHIP

CHAPTER 7: CONTEMPT OF COURT

TABLE OF CASES

All references are to paragraph numbers

TABLE OF STATUTES

All references are to paragraph numbers—references in bold are where that legislation appears in full

TABLE OF STATUTORY INSTRUMENTS

All references are to paragraph numbers

TABLE OF EC LEGISLATION

All references are to paragraph numbers

TABLE OF INTERNATIONAL TREATIES AND CONVENTIONS

All references are to paragraph numbers

Chapter 1

THE PHILOSOPHICAL, POLITICAL AND LEGAL EVOLUTION OF HUMAN RIGHTS: INTERNATIONAL AND CONSTITUTIONAL PROTECTIONS[1]

Individuals within society have become more rights conscious in recent 1–001 years. People speak in terms of "rights", "freedoms" and "civil liberties". They are more likely to place demands on government and institutions, be it in matters of criminal due process or in the guarantee of everyday essential services such as education and health care. Today they are more likely to demand minimal standards of care and treatment as citizens of the state. They want to be protected from decision-making procedures which appear arbitrary and unreasoned, as well as discretionary actions which may be biased against them.

Whilst the term "human rights", *per se*, is a relatively contemporary one, the concept is not. Theologians, philosophers and political theorists alike have been discussing these ideas for centuries. It is safe to say that an interest in human rights is as old as civilisation itself. Historical perspective is important for gaining a better understanding of human rights. A brief walk through the halls of history highlights the evolution of human rights and their subsequent protection under international and domestic law. This introductory chapter examines some of the leading philosophers and theorists who have contributed to the human rights debate, leading up to modern times and the enactment of instruments aimed at protecting human rights. The chapter concludes by examining some criticisms of the recently-enacted Human Rights Act 1998.

THE DEVELOPMENT OF RIGHTS THROUGHOUT THE AGES

Early notions of human rights were based on the recognition of basic needs. 1–002 The concept of natural law grew as time evolved and soon became inextricably linked to that of natural rights. Scholars of the day philosophised on the laws of rights, analysing their bases and credence owing thereto. What follows is a quick précis of some major thoughts on rights throughout the ages, leading up to the more important developments which were instrumental in shaping the concept of human rights as accepted in the Western World today.

Ancient Times and Natural Rights

1–003 Humans quickly distinguished themselves from other animals in the world, relying on their ability to think and reason, questioning their basic instincts. More cerebral in nature, humans questioned what they were taught, thus developing more sophisticated methods of getting on in the world. Coupled with technological advances and scientific thought were questions of morality and ethics.

Indeed, this author would contend that the search for human dignity is the very root of civilisation itself. By virtue of having advanced thought processes, humans quickly realised they were unique to other species. Once they distinguished themselves from other animals, they saw the need to protect this uniqueness by recognising basic rights; rights that people have by virtue of their being human. Violations of these natural rights were construed as contravening what came to be known as "natural" law. Thus, the concept of human rights has grown out of the natural rights of people which in ancient times, and for centuries thereafter, are known as natural rights. Natural rights are rooted in the moral and rational nature of humans and their common capacity to reason. The denial of these rights was, and still is to some extent, regarded as an affront to natural law.

Natural Law and Natural Rights

1–004 Today's notion of human rights has grown out of the concept of natural rights, which in turn became synonymous with natural law. Henry Campbell Black, a noted authority in definitions of the terms and phrases of American and English jurisprudence, defines natural law as:

> ". . . a condition of society in which men universally were governed solely by a rational and consistent obedience to the needs, impulses, and prompting of their true nature, such nature being as yet undefaced by dishonesty, falsehood, or indulgence of the baser passions".[2]

The notion of natural law remains today as one of the two major schools of jurisprudence, the other being positivism (state-made laws).

Black recognises that natural rights are derived from natural law and are not based on positive schools of thought. He defines natural rights as:

> ". . . those which grow out of nature of man and depend upon his personality and are distinguished from those which are created by positive laws enacted by a duly constituted government to create an orderly civilized society".[3]

In other words, the positivistic legal mechanisms in place today, although unnatural themselves, have been created to uphold and protect natural rights which are grounded in natural law.

Similarly, David Hume (1711–76), a theorist of justice, believed that although the rules which govern humanity may be artificial in that they are fabricated, "man-made", he contended that the principles behind them are in themselves natural:

> "Though the rules of justice be *artificial*, they are not *arbitrary*. Nor is the expression improper to call them *Laws of Nature*; if by natural we understand what is common to any species, or even if we confine it to mean what is inseparable from the species".[4]

Cicero (106–43 BC) stated, in reference to natural law, that it was **1–005**
"unchanging and everlasting" and "one eternal and unchangeable law which was valid for all nations and for all times". Ancient Greek and Roman philosophers such as Plato (c. 427–347 BC),[5] Aristotle (384–322 BC),[6] and Socrates (469–399 BC) were scholars of natural law:

> "The philosophers of Ancient Greece, where the idea of natural law originated, considered that there was a kind of perfect justice given to man by nature and that man's laws should conform to this as closely as possible".[7]

This author contends that the present day concept of equality rights, for example, may be traced to Aristotelian arguments relating to the Greek city-states. Such concepts continued into Christian Europe, where it was purported that all people were considered equal in the eyes of God.[8]

The Middle Ages

Human rights recognition grew throughout the Middle Ages (c. 600 to 1500 **1–006**
A.D.). Theologians and philosophers, such as Averroes, a Spanish Muslim, reflected on topics concerning rights and moral behaviours with respect to law. St. Thomas Aquinas (1224–74), inspired by Aristotle, dominated the thinking of this period. He emphasised that "natural law was a superior law". Further, he developed a natural law theory which was based upon Christian theology. Specifically, in his work *Summa Theologica*, St. Thomas Aquinas stated that "an unjust and unreasonable law and one which is repugnant to the law of nature, is not law but a perversion of law".

Note that during this period a major step forward was made in sowing the seeds of liberty in England, which would have a profound influence in shaping human rights and freedoms for the remainder of time. On June 15, 1215 the Magna Carta (also known as the Great Charter) was granted by King John to the barons at Runnymede and later confirmed in Parliament (with some amendments) by Henry III and Edward I.

> "This Charter is justly regarded as the foundation of English constitutional liberty. Among its thirty-eight chapters are found provisions for regulating the administration of justice, defining the temporal and ecclesiastical jurisdictions, securing the personal liberty of the subject and his rights of property, and the limits of taxation, and for preserving the liberties and privileges of the church".[9]

The Reformation

1–007 During the sixteenth century, the Reformation brought changes to the Roman Church. From these reforms came the need for protecting the freedom of religious beliefs. Such reforms led to a balkanisation of thinking and opinions regarding both law and religion. These variations followed throughout the seventeenth century and continued into the eighteenth century. Throughout the Reformation and after, many theorists and philosophers including Petrarch (1304–1374),[10] Machiavelli (1469–1527),[11] Erasmus (1466–1536),[12] Bacon (1516–1626),[13] Spinoza (1632–77),[14]§ More (1478–1535),[15] Montesquieu (1689–1755)[16] and Grotius (1583-1645)[17] emphasised that reason is the source of the natural law, placing less reliance on a theological content in the natural law itself. Discussion of rights soon became framed in social contract theories, which marked a turning point in how we view the protection of rights under domestic law. The influence of Hobbes (1588–1679), Locke (1632–1704), and Rousseau (1712–1778) linger today in many modern constitutions and to an extent in international law.

The English Experience: A Bill of Rights

1–008 The English experience has played an important role in the development of human rights; some time after the granting of the Magna Carta there was another large leap towards protecting individual freedoms, proving absolutism could be conquered. Under the reign of Charles II the Habeas Corpus Act was proclaimed in 1679. This Act served to regulate in a more precise manner the use of the writ of habeas corpus in order to secure a trial for confined suspects and to combat more effectively arbitrary imprisonment. Sir William Blackstone called this "the most celebrated writ in the English law".[18]

Shortly thereafter, 1688 marked the Glorious Revolution in England from which the people gained the right to limited control of governance. The Revolution saw the introduction of the Bill of Rights 1689 into which the Habeas Corpus Act was incorporated. Moreover, the Bill highlighted the respective powers of the Monarchy and Parliament.

The Age of Enlightenment

1–009 During the later part of the seventeenth century and throughout the eighteenth century recognition of the rights of the individual increased. Tyrannical governance based on the harsh and unjust treatment of the citizenry was criticised. Notions of oppression and subservience were foremost in the minds of many political and social theorists, such as Hobbes, Locke and Rousseau. It was at this time that the concept of "the social contract theory" of government developed. Social institutions slowly began to change and individuals became more aware of the need for equality and fairness. The idea of public representation emerged as people began demanding rights and freedoms.

Theorists questioned the notion of governance and the legitimate grounds pertaining thereto. Locke[19] and Rousseau, for example, believed that a government which did not respect natural rights should legitimately be opposed through civil disobedience and rebellion. Specifically Locke contended:

> "If Man in the State of Nature be so free, as has been said; If he be absolute Lord of his own Person and Possessions, equal to the greates, and subject to no Body, why will he part with his Freedom? Why will he give up this empire, and subject himself to the Dominion and Control of any other Power? To which 'tis obvious to Answer, that though in the state of Nature he hath such a right, yet the Enjoyment of it is very uncertain, and constantly exposed to the Invasion of others. For all being Kings as much as he, every Man his Equal, and the greater part no strict Observers of Equity and Justice, the enjoyment of the property he has in this state is very unsafe, very unsecure. This makes him willing to quit a Condition, which however free, is full of fears and continual dangers: And 'tis not without reason, that he seeks out, and is willing to join in Society with others who are already united, or have a mind to unite for the mutual *Preservation* of their Lives, Liberties and Estates".[20]

Rousseau coined the well-known phrase: "Man is born free; and everywhere he is in chains". At that time Montesquieu wrote his great philosophical work *L'esprit des Lois*, in which he addresses issues relating to principles of rights and justice.[21] Voltaire pleaded against intolerance and abuse of power. From these and similar works of the time came many revolutionary movements and perhaps two of the greatest social/political revolutions ever, in the plight of rights and equality, namely, the American and the French revolutions.[22]

The American Declaration of Independence

> "When Locke, near the end of the seventeen century, and Rousseau, in the eighteenth, argued that equality derived from the state of nature, Thomas Jefferson combined the spirit of these historical antecedents into the justification for [the American Declaration of Independence 1776]".[23] **1–010**

Janis and Kay state that "the intellectual influences of Locke, Montesquieu and Rousseau on Thomas Jefferson's document were plain to see".[24] On July 4, 1776 came the historic American Declaration of Independence. The Declaration specifically states:

> "We hold these truths to be self-evident, that all men are created equal, that they are endowed by their creator with certain unalienable rights, that among these are life, liberty and the pursuit of happiness. That to secure these rights Governments are instituted among men deriving their just powers from the consent of the governed; that whenever any form of government becomes destructive of these ends, it is the right of the people to alter or abolish it and

institute new government, laying its foundation on such principles and organizing its powers in such form, as to them shall seem most likely to effect their Safety and Happiness".

The events in America served as inspiration for the French.

The French Declaration of the Rights of Man and of the Citizen

1–011 In the same revolutionary era, a few years after American Independence, the French made a similar declaration entitled: The French Declaration of the Rights of Man and of the Citizen, 1789, which states:

> "In the presence and under the auspices of the Supreme Being, the following rights of man and citizen:
>
> Men are born and remain free and equal in respect of rights . . . The purpose of all civil associations is the preservation of the natural and imperescriptable [*sic*] rights of man. These rights are liberty, property and resistance to oppression".

The United States Bill of Rights

1–012 In September 1789, a few weeks after the signing of the French Declaration, at the first Congress of the United States of America, the first eight amendments of what now constitutes the United States Bill of Rights were presented. The American Revolution, and the subsequent signing of the Bill of Rights, made an impact on European governments and its peoples, instilling in many courage and faith. The French revolution, instrumental in social reform to this day prevails in France, and other countries throughout the world. The ramifications of the French and American revolutions were, and remain today, far-reaching.

Reverberations of such powerful statements of equality and human rights stand as precedent to past and present movements for democracy. In short, these revolutions advanced the notion of "liberty": "This is a manifestation of the belief that men should be ruled by laws, not men; that a government has no more power than the people have agreed to delegate to it".[25]

Moreover, these revolutions instill the hope that a recognition of human rights is indeed possible. But Black-Branch[26] contends that in order to achieve this end, it takes both the will of the people and the support of governing régimes, *i.e.* a marriage between popular and political support, as in the French and American examples. Constitutional guarantees placed in both the French declaration and the United States Bill of Rights were fundamental to establishing democracy, recognising the dignity of the person and the worth of the individual consistent with basic human rights principles whereby certain civil liberties are granted. It is in this spirit that monarchies and republics have come to limit the authority of their leaders.

But, one must bear in mind that guarantees themselves do not ensure the realisation of rights for all. Examining the plight of, *inter alia*, minorities, women, the disabled and homosexuals under these supposedly "free" and "equal" constitutions one sees that freedom and equality must be enforced. An independent and impartial judiciary must enforce the rights of "all" people even when there are competing interests between the minority and the majority groups.

The Nineteenth Century

The nineteenth century marked the demand for constitutional freedoms **1–013** and the allocation of powers to elected Parliaments in several European nations. This was realised through revolutions in some countries. The revolution of 1830 in Belgium, for example, led to its independence and the subsequent adoption of a constitution which includes an important chapter on rights and liberties which served as an example for other countries. Others, such as the Netherlands and the Scandinavian countries, adopted constitutions with protections for individuals without revolutions as such. But, issues concerning human rights as we know them today only gained considerable world-wide attention in the wake of the Second World War.

World War II

Many individual rights were withdrawn during World War II, in countries **1–014** around the world.[27] There were many atrocities committed against particular groups and classes of peoples, thus illustrating the precarious nature of human rights. Lessons from this era, particularly in regard to Nazi Germany, reiterate that the power of government can be abused. Dominant world leaders sought to address such abuses.

The Atlantic Charter

The notion of protecting basic rights and fundamental freedoms heightened **1–015** in the early 1940s. Discussion focused on issues involving political rights and civil liberties as questions regarding humanity and the dignity and worth of the individual took a world focus. In 1941 Winston Churchill and Franklin D. Roosevelt spelled out four essential freedoms in what was called the Atlantic Charter. These freedoms were: freedom of life; freedom of religion; freedom from want; and, freedom from fear.

But, it was not until after World War II that commitment on an international level took hold. At that point there was both political resolve and popular support for having stronger monitoring and enforcement of minimal international standards of human rights. From such dialogue came the establishment of the United Nations (which grew out of the League of Nations) and the enactment of the Universal Declaration of Human Rights.

UNITED NATIONS & THE UNIVERSAL DECLARATION OF HUMAN RIGHTS

1–016 The United Nations was formed with the intent of establishing an international commitment to protecting human rights on an global scale. On December 10, 1948, one of its first acts was the adoption of the Universal Declaration of Human Rights. This declaration came about largely in response to governmental abuses of power and atrocities committed during World War II. It was considered "a significant milestone"[28] in protecting human rights.

This declaration provided a set of standards, a model for countries to follow. It served as a precedent for individual countries to establish their own stand on human rights. The United Nations declaration states that "the inherent dignity" and "the equal and inalienable rights" of all people are "the foundation of freedom, justice and peace in the world". It repudiates "barbarous acts which have outraged the conscience of mankind" and encourages "the advent of a world in which human beings shall enjoy freedom of speech and belief and freedom from fear". Further, the declaration proclaims that "human rights should be protected by the rule of law", whilst promoting "the development of friendly relations between nations".

In short, the UN declaration is said to serve as an affirmation of faith in "fundamental human rights, in the dignity and worth of the human person and in the equal rights of men and women", whilst working to "promote the social progress and better standards of life". One of the United Nation's mandates is to promote "universal respect for and observance of human rights and fundamental freedoms". The enclosed preamble of the declaration expands upon its rational. Although it is somewhat lengthy, it is worth citing in its entirety.

THE UNIVERSAL DECLARATION OF HUMAN RIGHTS

1–017 "Whereas recognition of the inherent dignity and of the equal and inalienable rights of all members of the human family is the foundation of freedom, justice and peace in the world,

Whereas disregard and contempt for human rights have resulted in barbarous acts which have outraged the conscience of mankind, and the advent of a world in which human beings shall enjoy freedom of speech and belief and freedom from fear and want has been proclaimed as the highest aspiration of the common people,

Whereas it is essential, if man is not to be compelled to have recourse, as a last resort, to rebellion against tyranny and oppression, that human rights should be protected by the rule of law,

Whereas it is essential to promote the development of friendly relations between nations,

Whereas the peoples of the United Nations have in the Charter reaffirmed their faith in the fundamental human rights, in the dignity and worth of the human person and in the equal rights of men and women and have determined to promote the social progress and better standards of life in larger freedom,

Whereas member states have pledged themselves to achieve, in cooperation with the United Nations, the promotion of universal respect for and observance of human rights and fundamental freedoms,

Whereas a common understanding of these rights and freedoms is of the greatest importance for the full realisation of this pledge,

NOW THEREFORE THE GENERAL ASSEMBLY PROCLAIMS THIS UNIVERSAL DECLARATION OF HUMAN RIGHTS".

THE BRITISH POSITION

Britain was an active participant in the discussions in and around the establishment of the United Nations and the subsequent enactment of the Universal Declaration of Human Rights. Although a milestone in human rights recognition, the UN Declaration was limited in many respects. Notably, individuals cannot enforce these rights against a government, *i.e.* a member of the United Nations. So it is not enforceable in a court of law as such. Beyond this international treaty, many British people were reluctant to see these same guarantees entrenched into national laws. **1–018**

THE EUROPEAN COMMITMENT

Parallel to the international developments regarding human rights, important initiatives were being taken at the European level. European neighbours sought to institute a more profound recognition of rights and freedoms. **1–019**

> "Within Western Europe the ravages and destruction of its second catastrophic war within half a century had convinced its leaders and statesmen of the need to forge a new Europe built on a greater degree of unity and understanding. By doing so they would guard against the rise of further dictatorship, and lessen the risk of relapse into disastrous war".[29]

In May 1948 the International Committee of the Movements for European Unity organized a "Congress of Europe" in The Hague at which the Council of Europe was conceived.[30] An important resolution, regarding the establishment of an interstate regional body with the aim of protecting human rights, was adopted at the Congress which was the genesis of the now European Convention.[31] To that effect, this resolution stated:

> "The Congress:
>
> Considers that the resultant union or federation should be open to all European nations democratically governed and which undertake to respect a Charter of Rights;
>
> Resolves that a Commission should be set up to undertake immediately the double task of drafting such a Charter and of laying down standards to which a State must conform if it is to deserve the name of democracy".

These two important points, regarding the drafting of a Charter (now called The Convention) and laying down standards to which a state must conform, dominated the agenda of the first session and subsequent sessions of the Consultative Assembly (now referred to as the Parliamentary Assembly) of the Council of Europe. Hence, a commitment was made towards a greater protection of human rights within the larger European Community.

1–020 In that regard, in February 1949 the International Council of the European Movement, meeting in Brussels, advised its Legal Committee to prepare a preliminary draft of a Convention for the protection of human rights. It was intended that this draft would be submitted to prospective member countries interested in joining the Council of Europe. On May 5, 1949, 10 European states signed the Statute of the Council of Europe in London.[32]

Member States under the newly formed Council of Europe used the UN Declaration as a framework document, modeling the European Convention for the Protection of Human Rights and Fundamental Freedoms after this declaratory stand. They thus set thc stage for deeper commitment to guarantee individual rights and fundamental freedoms, going one step beyond the United Nation's Universal Declaration of Human Rights.

As stated in the preamble of the European Convention:

> "The Governments signatory hereto [the Convention], being Members of the Council of Europe, [and] Considering the Universal Declaration of Human Rights proclaimed by the General Assembly of the United Nations on 10th December 1948; [and] Considering that this Declaration aims at securing the universal and effective recognition and observance of the rights therein declared; . . . [and] Being resolved, as the Governments of European countries which are like-minded and have a common heritage of political traditions, ideals, freedom and the rule of law, [are] to take the first steps for the collective enforcement of certain of the rights stated in the Universal Declaration".

The European Convention and Court of Human Rights

1–021 European leaders moved to go beyond merely recognising the principles of human rights enshrined in the UN Declaration. They set out to entrench these principles in an international treaty which was open for nations to sign and hopefully adopt as national law. Such rights include: Right to life; Freedom from torture or inhuman or degrading treatment or punishment; Freedom from slavery, servitude, and forced labour; Right to liberty and security of person; Right to a fair hearing within a reasonable time by an independent and impartial tribunal established by law; Freedom from retroactive criminal law; Right to respect for private and family life, home and correspondence; Freedom of thought, conscience, and religion; Freedom of expression; Freedom of assembly and association; Right to marry and found a family; Right to an effective remedy before a national authority; Freedom from discrimination.

Most importantly, they instituted a Commission and a Court of Human Rights to enforce this European Convention. On behalf of the United Kingdom, Winston Churchill endorsed the notion of this court. Speaking at the first session of the Consultative Assembly of the Council of Europe in August 1949, Churchill stated:

> "Once the foundation of human rights is agreed on the lines of the decisions of the United Nations at Geneva . . . we hope that a European Court might be set up, before which cases of the violation of these rights in our own body of twelve nations might be brought to the judgement of the civilised world".[33]

The Right of Individual Petition

Seeking to protect individuals from arbitrary abusive acts or omissions and **1–022** misuses of power by officials and governments, the Council of Europe endeavours to establish an enforceable code of human rights whereby remedies can be available for victims of human rights violations. In particular, the Council accords individuals the right of petition the European Court of Human Rights in Strasbourg, in relation to alleged human rights abuses. The right of individual petition itself was clarified in the case *Lawless v. Ireland*.[34] In 1968 the Directorate of Information of the Commission of the Council of Europe stated that this right of petition is ". . . undoubtedly the cornerstone . . . the most original feature of the entire mechanism of the [European] Convention . . . a most effective shield for human rights".

At its inception, the Council of Europe established a European Commission and Court of Human Rights to deal with admissibility and hearings of cases, respectively. The system was recently replaced with a new and permanent Court of Human Rights.[35] Although the European Convention of Human Rights came into force, internationally on September 3, 1953, it was far from an effective means of redress for British citizens alleging human rights violations. Specifically, each member country to the Council of Europe had to expressly recognise the jurisdiction of the court. Britain refused do that for some time.[36]

Contemporary Times: The 1960s

The early 1960s saw a heightening of awareness of rights and freedoms **1–023** within the United Kingdom. On the one hand there were those (*i.e.* activist groups) who called on the government for greater protections of rights and freedoms, such as in the form of anti-discrimination legislation. But, on the other hand, such demands were equally matched by reluctant politicians who believed the common law system offered the ultimate protection of human rights through tradition, convention and legal precedent.[37] They subscribed to the traditional views of A. V. Dicey and Jeremy Bentham, who did not agree with expressly stated bills of rights. Hence calls for a bill of rights and further rights protection were largely dismissed.

In January 1966, under the Labour Government of Prime Minister Harold Wilson, the Government recognised the jurisdiction of the European Court, agreeing to allow individuals the right to petition the court regarding alleged violations of their rights and freedoms listed in the Convention. This put the issue of human rights squarely on the table, marking the beginnings of a new "rights culture" in Britain. The right to petition the Court has lead to an ever-increasing number of legal cases regarding violations of basic rights and fundamental freedoms listed in the Convention.[38] Concomitant to this move, the year 1968 was declared by The General Assembly of the United Nations as International Human Rights Year, thus contributing to general awareness of individual rights and liberties. The United Nations staged international awareness campaigns creating sensitivity on a world-wide scale to human rights abuses.

The 1970s, 1980s and Onward

1–024 During the 1970s and 1980s there was a plethora of articles, texts and commentaries on human rights in general but also on the cases taken to the European Court in Strasbourg under the Convention on Human Rights. Many cases have come forward wherein academics, lawyers and lobbyists alike have been quick to push their agendas via litigation. It is fair to say that the first cases, in particular the cases of *Golder*,[39] *The Sunday Times*,[40] *Tyrer*[41] and so forth, assisted in developing a rights consciousness amongst the British.

The literature reflects this historic change which in many respects marked the beginnings of a paradigm shift in the manner in which British citizens actually perceive rights in relation to state power and potential abuses thereof. Broadsheet newspapers now report rulings of this "European Court", contributing to greater public awareness and interest in basic human rights and civil liberties. Public interest and lobby groups numbers have grown, placing pressure on the government to reform practices and introduce human rights and anti-discrimination legislation.

The literature indicates that both academics and lawyers are busy analysing this shift in policy, many contributing directly to the causes of fledgling groups. As a result, the cumulation of the right to petition the European Court in 1966, coupled with greater public awareness throughout the 1970s and 80s, seem to have led to an increased "rights talk", which in turn has led to a more "rights-conscious culture" in the United Kingdom today. This has been a gradual build-up, which in turn has led to the establishment of human rights as a legitimate subject within the legal community at large.

Questions of rights and freedoms remained popular and many lobby groups and civil libertarians have sought to have greater rights recognition in British law. Whilst some sought changes to specific legislation and the introduction of anti-discrimination and equal rights laws, others lobbied for a bill of rights proper.[42] Helena Kennedy [now Baroness Kennedy] contends that,

> "Following World War II, Britain helped draft a Convention on Human Rights that it subsequently refused to incorporate into its own law. Such arrogance was based on the great British tradition that other people need rule, we don't".[43]

But such an attitude recently changed with the election of a *New* Labour Government.

The Human Rights Act 1998

In October 1997, under the *New* Labour Prime Minister, Tony Blair, the **1–025**
Government announced its intention to adopt the European Convention as a bill of rights.[44] This announcement prompted much debate and discussion regarding the wisdom of protecting rights in this fashion. Following its passage in the Houses of Parliament, the Human Rights Act subsequently came into force throughout the U.K., incorporating the European Convention on Human Rights into British law. As domestic law, individuals can seek remedy for alleged human rights breaches in home courts, without having to rely solely on the European Court in Strasbourg as in the past. Those aggrieved may still petition the European Court, after having failed to acquired a remedy at home. That said, it is anticipated that most cases will be exhausted in domestic courts, effectively stemming the flow of cases to Europe.

A Monumental Constitutional Change

The Human Rights Act changes forever the nature of British society, marking a major turning point in British constitutional history.[45] This author would argue it is one of the most important legislative changes since the introduction of the 1689 Bill of Rights following the Glorious Revolution. Moreover, it is as important as the Magna Carta 1215 and the recognition of the writ of habeas corpus. Sedley L.J. has said that whereas Lord Denning:

> ". . . likened the Treaty of Rome . . . to an incoming tide, flowing into the estuaries and up the rivers of our geographical and political island. The Human Rights Act deserves a different metaphor—perhaps that of a dye that will colour the fabric of our law except in those places where the fabric is impervious to it".

Deficiencies of the Human Rights Act

There is little doubt that the Human Rights Act is a progressive step **1–026**
towards protecting individual rights and freedoms. But, amid the fanfare of its enactment one must confront the reality of its shortcomings. Although a triumph for those seeking more stringent protections of rights, the Human Rights Act suffers from a number of deficiencies. Three in particular stand

out: its constitutional position in relation to the entrenchment of rights; the limited powers accorded to judges; and its weak equality rights clause.

Non-entrenchment and Limited Powers To Judges

1–027 This author contends that the degree to which rights are protected and upheld firstly depends on their position within the constitution of the country (its soul, so to speak). Effectively, this involves two components, the place of the Bill of Rights in the domestic legal fabric and the powers allocated to judges in relation thereto. Firstly, the place of the rights Bill within the constitutional fabric refers to its position in regard to government power and its authority over other legislation. A Bill that can be repealed or amended with a majority vote in Parliament, for example, is a weaker protector than one that is removed from the day-to-day affairs of government business, *i.e.* entrenched into the constitution, such as the Bill of Rights in the United States and the Canadian Charter of Rights and Freedoms.

Secondly, the strength of rights-protection also relates to the powers granted to the judiciary in deciding rights cases. The power to hold Parliament accountable by allowing judges to strike down or disapply legislation that is incompatible with rights is a powerful tool for protecting them. Allowing them simply to alert government of inconsistencies is a weaker model.

In the present case, this author would argue that the Human Rights Act is a weak protector of human rights. After examining a number of constitutional models, focusing mainly on New Zealand and Canada, the Government finally adopted a strengthened version of the New Zealand system. The Human Rights Act 1998 is not constitutionally entrenched and judges have powers to strike down secondary legislation but not primary legislation. They can issue declarations of incompatibility if they feel there is an incompatibility between the legislation and the rights in question, leaving it for Parliament to act on the issue if deemed appropriate to do so. Specifically,

> "The Government has reached the conclusion that courts should not have the power to set aside primary legislation, past or future, on the ground of incompatibility with the [European] Convention. This conclusion arises from the importance which the Government attaches to Parliamentary sovereignty. In this context, Parliamentary sovereignty means that Parliament is competent to make any law on any matter of its choosing and no court may question the validity of any Act that it passes. In enacting legislation, Parliament is making decisions about important matters of public policy. The authority to make those decisions derives from a democratic mandate. Members of Parliament in the House of Commons possess such a mandate because they are elected, accountable and representative. To make provision in the Bill for the courts to set aside Acts of Parliament would confer on the judiciary a general power over the decisions of Parliament which under our present constitutional arrangements they do not possess, and would be likely on occasions to draw

> the judiciary into serious conflict with Parliament. There is no evidence to suggest that they desire this power, nor that the public wish them to have it. Certainly, this Government has no mandate for any such change".[46]

In its Paper, the Government made it clear that the Human Rights Act is intended to provide a new basis for judicial interpretation of all legislation, but "not a basis for striking down any part of it".[47] The courts are, however, empowered "to strike down or set aside secondary legislation which is incompatible with the Convention, unless the terms of the parent statute make this impossible".[48] In this regard the Government were quick to defend this position by stating that:

> "The courts can already strike down or set aside secondary legislation when they consider it to be outside the powers conferred by the statute under which it is made, and it is right that they should be able to do so when it is incompatible with the Convention rights and could have been framed differently.[49]

In summation, the Human Rights Act may be repealed or amended at any time with a simple majority vote in Parliament. Moreover, judges have very limited powers to affect direct change in their review of human rights matters. While they are empowered to issue declarations of incompatibility placing rights issues on a "fast-track" procedure for Governmental change, close examination reveals it to be an inadequate means of protecting human rights. **1–028**

Aside from being a cumbersome procedure which may impede rights recognition rather than enhance them, it serves to politicise rights when it should strive to remove them from political debate. It politicises rights in that a politician will be forced, virtually on the spot, to reach decisions on often controversial issues. Depending on the day, the issue at hand, and the politician in question, the wrong decision regarding rights-protection may be reached for the wrong reasons.

As a result, from a political perspective, the constitutional position of the Human Rights Act is adequate, for it upholds the doctrine of Parliamentary sovereignty and political control. From a human rights perspective, however, the framing of the Act is flawed. While the existing system appears to grant rights and freedoms to the citizenry, in reality it allows Parliament to hold the reins of power over all rights matters. The mechanisms and procedures for ensuring rights-protection throughout the United Kingdom are weak, ultimately allowing basic rights and freedoms to be trampled over in the name of political expediency.[50]

Non-discrimination, a Parasitic or Symbiotic Existence

Additionally, this author would argue that the heart of any bill of rights is its guarantee of equality rights and non-discrimination. Protection against discrimination is protected under Article 14 of the Act, which states: **1–029**

> "The enjoyment of the rights and freedoms set forth in this Convention shall be secured without discrimination on any ground such as sex, race, colour, language, religion, political or other opinion, national or social origin, association with a national minority, property, birth or other status".

Article 14 sets out the scope of the right. It is carefully worded so as to encompass a wide variety of issues. Firstly, it calls for the enjoyment of rights and freedoms in the Convention without discrimination on any ground. It then lists specific grounds, as listed above. Note that this list is not exhaustive and could very well include other relevant grounds such as sex orientation or disability.

Prima facie, Article 14 is a weak guarantee as it only protects the right to non-discrimination in conjunction with another right or freedom in the Convention. It is thus limited in its scope. It is not what one would call a "free-standing" clause. It does not on its own offer a guarantee of equal rights or equal treatment.[51] It offers guarantees of non-discrimination in accordance with the "enjoyment" of other rights and freedoms set forth in the Human Rights Act. Indeed, the European Court of Human Rights has made it perfectly clear that Article 14 is not an "autonomous" provision.[52]

It does not prohibit against discrimination generally, it simply serves to enhance other provisions set forth in the Act. Commentators see it as living a "parasitic" existence.[53] It does not stand alone. Black-Branch argues that "it is not parasitic, living indulgently off other articles in the Convention. It is, indeed, "symbiotic" in its relationship to other provisions".[54] Specifically, Article 14 has been instrumental in assisting the court to find the Government in breach of human rights obligations in a number of cases where one substantive provision alone (such as Article 8, the right to family and private life) was insufficient to render an adverse ruling.

1–030 Article 14 thus strengthens the case at hand, serving not only a useful purpose, but indeed, a necessary function that is symbiotic in its relationship thereto. A case in point is *Abdulaziz, Cabales and Balkandali*.[55] Here the court was unwilling to find the British Government in violation of Article 8 (right to respect for family life) alone, in relation to its immigration rule prohibiting a specific category of women from bringing husbands into the United Kingdom. The court was prepared, however, to find a breach of these same rules in conjunction with Article 14. In this case the three applicants were lawfully and permanently settled in the United Kingdom. In separate circumstances, each woman married with the intent of bringing their respective husbands into the United Kingdom. Each of the applicants' husband was refused permission to remain with or join them as their legal spouse. In accordance with the immigration rules in force at the material time, men in the same category of applicants could bring wives into the United Kingdom but women were not permitted to bring husbands. The applicants maintained that, on this account, they had been victims of a practice of discrimination on the grounds of sex, race and also, in the case of Mrs. Balkandali, on grounds of birth.[56] The court held (unanimously) that although Article 8 was applicable in the present case, taken alone it had not been violated. But, taken in conjunction with Article 14 there had been a violation by reason of discrimination against the respective applicants on the ground of sex (but not on grounds of birth or race).[57]

In summary, whilst this author would not go as far as some commentators and say that Article 14 lives a parasitic existence, he would say it is weak in its protection of the individual. Indeed, it is an embarrassment to Britain compared to equality rights protections in other modern constitutions. Article 14 is dated in its approach, having been instituted in the wake of World War II. Since that time the world has seen major changes in relation to providing equal rights and protecting individuals from discrimination. It is necessary to guarantee a firm anti-discrimination clause, replacing the impotent one now in place.[58]

Conclusion: A Rights Culture in a Rights Conscious Society

Despite this author's views that the Human Rights Act is a deficient means **1–031**
of adequately protecting the rights of citizens in its current form, as it stands it does indeed mark a major step forward in protecting human rights. After a long struggle for human rights recognition, the Act sows the seeds for a better society. Although a rights consciousness has slowly taken hold, the degree to which individuals will actually benefit in this new era will depend largely on three main variables. Firstly, whether the people themselves, from all walks of life, will take the gauntlet and argue human rights cases in their home courts. Secondly, the degree to which the judiciary will enforce their rights when argued. And thirdly, the degree to which the Government will act to insure compliance with the Convention as a new set of legal principles embedded in domestic law.

After all, rights on paper that are not cherished by local people will surely lay dormant. Rights legislated but ignored by the judiciary will become disused tools of progress. Rights enacted by governments who refuse to comply with them will become symbols of oppression in a supposedly free world.

Endnotes

[1] This chapter has been written by Dr. Jonathan L. Black-Branch, MA, DPhil, (Oxon), PhD, (Toronto), Barrister (Lincoln's Inn) of One Garden Court, Temple, and Course Tutor, LLM International Law, at Oxford Brookes University, and of Wolfson College, Oxford.
[2] *Black's Law Dictionary* (5th ed., 1979, West Publishing, St. Paul), p. 925.
[3] *ibid.*
[4] David Hume, *A Treatise of Human Nature* (A.D. Lindsay ed., London, 1911), Vol. ii, p.190. Refer also to Edmund Burke (1729–97) whose contribution remains disputed today.
[5] Plato contributed to classical Hellenistic legal theory.
[6] Aristotle also contributed to classical Hellenistic legal theory.
[7] *Oxford Dictionary of Law*, (3rd ed., Oxford University Press), p. 261 (*natural law*).
[8] For further analysis of natural law refer to H. L. A. Hart, *The Concept of Law*, (2nd ed., Clarendon Press, Oxford), particularly Chap. IX, Law and Morals, which has extended discussion on natural law and legal positivism, the minimum content of natural law, and legal validity and moral value. See also J. Finnis, *The International Library of Essays in Law & Legal Theory Natural Law* (Dartmouth Press, Aldershot, 1991), Vol. I and Vol. II.
[9] *Black's Law Dictionary* (5th ed., 1979, West Publishing, St. Paul), p. 858.
[10] Italian poet and humanist who developed a strong sense of belief in the role of a unified Italy.
[11] Often associated with corrupt, totalitarian government (*The Prince*); but was truly a man who wanted both politics and patriotism, demonstrated in "Discourses on Livy".
[12] Sometimes referred to as the father of the Reformation; engaged in battles with Luther; works banned by the Council of Trent; first and foremost a humanist, not a religious reformer.
[13] His philosophy emphasised the belief that people are the servants and interpreters of nature, that truth is not derived from authority, and that knowledge is the fruit of experience; ampliative inference, a technique of inducing reasoning.
[14] Dutch philosopher.
[15] Refused to grant Henry VIII's request for a divorce from Catherine of Aragon; decapitated in 1535 for refusing oath of supremacy; canonised by Roman Catholic Church in 1935; best known for *Utopia* (1516).
[16] He addresses issues of rights and justice in his work *L'esprit des Lois*. He is discussed in greater detail later in this chapter.
[17] It was he who was first to propound a system of international law. His noted works is *De Jure Belli ac Pacis* (The Law of War and Peace), 1625. Although, some argue that a system of international law was implicit in the writings of Vitoria.
[18] See *Black's Law Dictionary* (5th ed., 1979, West Publishing, St. Paul), p. 639.
[19] See also *Locke and the Compass of Human Understanding* (J.W. Yolton ed., Cambridge University Press, Cambridge, 1970).
[20] J. Locke, Two Treatises of Government 395 (Laslett rev. ed., 1963, 3rd ed. 1698). J. J. Rousseau, The Social Contract 3 (Cole ed., 1950). See also J.B. Noone, Jr., *Rousseau's Social Contract, A Conceptual Analysis* (George Prior Publishers, London, 1980).
[21] For a more complete works on Montesquieu refer to Gonzague Truc, *De L'Esprit des Lois, Texte Établi avec une Intoduction, Des Notes et des Variantes*, (Librairie Garnier Frères, Paris, 1944).
[22] See also T. Paine, *The Rights of Man* (Dent, London, 1979); E. Burke, *Reflections on the Revolution in France* (1790) and, Conor Cruise O'Brien, *The Great Melody* (Minerva, London, 1993.
[23] W.S. Tarnopolsky & G-A Beaudoin, *Canadian Charter of Rights and Freedoms Commentary*, (Toronto, Carswell, 1982).
[24] M.W. Janis and R.S. Kay, *European Human Rights Laws* (University of Connecticut Press, Hartford 1990), p. 2.
[25] P.E. Trudeau, *A Canadian Charter of Human Rights* (Ottawa, Queen's Printer, 1968), p. 10.
[26] See: *Rights and Realities: The Judicial Impact of the Canadian Charter of Rights and Freedoms, Case Law and Political Jurisprudence* Ashgate-Dartmouth Publishing, Aldershot, England, 1997).
[27] Note that is was not just the warring countries affected. For example, those of Japanese background were detained in camps in North America and deemed a threat to national security in the US and Canada, even though they were long-standing citizens of those respective countries.

[28] See P. van Dijk & G.J.H. van Hoof, *Theory and Practice of the European Convention on Human Rights* (2nd ed., Kluwer, Deventer, 1992).
[29] *The Protection of Human Rights in Europe* (The Council of Europe,1981).
[30] This precis is based on the general information and background to the Convention provided in *European Commission of Human Rights: Documents and Decisions 1955–1956–1957*, pp. 92–100. A more complete synopsis on the drawing up of the Convention and Protocol may be seen in the booklet entitled *The European Convention on Human Rights* (2nd ed., Council of Europe Directorate of Information, 1958).
[31] European Convention for the Protection of Human Rights and Fundamental Freedoms, 213 U.N.T.S. 221, E.T.S. 5, U.K.T.S. 71 (1953) [hereinafter cited as: (the) "Convention" or "European Convention"].
[32] These were: (1) United Kingdom; (2) Norway; (3) Sweden; (4) Federal Republic of Germany, including West Berlin; (5) the Saar; (6) Ireland; (7) Greece; (8) Denmark; (9) Iceland; and (10) Luxembourg. Also signed on that date was the Preamble of the European Convention along with several Articles thereof, specifically, numbers 1, 3, 4, 5 and 8. Key players in this initiative were Pierre-Henri Teitgenm, Sir David Maxwell-Fyfe and Professor Fernand Dehousse.
[33] Council of Europe (1957). *Travaux Préparatoires* (Council of Europe, Strasbourg), p. 34.
[34] [1961] 1 E.H.R.R. 15.
[35] Note that the court encourages "friendly settlements".
[36] For further reading on the European Convention see "Observing and Enforcing Human Rights under the Council of Europe The Creation of a Permanent European Court of Human Rights", *Buffalo Journal of International Law*, July 1996.
[37] "Who Needs a Bill of Rights?", *Index on Censorship* 2, 1995.
[38] Applications to the Commission have reached the rate of over 200 per year on average (Survey of Activity and Statistics 1991). It should be noted that not all of theses applicants actually reach the European Court.
[39] *Golder v. United Kingdom* (1975) 1 E.H.R.R. 524.
[40] *Sunday Times v. United Kingdom* (1979) 2 E.H.R.R. 245.
[41] *Tyrer v. United Kingdom* (1978) 2 E.H.R.R. 1.
[42] For example, a past attempt by Lord Lester of Herne Hill. See *Jaconelli* (1980) for an extended discussion on legal problems and the logistics of enacting a bill of rights in the United Kingdom.
[43] See authors A. V. Dicey (*Law of the Constitution*) and Jeremy Bentham (*Principles of Morals and Legislation*).
[44] Government White paper entitled *Rights Brought Home: The Human Rights Bill*, October 1997.
[45] Many of the Commonwealth countries which have inherited the British tradition of parliamentary democracy have since modernised their respective constitutions, introducing their own bills of rights. Recent examples are Canada and New Zealand. For commentary on the *Canadian Charter of Rights and Freedoms*, for example, see J. L. Black-Branch, "Entrenching Human Rights Legislation under Constitutional Law: The Canadian Charter of Rights and Freedoms", *European Human Rights Law Review* No. 2 or 3 (in press) (1998); "Rights and Realities: The Judicial Impact of the Canadian Charter of Rights and Freedoms", *Case Law and Political Jurisprudence* (Ashgate Dartmouth Publishing, Aldershot, England, 1997); "Judging Education: Legal and Judicial Implications of the Canadian Charter of Rights and Freedoms", *Oxford Comparative Series in Education, Special Edition on Change in the Pacific Rim: Meeting the Challenges* (1997). For New Zealand see: A. Butler, *The Bill of Rights Debate: Why the New Zealand Bill of Rights Act 1990 is a Bad Model for Britain*. Another important example is the recent development in South Africa; see Johan De Waal, Iain Currie and Gerhard Erasmus (in Association with Lawyers for Human Rights and the Association of Law Societies of the Republic of South Africa), *The Bill of Rights Handbook* (1998).
[46] White Paper, *Rights Brought Home: The Human Rights Bill* (1997) (Cm 7382) para 2.13.
[47] *ibid.*, para 2.14.
[48] *ibid.*, para 2.15.
[49] *ibid.*, para 2.15.
[50] See also the article by Jonathan Black-Branch, "The Derogation of Rights under the Human Rights Act in Britain: Diminishing International Standards", *Statute Law Review* (2001) Vol. 22, No.1.
[51] For a complete contrast to this rather weak provision compare with the equality rights provision of the Canadian Charter of Rights and Freedoms, which offers equal rights and non-discrimination under four guises.

[52] In the *Belgian Linguistics Case (No. 2)* (1979–80) 1 E.H.R.R. 252, it was held by the European Court that: "While it is true that this guarantee has no independent existence in the sense that under the terms of Article 14 it relates solely to 'rights and freedoms set forth in the Convention', a measure which in itself is in conformity with the requirements if the Article enshrining the right or freedom in question may however infringe this article when read in conjunction with Article 14 for the reason that it is of a discriminatory nature". (at para. 9).
[53] Harris, O'Boyle and Warbrick, *Law of the European Convention on Human Rights* (1995), p. 463.
[54] "Equality, Non-Discrimination and the Right to Special Education: From International Law to the Human Rights Act", *European Human Rights Law Review* 3 (2000), pp. 297–314.
[55] *Abdulaziz, Cabales and Balkandali v. United Kingdom* (A/94): (1984) 7 E.H.R.R. 471.
[56] They further alleged violations of Art. 3 (prohibition of inhuman or degrading treatment) and Art. 13, that no effective domestic remedy existed for their claims.
[57] The court held there had not been a breach of Art. 3, but there had been a violation of Art. 13 in regard to the complaint of discrimination on the ground of sex. Based on the said violations the U.K. was to pay the applicants jointly for costs and expenses.
[58] For the strengths and positive aspects of Art. 14, see Chap. 9.

Chapter 2

THE EUROPEAN CONVENTION ON HUMAN RIGHTS, THE HUMAN RIGHTS ACT 1998 AND A NEW ERA OF DOMESTIC HUMAN RIGHTS?

INTRODUCTION

The beginning of the twenty-first century marks an important stage in the recognition and status of human rights in English law. The Human Rights Act 1998, which came into force on October 2, 2000, incorporated the European Convention on Human Rights into English law so that the rights which it contains are now directly enforceable in English courts. Domestic courts are now grappling with the Convention rights in a new way, with results which were not always foreseen. Regardless of whether there develop far-reaching and radical changes in domestic law as a result of the 1998 Act, we are now at the beginning of a period of re-evaluation and assimilation which, at the very least, will result in a new human rights perspective from which old laws will be examined and will stand or fall. Thus, the European Convention on Human Rights merits detailed discussion as a topic in its own right, although its provisions are discussed wherever relevant in each of the chapters of this book. The implications and potential consequences of incorporation will be discussed below, including the early signs from the first rash of cases decided in domestic courts after incorporation, but first the historical and theoretical background will be examined. 2–001

HISTORY

The ECHR is an international treaty which was signed in 1950 and came into force in 1953. Its full, but seldom used, title is the European Convention on the Protection of Human Rights and Fundamental Freedoms, which reflects its scope and the contracting parties' determination to avoid future abuses of human rights within the new and more unified Europe. Its aims are all the more understandable when counterposed against the events which immediately preceded it: the Second World War and the Nuremberg trials which revealed some of the human rights 2–002 atrocities which had taken place. There was also widespread fear of the rise of communism in Europe. In practice, however, such fears have not materialised or have faded into history, and so its operation has been on the level of civil liberties rather than fundamental rights. The original members of the Council of Europe drafted the Convention and signing the Convention is a requirement for membership of the Council of Europe. It is a document aimed at fostering and extending the protection of human rights and civil liberties within Europe, but it must be recognised that the document was produced after a process involving much discussion and compromise between countries with widely different backgrounds, legal systems and legal philosophies. It is thus understandable that the protection offered by the rights in the Convention is patchy, partial and focused upon the prevention of the worst abuses of the rights of citizens rather than upon the extension of social and economic rights. However, the weaknesses of the Convention are an issue which will be raised later in this chapter when discussing its incorporation into English law.

Procedure

2–003 The procedure by which the rights guaranteed by the ECHR may be enforced has recently been the subject of considerable change, and so needs some explanation.

One point which must be understood is that the rights confirmed by the ECHR only apply as against a state; neither a state nor an individual may bring an action to the European Court of Human Rights alleging breach of the Convention by an individual or by an organisation which is not an organ of government. This limitation means that the rights protected by the ECHR are partial; individuals and non-governmental groups are left free to (for example) invade the privacy of, or discriminate against, others within a state which is a party to the Convention, unless such behaviour happens to be prohibited by the domestic law or other international obligations of that state. But there is an oblique method by which the breaches of individuals within party states may be addressed: Article 1 provides that the "Contracting parties (States) shall secure to everyone within their jurisdiction the rights and freedoms within" the Convention; so, if the breach by an individual is attributable to a state's failure to legislate in order to secure the observance of the rights within the Convention, then an action may be commenced against that state for this failure. Thus it has been possible for some time that there would be a successful challenge of the lack of a right to privacy in English law, since the United Kingdom is obliged to secure respect for the private life of individuals by Article 8 of the Convention; reasons for the lack of such a successful challenge will be discussed below.

There is no method however, of ensuring that individuals or non-governmental organisations obey any such legislation within a party state, and the choice of how to protect the Convention rights is a matter for each party state to decide. There is no requirement that a party state should pass legislation in order to protect the Convention rights, nor that any right should be enforced by a specific and clear law; it is enough if a state's law does in fact protect the relevant rights, even if the protection comes from a variety of sources, as is often the case in English law.

Further, a state is in fact free to breach, or to allow the breach of, the rights protected by the Convention, unless and until an aggrieved party or individual brings a complaint against it. As will be seen, there are many practical factors which deter or delay actions under the Convention, and so its enforcement procedures have come under heavy criticism.

I. The former procedure

The Eleventh Protocol to the Convention came into force on November 1, 1998, creating a single, permanent European Court of Human Rights. The advantages of the new court and the accompanying modifications to procedure will be discussed below; but first the original bodies and procedure will be explained briefly. **2–004**

The method for enforcement of the ECHR rights in Strasbourg is, and always has been, twofold. Either a Member State or an individual may bring an action against a state which is a party to the Convention. If a state alleges that another state has broken one of the Convention's provisions then it may bring an action under Article 24; this is a "watchdog" function which is always possible regardless of whether the state commencing the action has been affected in any way by the alleged breach. If an individual, a group or a non-governmental organisation has a grievance relating to the behaviour of a state bound by the Convention then Article 25 provides a method of "individual application". But there used to be two requirements before an individual application could be commenced. First, the individual or group who wished to bring the action had to claim to have been a victim of the alleged breach by the state in question. Secondly, individual application was not a universal right: States were free to choose whether or not an individual application was possible against them. The United Kingdom has allowed individual applications against itself since 1966, and is to continue to do so for the foreseeable future in spite of the incorporation of the Convention into domestic law; this is a desirable measure since, if domestic courts become at variance with the Strasbourg court on the interpretation of any Convention provision, then an aggrieved individual will still be able to seek redress through the European Court of Human Rights, even if all attempts to do so in the United Kingdom fail. Further, the very validity of the Human Rights Act 1998 itself might be challenged by taking an action to Strasbourg on the basis of its exemptions, enforcement mechanisms or omissions such as Article 13.[1] Allowing individual applications was a brave measure for a state, since these are by far the more common type of complaint; for example, if the United Kingdom had not allowed individual applications then its "record" under the ECHR would be almost unblemished.[2]

Before the Eleventh protocol came into force, whether a state or an individual was the complainant, the same three bodies came into play: the court; the Commission; and the Committee of Ministers.

The Commission

2–005 The Commission was constituted of one member drawn from each of the states which are parties to the Convention, but a member did not represent his "home" state while sitting on the Commission; each member acted and decided according to his own conscience.

A complainant lodged a petition which was first considered by the Commission, which determined admissibility; not only must one of the rights protected by the Convention have been at issue, but the complainant must also have exhausted all applicable domestic remedies, unless the complainant is a state (Article 26). This means that the ECHR was and is a final resort for a complainant, and is not capable of having an advisory function for an individual. But it is by no means necessary for a complainant to have had his case heard by the House of Lords before he can have recourse to the ECHR, simply that there is no further action he could take in a domestic court which would be of use to him. Thus, it will be enough that there is an existing binding precedent which would cause the applicant to lose a domestic court case, since only "effective" remedies must be exhausted, and an unwinnable case is not an effective remedy. Indeed, a complainant need not have even commenced domestic proceedings if, for example, he has been denied legal aid on the basis that he does not have a prima facie case. But any available administrative remedies must also have been tried, for example where a Government Minister hears appeals.[3]

Further, an individual application may be admissible in spite of the lack of exhaustion of domestic remedies if an administrative practice has made such remedies ineffective.[4] Once a final decision had been made in the domestic legal system on the complainant's case, he had six months from the date of that final decision in which to bring his complaint to the Commission (Article 26). But this was only the first stage in the determination of admissibility where the applicant was an individual, a group or a non-governmental organisation using the individual petition mode of complaint; Article 27 provides several grounds upon which the Commission could declare a petition to be inadmissible:

- (i) the Commission was not able to allow anonymous claims to be considered;
- (ii) a claim was inadmissible if it was substantially the same as one which has already been considered by the Commission or which has been sent for consideration by "another procedure of international investigation or settlement".[5]
- (iii) the Commission could declare an application to be inadmissible if it considered the application to be incompatible with the provisions of the Convention, or "manifestly ill-founded" in the sense

of showing no prima facie case, or "an abuse of the right of petition" (Article 27(2)).

There was no right of appeal against a decision by the Commission that an application was inadmissible. Under Article 34, a majority decision on admissibility would normally suffice; but if an application was originally accepted and it was only later in the stages of its consideration that it became apparent that one of the grounds of inadmissibility might apply, then it was necessary for any decision to dismiss the application at that stage to be made unanimously (Article 29). The Commission acted as an important filter for applications, rejecting upwards of 90 per cent; whilst this was a necessary function in order for the other ECHR organs to be able to operate effectively, there was also a likelihood that many worthwhile applications were being dismissed at an early stage. This remains the case under the new procedure; see discussion below. Once an application had cleared the admissibility hurdle, it would be investigated by the Commission, which would either accept written (or sometimes oral) evidence from the parties or might obtain its own evidence (Article 28). Once it had collected the "facts", the Commission attempted to mediate between the two parties and to conciliate them, thus acting as a further filter upon cases. Sometimes a Government would offer to pay compensation to the complainant, and sometimes a state would agree to amend the law to some extent; both of these possibilities remain under the new procedure. Only about 10 per cent of admissible applications were (and still are) the subject of such "friendly settlements".

For the remainder, the Commission would prepare a report which contained its findings of fact and gave its own opinion on whether there had been a breach of the Convention (Article 31); copies of this report were sent to the state against whom the complaint was made (under a duty of confidentiality) and to the Committee of Ministers. But an individual complainant was not entitled to receive a copy of the report at this stage. The report was not legally binding but could be used by the court in making a ruling at a later stage.

The European Court of Human Rights

The next opportunity for an application to be addressed was by referral to **2–006** the European Court of Human Rights. Referral to the Court could be made by the Commission after it had made its report, or by a party state which referred the case to the Commission in the first place, or by a state who claimed that one of its nationals had been a victim of the alleged breach (Article 48); an individual applicant could not refer his case to the court, but would be informed if this has been done by the Commission or a state and would be able to appear in the court to give evidence either in person or through legal representation. When dealing with an application, the court would hear the arguments of the applicant, the Commission, and the relevant state(s) and then would decide on the evidence before it whether the Convention had been breached. It would then issue a judgment, which need only be by majority, and indeed a unanimous judgment was and is rare. If the court's judgment was that a state had indeed breached the Convention, then the state in question would be obliged to take positive steps in order to bring its law into compliance with the obligations of the Convention, and the court might also order the state to give compensation to the victim, either as damages or as costs.

If no one had referred an admissible application to the Court within three months of the relevant report being made by the Commission, then it would be considered by the Committee of Ministers, which is a body comprised of the Foreign Ministers of the party states (Article 32). There was no further hearing for consideration of the facts or evidence; the Committee simply decided by at least a two-thirds majority whether there had been a breach of a state's obligations under the Convention. If the answer was affirmative, then the Committee of Ministers would decide what should be done by the state which was in breach of the Convention, and would impose a date by which the remedial action must be taken by that state. If the state did not meet this deadline then the Committee would publish the Rcport sent to it by the Commission on the matter in question, and would make a further two-thirds majority decision as to what the breaching state should do. It should be noted that the Committee member for the state whose conduct is under scrutiny was permitted to vote.

If the State still refused to amend its law or practice, then the only sanctions which could be imposed upon it by the Committee were those of international disapproval and pressure, with the final threat of expulsion from the Council of Europe. The Committee of Ministers had this somewhat strange and unenforceable function because some of the Member States were not willing to have every potential breach of the ECHR decided by a full court procedure, but the side-effect of the uneasy dual system of deciding cases was that inconsistency and plurality of decisions might result, leaving the interpretation of the Convention unclear in many specific areas. In addition, it was arguably undesirable that important human rights and civil liberties issues should reach a final hearing in front of a group of Ministers without judicial safeguards.

II. The new procedure: the Eleventh Protocol

2–007 It was noted above that there is now a new improved procedure for the enforcement of the ECHR. For some time there had been calls for reform of the procedure for bringing cases alleging a breach of the ECHR: criticisms centred upon the length of the process (it could take upwards of five years for a final decision to be reached), the unnecessary duplication of effort between the court and the Committee of Ministers, the potential for inconsistency between individual cases and the lack of effective sanctions against a breaching state. As more states became parties to the Convention, public awareness about the possibility of making a complaint grew and the number of states which allowed individual applications increased, the resulting pressure upon the ECHR institutions has been intense. In response to these problems, there is now a new "fast-track" procedure which, it is hoped, will operate to streamline the application and decision process.

The new procedure is contained within the Eleventh Protocol, which was opened for signature by Member States in May 1994 (the United Kingdom was the first state to ratify the Protocol, in December 1994), and came into force fully on November 1, 1998. The changes and improvements which it introduced include the following:

(1) The Commission and the old-style court have been abolished and replaced by a single institution, the European Court of Human Rights. The new permanent body decides on both the admissibility of applications and the merits of each case. All cases are decided by the new court; the Committee of Ministers has lost its role of adjudicator.

(2) The individual application is now a right; it is mandatory for every Member State to allow its citizens to take a complaint to Strasbourg.

(3) The new court has multiple Chambers, each containing seven members, and more than one Chamber of the court sits at a time, with the aim that more cases may be heard simultaneously. The court sits in Committees of three judges, in Chambers of seven judges, and in a Grand Chamber of 17 judges (Article 27). Declarations of inadmissibility are made unanimously by the Committees, which are final arbiters as to this issue and may strike out any action (Article 28). If no such unanimous decision can be made then a Chamber will decide as to the admissibility and then the merits of individual applications (Article 29) and may also determine whether an inter-state application is admissible. The methods by which admissibility is determined are similar to those used by the old Commission. If a case involves important issues such as the interpretation of the Convention or any of its Articles or Protocols, or the decision may deviate from those in previous similar cases, then the Chamber may refer the case up to the Grand Chamber, subject to an objection to this from one of the parties to the case (Article 30). After a Chamber has delivered its judgment, then there is a limited appeal possible to the Grand Chamber, but only in exceptional cases (Article 43). Such an appeal may be requested by either of the parties to the case within a three-month time period from the original judgment. Applicants are now able to take part in the proceedings before a Chamber or the Grand Chamber; further, the President

of the court is able to invite any relevant person to take part in the proceedings (Article 36). The new court has broad powers to continue to examine any case so long as "respect for human rights as defined by the Convention and the Protocols thereto so requires" (Article 37), and can both strike out applications and restore those which have been stricken out at an earlier stage. No appeal is possible from a decision of the Grand Chamber.

(4) The court now undertakes the investigatory function which previously belonged to the Commission, and may employ experts and delegate fact-finding to specialists. These powers should greatly facilitate the court's function in cases which involve complex issues based on contested facts, such as the torture and disappearance cases which have been brought against Turkey in recent years.[6] Friendly settlements are still strongly encouraged (Article 38) and will avoid adverse publicity for the state concerned, since there is publication of only a brief summary of facts and of the solution reached. In contrast, court hearings are usually conducted in public now and there is a right of public access to documents held by the Registrar (Article 40), except in exceptional circumstances.

(5) The court must give reasons for its decisions and judgments, and any dissenting judge is entitled to give a separate opinion (Article 45).

(6) Once a violation is held to have occurred, the court will order "just satisfaction" for the applicant as before (Article 41), which may include compensation awards. The court cannot compel a state to change its law or to act in any particular way to redress a violation, but all contracting states do undertake to abide by the final decision of the court in any case to which they become a party (Article 46). The Committee of Ministers is still responsible for ensuring the execution of judgments (Article 46). The court may now give an advisory opinion on a legal question concerning the interpretation of the Convention or its Protocols, if the Committee of Ministers so requests (Article 47).

Thus the Eleventh Protocol has simplified the mechanics of bringing a claim to Strasbourg and has reduced the delays involved for applicants, albeit not to a significant extent so far since cases are still taking around four years to receive a hearing. But it has also resulted in an explosion of judgments by the Strasbourg court, the sheer volume of which has made the task of keeping up to date with ECHR law more difficult for states, practitioners and students. It is thus possible that the significance of potentially useful persuasive precedents for domestic courts will be missed. Further, cherry-picking of authorities will doubtless occur, since to a far greater degree than ever before there will always be many prior cases on any given Convention point, with subtle differences between them, and any practitioner will of course wish to rely upon the most advantageous to his argument. If any serious divergence between domestic and Strasbourg interpretations of the Convention does occur, then this would fall to be challenged in Strasbourg, subject of course to a willing "victim" of a Convention breach having the resources and inclination to bring a claim.

Before the Human Rights Act 1998 came into force, the Convention had **2–008** a very limited effect upon United Kingdom law; apart from situations where political and public pressure forced changes in domestic law as a result of a finding of a violation in Strasbourg, the Convention was used only as an aid to interpretation of statute or of common law. However, the extent to which it could be used in this way was limited to a few narrow situations. These were considered in the case of *Derbyshire County Council v. Times Newspapers*,[7] where Balcombe L.J. stated that a domestic court could only take the ECHR into account when deciding on a relevant case if:

(i) this was necessary in order to resolve an ambiguity in a statute; or

(ii) this would aid the court when deciding whether to exercise a particular discretion, such as whether to grant an equitable remedy; or

(iii) there was an uncertainty in the common law.

Thus, there have always been situations in which the provisions of the ECHR could be considered when an English court is applying English law, but this could not be done when the English law had a clear rule on the issue in question, even if that rule clearly conflicted with the provisions of the ECHR. There were some cases in which English courts appeared more willing than usual to employ the Convention as a tool.[8] As will be seen below, the Human Rights Act 1998 marked the beginning of complete change on this point, the full effects of which it will not be possible to assess for many years to come.

Content

The title of the Convention does not give much accurate guidance as to the **2–009** rights which it in fact protects; it deals as much with liberties as with rights, and does not cover social or democratic rights.[9] There are some rights which remain unprotected, and equally there is a need to balance competing rights, such as privacy and freedom of expression.

The rights which are enshrined in the Convention are mainly political rights, but there is also important declaratory protection of basic human rights such as the right to life. The main content of the ECHR concerns the following:

(1) Article 2: the right to life;

(2) Article 3: freedom from torture, and from inhuman and degrading treatment or punishment;

(3) Article 4: freedom from slavery and forced labour;

(4) Article 5: the right to liberty and security of the person;

(5) Article 6: the right to a fair and public trial of a criminal or civil case by an impartial court;

(6) Article 7: the principle of non-retroactivity in criminal trials;

(7) Article 8: the right to privacy;

(8) Article 9: the right to freedom of conscience, thought and religion;

(9) Article 10: freedom of expression;

(10) Article 11: freedom of association and assembly;

(11) Article 12: the right to marry and have a family;

(12) Article 13: the right to an effective remedy in a member nation for breach of the Convention;

(13) Article 14: freedom from discrimination.

This list raises several issues. First, it may be noted that democratic rights are not directly protected; there is no right to participate in the election of a government, for example. Secondly, in many cases there will be a need to balance two or more competing Convention rights. Thirdly, very few of the above protected rights are given in an unqualified form; there are many express exceptions which limit the practical effect and enforceability of the rights, which are thus given less protection than might otherwise be thought. For example, Article 11 allows a state to place restriction on the freedoms of association and assembly where this is necessary for a variety of interests, including national security. Fourthly, the Convention does not protect social rights such as the right to a home or to a job, although the First Protocol to the Convention does protect the rights to possessions and to education. Fifthly, Article 15 permits Member States to derogate from their Convention obligations in times of war or of public emergency. Finally, the list of protected rights and freedoms is the result of much compromise between many very different states with widely differing laws and legal systems, and thus it would be impractical to word the Convention in stronger or less vague terms.

In addition to the rights and freedoms enshrined in the Convention itself, there are also a number of Protocols to the Convention which increase its ambit. However, not all Member States adopt the Protocols, and so the rights which they protect are more vulnerable. Also, it is possible for a state to adopt a Protocol in a limited form by imposing a "reservation" upon the extent to which the rights or freedoms contained within the Protocol will be enforced.

First Protocol

The First Protocol to the Convention was passed in 1952 and came into force in 1954; it was almost universally adopted, and the United Kingdom is a party. However, the United Kingdom has not accepted the rights enshrined in the Protocol without reservation, as will be seen. **2–010**

Article 1 of the Protocol states that:

> "Every natural or legal person is entitled to the peaceful enjoyment of his possessions. No one shall be deprived of his possessions except in the public interest and subject to the conditions provided for by law and by the general principles of international law".

However, Article 1 also allows a State to interfere with property rights "in accordance with the general interest or to secure the payment of taxes or of other contributions or penalties".

Article 2 of the Protocol states:

> "No person shall be denied the right to education. In the exercise of any functions which it assumes in relation to education and to teaching, the State shall respect the rights of parents to ensure such education and teaching in conformity with their own religious and philosophical convictions".

But the United Kingdom has not accepted Article 2 of the First Protocol in full; the right to parental choice in education is accepted by the United Kingdom "only so far as it is compatible with the provision of efficient instruction and training, and the avoidance of unreasonable public expenditure". If parental choice of school and teaching methods were to be made paramount, then the expense would be high indeed in a multicultural and multi-faith society. The reservation will remain after the incorporation of the ECHR into United Kingdom law, so that the Education Acts' balancing of parental rights against costs in education may be maintained. The Human Rights Act does, however, require the Secretary of State for Education and Employment to review the reservation at five-yearly intervals and to lay reports before Parliament.

Fourth Protocol

The United Kingdom is not a party to the Fourth Protocol, and the Government is not planning to ratify it for the foreseeable future. But the Government does recognise that the rights within this Protocol are important, and the White Paper states that formal recognition of the rights within United Kingdom law is desirable, and may happen when potential **2–011** conflicts with domestic immigration law have been resolved. The rights which would become part of United Kingdom law if the Fourth Protocol were adopted are: Article 1:

> "No-one shall be deprived of his liberty merely on the ground of inability to fulfil a contractual obligation".

Article 2:

> "(1) Everyone lawfully within the territory of a State shall, within that territory, have the right to liberty of movement and freedom to choose his residence.
> (2) Everyone shall be free to leave any country, including his own.
> (3) No restrictions shall be placed on the exercise of these rights other than such as are in accordance with law and are necessary in a democratic society in the interests of national security or public safety, for the maintenance of order public, for the prevention of crime, for the protection of health or morals, or for the protection of the rights and freedoms of others".

Article 3:

> "(1) No one shall be expelled, by means either of an individual or of a collective measure, from the territory of the State of which he is a national.
> (2) No-one shall be deprived of the right to enter the territory of the State of which he is a national".

Article 4:

> "Collective expulsion of aliens is prohibited."

It is Article 3(2) which is perceived as the source of the most potential problems if the Protocol were adopted, since the current legal position concerning the entry rights of different categories of British nationals might not be tenable.

Sixth Protocol

2–012 The Sixth Protocol came into force in 1985. The United Kingdom was not a party but ratified the Protocol after the Human Rights Act 1998 was passed.[10] Article 1 states that the death penalty is to be abolished, and that no one is to be condemned to death or executed. Article 2 allows a state to "make provision in its law for the death penalty in respect of acts committed in time of war or imminent threat of war".

The reasons why the United Kingdom was not a party to this Protocol are complex. It is often forgotten that the death penalty did, until recent changes, still exist in English law, albeit in a small and unused form. In 1965 the death penalty was abolished as the punishment for murder, but it remained, in theory at least, the maximum penalty for violent acts of piracy, for treason, and for some armed forces offences. Although no one had been executed for the remaining death penalty offences since "Lord Haw-Haw" in 1946, the Government's White Paper took the view that ratification of Protocol 6 would make it impossible for a future Parliament to reintroduce the death penalty for offences such as murder without "denouncing the European Convention". Against this it can be argued that, first, reintroduction of the death penalty is extremely unlikely and so is not a real ground for failing to make such an important statement of a fundamental human right; and, secondly, that there may well be constitutional methods by which derogation from the Protocol could occur without damaging the status of the entire Convention once adopted into United Kingdom law. Once the Human Rights Act came into force it was very difficult to maintain such "justifications".

Seventh Protocol

The Seventh Protocol came into force in 1988, but the United Kingdom is **2–013** not a party and is unlikely to become one at present, largely due to fears and uncertainty about its potential impact upon domestic law and procedure:

(1) Article 1 would prevent expulsion of aliens without legal action and would create a right to review of any decision on expulsion.

(2) Article 2 would give a right of appeal against any criminal conviction except for a "minor" offence.

(3) Article 3 concerns the provision of compensation in miscarriage of justice cases.

(4) Article 4 states that no person should be tried twice for the same offence, save where the case has previously been abandoned and then reopened.

(5) Article 5 regulates the rights of married couples and states that they should have equal rights and responsibilities in relation to their marriage, their children, and any divorce, save where this is against the interests of the children.

As can be seen, much of the content of the Protocol is already in place in English law, and so arguments against its incorporation may dwindle in future. However, one point of interest is that of the double jeopardy restriction in Article 4 of the Seventh Protocol, which might be infringed by current proposals to amend domestic law in the light of the MacPherson Report on the murder of Stephen Lawrence.[11]

The Drive Towards Incorporation

Why has the ECHR been incorporated into U.K. law?

For a long time there has existed a movement towards the increased **2–014** recognition of civil liberties and human rights in the law of the United Kingdom, via a Bill of Rights. The method eventually chosen to effect the declaration and enforcement of such rights has been the incorporation of the European Convention on Human Rights. But, in order to understand the implications and the strengths and weaknesses of the new law, it is necessary to examine the stages which preceded it and to weigh up the alternatives which were not chosen.

1. The history of the Bill of Rights debate[12]

2–015 Few would argue that a Bill of Rights is necessary in Britain because civil liberties or human rights are under great threat of systematic abuse; the aim is rather to improve the methods by which such liberties and rights are declared, upheld and enforced. As has been argued throughout other chapters of this book, there are deficiencies in the protection of the rights and liberties of citizens under the domestic law, and no one body exists to ensure that the interests of the individual are balanced fairly against those of the state. Even if the current domestic law, post-Human Rights Act, were perfect in its protection of civil liberties, a further declaratory document could serve a useful purpose in concentrating and clarifying the extent of individual freedoms; English law is drawn from so many and such different sources that at the very least a Bill of Rights would remove confusion and conflicts. So, a Bill of Rights would be a gloss on the current law, rather than a total replacement for it.

It may not be immediately obvious why the ECHR in its original form was not a sufficient step to end calls for a Bill of Rights. Certainly, since the introduction of the ECHR and, in particular, the United Kingdom's decision to allow the right of individual application, there have been some notable changes in United Kingdom law as a direct result of its conflict with the ECHR. For example, the law relating to the interception of communications was changed and corporal punishment was abolished as a result of cases brought by individuals to enforce their ECHR rights. But, there have equally been many failures and disappointments for those who sought to enforce their rights via Strasbourg. Many of the criticisms of the ECHR centre upon the application procedure: the five years or longer which is required before a case reaches the court must operate as a serious deterrent against an action; even once a ruling has been made by the court, the state may take some time to give effect to a change in the law by statute; and, before any application may be considered, local remedies must have been exhausted, which may have involved considerable cost to the applicant as well as exacerbating the cycle of delay. The overlapping roles of the Strasbourg court, Commission and Committee of Ministers were the cause of confusion and waste of resources in the past. But such problems are only the beginning, since further criticisms concern the nature of the protection offered by the ECHR itself.

First, the Convention does not provide clear, uncontroversial or unequivocal protection for the full range of civil liberties and human rights; it covers political rights fairly well, but does not stray into the sphere of social and economic rights, and so is open to attack on the basis that it seeks to protect only the rights which are generally accepted and upheld rather than those which truly require protection and promotion. Some rights are already far better protected in British law or by other means than under the balance of competing rights accepted by the ECHR, and so it is of limited help in fields such as discrimination law or police powers. Secondly, the Convention is only concerned with how each state and its organs uphold the rights of citizens; it does not extend to abuses carried out by individuals, except indirectly by leading to changes in domestic law which will affect such individuals. Thus, there is no application to Strasbourg for an individual whose home has been bugged by a resident landlord, for example. Thirdly, the enforcement procedure for the ECHR depends upon aggrieved individuals and states making applications; breaches will not be addressed unless and until an application is made, since there is no body with the general function of investigating whether the Convention is being upheld. Fourthly, each case is dealt with on its facts rather than as an example of a generally-applicable principle, and so the court does not lay down general guidelines for the type of activity concerned; "test cases" on the protection offered by the Convention in relation to a particular right occur rarely and largely by accident, since the culture is towards settlement of cases before they even reach the court and many of even the strongest cases do not survive the lengthy application process. The rewards for an individual applicant are unpredictable due to the basis upon which compensation may be paid, and may compare unfavourably against the costs and effort involved in pursuing an application.

So, there are clear deficiencies in the effectiveness of the ECHR as a Bill of Rights without its incorporation into domestic law. The two basic aims of reformers are providing a process by which the rights of individuals may be upheld and also enabling the supervision of the application of the general principles of individual freedom by the state. Before we assess whether incorporation of the ECHR is likely to achieve these aims, there are some general problems related to the introduction of any Bill of Rights which require examination.

2. *Problems with a Bill of Rights*

The arguments for and against the introduction of a Bill of Rights for Britain were well summarised by the Standing Advisory Commission on Human Rights in 1976, which forms the basis of the following categories[13]: **2–016**

(i) *Positive arguments* **2–017**

- There is a need for fresh legislative safeguards against state-use of power in the United Kingdom because those which exist in the law are "less comprehensive and effective than those in many advanced democratic countries" (paragraph 10(1)). This argument may also be backed statistically by looking at the comparatively large number of successful claims against the United

Kingdom in Strasbourg; it is likely that this could be reduced substantially if United Kingdom courts could apply the ECHR directly, and thus the reputation of the United Kingdom might be improved in the international sphere.

- A Bill of Rights would prevent the fundamental rights and freedoms from being vulnerable to changes in government or attack by bureaucrats, by placing such rights and freedoms under the scrutiny and protection of the courts (paragraph 10(2)). It would also allow the courts to take a more active role in protection of rights than is possible at present (paragraph 10(4)). In the increasingly topical process of devolution, a Bill of Rights would be a source of continuity of citizens' rights throughout the United Kingdom (paragraph 10(3)).

> "The enactment of a Bill of Rights in this country would enable the United Kingdom to be manifestly in conformity with its international obligations and would also enable the United Kingdom citizen to obtain redress from United Kingdom courts without needing, except as a last resort, to have recourse to the European Court of Human Rights in Strasbourg" (paragraph 10(5)).

- A Bill of Rights need not be seen as a threat to strong and effective democratic government since it could contain provisions and qualifications to rights which would apply where justifiable on the basis of national security, prevention of crime, public safety or order or for the protection of the rights and freedoms of other persons (paragraph 10 (6)); this is of course already the position both under the ECHR and in many areas of domestic law.
- Because the rights stated would be broadly and generally drawn, it would be possible for their interpretation to be altered to reflect and to respond to changes in society and in the needs of individuals, thus allowing the document itself to be largely timeless (paragraph 10(7)). But where particular rights and freedoms require tightly-worded and specific protection, a Bill of Rights would not affect the extent to which safeguards already exist in domestic law or elsewhere, for example E.C. anti-discrimination law would merely be supplemented where appropriate (paragraph 10(8)).

2–018 *(ii) Negative arguments*

- The necessarily general nature of the rights stated would mean that the increased need for judicial law-making could render a Bill of Rights unpredictable, uncertain and open to excessively creative interpretation (paragraph 11(1)).
- It would also create increased expectations for citizens which would potentially be unmet since it would protect only the most

basic rights and freedoms rather than those which give rise to most citizens' grievances (paragraph 11(2)).

> "A Bill of Rights might be interpreted by the courts in a manner which would hamper strong, effective or progressive government, and the role of the courts would result in important public issues being discussed and resolved in legal or constitutional terms rather than in moral or political terms. It would risk compromising the necessary independence and impartiality of the judiciary by requiring the judges to work in a more political arena" (paragraph 11(3)).

- Involving the courts in assessing whether legislation complies with a constitutional document would allow the courts to effectively make the definitive rules on such controversial and politically sensitive issues as abortion and privacy. The legal profession would also have to change in response to new types of action in the United Kingdom.
- Most Bills of Rights are created by countries which have just undergone such important constitutional changes as revolution or independence and so have a large degree of political consensus about the content of the document in question; it is not always the case that the declaratory documents are respected or enforced even in such countries. The United Kingdom has no such consensus and does not need a declaratory document since the protection of rights in the United Kingdom is at least as strong and effective as in countries which do have a Bill of Rights; the protection is simply provided by other methods (paragraphs 11(4) and (5)).
- Bills of Rights belong in countries which have written constitutions, a codified legal system and many other differences from the United Kingdom, and so might sit uncomfortably on top of its basis of United Kingdom law and legal system (paragraph 11(6)). There is also a risk of wasteful duplication of safeguards which already exist in domestic law and the creation of unnecessary litigation (paragraph 11(8)) for what is essentially an image exercise.
- There are also some practical problems in creating an effective and enforceable Bill of Rights in the United Kingdom. Constitutionally, the entrenchment of a Bill of Rights is very difficult to achieve and so has not been attempted with the incorporation of the ECHR (see discussion below). Without entrenchment, any statutory declaration of rights and liberties is vulnerable to amendment or repeal by Parliament in the future, since the principle of parliamentary sovereignty prevents any one statute from being given a specially protected status. Of course, there would be great negative publicity and backlash against any

government which repealed such an important document. In any case, the Human Rights Act requires all Acts of Parliament and delegated legislation, both new and existing, to be made and interpreted in accordance with the rights under the Convention as far as this is possible; parliamentary sovereignty is thus preserved, but would only be exercised contrary to the provisions of the ECHR, where the need for this to be done could be held to outweigh the negative publicity which would arise.

Separate problems concern the nature of remedies to be available if rights are breached, and the method by which remedies are to be obtained. Stone argues[14] that there are two complementary functions for a Bill of Rights:

> "it should provide a mechanism whereby an individual whose freedom has been infringed can obtain compensation. It should, however, also provide a basis for a more general challenge to laws, or activities, which appear to be in conflict with the Bill, without the need to identify specific victims".

Thus individuals should be able to obtain the full range of civil remedies against whoever had broken the rules, regardless of whether the breach is carried out by a public body or a private individual; it will be seen that this is a deficiency of the Human Rights Act, which will impact upon breaches of rights by private individuals only indirectly.

2–019 As far as a general role of overseeing the implementation and enforcement of rights is concerned, Stone is among those who advocate the creation of an independent Commission charged with both the supervision of existing rights legislation and the examination of proposed legislation in order to ascertain whether it has the potential to conflict with civil liberties. Such a Commission could either run parallel to existing bodies such as the Commission for Racial Equality, the Equal Opportunities Commission and the new Disability Rights Commission, or it could encompass and subsume the roles currently played by such organisations. It will be seen that the Human Rights Act does not contain proposals for any such Human Rights Commission, but the White Paper advocated that Parliament should consider its introduction in the future, once possible drawbacks have been addressed.

The Human Rights Act

2–020 *(a) History* There have been many attempts to introduce a Human Rights Bill which would incorporate the provisions of the European Convention[15] on Human Rights into the law of the United Kingdom, with support being regularly expressed by British judges, and success has finally been achieved. The current Labour Government made an election pledge to incorporate the ECHR, but the details of how this was to be achieved were left sketchy until late 1997. In 1994 there had been a Private Members Bill introduced by Graham Allen, the then Labour Party Front Bench Spokesperson on Democracy and the Constitution, which reached a first reading in the House of Commons as the Human Rights (No. 3) Bill 1994, but was unsuccessful in achieving further progress. It was thought at the time that a future Labour Government would reintroduce very similar provisions, but in fact this has not been the case: the 1994 Bill did propose to incorporate the ECHR, but this was only to be the first stage in a process towards the creation of a Bill of Rights designed specifically for the United Kingdom by a United Kingdom Bill of Rights Commission. The Bill of Rights would cover social and economic rights as well as political rights, and so would stretch far beyond the reach of the Convention. A Human Rights Commission would be established and would have power to bring proceedings and interrupt court cases where such rights were involved, and would create Codes of Practice which would be part of a package aimed at the general promotion of civil liberties and human rights. The 1997 Human Rights Bill did not attempt such far-reaching and imaginative change, but went little further than incorporation; it remains to be seen whether any further steps will be taken after incorporation is complete, although signs in 2001 are hopeful.

The Human Rights Bill 1997 was introduced in order to give effect to Labour's manifesto pledge to incorporate the Convention, after the publication of a consultation paper entitled "Bringing Rights Home". The White Paper accompanying the Bill regarded the ECHR as an "excellent basis" for the protection of human rights in Britain because of its long-term success and the "tried and tested" nature of the rights and freedoms which it contains. Incorporation was also advocated so that the United Kingdom would not become the only Member State which had not incorporated the Convention, and in recognition of the fact that the domestic law of the United Kingdom is not sufficient alone to guarantee that rights and liberties are upheld. The main case for incorporation was stated as follows (paragraphs 1(14)–1(19)):

- Practical improvements will be made in terms of drastically cutting the amount of time which it takes to bring a claim based upon the Convention. "Bringing rights home" could shorten cases by years, cut costs greatly and encourage applicants to continue with worthy cases which would otherwise have been dropped or settled.

- Since the Convention rights will become part of United Kingdom law, there will be two complementary effects in terms of development of the law: United Kingdom law will benefit from a fresh and powerful source; and British judges will be able to make a stronger contribution to the development and implementation of the ECHR in Strasbourg.

- The relatively large number of cases in which the United Kingdom has been found to have violated the Convention's provisions serve to show that the previous method of implementation of the ECHR was not adequate and did not reflect the status of the Convention. Sometimes United Kingdom law was plainly in conflict with the Convention; sometimes practices of public authorities were lawful but breach Convention rights; and sometimes there was simply no method by which an action or decision could be challenged. Thus, there are many cases in which an individual felt aggrieved, rightfully, that he has been the victim of the breach of a Convention right by a public body, yet he could not obtain redress in United Kingdom courts and so would have to be committed enough and have sufficient resources in order to make an application to Strasbourg. Convenience was greatly served by incorporation.

Thus, the White Paper argued that rights should be "brought home" in the sense that individuals should be able to enforce their Convention rights directly in domestic courts, and United Kingdom courts should be able to rule on whether and how the Convention applies to a case before them. It was hoped that this would in turn:

> ". . . help to influence the development of case law on the Convention by the European Court of Human Rights on the basis of familiarity with our laws and customs and of sensitivity to practices in the United Kingdom. Our courts' decisions will provide the European Court with a useful source of information and reasoning for its own decisions . . . Enabling the Convention rights to be judged by British courts will also lead to closer scrutiny of the human rights implications of new legislation and new policies. If legislation is enacted which is incompatible with the Convention, a ruling by the domestic courts to that effect will be much more direct and immediate than a ruling from the European Court of Human Rights" (paragraph 1.19).

2–021 *(b) Content* The main effect of the new legislation is that courts in the United Kingdom are bound to consider the Convention rights where relevant and apply them directly. An applicant is able to seek the enforcement of his rights under the Convention through an ordinary domestic court action. But the changes go further than this. Before incorporation, the Government and other public authorities were free to exercise their powers in a manner which infringed Convention rights, but incorporation requires all public authorities to act in a manner which is compatible with Convention rights. A public authority is defined widely, including: central government and its agencies; local government; the police; courts and tribunals; prisons; immigration officers; public sector companies which exercise public functions, such as privatised utility companies. Thus, an individual who has a grievance against any such public authority is now able to challenge the decisions, actions or omissions of that authority without much of the delay of the previous process; equally, where a public authority brings either criminal or civil proceedings against an individual then the conduct of the authority may be compared against the standards of the Convention.

The right to bring an action concerning breach of Convention rights exists even if the claimant has no other legal action which he could pursue, but it is likely that most challenges will occur in the context of an action to enforce another right. The issue of whether the Convention has been breached is considered during the ordinary court proceedings, rather than any distinct "constitutional court" being introduced. So, the application of the Convention is direct rather than a review of decided cases. Previous decisions of the Commission and the Court of Human Rights are strongly persuasive authority for a United Kingdom court deciding upon the applicability of the Convention to a particular situation, but are not binding upon the United Kingdom courts. The interpretation to be given to Convention rights will be open to change according to changes in society and its values, and will be subject to balance against "the general interest of the community"; thus the individual's rights will not always be paramount.

Once it has been held by a court that a public authority has breached the Convention, the court is able to award the aggrieved party "any remedy which is within its normal powers to grant and which it considers appropriate in the circumstances".[16] The public authority's decision might be overturned, or an injunction granted to compel the authority to deal with the aggrieved party according to his rights, or damages might be awarded, depending upon the circumstances. If damages are awarded, the court is able to give the same amount which would have been granted as compensation in Strasbourg; thus there will be little advantage to be gained by seeking to enforce Convention rights through the European Court of Human Rights unless a domestic court has failed to provide a remedy for the alleged breach.

A second effect of incorporation relates to the interpretation of legislation by United Kingdom courts. As stated above, prior to incorporation the courts were only able to take Convention rights into account in narrowly-defined circumstances, principally to resolve an ambiguity in a statute or in the common law. But the new Act requires courts to interpret all previous and future legislation, whether Acts of Parliament or delegated legislation, in accordance with the Convention "unless the legislation itself is so clearly incompatible with the Convention that it is impossible to do so" (paragraph 2.7). This rule applies even if a particular piece of legislation has previously been interpreted in a way which is incompatible with the Convention rights, and so a new line of cases will be developed by the United Kingdom courts in relation to the interpretation of the Convention. It is however possible for the interpretation made by United Kingdom courts to differ from that made by the European Court of Human Rights in relation to the same right; an individual who believes that this has happened is still able to take his case to Strasbourg. If a court decides that a statute is clearly incompatible with the Convention, then any of the higher courts is able to make a formal declaration of incompatibility. Such a declaration does not in itself affect the validity of the legislation in question, but is expected to prompt the Government and Parliament to change the law accordingly.

The United Kingdom courts are not able to set aside an Act which is incompatible with the Convention, but there is such a power in relation to incompatible delegated legislation. This position was justified in the White Paper by reference to parliamentary sovereignty, and entrenchment of the Convention was rejected on the same basis. Since the general methods for amending legislation are cumbersome and often protracted, there is a new "fast-track" method of amending legislation which has been declared incompatible with Convention rights by either the higher United Kingdom courts or Strasbourg. A Government Minister is able to amend the offending legislation by means of an Order, subject to approval by both Houses of Parliament.

Now that Scotland, Wales and Northern Ireland have their own Parliaments or Assemblies, their position in relation to the Convention is slightly different from that in England. Scottish courts are under a duty to interpret legislation so far as is possible in accordance with the Convention, and the higher Scottish courts are able to make declarations of incompatibility. However, the new Scottish Parliament is not able to pass legislation which is incompatible with the Convention, and the Scottish Executive is restricted in the same way in relation to delegated legislation and executive action. Any primary or delegated legislation which does appear to conflict with Convention rights is open to challenge on the basis that the authority in question has failed to act within its is be held to be unlawful. The Welsh Assembly is similarly unable to make delegated legislation or take executive action which is Convention-incompatible.

2–022 The third area of reform introduced by the Human Rights Act concerns methods for improving and ensuring compliance with the rights under the Convention. It will obviously be easier to enforce the Convention in United Kingdom courts now that at least all new legislation is checked for compatibility before being passed, and so Parliament is under a duty to consider the compatibility of all new proposed legislation. As far as draft Government legislation is concerned, the Minister responsible for the Bill now has to make a statement that he believes that the Bill is compatible with the Convention. The statement is placed among the paperwork which accompanies the Bill to Parliament. If, however, the government wishes to introduce legislation which by its nature may conflict with the Convention, then the responsible Minister will have to both explain his situation outside Parliament and also give reasons during parliamentary debate as to why the government wishes to proceed with the Bill in spite of its potential incompatibility. Thus Parliament will have an opportunity to consider whether the need for or benefits of the proposed legislation outweigh the potential restriction of liberties.

The Government intends that the requirement of such ministerial statements concerning compatibility will raise the profile of civil liberties and human rights in the eyes of all government officials and will promote far greater vigilance among those involved in the preparation and drafting of legislation. In addition, the Government intends to "strengthen collective Government procedures so as to ensure that a proper assessment is made of the human rights implications when collective approval is sought for a new policy" (paragraph 3.4), and written guidance will be made available as to how this may take place. Although the details of how many of the new procedures are to operate in practice are still somewhat vague, the White Paper considered it likely that the implementation of the changes in procedure would:

> ". . . require an inter-departmental group of lawyers and administrators meeting on a regular basis to ensure that a consistent approach is taken and to ensure that developments in case law are well understood by all those in Government who are involved in proceedings on Convention points" (paragraph 3.5).

However there are no plans for the creation of a Minister for Human Rights. There is now a Parliamentary Joint Committee on Human Rights which has the portfolio of considering human rights issues in the United Kingdom (but not individual cases) and recommends legislative changes. It is currently considering whether a Human Rights Commission should be established. Its terms of reference include that it will:

> ". . .conduct enquiries on a range of human rights issues relating to the Convention, and produce reports so as to assist the Government and Parliament in deciding what action to take. It might also want to range more widely, and examine issues relating to the other international obligations of the United Kingdom such as proposals to accept new rights under other human rights treaties" (paragraph 3.7).

The New Act

The main provisions of the Human Rights Act 1998, are as follows: **2–022A**

Section 1 explains the scope of the rights to be incorporated into United Kingdom law as Articles 2–12 and 14 of the Convention, and Articles 1–3 of the First Protocol, subject to any derogations or reservations which may be made by the United Kingdom. The list of protected rights may be amended by the Secretary of State in order to reflect the ratification of any Protocol by the United Kingdom. Articles 1 and 2 of the Sixth Protocol are also included.

Section 2 states that when any court or tribunal is determining a question involving any Convention right, it must take into account any:

> "(a) judgment, decision, declaration or advisory opinion of the European Court of Human Rights,
>
> (b) opinion of the Commission given in a report . . .

(c) decision of the Commission . . . or

(d) decision of the Committee of Ministers . . . whenever made or given, so far as, in the opinion of the court or tribunal, it is relevant to the proceedings in which that question has arisen".

Section 3(1): "So far as it is possible to do so, primary legislation and subordinate legislation must be read and given effect in a way which is compatible with Convention rights", but this "does not affect the validity, continuing operation or enforcement of any incompatible primary legislation" (Section 3(2)(c)). According to *section 4*, if a court of the level of High Court or above is satisfied that a provision in primary or secondary legislation which it is considering is incompatible with one or more Convention rights, then it may make a declaration of incompatibility (section 4(2) and (3)), but a declaration of incompatibility "does not affect the validity, continuing operation or enforcement of the provision in respect of which it is given" (section 4(6)(a)) and "is not binding on the parties to the proceedings in which it is made" (section 4(6)(b)). *Section 5* requires a court which is considering the compatibility of particular legislation to give notice to the Crown, which has a right to intervene in the proceedings.

Section 6(1) states that "it is unlawful for a public authority to act in a way which is incompatible with one or more of the Convention rights", but there are exceptions if:

". . . as a result of one or more provisions of primary legislation, the authority could not have acted differently; or

(b) in the case of one or more provisions of, or made under, primary legislation which cannot be read or given effect in a way which is compatible with Convention rights, the authority was acting so as to give effect to or enforce those provision".

"Public authority" includes (section 6(3)) a court, a tribunal, and any person who has public functions. But "public authority" does not include either House of Parliament, any person exercising functions in connection with proceedings in Parliament, or a person who has some public functions but whose challenged act was the exercise of a private function. The Lord Chancellor Lord Irvine stated that there is a "disposition on the part of the courts to regard the Press Complaints Commission as a public authority",[17] and it is submitted that this is correct.

2–023 *Section 7* deals with the right of an individual who believes that his rights may have been infringed by a public authority to either bring court proceedings on that basis (section 7(1)(a)) or rely upon the Convention in any proceedings to which he is a party (section 7(1)(b)) where he is a victim of the unlawful act. But if the proceedings are by way of a judicial review of an act by a public authority, then a person may only bring proceedings if he is, or would be, a victim of that act (section 7(3)). The time-limit for commencing proceedings under section 7(1)(a) is one year from the date of the act giving rise to the claim, unless the court or tribunal thinks it just and equitable in all the circumstances to allow a claim to be brought after the lapse of a longer period (section 7(5)). The definition of "victim" throughout the Human Rights Act is that under Article 34 of the ECHR.

Section 8(1) states that "In relation to any act (or proposed act) of a public authority which the court finds is (or would be) unlawful, it may grant such relief or remedy, or make such order, within its powers as it considers just and appropriate". Thus, any remedy available to that court or tribunal may be granted; the claim is not limited to one for damages alone. In determining whether to award damages and the amount which should be given, "the court must take into account the principles applied by the European Court of Human Rights under Article 41 in relation to the award of compensation" (section 8(4)).

If it is a court's conduct which is being questioned, then *section 9* allows this to be done only by means of an appeal against the court's decision or by an application for judicial review, and damages may not be awarded otherwise than to compensate a person under Article 5(5) of the Convention for wrongful arrest or detention (section 9(3)); courts are thus treated differently from other public authorities.

Section 10 applies once there has been a declaration by a court that a legislative provision is incompatible with the Convention, or a Minister finds this to be the case after a finding on the issue by the European Court of Human Rights. On finding that there is a compelling case to do so, the Minister may amend the legislation as he considers appropriate by Order, and this power includes the ability to repeal primary legislation (section 10(3)(b)). But any such Order's effect may be delayed and no Order is to be made unless a draft of it has been approved by both Houses of Parliament (Schedule 2, section 2(1)) unless it appears to the Minister that the matter is so urgent that this is inappropriate, in which case the order must be considered by Parliament after being made. *Section 11* states that a person's reliance on any Convention right does not restrict any other rights or freedoms which he may have under domestic law, nor the availability of any other type of claim.

Where a person wishes to prevent the publication of any item, *section 12* **2–024**
was introduced into the final version of the Act to enhance the right to freedom of expression in certain circumstances at the expense of, it would seem, the right to respect for privacy. This section applies to the media in general, as well as to individuals and is not restricted to public authorities only.[18] Section 12 states:

> "(1) This section applies if a court is considering whether to grant any relief which, if granted, might affect the exercise of the Convention right to freedom of expression.

(2) If the person against whom the application for relief is made ('the respondent') is neither present nor represented, no such relief is to be granted unless the court is satisfied—

(a) that the applicant has taken all practicable steps to notify the respondent; or

(b) that there are compelling reasons why the respondent should not be notified.

(3) No such relief is to be granted so as to restrain publication before trial unless the court is satisfied that the applicant is likely to establish that publication should not be allowed.

(4) The court must have particular regard to the importance of the Convention right to freedom of expression and, where the proceedings relate to material which the respondent claims, or which appears to the court, to be journalistic, literary or artistic material (or to conduct connected with such material), to—

(a) the extent to which—

(i) the material has, or is about to, become available to the public, or

(ii) it is, or would be, in the public interest for the material to be published;

(b) any relevant privacy code.

(5) In this section—
'court' includes a tribunal, and
'relief' includes any remedy or order (other than in criminal proceedings)".

2–025 Thus subsection (1) refers to a situation where the court is considering granting relief to a party, *e.g.* an injunction, which if granted would result in the freedom of expression being stifled.

Under subsection (2) relief will only be granted where the respondent is present or represented, unless under subsection (2)(a) all practicable steps were taken to notify the respondent or under subsection (2)(b) there were compelling reasons for not notifying the respondent. Therefore as a general rule, without notice injunctions would not be granted without evidence that subsection (2)(a) and (b) had been complied with. An exception to this would include a situation where it was vital not to inform the respondent, because of the issues involved, for instance, national security, and the applicant wished to avert the danger of a possible damaging publication taking place prior to the *inter partes* hearing and thus before the possible granting of an injunction.

Under subsection (3) no relief will be granted to prevent publication unless it is likely that the applicant will succeed later at a full trial. One of the reasons given for this is to prevent delay in publication reaching the public at the earliest opportunity, instead of waiting until trial, by which time the publication itself may have become stale news. Thus, the freedom of expression will take precedence over the respect for privacy, leaving the applicant (if the publication is untrue, or is a breach of confidentiality, or for some other reason) with a claim for damages via the court.

Under subsection (4) special mention is given to journalistic, literary and artistic material such that the court, when considering freedom of expression must have "particular regard" to the extent of prior publication and whether or not the publication is in the public interest or any relevant privacy code (*e.g.* Press Complaints Commission): "The fact that a newspaper has complied with the terms of the code operated by the PCC—or conversely that it has breached the code—is one of the factors that we believe the courts should take into account in considering whether to grant relief".[19]

Under subsection (4)(a)(i) of section 12, there is no definition given to the word "public". Ultimately, it will be a matter for the courts to decide based on common sense and proportionality. Mr Jack Straw, the then Home Secretary stated that the courts "would take into account the extent to which the information was available in another country or on the Internet, but in each case, the courts would have to apply balance and proportionality" (col. 543). On the general issue of self-regulation, the then Home Secretary made it plain that he was in favour of the press effectively regulating itself and did not consider it necessary to legislate for any general law of privacy. However, he did emphasise that where there is a clash between Article 8 and Article 10 "they (the courts) must pay particular attention to the Article 10 rights" (col. 543). The result of this section is that in the future it will be even harder for individuals, companies and the like to successfully apply for an interlocutory injunction against any form of publication unless at the application stage it can be proved that he is "likely" to win at trial. As far as the media is concerned Mr Straw has shown that freedom of expression may well take priority over matters of privacy, at least as far as publications are concerned. For early indications of the courts' attempts to strike the correct balance, see the cases discussed in Chapter 8 on privacy.

Section 13 is a compromise reached with various religious groups who **2–026**
were worried about the consequences of being within the definition of "public authorities" for the purposes of the Act. Although a claim may be brought against a religious organisation, section 13(1) provides that:

> ". . . if a court's determination of any question arising under this Act might affect the exercise by a religious organisation (itself or its members collectively) of the Convention rights to freedom of thought, conscience and religion, it must have particular regard to the importance of that right".

Section 14 deals with derogations from Convention rights, and labels as "designated derogations" the United Kingdom's derogation from Article 5(3) of the Convention was withdrawn on February 26, 2001 to reflect the implementation of the Terrorism Act 2000. Section 16 states that, if a designated derogation is not otherwise withdrawn by the United Kingdom, it will cease to have effect after five years from the date at which it was made, unless it has been extended for a further five years prior to expiry. *Section 15* labels as "designated reservations" the United Kingdom's reservation from Article 2 of the First Protocol and any others which may be in force. *Section 17* requires the Minister to review designated reservations within five years of their coming into force or being renewed, and to write a report on his findings which will be presented to Parliament.

Section 19 requires a Minister in charge of a Bill in either House of Parliament to make a written statement, before the Second Reading of the Bill; that either,

(a) in his view the Bill is compatible with Convention rights, or

(b) although he is unable to state that the Bill is so compatible, the Government wishes to proceed with the Bill.

Criticism of the Human Rights Act 1998

2–027 "The touchstone of success is whether or not, at an administrative rather than a judicial level, decision-makers are acting more fairly, less disproportionately, and recognising and respecting the human rights enshrined in the Convention".[20]

Lord Hope in *Kebilene*:

". . .in the hands of the national courts the Convention should be seen as an expression of fundamental principles rather than a mere set of rules. The questions which the court will have to decide in the application of these principles will involve questions of balance between competing interests and issues of proportionality. In this regard difficult choices may have to be made by the executive or the legislature between the rights of the individual and the needs of society. In some circumstances it will be appropriate for the courts to recognise that there is an area of judgment within which the judiciary will defer, on democratic grounds, to the considered opinion of the elected body or person whose act or decision is said to be incompatible with the Convention".[21]

The two quotes above demonstrate that a difficult exercise has begun for all those involved in the political and legal arenas of the U.K., and that little will be certain about the effect of the Human Rights Act 1998's incorporation of the ECHR into U.K. law for some time to come. But the first indications have been that courts at least are likely to use their new powers with restraint. This is to some extent due to concerns about the possible effects of an expansive interpretation of the new law and the powers which it creates.

2–028 Although incorporation of the ECHR into United Kingdom law is a positive step towards the increased recognition and enforcement of civil liberties and human rights in the United Kingdom, the Human Rights Bill 1997 had hardly been announced before criticisms began. Some of the main reservations which have been expressed may be summarised as follows:

(i) The implementation and enforcement of the new law will be expensive when compared against the limited improvements which are likely to result in domestic law. Training has been required by judges, members of the legal professions, and public authorities. Guidance packs have had to be produced and legal advice will be necessary before public authorities change policy or make decisions. The legal aid budget may face extra strain at a time when efforts are being made to restrict it. The courts' workload will also be increased, particularly while a body of case law authority is being developed. However, early indications are that the expense has not been disproportionate: a Press Release from the Lord Chancellor's Department on March 20, 2001 stated that there had been "no significant impact" upon the court system due to incorporation and attributed this firmly to the training, evaluation, monitoring and information programmes of the LCD.

(ii) The Act does not go far enough for many critics. Its status is no less, and no more, important than any other statute. Exceptions introduced by amendment for, amongst others, religious bodies from the scope of the Act can be regarded as an unwarranted concession to lobbying pressure. The failure to incorporate the remaining Protocols to the Convention may be seen as a missed opportunity, and so may the lack of a supervisory Human Rights Commission. A Human Rights Commission could have had a powerful advisory, research and educative role and might also have acted as a claimant in cases testing the scope and application of Convention rights. Some would have preferred it if the courts had been given a power to strike down legislation which is incompatible with Convention rights, in spite of the parliamentary sovereignty implications which such a change would have. The Bill also omitted Article 13 of the Convention, which guarantees an effective remedy for breach of a Convention right. The organisation Liberty welcomed the Act as a first step, but wished that the Government would have gone much further by introducing a British Bill of Rights with a far wider scope of protection than the Convention's somewhat limited and counterbalanced rights.[22] Such concerns can only be increased when other legislation making its way through Parliament at the same time as the Human Rights Bill appeared to breach the Convention; for example the Crime and Disorder Act 1998 created offences of "anti-social behaviour" which might well be vulnerable to a declaration of incompatibility on the ground of breach of Article 6 (right to fair and impartial trial). Further such offences have been added by the Criminal Justice and Police Act 2001 (see Chap. 3).

(iii) Many of the problems concerning the ECHR have not been solved by incorporation; indeed, the problems have actually been incorporated into United Kingdom law. The delicate balance of rights under the Convention already means that United Kingdom courts will be faced with denying individuals, for example, an effective right to privacy in the same way as the Strasbourg court and Commission have done so; and some aggrieved persons will be unable to fund any court case at all, regardless of whether it is in Strasbourg or the United Kingdom, and so may be unable to enforce their newly-strengthened rights. There also remains the possibility that United Kingdom courts and parliament may form a fundamentally different opinion as to the nature and scope of ECHR rights from that formed by the European Court of Human Rights, with conflict as a result. Of course, economic and social rights remain outside the scope of the protection afforded by incorporation. The HRA falls short of being a true Bill of Rights with as much value as those in countries which have written constitutions, and does not definitively entrench rights since they are vulnerable both to interpretation and to the long-term fate of the HRA itself.

(iv) The ECHR is already out of date and some of its provisions do not easily adapt to modern requirements, *e.g.* right to know (compare with Freedom of Information Act 2000—see Chap. 8 for discussion). It is a product of its times, the post-war period, and so contains no real social or economic rights and also fails to protect the rights of growing minority groups. Thus, it is a poor model for twenty-first century Britain's human rights protection.

(v) The new procedures could be seen as giving courts too much power, and allowing them to interfere with the legislative process and legislative supremacy if they reinterpret existing law to be compatible with the Convention, rather than issuing declarations of incompatibility: This would be a step towards a greater degree of judge-made law.

(vi) The HRA has already created uncertainty throughout domestic law, *e.g.* we do not know whether, when or how any privacy-related right will be created by judges or Parliament in order to ensure that domestic law complies with Article 8.

2–029 But, against this background of reservations, it must be noted that there have clearly already been a number of positive implications and results of the HRA 1998. Although not in itself necessarily a "positive" point, it is clear that fears of a radical revolt and catastrophic effects upon the legal system were exaggerated. Change on a massive scale is unlikely, if the rest of the United Kingdom follows a similar pattern to that seen in Scotland after incorporation: in the first 600 human rights cases in Scotland, only 20 succeeded. Lord Steyn has advocated a realistic approach to the role of courts post-incorporation, and the avoidance of scaremongering about the potential for causing judicial chaos;

"The premise of this hysteria is that the courts will accede to every impractical and implausible claim, ignoring the balance inherent to the

Convention between individual rights and conditions of stability and order required even in a liberal democracy. This ignores the fact that the direct application of the Convention has caused no such chaos in other European democracies. The truth is that our highly trained, independent and impartial judiciary, carrying out its task in accordance with principles of institutional integrity, will approach the more extravagant claims made in the name of human rights with the scepticism which they deserve. Common sense has not been banished".[23]

This viewpoint is borne out by the first batch of cases decided just before and after incorporation. For example, in *Re F*,[23A] one judge based his decision on human rights principles but came to the same conclusion as did the other two judges, deciding on the basis of the common law alone. Further:

- The HRA gives us a chance to re-examine dusty old principles of law and precedent in a fresh and potentially radical light; even if the old rules survive unchanged, the human rights challenge serves a valuable purpose, that of adaptation to changing times, even if it is only the reasoning behind the rules which adapts. Any move which gives rights a significant status in everyday legal and political decisions is laudable.
- Many of the good points of the ECHR may "rub off" onto domestic law: statutes will have to be phrased less vaguely in order to ensure their compatibility with the HRA, and so domestic law should become more certain; the interplay between existing domestic law and new rights-driven cases may encourage development in the Convention rights, since it is a two-way process; its status as a living instrument should encourage statutes to be treated in the same way.
- One of the limitations of the HRA will lessen over time. Although only a public authority may be liable under the HRA, there is a possibility of "horizontal effect" developing so that the Convention rights become applicable in all cases, in all courts, even where all parties are private individuals. This is likely because section 6's effect will be that, even where no public authority is involved in a situation, as soon as the dispute reaches a court or tribunal, the Convention rights come into play, so eventually the "public authority" status may become redundant as human rights filter through into all aspects of domestic law.

According to Lord Hope of Craighead[24]:

"In particular the opportunity now exists for our judges to demonstrate, by means of reasoned judgments based upon established Convention law principles, how the basic human rights which are enshrined in the Convention can be respected without risk to the rule of law or to the established values of our democracy. Striking the balance is likely in many cases to be the crucial issue, as will be the development of the concept of proportionality".

He recognises that the balance between the new enshrined rights and the pressure for restraint in their interpretation and application is a difficult one, but suggests that it is neither an insurmountable problem nor one which can be left alone. It is certain that the number of cases brought to court in the United Kingdom will increase greatly, at least in the short term. But, he argues, this does not necessarily mean that human rights cases should be dealt with in any way differently from other cases, and certainly not more "robustly". The duty of care owed by lawyers to their clients requires them to make human rights arguments, not to sideline them, and the continued existence of the route to Strasbourg via individual petition holds a danger that "restraint" by domestic courts and lawyers will result in domestic law being demonstrated to be in violation of the Convention, with the associated embarrassment.

It remains to be seen to what extent incorporation of the ECHR into United Kingdom law serves more than a declaratory and time-saving function, and also whether further steps are to be taken towards increasing the level and range of rights protected in United Kingdom law. However, it must always be borne in mind, as was stated in *The Sunday Times v. U.K.*,[25] that:

"... [the] main purpose of the Convention is to lay down certain international standards to be observed by the contracting states in their relations with persons under their jurisdiction. This does not mean that absolute uniformity is required and, indeed, since the contracting states remain free to chose the measures which they consider appropriate, the Court cannot be oblivious of the substantive or procedural features of their domestic laws".

Synthesis: a work in progress

2–030 Since the Human Rights Act came into force, domestic courts have had to struggle not only with the application and interpretation of the rights under the Convention as incorporated, but also with the interpretation of the Human Rights Act itself. Certain sections have already caused considerable difficulties; two particular problems will be highlighted here, and others are dealt with in later chapters of this book. Firstly, the House of Lords has interpreted a statutory provision almost out of existence in using its interpretative powers under section 3(1) of the HRA to uphold a defendant's right to a fair hearing under Article 6(1); is this the beginning of a new power struggle between the courts and Parliament? In *R v. A*[25A]:

Facts. In December 2000 the respondent was to be tried for rape, and his defence would have been either that the complainant consented, or that he had honestly believed that she had consented. At a preparatory hearing defence counsel applied for leave to cross-examine the complainant about her alleged prior sexual relationships with both himself and his friend, and to adduce evidence about them. In accordance with section 41 of the Youth Justice and Criminal Evidence Act 1999, the judge ruled that:

(i) the acts of consensual sex with the friend could be put to the complainant in cross-examination;
(ii) the complainant could not be cross-examined, nor could evidence be led, about her alleged sexual relationship with the defendant; and
(iii) the defendant's prepared statement, which referred in general terms to his alleged sexual relationship with the complainant, could not be used in evidence.

Section 41(1) provides that, at a trial for a sexual offence, it is only with leave of the court that evidence about sexual behaviour of the complainant may be brought, or any question asked in cross-examination, by or on behalf of the accused. Leave may only be given where one of the exceptions under subsection (3) or (5) applies, and the court is satisfied that refusal of leave might render the jury's conclusion on any relevant issue in the case unsafe. The exceptions are that the evidence or question:

— relates to an issue other than consent (s.41(3)(a)); or
— relates to consent, and the sexual behaviour of the complainant referred to is alleged to have occurred at or about the same time as the event on which the charge is based (s.41(3)(b)); or
— relates to consent, and the evidence or question concerns sexual behaviour of the complainant which is alleged to have been so similar in any respect to sexual behaviour of the complainant which either, according to defence evidence, was part of the event on which the charge is based, or took place at or about the same time as that event, that it cannot reasonably be explained as a coincidence (s.41(3)(c); or
— goes no further than is necessary in rebuttal of evidence adduced by the prosecution about a specific instance of sexual behaviour by the complainant (s.41(5)).

Mindful that his ruling could breach the defendant's right to a fair trial under Article 6 of the ECHR, the judge gave leave to appeal. The Court of Appeal focused on the finding that the complainant could not be asked, and evidence could not be brought, regarding her having had sex with the defendant during the three weeks before the alleged offence. The Court of Appeal concluded that such questions and evidence were permissible as to the issue of whether the defendant had honestly believed that the complainant consented and so should have been allowed under section 41(3)(a). However, such evidence of a previous sexual relationship between the parties was inadmissible on the issue of whether there actually was consent (s.41(3)(b)) since it was not sufficiently close in time to the alleged offence. Pointing out the paradox in this situation and stating that the necessary direction might lead to an unfair trial, the court thus allowed the appeal, gave leave to appeal to the House of Lords and certified for the House of Lords the question:

> "May a sexual relationship between a defendant and complainant be relevant to the issue of consent so as to render its exclusion under section 41 of the Youth Justice and Criminal Evidence Act 1999 a contravention of the defendant's right to a fair trial?"

Decision. It was held, dismissing the appeal, that section 41 must be read as compatible with the fair trial requirements under Article 6 of the European Convention on Human Rights, as required by section 3 of the Human Rights Act

1998. In this way a declaration of incompatibility could and should be avoided. Although merely excluding some relevant evidence would not violate Article 6, there was the potential that in a significant number of cases section 41 would prevent a defendant from putting forward a full defence. The language of section 41(3)(b) could not be read in such a way as to admit relevant evidence of previous sexual relations between the defendant and the complainant. Thus, in order to uphold defendants' rights, section 41(3)(c) should be read in such a way as to allow the admission of evidence or questioning on a relevant issue whenever this was considered necessary by the trial judge in order to ensure a fair trial. Whilst complainants must be protected from humiliating and undignified treatment in court, evidence which is so relevant to the issue of consent that to exclude it would endanger the fair trial requirement of Article 6 of the Convention, should not be excluded. Lord Steyn stated that "Whilst the statute pursued desirable goals (*i.e.* the protection of vulnerable complainants and upholding the rights of victims), the methods adopted amounted to legislative overkill". By implying that all relevant evidence or questioning required to ensure a fair trial should not be treated as inadmissible under section 41, that section "will have achieved a major part of its objective but its excessive reach will have been attenuated in accordance with the will of Parliament as reflected in section 3 of the 1998 Act". Lord Hope, dissenting, thought that section 41 was a proportionate response to the rights of the complainant, and that any cases where the fairness of the trial might be affected should be dealt with individually as they arose. Parliament had drafted the section carefully, and it was not for judges to effectively overrule that decision.

Once again, Parliament's attempt to significantly limit the admissibility of evidence or questions relating to previous sexual behaviour of complainants in sex offence trials has fallen foul of the courts. Section 2 of the Sexual Offences Act 1976, which s.41 replaced and improved, was widely criticised for leaving too much discretion to the trial judge and allowing irrelevant considerations to be put to the jury. The present case has swayed the balance back in favour of judicial discretion as to admissibility of evidence, but it remains to be seen where the final balance will lie between the rights of the defendant and the complainant. Although each judge agreed that such evidence and questions were generally irrelevant as to the complainant's credibility or character, the end result of the decision is that in many cases evidence will be admitted and questions asked which will be used by the defence as an attack on just those factors of the complainant. Section 3 of the Human Rights Act gives much wider powers of statutory interpretation than those which were previously available to judges, and full use was made of them in this case

2–031 Whilst each judge in the House of Lords spoke eloquently of the terrible nature of the crime of rape, the need to protect complainants in the courtroom and the need to improve the conviction rates, the rights of the alleged victim clearly came second in their decision. It was open to the court to find that, whilst section 41 did restrict the admission of evidence and questions which might be relevant to the defendant's case, this by itself did not prevent a fair trial. The court did not refer in any detail to ECHR cases on "equality of arms", although this is the principle to which they are impliedly giving such primacy; in fact, as stated in *Dombo Beheer B.V. v.*

The Netherlands[25B] (a civil case), equality of arms requires only that "each party must be afforded a reasonable opportunity to present his case — including his evidence—under conditions that do not place him at a substantial disadvantage vis-à-vis his opponent". It is interesting that only Article 6 was referred to in this case. The Convention rights of the complainant, as an alleged victim of crime, were not addressed; the victim also has a right to a fair trial (see *X and Y v. The Netherlands*[25C]); the extremely low conviction rate for rape could be argued to show that the victim had no effective remedy as required by Article 13; and it is arguable that conditions for the complainant in many rape trials amount to at least degrading treatment under Article 3 and may violate the right to respect for private life under Article 8 (see again *X and Y v. The Netherlands*). The predictable outcry from women's rights and human rights organisations has begun.

The ball is now back in the Government's court as to whether they decide to reform section 41 in line with the opinion of the judiciary, to reverse the robust statutory interpretation in the present case by statute, or perhaps to take the simplest approach by requiring a direction by judges that the fact that the complainant may have consented to sexual activity with either the defendant or another person at another time does not mean that s/he consented on the facts of the alleged offence.

Secondly, the extent of the retroactive effect of the HRA upon criminal law has been debated in two recent decisions, and it appears that there remains a divergence between the cases concerned. The somewhat absurd result is that, where an appeal is brought by the convicted person, he can only rely on Convention rights if the alleged breach occurred after October 2, 2000; yet, if his case was referred to the Court of Appeal by the Criminal Cases Review Commission, this time limit does not apply and so the Act will have retroactive effect upon his original trial. Both the Court of Appeal in *Kansal* and the House of Lords in *R v. A* (each of which is studied below) have found this to be an undesirable result and one which is unlikely to have been intended by Parliament, but it is the latter body who must resolve the problem.

In *R. v. Kansal*[25D]: **2–032**

Facts. The appellant was convicted in February 1992 of various offences, including obtaining property by deception contrary to section 15 of the Theft Act 1968 and bankruptcy-related offences under the Insolvency Act 1986, and was sentenced to 15 months imprisonment. His appeal was unsuccessful and leave to appeal further was refused. In 1998 the Criminal Cases Review Commission referred the case to the Court of Appeal on the basis of *Preddy*,[25E] then in June 2000 the reference was widened. The grounds of appeal were, *inter alia*, that the judge should not have admitted into evidence the transcript of the defendant's examination at his bankruptcy proceedings, in the light of the decision of the European Court of Human Rights in the case of *Saunders v. U.K.*[25F] Thus the grounds of appeal relied upon cases which had been decided after the appellant's conviction. Two provisions of the Human Rights Act 1998 were relevant. Section 7(1)(b) allows a person who is or would be a victim of a breach of a Convention right by a public authority to rely on that right in any legal proceedings, including an appeal against the decision of a court. Section 22(4) states that this is the case regardless of when the act in question took place, if the proceedings are brought by or at the instigation of a public authority (which all criminal proceedings are): otherwise only acts occurring after section 7 came into force may be the subject of a human rights challenge.

Decision. The Court of Appeal found that the long-established practice of the Court of Appeal neither to re-open convictions nor to allow an extension of time or leave to appeal because of a change of law since the trial could no longer hold. The combined effect of the provisions of the Criminal Appeal Act 1995 and section 22(4) of the Human Rights Act 1998 was that:

(1) the CCRC could refer a conviction to the court of Appeal regardless of how long it was since the trial occurred; and
(2) once such a reference had been made, the Court of Appeal had to declare the conviction unsafe if it resulted from the admission of evidence in breach of Article 6 of the ECHR, or from a change in the common law (which is deemed to have always been that which it is authoritatively declared to be).

At his trial, the judge had allowed the admission of the answers given under compulsion by the appellant in his bankruptcy proceedings, via section 433 of the Insolvency Act 1986. A full transcript of the appellant's examination by thc Official Receiver from the bankruptcy proceedings was placed before the jury, and the judge when summing up stated that the transcript could be "very important". The admission of evidence given under compulsion now clearly violates the presumption of innocence guaranteed by Article 6(2) of the Convention. Applying the decision of the European Court of Human Rights in *Saunders v. U.K.*, and mindful of the fact that Schedule 3, paragraph 7 of the Youth Justice and Criminal Evidence Act 1999 now generally renders compelled statements inadmissible on behalf of the prosecution in criminal proceedings, the appeal was allowed since the trial was unfair by the new standards and the conviction could not be regarded as safe.

The Court of Appeal was clearly very reluctant to reach the conclusion which it did: "We reach this conclusion with no enthusiasm whatever". Now that the filter provided by the blanket refusal to extend time for appeal has been removed, the potential for new cases flooding in to the CCRC is enormous, with consequent impact on both the public interest in finality in litigation and the most efficacious use of limited resources. The Court pointed out that Sir Thomas More, Guy Fawkes and Charles I would all have benefited from Convention rights, and that every defendant before the Criminal Evidence Act 1898 had his right to a fair trial breached by his inability to give evidence on his own behalf. Whilst it has been accepted, from decisions such as *ex parte Kebilene*[25G] and *Lambert and Others*,[25H] that sections 7(1)(b) and 22(4) of the Human Rights Act 1998 do have a retrospective impact upon trials and appeals, those cases also found (*per* Lord Steyn in *Kebilene*) that "It should not however be assumed that non-compliance with the Convention before the Act came into force will be regarded as a ground for extending time for appealing". It was the lack of any time limit within the Criminal Appeal Act 1995 for references by the

CCRC which forced the Court of Appeal to make their decision in the present case. Statutory reform is, it is submitted, extremely likely. But the House of Lords appears to have a different opinion as to the retroactivity of sections 7(1)(b) and 22(4). In *R. v. Lambert*,[251] the court took a restrictive or "floodgates" approach and argued that Parliament could not possibly have intended all defendants convicted prior to October 2, 2000 to be able to appeal on HRA grounds. *Kansal* was not overruled, and it was only in fact mentioned in passing.

Facts. The defendant had been convicted of possessing cocaine with intent to supply, contrary to section 5 of the Misuse of Drugs Act 1971, and sentenced to seven years' imprisonment. He had relied upon the statutory defence under section 28(3)(b)(i), *i.e.* that he neither knew nor suspected nor had reason to suspect, that what he was possessing was a drug. This statutory defence placed a burden upon the defendant to "prove"' it. He appealed to the Court of Appeal, who found that the reversed burden of proof did not contravene the presumption of innocence as guaranteed by Article 6(2) since it placed only an evidential and not a legal burden upon the defendant: in other words he only had to supply some evidence to support his belief, and then the prosecution had to disprove it beyond reasonable doubt in order to convict him. Lambert was given leave to appeal to the House of Lords as to whether Article 6 had been violated at his trial. Three questions were certified for the House of Lords:

1. Whether it was an essential element of the offence in question that the accused knew that he was possessing a drug.
2. Whether the section 28 defence imposed a legal rather than an evidential burden upon the accused.
3. Whether, on appeal of a case decided before the Human Rights Act came into force, the appellant could rely upon a breach of Convention rights at his trial.

Decision. The Court of Appeal found that section 28 of the 1971 Act did violate the presumption of innocence in Article 6(2) by requiring the defendant to prove his defence, *i.e.* by imposing a legal rather than a purely evidential burden upon him. Thus, according to section 3 of the HRA, the court must construe that section, so far as it is possible, so that the defendant need only raise the evidential burden of initially establishing some facts in support of his argued defence. The burden of actual proof remains on the prosecution. But, since the defendant had been convicted before the Human Rights Act came into force, he could not rely on the rights which it created and so his appeal was dismissed. *Per* Lord Slynn,

> "It is clear that the 1998 Act must be given its full import and that long or well entrenched ideas may have to be put aside, sacred cows culled. Since, however, the Act did not come into force (apart from limited provisions) until [October 2, 2000]. . ., and since there is a presumption against retroactivity in legislation, it is not to be assumed *a priori* that Convention rights, however commendable, are to be enforceable in national courts in respect of past events".

Where an appeal is brought by the unsuccessful defendant, it is not within section 7(1)(b) and so only Convention breaches which occurred after October 2, 2000 can be judged by the court. Thus it is only where proceedings are brought by a public authority that section 22(4) gives section 7 retrospective effect over criminal appeals: all defendants who do not fit this category will have to take the Strasbourg route to vindication of their rights.

THE ECHR RIGHTS AND FREEDOMS AND THE GENERAL PRINCIPLES OF THE CONVENTION

2–032A There are a number of general principles of the ECHR which have no direct equivalent in domestic law, and hence which require brief elaboration at this stage. It is difficult to judge how domestic courts will apply and interpret them in future cases.

(i) The margin of appreciation

2–032B Although all contracting states must not only refrain from breaching the Convention rights but also must ensure that they are upheld within their boundaries, the European Court of Human Rights has always allowed states a degree of discretion as to the methods by which the specific rights are protected and the reasons for which they may be limited. It is thought that each individual state is in a better position than the ECHR to judge whether the circumstances within its boundaries necessitate limitations upon a right or freedom in a particular factual situation. This respect for the sovereignty of states gives rise to the margin of appreciation, *i.e.* the scope of the discretion which a state may employ in that respect. But it is not a static concept: its breadth varies between, and even within, Articles, and so the margin of appreciation must be considered separately for each right and freedom. Further, it is not enough for a state to simply rely upon its margin of appreciation to justify limitations upon any right or freedom: it must also show that its actions are both *reasonable* in the circumstances and *proportionate* to the legitimate aim argued for the limitation of the rights concerned. Although there is no margin of appreciation in domestic law and it plays no part in the Human Rights Act itself, similar reasoning is likely to be employed by domestic courts, for example in the form of statements that "Parliament is best placed to judge whether restrictions on the right to demonstrate are necessary".

(ii) Proportionality

2–032C If a state wishes to limit the scope of any of the Convention rights or freedoms within its territory, it cannot simply argue that it has a legitimate reason for doing so. The principle of proportionality requires, firstly, that any interference with a Convention right or freedom must not be disproportionate to the legitimate aim which the state argues for the interference; and, secondly, that the rights of the individual are weighed up fairly against the rights of society and the community in general. There is no formula by which these competing rights may be balanced; it is a question to be decided in each separate case.

(iii) Positive obligations

It has been stated elsewhere in this book, but a reminder may be timely: a state will not comply with its Convention obligations simply by refraining from breaching the rights and freedoms contained therein (a negative obligation): a state must also, in certain circumstances, positively uphold Convention rights within its territory. This positive obligation does not apply to all Convention rights and freedoms but, where a positive obligation has been found to exist by the ECHR in particular circumstances, a state will be required to uphold that right by positive action. This means that in effect a state may be indirectly held responsible for rights violations by private individuals, where for example the domestic law does not support the right in question and allows violations to go unpunished. But any positive obligation is only to *take steps* to ensure that a right is upheld, not to *achieve that result;* a state need only show that it has tried, not necessarily that it has succeeded. **2–032D**

Article 1: Obligation to Respect Human Rights

The High Contracting Parties shall secure to everyone within their jurisdiction the rights and freedoms defined in Section 1 of this Convention.[26] **2–033**

This Article was historically the basis upon which the "positive obligations" upon states were developed (see above). But nowadays the justificatory basis for each positive obligation is to be found within the detailed case law on each Article.

Article 2. Right to Life

1 Everyone's right to life shall be protected by law. No one shall be deprived of his life intentionally save in the execution of a sentence of a court following his conviction of a crime for which this penalty is provided by law. **2–034**

2 Deprivation of life shall not be regarded as inflicted in contravention of this Article when it results from the use of force which is no more than absolutely necessary:

(a) in defence of any person from unlawful violence;
(b) order to effect a lawful arrest or to prevent the escape of a person lawfully detained;
(c) in action lawfully taken for the purpose of quelling a riot or insurrection.

The right to life may be the most fundamental human right, but it is by no means absolute under the ECHR: in fact it has been surprisingly easy for states to justify killings of citizens. It is a positive obligation and so states must take positive steps to ensure that the right is upheld within their territory, but there are various sensitive issues involved which have led to guarded decisions by the ECHR. The issue of whether abortion should be allowed has been left within the domain of the states themselves (see *Paton v. U.K.*[26A]). State deprivations of life have often been found to be justified by being absolutely necessary and a proportionate response to the state's aim: for example in *Kelly v. U.K.*[26B] The right to life is discussed in full in Chapter 3.

Article 3: Ill-Treatment

2–035 No one shall be subjected to torture or to inhuman or degrading treatment or punishment.

The freedoms from torture and from inhuman or degrading treatment or punishment have given rise to complex case law. These freedoms are unlimited in the sense that there are no exceptions, and it is impossible for a state to derogate from Article 3. Again, Article 3 creates positive obligations upon a state. The difference between torture and the other types of ill-treatment is merely one of degree, with torture having to attain a much higher standard of severity. But there have been few cases where the ill-treatment has been severe enough to qualify as torture, and so a misleading impression may be conveyed by the low level of harm in some of the degrading treatment cases, for example smacking (see *Y v. U.K.*[26C]). Article 3 is discussed fully in Chapter 3.

Article 4: Right to Freedom From Slavery

2–036

1 No one shall be held in slavery or servitude.

2 No one shall be required to perform forced or compulsory labour.

3 For the purpose of this Article the term "forced or compulsory labour" shall not include:

(a) any work required to be done in the ordinary course of detention imposed according to the provisions of Article 5 of this Convention or during conditional release from such detention;
(b) any service of a military character or, in case of conscientious objectors in countries where they are recognised, service exacted instead of compulsory military service;
(c) any service exacted in case of an emergency or calamity threatening the life or well-being of the community;
(d) any work or service which forms part of normal civic obligations.

Freedom from slavery is of course one of the most fundamental human rights, and Article 4 therefore performs an important declaratory function.

But the exceptions to the Article do allow particular categories of persons to be compelled to perform particular work: citizens may be required to perform national service in states which (unlike the United Kingdom) still so require; prisoners may be expected to work; jury service may be compulsory; and community service is a valid method of official punishment. Detailed consideration of Article 4 is beyond the scope of this book.

Article 5: Right to Liberty

1 Everyone has the right to liberty and security of person. No one shall be deprived of his liberty save in the following cases and in accordance with a procedure prescribed by law: **2–037**

(a) the lawful detention of a person after conviction by a competent court;
(b) the lawful arrest or detention of a person for non-compliance with the lawful order of a court or in order to secure the fulfilment of any obligation prescribed by law;
(c) the lawful arrest or detention of a person effected for the purpose of bringing him before the competent legal authority on a reasonable suspicion of having committed an offence or when it is reasonably considered necessary to prevent his committing an offence or fleeing after having done so;
(d) the detention of a minor by lawful order for the purpose of educational supervision or his lawful detention for the purpose of bringing him before the competent legal authority;
(e) the lawful detention of persons for the prevention of the spreading of infectious diseases, of persons of unsound mind, alcoholics or drug addicts or vagrants;
(f) the lawful arrest or detention of a person to prevent his effecting an unauthorised entry into the country or of a person against whom action is being taken with a view to deportation or extradition.

2 Everyone who is arrested shall be informed promptly, in a language which he understands, of the reasons for his arrest and of any charge against him.

3 Everyone arrested or detained in accordance with the provisions of paragraph 1(c) of this Article shall be brought promptly before a judge or other officer authorised by law to exercise judicial power and shall be entitled to trial within a reasonable time or to release pending trial. Release may be conditioned by guarantee to appear for trial.

4 Everyone who is deprived of his liberty by arrest or detention shall be entitled to take proceedings by which the lawfulness of

his detention shall be decided speedily by a court and his release ordered if the detention is not lawful.

5 Everyone who has been the victim of arrest or detention in contravention of the provision of this Article shall have an enforceable right to compensation.

2–038 The main focus of Article 5 is upon preventing arbitrary arrest and detention. The right to liberty and security of the person may only be interfered with in limited circumstances such as, *inter alia*, following conviction by a competent court, after arrest on reasonable suspicion of having committed an offence, or pending deportation. Article 5 also contains a number of specific rights for a person after arrest which operate as basic safeguards of a citizen's rights and fair treatment. Many of the cases involving the United Kingdom have had terrorist suspects as applicants, since the pre-trial rules and procedures in such cases are more restrictive of a suspect's rights. Article 5 is dealt with fully in Chapter 3.

Article 6: The Right to a Fair Hearing

2–039 1 In the determination of his civil rights and obligations or of any criminal charge against him, everyone is entitled to a fair and public hearing within a reasonable time by an independent and impartial tribunal established by law. Judgment shall be pronounced publicly but the press and public may be excluded from all or part of the trial in the interests of morals, public order or national security in a democratic society, where the interests of juveniles or the protection of the private life of the parties so require, or to the extent strictly necessary in the opinion of the court in special circumstances where publicity would prejudice the interests of justice.

2 Everyone charged with a criminal offence shall be presumed innocent until proved guilty according to law.

3 Everyone charged with a criminal offence has the following minimum rights:

(a) to be informed promptly, in a language which he understands and in detail, of the nature and cause of the accusation against him;

(b) to have adequate time and facilities for the preparation of his defence;

(c) to defend himself in person or through legal assistance of his own choosing or, if he has not sufficient means to pay for legal assistance, to be given it free when the interests of justice so require;

(d) to examine or have examined witnesses against him and to obtain the attendance and examination of witnesses

against him and to obtain the attendance and examination of witnesses on his behalf under the same conditions as witnesses against him;

(e) to have the free assistance of an interpreter if he cannot understand or speak the language used in court.

Article 6 has become one of the most-argued Convention rights, and the same is happening in the domestic sphere post-HRA. This is hardly surprising because of its scope: it aims to ensure a fair hearing in both civil and criminal trials (Article 6(1)), and also provides a number of basic minimum fairness criteria for criminal trials (Article 6(2) and (3)), including: the presumption of innocence; right to be informed of charge; right to have time and facilities for preparing a defence; a limited right to legal aid; right to cross-examine; right to an interpreter. But, since the minimum fairness criteria operate at a very basic level, they will not often be triggered in domestic cases. Article 6 is discussed in full in Chapter 3.

Article 7: The Principle of Non-retroactivity in Criminal Trials

1 No one shall be held guilty of any criminal offence on account of any act or omission which did not constitute a criminal offence under national or international law at the time when it was committed. Nor shall a heavier penalty be imposed than the one that was applicable at the time the criminal offence was committed. **2–040**

2 This Article shall not prejudice the trial and punishment of any person for any act or omission which, at the time when it was committed, was criminal according to the general principles of law recognised by civilised nations.

The principle of non-retroactivity of criminal law is a very basic one indeed, and is founded upon the theory that criminal behaviour is freely willed: if the law may change retrospectively, then a person cannot make decisions about his conduct in order to stay within the confines of legality. One particular problem for the U.K. is that the common law never technically "changes", but is declared to have always been whatever a court of high ranking in terms of precedent declares it to be: from the perspective of a defendant, this is no consolation. As in *CR and SW v. UK*,[26D] at the time of the act which gave rise to his criminal conviction a person may have been outside the definition of an offence, but by the time his case came to trial a court may "declare" the common law to have been different all along. Article 7 is discussed in more detail in Chapter 3.

Article 8: Right to Respect of Privacy

1 Everyone has the right to respect for his private and family life, his home and his correspondence. **2–041**

2 There shall be no interference by a public authority with the exercise of this right except such as in accordance with the law and is necessary in a democratic society in the interests of national security, public safety or the economic well-being of the country, for the prevention of disorder or crime, for the protection of health or morals, or for the protection of the rights and freedom of others.

Article 8 has already caused a rethink in many areas of domestic law, since the protection of the so-called right to privacy in England and Wales is weak. Whether a great deal of change will occur or whether the existing diverse and disparate rules related to private life will simply receive the badge of being HRA-compatible will be decided over years to come, but early indications are discussed in full in Chapter 8. ECHR cases have covered a very wide range of situations indeed, including sexuality, the treatment of victims of sex offences and immigration law, as well as its more obvious applications. But it should be noted that:

(i) the four rights in this Article only have to be *respected,* and so are not as strong as they may appear; and

(ii) the list of legitimate aims which justify interference with the Article 8 rights is long and broad indeed.

Article 9: Right to Freedom of Thought, Conscience and Religion

2–042 1 Everyone has the right to freedom of thought, conscience and religion; this right includes freedom to change his religion or beliefs and freedom, either alone or in community with others and in public or private, to manifest his religion or belief, in worship, teaching, practice or observance.

2 Freedom to manifest one's religion or beliefs shall be subject only to such limitations as are prescribed by law and are necessary in a democratic society in the interests of public safety, for the protection of public order, health or morals, or for the protection of the rights and freedoms of others.

Every democratic society must respect freedom of thought, conscience and religion, but this is not a straightforward area. Many of the cases have involved delicate balancing exercises between the competing rights of individuals with differing beliefs; one man's demonstration of his religious beliefs may be viewed by another as harassment (see *Kokkinakis v. Greece*[26E]). Thus the *right* to freedom of religion, etc., is absolute, but the *manifestation* of beliefs, thought, conscience and religion may be interfered with to the extent that it is necessary in a democratic society for one of the listed legitimate aims. Article 9 is discussed in Chapter 6.

Article 10: Right to Freedom of Expression

1 Everyone has the right to freedom of expression. This right shall include freedom to hold opinions and to receive and impart information and ideas without interference by public authority and regardless of frontiers. This Article shall not prevent States from requiring the licensing of broadcasting, television or cinema enterprises. **2–043**

2 The exercise of these freedoms, since it carries with it duties and responsibilities, may be subject to such formalities, conditions, restrictions or penalties as are prescribed by law and are necessary in a democratic society, in the interests of national security, territorial integrity or public safety, for the prevention of disorder or crime, for the protection of health or morals, for the protection of the reputation or rights of others, for preventing the disclosure of information received in confidence, or for maintaining the authority and impartiality of the judiciary.

Freedom of expression is one of the most fundamental Convention rights and often takes priority over other rights, particularly the right to respect for private life under Article 8. The Human Rights Act preserves this priority in s.12. Freedom of expression includes the right to have an opinion and the right to receive information, even when such information may be shocking or unpleasant (see *Handyside v. UK*[26F]) and the state is under a positive obligation to ensure that its citizens have freedom of expression. The right may be interfered with to the extent that this is necessary in a democratic society for one of the legitimate aims listed, but the margin of appreciation in this respect is narrow, particularly where the public right to know is invoked. Article 10 is discussed fully in Chapter 6.

Article 11: Right to Freedom of Assembly and of Association

1 Everyone has the right to freedom of peaceful assembly and to freedom of association with others, including the right to form and join trade unions for the protection of his interests. **2–044**

2 No restrictions shall be placed on the exercise of these rights other than such as are prescribed by law and are necessary in a democratic society in the interests of national security or public safety, for the prevention of disorder or crime, for the protection of health or morals or for the protection of the rights and freedoms of others. This Article shall not prevent the imposition of lawful restrictions on the exercise of these rights by members of the armed forces, of the police or of the administration of the State.

Although Article 11 does recognise the rights to freedom of association and freedom of peaceful assembly, the exceptions in Article 11(2) mean that there is little extra benefit to be gained by incorporation of this Article into United Kingdom law. Even the most restrictive public order offences may be justified by reference to the needs of national security, prevention of crime or public safety; for example, in *DPP v. Jones*,[27] the court was of the opinion that the English law's limited and negatively-defined recognition of the right to public assembly is in compliance with Article 11, since:

(i) the right of assembly exists in English law wherever it is not expressly denied;

(ii) where citizens' assemblies do not obstruct the highway or involve actual or threatened disorder then they are not prohibited; and

(iii) the requirement of authorisation before a public demonstration may take place does not conflict with Article 11.

Article 12: Right to Marry

2–045 Men and women of marriageable age have the right to marry and to found a family, according to the national laws governing the exercise of this right.

Although Article 12 allows a State to make its own laws regarding marriage and the having of a family and the age limits for both of these, a line of cases has concerned the eligibility of transsexuals for marriage. English law does not allow a transsexual to marry a person of the opposite sex to their own new sex; thus a male-to-female transsexual, for example, may only marry another woman under English law, since her birth certificate will state that she is male. There are ways of obtaining other documents which state the owner's new sex, (*e.g.* by applying for a passport in another state which will register the bearer's new rather than original sex) but this will not allow a legal marriage in the United Kingdom. In *Cossey v. United Kingdom*,[28] the applicant was a male-to-female transsexual who lived successfully as a woman and was stated to be female on her passport, but her marriage to a man was held to be void by the High Court. The Commission found (*inter alia*) that there had been a violation of Article 12 by a majority of 10 to 6, but the United Kingdom government referred the case to the court, who held by 14 to 4 that there was no breach of Article 12. The decision was based upon a belief in the traditional concept of marriage as between a biological male and a biological female; the fact that some Member States would allow a marriage such as the applicant's was not enough to render United Kingdom law a breach of the applicant's rights.[29]

Article 13: Right to an Effective Remedy

2–046 Everyone whose rights and freedoms as set forth in this Convention are violated, shall have an effective remedy before a national authority notwithstanding that the violation has been committed by persons acting in an official capacity.

A party state must ensure that any person whose Convention rights are infringed has an effective remedy for the breach, but Article 13 does not make explicit the form which the remedy is to take. A remedy must be provided wherever the applicant has an "arguable claim" of breach of one of the ECHR rights.[30] After incorporation of the ECHR into United Kingdom law, the likelihood of challenges on the basis of Article 13 should decrease; it is however strange that the Human Rights Act did not include Article 13 within the terms to be incorporated.

Article 14: Right not to be Discriminated Against

The enjoyment of the rights and freedoms set forth in this Convention shall be secured without discrimination on any ground such as sex, race, colour, language, religion, political or other opinion, national or social origin, association with a national minority, property, birth or other status. **2–047**

Some caution needs to be exercised in the interpretation of Article 14, since it is different in scope and method of application from United Kingdom and E.C. law on discrimination. First, this Article does not create an absolute right to freedom from discrimination; it merely prohibits discrimination as far as the rights and freedoms protected by the Convention itself are concerned. So, if a right is not recognised by the Convention, then Article 14 cannot be used. But once it has been established that the facts of a case do fall within the scope of one of the Convention rights, Article 14 forbids discrimination in the application of that right on a far wider basis than does English law, and the list of prohibited grounds for discrimination is not closed. Nor does Article 14 contain any list of exceptions where discrimination is lawful, but the Court has interpreted the Article to require any discriminatory treatment in the application of Convention rights and freedoms to have some kind of objective and reasonable justification. In the *Belgian Linguistic case* (1968)[31] it was stated that:

> ". . . the Court, following the principles which may be extracted from the legal practice of a large number of democratic States, holds that the principle of equality of treatment is violated if the distinction has no objective and reasonable justification. The existence of such a justification must be assessed in relation to the aim and effects of the measure under consideration, regard being had to the principles which normally prevail in democratic societies. A difference of treatment in the exercise of a right laid down in the Convention must not only pursue a legitimate aim: Article 14 is likewise violated when it is clearly established that there is no reasonable relationship of proportionality between the means employed and the aim sought to be realised".

Thus, before an application based upon discrimination can succeed, it must be established: that the discrimination relates to one of the rights or freedoms protected by the Convention or applicable Protocols; and that there is no legitimate aim towards the realisation of which the discrimination is proportionate ("objective and reasonable justification"). Sexual discrimination is treated with the greatest scepticism; in *Abdulaziz, Cabales and Balkandali v. United Kingdom*[32] the Council stated that there must be "very weighty reasons" why differential treatment on the basis of sex should be allowed in application of the Convention, since all the party states to the Convention see equality of treatment of the sexes as a fundamental aim. But racial discrimination has not been treated in the same way, and is not generally within the scope of the Convention (since the Convention does not apply to discrimination in the fields of housing, employment, goods and services).

Incorporation of the Convention is likely to have some impact upon United Kingdom discrimination law. There are some kinds of sexual, racial and disability discrimination which are expressly authorised by statute; the provisions which allow such discrimination will now be open to challenge in United Kingdom courts on the basis that, and to the extent that, they are incompatible with the Convention. Further, English law permits discrimination on any basis other than race, sex or disability, whereas after incorporation it will be possible to challenge any type of unjustifiable discrimination related to one of the Convention rights.

Article 15: Right to Derogate

2–048 1 In time of war or other public emergency threatening the life of the nation any High Contracting Party may take measures derogating from its obligations under this Convention to the extent strictly required by the exigencies of the situation, provided that such measures are not inconsistent with its other obligations under international law.

2 No derogation from Article 2, except in respect of deaths resulting from lawful acts of war, or from Articles 3, 4 (paragraph 1) and 7 shall be made under this provision.

3 Any High Contracting Party availing itself of this right of derogation shall keep the Secretary-General of the Council of Europe fully informed of the measures which it has taken and the reasons therefor. It shall also inform the Secretary-General of the Council of Europe when such measures have ceased to operate and the provisions of the Convention are again fully executed.

Article 15 deals with the circumstances where a contracting state may be permitted to derogate from its normal responsibilities owed under the Convention, because of some exceptional crisis prevailing in that country. However, before the Commission or court would regard the derogation as justified there are four main requirements which must be adhered to:

(1) It must be in time of war or other public emergency threatening the life of the nation, and;

(2) The actions taken by the state did not exceed those strictly required by the exigencies of the situation; and

(3) Those actions were not at variance to existing obligations under international law; and

(4) If the state has already declared its derogation, that derogation should end when the emergency situation itself has subsided.

There is no absolute right to derogate from all the articles under the Convention; no derogation is permitted under Articles 2, 3, 4(1) and 7. Although each contracting state has a certain degree of flexibility (the "margin of appreciation" principle) whether or not to invoke Article 15(1), it is ultimately for the court to decide whether the requirements of (1) to (4) above have been discharged in the particular circumstances.

Thus in *Lawless v. Ireland (No. 3)*[33]:

Facts. The applicant was arrested under The Offences against the State (Amendment) Act 1940 ("The 1940 Act") and detained for some five months without trial on suspicion of being a member of a proscribed organisation, namely the IRA. Due to the volatile situation prevailing at that time in the Republic of Ireland, which could not be sufficiently contained by ordinary domestic law, section 3(2) of the 1940 Act gave special powers to detain persons without trial where it was "necessary to secure the preservation of public peace and order". During the applicant's period of detention he complained to the Commission for his release and claimed damages as a consequence of his detention, which he argued was contrary to the Convention. The respondent government argued that at the time of the applicant's arrest there was the "gravest suspicion" that he was, at least, involved in IRA activities, if not an actual member of the organisation itself, and that those activities were aimed at the destruction of the rights and freedoms afforded by the Convention. The Government submitted that a public emergency existed such that they were entitled to derogate from the ordinary domestic law and introduce emergency legislation to deal with the situation, via the 1940 Act.

Findings of the court. The court said that the words "other public emergency threatening the life of a nation" refer to "an exceptional situation of crisis or emergency which affects the whole population and constitutes a threat to the organised life of the community of which the State is composed".[34] Whether such an emergency situation actually existed at the time, the court considered the overall situation including:

a) The means by which the IRA sought to achieve its aims, *i.e.* by unlawful violence and destruction;
b) The IRA's activities involved both the Republic of Ireland and Northern Ireland, thus endangering relations between both sides; and
c) The increase in terrorism during the period from 1956 to 1957.[35]

The court held that as a result of the above factors the Irish Government were justified in considering that a public emergency existed and to legitimately derogate from its normal obligations under the Convention. The next question was whether the action taken by the Government, *i.e.* the introduction of the 1940 Act, was necessary under the circumstances or was it, as the applicant argued, disproportionate such that the measures taken outweighed the seriousness of the situation. In other words, were the legal provisions already in place sufficient enough to control the illegal endeavours of the IRA? The court having examined the difficulties arising out of the particular circumstances concluded that the action taken by the authorities did not overstep the line when the Irish Government introduced the 1940 Act. Further, all such detainees under the 1940 Act were afforded sufficient protection to prevent any arbitrariness by the authorities. For example,

(i) The Act was continually reviewed and could be repealed when no longer appropriate;
(ii) A Detention Commission was set up to hear appeals for release from detainees; and
(iii) Any detainee who gave a written assurance to the Government that in the future he would desist from any involvement in unlawful terrorist activities would be set free.[36]

Accordingly, in view of the existing safeguards and prevailing circumstances, the court decided that the government's action was not disproportionate to the requirements necessitated by the gravity of the situation. Therefore, since the Irish Government had properly informed the Secretary-General of the Council of Europe of its intention to derogate under Article 15(3), they were not in violation of their obligations under the Convention.

Article 16

2–049 Nothing in Articles 10, 11 and 14 shall be regarded as preventing the High Contracting Parties from imposing restrictions on the political activity of aliens.

Article 17

2–050 Nothing in this Convention may be interpreted as implying for any state, group or person any right to engage in any activity or perform any act aimed at the destruction of any of the rights and freedoms set forth herein or their limitation to a greater extent than is provided for in the Convention.

Article 18

2–051 The restrictions permitted under this Convention to the said rights and freedoms shall not be applied for any purpose other than those for which they have been prescribed.

Articles 16 to 18 put certain limitations on those parties wishing to apply the Convention, for whatever purposes. For instance, Article 16 relieves a Member State from its duties and obligations under Article 10, 11 and 14, but only to the extent where the contested matters refer to the political conduct of non-nationals; this includes nationals of other Member States involved in political speeches, demonstrations and the like and consequently permits discrimination against such aliens. In its present form the width of the restrictions seem at odds with the very purpose and spirit of the Convention. In practice, Article 16 has been seldom employed, even at the initial stages, as a ground for a breach of the Convention.

Article 17 is self-protective. In *Lawless v. Ireland (No. 3)*[37] it was stated that "the general purpose of Article 17 is to prevent totalitarian groups from exploiting in their own interest the principles enunciated by the Convention".[38] In the above case the Government argued, *inter alia*, that the applicant was associated with the IRA and since this was a proscribed organisation, because its purpose was the destruction of the rights laid down in the Convention, he could not therefore claim a breach of Articles 5, 6 or 7 or indeed any of its Articles. The court said that the applicant was not using the Convention "to justify or perform acts contrary to the rights and freedoms recognised therein"[39] but has complained only of having been deprived of the guarantees expressed in Articles 5 and 6. This he was entitled to do. Therefore the use of Article 17 is restricted to those particular Articles for which the applicant is seeking to obtain justice provided the purpose was not to destroy the very essence of the Convention itself.

The purpose of Article 18 is to restrict a party, normally a state, from claiming justification for an interference when in fact the reasons given were outside the particular rights and freedoms set down in the Article in question. It is a method of controlling arbitrary intervention. For instance, a respondent who wishes to rely on one of the exceptions within Article 8(2) must prove that the particular exception applies. It has been found, in practice, that it is easier to prove the interference in question fell within one of the exceptions laid out in the Article under consideration than for the other party to demonstrate the contrary:

> "Article 18 must be applied in conjunction with, at least, one other Article . . . (and) that a violation can only arise where the right or freedom concerned is subject to restrictions permitted under this Convention; unlike the "right of security" which is guaranteed in absolute terms".[40]

Article 50: Remedies

Under Article 50 of the Convention:

> "If the court finds that a decision or a measure taken by a legal authority or any other authority of a High Contracting Party is completely or partially in conflict with the obligations arising from the . . . Convention, and if the internal law of the said Party allows only partial reparation to be made for the consequences of this decision or measure, the decision of the court shall, if necessary, afford just satisfaction to the injured party". **2–052**

Once a breach of the Convention has been established and the domestic courts only allowed a partial reparation for the violation, then the applicant is entitled to apply for compensation, generally by way of damages, under Article 50. Any application must be made in accordance with the Rules of

Court and take the form of a memorial, made, at least, one month before the date fixed for the hearing.[41]

The words "just satisfaction" generally concern the refusal of the domestic State to award the appropriate damages to the victim. The damages awarded may be for material loss, non-pecuniary damage and for legal costs and expenses, including interest but ultimately "the court has to be satisfied that the costs and expenses were actually incurred, were necessarily incurred and were also reasonable as to quantum".[42] Further, the applicant must prove that there was a casual connection between the claim and the breach.[43] Whether the court awards damages or not is based on an equitable consideration and in practice the amounts awarded may differ considerably from the applicant's claim. For instance, in *Halford v. United Kingdom*[44] the applicant claimed £119,500 for legal costs and expenses. The court determined after having recalculated the solicitors hourly rates, irrelevant costs, etc., that £25,000 plus VAT was an appropriate sum.[45] There is no right to damages and the words "if necessary" in Article 50 confirms this. Thus, even where the court determines that a breach has occurred, that by itself may be sufficient to amount to "just satisfaction" without any compensation being given for the breach.

Conclusion

2–053 After the incorporation of the ECHR into domestic law, the individual who cries out "I know my rights" is now at last able to point to those specific rights which he alleges are to be protected. However, the Human Rights Act does not render previous case law on the scope of Convention rights redundant; all relevant prior and subsequent decisions of the Court and Commission must be considered by a United Kingdom court when it is deciding a case involving a Convention issue.

It is too early to forecast to what extent domestic law (whether it be statute or common law) will change as a result of incorporation but no doubt new incompatibility issues will arise which will test the court's skills and ingenuity when deciding future cases. For instance, it is not too difficult to forecast that for some time to come the continual competing issues of privacy (Article 8) and freedom of expression (Article 10) will raise particular dilemmas in our domestic courts. Also, the real danger of existing statute law being incompatible with the Convention is a particularly worrying aspect. For example, any member of the security or intelligence services charged under section 1(1) of the Official Secrets Act 1989, which at present is a strict liability offence, may in future be acquitted if no actual or foreseeable damage is caused by the disclosure. Further, as a result of the decisions in *Murray (John) v. United Kingdom*[46] and *Condron v. U.K.*[47] there must now be a question mark over whether adverse inferences may be drawn as a result of silence during police questioning where a suspect is refused access to legal advice at the initial stages of an interview. Other examples which may be ripe for consideration include where the defendant is legally compelled to make incriminating statements as in *Saunders v. United Kingdom*[48] or the procedures for the deportation of an individual on national security grounds as in *Chahal v. United Kingdom*.[49]

It is clear that judges will have to re-educate themselves to some extent on the different "foreign" concepts which will have to be considered when reaching a decision. For instance, phrases such as "prescribed by law", "necessary in a democratic society", "margin of appreciation", etc., will all require strict judicial interpretation and analysis with the aid of previous Convention case law. Further, phrases and words such as "pressing social need", "legitimate aims" and "proportionality", although recognisable in conceptual terms by our own courts, may still create problems in clarification when one considers that the rulings on these specific words were made by judges from various countries with different legal systems and perhaps contrasting social and cultural backgrounds.

No doubt we are in for an interesting time ahead. The transitional period may emphasise the "warts-and-all" dilemmas that are already foreseeable and Parliament and the courts themselves should commence preparation for some (but it is optimistically hoped not too much) realignment work to be done to existing national laws.

Brief Outline and Germane Cases

(Article 2)

Under Article 2(1) everyone is entitled to a right to life: 2–054
Paton v. U.K. [1980]; *Cyprus v. Turkey* [1976]; *X v. Ireland* [1973]
There are four main exceptions to the right to life which are set out in Article 2(2)(a), (b) and (c), and Article 2(1) concerning the death penalty: The authorities must take all necessary positive action to safeguard the lives of its citizens.
Kelly v. U.K. [1993]; *Stewart v. U.K.* [1982]; *McCann and others v. U.K.* [1996].

(Article 3)

Under Article 3 no persons should have to submit to torture or ill treatment:

(a) Torture: 2–055
Ireland v. U.K. [1978]; *The Greek case* [1969] 12 Yearbook 1.

(b) Inhuman and degrading punishment\corporal punishment:
Tyrer v. U.K. [91992]; *Costello-Roberts v. U.K.* [1993]; *Campbell and Cozans v. U.K.* [1982].

(c) Inhuman and degrading treatment:
Tomasi v. France [1992]; *Soering v. U.K.* [1989]; *Klass v. Germany* [1993].

(d) Expulsion of asylum seekers may amount to a breach of Article 3:
Cruz Aras v. Sweden [1991]; *Vilarajah v. U.K.* [1987]; *Rhmet Khan v. U.K.* [1995]; *Soering v. U.K.* [1989]; *D. v. U.K.* [1996]; *Chahal v. U.K.* [1995].

(Article 5)

2–056 Article 5(1)(a)–(f) deals with the circumstances whereby a person may be lawfully arrested or detained. Under Article 5(1)(a) in order for there to be a lawful detention there must be a causal link between the detention and the court conviction:
Weeks v. U.K. [1987]; *Monnell and Morris v. U.K.* [1987].
Under 5(1)(b) there may only be a lawful arrest or detention where there was a failure to fulfil an existing legal obligation.
Engel v. Netherlands [1976]; *McVeigh, O'Neill and Evans v. U.K.* [1981].
Under 5(1)(c) "reasonable suspicion" of having committed an offence is a precondition before arrest or detention is lawful.
Fox, Campbell and Hartley v. U.K. [1990]; *Murray (M) v. U.K.* [1994].
Under 5(1)(e) certain persons including those who are of unsound mind, or drug addicts, or carry diseases which may infect others may be lawfully arrested or detained. For the legal requirements of hospitalisation where appropriate, see:
Winterwerp v. Netherlands [1979]; *Ashingdane v. U.K.* [1985].
Under 5(1)(f) unauthorised persons entering a country or persons being expelled from a country may be lawfully arrested or detained.
Bozano v. France [1987]; *Chahal v. U.K.* [1995].
Article 5(2)–(4) deals with a person's rights after arrest or whilst in detention. Under 5(2) the suspect must be promptly made aware of the reasons for his arrest:
Fox, Campbell and Hartley v. U.K. [1989].
Under 5(3), First Limb: The suspect is entitled to a prompt judicial hearing.
Brogan v. U.K. [1989]; *Brannigan and McBride v. U.K.* [1994].
Under 5(3), Second Limb: The accused is entitled to a trial within a reasonable time or be released pending trial:
Neumeister v. Austria [1968]; *Muller v. France* [1997]; *Letellier v. France* [1991]; *Mattznetter v. Austria* [1969]; *Scott v. Spain* [1996].
Under 5(4) the suspect is entitled to question the validity of his arrest or detention:
Winterwerp v. Netherlands [1979]; *Weeks v. U.K.* [1987]; *Thynne, Wilson and Gunnell v. U.K.* [1986]; *Hussain v. U.K.* [1996]; *Singh v. U.K.* [1996]; *Herczegfalvy v. Austria* [1993].
Under 5(5) a person is entitled to compensation for wrongful arrest or detention:

Murray v. U.K. [1995]; *Brogan and others v. U.K.* [1989].

(ARTICLE 6)

Under Article 6 every person has the right to a fair hearing in both civil proceedings and criminal offences. What is a criminal charge? See: **2–057**
Engel v. The Netherlands (No. 1) [1976]; *Campbell and Fell v. U.K.* [1985]; *Putz v. Austria* [1996].
A fair hearing will include the following:

(a) Balanced procedures ("quality of arms"):
Dombo Beheer B.V. v. The Netherlands [1994]; *Neumeister v. Austria* [1979]; *Borgers v. Belgium* [1993].

(b) Trial commencing within a reasonable time:
Stogmuller v. Austria [1979]; *Zimmermann and Steiner v. Switzerland* [1984]; *Buchholz v. Germany* [1981].

(c) An impartial and independent tribunal:
DeCubber v. Belgium [1985].

(d) The right of access to a court:
Golder v. U.K. [1979]; *Ashingdane v. U.K.* [1985]; *Keegan v. Ireland* [1994]; *Airey v. Ireland* [1979].

(e) The presumption of innocence:
Murray (John) v. U.K [1996]; *Funke v. France* [1993]; *Saunders v. U.K.* [1996].

(f) Being informed of the charges against him:
Colozza v. Italy [1985].

(g) The right to be present and to be legally represented:
Monnell and Morris v. U.K. [1987]; *Murray (John) v. U.K.* [1996]; *Kamasinki v. Austria* [1989].

(h) The right to examine witnesses:
X v. U.K. [1993].

(ARTICLE 7)

Under Article 7 a person is not entitled to be tried for a criminal offence which did not exist at the time the act was committed. The law regarding any offence must be sufficiently clear and cannot be applied retrospectively. One of the problems under this Article is distinguishing between the "development" of existing law and adapting it to new situations, which would probably not contravene the Convention; and "new law" which hitherto was not in force when the act was carried out: **2–058**
SW v. U.K. [1995]; *R. v. R* [1991].

(Article 8)

2–059 Article 8 concerns a person's right to respect for his (i) private life; (ii) family life; (iii) home; and (iv) correspondence.

(i) Private life:
X and Y v. The Netherlands [1986] *X v. U.K.* [1979–80]; *Dudgeon v. U.K.* [1982].

(ii) Family life:
Marckx v. Belgium [1979–80]; *Johnston v. Ireland* [1987]; *Abdulaziz, Cabales and Balkandali v. U.K.* [1985].

(iii) Home:
Buckley v. U.K. [1995]; *Gillow v. U.K.* [1990]; *Niemietz v. Germany* [1993]; *Leander v. Sweden* [1987]; *Gaskin v. U.K.* [1990].

(iv) Correspondence.
Golder v. U.K. [1979–80]; *Campbell v. U.K.* [1993]; *Silver v. U.K.* [1983].

Before any interference by the national authorities can be deemed justified, the following hurdles will have to be overcome (similar requirements occur in Articles 9, 10 and 11):

(a) Any interference must be in accordance with the law:
Klass v. Germany [1979]; *Malone v. U.K.* [1985]; *Halford v. U.K.* [1997]; *The Sunday Times v. U.K.* [1979–80].

(b) The State must be pursuing a legitimate aim, *e.g.* national security, prevention of disorder or crime, protection of health or morals, etc. (see Article 8(2)):

(c) The interference must be necessary in a democratic society:
Leander v. Sweden [1987]; *Gillow v. U.K.* [1986]; *Hewitt and Harman v. U.K.* [1992]; *The Sunday Times v. U.K.* [1979–80]; *Chappell v. U.K.* [1990]; *Malone v. U.K.* [1985].

(Article 10)

2–060 The right to freedom of expression involves the disclosure and receiving of information and ideas, but this freedom is not unrestrained. It is restricted via the legitimate aims set out in the exhaustive list in 10(2). As a result, any interference by the national authorities may be justified if it comes within one of the exceptions and is (i) prescribed by law and (ii) necessary in a democratic society.

(i) Prescribed by law:

The Sunday Times v. U.K. [1979]; *Handyside v. U.K.* [1979]; *Gay News Ltd and Lemon v. U.K.* [1983]. See also Article 8.

(ii) Necessary in a democratic society:
The Sunday Times v. U.K. [1979]; *Handyside v. U.K.* [1979]; *De Haes and Gijsels v. Belgium* [1998]; *Lingens v. Austria* [1986]; *Otto-Preminger Institute v. Austria* [1995]. See also Article 8.

Legitimate aims examples:
Handyside v. U.K. [1979] (for the protection of morals); *The Sunday Times v. U.K.* [1979] (for maintaining the authority and impartiality of the judiciary); *Gay News Ltd and Lemon v. U.K.* [1983] (for the protection of the rights of others); *Lingens v. Austria* [1986], *Tolstoy Miloslavsky v. U.K.* [1995]; and *Goodwin v. U.K.* [1996] (for the protection of the reputation or rights of others); *Observer and Guardian v. U.K.* [1992] (in the interests of national security and for maintaining the authority of the judiciary).
The interference itself must not be disproportionate to the legitimate aim pursued:
Lingens v. Austria [1986]; *Jersild v. Denmark* [1994]; *Oberschlick v. Austria* [1998]; *Tolstoy Miloslavsky v. U.K.* [1995]; *Observer and Guardian v. U.K.* [1992].

(ARTICLE 15)

The power to derogate under Article 15 should only be used in exceptional **2–061**
circumstances and only then when all normal legal avenues have been tried and failed. Above all it must be applied sparingly. Even then the court may conclude that measures taken by the national authorities were disproportionate or too extreme to combat the particular crisis which existed at that time. In order for the derogation to be justified during a public emergency, the special steps taken by the State to alleviate the problem must be shown to have been necessary in the circumstances because (i) the situation was life threatening, nationally; (ii) the measures used were not excessive and were compatible with the prevailing state of affairs; and (iii) were not contrary to existing international law obligations:
Brogan v. U.K. [1988]; *Lawless v. Ireland* [1961]; *Brannigan and McBride v. U.K.* [1993]; *Ireland v. U.K.* [1978].

Endnotes

[1] See discussion of the Human Rights Act 1998 below at para. 2–032A.
[2] With the obvious exception of the case of *Ireland v. United Kingdom* (A/25): 18/1/1978, below.
[3] Such as those from prisoners to the Home Secretary; see *Golder v. United Kingdom* [1971] 14 Y.B. E.C.H.R. 416.
[4] See *Donnelly v. United Kingdom* [1973] 16 Y.B. E.C.H.R. 212.
[5] Such as the International Covenant on Civil and Political Rights (Art. 27(1)).
[6] See *Akkoc v. Turkey* [2000] App. Nos. 22947/93 and 22948/93.
[7] [1993] 1 All E.R. 1011.
[8] See *Attorney General v. Blake* [1996] 3 All E.R. 903; *R. v. Advertising Standards Authority, ex parte Vernons Organisation* [1993] 2 All E.R. 202.
[9] Other international treaties cover such rights, notably the European Social Charter, but do not have direct enforceability through a judicial process.
[10] Came into force on October 2, 2000.
[11] MacPherson Report, Cm.4262 see further de Than and Shorts, "Double Jeopardy, Double Trouble", *Journal of Criminal Law December* 2000, p.000.
[12] For a detailed discussion of the issues involved in the Bill of Rights debate, see Zander, *A Bill of Rights?* (4th ed., 1997).
[13] "Bill of Rights: a Discussion Paper", reprinted in *The Protection of Human Rights by Law in Northern Ireland*, Cmnd 7009.
[14] (2nd ed.), pp. 398–399.
[15] Most notably in 1976–7, 1979–81, 1985, 1987 and 1996; see Zander, *A Bill of Rights?* (4th ed., 1997), Chap. 1.
[16] White Paper, para. 2.6.
[17] Official Report, HL, Vol. 583, 784 (November 24, 1997).
[18] See Weekly *Hansard* Issue no. 1794, col. 534 *et seq.* (June 29–July 3, 1998).
[19] *ibid. per* Mr Jack Straw, the then Home Secretary, at cols 538 and 539).
[20] Pleming, "Assessing the Act: a firm foundation or a false start" [2000] E.H.R.L.R. 6 at 561.
[21] So, even though the "margin of appreciation" doctrine has no place in domestic law, its function may be preserved by judges, with the result that state actions are readily defended if interests such as national security are claimed to be at risk if a right should be upheld. Undue deference to the legislature and executive is possible.
[22] *The Lawyer*, November 4, 1997, p. 9.
[23] Lord Steyn, "The new legal landscape" [2000] E.H.R.L.R. 6 at 553.
[23A] [200] W.L. 774994.
[24] "Human Rights—Where we are now": a speech given by Lord Hope of Craighead at the JUSTICE annual lecture on October 3, 2000, the day after the Human Rights Act came into force in England.
[25] [1979] 2 E.H.R.R. 245 at para. 61.
[25A] [2001] U.K.H.L. 25, May 17, 2001.
[25B] [1994] 18 E.H.R.R. 213.
[25C] [1985] 8 E.H.R.R. 235.
[25D] unreported, CA (Criminal Division), May 24, 2001.
[25E] [1996] 8 A.C. 815.
[25F] [1997] 23 E.H.R.R. 313.
[25G] [2000] 2 A.C. 326.
[25H] [2001] 1 Cr. App. R. 205.
[25I] unreported, HL July 5, 2001; *The Times*, July 6, 2001.
[26] *i.e.* Arts. 2–18 of the Convention.
[26A] [1980] 3 E.H.R.R. 408.
[26B] [1993] 8 E.H.R.R. C.D. 20.
[26C] [1992] 17 E.H.R.R. 238.
[26D] [1995] 21 E.H.R.R. 363.
[26E] [1993] 17 E.H.R.R. 397.
[26F] [1976] 1 E.H.R.R. 737.
[27] [1997] 2 All E.R. 119.
[28] [1991] 13 E.H.R.R. 622.
[29] See Feldman, Ch. 11 for detailed consideration of the ECHR in relation to sexuality.

[30] *Silver v. U.K.* [1983] 5 E.H.R.R. 347.
[31] 1 E.H.R.R. 252.
[32] [1985] 7 E.H.R.R. 471.
[33] [1961] 1 E.H.R.R. 15.
[34] para. 28.
[35] *ibid.*
[36] para. 37.
[37] [1961] 1 E.H.R.R. 15 at para. 6.
[38] *ibid.* at para. 6.
[39] *ibid.* at paras 6 and 7.
[40] *Kamma v. The Netherlands* [1975] 18 Yearbook 300 at 316, Resolution of the Committee of Ministers.
[41] See rule 52(1) of Rules of Court B and see *Ferrantelli and Santangelo v. Italy*[1996] 23 E.H.R.R. 288 at para. 65.
[42] See *Eckle v. Germany* [1991] 13 E.H.R.R. 556 at para. 25.
[43] *ibid.* at para. 19.
[44] [1997] 24 E.H.R.R. 524.
[45] *ibid.* at paras 80–82.
[46] [1996] 22 E.H.R.R. 29.
[47] [1996] 23 E.H.R.R. 313.
[48] [1996] 23 E.H.R.R. 413.

Chapter 3

POLICE POWERS AND INDIVIDUAL FREEDOM

Introduction

Until the nineteenth century, law and order was largely a local matter. Crime was widely regarded to be out of control, and this situation was not helped by the lack of any systems of co-operation between neighbouring authorities or co-ordination of resources. Even as specialised and, eventually, professional police forces came into existence, the powers and duties of constables came from the common law and were, with few exceptions, no greater than the powers and duties which applied to ordinary citizens; every citizen had, and indeed continues to have, a duty to maintain the peace and a power of arrest. Thus, while the police were little more than private citizens grouped together for a common purpose and sometimes paid for doing so, there was no perceived need to give them any greater protection than the ordinary citizen would have in the same situation. 3–001

However, in the nineteenth century a series of statutes created new full-time professional police forces with a management and supervision structure, first in London and then in each municipal area of England and Wales, and finally in rural areas. As professionalism began, so did the creation of statutory offences of assaulting or obstructing the police. The police gained in strength, image, efficiency and powers, and it was recognised that the new forces required official support. Now that crime could realistically be prevented or detected, the peace maintained and offenders apprehended, the balance between individual freedom and public interest had changed; the scales tipped towards the furtherance of the public interest.

Subject to arrest, at common law a citizen is ordinarily under no legal positive duty or obligation to assist the police. Under the common law an individual is perfectly entitled to refuse to answer questions put to him by the police.[1] Nor may a police officer require a passer-by to stop and be detained without that person's consent. In addition, should a police officer physically prevent a person from going about his business, that officer may be liable to an action for assault.[2] But, it should be recognised that society requires the freedom of the individual to be balanced against the public interest in the maintenance of peace, the prevention and detection of crime and the apprehension of offenders. A police officer's tasks in pursuit of such public interests may be somewhat hazardous and so individual freedom is limited in particular circumstances in order to support and safeguard the police. As a result, statutory interventions have created various offences of confrontation against the police.

3–002 Historically, the creation of statutory criminal offences intended to support and enable the police function is tied to developments in the nature and form of the police themselves as an institution. For instance, section 12 of the Prevention of Crimes Act 1871 (as amended by section 2 of the Prevention of Crimes Amendment Act 1885) and section 38 of the Offences Against the Person Act 1861, created offences against the police and other law enforcers which are the ancestors of those to be discussed in this chapter. A consolidation of these offences took place in section 51 of the Police Act 1964; arguably this was a symbolic reorganisation of existing offences in order to increase their visibility to the police themselves. While police structure, management and accountability were re-examined and reorganised in the 1964 Act, the offences of assaulting or obstructing a constable in the execution of his duty were simply restated. Section 89(1) of the Police Act 1996 again restates these existing offences:

> "Any person who assaults [(resists or wilfully obstructs) section 89(2)] a constable in the execution of his duty, or a person assisting a constable in the execution of his duty, shall be guilty of an offence . . ."

I ASSAULT AND OBSTRUCTION OF A POLICE CONSTABLE

3–003 The offences under section 89 of the Police Act 1996 will be examined separately, although the contentious issue of when and in what circumstances a constable is acting in the execution of his duty is a common element of all three offences (assault, resisting or obstruction) and thus merits special attention. As with all criminal offences, it is possible to break this offence down into its constituent elements of definition.

A. Assaulting A Police Officer in the Execution of his Duty

The *actus reus* of the offence under section 89(1) requires proof of three elements: (i) an assault (ii) upon a constable (iii) in the execution of his duty.

(i) Assault

3–004 Assault here has its general meaning in English criminal law, and includes both common assault and common battery. Thus the offence may be committed either by causing a constable to apprehend the application of immediate unlawful physical violence from the defendant's words or actions,[3] or by causing the application of unlawful physical force to a constable, whether directly or indirectly.[4] If a greater degree of harm is caused by the defendant's actions, then a charge of an aggravated assault under the Offences Against the Person Act 1861 may be more appropriate.

(ii) Constable

"Constable" refers to a person holding the office of constable, and so includes all police ranks and some other officials such as prison officers.[5] Any person assisting a constable in the execution of his duties is given the same protection. **3–005**

(iii) In the execution of his duty

This element, common to all three of the offences under discussion, has been the source of considerable problems and debate. A police officer's duties are wide, varied and open to interpretation and in particular it is sometimes difficult to distinguish between the powers and duties of the police. It can be argued that leading cases have failed to provide a consistent rule on this issue and that the line between powers and duties has become somewhat indistinct. Generally speaking, if the constable's conduct is lawful and can be considered to fall within his powers in relation to the prevention and detection of crime and apprehension of offenders, then he is considered to be executing his duty. If, however, the constable for any reason exceeds his statutory or common law powers then he will no longer be considered to be acting in the execution of his duty for present purposes, *e.g.* physically detaining someone to ask questions without arresting that person, regardless of the fact that he may be "on duty" at the relevant time and may be performing tasks commonly carried out by the police.[6] Merely because a constable is on duty does not necessarily mean that he is "in the execution of his duty". Thus, in *Coffin v. Smith*,[7] the court said that . . . If the above case is correct, then a constable standing outside a store, blocking a person's entrance to that store could be considered to be acting in the execution of his duty, which would seem rather a wide interpretation of the words "execution of his duty". **3–006**

R. v. Waterfield[8] is considered to be a leading case on this issue: **3–007**

Facts. A constable, having been informed that a particular car had been involved in a serious offence and having received instructions from a superior officer, tried to prevent L, the owner of the car, from removing it from its parking space on a road (he was not arrested or charged at this stage). L assaulted the constable by driving the car at him in the course of removing it. L was later charged with assaulting a constable in the execution of his duty.

Decision. The court held that the constable had no entitlement to prevent the removal of the car in the circumstances and thus could not be considered to be executing his duty at the moment of the assault against him. This decision has been questioned on its facts[9] but the test formulated by Ashworth J. in *Waterfield* has been followed in many cases. Ashworth J. stated at page 170:

> "In the judgement of this court it would be difficult, and in the present case it is unnecessary, to reduce within specific limits the general terms in which the duties of police constables have been expressed. In most cases, it is probably more convenient to consider what the police constable was actually doing and in particular whether such conduct was prima facie an unlawful interference with a person's liberty or property. If so, it is then relevant to consider (a) whether such conduct falls within the general scope of any duty imposed by statute or recognised by common law, and (b) whether such conduct, albeit within the general scope of such a duty, involved an unjustifiable use of powers associated with that duty".

3–008 This test is easier to evaluate if split into two limbs:

(a) The first limb of the Ashworth test requires the court to outline (but not to define precisely) a constable's duty. This was attempted in *Coffin v. Smith*,[10] where the duties were considered to include detecting crime, bringing offenders to justice, keeping the peace and preventing crime. It is unusual for the courts to examine a constable's duty in isolation from his powers, because any prima facie infringement of a person's liberty or property must involve the exercise of some purported power. A duty may be defined as that which a person is under a general obligation or responsibility to do as part of his role as a police officer, imposed upon him by law and the police authorities. A power may be defined as that which a person may do, granted to him by law as a police officer to use at his discretion when the circumstances require, *e.g.* arrest. A police officer has many general duties, *i.e.* things which he must do, but also many specific powers, *i.e.* things which he may do in the furtherance of his role. This definitional difference is crucial yet often missed. It is rare for a case to fail the first limb of the Ashworth test, but this did happen in *Hoffman v. Thomas*,[11] where the court decided that the constable's act of stopping traffic for the purposes of a census did not fall within his general duties since his power at common law to regulate traffic derives only from his duty to protect life and property, neither of which were under threat. This case would also in fact have failed the second limb of the Ashworth test, but statute has superseded this particular problem.[12]

Most cases which involve only an analysis of a constable's duties and not of his powers pose few problems to the courts. The courts would consider that an on-duty constable was acting in the execution of his duty in most circumstances, even if not purporting to use any powers; for example, simply walking the beat is executing a duty. Many situations where the constable is not executing his duty are clear-cut, for example, stopping a passer-by for no reason whatsoever. It is the purported exercise of police powers which has caused the greatest difficulty. In two cases, a constable's act was regarded as falling within his duties, but he was found to have no power to perform that act.[13] In *Rice v. Connolly*,[14] it was decided that while a constable has a duty to ask questions of a suspect, he has no power to require answers. In *Waterfield* itself, it was stated that a constable has a duty to preserve evidence for the court, but no power to detain a car for this reason alone.

(b) The second limb of the Ashworth test requires the court to decide whether there was an excessive use of power associated with the performance of duty. The police can only exercise their powers if they are acting within their duties, because the police have no powers which do not derive from their duties and exist to enable the performance of those duties. Circumstances where the police may take themselves outside the execution of their duty by exceeding their powers include the entry of premises, searches, and, detention and arrest. In both the cases of *McLorie v. Oxford*,[15] and *D'Souza v. DPP*,[16] it was decided that the police had surpassed their powers of entry, and so taken themselves outside the execution of their duty.

It is generally the case that a police constable is not acting in the execution of his duty by, for instance, physically putting a hand on an individual. It was stated in *Ludlow v. Burgess*,[17] "the detention of a man against his will without arresting him was an unlawful act and a serious interference with the citizen's liberty".[18]

The case of *Lodwick v. Saunders*[19] illustrates the above difficulty:

Facts. A lorry driver was stopped by the police for failing to display an excise licence, failing to have a tachograph installed and not having any brake lights. When asked by the police whether he owned the vehicle he replied: "maybe, maybe not, I am in a hurry", then started the engine intending to drive away. The constable then entered the cab and grabbed the ignition key. As he did so, the driver pushed the constable's hand against the wheel, causing him to drop the key. The driver was arrested for assaulting a constable in the execution of his duty. **3–009**

Decision. It was held by the court that under section 159 Road Traffic Act 1972,[20] a driver is obliged to stop when required to do so by the police, and to cause his vehicle to remain at rest for a reasonable period. However, this section does not empower the police to do any act, without reasonable excuse, which interferes with a person's liberty and prevents him from driving off. So, if the driver refuses to answer questions, this in itself is not an arrestable offence and so the police constable has no right to prevent the vehicle from moving off; and if he does so, he is acting outside his duty as a police constable. Nevertheless, a vehicle must remain static until the police have made all proper inquiries under the law, such as asking for a driver's licence and insurance details. In addition, if the police reasonably suspect, as was the case here, that the vehicle has been stolen then they are entitled to prevent the vehicle from being driven away. Thus the constable was acting in the execution of his duty when he grabbed the keys in order to detain the vehicle.[21]

However, whether physical contact is considered to be outside the realms of a police constable's authority will depend on the particular circumstances.

For instance, in *Donnelly v. Jackman*[22]:

3–010

Facts. A police officer approached the defendant in the street to make inquiries about a particular offence the latter may have committed. The defendant refused to answer any questions and walked away. The officer repeatedly asked the appellant to stop, but without success. He then tapped the defendant on the shoulder in order to stop and speak to him. The defendant then turned around and struck the officer. He was convicted of assault.

Decision. The justices treated the "touching" as something so minimal and trivial that the officer was still acting within the scope of his duties, even though the officer had persistently harassed the individual by repeatedly requesting him to stop and physically touched him on two separate occasions.

Accordingly, minimal touching may be permitted to attract a suspect's attention without arrest and still remain in an officer's duty. Anything which goes beyond that would probably constitute an unlawful interference upon the freedom of the individual. However, in the recent case of *Mepstead v. DPP*[23]:

3–011 **Facts**. A police officer took hold of the defendant's arm, not to detain him or to arrest him, but just in order to draw his attention more strongly to what was being said to him and to calm him down. The defendant was abusive and violent and was arrested and convicted for assault on a constable in the execution of his duty. He contended on appeal that when he assaulted the officer, the latter was no longer acting in the execution of his duty but was in fact assaulting (battering) the appellant.

Decision. The Divisional Court followed *Collins v. Wilcock*[24] and found that the police officer's actions were within generally acceptable standards of conduct since the physical contact continued for no longer than was reasonably necessary for legitimate purposes; thus the police officer was acting in the execution of his duty and the defendant's conviction for assault occasioning actual bodily harm upon a constable was upheld.

At what point in time is the constable's conduct to be judged?

3–012 The point in time at which the court must decide whether the constable was acting in the execution of his duty is precisely when the constable commits the act or performs the conduct in question.[25] In *Lamb*,[26] although the constable entered premises as a trespasser, because he reasonably apprehended a breach of the peace, his presence was immediately justified by his common law powers to prevent a breach of the peace, and he was therefore no longer a trespasser. This case shows that the courts will determine the legality of a constable's act at the precise moment when he commits the act, and not by reference to what occurred before or afterwards.[27] If not a trespasser, and if told to leave, the police constable is entitled to satisfy himself that the person asking him to vacate the premises has the authority to do so. In *Jones and Jones v. Lloyd*,[28] it was held that a guest at a party does have the authority to invite the police into the owner's house, in order to confirm the guest's innocence. If the offence is based upon assault or battery, then intention or subjective recklessness are required; that is, it must be proved either that the defendant intended to cause the unlawful application of force to the victim, or that the defendant foresaw the risk that such force would be so applied.

The remaining elements of the offence under section 89(1) are of strict liability. Thus, it will be no answer to a charge of assaulting a constable in the execution of his duty, that the defendant did not know that the victim was a constable; nor will it assist the defendant if he claims that he did not know that the constable was acting in the execution of his duty. Even if the defendant has reasonable grounds for his belief, this will not aid his defence.

This was held in *Forbes*[29] and is the explanation of *McBride v. Turnock*[30]:

Facts. The defendant aimed a blow at X, who was not a constable, but missed and struck the victim, a constable. He was found guilty of assaulting a constable in the execution of his duty, even though he neither intended to hit the constable nor saw the risk of doing so.

Decision. The only *mens rea* for the offence is that of assault, which the defendant did have, and it made no difference in law that the wrong victim was struck. This situation should be contrasted with that concerning the offence of obstruction under section 89(2), which is a *mens rea offence*, not one of strict liability.

There are, however, some circumstances in which the defendant's lack of knowledge that the victim is a constable may be relevant in terms of defence to a charge under section 89(1); this is examined below.

Defences

The usual general defences will, of course, apply to section 89(1). Thus if the defendant is acting in self defence, defence of another, or prevention of crime by repelling an unlawful attack by the constable, he will be able to plead self defence. However, particular problems have arisen in relation to mistaken beliefs held by the defendant; the legal situation is both complex and lacking in case authority in some areas. There are many different types of belief which a defendant may possess at the time of assaulting a constable, but only a few such beliefs will enable him to escape liability. **3–013**

Since section 89(1) requires proof of an assault, a defendant could raise the defence of self defence or prevention of crime as with any other assault offence. If a constable used unlawful or excessive force against the defendant, then such a defence would be available, but would be unnecessary if only section 89(1) were charged since the constable's act would in any event take him outside "the execution of his duty"; a constable has no power to assault or to use excessive force.

Example 1: Bill, while being arrested, is hit by the constable restraining him. Bill pushes the constable away, knowing that he is a constable. Here, the constable is using excessive force and so is not acting in the execution of his duty; thus Bill cannot be convicted of section 89(1). Bill could also argue that he was acting in self defence. But if the constable used only lawful force, a defendant may nevertheless claim to have had a mistaken belief in the necessity of self defence.

As stated above, if the defendant was unaware that the person he assaulted was a constable, this makes no difference to his liability.

Examples of this situation may occur if the defendant repels what he perceives to be an attack from a plain clothes constable who fails to properly identify himself; or if a defendant repels a perceived attack from a uniformed constable in a melee or dark environment, and the constable is unable to identify himself or the defendant to properly observe the constable's uniform. In these circumstances, there is no mistake as to the constable's status because the defendant's mind was not focused upon that fact at all. It is irrelevant that the constable is in fact a constable because in deciding if an assault occurred, the constable's status is not material to the defendant's state of mind. But in such situations, the usual rules of mistaken belief in the necessity of self defence will apply.

Example 2: Jack turns a corner and sees a struggle during which one person, Nick, is restraining another, Karl. Jack, believing that Karl is being attacked, pulls Nick away so that Karl can escape.

Jack, if charged with section 89(1), could argue a defence based on his mistaken belief that he was acting in defence of another.

The standard principles of mistaken belief in the necessity of self defence or the prevention of crime, as stated in the leading case of *Williams (Gladstone)*[31] (below), were applied in *Blackburn v. Bowering*[32] to a charge of assaulting an officer of the court in the execution of his duty. The Court of Appeal likened this offence to assaulting a constable in the execution of his duty. Therefore, a defendant may raise mistaken belief in the necessity of self defence to a charge under section 89(1). The test which was laid down in *Williams (Gladstone)* is a mixture of a subjective and objective test, and may be summarised as follows: looking at the facts as the defendant believed them to be (subjective), did the defendant use reasonable force to repel an unjustified attack (objective)?

3–014 In *Williams (Gladstone)*[33]:

Facts. The defendant witnessed part of a struggle between X and a youth, during which X knocked the youth down. X told the defendant that he was a police officer and that he was arresting the youth for a street robbery. The defendant, suspicious, asked to see X's warrant card; X did not have one since he was not in fact a police officer. In the ensuing fight, the defendant punched X in the face; he was charged with assault occasioning actual bodily harm contrary to section 47 of the Offences Against the Person Act 1861. His defence was that he honestly believed that X was assaulting the youth, and so the defendant was acting in self defence or prevention of crime.

Unknown to the defendant, X had witnessed the youth committing the street robbery and was attempting a citizen's arrest; thus X was acting lawfully. The defendant was convicted and appealed on the ground that the jury had been misdirected when the judge told them to assess whether the defendant was acting in defence of another by looking at whether he had an honest belief based on reasonable grounds that reasonable force was necessary in the circumstances.

Decision. Appeal allowed. It was held that, if the defendant may have been acting under a mistake of fact, then he was entitled to be judged on the facts as he believed them to be, whether or not his belief was reasonable. Thus an honest belief that he was acting in the defence of another is sufficient to acquit the defendant.

The reasonableness of the defendant's mistaken belief is relevant only as to whether in fact he did see the situation as he claimed.[34] But it must be remembered that the defence of mistaken belief must relate specifically to the *mens rea* for the assault; the mistaken belief must cause the defendant to lack *mens rea*.

If a plain clothes officer has identified himself, but is not believed[35] then **3–015** the problem is more complex. The mistake in that situation is not a mistake as to the necessity of self defence, but a mistaken belief that the constable was not a constable. Can the normal rules of mistake in the need for self defence, found in the case of *Williams (Gladstone)*,[36] be applied to such a mistake? The difficulty lies partly in whether the status of a constable is a question of fact or of law. If it is a question of fact then the mistake may form a defence; following the authority of *Morgan*,[37] a mistake as to an element of the *actus reus* of the offence which results in the defendant lacking *mens rea* for the offence will be a defence as long as it is honest; it does not have to be a reasonable mistake. The case of *Ostler v. Elliott*[38] seemed to treat the status of the constable as a question of fact. But if it is a question of law then more questions need to be asked. A mistake of civil law may be a defence in this manner, but not a mistake as to the criminal law.[39] So, if a constable's status is a question of civil law, mistake as to this may be a defence; but if the status is a question of criminal law, then it cannot.

A further complication is that the constable's status is an issue of strict liability; since no *mens rea* is required, not even the low standard of "knowledge", then according to the authority of *Prince*,[40] not even an honest and reasonable mistake as to that status will form a defence. It is submitted that this is the best position; regardless of whether the constable's status or the issue of whether he is acting in the execution of his duty are questions of fact, law, or mixed fact and law, since both these elements are of strict liability, then there is no *mens rea* requirement; and thus there is no possibility that the defendant lacked *mens rea* due to a mistake about either of these two elements. It is since assault does have a *mens rea* requirement (as discussed above) that a mistaken belief in self defence/prevention of crime will form a defence; an assault must be "unlawful", and the defendant's *mens rea* as to this element of the *actus reus* will be negatived by proof that he honestly believed that he or another was under attack.

In summary, the following types of mistake will have the following results in terms of a defence:

(a) D mistakenly believes that the constable is not a constable; D has no defence.

(b) D mistakenly believes that he is repelling an unjustified attack, whether or not he knows that the other party is a constable: D has a defence if his belief is honest and, if the facts were as he believed them to be, he would have succeeded in arguing self defence/prevention of crime as a defence.

(c) D, knowing that the other is a constable, mistakenly believes that the constable is not acting in the execution of his duty because he is exceeding his powers; even if D's mistaken belief is both honest and reasonable, he will not always have a defence. In *Fennell*,[41] the court decided that the defendant, a father, might lawfully use reasonable force to free his son from an illegal police arrest; but if the arrest was shown to be lawful, then the father would have no defence regardless of whether his mistaken belief was honest and reasonable. Any mistake as to what a constable's duties or powers are would be a mistake of law, and so no defence would be available. But in *Fennell*, the mistake was as to whether the constable's actions fell within those powers/duties; this is a mistake of fact and so may form a defence if reasonable. For example, it would be a defence to claim that a defendant believed that the constable was using excessive force, but not a defence if the defendant claimed that he believed that the constable had no right to arrest him. This issue is in need of clarification by the courts or by legislation.[41A]

B. Resisting or Obstruction of a Constable in the Execution of his Duty; Section 89(2)

3–016 Resisting a constable in the execution of his duty will not be dealt with in detail here. "Resistance" does not necessarily involve an assault. An example of where it would not do so is where D, having been arrested by a constable, pulls away from the constable's grip and escapes.[42] "In the execution of his duty" has already been discussed above. The *mens rea* for resisting is intention to resist. The discussion already made as to the effect of mistake and the applicability of other defences also largely applies to this second offence. Obstruction does, however, require further elaboration since the definition of the offence is uncertain and nebulous.

(i) Obstruction

3–017 The *actus reus* of obstruction under section 89(2) is obstruction of a constable in the execution of his duty. The mens rea requirement is that the obstruction must be wilful.

In *Rice v. Connolly*[43]:

Facts. Two police officers, who were on duty in a particular neighbourhood where there had been several break-ins that same evening, noticed the defendant Rice, acting in a suspicious manner. They approached and asked him where he was going and for his name and address. He replied "Give me one reason why I should". The police repeated the question, to which the defendant replied "Rice, Convamore Road". They asked him to come with them to a police box in order to verify his statement. He refused, saying, "I am not moving . . . if you want me you will have to arrest me", which they accordingly did. He was charged with wilfully obstructing the police in the execution of their duty. He was convicted and thereafter appealed.

Decision. Lord Parker C.J. stated that the prosecution had to overcome three hurdles for the offence under section 51(3)[44] to be proved. First, that there was an obstruction of a constable. Secondly, that the constable was at the time acting in the execution of his duty and finally, that the person obstructing did so wilfully.[45] There was little doubt that the first two obstacles could be answered in the affirmative. However, with regard to the words "wilful obstruction", his Lordship interpreted these words to mean in this context, "something which is done intentionally and without lawful excuse." It was held that even though a person is under a moral or social duty to assist the police, there is no legal duty to that effect and therefore the defendant had a lawful excuse to refuse to answer questions put to him by the police constable.[46]

In *Hinchcliffe v. Sheldon*,[47] Lord Goddard defined obstruction as "making it more difficult for the police to carry out their duties".[48] There does not have to be actual physical obstruction for the police to be so hampered. Thus, in the above case, it was held to be obstruction to warn a landlord suspected of serving after-hours drinks that the police were planning to raid his public house. The same principle was enunciated in *Moore v. Green*.[49] Thus, giving warnings to others of a police presence has in some cases been held to be an obstruction. The "warning" cases have occurred in two particular situations; warning drivers of impending police speed traps, and warning landlords of public houses of impending police raids. In *Betts v. Stevens*[50] it was held to be an obstruction to warn speeding motorists of a police speed trap ahead. Whereas, in *Bastable v. Little*[51] the defendant was found not guilty in similar circumstances because the motorists he had warned had not been proved to be speeding; thus the police had not in fact been obstructed.

The court in *Moore v. Green* was not keen on the interpretation of the law taken in *Bastable v. Little*, and thought that it should be confined to its facts. But the court did draw a distinction between the following two situations: first, where the defendant made his warning in order to prevent the other person from ever committing an offence; and secondly, where the warning aimed at stopping the other person from acting in a particular way for a short period of time. Only the second of these two situations was thought to be obstruction. This decision has been criticised; see *Smith and Hogan*.[52] Most cases of obstruction do involve a physical element. A sequence of cases has revolved around the police giving orders in anticipation of a breach of the peace in public order contexts. In *Duncan v. Jones*,[53] the defendant was convicted of obstruction when he held a meeting despite police instructions to hold it elsewhere. It was held that if a constable reasonably apprehends a breach of the peace, any act which impedes him is an obstruction. In *Moss v. McLachlan*,[54] miners refused to turn back from a picket when the police tried to limit the number of strikers in the area. It was held that a senior constable could do whatever was reasonably necessary to prevent a breach of the peace. This generous donation of power to the police has been criticised because there was no proximity between the defendant's acts of refusal and the location of the feared breach of the peace.

As a matter of policy, it has been decided that a refusal to answer police questions is not an obstruction,[55] and neither is it obstruction to tell another not to answer questions.[56] Even if such a refusal is expressed in colourful language, the weight of academic opinion asserts that it should still not be an obstruction.[57] Commentators have therefore heavily criticised *Ricketts v. Cox*[58] where the "totality" of the defendant's abusive refusal to answer questions was held to be obstruction. *Ricketts v. Cox* could be justified on the basis that the abusive response obstructed the police actually asking the questions. In *Rice v. Connolly*,[59] it was stated that deliberately lying to the police or using threatening and abusive language when asked a question by them may constitute a wilful obstruction in that it makes it more difficult for the police to carry out their duties. Giving the police wrong answers will clearly be obstruction.[60]

(ii) Wilfulness

3–018 The term "wilful" is defined differently in its various legal contexts. For the purposes of section 89(2) it was traditionally defined to mean intention to actually obstruct,[61] and not just intention to do the act which does obstruct. This approach is consistent with the leading case on the definition of "wilful", *Sheppard*,[62] which pointed out that if wilful is only defined to mean intention to commit the act which does obstruct, then it adds nothing to the usual requirement that an act must be voluntary if it is to result in criminal liability. Some cases have nevertheless interpreted "wilfulness" in the context of obstruction to mean intention to commit the act, and not intention to obstruct. For example in *Hills v. Ellis*,[63] the defendant laid his hand upon a constable's arm to try to attract his attention during an arrest, and this was held to be obstruction despite the fact that the defendant thought that he would be helping the police, not obstructing them. The defendant's actions need not be "aimed at" the constable, nor need the defendant show hostility towards the police. A defendant may wilfully obstruct even if he means to be helpful (as in *Hills v. Ellis* above) as long as (i) his actions do result in a situation which in fact makes the constable's duties more difficult to perform, and (ii) he intends that his conduct should create such a situation.

An example of this can be seen in Lewis v. Cox[64]:

Facts. The defendant opened the rear door of a police van to ask his friend, who had been arrested, where he was going. The constable closed the door and warned the defendant not to repeat his act. When the defendant did open the door again he was arrested and charged with obstruction. The magistrates acquitted him on the basis that his act was not aimed at the police and he did not intend to obstruct the police. The Divisional Court allowed the Prosecution's appeal.

Decision. The defendant was guilty according to the standard definition of intention; *per* Kerr L.J., ". . . if the defendant intentionally does an act which he realises will, in fact, have the effect of obstructing the police . . ., he will in my view be guilty of having done so 'wilfully', with the necessary *mens rea*".

It is submitted that this definition of wilful is preferable to earlier ones mentioning hostility. *Lewis v. Cox* uses a more workable definition of wilfulness: a defendant must commit a deliberate act which he knew would bring about consequences which did in fact obstruct. Whether the defendant realised that the act amounted to obstruction is irrelevant. In *Rice v. Connolly*[65] the words "wilful obstruction" were interpreted to mean "something which is done intentionally and without lawful excuse."[66] Similar statements were made in *Lewis v. Cox*. This is somewhat confusing since the absence of lawful excuse is generally treated as part of the *actus reus* of an offence, whereas "wilfulness" is clearly *mens rea*.

Defences

It is a defence to section 89(2) if the defendant believed that the person he obstructed was not a constable, since this mistake will mean that his obstruction was not wilful. The case of *Forbes* does not apply to obstruction, since the offence of obstruction is not one of strict liability; the *mens rea* requirement is expressly stated in the statute. In *Ostler v. Elliot*,[67] the defendant reasonably believed that the police officers he obstructed were robbers; this belief was held to be a defence to a charge of obstruction. *Ostler* was decided before *Williams (Gladstone)*; now the defendant's belief would exculpate him if honestly held, and whether it was a reasonable belief would be irrelevant, since he would be acting to prevent crime (*Williams (Gladstone)*), and also, on the authority of *Morgan* (above) his mistake of fact would result in a lack of *mens rea* for the offence. **3–019**

Reform Proposals

In addition to criticisms made or discussed in this chapter, the recommendations of the Law Commission in "Legislating the Criminal Code Offences Against the Person and General Principles"[68] are relevant to the offence under section 89(1). Current proposals would introduce a further *mens rea* requirement into the offence of assaulting a constable in the execution of his duty: knowledge or recklessness that the victim was a police officer. This would eliminate some of the problems referred to above. The proposals would also adopt *R. v. Fennell*,[69] with the modification that the defendant's belief would be subjectively assessed. **3–020**

II. THE POLICE AND CRIMINAL EVIDENCE ACT 1984

Introduction

The Police and Criminal Evidence Act 1984 (PACE) is the result of decades of calls for police powers to be reformed and placed upon a statutory footing. The balance between the rights of the individual and **3–021** police powers was altered by the Act, which was the first attempt to place all the powers of all police forces on a statutory basis and to control the circumstances in which such powers could be exercised. In order to understand the significance of the introduction of PACE, some knowledge of the previous system of police powers and their regulation is necessary.

Just as there was no comprehensive system of police forces and their regulation until the late nineteenth century, police powers and their regulation before PACE were governed by the common law, with limited, specific statutory intervention; many such statutes applied only to the larger cities and to situations involving the commission of particular offences. Some police forces had far greater powers than others. This interplay of case-led common law and issue-specific statute gave rise to a patchwork of powers containing confusion, uncertainty and contradiction. Parliament had never taken the opportunity to consider all police powers and to develop a single body of rules to govern the exercise of such powers.

The pressure towards reform which resulted in PACE came from a variety of sources. The police and judiciary called for the extension of police powers and a corresponding limitation of existing civil liberties. It had become a major source of frustration that vital police powers such as those of arrest, stop and search, entry of premises and seizure of property had their roots in the nebulous common law and so had no firm definition. Without such definitions, the precise extent of a power is hard to predict yet gives rise to a risk of a civil action against the police if it is exceeded. Clear, comprehensive definitions are of advantage not only to the police but also to suspects, defendants and the court system. In contrast, notorious miscarriages of justice involving the abuse of police power gave rise to calls for the introduction of statutory safeguards to prevent the reoccurrence of such abuses. It was considered important that such safeguards should take the form of rules with the threat of sanctions for their breach. It was one such miscarriage of justice, the *Confait* case,[70] and the subsequent report to the House of Commons in 1977, which was the immediate trigger for the establishment of the Royal Commission on Criminal Procedure.

3–022 In February 1978 the above concerns were addressed by the establishment of the Royal Commission on Criminal Procedure, which was set up to examine the whole of the criminal process, from pre-trial investigation to prosecution. In so doing the Commission were asked to give full attention to the "interests of the community in bringing offenders to justice and to the rights and liberties of persons accused or suspected of crime",[71] and to make recommendations on "the powers and duties of the police in respect of the investigation of criminal offences and the rights and duties of suspect and accused persons, including the means by which they are secured".[72] The overall purpose of the Commission was to lay the ground for police powers to be put on a statutory footing. The police lobbied the Commission extensively for the introduction of nine new powers and the clarification of the circumstances in which existing powers could be exercised. The police demands were largely accepted by the Commission, leading to criticisms that the balance of the Report had swayed away from individual rights. As a result of the Commission's Report, a Police and Criminal Evidence Bill was drafted; this first Bill was dropped due to the calling of a General Election in May 1983, but it had already received fierce criticism; several of the proposed police powers went far beyond those recommended by the Commission, and after much negative feedback from a variety of sources, the Law Society had published a list of serious objections to the powers included in the Bill. After approximately 650 amendments, dealing to some extent with the concerns voiced by the Law Society and others, the second Police and Criminal Evidence Bill was passed.

In 1984, the Police and Criminal Evidence Act received the Royal Assent, although most of its provisions did not come into force until January 1, 1986. The main provisions of the Act included the following powers: to stop and search individuals and vehicles; entry and search of premises; seizure and retention of stolen goods and various other property; arrest; detention; questioning and treatment of arrested persons; evidence in criminal proceedings and procedures regarding complaints made against the police. Each of these areas deserves separate consideration, and so the provisions of PACE will be discussed in turn in the following sections.

Included, as an integral part of the Act, are the Codes of Practice which **3–023** set out the structure whereby police conduct is regulated towards suspected persons. This marks a significant departure from the pre-PACE situation in terms of individual rights, since there are disciplinary procedures for breach of the Codes of Practice and this may also give rise to civil actions by the suspect.

> "The main object of the . . . Codes of Practice is to achieve fairness to an accused or suspected person so as, *inter alia*, to protect his legal rights; but also fairness for the Crown and its officers so that there might be reduced the incidence or effectiveness of unfounded allegations of malpractice".[73]

There are five such Codes presently in operation, namely[73A]:

(a) Code A, which deals with powers of stop and search;

(b) Code B, searching of premises and seizure of property;

(c) Code C, detention, treatment and questioning of persons;

(d) Code D, identification issues; and

(e) Code E, tape recording of interviews of suspects.

Surprisingly, there is no Code of Practice concerning arrest, which is dealt with only in the statutory provisions of PACE itself.

Included within the Codes, but without the standing of provisions of the Codes, are the "Notes for Guidance". These are guidelines, without legal enforceability, for police officers to follow when exercising their authority. For example, under paragraph 1A of the Notes, regardless of the power being exercised, all police officers should be careful to ensure that the selection and treatment of those questioned or searched is based upon objective factors and not upon personal prejudice;

> ". . . an officer should bear in mind that he may be required to justify the authorisation or use of the powers to a senior officer and in court, and that misuse of the powers is likely to be harmful to the police effort in the long run and can lead to mistrust of the police by the community".

It is important to recognise the implications of the differing standing of the statutory PACE rules, the Codes of Practice and the Notes for Guidance. Breach of the rules created by PACE itself may give rise to civil or even criminal liability for the police officer concerned. Where a police officer has committed a breach of the Codes, that in itself will not render that particular officer liable to criminal or civil proceedings. It was the case at one time that if there was an infringement of the Codes, the officer responsible would be liable to disciplinary proceedings. This is no longer automatically so, and new procedures are soon to be implemented. PACE, s. 67(10) provides that a breach of the Codes is not to give rise to any civil or criminal liability. Of course, where a police officer has committed an illegal act, then he may be prosecuted through the courts in the usual manner. Where both PACE and Codes of Practice are concerned, evidence which has been obtained in breach of the rules may not be admissible in court. Since the Notes for Guidance are not binding but merely an aid to interpretation, a breach of Notes has no legal significance for the police officer concerned, and is also unlikely to taint evidence in court. The Secretary of State has the power to amend, modify or supplement the Codes wherever necessary. However, any changes must be put before both Houses of Parliament for consideration prior to their introduction. [74]

3–023A In recent years there have been relatively few distinctive changes made to PACE, and the introduction of the Human Rights Act 1998 has not led to any fundamental transformation of other statutory law relating to the area of police powers, with the possible exception of the Regulation of Investigatory Powers Act 2000. However, the recent introduction of the Criminal Justice and Police Act 2001 (CJPA) does makes a number of important amendments to domestic human rights. The CJPA received the Royal Assent on May 11, 2001. The Act is divided into six parts involving 138 detailed sections and seven Schedules. The Preamble states that the Act is:

> ". . .to make provision for combating crime and disorder. . .and about powers of search and seizure; to amend the Police and Criminal Evidence Act 1984, the Police and Criminal Evidence (Northern Ireland) Order 1989 and the Terrorism Act 2000; to make provision about the police.. . .and about the powers of the courts in relation to criminal matters; and for connected purposes".

At the time of writing many of the provisions were not yet in force. However, it is expected that by September 2001 the majority of the Act will be fully operational.[74A] This particular piece of legislation is wide-ranging and encompasses many changes via amendments, partially repealing and in some cases by totally repealing various sections of other statutes. In particular many sections of the Police and Criminal Evidence Act 1984 have been amended, for example arrest, detention, the taking, preservation and destruction of fingerprints or samples, the introduction of "on the spot" penalty notices for certain existing offences, and so forth. The list of various new provisions and changes to existing law is considerable. For instance, Part I of the Act includes provisions for dealing with disorderly conduct in various public places, harassment in the home, licensing laws, travel restrictions for drug trafficking offenders, restricting advertisements for prostitutes, and child curfew schemes. Part II relates to various search and seizure powers. Part III contains measures to deal with arrestable offences, detention, the codes of practice, fingerprinting and samples, and the powers of the investigating officers of the Department of Trade and Industry.

One example relating to the workings of the Act concerns the introduction of penalty notices for various existing so-called minor offences. Sections 1–11 deal with such penalty offences. Penalty offences involve a uniformed police officer issuing an "on the spot" penalty notice against a person he has reason to believe has committed disorderly conduct offences; for example under section 1, being drunk or disorderly in a public place; trespassing on a railway; buying or attempting to buy alcohol in a bar in licensed premises by a person under the age of 18; or consuming alcohol in a designated public place.[74B] With regard to the consumption of alcohol, the police officer must have reasonable grounds to believe that the person is consuming or intends to consume alcohol in a designated public place (section 12).[74C] In such circumstances the uniformed police officer has discretion whether or not to issue such notices. The accused person may accept the penalty notice, or if he so chooses be tried for the alleged offence (section 4(2)). If he chooses the latter option, he risks conviction. If he chooses the former, this will not constitute a criminal conviction or admission of guilt (section 2(4)).

Under section 6 the Secretary of State may issue guidance to police officers on matters to be considered before he exercises his discretion to issue a penalty notice. One of the reasons behind the introduction of such penalties is to alleviate the court's time dealing with minor offences of this kind. However, there exists the inherent danger that if the police do not use these discretionary powers in a proper manner, individuals may choose their right of option to a court hearing, which in turn may further exacerbate an already over-burdensome court calendar. Further discussion of the CJPA will take place in this and other Chapters where relevant and applicable.

III STOP, SEARCH AND DETAIN

3–024 The following imaginary situation will be used throughout this chapter in order to illustrate the practical implications of the rights created by PACE:

> Marcus is seen at 3 a.m. outside a nightclub by two police officers who are responding to a report that a violent disturbance is occurring. He appears to be angry and hostile. Can the police officers stop Marcus, search him for evidence and question him?

Section 1 of Pace

3–025 The power to stop and search a citizen without arrest or proof that an offence has been committed is potentially a great limitation on the freedom of the individual to go about his everyday business without interference. Such a power would clearly be an infringement of civil liberties if it could be exercised arbitrarily; to prevent a person from moving freely would in normal circumstances be actionable as a tort. Thus, if the police are to be given power to detain individuals and to search their clothing, bodies or vehicles, then such a power should be limited to situations in which it is strictly necessary and safeguards should also be provided to prevent misuse of the power.

Thus the new general power to stop individuals and search for certain prohibited articles created by section 1 of PACE is balanced by procedural requirements in section 2; rules in Code A, and guidelines in the Notes for Guidance. From the police point of view, a general power to stop and search can save time and resources, may be of help in preventing crime, and removes potential civil liability if exercised correctly.

Before PACE, the common law did not bestow any general power on the police to stop and search a person without a warrant. A citizen could, and still may, consent to such a search at common law; as will be seen PACE has done nothing to affect searches by consent. There were many statutes which conferred such a power locally; for example the Metropolitan Police Act 1839 gave a power to search for stolen goods and the Firearms Act 1968 gave powers to search for and seize firearms. The first statute to confer stop and search powers of national applicability was the Misuse of Drugs Act 1971. Section 23(2) of that Act gave a police officer the power to detain and search any person or vehicle for controlled substances (as defined by the Act), provided that he had reasonable grounds to suspect that such substances were in the suspect's possession or contained within or upon the vehicle.

That power has now been extended by various statutes to deal with other situations, principally by section 1 of PACE 1984, whereby the police may now stop, search and detain any person or vehicle in a public place in order to uncover stolen or prohibited articles, or offensive weapons, provided that the officer has reasonable grounds for suspicion that such articles or weapons will indeed be found.

Each of these requirements will be examined in turn.

(i) Stop

Despite the heading in Part One of PACE, "Powers to Stop and Search", section 1 does not mention the word "stop". This seems somewhat misleading. Under section 1, a constable has no explicit power to order an individual to stop, unless there are reasonable grounds for suspicion that offensive, prohibited or stolen articles may be found. However, under section 1(2)(b), a constable may detain a person or vehicle for the purposes of such a search. Therefore, it seems that the power to detain necessarily implies the power to stop. There does exist a power to stop a vehicle under other legislation, for example section 163 of the Road Traffic Act 1988. Thus it may be possible to find reasonable grounds for suspicion after the vehicle has been stopped. Whereas, with regard to the stopping of an individual, there must be pre-existing grounds for suspicion before any stop and search action may be taken under section 1. **3–026**

(ii) Search

Many safeguards and preconditions exist for a valid section 1 PACE search of a person or vehicle. According to section 2(9) of PACE, a search of an individual in public may only involve requiring the suspect to remove outer clothing; his coat, jacket or gloves but not headgear.[71] If a more thorough search is required, Code A, paragraph 3.5 stipulates that it should be conducted out of public view, by an officer of the same sex as the suspect, with no one else present. Effort should be taken to minimise a suspect's embarrassment during any search (paragraph 3.1) and "the co-operation of the person to be searched shall be sought in every case, even if he initially objects to the search . . . Force may only be used as a last resort" (paragraph 3.2). The search, and therefore the suspect's detention, should be completed as quickly as possible (Notes for Guidance 3B). An important safeguard for the suspect's rights, intended to prevent arbitrary, groundless search, is found in section 2 of PACE, which applies not only to stop and search under section 1 of PACE but also to the exercise of any other power to search a person or a vehicle without first making an arrest. Before the search is commenced (unless it is of an unattended vehicle), the constable must take reasonable steps to bring to the suspect's attention a number of relevant facts: **3–027**

(a) if he is not a uniformed constable, evidence that he is a constable (s.2(2)(i));

(b) the constable's name and the police station to which he is attached (s.2(3)(a));

(c) the object of the proposed search, (s.2(3)(b));

(d) the grounds for the search (s.2(3)(c));

(e) that a record of the search will be kept, of which the suspect has the right to request a copy, unless the constable believes that it will not be practicable in the circumstances to make such a record (section 2(3)(d), section 3(7) and 3(8)).

These requirements have useful consequences for the suspect, particularly if they are not followed. The provision of evidence that a plain clothes officer is a constable prevents fraud and confirms identity. Provision of the constable's personal details enables him to be traced if necessary for complaint. The requirements of providing the object of the search and the grounds upon which it is being made will enable a court to judge whether the object was within the constable's powers and the grounds constituted a relevant reasonable suspicion. The record of the search is to be made as contemporaneously as possible, weather and other circumstances permitting, on a national form, thus enabling police searches to be monitored and their reasonableness assessed by the authorities; it also is hoped to rule out personal prejudice as a motive. If an unattended vehicle is searched, the constable must leave a notice stating that it has been searched, giving the name of the police station to which he is attached, and stating that compensation may be claimed for any damage (section 2(6)).

(iii) Prohibited articles and offensive weapons

3–028 What constitutes a "prohibited article" is any object made or adapted for use in, or connected with, certain criminal offences, *e.g.* burglary, theft, obtaining property by deception, taking a motor vehicle without authority.[76] An "offensive weapon" is any object made or adapted for use for causing injury to persons or intended to be put to such use.[77] It includes any type of blade, knife or other implement but excludes a folding pocket knife whose blade is less than three inches.[78] However, if the pocket knife has a locking mechanism when opened and a trigger device to return the blade back into the handle, then even if the blade is under three inches (a "flick knife"), it is not deemed to be a "folding pocket knife" within the meaning of the Act.[79]

If the article itself is offensive or it was made or adapted for that purpose, (*i.e.* its purpose is to attack another person), then all the prosecution is required to prove is that it was in the accused's possession, which in the majority of cases is not too difficult. The burden of proof then falls upon the accused to prove that he had a lawful reason for carrying it, *e.g.* for use in intended work, recreational or religious purposes. However, being in possession of an offensive weapon for defensive reasons is no defence; for example, even if a woman has good reason to fear being attacked, she may not carry mace for protection.[80] If the purported offensive weapon is not "offensive" *per se*, (*e.g.* a pair of scissors or a screwdriver), then the prosecution have the additional burden of proving that the defendant intended using the article for some illegal activity. If there is doubt about the "offensiveness", then it is left up to the jury to decide the matter.

The Offensive Weapons Act 1996, s.4 inserts a new section 139B into the Criminal Justice Act 1988, whereby (*inter alia*) police are given a power to search any person on school grounds if he has reasonable grounds to suspect that they may be in possession of any offensive weapon or article with a blade or a point.

(iv) Public places

Stop and search powers under section 1 are restricted to areas where the **3–029** public have access by section 1(1), *e.g.* public highways, public parks, shopping malls, presumably religious buildings and the like. Also included in the list are places where the public must pay to enter, *e.g.* cinemas, museums, amusement centres, sports grounds and so on; but the powers cannot be exercised when such places are closed. Private gardens and dwellings are exempted from the list. However, an officer may enter private land to carry out a search of any person whom he has reasonable grounds to believe is a trespasser; having neither express nor implied permission to be there [section 1(4)].

(v) Reasonable grounds for suspicion

In order for a police constable to be permitted to stop and search an **3–030** individual or vehicle, he must have "reasonable grounds" for suspecting that he will find stolen or prohibited articles, or offensive weapons.[81]

There are problems of implementation when relying upon the grounds of "reasonable suspicion" within the meaning of PACE. If the words are applied too narrowly and rigorously, then most searches would probably be considered illegal and thus make the police officer's task more difficult and ultimately too impracticable to carry out. On the other hand, if the words are defined too widely, then the police could stop and search anyone indiscriminately. As a consequence, individuals would suffer a serious infringement on their liberties to go about their daily routine without police interference. Therefore, a precise interpretation of "reasonable suspicion" is a key determinant in attempting to limit most statutory stop and search powers. For there to be a valid reasonable suspicion, and therefore a legal stop and search, it is essential that the police officer has more than a mere suspicion, hunch or feeling. Suspicion, by itself, *e.g.* seeing a suspect with other known criminals, is not enough; it must be based on reasonable grounds. Further, the reasonable suspicion itself must exist as a precondition to the actual stopping, searching and detaining of a person rather than as a consequence. Therefore, a refusal to answer questions when there were no prior facts which could constitute a reasonable suspicion would not be enough in itself to create grounds for a search, and any detention would be deemed to be illegal.[82] An officer proceeding to search on such grounds would be conducting an unlawful search and could be liable to a charge of false imprisonment or assault.

In *King v. Gardiner*[83]:

Facts. A constable received a radio message that two men and a woman with a dog were loitering in the street. The constable stopped Gardiner, who was with a woman and a dog. Gardiner refused a request by the constable to open his bag. Gardiner was alleged to have assaulted the constable when he was subsequently detained in the police van. On a charge of assaulting a constable in the execution of his duty, it fell for the Divisional Court to decide whether the constable was acting in the execution of his duty; *i.e.* whether the constable had lawfully stopped and detained the defendant.

Decision. On the facts the court decided that there was no basis for the constable to reasonably suspect that Mr Gardiner's bag contained anything illegal. Simply receiving a radio message that a person was "loitering" did not justify a suspicion that a person roughly fitting the description was involved in any criminal activity.[84]

King v. Gardiner emphasises that the existence of a reasonable suspicion in a constable's mind is a question of fact for the court to determine; the suspicion's "reasonableness" is assessed objectively, and not merely by reference to the constable's own opinion. On the facts the court was entitled to consider that there was no reasonable suspicion on the constable's behalf that he would find in Mr Gardiner's bag any prohibited item. Some guidance to the difficulties surrounding "reasonable suspicion" is now largely encapsulated within the Code of Practice for the Exercise by Police Officers of Statutory Powers of Stop and Search (Code A), which supplemented the enactment of PACE. The Notes for Guidance also provide (at 1A) that "regardless of the power exercised, all police officers should be careful to ensure that the selection and treatment of those questioned or searched is based upon objective factors and not upon personal prejudice".

The provisions of Code A itself attempt to describe what does not constitute reasonable suspicion. Paragraph 1.6 suggests that circumstances will differ in each case and consideration should be given to time, place, nature of the article and the suspect's behaviour, *e.g.* where the suspect is seen attempting to hide something. Reasonable suspicion must also not be based upon wholly subjective grounds. Paragraph 1.7 outlines a list of factors which cannot be used to support a reasonable suspicion. These include a suspect's personal appearance, colour, age and any known prior convictions.[85] There must be some objective reason in existence which convinces the police officer that the search is justified. The Code, therefore, is only of some assistance to support a negative definition without detailing any positive rules which govern a legal stop and search.

(vi) Stop and search by consent

A search to which the suspect voluntarily consents is outside the provisions of sections 1, 2 and 3 of PACE and is not governed by Code A. It remains the case that any police officer may ask a citizen to stop and then to consent to a search. The officer does not need to have reasonable grounds for suspicion; he may simply be curious as to what the person is doing, where he is going or what he may be carrying on his person or in his vehicle. One potential problem is that police officers may attempt to obtain consent to a search in order to avoid the requirements of PACE and the Code, and that the suspect may feel pressurised into giving a consent which is not truly voluntary; another problem is that a suspect is unlikely to be fully aware of his rights under PACE and thus may not realise that consenting to a search removes the protection which he would otherwise have. There is evidence to suggest that consensual searches are indeed misused; it is difficult to assess the extent of this since of course no record of the search or the reasons for it need be made. **3–031**

The Notes for Guidance do have a little to say about searches by consent, although not of a binding nature. Note 1D(b) states that, although nothing in Code A affects the power to conduct voluntary searches,

> "In these circumstances an officer should always make it clear that he is seeking the consent of the person concerned to the search being carried out by telling the person that he need not consent and that without his consent he will not be searched".

Note 1E continues:

> "If an officer acts in an improper manner this will invalidate a voluntary search. Juveniles, people suffering from a mental handicap or mental disorder and others who appear not to be capable of giving an informed consent should not be subject to a voluntary search".

Thus, returning to our example, it must be shown either that Marcus consented to being stopped and searched, or that the officers formed a reasonable suspicion, based upon some objective evidence (such as the fact that Marcus fits the description given by witnesses). The reasons for the stop and search must be explained, as must its legal basis (section 2 of PACE). Marcus is in a public place; he may be stopped and searched for any offensive weapon (PACE, s.1) but Code A must be complied with. In addition, Marcus may be asked to "consent" to a search.

Other Statutory Powers to Stop and Search

Various other statutory powers to stop and search persons and vehicles exist under other statutory provisions, although many were repealed by PACE. Some, but not all, share PACE, s.1's requirement of reasonable grounds for suspicion before such action can be taken. **3–032**

Section 4 PACE 1984 gives a superintendent (or, in an emergency, any officer) a power to conduct road checks, *i.e.* to set up road blocks and stop traffic in order to search for a person who has committed a serious arrestable offence, is a witness to such an offence, or an escaped prisoner. Road checks are only authorised when the officer reasonably suspects that such a person is in or about to be in the area. The police may either stop all vehicles in the area or all vehicles which fit a particular description.

Section 163 of the Road Traffic Act 1988, authorises a police constable to stop vehicles whether or not a serious arrestable offence has been committed or is suspected. It requires a driver to stop when a constable in uniform requires them to do so; no power to search the vehicles for evidence is given by either this provision or section 4 of PACE. No detail was given in section 163 of the reasons for which the power could be exercised; it can be used for simple practical reasons such as traffic control or to warn of danger ahead or to check the driver's documents.

Section 60 of the Criminal Justice and Public Order Act 1994, gives a power to search persons or vehicles to a police officer in uniform. The search is to be for offensive weapons or dangerous articles, as in section 1 of PACE, but no reasonable grounds for suspicion need exist or be demonstrated by the officer. Such a power only exists when it has been pre-authorised by a superintendent who reasonably suspects that incidents involving serious injury may occur in a particular area. The authorisation only lasts for 24 hours and relates only to the specified locality.

3–033 The Misuse of Drugs Act 1971, s. 23 provides a power to stop and search any person or vehicle (*inter alia*) if a constable has reasonable grounds for suspicion that any person is in possession of a controlled drug, as defined by that Act. A person's belongings may also be searched under this power. The power may be exercised in any location.

The Firearms Act 1968, s. 47 gives a constable power to require a person to hand over a firearm for examination, or to stop and search a person or vehicle. The constable must have reasonable grounds for suspicion that a person has a firearm in a public place or is in possession of a real or imitation firearm with intent to commit one of the listed serious offences. The power may be exercised in any location, and the constable may enter any premises in order to use it.

The Sporting Events (Control of Alcohol, etc.,) Act 1985, s. 7 provides that a constable in uniform may search persons, coaches and trains for intoxicating liquor; the power can be exercised at all designated sports grounds or in coaches or trains travelling to or from designated sporting events. The constable must have reasonable grounds to suspect that alcohol is, or has been, present.

The Offensive Weapons Act 1996, s. 4 creates a new section 139B of the Criminal Justice Act 1988, giving a constable power to search (*inter alia*) any person on school grounds for offensive weapons and articles with blades or points. The constable must have reasonable grounds for suspicion that an offence is being, or will be committed (including any offence of possession of an offensive weapon). It applies to all buildings and land belonging to any school or college catering for students aged under 19.

IV ARREST AND CAUTION

Introduction

As has been seen, the police power to stop and search impinges upon the freedom of movement of the individual citizen. The power of arrest interferes with the individual freedom to a far greater extent and has further implications at a key stage in the chain of events which may lead to loss of liberty. The fact of an arrest changes the rights of the arrested person; he is deprived of the permission to use reasonable force to resist detention or to escape, and must himself submit to lawful reasonable force. Any arrest is regarded by the law as unlawful unless it can be justified by a particular power, either at common law or under a statute (now principally PACE). When subjected to an unlawful arrest, a person may resist the arrest by use of reasonable force and, if the arrest takes place, may seek both criminal and civil remedies for assault or false imprisonment.[86] Since arrest has such an impact upon the citizen, it has always been subject to a body of strict rules. PACE now provides such rules concerning grounds for arrest, necessary formalities and arrest procedures. **3–034**

Any person who is not under arrest is "helping the police with their inquiries" and may leave whenever he wishes, even if he has accompanied an officer to a police station and is being questioned, since his status is that of voluntary assistance through public spiritedness. PACE, s.29 and Code C paragraphs 3.15 and 3.16 provide safeguards for such a person's rights: when questioned at a police station, a person is free to leave at any time unless the police decide to arrest him; and if he asks about legal advice, he must be given information about its availability.

What is an arrest? Normally, it constitutes a loss of liberty on the part of the arrestee—freedom to move about is restricted or removed and, ultimately, it involves the suspect being taken into custody. The act of arrest consists of the touching or seizure of a person's body in order to facilitate his restraint, or words may suffice if the arrestee submits voluntarily. There are two methods of making an arrest: arrest with a warrant (or summons) and arrest without a warrant. It used to be the case historically that the police required an arrest warrant before almost any arrest would be deemed lawful. Nowadays, it is less common for the police to go before a magistrate and ask for such a warrant, *e.g.* bail jumping and refusing to obey a court order. Although PACE has done much to change statutory arrest powers, it should be recognised that the common law created powers of arrest which continue despite PACE's implementation and are only affected by PACE in terms of the arrested person's treatment and rights. In addition, certain other statutes create powers of arrest for particular offences.

After stopping Marcus and searching his pockets, the officers find a weapon which they believe has been used in an assault earlier that night. At this point, Marcus becomes angry and swears at the officers, then repeatedly kicks the police car. Do the officers have sufficient grounds on which to arrest him?

Power of Arrest at Common Law

3–035 Since the Middle Ages, every citizen has had a duty to keep the peace. Any citizen has always been permitted to arrest an offender in certain circumstances, but constables have been given a special duty to do so since the idea of watchmen first developed. At common law most types of arrest required a form of warrant, but arrest for breach of the peace did not, and still does not. In many situations where arrest is permitted at common law it will also be available under PACE, but in certain respects the common law power is wider than the statutory power of arrest. Arrest for breach of the peace can occur in any location, even on private premises, and no specific criminal offence need have been committed, attempted or feared. An arrest at common law may be preventative, whereas under statute it is a sanction.

The leading case is now Howell,[87] where the Court of Appeal stated that the power to arrest at common law exists in any of three situations:

(1) Where the person making the arrest has actually witnessed a breach of the peace;

(2) Where, although no breach of the peace has yet occurred, the person making the arrest reasonably believes that a breach of the peace will occur in the imminent future;

(3) Where a breach of the peace has already been committed by the person being arrested, and the person making the arrest now has a reasonable belief that a further breach of the peace will occur.

In each of these situations, a breach of the peace must be committed or threatened. It is therefore necessary to have a working definition of "breach of the peace". In *Howell*, the Court of Appeal stated that;

> "There is a breach of the peace whenever harm is actually done or likely to be done to a person or in his presence to his property, or a person is in fear of being so harmed through an assault, an affray, a riot, an unlawful assembly or other disturbance".

There are two important consequences of this definition. First, it will be seen that under PACE there is no power of arrest without warrant for common assault, assaulting a constable in the execution of his duty, or obstruction of a constable in the execution of his duty, unless one of the general arrest conditions (discussed below) is satisfied,[88] since none of these offences are arrestable. However an arrest may be made at common law for certainly the first two of those offences and often the third, since a breach of the peace is entailed. Secondly, at common law an arrest is justified in any situation where the person arresting reasonably believes that some violence or harm is likely to occur in the immediate future, even if the person arrested is behaving lawfully until the time of the arrest. An arrest can be used to prevent such harm or violence and to allow the persons concerned to calm down. This is not possible with a statutory arrest governed by PACE, as will be seen below. Thus the power to arrest at common law may be extremely useful to the police, and is often exercised.

Authority to Arrest Under PACE

Beginning with the premise discussed above that normally an individual has **3–036** the freedom to go where he pleases without state interference, any unjustified intrusion into that liberty must be considered to be a serious matter. Thus, a statutory power to arrest a citizen should only be exercised under stringent supervision and within strict principles.

Arrestable Offences

Today, the more common method of arresting a person is without a **3–037** warrant. PACE, s.24 and s.25 set out the circumstances in which a police officer has power to arrest a suspect without a warrant. Section 24 designates certain offences as "arrestable offences". The main categories are as follows[89]:

(a) Where the sentence for the offence is fixed by law (principally, murder);

(b) Where the offence carries at least five years' imprisonment, *e.g.* theft, indecent assault, burglary;

(c) Specified statutory offences in section 24(2), including going equipped to steal, taking a motor vehicle without authority, publishing obscene matter or material likely to stir up racial hatred.

Thus arrestable offences are, broadly, the most serious offences, and also those where it is either in the public interest to remove a suspect from the community as quickly as possible or where there is a distinct possibility that a suspect may flee or continue to offend if an arrest is not made immediately. However, under section 71 of the recently introduced Criminal Justice and Police Act 2001, the statutory offences of kerb-crawling and failure to stop and report an accident involving personal injury, are now also arrestable offences under section 24(2) of PACE.

There are many offences which perhaps should be, but are not, arrestable offences. For instance, not all assault offences are arrestable offences. The nature and seriousness of the assault and its consequences are vital to a conviction. For example, common assault is not an arrestable offence. However, assault occasioning actual bodily harm contrary to section 47 of the Offences Against the Person Act is arrestable, as is the intentional or reckless infliction of grievous bodily harm contrary to sections 18 and 20 of that Act. Statute has recently interfered to some extent here since, if a common assault occurs on more than one occasion, it may well fall within the new "stalking" offences under the Protection from Harassment Act 1997, in which a power of arrest is given (it should also be remembered that a common law arrest could be made for actual or threatened breach of the peace in all assault situations, except where the assault has already occurred and no further violence is reasonably believed to be likely). Subject to the above, assaulting a police constable in the execution of his duty under section 89(1) Police Act 1996 is not, by itself, an arrestable offence, mainly because it only carries with it a maximum sentence of six months. If the police constable comes across a situation whereby the offence of obstruction or a breach of the peace is involved and makes it clear to the suspect that he is arresting him for obstruction, any reasonable force used by the suspect to resist arrest will be lawful.

In *Chapman v. DPP*[90]:

Facts. Constable Sneller, whilst on duty, received a radio message that a fellow officer had just been attacked by six youths. S immediately went to his aid. He saw what he believed to be one of the youths go into a block of flats on an estate. S went with the constable who had been assaulted to the flat. He knocked at the door and explained to the defendant that he believed that one of the youths who had assaulted his colleague was inside and that he would like to come in and have a look. The defendant replied, "Not fucking likely, now fuck off". S tried to push past him whereupon the defendant punched S in the eye. The defendant was charged with assault contrary to section 51(1) of the Police Act 1964. He was convicted and appealed.

Decision. Whether the conviction could be upheld depended upon whether S was acting lawfully "in the execution of his duty" when he attempted to enter the flat. Under section 17(1)(b) of PACE, subject to certain exceptions, "a constable may enter and search any premises for the purpose of arresting a person for an arrestable offence". The question which the court had to consider was whether S had a statutory power to enter the flat and make an arrest. Since the arrest can only be lawful if the offence is an "arrestable offence", it must first be determined whether the "assault" came within section 24. There was no evidence for S to reasonably suspect that his colleague had suffered serious harm, or indeed any physical injury. He may have suspected an assault under section 51(1), but, as was stated above, that is not an arrestable offence. As Bingham L.J. stated,

> "what is . . . inescapable and fatal to this conviction is that the justices have not found as a fact that S reasonably suspected this, or any other arrestable offence, to have been committed, or any facts amounting to an arrestable offence to have occurred".

Therefore, the appeal was allowed.

Whether an offence is arrestable is vital to whether the statutory power of arrest can be exercised under PACE, s.24.

Under section 24(4), any person (including a police officer) may arrest without warrant: **3–038**

(a) Any person who is in the act of committing an arrestable offence; or

(b) Any person whom he has reasonable grounds to suspect to be committing such an offence.

Under section 24(5), where an arrestable offence has been committed, any person (including a police officer) may arrest without warrant:

(a) Any person who is guilty of the offence; or, importantly

(b) Anyone whom he has reasonable grounds for suspecting to be guilty of the arrestable offence.

Section 24(6) goes even further, covering the situation where there is no proof that an arrestable offence either has already been committed or is in the process of being committed:

> "Where a constable has reasonable grounds for suspecting that an arrestable offence has been committed, he may arrest without a warrant anyone whom he has reasonable grounds for suspecting to be guilty of the offence".

Finally, section 24(7) provides that a constable may arrest without warrant:

(a) Any person who is about to commit an arrestable offence; or

(b) Anyone whom he has reasonable grounds for suspecting to be about to commit an arrestable offence.

Sections 24(6) and section 24(7) are the only two of the four powers of arrest in section 24 which apply solely to a constable; the others expressly apply to any person, following the pattern of the common law. Each of the crucial terms in these powers will be defined separately in this chapter.

Citizen's Arrest

As has been observed, sections 24(4) and 24(5) give any member of the public the power to arrest, without a warrant, anyone who is committing or guilty of an arrestable offence or anyone whom he has reasonable grounds for suspecting to be committing or guilty of an arrestable offence. These powers, known as the power to make a "citizen's arrest", are in addition to the common law power to arrest for actual or threatened breach of the peace, but there is some overlap. It should however be noted that under **3–039** section 24 a citizen has no power to arrest in order to prevent a crime; such a power does in fact exist independently of PACE both at common law and under section 3(1) of the Criminal Law Act 1967, which provides that:

> "A person may use such force as is reasonable in the circumstances in the prevention of crime, or in effecting or assisting in the lawful arrest of offenders or suspected offenders or of persons unlawfully at large".

Thus, in parallel to a constable's powers under section 24(6) and 24(7), a citizen may at common law act reasonably to prevent crime, even if he only believes the suspect to be about to commit an offence. The citizen need only honestly believe that reasonable force is necessary to prevent a crime; his belief need not be based upon reasonable grounds. This contrasts with the demand for reasonable grounds placed upon the arresting person when the powers under PACE, s. 24 are being used. Another contrast is that, at common law, the offence which has been committed or is believed to be about to be committed need not be "arrestable". The powers of citizen's arrest given by section 24 are often used by store detectives when a person has committed theft or is reasonably suspected of having done so.

In *Graham Self*[91]:

Facts. A police constable was seen by a store detective leaving Woolworths with a bar of chocolate without paying for it. The store detective and his assistant followed the P.C. and accused him of shoplifting, whereupon the P.C. hit the detective and tried to run off. He was apprehended and charged with theft and assault. He was acquitted of theft, but convicted of assault. He appealed.

Decision. Allowing the appeal, the court held that the commission of an arrestable offence was a precondition to the making of a citizen's arrest under section 24(5). Since the appellant had been acquitted of theft, the citizen's arrest had been invalid because no offence had in fact been committed. Thus the defendant had been entitled to attempt to escape, and the assault conviction could not be sustained.

Section 24(4) can only be used where the defendant is actually in the act of offending, or if the citizen reasonably suspects that he is in the act of offending. In *R. v. Self* the arrestor was using section 24(5), where for a citizen's arrest to be lawful after the offence has been committed, it must be proven that an offence was in fact committed. The court rejected the Crown's contention that in escaping the appellant was still in the act of what might reasonably be believed to be an offence. It would be a question of fact whether the defendant had completed the *actus reus* of the offence. If the offence were not completed, then section 24(4) would be the more appropriate section to use.

Police Arrest

3–040 The power of a citizen to arrest under sections 24(4) or 24(5) of PACE is more limited than a constable's power under sections 24(6) or 24(7). Under sections 24(6) and 24(7), as mentioned above;

(a) Where a constable has reasonable grounds for suspecting that an arrestable offence has been committed, he may arrest without warrant any person whom he has reasonable grounds for suspecting to be guilty of that offence; and

(b) A constable may arrest any person who is about to commit an arrestable offence or any person whom he has reasonable grounds for suspecting to be about to commit an arrestable offence.

The necessary implication of this is that a constable may have made a lawful arrest even where no arrestable offence was in fact committed, or where an arrestable offence was committed by a different person to the suspect, as long as the constable had reasonable grounds for his relevant suspicion at the time of the arrest. These powers of course apply in addition to those powers, under sections 24(4) and 24(5) of PACE and elsewhere, which a police officer possesses by virtue of falling within the decision of "any person" or "a citizen".

General Arrest Conditions

Under section 25, if a police officer has reasonable grounds for suspecting **3–041**
that an offence, not included within section 24, has been committed or attempted, or is being committed or attempted, he may arrest the person he suspects of committing the offence if it appears to the constable that service of a summons is impracticable or inappropriate because one of the following "general arrest conditions" is satisfied:

(a) The suspect's name is unknown to the constable and cannot be readily ascertained; section 25(3)(a);

(b) The constable has reasonable grounds for doubting whether the name given to him by the suspect is his real name; section 25(3)(b);

(c) The suspect has failed to provide a satisfactory address at which a summons could be served; section 25(3)(c)(i);

(d) The constable has reasonable grounds for doubting whether the address provided by the suspect is satisfactory for service of a summons, (*e.g.* it is a temporary address); section 25(3)(c)(ii);

(e) The constable has reasonable grounds for belief that the suspect, if not arrested, will; injure himself or another person; suffer physical injury; cause the loss or damage of property; commit an offence against public decency; or obstruct the public highway; section 25(3)(d); or

(f) The constable has reasonable grounds for believing that arrest is necessary to protect a child or other vulnerable person; section 25(3)(e).

Thus a police officer does have the power in any of the circumstances stated above to arrest without warrant in spite of the fact that the offence which has been committed or attempted, or which the police officer has reasonable grounds to suspect has been committed or attempted, is not an arrestable offence. The general arrest conditions divide into those which exist for practical reasons (*e.g.* there is no point in serving a summons at a fictitious address) and those which exist to protect the public or the suspect (*e.g.* the suspect may be arrested to prevent harm to himself, another or property).

Section 25 has been criticised since it creates a general power of arrest in the circumstances to which it applies which far exceeds the power proposed by the Royal Commission. The first PACE Bill would have created a power to temporarily detain a suspect while the name and address which he had provided were checked, but this provision was dropped; arguably a strictly limited power along such lines would be preferable to the existing wide section 25 arrest power. If a name and address are given, there must be a genuine belief in the officer's mind that they are dubious. In *G. v. DPP*,[92] an arrest was held to be unlawful because the constable gave as his reason for doubting the appellant's name and address that people who commit offences often do not tell the truth. Because the name and address were furnished before the appellant was suspected by the constable of an offence (in this case, a non-arrestable offence of obstruction), the constable could not use that reason to doubt the appellant's honesty. Arrest for giving an incorrect name and address is not, by itself, a lawful arrest. In *Nicholas v. Parsonage*[93]:

3–042 **Facts**. The defendant was seen to make an obscene gesture to a constable after being told to hold the handlebars of his bicycle, whereupon the constable asked the defendant for his name and address. The defendant refused, and attempted to ride off. The constable informed him that he was arresting him under PACE, whereupon the defendant assaulted the constable whilst trying to escape. He was charged and convicted under section 51(1) of the Police Act 1964.

Decision. Dismissing the appeal, Glidewell L.J. stated,

> "It is sufficient if the constable says, as the prosecutor did, 'what is your name?' and then later 'what is your address?'. If the person refuses to give them, being reasonably suspected of having committed an offence, then that satisfies the relevant provisions of section 25 in my view . . . If there has been no prior indication at any time of the nature of the offence which the constable suspects has been committed, in my judgement it does not suffice to satisfy section 28(3)[94] to ask for a name and address and then say 'I am arresting you because you have not given your name and address.' In other words, I reject the submission that of itself the failure to give the name and address is a ground for arrest."[95]

The defendant had been arrested in accordance with PACE ss. 25 and 28. All that is required is that the constable reasonably suspects a person of committing any offence (not an arrestable offence which comes under section 24) and the defendant refuses to answer the question "what is your name and address?" Under section 28(3) the constable must not only tell the defendant of which offence he is suspected, but also that the reason why he is being arrested is both for the offence and for refusing to give his name and address. The defendant must still be told the reason for his arrest even where it is obvious, under section 28(4).

At the time of the arrest, the constable must be aware that there is a likelihood of a prosecution against the suspect. If there is no possibility of a prosecution, and the constable is aware of this, then the arrest would probably be unlawful. If, prior to arrest, the constable is not aware of a prosecution being set aside by, for example, the charges being dropped, then the arrest would nevertheless still be lawful. If, however, the constable was aware of the circumstances then the arrest would be unlawful.[96]

Thus Marcus may be arrested, either for breach of the peace or under PACE. A common law arrest may be made on wider grounds than those under sections 24 and 25, for example to give Marcus time to calm down, or to prevent him from causing a feared breach of the peace. But if PACE arrest powers are used, Marcus could be arrested without warrant:

(a) Under section 24 if a serious arrestable offence is reasonably suspected (*e.g.* if the assault victim is in hospital, or the police car has been damaged);

(b) Under section 25 if one of the "general arrest conditions" is satisfied, for example if the officers reasonably doubt that Marcus has given them his correct name and address, or have reasonable grounds for belief that he will be a danger to a person or to property unless arrested.

In any of the above situations, reasons must be given for the arrest.

Reasonable Grounds for Arrest

As has been seen, many of the situations in which an arrest can be made under sections 24 and 25 of PACE depend upon the concept of "reasonable grounds for suspicion". PACE gives no guidance as to which facts may be or are not capable of being reasonable grounds for suspicion in the context of arrest, and there are no Code of Practice or Notes for Guidance to help here. Thus it has fallen to the common law to develop guidelines as to which grounds for suspicion are permissible; such guidelines, of necessity, are created in response to the facts of the case before the court and so lack generality; each case is to be judged on its own facts. **3–043**

In the case of *Holgate-Mohammed v. Duke*[97]:

Facts. Mrs Holgate-Mohammed was arrested on suspicion of theft and questioned at a police station, but was released without charge. The trial judge decided that because the arrest was made in order to induce a confession, rather than simply questioning the suspect under caution, there had been a wrongful arrest. The Court of Appeal overturned this decision; provided that there was a reasonable suspicion, it is not a wrongful arrest just because one motive of the arrest was that a confession was more likely to result after arrest than through simple questioning. Mrs Holgate-Mohammed appealed to the House of Lords.

Decision. Dismissing the appeal, it was held that since an arrestable offence had been committed, and the constable had reasonable cause for suspecting the appellant to be guilty of the offence, he was entitled to arrest her (under previous statutory provisions). The interrogation of a suspect in order to dispel or confirm a reasonable suspicion was a legitimate cause for arrest. So, the fact that the constable, when exercising his discretion to arrest the appellant, took into consideration that she might be more likely to confess her guilt if arrested and questioned at the police station was a relevant matter and therefore did not render the exercise of his discretion *ultra vires*. The House of Lords stated that the statutory powers of the police are subject not only to their own statutory regulation, but also to the principle of "*Wednesbury* unreasonableness" applied in administrative law. The constable must not account for irrelevant factors, or ignore relevant factors when using his discretion, and his decision must not be so unreasonable that no reasonable constable would have made the same decision. Using the principles of *Wednesbury* unreasonableness, the Lords considered that the constable was entitled to arrest the suspect if he believed that she might be more likely to confess guilt when arrested. Clearly, it would be an improper arrest for different grounds if there was no reasonable suspicion.

In *Castorina v. Chief* Constable of Surrey (see below), Wolf L.J. introduced a helpful formula to assist the court in determining whether or not reasonable grounds for suspicion existed. The three-stage test expounded is as follows:

(1) Did the constable suspect that the arrested person was guilty of the offence? (subjective test)

(2) If yes, did the constable have reasonable proof of that suspicion? (objective test)

(3) If yes to both (1) and (2), then the constable has discretion to arrest provided that the arrest did not constitute unreasonableness under *Wednesbury* principles.

In *Castorina v. Chief Constable of Surrey*[98]:

3–044 **Facts**. The defendant was an ex-employee of a company which had just been burgled. The burglary took place in circumstances which suggested an "inside job". The police had been informed by the manager that the defendant had recently been dismissed and might possibly hold a grudge. Without making any further investigations, they went to the defendant's home and arrested her. She had no previous convictions and there was no definite evidence that she bore any resentment at being dismissed. She was detained at the police station for nearly four hours before being released. She took an action against the police for false imprisonment and arrest. The judge, at first instance, defined reasonable cause as: "the honest belief founded on reasonable suspicion leading an ordinary cautious man to the conclusion that the person arrested was guilty of the offence" and found that the police did not have reasonable cause for the arrest and she was awarded four thousand pounds. The Chief Constable appealed.

Decision. On appeal by the Chief Constable, the Court of Appeal declared that the judge's definition was too strict and implied a subjective test. The Court of Appeal emphasised that "reasonable cause" was objective and that in order to decide on the matter, emphasis must be placed upon the arresting officer suspecting the person to be guilty of the offence, not upon the person actually being guilty of the offence. Purchas L.J. stated that it was not necessary "for the officer to conclude that the person was guilty of the offence; it was enough that a reasonable man would suspect that that was so".

Whilst reasonable grounds for suspicion are generally required under section 24, sections 24(4)(a) and 24(7)(a) are an exception for practical reasons; under the former, all that is required is anyone actually committing the arrestable offence (arrest may be by an ordinary individual or a constable). Under the latter, anyone who is about to commit an arrestable offence (arrest may only be made by a constable).

Inform of the Reasons for Arrest

Pre-PACE, in *Christie v. Leachinsky*[99] the following five main propositions for a lawful arrest after reasonable suspicion, were set out: **3–045**

(1) The police constable must inform the suspect of the true grounds for arrest. If not so informed, then;

(2) The police officer may be liable for false imprisonment;

(3) The reason for his arrest may not be given if he already is aware of the general nature of the offence (but see PACE, s. 28 now where reasons must be given);

(4) The reasons need not be given to the suspect in technical or precise language;

(5) The grounds for arrest need not be given at that time if the situation makes it practically impossible to inform him, *e.g.* by the suspect absconding or during a violent struggle, etc.

Now under section 28(3) of PACE it is stated that "no arrest shall be lawful unless the person arrested is informed of the ground for his arrest at the time of, or as soon as practicable after the arrest". Under section 28, where a person is arrested in a situation where he was not informed that he is under arrest, *e.g.* where he is simply physically detained, then he must be informed of his arrest as soon as it is practicable. No exact words need be used to constitute an arrest, such as "you are under arrest" or "I am arresting you for . . .". Words such as "stay there"[1] would suffice. Indeed, any verbal communication is sufficient provided that the arrestee is aware that he is no longer free to leave. But what happens if, due to the circumstances, reasons for the arrest cannot be given?

In *DPP v. Hawkins*[2]:

Facts. The defendant threw a drinks carton which struck a P.C. on the back of the leg. The P.C. said to the defendant, "you are under arrest" and took him by the arm. A struggle ensued during which it was impossible for the P.C. to give the defendant reasons for the arrest. The defendant then kicked two other police officers in the face and the groin. He was taken to the police station, where he continued to struggle. Even at the police station he was not informed of the grounds for his arrest. He was charged under section 51(1) of the Police Act 1964. The defence argued that, since he was not informed of the reasons for the arrest as soon as practicable, the arrest was unlawful and therefore there was no case to answer. The court at first instance agreed. The DPP appealed.

Decision. Whilst it is true to state that he should have been informed of the grounds of his arrest, as soon as was practicable, this does not retrospectively make the arrest unlawful. Parker L.J. stated ". . . that does not mean that acts, which were previously done and were, when done, done in the execution of duty, become retrospectively, acts which were not done in the execution of duty". Therefore, the appeal was allowed.

However, any action against the police for false imprisonment may well succeed on the grounds that the arrestee's detention became unlawful after such time as it was practicable to give reasons for the arrest, and the reasons were not given. Whether this "practicable time" was inside or outside the police station is a question of fact.[3] It has also been stated that where the initial arrest was unlawful, due to reasons for the arrest not being given, and then some time later reasons were given, the arrest became lawful after that later period.[4] If the reasons given to the suspect for the arrest under section 28(3) are invalid or the wrong reasons,[5] then the arrest itself is unlawful.

Thus in *Edwards v. DPP*[6]:

3–046 **Facts**. Three police officers in plain clothes who were on duty in Shaftesbury Avenue noticed three men each with unrolled cigarette papers in their hands. One of them was burning a brown resinous substance from underneath. Suspecting that all three were in possession of cannabis, the officers exercised their powers under the Misuse of Drugs Act 1971 and insisted on searching them. One of the men, Fox, put something into his mouth and struggled violently when the P.C. went to take it. The P.C. then said, "You're nicked of obstruction". The defendant then intervened by trying to push one of the police officers away. She in turn was arrested and charged under section 51(3) of the Police Act 1964 with wilful obstruction.

Decision. The main question is, was this a lawful arrest? The offence of obstruction is not an arrestable offence under the Misuse of Drugs Act 1971, nor under the then section 51(3) of the Police Act 1964. So, could it be a lawful arrest under section 25? Only if the service of a summons is impracticable or inappropriate because the general arrest conditions apply. Section 25 was not referred to or relied upon by the police officer and the reason for the arrest was invalid, therefore the arrest itself was unlawful. Accordingly, the conviction was quashed. Evans L.J. said that, although he had great sympathy with the police in these circumstances,

> "nevertheless it has to be borne in mind that giving correct information as to the reason for an arrest is a matter of the utmost constitutional significance in a case where a reason can be and is given at the time".

Evans L.J. also stated that for an arrest to be lawful under section 25 (citing Woolf L.J. in *Castorina v. Chief Constable of Surrey*) two questions must be answered; (1) What was the state of mind of the arresting officer, *i.e.* what arrest conditions did he consider? (2) Was there justification for that state of mind in the eyes of the court? In this instance the officer only had in his mind an arrest for the non-arrestable offence of obstruction, although he could have, had he thought of it at the time, legally arrested the appellant for unlawful possession of drugs.[7]

However, if the reasons are somewhat imprecise, but nevertheless the suspect understands why he has been arrested, then the arrest is still valid.[8]

Caution—Code C, Paragraph 10.1

The caution which is administered by a police officer to a person who is **3–047**
suspected of an offence has an important function as a safeguard and reminder of the suspect's rights, but also shows the limitations of those rights, in particular the right of silence. PACE worked in favour of the suspect's rights by bringing forward the time at which a caution must first be administered to the stage of mere suspicion that the suspect has committed an offence; previously no caution was required until the officer's suspicion could be shown to be based upon reasonable grounds. However, since PACE the caution has been modified by the Criminal Justice and Public Order Act 1994, which adds to the previous caution a warning that silence may incriminate. The original PACE caution was as follows: "You are not obliged to say anything unless you wish to do so but what you say may be put into writing and given in evidence". The new caution, which must be administered when a constable has grounds to suspect a person of an offence, consists of the following words; "You do not have to say anything. But it may harm your defence if you do not mention when questioned something which you later rely on in court. Anything you do say may be given in evidence". (Code C, paragraph 10.4)

Minor deviations are permitted to the actual words, and if a person does not understand the meaning, then the officer may explain it in his own words (Code C, Note 10C). But it is essential that the suspect is made fully aware of all the main ingredients of the caution. Prior to the giving of the caution no questions may be put to the suspect regarding that person's involvement or suspected involvement in that particular offence if his answers or his silence may be given in evidence in a prosecution (paragraph 10.1).

3–048 In *R. v. Purcell*[9]:

Facts. The defendant, some 12 months previously, had escaped from police custody after being arrested for rape. He was now arrested again for burglary. He was taken to the interview room and the following conversation was alleged to have taken place, prior to any caution being given;

> Purcell: "I'm Patrick Purcell and I'm wanted for something, something very bad".
>
> Officer: "What is it Pat?"
>
> Purcell: "I'm ashamed. I done a rape . . . I'm so ashamed"
>
> Officer: "I know nothing of this. Just calm down and take it easy for a moment. I want to speak to you about the other matters".

After being cautioned and then interviewed regarding the burglaries, the defendant read and signed a note made by the officer of the whole conversation. Three days later, the police went to the defendant's cell and arrested him for rape. After being cautioned it was alleged that he said that his family would be ashamed of him for what he had done. No contemporaneous record was ever shown to the defendant. There then followed a taped interview where he admitted to sexual intercourse with the girl but claimed it was with her consent.

Decision. The defendant was convicted and appealed on the ground that the judge should not have allowed admissions of the two oral statements since (1) he was not cautioned prior to the police officer asking "What is it Pat?" and therefore was a breach of Code C, paragraph 10.1 and (2) no contemporaneous record was taken of the interview in the cell, and thus there was no opportunity for the defendant to read and sign it—this was a clear breach of paragraphs 11.3 and 12.12 (now paragraphs 11.5 and 11.10). As to (1) the Court of Appeal held that a caution must be given prior to any questions which are "for the purpose of obtaining evidence which may be given to a court in a prosecution". The judge at first instance, ruled that there was no breach of paragraph 10.1. The judge accepted the police officer's evidence that he was not trying to obtain evidence, but merely wanted to know what was disturbing the defendant, hence the question, "What is it Pat?".

As to (2), the court ruled that since no questions were put to the defendant and since the officers were there, not to obtain evidence, but merely as a preliminary to the formal interview, there was no need to record any comments made by the defendant. Therefore there was no breach of the Codes as they then were. Thus, the appeal was dismissed.[10]

However, no caution is necessary where questions are asked for other unrelated purposes, *e.g.* establishing the identity of the person, or proof of ownership of a vehicle, or required under statute to answer questions, or to make a lawful search, etc., (paragraph 10.1). A person may be cautioned before or after arrest. If before, then that person is under no obligation to remain with the officer and be informed that he is not under arrest (paragraph 10.2). If not arrested, the suspect is entitled to walk off, despite being cautioned. If that occurs then the police are more likely than not to then arrest him. However, if there were grounds to suspect that an offence had been committed at that time, the mere walking off will not turn that into reasonable grounds and the suspect may well have a claim for wrongful arrest if no other reason is given for the arrest. Immediately after arrest he must, of course, be cautioned unless either of the following requirements are satisfied (paragraph 10.3):

(a) It is impracticable to administer a caution because of the suspect's condition or behaviour at the time; or

(b) He has already been cautioned immediately prior to arrest.

As stated above, the officer must have "grounds to suspect" a person in order to give a caution and not necessarily "reasonable grounds." The test is an objective one. Thus, the standard required for the giving of the caution is less than that for arrest or stop and search. Where there are no grounds to suspect the person, or no real evidence to show that an offence has been committed, any conversations between the police and that person, at that time, will not come within paragraph 10.1. At any subsequent trial, the defendant will not be able to exclude those previous conversations by reason of section 78.10. Cautions must be repeated during a break in questioning a suspect under caution, so that he is reminded of his right to silence and its limitations (paragraph 10.5).

V ENTRY, SEARCH AND SEIZURE

Introduction

In many jurisdictions, a person's home, property, documents, and business are protected by the legal or constitutional recognition of a general right to privacy. In Britain no such right has yet been recognised, and so it has historically fallen to the common law to prevent and regulate state interference with a person's private life and possessions by means of upholding rights to property and confidentiality. Most of these rights have been developed by the common law disciplines of contract and equity, with both extensions to and exceptions from the rights being introduced by specific statutes. The result is that police and other state officials have greater powers in this field than do their counterparts in both civil and even other common law jurisdictions. The rules of entry, search and seizure represent a compromise between an individual's rights to confidentiality and property, and the needs of the state in pursuit of justice or security. In spite of Sir Edward Coke's pronouncement that "Every man's house is his castle", the common law did allow police officers to enter a citizen's home or other premises and search there, seizing what they found. But a search warrant was generally required by the common law, which had also developed comparatively early a rule that a private home may not be entered without either the consent of the occupier (express or implied) or a strong legal justification for such an invasion. **3–049**

The famous cases of *Leach v. Money* and *Entick v. Carrington*[12] had entrenched these two aspects of the rule by the eighteenth century; before that time, general search warrants were granted by the Secretary of State, for example to prevent the publication or dissemination of blasphemous documents. But the common law was always hostile to the recognition of any general right to enter, search and seize, and regularly rejected arguments either that such a right had been recognised in earlier cases or that such a right was justified on the ground of state necessity. One of the great concerns has always been that a person's home and possessions could be invaded, without true justification, in order to see whether that person might be involved in any illegal activity. Such "fishing expeditions" were strongly disapproved at common law: in the words of Lord Denning, unless a search warrant has been granted, "the common law does not permit . . . police officers to ransack anyone's house or to search for papers or articles therein, or to search his person simply to see if he has committed some crime or other".[13]

Immediately before the passing of PACE the common law permitted entry and search of premises either with or without a warrant, but only in limited circumstances. With a warrant, entry was originally only permitted in order to search for stolen property on the premises; the Theft Act 1968 converted this power to statutory status. Over the centuries this right was extended so that, with a warrant granted by a magistrate, the police could enter and search premises for substances or articles which it was illegal for any citizen to own or possess. Seizure of property without arrest or charge was permitted only in very limited circumstances, at first by warrant and later without a warrant, provided that there were reasonable grounds at the time of the seizure for belief that the property was related to a serious crime and that the article was kept for only as long as required for the purposes of investigation and evidence. At common law, without a warrant or the consent of the occupier, a power of entry of private premises existed only for three reasons: to prevent or stop a breach of the peace, including harm to persons or serious damage to property; to arrest persons known to be on those premises; or to capture a person who had escaped following a lawful arrest.

3–050 Before PACE, it was uncertain to what extent the common law allowed search without warrant of the premises of an arrested person; cases conflicted, with unpredictable results. Many statutes since the seventeenth century extended the circumstances in which entry and search powers existed, with or without warrant, for a wide variety of reasons including fraud, firearms, terrorism and licensing offences. Many officials, including customs officers and utilities such as electricity companies, were given such statutory powers of entry, which were thus not limited to the police.

The Royal Commission proposed the retention and extension of existing powers of entry and search with a warrant, provided that reasonable grounds could be shown for suspicion that prohibited items would be found on the premises. They also proposed that the existing powers of entry and search without a warrant, and of seizure of property without a warrant, should be maintained and become statutory; this is what in essence was done by PACE, with extensions of powers to cover previous gaps or grey areas. In addition, safeguards should be and were introduced for the rights of the individual concerned in the exercise of any such police power. However, it must be recognised that historically many entries to premises and searches of those premises have been carried out with the "consent" of the occupier or owner, whether or not such consent was in fact freely given, and that such a trend continues in spite of the passing of PACE. Thus Code B contains rules and procedures for searches "by consent", breach of which will affect the validity of the search and the admissibility of any evidence obtained.

1. Entry and Search with A Warrant

Section 8 of PACE: applications to magistrates for search warrants

Under section 8 of PACE, magistrates may issue warrants to enter and **3–051** search premises for evidence of serious arrestable offences. A magistrate must first be satisfied (section 8(1)) that there are reasonable grounds for belief that all of the following five elements exist: that a serious arrestable offence (defined in section 116 and Schedule 5)[14] has been committed; that there is material on the specified premises which is likely to be of substantial value to the investigation of that offence; that the material is likely to be relevant evidence; that the material is not subject to legal privilege (defined in section 10) and is not excluded material (defined in section 11) or special procedure material (defined in section 14); and that one of the conditions set out in section 8(3) applies. Section 8(2) provides that a constable may seize and retain any item for which a search has been authorised under section 8(1).

The conditions under section 8(3) are as follows: it is not practicable to communicate with any person who could consent to entry to the premises; or, although a person could grant entry to the premises, it is not practicable to communicate with any person who could grant access to the evidence; or, entry to the premises will not be granted unless a warrant is produced; or, the purposes of the search may be frustrated or seriously prejudiced unless a constable can gain immediate entry upon arrival at the premises. Thus, it is of the utmost importance in section 8 that a magistrate must be satisfied that there exist reasonable grounds for believing, before a search warrant is issued, that the requirements set out in section 8(1) have been adhered to and that the police have satisfied one of the conditions of section 8(3). If not so satisfied, the magistrate is not entitled to issue the warrant.

For instance, in *R. v. Guildhall Magistrates Court, ex parte Primlaks Holding Co.*[15]:

Facts. The City of London Police Company Fraud Department applied *ex parte* to the magistrate for the issue of two search warrants against two highly reputable law firms to seize certain correspondence between the applicant, Primlak, and one of the law firms concerning the purchase of five vessels. After a hearing lasting approximately ten minutes, the warrants were issued. The applicant sought:

(1) judicial review of the justice's decision and to have the warrants quashed; and

(2) declarations that the correspondence was subject to legal privilege[16] and/or constituted special procedure material.[17]

Decision. The applicant advanced two questions for the court to decide: did the justice properly satisfy himself that (a) there were reasonable grounds for believing that the correspondence was not subject to legal privilege or special procedure material; or (b) that any of the conditions set out in section 8(3) applied? The police contended that, even though prima facie the material was subject to legal privilege, that privilege was lost because the material was held with the intention of furthering a criminal purpose under section 10(2). This was rejected by the courts. It was held that there were no grounds upon which the justice, properly directing himself, could reasonably believe that the correspondence was neither subject to legal privilege nor special procedure material. Parker L.J. stated[18] that "the fact that a police officer who has been investigating the matter, states in the information that he considers that there are reasonable grounds is not enough. The justice himself must be satisfied". Parker L.J. gave short shrift to the second contention by the police that the conditions in section 8(3) applied. He regarded such accusations as "ludicrous" and "wholly without substance". As a result, both warrants were quashed.

Section 9 and Schedule 1: access provisions

3–052 Section 9 governs access by police to material which is held confidentially. A constable may apply to obtain access to such material for the purposes of a criminal investigation by following the procedure laid down in Schedule 1. Under Schedule 1, a circuit judge may grant an order that the possessor of the material should give access to such material if one of the two following sets of conditions are fulfilled. Either:

(i) There are reasonable grounds for belief that a serious arrestable offence has been committed, and special procedure material which is likely to be relevant evidence and to be of substantial value to the investigation is on the specified premises. Other methods of obtaining the material must have failed or not have been worth trying, and it must be considered that it is in the public interest to grant access to the material; or

(ii) There are reasonable grounds for belief that excluded material or special procedure material is on the specified premises, and if the material were not excluded or special procedure, then a search of the premises for that material could have been authorised by issue of a warrant under previous legislation. It must also be shown that issue of such a warrant would have been appropriate.

If a circuit judge grants an order of access to such material on the second set of the above grounds but the possessor does not grant access to the material, then the circuit judge may grant a search warrant and start proceedings for contempt of court. If the first set of access conditions were used, then only contempt of court is available as a remedy for refusal of access to the material. The decision to allow police access to confidential material was a difficult one:

> "Two conflicting public interests had to be weighed—investigating crime and the maintenance of confidentiality of communication and their legal advisers. Maintaining confidentiality was of the greatest importance as vital for the maintenance of confidence in the legal system".[19]

This section concerns specialised confidential information which cannot be obtained through the normal procedures for search warrants undertaken in section 8, but instead must go through the special procedures set out in Schedule 1 to PACE. There are three such "specialised confidential" categories, namely:

(1) Items subject to legal privilege (section 10);

(2) Excluded material (section 11); and

(3) Special procedure material (section 12). Legally privileged material is generally exempted from police access, whereas access may be granted to the other two categories of confidential material, providing that stringent rules and safeguards have been satisfied.

Under section 9(1), a constable when seeking to have access to excluded material or special procedure material is not under a compulsion to use Schedule 1. The police may simply ask the holder of the relevant material to hand it over. If that request is complied with then Schedule 1 is no longer required. This was held in *R. v. Singleton*,[20] where, in a murder trial, a dentist voluntarily handed over the accused's dental records to the police. The words in section 9(1) "a constable may obtain access . . ." under Schedule 1 do not mean that he has to do so. The Court of Appeal stated in that case that had the dentist not disclosed the records voluntarily, an application under section 9 would not have been successful.

Section 10: legal privilege

Legal privilege exempts items from police access by means of a production order or search warrant; they may neither search for such material nor seize it. The privilege is restricted to three situations: **3–053**

(1) Communications relating to purely professional legal advice.

(2) Communications which deal with legal proceedings, or the anticipation of such proceedings.

(3) Items enclosed with or referred to in any of the communications in (1) or (2) above, except that any items held with the intention

of furthering a criminal purpose are not items subject to legal privilege.

The word "communication" is used here in a wide sense, *e.g.* most files including correspondence, letters, memoranda, notes, records of telephone conversations etc., provided that they relate to legal advice and/or legal proceedings. The legal advice itself does not necessarily have to be confined to purely legal issues. Certain types of communications do not come within the scope of legal privilege, *e.g.* conveyancing documents would not normally attract legal privilege.[21] Correspondence which did refer to the conveyance would, however, be privileged if it contained some legal advice issues.[22] In *Francis and Francis v. Central Criminal Court*[23] it was decided that conveyancing documents which were intended for the purpose of furthering a criminal purpose were not items subject to legal privilege. Here, the police suspected that drug money was being laundered through the purchase of various properties. Since the conveyancing documents were a vital part of the police investigation, the exception in section 10(2) applied. Further, in that case, the House of Lords (by a 3:2 majority) stated that under section 10(2) it is not necessary for the solicitor or client to be involved in any criminal activity; it is enough that there is some third party in the chain who intends to use the client or solicitor for some criminal purpose. Finally, the common words of "made in connection with" in section 10(1) mean that legal privilege is restricted to documents and items which exist only from the time the legal adviser/client relationship was entered into. Communications prior to that relationship would probably not be regarded as "made in connection with" legal advice or proceedings.

Section 11: excluded material

3–054 There are three separate categories under the term "excluded material":

(1) Personal records [section 11(1)(a)].

(2) Human tissue or tissue fluid [section 11(1)(b)].

(3) Journalistic material [section 11(1)(c)].

A common requirement to all three categories here is that the material is "held in confidence" by a person. This means under (1) and (2) above that there is an express or implied undertaking to hold it so, or that there is a restriction of disclosure under some Act. Under section 11(3), journalistic material is held in confidence if the person holding it is subject to such a restriction, undertaking or obligation and it has been held continuously in this way ever since it was first acquired or created for the purposes of journalism. Excluded material cannot be the subject of any production order or search warrant unless a search warrant would have been available before PACE.

Section 12: personal records

In Section 12 personal records refer to "identification" documents and records relating to a person's physical or mental health, spiritual counselling or personal counselling given by a professional, (*e.g.* psychologist, social worker or the like). Personal records within this definition are completely excluded from police access; thus no production order or search warrant can be obtained for items such as medical records or student record files held by universities, schools or colleges. Even the dead receive this protection. **3–055**

Section 13: journalistic material

Journalistic material is defined as material which has been acquired or created for the purposes of journalism, and is in the possession of a person who acquired or created it for such purposes. As stated above, section 11(2) and 11(3) require that the material has been continuously held in confidence, with an obligation to so hold it; logically, therefore, journalistic material intended for publication does not qualify as excluded material. Journalism is not confined to print or visual media, but includes any kind of publication. **3–056**

Section 14: special procedure material

The definition of special procedure material for the purposes of section 9 and Schedule 1 includes all material, other than material subject to legal privilege or excluded material as defined above, which is in the possession of a person who acquired or created it in the course of a trade, business, profession, occupation or unpaid employment, and who holds it subject to an undertaking, restriction, or obligation of confidence. In other words, all confidential material connected with an occupation will be special procedure material, unless it qualifies as legally privileged or excluded material. Examples of special procedure material would include a company's bookkeeping records held by an accountant, any business records of a company or individual held by a bank, and much journalistic material which does not qualify as excluded material. In fact, the police very often seek, and obtain, access to special procedure material. **3–057**

Section 15 and Code B, paragraph 2: safeguards for search warrants

Under section 15, when a constable applies for any warrant to enter and search premises, the use of the warrant will be unlawful unless it complies with the safeguards and procedures stated in sections 15 and 16. Section 15 imposes upon the constable a duty to state, when applying for the warrant: **3–058**

(i) The ground for his application,

(ii) The statute under which the warrant is to be issued,

(iii) The premises which are to be entered and searched, and

(iv) To identify as far as possible the articles or persons to be sought.

The warrant when issued will authorise only one entry and will state the name of the applicant, the date of issue, the statute under which it is issued, the premises to be searched and, so far as is practicable, whom or what is being sought. Two copies must be kept, and an "information" in writing containing the same details as are required for the warrant must accompany the application for the warrant.

Code B, paragraph 2.1 requires the officer wishing to apply for a search warrant or production order on the basis of information received to "take reasonable steps to check that the information is accurate, recent and has not been provided maliciously or irresponsibly" and prevents an application from being made merely on the basis of an uncorroborated anonymous source. Paragraphs 2.2 and 2.3 impose further duties before an application is made; the officer must make reasonable enquiries to gather information about the articles sought and their location, the details of the occupier of the premises and of any other previous searches of the premises. Under paragraph 2.4, the authority of an officer of at least the rank of inspector must normally be sought before an application; a senior officer's approval will suffice in circumstances of urgency.

R. v. Leeds Crown Court, ex parte Switalski[24]:

Facts. The police applied, *ex parte*, for a search warrant against a firm of solicitors under investigation for fraud. The police wished to seize all the files and documents of the firm. The applicant solicitor sought judicial review on the grounds that paragraph 14(a) of Schedule 1 had not been complied with by the police and therefore the warrant should be set aside.

Decision. The application was dismissed. What was rare in this case was that the search warrant did not specify what documents were to be sought. However, the Court took the view that because of the unusual and serious circumstances, *i.e.* investigation of a solicitor for legal aid fund fraud, it was not possible to decide in advance what items were subject to legal privilege and what were excluded by reason of section 10(2). Further, if the information does not agree with the warrant, then the warrant itself is more likely to be adjudged invalid.[25]

It is therefore of the utmost importance that the warrant to be issued shall identify, so far as is practicable, the articles or persons to be sought. If not properly identified, then the warrant itself may be invalid, despite the other conditions of the warrant being adhered to.

For instance, in *R. v. Central Criminal Court and BRB, ex parte AJD Holdings*[26]:

Facts. The applicant, AJD, had a subsidiary company which contracted with BRB to do various construction work. Fraud, involving false accounting and fake invoices, against BRB was alleged by some employees of the subsidiary company. A warrant was issued to the British Transport Police under section 9 and Schedule 1 for the entry of premises and seizure of various company documents.

Decision. The applicant contended that the warrant failed to comply with section 15(6)(b), in that the warrant failed to identify, as far as practicable, the proper documents sought. The police information referred to "all records of business details relating to the finances of the company, namely letters, notes . . .", whereas the warrant referred to letters and notes but omitted to identify them as records of financial business details of the company. This omission was of the utmost importance since it would permit the police to seize all the documents they wished, irrespective of whether it was set out in the information or relevant to the investigation. As a result of this omission, the warrant was declared invalid.

Thus, unless the warrant is able to specify with some degree of exactness, which is in the knowledge of the police, it will be deemed to be too general for a warrant to be granted. Further, if the information does not agree with the warrant, then the warrant itself is more likely to be adjudged invalid.[27]

In section 15(1) it is stated that ". . . an entry on or search of premises under a warrant is unlawful unless it complies with this section and section 16 below". What does "it" refer to in section 15(1); a warrant or entry and search of premises?[28] In Bevan and Lidstone's *The Investigation of Crime* it is stated that the clearer formulation is in article 17(1) of the PACE(N.I.) Order 1989, which states that "an entry on or search of premises under a warrant is unlawful, unless the warrant complies with the Article and is executed in accordance with Article 18" [equivalent to PACE, s.16]. This makes it clear that it is the entry on or search of premises which is unlawful if sections 15 and 16 are not complied with.[29] The preferred meaning, it is suggested, is that "it" encompasses the words "entry on or search of premises under a warrant", and that the whole of these words must comply with section 16.

Section 16: execution of warrants; notice of powers and rights

Section 16 provides further procedures for the execution of search war- **3–059**
rants, which are designed to protect the occupier of the premises and ensure that the entry and search are conducted responsibly. A warrant remains valid for one month after its issue (section 16(3)). The entry and search under the warrant must be carried out at a reasonable hour unless the constable believes that to do so would frustrate the purposes of the warrant (section 16(4)). If the occupier of the premises (or any other person who appears to the constable to be in charge of the premises under section 16(6)) is present at the time when the warrant is to be exercised, then the constable must identify himself to the occupier, produce the warrant and hand over a copy of it to the occupier (section 16(5)). If no one is present on the premises at the time of the entry and search, then a copy of the warrant must be left in a prominent place on the premises (section 16(7)). Once the search is completed, the constable who carried it

out must endorse the warrant with details of whether the articles or persons sought were found, and whether any other articles were seized.

Code B adds further rules for the valid execution of a search warrant and the seizure of property (it also applies to searches without a warrant under sections 17 and 18 and elsewhere). The relevant paragraphs here are Code B paras 5 and 7. Under paragraph 5.4, the police officer conducting the search must attempt to communicate with the occupier of the premises and explain under what authority the search is to be conducted; permission to enter the premises should be requested. Exceptions to this exist where the premises are unoccupied or there are reasonable grounds for belief that alerting the occupier would frustrate the purposes of the search or endanger a person. Paragraph 5.6 allows reasonable force to be used to effect an entry to the premises if access has been refused by the occupier, or it is impossible to communicate with the occupier or if the officer believes that to do so would frustrate the purpose of the search or endanger a person. Code B also requires the officer, unless it is impracticable to do so, to supply the occupier, before the search begins, with a notice which: specifies the type of search being conducted; summarises the powers of search and seizure under PACE; explains the occupier's rights in the situation relating both to the search and to any seizure of property; states that compensation may be available for any damage caused; and states that a copy of Code B is available at any police station. If the occupier is not present then the notice and a copy of any warrant should be left in a prominent place on the premises.

Section 16(5)(b) states that the constable "shall produce the warrant to him; and (c) shall supply him with a copy of it". Code B, paragraph 5.8 states that if the occupier is present a copy of the warrant "should if practicable be given to the occupier before the search begins . . .". Thus, by not handing over a copy of the warrant, prior to the search, there is technically a breach. But in *Heagren and Heagren v. Chief Constable of The Norfolk Constabulary* [1997] (unreported) the Court of Appeal ruled that even if there was a contravention of the Code, the practical approach is to be preferred, that is, serving the copy after the search was completed in order to endorse what, if any, articles or persons were found and/or seized under section 16(9). Paragraphs 5.9–5.12 relate to the conduct of the search itself. Once all the items specified in a warrant have been found, the search should stop. Due consideration should be shown for the privacy and property of the premises' occupier, who must be allowed to have a witness present during the search if he so wishes, unless the officer in charge has reasonable grounds for belief that this would seriously hinder the investigation or endanger a person. If force has been used to enter the premises then they must be left secure.

3–060 Under both section 16(5) and Code B, paragraph 5.5, the constable must identify himself. The question is, must it be done before entry to the premises or are there circumstances where identification is permitted after entry? In *R. v. Longman*[30] the Court of Appeal stated that a constable executing a search warrant may effect entry to premises before identifying himself or producing the warrant, if he had reasonable grounds to believe that by identifying himself, the purpose of the search would be frustrated or the constable might be injured. Under Code B, paragraph 5.4(iii), it may be permissible to use force or subterfuge to gain entry. However, the police must still make the warrant available for inspection (and not simply flash it at the occupier) before the search itself is conducted. Further, the Divisional Court decided in *R. v. Reading Justices, ex parte SW Meat*[31] that the search itself must be under the control of the police (and not the Meat Intervention Board as in that case). The warrant in that case was also invalid because there was no reason to consider that the search would be prejudiced unless immediate access were gained, and the warrant did not specify with sufficient particularity the object of the search. In *R. v. SW Magistrates, ex parte Cofie*[32] the Divisional Court added that if premises are internally divided, then the warrant must specify which parts of the premises are to be searched. Code B, paragraph 7 contains the procedures to be followed after a search has been carried out. On return to the police station, the officer in charge of the search must complete a record of the search which contains details of the entire conduct of the search, the details given on the warrant, the names of all police officers involved in the search and what, if anything, was seized, amongst other details.

2. Entry and Search Without a Warrant

Section 17: entry for purposes of arrest

Under section 17(2), a police officer may enter and search premises without a warrant where he has reasonable grounds for believing any of the following needs exist: section 17(1)(a) to arrest a person under a warrant of arrest; section 17(1)(b) to arrest a person for an arrestable offence[33]; section 17(1)(c) to arrest a person for certain statutory public order offences; section 17(1)(d) to recapture a person who is unlawfully at large and whom the officer is pursuing; section 17(1)(e) to save life or prevent serious damage to property. This section deals with situations where the constable may enter and search premises without the need of first applying for a warrant. The main purpose, though by no means exclusive, is in order to make an arrest. This section is generally used for the purpose of seeking out persons, save under section 17(1)(e) where the reason is preventing serious damage to property. Section 17(1)(d) permits the constable to recapture a person who is unlawfully at large and whom he is pursuing. "Unlawfully at large" refers to escapees from prisons, legal custody, mental hospitals and the like, as well as those persons who have escaped from an ordinary lawful arrest. However, an important stipulation in section 17(1)(d) is that the constable must be in pursuit of the escapee. 3–061

The meaning of this was considered by the courts in *D'Souza v. DPP*[34]:

Facts. The mother of the appellant was unlawfully at large after leaving a psychiatric hospital without permission. The police believed the mother of the appellant to be in the appellant's house, and when entry was refused by the appellant, the police forced entry under PACE, s. 17(1)(d). The appellant was convicted of assaulting the constables in the execution of their duty, and appealed to the House of Lords on the basis that the police had no power to enter the house without a warrant, and thus were not "in the execution of their duty".

Decision. Under PACE, s. 17(1)(d) a constable can enter and search premises for a person who is "unlawfully at large and whom he is pursuing". There must be evidence of the pursuit. The entry of the person at large into the premises must be almost contemporaneous with the pursuit. On the facts of the case, whilst the person was unlawfully at large, the police had not been "pursuing" the person and so there was no power of entry under section 17(1)(d).

Unless the police are physically chasing the person "at large", they cannot enter premises without a warrant to arrest them under section 17(1)(d). *Zander* states[35] that an escaped convict may be regarded as being "pursued" at all times, but the person at large in the above case had simply left a psychiatric hospital without permission. Had the police not been in pursuit, they would still have been able to enter under section 17(1)(b) had it been an arrestable offence that had been committed. Since it was not, they should not have entered without first obtaining an arrest warrant. Under the general statutory provisions of section 17, a police officer, in the absence of consent, may use reasonable force, if necessary, to gain entry for the purposes of section 17(1)(a)-(e), but the police must have lawful authority or excuse to take such action. Thus, in *O'Loughlin v. Chief Constable of Essex*,[36] the court said that entry by reasonable force should not be permitted unless legally justified and the occupant is given reasons for the entry.

Section 17(6) is the only common law power of entry preserved by PACE; all others are abolished in section 17(5). The power is restricted in its application to where the police hold a "genuine belief" that a breach of the peace is "a real and imminent risk", although the breach need not be of a particular type and the power can be used on private residences.[37]

3–062 *Section 18, section 32 and Code B, paragraph 5: entry and search after arrest*

Section 18(1)(a) allows a constable, after an arrest for an arrestable offence, to enter and search premises occupied or controlled by the arrested person if he has reasonable grounds to suspect that he may find there evidence which relates to that offence. Any such evidence found may be seized under section 18(2).

Under section 18(1)(b), after an arrest, a constable may search for and seize anything which relates to some arrestable offence which is connected to, or similar to that offence. The words "connected to" or "similar to" have not been defined under the Act, but searching premises for drugs where a person has been arrested for stealing a sandwich would not constitute a valid search.[38] Thus, in *Jeffrey v. Black*,[39] a non-consensual search of premises for drugs was held to be unlawful for that precise reason.

Under section 18(4) the power granted to a constable under this section may only be authorised in writing by an officer of the rank of inspector or above, subject to section 18(5). Merely giving a verbal authorisation is not sufficient. Even making a written record of the verbal authorisation will still not constitute "authorisation in writing". It must be an independent document. Although the Act does not provide any definition or guidelines as to the form of the written authorisation, a document which clearly denotes authority and which is specific enough to the request in question would probably suffice.

Section 32: search away from the police station

Section 32 deals both with searches of a person away from a police station **3–063** (see section on detention) and searches of premises which were either the venue of the arrest, or from which the suspect had left shortly before being arrested. section 32(2)(b) gives a constable a power:

> ". . . to enter and search any premises in which he (the suspect) was when arrested or immediately before he was arrested for evidence relating to the offence for which he has been arrested".

The police may only search the premises (or indeed the suspect) for items which either might be useful to him for the purpose of escaping from lawful custody, or might be evidence relating to an offence (section 32(2)).

Thus the search is limited both in terms of the venue which may be searched and the purpose for which the search may be made; there should not be any "fishing expeditions". In addition, the section 32 power to search premises only applies "to the extent that it is reasonably required for the purpose of discovering any such thing or any such evidence" (section 32(3)). The constable who carries out the search must be able to demonstrate that he has reasonable grounds for belief that there is relevant evidence on the premises (section 32(6)).

Code B, paragraph 5 adds further requirements before a search carried out under the authority of section 32 will be valid. These requirements in fact apply to all searches, including those carries out under section 18. First, the search should take place at a "reasonable hour"; this term is left undefined by the Code, which simply states that the police should have regard to whether there is likely to be anybody on the premises (Note 5A). The officer carrying out the search should identify himself on reaching the premises and should attempt to speak to someone who could allow him permission to enter (paragraph 5.4). The officer should state the reasons for the search (paragraph 5.5). But if it is known that the premises are empty, then the identification and notification rules do not apply; this is also true if it is believed by the officer on reasonable grounds that to notify the occupiers of the premises of an impending search would endanger the existence of the evidence or the safety of the officers (paragraph 5.4). An officer may use reasonable force in order to gain entry to the premises to be searched if the latter reasons apply, or if the occupier of the premises refuses entry or is unobtainable (paragraph 5.6).

When the search is about to take place, the officer must give to the occupier of the premises, if are he is available, a Notice of Powers and Rights which is detailed in paragraph 5.7. The only exceptions to this duty are if the search would be hampered, or officers endangered, by so doing. (paragraph 5.8). In the Notice are stated the reasons for the search, the authority upon which it is being made, the rights of the occupier and the potential for compensation for any damage or seizure of property. It also explains the PACE Codes available from any police station (paragraph 5.7). According to paragraph 5.10, the search must be carried out in a manner which causes the least disturbance necessary, and shows due consideration for the occupier's property and privacy. A witness may attend the search if the occupier so wishes (paragraph 5.11), unless such a person's presence would be likely to hamper the investigation. If the premises have been subject to a forced entry, then they must be secured before the officers leave (paragraph 5.12).

> Returning to our example, do the police have sufficient justification for visiting Marcus' home and searching it for evidence related to the assault earlier that evening? Or alternatively, what if one of the officers realises that the arrestee fits the detailed description of a man wanted for other serious offences? It can be seen that a search of premises could be made either with (section 15 and 16) or without a warrant. The police may search a private residence for anything connected to an arrestable offence (section 18) without a warrant. The provisions of Code B will apply to any search. But, unknown to the police, Marcus is a journalist: care will therefore have to be taken to comply with sections 11–14.

Section 19 and Code B, paragraph 6: seizure of articles

3–064 Section 19 confers powers upon a constable who is lawfully on any premises to seize items in the following three situations. Under section 19(2) a constable may seize anything on the premises if he has reasonable grounds for belief that the item was obtained through the offence; or that it is necessary to seize the item in order to prevent it from being damaged, destroyed or otherwise disposed of.

Section 19(3) allows a constable to seize anything which is on the premises if he has reasonable grounds for belief that it is evidence in relation to any offence, and in addition that it is necessary to seize the item to prevent its disposal, damage or destruction.

Section 19(4) states that a constable may require any information held on a computer and accessible from the premises to be handed over, if he has reasonable grounds for belief that the information is evidence in relation to any offence; or that it has been obtained through an offence; or that it is necessary to seize the information in order to prevent its disposal, damage or destruction:

(1) Items subject to legal privilege cannot be seized (section 19(6)).

(2) Other pre-existing powers of seizure are expressly preserved by section 19(5).

(3) It should be noted that items may be seized even though a search warrant would not have been available for them; for example, excluded and special procedure material.

Code B paragraph 6.3 states that, if an officer decides that it is inappropriate to seize property because of an explanation given by a person holding the property, but the officer has reasonable grounds for belief that the property is related to an offence, the officer shall inform the holder of that belief and explain the civil and criminal consequences which may follow if the holder disposes of the property. Paragraph 6.4 allows for the copying or photography of any document or article which the officer has power to seize.

According to paragraphs 6.6 and 6.7, items which have been seized may be retained only as long as is necessary in the circumstances, and may not be retained if a photograph or copy or the item would suffice in its place for the purposes of evidence or investigation.

A particular problem facing those persons authorised to seize various materials is that in many cases it is impossible to discover immediately what property is relevant and within the remit of the warrant. In many instances it is impracticable to examine everything on particular premises. There is always the ever-present danger that if the seized material or property is later on discovered to be outside the scope of the warrant then the police could be sued for damages for unauthorised and unjustified seizure. Examples of the types of material likely to cause problems in this area include the various different kinds of computer disks, or documents which are so detailed or vast in quantity that it is not practical to examine them there and then. However, sections 50 and 51 of the Criminal Justice and Police Act 2001 entitle those persons in possession of a warrant to search and seize material where "he has reasonable grounds for believing may be or may contain something for which he is authorised to search on those premises",[39A] in order to make such a determination. Thus where there is discovered any material or property which is not reasonably practical to separate on the premises, then the authorised person is entitled to remove it for examination.[39B] Under section 50(3) the confines upon which this power is based involves consideration of the following factors, including:

(i) How long it would take to carry out the determination or separation on those premises (section 50(3)(a));

(ii) The number of persons that would be required to carry out the determination or separation on those premises within a reasonable time (section 50(3)(b));

(iii) Whether the determination or separation would involve damage to property (section 50(3)(c)).[39C]

VI DETENTION AND TREATMENT IN CUSTODY

INTRODUCTION

3–065 There are strong reasons why the police should have a power to detain a suspect after arrest, without first charging him with an offence. If such a power did not exist, arrest would often have to be delayed until the police were absolutely sure that sufficient evidence had been obtained to sustain a specific charge and that the chosen charge was the most appropriate to the evidence. Questioning of a suspect at the police station would be impossible without his consent if the power to detain without charge did not exist; such questioning is a vital stage in many cases which establishes the strength or weakness of the evidence against the suspect, and is often the first opportunity to ascertain whether he has an alibi or defence. Detention may avoid wrongful charges and prosecutions, and allows some time to assess whether and what charges should be brought. Of course there have been many criticisms that detention powers are used as leverage to sway a suspect towards a confession, but if the safeguards in PACE are followed this should not be a substantial concern in most cases. These arguments must be weighed against the obvious interference with a citizen's liberty which occurs when he is detained without charge.

As has been discussed above, an arrest can be made where a relatively trivial offence has been committed or is merely threatened, and even where it has not been proven that any offence has been committed at all; thus some detentions without charge will be of innocent individuals against whom no prosecution will be taken and who therefore are being deprived of their liberty without justification. A distinction can be drawn between situations where a serious offence has been committed or is at least reasonably suspected to have been committed by the suspect, and situations where this criterion cannot be established. In the former it can be argued that the public interest in the detection and prosecution of offenders temporarily outweighs the suspect's right to liberty; this type of argument is difficult to sustain if the person is suspected of a trivial offence, there is little evidence remaining to be collected by the police, or the arrest and detention are arguably a "fishing expedition" and no charges may ever be brought.

Before PACE, the extent of the police power to hold a suspect for questioning was ill-defined both at common law and under existing statutes.

The statutory authority for detention dated back to the second half of the nineteenth century, and was re-enacted in successive Acts until the Magistrates' Courts Act 1980. Under section 43 of that Act, a suspect could be detained without charge if the offence was a serious one and it "would not be practicable to bring him before a magistrates' court within twenty-four hours after his being taken into custody". He should then be brought before the magistrates "as soon as practicable". What was meant by "as soon as practicable" was a source of much controversy, with some cases holding that this encompassed indefinite detention, but some courts stating vigorously that it did not. But neither in section 43 nor in any other statute was there an express power to detain a suspect for the purpose of questioning; for this it was necessary to look to the common law. The Court of Appeal in the case of *Mohammed-Holgate*[40] (discussed above) held that detention for questioning was not unlawful; but the extent of this power and the rules according to which it should be exercised were never fully explored or defined by the courts. The Royal Commission was critical of the existing law and considered it to have too great a degree of uncertainty. Whilst agreeing that detention for questioning without charge was lawful and an important part of the police function, they considered that a framework of safeguards should be introduced and the parameters of the power should be set firmly. The length of detention should be limited by strict rules which would compromise between police needs and suspects' rights. Detailed records should be kept of the detention and the reasons behind it. A detention should be monitored both in this way and by appearances before a magistrates' court if the police should wish to extend the original period of detention. Most of the Royal Commission's recommendations were embodied in PACE, but the Act also imposes a mandatory maximum length of detention without charge and extends the length of time in detention which can elapse without a court appearance being required.

PACE provides detailed rules and procedures for the treatment during detention in police custody of a person who has been arrested but has not yet been charged with a criminal offence. The PACE powers go far beyond previous common law and statutory provisions in relation to detention, but new safeguards are also provided. Code C and the related Notes for Guidance play an important role in the imposition of these safeguards. Each of the sections of PACE which concern detention without charge will be discussed in turn.

The following forms, *i.e.* Notice to Detained Person and Notice of Entitlements, must be given to suspects at the police station in order that they are aware of their rights during police detention.

METROPOLITAN POLICE SERVICE

Form 3053

Notice to Detained Person

The section in capital letters is to be read to the detained person by the Custody Officer before giving the notice to the detained person.

YOU HAVE THE RIGHT TO:

1. SPEAK TO AN INDEPENDENT SOLICITOR FREE OF CHARGE
2. HAVE SOMEONE TOLD THAT YOU HAVE BEEN ARRESTED
3. CONSULT THE CODES OF PRACTICE COVERING POLICE POWERS AND PROCEDURES

YOU MAY DO ANY OF THESE THINGS NOW, BUT IF YOU DO NOT, YOU MAY STILL DO SO AT ANY TIME WHILST DETAINED AT THE POLICE STATION.

If you are asked questions about a suspected offence,you do not have to say anything. But it may harm your defence if you do not mention when questioned something which you later rely on in court. Anything you do say may be given in evidence.

More information is given below.

Free Legal Advice.

You can speak to a solicitor at the police station at any time, day or night. It will cost you nothing.

Access to legal advice can only be delayed in certain exceptional circumstances (see Annex B of Code of Practice C).

If you do not know a solicitor, or you cannot contact your own solicitor, ask for the duty solicitor. He or she is nothing to do with the police. Or you can ask to see a list of local solicitors.

You can talk to the solicitor in private on the telephone, and the solicitor may come to see you at the police station.

If the police want to question you, you can ask for the solicitor to be there.

If there is a delay, ask the police to contact the solicitor again. Normally, the police must not question you until you have spoken to the solicitor. However, there are certain circumstances in which the police may question you without a solicitor being present (see paragraph 6.6 of Code of Practice C).

If you want to see a solicitor, tell the Custody Officer at once. You can ask for legal advice at any time during your detention. Even if you do tell the police you do not want a solicitor at first, you can change your mind at any time.

Your right to legal advice does not entitle you to delay procedures under the Road Traffic Act 1988 which require the provision of breath, blood or urine specimens.

THE LAW SOCIETY

Legal Aid

The right to have someone informed of your detention.

You may on request have one person known to you, or who is likely to take an interest in your welfare, informed at public expense as soon as practicable of your whereabouts. If the person you name cannot be contacted you may choose up to two alternatives. If they too cannot be contacted the Custody Officer has discretion to allow further attempts until the information has been conveyed. This right can only be delayed in exceptional circumstances (see Annex B of Code of Practice C).

The right to consult the Codes of Practice.

The Codes of Practice will be made available to you on request.
These Codes govern police procedures. The right to consult the Codes of Practice does not entitle you to delay unreasonably any necessary investigative and administrative action, neither does it allow procedures under the Road Traffic Act 1988 requiring the provision of breath, blood or urine specimens to be delayed.

The right to a copy of the Custody Record

A record of your detention will be kept by the Custody Officer.
When you leave police detention or are taken before a Court, you or your legal representative or the appropriate adult shall be supplied on request with a copy of the Custody Record as soon as practicable. This entitlement lasts for 12 months after your release from police detention.

METROPOLITAN POLICE SERVICE

PERSON ATTENDING VOLUNTARILY AT POLICE STATION AND NOT UNDER ARREST

You can speak to a solicitor at the police station at any time, day or night. It will cost you nothing.

If you do not know a solicitor, or you cannot contact your own solicitor, ask for the duty solicitor. He or she is nothing to do with the police. Or you can ask to see a list of local solicitors.

You can talk to the solicitor in private on the telephone, and the solicitor may come to see you at the police station.

If the police want to question you, you can ask for the solicitor to be there. If there is a delay ask the police to contact the solicitor again. You can ask the police to wait for the solicitor to be at the interview.

THE LAW SOCIETY

Legal Aid

M.P. 1101/96

METROPOLITAN POLICE SERVICE Form 3053A

NOTICE OF ENTITLEMENTS

This notice summarises provisions contained in Codes C and D of the Codes of Practice regarding your entitlements whilst in custody. The letters and numbers in brackets relate to appropriate Code and paragraph references. If you require more detailed information please ask to consult the Codes.

All persons should read parts A and B of this notice. Part C explains provisions which apply to juveniles and persons suffering from mental disorder or mental handicap and Part D explains additional provisions which apply to citizens of independent commonwealth countries and nationals of foreign countries.

PART A—GENERAL ENTITLEMENTS

Whilst in custody you are entitled to the following:—

1. **Visits and contact with outside persons**

   In addition to your rights to have someone informed of your arrest, and legal advice, you may receive visits, at the custody officer's discretion. Unless certain conditions apply you may also make one telephone call, and be supplied with writing materials ('C' 5.4 and 5.6).

2. **Reasonable Standards of Physical Comfort**

   Where practicable you should have your own cell ('C' 8.1), which is clean, heated, ventilated and lit ('C' 8.2). Bedding should be clean and serviceable ('C' 8.3).

3. **Adequate Food and Drink**

   Three meals per day. Drinks with and, upon reasonable request between meals ('C' 8.6).

4. **Access to Toilets and Washing Facilities** ('C' 8.4).

5. **Replacement Clothing**

   If your own clothes are taken from you, you must be given replacements that are clean and comfortable ('C' 8.5).

6. **Medical Attention**

   You may ask to see the police surgeon (or other doctor at your own expense) for a medical examination, or if you require medication. You may also be allowed to take or apply your own medication at appropriate times but in the case of controlled drugs the police surgeon will normally supervise you when doing so ('C' 9.4—'C'9.6).

7. **Exercise**

   Where practicable, brief outdoor exercise every day ('C' 8.7).

8. **If in 'Police Detention' to make representations when your detention is reviewed**

   When the grounds for your detention are periodically reviewed, you have a statutory right to say why you think you should be released, unless you are unfit to do so because of your condition or behaviour ('C' 15.1).

PART B—CONDUCT OF INTERVIEWS

1. Interview rooms should be adequately heated, lit and ventilated ('C' 12.4).

2. Persons being interviewed should not be required to stand ('C' 12.5).

3. Unless certain conditions apply in any 24 hour period you must be allowed at least eight hours rest, normally at night ('C' 12.2).

4. Breaks should be made at recognised meal times, and short breaks for refreshments should normally be made at intervals of approximately two hours ('C' 12.7).

5. Interviewing officers should identify themselves by name and rank (or by warrant or other identification number in terrorism cases) ('C' 12.6).

PART C—APPROPRIATE ADULTS

If you are under 17 years of age or suffering from a mental disorder or mental handicap, you should be assisted by an "appropriate adult" as explained in Code C, paragraph 1.7. A solicitor or lay visitor present at the station in that capacity may not act as the appropriate adult ('C' Note 1F). The appropriate adult will be present when you are:—

1. informed of and served with notices explaining the rights of detained persons, and when informed of the grounds for detention ('C' 3.11);
2. interviewed (except in urgent cases), or provide or sign a written statement ('C' 11.14);
3. intimately or strip searched ('C' Annex A, Paragraph 5 and 11(c));
4. cautioned ('C' 10.6);
5. given information, asked to sign documentation, or asked to give consent regarding any identification procedure ('D' 1.11, 1.12, 1.13); or
6. charged ('C' 16.1); or
7. when the grounds for detention are periodically reviewed ('C' 15.1).

You should always be given the opportunity, when an appropriate adult is called to the police station, to speak privately to a solicitor in the absence of the appropriate adult should you wish to do so.

PART D—FOREIGN NATIONALS/COMMONWEALTH CITIZENS

If you are a citizen of a foreign or commonwealth country, you are entitled to the following:—

1. To communicate at any time with your High Commission, Embassy or Consulate, and have them told of your whereabouts and the grounds for your detention ('C' 7.1).
2. To private visits from a consular officer to talk, or to arrange for legal advice ('C' 7.3).

M.P. 95/28173

Section 30

3–066 Once a person has been arrested at a venue other than a police station, he must be taken to a police station by a constable "as soon as is practicable" after the arrest (section 30(1)). It should generally be a "designated police station" to which he is taken (section 30(2)) (see below). But if at the time of arrest it appears to the constable that it may be necessary to detain the suspect for longer than six hours, then he should take the arrestee to a designated police station (section 30(5)). However there is a major exception to the section 30(1) requirement that the arrestee should be taken to a police station as soon as is practicable; section 30(10) allows a delay if the suspect's presence elsewhere "is necessary in order to carry out such investigations as it is reasonable to carry out immediately". So, if an element of surprise or the existence of evidence might be lost in the time involved in taking the arrestee immediately to the police station, a detour may be made, but a record of this fact and the reasons behind it must be kept (section 30(11)). An example of a situation where section 30(10) might apply would be if the arresting officer believes on reasonable grounds that it is necessary to carry out an immediate search of the arrestee's home for evidence and wants the arrestee to be present; or if there are reasonable grounds for belief that a further offence is about to be committed by an accomplice of the arrestee, who may be arrested if caught in time.

> Returning to our example, Marcus has been arrested on reasonable suspicion of an offence. Evidence was found at his home which may relate to several ongoing investigations. What are his rights in relation to being taken into custody?

Section 34: The Limits of Detention

3–067 Under section 34, a person arrested for any offence may only be detained in police custody without charge if the conditions in Part IV of PACE are satisfied. If a custody officer becomes aware that the grounds for detention of any person no longer apply, or is not aware of any grounds which justify the continued detention of that person, then he must release the suspect from custody immediately, unless the suspect appears to the custody officer to have been unlawfully at large at the time of his arrest. Only the custody officer at the police station where the suspect's custody was authorised has authority to release him. When a detained suspect is released from custody, his release is to be without bail unless it appears to the custody officer that either: any matter related to the reason for which he was detained requires further investigation; or that proceedings may be taken against the suspect for any offence; in each of these cases the suspect is to be released on bail.

So, Marcus must be taken as soon as is possible to a police station, preferably a "designated police station". He must be charged with an offence as soon as possible, unless Part IV of PACE is satisfied (s.34), in which case he may be detained without charge. He will be brought as quickly as possible before a custody officer.

Sections 35 and 36: The Function of Custody Officers at Designated Police Stations

A distinction is drawn for the purposes of detention between "designated police stations" and other, smaller or rural stations. Section 35 requires the chief officer of police for each police area to designate which police stations in that area are to be used for the detention of suspects, on the basis that they have suitable accommodation for that purpose. However, a suspect may be taken on arrest to any police station if it appears to the arresting officer that it will not be necessary to detain the suspect for a period of more than six hours (section 30(3)); or if the arresting officer is alone and it appears to him that he will be unable to take the suspect to a designated police station without the suspect injuring himself, the constable or some other person. A person detained at a non-designated police station who is not released within six hours must be taken to a designated station (section 30(5) and (6)). **3–068**

Section 36(1) requires the appointment of at least one custody officer for each designated police station, who must be of at least the rank of sergeant, but his functions may be performed by another officer if he is not available at a particular time (section 36(4)). Generally an officer may not be the custody officer in relation to a case which he is investigating (section 36(5)), but he may perform some normal police roles in relation to the suspect, such as searching him or carrying out a breath test, and may do anything else authorised by PACE or the Codes (section 36(6)).

In a non-designated police station, there must be an officer available in the event of a custody officer being required. A gap exists in relation to the separation of a custody officer's role from investigation of the case; in a non-designated police station it is possible for the same person to be both custody officer and involved in the investigation if no other officer is readily available to act as custody officer; if this problem should arise then the officer who accompanied the suspect to the station, or any other officer, may act as custody officer (section 36(7)(b)). Under sections 36(9) and (10), an officer of at least the rank of Inspector at a designated station must be informed as soon as is practicable that this is the case; the reason behind this is that the senior officer may then order the transfer of the suspect to the designated station. PACE does not regulate the duration of a custody officer's role nor how it is to be assigned; such matters fall to the discretion of particular stations.

Section 37: The Duties of the Custody Officer Before Charges are Brought

3–069 The intention behind the safeguards in section 37 is to hasten the charging of a suspect as soon as possible after he is brought to a police station, provided of course that there is sufficient evidence upon which to justify the charge. Detention of a suspect is only permitted to continue without charge if the custody officer believes on reasonable grounds that further detention is necessary for one of certain narrowly defined reasons. The rights and duties created by section 37 apply where any of the following persons are brought to a police station: a person arrested without a warrant; a person arrested on a warrant which is not endorsed for bail; or a person who has returned to a police station to answer to bail (section 37(1) of the PACE, section 29(3) of the Criminal Justice and Public Order Act 1994).

A custody officer at a police station where a suspect has been brought and is being detained after arrest must determine whether sufficient evidence exists to charge the suspect with the offence for which he has been arrested; while the custody officer is making his decision, the suspect may be detained at the police station for "such period as is necessary to enable him to do so" (section 37(1)). According to section 37(2), a custody officer shall release any suspect who has not been charged if insufficient evidence to charge exists, unless:

(i) The custody officer has reasonable grounds for belief that the suspect's detention without charge "is necessary to secure or preserve evidence relating to an offence for which he is under arrest"; or

(ii) The custody officer has reasonable grounds for belief that the suspect's detention without charge is necessary to obtain evidence for the offence by questioning the suspect. Thus there is now a general police power to detain a suspect for questioning without first charging him with an offence.

If either of these two reasons exist, then the custody officer may authorise the suspect to be kept in police detention. In such a case, the custody officer must, as soon as is practicable, make a written record of the grounds for the detention (section 37(4)). The suspect should be present while this is done and should himself be informed of the grounds, unless the suspect is incapable of understanding what is being said to him, is or may become violent, or is in urgent need of medical attention (section 37(5),(6) and (7)). Code C increases the protection for the suspect in this situation, but also allows some flexibility within the rules. Under paragraph 1.1, all detained suspects "must be dealt with expeditiously, and released as soon as the need for detention has ceased to apply". However, a custody officer will not be in breach of the Code by a simple delay in the exercise of his duties "provided that the delay is justifiable and that every reasonable step has been taken to prevent unnecessary delay".

In *R. v. Davison*[41]: **3–070**

Facts. The defendant was arrested for handling stolen property and brought to the police station at 7 a.m. where the following events took place:
9:12 a.m.—Interviewed by police—no evidence against him.
11:00 a.m.—Should have been released by this time. Custody officer not informed.
1:15 p.m.—Custody record showed "Further detention authorised . . .". After 1:15 p.m., police receive information to connect the defendant with a robbery in 1994.
3:00 p.m.—Authority to have access to solicitor delayed for reasons that (a) defendant might warn off accomplice (b) proceeds of robbery might be removed and (c) firearms still not found.
4:30 p.m. (approx.)—questioned about robbery, but not arrested (breach of section 31).
Notes of questions not shown to defendant (breach of then C12:12).
5:10 p.m.—interviewed, access to solicitor denied. Defendant makes a full confession.
8:00 p.m.—interview terminated. Defendant allowed phone call and access to solicitor.

Decision. The court held that the defendant should have been released from detention at 11.00 a.m. and any detention after that was unlawful (breach of section 34). The custody officer was in breach of section 37 for not properly adhering to procedures as set out therein. The court also found that the police did not have sufficient grounds for refusing the defendant access to legal advice. Since the defendant had not named a particular solicitor to be contacted, there were no reasonable grounds to suppose that outside accomplices would be warned. The court said that in order to delay access "the police in proving the reasonableness of withholding access to a solicitor must go beyond showing a substantial risk of their fears being realised". As a consequence of the above stated breaches of the Act and the Codes, the court held that the police had used their powers in a way which was capable of amounting to oppression, *i.e.* it was "exercised in a wrongful manner", and therefore constituted a breach of section 76 (see below at para. 3–095, *et seq.*). Accordingly, the defendant was discharged.

Any delay and the reason behind it must be noted on the custody record (see below); the delays which are envisaged as reasonable include practicalities such as the police station being overloaded with suspects, an interpreter needing to be found or a parent to be traced (paragraph 1.1A, Notes for Guidance 1H).

Paragraph 2.1 of Code C requires a separate custody record to be created for each person who is under arrest and at a police station. All information which PACE and the Code require to be placed on the custody record must be recorded as soon as practicable. The custody officer is responsible for the accuracy and completeness of the custody record and must make sure that a copy of the record goes with the suspect if he is transferred to another police station. The time of a suspect's release must be entered on the record (paragraph 2.3). The detained person and his legal representative (or appropriate adult, if applicable) may inspect the custody record on request as soon as is practicable after arrival at the police station, and may request a copy after release or a court appearance (paragraph 2.4, 2.5). All entries on the custody record must be accompanied by a signature and the time noted, or user identification and time if the record is held on computer (paragraph 2.6).

Paragraph 3 of Code C contains the normal procedure to be followed when a suspect is being detained at a police station. The custody officer must promptly explain the suspect's rights which follow, and those rights exist throughout his detention. The relevant rights are as follows: the right to have another person informed that the suspect has been arrested; the right to consult a solicitor in private; the right to independent legal advice without cost to the suspect; the right to consult the Codes of Practice. These rights and how to exercise them are also explained in a written notice which the custody officer must give to the suspect, in addition to a written notice which explains in summary the suspect's rights during detention (including such matters as visits, physical comfort, adequate food and drink, access to bathroom facilities, clothing, medical treatment and exercise—Notes for Guidance 3A). The suspect is expected to sign for receipt of these notices and if he refuses this fact is to be noted on the custody record. If the suspect makes any comment then this is to be entered on the record, but no comment is to be expected, nor may the custody officer question the suspect about his involvement in any offence; if this rule is breached then the conversation is likely to constitute an interview for the purposes of certain safeguards required elsewhere in PACE and the Code, which will be discussed at a later point. The suspect must also be asked at this early stage whether he requires legal advice, and is to be asked to sign the custody record in confirmation of his decision (paragraphs 3.4 and 3.5).

3–071 Code C paragraph 4 gives the custody officer the remit of taking possession of a detained suspect's personal property when the suspect arrives at the police station and keeping safe any such property during the person's detention. He may search the suspect's body and clothing or authorise another person to do so (see discussion below of requirements for intimate searches and body searches). But a custody officer cannot force the suspect to hand over clothing or personal property (other than cash or valuables), unless it is feared that the suspect may use items to harm himself or others, to cause damage to property, to interfere with evidence or to attempt an escape. If any property is confiscated on these grounds then the suspect must be informed why.

So, for how long may Marcus be detained without charge? Which safeguards apply to him?

According to section 37, the custody officer must determine whether there is sufficient evidence upon which to charge Marcus with an offence at this stage. He may only be detained without charge if: there are reasonable grounds for belief that this is necessary to protect evidence; or there are reasonable grounds for belief that detention is necessary to obtain evidence, for example by questioning the suspect. The custody officer may authorise detention without charge for either of these reasons, making a written custody record, and complying with Code C. Marcus will be entitled to receive the standard form "Notice of Entitlements".

Section 38: The Duties of the Custody Officer After Charges are Brought

Section 38 deals with the custody officer's decision whether to detain a suspect in custody after charge, and establishes rules upon which this decision is to be made. This section has to be read in conjunction with section 25 of the Criminal Justice and Public Order Act 1994, which created a category of serious offences for which bail cannot be granted if the suspect has already been convicted of one of those offences, including homicide and some sexual offences. The custody officer faced with a charged person must make a decision whether that person is suitable for bail, either with or without conditions being attached to the bail. Section 38 stresses that the suspect should be released after police detention, either on bail or without bail, unless he falls into one of the categories of special risk which allow further detention. Thus the pressure is towards releasing the suspect from custody in some form. **3–072**

The special risks which allow further police detention of an adult suspect are as follows (section 38(1)(a)):

(i) The suspect's name and address cannot be obtained or the custody officer has reasonable grounds for doubting that the details provided by the suspect are correct.

(ii) The custody officer has reasonable grounds for belief that the suspect will fail to appear in court to answer bail.

(iii) If the offence for which the suspect was arrested carries a prison sentence, and the custody officer has reasonable grounds for belief that it is necessary to detain the suspect to prevent him from committing an offence.

(iv) If the offence charged does not carry a prison sentence, and the custody officer has reasonable grounds for belief that the suspect's detention is necessary to prevent him from causing physical injury to another person or damaging property.

(v) The custody officer has reasonable grounds for belief that detention is necessary to prevent the suspect from interfering either with the administration of justice or with the investigation of an offence.

(vi) The custody officer has reasonable grounds for belief that detention is necessary for the suspect's own protection.

If the suspect is a juvenile, then in addition to the above reasons the custody officer may order his detention on the basis of reasonable grounds for belief that the juvenile should be detained "in his own interests" (section 38(1)(b)).

When making his decision (apart from grounds (i) and (vi) above and section 38(1)(b)), the custody officer is to have regard to the same points which a magistrate would have to consider in relation to an application for bail, namely: the nature and seriousness of the offence alleged and the likely penalty if convicted; the suspect's character, previous criminal record, community ties; whether the suspect has complied with any previous bail; and the strength of the evidence against the suspect, in addition to any other relevant considerations (section 38(2A)). As soon as is practicable the custody officer is to make a written record of the grounds for detention and this is to be done in the presence of the suspect, unless the suspect is incapable of understanding; actually or potentially violent; or in urgent need of medical treatment at that time.

Section 39: Treatment of Detained Persons

3–073 Custody officers are given a duty to ensure that detained suspects are treated in accordance with PACE. Section 39(1) states that a custody officer at any police station must ensure that all persons in police detention are treated in accordance with PACE and the Codes of Practice, and is also responsible for the recording of all required matters in custody records. If any detained person is transferred to another police station or to the custody of a person outside the original police station, then these obligations are transferred with him to the officer who becomes in charge of him (section 39(2)). If a superior officer gives orders in relation to the treatment of a detained person which conflict with any PACE or Codes of Practice rules, or go against a decision which the custody officer would have made himself, then the custody officer has a duty to refer the matter to an officer of at least the rank of superintendent (section 39(6)).

Section 40: Reviews of Police Detention, Whether or not the Suspect has been Charged with an Offence

3–074 A change from the previous law can be seen in section 40, which requires even more frequent reviews of a suspect's detention than were recommended by the Royal Commission. These reviews exist in order to ensure that a suspect is detained no longer than is reasonably necessary, but also serve the function of confirming that the suspect's treatment has been appropriate. Reviews of a suspect's detention are carried out by the custody officer in respect of those who have been arrested and charged, or by an officer of at least the rank of inspector who is not involved in the investigation if the suspect has been arrested but has not been charged (section 40(1)). The officer carrying out a review of detention is referred to as a "review officer." The first review of a suspect's detention must be carried out within six hours of his detention first being authorised. A second review must follow within another nine hours, and must be repeated throughout the suspect's detention at least every nine hours (section 40(3)). The exception to this is that a review may be postponed if in all the circumstances it is not practicable to carry out the review at that time; or if the suspect is being questioned when a review of detention is due and the review officer is satisfied that interrupting the interview would prejudice the investigation; or if no review officer is readily available at the time when a review is due (section 40(4)). But a postponed review must be carried out as soon as practicable, and the reasons for postponement must be noted on the custody record. However, it is now possible under the Criminal Justice and Police Act 2001 for a review to take place despite the fact that the review officer is absent from the police station where the arrested person is detained. Under section 73, amending section 40 of PACE, an officer of at least the rank of inspector may review, by telephone, the detention conditions of a person arrested but not yet charged, but only under the following circumstances:

(i) Where it is not reasonably practicable for the review officer to be present at the particular police station (section 73(1)(a)), and

(ii) "the review is not one which regulations under 45A (see below) authorise to be carried out using video-conferencing facilities, or is one which is reasonably practicable, in the circumstances, to carry out using any such facilities".[41A]

Further, section 73(3)[41B] enables the Secretary of State to permit a police officer who is not present at the same station as the arrested person to perform various functions where he has access to video-conferencing facilities that enable him to communicate with persons in that station (section 73(3)(1)(a) and (b)), including carrying out reviews as set out in section 40(1)(b) of PACE and the duties of a custody officer under sections 37, 38 or 40 of PACE. Before authorising any suspect's continued detention, the review officer must allow him or a solicitor representing him to make representations, either orally or in writing, about the detention (section 40(12),(13)). Code C, paragraph 15.1 states that the review officer has a discretion to allow other persons "having an interest in the person's welfare" to make representations.

The officer conducting the review of detention must not ask the suspect any questions related to the offence, since to do so would constitue an interview (paragraph 15.2A). A record is to be kept of any representations made before a review and of the outcome of each review. If further detention is required then either an authorisation of continued detention, a warrant of further detention or extension of detention must be applied for. Any period of police detention will be deducted from any sentence to be served for the same offence if the suspect is later convicted (section 49). It should be noted that a suspect who has been arrested for breach of the peace, or a suspect who attends a police station voluntarily without being arrested, is not in "police detention" and therefore is not entitled to section 40 reviews. However, such suspects are in "police custody" and so are entitled to certain of the rights under PACE; principally to have another person informed of his situation, to receive legal advice, and to be treated in accordance with the whole of Code C. A further problem is that, if an arrest is in fact unlawful, the PACE detention rules do not appear to apply; we are waiting for a court decision on this issue. The most sensible approach might be to interpret PACE rules as covering those arrested either unlawfully or by use of a common law power of arrest, since to do otherwise would contradict the purpose of the introduction of PACE and would create an unregulated area in the law.

Section 41: Time Limits for Detention without Charge

3–075 Section 41 contains the time limits for detention without charge which were introduced in order to give effect to the general spirit of the reforms recommended by the Royal Commission, but which differ from the Commission's recommendations in certain respects. Section 41(1) provides that a person shall not be held in police detention for longer than 24 hours without being charged, unless one of the exceptional grounds for an extension exists. The period of detention is to be calculated from the moment of arrival of the suspect at the police station, or as 24 hours after his arrest, whichever is the earlier (section 41(2)). The period of detention includes any time during which any suspect in police custody is being questioned, but not any other time in hospital or journeys there and back (section 41(6)). Section 41(7) emphasises that when the first 24 hours of detention expires, the suspect is to be released either with or without bail, unless he is to be charged with an offence or further detention has been authorised.

Returning to Marcus, if he was originally arrested for breach of the peace then in theory he has no right under PACE to a section 40 detention review. But Code C rights and the right to legal advice will apply. As has been seen, a further problem would arise if the original arrest appears to be unlawful.

SECTION 42: AUTHORISING CONTINUED DETENTION WITHOUT CHARGE

Under section 42, the basic 24-hour period may be extended up to a maximum of 36 hours' detention by an officer of the rank of superintendent or above at the relevant police station, if he believes on reasonable grounds that: 3–076

(1) The suspect's continued detention without charge is necessary to secure, preserve, or obtain by questioning some evidence relating to an offence for which he has been arrested; and

(2) The offence for which the suspect has been arrested is a serious arrestable offence; and

(3) The investigation "is being conducted diligently and expeditiously".

If the senior officer then authorises further detention, he must inform the suspect or where appropriate his solicitor of the grounds for the continued detention and must add these details to the custody record. The provisions under section 42(6) are mandatory and the accompanying procedures must be strictly adhered to.[42] The suspect or his legal representative must again be allowed to make representations and these must be recorded on the custody record. Therefore, by elimination, a suspect who is held in police detention without charge in relation to any offence which is not a serious arrestable offence must be released, either with or without bail, within 24 hours.

> What if the initial maximum of 36 hours' detention is about to expire, but the police have not yet amassed sufficient evidence upon which to charge Marcus with an offence? If the custody officer is convinced that one of the "special risks" under section 38(1)(a) continues to apply, and has considered bailing or releasing Marcus without charge, he may apply to a magistrates' court for extensions of detention, up to a potential maximum of 96 hours without charge. In this time Marcus may be interviewed and identification measures may take place, such as an identity parade. He may also be searched (see section 54, 55 and Code C, Annex A, below)—the rules for this will depend upon the amount of indignity involved in the search method chosen.

SECTIONS 43 AND 44: WARRANTS OF FURTHER DETENTION

Section 43 requires that after the initial maximum of 36 hours in police detention, there must be a hearing before a magistrates' court if the police wish to extend the suspect's detention any further. The suspect must be 3–077 present at the hearing and have been given a copy of the "information" upon which the application for a warrant of further detention is based, and he is entitled to be legally represented. The court may issue the warrant if it is satisfied that the suspect's further detention is "justified", according to the same grounds (1), (2) and (3) above which were used by the senior police officer to grant the initial extension to 36 hours. In all cases, the magistrates' court hearing must be conducted before the expiry of six hours after the 36 hours have passed. If the magistrates are of the opinion that the hearing could reasonably have been conducted before the expiry of the initial 36 hours and this was not done, then they must dismiss the application.[43] If satisfied that further detention is necessary on the appropriate grounds, then the court may issue the warrant of further detention for a period of up to a further 36 hours.

Once a warrant of further detention has been granted, the magistrates' court may extend the warrant for up to a further 36 hours, provided that it is satisfied that there are reasonable grounds for belief that further detention is justified (section 44). The total maximum detention period for a suspect is 96 hours, including the initial detention and all extensions. If the suspect is not charged within that time, he must be released.

Section 46: Detention After Charge

3–078 After a suspect has been charged with an offence, the general rule is that he must make his first court appearance within 36 hours, except where practicalities such as public holidays prevent this, in which case the next day will suffice. Thus, police detention of such a person will generally end with the court appearance, unless he is remanded in police custody (see below).

Section 47: Bail After Arrest

3–079 A custody officer may grant a suspect bail at the police station, requiring him to return to the station or to the court at a designated time unless he should subsequently be informed that such attendance is no longer required. The police may also impose conditions upon the bail such as requiring the suspect to hand over his passport, to pay a surety, to report regularly to the police station, to live at a specified address or to keep away from particular people. Bail conditions may be varied by either a custody officer or the court. If the suspect fails to keep to the rules of his bail, absconds or fails to appear in court, then the police have a power to arrest him without a warrant and take him to the police station at which he was supposed to report.

Section 48: Remands in Police Custody

3–080 In order to facilitate police inquiries into other offences which a suspect may have committed, section 128(7) of the Magistrates' Courts Act 1980, grants magistrates a power to remand a suspect who has already been charged with an offence in police custody for a period of up to three days, provided that such detention is considered to be necessary for the purposes of such inquiries. Any detention permitted in this way must comply with the PACE rules under section 40 (above) regarding reviews of detention.

SECTION 50: RECORDS OF DETENTION

Section 50(1) provides that each police force must keep written records which show the annual figures for the number of persons kept in police detention without charge for more than 24 hours and then released without charge; the number and outcomes of applications for warrants of further detention; details of the authorised and actual detention of each individual suspect, and whether he was charged or released without charge. These annual figures are published, but are not always useful since there is no standard method of data collection or centralised set of rules upon how to present the data collected.[44] **3–081**

SPECIAL CATEGORIES: RULES FOR THE DETENTION OF JUVENILES AND OTHER PERSONS AT RISK

It should be noted that throughout PACE and the Codes of Practice there are certain special rules for the treatment of the above categories of persons. In relation to detention, Code C paragraphs 3.6–3.14 are particularly relevant. In summary, a custody officer must provide an interpreter for any detained suspect who appears to need one, whether due to hearing or language difficulties, if the suspect is a juvenile then the custody officer must obtain the details of a person responsible for the juvenile's welfare and inform that person of the detention; if the suspect is a juvenile, mentally handicapped or has a mental disorder then the custody officer must as soon as is practicable inform an "appropriate adult" of the detention and the grounds for it, and ask the appropriate adult to come to the police station. The PACE rules and guidelines are to some extent open to interpretation. For example, time limits are not held to be breached if the overrun of detention is a matter of minutes. However, some of the rules concerning detention are interpreted more strictly. **3–082**

In *R. v. Canale*[45]:

Facts. The defendant was arrested and interviewed at the police station on four separate occasions. At the first two interviews, he allegedly made various admissions. However, those admissions were not contemporaneously recorded as required by paragraph 11.3 (now 11.5) of Code C which states that "the record must state the place of the interview, the time it begins and ends, . . . on the forms provided for the purpose, and the names of those present . . .". No reasons were given by the police for the lack of record, as set out in paragraph 11.6 (now paragraph 11.9). At two later interviews, the defendant repeated the admissions made previously. At his trial the judge, nevertheless, allowed all four interviews to be admitted in evidence. The defendant alleged that he had been induced by a trick and promises from the police to make the admissions. He was convicted and appealed on the grounds of the irregularities in the interviews, which, it was alleged, rendered the conviction unsafe and unsatisfactory.

Decision. The appeal was allowed. In the Court of Appeal, Lord Lane C.J. stated that the object of Code C is twofold: ". . . to ensure, as far as is possible, that the suspect's remarks are accurately recorded and . . . (as) a protection for the police to ensure that, as far as is possible, it cannot be suggested that they induced the subject to confess by improper approaches or improper promises". The court stated that there had been "flagrant breaches" and a "cynical disregard of the rules". Under section 78(1), "the court may refuse to allow evidence if, in all the circumstances, the evidence would have such an adverse effect on the fairness of the proceedings that the court ought not to admit it." Since no contemporaneous record had been made of the first interview, at which the appellant alleged promises were made in exchange for his admissions, the judge was not in a proper position to decide from the evidence whether to exclude those admissions.[46] Since the confession was the only real evidence against the defendant, and should have been excluded, the conviction was quashed.[47]

Fingerprinting and Intimate and Other Samples (Sections 60–65)

3–083 Fingerprinting rules are to be found in section 61. A person's fingerprints may not be taken without consent of either the suspect or an officer of at least the rank of inspector, unless the suspect has been charged with a recordable offence or has been informed that this will happen, and his fingerprints have not already been taken during the police investigation. The authorising officer must have reasonable grounds for belief that the suspect is involved in a criminal offence, and that taking the fingerprints will enable his involvement to be either confirmed or disproved (section 61(3),(4) and (5)). Reasons for taking the fingerprints must be recorded and given to the suspect (section 61(7)). If a person has been convicted of a recordable offence then his fingerprints may be taken without his consent. Section 78 of the Criminal Justice and Police Act 2001 (CJPA) lays down extended conditions for fingerprinting under section 61 of PACE and in particular matters relating to compulsory fingerprinting.[47A] Thus after section 61(4) of PACE there is to be inserted 4A which states that:

> "The fingerprints of a person who has answered to bail at a court or police station may be taken without the appropriate consent at the court or station if—
>
> (a) the court, or
> (b) an officer of at least the rank of inspector,
>
> authorises them to be taken."

The conditions of such an authorisation occurs where:

(a) there are reasonable grounds for believing that he is not the same person, or

(b) claims to be a different person from a person whose fingerprints were taken on a previous occasion.[47B]

Further, section 78 of the CJPA amends section 61(6) of PACE by stating that the words "he has been convicted of a recordable offence" are to be substituted for:

> "(a) he has been convicted of a recordable offence;
> (b) he has been given a caution in respect of a recordable offence which, at the time of the caution, he has admitted; or
> (c) he has been warned or reprimanded under section 65 of the Crime and Disorder Act 1998 for a recordable offence".

The taking of both intimate and non-intimate samples from a suspect are governed by section 62 and section 63, as amended by the Criminal Justice and Public Order Act 1994, which takes account of advances in DNA technology and its use in court as evidence, and also reclassified certain samples.

An intimate sample is defined in section 65 to include: a sample of blood, semen, urine, any other tissue fluid; pubic hair; dental impressions; and swabs taken from any body orifice other than the mouth. A non-intimate search is defined in section 65 to include: a sample of hair other than pubic hair; samples taken from, or from under, nails; swabs taken from any part of the body, including the mouth but excluding any other orifice; saliva; footprints or impressions of any other body part other than a hand. Section 80(5) of the CJPA had amended section 65(e) of PACE (Part V — supplementary) relating to non-intimate sample, the words footprints, etc., shall be substituted with "a skin impression". The definition of "skin impression" is "any record (other than a fingerprint) which is a record (in any form and produced by any method) of the skin pattern and other physical characteristics or features of the whole or any part of his foot or of any part of his body" (section 80(5)(c) of the CJPA). An intimate sample may only be taken from a person in police detention if (section 62): an officer of at least the rank of inspector authorises the taking of the sample and the written consent of the suspect or, if a juvenile, that of an appropriate adult has been given. In relation to the taking of samples under section 62 of PACE, under section 80(2) of the CJPA, section 62(9) has been amended to include "a registered nurse" as a person authorised to take an intimate sample. If the suspect refuses consent, then he must be warned that his refusal to provide the intimate sample may harm his case in court. The suspect must also be reminded that he has a right to free legal advice. If, however, the suspect is not in police detention, then an intimate sample may only be taken from him if, in addition to the above requirements, two or more previous samples have been taken from him but have proved to be insufficient for analysis purposes.

A non-intimate sample may also not generally be taken from a suspect without the relevant written consent (section 63). However, there is an exception where the suspect is in police detention and an officer of at least the rank of inspector authorises the taking of a non-intimate sample without consent where the offence concerned is recordable, and the officer has reasonable grounds for belief that the sample will either confirm or disprove the suspect's involvement in an offence. The suspect must be informed of the grounds for taking the sample and these must also be recorded on the custody record. If the suspect is not in police detention but is merely in police custody and has been charged with a recordable offence, then a non-intimate sample may be taken from him, subject to the above requirements; and the possibility of taking non-intimate samples from a person who is neither in police detention nor custody exists, where previous samples have proved insufficient for analysis, in the same circumstances as discussed above in relation to intimate samples.

3–083A Section 63A, which was added by the 1994 Act, allows the speculative searching of existing records for comparison with a suspect's fingerprints or samples. A suspect from whom a sample of whatever kind is being taken must be informed that a speculative search and comparison may occur. Section 63A also gives the police the power to require a person to attend a police station in order to give a sample if he has been charged with a recordable offence, or if he has been convicted of a recordable offence, and has either not had a sample taken or the sample has proved unsatisfactory for analysis.

Section 64 of PACE deals with the restriction on use and the destruction of fingerprints and samples. Now, under section 82(1), (2) and (3) of CJPA, section 64 of PACE has been amended to include the following:

> "For subsections (1) and (2) (obligation to destroy fingerprints and samples of persons who are not prosecuted or who are cleared) there shall be substituted—
>
> (1A) where—
>
> (a) fingerprints or samples are from a person in connection with the investigation of an offence, and
> (b) subsection (3) below does not require them to be destroyed,
>
> the fingerprints or samples may be retained after they have fulfilled the purposes for which they were taken but shall not be used by any person except for purposes related to the prevention or detection of crime, the investigation of an offence or the conduct of a prosecution".[47C]

Under section 82(3) of the CJPA, subsections 3A and 3B of section 64(3) of PACE (power to retain samples for elimination purposes and restriction on use) shall be substituted by—

> "(3AA) Samples and fingerprints are not required to be destroyed under subsection (3) above if—
>
> (a) they were taken for the purposes of the investigation of an offence of which a person has been convicted; and

(b) a sample or, as the case may be, fingerprint was also taken from the convicted person for the purposes of that investigation".[47D]

The consequences of the above section are that in future, once fingerprints and samples have been provided by a person and that person is thereafter released without charge, or no further action by the police will be taken, or no proceedings issued, then there is no legal compulsion for the authorities to destroy those particular fingerprints or samples. They may be retained and used against that person in future police investigations not yet contemplated. Further, under section 82(6) when this particular section comes into force, all previously held fingerprints and samples which should have been destroyed but were not, will be retained for future use.[47E]

VI(i) QUESTIONING AND TREATMENT OF PERSONS IN CUSTODY

Introduction

Once arrested, a person's rights and freedoms are to some extent curtailed, but this does not mean that an arrestee's dignity and bodily integrity may be infringed without good reason and stringent safeguards. The searching of an arrestee's clothing is an invasion of privacy which is justified in many situations by reference to the need to find evidence of offences and to prevent harm to people or property from a concealed weapon. Searches which involve the removal of more than outer clothing are an increased invasion of privacy, a source of embarrassment and of distress, so should never become a matter of course. Even greater safeguards and caution are required if the search is to be of intimate or private parts of the body, since the degradation involved should be rare if it is to be allowed at all. An intimate search of a person without his consent is prima facie both a tort and a criminal offence, battery or indecent assault, which is not only humiliating but may also cause serious physical injury; so, in order to justify such an invasive procedure, the threatened harm and the grounds for suspicion of concealment of an article must be great. 3–084

Searches in Detention

Police powers to stop and search a suspect without arrest have already been discussed; but the police also have a range of powers to search a person who is under arrest in certain circumstances. At common law, prior to PACE the police were permitted to search an arrested person's body, clothing and possessions, but only as a means of ensuring that the suspect did not commit further wrongs such as harming himself or another person, or destroying evidence. These common law powers to search were largely abolished by PACE, but some still exist, principally where a suspect has been taken to a police station after being arrested other than for an 3–085 offence. There was no general statutory power to search an arrested person before PACE, although various statutes introduced limited powers to search any person's clothing, regardless of his status or location, for particular prohibited articles such as offensive weapons or drugs. All such statutory powers to search an arrestee at a police station were abolished by PACE, and so other statutes are relevant only outside the police station or where a person has not yet been arrested.

It is a matter of debate whether there was in fact a common law power to conduct intimate searches without the arrestee's consent prior to the enactment of PACE, but it is a fact that these searches were performed and justified by reference to a claimed common law power. The lack of certainty at common law and the limited scope of statutory powers prompted a re-examination of the issue by the Royal Commission, who proposed that intimate searches should be conducted only by doctors and only where the offence charged was very serious. The Government expanded the scope of the power, and originally the Bill included a power to search for evidence, but policy issues and intense criticism about the potential impact on civil liberties led to the withdrawal of that specific power from the final version of PACE. This leads to an illogical situation since Customs officers may conduct intimate searches in the hope of finding evidence,[48] and so have greater powers in this area than do the police. Intimate searches are highly regulated by PACE and may only be carried out in very limited circumstances. The pressure to regulate intimate searches and to introduce safeguards came in the main from the medical profession, who refused to be involved in intimate searches unless certain of the limitations were enacted.

Searches of a person under PACE may only be carried out in the following circumstances. First, section 32 authorises a search without consent after a person has been arrested at a location away from a police station. The search may be performed if the police have reasonable grounds for belief that the suspect may be a danger to any person, including himself; or if the police have reasonable grounds for belief that the arrested person may have an article which could enable him to escape, including a weapon, or which might be evidence relating to any offence. This is wider than the previous common law powers, and goes beyond the Royal Commission's recommendations. Only outer clothing may be removed, but the suspect's mouth may be searched. The premises at which the arrest took place may also be searched. A section 32 search may only be carried out at the time of the arrest, not several hours later.[49] Secondly, a person who has been arrested may be searched at a police station under section 54 of PACE, which deals with non-intimate searches. Thirdly, section 55 of PACE authorises intimate searches at a police station but only according to strict rules. Fourthly, strip searches are permitted at a police station if the rules of Code C, Annex A are followed. Each of these three types of search will be discussed individually below. Finally, there are powers of search under statutes which have come into force since PACE, such as the Prevention of

Terrorism (Temporary Provisions) Act 1989, which will be discussed in a separate chapter.

SECTION 54: NON-INTIMATE SEARCH

Under section 54 and Code C, paragraph 4, a custody officer has a duty to create a record of all property which an arrestee at a police station has on his person. Linked to this duty is a power (section 54(3) and (4)) to search the suspect and to seize and retain any items, including clothing and personal property, which the custody officer honestly believes that the arrestee may use for any of the following purposes: **3–086**

(i) To cause physical injury to any person, including himself;

(ii) To damage property;

(iii) To interfere with evidence; or

(iv) To assist him to escape.

Section 54(4)(b) also allows the custody officer to seize even clothing or personal effects if he has reasonable grounds for belief that they may be evidence related to an offence.

Section 54(6A) allows the searching of a person in custody at a police station at any time in order to ascertain whether that person has with him anything which could be used for the above purposes. Subsection (7) prohibits intimate searches from being carried out under this power. Any search under section 54 must be carried out by a constable who is of the same sex as the person who is being searched (section 54(9)). Reasonable force may be used if necessary to carry out the search (section 117). It seems that any policy of searching all persons under arrest at a police station is invalid, but cases have stated that such a policy would not be enough in itself to render unlawful any search performed under the policy; each search must be justified on the facts before the custody officer at the time and related to the particular arrestee.[50] Code C, Note for Guidance 4A, states that section 54 does not "require every detained person to be searched". Strip searches, that is searches which require the removal of more than outer clothing, may be carried out under section 54, and are discussed below.

SECTION 55: INTIMATE SEARCH

An intimate search is defined in section 65 as "a search which consists of the physical examination of a person's body orifices other than the mouth", *i.e.* anus, nostrils, vagina, ears. Some kind of physical intrusion into the orifice is required before the search is considered to be intimate; mere visual inspection is considered to be a strip search. Under section 55, **3–087** intimate searches are permitted for either drugs or weapons, and the rules for each differ. The basic rule is that an officer of at least the rank of inspector may authorise, either orally or in writing, an intimate search of a person if he has reasonable grounds for belief that:

(i) A person who has been arrested and is in police detention may have concealed on him anything which he could, and might, use either to cause physical injury to any person, including himself; or

(ii) Such a person may have a Class A drug concealed on him, and was in possession of it with the appropriate criminal intent before his arrest (section 55(1)).

If there is any reasonable alternative way of finding the object, an intimate search should not be authorised (section 55(2)). An oral authorisation of an intimate search must be confirmed in writing as soon as is practicable (section 55(3)).

If the intimate search is for drugs, it can only be carried out by a "suitably qualified person", meaning a doctor or registered nurse, and cannot be carried out in a police station (section 55(4),(9)). If the search is for weapons, it must be made by a "suitably qualified person" unless an officer of at least the rank of inspector considers that this is not practicable (section 55(5)); thus it may be performed by a police officer in such circumstances, although this is seen as undesirable and the medical profession has grave concerns about the potential harm of this practice. Examples of where an intimate search for weapons may be carried out by a police officer include where a doctor has been approached but has refused to carry out an intimate search without the arrestee's consent; or where the arrestee is believed to have concealed an article which is endangering his life and time is of the essence. If a police officer conducts an intimate search, he must be of the same sex as the person being searched (section 55(7)). The meaning of the words "not practicable" is not given, but presumably refers to the situation where a suitably qualified person cannot be contacted, or due to circumstances it becomes impracticable to delay the search any longer. An intimate search by a constable need not be a "last resort". However, undoubtedly, efforts must be made to find a suitably qualified person to conduct the examination. Intimate searches may only be carried out at a police station (except for drugs), hospitals, registered medical practitioners' surgeries, or other places used for medical purposes (section 58(8)). An interesting point to note is that, unlike police officers, doctors or nurses who conduct intimate searches have no statutory authority for doing so; the procedure is not medically necessary and so, on general principles of both law and medicine, should not be conducted without the consent of the person to be searched. Thus the doctor or nurse is vulnerable to an action for trespass against the person, or to more serious actions if any physical harm is caused during a search. This problem may help to explain the medical profession's reluctance to be involved in the process.

When an intimate search has occurred, the arrestee's custody record must state which parts of the body were searched, and for what purpose, and this record must be made as soon as practicable after the completion of the search (section 55(10) and (11)). As a monitoring exercise, annual reports made by police forces must contain statistical details about intimate searches. The total number rarely exceeds 100 per year.

Code C, Annex A gives further requirements for intimate searches. Paragraph 6 requires that, except in the case of a juvenile or mentally impaired arrestee being searched, no person who is not a medical practitioner or nurse shall be present, nor shall anyone whose presence is unnecessary; however a minimum of two persons other than the arrestee must be present during the search. This is intended to guarantee that a witness is available to confirm or deny the validity of the search and its results. The search must be "conducted with proper regard to the sensitivity and vulnerability of the person in these circumstances". If the person being searched is a juvenile or mentally impaired, then an intimate search may only take place in the presence of an appropriate adult of the same sex, unless a juvenile wishes otherwise and the appropriate adult agrees (paragraph 5). The results of the search, who was present, and who performed it must be recorded on the custody record (paragraph 7); this is in addition to the requirement (section 55(10) and (11)) of recording which parts of the body were searched and the purpose of the search. If an intimate search has been carried out by a police officer, then the custody record must also state the reason why it was impracticable for a suitably qualified person to conduct the search (paragraph 8). Thus, the police may be brought to account for any non-justifiable reason why, for instance, a doctor was not consulted for examination of the suspect. But even after a doctor is contacted, he is not bound to conduct the examination and may refuse. It should be noted that there is no power to conduct an intimate search merely in the hope of finding evidence.

Strip Search

Until recently, strip searches were not fully distinguished from intimate **3–088** searches. Now, under the 1995 revised Code C, Annex A, the two types of search have different rules and authorisation procedures.

In Code C, Annex A, paragraph 9, a strip search is defined as "a search involving the removal of more than outer clothing".[51] This search is for articles which a person would not be allowed to keep during detention. The officer must consider it necessary to remove these articles and that the person has concealed such an article (Annex A, paragraph 10). This power again seems very wide and may be abused by the police, if the only reason for the strip search is to humiliate or degrade the suspect. However, under Annex A, paragraph 12 a record of the search must be made, stating the reasons why it was considered necessary. Thus, in practice, such circumstances do have their limitations and if abused, will be considered a breach of the Codes.

A strip search may be carried out by any police officer; until 1995, authorisation was required from a custody officer. The procedures to be followed when conducting a strip search are to be found in Code C, Annex A, paragraph 11. The police officer conducting the strip search must be of the same sex as the person being searched. The search must be conducted in a location which is not visible to any person whose presence is unnecessary or who is of the opposite sex to the person being searched. If intimate parts of the body are to be exposed, except in urgent cases where there is "a risk of serious harm to the person detained or to others", at least two persons must be present other than the person being searched. Where the search is of a juvenile, an appropriate adult must be present unless the juvenile wishes otherwise and the appropriate adult agrees. It is only in exceptional circumstances that more than two persons, other than an appropriate adult, should be present during a strip search (paragraph 11(a),(b) and (c)). The search shall be conducted "with proper regard to the sensitivity and vulnerability of the person in these circumstances and every reasonable effort shall be made to secure the person's co-operation and minimise embarrassment" (paragraph 11(d)). Total nudity should not be required at any time. But a person may be required to raise his arms, stand with legs apart, or bend over "so that a visual examination may be made of the genital and anal areas provided that no physical contact is made with any body orifice" (paragraph 11(e)); however these steps should only be taken where necessary to assist the search. Articles found in an orifice other than the mouth during a strip search cannot be removed except by the procedures for an intimate search; the practical solution is to ask the person being searched to hand over any such article. Strip searches must be conducted as quickly as possible to minimise the discomfort.

VI(ii) NOTIFICATION AND ACCESS TO LEGAL ADVICE

3–089

> Some of Marcus' most important rights have not yet been considered. By this stage, he will have been given information about the reasons for his arrest and detention; he also has the right to have someone notified (section 56 and Code C) and the important right of access to legal advice (section 58 and Code C). But both of these rights may be delayed in certain circumstances. Marcus' rights in relation to interviews and cautioning must also be considered.

Notification of Detention: Section 56 and Code C, Paragraph 5

3–090 In accordance with the recommendations of the Royal Commission, the suspect's right to have another person informed that he has been arrested has been preserved by PACE and given more detailed rules. The general rule is that an arrestee who is being held in police custody[52] is entitled on request to have one person informed, as soon as is practicable, that he has being arrested and is being detained at a specific location (section 56(1)). If the person requested cannot be found, then the arrestee may choose up to two alternatives (Code C, paragraph 5.1). The custody officer or investigating officer have discretion to allow further attempts until someone has been notified. Visits are allowed at the custody officer's discretion (paragraph 5.4). If a friend, relative or other person with an interest in the arrestee's welfare inquires as to the arrestee's whereabouts, then if the arrestee agrees, that person should be given the information (paragraph 5.5). Code C, paragraph 3.1 and 3.2 require a custody officer to inform the suspect of the right to notification when he authorises detention. Notification of a person, once requested, may be delayed for up to 36 hours, provided that the grounds for delay detailed below are satisfied (section 56(5)). If a delay in notification is authorised, then the suspect must be informed of the reason for the delay and the reason must also be entered on the custody record (section 56(6)). The officer can only delay notification of a named person; blanket bans are not permitted.

The arrestee has a separate right to make one telephone call for a reasonable amount of time, and to have access to writing materials on request (paragraph 5.6); thus the expression "You are allowed to make one telephone call" applies to this situation. But, in contrast to the right to have someone notified, the right to use the telephone or writing materials can not only be delayed but can be withdrawn altogether. The grounds for either delaying notification, or for delaying or denying a telephone call are the same, and are as follows. If the person is detained as a consequence of a serious arrestable offence, and has not been charged, and an officer of at least the rank of Superintendent (re notification) or Inspector (re telephone calls or letters) has reasonable grounds for believing that allowing notification or the telephone call or letter will:

(a) Lead to interference with or harm to evidence, or physical injury to other people including witnesses; or

(b) Lead to the alerting of other people suspected of having committed such an offence; or

(c) Hinder the recovery of property obtained as a result of such an offence.[53]

"Serious arrestable offences" are defined in section 116 and Part 1, Schedule 5 and include murder; rape; drug offences under the Drug Trafficking Act 1993, s.1(3)(a)–(f); various terrorist offences under the Prevention of Terrorism (Temporary Provisions) Act 1989, ss. 2, 8, 9, 10 and 11; causing, intending or threatening death, serious injury or serious financial loss to any person. In any case, before a letter is sent or a telephone call made, the arrestee must be informed that what he writes or says may be monitored and may be given in evidence (paragraph 5.7). Records must be kept of requests for notification, letters and telephone calls and whether they were permitted (paragraph 5.8).

Section 58: Access to Legal Advice

3–091 Before PACE, there was no obligation on the police to inform a suspect that he had a right to legal advice, and the right could also be withheld on broad grounds. There was no statutory recognition of the right to legal advice, and case law was both lacking in generality and unsatisfactory in enforcing the rights of the suspect. The Royal Commission recommended that an arrestee should have a right of unlimited private access to his legal advisor and that there should be a duty to inform him of this right.[54] It should be a rare and exceptional set of circumstances which would allow the denial of this right. This is more or less the situation as enacted in PACE.

Section 58(1) provides that a person who has been arrested and is being held in police custody has the right to consult a solicitor privately at any time.[55] If the arrestee makes such a request, it must be recorded on his custody record (section 58(2)). Access to a solicitor must be provided as soon as is practicable after the request is made, unless delay is authorised on the grounds permitted.[56] Delay of access to legal advice cannot exceed 36 hours, and the arrestee must be informed of the reason for any delay as well as it appearing on his custody record (section 58(9)). Code C, paragraph 6.1 adds that, subject to the provisions on delay,

> "all persons in police detention must be informed that they may at any time consult and communicate privately, whether in person, in writing or by telephone with a solicitor, and that independent legal advice is available free of charge from the duty solicitor".

Code C, paragraph 3.5 ensures that a suspect is told that he has this right as soon as he first meets the custody officer, who must obtain the suspect's signature on the custody record to show whether he wishes to have legal advice at that point. Posters must be placed prominently in the police station to advertise that there is a right to legal advice (paragraph 6.3); police officers must never attempt to dissuade a suspect from exercising the right (paragraph 6.4); and custody officers must give a suspect repeated reminders of the right (paragraph 6.5). If a suspect does want legal advice, he is not to be interviewed until he has received it, unless: the grounds for delay in provision of the advice apply (see below); or an officer of the rank of superintendent or above has reasonable grounds for belief that waiting for a solicitor who has been contacted would unreasonably delay the investigation, or that there is an immediate risk of harm to persons or serious damage or loss of property; or neither a nominated solicitor nor the duty solicitor can or is willing to attend. Even if a suspect has stated that he does not want legal advice, if a solicitor arrives at the police station to see him (perhaps sent by a well-meaning relative or friend), then the suspect must be informed of this and asked whether he wishes to see him (paragraph 6.15).

Access to legal advice may only be delayed where the suspect has been arrested and is being detained in connection with a serious arrestable offence. The grounds for delay are to be found in section 58(8) and Code C, paragraph 6, Annex B. Delay may be authorised by an officer of at least the rank of superintendent where he has reasonable grounds for belief that allowing access to legal advice at that time would:

(a) Lead to interference with or harm to evidence or physical injury to other people, including witnesses; or

(b) Lead to the alerting of other people suspected of having committed such an offence; or

(c) Hinder the recovery of property obtained as a result of such an offence.

Two observations can be made here. First, the grounds for delay here are the same as those for delaying notification under section 56. Secondly, it is difficult to justify delay of access to legal advice in all but the most extreme cases since to do so is to allege that reasonable grounds exist to suspect that the solicitor would either intentionally or inadvertently give information to another who would use it to commit a crime, intimidate witnesses, or interfere with evidence; or even that the solicitor would do any of these things himself. Annex B paragraph 3 makes it clear that delay cannot be authorised simply because a solicitor may tell his client that he should not answer questions; what is necessary to justify delay of access is a fear, based on reasonable grounds, that the solicitor will either act negligently or commit misconduct in one of the relevant ways.

The most important function of a solicitor at a police station is related to interviews with his client conducted by the police. Solicitors are normally allowed to attend any interview with the suspect if they are available to do so, and may only be prevented from doing so if the solicitor's conduct is such that it prevents the investigating officer from questioning the suspect (paragraphs 6.8 and 6.9). Note for Guidance 6D stresses that "the solicitor's only role in the police station is to protect and advance the legal rights of his client. On occasions this may require the solicitor to give advice which has the effect of his client avoiding giving evidence which strengthens a prosecution case". During an interview, the solicitor can interrupt for clarification of what is being said or asked, to challenge improper questioning or tactics, to advise his client that he should not answer particular questions, or to provide further legal advice to the suspect. None of these interruptions will justify exclusion of the solicitor from the interview unless he unreasonably obstructs proper questions.

It can be seen from the following cases that breach of the suspect's rights under section 58 is no trivial matter and often leads to the courts excluding evidence or overturning a conviction, provided that the denial or delay of access to legal advice made a difference to the suspect. Relevant considerations include the suspect's level of knowledge of his legal rights, his mental capacity and suggestibility, and whether in the circumstances a solicitor would have advised silence but the suspect answered questions.

In *R. v. Samuel*[57]:

3–092 **Facts**. The defendant was recognised by a cashier at the Leeds Building Society while depositing money as a member of a gang who had previously robbed the Building Society. The next day, the defendant was arrested and questioned about the offence. At 8.30 p.m. the defendant requested access to a solicitor, which was denied on the grounds that there was a likelihood of other suspects being inadvertently warned. The defendant was only allowed to see his solicitor after he had confessed to the robbery. The defendant appealed on the basis that the confession should have been excluded under section 78 of PACE because there were no "reasonable grounds for believing" that the defendant's solicitor would deliberately or intentionally alert other suspects, or hinder the recovery of property.

Decision. The appellant's first main argument was that the circumstances for delay are set out in Annex B, paragraph 1, *i.e.* delay cannot be maintained once the accused has been charged with an offence. Thus, when the appellant was charged with the burglary offences, the right to legal advice could no longer be delayed, and therefore any such refusal was unlawful. The appellant's second argument was centred around the correctness of the superintendent's judgement in delaying access to a solicitor. Whether the delay was lawful should be decided by the reasons given in section 58(8) and especially interpreting the words "reasonable ground for believing" that the superintendent exercised that right to delay access justifiably. Here the relevant "reasonable grounds for believing" put forward by the superintendent for refusing access were that the solicitor would either deliberately or unintentionally alert the other suspects, or hinder the recovery of stolen property. Hodgson J. stated that in deciding whether refusal was justified the court would have to decide two questions: "Did the officer believe?"—a subjective test; "were there reasonable grounds for that belief?"—an objective test. Hodgson J. thought that to refuse access on these grounds would be rare. Solicitors are officers of the court and intelligent professional men. In order for a refusal to be upheld, there must be evidence "by reference to specific circumstances to the actual person detained or to the actual solicitor consulted". Here, no such grounds existed and therefore the appeal was allowed.

The grounds for delaying access to a legal representative are precise, as set out in section 58(8). Any deviation from these grounds will not constitute proper reasons for delaying access.

In *R v. Alladice*[58]:

Facts. Five men, one carrying a gun, robbed a post office of some £2,900,000. The appellant was arrested in the public gallery of the Crown Court and his house was searched in the presence of his mother. He later confessed to being one of the robbers. The appellant appealed that his admissions ought to have been excluded on the grounds that he was denied access to a solicitor, when requested. Such a denial was not based on a proper construction of the Act or Codes of Practice.

Decision. The reasons given for the refusal to allow access to a solicitor were:

(1) the offence was a serious arrestable offence;
(2) four men only were arrested—there was still one at large, although his identity was known;
(3) neither the money nor the firearm had been recovered; and
(4) the solicitor could unintentionally alert others.

It was contended by the appellant that the real reason was that the solicitor might advise the appellant to say nothing, thereby preventing the confession. This was not a lawful ground for refusal under Annex B of the Codes. It was further stated that:

> ". . . we do not share the Court's (in *R. v. Samuel*) apparent scepticism about solicitors being used as unwitting channels of communication. That such things do happen is within the experience of members of this Court".

In this case, access to a solicitor could not have done any further damage since the damage was probably already done. Thus, there were no reasonable grounds for that belief. Therefore, there was a breach of section 58. However, the appellant himself gave evidence to the effect that he was well able to cope with the interviews, knew his rights, and that the interviews had been conducted properly. Indeed, he maintained he said nothing at all after the first four questions and that his confession had been invented by the police. The judge rejected that last allegation. The only difference the presence of a solicitor would have made would be to advise him to say nothing—a right which the appellant already knew and in fact exercised on a number of occasions. Therefore, despite there being a breach of section 58, the presence of a solicitor would not have enhanced the appellant's case, and accordingly the confession was still admissible. Similarly, in *R. v. Dunford*,[59] even though section 58 had been breached, the interview was nevertheless admissible because the solicitor's advice would have added nothing to the defendant's knowledge of his rights.

In *R. v. Parris*[60]:

Facts. The appellant was arrested for armed robbery. At:
Interview 1—He remained silent. Access to legal advice was denied.
Interview 2—He allegedly made oral admissions, but nothing was written down.
Interview 3—Solicitor was present. He refused to answer questions.

At his trial, he pleaded not guilty and denied making any confession. Counsel for the appellant argued that there had been a breach of section 58 and Code C, paragraph 5.1. This was rejected by the judge and therefore the issue of section 78 did not arise. The appellant was found guilty.

Decision. On appeal, the Crown acknowledged that there had been a breach of section 58 and Code C, paragraph 5.1 and therefore, the question whether to exclude the confession in the second interview under section 78 should have been contemplated. There were no grounds for believing that the exceptions to delay legal advice in section58(8) were relevant in this case. The court decided that had the appellant been allowed to see a solicitor, no admissions would probably have been made at the second interview and he would have remained silent. In deciding whether to accept the police or the appellants testimony at trial, the court decided that had section 58 been complied with and a solicitor present during the second interview, then what was said then by the appellant and police could have been confirmed by the solicitor's evidence. Since there was no real case against the appellant, apart from the alleged confession, the appeal was allowed.

In *R v. Kerawalla*[61]:

3–093 **Facts**. J was arrested by customs officers for illegally importing heroin into England. She was taken to a hotel, where she telephoned K regarding the collection of the drugs. When K arrived at the hotel two days later, he was arrested and questioned. At the first interview, he denied any involvement or talking with J on the telephone. He was refused access to legal advice. At a second interview at a customs office, he again gave innocent reasons for being in England; this time, in the presence of his solicitor. At K's trial, he admitted talking with J on the telephone, but denied it was about drugs. K sought to exclude evidence of his denials at the first interview on the grounds of breaches of section 30 (interview not at a designated place) and section 58. The judge refused to exclude the evidence on the grounds that under section 30(10), it was necessary to carry out the investigation immediately, lest others would be alerted if they spotted K in the company of customs officers at the hotel. He was convicted and appealed on the grounds that the evidence should have been excluded under section 78.

Decision. The Court of Appeal held that (1) the customs officers had conducted the interview in a fair manner and in good faith, (2) the customs officers were justified under section 30(10) to conduct the interview in the hotel room. Had K been granted access to legal advice initially, he would most likely have been advised to remain silent. Since this did not affect the overall fairness of the proceedings under section 78, the appeal was dismissed.

However, in *R. v. Sanusi*, where the customs officers suspected the defendant of illegally importing heroin, he was questioned at length at Gatwick Airport. He was not informed of his right to legal advice. This was a serious infringement of section 58 and the Codes. When eventually he was told that he could have a solicitor present, at the subsequent interview, he refused to answer further questions. Here, the court took into account that he was foreign, with no previous criminal record and unfamiliar with his legal rights. Therefore, the judge should have taken into account these factors when considering to exclude the evidence and therefore, the appeal was allowed. Because of the intricacies and complexities of the new caution, it is suggested that access to legal advise is even more important now than under the old one. The police may take advantage of the suspect not fully comprehending, even if after explanation, the meaning of the caution, especially when the suspect is below average intelligence or is overawed by the whole experience of being taken to a police station or is a "first-time interviewee".

VII ADMISSIBILITY OF CONFESSIONS AND EVIDENCE

3–094 Immediately after arrest, it is claimed that Marcus confessed his involvement in a number of serious arrestable offences to one of the arresting officers. To what extent will his "confession" be admissible in court?

Admissibility of Confessions and Other Evidence in Court—Section 76 and Section 78

The admissibility of evidence may be affected by breach of the rules of PACE or the Codes of Practice. PACE reformed, consolidated and tightened many of the rules of criminal evidence, and two of its provisions have particular application to the treatment of suspects in detention and their questioning. Section 76 is a striking reform to the law concerning confessions and their admissibility in court. Confessions have always been very important to the police and the percentage of interviews with suspects which lead to confessions has consistently remained at 50–60 per cent even since the enactment of PACE. Before PACE, the common law strictly required a confession to have been made voluntarily, without any hint of coercion, threat, bribery or other improper methods if it was to be admissible in evidence. Successive criticisms from law reform bodies and other sources had been recommending since the early 1970s that the common law restricted police methods excessively, culminating in the Royal Commission stating that it was not possible to judge the voluntariness of a confession even if present when it was made; what should be examined was not whether the confession was made voluntarily, but whether the police officer to whom the confession was made had behaved within the boundaries of permissible conduct. Minor deviations from the rules of interviewing should not render a confession inadmissible, but violence, threats and degradation should. Minor breaches might only lead a judge to warn a jury that the confession, unsupported by any other evidence, formed a weak case against the suspect. **3–095**

Excluding Confessions Under Section 76

Section 76 of PACE enacts the Royal Commission's reforms. Subsection (1) provides that a confession made by the accused in any proceedings may only be given in evidence against him where it is relevant and is not excluded by section 76. Thus a confession must be held inadmissible if it falls within either of the two categories in section 76. Confessions are excluded if they are the result of oppression (section 76(2)(a)) or result from conduct which is likely to make a confession unreliable (section 76(2)(b)). Once the possibility of either of these situations existing has been raised in court, the confession may not be given in evidence unless the prosecution discharges the heavy burden of proof beyond reasonable doubt that the confession was not the result of either of the two prohibited types of conduct. The truth of the confession makes no difference; it will be inadmissible if it was obtained improperly within section 76. But the prosecution may still rely on any evidence which was obtained as a result of an inadmissible confession.[60] It is therefore necessary to define "confession", "oppression" and "unreliable". Section 82(1) provides that a confession "includes any statement wholly or partly adverse to the person **3–096** who made it, whether made to a person in authority or not and whether made in words or otherwise".

OPPRESSION

3–097 Section 76(8) defines oppression to include torture; inhuman treatment; degrading treatment; the use of violence and the threat of violence—other types of conduct may also qualify.[63] Questioning by the police which involves either physical or extreme mental pressure as defined by section 76(8) certainly would amount to oppression and any confession subsequently obtained would probably be excluded. However, less direct and open approaches to questioning may also come also under the guise of oppression if carried out by the police. Examples such as, raising voices and using foul language by the police during questioning,[64] would probably not amount to oppression. However, using such overbearing tactics as constant shouting at the suspect after repeated denials of any involvement in the particular crime, may very well constitute oppression under PACE.[65] Making derogatory statements and telling lies to the suspect in order to get a confession, may also be deemed oppression although, for instance informing the suspect's wife that he is having an affair with the woman next door would, by itself, not amount to oppression, since though hurtful, would probably not reach the standard of impropriety required for a confession to be inadmissible.

In *R. v. Paris, Abdullahi, Miller*[66]:

Facts. The three defendants were charged with the murder of a woman with whom Miller had until recently been living. During tape-recorded interviews with Miller, he initially denied any involvement with the crime. To questions put to him by the police, he repeatedly replied "I wasn't there"; some three hundred times he denied the accusations put to him by the police. However, after tape number 18, and 13 hours of interviews, Miller finally made a confession and stated "I just stabbed her, not stabbed her just fucking thumped her in her face, I mean". The police shortly after asked him "You were so blocked up (full of drugs) you didn't know what you were doing". Miller then says "That's what I say, I don't know. I might have done, I might have done". They were all convicted and appealed on the grounds that the confession should have been ruled inadmissible under section 76(2) and section 78.

Decision. The Court of Appeal (Lord Taylor L.C.J.) stressed the issues relating to section 76(2);

(1) Once the oppression issues have been put forward by the defence, it is then for the prosecution to prove that the confession was not obtained by such means.
(2) The emphasis is on how the confession was obtained, not whether it was true.
(3) If the confession was obtained by oppression, then the judge has no discretion and must exclude the evidence.

The court, having heard the tapes, were shocked by the police tactics in trying to "get a result". They said that Miller was shouted at, bullied, intimidated, and brainwashed. They finally came to the conclusion that this constituted oppression within section 76(2) and as a consequence was unreliable. Added to this was the evidence that Miller had an IQ of 75, a mental age of 11, and a reading capacity of a child of eight. Since the prosecution could not discharge the burden of proving that the confession was not obtained by oppression, their Lordships allowed the appeal. In conclusion, their Lordships emphasised "the circumstances of this case do not indicate flaws in these provisions (PACE). They do indicate a combination of human errors".

In *R. v. Fulling*[67] it was stated that "oppression" is to be given its ordinary dictionary meaning, *i.e.* "Exercise of authority or power in a burdensome, harsh or wrongful manner; unjust or cruel treatment of subjects, inferiors, etc.; the imposition of unreasonable or unjust burdens". The words "Exercise of authority in a burdensome, harsh or wrongful manner", do not at first inspection seem to be serious enough to be elevated to the level of a legal oppression. Indeed, using a power in a "wrongful manner" may not, by itself, if not serious enough, establish oppression. In order to exclude a confession under the above phrase, the court will look at all the circumstances surrounding the confession in order to decide whether the treatment by the police amounted to a breach of section 76.[68] The phrase or definition is not severable and must be considered as a whole. Thus, in *R. v. Parker*[69] it was stated that the word "wrongful" should be combined with the words immediately proceeding it and the immediate words following it. Otherwise, any breach of the Code, which might be said to be wrongful, could be said to amount to oppression, which clearly was not so.[70] Of course, if the test for oppression under section 76 fails, section 78 may still be used to exclude the confession.

In deciding whether or not to allow a confession to be admitted, the **3–098**
judge must have access to all the relevant material before him, including not only evidence to any breaches of the Act which may have occurred, but also to any breaches of the Code—especially Code C. If, for instance, the judge is deprived of the notes of a previous interview which was not contemporaneously recorded, despite the fact that the defendant only made his confession in a later interview, this:

> ". . . may tip the scales in favour of the defendant in these circumstances and make it impossible for the judge to say that he is satisfied beyond reasonable doubt, and so require him to reject the evidence".[71]

Thus, in these circumstances, any confession thereafter may be unreliable.[72]

Sometimes, the questioning involved does not amount to physical or mental pressure and even though there may be some impropriety that does not, in itself, amount to oppression. Oppression has been used in a wider sense than merely pure interviewing technique. In *R. v. Beales*[73] the defendant was charged with assaulting a two year old boy. During a 35 minute interview at the police station, the officer made false statements and in general distorted and deliberately tried to confuse the defendant in order to extract a confession from him. It was held that the resulting confession was to be excluded on the grounds that treatment of the suspect came within the bounds of oppression. But even if not oppressive, the confession was to be considered unreliable, for the interview by the police was such that the defendant was ultimately "hectored and bullied from first to last".

Unreliable

3–099 A confession may be held to be "unreliable" where, for example, a witness is falsely stated to have identified the suspect, or the suspect was denied legal advice, or the procedures for interviews were not followed; but none of those breaches will necessarily result in a confession being inadmissible. In *R. v. L*[74] it was stated that "where there is aggressive and hostile questioning, it becomes a matter of degree as to whether the threshold is passed beyond which the behaviour of the officers had made the so-called confession unreliable in all the circumstances".[75] The defence under section 76(2)(b) may wish to exclude a confession "in consequence of anything said or done which was likely in the circumstances existing at the time, to render unreliable any confession which might be made by him in consequence thereof . . .". Breaking down this subsection into its component parts, the court will examine (1) what was actually said or done by the police during the whole period of questioning (2) as a result of what was said or done, the court should then consider whether in the circumstances the confession is reliable or not—objective test is used[76] and (3) the burden of proof is on the prosecution to show that the confession was not obtained due to what was said or done.

In *R. v. Chung*[77]:

Facts. The defendant was charged with handling stolen goods. He was alleged to have made certain admissions at his flat, while a search was being conducted by police officers. The officers did not record these admissions at the flat. Later on, at the police station, a police constable did make a record of the alleged admissions. The defendant was held incommunicado for some 14 hours before being allowed, despite earlier requests, to see a solicitor. He was convicted and appealed that the judge had erred in allowing the confession to be admitted at trial.

Decision. The Court of Appeal ruled that:

(1) the questioning of the appellant at the flat amounted to an interview, the purpose of the questions being to elicit evidence of his guilt in this matter;
(2) no effective reasons were given by the police as to why it was not practicable to make any written record at the flat;
(3) when a record was finally made, it was not shown to the appellant to read or sign it;
(4) the solicitor was not informed of the record, which the court found to be "quite astonishing;" and
(5) there was an unwarranted delay of access to a solicitor.

Taken altogether, with other minor breaches of the Code, the court concluded that the confession was unreliable under section 76(2)(b).[78]

"In Consequence of Anything Said or Done"

The words in this subsection refer to anything said or done by the police, not by the accused, whether directly or indirectly, *e.g.* the police talk to the wife of a suspect and tell her to persuade her husband to confess, otherwise he will never see her again, or if the police know that the accused is a drug addict, for instance, and is more likely to confess in order to be released early so as to get a "fix"; such cases could amount to any confession being inadmissible for unreliability.[79] Silence still cannot form a confession, in spite of reforms to the right of silence. **3–100**

It has been recognised since *R. v. Sang* that evidence improperly or illegally obtained may still be admissible at trial. There are exceptions, *e.g.* confessions and admissions, where the judge does have a discretion to prevent such evidence from being admitted. Thus, in *R. v. Khan (Sultan)*,[80] the police installed an electronic listening device on the outside of a house, at which the defendant was visiting. The defendant made various statements which were unknowingly recorded by the police including admissions that he was involved in illegal drugs importation. He was later charged with various drug offences. At trial, it was conceded by the prosecution that the only real evidence was the tape recordings. He pleaded guilty and appealed. He argued that the police had no statutory powers or authority to place the listening devices without the knowledge of the occupants. Hence, their actions were illegal and amounted to a civil trespass and, as it happens, damage to property. The main issues for the Court of Appeal to decide were (1) whether the tape recording evidence was admissible, and if so then (2) whether it should have been excluded at common law or under section 78 PACE. Having discarded the right to the exclusion of improperly obtained evidence under *R. v. Sang* principles, the House of Lords (Lord Nolan) contended that the recordings could then only be excluded if (a) the appellant had a right to privacy and (b) evidence obtained as a result of an infringement of the right to privacy was inadmissible. Since the proposition in (b) relies on (a), and since the right to privacy does not exist in English law, the whole question was otiose. Thus, in answer to the first question the tape recordings were properly admitted. Whether, on the second question, regarding exclusion under section 78 PACE, Lord Nolan stated that what is important is the significance of the breach[81]:

> "Its significance, however, will normally be determined not so much by its apparent unlawfulness or irregularity, as upon its effect, taken as a whole, upon the fairness or unfairness of the proceedings".[82]

Here, the House of Lords stated, in effect, that the domestic law would be perverse if it allowed a confessed drug dealer to be set free, purely on the basis that his privacy had been infringed. Accordingly, the appeal was dismissed.

The applicant brought his case to the European Court of Human Rights:

Khan v. U.K.[83]:

The applicant complained that, *inter alia*, his right to respect for privacy had been infringed under Article 8 of the Convention. Although there was no doubt that the surveillance techniques used by the police constituted a violation of Article 8(1), the court had to consider whether such actions by the police were in accordance with the law, and if so, whether their actions were necessary in a democratic society, in particular, for the prevention of crime.[84] To be in accordance with the law, the police action not only has to adhere to existing domestic law but also it must relate to the quality of that law, in order to ensure against any arbitrariness by the authorities. The court noted that at the time of the applicant's conviction domestic law lacked legislation to cover the surveillance used by the police.[85] Therefore, it could not be successfully argued by the respondent that what the police did was in accordance with the law. Since the government failed at the first hurdle, it was not incumbent on the court to consider the second proposition, *i.e.* whether or not it was necessary in a democratic society.

The applicant also submitted that since the tape-recordings were in breach of Article 8 and since they were the only evidence against the accused, their admissibility amounted to a violation of Article 6(1), *i.e.* absence of a fair hearing. The court confirmed that it was not their role "to determine, as a matter of principle, whether particular types of evidence, for example, unlawfully obtained evidence, might be admissible or indeed, whether the applicant was guilty or not". Neither would it exclude, as a matter of principle, that such illegally obtained evidence might be allowed in evidence at trial. Despite the fact that the evidence had been obtained in violation of Article 8, "it had not been unlawful in the sense of being contrary to domestic criminal law". The question ultimately was, did the applicant receive a fair trial? The authenticity of the tape-recordings had not been called into question, only their admissibility. Since the domestic courts had a discretion under section 78 PACE whether or not to admit such evidence and concluded that their admissibility would not give rise to unfairness of the trial itself, the court found that the admissibility element did not conflict with the requirements of fairness guaranteed by Article 6(1).[86]

3–101 Despite settled European Court case law regarding the refusal of the court to enquire into unlawfully obtained evidence, Loucaides J. (dissenting) in the above case forcibly argued that where evidence had been secured in breach of the Convention, and subsequently admitted in court proceedings, those proceedings could not thereafter constitute a fair hearing.

Exclusion of Evidence Under Section 78

3–102 Section 78 deals with situations where the court is to have a discretion to exclude evidence from the proceedings. Under section 78(1), a court may refuse to allow evidence upon which the prosecution wishes to rely if:

> ". . . it appears to the court that, having regard to all the circumstances, including the circumstances in which the evidence was obtained, the admission of the evidence would have such an adverse effect on the fairness of the proceedings that the court ought not to admit it".

Any evidence may be excluded in this way, including confessions. Thus section 78 can be useful where the breach committed in obtaining a confession was not serious enough for section 76 to be satisfied. There are some types of breach which are almost always held to justify exclusion of evidence, for example a failure to caution the suspect when required, failure to record a confession alleged to have been made during an interview, or failure to inform a suspect of his right to legal advice before questioning him. Any breach of code C may trigger a section 78 exclusion of a confession or other evidence, but will not necessarily do so; each case must be judged on its own facts.

Although confessions are the prime example of evidence which may be excluded under section 78, some others are worthy of mention. Evidence obtained by entrapment may be excluded if, for example, in the circumstances the defendant would not have committed the offence but for the actions or persuasion of the police officer involved. Identification evidence might be excluded if the procedural rules of Code D were infringed. Or in a case involving a charge of driving whilst intoxicated, scientific evidence has been excluded because of the manner in which it was obtained.[87] Courts often refer to "significant" or "substantial" breaches of PACE rules or the Codes of Guidance when exercising the section 78 discretion in favour of the defendant and ruling that the tainted evidence is inadmissible. Unfortunately, there is no consistent approach or guideline as to when the discretion should be exercised or when a breach is significant or substantial enough to make admission of the evidence "unfair". Further discussion of when PACE and Code of Practice breaches will affect the admissibility of evidence will take place below in connection with the procedures for interviewing suspects at a police station.

Lies and Tricks Used by The Police to Obtain Confessions

The courts are generally not concerned with how the evidence was **3–103** obtained, and this may include the information being gathered by means of subterfuge. What matters is the fairness of the trial, and only if the evidence admitted produces unfairness will the court exercise its discretion to exclude such evidence. The common law direction to exclude evidence so as to ensure a fair trial is still maintained under section 82(3). Entrapment, agent provocateur or tricks used by the police against a suspect does not constitute a defence for any criminal offence at common law.[88] The question is, whether the introduction of section 78 has changed that rule or whether, now, if there is an agent provocateur involved can the defendant submit that any evidence, including admissions, gathered as a result of the methods used, be excluded at trial. Agent provocateur is defined as ". . . a person who entices another to commit an express breach of the law which he would not otherwise would have committed and then proceeds to inform against him in respect of such an offence",[89] (*e.g.* undercover police, persuading an otherwise innocent person to commit an offence). The attitudes of the court since *R. v. Sang* is that merely proving that the offence involved an agent provocateur does not, by itself, amount to a defence, so that the court ought to exclude the otherwise admissible evidence. Part of section 78(1) refers to ". . . Having regard to all the circumstances, including the circumstances in which the evidence was obtained . . .", and if the evidence was gathered in such a way so as to produce an adverse effect, and resulted in unfairness at trial, only then ought the judge to exclude it.

In the case of *R. v. Smurthwaite and Gill*[90]:

Facts. This was an appeal against conviction by the appellants Smurthwaite and Gill. The facts with regards to Smurthwaite were that he had decided to murder his wife. Unfortunately for him, he decided to engage the services of an undercover police officer, posing as a contract killer. During their two meetings, the "hit-man" secretly tape-recorded their conversations. At the second meeting the appellant handed over half the agreed amount (£20,000) and said, "I want me wife killed basically", and suggested how it might be carried out. The appellants' main appeal was that:

(1) the police officer had acted as an agent provocateur, and if it had not been for him, the appellant would never have murdered his wife.
(2) The tape recording evidence had been obtained by a trick.

Decision. It was held in (1) above that the court having listened to the unchallenged evidence of the tapes, were not convinced that the police officer was in fact acting as an agent provocateur, and (2) despite tricking the appellant by masquerading as a contract killer, the evidence showed that the police officer remained mostly silent and did not influence the appellant on how the murder was to be carried through. It was the appellant who came forward with the ideas and suggestions of the overall planning of the murder. There was therefore no pressure, incitement or persuasion used by the police officer on the appellant to commit a crime he was not already intent on doing. As a result, the appeal (and for the similar reasons given in Gill) was dismissed.

Where the police have not identified themselves intentionally, in order to trick or entrap the suspect, it may still be the case that such evidence will still be admissible, despite breaches of the Codes. Indeed, the Codes may not be applicable at all.

For instance in *R. v. Christou and Wright*[91]:

Facts. The police set up a type of "sting" operation, whereby they opened up a fake jewellery shop. They let it be known that they were interested in purchasing stolen property. Video and sound equipment were installed to record such dealings. As a result of this operation and evidence gathered, the defendants were charged with handling stolen goods. Since the judge allowed evidence obtained during the operation, the defendants pleaded guilty.

Decision. The defendants appealed on the grounds, *inter alia*, that since the police suspected the appellants of the offences, they should have issued a caution under Code C, paragraph 10.1, and that the operation of the Codes should not be circumvented to allow an investigation to succeed. The judge, at first instance, decided that the Code did not apply in a situation such as this. The Court of Appeal agreed. Lord Taylor of Gosforth C.J. stated that the Code applies where the suspect is being questioned about an offence by a police officer acting as a police officer for the purpose of obtaining evidence. In that situation, the officer and the suspect are not on equal terms, but that was not the case here. Here, dealings between the police and the criminals were on equal terms, and the Code was not intended to be used for this purpose. His Lordship went on to say that had questions in the shop concerned the offence itself, and were not merely about conducting everyday business, then it would be up to the judge to exclude such questions under section 78. However, the judge found that the only questions and answers were the sort normally associated with dealing with a shady jeweller.
Therefore the appeal was dismissed.[92]

However, in *R v. Bryce*[93]:

Facts. The defendant was arrested for handling stolen property, after trying to sell a stolen car to an undercover police officer named Pearson. During their negotiations Pearson was alleged to have asked the defendant "How long has it been nicked", to which the defendant allegedly replied, "two or three days". At the police station the defendant remained silent throughout the interview, but after the questioning finished and the tape recorder was switched off, the police alleged that the defendant made a confession. At trial, the judge allowed evidence of these alleged conversations and the defendant was convicted. He appealed. **3–104**

Decision. The appeal was based on two grounds, in that the judge erred in (1) allowing the alleged discussion between Pearson and the appellant and (2) allowing evidence of the alleged confession to be admitted. As to (1), the court stated that the question asked by Pearson went directly to the issue of the appellant's guilt. Such questions constitute an interview and thus require a caution under Code C. In *Christou v. Wright*, it was said that "it would be wrong for police officers to adopt or use an undercover pose or disguise to enable themselves to ask questions about an offence uninhibited by the requirements of the Code and with the effect of circumventing it".[94] Further, no record, written or recorded, was made by Pearson of these alleged conversations which were, in any event, vigorously challenged by the appellants. In the circumstances, the judge ought not to have admitted such evidence. In (2), there were a number of serious breaches of the Code. Once the taped no-comment interview was over, the police when asking the appellant, "Well, what happened, then?", should have re-cautioned the appellant before answers were given (under the then C10:5, a caution must be given again when there is "a break in questioning"). The appellant was not prepared to speak if his answers were going to be recorded, and indeed, the alleged confessions were not contemporaneously recorded. The court held that if such a confession was allowed to be admitted, it would completely negate the whole purpose of concocted interviews. Not to exclude it could cause an adverse effect on the whole fairness of the trial. As a result, the conviction was held to be unsafe and unsatisfactory and the appeal was allowed.

The courts do not look lightly upon the situation where the police intentionally deceive or lie to a solicitor whose presence there, at the police station, is not only to safeguard the interests of his client, but also to see that what information he receives from the police is honestly given in the interest of justice, overall.

Thus in *R. v. Mason*[95]:

Facts. The defendant was arrested for arson. During an interview, the defendant and his solicitor were informed by the police that the defendant's fingerprints had been found on the fragments of a bottle used to start the fire. After this finding the solicitor advised his client to answer all the police officer's questions. Thereafter, he admitted filling the bottles with petrol. In fact, no fingerprints had been found—the police had lied. The judge, at first instance, nevertheless allowed the confession to be admitted as evidence and the defendant was convicted.

Decision. The "fingerprint information" was totally without foundation. The police had deliberately lied and deceived not only the appellant, but more importantly his solicitor, "whose duty it is to advise him, unfettered by false information from the police".[96] The court when admonishing the police used such expressions as "reprehensible", "misbehaviour of a serious kind", and "deliberate falsehood" to describe their distaste for such underhanded behaviour and accordingly allowed the appeal.

Tape-Recordings Used to Obtain Confessions

3–105 Tape-recording by the police of a confession, without the knowledge of the suspect, does not automatically amount to the confession being excluded at trial, unless there is evidence to suggest that the police used tactics which the court feels to be so abhorrent so as to affect the fairness of the trial. Even some forms of tricks or subterfuge practised by the police in this area will not excuse the evidence from being admitted. For example, tape-recording confessions of suspects shouting to each other self-incriminating statements from separate cells is admissible, since the police played no part in this action, save using an apparatus to record their conversations.[97]

In *R v. Bailey and Smith*[98]:

Facts. The police, by a ruse, convinced the defendants, who were charged with robbery, that they had to share a police cell. The police in order to dampen the defendant's suspicion that the cell was bugged, acted out an argument between themselves protesting that the defendants should be placed in the same cell. Having satisfied the defendants fears that the cell was not bugged, the police then tape-recorded their conversations which led to various admissions. They were convicted.

Decision. The appeal, *inter alia*, was based on the fact that the appellants had remained silent when questioned and then subsequently charged. Thus, no further questioning could be put to them regarding the offences. They were in fact being tricked into speaking to the police without their knowledge or consent and that this was not done voluntarily. The Court of Appeal rejected these submissions. The court referred back to a number of cases on tape-recording suspects and stated that despite the trickery used to record the conversations, the verbal exchange between the defendants was done voluntarily. There had been no oppression used so as to make the admissions unreliable. Thus, the appeal was dismissed.

Tape-recording need not necessarily be restricted to verbal exchanges between the suspect and other criminals, family or friends, but can be extended to eavesdropping on telephone conversations to gather evidence against a suspect.[99] There are no hard and fast rules in this area regarding when to admit or reject the evidence under section 78, save the judge considering the adverse effects on the fairness of the trial, if the evidence was admitted. Each case must be judged on its own particular facts and the judge has a very wide discretion whether to admit or exclude the relevant admissions. It is suggested that the law in such instances may be summarised as follows: the police may surreptitiously tape-record conversations at the police station, and it does not necessarily matter that:

(a) The suspect was unaware of the recording;

(b) The suspect unwittingly volunteered the self-incriminating statements;

(c) The police used deception by bugging a prison cell at the request of one of the suspects;

(d) The police persuaded one of the suspects to entrap his accomplice into making a confession;

(e) The suspect had already been charged and then subsequently made the admissions;

(f) The police persuaded some person to go into the already bugged-cell in order to induce another prisoner to admit the offence;

(g) Those inside the cell knew, or did not know, that the cell was bugged.

Entrapment is not a defence under English law and it is very difficult for the accused to successfully argue that evidence of entrapment would have such an adverse effect on the fairness of the proceedings that it ought to be excluded under section 78 of PACE. This difficulty was shown in the case of *Nottingham County Council v. Amin*[99A] where two plain clothes police officers stopped a taxi in the Nottingham area, an area for which that particular taxi was not licensed. The taxi driver drove the police officers to another part of Nottingham. He was then charged with plying for hire without a license. At first instance the case was dismissed on the grounds that the police evidence was inadmissible under section 78 having regard to the previous decisions of the European Court of Human Rights and the forthcoming introduction of the Human Rights Act 1998. On appeal by the city council, the Divisional Court considered that on the facts of the case the respondent had not been "prevailed upon, or overborne, or persuaded, or pressurised, or instigated or incited to commit the offence". Accordingly, the appeal was allowed. However, not all entrapment is carried out at the instigation of, or even with the knowledge of, the police; media "stings" on celebrities are bcoming increasingly common and are a fruitful source of column inches. Where evidence is acquired by entrapment via an agent provocateur, that fact by itself is not sufficient to result in the exclusion of such evidence under section 78 of PACE or the common law, but merely one factor which the judge will consider when deciding whether or not that evidence should be admitted. In *R. v. Shannon*[1]:

Facts. The appellant was convicted of supplying cocaine to a *News of the World* newspaper journalist, who was posing as an Arab Sheikh, in order to produce evidence that the appellant was dealing in drugs. At trial, the appellant's argument that the evidence should be excluded under section 78 of PACE 1984 or alternatively, that he was deprived of a fair trial under Article 6 of the ECHR, was rejected by the judge. The appellant appealed on the following grounds:

(i) that the failure to exclude evidence under section 78 of PACE or at common law, obtained through deception by the journalist, was unreasonable;
(ii) that the judge erred in ruling that there had been no entrapment or the use of agents provocateurs; and
(iii) that the case of *Teixeira de Castro v. Portugal*[2] should have been applied to exclude agent provocateur evidence on the grounds that it prevents a fair trial.

Decision. The Court of Appeal held that the judge had not erred in his discretion to allow the evidence to be admitted. Cases such as *R. v. Chalkley*[3] showed that entrapment is only one factor to be considered where deciding whether or not to admit evidence. Principally, the judge should examine:

(a) the procedural fairness of the trial;
(b) the reliability of the prosecution evidence; and
(c) the fullness and fairness of the opportunity available to the defendant to deal with the evidence which the prosecution sought to produce.

Although it was correct for the judge to evaluate whether or not the appellant had been persuaded or enticed to commit an offence by entrapment (see above *R. v. Smurthwaite and Gill*[4]) the main consideration was whether the fairness of the trial would be adversely affected by admitting the evidence obtained by entrapment or via an agent provocateur. Since English criminal law does not permit entrapment to be used as a defence, evidence obtained by such means is not unlawful. Even if some encouragement or enticement existed, it did not impede on the overall fairness of the trial. The only exception to this would be where the behaviour of the police, or of someone acting for or on behalf of them, had been such as to justify a stay of proceedings on the grounds of abuse of process.

The Court of Appeal acknowledged the principle stated in *Teixeira de Castro v. Portugal*[5] that the admissibility of evidence is primarily a matter for the national courts to determine and that, in doing so, their task under Article 6 is to determine whether the proceedings as a whole, including the manner by which the evidence was obtained, were fair. This principle is in line with English law, although the facts in *Teixeira* were different from that of *Shannon*. *Teixeira* was concerned with police entrapment, not media involvement.[6] Does it make any difference whether the entrapment is carried out by the police, media or some private individual? Apparently not, it does not seem to matter how the evidence is obtained, provided the proceedings themselves are fair and the adduced evidence reliable. In *Teixeira* it was found that the police enticed the defendant to commit an offence, a factor which was not present in the *Shannon* case; but from another perspective the *Shannon* case is worse, since the offence was entirely set up and created by the insistence of the instigating reporter. It thus remains uncertain whether the effect would have been the same if *Shannon*'s offence had been instigated by a police operative; presumably the Court of Appeal would then have had to give far more weight to the *Teixeira* arguments.

Breach of the Codes

One of the most common dilemmas confronting the courts is the situation in an interview where the accused makes various admissions or confessions in the absence of a legal adviser.[7] The problem is, that assuming there was a breach of section 58(1) and the Codes, should the evidence of the confession be admissible at trial or excluded on the grounds of section 78? As was stated previous, not every breach of section 58 or the Codes will automatically mean that the evidence of the confession will be ruled inadmissible. **3–106**

In *R. v. Walsh*[8]:

Facts. The appellant was charged and convicted of robbery and various firearm offences. At the police station, he was refused access to legal advice. At the first interview, the police failed to keep contemporaneous records, or give reasons for not making a record, or give the appellant the chance to read or sign the record (the prosecution did not contest the issue that there was a breach of section 58 and the Codes). The interview took place in a police cell as opposed to an interview room—a breach of the Code. On appeal, the prosecution did not accept this particular breach on the grounds that it was not practicable in the circumstances. Although there were a number of serious breaches, the judge at first instance, found that the police had acted in good faith, and that whether a solicitor was present at the interview or not, would not have made any difference to what was said during the interview.

Decision. On appeal, Saville J. stated that:

> ". . . if there are significant and substantial breaches of section 58 or the provisions of the Code, then prima facie at least the standards of fairness set by Parliament have not been met. . . . This does not mean, of course, that in every case of a significant or substantial breach of section 58 or the Codes of Practice the evidence concerned will automatically be excluded. Section 78 does not so provide. The task of the court is not merely to consider whether there would be an adverse effect on the fairness of the proceedings, but such an adverse effect that justice requires the evidence to be excluded".

The court expressed the view that it could have made a difference had the appellant been allowed legal advice, since on the facts, after consulting with a solicitor he declined to answer any questions. Just how major a difference it would have made the court did not comment upon, other than that it was perhaps "uncertain" whether or not the presence of a solicitor would have made any difference. The appeal was allowed.

In *R. v. Walsh*, the question whether the proviso under section 2 of the Criminal Appeals Act 1968 should be applied, was also considered. Saville J. said:

> ". . . proceedings are not rendered fair by the fact that other evidence is available, while the absence of any other such evidence merely reinforces the unfairness that already exists. Where the strength or otherwise of the other evidence is relevant, is in considering the proviso, for if this court concludes that notwithstanding the unfairness of the trial, the appellant would have been convicted anyway had the trial been wholly fair, then at the end there may have been no real miscarriage of justice at all".

In this case, the other evidence was not overwhelming and in these circumstances the appeal was allowed.

Despite refusal of access to legal advice, the court will not only look at the relevant breaches to decide whether any evidence should be excluded, but also the behaviour and personal attributes of the accused whilst being interviewed. If it was shown that the person was streetwise as well as "lawwise", the judge should take that into consideration when deciding to employ section 78. For instance, if the accused knew that he could remain silent and further did not need to sign the interview record, *i.e.* he had "experience of arrest",[9] the judge would be entitled to conclude that a solicitor present at an interview would make no difference to the accused's behaviour Where there is a breach of the Codes, especially Code C, many scenarios exist which may or may not result in the particular admission being excluded. For instance, the police may wish to introduce evidence of the accused's guilt and he denies ever making such statements. Alternatively, the accused admits making the confession but maintains that it should have been excluded at trial because of the breaches of the Act and/or Code. Some breaches are considered so serious that the only remedy, in order to retain the fairness of the trial, is to exclude the otherwise admissible evidence; whilst other breaches, even if admitted, would have such little consequence on the accused's guilt that no harm would be had by including such evidence. Then there is the grey area, whereby before the judge exercises his discretion he should take account of all the other relevant factors under section 78. For example in *R. v. Delaney*,[10] the whole prosecution case was based on admissions made by the defendant (and later interviews), on a charge of indecent assault, after having been interviewed for approximately one and a half hours. The record of the first interview was not recorded until the following day; in breach of the then Code C 11:3 and 11:4 (now C 11:5 and 11:7 respectively), in that the record must be made as soon as practicable and contemporaneously. The judge at first instance ruled out the defence under section 76(2) and admitted the confessions, whilst at the same time recognising that the reasons for not making a record as soon as practicable was utter nonsense and a flagrant breach of Code C. The appellant was a man of below normal intelligence, and indeed there was evidence from a psychologist to state that he was likely to confess in order to end the interview as quickly as possible. Indeed, the police during their interviews stressed that the person who committed this offence was in need of treatment rather than punishment. This, coupled with the various breaches of the Code itself, satisfied the court that the conviction was unsafe and unsatisfactory and therefore the appeal was allowed.

Mentally Disadvantaged Under Section 77

"Mentally handicapped" is defined in section 77(3) as ". . . a state of arrested or incomplete development of mind which includes significant impairment of intelligence and social functioning". Special care must be taken with confessions made by those who are mentally impaired. Section 77 requires judges to remind juries that reliance upon such a person's confession is inadvisable if there is a lack of other corroborating evidence and the confession was made without any independent person being present.[11] *In R. v. Bailey*,[12] the prosecution relied wholly on the confession by the accused who suffered from a severe personality disorder and a mild form of mental handicap. The main question for the court to decide was whether the accused's confession was so unconvincing that a jury properly directed could not safely convict on it. In reaching a decision the judge is at liberty to take into account all the evidence including the surrounding circumstances. The jury should be informed that: **3–107**

(1) Such persons are apt to make false confessions in these circumstances, giving examples;

(2) That there was no prosecution case without the confession;

(3) There may have been facts which induced the accused to make the confession; and

(4) Special facts about the case which the accused knew might have been obtained innocently, *e.g.* by newspaper articles, media or from other people.

Expert evidence in circumstances such as this is vitally important. It is this evidence which must be examined by the judge in determining the reliability of the confession in conjunction with other circumstances existing at the time. In *R. v. Everett*,[13] it was stated that whether or not the police when interviewing the defendant took into account the defendant's mental condition is not relevant, but the doctor's evidence is, viewed objectively. The judge in this case wrongly considered only the taped confessions and therefore erred in not examining all the circumstances surrounding the confession, including the defendant not having an independent adult present and therefore the appeal was allowed.

With regard to section 77, there is an even greater need to protect the individual who might otherwise not receive a fair trial. It is all too easy for the police to extract a confession in such cases, through interviewing techniques which in normal circumstances would constitute a valid and admissible confession. Here, because of the mental condition of the accused there is a wider need for protecting such an individual. This is emphasised by Code C Annex E Notes for Guidance E3:

> ". . . although mentally disordered or mentally handicapped people are often capable of providing reliable evidence, they may, without knowing or wishing

> to do so, be particularly prone in certain circumstances to provide information which is unreliable, misleading or self-incriminating. Special care should therefore always be exercised in questioning such a person, and the appropriate adult involved, if there is any doubt about a person's mental state or capacity".

Any confession made by a mentally handicapped person must be made in the presence of an independent person.[14] In *R. v. Bailey* (above), the accused was interviewed in the absence of her solicitor and independent person and confessed to manslaughter and arson. She later retracted her confession during an interview, in front of her solicitor and social worker. The jury should have been directed on the initial confession as to the inherent problems associated with convicting under these circumstances. Further, the question in cases such as this is, not whether the confession was true, but whether taking all the circumstances into account, it was made in consequence of anything done or said which was likely to render it unreliable.[15]

Section 82(3) states that where a discretion to exclude evidence existed before PACE, it will continue to do so. Thus, confessions (and any other evidence) may be held inadmissible at the discretion of the court if it is deemed necessary to so act in order to ensure a fair trial. This common law discretion is quite narrow and will only apply if the evidence is more likely to prejudice the trial than it is of value in proving the prosecution case.

VIII POLICE INTERVIEWS

Introduction

3–108 Since the establishment of full-time police forces in the early nineteenth century, it has been part of the function of a police officer to investigate offences which have, or may have, been committed. Even before this occurred, there was an established common law principle that a suspect should not be induced to incriminate himself; questioning or interrogating a suspect should have the elucidation of the truth and the finding of evidence as its only purposes, and should be carried out in circumstances and conditions which were likely to produce these desired results and were fair to the suspect. As early as the seventeenth century the courts were dubious about convicting a person where the only evidence presented against him by the prosecution consisted of an uncorroborated confession, particularly where there was any suspicion that the suspect had been "persuaded" to confess. By 1912, the Judges' Rules contained four provisions governing the police questioning of suspects, and these were amended and expanded in 1918 and 1964. The 1964 Judges' Rules and Appendix contained many stipulations which were preserved by PACE, but took the form of instructions rather than strict rules and so their breach did not regularly lead to the relevant evidence being excluded in court. According to the 1964 Rules, the police had a right to question any person, and should caution a suspect once there were reasonable grounds for suspicion that an offence had been committed, or on charging a suspect, or when a written statement was made. Suspects could expect a level of comfort and proper treatment, and separate provisions were made for the interrogation of juveniles, the mentally impaired and those suspects who required an interpreter. The right to silence and the necessity of a statement being made voluntarily if it was to be admissible in evidence were among those rights mentioned in the Preamble to the 1964 Rules and supported therein:

> "It is a fundamental condition of the admissibility of evidence against any person, equally of any oral answer given by the person to a question put by a police officer and of any statement made by that person, that it shall have been voluntary, in the sense that it was not obtained from him by fear of prejudice or hope of advantage, exercised or held out by a person in authority, or by oppression".[16]

This paragraph was based upon the established common law.

The Royal Commission recommended that the right to silence, amongst other rights, should be retained, since it is a burden placed upon the prosecution to prove that the defendant is guilty—the defendant should not be forced either to implicate himself in the offence or to assist the prosecution. The Commission criticised the lack of accuracy in police records of interviews and statements, and suggested ways of improving this. Tape recording of interviews was also recommended in order to allow the conduct of the officers concerned to be monitored and to enable the court to physically hear evidence verbatim, rather than to hear an officer's recollection of what was said and done. Evidence could then be from a primary source rather than being hearsay. The requirement of video recording of interviews was rejected by the Commission on the ground of cost, but was regarded as advantageous if any police force or station should wish to use it in particular circumstances.

PACE largely adopts the recommendations of the Royal Commission, although certain amendments have been made since, principally in relation to the right of silence, and will be discussed later. The rules governing the conduct of interviews are to be found in Code of Practice C. Section 60 requires the Secretary of State to issue a Code of Practice covering the tape recording of all interviews with suspects conducted at police stations, and to make mandatory the tape recording of all such interviews. This requirement is satisfied by Code of Practice E, which states that interviews must be tape recorded in the following situations (paragraph 3):

(1) Where the interviewee has been cautioned for an offence which is either indictable or triable either way;

(2) Where a suspect has been charged with an offence, or informed that he may be prosecuted for such an offence, and the police need to ask additional questions about an offence which is

indictable or triable either way (this situation is permitted only rarely); and

(3) Where another person has been interviewed or has given a statement and the police wish to bring this to the attention of the suspect, who has either been charged with an indictable offence or one which is triable either way, or has been informed that he may be prosecuted for such an offence.

Tape Recording

3–109 It is now general practice to record all interviews, although those with terrorist suspects or persons suspected of Official Secrets offences need not be recorded (paragraph 3.2). The custody officer has a discretion to authorise the interviewing officer not to tape record an interview if it is not reasonably practicable to do so, due to equipment failure or inadequate resources, if the custody officer believes on reasonable grounds that the interview should not be delayed. If an interview is not taped then a written record must be taken, including the reason why taping did not occur (paragraph 3.3), and the decision not to tape the interview may have to be justified in court. The recording must be made openly, a new cassette being opened and inserted into the recorder in the suspect's presence (paragraph 4.1). Then the suspect must be formally told about the tape recording, given the names of all officers present at the interview and given a notice about what will happen to the tape. The suspect must be cautioned, informed of his right to free legal advice and asked to confirm or deny on the tape any earlier statements or silences which are considered to be significant (paragraph 4.3). If the suspect is or may be deaf or hearing-impaired, then a contemporaneous note must be taken of the interview as well as the tape (paragraph 4.4). If the suspect objects or complains about the interview being recorded during the interview, this must be recorded on the tape and then the recorder may be switched off. A written record of any continuance of the interview must then be made (paragraph 4.5). If a break is taken during an interview, this fact must be recorded on the tape and the tape must be removed from the machine. At the end of the interview, the suspect must be allowed an opportunity to speak, when he may clarify what he has said and add anything further (paragraph 4.12). Tapes must be sealed, labelled and signed after the interview, and arrangements for tape security at police stations are also stringent. Apart from the present conditions relating to tape recording interviews, section 60 of PACE has been amended by section 76 of the Criminal Justice and Police Act 2001 which grants the Secretary of State powers "to issue a code of practice for the visual recording of interviews held by police officers at police stations" (section 76(1)),[16A] as well as to issue an order requiring certain cases to be dealt with using visual recordings in line with the Code (sections 76(2) and (3)).

The Interview

Interviewing a suspect is a vital tool for police in making the decision whether or not to prosecute that person for an offence; without a power to question a suspect who is detained at the police station, the obtaining of evidence would be an extremely difficult task. This significance of the interview has two major consequences: first, many safeguards have been developed under PACE, the Codes of Practice and the common law to govern the conduct and content of interviews with suspects; and secondly, the definition of "interview" has become highly important due to the fact that these safeguards apply only during interviews and not during mere "discussions" or "off the record questions". **3–110**

Returning to Marcus for the last time, when and where may he be interviewed concerning the offences of which he is suspected? An "interview" is itself a contentious issue (see below). But it will be important to determine where the interview took place, and whether the requirements of Code C were met. Again, Marcus is entitled to formal procedures, legal advice and written notification. If he answers questions in the back of the police car which takes him to the designated police station after his arrest, the information will be treated differently from information given in a police interview suite with legal advice and tape-recording facilities.

What Exactly Constitutes an Interview?

"An interview is the questioning of a person regarding his involvement or suspected involvement in a criminal offence or offences which, by virtue of paragraph 10.1 of Code C, is required to be carried out under caution" (Code C, paragraph 11.1A). The difficulty in deciphering, in varying circumstances, what is an interview and what is merely an informal talk has caused the courts more problems than was ever envisaged. The abundance of past case law on this subject has shown the innumerable practical problems involved in explaining, with sufficient clarity, the exact meaning of the word, despite the new definition in paragraph 11.1A. At the end of the day where the position is unclear, it is for the court to decide using an objective test. In *R. v. Weekes*[17] the court said that ". . . it was a question of fact, bearing in mind the nature of the questioning, its length, sequence, and the place where such enquiries were conducted, whether it then became an interview". **3–111**

Before an interview can take place an individual must be cautioned. If not, this will constitute a serious breach of the Code and any evidence of admissions made during such an interview may well be excluded under section 78. For instance, in R. v. Absolam[18]:

Facts. The defendant had been arrested for using threatening behaviour. Whilst at the police station he was asked by the custody officer to put any drugs in his possession on the table. He produced some cannabis resin from inside his trousers. The custody officer reminded him of the caution and then asked him some questions which included, "Were these bags ones that you have left over from selling today?". The defendant allegedly replied "Yes". No record was made of this conversation until much later, and was never shown to the defendant. The defendant denied the conversation took place. Further, it was only after the alleged conversation that he was advised of his right to seek legal advice. The custody officer admitted that he was trying to obtain admissions from the defendant. He was convicted of possession of the drugs with intention to supply and appealed on the grounds that the judge ought to have excluded the questions put to him by the custody officer.

Decision. The Court of Appeal allowed the appeal. The lack of informing the appellant as to his right to legal advice at the moment when the custody officer was fully aware that an offence had been committed, amounted to a serious breach. Further, not making a contemporaneous record, nor showing that record to the appellant were significant and substantial breaches of the Code. Thus, any admissions ought to have been excluded. The lesser offence of possession of drugs was substituted for the more serious one of supplying.

Even if the evidence should have been excluded, due to a serious or significant breach of a Code, it may still remain the case that the appeal will not be allowed, if having excluded the "breached interview" from admission, there was other evidence which made the conviction safe and satisfactory.[19]

For example in *R v. Okafor*[20]:

Facts. The defendant, who arrived at Gatwick airport from abroad, was searched by customs officers. Cocaine with a street value of £200,000 was found hidden in snails, as part of a snail stew. The custom officers, hoping to entrap other accomplices, did not immediately alert the defendant to their findings or arrest him. Instead, they allowed him to proceed to his train after he had agreed to answer some further questions during a body search. The questions included, whether he had caught the snails himself. To which he replied, "No, from the market". The judge, at first instance, ruled that despite there being breaches of the Code and no contemporaneous record of the conversation, the defendant was not unfairly prejudiced and admitted the dialogue evidence.

Decision. He was convicted and appealed on the grounds that the conversation about the snails should have been excluded since:

(1) That conversation constituted an interview and no caution was given at the appropriate time;
(2) He was not informed of his right to legal advice prior to the interview; and
(3) The interview was not contemporaneously recorded and therefore there was a serious breach of the Code.

The Court of Appeal stated that the relevant conversation was an interview which ought to have been excluded. The customs officers are bound by the Codes, as are the police. The court said that in a future similar case such as this, the customs officer should either avoid asking questions related to the offence or give a caution. The court further considered whether the proviso should be applied in this case and decided that on the overwhelming evidence, even after excluding the interview, the whole story was quite incredible. The jury would still have come to the same verdict and thus, the court applied the proviso in the present case.

QUESTIONING

The interview must involve questioning. So that if, without questioning the suspect volunteers information or an admission, that will not constitute an interview.[21] Even one question will bring it within the bounds of an interview.[22] Furthermore, the questioning must take place between a police officer and the suspect, and relate directly to the offence to which the police have reasonable grounds of suspicion.[23] If, for instance, a police constable notices a person putting an offensive weapon, *e.g.* a knife, into his pocket in suspicious circumstances, and asks "What's this for?", this may well amount to an interview and a caution should be given before such a question is asked.[24] In *R. v. Weerdesteyn*,[25] W was charged with the importation of cannabis. After the formal interview was concluded, W asked the customs officer, S, "How many kilos had been found?", S replied, "I don't know, how much should there be?", W responded, "There are forty boxes. They told me there was two kinds". W was convicted. It was decided, on appeal, that since at least one question suggested W's involvement in the offence, this amounted to an interview. As no caution had been given prior to this new conversation, there was a serious breach of the Code. As a result, the appeal was allowed. But, what is the position if the suspect is unaware that the person to whom he is speaking is a police officer, because they do not want their identity to be known? In such circumstances, since no caution or formal interview under Code C could possibly be administered, would the evidence, including any admissions, be admitted in court? Beginning with the established law that merely because there is a breach of the Codes that, by itself, does not automatically exclude relevant evidence acquired. The court, under both section 76 and section 78 will still have a discretion whether to allow such evidence to be admitted. **3–112**

CODE C, PARAGRAPH 11: GENERAL INTERVIEWING RULES

Paragraph 11.3 forbids a police officer from attempting "to obtain answers to questions or to elicit a statement by the use of oppression". Generally, "no police officer shall indicate, except in answer to a direct question, what action will be taken on the part of the police if the person being interviewed answers questions, makes a statement or refuses to do either". Under paragraph 11.4, when an officer who is "making enquiries" believes that a suspect will be prosecuted and that there is sufficient evidence for the prosecution to succeed, then the officer must ask the suspect whether he has anything further to say. If the suspect replies that he does not, then the officer must immediately stop questioning him about the offence. **3–113**

Paragraph 11.14–11.16 concern the interviewing of juveniles, mentally disordered persons and mentally handicapped persons. None of these persons may be interviewed or asked to give or sign a written statement unless an appropriate adult is present. Juveniles should only be interviewed (or indeed arrested) at school in truly exceptional circumstances. If an appropriate adult is present at an interview, he must be informed that his role is not simply to observe but also: to advise the interviewee and assess whether the interview is conducted properly and fairly; and to aid communication between the police and the interviewee. Note for Guidance 11B is a reminder that the persons in these categories may be particularly susceptible to self-incrimination or to giving unreliable or misleading evidence. Thus special care should be taken during interviews and corroborating evidence should also be obtained whenever possible.

Interview Records

3–114 Paragraph 11.5 of Code C deals with the records which must be kept of any interview with a suspect. A full and accurate record must be taken of all interviews, whether or not they occur at a police station, if the interviewee is suspected of an offence. This record must contain details such as the venue, the start and finish times, whether the interview was interrupted for a break, the names of all persons present; and the record must either be made on a standard form, in the police officer's notebook, or on tape. The record must be made during the interview, not afterwards, "unless in the investigating officer's view this would not be practicable or would interfere with conduct of the interview", and should preferably be verbatim. An accurate summary is otherwise permissible. If the interview record is not made during the interview for one of the permitted reasons, it must be made as soon as practicable afterwards (paragraph 11.7). Written interview records must be timed and signed (paragraph 11.8). A general principle is that the interviewee (or, if relevant, an appropriate adult) should be given the opportunity to read and sign the interview record and indicate whether he considers it to be accurate, unless "it is impracticable" to allow him to do this (paragraph 11.10); no guidance is given as to what type of circumstances would be impracticable. If an interviewee refuses to sign an interview record, then the refusal must be recorded. If the suspect, while not being interviewed, makes any other comments, including unsolicited comments, which may be relevant to the offence then a written record must be made of these comments. Where practicable, the person shall be given an opportunity to read and sign this record (paragraph 11.13).

In *Batley v. DPP*[26] the police enquired from a publican what the arrangements were regarding drinking hours at the pub. This was held to be an interview, since the reason behind the questioning was for the publican to incriminate himself into admitting that after hours drinking had taken place there. Under the circumstances, a caution should have been given prior to this questioning. Further, although a note had been made of the conversation by the police, this was not shown to the defendant in order that he might verify its contents. Hence, "there was a real risk that the fairness of the proceedings against the defendant would be adversely affected". Accordingly the appeal was allowed.

Interviews at the Police Station

Most interviews are carried out at a police station, and Code C strongly advocates that this should be the case. If an officer wishes to interview a suspect who is being detained, the custody officer is responsible for deciding whether this should happen (paragraph 12.1). Before any interview begins at a police station (or other authorised place of detention) or is continued there after commencing somewhere else, the interviewing officer shall remind the suspect that he is entitled to free legal advice and that the interview may be delayed to enable this. The fact that these reminders have been given must be entered in the interview record by the interviewing officer (paragraph 11.2). When an interview in a police station is about to begin, the interviewing officer, having cautioned the suspect, must ask him to confirm or deny any significant statement or silence which took place before the suspect arrived at the police station, and ask whether the suspect wishes to add anything. A "significant statement or silence" is one "which appears capable of being used in evidence against the suspect, in particular a direct admission of guilt, or failure or refusal to answer a question or to answer it satisfactorily".[27] (paragraph 11.2A). **3–115**

Para. 12 also contains a number of rules which concern the treatment and comfort of the detained interviewee. At least eight hours in each 24 must be continuous rest without questioning or any other interruption. This should normally be at night. The only grounds for interruption or delay of the rest period are reasonable grounds for belief that otherwise: people or property would be harmed; the suspect's release from custody would be unnecessarily delayed; or the outcome of the investigation would be prejudiced (paragraph 12.2). Interviewing rooms must be adequately heated, lit and ventilated, unless impracticable, and a seat must be provided for the interviewee (paragraph 12.4, 12.5). There must be meal breaks at usual times, and short breaks at about every two hours. The short breaks may be delayed on the same grounds as for rest breaks (above), but if this happens then a longer than usual break should be provided afterwards (paragraph 12.7). If an interviewee makes a complaint about any Code C provision during an interview, then the complaint shall be noted in the interview record and the custody officer must be informed and shall deal with the complaint (paragraph 12.8). Where any written statement is made under caution, it must be on the standard form provided (paragraph 12.12).

Interviews away from the Police Station

Although under paragraph 11.1 the suspect should be interviewed at a police station or other place of detention nevertheless, a formal interview may take place away from the police station if the delay involved in transferring him from his present location would be likely to lead to: **3–116**

(a) Interference with or harm to the evidence connected with an offence, or interference with or harm to other people; or

(b) The alerting of other people suspected of having committed an offence but not yet arrested for it; or

(c) The hindering of the recovery of property obtained because of the commission of an offence. (Code C 11.1).

Once the risk of any of the above situations has been averted then all interviews must cease.[28]

In *R. v. Cox*[29]:

Facts. Detectives went to the home of the defendant to investigate the theft of a lorry which had been involved in a burglary. The detectives informed the defendant that they had seen him the previous Thursday evening driving the lorry, which contained stolen furniture and that when they had then tried to arrest him he ran off and escaped. The following exchange of dialogue then took place:
Detective: "What have you got say about that?".
Def.: "If you think you can prove it, go ahead".
The defendant was then arrested and cautioned.
Detective: "Where is the clothing that you were wearing last Thursday?".
Def.: "You have two chances of finding it".
Detective: "But you are not doubting that we saw you last Thursday in Hazel Close in the lorry?".
Def.: "If you saw me it's up to you to prove it, but I'll give you six to four I'll get off".
He was then taken to the police station where he was interviewed. He refused to make any comment. After the interview, the defendant was shown a note, made prior to the interview, of the conversation at his home, but the defendant refused to sign it. This was all done in the absence of his legal representative. In evidence at his trial the defendant denied the conversation or that he was shown the note.

Decision. The recorder ruled that the "three questions" fell short of being a formal interview, and that there was no breach of paragraph 11. He also decided that the admission of the three questions would not have such an adverse effect on the fairness of the proceedings and was of sufficient probative value that it ought not be excluded, under section 78. The defendant was convicted of handling stolen goods and driving a conveyance without lawful authority. He appealed on, *inter alia*, two main grounds; (1) since the police had attempted to arrest him on the previous Thursday, a caution should have been given at his home prior to any questions and therefore there was a breach of paragraph 10.1, and (2) the three questions constituted, in reality, an interview, and therefore required the relevant procedures set out in paragraph 11. Since this was not done there was a breach of paragraph 11.

The main question for the Court of Appeal to decide was, did the three questions amount to an interview? The detective gave evidence at the trial, which the recorder accepted, that the purpose of question (1) and (3) were purely for identification reasons and not about the offence. McCullough J. doubted this to be the reason, since the detective knew the appellant by sight. The real purpose was to get the appellant to accept that he was driving the lorry. Hence, questions relating to (1) and (3) amounted to an interview and therefore the relevant requirements of paragraph 11 applied. Thus, there were serious breaches of, *inter alia*, paragraph 11.1, 11.5, 11.9 and 10.1. It was conceded by Counsel for the Crown that had question (2) stood alone, the Crown would not have relied upon it. The court, therefore, decided that the evidence should have been excluded. However, they were not willing to quash the convictions and applied the proviso, since as all the surrounding evidence pointed to the appellants guilt there had been no miscarriage of justice. As a result, the appeal was dismissed.[30]

The normal sequence of events leading up to a formal interview are as follows:

(a) An offence has been committed,

(b) The police have grounds to suspect a particular person,

(c) A caution is given before or after arrest; (if after arrest, there must be reasonable grounds for suspicion),

(d) The suspect is then taken to the police station,

(e) The suspect is informed of his rights and entitlements,

(f) The suspect is given access to legal advice,

(g) A caution is given again prior to interview,

(h) The interview commences.

Conclusion

What can be concluded from the above discussion and case law is that the courts are willing to take a flexible approach to the whole area of interviews. Indeed, Bingham L.J. in *R. v. Marsh*[31] stated: **3–117**

> ". . . it is plainly desirable that these provisions should not become so highly technical and sophisticated in their construction and application that no police officer, however well intentioned and diligent, could reasonably be expected to comply with them. There has to be a reasonable commonsense approach to the matter such that police officers, confronted with unexpected situations, and doing their best to be fair and to comply with the Codes, do not fall foul on some technicality of authority or construction".

VIII(i) RIGHT OF SILENCE

Introduction

The right of silence, and the limitations of that right, are probably the greatest source of controversy and legal debate as far as the rights of the suspect are concerned. Recent changes have served to fuel the debate and heighten concern for the rights of the vulnerable; yet there are those who believe that the existence of any such right or privilege interferes with and hampers the running of the entire criminal justice system. Yet even the term "right of silence" or "right to silence" has no single, definite meaning. **3–118**

In the case of *Smith v. Director of SFO*[32] Lord Mustill identified at least six established legal meanings for the term, four of which are relevant to the present discussion, and only one of which has been affected by the limitations imposed under the Criminal Justice and Public Order Act 1994, to be discussed below. At its most basic, the right of silence may be defined as the immunity possessed by all persons from being compelled to answer questions; but we are more concerned with specific applications of this general principle. As has already been discussed, a suspect who is being questioned by a police officer has the right to refuse to answer any question whatsoever. Secondly, a person who is undergoing trial cannot be compelled to give evidence or to answer any questions in court. Thirdly, a person who has been charged with a criminal offence cannot be compelled to answer questions addressed to him by a police officer. Finally, a person who is being tried for a criminal offence had, at common law and under PACE, an immunity from having adverse comments made about the fact that he has chosen either not to give evidence at the trial, or not to answer questions asked of him before his trial. Only the last of these immunities was changed by the 1994 Act; thus, although it is a matter of common belief, the right of silence has not been "abolished". However, this change has had an impact on the other three immunities, since they may now seem somewhat hollow rights; what use is a right to remain silent and refuse to answer questions when being interrogated at a police station, if there is the potential of such a refusal leading to the jury at any later trial of the suspect drawing adverse conclusions from that refusal to talk?

Before the important recent changes to the right of silence are discussed, a short detour into the history of the right may be useful in order to explain why and how the amendments came about. At common law, a suspect's right to silence was well established[33] and had its basis in two separate entrenched general principles: that the accused is innocent until proven guilty beyond all reasonable doubt by the prosecution, upon whom the burden of proof rests,[34] and secondly that a person cannot be forced to incriminate himself by making any statement—this is widely referred to as the privilege against self-incrimination, and still applies in civil cases. Both of these principles have been seen as vital to the English system of criminal justice for several centuries, as its guarantees of fairness both at the stages of investigation and of trial,[35] and so it is understandable that any proposals for change would create an outcry. Yet there had long been concern that the right was either worthless or abused; for example, Jeremy Bentham stated in his Treatise on Evidence that the privilege of silence at trial was of help only to the guilty:

> "If all criminals of every class had assembled, and framed a system after their own wishes, is not this rule the very first which they would have established for their security? Innocence never takes advantage of it. Innocence claims the right of speaking, as guilt invokes the privilege of silence".

These views are still current, even though most sets of statistics indicate both that the right of silence is used relatively infrequently and is often used by suspects who are vulnerable due to their youth, below average intelligence or mental disorder, or who are simply either waiting for, or acting according to, legal advice.

Arguments for and against the existence of the right of silence can be examined in the context of recommendations and legislation since the reports of the Criminal Law Revision Committee in 1972 and the Phillips Royal Commission. The CLRC had recommended that the right of silence should be abolished[36] and, eventually, their proposals became law in 1994. However, in the meantime the Phillips Royal Commission had recommended by a majority that the right of silence should be maintained in its existing form, for two main reasons: the danger that the number of false confessions would be increased if suspects were required to make statements or give evidence; and the conflict which would exist between the abolition of the right and the burden of proof "To use a suspect's silence as evidence against him seems to run counter to a central element" in the criminal justice system, since it is inconsistent:

> "... in requiring the onus of proof at trial to be upon the prosecution and to be discharged without any assistance from the accused, and yet in enabling the prosecution to use the accused's silence in the face of police questioning under caution as any part of the case against him at trial".[37]

Originally the recommendations and reasons from the Phillips Royal Commission were accepted by the Government and were reflected in PACE, Code C as regards the caution (see discussion above). But within three years it had been announced that a Home Office Working Group was to be set up to consider, not whether the right to silence should be abolished, but what manner of changes in the law would be the best method of abolishing the right. The Working Group produced its report in 1989, but in the meantime the right to silence had been abolished in Northern Ireland for those suspected of any offence, not merely of terrorist offences as previously expected. The Criminal Evidence (Northern Ireland) Order 1988 allows a court to draw adverse inferences from the suspect's failure to mention, either before or after charge, any fact upon which his defence relies at his trial; and objects or marks found on the suspect's person or in his possession at the time of his arrest which he does not explain when asked to do so by a police officer may again lead to adverse inferences being drawn in court. A suspect found at or near the scene of a crime may be asked to explain his presence, and failure to do so will allow an inference to be drawn. Any of these three types of failure to speak may amount to corroboration of any other evidence which exists. **3–119**

The 1989 Report of the Home Office Working Group contained recommendations which were very similar to the law which had just been passed for Northern Ireland, and expressly approved the recommendations of the CLRC which had been out of favour since 1972. A suspect's failure to answer questions or to mention a fact later relied upon at his trial should be capable of giving rise to an inference in the eyes of the jury that the defence which he was arguing was false; but it should not be capable of acting as corroboration of any other evidence, unlike the Northern Ireland provisions. As an additional difference, the safeguards for the suspect should be increased so that statutory guidelines would list the factors which a jury would have to consider when deciding whether to draw an adverse inference, including whether the failure was reasonable in the circumstances, whether an innocent explanation might exist, and whether any of the rules of PACE or the Codes of Practice had been breached or stretched. These recommendations were short-circuited by the discovery of a series of miscarriages of justice in which false confessions had played a pivotal role, and the subsequent establishment of the Runciman Royal Commission on Criminal Justice. This Royal Commission was expressly asked to consider, amongst many other issues, whether the right of silence should continue in its present form. Its recommendation, again by a majority, was that the right of silence should continue unamended, with the principal reason being given as the greater risk of miscarriages of justice which would result from its abolition. The minority however was of the opinion that the right to silence should be amended into the form which it is today, arguing that the safeguards which exist for the suspect's welfare during detention and questioning are now sufficient to ensure that the rights of the innocent and the vulnerable are protected. It was the minority view which was adopted by the Government, resulting in sections 34–39 of the Criminal Justice and Public Order Act 1994, which will be discussed below. The 1994 Act broadly followed the recommendations of the 1989 Home Office Working Group, and also introduced some amendments to the Northern Ireland rules in order to bring it into line with the new English law.

Silence Under Police Questioning—Section 34

3–120 No individual may be forced physically or otherwise to answer questions put by the police or make admissions of any kind. However, now under sections 34 and 35 failure to do so may result in adverse inferences being drawn by the court in any proceedings.[38] The key purpose of section 34 (and indeed sections 35, 36 and 37) is to prevent the accused from fabricating a defence, after he has had time for reflection, at a later stage in the proceedings. Section 34(1) states that:

> "(1) Where, in any proceedings against a person for an offence, evidence is given that the accused—
>
> (a) at any time before he was charged with the offence, on being questioned under caution by a constable trying to discover *whether or by whom the offence had been committed, failed to mention any fact relied on in his defence* in those proceedings; or

(b) on being charged with the offence or officially informed that he might be prosecuted for it, failed to mention any such fact, being *a fact which in the circumstances existing at the time the accused could reasonably have been expected to mention* when so questioned, charged or informed, as the case may be, subsection (2) below applies" (all italics are added).

The consequences of section 34 are that, if the accused relied on in his defence some fact or facts which he did not mention when questioned by the police under caution at least, then the court is entitled to draw inferences from his failure to mention that defence at the relevant time. In order for such evidence to be admitted a number of conditions should be adhered to. For instance, there must be questions asked by the police and not merely voluntary statements made by the accused. The questions themselves must be understood and not ambiguous in any way, else it could be argued that the reason for the silence was not a refusal to answer, but related directly to not comprehending what was being asked. Further, any questioning must be done under caution, and therefore, evidence of silence may be admissible even prior to arrest.[39] Thus, since the police only require grounds for suspicion to administer a caution, as opposed to reasonable grounds in order to arrest, there may be a danger that an individual, not under arrest, may not mention a fact because he feels it is not necessary at that stage, the failure of which could ultimately be used against him in court.

"Whether or by whom the offence had been committed"

Under section 34(1)(a), adverse inferences may only be applied to an interview which contained questions to discover specifically "whether or by whom" the offence had been committed. If the interview concerned other material which was not relevant to the above question, then section 34(1)(a) will not apply, despite the fact that the jury may be aware that an interview took place. This problem arose in *R. v. Pointer*,[40] where the appellant was convicted of selling a class A controlled drug. The interview in question had taken place after the police had already found sufficient evidence to charge the suspect (Code C:16.1) but did not so charge. One of the questions for the Court of Appeal was whether the later questioning after the police had gathered sufficient evidence for a prosecution, constituted an interview. Under Code C:11.4 once the police have sufficient evidence for a prosecution, "he shall then ask the suspect if he has anything further to say". That further question was found to constitute an "interview" within Code C:11.1(a) and therefore theoretically, section 34 should have applied. But once the "sufficient evidence" factor has been established, then the police are only entitled to charge and not enter the realms of whether or by whom the offence had been committed. Therefore, section **3–121**

34 did not apply in this case. When analysing the transcript of the trial the Court of Appeal found that the judge in fact directed the jury not to draw adverse inferences because in the circumstances it seemed more fair and appropriate. As an addendum, the appeal was dismissed on other grounds (identification evidence) which resulted in the decision at first instance not being unsafe in the circumstances. Once the suspect has been charged, however, no further questions related to the offence should be asked (C:16.5).

"Failed to mention any fact"

3–122 It is not the case that all facts may adduce adverse inferences in any subsequent proceedings. It is restricted to those facts which the defence relied on at trial. If not relied on as a defence then section 34 may not be applied.[41] First and foremost, it is up to the prosecution to prove their case. In theory, the defence is entitled to remain silent throughout the trial. However, once the prosecution have made their case, section 34 can only be used when the defence rebutts the prosecution evidence, and at that stage introduces evidence which he failed to mention previously when cautioned. Only then may the court or jury draw adverse inferences from the accused's failure to mention his defence at the time of the caution or upon being charged. Section 34(1)(a) states that "under caution" the accused "failed to mention any fact relied on in his defence", whereas section 34(1)(b) refers to "on being charged or . . . officially informed that he might be prosecuted", and states that he, "failed to mention any such fact, being a fact . . . the accused could reasonably have been expected to mention when so questioned, charged or informed . . .", which seems to be a narrower condition than when cautioned in section 34(1)(a). This distinction may be important because if the police adduce evidence of silence under caution, the accused cannot then submit that he could not reasonably have mentioned certain facts which the court have now drawn adverse inferences from, although it seems that the words "when so questioned", in section 34(1)(b) probably also refers to section 34(1)(a) and not restricted to on being charged or being informed of a possible prosecution. Thus, is "facts" in section 34(1)(a) and (b) disjunctive, or meant to be taken together in conjunction with each other?

"Relied on in his defence"

3–123 Section 34 is limited to questions put to the accused which he ultimately uses in his defence. However, if the accused remains silent on questions which are not relevant to his defence, then section 34 cannot be applied and no adverse inferences may be drawn on those particular questions. Before any adverse inferences may be drawn, the prosecution must present, at least, a prima facie case to begin with.[42] It is no longer questionable that if the defendant refuses to put forward a defence, or refrains from rebutting any allegations and leaves it up to the prosecution entirely to prove their case, the court is entitled to draw adverse inferences under these circumstances. In *R. v. Bowers*[43] the Court of Appeal stated that for section 34 to become a relevant issue, two questions must be considered; (i) did the defendant rely on a particular fact and (ii) did he fail to mention that fact when questioned? If the answers to these questions are in the negative, then it is preferrable for the judge to direct the jury that no adverse inferences should be drawn from the defendant's refusal to answer questions during the interview. Notwithstanding this, it is not unthinkable that once the jury are made aware of the "silent interview", they may give some weight, no matter how little, to the defendant's failure to answer the intereview questions.

If the accused remains silent at the first interview, but then answers questions at subsequent interviews, adverse inferences may be drawn from the refusal to answer questions at the previous interviews. The court is entitled to draw the conclusion that the accused had the opportunity to fabricate a defence in the meantime. But, it is suggested that the court should take into account the length of time between the initial interview and any interviews thereafter.

"Facts which the accused could reasonably have been expected to mention"

The accused must reply to all questions which he could reasonably have **3–124** been expected to answer at the relevant time. However, there may be circumstances which prevent the accused from answering certain questions. For instance, the questions put to him may be incoherent or incomprehensible. In that case the court may well decide that there was no real justification to answer such questions. Other reasons may include the accused being dazed, traumatised or in a temporary mentally unstable condition. Further, the accused may prefer to remain silent, because to answer might seriously compromise his position at work, or jeopardise his home life, even though what he was actually doing at the relevant time was quite legal or his solicitor advised him to remain silent. Nevertheless, the court may consider the reasons why he remained silent insufficient or not convincing enough to warrant adverse inferences not to be considered. It has not, as yet, been decided whether the courts will use an objective or subjective test when referring to the words "reasonably have been expected to mention". An indication as to why a subjective view is to be preferred is because the phrase itself refers back to "the accused". However, there are reservations that the court would accept the accused's word alone, even if honestly held, that in the particular circumstances he saw fit to remain silent. It is suggested that the better view would be to treat the phrase both objectively and subjectively, by first taking into account the accused's demeanour (subjective) and then deciding whether a reasonable person would have acted as the accused acted in his condition (objective).

In R v. Argent[44]:

Facts. A man was stabbed to death during a fight outside a night-club during the early hours of the morning. The same day, following an anonymous phone call, the defendant was arrested and interviewed by the police, and after taking legal advice he remained silent. Some three months later, he was picked out of an identification parade by a number of eye witnesses. Later, at a second interview, he refused to answer any questions, and thereafter was charged with manslaughter. His defence was that he had already left the night-club prior to the fight taking place. The judge directed the jury that it was open to them to draw an adverse inference from the appellant's silence in the second interview under section 34(2)(d). He was convicted and appealed.

Decision. He appealed, *inter alia*, on the grounds that the second interview should have been excluded. As to whether adverse inferences could be drawn, this was a question of fact for the jury to determine after having been given the correct directions by the judge regarding the relevant evidence. The Court of Appeal stated that six conditions had first to be adhered to before the jury can draw any such inference:

(1) There had to be proceedings against a person for an offence. (This had been complied with).
(2) The alleged failure to answer questions had to occur before the defendant was charged. (This also had been complied with).
(3) The alleged failure had to occur during questioning under caution by a constable or other person authorised under section 34(4). (This had been fulfilled).
(4) The questioning had to be directed at trying to discover whether or by whom the alleged offence had been committed. (This had been adhered to).
(5) The alleged failure by the defendant had to be to mention any fact relied on in his defence in those proceedings. This raises two questions of fact: (i) is there some fact which the defendant has relied on in his defence? (ii) did the defendant fail to mention relevant facts or matters to the constable when he was being questioned in accordance with this section, *e.g.* he left before the fight commenced; he was not involved in the fight; he went home; he did not carry a knife, etc.? These were matters for the jury to decide.
(6) The fact which the defendant failed to mention was a fact which, in the circumstances existing at the time, he could reasonably have been expected to mention when so questioned. "Circumstances" included the defendant's age, experience, sobriety, state of health, legal advice, etc. Again, this was a question for the jury using "their collective common sense, experience and understanding of human nature".[45] Since the judge's directions to the jury in this case were clear, concise and comprehensive the appeal was dismissed.

Lord Bingham C.J. said in *R. v. Argent* that it would only be on rare occasions correct for the judge to direct the jury that they should, or should not, draw the appropriate inference. Sadly, his Lordship did not elaborate on what these rare occasions might be. The judge at first instance in that case decided that it would be perfectly reasonable to remain silent without any adverse inference being drawn at trial, where the only proof that he committed a crime was an anonymous tip-off, without more. His Lordship thought that "the judge may have overstepped the bounds of his judicial function" but nevertheless, since it had not disadvantaged the defendant no further comment was made.[46]

SILENCE IN COURT—SECTION 35

Section 35 concerns the circumstances in which adverse inferences may be drawn from the accused's failure to give evidence in court. It only applies where the accused is over fourteen, his guilt is at issue, and the accused's mental or physical condition does not, in the eyes of the court, make it undesirable for him to give evidence (section 35(1)). Once the prosecution's evidence has been presented: **3–125**

> ". . . if he (the accused) chooses not to give evidence, or having been sworn, without good cause refuses to answer any question, it will be permissible for the court or jury to draw such inferences as appear proper from his failure to give evidence or his refusal, without good cause, to answer any question" (section 35(2)).

But the accused cannot be compelled to give evidence, nor will his failure to do so render him liable for contempt of court (section 35(4)).

"May draw such inferences from the the failure as appear proper"

The words "may draw such inferences", etc. appear in both section 34 and section 35. Under section 35 their purpose is to allow the court or jury to draw adverse inferences in a case where the accused refuses to testify. Should the defendant refuse to give evidence, he must, at the end of the prosecution case be made aware by the judge, in the presence of the jury, of the consequences of remaining silent.[47] **3–126**

Soon after the CJPOA 1994 came into force, the case of *R. v. Cowan and Others*[48] came before the Court of Appeal on the question of how a judge should direct or advise a jury when considering the issue of "adverse inferences" in section 35. The above case will now be examined in detail. Each appellants case will be taken in turn and the reasons for their Lordships decision. The appellants based their appeals on the grounds of a misdirection by the judge as to the circumstances when the jury could draw adverse inferences under section 35. What directions or advise should the judge give the jury when deciding whether section 35 applies? Taking guidance from a specimen direction by the Judicial Studies Board, the court itself laid down certain general conditions which should be given by a judge to a jury in his summing up. They are as follows:

(1) The judge will have told the jury that the burden of proof remains upon the prosecution throughout and what the required standard is (this direction is nothing new and is standard practice).

(2) It is necessary for the judge to make clear to the jury that the defendant is entitled to remain silent. That is his right and his choice. The right of silence remains.[49]

(3) An inference from failure to give evidence cannot on its own prove guilt; section 38(3) of the Act.

(4) Therefore, the jury must be satisfied that the prosecution have established a case to answer . . . before drawing an adverse inference from the defendant's silence.

(5) If . . . the jury conclude the silence can only sensibly be attributed to the defendant's having no answer or none that would stand up to cross-examination, they may draw an adverse inference.

The above "direction conditions" are a general guideline. Individual cases will, of course, vary in substance and circumstance. At the end of the day, it is up to the jury to decide, having been given proper guidance, whether, in fact, adverse inferences will be drawn or not.

In *R v. Cowan*[50]:

Facts. The defendant, who had a criminal record, was convicted at two separate trials for unlawful wounding and assault, culminating with a sentence of four years in total. During the first trial for unlawful wounding, during cross-examination of the victim, the appellant's counsel suggested to the victim, *inter alia*, that he had been mistaken and let the jury know of the victim's previous record. The judge did not direct the jury that:

(1) Failure by the accused to testify could not, by itself, infer guilt, and;
(2) If they wished to draw any adverse inferences, they could do so provided they decided that the only reasonable explanation for the appellant's failure to testify was that he had no answer to the case against him, or none that could have stood up to cross-examination.

Decision. The Court of Appeal allowed the appeal on the grounds that since there was a clear conflict of evidence, without the two directions given above, the jury might attach too much unnecessary weight to the appellant's failure to testify.

In *R. v. Gayle*[51]:

Facts. The defendant threatened a witness with violence if he testified against him on a criminal damage charge. The defendant was convicted of perverting the course of justice and sentenced to nine months imprisonment. For similar reasons given in *R. v. Cowan* above, their Lordships allowed the appeal.

Decision. The judge in that case did not give directions that the defendant has a right not to give evidence. Further, although the jury were entitled to draw adverse inferences from the failure of the defendant to testify, it was up to the prosecution to prove at least a prima facie case against him. Finally, the judge should have further directed the jury in terms similar to (2) above.

In *R. v. Cowan. R. v. Ricciardi:*[52]

Facts. The defendant was charged and convicted of attempted theft. He appealed on the grounds that the judge should have advised the jury, that in addition to the specimen direction, there were many innocent reasons why the defendant did not give evidence at trial.

Decision. The court held that since no evidence was adduced as to what these innocent reasons were, there was no need to give the jury any direction on this matter. Hence, the appeal was dismissed.

Legal Advice to Remain Silent

What is the position where the suspect's solicitor advises his client to remain silent during an interview? May the court still draw adverse inferences from the accused's silence at trial, despite accepting that legal advice? It would be extremely easy to circumvent section 34 if the defendant could successfully put forward a defence that his solicitor advised him to remain silent, without more. The advice given by the solicitor to remain silent is not the deciding issue; it is the reason behind that advice which is the determining factor. At the conclusion of the prosecution evidence, if the accused submits that no adverse inferences should be drawn from the solicitor's "advice to remain silent" at interviews, he or his solicitor may be asked to give evidence in court to explain the reasons behind that advice. This is done in order to ascertain whether the advice was justified in order to negative the strong possibility that the defendant invented his story some time later. **3–127**

In *R v. Condron*[53]:

Facts. The defendants were convicted of supplying and intent to supply class A (heroin) drugs. After four days of police observation of the defendant's flat, they were arrested. Their solicitor considered them unfit to be interviewed at the police station due to drug withdrawal symptoms, and accordingly advised them to remain silent. The force medical examiner considered them fit for interview. They gave evidence denying supplying drugs. In cross-examination concerning their no-comment interviews, they stated that they did so on their solicitor's advice. In his summing up, the judge gave the Judicial Studies Board specimen direction, *inter alia*, stating that it was a matter for the jury to decide whether any adverse inferences should be drawn by the defendant's silence at the interviews.

Decision. The defendants appealed on the grounds of a misdirection by the judge. Stuart-Smith L.J. stated that where the appellant had reasons why he remained silent at interview and therefore why the jury should not make any adverse inferences, those explanations should be put to the judge at the conclusion of the evidence, in the absence of the jury, prior to the adverse inference direction being given. Where the appellants' solicitor advised them to remain silent, that by itself, did not constitute a waiver of legal professional privilege. But neither was it "sufficient reason". Equally, that bare assertion was unlikely by itself to be regarded as a sufficient reason for not mentioning matters relevant to the defence. The appellants would need to explain and have good reason why they remained silent. In conclusion, there was no miscarriage of justice in this case.

Just what "sufficient reasons" are will depend on all the circumstances, but will no doubt include the extent of knowledge which the solicitor possesses about the case in order to properly advise his client. In *R. v. Roble*[53A] during an interview by the police, the defendant's solicitor advised the suspect to remain silent. The defendant only put forward his defence of self-defence at trial. The Court of Appeal held that merely being advised by a solicitor not to answer questions by the police was not in itself sufficient reason to remain silent such that adverse inference are not entitled to be drawn at trial. There must be further reasons submitted why that advice was given, *e.g.* the solicitor may not have received the sufficient relevant facts of the case or the case was too complex or it was too long after the offence[53B] to give proper advice at the interview stage.[53C]

3–128 Having been unsuccessful in the national courts the applicants then brought their case to the European Court of Human Rights: in *Condron v. U.K.*[54]:

Facts. The applicants complained that "the absence of basic safeguards against the drawing of adverse inferences from their silence during police interviews, coupled with the failure to take into account the particular circumstances of their case, undermined that right" (at paragraph 55) and therefore was a violation of Article 6, *i.e.* the right to a fair trial.

Decision. The court once again reiterated their decision in *Murray (John) v. U.K.*[55] by stating that the right to silence was not absolute. However, it was necessary in order for the applicants to receive a fair trial under Article 6(1) that a proper balance be apportioned between the right of an accused to remain silent during interviews and the drawing of adverse inferences from that silence at trial. In order to achieve this balance a proper direction to the jury by the judge must be given such that there is sufficient reason why the accused's right to silence is no longer sustainable. In this case the explanation to remain silent was on the instructions of their solicitor. The court noted that in these circumstances the direction by the judge to the jury did not attain the required balance, despite the jury having been informed of the reasons behind the applicants' silence and informed that silence by itself did not prove guilt. The court noted that a particular caution was required before a domestic court could invoke an accused's silence against him (at paragraph 56). The court stated that it would be incompatible with the right of silence to base a conviction solely or mainly on the accused's silence or on a refusal to answer questions or to give evidence himself. Nevertheless, the court found that it is obvious that the right cannot and should not prevent that "the accused's silence, in situations which clearly calls for an explanation from him, be taken into account in assessing the persuasiveness of the evidence adduced by the prosecution" (at paragraph 56). The court took issue with the Judicial Studies Board guidelines direction to the jury, regarding the question of silence, which states, *inter alia*, that:

> "(T)he law is that you may draw such inferences as appear proper from his failure to mention it at that time. You do not have to hold it against him. It is for you to decide whether it is proper to do so. Failure to mention such a fact at that time cannot, on its own, prove guilt, but depending on the circumstances you may hold that failure against him when deciding whether he is guilty, that is, take into account as some additional support for the prosecution's case, It is for you to decide whether it is fair to do so".

Accordingly,

> "the jury should have been directed that it could only draw an adverse inference if satisfied that the applicants' silence at the police station could not sensibly be attributed to their having no answer or none that would stand up to cross-examination" (at paragraph 61).

The court also noted that the court of Appeal was concerned with the safety of the applicants' conviction, not whether they had received a fair trial. Since the jury had not been properly directed the applicants had not received a fair trial under Article 6(1).

Thus, the present position seems to be that if the jury are satisfied that the defendants would have been able to put forward a reasonable explanation at the police station, but only refrained from making a statement because they had been advised by their solicitor to remain silent, then they should not be permitted to draw any adverse inferences. In the *Condron* case, since the court considered the judge's direction to the jury to be incomplete and insufficient on this issue, a violation of Article 6(1) had resulted. Although section 34 of the Criminal Justice and Public Order Act 1994 is not *per se* incompatible with the Convention, nevertheless to prevent a similar reocurrance in the future a change in the Judicial Board guidelines will need to be introduced to give effect to this decision in order to prevent future violations of a fair trial.

Comparisons were made in the *Condron* case with that of *Murphy (John) v. U.K.* However, the two cases are distinguishable in many respects. It was noted by the court in the above case that whereas in *Murray (John) v. U.K.* it was the judge who was deciding the issue of whether or not adverse inferences should be drawn, and ultimately required to reasons for his decision, in *Condron* it was the jury who had to make the decision, without giving reasons for their decision.

Past decisions of the European Court of Human Rights have shown that **3–129** they are apt to take a more restrictive approach than domestic courts when deciding whether or not to allow adverse inferences to be drawn from a defendant's silence during police questioning. The question concerning adverse inferences is a developing one. New cases involving new facts and situations arise continually, and it is becoming more difficult to state precisely under what circumstances a domestic court should or should not be allowed to draw adverse inferences in any given situation.

In the recent case of *Averill v. U.K.*[55A] the applicant was arrested in connection with a double murder in Northern Ireland under section 14(1)(b) of the Prevention of Terrorism (Temporary Provisions) Act 1989. Access to a solicitor was denied for the first 24 hours of his detention. He declined to answer questions concerning his whereabouts at the time of the murder; nor was he prepared to answer questions relating to fibres discovered on his hair and clothing which matched those found in a burnt-out car used by the gunmen. At trial he testified and provided alibis and explanations for the above questions. The trial judge drew strong inferences from the applicant's refusal to answer police questions and he was eventually convicted of the murders. He thereafter complained to the Commission that he had been denied a fair trial under Article 6(1). The ECHR noted that the trial judge gave particular weight to the forensic evidence directly linking the applicant to the murder scene. Further, the court stated that the trial judge drawing adverse inferences from the applicant's silence was only one element upon which he had reached his decision. The applicant's failure to give any explanation, when he could have been expected to provide one, showed, as a matter of common sense, that he could not put forward any innocent explanation. Accordingly, there had been no violation of Article 6(1). The applicant also argued that since he had been denied access to a solicitor this was incompatible with Article 6(1) in conjunction Article 6(3)(c). In this respect the court found (following *Murray v. U.K.*) that the applicant was entitled to a solicitor from the initial stages of his detention. Once it was accepted that there was the danger of adverse inferences been drawn against him under Articles 3 and 5 of the Criminal Evidence (Northern Ireland) Order (1988), as a matter of fairness he was entitled to legal advice. Since this was refused his rights under Article 6(3)(c) taken in conjunction with Article 6(1) had been violated.

The above case reiterates two fundamental important rights. Firstly, the right to immediate legal representation to those persons arrested and in detention is essential. It would only be in very exceptional cases that the right to legal advice would be withheld. Coupled with this is the importance the European Court places on the legal advice given.[55B] Secondly, the right to silence still remains a crucial right, if not absolute However, in order not to devalue the right to silence it is still the case that a conviction based solely or mainly on the accused's refusal to answer questions during police interviews is not permitted. There must exist some other evidence, upon which the accused remained silent, where it would have been expected of him to provide some plausible exculpatory explanation, as in the above case of *Averill v. U.K.* Recalling the judgment in *Murray (John) v. U.K.*, the court there noted that whether or not adverse inferences could be drawn depended 'on all the circumstances of the case, having particular regard to the situations where inferences might be drawn, (and) the weight attached to them by the national courts. . .". [55C]

Section 36

3–130 Section 36 deals with objects, substances, or marks which were found in the defendant's possession or in any place in which he was at the time of his arrest, and which he refuses, under questioning, to explain. Under section 36, where the accused remains silent, then the jury may draw adverse inferences. The failure to explain at interview the objects, marks, etc., must, however, take place after arrest, unlike section 34(1) where it could be upon caution only. Also under s. 36(1)(d), the inferences can only be drawn in the proceedings in which the accused is charged, not necessarily arrested.

Under section 36, there are a number of prerequisites before the court may draw adverse inferences in these circumstances:

(1) The accused must have been arrested (section 36(1)(a)), and
(2) The police must reasonably believe that the particular objects, etc. were found near or on the person and related to an offence(section 36(1)(b)), and
(3) The police must ask the suspect to explain the presence of the objects (section 36(1)(c)), etc. and
(4) The suspect must be informed in ordinary language of the consequences of his refusal to answer questions related to the

objects, etc. including that a court may draw adverse inferences and that a record of the interview may be given in evidence at trial (Code C, 10.5 B (d) and(e)).

Similar conditions operate under section 37 when questioning refers to a person "found at a place at or about the time of the offence". However, under section 58(1) of the Youth Justice and Criminal Evidence Act 1999, when dealing with inferences from silence, sections 34(1) and (2), 36(1) and (2) and 37(1) and (2) of the Criminal Justice and Public Order Act 1994 have been amended such that no inferences may be drawn from an accused's silence if he had not been allowed an opportunity to consult a solicitor prior to being questioned.[56] Further the *Saunders v. U.K.*[57] has been given effect, such that compelled evidence will rarely be admissible.

VIII(ii) IDENTIFICATION OF PERSONS BY POLICE OFFICERS: CODE D

Even if a suspect is "caught in the act" of committing a crime, it may be **3–131** necessary to obtain confirmation of his identity from the victim or a witness to the crime. The need for identification is obviously greater when all that is known of the offender is a general description. The rules by which identification of the offender is to be made are to be found in Code D and Annexes A-E, although some of these provisions are repeated in Code C. Before any attempt at identification is made, a record must be made which details the initial description of the suspect (Code D, paragraph 2.0). The officer in charge of the identification is called the identification officer, and must hold at least the rank of Inspector and be unconnected with the investigation (D, paragraph 2.2). Whichever kind of identification is to be attempted, a suspect must be given a written notice, which he should read and sign, and indicate whether he is willing to take part in the chosen method of identification (D, 2.16). The notice must contain the information below:

(i) The purpose of the identification;

(ii) His entitlement to free legal advice;

(iii) The relevant procedures;

(iv) Different arrangements for juveniles or the mentally disadvantaged, where relevant;

(v) His right to refuse consent to the identification, and the limited police power to override his wishes;

(vi) Warning that failure to give consent may be mentioned in court;

(vii) That videos and photographs may be taken of him;

(viii) Whether the witness has already seen photographs or a description of the suspect;

(ix) That he should not significantly change his appearance before an identification, or he will risk an adverse inference in any trial; and

(x) That he and his solicitor will be provided with details of the suspect's description as originally made by the witness.

There are two broad categories of situation in which an identification may be made: first, where the suspect is "known" to the police; and secondly, where the suspect's identity is not known. Under Code D:2.1 where the suspect is "known" to the police, and is available, the following methods of identification may be used;

(i) a parade;

(ii) group identification;

(iii) video film and

(iv) confrontation.

Under Notes for Guidance 2E, "known" means "the arrestee", *i.e.* sufficient information must be gathered by the police to justify the particular suspect being arrested. Where descriptions given by witnesses to the police are too broad for a specific identification, and could apply to various people, then there is no "known" suspect. It would seem that the level of evidence required before an arrest takes place ought to be very high, since it would not be practical, considering the cost, manpower and organisation to hold an identification parade, every time a general description was given by a witness.[58–59] The more pragmatic approach is to either request the possible offender to go before the witnesses to be identified or vice versa without actually being arrested.[60]

1. Suspect is "Known"

a) Identification parade

3–132 An identification parade is seen as the best method of identification since it is formal and more reliable than most other methods. It will not usually be necessary to hold an identification parade if the suspect confirms that he committed the offence, but one may be held if the officer in charge of the investigation "considers that it might be useful" (Code D 2.3). But a parade is only possible if the suspect consents (D 2.3). Although desirable, a parade is not required to be held. A situation where a parade is undesirable is when the suspect has an unusual appearance and thus it would be difficult to collect together enough persons who matched the suspect's description in order to allow a fair parade (D 2.4). If the suspect does not consent to attend a parade or fails to attend, then one of the other three identification methods should be followed (D 2.6).

Annex A to Code D contains the rules which must be followed for a fair identification parade. The parade may take place either in an ordinary room or in a suite which shields the witness from the suspect's view (Annex A D.2). The suspect is to be given a reasonable opportunity to have a solicitor or friend present (A, D.1) and before the parade happens the suspect or his solicitor is to be given a copy of initial description made by the witness, together with any press release giving a description. The only exception to this is if to do so is not practicable or would unreasonably delay the investigation (A, D.2A). If the suspect is already in prison, then a parade may take place either at the prison or elsewhere, but the prisoner must be dressed in a similar manner to the other parade members, since leaving him alone in a prison uniform would render the parade useless (A, D.4). When a parade is about to commence, the identification officer must remind the suspect of the rules concerning identification and give him a Code C caution (A, D.5). The parade must consist of at least eight persons as well as the suspect "who so far as possible resemble the suspect in age, height, general appearance and position in life". Only one suspect shall be included in a parade unless two suspects happen to be similar in appearance (A, D.8). The suspect is entitled to legal advice before the parade begins and must be asked whether he objects to the parade being held. If he does and the grounds for the objection can be corrected, (*e.g.* one of the other parade members is thought to be dissimilar to the suspect and can be replaced), then this should be done (A, D.10). The suspect can choose where he stands in the line-up and if there is more than one witness who will view the parade, then the suspect may move his position (A, D.11). The identification officer must make sure that, before the parade, the witnesses do not communicate with each other, see any of the line-up, see any photograph or description of the suspect or see the suspect (A, D.12). If necessary during the parade, the witness may ask to have any member of the parade speak or move (A, D.17). A video or colour photograph of the parade must be made, and a copy supplied to the suspect or his solicitor within a reasonable time (A, D.19), then destroyed if the suspect is not tried or is acquitted (A, D.19, D.20).

b) Group identification

A group identification is less formal, and involves the witness viewing the **3–133** suspect among an informal group of people, either with the suspect's knowledge or secretly (D, 2.7). The suspect should be asked whether he consents, but the identification officer has discretion to carry out a group identification without consent (D, 2.8). Annex E contains the detailed rules for group identifications, which must be carried out in as public and busy a place as is practicable (*e.g.* a shopping centre). The suspect's rights and the procedural fairness rules are very similar to those relating to identification parades.

c) Video identification

3–134 A video identification will only take place when the investigating officer considers this to be the best course of action, usually because the suspect has refused to take part in an identification parade or group identification (D, 2.10). The suspect's consent should be sought, but is not necessary (D, 2.11). Annex B gives rules for the procedure of video identification. The general fairness provisions are the same as for the two previous methods of identification, (*e.g.* at least eight other members in the line-up, lack of contact between witnesses, etc.), except that the suspect has no right to attend the identification (Annex B, D.8) but may view the video of himself and the other persons selected before it is shown to any witnesses, and may record any objection which he has. His solicitor should attend the viewing of the video by the witness.

d) Confrontation

3–135 Where none of the other permissible identification methods are practicable, then as a last resort the suspect may be confronted by the witness (D 2.13). Annex C provides the rules for conduct of a confrontation, which again are similar attempts to guarantee fairness to those which apply to the other identification methods, except that a confrontation should only normally be held in a police station and the suspect's solicitor should attend.

2. Where the Suspect is "Not Known"

3–136 If no-one has been arrested for the offence, then somewhat different procedures apply. The police may take a witness back to the crime scene or to any other place in order to see whether he can spot the offender, but must not point anyone out to the witness (D, 2.17). Alternatively, the witness may be shown photographs, photofits or other pictures, provided that the safeguards in Annex D and paragraph 2.10 are followed.

Formal versus informal identification

3–137 In many instances, because of the seriousness of the offence, the police will often request potential witnesses to accompany them in their patrol cars around the particular area in search of the offender. This inevitably leads to problems, especially where there may be differences of opinions as to the description given by those witnesses. For example, in *R. v. Hickin*,[61] two men were seriously assaulted by seven members of a group. Within a few minutes of the attack, witnesses were assisting the police with identifying the offenders. Eventually, possible suspects were spotted, arrested and identified without a formal identification being held. Since the descriptions of the possible assailants was based mainly on clothing and other general features, the appellants argued that the identification evidence should have been excluded. In this case, there were several possible offenders and there was a real possibility of mistaken identity if the evidence was not of a specific nature, such that the defendants might be unfairly prejudiced under section 78. It was decided that formal identification procedures were impractical under the circumstances, taking into account the danger that witnesses' memories could fade in the interval. The question for the court was whether those informal practices (as opposed to a formal identification parade), amounted to having such an adverse effect on the proceedings that it ought not to have been admitted under section 78 PACE.

The Court of Appeal emphasised that each case must be considered on its own facts. Here, there was a danger that the witnesses, when together, would discuss amongst themselves the identification issue and might influence the other witnesses or worse still confuse the whole matter. To alleviate this problem, to a great extent, it was suggested by the court that a statement be taken by a witness of the description of the offender(s) before identification took place, thus retaining some consistency and fairness throughout the informal procedure. Such a practice would diminish the possibility of variable and conflicting descriptions given by witnesses and a record should be kept of anything said by those witnesses in these situations. As a result of the particular circumstances and of the danger of convicting on "non-detailed descriptions", all but two of the appellants appeals were allowed.

In *R. v. Conway*,[62] the defendant was convicted of stabbing a person called G. P and her son D (who were living with G) identified the defendant as one of three men who had visited her home just prior to the attack. Although P and D had recognised the defendant from seeing him on other occasions, and that he had been to the house previously, they did not until later discover his name. D, but not P, was a witness to the stabbing; P only saw the back of the defendant. The defendant requested an identification parade on the grounds of mistaken identity and denied knowing the victim or P. The police regarded it as unnecessary because he was "a named person". At the committal proceedings, P and D were allowed to make a dock identification by the magistrates. On appeal, the appellant argued that the identification parade should have been held where the identification evidence was in dispute. The Court of Appeal held that:

(i) There was no problem in arranging such a parade, nor any practical reason why it should not have been proceeded with;

(ii) He was not a named person, since the witnesses did not know his name at the time of the attack;

(iii) The dock identification seriously prejudiced the appellant; and

(iv) The peculiar facts of this case and the not altogether reliable descriptions given by P and D, had also to be considered.

Therefore, the appeal was allowed.

An identification parade should be held, for the protection of the defendant, where a witness states that he/she will be able to identify the offender, or there is a reasonable chance of him/her doing so. In *R. v. Rutherford and Palmer*,[63] the defendants forced their way into the victim's home, after having pushed the victim aside and stole jewellery and money and some Indian rupees, and then drove away. The defendants' car was later stopped by the police. They discovered the victim's jewellery, money and Indian rupees. Of the four main witnesses to the event, only one could say with any certainty that she would recognise the robbers again. The defendants each requested that identification parades be held, but none were. The appellants appealed on the grounds that there was a breach of Code D:2.3 and had argued that since there was no identification parade and the evidence was weak and circumstantial, the trial should have been stopped. It was acknowledged by the Court of Appeal that the appellants were entitled to an identification parade (one of the witnesses failed to identify the defendants at trial, and the other two were not called), and therefore the Codes applied. The court then examined whether despite the breach, the judge at first instance was right to continue the trial, as he believed the fairness of the proceedings would not, in any event, be impaired. The Court of Appeal, having looked at the existing evidence decided that although circumstantial, it was very strong, despite the absence of identification evidence. In the circumstances, the breach did not have an adverse effect on the proceedings, and the judge was correct in permitting the trial to proceed. Accordingly, the appeals were dismissed.

Improperly conducted identification parades

3–138 Although a breach of the Codes does not automatically interpret into the trial itself being stopped or the evidence being excluded, a breach is nevertheless a serious matter. Indeed, in *R. v. Quinn*,[64] Lord Taylor C.J. said that "where a detailed regime is laid down in a statutory Code, it is not for police . . . to substitute their own procedures and their own rules for that which is laid down".[65] In that case, the defendant was convicted of, *inter alia*, two robberies; one at a hotel and the other at a travel agents. Two receptionists from the hotel picked out the defendant at an identification parade; one describing the robber as having big brown eyes, and that his hair was lightish in colour (in fact, the defendant's eyes were blue and his hair dark brown). The other receptionist described his hair as blond. Two other witnesses from the travel agents also picked out the defendant. On appeal, it was argued that because of the breaches of Code D, the identification evidence should have been ruled inadmissible, or if included, because of the breaches, could not be regarded as safe under section 78 PACE. The appellant specifically argued that:

(1) Code D Annex A D:8, was contravened in that the other persons in the line-up did not "so far as possible resemble the suspect in

age, height, general appearance and position in life," and because of the differences, "he stuck out like a sore thumb". This argument was rejected by the judge at first instance since the defendant and his solicitor had some involvement in the arrangement and composition of the parade, and no complaint about the parade was made at that time.

(2) Code D Annex A D:12 states that "witnesses are not able to (i) communicate with each other about the case . . .". The appellant submitted that the supervising police officer left the witness room for a few minutes, thus allowing the possibility for the witnesses to discuss the events amongst themselves. The Court of Appeal found that although there was technically a breach, the witnesses at first instance gave evidence that the defendant's appearance was not discussed.

(3) Code D:2.2 states that "no officer involved with the investigation of the case against the suspect may take part in these procedures".[66] The Crown accepted that such a breach occurred. An investigating officer involved in the case demonstrated how a parade of this kind would be conducted, prior to the actual parade. However, the Court of Appeal found as a fact that the officer in question behaved quite properly and impartially throughout that whole demonstration. Notwithstanding that, there remained a breach of the Code.

(4) Code D Annex A D:6 states that "all unauthorised persons must be excluded from the place where the parade is held". There was contradictory evidence as to whether a police officer only brought the witnesses to the door of the parade room or was actually present during the identification parade. Although, the judge found the whole situation to be unsatisfactory, the police officer was nevertheless considered to be "an honest witness".

The main submissions by the appellant were that since there were various breaches of the Codes, with regard to the identification procedures, it should have been left to the jury to evaluate whether the breaches were so serious as to cast doubts on the correctness of the witnesses identification. The Court of Appeal stated that the "only real direct evidence," on the hotel charge, was that of identification. Taking into account the inconsistent descriptions given by the witnesses, and the numerous violations of the Code itself, the judge should have informed the jury regarding these breaches, and left it to them to decide what weight should be attached to them. Therefore, The Court of Appeal allowed the appeal regarding the hotel charge, but dismissed the "travel agent" appeal as there was other relevant evidence apart from identification which connected him with that offence.

Consequences where no identification parade is held

3–139 Unless exceptional circumstances arise,[66A] whenever a suspect disputes an identification, an identification parade must take place if the suspect consents to it (section D.2.3). Even when the eyewitness knows the identity of the suspect, it is preferable, under the codes, that an identification parade take place. Thus in *R. v. Forbes*[66B] an attempt was made to rob the complainant, after he had withdrawn money from a cashpoint machine. As the assailant made off in a nearby vehicle, the complainant saw him. He notified the police. Later on, after a search of the streets with the police he identified the assailant, who was subsequently arrested and charged. Despite repeated denials that he was the assailant, his requests for an identification parade were refused. At trial it was held that since the complainant had made a full and complete identification of the defendant an identification parade was unnecessary. No statement to the jury had been given that there had been a breach of section D.2.3 nor any direction on the effects of that breach. He was convicted. His appeal to the Court of Appeal was dismissed and thereafter he appealed to the House of Lords. The court said that an appropriate direction to the jury regarding a breach of section D.2.3 should be given in terms of being told that:

> ". . .an identification parade enables a suspect to put the reliability of a witness's identification to the test, that the suspect had lost the benefit of that safeguard and that the jury should take account of that fact in its assessment of the whole case, giving it such weight as it thought fair".

In the present case the court held that "failure to direct the jury on the breach of D.2.3 and its consequences did not lead them to regard the defendant's trial as unfair or his conviction as unsafe".

Voice identification

3–140 Visual identification is rarely fool-proof; there is always the possibility of an honest yet wholly mistaken identification occurring. Whatever difficulties exist for an eyewitness recognising the facial and other features of a particular person, there is no doubt that there is even more likelihood of mistake when it comes to voice recognition. All the more reason why special procedures should be in place and proper directions given to a jury in order to lessen the possibility of a wrongful voice identification. In *R v. Hersey*,[66C] a shopkeeper, W, was robbed by two men wearing balaclava helmets. W was convinced that he recognised the defendant's voice as one of the robbers, whom he knew as a long-standing customer. During a voice identification parade at which eleven people read from a text of a previous unrelated interview with the defendant, W picked out the defendant's voice. Two other witnesses failed to identify the defendant's voice. Although expert evidence was given on the *vire dire*, favourable to the defendant, the judge refused the evidence to be heard by the jury. The defendant was subsequently convicted of robbery. On appeal, he argued, *inter alia* (1) that the judge erred in admitting the voice identification evidence and (2) that the judge failed to adequately deal with the identification evidence in his summing up. As to (1) the court stated that an identification parade was necessary, not only to test the identification but also "out of fairness to the accused to give him the opportunity to be excluded if the original identification was erroneous". Dealing with (2) above the court said that although there lacked authority on how a judge should direct a jury on voice identification, any direction should be in given in similar terms as visual identification as already laid down by law, for example, stating the risks involved in mistaken identification, and how an honest witness may nevertheless be wrong, and the strengths and weaknesses of the case. The court said that the judge dealt fully with the issues in his summing up and therefore the appeal was dismissed.

Whilst it is up to the judge to decide whether, in the absence of an identification parade, the testimony of an eyewitness should still be admissible (under section 78 of PACE), in the interests of justice the jury should be informed that a breach of the codes did occur and be permitted to consider the consequences of that breach.

RELEVANT ECHR PROVISIONS: ARTICLES 2, 3, 5, 6 AND 7

In order to understand those Articles of the ECHR which will often be relevant to the exercise of police powers, it is necessary to also consider some cases which have a very different subject matter. Thus when examining the application of Article 2 (right to life), as well as "*Death on the Rock*" we shall also look at the *Conjoined Twins* case. It is indicative of the nature of the Convention that the Articles discussed in this section have given rise to such breadth of application to wildly different factual situations. **3–141**

ARTICLE 2: RIGHT TO LIFE

1 Everyone's *right to life* shall be *protected by law*. No one shall be deprived of his life *intentionally* save in the execution of a sentence of a court following his conviction of a crime for which this penalty is *provided by law*. **3–142**

2 Deprivation of life shall not be regarded as inflicted in contravention of this Article when it results from the use of force which is no more than *absolutely necessary*

(a) In defence of any person from unlawful violence;
(b) Order to effect a lawful arrest or to prevent the escape of a person lawfully detained;

(c) In action lawfully taken for the purpose of quelling a riot or insurrection. (italics added)

Beginning with the general premise under Article 2 that everyone is entitled to the right to life, and that that right ought to be protected by the state, there are, nevertheless, four main circumstances which may obviate that right. The first is set out in Article 2(1) regarding the death penalty for a crime (the others being set out in Article 2(2)(a)(b) and (c)). Since very few Member States have at present the death penalty in force, this exception is somewhat redundant, although a contracting country who has not ratified the Sixth Protocol is still at liberty to reintroduce the death penalty into their domestic law at any time in the future.[67] Although Article 2 itself does not sanction the taking of life during war or a national emergency, under Article 15(2) a Member State may derogate from its obligations in respect of deaths resulting from "lawful acts of war". However, deaths caused by "unlawful" acts of war will always constitute a violation of the Convention. For instance, in *Cyprus v. Turkey*,[68] after the invasion of Cyprus by Turkey in 1974, the Cypriots complained to the Commission regarding certain atrocities committed by the Turks during that period. Amongst the complaints were violations of Article 2, whereby the applicant alleged that the Turkish Army killed civilians who were unconnected with the war; *i.e.* children, old and paralysed people, and that some 3,000 civilians were missing, presumed dead. The respondents refused to participate on the merits of the above claims by the applicants.[69] Various statements given as evidence by eyewitnesses to the killing of civilians were declared by the Commission to be trustworthy and accurate.[70] The Commission declared that the Turkish Government owed a duty of responsibility to those persons who, after July 20, 1974, were in their custody. However, since the Commission Delegation was refused admittance to the northern part of Cyprus to investigate the complaints, the Commission was unable to make a declaration concerning the missing Greek Cypriot prisoners and whether they were alive or dead.[71] They found there to be a violation of Article 2(1) by the killing of 12 civilians in one particular town, and no evidence of justification was put forward by the respondents under the exceptions in Article 2(1) and (2),[72] nor did the respondents' actions come within Article 15.

The right to life

3–143/ 144 As far as the United Kingdom is concerned, the main "right to life" issues involve acts of terrorism, withdrawal of medical treatment, euthanasia, damage caused by nuclear testing, abortion and the rights of the unborn child.

In relation to some of the above categories, it is not uncommon for the domestic laws between states to differ considerably, when deciding on the basic rights, especially on such life matters as euthanasia and abortion (discussed below). In this respect the ECHR has in many such cases permitted states a wide margin of appreciation when interpreting Article 2.

The question whether an unborn child has a right to life and comes within the meaning of the word "life" has not until now been settled under the Convention. It has been argued that "everyone" connotes a person who comes within the exceptions laid out in Article 2 above, and thus assumes that such a person is already born. Cases which have come before the European Court in this area usually involve abortion. In these instances, the European Court has avoided answering the question directly but has instead considered the domestic law on abortion in individual states, without expressly stating where life begins. In *Paton v. U.K.*,[73] the Commission examined the laws and constitutions of various states including, The American Constitution on Human Rights 1969, where it is stated under Article 4(1) that life begins from the moment of conception. However, in Germany, for instance, when considering Article 2, the Federal Constitutional Court stated that life began from the fourteenth day after conception (nidation).[74] The meaning of the word "life" is further complicated by its use in individual states according to whether the issue comes under the criminal or civil law. **3–145**

In *Paton*, the Commission stated that there were three options;

(i) no "right to life" recognition of the foetus;

(ii) recognised, but with limitations;

(iii) absolute recognition.

The Commission refused (iii) above on the grounds of the foetus's interconnection with the pregnant woman. If otherwise, abortion would be disallowed, even at the expense of seriously damaging the health of the pregnant woman. Such an interpretation would be "contrary to the object and purpose of the Convention".[75] In (ii) above the Commission were of the opinion that even if some protection was to be given, it would be limited to protecting the life and health of the pregnant woman, which must remain paramount. Because of the sensitivity of the issue, *i.e.* the different moral, ethical and religious attitudes in the various Contracting States, the European Court is inclined to give a greater degree of latitude to particular domestic laws when considering whether an application is justified to go before the court.

"Protected by law"

All persons under Article 2 are entitled to be protected by law. This protection includes undertakings by the state authorities to effectively investigate unlawful acts against its own citizens by the police, government security services, army and so forth. The European Court of Human Rights has held repeatedly that a state may be under a positive obligation to **3–146** uphold the rights of its citizens, even where the threatened interference would come from a private individual or other non-state actor. Such positive obligations have been found to exist, inter alia, in relation to Articles 2, 3 and 8. Thus in *Akkoc v. Turkey*[76]:

Facts. The applicant, a teacher, made a statement to a newspaper concerning a teachers' meeting attended by the National Education Director. In the published article she alleged that at the meeting she was verbally abused, harassed and that in some cases teachers were assaulted by the security services. She later received death threats against her and her husband, a man of Kurdish origin and a trade union activist. She complained to the authorities on a number of occasions, but nothing was done. During this time killings were taking place against supporters of the PKK ("Kurdish Workers Party"). On January 13, 1993, the applicant's husband was shot dead by, she alleged, the security forces. Although a student was eventually arrested for the crime, he was subsequently released through lack of evidence. On February 1994 the applicant was taken into custody by the police and held in detention for ten days. During this period she was blindfolded, stripped naked and sexually abused; hosed down in cold water; subjected to electric shock treatment; beaten; subjected to loud music; handcuffed; her hair was pulled and she was told that her children were being tortured. On February 18, 1994 she signed a statement that she was a member of the PKK. The medical doctor signed a report that she had not suffered any physical blows, although she showed him various injuries over her body. After her release she continued to suffer from physical and psychological problems as a result of her ill-treatment. The applicant thereafter lodged a complaint claiming that, *inter alia*, the state had failed in its obligations, under Article 2, to protect her husband's life and to carry out an effective investigation into his death.

Decision. One question facing the court was whether the Turkish authorities took reasonable measures to avert the murder of the applicant's husband, as required by Article 2(1), *i.e.* to be protected by law. The court stated that "the scope of the positive obligation must be interpreted in a way which does not impose an impossible or disproportionate burden on the authorities" (paragraph 77). Citing *Osman v. U.K.*,[77] the court said that in order for a positive obligation to exist in these circumstances it must be established that the authorities knew or ought to have known at the time of the existence of a real and immediate risk to the applicant's husband. Here, it had not been proved beyond reasonable doubt that the authorities themselves were in some way connected with the murder. However, since the applicant's husband was involved in trade union activities perceived as unlawful by the authorities, there existed, in the circumstances, a risk to his life that was real and immediate. The authorities must have been aware of such a risk and still did not take any action regarding the complaints made by the applicant and her husband. In a number of previous cases which came before the court regarding complaints made against the security forces for unlawful acts, it was found that investigations made into such allegations were either not properly conducted, *e.g.* not interviewing nor taking statements from those persons suspected of being involved; accepting the reports made by security services as fact without further scrutiny; laying blame on the PKK where there was little or no substantive evidence; or in many cases, making no inquiries at all. (see *Kurt v. Turkey*[78]; *Tanrikulu v. Turkey*[79]). Where investigations did take place, the decision to prosecute in certain circumstances was handed over to administrative councils which consisted of civil servants. In such cases, there was evidence of bias in favour of the security forces. In consideration of all of these factors, which resulted in the lack of reasonable measures being taken by the authorities to protect the life of the applicant's husband, the court found there to be a violation of Article 2. Further, taking into account the length of the active investigation into the husband's death, *i.e.* only twelve days, and the manner by which the whole inquiry was conducted, *i.e.* one statement from a witness who was at the scene of the crime, the court concluded that the investigation was wholly inadequate and ineffective. Accordingly, under these circumstances, there was also here a violation of Article 2.

In the case of *Keenan v. U.K.*[79A]: **3–146A**

Facts. On April 1, 1993 the applicant's son, Mark Keenan (aged 28), was sentenced to four months imprisonment on assault charges. For the previous seven years he had undergone intermittent anti-psychotic medical treatment for symptoms which included aggression, violence and deliberate self-harm. On May 1, 1993, whilst in prison he assaulted two prison officers. He was sent to a segregation unit for seven days and had his sentence increased by 28 days. On May 15, he committed suicide by hanging himself in his cell. The applicant complained that the authorities had breached Article 2 of the Convention in respect of her son's right to life, and further that her son had been subjected to inhuman and/or degrading treatment in violation of Article 3.

Decision. One of the questions considered by the European Court was whether the authorities had done all that was reasonable expected of them in the circumstances to safeguard the victim's life under Article 2. The court found that by the authorities providing appropriate hospital care and continually monitoring his medical condition when he showed signs of self-harm, they had taken all reasonable steps required under the circumstances. Accordingly, since there was no evidence of the prisoner likely to commit suicide on May 15, the court unanimously decided that the authorities were not in violation of Article 2. In relation to Article 3 the court noted that the word "degrading" included the prisoner being treated in a manner which humiliated and debased him and which would possibly break his physical or mental resistance or drive the victim to act against his will or conscience, and therefore be incompatible with prohibitions of Article 3. Where mentally ill persons are concerned it was necessary to consider further the vulnerability and inability to complain about their treatment. In this case the court found that:

(1) no medical notes were available from May 5–May 15, when it was known that the prisoner was a suicide risk;

(2) after April 29 no reference as made to any psychiatric advice or recommendation that because of his mental condition the prisoner should not be permitted to associate with others;

(3) no psychiatrist was consulted as to his fitness for adjudication and punishment when his sentence was increased for the assault on the two prison officers.

Due to the above lack of proper psychiatric treatment and consultation, the court found that the prisoner had not been provided with the appropriate medical care required for a mentally-ill person under the circumstances. Accordingly, by a majority of 5 votes to 2, the court concluded that the authorities were in violation of Article 3.

However, continual protection for an individual by the state, under certain circumstances, over an indefinite period, may prove to be unrealistic, however much required. For instance, in *X v. Ireland*,[80] the applicant received for three and a half years full police protection from attempts on his life by the IRA. Once this protection stopped, he alleged that this amounted to a breach of Article 2. The Commission formed the opinion that there was no duty on the state to provide unlimited protection of this kind (in this case, it could have amounted to a permanent bodyguard), therefore there was no violation. This was a case of one person's protection. However, the state does have an obligation to take all reasonable steps to protect its citizens against threats, such as terrorism and including, where necessary, all forms of life-threatening situations which affect the safety of its population and includes press publication of information about persons likely to suffer serious injury or death by others should their identities become public. A recent example of this concerned the well-publicised case of the two youths convicted of the murder of the infant James Bulger in 1993. In *Jon Venables and Robert Thompson v. GN Ltd Associated Newspapers Ltd et al.*,[81] such was the public outcry and the ensuing death threats to the youths upon their release from detention that they applied to the court for an indefinite injunction to restrain the press from publishing their identities, their change in physical appearance, their new addresses and all information relating to their period spent in secure units. The press opposed the application. The main questions to be considered by the court was whether jurisdiction existed to grant such an injunction, and if so, was there a real possibility of serious injury or even death if the injunction was not granted, and if, in the circumstances the court did decide to grant the injunction, over what period? The respondents argued that the claimants had no cause of action and that there was a presumption in favour of freedom of expression. The court recognised that a serious future threat did exist to the claimants' lives from certain members of the public as well as from the relatives of the victim, and indeed upon their release they were to be given new identities. Thus, under these exceptional circumstances and in line with Article 2 the order for an indefinite injunction would be granted for the protection against the claimants lives.

What is reasonable will depend upon such factors as the resources available, including manpower, the seriousness of the threat, feasibility, etc., as well as the age, sex, and circumstances of each individual case. For instance, in the case of *T and V v. U.K.*,[81A] the applicants, both aged 10, were tried and convicted for the murder of a young boy, in an adult court, amidst surrounding wide-spread publicity. Such treatment of children was found by the European Court to be both inhuman and degrading. The ECHR stated that special protection and treatment should be provided by the authorities in cases where children appear in court as witnesses or defendants. Protection also includes:

> ". . . putting in place effective criminal law provisions to deter the commission of offences against the person backed up by law enforcement machinery for the prevention, suppression and sanctioning of breaches of such provisions, and may also imply in certain well defined circumstances a positive obligation on the

authorities to take preventive operational measures to protect an individual whose life is at risk from the criminal acts of another individual" (see *Osman* (below) at paragraph 115).

In *Osman v. U.K.*[82]: **3–147**

Facts. The applicants, Mrs Mulkiye Osman and her son, Ahmet, claimed that the police did not take adequate or appropriate measure required under Article 2 (1) to protect the lives of the second applicant, nor his father, who had been shot dead by Mr Paget-Lewis, a school teacher. The second applicant had been severely wounded by the teacher. Prior to the shooting, the applicants maintained that the police had been informed on several occasions that the lives of Ali and Ahmet Osman were at real risk from the threat posed by Mr Paget-Lewis.
In 1988, Mr Paget-Lewis pleaded guilty to two charges of manslaughter (he had also shot dead the deputy head-master) on the grounds of diminished responsibility. He was sentenced to be detained in a secure mental hospital without limit of time. In 1989, the applicants commenced a civil action against, *inter alia*, the Commissioner of Police of the Metropolis (*Osman and another v. Ferguson and another*[83] alleging negligence in not taking any action against Mr Paget-Lewis. But on grounds of public policy, the claim was struck out, *i.e.* no action may be sustainable against the police for negligence when carrying out their duties in the investigation and suppression of a crime.

Decision. Whether, in this case, the police were in breach of these positive obligations, ". . . it must be established to its (the court's) satisfaction that the authorities knew or ought to have known at the time of the existence of a real and immediate risk to the life of an identified individual or individuals from the criminal acts of a third party and that they failed to take measure within the scope of their powers which, judged reasonably, (confirmed in *Akkoc v. Turkey*[84]) might have been expected to avoid that risk" (see paragraph 116).

Did the police do all that was reasonably expected of them in the given situation? Despite Mrs Osman's allegations of persistent threats, intimidation and unlawful actions by Mr Paget-Lewis, the court found, as a matter of fact, that it could not be said that the police knew or ought to have known that the lives of the Osman family were in immediate danger. Under the circumstances, the police could not be blamed for not arresting Mr Paget-Lewis on a prior occasion; the evidence for such an arrest was, the court considered, not sustainable.
Whether such a positive obligation exists will depend on all the circumstances of the individual case. In *Osman*, it was held, that on the facts the police behaved reasonably and therefore were not in violation of Article 2.

"Absolutely necessary"

In order that the resulting death be considered a violation of Article 2, the amount of force used in Article 2(2)(a), (b) or (c) must have been more than was absolutely necessary. The meaning of "absolutely necessary" indicates that a stricter and more compelling test of necessity must be employed from that normally applicable when determining whether state action is "necessary in a democratic society" under paragraph 2 of Articles 8–11.[85] For instance, in *Kelly v. United Kingdom*,[86] five joyriders went on the rampage in a car in Belfast. Upon approaching a military road block, the **3–148** driver, after causing considerable damage to other vehicles, broke through the road block in an attempt to escape. The soldiers tried to stop the car by firing at the driver. The driver was killed. The applicant, the driver's father, brought an action against the Ministry of Defence for assault and negligence by the soldiers, for using excessive and unreasonable force in the situation. The trial judge found that the soldiers reasonably believed that the car contained terrorists, and in order to prevent crime the soldiers believed that if not stopped they would commit further terrorist offences. Therefore, under those circumstances, the use of force was justified. The applicant complained to the Commission that the use of force by the soldiers was not justified under Article 2(2)(a), (b) or (c). The Commission when analysing the words "absolutely necessary" said, "that the test of necessity includes an assessment of whether the interference was proportionate to the legitimate aim pursued", and in conjunction with the word "absolutely" denotes a very strict limitation when the use of force, which results in the loss of life, is acceptable or permissible. The force used must be "proportionate to the achievement of the permitted purpose", taking into account such factors as:

> ". . . the nature of the aim, the dangers to life and limb inherent in the situation and the degree of risk that the force employed might result in loss of life, and all the relevant circumstances surrounding the deprivation of life"[87] (the "proportionality test").

Although the domestic court found in favour of the defendants due to the action taken to be "reasonable in all the circumstances" to prevent crime, the Commission did not, however, examine this aspect of the case because such a defence does not exist under Article 2. Nevertheless, the Commission found the soldiers' reactions "absolutely necessary" for the purpose of "effecting a lawful arrest" under Article 2(2)(b). They said that "it was strictly proportionate, having regard to the situation confronting the soldiers, the degree of force employed in response and the risk that the use of force could result in the deprivation of life".[88]

Does the killing have to be "intentional"?

3–149 *Kelly*[89] was a case involving intentional killing where the only means at the disposal of the soldiers to prevent the car from escaping (unless they allowed the driver and others to evade capture) was to deliberately aim in order to kill or at least cause serious injury. Although Article 2(1) states that "no one shall be deprived of his life intentionally", the exceptions under Article 2(2) do not mention whether the act must be intentional or whether death can be brought about unintentionally, accidentally, recklessly, negligently or otherwise. In *Stewart v. United Kingdom*,[90] a 13 year old boy had been fatally shot accidentally by a soldier using "plastic bullets" during a riot in Northern Ireland. The applicant, the mother of the boy, argued before the Commission that since the situation was not life threatening, the use of such means was more than absolutely necessary in the circumstances and that this constituted a disproportionate response to the situation which existed at the time. The respondents argued that; (i) Article 2 only deals with acts which are only intentional; and (ii) even if the act was unintentional, the use of plastic bullets by the soldiers "constituted the use of force which was no more than absolutely necessary" under Article 2(1)(a) or (c). The Commission stated that Article 2 "should not be restricted to merely intentional acts and that any other interpretation would not be consistent with the object and purpose of the Convention . . ."[91] They then examined whether the force actually used was "absolutely necessary", by considering whether the force was proportionate to the event which existed at the time. They concluded that under Article 2(2)(c);

(1) The Government was entitled to quell a riot without having to retreat or directly avoid confronting the rioters.

(2) The use of "plastic bullets" may cause serious injury and even death occasionally, however, judged by the amount of rounds fired, the Commission considered them to be "less dangerous than alleged".

(3) The soldier involved did not deliberately aim to kill the boy. The ensuing death was caused by his aim being diverted after he had been hit by a stone thrown by the rioters.[92] As a result, the Commission rejected the application.[93]

There is a positive obligation on the state not only to take the necessary measures to protect the lives of its citizens, but to ensure that whatever procedures are instigated, they must attain a reasonable and effective standard. There may well be a breach of Article 2 if the state falls below that standard such that lives are lost as a result. Included in this obligation are the methods and procedures by which a thorough examination into the circumstances which resulted in the death of a person can be properly investigated.[94]

In *McCann v. United Kingdom*[95]:

Facts. A number of SAS (Secret Air Services) officers arrived in Gibraltar on March 4, 1988 to prevent an IRA Active Service Unit (ASU) from carrying out a terrorist attack, by the use of a car bomb, on the Royal Anglian Regiment on the March 8, 1988. When the ASU arrived (two men and a woman) in Gibraltar on March 6, they were spotted and a surveillance operation of the suspects was embarked upon. One of the suspects later parked a car. He was then joined by the other two suspects. Soon after they departed (one of the suspects heading off in a different direction to the other two), a member of the SAS team approached the parked car. He described it as a "possible car bomb", without making any detailed examination of the inside or underneath of the car. The SAS were then given orders to arrest the suspects which they set about doing. However, when they approached the suspects in the street, the latter moved in such a way that the SAS interpreted this as attempting to detonate the car bomb by remote control. The SAS immediately started shooting and eventually all three suspects were killed. It was later discovered that the suspects carried no guns or concealed any type of detonating devices, nor did the car contain any bomb. After all domestic remedies had been exhausted[96] the applicants complained to the Commission that the killing of the three suspects was a violation of Article 2.

Opinion of the Commission. The Government argued that the force used was no more than was absolutely necessary in defence of the people of Gibraltar from unlawful violence. The applicants contended that there was "a shoot to kill" policy in force whereby the SAS were ordered to kill the suspects in Gibraltar. The Commission concluded there was no evidence to support that claim. Alternatively, the appellants argued that the SAS were negligent, and totally disregarded the suspects' right to life. The Commission stated that the deliberate shooting of the three suspects was absolutely necessary in the circumstances as the SAS perceived the situation at the time, since if the bomb could be detonated by the pressing of a button by remote control and havoc and death would result, then the SAS actions could not be considered to be disproportionate to the eventual consequences, *i.e.* protecting the citizens of Gibraltar against those persons engaged in unlawful violence under Article 2(2)(a). The Commission said that once the risk existed, it was right to act on that risk, disregarding "the degree of probability of that risk, *i.e.* whether detonation of a bomb was possible or highly likely".[97] Accordingly, by 11 votes to 6, the Commission found there to be no violation of Article 2.

Findings of the Court. Against the applicants' allegation that there was a "shoot to kill" policy in force, the Court concluded, on that issue, that there was no evidence to suggest that there was a predetermined plan to kill the suspects (the jury at the Inquest also seemed to have reached such a conclusion). The court appreciated the SAS dilemma, *i.e.* the duty to protect the people of Gibraltar, on the one hand, and the confines and restraints of national and international law of using lethal force against the suspects on the other hand.[98] The court took into account not only the "proportionality test" with regard to unlawful violence, but also considered whether the operation itself was so co-ordinated, organised and planned so as to minimise the chances of using lethal force. They accepted that the SAS honestly believed that it was necessary to kill the suspects in order to prevent them from detonating the bomb.[99] Thus, the SAS actions were not considered to be a violation of Article 2 on that issue. However, regarding the organisation of the operation itself, the court had serious doubts. Could the suspects not have been arrested when they reached Gibraltar (they knew their identities), thus averting a bloodbath in the streets of Gibraltar? The Government argued that at that stage, they had insufficient evidence for a conviction. Notwithstanding that, the court said that the safeguarding of the Gibraltar people was paramount and took priority over the convictions of the suspects.[1] The court also made assertions that the Government's view of the situation was somewhat blinkered in that whilst they thought that a bomb existed they had not considered the other possibilities, *e.g.* that the intelligence information might be incorrect, or the suspects were merely on a reconnaissance mission. Also, the conclusion by an SAS member that it was a "suspect car bomb", in the absence of any real examination of the car, was itself alarming, and passing this information on to other members and trying to make an arrest without using lethal force was "almost unavoidable".[2] When confronted with the arrest of the suspects it was highly likely that any sudden or quick movement by the latter would result in the SAS shooting to kill. The court concluded (by 10 votes to 9) that they were not persuaded that the use of force involved was no more than absolutely necessary under Article 2(2)(a), *i.e.* in defence of any person from unlawful violence. As a result, there was a breach of Article 2.[3]

A recent, and very difficult, balancing exercise under Article 2 was found in *Re A (children)* (conjoined twins: surgical separation)[4]: **3–150**

Facts. The parents of two conjoined twins, Jodie and Mary, refused to give their consent to an operation to surgically separate the twins. The consequence of such an operation would result in the inevitable death of one of the twins, Mary, who was alive solely because a common artery enabled Josie to circulate oxygenated blood to them both. Without the operation both Jodie and Mary would die within three to six months. The hospital sought a declaration from the court that the operation may lawfully be performed. Johnson J. granted the declaration and thereafter the parents appealed against the order on the grounds that the judge erred in holding that the operation was:

(i) in Mary's best interests;
(ii) that it was in Jodie's best interest; and
(iii) that it would be unlawful.

Decision. Because of the extraordinary facts and dilemma facing the Court of Appeal,[5] their Lordships decided to thoroughly examine the impact their decision would have on the various legal areas involved including; the medical law, family law, criminal law and human rights.
There were two independent crucial questions to be answered in this case. Firstly, was the operation itself in the best interests of the twins? And secondly, can such an operation be performed lawfully? In relation to Mary's "best interests", Ward L.J. said that this means:

> "the Court must decide what is best for her, taking all her interests and needs into account, weighing and then bringing into balance the advantages and disadvantages, the risks of harm against the hopes of benefit which flow from the course of action under consideration" (at page 997).

But can it be said that an operation which terminates a person's life can be of benefit to that person? In this respect the court considered the case of *Airedale NHS Trust v. Bland*,[6] which concerned the withdrawal of all life supporting medical treatment from a patient who had been in a vegetative state for some three years. It was held by the House of Lords not to be an intentional killing in relation to murder, since, *inter alia*, the doctors concerned did not owe a duty to the patient to prolong his life, if the treatment was not in the best interests of the patient. Since there was no possibility of improvement, sustaining the patient artificially would not be in the interests of that particular patient.[7]

Although the parents' wishes and opinions were extremely important and influential, their views became subordinate where the welfare of the children was at issue. For health purposes, the operation served no advantage; Mary would inevitably die as a result. Although Johnson J. found that because of Mary's condition, her life was worth nothing to her, Ward L.J. disagreed. He stated that all life has an equal inherent value irrespective of how gravely an individual is impaired. Accordingly, it was not in Mary's best interests to undergo an operation, but only in Jodie's best interests. His Lordship noted that the case of *Birmingham City Counsel v. H (a minor)*[8] advocated balancing the interests of one against the other and to chose the least detrimental alternative. This would ultimately mean choosing "the lesser of two evils". In this case, it was a question of balancing the weight given to the treatment of each of the twins, *i.e.* performing or not performing the operation. Although each twin equally had the right to life, the quality of that right had to be a consideration. In Jodie's case, there was an expectation of a relatively normal life, but with its own inherent mental and physical difficulties, should the operation go ahead. On the other hand, the operation would shorten Mary's life, and she would die within a very short time of the commencement of the operation. Hence, overwhelmingly, the balance lay in Jodie's favour. Accordingly, in Ward L.J.'s judgment, the operation could be performed, and lawfully so, agreeing with the conclusions in this respect of Brooke L.J. (see below). In his conclusion Ward L.J. stated the uniqueness for which this case is authority are as follows:

> "They are that it must be impossible to preserve the life of X without bringing about the death of Y that Y by his or her very continued existence will inevitably bring about the death of X within a period of time, and that X is capable of living an independent life but Y is incapable under any circumstances (including all forms of medical intervention) of viable independent existence".

The Court of Appeal also considered, *inter alia*, if the operation went ahead whether there would be:

(i) an unlawful;
(ii) killing of a person;
(iii) with intent to kill or cause grievous bodily harm.[9]

Despite Mary possessing a dysfunctional heart, brain and lungs, it would, in the court's judgment, be an act of murder if someone deliberately acted so as to extinguish that life unless a justification or excuse could be shown which English law is willing to recognise. The word "intentionally", the court stated, "should be given its natural and ordinary meaning", and continued, that the word, construed in that way, applies only to cases where the purpose of the prohibited action was to cause death. The acknowledged question in this case is whether circumstances could ever be extreme enough for the law to confer a right to choose that one innocent person should be killed rather than another. The surgeons performing the operation are in an impossible dilemma. On the one hand, performing the operation will kill Mary, and on the other hand, if they do not operate both Mary and Jodie will die.

Since both babies have an equal right to life, is there some exception which would prevent the operation and its consequences, to go ahead? Having examined established authority on the meaning of the words "unlawfully", "kills", "any reasonable creature" and "with intent to kill", Brooke L.J. concluded that the intention to kill in English law in these circumstances meant that the surgeons intended to kill Mary, however little they desired that end (at page 1029), since Mary would inevitably die as a result. However, his Lordship, also considered in great detail[10] the doctrine of the defence of necessity[11] (FT despite that hitherto necessity is not a defence to murder or attempted murder; see *R v. Howe* (1987) 1 AC 417 and *R v. Gotts* (1992) 2 AC 412) and concluded that in order for the doctrine to apply, and hence justify the operation, there were three requirements:

(1) The act is needed to avoid inevitable and irreparable evil;
(2) No more should be done than is reasonably necessary for the purpose to be achieved; and
(3) The evil inflicted must not be disproportionate to the evil avoided.

His Lordship considered that in this case, all three conditions had been met[12] (page 1061). Accordingly, he dismissed the appeal (at page 1052).

3–151 The court when considering Article 2 of the Convention reaffirmed Mary's right to life, and that right extends to "rights of bodily integrity and autonomy, the right to have one's own body whole and intact and (on reaching an age of understanding) to take decisions about one's own body" (at page 1070), and that it would be unlawful to intentionally kill her by operating on her. However, Jodie also has a right to life. The purpose of the operation would be to separate the twins and so give Jodie a reasonable good prospect of a long and reasonably normal life. Mary's death would not be the purpose of the operation, although it would be its inevitable consequence (*per* Robert Walker L.J.). She would die, not because she was intentionally killed, but because her own body cannot sustain her life. The proposed operation would not be unlawful. It would involve the positive act of invasive surgery and Mary's death would be foreseen as an inevitable consequence of an operation which is intended, and is necessary, to save Jody's life. But Mary's death would not be the purpose of the surgery and she would die because tragically her body, on its own, is not and never has been viable (at page 1067). Robert Walker L.J. concurred and stated, that this case is a case of doctors oweing conflicting legal (and not merely social or moral) duties. He stated that it is not a case "of evaluating the relative worth of two human lives, but of undertaking surgery without which neither life will have the bodily integrity (or wholeness) which is its due" (page 1067). As a consequence, the appeal was dismissed.

Article 3: Ill-Treatment

No one shall be subjected to torture or to inhuman or degrading treatment or punishment. **3–152**

Introduction

Article 3 is a doubly unusual provision of the Convention which operates as an especially strong guarantee of the rights which it protects. It places freedom from torture and inhuman treatment as one of the most fundamental rights of a citizen, and in fact puts these rights at a higher priority than the right to life. As has been seen, Article 2 allows States to have the death penalty and also places the right to life in the balance against other lawful interests. By contrast, the rights under Article 3 are given unqualified protection. Unlike almost all the other Articles, there are no exceptions stated in Article 3, and derogation from these rights is impossible for a state even in times of war or national emergency. Thus there is no reason or excuse which will permit torture or inhuman or degrading treatment, no matter how desperate the situation may be at the time, and the United Kingdom cannot use the situation relating to terrorism in Northern Ireland as a justification for derogating from this Article. Therefore the United Kingdom is in a confusing and often contradictory position in relation to Convention rights in cases concerning Northern Ireland or mainland terrorism. Under Article 15 there was a permitted derogation in force from Article 5(3) so that suspects could be detained without charge for extended periods. However, after the Terrorism Act 2000 removed the need for this **3–153** provision, the derogation was withdrawn on February 2001. But derogations from some other Articles are not possible (Articles 2, 3, 4(1) and 7).[13] with the result that one set of facts may give rise to challenges on the basis of several different Convention rights, with different results in each case.

Torture and ill-treatment

3–154 In order to qualify an act as torture, a distinction must be made between that type of ill-treatment with that of inhuman or degrading treatment or punishment.[14] It was specified in *Ireland v. United Kingdom*[15] that "ill-treatment",

> ". . . must attain a minimum level of severity . . . The assessment of this minimum . . . depends on all the circumstances of the case, such as the duration of the treatment, its physical or mental effects and, in some cases, the sex, age and state of health of the victim, etc".[16]

The Article intentionally distinguishes between "torture and inhuman and degrading treatment"; the first of these being considered the most detrimental and serious. "Torture" may be defined as "deliberate inhuman treatment or punishment causing very serious and cruel suffering."[17] It is the level of intensity and cruelty which will determine whether or not the treatment amounted to torture.[18] In *Ireland v. United Kingdom*, as a result of the increasing acts of terrorism in 1971 by the IRA and violence by Loyalists, internment was introduced as a means of alleviating the hostile situation. Thus, an individual could be arrested and detained without trial if suspected of being involved in terrorist activities (Loyalists were excluded from these internment provisions). The main reason given by the Northern Ireland Government for the introduction of internment was:

(1) Normal methods of investigations into the workings of the IRA produced very few effective results;

(2) Intimidation and threats by the IRA, meant that few witnesses came forward in prosecution cases against the offenders; and

(3) It was difficult to effectively patrol the border area between Northern Ireland and the Republic of Ireland; thus allowing IRA members to slip over the border surreptitiously from one part of the country to the other, without too much problem.

On August 9, 1971, some 350 suspects were arrested and detained at various holding centres (in less than a year some 3,276 persons were in custody). The IRA retaliated and violence intensified over this period. Whilst in detention at these various centres, the arrestees were subjected to "interrogation in depth". This type of questioning involved, what became known as, "the five techniques". The object of these techniques was to illicit certain information from the arrestees, *e.g.* to obtain confessions, their affiliation with the IRA, and other secret information about that organisation. Fourteen of the internees were subjected to this treatment which consisted of

(a) Wall-standing: standing on their toes with their legs and feet apart for hours against a cell wall;

(b) Hooding: putting a bag over the internee's head throughout most of their period of imprisonment;

(c) Noise: subjecting the person to continuous loud and hissing noises;

(d) Sleep: depriving the person of continual sleep;

(e) Food and drink: depriving the person of sufficient nourishment.

The Government admitted that the order for such techniques was authorised by those at "high level". Indeed, the interrogating officers (mainly the Royal Ulster Constabulary) were shown how to implement these five techniques by the English Intelligence Centre. This form of questioning proved valuable in discovering more information about IRA operations.[19]

The Irish Government complained to the Commission of violations under Article 3 against the practices operated by the respondents. The Commission examined some eight cases. They ruled that the practices of the "five techniques" constituted, not only inhuman and degrading treatment, but also torture. The Commission also found that it was probable that physical violence accompanied the five techniques in certain cases, however, they ruled that in only one case (out of a possible 14) was it actually shown. The court declared such practices to be degrading, and by causing intense physical and psychological suffering during questioning constituted inhuman treatment under Article 3. They found that although the treatment which the detainees received was of an inhuman and degrading nature, however, this did not escalate to the intensity required for the treatment to be considered "torture". They considered the treatment of detainees at various detention centres and concluded that, although the arrestees suffered from "extreme discomfort and had to perform irksome and painful exercises" for a few days, and that although the practice was discreditable and reprehensible, nevertheless, the level of severity of the suffering did not amount to torture. Notwithstanding, the court concluded, by an overwhelming majority (16 votes to 1), that in those detention centres where the practice of the "five techniques" was in operation, there was a violation of Article 3.

In order for ill-treatment to be established under Article 3, a minimum level of severity against an applicant must exist and this may include the court looking to the long-term effects as a result of the actions taken against the applicant. In *Selcuk and Asker v. Turkey*[20] the two applicants,

Turkish citizens of Kurdish origin, complained to the Commission that their homes in the south-east of Turkey had been destroyed by government security forces, allegedly because the houses were being used by the PKK (Kurdish Workers' Party), an illegal organisation. The respondent government disputed the events. An investigation by the Commission concluded that security forces did indeed burn down their houses and business premises partly owned by Selcuk, and in front of the two applicants, despite pleadings to the security forces to refrain from such action. Whether this severity of the ill-treatment amounts to a violation depends on all the circumstances of the case, such as the duration of the treatment, its physical and/or mental effects, and in some cases the sex, age and state of health of the victim (paragraph 76). The applicants were aged 54 and 60 respectively; their homes and property were destroyed; they could only stand by and watch as this was going on. They subsequently had to leave the village where they had lived all their lives; their protests to the security forces were ignored; very little protection from smoke or flames was given to the applicants, and no assistance was provided after the destruction of their property (paragraph 77). The court concluded that the particular circumstances amounted to inhuman treatment and therefore a violation of Article 3. Whether each of the events, taken by themselves, would have amounted to such severity so as to constitute inhuman treatment not only depended on the acts done by the security forces, but also on the effect that such acts had on the applicants. In *Selcuk* the catalogue of events which ensued, although, in themselves would normally be considered serious, together established ill-treatment of such a nature so as to constitute a violation of Article 3. It seems in the above case that the court not only looked at the acts themselves and the immediate results, but also at the long-term consequences, *i.e.* having to leave the village and start their lives afresh elsewhere, in deciding whether or not there had been a violation of Article 3.

Inhuman and degrading punishment

3–155 Inhuman punishment generally involves some form of legally authorized assault on the victim, but whether or not the particular violence will constitute a breach of Article 3 may be a question of degree. A series of corporal punishment cases illustrate very well the difficulties surrounding what amounts to inhuman or degrading punishment. For example, in *Tyrer v. United Kingdom*,[21] a boy of 15, who was a resident of the Isle of Man, pleaded guilty to assault charges and was sentenced to receive three strokes of the birch.[22] The punishment was carried out by the police at a police station. The applicant claimed before the Commission that this was a violation of Article 3. The issue in this case was not one of torture (the suffering did not in fact reach the required threshold) nor did the punishment attain the degree of severity to constitute inhuman punishment; the question here was, whether the punishment amounted to "degrading", such that it violated Article 3. Generally, mere legal punishment, although *per se*, is humiliating, is not to be construed as degrading within Article 3. In order for it to be degrading:

> "... the humiliation or debasement involved must attain a particular level of severity ... it depends on all the circumstances of the case, and in particular on the nature and context of the punishment itself and the manner and method of its execution".[23]

A factor which the court will not take into account is its deterrent effect; that is not considered a defence to a violation within Article 3. The court said that the legal inflicting of corporal punishment by those in authority constituted an attack on "a person's dignity and physical integrity", which Article 3 sought to protect. Added to this, the possible psychological problems from having to wait six weeks before sentence was carried out and the bending over a table with his buttocks naked to receive his punishment from strangers, all contributed to the Court's conclusion that "the element of humiliation attained the level inherent in the notion of degrading punishment"[24–25] under Article 3.

In *Y v. United Kingdom*,[26] a 15 year old boy was given four strokes of the cane on his trouser-covered bottom by a headmaster at a private school. Having lost a civil claim at the county court for damages for assault, and being advised of no prospects of success on appeal, the parent complained to the Commission alleging a breach of Article 3. The Government responded that the punishment "was moderate and reasonable and did not attain the high level of severity condemned by the Court in the *Tyrer* case"[27] (see above). The Commission considered, however, that the severity of the caning itself, which caused physical injury (four raised streak marks on his buttocks) and the humiliation, amounted to degrading treatment and punishment under Article 3. The case eventually ended with a friendly settlement (£8,000 plus costs) prior to the court's judgement. However, in *Costello-Roberts v. United Kingdom*[28] where a seven year old schoolboy was given three smacks with a slipper on his fully clothed bottom, the Commission in examining the above cases, found that such mild chastisement which caused no injury, did not reach the harshness required for a violation under Article 3—but only just (by five votes to four). Two of the dissenting judgments in this case, said that merely because the punishment was mild was not in itself the deciding factor, other issues pointed to the punishment reaching the level of severity, *e.g.* the boy being a seven year old and having to wait three days for the punishment—a long time in this instance. Further, the court should have considered the vulnerability, sensitivity and lack of maturity in one so young, and of the effects of any physical force on his being by someone in authority. Thus, having considered the full circumstances, the minority concluded that the boy suffered inhuman and degrading punishment in violation of Article 3.

These two cases illustrate the practical problems involved in interpreting the Convention before incorporation; the stronger case was settled out of court, and the weaker case proceeded to judgment—stronger cases may have fallen at earlier fences. The pressures which discourage applications and encourage settlements result in an arbitrariness which may belie the true state of civil liberties in a country. It is hoped that incorporation of the ECHR will go some way towards this situation. Another factor which was highlighted in the following case, was whether the mere threat of punishment, without it actually being carried through, constituted "degrading" within Article 3. In *Campbell and Cozans v. United Kingdom*,[29] the court did not rule out the possibility of threats alone reaching the required level of severity in order to amount to a breach. In this case, one of the boys was due to be caned, but he did not suffer the actual physical punishment although he had this threat hanging over him for some four months before it was finally suspended. The court found, on the facts, that he did not suffer any psychological effects from the experience.[30]

Degrading and inhuman treatment

3–156 Everyone, at some time or other, has suffered some degree of degradation or humiliation by some person in public authority, and no doubt stress, anxiety, despair, etc. has resulted as a consequence. Whether, the Commission (if it reaches that stage) would entertain a complaint under those circumstances, will depend, *inter alia*, on the level of severity which the complainant has suffered:

> "Inhuman treatment covers such acts as intentionally conflicting severe mental or physical suffering or if the treatment inflicted humiliates the person before others or drives him to act against his own will or conscience".[31]

What may distinguish this form of treatment from actual severe punishment is that here psychological damage is more likely to result, *i.e.* humiliation, demoralisation, a person's self respect and free will may have been sapped due to the degrading treatment carried out. For instance, in *Tomasi v. France*,[32] the applicant had been charged and remained in detention for five years and seven months before eventual acquittal. He complained to the Commission that whilst in custody, he had been beaten by the police on a number of occasions, which resulted in not only physical and mental pain, but he had suffered "fear, anguish and inferiority capable of humiliating him and breaking his physical and moral resistance".[33] Medical reports by four doctors indicated that the injuries could only have been sustained during a specified 40-hour interrogation whilst in detention. The Commission was of the opinion that although the injuries themselves were "relatively slight", the assault in combination with the detention element (depriving the person of his freedom) led to a state of inferiority, and therefore constituted both inhuman and degrading treatment.[34] The court put great emphasis on the medical reports on the number of blows inflicted and their intensity. Coupled with this was the lack of evidence by the respondents for alternative reasons for the injuries sustained by the applicant.[35] As a result, the court unanimously held that there had been a violation of Article 3 in this case.[36]

As was stated in the above case of *Tomasi v. France*, where a suspect is detained at a police station and is in good health upon his arrival, and upon his release is found to have sustained injuries, it is up to the police to account for those injuries. Whether or not the police are subsequently prosecuted the state will not be absolved from responsibility under the Convention. In *Selmouni v. France*[37] the applicant was arrested on suspicion of drug-trafficking and taken to a police station where, he alleged that he was beaten repeatedly, hit with objects, urinated upon, threatened with a blowlamp, dragged by the hair and suffered physical and mental injuries as a result of this ill-treatment. Having examined the medical evidence the Commission found these allegations to be established. The court stated that it was "incumbent on the state to provide a plausible explanation on how those injuries were caused, failing which a clear issue arises under Article 3 of the Convention" (at paragraph 87). Having considered all the evidence the court found that the pain and suffering undergone by the applicant attained the "severity" necessary for it to constitute torture, not merely inhuman or degrading treatment. The court further noted that, because:

> "the Convention is a living instrument and must be interpreted in the light of present day conditions, certain acts which were classified in the past as 'inhuman and degrading treatment' as opposed to 'torture' could be classified differently in future. It takes the view that the increasingly high standard being required in the area of the protection of human rights and fundamental liberties correspondingly and inevitably requires greater firmness in assessing breaches of the fundamental values of democratic societies" (at paragraph 101).

ARTICLE 5: RIGHT TO LIBERTY

1 Everyone has the right to liberty and security of person. No one shall be deprived of his liberty save in the following cases and in accordance with a procedure prescribed by law: **3–157**

- (a) The lawful detention of a person after conviction by a competent court;
- (b) The lawful arrest or detention of a person for non-compliance with the lawful order of a court or in order to secure the fulfilment of any obligation prescribed by law;
- (c) The lawful arrest or detention of a person effected for the purpose of bringing him before the competent legal authority on a reasonable suspicion of having committed an offence or when it is reasonably considered necessary to prevent his committing an offence or fleeing after having done so;
- (d) The detention of a minor by lawful order for the purpose of educational supervision or his lawful detention for the

purpose of bringing him before the competent legal authority;

(e) The lawful detention of persons for the prevention of the spreading of infectious diseases, of persons of unsound mind, alcoholics or drug addicts or vagrants;

(f) The lawful arrest or detention of a person to prevent his effecting an unauthorised entry into the country or of a person against whom action is being taken with a view to deportation or extradition.

2 Everyone who is arrested shall be informed promptly, in a language which he understands, of the reasons for his arrest and of any charge against him.

3 Everyone arrested or detained in accordance with the provisions of paragraph 1(c) of this Article shall be brought promptly before a judge or other officer authorised by law to exercise judicial power and shall be entitled to trial within a reasonable time or to release pending trial. Release may be conditioned by guarantee to appear for trial.

4 Everyone who is deprived of his liberty by arrest or detention shall be entitled to take proceedings by which the lawfulness of his detention shall be decided speedily by a court and his release ordered if the detention is not lawful.

5 Everyone who has been the victim of arrest or detention in contravention of the provision of this Article shall have an enforceable right to compensation.

The whole essence of Article 5(1) is that any arrest or detention must be "lawful" and "in accordance with a procedure prescribed by law".[38] The right to liberty in Article 5(1) refers to the fundamental right of unhindered physical freedom[39] which should not be taken away through any arbitrary manner.[40] In determining whether or not a person has been lawfully deprived of this liberty, the court will consider such factors as "the type, duration, effects, and manner of implementation of the measure (or penalty) in question".[41] Article 5 (1) does not bestow on everyone an absolute right to liberty. There is an exhaustive list ((a)-(f)) whereby a person's liberty may be justifiably taken away without there being a breach of Article 5(1), provided it was done "in accordance with a procedure prescribed by law." The exceptions to "liberty" in Article 5(1)(a)-(f) revolve around the issues of arrest and/or detention and these will now be examined in turn.

Article 5(1)(A): Detention After Conviction

3–158 In Article 5(1)(a), arrest by itself is not sufficient; there must be detention and conviction of an offence.[42] Further, there must also be a causal connection between the conviction and the deprivation of liberty of the person. For instance, in *Weeks v. United Kingdom*,[43] the applicant (an immature 17 year-old boy) pleaded guilty to armed robbery in 1966 (he robbed a pet shop with a starting pistol and stole 35 pence, which he later dropped) and was sentenced to life imprisonment—the sentence to be indeterminate.[44] In 1976, he was released on licence, but after a few minor offences, he was re-detained in June 1977 on the order of the Home Secretary on the grounds that the applicant's continued liberty constituted a danger to the public or to himself; there was also a question mark over his state of mind. Again, in 1982, he was released on licence, but after a number of offences was again returned to prison in 1984. He argued before the Commission that his re-detention in 1977 was a breach of Article 5(1)(a) because when he was released in 1976, that fulfilled the objectives of the sentencing court, so that he had "his full rights restored to him", at that time. When recalled in 1977, the causal link, he maintained, between the original conviction and sentence had evaporated. The court did not agree. The applicant, because of the life sentence imposed, was throughout the remainder of his life at the mercy of the Home Secretary whether the applicant was inside or outside prison. The court regarded the applicant's recall in 1977 as not amounting to arbitrariness or unreasonableness, and was within the bounds of the object and purpose of the original sentence.[45] The applicant's subsequent releases and recalls in 1982 and 1984 and again in 1985 and 1986, after having committed a number of further offences including violence, fell within the discretionary power of the Home Secretary to order his reimprisonment. The court concluded that there was no breach of Article 5(1)(a).

The causal link between conviction and sentence could be broken if a position were reached by which a decision not to release or re-detain a convicted person was based on grounds that were inconsistent with the objectives of the sentencing court.[46] In *Monnell and Morris v. United Kingdom*[47] the first applicant was convicted of a number of burglary offences, receiving a total of three years and nine months imprisonment. He appealed against his conviction and sentence, in spite of receiving legal advice that it was completely futile. The Court of Appeal dismissed his application as without foundation and with no prospects of success. Under section 29(1) Criminal Appeal Act 1968, the Court of Appeal has a discretion, if it thinks fit, to order that the period spent awaiting an appeal outcome should not count towards the original prison sentence, if leave to appeal is refused. They decided that because of the first appellant wasting the court's time, his 28 days in custody, should not count towards his original sentence. In Morris's case, for making a hopeless application, the Court of Appeal concluded that the 56 days spent in custody awaiting the verdict of the appeal was also not to count towards his time already served in prison. Both applicants argued before the Commission a breach of Article 5(1)(a) on the basis that those periods already spent in prison should be taken into account and be included in their sentencing periods. The Commission expressed their opinion that there had been a breach of

Article 5(1)(a). The question for the court was whether the applicants' further sentence occurred after the original convictions. The applicants argued that since the further sentence was not for an offence but for an appeal, there was no link between the conviction at trial and the subsequent Court of Appeal order. The court contended that in English law, it is accepted that where there are proper grounds for appeal, the time served awaiting the outcome of the decision should be counted in the appellant's favour. But, if the appeal is frivolous and without merit, then the discretionary power may be invoked so as not to include the time served awaiting the appeal decision. Whatever the actual outcome of the individual cases, the appeal process is "an inherent part of the criminal appeal process following conviction of an offender and pursues a legitimate aim under Article 5(1)(a)"[48]. Thus, the court concluded that there was no breach of that particular paragraph of the Article.

Article 5(1)(B): Arrest or Detention for Breach of Court Order or Fulfillment of Legal Obligation

3–159 Under the second part of Article 5(1)(b) ". . . to secure the fulfilment of any obligation prescribed by law," it was stated in *Engel v. The Netherlands*[49] that these words "concern only cases where the law permits the detention of a person to compel him to fulfil a specific and concrete obligation which he has until then failed to satisfy",[50] for example, failure to carry a valid passport, unpaid taxes,[51] fines or custom duties, refusal to do military service, if legally required, etc. In *McVeigh, O'Neill and Evans v. United Kingdom*,[52] the three applicants, after having arrived at Liverpool from Dublin by boat, were arrested and detained by the police under the Prevention of Terrorism (Supplemental Temporary Provisions) Order 1976. They were detained for 45 hours prior to release without charge. During that period they were questioned, searched, photographed and fingerprinted. The first two applicants alleged that they were not permitted to telephone their wives. Amongst the applicants' submissions before the Commission were that the arrest and detention were unjustified within Articles 5(1)(b), (c) or (f). The Government argued that they were entitled to detain them for further examination under section 5(2) of the 1976 Order (examination of persons arriving in or leaving Great Britain. . . may be required to submit to further examination).

> "In the Commission's opinion, the person concerned must normally have had a prior opportunity to fulfil the specific and concrete obligation incumbent on him and have failed, without proper excuse, to do so before it can be said in good faith that his detention is 'in order to secure the fulfilment' of the obligation".[53]

The applicants argued that since there was no prior legal obligation on them to fulfil any existing law, there was no justification for the authorities to arrest and detain them. In this case, the 1976 Order was of such specific and concrete character and importance that there was an obligation on the applicants to fulfil it there and then, *i.e.* to submit to further examination. Hence, there was no breach of Article 5(1)(b):

> "The McVeigh case establishes that in certain 'limited circumstances of a pressing nature' Article 5(1)(b) extends not only to cases in which there has been a prior failure to comply with an obligation, but also to cases in which short-term detention is considered necessary to make the execution of an obligation effective at the time that it arises".[54]

Article 5(1)(c): Arrest or Detention in Order to Bring to Justice a Person who has Committed an Offence, or About to do so, or to Evade Capture

Where a complaint is brought under Article 5(1)(c), "reasonable suspicion" is a fundamental ingredient before a lawful arrest may be made. Further, the arrest and detention must be for the purpose of bringing the suspect before a judge or other judicial authority. Normally, under domestic law, for an arrest to be lawful, there must be "reasonable suspicion". However, there may be a conflict between what the national law deems "reasonable" and how the court interprets the word. **3–160**

For example, in *Fox, Campbell and Hartley v. United Kingdom*[55]:

Facts. The first and second applicants were arrested under section 11(1) Northern Ireland (Emergency Provisions) Act 1978, *i.e.* any constable may arrest without warrant anyperson whom he suspects of being a terrorist, and under section 11(3) be detained for up to 72 hours. They were both questioned about their involvement with the IRA, and detained for 44 hours each. The third applicant was arrested and detained for 30 hours and 15 minutes. One of the main arguments put by the applicants to the Commission was that the police did not possess the necessary "reasonable suspicion" for their arrest and detention. Previously, the House of Lords said that "an honestly held suspicion" by the police would suffice for an arrest, *i.e.* a subjective test. The absence of the word "reasonable" was a minimising of the "suspicion" required in Article 5(1)(c).

Findings of the Court. The court said that the words "reasonable suspicion" formed "an essential part of the safeguard against arbitrary arrest and detention which is laid down in Article 5(1)(c)". The words presuppose the existence of facts or information which would satisfy an objective observer that the person concerned may have committed the offence and further must be judged against all the circumstances of the case.[56] Because of the inherent dangers of offences involving terrorism the police have to act promptly and attempt, amongst other things, to amass information from reliable informants. The Government argued that, in these urgent circumstances, it is not always easy to possess such a high degree of suspicion before an arrest can be made. Where terrorism is concerned, it may be the case that the justification for an arrest may not be of the same standard as in an ordinary domestic crime. They further argued that they were disadvantaged in not being able to divulge the source of their information, on national security grounds, and anyway, disclosure would obviously endanger their informants lives. Nevertheless, they maintained that they could prove via other evidence that they had the necessary "reasonableness" for an arrest. They said that not only had the applicants previous convictions for terrorist offences but also that the questioning was limited to the areas of acts of terrorism and their IRA connections, all of which formed the "genuine" suspicion required.[57] The court stated, however, that some additional relevant material must be presented to substantiate the legality of the applicants' arrest, otherwise they might not be properly protected under section 5(1)(c). The court concluded under Article 5(1)(c) that, (1) it was not sufficient to make an arrest where the only evidence was that the applicants had previous convictions for terrorist offences, especially some seven years previously; (2) although the police had a genuine suspicion (a subjective test) for their arrest, and subsequent questioning involved only issues of terrorism alone, that was not sufficient. The court found that the facts would not have satisfied an objective observer that the applicants may have committed these acts.[58] On the grounds of (1) and (2) above, the police failed to produce the necessary evidence to support the arguments that there was a reasonable suspicion for the arrest and detention. As a result, the court found that there had been a violation of Article 5(1)(c).

The court, may however, find the necessary "reasonable suspicion" proved, if all the surrounding evidence taken together provides the required level of suspicion. Thus, in *Murray "(Margaret)" v. United Kingdom*[59] the applicant, a Mrs M. Murray, complained to the Commission that her arrest and detention were a violation of Article 5(1). She had previously been arrested under section 14 of the Northern Ireland (Emergency Provisions) Act 1978 on suspicion of being engaged in unlawful fundraising activities for the IRA. She was in detention for some two hours before being released without charge. She argued, *inter alia*, that there was a lack of reasonable suspicion for any criminal offence. The Commission formed the opinion that there were no "material distinguishing features" between the present case and *Fox, Campbell and Hartley v. United Kingdom* (see above) and concluded that since the Government did not present any further evidence to support the reasonable suspicion requirement under Article 5(1)(c), a breach of that Article was established. The Government argued that they possessed the necessary high standard of reasonableness required, because their information was gathered through a reliable source, whose identity could not be revealed to the court on security grounds. They submitted that this, nevertheless, should be considered by the court, along with other evidence which included (a) the findings of the domestic courts and (b) her visits to the USA to see her two brothers who were recently convicted of purchasing weapons for the IRA. They argued that combining all of these matters reached the necessary reasonable suspicion for a lawful arrest. The court in applying the same principles as laid down in *Fox* found that:

(1) The lower standard, *i.e.* honest belief suspicion (a subjective test), established in the domestic courts whilst not constituting "reasonableness" itself, nevertheless amounted to "One indispensable element of its reasonableness"[60];

(2) The subsequent questioning at the Army centre was limited to the suspicion that she was involved in a specific terrorist activity; and

(3) Her visits to her recently convicted brothers in the USA. The court concluded that when combining all the available factual

evidence as well as "the special exigencies of investigating terrorist crime",[61] the objective standard of suspicion had reached its required reasonableness for the arrest to be lawful under Article 5(1)(c).

Article 5(1)(E): Detention of Persons of Unsound Mind or for Medical Purposes

There is no definition of "persons of unsound mind" in the Convention, but those words are to be given the same meaning and conformity as if the phrase referred to "mentally ill persons"; the interpretation of which is to be gathered from domestic law. In *Winterwerp v. The Netherlands*[62]: **3–161**

Facts. In 1968, the applicant was compulsorily admitted to a psychiatric hospital under section 14 Mentally Ill Persons Act 1884. Shortly after, his wife applied, with medical evidence, to the court for an order that he remain there, on the grounds that he was a danger to his family, the public and himself. In his absence, the court granted the order. Extension of this order was granted from 1968 until 1977 based on medical records showing schizophrenic and paranoiac tendencies. In between these years, the applicant made four requests for discharge to the public prosecutor, who repeatedly rejected his applications. The applicant's last three requests were not forwarded to the Regional Court. On a number of occasions throughout this period, he had been allowed to live outside the hospital, but due to bouts of psychological problems, had to be re–admitted. In 1972 he complained, *inter alia*, to the Commission that he had been arbitrarily deprived of his liberty.

Opinion of the Commission. The Commission stated that, apart from the special circumstances of emergency cases, no detention which is arbitrary can ever be lawful. The following conditions must be adhered to before hospitalisation can be deemed lawful:

(1) Objective medical expertise must be introduced to show the true medical disorder.
(2) The medical disorder must be of a kind or degree warranting compulsory confinement.
(3) The validity of continued confinement depends upon the persistence of such a disorder. The Commission, to which the court and the respondent Government agreed, expressed the opinion that "no one may be confined as a person of unsound mind, in the absence of medical evidence establishing that his mental state is such as to justify his compulsory hospitalisation".[63]

Findings of the Court. The medical evidence, which the court accepted, showed the applicant to be suffering from various psychological conditions which caused him to commit serious acts, without consciously realising the consequences. Further, the crucial emergency hospitalisation in 1968 was not considered unlawful (although it was for a lengthy period of six weeks). The court concluded that the objectivity and reliability necessary in such cases had been adhered to and thus, there was no breach of Article 5(1)(e), at least, as far as the lawful detention of a person of unsound mind was concerned.

In *Ashingdane v. United Kingdom*,[64] the applicant was compulsorily admitted to a psychiatric hospital in 1970 under section 60 Mental Health

Act 1959, and without limit of time (section 65). He was later in 1971 transferred to Broadmoor Hospital, a "special hospital", for those with serious psychological problems. By 1978, he had been refused discharge on four occasions. However, towards the end of 1978, recommendations were made that he had improved such that he could be treated in an "open hospital". The Home Secretary (who was responsible for him under the 1959 Act) gave his consent to this. However, the open hospital refused to accept him due to union restrictions on certain patients, and since nowhere else could be found, he remained at Broadmoor. He stayed there for some two years before he was eventually moved to the original open hospital. The applicant complained, *inter alia*, to the Commission, that his period at Broadmoor from October 1978 was in breach of Article 5(1)(e). The court, extracting the three conditions set out in the *Winterwerp* case above, and examining the medical evidence and the doctors' conclusions, agreed with the "objectivity and reliability" of their judgement, that the applicant's confinement had been warranted and therefore there had been no breach of Article 5(1)(e). There was a difference between a "special" and "open" hospital (the latter being more relaxed), and therefore it would seem that the applicant suffered more than he needed to. However, the reality of the situation was that had he gone to the open hospital at the appointed time, he would still have had to remain in a closed ward for 10 months before being transferred to an open ward. As a consequence, his liberty was still being deprived whether it be at the special or open hospital. The court therefore concluded that there was no breach of Article 5(1)(e).

Article 5(1)(f): Arrest or Detention to Prevent Entry into the Country, or for the Purposes of Deportation or Extradition

3–162 The theme running throughout Article 5(1) is that the suspect must at all times be protected against arbitrariness, i.e. the detention itself must abide by the rule of law. Thus, in *Bozano v. France*,[65] the applicant was found guilty of murder and other crimes of violence in Italy, *in absentia*, and sentenced to life imprisonment. He was at this time in France under an assumed name, but was eventually arrested. The French Court of Appeal rejected, for various reasons, the Italians' request for his extradition. This decision was binding on the French Government. Nevertheless, a deportation order was issued by the Minister of the Interior.[66] Without being allowed to notify a lawyer or his wife, he was within 12 hours of his arrest taken forcibly by the police to Switzerland (Spain would have been closer). After a request from the Italians to extradite the applicant, the Swiss agreed and he was returned to Italy to serve his life sentence.

The applicant complained to the Commission that he had been deprived of his liberty unlawfully. The main question was whether the French Government's action was "lawful". It was stated in this case that the Commission's responsibility was not to interfere with decisions properly taken by domestic courts, but "it can and must take account of any national decisions on the ordering of disputed measures from which it might possibly be inferred that there had been unlawful deprivation of liberty".[67] Here, the Minister's decision to deport was in direct contravention to the Court of Appeal's decision not to extradite: what the Commission called a "manifest error of judgement".[68] Such a decision was considered to be an ousting of the jurisdiction of the court and an abuse of power, and was thus unlawful. Taking into account the circumstances, the irregularities and the manner by which the applicant was deported, the court found that the arbitrariness of the appellant's removal was a breach of Article 5(1)(f).

Articles 5(2)–5(5) create a series of rights for a person under arrest or detention.

Article 5(2): Reasons for Arrest

Under Article 5(2), the arrested person must be given the reasons for his **3–163** arrest promptly. The reasons themselves do not have to be exact, but nor can they be too general. It is generally a question of whether the reasons given for the arrest had sufficient substance, taking into account all the material circumstances of the arrest, and may seemingly, include any subsequent questioning. In *Fox, Campbell and Hartley v. United Kingdom*[69] (see above) the arrestees were merely informed that they were being taken into custody under section 11(1) of the 1978 Act, on suspicion of being terrorists. This, by itself, would not normally constitute "sufficient reasons". However, the questions put to them whilst in custody were restricted to specific terrorist activities and whether they were members of a proscribed organisation. Under these circumstances, it was reasonable to suppose that the applicants realised the reasons for their arrest. Therefore, there was no breach of Article 5(2).

However, the word "promptly" would indicate that the reasons for the arrest need to be conveyed, circumstances permitting, "at once" or at least within a very short time. But, there may be circumstances which prevent reasons for an arrest being given immediately, *e.g.* the suspect at the time resisted arrest or was not in a fit condition, *i.e.* drunk, injured, mentally disadvantaged, or was devoid of understanding, etc. But the reasons should be conveyed to the suspect as soon as normal conditions resume. Being questioned later at the police station, as in the case of *Fox, Campbell and Hartley* above, should only be relevant as to the reasons why the individual was arrested in the first place, not to substantiate an arrest. After all, deprivation of liberty begins from the moment of arrest.

Article 5(3), First Limb: Prompt Court Appearance

Under this particular Article, once the suspect is not released, then he must **3–164** be brought "promptly" before a competent legal authority. The reason why the word "promptly" in this context is given such importance lies in safeguarding an individual's right to liberty against any arbitrary interference by the national authorities.[70] Once his liberty has been forfeited, whether there was a lack of promptness involved such that the suspect suffered an unduly lengthly detention before his court appearance will depend upon all the circumstances of the case.

In *Brogan v. United Kingdom*[71]:

Facts. The four applicants were arrested and detained on suspicion of being involved in terrorist activities contrary to section 12 of the Prevention of Terrorism (Temporary Provisions) Act 1984 (PTA).[72] The following detention periods for each applicant were five days 11 hours, six days 16 hours, four days and six hours and four days 11 hours. Under Northern Ireland's domestic law, 48 hours was the maximum detention time before being either released or brought before a competent legal authority. However, under section 12(4) of PTA 1984, this period can be extended for a further five days (with the authority of the Secretary of State for Northern Ireland). All the applicants were released without charge, and at no stage were they brought before a judge or other officer exercising judicial power within section 5(3).

Opinion of the Commission. The Commission found on the facts that the applicants had been lawfully arrested under Article 5(1)(c); there being the required "reasonable suspicion" in existence. Under Article 5(3), the main issue of contention was that of "promptness", *i.e.* whether the periods of detention in this case exceeded the time period for being brought before a judicial authority under that Article. The Commission (but not the court) stated that previous case law in normal criminal offences suggested that four days was permissible for detention, and in exceptional cases even five days would be acceptable. The Commission formed the opinion that the two applicants who had been held in detention for just over four days did not amount to a breach, but the other two applicants' detention did constitute a violation of Article 5(3).[73] There were four dissenting opinions of the Commission who regarded all the periods of detention as exceeding the sufficient promptness under Article 5(3).

Findings of the court. Since at no time were the applicants taken before a judge, the question for the court was whether they were released "promptly" in the circumstances. It was for the court to decide whether there existed in this case "special features" which amounted to their release being regarded as prompt within Article 5(3). The word "promptly" also appears in Article 5(2) and connotes the meaning of "at once" or "immediate". However, under Article 5(3), the detention may be for a criminal offence which is outside that of the norm and comes under the title "special feature", *e.g.* war, or in this instance, terrorist offences. Here, since the reasons for the arrest were under the PTA, the authorities, because of the inherent dangers associated with terrorism, ought, in certain circumstances, to be given some latitude when dealing with offences of this kind. In this respect, the investigation and questioning of those in detention may need to take further time before they either go before a judge or be released. However, the court decided that even four days six hours detention fell "outside the strict constraints as to time permitted by the first part of Article 5(3)". To attach such importance to the special features of this case as to justify so lengthy a period of detention without appearance before a judge or other judicial officer would be an unacceptably wide interpretation of the plain meaning of the word "promptly".[74]

The Government could have, of its own volition, derogated from its obligations under Article 15, from Article 5(3), but, instead decided against such action and suffered the consequences. Thereafter, the Government, having learned its lesson, took the "derogation" route when defending similar actions in terrorist cases. For instance, in *Brannigan and McBride v. United Kingdom*[75] where the two applicants had been detained for six days four hours and four days six hours respectively, the Government decided to serve notice of its derogation under Article 15,[76] *i.e.* to derogate from the requirement of Article 5(3). The main issue was whether it was correct to give some extra latitude to the emergency situation existing in Northern Ireland, whereby the Secretary of State for Northern Ireland was empowered to extend the detention period in terrorist cases (for up to seven days), rather than bringing them before the judiciary to decide the matter.[77] In the special circumstances, the Commission agreed that the derogation requirements had been achieved, *i.e.* in order for the Government to be able to combat terrorism and make further investigations, and therefore Article 5(3) had not been breached. Although, this would seem to involve, to some extent, arbitrary intervention which would go against the whole essence of the Convention, the court nevertheless held that the applicants were protected against such arbitrary measures by having at their disposal the following available lawful remedies:

(1) The remedy of habeas corpus to ensure the lawfulness of their arrest and detention.

(2) The access to legal advice within 48 hours of their detention.

(3) Permitted to institute proceedings for judicial review, if the request under (2) above was refused or delayed.[78]

Added to the above, with regard to an individual's protection, was the fact that the operation of the legislation in question, (*i.e.* the PTA), had been continually independently reviewed. Therefore, there was no unreasonable arbitrariness involved in this case. As a consequence, the court decided that the United Kingdom had satisfied the requirements under Article 15 and that there was no breach of Article 5(3).

Article 5(3), Second Limb: Trial within a Reasonable Time or Released Pending Trial

Reasonable Time

Is the period spent in detention to be measured against the commencement of the trial itself or when the trial has been concluded and the judgment given or even at a later period, *i.e.* if convicted when all the appeal proceedings have been exhausted? In *Wemhoff v. FRG*[79] the court determined that the application of Article 5(3) was restricted to detention periods after judgment had been delivered at the trial.[80] Should the **3–165** applicant wish to question the reasonableness after that period, for instance, through to the end of the appeal process then the complaint should be brought under Article 6(1).

The Convention does not fix a definite time for a detention period. Instead the words "reasonable time" are used to convey the permissible duration period. In determining whether the detention period has exceeded a reasonable time the court will examine the reasons given by the national authorities to justifythe continued detention. If the reasons are not relevant and sufficient and the accused is not released then there is a violation of Article 5(3). In *Wemhoff* the applicant's detention was necessary, for the authorities feared that if he was freed he would abscond and destroy the evidence. By the commencement of the trial, at least one of those reasons stated above was still relevant. Further, since the investigation itself had been conducted expeditiously and with "special diligence" and considering the complexities of the case the court did not regard the period from detention to trial as unreasonable.

It was stated in *Neumeister v. Austria (No. 1)*[81] that:

> ". . . until conviction the accused must be presumed innocent, and the purpose of the provision under consideration is essentially to require his provisional release once his continuing detention ceases to be reasonable".[82]

But in certain circumstances the presumption of innocence may be somewhat disregarded, if there is a likelihood that if released prior to trial, the suspect would, for instance, commit further offences.[83] Thus, whether the respondent state exceeded the "reasonableness" requirement by not releasing the suspect, the court will consider such factors as:

(i) The complexity of the case, *i.e.* has the investigation taken an unusual amount of time due to the complicated issues involved,[84] *e.g.* fraud cases;

(ii) The risk of collusion, *i.e.* was there a possibility of those involved conniving together to interfere with the investigation?

(iii) The risk of the suspect fleeing the country; does the suspect have strong family connections, a home, business which prevent him from absconding?

(iv) The risk of the suspect reoffending.[85] Here, the court will take into account such factors as his previous record and character, and whether he is already on bail for another offence.[86]

In (iii) (above) release may be refused where there is a danger of the suspect absconding to another country. For instance, in *Neumeister v. Austria (No. 1)*[87] the applicant was arrested and detained on remand on tax fraud charges. He was then released and rearrested and was imprisoned from July 12, 1962 until September 16, 1964, on the grounds that there was a danger he might abscond. All appeals by the applicant for release were rejected. Thus he had served some two years and four months in custody prior to his trial, which after various adjournments eventually began in November 1964. The applicant complained to the Commission, that, *inter alia*, he had not been brought to trial within a reasonable time, nor released pending trial. One of the reasons given by the respondent Government for his continued detention was the fear of the applicant fleeing to Finland, due to further incriminating evidence being discovered against him in the meantime. However, other factors must be taken into account, *e.g.* his family ties, his home, his occupation, etc.—all go to decide whether there was a real danger of him absconding; added to this was the time spent on remand which would eventually go towards his prison sentence, as time served, if subsequently convicted. The Investigating Judge gave his opinion that he did not believe that the applicant would flee. The court also considered that the applicant offered a guarantee of an amount of money as security for his attendance at trial. This was rejected by the Austrian authorities. Eventually, bail was fixed at one million Austrian schillings, being a similar amount to that which he was accused of defrauding. This method of calculation was rejected by the court as an improper means by which to fix bail. They said that the guarantee "must be assessed principally by reference to him, his assets and his relationship with the persons who are to provide the security . . .," such that it should act as a sufficient deterrent against his non-attendance at trial.[88] Accordingly, the court found his prolonged detention to be a breach of the second limb of Article 5(3).

Article 5(4): Right to Question Validity of Arrest or Detention

Under Article 5(4), any person deprived of his liberty has a right of **3–166** recourse either personally or through legal representation to a court on the issue of the "lawfulness" of his or her detention. "Any person" includes someone who, through mental illness, may not be in a position to defend himself properly. In the *Winterwerp* case above, for instance, the applicant was neither informed nor represented in any proceedings when orders were made against him for his continued detention in a psychiatric hospital. Such lack of procedures by the relevant court contravened the guarantees under Article 5(4) in the absence of that individual being permitted to argue his case. Where a sentence is indeterminate, as in the case of *Weeks v. United Kingdom*,[89] special problems arise. In this case, the applicant was convicted of armed robbery and was given an indeterminate life sentence by the court. This sentence was considered appropriate because of his mental instability, aggressive personality and that he was likely to be a danger to the public. He could only be released after his tariff period had been served and then only on licence with the authority of the Home Secretary. On being released, any further redetention had to be in keeping with the objectives of the original sentencing court. If that link was broken, as was the case here, then he was entitled to argue that his detention was no longer lawful before a court. The court decided that this entitlement should have been exercisable by him at the moment of any return to custody after being at liberty and also at reasonable intervals during the course of his imprisonment.[90]

Meaning of "court"

3–167 It is not enough that a "court" exists; that court must provide an outlet whereby the detainee can put forward his side of the case on the lawfulness of the detention. "Court" denotes "bodies which exhibit not only common fundamental features, of which the most important is independence of the executive and of the parties of the case, but also the guarantees of judicial procedure."[91] In order to determine whether a proceeding provides adequate guarantees, regard must be had to the particular nature of the circumstances in which such proceedings take place.[92] For example, a Parole Board may constitute a "court" for the purposes of Article 5(4) provided it fulfils the necessary conditions of a judicial body. Therefore, it must be (i) independent and impartial (normally they possess this characteristic); (ii) it must possess the necessary powers and procedural guarantees (normally they are only there in an advisory capacity to the Home Secretary on whether to release the detainee or not—therefore they lack the necessary judicial powers). Consequently, Parole Boards are generally not to be construed as a "court" for the purposes of Article 5(4).

Thus, in *Thynne, Wilson and Gunnell v. United Kingdom*,[93] the three applicants, at different times, were convicted of particularly serious offences including rape, buggery and indecent assault. They were all given discretionary life sentences because unlike a normal sentence, which is purely punitive, they were also considered to be danger to the public due to their unstable mental state (ultimately, via a Parole Board, it is up to the Home Secretary to decide when it is safe to release such persons on parole). The "punitive" part of the sentence was solely handed down for the crime itself as a punishment and for deterrent purposes, and such persons are entitled to be released after serving a definite number of years (the "tariff" period).[94] The other "security" part of the sentence exists because of the applicant's mental conditions and such persons will only be allowed out on parole when the Home Secretary regards those individuals as no longer being a danger to the public. The three applicants complained that the continued lawfulness of their detention should be decided by a court at reasonable intervals throughout their imprisonment (and in two of the applicant's cases, the lawfulness of their redetention was not decided by the court). The court was satisfied that all three applicants had served their punitive period. The Government argued that unlike the *Weeks* case (see above) "the gravity of the offences remains the continuing justification for the second and third applicant's redetention and the first applicant's detention".[95] The court, applying the *Weeks* case, said that "the factors of mental instability and dangerousness are susceptible to change over the passage of time and new issues of lawfulness may thus arise in the course of detention".[96] Thus, the three applicants were entitled to have the lawfulness of their detention and redetention examined by a court. Accordingly, there had been a breach of Article 5(4).[97] Finally, under Article 5(4) any decision by the court must be given "speedily". Whether or not this has been accomplished will depend on "the substantive and procedural rules of the national legislation and moreover be conducted with the aim of Article 5, namely to protect the individual against arbitrariness".[98]

Article 5(5): Compensation for Breach of Article 5

Under Article 5(5), only the victim may recover compensation (normally an award of damages) where applicable. The damages are restricted to where there has been an unlawful arrest or detention. Where the arrest and detention is unlawful under national law, and there is no domestic entitlement to damages, under the Convention, the victim still has a rightful claim to damages[99] under Article 5(5) or under the "just satisfaction" of Article 50. Any claim under Article 5 must be as a result of a violation under Article 5(1)–(4). Further, the victim may have to show that he has suffered at least some damage or injury whether it be financial, physical or mental. Compensation is not limited to arrest or detention itself but extends to procedural or other guarantee matters which the detainee should have benefited from under Articles 5(2)–(4). **3–168**

Article 6: The Right to a Fair Hearing

1 In the determination of his *civil rights and obligations or of any criminal charge* against him, everyone is entitled to *a fair and public hearing within a reasonable time* by an *independent and impartial tribunal* established by law. Judgment shall be pronounced publicly but the press and public may be excluded from all or part of the trial in the interests of morals, public order or national security in a democratic society, where the interests of juveniles or the protection of the private life of the parties so require, or to the extent strictly necessary in the opinion of the court in special circumstances where publicity would prejudice the interests of justice. **3–169**

2 Everyone charged with a criminal offence shall be *presumed innocent* until proved guilty according to law.

3 Everyone charged with a criminal offence has the following minimum rights:

(a) to be *informed promptly*, in a language which he understands and in detail, of the nature and cause of the accusation against him;

(b) to have adequate time and facilities for the preparation of his defence;
(c) to defend himself in person or through *legal assistance* of his own choosing or, if he has not sufficient means to pay for legal assistance, to be given it free when the interests of justice so require;
(d) to examine or have examined witnesses against him and to obtain the attendance and *examination of witnesses* against him and to obtain the attendance and examination of witnesses on his behalf under the same conditions as witnesses against him;
(e) to have the free *assistance of an interpreter* if he cannot understand or speak the language used in court. (italics added).

Article 6(1): Right to Fair Civil or Criminal Hearing

3–170 Article 6 creates a series of rights for both the parties to civil court cases and defendants in criminal cases. The rights concern the conduct of the trial and issues of access to justice. Thus, the question is not whether or not the domestic court properly evaluated the evidence put before it, but whether the proceedings themselves were conducted in a proper manner such that the defendant received a fair hearing.

Civil rights and obligations

3–171 Taking the words "civil rights and obligation" in their widest sense, their meaning is that all individuals are entitled to a fair hearing where the issues to be resolved fall into the categories of private law as well as those private claims which may overlap with administrative law, within a Contracting State's domestic legal system. However, it is now well established that the words "civil rights and obligations" do not refer to purely public law actions. Further, the court has, in past decisions, interpreted the words "civil rights" to possess the characteristics of autonomy, *i.e.* independent of the category the Member State gives to those specific words.

The question is not whether the trial itself is based upon private or public issues, nor whether the action is based in administrative or "civil" law, but whether the aggrieved individual's claim was based upon a private, civil right which he could have asserted against anyone; the identity of the defendent being irrelevant under Article 6(1). It matters not that the applicant is proceeding against the state. The question is, was the applicant's original claim based on a breach of a private civil right[1] or was it based upon purely public law. If the latter then Article 6(1) will not apply. For example, the payment of income tax is within the sole territory of the national authorities and hence a public law issue. If, however, there is an agreement between the state and an individual which permits that person to pay an amount outstanding by, for instance, monthly instalments, then that contract is a private issue which would come within Article 6(1). There is a two stage process involved:

(1) What was the factual basis upon which the aggrieved party found himself in? If it involved any civil claim, private in nature, which he had as an individual, then it falls within the phrase "civil rights and obligations".

(2) Did he receive a fair trial in determination of that right?

The word "determination" refers to the legal adjudication of the dispute, not necessarily the forum by which that decision was reached. Thus in *Ringeisen v. Austria (No. 1)*,[2] the court stated that "The character of the legislation which governs how the matter is to be determined (civil, commercial, administrative law, etc.), and that of the authority which is invested with jurisdiction in the matter (ordinary court, administrative body, etc.), are therefore of little consequence". In *Fayed v. U.K.*,[3] Government Inspectors investigated and published a report on the business affairs of the applicants and found that they had misrepresented and lied about their personal backgrounds; thus damaging the applicants civil right to a good reputation. The court decided that the Government inquiry did not adjudicate or "determine" any dispute; its purpose was purely investigative and therefore did not fall within the boundaries of Article 6(1).

A fair hearing

As has been written on numerous occasions, what would be the point of **3–172**
having all those efficient safeguards enunciated in Article 5 for arrest and detention, if at the end of the day there was no effective protection for the individual when the case eventually comes to trial? In the interests of justice, every person has the right to a fair hearing, including the right to:

(i) be present;

(ii) have balanced procedures ("equality of arms");

(iii) an impartial and independent tribunal;

(iv) access to the court;

(v) be heard within a reasonable time;

(vi) permitted to examine and cross-examine witnesses.

The different procedural systems for judicial hearings in various Contracting States make the issue of "fairness" extremely difficult to evaluate. Because of this, it would be almost impossible to state with any degree of exactness within the confines of an particular Article the detailed concept of a fair hearing, although some generalities such as independent, impartial, open justice, etc. are included. As against this, it was stated in *Colozza v. Italy*[4] that:

> ". . . the Contracting States enjoy a wide discretion as regards the choice of the means calculated to ensure that their legal systems are in compliance with the requirements of Article 6(1) in this field. The court's task is not to indicate those means to the States, but to determine whether the result called for by the Convention has been achieved".[5]

Criminal charge

3–173 Article 6(1) covers both civil and criminal hearings whilst Article 6(2) and (3) concerns solely those persons charged with a criminal offence. In Article 6(1), the "determination" of any criminal charge does not necessarily end with the actual trial itself; it may only become final when the decision itself, if appealed, has gone through all the appeal procedures. The appellant then is entitled to the same "fair hearing" at all the appropriate stages of appeal where it will eventually end up either in being allowed or rejected.[6] It is not always easy to classify an offence as "criminal". Different contracting countries may designate some offences as criminal whilst others either do not give the title "criminal" to the activity or determine that such behaviour is not criminal at all. Certain proceedings therefore do not come within Article 6. For instance, "disciplinary action" alone against an individual does not constitute the required relevancy under Article 6, unless it can also be brought under another Article or the punishment is designated to be criminal under the Convention. There is always the risk of a Contracting State designating an offence disciplinary and not criminal, which may have the consequences of Article 6 being attempted to be circumvented. However, the court will not necessarily hold the offence to be disciplinary if it leads to results incompatible with the object and purpose of the Convention.[7] On the other hand, if the respondent state determines that the offence is criminal, then it will certainly come within Article 6.

In *Engel v. The Netherlands (No. 1)*[8] the applicants were all conscripted soldiers who had been punished for various offences arising out of their duty in the armed forces. The applicants complained to the Commission that, *inter alia*, the proceedings before the military authorities and the Supreme Military Court were in contravention of Article 6. One of the main questions for the court was whether the penalties suffered by the applicants were purely part of the disciplinary proceedings or due to a criminal offence, or a mixture of both. In unravelling the dilemma as to whether the charge was in fact criminal, the court considered the following:

(1) It is first necessary to know whether the provision(s) defining the offence charged belong, according to the legal system of the respondent state, to criminal law, disciplinary law or both concurrently.

(2) The very nature of the offence—a factor of greater import.

(3) The degree of severity of the penalty which the person concerned risks occurring.[9]

Since the applicants were under the control of the army, they were subject to certain disciplinary measures, rather than criminal. The court said that:

> "In a society subscribing to the rule of law, there belong to the 'criminal' sphere deprivations of liberty liable to be imposed as a punishment, except those which by their nature, duration or manner of execution cannot be appreciably detrimental".[10]

The first and second applicants were under "light" arrest (confined when off-duty to their barracks). The first applicant also served two days imprisonment. Although this was a deprivation of liberty, the court considered this period to be "too short a duration to belong to the criminal law" in all the circumstances.[11]

In *Campbell and Fell v. United Kingdom*[12] the two applicants were convicted of various offences and sentenced to 10 and 12 years respectively. During a violent protest at the prison the applicants were found guilty by the Prison Board of Visitors of disciplinary offences under the Prison Rules 1964. The first applicant was denied legal representation at the hearing. For this incident and other disciplinary offences, he lost a total of 720 days remission and privileges. He was released in 1982 after having served eight years and eight months of his 10 year sentence. He complained to the Commission that, *inter alia*, the disciplinary charges against him were in reality criminal charges and that he had been convicted by the Board Visitors in the absence of a proper hearing under Article 6. Under domestic law, the offence was under Prison Rule 47, a disciplinary offence and "designed and pursued with the limited objective of maintaining order within the confines of the prison".[13] But by no means does that settle the matter. Next, the nature of the offence in this instance was one of assaulting a prison officer, this being a crime of assault occasioning actual bodily harm, which is a serious offence in ordinary domestic criminal law. But even if not wholly criminal, it could, the court said, be subjected to both criminal and disciplinary proceedings, which although not conclusive gives them "a certain colouring which does not entirely coincide with that of a purely disciplinary matter".[14] With regard to the severity of the penalty, it was within the Board's power to take away his remission and privileges. Despite the fact that the applicant did not receive an extension to his actual prison sentence, the court examined the remission aspect of his case and stated that the two years he lost were sufficiently serious to constitute the offence for the purposes of Article 6 as "criminal". Combining this with the serious assault offence laid against him, the offences were to be classified as criminal and therefore within Article 6.

Apart from disciplinary sanctions, there are in existence other legal **3–174** actions which may or may constitute a "criminal offence" under the Convention. For instance, does contempt of court or imposed fines come within Article 6, if not specifically designated a criminal offence within a Contracting State? In *Putz v. Austria*,[15] the applicant disrupted court proceedings by calling into question the fairness of the trial, and by insulting the trial judge. He was fined. However, since the penalty was not imposed under the respondent's state Criminal Code, nor entered as part of a criminal record, the court declared that this tended to show that the fine was not considered as a criminal penalty under Austrian law. Fines for such disruptive behaviour were considered to be more of a disciplinary measure rather than a criminal offence. At the Commission stage, they were of the opinion that the "severity" of the penalty, in terms of the amount, constituted the offence being classified as "criminal". However, the court said that since:

(i) the fines are not entered in the criminal record;

(ii) if failure to pay resulted in a prison sentence, an appeal was available; and

(iii) in any event, the maximum term in prison was 10 days, thus what "was at stake for the applicant was not sufficiently important to warrant classifying the offences as criminal".[16]

Therefore, Article 6 did not apply.

Once the offence has been classified as criminal then Article 6(1) will only apply in this instance from the time the suspect has been charged. What is meant by the word "charge"? This has been defined as "the official notification given to an individual by the competent authority of an allegation that he has committed a criminal offence"; a definition that also corresponds to the test whether "the situation of the [suspect] has been substantially affected".[17] Although it is relevant what meaning the particular Member State gives to the word "charge", it is not decisive; ultimately it is subject to re-evaluation by the Commission and Court.[18] In *Deweer v. Belgium*,[19] the court said that "charge" is to be given "a substantial rather than a formal conception. The Court is compelled to look behind the appearances and investigate the realities of the procedure in question".[20]

Equality of arms

3–175 The words "equality of arms" import the proposition that for a fair trial to exist, one party must not be put at such an advantage that the "scales of justice" are tilted in his favour, *e.g.* the prosecution being allowed to present evidence in the absence of the defendant or legal counsel.[21] In other words, there must exist parity or at least a "level playing field". However, lack of "equality of arms" alone may not necessarily constitute a breach of Article 6(1); it is but one factor to take into consideration, along with other matters which prevent a fair hearing from taking place. There is a definite overlap here between the equality of arms, and the independence and impartiality factors involved in conducting a fair trial[22] The principle behind "equality of arms" was stated in *Dombo Beheer B.V. v. The Netherlands*,[23] to be that the words imply "that each party must be afforded a reasonable opportunity to present his case—including his evidence—under conditions that do not place him at a substantial disadvantage *vis-à-vis* his opponent".[24] This case involved a civil dispute between the applicant, who was a managing director of a company, and a bank, whereby the applicant claimed that the bank orally agreed to increase the company's financial credit limit. Under Dutch law at that time, a person who was party to the proceedings was not permitted to give evidence in those proceedings. However, the bank manager in question was allowed to testify. The applicant complained to the Commission that the domestic courts were in breach of the "equality of arms" principle and therefore in violation of Article 6(1). The court stated that the primary purpose was to decide only on whether the whole proceedings were "fair", not to examine the domestic law. They held that since the director and branch manager were the only two persons present when the alleged oral agreement was made, it could not be considered a "fair balance" to hear only the bank manager; thereby resulting in the company being put at a substantial disadvantage towards the bank.[25] Therefore, there was a breach of Article 6.

Reasonable time

Under Article 6(1), a person must be brought before a tribunal within a **3–176** reasonable time. The explanation for introducing "reasonableness" is that the person should not have to wait for a longer period than necessary before the commencement of the hearing, so as not to suffer the stress and apprehension and in some cases public humiliation often associated with court proceedings. Article 6 is designed to avoid the situation of defendants remaining too long in a state of uncertainty about their fate. Its aim is to protect them against excessive procedural delays; especially in criminal matters.[26] Whether the length of the proceedings are themselves reasonable is to be determined according to the particular circumstances of each case, taking into account such factors as the complexity of the issues involved,[27] as well as how all parties conducted themselves during this period. Time begins to run from the accused being charged.[28] The "reasonable time" issue also relates to the period between lodging an appeal and the decision of an appeal.[29] In *Zimmermann and Steiner v. Switzerland*,[30] the appeal judgment was given some three years six months from the date of application. The court in that case said on the question of reasonableness that they have to consider all the circumstances including;

(i) the complexity of the factual or legal issues raised in the case;

(ii) the conduct of the applicants;

(iii) the conduct of the competent authorities and

(iv) what was at stake for the applicant.[31]

In (i), the case was straightforward and uncomplicated. In (ii), no fault lay with the applicants; indeed, they wrote to voice their concern about the lack of progress of the appeal. In (iii) the court found total inactivity and stagnation on behalf of the Federal Court.[32] The Government argued that unusual increases in the workload of the Federal Court contributed to the delay. The court however, found that the measures taken to alleviate that particular problem were unsatisfactory and insufficient. Accordingly, there was a breach of Article 6(1). Of course, if the applicant himself is responsible for any unreasonable delay, then the court will take this into account when deciding whether or not a violation occurred.

Impartial tribunal

3–177 The common thread throughout Article 6 in respect of a "fair hearing" is that the proceedings must be guaranteed to be impartial. The defendant must not be allowed to suffer the dangers of bias of a tribunal such that it prejudices a fair trial, and that includes the conduct, organisation and composition of the court itself. For instance, the court may be made up of judges who have also acted for the prosecution at the investigation stage, and thus may not be impartial. In *De Cubber v. Belgium*,[33] the investigating judge and the trial judge were the same person and the question was whether, by an objective test, the accused could still obtain an impartial hearing. The court considered that (i) the investigating judge was under the auspices of the state prosecutor, although the former's task was both to gather evidence against the accused and also to find proof in favour of the accused (ii) the court also considered the degree of involvement by the judge in the case—the more involvement, the more likely the bias, although perhaps unwittingly. In this case, the judge had ordered the applicant's arrest and interviewed him on several occasions regarding the relevant criminal offences. The court considered that, prior to any trial the judge would have made extensive enquiries such that he would have acquired much more knowledge than any other judge coming to the case for the first time. There was a real danger that the accused might thus suspect that the judge had already formed an opinion as to his guilt[34] and therefore constitute a form of "judge in his own cause". The court decided that "his (the judge's) presence on the bench provided grounds for some legitimate misgivings, on the applicant's part".[35] The test of impartiality is both a subjective and an objective one, taking into consideration all the circumstances of the particular case. This is not necessarily restricted directly to the proceedings themselves but may also include statements made by the judiciary outside of the court. For example in *Hoekstra v. HM Advocate*[35a] a judge, shortly after hearing an appeal, published an article in a national newspaper giving a critical and negative opinion of the ECHR. The HCJ (High Court of Justiciary) said that such an article "would create in the mind of an informed observer an apprehension of bias on the part of the author against the Convention. . .". The ECHR further stated that such criticism could not be seen as impartial when the author's duties as a judge involve applying that particular branch of the law. Accordingly, a fresh appeal was granted, to be heard in front of three different judges.

Is there a right of access to the court?

Does Article 6(1) relate solely to the conduct and restrictions of court proceedings or may it be inferred that there is an inherent right for all persons to have their "day in court"? In *Golder v. United Kingdom*,[36] during a prison disturbance, a prison officer who had been assaulted, suggested that the applicant, a prisoner, was one of those who attacked him. The prison officer later retracted this statement. Nevertheless, details of the incident were entered into the applicant's record. The applicant petitioned the Home Secretary to consult with a solicitor regarding a possible libel action against the prison officer, but was refused. By prohibiting the applicant this request, the Home Secretary was in reality preventing the applicant from properly pursuing his intended legal libel action. The applicant complained to the Commission on the basis of that refusal. The court considered that there were two questions to be answered. **3–178**

(1) Is access to the court limited to cases which are pending, or does it extend to commencing an action in order to have the applicant's civil rights and obligations determined?
(2) If yes to the second part, are there any implied limitations to the right of access?

The court declared as to (1) above, that by prohibiting communication with a solicitor, this amounted to preventing the instigating of a legal action against the prison officer. They said that "the principle whereby a civil claim must be capable of being submitted to a judge ranks as one of the universally 'recognised' fundamental principles of law".[37] Although in (2) above, there are limitations to the inherent right of access, *e.g.* mentally ill patients,[38] minors, frivolous claims, etc., the court found that such restrictions did not apply in this case. It was not up to the Home Secretary to assess the possible libel action, that was up to the court itself. In refusing the applicant's request and denying his "right", the Home Secretary was in breach of Article 6(1).[39] In a dissenting judgement, Judge Zekia stated that the opening words of Article 6(1), *i.e.* "in the determination of his civil right and obligations or of any criminal charge against him, deal exclusively with the conduct of proceedings . . .". Article 6(1) deals only with court proceedings already instituted before a court and not with a right of access to the court.[40] In other words, Article 6(1) is directed at the incidents and attributes of a just and fair trial only. If the Convention meant otherwise, he said, it would have expressly stated "access to the courts".

An individual merely having the right to attend a court without having legal representation present may in certain cases, still constitute a breach of Article 6(1). The question for the court will be, could the defendant present his case "properly and satisfactorily".[41] In *Airey v. Ireland*,[42] the applicant attempted to secure a judicial separation from her husband.[43] She had suffered physical and mental cruelty during her marriage. At that time, legal aid was not available for this particular type of action and she complained to the Commission that, *inter alia*, she was denied access to a court, since under the circumstances, she could not afford the legal costs involved. The Commission, unanimously, were of the opinion that there was a violation of Article 6(1). Although the Government argued that she was permitted to present her own case at the High Court without legal counsel, the court found that due to the legal complexities of this type of action, *e.g.* expert evidence, witnesses, points of law, and the inherent problems of presenting such a case, it was most improbable that a lay person could conduct such a trial, and effectively receive a fair hearing. Thus, the court concluded that she was denied the effective right of access. This right had to be neither theoretical nor illusory but practical and effective.[44] The Government argued that if found in breach they would be under a duty to provide legal aid for all cases determining a civil right. The court disagreed. They stated, *inter alia*, that in civil actions; "Article 6(1) may sometimes compel the State to provide for the assistance of a lawyer when such assistance proves indispensable for an effective access to court . . ."[45] It all depends on the particular circumstances of the case. Notwithstanding this, appearing before a High Court without legal counsel, may suffice, where, for instance, the issues are fairly uncomplicated and do not involve lengthy and intricate examination of evidence, witnesses, etc.

Article 6(2) Presumption of Innocence

3–179 Under Article 6(2), the presumption of innocence lies with the accused. It is for the prosecution to prove their case. In *Murray (John) v. United Kingdom*,[46] the applicant was arrested under section 14 of the Prevention of Terrorism Act 1989 in Northern Ireland for terrorist offences relating to the unlawful imprisonment in a house of an alleged IRA informer. He was given the appropriate arrest caution, which included the possible consequences of adverse inferences being drawn against him by the court should he refuse to answer any questions, under Article 3 of the Criminal Evidence (Northern Ireland) Order 1988.[47] Throughout his entire detention period, he chose not to say anything, and in particular refused to make any statements as to the reasons why he was at the particular house when the police arrived. He was also denied access to a solicitor for 48 hours. At his trial, he refused to give evidence and was eventually found guilty of aiding and abetting the unlawful imprisonment of a person and sentenced to eight years imprisonment. He complained to the Commission that, *inter alia*, (i) under Article 6(1) and 6(2) he was denied his right to silence as well as the right not to incriminate himself and (ii) under Article 6(3)(c), he was refused access to legal advice entitled to him whilst in custody, under section 15 of the Northern Ireland (Emergency Provisions) Act 1987.[48] The applicant argued that he had an inherent right not to answer questions during police interviews, nor to give evidence at trial, and accordingly, the judge was not entitled to draw any adverse inferences from his silence. To do otherwise, he maintained,

> "amounted to subverting the presumption of innocence and the onus of proof resulting from that presumption: it is for the prosecution to prove the accused's guilt without any assistance from the latter being required".[49]

The Government argued that the right of silence and refusal to testify had not been taken away but merely permitted the judge to make inferences from the accused's silence once the following state of affairs had been affirmed[50];

(a) The prosecution must have first established, at least, a prima facie case;

(b) The accused must have failed to give a plausible innocent explanation for his silence when questioned; and

(c) The accused must be informed of the consequences of maintaining his silence.

As a result of the above, the judge is entitled to take an ordinary common sense approach when deciding what inferences, if any, are to be drawn from the accused's silence. The court's principal task in this instance was to consider whether the applicant received a fair hearing or not. The court refused to accept that the right of silence was absolute. There may be certain circumstances where an explanation is called for by the accused, and if none is forthcoming, the court may take into account that silence in assessing the persuasiveness of the evidence adduced by the prosecution.[51] They stated that whether the drawing of adverse inferences from the accused's silence infringed Article 6 depended on all:

> ". . . the circumstances of the case having particular regard to the situation where inferences may be drawn, the weight attached to them by the national courts in their assessment of the evidence and the degree of compulsion inherent in the situation".[52]

There was no compulsion in this case on the accused to speak,[53] *i.e.* the accused was not coerced or oppressed by the investigating authorities in some way, so that he involuntarily gave up the right of silence and incriminated himself. However, in this case the court found on the facts that a very strong case against the accused had been established. Since the accused offered no innocent explanation at all, and in the light of very strong evidence against him and all the surrounding circumstances, the drawing of inferences was a matter of common sense which could not be regarded as "unfair or unreasonable".[54] Therefore, Article 6(1) and 6(2) had not been breached.

As part of a fair hearing under Article 6(1), and the presumption of innocence under Article 6(2), the applicant has the right not to be legally compelled into making statements or handing over documents which may be self-incriminating. In *Funke v. France*,[55] the applicant was asked to pass over his bank statements from accounts held abroad and other foreign business documents to customs officials and was informed that if he did not produce them, he would be fined or possibly imprisoned.[56] He refused and was fined. The court said that "the special features of customs law cannot justify such an infringement of the right of anyone "charged with a criminal offence", within the autonomous meaning of this expression in Article 6, to remain silent and not to contribute to incriminating himself".[57] Thus, there had been a violation of Article 6(1). This case concerned an investigation at the pre-trial stage. The applicant was not subsequently charged with any offencc relating to the possible illegal activities in the undisclosed documents.

The question then is, is the position the same where the accused is compelled to make statements and those statements are ultimately used by the prosecution as evidence against the accused at his trial? In a much publicised case, *Saunders v. United Kingdom*,[58] the Department of Trade and Industry were investigating the misconduct of a company (Guinness plc) which they alleged, were falsely inflating the price of their shares as part of a successful takeover of another company (Distillers plc). During a number of interviews with the applicant (the chief executive of Guinness), he made certain involuntary statements which he was legally compelled to do; refusal would have constituted contempt of court under the Company's Act 1985. In the subsequent trial for various fraud offences, these statements were used by the prosecution as evidence of the applicant's guilt. The applicant complained to the Commission that being legally compelled to make statements which may incriminate himself if used at trial, amounted to an unfair hearing under Article 6(1). Once it was conceded that the statements were made under legal compulsion, the issue for the court was whether such statements could be used by the prosecution at the applicant's trial, and if so, whether this constituted an unfair hearing. The court said that the statements themselves did not have to be incriminating, it was enough if they were used in such a way as to question the innocence of the applicant. Since the involuntary statements made by the applicant at the interviews were a major part of the prosecution case, and were put before the jury as evidence of his guilt, that infringed the applicant's right not to incriminate himself. Therefore, there was a violation of Article 6(1). Lest it be thought that this decision means that all legally compelled evidence", *e.g.* fingerprints, blood, breath, urine samples, etc., taken from a suspect is now inadmissible in a court of law, the court quashed this notion by emphasising that it was the interference with the accused's "will" not to incriminate himself in criminal proceedings which must be respected, and this did not extend to the "physical" legal taking of incriminating evidence, or any other legally obtained relevant material.

Article 6(3)(A) Right to be Informed of the Accusations Against him

Under this particular paragraph every person must be aware of the charges laid against him as part of the "fair hearing" process. In *Colozza v. Italy*[59] the applicant had been found guilty of fraud charges, in absentia, and sentenced to five years imprisonment. He had been declared untraceable by the court. When eventually arrested, he complained to the Commission of a violation of Article 6(3)(a) on the grounds that he was not "latitante", *i.e.* wilfully evading the execution of a warrant issued by a court.[60] He was unaware of the charges against him. The court held that the procedures instigated to trace him were inadequate. (He had, in the meantime, been traced by the Rome police to his new address for other criminal offences). The court was not satisfied that the efforts made by the authorities were conducted expeditiously and with all due diligence. Therefore, there had been a breach of Article 6(1). **3–180**

Article 6(3)(C) Right to be Present and Right to Legal Assistance

Generally, in criminal cases, the accused should be present at his own appeal hearing. However, there may be other circumstances existing which override that right such that the absence of the appellee will not automatically constitute a breach of Article 6(1). In *Monnell and Morris v. United Kingdom*,[61] the Court of Appeal considered that the applicant's appeal against conviction and sentence was so unmeritorious and futile that the court refused to deduct the time spent in detention awaiting the verdict.[62] The applicants complained to the Commission that inter alia, the procedures adopted by the Court of Appeal were not in accordance with Article 6(3)(c). They argued that they should have been present at the appeal hearing. The court, on the issue of whether fairness had been met, said that: **3–181**

> ". . . it is necessary to consider matters such as the nature of the leave-to-appeal procedure and its significance in the context of the criminal proceedings as a whole, the scope of the powers of the Court of Appeal and the manner in which the two applicants' interests were actually presented and protected before the Court of Appeal".[63]

The court, when evaluating whether the applicants presence were required to argue their case against "loss of time" under section 29(1)

Criminal Appeal Act 1968, so as to constitute fairness, found that the following procedural factors to have existed:

(1) The "equality of arms" factor was present, in that neither side was physically represented at the Court of Appeal stage.[64]

(2) The applicants were aware of the "loss of time" possibility which was printed in the Form AA, "Advice on appeal".[65] They had previously been advised by counsel of the hopelessness of any prospect of success. Nevertheless, after being refused leave to appeal by a single judge, they continued their appeal.[66]

(3) All relevant documents, the transcript of the trial, social enquiry and psychiatric reports were in the hands of the appeal judges. Notwithstanding this, the applicants still had the right to instruct counsel to appear on their behalf.[67]

(4) Under Article 6(3)(c), the applicants were guaranteed the right to legal aid but "only so far as the interests of justice so required". The court said that:

> ". . . the interests of justice cannot, however, be taken to require an automatic grant of legal aid whenever a convicted person, with no objective likelihood of success, wishes to appeal after having received a fair trial at first instance in accordance with Article 6".[68]

Thus, the interest of justice and fairness, could, in the circumstances, be met by the applicants being able to present relevant considerations through making written submissions".[69] Accordingly, the court found that the procedures for a fair hearing had been followed and therefore there had been no violation of Article 6(1) or (3)(c).

A vital part of the process of a fair hearing is the availability of legal assistance to the accused. Although it is expressly stated within Article 6(3)(c) that the accused has the right to legal advice for defence purposes and only then when he has been charged, it is recognised that this right extends to the pre-trial stages also. The question then becomes, does this right have its limitations, or must a request for legal assistance be always granted? The answer is, it depends on all the circumstances of the individual case. Due to the "dilution" of the right of silence in some Contracting States, it is of the utmost importance that legal advice should be made available to the suspect at the earliest stages of his arrest and detention. This is so because of the adverse inferences which may be drawn at trial on the accused's silence during police questioning. In *Murray (John) v. United Kingdom*,[70] the accused was denied immediate legal representation and had to wait 48 hours before being granted access to a solicitor. The Government argued that it would not have made any difference if access had been granted; he would still have refused to answer police questions and thus the accused did not suffer any prejudice so as to make the trial unfair under Article 6(1). The court said that despite the police having the appropriate reasonable grounds for denying the accused legal advice (fear of interference with evidence or information which could be relevant to terrorist offences), "it is of paramount importance for the rights of the defence that an accused has access to a lawyer at the initial stages of police interrogation".[71] There may, however, be influential factors which may override this right, "including the nature, duration and effect of any restriction, to determine whether, in the context of the proceedings as a whole, an accused has been deprived of a fair hearing".[72] In this case, because of the probable prejudicial effects to the accused at trial, due to his remaining silent throughout, he should have been entitled to legal advice at the initial stages of the police interviews. As a result there was a violation of Article 6(3)(c). The ramifications of this decision seem to be that, apart from the narrow restrictions, all suspects are now entitled to immediate legal assistance, if so requested.

Merely a Contracting State appointing legal assistance to an accused is not enough, it must be such that it is of "practical and effective" benefit.[73] If the domestic court finds that the appointed counsel is not conducting the defence adequately or worse, negligently, and they are aware of this, then they are under an obligation under Article 6(3)(c) to rectify this situation. In *Kamasinki v. Austria*,[74] the applicant, who was American, was charged with fraud offences in Austria. Since he could not understand the German language he requested an interpreter and legal representation. He was eventually convicted. Amongst the many complaints to the Commission by the applicant was the lack of effective legal representation throughout the course of his detention and trial. He alleged violations including Article 6(1) and Article 6(3)(c) on the basis of not properly being defended by the appointed lawyer, and in particular was unhappy with the lawyer's preparation of his defence, including not having the opportunity to inspect all relevant documents. However, the court found on the facts that the applicant had been properly legally represented prior to and at trial, and that it was enough that the accused's defence counsel inspected the documents in question. Therefore there was no breach of Article 6(3)(c).

Article 6(3)(D) Examining Witnesses

As a general rule, in Article 6, all court proceedings must be held in public **3–182**
and held under "adversarial" conditions.[75] A fair hearing includes the right for the defendant to examine and cross-examine witnesses,[76] and this includes being able to see those witnesses. However, this is not always the case. In certain instances, due to the danger of witnesses being intimidated by the accused, the judge has a discretionary power to "screen" witnesses, *i.e.* to prevent the defendant from seeing the witness, whether by use of a physical barrier, such as a screen around the witness box or by use of a video link whereby the witness gives evidence from a separate room. This normally occurs during trials of serious assault, blackmail, where children

are witnesses, custody cases and especially terrorist offences, where there is a reluctance for prosecution witnesses to come forward for fear of reprisals. In *X v. United Kingdom*,[77] the applicant was convicted of terrorist offences. At his trial, the judge permitted certain witnesses to be screened. The applicant himself could not observe his accusers and he complained to the Commission on that basis. The Commission, reiterating past authorities, said that:

> ". . . in principle, all evidence must be adduced in the presence of the accused at a public hearing with a view to adversarial argument, but this does not mean that a statement from a witness must always be made in court and in public if it is to be admitted in evidence".

Indeed, the evidence from these witnesses did not prejudice the applicant in any way. Further, these witnesses could be cross-examined even though their names were not known to the applicant. The Commission found that screening was "in the interest of public order or national security and to the extent strictly necessary in the opinion of the court in special circumstances where publicity would prejudice the interest of justice". Accordingly, they found that the applicant's rights had not been interfered with under Article 6(1) or 6(3)(d).

Article 6(3)(E) Right to Interpreter

3–183 In *Kamasinki v. Austria* (for facts, see above) the applicant complained that because of the language problem, he was not given proper interpretation of oral statements nor translations of relevant written documents under Article 6(3)(e). The court said "the interpretative assistance provided should be such as to enable the defendant to understand the case against him and to defend himself, notably by being able to put before the court his version of the events".[78] Thus, it is not every written statement or document which ought to be translated. However, in order that a fair trial ensues, the accused is entitled to, at least, a written translation in his own language of the indictment against him and any other relevant documents which enable him to advance a proper defence.[79]

Article 7: The Principle of Non-Retroactivity in Criminal Trials

3–184

> 1 No one shall be held guilty of any criminal offence on account of any act or omission which did not constitute a criminal offence under national or international law at the time when it was committed. Nor shall a heavier penalty be imposed than the one that was applicable at the time the criminal offence was committed.
>
> 2 This Article shall not prejudice the trial and punishment of any person for any act or omission which, at the time when it was

committed, was criminal according to the general principles of law recognised by civilised nations.

It is one of the basic principles of criminal law that a person should not be punished for an act which did not constitute a crime at the time when it was committed. A person cannot regulate his behaviour in order to avoid breaking the criminal law if the law may be retroactively changed. But from time to time there is a criminal case which appears to breach this principle of nonretroactivity. In *Shaw v. DPP*,[80] the defendant was convicted of a common law offence which does not appear to have existed prior to that case itself; thus at the time there was a potential breach of Article 7, but of course in subsequent cases there would be no such problem. Again, in the case of *R. v. R*,[81] there was a similar problem: the defendant was convicted of rape of his wife, and in a landmark decision the House of Lords upheld his conviction on the basis that the previous common law rule that a woman could not refuse to consent to sex with her husband[82] was anachronistic and wrong. However, at the time when the defendant had carried out the conduct in question, courts were still holding that a husband could not be convicted of rape of his wife. Nevertheless, up until that time, the immunity against rape within marriage was being steadily eroded through domestic legal decisions during the previous 50 years.

In *SW v. United Kingdom*,[83] the applicant, having been informed by his wife that the marriage was over, ejected her from the home. After police were called, she returned. Later that evening she was raped by the applicant. He was eventually convicted of rape and assault. He argued before the Commission that since there was no offence of marital rape in English law, no law had been broken and therefore the Court of Appeal wrongly considered itself to be bound by the decision in *R. v. R* and that such a law was made retrospectively which directly contravened the whole purpose of Article 7. The Commission recognised that, in a number of cases the immunity in this area had been somewhat diluted over the years[84] and there was reason to believe that further "inroads on the immunity was probable". Apart from this, they considered the "progressive development" of equal rights for women generally within marriage, and hence, due to the above, the offence of rape within marriage was reasonably foreseeable in the circumstances. The Court stated that a law prohibiting particular behaviour must exist before a prosecution can be brought for that specific crime. However, although the law must be clearly defined, it need not necessarily take into account all variations and situations, such that it allows the defendant a defence by arguing that since a law is not exact in these circumstances, no crime has been committed. In this case it was stated that:

> "Article 7 of the Convention cannot be read as outlawing the gradual clarification of the rules of criminal liability through judicial interpretation from case to case provided that the resultant development is consistent with the essence of the offence and would reasonably be foreseen".[85]

The court agreed with the Court of Appeal and the House of Lords that their decision did "no more than continue a perceptible line of case law development dismantling the immunity of a husband from prosecution for rape upon his wife"[86] and in general was in accordance with the object and purpose of the Convention, namely "respect for human dignity and human freedom". Hence, there was no violation of Article 7.

The second part of Article 7 allows the trial of persons whose conduct, viewed objectively, ought to be criminal, but may not be so viewed by the law of his home state. For example, War Crimes Tribunals could not exist if they were forced to apply the law of the state in which the crimes were committed; domestic law must sometimes be subjected to international law in order to uphold the common good.

A recent conflict between public interest human rights has arisen in relation to double jeopardy. The proposals founded by the Government in the Queen's Speech in Parliament in 2001, potentially violate the principle against retroactivity. Further, although the United Kingdom has not ratified Protocol 7 of the ECHR which contains the double jeopardy ban, cases do treat the *autrefois acquit* and convict rules as part of the right to a fair hearing under Article 6(1). Therefore it is possible should the acquitted in the Stephen Lawrence case be retried under a new law they could argue that any fresh trial would be an unfair one.[87]

BRIEF OUTLINE AND GERMANE CASES

Offences Against the Police

3–185 *Police Act 1996, s.89(1): It is an Offence to Assault A Constable in the Execution of his Duty.
Definition: *Waterfield* [1964]; *Donnelly v. Jackman* [1970]; *Mepstead v. DPP*[1996].
Defences: self defence/prevention of crime; mistaken belief in self defence—*Williams (Gladstone)* [1987]; mistaken belief that constable is exceeding his powers—*Fennell* [1971].

*Police Act 1996 s.89(2): It is an Offence to Resist or to Wilfully Obstruct A Police Officer in the Execution of his Duty
Definition: resisting—*Sherriff* [1969]; obstruction—*Rice v. Connolly* [1966], *Hinchcliffe v. Sheldon* [1955], *Green v. DPP* [1991]; obstruction must be wilful—*Wilmott v. Atack* [1977], *Lewis v. Cox* [1985].
Defences: mistaken belief that the victim was not a constable—*Ostler v. Elliot* [1980]; mistaken honest belief in self defence/prevention of crime—*Williams (Gladstone)* [1987].

Stop and Search Powers Prior to Arrest

3–186 *PACE 1984, s.1: power to stop, search and detain any person or vehicle in a public place in order to uncover stolen or prohibited articles or offensive weapons.

Definition: search—s.2(9) PACE, Code A para. 3.1–3.5, Notes for Guidance 3B, ss.2(2),(3),(6) PACE; public place—s.11(1) and 1(4) PACE; prohibited articles—ss.1(7) and 1(8) PACE; offensive weapons—s.1(9) PACE, s.139 CJA 1988; constable must have reasonable grounds for suspicion—Code A para. 1.6, 1.7, Notes for Guidance 1A; *Rice v. Connolly* [1966]; *King v. Gardiner* [1979].
Exceptions: stop and search by consent—Notes for Guidance 1Db, 1E; other statutory stop and search powers (see list in text).

Powers of Arrest Under ss.24 and 25 Pace

*PACE 1984, s.24(4): any person may arrest without warrant a person who **3–187**
is in the act of committing an arrestable offence, or a person whom he has reasonable grounds to suspect to be committing an arrestable offence:
Arrestable offence—*Chapman v. DDP* [1989].
Reasonable grounds for suspicion—*Holgate-Mohammed v. Duke* [1984]; *Castorina v. CC of Surrey* [1988].

*PACE 1984, s.24(5): any person may arrest without warrant a person who has committed an arrestable offence, or a person whom he has reasonable grounds to suspect to be guilty of an arrestable offence which has already been committed. *Self* (*Graham*) [1992].

*PACE 1984, s.24(6): a constable may arrest without warrant any person whom he has reasonable grounds to suspect has committed or is committing an arrestable offence. Under the CJPA 2001 kerb crawling and failure to stop and report an accident involving injuries are now arrestable offences.

*PACE 1984, s.24(7): a constable may arrest without warrant any person who is about to commit an arrestable offence or whom he has reasonable grounds to suspect is about to commit an arrestable offence.

*PACE 1984, s.25: a constable may arrest without warrant any person where any offence has been committed or attempted, or is being committed or attempted, and it appears to him that service or a warrant is impracticable or inappropriate because any of the general arrest conditions are satisfied.
Nicholas v. Parsonage [1987].

*PACE 1984, s.28: an arrest is unlawful unless the arrestee if informed that he is under arrest as soon as practicable after his arrest, and informed of the ground for the arrest at the time of the arrest or as soon as is practicable.
DPP v. Hawkins [1988]; *Edwards v. DPP* [1993].
Exceptions:

power of arrest at common law for actual or anticipated breach of the peace; arrest by warrant;
powers of arrest under other specific statutes.

ENTRY, SEARCH AND SEIZURE

3–188 *PACE, s.8: entry and search with a warrant.
A search warrant will be available if there are reasonable grounds for belief that:

—serious arrestable offence

—not legal privilege (s.10)

—not excluded material (s.11)

—not special procedure (s.14)

—condition from s.8(3) applies.

ex p. Primlaks [1989].
Safeguards for search warrants: PACE, s.15 and Code B, para. 2
ex p. Switalski [1991]; *ex p. AJD Holdings* [1992].

Procedure for execution of warrants; notice of powers and rights: PACE, s.16 and Code B, para. 5

*PACE s.17: entry and search without a warrant for the purposes of arrest *D'Souza v. DPP* [1992].

*PACE, ss.18 and 32: entry and search without a warrant, following an arrest, where there are reasonable grounds to suspect that evidence may be found. Power to seize articles related to arrestable offence.

*PACE, s.19 and Code B, para. 6: seizure of articles where there are reasonable grounds for belief that the item was;
obtained through the offence;
will be disposed of;
or evidence will be destroyed. Also see sections 50–66 of the Criminal Justice and Police Act 2001.

DETENTION

3–189 *PACE, s.34: limits of detention without charge.

*PACE, ss. 35 and 36: function of custody officer.

*PACE, s.37 and Code C paras. 3, 2: duties of custody officer before charge; custody records; treatment.

R. v. Davison [1988]

*PACE, s.38: duties of custody officer after charge; decision on detention; special risks.

*PACE, s.39: treatment of detained persons in accordance with PACE.

*PACE, s.40: reviews of police detention; authorisation or extension of further detention. See also the (JPA 2001, section 73 (amending s.40 *PACE) for reviews when police officer is absent from station.

*PACE, s.41: time limits of detention without charge.

*PACE, s.42: authorising further detention without charge—serious arrestable offence, authorization from superintendent.

*PACE, ss.43 and 44: warrants of further detention.

*PACE, s.46: detention after charge.

*PACE, s.50: records of detention.
R. v. Canale [1990]
Special categories of detained persons: Code C Paras 3.6–3.14.
Fingerprinting and intimate other samples: PACE ss.60–65.

Searches in Detention

*PACE, s.32: search without consent after arrest outside police station. Requires reasonable grounds for belief that the person is in danger, or has a concealed tool for use in escape. **3–190**

*PACE, s.54 and Code C, para. 4: non-intimate search at police station after arrest. Carried out by same-sex constable. Search for prohibited articles. Power to seize.

*PACE, s.55 and Code C, Annex A: intimate search after arrest. Must be authorised by superintendent. Requires reasonable grounds for belief that either an offensive weapon or drugs may be concealed. If search for drugs, must be carried out by a suitably-qualified person of the same sex at police station.
*Code C, Annex A para. 9: strip search after arrest. Search for prohibited articles by same-sex constables at police station.

Notification, Communication and Access to Legal Advice

*PACE, s.56 and Code C: right to have one person notified of arrest; but power to delay notification. Right to make telephone call/have access to writing materials; but power to delay or deny communication. **3–191**

*PACE, s.58 and Code C, para. 6: right of access to legal advice. Right to consult solicitor free of charge at any time if held in custody. But power to delay access. Legal advice during interviews and effect of breach:
R. v. Samuel [1988]; *R. v. Alladice* [1988]; *R. v. Dunford* [1990]; *R. v. Walsh* [1989]; *R. v. Parris* [1988].

Admissibility of Confessions and Other Evidence in Court

3–192 *PACE, s.76: a confession made by a suspect may only be given in evidence against him where it is relevant and is not excluded. Confessions are excluded if they are the result of either:

—oppression s.76(2)(a), s.76(8): *R. v. Paris, Abdullahi, Miller* [1993]; *R. v. Fulling* [1987] or;

—conduct likely to render confession unreliable s.76(2)(b): *R. v. Chung* [1991].

*PACE, s.78: a court has discretion to exclude evidence where its admission would have an adverse effect upon the fairness of the proceedings. Usually due to breach of Codes.
R. v. Christou and Wright [1992], *R. v. Bryce* [1995], *R. v. Mason* [1988], *R. v. Bailey and Smith* [1993]; *Khan v. U.K.* [2000]

*PACE, s.82(3): common law jurisdiction to exclude evidence still exists where necessary to do so in order to ensure a fair trial.

Police Interviews

3–193 Tape recording: Code of Practice E. See s.76 of the CPJA 2001.
What is an interview? Code C, para. 11; *R. v. Weekes* [1992].
Breach of code and exclusion under s.78: *R. v. Absolam* [1988]; *R. v. Okafor* [1994] 3 All E.R. 741.
General interviewing rules: Code C, paras 11 and 12.
R. v. Cox [1992].

Right of Silence

3–194 *CJPOA 1994 s.34: drawing of inferences from silence where accused, when questioned before charge, failed to mention any fact which he later relied upon in his defence.
Code C, para. 11, para. 16; *R. v. Pointer* [1997]; *R. v. Bowers* [1998]; *R. v. Argent* [1996]; *Condron v. U.K.* [2001]; *Averill v. U.K.* [2000]. See also ss.58 and 59 at the Youth Justice and Criminal Evidence Act 1999.

*CJPOA 1994 s.35: inferences which may be drawn from accused's refusal to give evidence in court

R. v. Cowan [1995]; *R. v. Condron* [1997]

*CJPOA 1994 s.36: inferences which may be drawn from unexplained objects, substances and marks found in the accused's possession or on his property at time of arrest.

Identification of Persons by Police Officers

*PACE Code of Practice D and Annexes A-E **3–195**
Code D, para. 2: notice of identification arrangements.
Code D, para 2.1: where suspect is "known to" police, police can arrange:
identity parade (Code D, para 2.3–2.6, and Annex A); *R. v. Forbes* [2000];
group identification (Code D, para. 2.7, 2.8);
video film (Code D, para. 2.10, 11 and Annex B) or voice identification; *R. v. Hessey* [1998];
confrontation (Code D, para. 13, and Annex C).
Notes for Guidance.
R. v. Hickin [1996]; *R. v. Conway* [1990]; *R. v. Rutherford and Palmer* [1994]; *R. v. Quinn* [1995].

For summary of other ECHR cases see "Brief Outline and Germance Cases" in Chapter 2.

Endnotes

[1] *Rice v. Connolly* [1966] 2 Q.B. 414.
[2] There are statutory exceptions such as those under the Terrorism Act 2000; however the ca of *Lodwick v. Saunders* [1985] 1 All E.R. 577 shows that there are limits even to statuto requirements to co-operate with the police.
[3] Approved in *Fagan v. MPC* [1968] 3 All E.R. 442. Although this book is not the place fo detailed consideration of the offences of assault and battery, it should be noted that recen cases such as *Ireland* (1996) appear to have reduced the requirement for immediacy so that is satisfied if the victim apprehends personal violence at some time not excluding th immediate future. See also *R. v. Constanza* [1997] Crim.L.R. 576.
[4] See *Fagan v. MPC*, *ibid.*; allowing a car to remain upon a policeman's foot is a battery.
[5] Prison Act 1952, s. 8.
[6] *Ludlow v. Burgess* [1971] Crim.L.R. 238.
[7] (1980) 71 Cr.App.R. 221.
[8] [1964] 1 Q.B. 164, [1963] 3 All E.R. 659.
[9] *Ghani v. Jones* [1970] 1 Q.B. 693 at 707, CA; Fitzgerald, "The arrest of a motor car" [196 Crim.L.R. 23; Smith and Hogan *Textbook on Criminal Law* (Butterworths), p. 430–1.
[10] (1980) Cr.App.R. 221.
[11] [1974] R.T.R. 182, [1974] 2 All E.R. 233.
[12] Road Traffic Act 1988, s. 35.
[13] See Lidstone, "A policeman's Duty not to take Liberties" Crim.L.R. 617.
[14] [1966] 2 Q.B. 414.
[15] [1982] Q.B. 1290.
[16] [1992] 4 All E.R. 545.
[17] [1971] Crim.L.R. 238.
[18] See *Bentley v. Brudzinski* [1982] Crim L.R. 825.
[19] [1985] 1 All E.R. 577.
[20] Now Road Traffic Act, 1988, s. 163.
[21] See also *Bentley v. Brudzinski* (1985) 75 Cr.App.R. 217 and *Donnelley v. Jackman* (1970) 5 Cr.App.R. 229.
[22] [1970] 1 W.L.R. 562.
[23] (1996) 160 J.P. 475.
[24] [1984] 3 All E.R. 374.
[25] See *DPP v. Hawkins* [1988] 1 W.L.R. 1166.
[26] (1990) Crim.L.R. 58; See also *Robson v. Hallett* [1967] 2 All E.R. 407.
[27] See *McGowan v. Chief Constable of Kingston upon Hull* [1968] Crim.L.R. 34.
[28] [1981] Crim.L.R. 340.
[29] [1865] 10 Cox C.C. 456.
[30] [1964] Crim.L.R. 456.
[31] [1987] 3 All E.R. 411; see also *Owino* [1995] Crim.L.R. 743.
[32] [1994] 3 All E.R. 380.
[33] [1987] 3 All E.R. 411.
[34] For an analysis see *Forbes* [1865] 10 Cox C.C. 456.
[35] As in *Albert v. Lavin* [1981] 3 W.L.R. 955.
[36] [1987] 3 All E.R. 411.
[37] [1975] 2 All E.R. 347.
[38] [1980] Crim.L.R. 584.
[39] Smith [1974] 1 All E.R. 632.
[40] (1875) L.R. 2 C.C.R. 154.
[41] [1971] 1 Q.B. 428.
[41A] Also see discussion of *Brady v. U.K.* (2001), *re.* "Honest Mistakes" in Chap 2.
[42] See *Sherriff* [1969] Crim.L.R. 260.
[43] [1966] 2 Q.B. 414.
[44] Now s. 89(2).
[45] *ibid.* at 419.
[46] *ibid.* at 419.
[47] [1955] 3 All E.R. 406.

[48] A recent example of making it more difficult for the police to carry out their duties can be seen in *French v. DPP* [1996] Q.B.D., where the defendant swallowed a substance suspected to be a prohibited drug after being strip searched. It was held that, if the search was lawful and therefore the police officer was acting in the execution of his duty, then the defendant's acts were an obstruction.
[49] [1983] 1 All E.R. 663.
[50] [1910] 1 Q.B. 1.
[51] [1907] 1 K.B. 59.
[52] *Textbook on Criminal Law* (Butterworths).
[53] [1936] K.B. 318.
[54] [1985] I.R.L.R. 76.
[55] *Rice v. Connolly* [1966] 2 Q.B. 414.
[56] *Green v. DPP* (1991) 155 J.P. 816.
[57] See Smith and Hogan, *ibid.* p. 434; Lidstone [1983] Crim.L.R. 29.
[58] (1982) 74 Cr.App.R. 298.
[59] See above.
[60] *Ledger v. DPP* [1991] Crim.L.R. 439.
[61] *Wilmott v. Atack* [1977] Q.B. 498.
[62] [1981] A.C. 394.
[63] [1983] Q.B. 680.
[64] [1985] Q.B. 509.
[65] [1966] 2 Q.B. 414.
[66] *per* Lord Parker at 419.
[67] [1980] Crim.L.R. 584.
[68] Consultation Paper [1992] LCCP No. 122; also Law Comm. no. 218.
[69] [1970] 3 All E.R. 215.
[70] The *Confait Case*, Report of the Hon Sir Henry Fisher to the House of Commons (HMSO, 1977).
[71] RCCP Report Cmnd. 8092, para 1.11.
[72] RCCP Report Cmnd. 8092.
[73] *R. v. Walsh* (1990) 91 Cr.App.R. 161, *per* Saville J. at 163.
[73A] New versions published CJPA 2001. See discussion.
[74] s. 67(1)–(7).
[74A] Although much of the Act extends to England and Wales only, it is advisable to read s. 138 in order to discover which provisions may also be applicable to the rest of the U.K., or restricted to a part or parts of the U.K.
[74B] For a full list see s. 1(1).
[74C] For the definition of a "designated or non-designated public place" see ss. 13 and 14.
[75] Some people of certain religions, *e.g.* Jews, Muslims, would find removing their headgear a serious invasion of their religious beliefs. But under Code A, para. 3A, the police may ask a person to voluntary remove other clothing. Under s. 13A of the Prevention of Terrorism (Temporary Provisions) Act 1989, an individual may have anything which he is carrying, searched—the individual himself must not be searched (See Code A, para. 3.5A).
[76] s. 1(7),(8).
[77] s. 1(9).
[78] s. 139 of the Criminal Justice Act 1988.
[79] *Harris v. DPP, Fehni v. DPP* [1993] 1 All E.R. 562.
[80] Although the carrying of an offensive weapon for protection for fear of an imminent attack may constitute "reasonable excuse" (see *Evans v. Hughes* (1972) 56 Cr.App.R. 813 at 817).
[81] See Misuse of Drugs Act 1971, s. 23(2). See also Annex A in Codes of Practice A for list of stop and search statutory powers.
[82] *Rice v. Connolly* [1966] 2 Q.B. 414.
[83] (1979) 71 Cr.App.R. 13.
[84] Under Code A, para. 1.6A "reasonable suspicion may be based upon reliable information or intelligence which indicates that members of a particular group . . . habitually carry knives unlawfully or weapons or controlled drugs" (see also s. 60 of the CJPOA 1994 and Code A, para. 1.7AA).
[85] See also Code A para. 1.7AA and Code A:1 H.
[86] See above, "assaulting and obstructing a police officer in the execution of his duty".
[87] [1981] 3 All E.R. 383. See also Breach of the Peace.
[88] See ss. 24 and 25 of PACE.

[89] For an exhaustive list see s. 24(1), (2) and (3).
[90] (1989) 89 Cr.App.R. 190.
[91] (1992) 95 Cr.App.R. 42.
[92] [1989] Crim.L.R. 150.
[93] [1987] R.T.R. 199.
[94] See *Christie v. Leachinsky* [1947] A.C. 573 and see "reasons for arrest" at para. 3–043.
[95] *Nicholas v. Parsonage* (see above) at p. 203.
[96] *Plange v. Chief Constable of South Humberside Police*, *The Times*, March 23, 1992.
[97] [1984] A.C. 437.
[98] (1988) 138 N.L.J.R 180, Lexis.
[99] [1947] A.C. 573.
[1] *R. v. Brosch* [1988] Crim.L.R. 743.
[2] [1988] 1 W.L.R. 1166.
[3] For an unusual example of "practicable time" see *Dawes v. DPP* [1995] 1 Cr.App.R. 65.
[4] *Lewis v. Chief Constable of the South Wales Constabulary* [1991] 1 All E.R. 206.
[5] See *Mullady v. DPP* [1997] LTL July 3, 1997 where the arrest reasons were given as "obstruction" (a non-arrestable offence under s. 25) whereas a "breach of the peace" arrest would have made the police constable's action legal.
[6] (1993) 97 Cr.App.R. 301.
[7] Confimed by *Mullady v. DPP* [1997] see above, n.5.
[8] *Gelberg v. Miller* [1961] 1 W.L.R. 153.
[9] [1992] Crim.L.R. 806.
[10] But see para. 11.13 now, where "a written record must be made of any comments, including unsolicited comments which are outside the context of an interview".
[11] *R. v. James* [1992] Crim.L.R. 650; see also *Marsh* [1991] Crim.L.R. 56.
[12] 19 State Trials 1001; 19 State Trials 1029.
[13] *Ghani v. Jones* [1970] 1 Q.B. 693.
[14] Includes death; serious injury; serious harm to the state; substantial financial gain or serious financial loss to any person, etc.
[15] [1989] 2 W.L.R. 841.
[16] See s. 10(1) of PACE 1984.
[17] *ibid.*, s. 14(2).
[18] [1989] 2 W.L.R. 841 at 850.
[19] *R. v. Leeds Crown Court, ex p. Switalski* [1991] Crim.L.R. 559 at, 560.
[20] [1995] 1 Cr.App.R. 431.
[21] *R. v. Crown Court at Inner London Sessions, ex p. Baines v. Baines* [1988] Q.B. 579.
[22] *ibid.*
[23] [1988] 3 All E.R. 775.
[24] [1991] Crim.L.R.559.
[25] *R. v. Reading Justices, ex p. South West Meat Ltd* [1992] Crim.L.R. 672.
[26] [1992] Crim.L.R. 669.
[27] *R. v. Reading Justices, ex p. South West Meat Ltd* [1992] Crim.L.R. 672.
[28] See Richard Stone, Entry, Search and Seizure.
[29] See also Crim.L.R. [1992], Commentary 671.
[30] [1988] Crim.L.R. 534.
[31] [1992] Crim.L.R. 672.
[32] *The Times*, August 15, 1996.
[33] *O'Loughlin v. Chief Constable of Essex* [1998] 1 W.L.R. 374.
[34] [1992] 4 All E.R. 545.
[35] at p. 50. The Police and Criminal Evidence Act 1984.
[36] [1998] 1 W.L.R. 374.
[37] *McLeod v. MPC* [1994] 4 All E.R. 553.
[38] *Jeffrey v. Black* [1978] Q.B. 490.
[39] [1978] Q.B. 490.
[39A] See s. 50(1)(a)-(c).
[39B] See s. 50(2)(a)-(c). S. 50(2) does not apply to legally privileged material under s. 19(6) of PACE.
[39C] For the list of factors for consideration see s. 50(3)(a)-(e). For a full account of the additional powers of seizure under the CJPA see ss. 50–66 of the Act.
[40] *Mohammed-Holgate v. Duke* [1984] 1 All E.R. 1054.
[41] [1988] Crim.L.R. 442.

[41A] s. 73(1)(b); to be inserted after s. 40 of PACE as s. 40A.
[41B] To be inserted after s. 45 of PACE as s. 45A.
[42] *Matter of an Application for a Warrant of further Detention* [1988] Crim.L.R. 296. See also [1991] Crim.L.R. 541—identification parade held out of time, acceptable; it was going to take place anyway—ss. 41 and 42 irrelevant.
[43] See *R. v. Slough Justices, ex p. Stirling* [1987] Crim.L.R. 576.
[44] See Zander pp. 106–108 for further criticism; and McKenzie, Morgan and Reiner, "Helping the police with their inquiries" [1990] Crim.L.R. 22.
[45] [1990] 2 All E.R. 187.
[46] See A.A.S. Zuckerman, "Confession and the Observance of the Code of Practice", All E.R. Review 1990, p. 116.
[47] See also *R. v. Parris* [1989] Crim.L.R. 214, below.
[47A] "Fingerprinting" means a record "of the skin pattern and other physical characteristics or features of any of that person's fingers; or either of his palms", s. 65(1) of PACE as amended by s. 78 of the CJPA.
[47B] To be inserted as 4B of s. 61(4) of PACE.
[47C] See s. 82(2) of CJPA.
[47D] See s. 82(3) of CJPA.
[47E] Under ss. 83 and 84 similar amendments are set out in the Police and Criminal (Northern Ireland) Order 1989 and the Terrorism Act 2000.
[48] s. 164, Customs and Excise Management Act 1979.
[49] *Badham* [1987] Crim.L.R. 202.
[50] *Middleweek v. Chief Constable of Merseyside* [1990] 3 All E.R. 662.
[51] For non-intimate searches other than at a police station, see s. 2(9)(a) and Code A, para. 3.5.
[52] For a valuable interpretation of and distinction between the words "custody" and "police detention" See Ken Lidstone and Clare Palmer, *The Investigation of Crime—A Guide to Police Powers* (2nd ed., Butterworths) pp. 405 and 406.
[53] See Code C, Annex B, paras. 1 and 2.
[54] *R. v. Franklin, The Times*, June 16, 1994.
[55] s. 58 will not apply where the accused has been remanded in custody by a magistrates court, nor to persons attending a police station voluntarily.
[56] There still exists a common law right to a solicitor, as soon as is reasonably practicable. See *R. v. Chief Constable of South Wales, ex p. Merrick* [1994] Crim.L.R. 852.
[57] [1988] 2 All E.R. 135.
[58] (1988) 138 New L.J. 347, CA.
[59] (1990) 91 Cr.App.R. 150.
[60] (1988) 89 Cr.App.R. 68; [1989] Crim.L.R. 214.
[61] [1991] Crim.L.R. 451.
[62] However, proof that the evidence was obtained as a result of an inadmissible confession is normally excluded—s. 76(5) and s. 76(6).
[63] *R. v. Fulling* (1987) 85 Cr.App.R. 136.
[64] *R. v. Emmerson* (1991) 92 Cr.App.R. 284.
[65] *R. v. Paris* (1993) 97 Cr.App.R. 99.
[66] (1993) 97 Cr.App.R. 99.
[67] (1987) 85 Cr.App.R. 136.
[68] For example, in *R. v. Davison* [1988] Crim.L.R. 442—rearrested after release may constitute exercising powers in a "wrongful manner".
[69] [1995] Crim.L.R. 233.
[70] *ibid.* at 234.
[71] *R. v. Delaney* (1989) 88 Cr.App.R. 338 at 341, 342.
[72] *R. v. Conway* [1994] Crim.L.R. 839.
[73] [1991] Crim.L.R. 118.
[74] [1994] Crim.L.R. 839.
[75] *ibid.* at 840.
[76] *R. v. Barry* (1992) 95 Cr.App.R. 384.
[77] (1991) 92 Cr.App.R. 314.
[78] *R. v. Marsh* [1991] Crim.L.R. 455.
[79] See *R. v. Goldenberg* (1988) Cr.App.R., *R. v. Everett* [1988] Crim.L.R. and *R. v. Weeks* [1995] Crim.L.R. 52.
[80] [1996] 3 All E.R. 289.

[81] The House of Lords referred, not only to a breach of the national law, but also to the Convention especially under Articles 6, 8, and 13, but refused to base their decision on those Articles.
[82] [1996] 3 All E.R. 289 at 301.
[83] App. no. 35394/97, judgement May 12, 2000.
[84] See also the recent case of *R. v. P. & Others* (2001) 2 W.L.R. 463.
[85] The domestic version of this case was decided prior to the introduction of the Police Act 1997 and the Regulation of Investigatory Powers Act 2000.
[86] See also the earlier cases of *X v. Germany* (1989) 11 E.H.R.R. 84 and *Schenk v. Switzerland* (1998) 13 E.H.R.R. 232.
[87] *Sharpe v. DPP* (1993) 158 J.P. 595, where the suspect, who was clearly over the limit, was dragged off his own driveway after a police chase in order to submit him to a breath test.
[88] *R. v. Sang* [1980] A.C. 402.
[89] Royal Commission on Police Powers 1928.
[90] (1994) 98 Cr.App.R. 437.
[91] [1992] 3 W.L.R. 228.
[92] The appellants had not been tricked or entrapped into dishonest dealing. Even if the shop did not exist, they would have sold their property elsewhere. See also *R. v. Mason* [1988] 1 W.L.R. 139, where tricks and lies by the police led to acquittals since such evidence was seriously tainted and should have been excluded.
[93] (1995) 95 Cr.App.R. 320.
[94] *R. v. Christou and Wright* [1992] 3 W.L.R. 228 at 237.
[95] (1988) 86 Cr.App.R. 349.
[96] *ibid.* at 354.
[97] *R. v. Mills and Rose* (1962) 46 Cr.App.R. 336.
[98] (1993) 97 Cr.App.R. 365.
[99] *R. v. Jelen and Katz* (1990) 90 Cr.App.R. 456; but see *R. v. H* [1987] Crim.L.R. 47, where the court used their discretion and excluded a taped telephone conversation between the defendant and the victim where the defendant had already been interviewed under caution and released.
[99A] (2000) Crim.L.R. 174.
[1] (2001) 1 W.L.R. 51; *The Times*, October 11, 2000.
[2] (1999) 28 E.H.R.R. 101.
[3] (1998) Q.B. 848.
[4] (1994) 98 Cr.App.R. 437
[5] (1999) 28 E.H.R.R. 101.
[6] In *Teixeira* the court held that the action of undercover agents had to be restricted and sufficient safeguards put in place, *e.g.* legislation or judicial control to oversee the conduct of the police, so as to prevent officers from inciting and instigating an individual to commit an offence he would not otherwise have committed; such behaviour would not justify admitting evidence obtained in those circumstances. Accordingly, there was in that case a violation of Art. 6.
[7] For a detailed discussion on the specific problems on the relationship between s. 58 and s. 78 see "Delay to Legal Advice".
[8] (1990) 91 Crim.App.R. 161.
[9] *R. v. Dunford* (1990) 91 Cr.App.R. 150.
[10] (1989) 88 Cr.App.R. 338.
[11] *R. v. Mackenzie* (1993) 96 Cr.App.R. 98.
[12] *The Times*, January 26, 1995.
[13] [1988] Crim.L.R. 826.
[14] "Independent person" is negatively defined in s. 77(3) as a person who "does not include a police officer or a person employed for or engaged on police purposes," but does include such persons as, *e.g.* social workers, family or an appropriate adult. "Appropriate adult" is defined in Code C, Annex E, para. 2 as a relative, guardian or some other person responsible for his care or custody. Indeed, any adult would suffice providing they are not employed by the police.
[15] *R. v. Cox* [1991] Crim.L.R. 276.
[16] 1964 Judges' Rules, Appendix A, para.(e).
[16A] After s. 60 of PACE there is to be inserted s. 60A.
[17] *Times* Law Reports May 15, 1992.
[18] [1988] Crim.L.R. 784.

[19] *R. v. Sparks* [1991] Crim.L.R. 128.
[20] [1994] 3 All E.R. 741.
[21] *R. v. Menard* (1995), 1 Cr.App.R. 306.
[22] *R. v. Ward* (1993) 96 Cr.App.R. 1 and *R. v. Cox* [1992] 96 Cr.App.R. 464, see below.
[23] *R. v. Marsh* [1991] Crim.L.R. 455 and *R. v. Absolam* (1993) 88 Cr.App.R. 332.
[24] *R. v. Hunt* [1992] Crim.L.R. 582.
[25] [1995] Crim.L.R. 239.
[26] *The Times*, March 5, 1998.
[27] This point will be discussed further in connection with the right of silence and inferences which may be drawn from silence, below.
[28] *R. v. Joseph* (1993) Crim.L.R. 48; *R. v. Hunt* (1992) Crim.L.R. 582; *R. v. Gordon* (1995) Crim.L.R. 306; *R. v. Goddard* (1994) Crim.L.R. 46.
[29] (1992) 96 Cr.App.R. 464.
[30] See also *R. v. Oransaye* [1993] Crim.L.R. 772.
[31] [1991] Crim.L.R. at 455.
[32] [1992] 3 All E.R. 456.
[33] See Zander, *Cases and Materials on the English Legal System*, (6th ed. Butterworths, 1993), for detailed explanation of the former common law right, the exceptions to it and statistics.
[34] See *Woolmington v. DPP* [1935] A.C. 462.
[35] Indeed, until the Criminal Evidence Act 1898, an accused person was not allowed to testify at his own trial, as an extreme result of these principles.
[36] 1972 Cmnd. 491.
[37] Phillips Report, paras 4.50 and 4.51.
[38] Prior to the CJPOA 1994, there existed and still exists legislation whereby a refusal to answer questions could result in an offence punishable by imprisonment, *e.g.* s. 2 of the Criminal Justice Act 1987.
[39] See Code C, para. 10.1.
[40] [1997] Case 97/0051/Y3.
[41] Although evidence may still be excluded under s. 78 of PACE.
[42] In *R. v. Birchall*, *The Times*, February 10, 1998, the court said that it was "essential" the jury be informed that the prosecution must, at least, establish a prima facie case against the defendant.
[43] *The Independent*, March 24, 1998.
[44] (1996) 161 J.P. 190; (1997) 2 Cr.App.R. 27.
[45] *R. v. Argent* [1997] 2 Cr.App.R. 27 at 32–33.
[46] At 193 where evidence of the first interview was excluded.
[47] See Practice Direction (Crown Court: Defendant's Evidence) [1995] 1 W.L.R. 657 at para. 3.
[48] [1995] 4 All E.R. 939.
[49] This was also the case pre-CJPOA 1994. However, in the past, the courts have to a limited degree, commented on the defendants refusal to give evidence. But guilt alone could not be implied from such a failure.
[50] [1995] 4 All E.R. 939.
[51] *ibid.*
[52] *ibid.*
[53] [1997] Crim.L.R. 215.
[53A] [1997] Crim.L.R. 449.
[53B] See *R. v. Napper* (1997) 161 J.P. 16.
[53C] See Commentary at 449–450, in *R. v. Roble*.
[54] (2001) 31 E.H.R.R. 1.
[55] (1996) 22 E.H.R.R. 29.
[55A] App. No. 36408/97. *The Times*, June 20, 2000.
[55B] See *Condron v. U.K.*
[55C] at para. 47.
[56] See ss. 58 and 59 of the Youth Justice and Criminal Evidence Act 1999.
[57] (1996) 23 E.H.R.R. 313
[58–59] See *R. v. Oscar* [1991] Crim.L.R. 778 where identification of clothing alone may not by itself constitute the application of Code D.
[60] See *R. v. Rogers* [1993] Crim.L.R. 386.
[61] [1996] Crim.L.R. 584 For an illuminating discussion on the problems which the courts face in this area, see Commentary to *R. v. Hickin* [1996] Crim.L.R. 584 at s. 586–587.

[62] (1990) 91 Cr.App.R. 143.
[63] (1994) 98 Cr.App.R. 191.
[64] (1995) 1 Cr.App.R. 480.
[65] *ibid.* at 488.
[66] See *R. v. Jones (Terrence)* [1992] Crim.L.R. 365 and *R. v. Gall* (1989) 90 Cr.App.R. 64.
[66A] For exceptions see ss. D.2.4, D.2.7 or D.2.10.
[66B] *The Times*, December 19, 2000.
[66C] (1998) Crim L.R. 281.
[67] The remaining death penalty sentences for piracy and treason in the U.K. have recently been abolished.
[68] [1976] 4 E.H.R.R. 482.
[69] The Turkish Government failed to recognise the applicants as the legal representatives of the Republic of Cyprus. See para. 23.
[70] *ibid.* at paras 343–346.
[71] *ibid.* at paras 347–351.
[72] at 559.
[73] [1980] 3 E.H.R.R. 408.
[74] Judgment of February 25, 1975, Appendix VI to the Commissioner's Report in *Bruggemann and Scheuten v. FRG*, CI 1 b of the grounds; [1978] 10 D.R. 100.
[75] at paras 19–20.
[76] Application nos. 22947/93 and 229478/93, judgment October 10, 2000.
[77] (2000) 29 E.H.R.R. 245.
[78] (1999) 27 E.H.R.R. 373.
[79] (2000) 30 E.H.R.R. 950.
[79A] App.No. 27229/95; *The Times*, April 18, 2001.
[80] [1973] 16 Yearbook 388.
[81] *Times* L.R. January 16, 2001.
[81A] (1999) E.H.R.R.
[82] (2000) 29 E.H.R.R. 245.
[83] (1993) 4 All E.R. 344.
[84] App nos 22947/93 and 229478/93, judgment October 10, 2000.
[85] *Andronicou and Constantinou v. Cyprus* [1998] 25 E.H.R.R. 491.
[86] [1993] 16 E.H.R.R. CD 20.
[87] See *Stewart v. U.K.* [1984] 7 E.H.R.R. 453 at 458, para. 19.
[88] For a criticism of this case see J.C. Smith, "The right to life and the right to kill in law enforcement", 144 N.L.J. 354.
[89] *Kelly v. U.K.* (1993) 16 E.H.R.R. 1020.
[90] [1982] 7 E.H.R.R. 453.
[91] *ibid.* at para. 15.
[92] *ibid.* at 460, paras 28–30 inclusive.
[93] The Commission did not feel it necessary to examine Art. 2(2)(a).
[94] *Dawn Barrett v. U.K.* App. No. 30402/96.
[95] [1996] 21 E.H.R.R. 97.
[96] At the Inquest, the jury returned verdicts of lawful killing. An action against the Crown was excluded on the grounds that the liability claim did not arise "in respect of Her Majesty's Government in the U.K. or Northern Ireland". Judicial review was eventually withdrawn and the High Court action was struck out on October 4, 1991.
[97] [1996] 21 E.H.R.R. 97 at 248.
[98] *ibid.* at para. 192.
[99] *ibid.* at para. 200.
[1] *ibid.* at para. 205.
[2] *ibid.* at para. 210.
[3] For a recent, not too dissimilar case, which produced the opposite result (by a majority of 5 votes to 4), see *Andronicou and Constantinou v. Cyprus* [1998] 25 E.H.R.R. 491 and especially paras 171–194.
[4] (2000) 4 All E.R. 961
[5] On this rare occasion the Archbishop of Westminster and the Pro-Life Alliance were permitted to make written submissions to the court, which were thereafter commented upon in the judgment.

6 (1993) 1 All E.R. 821.

7 The Archbishop of Westminster, in his submissions made no distinction between taking a life by omission or by a positive act—both were wrong. In *NHS Trust A v. Mrs M: NHS Trust B v. Mrs H* (2001) 1 All E.R. 801, the court followed the decision in *Airedale NHS Trust v. Bland* (1993) and made a declaration granting the discontinuation of artificial nutrition and hydration to two patients who remained in a persistent vegetative state. The court did not consider the withdrawal of such treatment to be in violation of the states' negative obligation to sustain life where it was not in the best interests of the patient to do so.

8 (1993) 1 F.L.R. 883.

9 *ibid. per* Ward L.J. at 1012.

10 *ibid.* at 1032–1052.

11 Despite the fact that hitherto necessity is not a defence to murder or attempted murder; see *R. v. Howe* (1987) 1 A.C. 417 and *R. v. Gotts* (1992) 2 A.C. 412.

12 Counsel for the appellants argued that a separation surgery would be a positive act (unlike *Bland* which concerned an omission). It would be an invasive of Mary's body and it would cause her death. Necessity, they argued, was not a defence to murder, "nor is it a defence to say that the defendant did not wish to cause death, if it is for all practical purposes inevitable that that will be the result of his actions" (at 1061).

13 See Art. 15(2).

14 Under the United Nations Convention against Torture and other Cruel, Inhuman or degrading Treatment or Punishment (1987), Art. 1 states that torture "means any act by which severe pain or suffering, whether physical or mental, is intentionally inflicted on a person for such purposes as obtaining from him or a third person information or a confession, punishing him for an act he or a third person has committed or is suspected of having committed, or intimidating or coercing him or a third person, or for any reason based on discrimination of any kind, when such pain or suffering is inflicted by or at the instigation of or with the consent or acquiescence of a public official or other person acting in a official capacity".

15 [1988] 2 E.H.R.R. 25.

16 at 79, para. 162.

17 at 80, para. 167.

18 In *Aydin v. Turkey* [1998] 25 E.H.R.R. 251 at paras 83–85 where the court held that authorised rape constituted a torture and referred to the act as "especially grave and abhorrent". Apart from the physical injuries, consideration must be given to the mental problems which accompany such an horrific experience.

19 The British Government gave an undertaking to discontinue these techniques on February 8, 1977.

20 (1998) 26 E.H.R.R. 477.

21 [1978] 2 E.H.R.R. 1.

22 In accordance with s. 8 of the Summary Jurisdiction Act 1960, as amended.

23 para. 30.

24–25 para. 35.

26 [1992] 17 E.H.R.R. 238.

27 para. 40.

28 [1993] 19 E.H.R.R. 112.

29 [1982] 2 E.H.R.R. 293.

30 Since the Education Act 1986, corporal punishment in State schools has been abolished.

31 *Soering v. U.K.* [1989] 11 E.H.R.R. 439 at para. 104.

32 [1992] 15 E.H.R.R. 1.

33 at para. 112.

34 para. 113.

35 at para. 115.

36 But see *Klass v. Germany* [1993] 18 E.H.R.R. 305.

37 (1999) 29 E.H.R.R. 403.

38 For the meaning of "prescribed by law" see Arts 8 and 10.

39 *Engel v. The Netherlands* [1976] 1 E.H.R.R. 647 at para. 58.

40 *Guzzardi v. Italy* [1980] 3 E.H.R.R. 333.

41 para. 92.

42 *Van Droogenbroeck v. Belgium* [1980] 4 E.H.R.R. 443 at para. 35.

43 [1987] 10 E.H.R.R. 293.

44 The sentence may seem harsh, but was considered by the court to be in the interests of the boy himself, who, when found to be fully rehabilitated, would be released earlier, than if he had been given a fixed imprisonment sentence.

45 [1987] 10. E.H.R.R. 293 at para. 51.
46 *ibid.* at para. 49.
47 [1981] 10 E.H.R.R. 205.
48 *ibid.* at para. 46.
49 [1976] 1 E.H.R.R. 647.
50 *ibid.* at para. 69.
51 Detention for refusal to pay the poll tax. See *Beham v. U.K.* [1996] 22 E.H.R.R. 293.
52 [1981] 5 E.H.R.R. 71.
53 *ibid.* at para. 175.
54 D. J. Harris, M. O'Boyle and C. Warbrick, *Law of the European Convention on Human Rights* (Butterworths, 1995), p. 114.
55 [1990] 13 E.H.R.R. 157.
56 *ibid.* at para. 32.
57 *ibid.* at para. 33.
58 *ibid.* at para. 35.
59 [1994] 19 E.H.R.R. 193.
60 [1990] 13 E.H.R.R. 157 at para. 61.
61 *ibid.* at para. 63.
62 [1979] 2 E.H.R.R. 387.
63 *ibid.* at para. 39.
64 [1985] 7 E.H.R.R. 528.
65 [1987] 9 E.H.R.R. 297.
66 The Minister is entitled to deport a person but only in cases of urgency or where the individual fails to comply, in certain circumstances, with an order of the court, or by statute—none of which applied to this case.
67 [1987] 9 E.H.R.R. 297 at para. 73.
68 *ibid.* at para. 74.
69 [1990] 13 E.H.R.R. 157.
70 "Judicial control of interference by the excutive with the individual's right of liberty is an essential feature of the guarantee embodied in Article 5(3) which is intended to minimise the risk of arbitrariness": *Brogan v. U.K.* [1989] 11 E.H.R.R. 117 at para. 58.
71 [1989] 11 E.H.R.R. 117.
72 Now s. 14 of PTA 1989.
73 Under domestic law in Northern Ireland, the period was 48 hours, whilst in the remainder of the U.K., under PACE 1984, ss. 41–46, the maximum period is 36 hours, although this can be extended to 96 hours, but only with the authorisation of a judge.
74 [1989] 11 E.H.R.R. 117 at para. 62.
75 [1994] 17 E.H.R.R. 539.
76 For full discussion see Article 15.
77 [1994] 17. E.H.R.R. 539 at para. 62.
78 *ibid.* at para. 63–65.
79 [1979–1980] 1 E.H.R.R. 55.
80 See *B. v. Austria* [1991] 13 E.H.R.R. 20 at para. 36.
81 [1968] 1 E.H.R.R. 91.
82 *ibid.* at para. 4.
83 See *Scott v. Spain* [1996] 24 E.H.R.R. 391, where the court said that continued detention can only be justified if there are "specific indications" of a "genuine requirement of public interest" which outweighs the rule of respect for individual liberty (at para. 74).
84 See *Muller v. France* [1997] Judgment, March 17, 1997. An immediate admission of guilt, followed by a delay before coming to trial, may be taken into account to show that the investigation was not conducted with all due diligence; in this case four years on remand was considered to exceed the reasonable time within Art. 5(3).
85 In *Matznetter v. Austria* [1969] 1 E.H.R.R. 198, the court found it proper in this case to consider "the very prolonged continuation of reprehensible activities, the huge extent of the loss sustained by the victims and the wickedness of the person charged".
86 See *Letellier v. France* [1991] 14 E.H.R.R. 83. Release was refused for fear of resuming a public disturbance activity.
87 [1968] 1 E.H.R.R. 91.
88 *ibid.* at para. 14.
89 [1987] 10 E.H.R.R. 293.
90 *ibid.* at para. 58, and see *XVY* (1982) 4 E.H.R.R. 188 at para. 52.

[91] *DeWilde, Ooms and Versyp v. Belgium* [1979–80] 1 E.H.R.R. 373 at para. 78.
[92] *ibid.*
[93] [1986] 13 E.H.R.R. 666.
[94] The "tariff period" (the minimum period to be served) is communicated to the Home Secretary in order that he may fix the first review date. Even so, release is not automatic after the tariff period has been completed.
[95] [1986] 13 E.H.R.R. 666 at para. 75.
[96] *ibid.* at para. 76.
[97] See also *Hussain v. U.K.* [1996] (55/1994/502/584) and *Singh v. U.K.* [1996] (56/1994/503/585).
[98] *Herczegfalvy v. Austria* [1993] 15 E.H.R.R. 437 at para. 75.
[99] *Brogan v. U.K.* [1988] 11 E.H.R.R. 117 at para. 67.
[1] In *Fayed v. U.K.* [1994] 18 E.H.R.R. 393 at para. 55, the court said that "the result of the proceedings in question must be directly decisive for such a right or obligation, mere tenuous connections or remote consequences not being sufficient to bring Article 6(1) into play".
[2] [1971] 1 E.H.R.R. 455 at para. 94.
[3] [1994] 18 E.H.R.R. 393 at paras 55–63.
[4] [1985] 7 E.H.R.R. 516.
[5] See also *DeCubber v. Belgium* [1985] 7 E.H.R.R. 236 at para. 35 when deciding on an impartiality case.
[6] *Delcourt v. Belgium* [1970] 1 E.H.R.R. 335 at para. 25.
[7] *ibid.* at para. 68, see also *Campbell and Fell v. U.K.* [1985] 7 E.H.R.R. 165.
[8] [1976] 1 E.H.R.R. 647.
[9] *ibid.* at para. 82.
[10] *ibid.*
[11] *ibid.* at para. 85.
[12] [1984] 7 E.H.R.R. 165. Although this case considers the issues of prisoners, unlike *Engel* with military issues, the problems are nevertheless *mutatis mutandis*.
[13] *ibid.* at 13, para. 70.
[14] *ibid.* at 14, para. 71.
[15] [1996] 57/1994/504/586 judgment, February 22, 1996.
[16] *ibid.* at para. 37.
[17] *Eckle v. Federal Republic of Germany* [1982] 5 E.H.R.R. 1 at para. 7, and see also *Foti v. Italy* [1982] 5 E.H.R.R. 313 at para. 52, where it was stated that "charge" may "take the form of other measures which carry the implication of such an allegation and which likewise substantally affect the situation of the suspect".
[18] *Deweer v. Belgium* [1980] 2 E.H.R.R. 439 at para. 42: "The word must be given an autonomous meaning".
[19] [1980] 2 E.H.R.R. 439.
[20] *ibid.* at para. 44.
[21] See *Neumeister v. Austria* [1979–80] 1 E.H.R.R. 91 at para. 22.
[22] See *Borgers v. Belgium* [1993] 15 E.H.R.R. 92 and compare *Delcourt v. Belgium* [1979–80] 1 E.H.R.R. 355.
[23] [1994] 18 E.H.R.R. 213.
[24] *ibid.* at para. 33.
[25] *ibid.* at para. 35.
[26] *Stögmüller v. Austria* [1979] 1 E.H.R.R. 155 at para. 5.
[27] See *Neumeister v. Austria (No. 1)* [1980] 1 E.H.R.R. 91, where seven years was not considered unreasonable due to enormous complexities of the case.
[28] For the meaning of the word "charge" see above, n. 17.
[29] The Convention makes no demands on Member States to implement an appeal system as part of their judicial process.
[30] [1984] 6 E.H.R.R. 17.
[31] *ibid.* at para. 24.
[32] In *Buchholz v. Germany* [1981] 3 E.H.R.R. 597, five years was found to be reasonable since the case went through three separate courts and continued relevant evidence was being gathered during this period.
[33] [1985] 7 E.H.R.R. 236.
[34] *ibid.* at para. 29.
[35] *ibid.* at para. 30.
[35A] *The Times*, April 14, 2000.

[36] [1979–80] 1 E.H.R.R. 524.
[37] *ibid.* at para. 35.
[38] see *Ashingdane v. U.K.* [1985] 7 E.H.R.R. 528.
[39] See *Keegan v. Ireland* [1994] 18 E.H.R.R. 342. An unmarried father of a child had no right of access to a court to challenge the adoption procedure under domestic law. This was held to be a violation of Art. 6(1).
[40] [1977–80] 1 E.H.R.R. 524 at para. [8].
[41] *Airey v. Ireland* [1979–80] 2 E.H.R.R. 305.
[42] *ibid.*
[43] Divorce at that time was not possible under Art. 4 of the Irish Constitution, "No law shall be enacted providing for the grant of a dissolution of marriage".
[44] [1979–80] 2 E.H.R.R. 305 at para. 24.
[45] *ibid.*
[46] [1996] 22 E.H.R.R. 29.
[47] See s. 34 of the Criminal Justice and Public Order Act 1994.
[48] Legal advice may be withheld for up to 48 hours on reasonable grounds.
[49] [1996] 22 E.H.R.R. 29 at para. 41.
[50] see Arts 3, 4 and 6 of the Criminal Evidence (Northern Ireland) Order 1988.
[51] [1996] 22 E.H.R.R. at para. 47.
[52] *ibid.*
[53] see *Funke v. France* [1993] 16 E.H.R.R. 297.
[54] *ibid.* at para. 54.
[55] [1993] 16 E.H.R.R. 297.
[56] Under Art. 65–1 Customs Code—imprisonment maximum one month and a fine of up to 3000 French Francs.
[57] [1993] 16 E.H.R.R. 297 para. 44 The report states "itself" instead of "himself."
[58] [1996] 43/1994/490/572 23 E.H.R.R. 313. *The Times*, December 18, 1996.
[59] [1985] 7 E.H.R.R. 516.
[60] *ibid.* at para. 12.
[61] [1987] 10 E.H.R.R. 205.
[62] See s. 29(1) of the Criminal Appeal Act 1968.
[63] [1987] 10 E.H.R.R. 205 at para. 56.
[64] *ibid*, at para. 62.
[65] A form given to every prisoner contemplating an appeal to the Court of Appeal, see para. 11.
[66] [1987] 10 E.H.R.R. 205 at paras 63–65.
[67] *ibid.* at para. 66.
[68] *ibid.* at para. 67.
[69] *ibid.* at para. 68. The court also had no doubt that the Court of Appeal decision to refuse the applicant's leave to appeal, and to impose "loss of time" was based on a full and thorough evaluation of the relevant factors (at para. 69).
[70] [1996] 22 E.H.R.R. 29.
[71] *ibid.* at para. 66.
[72] *ibid.* at para. 70.
[73] *Artico v. Italy* [1980] 3 E.H.R.R. 1 at para. 33.
[74] [1989] 13 E.H.R.R. 36.
[75] *Barbera, Messegue and Jabardo v. Spain* [1989] 11 E.H.R.R. 360 at para. 78.
[76] There is no absolute right to call witnesses; that is a matter for the court to decide.
[77] 15 E.H.R.R. CD 113.
[78] *ibid.* at para. 74.
[79] See *Brozicek v. Italy* (1990).
[80] [1961] 2 All E.R. 446.
[81] [1991] 1 A.C. 599.
[82] Set out in (1736) Matthew Hale C.J., *History of the Pleas of the Crown*.
[83] [1995] 21 E.H.R.R. 363.
[84] See *R. v. Clarke* (1949) 33 Cr.App.R. 216—non-cohabitation orders; *R. v. O'Brien* (1974) 3 All E.R. 663—judicial separation orders of *decree nisi*; *R. v. Steele* (1976) 65 Cr.App.R. 22—non-molestation—orders.
[85] [1995] 21 E.H.R.R. 363 at para. 36.
[86] *ibid.* at para. 43.
[87] For more detailed discussion, comment and related issues, see Claire de Than and Edwin Shorts, "Double Jeopardy, Double Trouble" [2000] J.Crim.L.

Chapter 4

PUBLIC ORDER

INTRODUCTION

4–001 The Public Order Act 1986, as amended by the Criminal Justice and Public Order Act 1994, creates a framework of offences relating to both public and private behaviour. These offences are widely drafted with the result that public order offences are now almost entirely statutory; the only important exception is the residual common law police power to arrest for breach of the peace, whether real or feared. The 1986 Act, perhaps surprisingly, was met with far less controversy and backlash than the comparable changes introduced by the 1994 Act. Three distinct themes may be perceived in the 1986 Act: first, the regulation and control of public assemblies and processions; secondly, the creation of a set of criminal offences relating to disorderly behaviour such as riot, violent disorder and a modified version of affray; and thirdly, the creation of a range of offences concerning behaviour which causes harassment, alarm or distress. The third of these categories in particular has been subject to much expansion by later statutes including the Criminal Justice and Public Order Act 1994 and the Protection from Harassment Act 1997 (both of which will be discussed further below) and as a consequence has also been the source of detailed debate and criticism. It appears that further harassment offences are likely to be placed before Parliament in the near future; it is debatable whether there is any necessity for such a move when a comprehensive range of offences already exists, with much compromise to the personal freedom of the individual as a result. However, and to some extent contradictorily, it is also arguable that the growing collection of harassment offences is the early stages of a recognition of a right to privacy; this proposition will be discussed below and, in greater detail, at a later stage in this book.

A confusing aspect of the 1986 Act is that, whilst controlling public (and often also private) displays of violence, aggression, feeling and belief, it in no way confirms that there is a right to assemble or to demonstrate in public. Thus the freedom of assembly is protected only by omission and by the lack of any police power to control behaviour which falls outside the ambit of the specific statutory provisions. Without statutory recognition of a right to assemble and to demonstrate, it is relatively easy for the freedom which does exist to be further curtailed. Again, without a statutory right, it is easy for the widely-drafted statutory provisions to catch unintended victims; peaceable demonstrations by law-abiding citizens may be controlled in the same way as violent ones, and angry behaviour by an individual in the privacy of his own home when no other person is in fact distressed by his actions may be covered by the same offence as violence in public in front of a frightened victim. Greater clarity and limitation in the drafting of these offences would have prevented many of the cases which have provoked criticism from being brought in the first place.

4–002 Citizens, both individually and collectively, are recognised as having the freedom to protest peacefully and to assemble in public in order to do so. There is some level of disagreement about the nature of this freedom; some assert that it is a constitutional right, whereas others argue that it is at best a privilege—a limited concession made by the law in order to appease the public, but which could be further limited or even withdrawn fairly easily. In addition to, and often opposed to this, every citizen has a duty at common law to maintain the peace and uphold order. Strictly speaking, public order concerns the delicate balancing act between freedom of assembly and the maintenance of the peace. Therefore much of this chapter will deal with the legal limits placed upon citizens who wish to assemble in public, march or demonstrate in order to express themselves. However, the term "public order" is itself misleading: relevant statutes such as the Public Order Act 1986 and the Criminal Justice and Public Order Act 1994 regulate not only the above public demonstrations but also many types of behaviour which may be committed in private, in domestic premises, and even when the accused is alone. Thus this chapter will also discuss offences such as harassment, threatening behaviour, aggravated trespass, and affray, in order to examine the whole picture. There is wide agreement that behaviour such as rioting and violent disorder in public should be subject to criminal sanctions, but some of the newer offences are more contentious, straddling the boundary between criminal and civil liability uncomfortably. There is a potential that not only freedom of assembly but also freedom of expression and the right to privacy may be curtailed by these offences, especially if future case law interprets them to their fullest extent. A further problem is that the statutory offences and regulation in some cases draw no distinction between violent troublemakers intent upon causing harm to others or to property, and persons who wish to express peaceably a legitimate grievance.

Fear of public disorder and mob violence is not a new phenomenon; it was one of the main reasons for the formation of the first full-time professional police force in the nineteenth century, and indeed even in the middle ages a constable's oath would typically include the following pledge:

> ". . . (that I) shall keep the Peace of our Lord the King well and lawfully according to (my) power, and shall arrest all those who shall make any contest, riot, debate, or, affray, in breaking of the said peace, and shall bring them into the house or Compter of one of the Sheriffs".[1]

Throughout their history, police forces have been challenged by public demonstrations and riots; to supervise the former and quell the latter requires tactical skill, pragmatism and tact. It is perhaps unsurprising that mistakes have been made and that recurrent accusations of heavy-handed abuse of power and inflammatory behaviour have stalked the police for at least a century. Chartist riots in 1887 lasted for weeks and ended with outright battle in Trafalgar Square; Poll Tax riots and demonstrations in the 1980s looked little different. Criticisms of police methods of dealing with public disorder have always existed, but reached their height with the media coverage of events in recent years such as the 1974 Red Lion Square anti-National Front demonstration, riots in Brixton, Toxteth and elsewhere in the early 1980s, and the Miners' Strike of the mid-1980s. The distinguishing factor of public disorder since 1980 has been that in most cases where police behaviour has been criticised, the police were not a mediating party between two opposing groups of demonstrators; they were one side of the battle itself. Indeed, in the case of the Brixton riots in particular, and others since, it was allegations of police misconduct which ignited existing resentment and were seen as a cause of the rioting. Successive inquiries[2] recommended changes to public order laws, community policing methods and complaints procedures, but none were implemented immediately. The Brixton riot, the Miners' Strike and the 1983 Report of the Law Commission which reviewed public order offences and recommended statutory changes[3] led to the Public Order Act 1986, which introduced a new, entirely statutory scheme of public order offences and regulation, which will be discussed below in conjunction with more recent statutory developments. In recent years many policy initiatives have also been taken by police and government in order to foster and maintain better relations between police and communities, with varied amounts of success; community policing and education programmes are common examples which are thought to have had a positive effect. **4–003**

Public Order Act 1986

Section 1: Riot

A riot, under section 1(1), occurs where 12 or more people, acting for a common purpose, use or threaten unlawful violence, and the conduct of the group is such that it would cause a person of reasonable firmness if present at the scene (either a public or private place) to fear for his own safety. But an individual may only be guilty of riot if he actually uses violence rather than merely threatening violence. A riot is the most serious example of public disorder, and is an indictable offence which is punishable by up to 10 years' imprisonment (section 1(6)). The consent of the Director of Public Prosecutions is necessary before a prosecution for riot may commence. **4–004**

The mental element (*mens rea*) of the offence which must be proved is that it must be shown that each defendant intended to use violence or was aware that his conduct might be violent. Thus, it is not necessary to show that the defendant intended to cause anyone to fear for his personal safety, nor even that he knew that this might occur. The mental element relates only to the defendant's conduct; he does not have to consider or to be aware of its consequences.

Unlawful Violence

4–005 Violence, under section 8 includes any form of violent conduct which is capable of causing injury, *e.g.* throwing an object at someone even if the object misses the intended person completely (section 8(b)), but he must have intended or at least been aware that his conduct may be violent (section 6(1)). The word "unlawful" denotes that the defendant still has a legal justification to use reasonable force to defend himself in circumstances of an unwarranted attack.[4] Section 1 is restricted to those persons who actually use violence; merely threatening violence will not suffice under this section. Thus it is possible that a riot exists where only a few of those involved are liable for the offence, since the majority merely threatened violence. However, persons who incite or actively encourage violence may still be convicted of aiding and abetting violence, provided all the other ingredients of section 1 arc present.[5]

Common Purpose

4–006 The words "common purpose" relate to the conduct of those persons present at the scene. Thus, if the group in question were carrying weapons, displaying similar banners or were members of the same organisation, this may be evidence to show a common purpose by those present. It is up to the prosecution to prove a common purpose and after the judge has given the appropriate direction on the meaning in law of common purpose, it is then for the jury to decide whether in fact a common purpose existed. In *R. v. Tyler and Frost*[6] the defendants took part in a demonstration against the poll tax. Violence erupted through buildings being damaged and police being attacked. Some forty people were believed to be involved in the actual violence. One of the defendants admitted throwing a stone. The issue was whether it was done as part of a common purpose, *i.e.* the demonstration itself. The judge at first instance, stated that "it would not be sufficient to prove that it was done to further the common purpose if you (the jury) thought that there was at least room for a reasonable doubt as to whether he did that, or whether he did it for some other purpose—some purpose of his own".[7]

A person of reasonable firmness

4–007 In the midst of a riot, due to the overall confusion, it is often very difficult to extricate from the mêlée who committed particular violent offences at the scene. The purpose of this particular public order offence is to penalise threatening or violent behaviour emerging from a whole group of people, regardless of the identity of the actual victim. The reason for this lies in the fact that violent behaviour of a whole group represents a potential danger to the maintenance of public order and the protection of the innocent bystander, even if nobody is actually present at the scene, at that very moment. Hence, the introduction of the concept of the "person of reasonable firmness", who is a type of stand-in for the actual victim.

The meaning of the phrase in section 1(1) refers to "a person of reasonable firmness present at the scene to fear for his personal safety"; then section 1(4) states "no person of reasonable firmness need . . . be present at the scene"—somewhat confusing and seemingly contradictory drafting and in need of clarification. Where riot is concerned, the violence need only be directed against some theoretical person, not necessarily an actual person, who possesses all the attributes of reasonable firmness and who is in fear for his own safety. Juries are used to dealing with victims who can be identified. Here, the court is asking the jury to convict the defendant on conduct which "would cause a person" to fear for his own safety without the possibility of the victim necessarily being present to give evidence. It would seem then that evidence from others at the scene would have to hypothesise whether, had the theoretical victim been present, there was a danger that violence would have been used against him.

In *R. v. Davison*,[8] a case concerning affray (nevertheless, the issue of what is "reasonable firmness" remains equally relevant), the Court of Appeal stated that:

> ". . . there was a standard for the conduct which was to be set by a hypothetical person of reasonable firmness who could be, but not necessarily was, at the scene to fear for his personal safety if he was there".[9]

What are the characteristics of this theoretical person? Reasonable firmness suggests an ordinary, reasonable person who, under normal circumstances, would be able to withstand a normal amount of aggression, but who, under these particular conditions, would be in fear of his physical well-being when confronted by a group of rioters using violence against him. Thus, the purpose of using such a hypothetical person is to enable the jury to evaluate in an objective way whether the behaviour of the group was potentially dangerous or not, *i.e.* whether a "normal" third party would have felt fear for his own safety. It would be insufficient for the judge to direct the jury that it is enough if they found that the victim feared for his own safety, the judge must further instruct the jury on the effect a theoretical person at the scene would suffer.[10]

Section 2: Violent disorder

Section 2 created a new offence designed partly to replace the previous common law offence of unlawful assembly and partly to provide a lesser offence as a "safety-net" beneath riot. The immediate motivation behind **4–008** the offence was to control picketing which erupted into violence. A defendant may be guilty of violent disorder if:

(i) he is one of three or more persons who either used or threatened unlawful violence; and
(ii) his conduct was such that it would cause a person of reasonable firmness, present at the scene, to fear for his personal safety; and
(iii) he himself actually used or threatened violence.

The mental element (*mens rea*) required is that the defendant either intended or was aware that his conduct was or might be violent, or that it might threaten violence. Unlike section 1, there is no "common purpose" precondition to be considered here. Also, in contrast to section 1 merely threatening violence is sufficient for a conviction as opposed to the use of violence itself. Further, it is only necessary to have at least three persons present at the scene. It is not essential for at least three persons to be charged with violent disorder. However, if charges of violent disorder are brought against three persons and no others were involved in the offence, then all three must be convicted for the offence to be lawful. If only two are found guilty and one is acquitted, then the convictions of the other two will be quashed or substituted for a lesser offencc, if suitable.

4–009 In *R. v. Mahroof*[11]:

Facts. Four men, including the appellant and S, went to the home of the co-accused, B, to collect an overdue debt. Threats and violence occurred at B's home involving B, S and the appellant. The three were subsequently charged with violent disorder. The indictment only mentioned the three defendants, without including the other two men who were present. Both B and S were found not guilty of violent disorder. The appellant was convicted and appealed.

Decision. For violent disorder, there must be at least three persons present involved in the criminal activity associated with section 2, although, not necessarily those same persons stated in the indictment. Since two (B and S) out of the three accused had been acquitted the appellant must also be acquitted. If there was evidence of others involved, this should have been mentioned in the indictment. This was a material irregularity and the section 2 offence was therefore quashed, although in the appellant's case, a section 4 conviction was substituted.[12]

In *R. v. Fleming and Robinson*[13] it was stated that the judge should direct the jury that "if it could not be sure that three or more of the defendants were using or threatening violence, it should acquit every defendant of violent disorder, even if satisfied that one or more particular defendants were unlawfully fighting".[14]

Section 3: Affray

4–010 The offence of affray contrary to section 3 is committed by using or threatening unlawful violence so that a person of reasonable firmness would fear for their personal safety. The action does not have to take place in a public place, and indeed may occur where only the defendant is present. The offence can be committed if the hypothetical person of reasonable firmness would have feared for his safety (*R. v. Sanchez*[15]) and the requisite *mens rea* is either intention to use or threaten violence or alternatively awareness that his conduct may be violent, or threaten violence. The threat of violence itself may take various forms. For instance, the mere brandishing of offensive weapons or openly carrying objects likely to cause or threaten violence may, in certain circumstances, amount to a breach of section 3. In *R. v. West London Youth Court, ex parte M and Others*,[15A] some 40 youths were found to be in possession of unlit petrol bombs in the vicinity of residential flats. At the time there were no other persons present. Nevertheless, the court held that a hypothetical bystander of reasonable firmness (which included police officers not directly threatened) confronted by a group of youths carrying petrol bombs would be in fear of a threat of unlawful violence, and therefore, in the circumstances, constituted a breach of section 3 of the Public Order Act 1986. Their appeals to the Divisional Court were dismissed and they thereafter appealed to the House of Lords. The court said that in order for the conduct to amount to an offence under section 3(1) of the 1986 Act the threat must be directed towards another person or persons actually present at the scene. On the facts of this case, once the police had arrived the youths dispersed and since there was no unlawful violence or threat of such violence towards any persons in the vicinity, no offence of affray had been committed. Accordingly, their appeals were allowed.[15B] The offence is punishable by up to three years' imprisonment or an unlimited fine.

In this section only one person is needed to use threatening violence for the offence to be proved. Mere words alone cannot constitute the offence (section 3(3)). Even aggressive words which have the effect of frightening the other person, still will not amount to affray, without more.[16] However, in *R. v. Dixon*[17] a suspect called upon his untrained dog to attack two police constables with the words, "go on, kill". The words, combined with, as the court said, using the dog as a weapon, so that the police officers feared for their own safety, satisfied the term "threat of unlawful violence" in section 3. The use or threat of unlawful violence must be directed only against a person, and does not include property as in sections 1 and 2 (section 8(a)). Also, where a person of reasonable firmness was not in fear for his safety, then no affray is committed. For example, if a fight takes place in a pub and others in the pub carry on drinking and do not fear any apprehended threat of violence against them, that is evidence to support the conclusion that a person of reasonable firmness would not have so feared.[18]

For an offence of affray to be made out there must be some form of continuity of unlawfulness, for instance, where the fight takes place in a night-club and then afterwards the violence breaks out in the street. If the fighting stops and then begins again at some later stage, the prosecution must satisfy the jury that both incidents constituted an affray, if charged as a single count. However, if both events were not severable and the second event merely represented a continuation of the first, then the prosecution need only prove "the general nature and effect of the conduct as a whole and not on particular incidents and events which might take place in the course of it."[19] Unlike riot and violent disorder, the offence of affray does not come within the category of "arrestable offence". However, a constable may arrest without warrant anyone he reasonably suspects "is committing" the offence (section 3(6)). If the full offence has already been completed and peace has been restored, then it may well be too late to make an arrest under this section.

Section 4: Fear or provocation of violence

4–011 Sadly, in everyday life, it is a common occurrence that people are insulted, abused, or threatened, and as a result become stressed, angry or as a last resort retaliate through violence. Section 4 concerns violent reaction: fear of violent actions by the person using highly offensive words or behaviour towards the victim, or provoking violent reactions by the victim to the person using such words.

A lesser offence along similar lines to section 3 is created by section 4: using threatening, abusive or insulting words or behaviour to another person, or displaying/distributing threatening, abusive or insulting words. Under section 4(1), a person is guilty of an offence if he—

(a) uses towards another person threatening, abusive or insulting words or behaviour, or

(b) distributes or displays to another person any writing, sign or other visible representation which is threatening, abusive or insulting, with intent to cause that person to believe that:

(i) immediate unlawful violence will be used against him or another by any person, or to

(ii) provoke the immediate use of unlawful violence by that person or another, or whereby

(iii) that person is likely to believe that such violence will be used or

(iv) it is likely that such violence will be provoked (numbers in brackets added).

The offence is summary and the *mens rea* is complex requiring intention that the words or behaviour should be threatening, abusive or insulting, or knowledge that they might be; and either intention that the victim should believe that immediate unlawful violence would be used, or intention to provoke another to use such violence; or that it was likely that either the victim would believe that such violence would be used, or that, objectively viewed, such violence would be provoked. Thus, there are four different ways in which the offence may be committed and it is important that the defendant is charged with the correct particulars. In *Winn v. DPP*[20] a server attempted to serve a summons on the defendant. The server was threatened and abused by the defendant and the latter was subsequently charged and convicted under (iv) above, in that the defendant used threatening and abusive words and behaviour whereby it was likely that violence would be provoked. He appealed. The prosecution had to prove that it was likely that the server would be provoked to immediate unlawful violence. But on the facts there was no evidence of this and accordingly, the appeal was allowed. Had the charge been phrased in either (i) or (iii) terms, then it is suggested that the prosecution case would have been so strong as to warrant a conviction.

"Road rage" is a prime modern example of such behaviour whereby (i)– **4–012**
(iv) may all be used to satisfy the criteria of section 4. Taking all the different types of behaviour in section 4(1) into consideration, it can be seen that "threatening" is the word most likely to be understood as having such force that would either cause the recipient to fear some form of violence against him, or alternatively provoke that person to take immediate action against the person making the threat. Although threats which do not have the required results as in (i)–(iv) will not amount to an offence under this section, it is suggested that where the threat is of a very serious nature, in most cases, a charge of affray may be more appropriate; the maximum prison sentence being three years, whereas under section 4 it is only six months.

"Abusive and insulting words or behaviour"

The words "abusive" and "insulting" are generally considered to be **4–013**
interlinked, although there does exist a pedantic difference between them. Mere disrespectful behaviour, without more, does not amount to an offence under this section. In *Brutus v. Cozens*[21] the defendant was charged with insulting behaviour, under the old section 5 of the Public Order Act 1936. During a Wimbledon tennis match, the defendant along with others, distributed leaflets, displayed banners and sat down on the tennis court protesting against the apartheid policies of South Africa. The House of Lords said that it was a question of fact in each case whether the behaviour amounting to "insulting". Lord Reed stated that "distasteful or unmannerly speech or behaviour is permitted so long as it does not go beyond any of three limits (threatening, abusive or insulting)". Despite 13 pages of judgment and in-depth discussion by three of their most eminent Lordships, no definition narrow or wide was formulated to give any clearer meaning to the word "insult". The word must be taken to mean its ordinary common sense definition, but as was stated in this case, "an ordinary sensible man knows an insult when he sees or hears it".[22]

However, an insult must be personally addressed at another person and if the defendant is not conscious of any person present, then surely it cannot be said to be addressed at anyone.[23] But in *Masterson v. Holden*[24] the defendants, two gay men, were kissing in Oxford Street at approximately 2 a.m. in the morning, oblivious as to whether anyone was watching or not. Two men walking by with two women shouted at the defendants "You filthy sods. How dare you in front of our girls". The defendants were arrested and charged with using insulting behaviour whereby a breach of the peace might have been occasioned.[25] They were convicted and appealed. The court found that although the defendants did not deliberately aim their conduct at any particular person, nevertheless they must have been conscious of the fact that even at 2 a.m. in the morning, it was likely that there would be people in Oxford Street who would find their conduct objectionable and unacceptable and thus insulting. It is suggested that such conduct today would not be found to be so offensive to the ordinary person as to warrant a prosecution. But, other lawful acts which are at present legal, may nevertheless constitute behaviour which is abusive or insulting. For instance, a person smoking, whether in a restaurant or in the street may lead to violence by a non-smoker who feels threatened or even insulted by such behaviour, whereas a smoker would presumably consider the same situation quite acceptable. Should the "victim" fear or be provoked into violence, will the courts consider the characteristics of the intended victim, *i.e.* on a subjective basis, or will they consider the reactions of a reasonable person in the same predicament, on an objective basis?

4–014 In *Jordan v. Burgoyne*[26]:

Facts. The defendant gave a public speech in Trafalgar Square to about 5,000 people, amongst which were many Jews. The defendant advocated in his speech that "Hitler was right, our real enemies are not the Nazis, but world Jewry". Complete disorder ensued with part of the crowd pushing forward towards the speaker's platform. The defendant was arrested and convicted of using insulting words contrary to section 5 of the Public Order Act 1936. The appellant appealed to the Quarter Sessions which allowed the appeal on the grounds that, although the words were insulting, they were not likely to lead ordinary reasonable people to a breach of the peace by committing assaults.

Decision. The prosecutor appealed. Lord Parker L.J. held that the appellant "must take his audience as he finds them". Thus, if the present crowd were likely to be provoked by his speech so that a breach of the peace occurred, then he is guilty under section 5.

The test seems at first sight somewhat severe. In *Jordan*, the narrator was well aware that part of the crowd included Jews and other people opposed to his views. Indeed, his speech was such as to incite those others to violence and intended that to be the ultimate result. It is suggested that where the defendant does not know or is not aware that his activity would provoke an unusually sensitive audience, then no prosecution should be forthcoming. The reoccurrence of a *Masterson*–type situation should give the court the opportunity of examining all the surrounding circumstances, not only the victim as he or she was, but whether what the defendant was doing was:

(a) lawful, and

(b) if lawful, whether he realised the effect it would have on others in the surrounding area, having given some thought to it, and

(c) taking into account the persons likely to be so affected by his actions.

Behaviour towards another

Under section 4(1)(a) the offensive words or behaviour must be "used towards a person". In *Atkin v. DPP*[27] the court held that the words "uses towards a person" meant "addressed directly to another person who is present and in earshot". Any indirect message passed via a third party, even though insulting, will not be considered as words "towards a person", for the purposes of this section. **4–015**

Intention to commit the offence

The person whose conduct was threatening, abusive or insulting must have intended that the reaction by the victim would be to fear some form of violence being directed against him or from him to the person using the words or circulating some form of written material or reading which is threatening, abusive or insulting. **4–016**

Under section 6(3), he must intend his words, behaviour, etc., or at least be aware that his words, etc., may be threatening, abusive or insulting. It is no defence to say that he was drunk, or presumably, under the influence of drugs unless such substances were taken as part of a medically prescribed treatment (section 6(5)), or at least that they were not voluntarily self-induced. Despite the condition that the insulting words had to be addressed directly to another person, it is not necessary for the victim to give evidence that he believed immediate unlawful violence was to be used against him and that the defendant intended it so. It is enough if someone present at the scene were to give evidence to that effect. Further, the issue of intent could also be settled by any admissible evidence, without hearing from the victim himself.[28]

Immediate unlawful violence

Since some form of violence must be directed at another person is a precondition under section 4, it is necessary to show that any reaction to those specific words or behaviour must take place either immediately or at least at a very short time in the future. Whilst there is no problem in interpreting this condition in (i) and (ii) in section 4(1)(b), difficulties do arise where the word "immediate" is missing from (iii) and (iv) and the expression "such violence" is only written. Therefore, the question is, if charged under (iii) or (iv) and the violence is not imminent, can a conviction nevertheless be upheld under this particular section? **4–017**

In *R. v. Horseferry Road Metropolitan Stipendiary Magistrate ex parte Siadatan*[29]:

Facts. The applicant S laid an information against Penguin Books Ltd for the distribution of Salman Rushdie's *Satanic Verses*, for containing abuse and insulting writings whereby "it was likely that unlawful violence would be provoked". The applicant argued that the words "such violence" in (iv) meant only "unlawful violence" and not immediate unlawful violence, since the word "immediate" is missing from both (iii) and (iv). Penguin argued on the wider freedom of expression issues, that:

> "the statutory requirement of immediacy insures that writings containing ideas which are likely to offend, shock or disturb any section of the population may be freely published unless there is a clear and present danger of violence caused by publication. The requirement of immediacy is essential to prevent the exercise of the right of free speech from being unnecessarily restrained or punished even where the words are threatening, abusive or insulting".[30] The magistrate ruled that the words "such evidence" implied the word immediate into the expression. The applicant sought judicial review of this decision.

Decision. For the following reasons, the application was dismissed[31]:

(1) It was doubted whether Parliament would introduce a section, the conduct of which, although to have an immediate effect on a person, the violent reaction was to be at some unspecified time in the future.
(2) The words "such violence" in (iii) and (iv) must have been intended by Parliament to refer back to (i) and (ii) where the word "immediate" is used.
(3) Where in a penal statute, there are two possible interpretations, it is a basic rule that the restricted meaning which limits the scope of the offence is to be preferred. The court stated that it would be strange if in (ii), the prosecution had to prove intent to provoke immediate violence, whereas in (iv), no such proof of immediacy was required.

The court, however, was of the opinion that "immediate" does not mean instantaneous, but within a relatively short time of the offensive behaviour being used.

Under section 4(2), the offence may occur in a private or public place. However, the offence cannot be committed where both parties are in the same dwelling or one of the parties is in another dwelling.[32] Therefore, domestic quarrels which take place in the home are not included, but may still be caught for breach of the peace or other offences. Common parts, such as a landing and presumably lifts, common stairs, etc., do not come under the description of dwelling for the purposes of this section.[33]

Section 4A: Intentional harassment, alarm or distress ("HAD")

4–018 Section 4A of the Public Order Act of 1986 (introduced by section 154 of the Criminal Justice and Public Order Act 1994), makes it an offence to intentionally harass, alarm or distress another: the requirements of intention and that the victim did in fact suffer such consequences are a question of fact for the court. All offences under section 4 are arrestable without a warrant and punishable by up to six months' imprisonment or a level five fine or both (section 4A(5)). The wording of section 4A is similar to both that of section 4 and section 5.

Section 5—harassment, alarm or distress (HAD)

Under section 5(1), a person is guilty of an offence if he— **4–019**

(a) uses threatening, abusive or insulting words or behaviour or *disorderly behaviour*; or

(b) displays any writing, sign or other visible representation which is *threatening, abusive or insulting*, within the hearing or sight of a person likely to be caused *harassment, alarm or distress* thereby. (italics added)

This section makes it an offence to use threatening, abusive or insulting words or behaviour, or disorderly behaviour within the hearing or sight of a person who is likely to be caused harassment, alarm or distress (HAD) as a result. Although the offence only attracts a maximum penalty of a level three (currently £1,000) fine it can be a useful offence to charge in more minor cases and can provide evidence if subsequent behaviour demands that injunctions and/or more serious criminal charges are necessary. One advantage of this offence is that there is no need to prove that the person was in fact harassed, alarmed or distressed, only that the consequence is likely as a result of the actions of the defendant, which allows for more vulnerable victims to be considered when charging the offence (*i.e.* the person of reasonable firmness test, applicable to the more serious public order offences does not apply). The offence is also subject to defences which prevent defendants being convicted as a result of vexatious claims. Thus, one cannot be guilty if the action was reasonable or the defendant had no reason to believe that anyone might witness the behaviour who would be harassed, alarmed or distressed.

Definition of words in section 5—Threatening, abusive, insulting, words, or disorderly behaviour

The offensive words in section 5(1) are not defined elsewhere, and it is left **4–020** to the courts to indicate whether these words are to be given their normal everyday meaning or whether some special legal definition should be attached to them. Case law normally interprets these words as they are used in common practice. Although the words each have their own distinct, individual meaning, there is undoubtedly a closer relationship and overlap between some more than others. However, their use in section 5(1)(a) and (b) is restricted to remarks which fall short of turning the situation into one of violence. Hence, the penalty for the offence in section 5 is limited to a fine[34] whereas in sections 1 to 4 which do include the word violence, actual or threatened, carry with them terms of imprisonment.

Those likely to be caused harassment, alarm or distress ("HAD")

4–021 If, for example, a person shouts obscenities or threatens a person in the immediate area with such words, and no one hears, there is no offence under this or any other section.[35] No harm of any kind has been done. It only becomes an offence if the offensive remarks or behaviour are seen or heard by others likely to be HAD. Thus in *Vigon v. DPP*[36] the defendant was convicted of causing HAD under section 5 by installing a video camera in order to take films of women trying on swimwear at his clothing stall. He appealed. Normally, a section 5 offence was used when dealing with conduct which was open and at least within the sight of a person likely to be HAD. Here, the court held that by fixing up the camera and turning it on, this amounted to insulting behaviour within section 5. It made no difference whether he himself looked at the women undressing or whether he used a camera to observe the act. Accordingly, the appeal was dismissed.

One may argue that, if the only people within seeing or hearing distance are the police, it is highly unlikely that such persons would be HAD, since the use of rude or offensive language are a common occurrence in the everyday life of a police constable, and provided that violence is an unlikely consequence of such remarks, no offence will have been committed under section 5(1).[37]

4–022 However, in *DPP v. Orum*[38]:

Facts. The defendant and his girlfriend were standing in a street having a quarrel, the former using offensive and foul language. Two constables repeatedly requested him to desist. The defendant became abusive and uttered the time-honoured phrase, "I know my rights" and continued, "If you don't go away I am going to hit you." Upon being arrested for breach of the peace, he kicked and punched one of the constables. The magistrates having decided that, as the only persons present were the defendant's girlfriend and the two constables, no other persons were likely to be HAD. Thus, no offence was committed under section 5(1) and therefore it was an unlawful arrest.

Accordingly, the charges were dismissed.

Decision. On appeal by the prosecution, one of the main issues was whether it was possible for a police constable to be HAD. The court answered in the affirmative. It "is a question of fact (not law) for the magistrates to decide having regards to all the circumstances: the time, the place, the nature of the words used, who the police officers are and so on".

It would seem that the defendant must take his victim as he finds him. Thus, the victim of the abuse is not necessarily the ordinary reasonable individual but any person who possesses such characteristics which would be likely to cause him HAD. In *DPP v. Orum*, McCullough J. pointed out that what is important is not the physical impact which was to be had on any person under this section, but the mental impact suffered on account of the words used in section 5(1).

Defences under section 5

Under section 5(3) the accused does have a number of defences if he can prove the following: (a) that he had no reason to believe that there was any person within hearing or sight who was likely to be caused HAD, or (b) that he was inside a dwelling and had no reason to believe that the words, etc., would be heard or seen by a person outside that or any other dwelling, or (c) that his conduct was reasonable. **4–023**

In *DPP v. Clarke*[39]:

Facts. The defendants, anti-abortionists, took part in a demonstration outside an abortion clinic. They displayed photographs of abortive foetuses to passing motorists and in particular to the police constable on duty. After repeated requests to stop displaying the pictures, the defendants were arrested and charged under sections 5 and 6 of the Public Order Act 1986. The defendants put forward the defence under section 5(3) that their conduct was reasonable. The justices found that under section 5(1) the photographs were abusive and insulting and likely to cause those within sight to be HAD, and indeed the police constable present was found to be so. Thus, applying an objective test, the justices ruled that the defendants conduct was not reasonable.
However, under section 6(4) "a person was guilty under section 5 only if he intends the writing, etc., to be threatening, abusive or insulting, or is aware that it may be (so)". Thus, using a subjective standard, the justices found that on a balance of probabilities, the defendant did not intend the photographs to be threatening, abusive or insulting or was aware they might be so.

Decision. The prosecutor appealed on the grounds that the defendants must have been aware, at the very least, that the display of the photographs might be abusive or insulting; coupled with this was the justices findings that the pictures were likely to cause HAD and did in fact do so. The court stated that section 5(1) was made up of two distinguishing features; (1) the display, etc., must be threatening, abusive or insulting and (2) it had to be within the sight of a person likely to be caused HAD. Section 6(4) only concerns "intention to" threaten, abuse or insult; HAD is not mentioned. On the evidence, it was found that the defendants did not intend to threaten abuse or insult.

Even if the prosecution proved that the defendants intended the pictures to HAD, it does not necessarily mean that they also intended them to be threatening, abusive or insulting. Despite the fact that the pictures themselves were threatening, abusive or insulting, (the police constable found them so) the justices found that, according to the evidence, the defendants lacked the necessary *mens rea* under section 6(4) for the offence to be made out.

Sometimes the innocent get caught up in a march or demonstration. **4–024**
Merely being in the vicinity is not, in itself, proof of participation, but being a member of that protesting group, *e.g.* Animal Rights, may be sufficient to

establish a prima facie case against that person despite there being no proof that threatening behaviour, etc., was used by that person.[40]

Section 4A is very similar to section 5, *i.e.* the offensive words are threatening, abusive or insulting behaviour, and these words are connected by causation to the words harassment, alarm or distress. However, there are significant differences between the two sections. In section 4A(1), the offence can only be committed if there is "intent" involved to cause HAD by using threatening, abusive or insulting behaviour, whereas in section 5, no intent is required, merely using the words will suffice. Also in section 4A(1)(b), the intended person of the offensive words must be actually caused HAD, whereas in section 5(1)(b), the wording is a little different in that the offender needs to be within the hearing or sight of a person likely to be caused HAD. In *Chappell v. DPP*,[41] letters containing offensive words, were put through a private letter box. On the question whether this would come within section 5(1)(a) or (b), the court held that where the offensive words were not visible from within an envelope, they could not be considered as "displayed" for the purposes of section 5(1)(b). Further, the court stated that sending a letter to another person, who opens it in their absence, did not constitute "within the hearing or sight of a person" under that section. The court in that case looked at the wider issues and pragmatic purpose of the act and concluded that it was not meant to be applied in cases such as this. Thus, offences under the Act are primarily to be used for public order purposes, *e.g.* disorderly conduct outside pubs, verbally abusing or frightening the disabled, elderly or ethnic minorities, or displaying posters which were racially offensive. Indeed, for the Public Order Act to apply the offensive words should affect a certain section or group, no matter how small, of society.[42] Section 42 of the Criminal Justice and Police Act 2001 deals with the situation where HAD is likely to be caused by persons outside or in the vicinity of a dwelling, such as a home or other living accommodation, against residents living there. Under these circumstances, where there are reasonable grounds to believe that persons are likely to cause HAD, a police officer may order such persons to leave the vicinity of the dwelling; or he may, in order to prevent HAD, impose such conditions as he thinks fit to the location, distance, number or identity of persons who may remain in the vicinity of the targeted premises (section 42(5)). Failure to comply constitutes an offence for which the penalty, on summary conviction, may be a maximum of up to three months imprisonment or a fine (section 42(7)). Section 42 does not apply to the right to picket peacefully at a work place.

Processions and Assemblies

Section 11: Notice of processions

4–025 The Public Order Act 1986 contains no definition of "procession" and case law has little to add. It was defined in *Flockhart v. Robinson*[43] as "a body of persons moving along a route",[44] but this is merely a common sense definition. Any march or moving demonstration will be included, as long as at least two people are involved.

If a procession is intended to be held, then there is a requirement under section 11 that the police must be given notice by the organisers if the procession is to be public and in addition is intended to have any of the three following purposes:

(i) to demonstrate support for, or opposition to, the views or actions of any person or body of persons; or

(ii) to publicise a cause or campaign; or

(iii) to mark or commemorate an event.

A procession is a public procession if it takes place in a public place, that is on the highway, or anywhere to which the public has access by right or by express or implied permission, regardless of whether access is obtained by payment (section 16). Thus a football ground, library or cinema is a public place for this purpose.

There are, however, certain exceptions which will exempt some public processions which appear to fall within one of the three purposes above from the notice requirement. Customary processions such as long-established annual celebrations and official funeral processions are both exempt (section 11(2)). Regardless of the type of procession, notice is not required if it is not reasonably practicable for advance notice to be given, for example where a procession is a spontaneous and immediate reaction to an announcement of an event such as a deportation order where quick reaction is necessary if the protest is to have any chance at success.

Where notice is required, it must be given at least six clear days before the planned procession, either by post or by hand delivery, and must contain the date, starting time, proposed route and the name and address of at least one of the organisers of the procession. The notice must be delivered to a police station in the police area in which it is proposed that the procession will commence (sections 11(3)–(6)). If the required notice is not given satisfactorily, then a summary offence is committed.

It should be noted that the requirement is merely one of notice, not of permission; if the police wish to prevent a procession of which they have been given notice, then they must initiate separate proceedings for banning that procession. There is no need for the organisers to seek permission from the police or to wait for it to be granted.

Section 12—Imposing conditions upon a procession

Where any public procession is planned (whether or not it has one of the purposes listed in section 11), a senior police officer may impose conditions upon the procession where he has one of the specified grounds for doing so. The senior police officer is simply the most senior officer present if the **4–026** procession is about to commence, or the chief constable or Commissioner if the procession is still at the planning stage (section 12(2)). While the procession is still merely planned, any conditions imposed must be given in writing, but once the protesters are beginning to assemble then conditions may be imposed orally. The grounds for imposition of conditions are that the senior police officer reasonably believes that any of the following is true:

(i) the procession may result in serious public disorder, serious damage to property, or serious disruption to the life of the community; or

(ii) the organisers intend to intimidate others into complying with their wishes, so that the others either do an act which they have a right not to do, or do not do an act which they have a right to do (for example where striking workers follow non-striking colleagues towards the building and attempt to persuade them not to work).

Section 12(1) allows the senior officer to impose any conditions which appear to him to be necessary in order to prevent the feared harm. This is a subjective test; the officer does not have to be able to show that his choice of conditions was based on reasonable grounds. This wide discretion is potentially open to abuse since conditions may be imposed upon a procession in such a manner that it is deprived of any desired effect, for example, by diverting the route or preventing the entry of a particular public place. Failure to comply with conditions, if done with knowledge of the condition(s), is an offence which can be committed by an organiser or participant in the procession and which is arrestable without warrant if a constable in uniform reasonably suspects a person of committing such an offence (section 12(4), (5)). Section 12(6) creates an offence of inciting another to fail to comply with a condition. These offences and arrest powers are extremely wide and overlap greatly with other powers of arrest under section 25 of PACE and the common law of breach of the peace, thus leading to criticism.

Section 13(B): Banning processions

4–027 A chief officer of police may apply to a local council for an order which prohibits either all public processions or all public processions of a particular class, in that area, and for a specified period of up to three months. In order to obtain a banning order, the chief officer must believe on reasonable grounds that, due to circumstances existing in the police area at that time, his section 12 power to impose conditions will be insufficient to prevent serious public disorder. In London, a banning order may be granted by the Commissioner of the Metropolitan or City Police forces with the consent of the Home Secretary. Outside London, the procedure is for the chief constable to apply to the local council, which may issue the banning order with the approval of the Home Secretary, who may also modify it. In *Kent v. MPC*[45] members of the Campaign for Nuclear Disarmament wished to hold a peaceful protest march in London. The Metropolitan Police Commissioner applied for (with the consent of the Home Secretary) and was granted, an order prohibiting all public processions in the Metropolitan area (some 786 square miles) for 28 days in order to "prevent serious public disorder" under the then section 3 of the Public Order Act 1936. The organisers applied for judicial review against the order. They argued that the order was too wide. The Court of Appeal said that the decision whether there was a real risk of serious public disorder should be left up to the Commissioner, unless he was at fault or acted *ultra vires*, which was not considered to be the case here. There had in recent months been serious disturbances in Brixton and elsewhere resulting in serious damage to property and attacks on the police. The problem in this case was not the protestors themselves, whose intentions were purely non-violent, but a hooligan element bent on causing unrest and destruction. Any procession would be, the Court said, albeit unwittingly, provocative to that violent extremist minority. Since there was, under the present circumstances, a real risk of serious harm if the procession went ahead, the Commissioner had acted within his powers. Therefore the application was dismissed. In the above case, the order did not apply to those processions traditionally held, *e.g.* the May Day parade or religious processions; nor did it operate to prevent public meetings from taking place during this period.

Although there is no power to ban one particular procession, a banning order for a class of processions may in practice be worded so tightly that only one planned procession is affected. A banning order may be subjected to judicial review if practicable (see *Kent v. MPC* above). There are summary arrestable offences of organisation or participation in a procession which has been banned, and of inciting another person to do so (section 13(7), (8), (9)).

Section 14: Imposing conditions upon public meetings

The Public Order Act 1986 introduced for the first time a statutory method of controlling static public meetings or assemblies. Previously only moving processions could be regulated, yet a series of disturbances such as the vigorous picketing during the 1984–85 miners' strike demonstrated that a protest does not have to be mobile in order to raise public order implications. But, unlike processions, public meetings could not originally be banned under the 1986 Act. The police had a power merely to impose conditions before the meeting could go ahead. Public meetings are perceived as being a fundamental expression of freedom of speech, and they are of course an important part of the political process; thus it is with caution that any limitations are to be placed upon the citizen's freedoms of **4–028** expression and association. However, as will be seen below, the 1994 Criminal Justice and Public Order Act controversially inserted a new power to ban certain types of assembly or meeting; this will be discussed later.

Section 16 defines a public assembly widely as any "assembly of twenty or more persons in a public place which is wholly or partly open to the air". Public places are defined in the same way here as for section 11, that is the highway or "any place to which at the material time the public or any section of the public has access, on payment or otherwise, as of right or by virtue of express or implied permission" (section 16). But there is no reference to the purposes of the assembly; thus it is not relevant why the assembly has congregated when judging whether conditions may be imposed upon it. Section 14 provides a parallel system for imposing conditions upon public assemblies to that for imposing conditions upon public processions (section 12). Thus a chief constable or Commissioner may impose conditions before the assembly occurs, or the senior police officer present at the scene of an assembly which is underway may also do so (section 14(2)). Section 14(1) lists the grounds for imposing conditions, which are identical to those already discussed under section 12(1) above, *i.e.* the officer has a reasonable belief that the assembly may result in serious public disorder, or serious damage to property, or serious disruption to the life of the community; or that the assembly has the illegitimate purpose of intimidating others.

One difference between section 12 and section 14 relates to the precise conditions which may be imposed: as far as assemblies are concerned, there is a limited category of conditions, *i.e.* directions as to "the place at which the assembly may be . . . held, its maximum duration, or the maximum number of persons who may constitute it" which appear to the senior police officer to be required in order to prevent the threatened harm. A second difference between processions and assemblies is that there is no requirement of notice of an assembly. Again in parallel to processions, there are offences of organisation of or participation in an assembly while knowingly failing to comply with a condition under section 14(4) and 14(5), and of incitement to such participation under section 14(7).

Section 14(A): Trespassory assemblies

4–029 This section was inserted by section 70 of the Criminal Justice and Public Order Act 1994, and provides for the first time a power to ban certain categories of static assembly. A chief officer of police may apply for a banning order if: he reasonably believes that an assembly is likely to be trespassory and may result in serious disruption to the life of the community, or in serious property damage. There must be, or be likely to be, 20 or more persons congregating on the land in question. The land must be open to the air and the public must have either no right of access or a merely limited right of access to the land. If permission has been given for the assembly and any terms of such permission have not been exceeded or breached, nor is any such breach likely, then a ban cannot be issued.

A banning order, once granted, lasts for four days and covers a five mile area around the stipulated location. But these two restrictions do little to limit the power to ban; by comparison with the power to ban marches, section 14A is far wider, being based upon the police officer's belief of what may be "serious disruption to the community" rather than section 13's "prevention of serious public disorder". Section 71 of the 1994 Act added section 14C, which provides for a power to stop any persons within a five mile radius of an assembly if a police officer believes on reasonable grounds that a section 14A banning order has been granted and that the persons in question are travelling to the prohibited assembly.

Perhaps due to concerns about the civil liberties implications of section 14A, few such banning orders have in fact been granted and indeed the police appear reluctant to apply for such an order even where serious disturbances are feared. However, it may be simply that the power to ban is being used strategically as a bargaining tool whereby the police and local authorities negotiate with the organisers of planned marches or assemblies by using the threat of a ban to ensure compliance with conditions or to render them unnecessary.

In *DPP v. Jones*[46]: **4–030**

Facts. The police applied for, and were granted an order under section 14A(2) (see below) prohibiting the holding of trespassory assemblies within a four-mile radius of Stonehenge from May 29 until June 1, 1995. On June 1, some 21 persons assembled on the grass verge next to the roadside of Stonehenge. Although they assembled on the public highway and were peaceful and non-obstructive, nevertheless the police requested them to leave, under the section 14A order. They refused and the defendants were arrested. Section 14A(1) states that -

> "if . . . a chief officer of police reasonably believes that an assembly is intended to be held . . . on land to which the public has no right . . . or only a limited right of access . . . he may apply to the council of the district for an order prohibiting for a specified period . . . all trespassory assemblies." Under section 14A(2), ". . . a council may . . . with the consent of the Secretary of State make an order . . .". The defendants were convicted by the magistrates under section 14B(2) which states that—"a person who takes part in an assembly which he knows is prohibited by an order under section 14A is guilty of an offence".

On appeal to the Crown Court, the court ruled that the appellants had not exceeded their "limited" right of access to the highway as defined by section 14A(9) which states that—"limited . . . means that their [the public] use of it [the highway] is restricted to use for a particular purpose . . .". Since the appellants remained within these legal bounds, *i.e.* peaceful assembly, the appeal was allowed. Thereafter, the prosecution appealed to the High Court.

Decision. The main issues for deliberation were (1) where there is a section 14A(2) order in force, does a peaceful assembly exceed the public's right of access to the highway and thus, amount to a trespassory assembly under section 14A? (2) Must the prosecution prove that all those present (at least 20) exceeded the allowed limit within section 14A(9) or merely to those persons charged who exceeded the limit? The argument by the respondents, that provided the assembly was peaceful and no obstruction was caused then it was lawful, was rejected by the court. It did not take into account the prohibiting of the assembly by the section 14A(2) order and its legal consequences. The answer to the first question was yes. Very little argument was given to the second question, except that the court concluded in the final paragraph of the judgment that the answer was no because under section 14A(5), although the assembly must exceed the limit of the public's right of access, any one of that group who is aware of the prohibition section 14A order is liable under either section 14B(1) or (2).[47] The court examined the age-old problem of whether a person has the right of peaceful assembly on a public highway. First and foremost, there is no legal right to the freedom of public assembly on a public highway. McCowan L.J. cited the cases of *Harrison v. Duke of Rutland*,[48] to support the view that no such right exists, although a person is free to use the public highway in order to (a) pass or repass and/or (b) for any reasonable or ordinary purpose. Holding public meetings or assemblies would, it seems, not come automatically within the categories of (a) or (b) above. This view was endorsed by Collins J. who stated that:

> "the holding of a meeting, a demonstration or a vigil on the highway, however peaceable, has nothing to do with the right of passage. Such activities may, if they do not cause an obstruction, be tolerated, but there is no right to pursue them. A right to do something only exists if it cannot be stopped: the fact that it would not be stopped does not create a right to do it".[49]

4–031 In *DPP* v. *Jones*[50] the defendant thereafter appealed to the House of Lords. The two main questions for considerations were (1) what were the limits of the public's right of access to the public highway at common law; and (2) what was the particular purpose for which the public had a right to use the highway. If the public's right to use the highway was restricted to only "passing and repassing" and not for the purpose of peaceful assembly, then the decision of the Crown Court would no doubt have been upheld. However, the House of Lords recognised the principle of permitting "reasonable activities" to be conducted on the highway, in this instance, peaceful assembly. The Lord Chancellor stated that reasonable activities should be allowed provided they (i) did not involve the commission of a public or private nuisance, (ii) did not involve obstruction of the highway or the public's right to pass and repass, and (iii) did not involve trespass. It was a question of fact and degree in each case. Lord Clyde's approach was somewhat more cautious. He stated that a careful assessment of the nature and extent of the activity in question was required, and that a peaceful assembly that did not obstruct the highway did not necessarily constitute a trespassory assembly. Accordingly, the House of Lords (by a 3 to 2 majority) allowed the appeal.

Section 14A(2) applies to "trespassory assemblies", and the chief officer of police must have a reasonable belief that some form of trespass is likely to occur in the foreseeable future. The belief itself may be based on past experiences of similar situations. Once the order has been granted, its instigation should be reserved for those instances where a trespass is or is about to take place. However, in Jones it seems that there was in fact no trespass, unless as was described in the reports that "some banners were draped over the perimeter fence," could somehow constitute a trespass. This would indeed be stretching the definition of a legal trespass. The granting of the order itself may have been correct but its application in this instance is to be doubted. If that is the case, then it is submitted that the incorrect order was used and a section 14 order imposing conditions to the assembly would have been more appropriate. If the use of the order was legal, then it is possible to speculate that future peaceful assemblies will be considered prohibitory all too easily. The question will not arise whether the assembly was conducted in a peaceful and non-obstructive manner, but whether the police themselves decide to sanction such a gathering and thereby further the "inroads" into freedom to protest activities on the public highway.

Sections 63–67: Criminal Justice and Public Order Act 1994: preventing and controlling raves

As can be seen from the wording of these sections, they were drafted to **4–032** deal with the perceived harm of a very specific type of behaviour, the rave, which had been causing controversy for some years and which had proved difficult to control under existing legislation. A rave is a large gathering at which music is played and dancing takes place, often outdoors and usually with the permission of the landowner upon whose property the event is held, indeed, the landowner is often paid for the use of his land. Permission to use the land rules out the possibility of the rave being classified as a trespassory assembly, but the potential for excessive noise does mean that noise pollution offences may be committed and noise abatement sanctions may be taken by local authorities, the police, or neighbours if there are any. An added perceived threat of raves is the sheer number of people who will typically travel to and congregate at the event.

According to section 63(1), a rave is where at least 100 people gather, on open land, where "amplified music is played during the night" and the music, due to its volume, duration and the time at which it is played, "is likely to cause serious distress to the inhabitants of the locality". Section 63(1)(b) defines music widely so that it covers "sounds wholly or predominantly characterised by the emission of a succession of repetitive beats". This cumbersome definition is designed to catch rave and dance music, but has been seen by some as a sign of prejudice against modern music. If an officer of at least the rank of superintendent believes on reasonable grounds that two or more people are preparing for the holding of a rave, or that 10 or more persons are waiting for a rave to start, or that at least 10 people are at a rave which has already begun, then he may order those people to leave the land in question and to take with them any vehicles and property which they may have brought (section 63(2)). If any such person fails to comply with such an order, or returns to the land in question within seven days, then he is committing a summary offence under section 63(6), for which there is a power of arrest under section 63(8) which may be exercised by any uniformed constable.

In parallel to section 14C of the Public Order Act 1986, if a superintendent or officer of higher rank has made a section 63(2) order in relation to a particular rave, then any constable in uniform may stop any people who are within five miles of the rave whom he believes on reasonable grounds to be travelling to the rave, and he may then direct them that they should not proceed in travelling towards the rave (section 65). If any person fails to comply with such a direction, then they commit an arrestable summary offence.

Section 64 gives the police a power to enter land in order to seize sound equipment and vehicles if a rave is taking place. If a person is convicted of any of the offences relating to raves, then any confiscated equipment may be forfeited under section 66.

Section 68: Criminal Justice and Public Order Act 1994: aggravated trespass

4–033 Like sections 63–67, section 68 was designed to deal with a particular type of behaviour which was perceived to be an interference with lawful activity or behaviour. In this instance, the perceived harm is hunt sabotage, but the section is drafted so widely that other behaviour which disrupts any lawful activity in the open air may be covered, for example streaking or protesting against road building by digging and living in tunnels on land designated for the construction work. The offence under section 68 is committed by trespassing on land in the open air. The definition of land for these purposes does not include roads but does cover bridleways, footpaths and so on (section 61(9)). The required mental state is that of intention that one of the following three sets of circumstances will result from the relevant conduct: intimidation of any person or persons involved in lawful activity, in order to deter them from that activity; or obstruction of the lawful activity; or disruption of the lawful activity (section 68(1)). There is clearly an overlap between these three sets of circumstances.

An offence under section 68 is, in summary, punishable by up to three months' imprisonment, and carries a power of arrest by a constable in uniform (section 68(4)). Again in parallel to the provisions concerning raves, a constable may direct trespassers whom he reasonably believes to be involved in the commission of a section 68 offence, or to have already committed or to be about to commit a section 68 offence, to leave the land in question (section 69). It is a further offence to fail to leave the land, or to re-enter within three months, with knowledge that a direction to leave the land has been given, but there is a defence available to section 69 if the defendant can show that he was either (a) not a trespasser on the land, or (b) had a reasonable excuse for his failure to leave the land as soon as was practicable or his re-entry of the land.

4–034 Thus in *Winder v. DPP*[51]:

Facts. The defendants, along with some 200 to 400 protestors, went as trespassers onto a field where a fox hunt was taking place. Their intention was to disrupt the event. At the time of their arrest they were running across the field in the direction of the fox hunt. The defendants were charged and convicted of aggravated trespass contrary to section 68 Criminal Justice and Public Order Act 1994.

Decision. In order for the offence under section 68 to be sustained, the prosecution must prove (1) the defendants were trespassers and (2) they intended to disrupt the lawful activity of fox hunting and did some act towards that end. The appellants admitted that it was their intention to interfere with the hunt, but that merely running along with the hunt did not in itself obstruct the event in any way. However, it was found, as a matter of fact, that the running after the hunt was a means to an end, *i.e.* an intention to disrupt it. Thus, the act of pursuing the hunt was, it was decided, so closely connected with the intention to disrupt it that it was "more than merely preparatory" (Criminal Attempts Act 1989), and constituted the required offence and therefore the appeal was dismissed.

Section 61: Criminal Justice and Public Order Act 1994: controlling travellers

Another new perceived threat to public order in recent years which had **4–035** proved difficult to control under offences existing before 1986 was that of travellers, gypsies and new age convoys who may take over land belonging to third parties as trespassers for a limited amount of time, allegedly causing disturbance and damage and refusing to leave the land when asked to do so. Particular concern related to the damage caused by large numbers of vehicles being moved onto land. The opposite side of the argument points out that such groups have existed for centuries and arguably have established rights to their chosen ways of life. Long-established patterns of movement and use of land have been interrupted increasingly in recent years by restrictive policies controlling and limiting the number and size of official sites for travellers' use and limiting the length of permitted stay at some locations. The rights of landowners come into direct conflict with the freedom of movement of travellers and their freedom to live according to their chosen values. Again, it is arguable that one of the purposes behind this offence, the prevention of gatherings at ancient monuments such as Stonehenge for unofficial festivals and pagan celebrations, may be an overreaction and an interference with a legitimate use of ancient sites, although of course such sites and monuments must be preserved and protected.

These groups are a kind of moving assembly and so fell between several types of regulation, and section 39 of the Public Order Act 1986 was introduced into the Act at a late stage of its progress through Parliament in an attempt to deal with the problem. Section 39 was repealed and replaced by section 61 of the Criminal Justice and Public Order Act 1994, which in fact is not substantially different from its predecessor. Section 61 creates a limited criminal offence of group trespass on open land. Common land is covered by the definition, but trespass of buildings will not constitute the offence, with the exception of agricultural buildings and monuments; thus squatters in private or council residential accommodation will not commit this offence.[52] A "group" of trespassers need only in fact number two, although this is not the intention behind the creation of the offence; however there is a potential here for persons such as anti-road protesters to be caught by this offence in addition to those specifically designed for their activities, discussed above.

4–036 The offence is triggered by failure to comply with a direction issued by a police officer to leave the land. A police officer may make such a direction to leave the land if he believes on reasonable grounds that the occupier of the land, or his representative, has already taken reasonable steps to ask the trespassers to leave the land. In *Krumpa and Anderson v. DPP*[53] it was stated that the words "as soon as reasonably practicable" in section 39(2) are not to be judged by the police who made the order to move off the land, but instead referred to the actual practicalities of leaving the property. Further, it was best for all concerned that the police state in clear language and terms the precise time the trespassers are to leave, and to ask them to remove their belongings, *e.g.* caravans, vehicles, etc., so that there should be no misunderstanding as to the exact requirement orders.

In addition to his belief that the landowner has taken these reasonable steps, the police officer making the direction to leave must also have one of the following alternative beliefs, based upon reasonable grounds, before he may direct the trespassers to leave; either—

(i) that one or more of the trespassers has caused damage to property which is on the land; or

(ii) that one or more trespassers has used threatening, abusive or insulting words or behaviour towards the occupier or his family or representative; or

(ii) that the trespassers have brought at least six vehicles onto the land.

After a direction to leave the land has been given by a police officer according to the above requirements, any person who either fails to leave the land within a reasonable amount of time, or who re-enters the land or attempts to do so within three months, will commit the offence. Section 61(5) attaches a power of arrest which is exerciseable by a constable in uniform if he reasonably suspects any person of having committed a section 61 offence; thus it can be seen that it is relatively easy to empty the land of all trespassers and vehicles within a short time of a direction to leave being given. If vehicles are left on the land after a direction to leave, they may be seized (section 62).

The Public Order Act 1936 has all but been repealed. Section 1 states that ". . . any person who in any public or at a public meeting wears a uniform signifying his association with any political organisation . . . shall be guilty of an offence".

In *DPP v. O'Moran*[54]:

4–037 **Facts**. The defendants took part in a political funeral procession of a man who had recently died in prison. Each defendant wore a black or dark blue beret, dark glasses, black roll-necked pullovers, dark clothing and walked in front of the hearse, taking military commands from one of the defendants, O'Moran. They were arrested and charged under section 1(1) of the Public Order Act 1936. The defendants argued that (1) they were not wearing a uniform, since there were differences in dress between them. (2) No political organisation had been identified. (3) There was no evidence that the clothing worn was the uniform of any political organisation. The magistrates found that it was a question of fact and degree as to what constituted a uniform. They concluded that from the evidence, *e.g.* photographs, placing the Irish tricolour flag and black beret on the coffin, the clothing was distinctive enough to be a uniform, and as a fact signified association with an Irish political movement. It was not necessary to identify the particular political organisation. The defendants were convicted and appealed.

Decision. On appeal, it was held that "its power to show the association of the wearer with a political organisation can be judged from the events (and conduct) to be seen on the occasion when the alleged uniform was worn".[55] Since the defendants were taking an active part in a funeral service associated with a member of the Irish republican movement, this, together with the other evidence (cited above) amounted to a political gathering. But it was not necessary for the prosecution to prove exactly which political organisation the defendant belonged to. Accordingly, the appeals were dismissed.

RELEVANT ECHR DECISIONS

The very essence of Article 10(1) is its broad scope, taking in not only the freedom to express opinions and ideas via various mediums of communication, but also extending to the unrestricted freedom of all individuals, be they politicians, religious leaders, lawyers and so forth, to be permitted to put forward their views without fear of interference by the public authorities. Article 11 has been interpreted in a similar way. **4–038**

In *Ezelin v France*[56]:

Facts. The applicant, a Guadeloupe lawyer, took part in a procession involving about 1000 people. During the demonstration certain people chanted slogans, painted offensive graffiti on a number of buildings, made death threats against the Guadeloupe judiciary, and generally behaved in an aggressive manner. The applicant was eventually charged with breaches of professional duty and with "taking part in a public demonstration against the judiciary in circumstances likely to entail criminal liability under Article 226 of the Criminal Code". It was not disputed that the applicant himself acted in a peaceful manner during the demonstration. The Bar Council dismissed the action for disciplinary sanctions against the applicant. The Public Prosecutor appealed to the court of Appeal against the decision. The Court of Appeal reversed the Bar Council's decision and formally reprimanded the applicant for his misconduct.

Decision. The applicant complained to the Commission that there had been a breach of freedom of peaceful assembly guaranteed by Articles 10 and 11. The Commission found that since he had not disassociated himself with the aggressive behaviour of certain demonstrators, and by refusing to identify the perpetrators of various criminal acts committed during the demonstration, *e.g.* criminal damage, the disciplinary sanction of the applicant being reprimanded was not disproportionate to the seriousness of his professional misconduct. The applicant complained that the interference, which the court found to be legitimate for the prevention of disorder under Article 11(2), was not, however, necessary in a democratic society. The main question for the court to consider was whether or not the reprimand was proportionate to the legitimate aim pursued, having regard to the special importance of peaceful assembly and freedom of expression (para. 51). "The proportionality principle demands that a balance be struck between the requirements of the purposes listed in Article 11(2) and those of the free expression of opinions by word, gesture or even silence by persons assembled on the streets or in other public places. The pursuit of a just balance must not result in avocats being discouraged, for fear of disciplinary sanctions, from making clear their benefits on such occasions" (para. 52). Even though the reprimand was at the lower end of the disciplinary scale of penalties, the freedom to take part in a legally permitted peaceful assembly, even for a lawyer, should not be undermined. Accordingly, the court found that the reprimand was disproportionate and not necessary in a democratic society. Therefore there was a violation of Article 11 in this case.

4–039 There has also been scrutiny of specific uses of the United Kingdom powers to ban assemblies and processions: in *Rai, Allmond & "Negotiate Now" v. United Kingdom*,[57] the government refused to permit the applicants to hold a rally in Trafalgar Square for the purposes of promoting peace negotiations in Northern Ireland. The government gave their reasons that since 1972 it had been the policy of successive governments to ban all demonstrations taking place in Trafalgar Square relating to issues concerning Northern Ireland, although other venues may be used for such purposes. On application for judicial review, counsel for the Secretary of State stated that permission was refused on public order grounds. Although rallies in Trafalgar Square may be permitted for "uncontroversial" gatherings, the government stated that the present demonstration did not come within that category. Accordingly, leave for judicial review was denied. The applicants complained to the Commission that the ban was in breach of Articles 9, 10 and 11 (*i.e.* freedom to manifest their beliefs in public, freedom of expression and freedom of public assembly). Since it was established that there was an interference within Article 11(1), the Commission had to consider whether the restriction was prescribed by law, and if so, was the ban necessary in a democratic society? The applicants argued that the domestic law granting discretionary powers relating to the ban was "so broad and undefined as to render them unable to regulate their conduct or foresee the outcome of their request" (at page 97). The Commission stated that "provided that the scope of the discretion and the manner of its exercise are indicated with sufficient clarity to give the individual protection from arbitrary interference", no incompatibility with the law arises. The House of Commons had on many previous occasions made public statements refusing permission to grant demonstrations of this nature. Accordingly, individuals could foresee with sufficient clarity and certainty how to regulate their conduct, and therefore the first requirement of "prescribed by law" had been achieved. Whether or not the ban was necessary in a democratic society, the Commission reverted to the accepted case law that necessity must correspond to a pressing social need, *i.e.* that it is proportionate to the legitimate aim pursued. In this respect, the state is permitted a degree of flexibility ("a margin of appreciation"). This included the government being permitted to grant certain "uncontroversial" groups permission to use Trafalgar Square for peaceful demonstrations whilst refusing the applicants' rally, relating to the contentious issues of Northern Ireland, the same privilege and right. Since the government's decision was neither arbitrary nor biased, the restriction, under the circumstances, was regarded by the Commission as proportionate and justified as necessary in a democratic society and fell within the purpose of Article 11(2).

It appears that the Government is planning to "crack down" on unauthorised public assemblies and demonstrations, particularly those which have in the past been associated with violence, such as the May Day "Reclaim the Streets" event (which has been characterised variously as a demonstration or a riot, depending on the commentator's perspective). However any such move should be made with extreme caution since it could potentially fall foul of the Human Rights Act.

In *Hashman and Harrup v. U.K.* (1999) 30 E.H.R.R. 241:

Facts. The applicants, who were hunt saboteurs, attended a fox hunt and in order to disrupt the activities began blowing a horn and hallooing. Before the magistrates the applicants were bound over to keep the peace and be of good behaviour for a period of 12 months. On appeal, the Crown Court was of the opinion that there was no breach of the peace (there being no violence or threat of violence in this instance), but that the applicants' behaviour in attempting to interfere with the hunt was conduct amounting to *contra bonos mores.*[57A] Accordingly, the appeal was dismissed.

Decision. The applicants complained to the Commission and argued that "an order not to act *contra bonos mores* cannot be described as being 'prescribed by law' within the meaning of Article 10, as it does not state what the subject of the order may or may not lawfully do".[57B] Once the court had decided that there was an interference with their right to freedom of expression, the next question was whether the interference was "prescribed by law" under Article 10(2). The Government argued, *inter alia*, that by intending to disrupt the lawful activities of a hunt, the applicants were aware that their behaviour was unlawful and therefore their conduct was *contra bonos mores*. One important aspect of the "prescribed by law" expression is the requirement of foreseeability. Foreseeability involves the domestic law having "sufficient precision to enable the citizen to regulate his conduct".[57C] The court stated that

> "(the) level of precision depends to a considerable degree on the content of the instrument in question (in this instance the Justice of the Peace Act 1361 and the common law), the field it is designed to cover and the number and status of those to whom it is addressed".[57D]

The court, referring to the case of *Steel v. U.K.*,[57E] noted that the order "to be of good behaviour" was particularly imprecise. The applicants had not been charged with any criminal offence, nor had they been found to be in breach of the peace,[57F] therefore the order not to behave *contra bonos mores* was not evident or precise enough for the applicants to know over what they were being bound not to do. Accordingly, the order did not comply with the "prescribed by law" requirements within Article 10(2) and therefore it followed that there had been a violation of Article 10.

II RACIAL HATRED

4–040 Part III of the Public Order Act 1986 contains the criminal offences of incitement to racial hatred. These offences straddle several sections of the ambit of civil liberties, involving the competing claims of freedom of speech, freedom from harassment, abuse and defamation, and freedom from discrimination. However much it may be desired that no person should make racist statements or possess or publish racist material, to criminalise all such examples of conduct would constitute a serious inroad into freedom of speech or private behaviour. Thus further inflammatory motives, intentions or behaviour are required by the statutory offences in order to justify conviction. The offences were originally introduced under legislation concerning racial discrimination, but now clearly take the form of public order offences rather than a discrimination matter. It is not the effect on any victim which is of primary concern in relation to these offences, but the effect which the behaviour of the defendant either did have, or might potentially have, upon others who see, hear or otherwise witness it. The mischief addressed is the dissemination of racism rather than the practice of racism itself. Thus it is not an offence to hold racist beliefs, but it is an offence to attempt to influence others by such beliefs. Certain racist statements or material will not be covered by the offences, for example where the person concerned honestly believes that the material is factual, and it is presented in a manner which is not likely to foster racial hatred in others.

As a set of criminal offences, incitement to racial hatred is somewhat unusual in that it criminalises the incitement of behaviour which, if actually committed, is not in itself an offence. Generally speaking, incitement is only an offence where the conduct incited would itself be a criminal offence if committed by the incitee. It is therefore a measure of the importance placed upon the prevention of racism that this set of offences does exist. However, as a safeguard the consent of the Attorney-General is required before any prosecution may be brought for any of these offences.

The offences in Part III of the 1986 Act concern threatening, abusive or insulting words or behaviour, either conducted or published (or in one instance merely possessed[58]), in circumstances where the defendant either intends to encourage racial hatred, or his conduct is likely to have this effect.

Racial hatred in section 17 means "hatred against a group of persons in Great Britain defined by reference to colour, race, nationality (including citizenship) or ethnic or national origins". Religious groups are not included for the purposes of this section. However, in many cases there is an overlap between the terms "ethnic or national origins" and religion. Does, for instance, a person of the Jewish faith belong to a religion or an ethnic group or both? The answer, it has been suggested, is that it seems to fit the criteria of racial group as defined in the famous case of *Mandla v. Lee*,[59] which is discussed in detail in Chapter 9 on racial discrimination.

THE PERSON WHO "USES" OBJECTIONABLE BEHAVIOUR/DISPLAYS, ETC.

Under section 18(1): **4–041**

> "a person who uses threatening, abusive or insulting words or behaviour, or displays any written material which is threatening, abusive or insulting, is guilty of an offence if—
>
> (a) he intends thereby to stir up racial hatred; or
>
> (b) having regard to all the circumstances racial hatred is likely to be stirred up thereby."

Under section 18(1)(b) it is not necessary to prove an intention to stir up racial hatred; it will suffice that the inflammatory use was likely to result in such a consequence occurring. On the other hand, if the person using the words intended to create such an effect, then even if no hatred in fact resulted, or was even likely to result as a consequence, he may still be liable under section 18(1)(a). However, he may have a defence under section 18(5) if he can prove that he did not intend to promote racial hatred by his words, behaviour or written material, or was unaware that they might be threatening, abusive or insulting.

Under section 18 the objectionable behaviour/displays, etc., need not **4–042** necessarily be directed at any individual(s), it will suffice if the recipient happens to come across the racist or inflammatory material accidentally. The word "uses" means to a third party, inciting that person to racial hatred. It cannot be to a member of the racial group being vilified, since that would result in hatred against himself and this is not the purpose of the section. The objectionable behaviour/displays, etc., amount to an offence if committed in a public or private place, but no offence will be committed if the person responsible is in a dwelling and the only other person hearing or seeing the offensive material is also in that or another dwelling (section 18(2)). If a person inside a house is shouting abusive racial remarks and is overheard by somebody outside walking past, that would normally be an offence. But the offender has a defence if he can prove that he "had no reason to believe" that his remarks would be heard (section 18(4)). However, displaying for instance "a sign or other visible representation"[60] which is inflammatory next to an open window, within sight of a passerby, may well be difficult to discharge the burden of proof that he had no reason to believe that racial hatred would not be stirred up as a result of such actions. The problems with the "dwelling" section are all too obvious. It means in reality that it is possible for groups to congregate in a private home spouting anti-racial ideas and inciting racial hatred within earshot of their neighbours, without being caught under this section. Why, then, was such a privilege excluding dwellings introduced? The answer must surely have been to retain the freedom of expression, and to protect the intimacy of private conversations within our homes. Parliament have always taken very seriously any limitation on the freedom of speech and will only interfere where not to do so would cause widespread public disorder, hence, the enacting of this particular statute to deal with abhorrent behaviour likely to lead to national unrest. Freedom of expression should be protected in one's own home, and if not, this may ultimately result in the exchange of ideas and information being hindered in private which is unacceptable in a democratic society.

In section 19(1), a person who publishes or distributes written material which is threatening, abusive or insulting, is guilty of an offence[61] if;

(a) he intends thereby to stir up racial hatred; or

(b) having regard to all the circumstances racial hatred is likely to be stirred up thereby.

The distribution or publication of the written material must be to the public or at least to a section of the public. Distribution or publication to a private person only will be exempt for the purposes of this section.

In *R. v. Britten*[62]:

Facts. The defendant attached a pamphlet to the door of the house of an M.P. which read "blacks not wanted here", and showed a picture of a hand indicating "stop further immigration". He was charged under section 6 of the Race Relations Act 1965 (now repealed) with distributing written material likely to stir up hatred "against any section of the public". He was convicted.

Decision. On appeal, the question was whether the distribution to an M.P. was regarded as a distribution to a section of the public. It was said in this case that distribution must be to the public at large, distribution to members of the particular group or organisation by a member himself is not to be considered to be distributing to the public at large. Here, the M.P. is not a section of the public, even if his family see the pamphlet also. The appeal was allowed. The court said obiter that if the pamphlet could be seen from the road by passersby, then this may well amount to a publication, but this was not the case here.

III BREACH OF THE PEACE AT COMMON LAW

4–043 In spite of the many statutory amendments and new offences which have been introduced in the sphere of public order law, its fundamental basis remains that of the common law duty of each and every citizen to maintain and uphold the Queen's peace. Since every citizen must maintain the peace, he must balance within himself that duty and any desire to exercise his freedom of assembly, expression or protest. Whilst breach of the peace is no longer an offence in itself, and neither does it form a component of any of the new statutory public order offences, it is still a ground for arrest by a constable or an ordinary citizen, as discussed in the second chapter. Ironically, breach of the peace is in fact often preferred by the police as grounds for arrest rather than an arrest for a statutory public order offence, since the former is broader and more flexible than the latter, and avoids much of the regulation imposed by PACE.

For a concept with a thousand years of history, breach of the peace is somewhat lacking in a clear, concise and unambiguous definition. As will be seen, the generally accepted definition of breach of the peace involves the following elements—

> a positive act or words, either having already happened or now threatened, which:
>
> (1) is in the process of occurring and actually harms a person or property which is in his presence; or
> (2) causes a person to fear such unlawful violence; or
> (3) makes such unlawful violence likely to occur.
>
> the power of arrest is available not only when a breach of the peace is in the process of being committed, but also where the arrestor has reasonable grounds for belief that a breach is likely to occur in the near future; or
>
> where a breach of the peace has already been committed and the arrestor reasonably believes that a further act of violence is likely.

This definition will be discussed in relation to, and compared with, several important cases.

It is frequently cited in case law that part of a police constable's basic duty is to preserve the peace. It is preferably more correct to state that he has a duty to prevent a breach of the peace—the accepted norm being that people live in a peaceful society and therefore a positive duty is put on the constable to maintain the status quo. This is especially so since the common law permits a constable to arrest anyone without a warrant, on reasonable grounds, where there is an anticipatory breach of the peace as opposed to an actual breach and gives the police a very wide power to enter public or private[63] premises to do so. Notwithstanding the above, prevention of breach of the peace plays an important part in the responsibility of an ordinary police constable and it is in the public interest that the public be protected from those persons who wish to harm, threaten, obstruct or cause alarm to other members of an otherwise peaceful society. The question is how are the police meant to recognise an impeding breach of the peace so as not to overstep their legal duties?

In *Duncan v. Jones*[64]: **4–044**

Facts. On May 25, 1933, a public meeting was held outside an unemployed training centre, at which the defendant was one of the speakers. Immediately following the meeting, a ruckus occurred inside the training centre. The police were called to avert the danger of a breach of the peace (whether this was due to events taking place outside the centre is not clear). On July 30, 1934, a protest meeting was due to take place beside the same training centre. As the meeting was about to commence, the chief constable and a police inspector fearing a repetition of the events of 14 months previously, refused to permit the meeting to take place there and requested that it be held some 175 yards away. Present at the meeting was the defendant. The defendant refused to leave and was arrested and convicted for obstructing a police officer in the execution of his duty.

Decision. On appeal, despite there being no evidence that there was any real obstruction of the highway nor any incitement of those present to commit a breach of the peace, the court held that (1) the appellant must have realised the probable consequences of holding such a meeting; (2) the police inspector reasonably apprehended a breach of the peace; and (3) that therefore, he had a duty to prevent the meeting being held; and (4) that by persistently trying to hold the meeting, the appellant was obstructing the inspector in the execution of his duty. Therefore, the appeal was dismissed.

The court in *Duncan v. Jones* had, at that time, the opportunity to examine the rights and liberties of public assemblies in general, but refused in any detail to do so. Indeed, Lord Hewart C.J. took the opposite approach by denying that the present case was directly concerned with the issues of public meetings and free speech. Instead, he merely reiterated Professor Dicey's view that "English law does not recognise any special right of public meeting either for a political or any other purpose. The right of assembly is nothing more than a view taken by courts of individual liberty of speech."

Definition of Breach of the Peace

4–045 Nowadays, actual or impending violence is the main pre-existing criteria for police intervention for a breach of the peace. Whether the police should interfere when confronted with what may or may not be a breach of the peace is at present causing immense difficulties, hence the plethora of cases in this area. The problems stem from the circumstances themselves, the inherent danger from police interference, and the wider issues of conflict between preserving the peace and freedom of expression. In *R. v. Chief Constable for Devon and Cornwall ex parte Central Electricity Generating Board*[65] protesters blocked entrances, chained themselves to drilling rigs and generally created havoc for surveyors on a site to prevent them from working on the possible construction of a nuclear power station. In the Court of Appeal, Lord Denning M.R. said that "there is a breach of the peace whenever a person who is lawfully carrying out his work is physically prevented by another from doing it", and that once this occurs the obstructee is entitled to use any reasonable physical means to prevent any further hindrance. His Lordship seems to advocate that despite there being no violence or even the threat of violence by either workers or protesters, any interference will entitle the obstructee to remove the protesters. This rather harsh and wide declaration would seem to suggest that preserving the peace takes precedence over the right to peaceful protest.[66] Despite this, Lord Denning did go on to state that the decision was one for the police to act upon and the courts should not interfere. This last point was emphasised by Lawton C.J. in the same case. He said that he was not in favour of "self help" remedies in all situations. He advocated other remedies such as inviting the protesters to leave the site. Only then if there is resistance should the minimum amount of force be used to remove the demonstrators. It was also stated by Templeman L.J. that the obstructee should first seek an injunction against the protesters and if this does not succeed he may then, with the assistance of the police, use self help remedies to remove the protesters but only when there is a danger of a breach of the peace through "resistance, threatened or actual, passive or violent"; a more restrictive use of a breach of the peace remedy. In CEJB, the court stated that it was for the police to decide whether or not to intervene. They could not be forced to do so by the surveyors and then only if the police reasonably believed that a breach of the peace was likely to occur in the near future.

Mere abuse by words, without more, would not generally amount to a breach of the peace. Thus, a verbal confrontation between persons which resulted in direct interference with others would not permit the police to intervene, unless violence or threat of violence could reasonably be anticipated.[67]

In *R. v. Howell*[68]: 4–046

Facts. Police were called by neighbours to prevent continuing unruly behaviour by a small group who were attending a street party. When asked to leave, they shouted and swore at the police. When warned to desist from swearing, the defendant refused. The police attempted to grab hold of the defendant in order to arrest him. Thereupon, the defendant struck the police constable and was arrested. He was found guilty and appealed on the grounds that since there was no actual breach of the peace, the arrest itself was unlawful.

Decision. The question that the court had to consider was whether it was necessary for a breach of the peace to exist prior to arrest or would an impending breach of the peace suffice, providing of course, the police had reasonable grounds to believe that such a breach was likely to occur. Watkins L.J. discussed previous unsatisfactory common law definitions of breach of the peace and proposed the following;

> ". . . there is a breach of the peace whenever harm is actually done or is likely to be done to a person or in his presence, to his property or a person is in fear of being so harmed through an assault, an affray, a riot, unlawful assembly or other assembly. It is for this breach of the peace when done in his presence or the reasonable apprehension of it taking place that a constable, or anyone else[69], may arrest an offender without warrant—."

The court found in this case that since the constable had reasonable grounds for believing that the appellant's behaviour would probably end in some form of violence, the arrest was lawful and therefore the appeal was dismissed.[70]

Provocation by Others to Commit a Breach of the Peace

"Provocation to commit violence as a natural consequence of the defendant's behaviour" is a key determinant in deciding whether a breach of the peace is likely to occur in the near future. It is settled law that the 4–047 defendant's conduct itself is capable of causing a breach of the peace. No other party need be involved nor must the breach or the likelihood of the breach originate via some other person.[71] However, if people are lawfully protesting, will that nevertheless still amount to a breach of the peace if through their actions they interfere with others and provoke those others to use force in response to the behaviour of the former?

In *Nicol and Selvanayagam v. DPP*[72]:

Facts. During a fishing competition, animal rights protesters threw sticks into the water and at fishing lines. Police warned the protesters to desist from such action, but they refused, and were arrested. The court held that as a consequence of the protesters' behaviour, it was likely that a breach of the peace would ensue since their action would probably result in the anglers being provoked into some form of violence being taken against the protesters in retaliation. The protesters were ordered to be bound over to keep the peace. They refused and were sentenced to 21 days imprisonment under section 115 Magistrates' Courts Act 1980.

Decision. On appeal, the question the court had to consider was whether the actions of the protesters could amount to a breach of the peace by others, whose lawful activities were being interfered with. The court held, that despite the fact that the protesters were not doing anything unlawful *per se*, nevertheless their actions were to be considered unreasonable. They intended to disrupt the competition and took such steps as were necessary to frighten the fish away and as a consequence, would, if not prevented, provoke the anglers into taking some form of physical violence against them. Once this was recognised by the police, they were entitled to take some positive response against the protesters.

4–048 It is difficult to decipher whether the circumstances amounted to provocation of violence. Where the protest is unlawful, the issue of provocation may not be so important since the police may use other public order powers to quell any disturbance. On the other hand, where the courts have to decide whether the accused "acted lawfully but unreasonably", the facts may become blurred where the broader issues of freedom to protest and interference to others clash. For instance, in the Nicol case above, had day-trippers to the area played loud music or gone swimming in the lake, and as a result of their activities drove the fish away or made it more difficult for the anglers to continue their event, could this constitute "acting unreasonably" if this resulted in some form of violent response by the anglers? There is no clear answer, but it is suggested, that having examined all the relevant facts, a pragmatic approach should be used when deciding whether violence would be the net result should the police not intervene beforehand.[73]

The emphasis seems to be put on the defendants, whether they acted unreasonably. It is suggested that this approach may be somewhat restricted and unfair. The other party may be unusually sensitive and susceptible to violence, whereas an ordinary person in similar circumstances may not be so. In that case should the freedom to protest be curtailed merely because of the sensitivity of the other party or should the court take into account that an ordinary individual would not have been so provoked to violence in the circumstances? Again, the answer would seem to be how the police viewed the situation as it then was, taking into consideration all the relevant issues including the personal attributes of all the parties involved.

Facts. In *Redmond-Bate v. DPP*,[73A] the appellant, along with two other women, had been preaching to passers-by outside Wakefield Cathedral on topics such as morality, God and the Bible. Having received a complaint P.C. Tennant asked the women not to stop people, and since they had not, he left. Soon afterwards he returned to find that over a hundred people had gathered, some of which were conveying a hostile attitude towards the speakers. He requested the women to stop preaching and when they refused, he arrested them for a breach of the peace. The appellant was convicted under section 89(2) of the Police Act 1996 of obstructing a police officer in the execution of his duty. She thereafter appealed.

Decision. The first question for the court to consider was whether it was reasonable for P.C. Tennant, in light of what he perceived at the time, to believe that the appellant was about to commit a breach of the peace—this was an objective test. Secondly, where did the police officer perceive the threat coming from—the women or the crowd? The court stated that free speech included not only inoffensive but contentious and provocative issues, provided it did not tend to provoke violence. On this occasion, the women's preaching could not be viewed as provoking violence. The court said that "to conclude as the court below did that by preaching in this manner would lead to a reasonable apprehension that violence was going to erupt, was both illiberal and illogical". Accordingly, the action by the police officer to prevent the women from preaching was unjustified and not within the execution of his duty. Therefore her appeal for obstruction was allowed.

In *Bibby v. Chief Constable of Essex Police*[74], Mr Bibby, a bailiff, arrived at the home of Mr and Mrs Brannan with a court order for the removal of certain goods in respect of unpaid rates which were overdue. Mr Brannan threatened Mr Bibby into leaving without the goods and eventually the police were called. The police considered Mr Bibby's behaviour provocative and that a breach of the peace appeared likely if he remained, and ordered him to leave the premises. On his refusal to do so, he was arrested and detained at the police station for approximately an hour. At first instance, in a claim for damages for assault and false imprisonment by Mr Bibby against the police, the court found that the action taken by the police was reasonable to prevent probable violence if Mr Bibby attempted to remove any goods. On appeal by Mr Bibby, the Court of Appeal said that the police "had failed to identify whence the threat of violence was coming: implicit in Mr Brannan's attitude had been a threat to use violence if Mr Bibby persevered". The Court said that in order to exercise the common law power of arrest (i) only a sufficiently real and present threat justified depriving a citizen, not at the time acting unlawfully, of his liberty; (ii) the threat must come from the person to be arrested; (iii) the conduct must clearly interfere with the rights of others and its natural consequence must be "not wholly unreasonable violence" from a third party; and (iv) the conduct of the person to be arrested must be unreasonable. Accordingly, since the threat came from the debtor when the bailiff was only going about his normal lawful business, and his behaviour was at the time reasonable in the circumstances, the appeal was allowed.

Reasonable Cause for Breach of the Peace

4–049 The action of the police must be based on a reasonable belief that a breach of the peace is a real possibility. As part of the reasonable belief criteria will be the behaviour of the defendant throughout the period of the incident including, for instance, the reaction of the defendant when told to desist, his use of foul language, and his resistance upon being arrested. In-depth examination by the court into how the constable concluded that there was a breach of the peace, is seldom investigated. It was stated in *Kelly v. Chief Constable of Hampshire*[75]:

> "If there was conflicting evidence as to what happened, the jury had to resolve that conflict; but it was for the judge to rule whether the defendant's conduct was reasonable or unreasonable, and it was for the judge to decide what facts were relevant to that question. . . . It was a question for the judge whether, at that moment, the officer had reasonable cause to believe that a breach of the peace was likely to occur".[76]

In *Piddington v. Bates*[77]:

Facts. During a trade dispute at a printing firm, the police informed the pickets that it was sufficient to have only two pickets at each of the front and rear entrances of the premises. Another 18 pickets stood outside on the road. When the defendant decided to join the pickets at the rear entrance, the police warned him against doing this. The defendant said, "I can stand by the gate if I want to, I know my rights. If you don't want me to, you'd better arrest me". The defendant tried to proceed, whereupon he was arrested. Prior to the arrest, there had been no obstruction of the highway, no actual or feared breach of the peace, no disturbance of any kind. Nevertheless, he was convicted of obstructing a constable in the execution of his duty. He appealed.

Decision. On appeal, the appellant argued, *inter alia*, that since there was no obstruction or intimidation tactics of any kind or breach of the peace, the constable had no right in law to limit the number of pickets at the entrances. Lord Parker C.J. said that there must be facts from which a constable could on reasonable grounds anticipate a real possibility of a breach of the peace. Whether this is so is a question of fact in each case. The relevant evidence here showed that at the time there were only eight people working on the premises. There were 18 pickets "milling about in the street". This, taken together with a phone call to the police from the employer fearing trouble, meant that the police had reasonable cause to believe that more than a mere peaceful protest was afoot. Thus, since the police were under a duty to preserve the peace, they were entitled to take preventive action and issue instructions that no more than two pickets at each entrance was allowed.

4–050 A valid argument put by the appellants in the above case, but not discussed in any great detail by the court, was that two pickets were insufficient to communicate or persuade workers leaving the premises. Since there were in total 24 employees it would be difficult to speak to at least a majority of them under such tight restrictions. There was no evidence to suggest that the appellant knew that only eight employees were working there at the relevant time.

The wide power and discretion of the police was particularly prevalent in *Piddington v. Bates* (see above). The issue was one of sufficient numbers; sufficient enough for the police to keep control, but not large enough for an effective peaceful protest. Again, this is another instance of the preservation of the peace taking precedence over the freedom to protest.

Where two Opposing Groups Collide

What is the position where there is a peaceful procession and others **4–051** opposed to the march decide to unlawfully interfere by shouting, using threats or even physical violence? Should the peaceful procession be allowed to proceed, despite the reasonable apprehension that there will be as a consequence a breach of the peace?

In *Beatty v. Gillbanks*[78]:

Facts. During previous processions by the Salvation Army through the streets of Weston-super-Mare, there were confrontations with a group opposed to their religious views called the Skeleton Army. Fighting, shouting and general disorder was the usual result of any meeting between these two groups. To prevent any further confrontation the police issued a notice forbidding the Salvation Army to march at a forthcoming procession, led by the defendant William Beatty. The defendant refused to comply with the notice and proceeded to march. Thereupon he was arrested. The defendant used no force or violence. He was charged with unlawful assembly by the disturbance of the public peace. The magistrates found against the defendant.

Decision. On appeal, the crucial question for the court to decide was whether the defendant was involved in any unlawful act. The purpose of the procession was a wholly peaceful one. They were opposed to any form of violence or disorder. There was nothing in their conduct to show that what they were doing was against the public peace. It was argued that since on previous occasions the marches ended in physical conflict with the Skeleton Army, it was reasonable to believe that if the present march was allowed to go ahead there would be a recurrence of the violence. The court found as a fact that the conduct and intention of the appellants was not to cause a disturbance. Whatever unlawful consequences occurred was as a direct result of the Skeleton Army's interference. The court asked what right have others to interfere or molest those conducting a peaceful march? If they (Skeleton Army) are doing anything unlawful it was for the magistrates and police to interject. As a result, the appeal was allowed.

The European Court of Human Rights has debated the matter of clashes **4–052** between opposing groups in some depth. In Plattform *"Arzte fur das Leben" ("Doctors for Life") v. Austria*[79] the applicant, an association whose members were anti-abortionists, decided to march from a church to a hillside and hold a religious ceremony there. Whilst outside the church, pro-abortionists assembled and intermingled with the marchers and caused disruption by shouting abuse, chanting slogans, waving banners and throwing eggs. Previous encounters between the two groups had resulted in violence. The applicant complained to the Commission that their association had not received significant police protection during the demonstration, claiming violations of Articles 9, 10, 11 and 13 of the Convention. The Commission declared Articles 9, 10 and 11 inadmissible as manifestly ill-founded, but found the Government in violation of Article 13, *i.e.* lack of an effective remedy by a national authority.

Although it might seem strange that a state could be in violation of Article 13 and not be in breach of any of the other articles, both the Commission and the Court noted that if the applicant had an arguable case, even if ill-founded, under Article 11 it could still be admissible for the purposes of Article 13. The main question for consideration was whether the state has a positive obligation to protect legally permitted demonstration from those who may wish to interfere with them. The Court stated that persons must:

> "be able to hold a demonstration without having to fear that they will be subjected to physical violence by their opponents; such a fear would be liable to deter associations or other groups supporting common ideas or interests from openly expressing their opinions on highly controversial issues affecting the community. In a democracy, the right to counter-demonstrate cannot extend to inhibiting the exercise of the right to demonstrate" (para. 32).

The court further stated that "whilst it is the duty of contracting states to take reasonable and appropriate measures to enable lawful demonstrations to proceed peacefully, they cannot guarantee this absolutely and they have a wide discretion in the choice of the means to be used" (para. 34). In this instance, the police took appropriate measures to avert the dangers of violence between the two opposing groups by dispersing the crowds. Accordingly, there was no arguable claim that a breach of Article 11 had been committed and therefore Article 13 was not applicable in this case.

4–053 Thus, it would seem that in a *Beatty v. Gillbanks* type situation where two opposing groups confront each other, the courts would side with those advocating peaceful protest. Further, although there is a positive obligation on the police to take some form of affirmative action where unlawful acts are anticipated, the individual states are given a wide margin of appreciation when deciding what measures to undertake when dealing with a particular situation. However, the *Plattform* judgment above is limited to circumstances where one group initially creates the violence.

It was stated by Cave J. in *Beatty v. Gillbanks* that if the Salvation Army when opposed met force with force that would constitute an unlawful assembly. However, when confronted by the Skeleton Army, they used no violence in resistance. However, in *Wise v. Dunning*[80] public speeches made by a Protestant lecturer using provocative and abusive language against the Catholic Church amounted to a breach of the peace because of the natural consequence of using such insulting words. It was stated in this case that if the defendant does an act which although lawful in itself has the natural consequence of producing unlawful acts by others and a breach of the peace occurs,[81] then the court is entitled to make a binding over order against the narrator of those statements. Thus, a person may be in breach of the peace despite not intentionally inciting others if his own behaviour provokes a breach of the peace.

Preventing an Impending Breach of the Peace

The adage "an ounce of prevention is worth a pound of cure", is exceptionally pertinent to the issue of averting the danger of a breach of the peace before it has begun. However, preventative measures bring with them the inherent problems of the police correctly assessing a situation which will only occur some time in the future. This is not particularly easy for the ordinary police constable who very often may have to make a snap decision on whether a situation is about to turn nasty. With very little guidance available the police constable is left to his own devices, subject to the condition of "reasonable grounds for believing", whether his interference may result in fuelling an already volatile situation. Added to this, the danger of making an unlawful arrest and any claims which may follow by the arrestee against the police leaves little doubt that at present the law regarding this matter is deserving of clearer regulation. The courts themselves are not concerned with whether the police action at the relevant time was correct or not. More important is how the police constable on the spot reasonably viewed the situation there and then, and asking whether or not there were in existence reasonable grounds for believing that should the police constable not interfere, a breach of the peace could result as a probable consequence. Here, the evidence of the police constable may take precedence over the defendant's claim that a breach of the peace would not have resulted. This is a question of law for the judge to decide. **4–054**

Thus in *Moss v. McLachlan*[82]:

Facts. The defendants were part of a vehicle convoy (carrying between 60 and 80 men) on their way to support striking miners at four collieries. They were stopped by police on the M1, some two miles from the nearest pit. They were informed that they would not be permitted to proceed any further as the police had reasonable grounds to believe that a breach of the peace would result once the strikers reached their objective. Some 40 miners, including the defendants, attempted to go through the police cordon, and were arrested and convicted for obstruction. The magistrates concluded that there would be a breach of the peace if a mass demonstration was allowed to take place at any one of the collieries.

Decision. They appealed on the grounds that although there was no dispute as to the obstruction the police action itself was unlawful and therefore the arrest was invalid. Skinner J. held that in order for the police to make a valid judgment of the situation they must consider all the circumstances, including their experiences and knowledge gathered from what they had seen on television and read in the newspapers and "to exercise their judgement and common sense on that material as well as on the events which are taking place before their eyes".[83] "Provided they honestly and reasonably formed the opinion that there is a real risk of a breach of the peace in the sense that it is in close proximity both in place, and time, then the conditions exist for reasonable preventive acting . . ." The appeal was dismissed.

In order for the police to take preventative measures the breach itself must not be too remote. Just how far into the future this may be before any action is taken is difficult to ascertain. Using words such as "imminent", or "pending" presupposes that the breach must take place immediately or at least a very short time in the future. However, this is not necessarily so. What is certain is that there must be a real possibility at some stage in the future of the breach occurring. In *Moss v. McLachlan* above, the High court were reluctant to conclude that imminent meant necessarily "committed in the immediate future", for these purposes. The test is whether, having examined all the relevant conditions, there is a real possibility of a breach occurring before preventive action may be taken.

Breach of the Peace on Private Premises

4–055 It is a major part of a police constable's task to prevent crime from initially occurring. Indeed, he has a positive duty to intervene in those circumstances where any unlawful activity arises.[84] This is especially so where there is a likelihood of a breach of the peace. Police have always had the power at common law to enter private premises to quell existing breaches of the peace. In such cases, the breach must be one that was actually occurring at the time before the entry would be deemed lawful. However, it was decided in *Thomas v. Sawkins* that the police were entitled to enter a private hall where they reasonably believed that a breach of the peace was merely imminent or likely to occur.

In *Thomas v. Sawkins*[85]:

Facts. A public meeting was held in a private hall (entry was free of charge) to discuss the forthcoming Incitement to Disaffection Bill, and demands for the dismissal of the Chief Constable of Glamorgan. Three police officers, including a sergeant Sawkins entered the hall and sat in the front row. The hirer, Thomas, asked them to leave, but they refused. Thomas put his hand on the Inspector to eject him. Thereupon, Sawkins pushed Thomas' hand away. Other police officers arrived, and no further action was taken to remove them. Thomas laid an information against Sawkins for assault on the grounds that the police were trespassers, and therefore he was entitled to use reasonable force to remove them, and that in using resistance against removal, he was unlawfully assaulted by Sawkins.

Decision. It was stated that not only were the police entitled to go on to and remain on private premises where an offence has been committed, but also by their preventative powers had the right to do so when there were reasonable grounds for believing that an offence was imminent or likely to occur. Therefore, the appeal was dismissed. Despite the justice's findings that there were "ample materials" to conclude that disorder might result if there were no police presence, it is suggested that there was more of a likelihood, due to the subject of the meeting, of a breach of the peace with the police being there than through their absence. The police presence represented an antagonistic force, and whether their attendance was lawful or not, they themselves, could not be regarded as "acting reasonably" in the circumstances.

The above case has been criticised by various academics on different grounds. It has been said that it contravenes the basic law that there should be no interference by the police authorities unless or until an offence has been committed. Also, it has been argued that the case was to be restricted to instances involving public meetings and should not be extended to cover private dwellings.

The common law proposition of entry has now been given the stamp of approval by section 17(6) of PACE, which gives the police the power to enter private premises without a warrant to deal with actual or preventing an anticipatory breach of the peace.

In *McLeod v. Commissioner of Police of the Metropolis*[86]: **4–056**

Facts. The plaintiff's ex-husband, along with five others, including his solicitor and two police constables, went to the house of the plaintiff to remove his furniture, three days before the expiry date of a division of property order issued by the court. As the furniture was being loaded, the plaintiff arrived home and demanded that the furniture be put back. The police refused the request and permitted the loaded van to be driven off. The plaintiff took an action for trespass against those present, including the police. The judge at first instance decided, that since the solicitor and the husband had not been given permission to enter the home by the plaintiff, the entry was unlawful and therefore a trespass. Regarding the action against the police, they argued that since there were reasonable grounds to believe that a breach of the peace was likely to occur, the entry was therefore lawful. Tuckey J. relied on *Thomas v. Sawkins* and stated that the police were justified in their decision to be present. They gave evidence that in their experience altercations frequently occurred in similar situations such as this. In fact, the feared breach of the peace did occur when the plaintiff arrived home, and therefore the plaintiff's claim for trespass against the police was rejected. She appealed.

Decision. The Court of Appeal agreed with the judgment at first instance and decided that the police had ample grounds for believing that a breach of the peace would probably occur, thereby rejecting the appellant's appeal. They said two questions needed to be considered. (1) In what circumstances may police enter a private house to prevent a breach of the peace, and (2) if such a right does exist, did those circumstances exist here? Having discussed *Thomas v. Sawkins* (see above) the court ruled that "the officer must satisfy himself that there is a real and imminent risk of a breach of the peace, because if the matter has to be tested in court, thereafter, they may be scrutinised not only to his belief at the time but also of the grounds for his belief".[87]

This would seem to suggest a subjective test with regard to the police constable's initial belief, and an objective test on whether there existed sufficient grounds for that belief. Normally, a breach of the peace takes place in public areas where detection is easy and the constable is in as good a position as anyone else present to assess the situation and take the appropriate action. However, where a breach of the peace arises on private property, the question whether or not the police should enter is not so easy to evaluate. The police in such a situation are not usually in a position to see what is occurring inside the house. They may be called upon to rely on information given by, for instance, neighbours who may genuinely but mistakenly believe that a breach of the peace is taking place. Harder still, is showing that there were reasonable grounds for believing that more than just a "normal domestic quarrel" is about to result in violence or the threat of violence, before the police can take any preventive action.

4–057 The case went to the European Court of Human Rights, who found a violation of the Convention.

In *McLeod v. U.K.*,[88] the complainant submitted that (1) the entry by the officers into her home and (2) their failure to prevent her ex-husband from entering her home, were violations of Article 8 in that they constituted interferences with her right to respect for her private life and home. Once it was established that the police and her ex-husband did in fact enter her home, the next question for the court to consider was, was the infringement justified in accordance with the law? The government argued that the power of the police to enter private premises existed under section 17(6) of PACE, even without the consent of the owner or occupier, where a breach of the peace is apprehended. Accordingly, the court found that the law in this area was sufficiently defined to adhere to the requirement of "in accordance with the law". The next question was whether the infringement met with the legitimate aim requirement under Article 8(2), *i.e.* in this instance, prevention of crime or disorder. The government argued, as they did in the national courts, that domestic disputes often lead to disorder and occasionally serious violence, and therefore entry into the home by the police was necessary to avoid this. The court agreed, and hence the legitimate aim factor was found to be present here. However, were the measures taken by the police necessary in a democratic society, as provided by Article 8(2)? This implies that the interference corresponds to a pressing social need, and in particular that it is proportionate to the legitimate aim pursued. In this case this meant the police having to make an impartial decision between on the one hand the applicant's right to respect for her private life and home, and on the other hand the prevention of disorder and crime (para. 53). In these circumstances, the facts revealed that the solicitors of the ex-husband rightfully anticipated that the police were required to prevent a breach of the peace. However, the police were under an obligation to check the court order permitting the ex-husband to remove his property from the applicant's home. Had they done so properly, they would have discovered that it was the wife who was to deliver the property to her ex-husband, despite a genuine belief by him that a later agreement was reached between himself and his ex-wife that he should collect the property. Accordingly, since the wife was not at home when the police arrived, the latter should have realised that there was little or no risk of a breach of the peace occurring, and therefore the police should not have entered the applicant's home. The fact that a breach of the peace did occur upon her arrival was immaterial in justifying the police entering her home (para. 57). As a result, the court found (by seven votes to two) that the actions by the police were disproportionate to the legitimate aim pursued, and therefore in violation of Article 8. The applicant was subsequently awarded £15,000 in respect of costs and expenses.

This was not a case where the owner was at home at the time the police attempted to gain entry. It seems that had she been there, their entry would have been proper and proportionate to the legitimate aim pursued, *i.e.* to prevent a breach of the peace. The two dissenting judges in the above case stated that it was the duty of the police to maintain the peace, or at least remain in the house to prevent a breach of the peace. Accordingly, it was not disproportionate for them to enter the home in the wife's absence to prevent any likely trouble when she did eventually make an appearance, thereby disagreeing with the court's majority finding of a violation of Article 8.

Binding Over Orders

An archaic but often used possibility in many public disorder situations, **4–058**
real or merely threatened, is that of the binding over order under the Justices of the Peace Act 1361. A person may be arrested without warrant for breach of the peace, but that in itself is not a criminal offence and so cannot lead to a conviction, unless of course the arrestee has incidentally committed a separate criminal offence. If the police can find no other charge and are unwilling to release the arrestee without charge, then he may be taken to the magistrates court and bound over to keep the peace or to be of good behaviour for a specified period.

Sometimes the court will require other, more specific, promises or conditions to be made in conjunction with the order (for example that the arrestee will avoid particular persons or places for a specified period). The person may also be required to promise to pay a sum of money if he fails to comply with the terms of his binding over or good behaviour bond. Another person may be required to guarantee payment of this sum if the arrestee is unable or unlikely to pay. The person can be bound over regardless of whether he has been convicted of an offence. Binding over may be a sole or additional disposal. A person may only be bound over by consent—the arrestee will hear from the court that they intend to bind him over to keep the peace, and he has a right to address the court. If he refuses to consent to being bound over then it is impossible for this to occur, but the ultimate consequence of such a refusal is a potential prison term of up to six months, or until he changes his mind. During the miners' strike of 1984–85, many protesting miners were imprisoned in this way.

It should be noted that the power of arrest and binding over for breach of the peace can be used at any stage in a protest, from when it is first believed to be likely to occur until violence results. Thus it is possible for the police, once they know that a demonstration or other disturbance is intended, to pre-empt and even prevent it by use of these powers. Since breach of the peace is generally a wider concept than the comparable statutory offences, the powers of arrest and binding over may be used in this way in situations where the police are unable to use any statutory powers.

Obstruction of the Highway

4–059 The majority of the discussion above relates to public meetings and gatherings of one kind or another whereby a breach of the peace was imminent or actually occurred. However, there are in existence a number of statutory offences which specifically deal with using the public highway in an improper manner, whether it be for purposes of personal use, such as street selling or demonstrations or indeed any form of conduct which results in the interference of others to go about their normal everyday business. For instance, under section 137 of the Highway Act 1980 "If a person without lawful authority or excuse, in any way wilfully obstructs the free passage along a highway he is guilty of an offence . . .".

Passage along a highway

4–060 First and foremost, there is no right to freedom of assembly on a public highway in this country. The courts however, in numerous cases, have recognised a wide interpretation of the word "right" regarding the use of the highway, and stated that a person has the right to pass and repass along the highway. The words "pass or repass" include activities which are connected with, or incidental to, the actual movement along the highway. People assembling in the street, for whatever reason, do not generally come within this category. Any purpose, therefore, which is not used for passage is potentially unlawful. Stopping in certain instances would be considered to be within the area of activities incidental to the highway. For example, stopping to wait for the traffic lights to change before crossing the road would be permissible. Even stopping to converse with someone would be within a person's rights. However if through stopping, an obstruction was caused and as a result the pathway was even slightly blocked this may well constitute an offence under section 137.[89] Thus, even if the act is lawful in itself, an offence may still be committed if the conduct could not be considered reasonable. In *Waite v. Tyler*[90] the defendant, a street performer was entertaining the public in a pedestrian precinct which was some 40 feet wide. The public either stopped to see the act or merely side-stepped the defendant to avoid the performance. He was arrested under section 137 of the Highways Act 1980 and acquitted: the justice having decided that this particular activity in the circumstances was not an unreasonable use of the highway. On appeal by the prosecution by way of case stated, the court took a restricted meaning of the word "passage" and concluded that what the defendant was doing was not incidental to the lawful pursuit of the highway, *i.e.* passing or repassing.

Lawful authority or excuse

The words "lawful authority" refer to permission being granted to a person by some authority or under the law, entitling that person to use the highway for a particular purpose, *e.g.* a licence to set up a flower or food stall or a temporary news stand on the street. In reality the law is allowing that person the right to a limited obstruction of the highway. Nevertheless it is an obstruction which the law is prepared to tolerate in the circumstances. "Lawful excuse" in this section refers to a set of circumstances whereby even though the act itself was illegal and there was an actual obstruction, there were legitimate reasons why it should not constitute an unlawful act under section 137. For example, a car breaks down on the highway where no parking is allowed, thereby obstructing traffic. The driver could not be considered to be causing a "wilful obstruction" since there was no choice but to stop the car in the circumstances.[91] The word "excuse" seems to be synonymous with reasonable use. But there must be proof of reasonable use. Parker L.J. in *Nagy v. Weston* stated: **4–061**

> "It is a question of fact depending on all the circumstances, including the length of time the obstruction continues, the place where it occurs, the purpose for which it is done, and, of course, whether it does in fact cause an actual obstruction as opposed to a potential obstruction".[92]

It is suggested to this list should be added the number of persons involved, since this is often a common factor which in the past has determined whether in fact there existed an actual obstruction, especially regarding demonstrations and the like.[93]

In *Hirst and Agu v. Chief Constable of West Yorkshire*[94]:

Facts. The defendants, who were animal rights supporters, handed out leaflets and displayed banners outside a store, protesting against the sale of furs in a main shopping area in Bradford. They were arrested for obstruction of the highway under section 137 and for breach of the peace. At first instance, the defendants were convicted on the restricted legal grounds enunciated in *Waite v. Taylor*, *i.e.* their activity was not incidental to the legally accepted purpose of passage along a highway. They appealed.

Decision. The court, having examined in detail previous relevant authorities, affirmed the dictum of Parker L.J. in *Nagy v. Weston*, stating that magistrates should consider the following questions: (1) Is there an obstruction—more than merely *de minimus*, if yes, then (2) was it wilful—intentional or deliberate, if yes, then (3) have the prosecution proved lack of authority or excuse? Lawful excuse embraces activities otherwise lawful in themselves which may or may not be reasonable in all the circumstances mentioned by Parker L.J. (see above). In this case, the justices had not dealt with the issue of "reasonable user" and therefore the appeal was allowed.

4–062 Otton J. in *Hirst and Agu*, whilst totally agreeing with the judgment of Glidewell L.J., went on to discuss obiter the wider issues of free speech and specifically stressed that "the courts have long recognised the right of free speech to protest on matters of public concern and to demonstrate on the one hand and the need for peace and good order on the other". Both judges agreed with Lord Denning M.R. in his prolific dissenting speech, although obiter, in *Hubbard v. Pitt*[95] that:

> "These (rights to protest) are rights which it is in the public interest that individuals should possess; and indeed, that they should exercise without impediment as long as no wrongful act is done . . . Our history is full of warnings against suppression of these rights. Most notable was the demonstration at St Peter's Fields, Manchester, in 1891 in support of universal suffrage. The magistrates sought to stop it. Hundreds were killed and injured. Afterwards, the Court of Common Council of London, affirmed 'the undoubted right of Englishmen to assemble together for the purpose of deliberating upon public grievances'. Such is the right of assembly. So also is the right to meet together, to go in procession, to demonstrate and to protest on matters of public concern. As long as all is done peaceably and in good order without threats of incitement to violence or obstruction to traffic, it is not prohibited . . . It is time for the courts to recognise this, too".

Under section 137 the prosecution must prove at least two things (1) there was a wilful obstruction of the highway, *i.e.* the obstruction was caused intentionally or deliberately and (2) the defendant had no lawful authority.[96] Once the prosecution have proved that the issue of lawful authority is not relevant, the defendant, nevertheless, may have had a lawful excuse to obstruct the highway in the circumstances. The problem is whether "unreasonable use" should have to be proved by the prosecution or whether it is up to the defendant to put forward the defence of reasonable use. Given the wide guidelines expounded by Parker L.J. in *Nagy v. Weston*, and the equally wide definition of Gildewell L.J. as to what is unreasonable use of the highway:

> "it may be decided that if the activity rose to an extent that it is unreasonable by reason of the space occupied or the duration of time for which it goes on that an offence would be committed, but it is a matter on the facts for the magistrates, in my view."[97]

If the onus is on the defendant to prove reasonable use, then the burden, despite being one on a balance of probabilities, may well be a heavy duty to discharge. The reasons being that any defence is to be measured against existing established law in the particular area. Where the law is uncertain and the boundaries not clearly defined[98] it is suggested that it may be very difficult for a defendant at trial to know whether or not in the particular circumstances his actual behaviour was reasonable and amounted to a valid defence. This uncertainty remains. It is a question of fact in each case for the courts to decide. In Feldman[99] he states:

> "The reasonableness of the protesters' behaviour provides at best an uncertain defence to a prosecution, as it is dependant on the magistrates' view as to

> reasonableness. This may vary according to the ethos of particular benches, or perhaps the political or other causes which the protester espoused".[1]

Whatever the difficulties stated above, it is nevertheless suggested that the burden of proof as to reasonableness rests upon the defendant.[2] As one of the most basic principles of the criminal law, the burden of proof in a criminal case rests upon the prosecution. It is for the prosecution to prove beyond reasonable doubt that the necessary elements of the offence were committed by the defendant with the required mental state. But there are several distinct exceptions to this rule, whereby to some extent the defendant may have to satisfy a more limited burden of proof himself. Generally speaking, where a defendant wishes to plead a defence to a criminal charge, he will have to satisfy at least a limited proof requirement himself. At common law a principal example of this is where the defendant pleads insanity. He must discharge an evidential burden of proof by establishing, on the balance of probabilities, that he has the defence. Thus the defendant has only to satisfy the civil standard of proof, whereas the prosecution must disprove the defence argued beyond all reasonable doubt. In practice this means that the defendant need only raise the defence as a possibility, then challenge the prosecution to disprove it to the criminal standard of proof. Statutory defences have often followed the same pattern, for example diminished responsibility as introduced by the Homicide Act 1957, and many of the statutory offences discussed in this book state both the nature of the applicable specific defences and upon whom the burden of proof rests for such defences. However in the present context there has been debate as to the nature of the burden of proof which rests upon the defendant if he is to establish a defence based upon the argument that his behaviour was reasonable, since the statute is silent as to this point. It has not been decided for certain whether the defendant must merely raise the defence as a possibility, or whether he must go further to establish it on the balance of probabilities. Since establishing reasonable behaviour is a criminal defence, on general principle the defendant should at least have to satisfy an evidential burden if he wishes to have his behaviour excused. As reasonable use is properly regarded as a mere limited excuse for the defendant's behaviour, it is submitted that the defendant should establish the defence of reasonable use to the civil standard of proof, that is on the balance of probabilities. This is a difficult point which has caused problems in many other areas of the criminal law and has rarely been given a satisfactory conclusion.

Brief Outline and Germane Cases

Chapter 4: Public Order

*Public Order Act 1986, s.1: the offence of riot: use or threat, by group of 12 or more with common purpose, of unlawful violence which would cause person of reasonable firmness to fear for his safety. **4–063**

R. v. Davison [1992].

*POA 1986, s.2: violent disorder; use or threat of unlawful violence by group of three or more.

*POA 1986, s.3: affray; use or threat of unlawful violence such that hypothetical person of reasonable firmness would fear for his safety.
R. v. Dixon [1993]; *I and Others v. DPP* (2001).

*POA 1986, s.4: using threatening, abusive or insulting words or behaviour. *Masterson v. Holden* [1986]; *Jordan v. Burgoyne* [1963]; *R. v. Horseferry Rd ex p. Siadatan* [1991].

*POA 1986, s.4A: intentionally causing harassment, alarm or distress.

*POA 1986, s.5: using threatening, abusive or insulting words or behaviour, or disorderly behaviour; unlike s.4, no need to show that any person was in fact affected by the words or behaviour, nor that a person of reasonable firmness would have been. *Vigon v. DPP* [1997]; *DPP v. Orum* [1988].
Defences: s.5(3), *DPP v. Clarke* [1991].

*POA 1986, s.11: notice must be given to the police of any procession which is a demonstration and will take place in public.

*POA 1986, s.12 and s.13: police may impose conditions upon public processions or ban them in order to prevent serious public disorder.
Kent v. MPC [1981].

*POA 1986, s.14: police may impose conditons upon public meetings.

*POA 1986, s.14A: police power to ban trespassory assembly.
DPP v. Jones [1999].

*CJPOA 1994, s.61: offence of group trespass.

*CJPOA 1994, ss.63–67: police powers to prevent and control raves.

*CJPOA 1994, s.68: aggravated trespass.
Winder v. DPP [1996].

*POA 1986, Pt III: offences of incitement to racial hatred; ss.18 and 19.
R. v. Britten [1967].

Breach of the peace at common law: duty to preserve the peace. *Duncan v. Jones* [1936]; *R. v. Howell* [1982]; *Nicol and Selanayagam v. DPP* [1996]; *Piddington v. Bates* [1961]; *Beatty v. Gillbanks* [1882]. Relationship with

PACE: *McLeod v. Commissioner of Police for the Metropolis* [1994]; *Steel v. U.K.* (1999).

For the meaning of *contra bonos mores* see *Hashman and Harrop v. U.K.* (1999); *Plattfern v. Austria* (1988); *McLeod v. U.K.* (1997) Article II ECHR decisions; *Ezelin v. France* (1992); *Rai, Allmond and "Negotiate Now" v. U.K.* (1995).

Binding over orders.

Obstruction of the highway: *Hirst and Agu v. Chief Constable of West Yorkshire* [1987].

Endnotes

[1] From the *Liber Albus*.
[2] Notably those chaired by Lord Scarman in 1975 and 1981, Cmnd 5919 and Cmnd 8427 respectively.
[3] Law Com. No. 123 1983.
[4] *R. v. Rothwell and Barton* [1993] Crim.L.R. 626.
[5] *R. v. Jefferson and Others* [1994] 1 All E.R. 270.
[6] (1993) 96 Cr.App.R. 332.
[7] *ibid.* at 338.
[8] [1992] Crim.L.R. 31.
[9] *ibid.* at 32.
[10] *R. v. Sanchez* [1996] Crim.L.R. 572.
[11] (1989) 88 Cr.App.R. 317.
[12] Under s. 7(3) if acquitted of violent disorder or affray, a conviction under s. 4 may be substituted in the alternative, circumstances permitting. However, the judge must give the jury a proper direction on what part of s. 4 is relevant to the particular case. See *R. v. Perrins* [1995] Crim.L.R. 432.
[13] [1989] 153 J.P. 517.
[14] See *R. v. Guigan and Cameron* [1991] Crim.L.R. 719.
[15] [1996] Crim.L.R. 572 and see *R. v. Davison* [1992] Crim.L.R. 31.
[15A] *The Times*, July 7, 1999.
[15B] See *I and Others v. DPP* (2001) Crim.L.R. 491.
[16] *R. v. Robinson* [1993] Crim.L.R. 581.
[17] [1993] Crim.L.R. 579.
[18] *DPP v. Cotcher and Cotcher* [1993] C.O.D. 181.
[19] *R. v. Smith* [1996] Crim.L.R. 893.
[20] (1992) 142 N.L.J. 527.
[21] [1973] A.C. 854, HL.
[22] *ibid.* at 862.
[23] *Parkin v. Norman* [1983] Q.B. 92.
[24] [1986] 1 W.L.R. 1017.
[25] S.54(13), Metropolitan Police Act 1839.
[26] [1963] 2 Q.B. 744.
[27] (1990) 89 Cr.App.R. 199.
[28] *Swanton v. DPP*, *The Times*, January 23, 1997.
[29] [1991] 1 Q.B. 260.
[30] *ibid.* at 263.
[31] *ibid.* at 268 and 269.
[32] Dwelling is defined in s. 8 as "any structure or part of a structure occupied as a person's home or as other living accommodation". See *R. v. Va Kun Hau* [1992] Crim.L.R. 518.
[33] *Rukwira v. DPP* [1993] Crim.L.R. 882.
[34] "Disorderly behaviour"—do not necessarily incorporate the words threatening, abusive or insulting. See *Chambers and Edwards v. DPP* [1995] Crim.L.R. 896; "Insulting", see *Brutus v. Cozens*.
[35] See s. 5(3)(a).
[36] *The Times*, December 9, 1997.
[37] *Marsh v. Arscott* (1982) 75 Cr.App.R. 211.
[38] [1998] 3 All E.R. 449.
[39] (1991) 94 Cr.App.R. 359.
[40] *R. v. Fidler and Moran* [1992] Crim.L.R. 62.
[41] (1989) 89 Cr.App.R. 82.
[42] In *Chappell* the court stated that the correct charge should have been under the Malicious Communications Act 1988.
[43] [1950] 2 K.B. 498.
[44] *per* Lord Goddard.
[45] *The Times*, May 14, 1981.
[46] [1997] 2 All E.R. 119.
[47] See *ex parte Lewis* [1888] 21 Q.B.D 191.
[48] [1893] 1 Q.B. 142.

[49] *ibid.* at 125.
[50] *The Times*, 5 March 1999.
[51] [1996] 160 J.P.R. 713.
[52] Other statutory offences cover such conduct.
[53] [1989] Crim.L.R. 295.
[54] [1975] 1 Q.B. 864.
[55] Lord Widery C.G. at 874.
[56] [1992] 14 E.H.R.R. 362.
[57] [1995] 19 E.H.R.R. CD93.
[57A] The meaning of *contra bonos mores* has been expressed as "conduct which has the property of being wrong rather than right in the judgment of the majority of contemporary fellow citizens" *per* Glidewell L.J. in *Hughes v. Holley* (1988) 86 Cr.App.R. 130.
[57B] at para. 42 of the Commission's opinion.
[57C] at para. 31.
[57D] at para. 31.
[57E] (1999) 28 E.H.R.R. 81.
[57F] See *Steel v. U.K.* where the court found that the elements of breach of the peace were adequately defined and as such the binding over order in that case related to similar behaviour not being repeated.
[58] See s. 23 where a person in possession of written material or recordings or films, photographs and the like, with a view to display, publish, play or show any of the above, commits an offence if he intends to stir up racial hatred or racial hatred is likely to be stirred up.
[59] [1983] 2 A.C. 548.
[60] Definition of "written material" in s. 29.
[61] Now inserted as an arrestable offence in s. 24(2) PACE 1984 by s. 155 Criminal Justice and Public Order Act 1994.
[62] [1967] 2 Q.B. 51.
[63] see *McConnell v. Chief Constable of the Greater Manchester Police* [1990] 1 All E.R. 423.
[64] [1936] K.B. 318.
[65] [1982] Q.B. 458.
[66] *ibid.* at 470, Lord Denning stated that "English law upholds the right to demonstrate . . . as long as it is done peacefully". Here, he did not see the obstruction as being peaceful.
[67] *Brutus v. Cozens* [1973] A.C. 854 where "insulting" words did not amount to a breach of the peace.
[68] [1982] Q.B. 46.
[69] An ordinary citizen also has the power to arrest in such circumstances. See Chap.3, para. 3–039, "Citizen's Arrest"; also *Albert v. Lavin* [1982] A.C. 546 and compare *Lewis v. Chief Constable of Greater Manchester, The Independent*, October 23, 1991.
[70] The definition in *R. v. Howell* was endorsed in *Percy v. DPP* [1995] Crim.L.R. 714.
[71] But see *G v. Chief Superintendent of Police, Stroud, Gloucestershire* [1987] Crim.L.R. 269; (1988) 86 Cr.App.R. 92.
[72] [1996] 160 J.P. 155; (1996) Crim.L.R. 318.
[73] *R. v. Morpeth Ward Justices ex p. Ward* (1992) 95 Cr.App.R. 215.
[73A] *The Times*, July 28, 1999.
[74] *The Times*, April 24, 2000.
[75] *The Independent*, March 25, 1993.
[76] *per* Lloyd L.J.
[77] [1961] 1 W.L.R. 162.
[78] [1882] 9 Q.B.D. 308.
[79] [1988] 13 E.H.R.R. 204.
[80] [1902] 1 K.B. 167.
[81] *ibid.* at 176, *per* Lord Alverstone C.J.
[82] [1985] I.R.L.R. 76.
[83] *ibid.* at 78.
[84] *R. v. Dytham* [1979] Q.B. 722.
[85] [1935] 2 Q.B. 249.
[86] [1994] 4 All E.R. 553.
[87] *per* Neill L.J. at 560.
[88] [1997] 27 E.H.R.R. 493.
[89] Even if there is no actual obstruction it may, nevertheless, amount to a public nuisance if those assembled interfere with others conducting their normal lawful business activities—*Hubbard v. Pitt* [1976] Q.B. 142.

[90] [1985] 149 J.P.R. 551.
[91] However, under regulation 3 of the Removal and Disposal of Vehicles Regulations 1986 "a constable may remove or arrange for the removal of the vehicle". See *Carey v. Chief Constable of Avon and Somerset* [1995] R.T.R. 405.
[92] *Nagy v. Weston* [1965] 1 All E.R. 78 at 80.
[93] See *Duncan v. Jones* [1936] K.B. 318.
[94] (1987) 95 Cr.App.R. 143.
[95] [1975] 3 All E.R. 1 at 10–11.
[96] *Nagy v. Weston* [1965] 1 All E.R. 78 at 80.
[97] *Hirst and Agu v. Chief Constable of West Yorkshire* [1987] 85 Cr.App.R. 143 at 150.
[98] Otten J. states at 152 that "freedom to protest on issues of public concern" should be taken into consideration when deciding whether the defendant committed a criminal offence.
[99] D. Feldman, *Civil Liberties and Human Rights in England and Wales* (Clarendon Press).
[1] *ibid.* at p. 817.
[2] See 1987 Crim.L.R. pp. 331, 332 for commentary.

Chapter 5

OFFICIAL SECRECY AND FREEDOM OF INFORMATION

INTRODUCTION

Freedom of access to information may relate to either public or private information. The former where information of public interest is kept out of the public domain by government agencies; and the latter where private individuals wish to obtain access to information held about them. Access to private information will be dealt with in a separate chapter on privacy. This chapter is concerned with the delicate balance which is maintained between the citizen's right of access to information about the operation of government and the legitimate state or government need to withhold certain material from the public domain, at least temporarily. The competing claims for secrecy and openness will be examined, and the methods employed in order to ensure secrecy and minimise the damage caused by breaches of secrecy or confidentiality will be evaluated. In the light of the Human Rights Act 1998 and the new Freedom of Information Act 2000, which will come into force fully by 2005, some of the basic principles by which courts have upheld official secrecy require re-evaluation. It is now becoming increasingly difficult to justify the harshness of the offences under the Official Secrets Act 1989. **5–001**

THE CASE FOR ACCESS TO GOVERNMENT INFORMATION

It is one of the fundamental tenets of any democratic society that a democratic government must be open to public scrutiny. If a citizen is to have the right to scrutinise and to criticise the operation of the state and of government, then he should be given access to sufficient information and other material in order to make his assessment. Freedom of information is closely tied to freedom of expression; free speech is of far greater power if it is backed by the ability to support arguments with evidence, and further to publish the findings. If a citizen is to carry out his democratic duties, then the state or government cannot be allowed to withhold material without being able to show a strong public interest justification for doing so. Governmental mistakes and excesses should not be given the protection of a cloak of immunity by a blanket maintenance of secrecy. There have been **5–002** notable instances of blunders in the past which have remained secret for many years and only reached the public gaze once it was far too late to redress the situation. Avoidance of political or private scandal should be achieved by prevention rather than by cover-up. It is important that only legitimate interests are protected by official secrecy. Good, honest, fair government should be happy to be open and avoid unnecessary secrecy in instances and areas where national security would not be compromised by any revelation. In theory, open government should be an advantage to the state as well as to citizens since potential problems could be discussed in the public arena and avoided, thus saving resources and enabling the future to avoid the mistakes of the past.

But information held by the government may not only be of importance in scrutinising the operations of Government; it may also incidentally hold information which could benefit wider concerns such as research, science, public health, legal actions or the avoidance of many potential risks or harms to the public or individuals. If information is kept secret needlessly then harm may result and time, effort and money may be wasted.

As will be seen, official secrecy may impact at different levels of individual freedom. In civil liberties terms, it can be argued that there is a substantial difference between merely punishing unauthorised publication of confidential information, and preventing the publication of that information in the first place. A citizen may weigh up the potential consequences of speaking out, revealing the secret, or "whistle-blowing", and decide that the public interest in favour of publication of the information is of greater significance than any civil or even criminal sanction which he personally may incur for his behaviour. If the citizen is prevented from speaking out, he cannot make a rational evaluation of the public interest, since he is forced to remain silent. It is also arguable that the use of criminal sanctions in the field of official secrecy is inappropriate, and that a civil action would be more suitable; it will be seen in cases such as *R. v. Ponting* (below) that there is widespread public disapproval of the use of the criminal law against individuals who believe that they are acting in the public interest when they reveal secret information. What is the point of stigmatising whistle-blowers with criminal prosecution if juries in criminal trials then refuse to convict on policy grounds, in direct conflict with the evidence presented to the jury? Further, it may be to the Government's advantage that whistleblowers should feel able and willing to speak out against illegal or otherwise wrongful activities, since it is only by knowing about all such practices that the Government as a collective body may work to prevent them and to provide redress for any harm caused. It is secrecy which is at least partially responsible for allowing impropriety to continue unchecked.

The Case for Government Secrecy

5–003 Every government has areas of operation in which it has a legitimate need for secrecy. Obvious examples include defence/national security and foreign affairs. The "national security" argument is one of the most commonly given in justifying secrecy, but unfortunately no satisfactory definition has been given of this important term and in cases hinging on this issue courts have tended to accept with little criticism or investigation a Government's statement that national security was involved in a situation. Clearly, there are certain defence secrets of which disclosure could endanger the state or its operatives, and the following have been long accepted to fall within the term "national security": operations by security and intelligence services[1]; matters to do with movements of the armed forces[2]; war itself[3]; details of nuclear weapons[4]; and defending the country in general.[5] These can be summarised as security, defence and intelligence matters; few would argue that secrecy is unjustifiable in these areas, as long as the limits are defined. The security of the state must be more important than freedom of either information or expression.

Free access to all information held by the Government might lead to excessive bureaucracy and impede swift decisions on important matters of policy. Some would argue that, for example, discussions by the Cabinet would not be as uninhibited and honest if open to public display. Alarm might be caused unnecessarily if information about preliminary or exploratory discussions were revealed when in fact a different solution would eventually emerge from the debate. Many would claim that there is a need to preserve the facade of unity of Cabinet Government when in fact the Cabinet is comprised of individuals with differing opinions and tensions are inevitable, although rarely serious or lasting. Although it may sound paternalistic, the public do not need to know everything about the Government and its workings; and the public interest is not identical to those matters in which members of the public are interested. The Government itself is accountable to Parliament, and could in theory be ejected at any time if it oversteps or abuses its powers. If this system works then public scrutiny of Government should not be necessary. Many disclosures of confidential information are made by civil servants, who are not accountable or responsible to Parliament, whereas a Minister is responsible for actions taken in his name by those in his department—ministerial responsibility should act as a sufficient safeguard against government excesses. Parliament may require a Minister to provide information in its function as a court and in the final resort it may remove the government.

Some would further argue that secrecy is justified in the international field where negotiations and relations with the governments of other nations are concerned—the country's international standing and reputation could be damaged by certain revelations of sensitive information. A related argument is that unscrupulous individuals and companies can profit financially or otherwise from the publication of sensitive information concerning the economy or other domestic factors related to trade and industry. For example, if a Government is considering an economic policy which would be directly advantageous to a powerful multinational company, then if that company were to obtain this information before the final official policy decision had been made it might be able to encourage or influence the implementation of the policy by applying pressure upon the Government. It should however be noted that this argument, like the others in favour of secrecy, has a narrow and very specific application; none of these arguments can justify a wholesale policy of secrecy.

What is Secrecy?

5–004 The United Kingdom has a long-established tradition and framework of secrecy relating to many categories of Government information. In contrast to other comparable countries, a citizen of the United Kingdom has historically had no general "right to know". Until the Freedom of Information Act 2000 comes into force, freedom of information is a matter of omission in that the right to obtain information exists only where it is not restricted or completely forbidden. This culture of secrecy is almost unique and has its roots in constitutional and legislative history. Government is prima facie secret, hidden from public scrutiny, except where the veil has been lifted for practical or policy reasons. Courts have supported and to some extent created the culture of secrecy, by treating Government assertions uncritically. Although the Human Rights Act 1998 is likely to lead to a diminution in the extent to which official secrecy arguments may be upheld as will be seen, the leading ECHR cases have so far allowed considerable sway for "national security" arguments. It is true that the Government is usually in the best position to judge what the national interest is, but the Government is also ideally placed to judge how to avoid the disastrous or the embarrassing by means of secrecy. This monopoly can in fact be self-maintaining; if no other body is able to obtain the information, then no other body will be in possession of sufficient information upon which to base its challenge to the Government's assertions.

Arguments of secrecy may be involved at various stages in the legal process. In pre-trial civil proceedings a Government may argue that the public interest weighs in favour of keeping the confidentiality of certain documents or other sources of information which would otherwise form part of the evidence in the case. Thus "discovery" of the documents may be prevented[6] and the other party's evidence may be severely weakened. Even relatively insignificant preparatory paperwork related to the formation of Government policy may be protected in this manner[7] as may papers held by other bodies including the police, if discovery of those papers might well harm the reason for which the papers were produced.[8] This concept is known as public interest immunity, and will only prevent discovery if the court accepts that the public interest in secrecy is on the facts greater then that in favour of making the information publicly available.

Criminal proceedings may also be brought against a person who commits espionage or sabotage,[9] or against a crown servant or government contractor who communicates information about security or defence matters[10] or a person who intercepts communications.[11]

Civil proceedings may be brought against a person who is liable in equity for breach of confidence, *i.e.* taking unfair advantage of the position obtained by the receipt of confidential information, and censorship may be imposed upon the media either formally or informally by use of the system of DA notices.

Each of these arenas of secrecy will be examined separately below.

Freedom of Expression Versus Official Secrecy

Until the Human Rights Act 1998 came into force, the United Kingdom's unwritten constitution gave no specific protection to the individual's right of freedom of expression. The post-HRA situation can still be contrasted with the express protection given in many written constitutions, including for example the United States where it is mentioned in the First Amendment. In fact it is a right which is typically placed symbolically early in constitutional documents, probably in recognition of its importance both in itself and as a further means of safeguarding the other basic rights of a citizen. Freedom of expression is relevant to several chapters in this book, but official secrecy and self-expression form a particularly strong contrast and so it may be useful at this point to look briefly at the main issues raised by freedom of expression. **5–005**

In constitutions such as that of the United States, a citizen's right of freedom of expression is first stated to exist and then qualified by exceptions supported by the Supreme Court, which apply in situations where the particular instance of speech tends towards harming society to such an extent that there is a "clear and present danger" which the State has a duty to prevent. Thus, in theory at least, free speech is a constitutional right for every United States citizen in all circumstances, unless a greater and pressing need can be shown for a particular law which curtails free speech. However, in the United Kingdom, freedom of speech has been a fragmented right without any express constitutional backing. It has also been crucial to distinguish different methods of "speech" such as writing, oral words, forms of expression which do not involve words as such at all, and printed publications, and it will often matter who is making the words public and in what circumstances. The law of the United Kingdom further distinguishes between true expression and activities associated with protest, the latter being dealt with as a public order issue. These subdivisions and classifications create a complex situation from which freedom of expression does not emerge as a coherent right; rather it is a limited and much circumscribed right which exists only where it is not excluded by statute or common law—a negatively-worded freedom.

However, there were always a few narrow situations in which freedom of **5–006** expression is given express recognition in English law. First, statements made by any Member of Parliament, a member of the House of Commons or of the House of Lords, which are made during Parliamentary proceedings remain protected absolutely by privilege and cannot result in prosecution for the person who speaks. This privilege has existed since the seventeenth century, and has since been extended to the publishers of papers printed by parliamentary authority and to petitions received by M.P.s from their constituents. Secondly, there is a theoretical right of a citizen to petition the monarch (which includes for these purposes any Minister of the Crown) with any grievance; this right was recognised and protected by the Bill of Rights 1689, but has now fallen into disuse. Finally, there are various specific statutory provisions which recognise freedom of expression for certain classes of individuals in certain circumstances, and indeed create duties upon public or private bodies (and occasionally individuals) to enable such expression. Examples include the campaigning rights of parliamentary candidates, whether in terms of use of school and other buildings, leafleting or free use of the Royal Mail, and the convention that each political party receives a broadcasting airtime slot for the purpose of party political broadcasts. In summary, freedom of expression was not greatly supported by any of these limited recognitions of its existence, but parliamentary privilege is the most important of the exceptional cases.

The strongest evidence of the existence of the right to freedom of expression in English law before 2000 was in fact its express legal limitation or prohibition in certain defined situations. The implication is that the right continued to exist in all circumstances where it has not been regulated. Freedom of expression has been limited in the provision of education by schools and colleges, where the promotion of "partisan political views"[12] and the distribution of certain types of political material[13–14] are prohibited. Independent schools are exempted. A series of conventions, practices and rules, including those embodied in the Civil Service Code, discourage civil servants from engaging in politics and from public expression of views related to their employment or to government policy. Official secrecy legislation and the equitable rules of confidentiality form further constraints, and will be covered in depth in this chapter. There are numerous other examples of express legal limitations of freedom of expression, including such disparate rules as those forbidding local authorities from using their funds to promote prohibited causes, and criminal offences relating to harassment. Each of these rights of expression and limitations upon expression will have to be re-evaluated by future courts in the light of the Human Rights Act 1998, and in particular of section 12. This is a process which has already begun and some of the cases dealt with below give insight into the methods being used by judges to reconcile the old and new legal rules and policy requirements.

The Protection of National Security by Criminal Sanctions Official Secrets Act 1911

5–007 All the current statutory law governing official secrecy has involved the imposition of relatively high criminal sanctions upon those who, by speech or otherwise, reveal information which has the potential of threatening state security. Thus sanctions are imposed after the event of disclosure and the threat of such sanctions is intended to operate as a deterrent, or at least as a factor which may influence a person against speaking out. There is also a declaratory function served here by the criminal law, in delineating what is to be perceived as acceptable behaviour. The statutes enacted over the past century, in contrast to the approach taken by equity (see below), do not attempt to pre-empt or to prevent disclosure.

The Official Secrets Act 1911 was passed in great haste in response to widespread fear of espionage being carried out by Germany. Although its provisions are broad, vague and much-criticised, much of the Act is still in force. The changes which the 1911 Act introduced were sweeping, and so it is somewhat surprising that its long title was "An Act to re-enact the Official Secrets Act 1889, with amendments". While the 1911 Act was being debated and publicised, the Government promoted it in terms of providing protection for the state against espionage and other conduct which may aid the enemy and thus injure the state; little mention was made of its second role, that of preventing the unauthorised disclosure of information by state employees. Although the Act created a range of criminal offences, some have been repealed and others have been replaced by newer legislation or have fallen into disuse.

Section 1

Despite the heading "penalties for spying", the scope of the Act is not restricted to espionage activities or foreign agents, and as will be seen below may include sabotage, potential or otherwise, even where there is no intention of harming the country or the Government of the time. The most important remaining offence is section 1, which is potentially a great restriction upon freedom of expression for those whom it covers. However, it should be noted that the section is a problem more in terms of theory than of reality, since very few prosecutions are actually brought under this set of offences. **5–008**

Under section 1(1), it is an offence punishable by a prison sentence of up to 14 years if any person for any purpose prejudicial to the safety or interest of the State (a) approaches, is in the vicinity of, or enters any prohibited place, or (b) makes any plan, sketch, note or document, etc.,[15] which might be or intended to be useful to an enemy or, (c) obtains, or communicates that plan, document, etc., which might be or intended to be useful to an enemy. Thus section 1 is a set of thorough, if vague, anti-espionage offences for which it is not necessary to prove that the defendant intended to threaten the security of the State. It is enough if the defendant's purpose is in fact prejudicial to State safety, and further, the information or other secret item is capable of being useful to an enemy. The defendant may even be convicted if the secret information is factually useless, as long as the defendant himself believed that it could be useful to an enemy.

The word "State" does not necessarily mean government or the executive **5–009**
or indeed, as was argued in *Chandler*,[16] the individuals who inhabit these islands, since interests differ amongst individuals.[17] Lord Reid suggested the

words "the organised community" as an acceptable definition. "Prohibited place" refers to any defence establishment, whether it be naval, army, airforce, ammunition factory, etc. occupied by or on behalf of Her Majesty, or under contract with Her Majesty; or a place, including railway, road, electricity stations, etc. or any documents related to such areas, declared by the Secretary of State to be a prohibited place.[18] The words "useful to an enemy" do not necessarily mean useful to an existing or present enemy but a potential enemy with whom we might some day be at war.[19] The offence under section 1 is an arrestable offence and a prosecution may only take place with the consent of the Attorney-General. The quality of the information which is disclosed is not important.[20] If the purpose of the classified documents is to prejudice the safety of the State then the discloser is guilty of an offence under this section. The actual documents may, in fact, be ultimately useless to the enemy but that is not relevant. It is, further, not necessary that the purpose be detrimental to the safety of the nation. That the reasons were for the promotion or the conversion of others to British ideas is no excuse, but only goes to the seriousness of the offence.[21] Thus, the motive behind the disclosure is irrelevant.

Under section 1(2) it is not necessary for the prosecution to prove that the defendant's purpose was prejudicial to the safety or the interest of the State, it is enough if looking at all the circumstances, including the defendant's conduct and known character, it appears that his purpose was prejudicial to the State. Further, any plan document, etc. made without lawful authority is deemed to have been made for a purpose prejudicial to the safety or interest of the State. Thus it is for the defendant to prove that the particular purpose was not in fact prejudicial to the State.

5–010 For instance, in *Chandler v. DPP*[22]:

Facts. A peaceful demonstration took place at Wethersfield Airfield (at that time used as a U.S. air base) by members of the "Committee of 100", a pro-nuclear disarmament organisation. At that time, the air base was a prohibited place under section 3 of the OSA 1911. The purpose of the protest was to (a) prevent the aircraft from taking off by the protestors placing themselves in front of the aircraft, and to (b) sit outside at the entrance of the airfield thereby immobilising the surrounding area. In fact, the protestors were stopped by the police from entering the airfield. The defendants were arrested and charged with conspiracy to commit a breach of section 1 namely, for a purpose prejudicial to the safety or interest of the state to enter a Royal Airforce station. The defendants pleaded that (1) the acts did not constitute a breach of section 1; (2) that their acts were for the benefit of the State; and (3) the purpose was not in fact prejudicial to the safety of the State. The judge refused the defendants to admit evidence regarding (2) and (3) above, or to allow cross-examination of a witness, an Air Commodore, who testified that any interference with aircrafts amounted to a prejudicial affect on the safety of the State. The judge ruled that the defendants were not entitled to call evidence to establish that it would be beneficial for this country to give up nuclear armaments or that the accused honestly believed that what they were doing was not endangering the security of the State. The defendants were convicted and appealed.

Decision. They appealed on the grounds that (1) there was no conspiracy under section 1 OSA 1911; (2) the judge erred in refusing cross-examination of the Air

Commodore; and (3) the judge was wrong in excluding evidence on the issue of whether the appellants' purpose was prejudicial to the safety or interest of the State (the appellants believed that what they were doing was beneficial to the State). Their appeal was dismissed by the Court of Appeal and they appealed to the House of Lords. Lord Reid first of all examined the word "purpose" in section 1(1). Here, there was no doubt that the purpose (which included "any purpose") was to obstruct so as to render the aircraft completely inactive for a period of time and intended and desired that effect. It is for the jury to decide whether or not the purpose was prejudicial to the Safety of the state. The next question was, what is and what is not "prejudicial to the safety or interest of the State". Here, the court was dealing with "interference with a prohibited place". His lordship said that:

> "it is in my opinion clear that the disposition and armament of the armed forces are and for centuries have been within the exclusive discretion of the Crown and that no one can seek a legal remedy on the ground that such discretion has been wrongly exercised. If a place was legally declared a prohibited place, then any unlawful interference within that area must be treated as being useful to the enemy and therefore prejudicial to the safety or interests of the State."

Thus, it was not open to the appellants to adduce evidence that what they were doing, according to their beliefs, was of benefit to the state, and that they should be acquitted on those grounds. Accordingly, the judge was correct in refusing the Air Commodore to be cross-examined on matters, such as the dangers of possessing nuclear armaments, since this was irrelevant to the main issues, which were issues of politics to be decided upon by the Crown and therefore rendering the personal opinions of the appellants inadmissible.

SECTION 2

Before embarking on the OSA 1909 it is necessary to discuss the now **5–011**
defunct section 2 OSA 1911 in order to understand and appreciate the significant differences (if indeed there are any) between past and present law. Section 2 of the Act was called the "catch-all" provision, since the wording contained some 2000 different instances whereby a person could face prosecution for an offence under this section. Under section 2(1) of the Official Secrets Act 1911:

> "If any person having in his possession or control any sketch, plan, [etc.] . . . document, or information . . . which has been entrusted in confidence to him by any person holding office under [her] Majesty . . . communicates the sketch, plan, [etc.] . . . document or information to any person, other than a person to whom he is authorised to communicate it, or a person to whom it is in the interest of the State his duty to communicate it . . . he shall be guilty of a misdemeanour."

SECTION 2(2)

> "If any person receives any sketch, plan, [etc.] . . . or information knowing or having reasonable ground to believe that (it) was communicated to him in contravention of this act, he shall be guilty of a misdemeanour . . ."

Thus it was an offence to communicate to another, without authority, any confidential information received from a state employee who had obtained the information in his official capacity. It was also an offence to receive such information willingly, with either knowledge or reasonable grounds for belief that the information was being communicated in breach of the 1911 Act. It was not necessary for the information to be important, nor secret, nor indeed of any potential harm to state security; even the disclosure of insignificant clothing details has triggered the offence.

5–012 For instance, in *R. v. Crisp and Homewood*[23]:

Facts. Crisp worked as a clerk at the War Office, dealing with army uniform contracts. Having been transferred to another department he went back and copied certain data relating to clothing suppliers. Homewood, a tailor, tendered for clothing contracts. Some documents were found in Homewood's office in Crisp's handwriting relating to contracts and were handed over to the War Office. Crisp was arrested and charged under section 2. It was accepted that the disclosure of the information was not for monetary gain, but more out of friendship.

Decision. It was argued by the defendants that the information was not marked "confidential" and therefore not secret, thus no danger to the State or valuable to a foreign enemy. Avory J. said that it was not necessary to prove that the documents were confidential; merely showing that he obtained those documents by virtue of his position of holding office under his Majesty was enough. Finally, since Homewood must, at least, have reasonable grounds to believe that the information received was communicated to him in contravention of the Act, both parties pleaded guilty. The judge regarded the matter as a "technical breach" and fined them both 40s each.

If the offences under section 2 were interpreted naturally, no civil servant or government contractor could communicate to any other person any information gained at work or concerning his employment, without prior authorisation. Communication of the menu options in the staff canteen might constitute the offence. The section 2 communication offence is one of absolute liability; in other words, no *mens rea* is required whatsoever and neither motive nor explanation will make any difference to the defendant's conviction. The triviality of some of the instances which could constitute the offence, coupled with the severity of the maximum sentence, formed a combination which was ripe for either abuse or criticism, both of which could draw attention away from the true instances where the offence was needed to protect national security. Due to many such concerns about the unacceptably wide drafting of section 2, it was finally replaced by the Official Secrets Act 1989, which creates a more structured and classified series of offences although their scope may not be any narrower in effect. But before this restructuring took place, section 2 had been extended in scope twice by the Official Secrets Acts of 1920 and 1939, and had enjoyed a sudden surge of popularity, at least in terms of the number of prosecutions commenced, between 1978 and 1986 when there were as many trials as there had been in the previous 30 years.

5–013 A good example of the workings of the Official Secrets Act 1911 can be found in the case of a Miss Sarah Tisdall. Miss Tisdall[24] was employed as a clerk at the Foreign Office. She photocopied two documents marked "secret", made by the Secretary of State for Defence regarding the exact time of delivery of cruise missiles to the Greenham Common RAF base, and the security arrangements involved. She made extra copies and handed them over to *The Guardian* newspaper anonymously. *The Guardian* printed the document relating to the arrival time of the missiles. After a thorough investigation by the Ministry of Defence, Miss Tisdall confessed and was imprisoned for six months.

Up until this time, all prosecutions under section 1 and/or section 2 had been made against activities involving espionage and sabotage. Now for the first time the media was being targeted and especially journalists who had received so-called confidential information. Legal action was being taken against those journalists. For instance, in a case referred to as the *ABC case*, an article in *Time Out* had been written by a Mr Duncan Campbell and Mark Hossenball, entitled "The Eavesdroppers", detailing the activities of GCHQ (which had hitherto not been formally recognised as existing). Berry formerly worked for the Intelligence Corps for seven years, before leaving with the rank of lance-corporal. Aubrey, another journalist, and Campbell contacted Berry to talk about his work and the conversation was fully tape-recorded. After the meeting, all three were arrested by Special Branch. They were denied access to a solicitor for some 40 hours, and were eventually charged under section 2; B with communicating information to C without authority; C with receiving it; and A with aiding and abetting. Mars-Jones J. gave a strong recommendation to the prosecution that the charges under section 1 should be dismissed, and accordingly they were. With regard to section 2, Lord Hutchinson Q.C. for the defendants asked a prosecution witness, Colonel B, how secrets are classified. "What remains secret is what is designated secret by whoever makes the designation", he replied. "You mean the rules that are laid down for what is and what is not secret are themselves secret?". "Yes", was his unflinching reply.[25] B had definitely disclosed confidential information without authority and he was aware of this. He maintained that he was within his rights to act as he did. He regarded SIGINT (Signals Intelligence) to be illegal and in effect a form of espionage organisation. Lord Hutchinson Q.C. contended "that the role of the OSA is to prevent harm to the nation's safety and not to save the Government from embarrassment or to block Watergate-style newspaper investigations." The judge said "we will not tolerate defectors or whistle-blowers from our intelligence services who seek the assistance of the press and other media to publish secrets whatever their motives".[26] The judge said that section 2(1) is an absolute offence, and is committed whatever the document contains, whatever the nature of the disclosure and whether or not the disclosure is prejudicial to the state. The essence of the offence is the disclosure of confidential information.[27] The jury having retired for nearly 68 hours brought back a verdict of guilty for all the defendants under section 2. B was sentenced to six months, suspended for two years. A and C were conditionally discharged.

"In the interests of the state"

5–014 Under section 2 the defendant did have a defence if he could prove that the prosecution case should fail as the disclosure was made "in the interest of the State". Just how this expression should be interpreted was the main question involved in the case of *R. v. Ponting*.[28] There, the defendant was employed as head of the Ministry of Defences' "Secretariat 5". He sent two unauthorised documents to an M.P. regarding the sinking of the vessel, the General Belgrano, during the Falklands war. He was charged under section 2(2) of the OSA 1911. The defendant argued that it was his duty in the interest of the State that he communicate such information to the M.P. It was irrelevant that the documents did not endanger national security in any respect. Under section 2, it was not necessary for the prosecution to prove *mens rea* on the part of the defendant. It was part of the defendant's official duty as a civil servant to withhold all information from release unless otherwise officially authorised. As to the question, "what is in the interest of the state?" the judge directed the jury that it was for the Government of the day to decide what was in the interest of the State.[29] It was not for the jury to decide on Government policy. The defendant argued that "in the interest of the State" meant in the interest of the country, or the realm, or thc national interest. The jury were not convinced by the judge's direction and acquitted the defendant.

After Clive Ponting was acquitted, the Government became more wary in forging ahead with similar prosecutions in this area, even those which were likely to succeed. A good example of where the Attorney-General refrained from taking such a course, even though the "secret" was publicly made, involved an ex-security intelligence service employee named Cathy Massiter who gave an interview for a TV programme entitled "MI5's Official Secrets", to be transmitted on Channel 4 shortly afterwards. The statement given in the programme revealed certain, to say the least, iniquities, and at the very most, illegal operations carried on by MI5; including telephone tapping of trade union officials, alleged communists, and political activists as well as members of the Campaign for Nuclear Disarmament. All of this information was clearly confidential and whether legal or not, MI5 certainly did not want it publicised. On the day it was meant to be shown the then IBA decided that there was a grave risk of prosecution if the programme went ahead, so they decided to bar its transmission. Later, that same day journalists were shown a video of the programme. Videos were also sent to the DPP and other copies were made. Even Richard Branson began selling the video under the name "MI5's Official Secrets—The Programme that Couldn't be Shown". Ms Massiter also met with M.P.s to discuss the matter. In the light of all that was happening, no doubt influenced by the Ponting episode, the Attorney-General decided not to go ahead with any prosecution. Further, it was unlikely that Ms Massiter was going to give up without a fight, if prosecuted. The programme was eventually transmitted some three months later. In the wake of all this, Lord Bridge set up an inquiry into the phone tapping allegations and after only five days investigation decided that the proper procedures and guidelines had been followed by the security services.

OFFICIAL SECRETS ACT 1920[30]

The enactment of section 1 of the 1920 Act extended secrecy provisions to cover the unlawful retention of documents, but more importantly section 7 of the 1920 Act significantly widened the scope of the offences under the 1911 Act. Section 7 makes it an offence to attempt to commit, to be an accomplice to, or to suggest that another person should commit (amongst other such variants of inchoate liability) any of the offences under either the 1911 or the 1920 Official Secrets Acts. This may seem puzzling since, on general principles of criminal law, it is already an offence to be involved in the commission of any criminal offence in any of the ways listed in section 7; the section at first appears to do no more than to restate the rules of criminal law relating to accomplices and attempts. However, there is one important exception; under section 7 it is an offence to do "any act preparatory to the commission of an offence"[31] under either the 1911 or 1920 Act. **5–015**

In *R. v. Bingham*[32]:

Facts. The defendant approached the Soviet Embassy for the purposes of supplying them with confidential information in return for payment to her husband. She stated that such information would have been entirely useless to the Soviets, and thus would not have damaged national interests in any way. She was arrested and charged under section 1 of the Official Secrets Act 1911 and section 7 of the Official Secrets Act 1920. The jury were directed that if they thought that she realised that the handing over of confidential information was a possibility, they should convict. She was acquitted under section 1 but was convicted under section 7 and imprisoned for two and a half years. She appealed.

Decision. Her appeal was based on the grounds that she had not done "any act preparatory to the commission of an offence". The question for the Court of Appeal was as to the timing of the commission of the offence—was the offence committed when she realised that the passing over of confidential information might occur as a *possibility*, or did the offence take place only when she realised that the transferring of the information was *probably* going to happen? Lord Widgery concluded that mere possibility would suffice here. He said, this section existed to fill a gap in the law. "It contemplates something which is even more remote from the substantive offence than an attempt to commit it", *i.e.* it would take place some time in the future. Thus, as the prosecution said, if a person creates circumstances, (*i.e* approaches the Soviets) in which the possibility of an offence under the Act becomes a real likelihood, (*i.e.* the handing over of information) though it may not eventually end up in a crime being committed, nevertheless, the offence is made out. The Court of Appeal agreed and the appeal was dismissed.

This encompasses actions and conduct at a much earlier stage than would ever create criminal liability on usual principles. Under the Criminal

Attempts Act 1981, section 1, conduct must be "more than merely preparatory" in relation to the commission of a full offence before it will create liability. In other words, the defendant must be shown to have passed the stages of planning and preparation for the offence and to have engaged upon the course of conduct which, when complete, will constitute the full offence. Thus section 7 is a further example of an official secrecy provision which does not follow the usual rules which criminal law considers to be important. It is open to question whether the subject matter of the offences, that is national security or state secrecy, justifies such repeated deviation from the long-established and carefully considered principles of criminal law. If a defendant cannot be convicted of attempted murder, attempted rape or an attempt of any other serious offence when he is caught at the stage of preparation for the offence, then it seems anomalous and excessively harsh to require such a minimal amount of conduct to constitute a serious official secrets offence, particularly when the great breadth of the offences and the lack of necessity for proof of *mens rea* are also taken into consideration. In view of this, the safeguard that the consent of the Attorney–General is necessary according to section 8 before a prosecution can be brought may not appear adequate. One reason why there have not been more prosecutions under the 1920 Act is that even an unofficial or informal authorisation of disclosure of the information in question will operate to prevent liability, but in many circumstances such practices created even greater problems for journalists and publishers since it could be extremely difficult to assess which statements among "leaked" information were safe to use or publish, and which might involve criminal liability. Interestingly, the right to silence was removed in this area long before others: section 6 of the 1920 Act originally created an offence of refusing to disclose to a police officer on demand the details of the source from which information had been obtained in breach of the Acts.[33] Section 9 also gives powers of search and seizure: a magistrate may grant a search warrant which allows the police to enter and search premises, to search any person found on the premises, and to seize any evidence that an offence under the Act has been committed or is about to be committed. This section creates a much wider set of powers than would exist under PACE, and has led to extreme situations such as that of "the Zircon Affair".[34]

Official Secrets Act 1989: A New Scheme of Criminal Sanctions for Disclosure

5–016 As has been discussed above, problems with the Official Secrets Acts 1911–1939 had led to concerns about the scope and harshness of the offences and to calls for reform. In 1972, the Franks Committee[35] had criticised section 2 of the 1911 Act for the breadth of the offences which it created and its lack of discrimination according to the justice of the case. The Committee had recommended that section 2 should be replaced by a series of narrowly-defined offences which would form a coherent body of law within which fairness would be achieved by the law itself, not by the exercise of the prosecutorial discretion as to which offence to charge or whether to commence proceedings against a defendant. Criminal sanctions for disclosure should only attach to information in the following alternative categories:

(1) Classified information concerning defence, internal security, foreign relations, or the currency, where unauthorised disclosure could be proven to be capable of causing serious injury to the interests of the nation;

(2) Official information which is likely either to assist criminal activities or to impede law enforcement;

(3) Cabinet documents;

(4) Confidential information which has been entrusted to the Government by a private body or individual.

Thus the criminal law would still have a large role to play in the field of official secrecy, although its sanctions would be withdrawn from certain parts of the scope of section 2. Worthy of mention here is the proposal that the question of the definition of "serious injury" in category (1) above should be left to the Minister, and not to the jury, with the result that a certificate issued by the Minister prior to a prosecution for the proposed new offence, stating that the disclosed document had been categorised correctly as capable of causing serious injury to State interests by its disclosure, would form conclusive proof of that classification, the Government would thus have considerable power over the interpretation of the offence. In addition, the Franks proposals were weak in their provision of defences, making no concession to certain situations where disclosure might be justified or at least excusable, for example, where the information in question was already available to the public in some form, or where the disclosure was done in the public interest.

Several reform attempts followed the Franks Report, but it was only after **5–017** such high-profile cases as the ABC, Tisdall and Ponting trials that pressure towards reform escalated, largely as a response to the perceived Government overreaction and excessive sanctions in the ABC and Tisdall cases, and due to the jury's refusal to convict Ponting in spite of his legal guilt under section 2. There are arguments in favour of encouraging civil servants to alert the public and/or the authorities to instances of malfeasance, illegality or other wrongdoing in a government office, to criminalise such "whistleblowing" indiscriminately merely risks criticism and the discrediting of the law. Since section 2 had now become very difficult to charge and the issue of "whistleblowing" had been highlighted, there was a new opportunity to reform this area of law towards both fairness and workability. In 1988 a White Paper was published on reform of section 2 of the Official Secrets Act 1911,[36] from which a Bill was drafted which became the Official Secrets Act 1989. But, in contrast to most other European countries, the new Act did not take the opportunity to either create a "right to know" for citizens or to radically change the scope of official secrecy. Rather, the new Act followed the recommendations of the Franks Committee in creating narrowly-defined categories of information which are potentially damaging to the State, and introducing requirements of proof of both harm and fault before a conviction may be obtained. Thus the 1989 Act can be seen as a better-defined version of the old section 2, with less obvious shortcomings, but it is by no means a great departure and most defendants convicted under the former law could also be convicted under its replacement. However, the Government did claim at the time of the statute's enactment that it was a "great liberalising measure"[37]; this statement must be assessed in relation to the operation of the new Act as a whole.

The 1989 Act created six new categories of protected information to replace the "catch-all" definition from the old section 2. But it should be noted that these six categories remain widely drafted. The categories are:

(1) Security and intelligence (section 1)

5–018 Any information concerning "the work of, or in support of, the security and intelligence services or any part of them" (section 1(9)), or held by those services, falls within the definition. Clearly this covers bodies such as MI5 (counter-espionage) and MI6 (overseas intelligence), but it is not clear whether the Special Branch,[38] and army intelligence or British Embassy officials abroad are included here. But it does include those persons who are "notified" that they are subject to section 1(1) and may include any member of the public and certain prescribed organisations (section 12(1)(f) and (g)).[39] Judicial review is available to persons who are notified under section 1(6). Section 1 also refers to Crown servants and Government contractors; the former is defined in section 12 and includes every Government minister, all civil servants at every level of seniority, all members of the armed forces and police forces, civilians who work for the police, and many Members of Parliament.[40] Under section 12(1)(f) and section 12(1)(g), the Government is given power to widen this category by deeming other types of person or individuals to be regarded as Crown servants as far as official secrecy is concerned. This power has been exercised recently to broaden the scope of the 1989 Act; for example, the Parliamentary Ombudsman and those who work in nuclear energy have been so treated.[41] Government contractors include all persons who are concerned with or employed in the provision of goods or services to any government department, or to the armed forces (section 12(2)(a)). The Secretary of State may provide that suppliers under international agreements are to be treated as falling within this category (section 12(2)(b)).

(2) Defence (section 2)

Section 2(4) defines "defence" to include defence policy and other matters relating to the Ministry of Defence, strategy, military planning, military intelligence, information on the armed forces in general, their weapons and resources, and matters to do with war. **5–019**

(3) International relations (section 3)

Section 3(5) defines this category to include relations between states, international organisations, or a combination of the two, including internal issues which may affect relationships with an international body (for example the United Nations) or other state. **5–020**

(4) Criminal investigations (section 4)

This category concerns information which may have any of the following results: aiding/enabling the commission of an offence; aiding an escape from legal custody; impeding the prevention or detection of offences or the apprehension or prosecution of offenders. **5–021**

(5) Information gathered by a legal warrant for interception of communications (section 4)

This type of information is obtained by means of a warrant under the Regulation of Investigatory Powers Act 2000.[42] The new statute allows the Secretary of State to authorise security services to engage in conduct which, but for the authorisation, would otherwise be illegal, including bugging of premises, removal of documents from premises, photographing documents, and entry into premises in order to accomplish any of these ends. **5–022**

(6) Confidential communications from the British Government to other states or to international organisations (section 6)

Section 6 applies only to material concerning defence, security or intelligence, or international relations, and was intended to prevent information given by the British Government to overseas bodies from reappearing later in the British media after a "leak". The communication of the information to the other State or the international organisation must have occurred in confidence. It should be noticed that one of the Franks Committee's recommendations as to categories of information which should be protected was rejected by the Government. Cabinet documents do not receive protection as a category in their own right, although of course they may fall incidentally into another category in many circumstances. **5–023**

Damage Under the Official Secrets Act 1989

When must it be proven that the disclosure would be damaging? For most of the categories, the disclosure must be shown to be damaging before an offence can be committed, but the extent to which this is necessary also varies from category to category. **5–024**

Who commits the offence, and in what circumstances?

5–025 There are three categories of persons addressed by the offences under the 1989 Act: the intelligence/security services; those who are either Crown servants or government contractors; and private individuals, which will include by implication the media.

5–026 *(i) The section 1 offence* Crown servants (including, of course, members of the security and intelligence services) and government contractors may be convicted of any of the offences in sections 1–4. As discussed above, damage must generally be proved.

Under section 1(1) if the person making the disclosure is a member or past member of the security services,[43] then he faces an absolute ban upon disclosure and there is no need to prove either actual or foreseeable damage; presumably on the basis that those who work for the security or intelligence services have an absolute duty not to disclose any information whatsoever gained in the course of their employment, regardless of whether it is damaging or innocuous. But it must be questionable whether it is necessary to prohibit members of the security and intelligence services from parting with information such as the number of paperclips on their desks or the date of the staff Christmas party. The Public Interest Disclosure Act 1998 exempts government employees from the employment law protection which it gives to those who whistleblow in the public interest. However, the *Ponting* case and the recent *Tomlinson* and *Shayler* sagas (see below) have shown that judges and juries are not always keen to criminalise those who disclose information in the public interest or to ban publication of such information.

Section 1(4) contains the test for damage in relation to disclosures of information made by Crown servants and government contractors concerning security and intelligence: a disclosure is damaging if it either in fact causes damage to any aspect of the work of the security and intelligence services; or if an unauthorised disclosure[44] "would be likely to cause such damage . . .", or if it is part of a class of documents of which the unauthorised disclosure is likely to cause damage. It can be seen that this test is easy to satisfy if it is the second and third limbs which are applied. Since the section 1(3) offence applies only to Crown servants and contractors, there is the potential that proof of even foreseeable harm caused by a disclosure by such persons will be necessary only when the document in question does not fall within a class of documents which as a category of information are likely to cause harm if disclosed without authorisation. But even if the information in question does not fall within such a class of documents and so it must be shown that actual damage has been caused by the disclosure under the first limb of the test, no definition of harm is given and so it is impossible for a Crown servant to predict in this circumstance whether information which he is planning to disclose would attract liability. This comes close to the absolute prohibition on disclosure which faced Crown servants under the 1911 Act.

(ii) The section 2 offence The damage requirement for section 2, which concerns information relating to defence, is satisfied if the disclosure of the information either causes, or is likely to cause, any of the following results: **5–027**

(a) damage to the capacity of any part of the armed forces to carry out their tasks;

(b) death or injury to members of the armed forces;

(c) serious damage to equipment or installations of armed forces;

(d) endangers the United Kingdom's interests abroad;

(e) seriously obstructs the promotion or protection of interests abroad by the United Kingdom; or

(f) endangers the safety of British citizens abroad.

Although the wording of this section is again wide, it applies only to persons who are Crown servants or government contractors, or who gained the information in question when in such a capacity.

(iii) The section 3 offence Where the information relates to international relations, damage is satisfied by proof that the disclosure either caused, or is likely to cause, any of the results in (d), (e) or (f) above, discussed in relation to defence. In addition, if it needs to be decided whether the information was likely to cause one of these types of damage, then the fact that the information was received in confidence from either another state or from an international organisation may be enough in itself to satisfy the test (section 3(3)(a)). Section 3 applies only to Crown servants, government contractors, and those who formerly held such a role; the information must also have been gained in the course of such employment. **5–028**

(iv) Part 1 of section 4—section 4(1) and section 4(2) Where the information is related to crime, section 4 does not follow the general tendency of the offences under the Act by classifying disclosures by categories of information and using a general definition of damage within those categories; rather, it looks simply at the result of the disclosure, whether actual or potential. It is not necessary to prove that the disclosed information falls within any particular category of information or comes from any particular source. According to section 4(2), the offence may be committed by disclosure of any information which: **5–029**

> ". . . results in the commission of an offence; or facilitates an escape from legal custody or the doing of any other act prejudicial to the safekeeping of persons in legal custody; or impedes the prevention or detection of offences or the prosecution of suspected offenders; or which is such that its unauthorised disclosure is likely to have any of those effects."

The section seems unnecessarily complicated, since many of the instances could have been placed within one general category of assisting those suspected of an offence.

5–030 *(v) Part 2 of section 4—section 4(3)* Where special investigative powers created by the named statutes under the second part of section 4 are concerned, damage is defined in terms of content of the information rather than real or potential effect of disclosure. This contrasts strongly against the first part of section 4. But there is no definition of damage or requirement of proof of harm; any Crown servant, whether or not a member of the security and intelligence services, may commit the offence by disclosing any information about the interception of communications under the 1985 Act (before 2000) or information obtained by reason of warrants issued under the Security Services Act 1989 or the Intelligence Services Act 1994 (section 4(3))(before 2000) or under the new Regulation of Investigatory Powers Act 2000. Thus it appears that these categories of information are regarded as so intrinsically harmful to legitimate interests if disclosed that a blanket prohibition is justifiable. The White Paper (paragraphs 30 and 53) took that approach, stating that secrecy is paramount if interception of communications is to have the desired effect, and also that since the statutes in question invade the privacy of private individuals in order to obtain the information sought, the public interest will be served only if the privacy of those individuals is not further assaulted by disclosure of the information obtained as a result of the operation of those statutes. While these arguments are persuasive, they cannot justify the application of the section 4(3) offence to disclosure of any information obtained by operation of the Acts and warrants, for example, annual reports made which record the number of warrants issued for such purposes under any of the three statutes in question; these reports are submitted to Parliament and so should not be regarded as secret or damaging.

5–031 *(vi) The section 6 offence* This offence was added to the Act after the White Paper, in which it did not appear. It applies to information concerning security, intelligence, defence or international relations which has been entrusted by the British Government to another state or to an international body. The section excludes information covered by section 4 (crime and special investigations) and, unusually, contains a *mens rea* requirement; in addition to the requirement that the disclosure of the information must be damaging, it must be shown that the defendant knew, or had reasonable cause to believe, that the information was of the type covered by this section and that its disclosure would be damaging. Again unusually, it is a defence under section 6(3) to show that the information disclosed has already been made public with the consent of the foreign state or international organisation concerned; this is known as the defence of prior disclosure.

Private individuals, including the media

5–032 The 1989 Act also aims to prevent and to control unauthorised disclosures by private individuals and the media, although no specific provisions apply to the media *per se*. The key issue is how the information was acquired by the person disclosing it. Disclosure of information gained in any of the following ways may amount to an offence under section 5 of the 1989 Act:

(a) material acquired through a disclosure in breach of section 1 of the Official Secrets Act 1911 (section 5(6)). As previously discussed, the offence under section 1 of the 1911 Act concerns communication of information for purposes prejudicial to the state's interests or safety; the information must either be, or be intended to be, useful to an enemy. Disclosure of material of this type is an offence if done without lawful authority. The defendant must either know, or have reasonable cause to believe, that the information has been communicated in breach of section 1 of the 1911 Act.

(b) material acquired through an unauthorised disclosure by a Crown servant or government contractor (section 5(1)(a)(i)).

(c) material which was entrusted to the defendant in confidence, or in circumstances where there was a reasonable expectation of confidentiality, by a Crown servant or government contractor (section 5(1)(a)(ii)).

(d) material acquired through an unauthorised disclosure by an individual to whom it had been entrusted by a Crown servant or government contractor in confidence or in reasonable expectation of confidentiality (section 5(1)(a)(iii)).

For disclosures of material which fits any of categories (b), (c) or (d), a further test must be satisfied which relates to the type of material which has been disclosed. If the material concerns security and intelligence, defence, or international relations, then an offence will be committed if: the individual discloses it without lawful authority; the disclosure is damaging according to the test in the relevant section for the type of material disclosed; and the individual disclosing the material either knows or has reasonable cause to believe both that the material is protected under the 1989 Act and that disclosure would be damaging.

If the material concerns crime or special investigation powers, the elements required to be proved are reduced since it does not have to be shown that the disclosure was damaging, nor that the person disclosing the information knew or had reasonable cause to believe that it would be damaging. The remaining requirements discussed in the last paragraph do apply to this category.

(e) Information entrusted to other states or to international organisations in confidence (section 6). If an individual or the media obtain information which had been previously entrusted to such a body in confidence, then disclosure will be an offence if it is damaging, and the discloser knows or had reasonable cause to believe both the nature of the information and that disclosure would be damaging.

Additionally there is a specific defence to a section 6 offence; section 6(3) provides that no offence is committed if the information disclosed by the defendant had been disclosed previously to the public, with the authority of the state or organisation concerned. This defence is therefore one of prior disclosure, and is remarkable due to the general lack of such defences within the 1989 Act.

DEFENCES

5–033 The 1989 Act does not allow many defences, and those which do exist are relatively narrow in application. Generally a defendant to any particular charge under the Act will find that he does not have a range or defences from which to choose. There are two defences which are created by the Act itself: first, a denial of the necessary mental state for conviction; and secondly, lawful authority. Other defences were considered at the White Paper stage but were rejected on policy grounds. A public interest defence was thought to be too difficult to apply due to the wide range of situations in which disclosure could be argued to be in the public interest, and it was also thought that the reforms in the 1989 Act would operate in such a way that only disclosures which were in fact contrary to the public interest would attract criminal liability. If this were so, then there was no need for such a defence. A general defence of prior publication was also rejected, it being thought that prior publication of the material in question would already be a factor to be considered in the assessment of whether the disclosure was "damaging" and so did not require separate consideration; it was also argued that the fact that information has already been published elsewhere does not necessarily prevent the fresh disclosure from causing substantial damage, particularly if it adds weight to what was previously widely dismissed as gossip.[45]

(i) The mens rea (mental state) defence

5–034 Unless the person disclosing the information is or has been a member of the security or intelligence services, then there is a general requirement for each of the offences under the 1989 Act that the defendant must be shown to have had a prohibited state of mind at the time of the disclosure. Thus it will be a defence if the defendant shows that he neither knew, nor had reasonable cause to believe, that the information which he disclosed fell within one of the protected categories of information under sections 1–4 of the Act. Depending upon the offence charged, there may also be a defence that the defendant neither knew nor had reasonable cause to believe that the disclosure would be damaging (obviously this will only operate as a defence to offences which require damage to be proved).

The burden of proof relating to such defences varies, depending upon the identity of the defendant. If the defendant is a Crown servant or government contractor, then he must establish his lack of the required mental state, on a balance of probabilities. But if the defendant is a member of the public or the media charged under sections 5 or 6, then the burden of proof remains entirely upon the prosecution, who must establish guilt beyond reasonable doubt. Thus such a defendant is entitled to an acquittal if he raises lack of the required mental state as a defence and the prosecution fails to disprove it beyond all reasonable doubt.

(ii) Lawful authority

Each offence which has been discussed requires proof that the disclosure **5–035**
was made "without lawful authority". But in addition to this there is a defence under section 7(4) if the discloser of the information can show that, at the time he made the disclosure "he believed that he had lawful authority to make the disclosure in question and had no reasonable cause to believe otherwise".

The meaning of "lawful authority" depends upon the identity of the person making the disclosure. If the discloser is either a Crown servant or has been notified that he is subject to the restrictions under section 1(1), then he may only argue belief in lawful authority for a disclosure if he acts in accordance with his "official duty" (section 7(1)). If the discloser is a government contractor, lawful authority means either "in accordance with an official authorisation" or "for the purposes of the function for which he is a government contractor and without contravening an official restriction" (section 7(2)). If the discloser is a member of the public, including the media, then lawful authority only applies to disclosures made to a Crown servant or with official authorisation (section 7(3)).

Prior Restraint via the Civil Law

The Official Secrets Acts 1911–89 create a framework of criminal offences **5–036**
which provide serious criminal sanctions once a disclosure has been made, but which only incidentally prevent the disclosure of confidential material by means of deterrence. Thus the criminal law discussed so far in this chapter has little application to the prevention of disclosure of information, and so its limitations are apparent. In most situations where official secrecy is concerned, it is far more desirable to prevent any disclosure than to punish it once it has already occurred and caused damage. It is primarily for this reason that the civil law has been used so often and, generally, effectively in the field of official secrecy. The civil law will not only operate to punish disclosure by way of an award of damages or another civil remedy, it is possible to obtain an injunction to prevent disclosure or publication of the secret information. Injunctions may be granted quickly, without the defendant being present to argue his side of the facts, and as an

interim measure before the case reaches a full trial, and thus may be an extremely effective tool for the Government in the prevention of unauthorised or harmful disclosure. As an exercise in damage prevention or limitation, the civil law may operate as a "prior restraint" which prevents disclosure rather than simply an ultimate sanction. Further, if the injunction preventing disclosure or publication is breached, then a prison sentence is available. Some would argue that a person who is not deterred from disclosure by the threat of criminal sanctions under the Official Secrets Acts is unlikely to comply with an injunction for the same reasons, but injunctions are easier to obtain than criminal convictions, being based upon the lower civil standard of proof (balance of probabilities), and it is also likely that third parties such as the media will be concerned about breaching an injunction by publication and thereby incurring substantial damages and costs.

Obviously, such prior restraint has a serious impact upon freedom of expression and the right of a citizen to speak out against impropriety or injustice by preventing speech, and so the policy considerations discussed at the beginning of this chapter are heightened in relation to the civil law. Somewhat suprisingly, in this context the criminal law is less of an invasion of civil liberties than is the civil law, since the criminal sanctions attach only to those who have chosen to disclose and to face the consequences.

PUBLIC BREACH OF CONFIDENCE

Introduction

5–037 In order to obtain an injunction to restrain disclosure or publication of information, the Government must satisfy the general equitable principles upon which injunctions, being an equitable remedy, are granted. Whilst this is not the place for detailed explanation of the principles upon which injunctions are granted, some knowledge of this area is necessary. An injunction will only be granted where the plaintiff can establish on the balance of probabilities that he has an established legal (or equitable) right with which the defendant's conduct is interfering, or may in the future interfere. The most relevant established right in the present situation is that of confidentiality; thus the injunction sought by the Government will be one to restrain a breach of confidence. Although this is by no means the conventional terminology, it may be helpful to subdivide between public breach of confidence and private breach of confidence. The latter concerns disclosure of information communicated confidentially from one private individual to another, and is not relevant to the present chapter. It is public breach of confidence which is relevant to the current discussion; that is, where information has been conveyed from the State to an individual in circumstances of confidentiality and the individual goes ahead to disclose that information. Put at the most basic level, an injunction may be either interim (temporary) or perpetual (final/permanent). In the present context, most injunctions will be permanent since the Government will generally be aiming to prevent disclosure or publication of confidential material for all time, rather than simply delaying publication.

The principles relevant to granting an injunction to restrain a breach of confidence will be illustrated in the *Spycatcher* case, discussed below; but it should be remembered that all equitable remedies are discretionary and thus it is impossible to lay down exact rules for the granting of any type of injunction. It is also still uncertain to what extent future courts will use section 12 of the Human Rights Act and Article 10 of the ECHR to create a greater culture of official openness. Section 12 provides that: **5–038**

> "(1) This section applies if a court is considering whether to grant any relief which, if granted, might affect the exercise of the Convention right to freedom of expression.
> (2) If the person against whom the application for relief is made ('the respondent') is neither present nor represented, no such relief is to be granted unless the court is satisfied—
>
> (a) that the applicant has take all practicable steps to notify the respondent; or
> (b) that there are compelling reasons why the respondent should not be notified.
>
> (3) No such relief is to be granted so as to restrain publication before trial unless the court is satisfied that the applicant is likely to establish that publication should not be allowed.
> (4) The court must have particular regard to the importance of the Convention right to freedom of expression and, where the proceedings relate to material which the respondent claims, or which appears to the court, to be journalistic, literary or artistic material (or to conduct connected with such material), to—
>
> (a) the extent to which—
>
> (i) the material has, or is about to, become available to the public; or
> (ii) it is, or would be, in the public interest for the material to be published;
>
> (b) any relevant privacy code."

In *Att.-Gen. v. Times Newspapers, Kelsey and Leppard*[45A]:

Facts. Richard Tomlinson, a former Security Intelligence Services (SIS) officer, published *The Big Breach: From Top Secret to Maximum Security* in Russia in January 2001. The book, written in English, was an account of his time in SIS and appeared to constitute a breach of confidence by him. It was unclear by the time of the instant trial how many copies of the book had actually been published and how widely it had been circulated. The defendants were *The Times*, who intended to publish extracts from the book, and two of its journalists. In 1996 *The Sunday Times* had published articles which appeared to be based on information given to them by Mr Tomlinson: as a result of the latter's intention to make further disclosures, undertakings were given in September and November 1996 which restrained Mr

Tomlinson from making further disclosures and Times Newspapers Ltd from publishing or disclosing:

> 1.(a) "Any information relating to the identity of a former employee of the Secret Intelligence Service. . .(Tomlinson)
> (b) any information obtained by the Defendants . . .from T in relation to security or intelligence, that is in relation to the work of, or support of, the security and intelligence services, such information having been received by T in the course of or as a result of his employment in the SIS. . .
> Provided that:
> (a) Nothing in this undertaking prevents the defendants . . .from republishing anything which has previously been published in *The Sunday Times* or in any other national newspaper. . .".

In 1999, after the identity of Mr Tomlinson had become a matter of public knowledge, the Attorney-General released the defendants from the undertaking (a). In January 2001 Times Newspapers sought to have the undertaking amended so that they would be able to publish anything which was in the public domain through having been published in any country or made available to the public through electronic publication. Thus they would be able to publish extracts from the book once they had obtained a copy from Russia. The Attorney-General opposed the variation, arguing that it was possible for publication to be made to a tiny audience by publication in an obscure overseas magazine, possibly with the contrivance of a major domestic newspaper, simply so that the material would then be "in the public domain" and publishable in the U.K. with impunity. It was suggested that Times Newsgroup might have colluded with Mr Tomlinson to get the book published in Russia for the purpose of escaping their earlier court undertaking. The Court of Appeal stated that the first issue was the degree of publicity which would have to occur before Times Newspapers would be released from their undertaking. The answer was clearly to be found in *Spycatcher*; widespread publicity would suffice, or alternatively put, that the information was in the public domain. The undertaking was therefore varied so that:

> "A. Nothing in this undertaking prevents the Defendants or any of them from republishing anything which at the date of publication or intended publication by the Defendant. . .
>
> (ii) has previously been published in any other newspaper, magazine or other publication, whether within or outside the jurisdiction of the Court, to such an extent that the information is in the public domain (other than in a case where the only such publication was made by or caused by the Defendants. . .)
>
> (iii) has previously been published by or through the internet or other electronic media to such an extent that the information is in the public domain (other than in a case where the only such publication was made by or was caused by the Defendants. . .".

The second major issue was whether Times Newspapers should be obliged to seek clearance from the Attorney-General before publication that the material in question was in fact "in the public domain". Times Newspapers argued that this was both impractical and a violation of Article 10 of the ECHR and section 12(4) of the HRA, being an unjustified fetter upon the freedom of expression and the right to receive information. The restriction would be disproportionate to the aim of national security. The Court of Appeal found that:

> ". . .it is desirable that there should usually be consultation between a newspaper and representatives of the SIS before the newspaper publishes

information which may include matters capable of damaging the Service or endangering those who serve in it" (*per* Lord Phillips M.R. at para. 34).

However, it was not right to impose on Times Newspapers a requirement to seek clearance before publication, since to do so would not be consonant with Article 10 and section 12 of the HRA. The potential sanctions for contempt of court should Times Newspapers fail to comply with their undertakings were a sufficient fetter upon the freedom of expression alone.

Breach of confidence has a somewhat confused and obscure history as an equitable action, but this area is growing rapidly both in its "public" and its "private" aspects. There has certainly been availability of injunctions to restrain breach of confidence for at least 150 years, with early cases concerning such matters as private confidences, trade secrets or information communicated between employer and employee,[46] but injunctions for public breach of confidence have become important only in the last forty or so years. Fairness is of great importance in the equation of granting the injunction, and so it must be assessed whether the defendant has taken an unfair advantage of the information entrusted to him in confidence by the plaintiff. A further, and extremely important, factor is the balance of the public interest in favour of confidentiality against the public interest in favour of publication. This balance can prove very difficult to judge and has caused the courts great difficulty, as is illustrated by the cases below. Coupled with the above factors are the problems surrounding the definition of the word "confidentiality" itself, for which the cases do not provide a simple answer. **5–039**

For instance in *Att.-Gen. v. Jonathan Cape Ltd*[47]:

Facts. The Attorney-General applied for a permanent injunction against the defendants from publishing a book or further extracts already published in *The Times* entitled "The Diaries of a Cabinet Minister", written by the late Mr Richard Crossman, a former Cabinet Minister. The book contained details of Cabinet meetings and various conversations that went on between those Ministers and general debates on government policy. The existence of these diaries at the time were common knowledge amongst his colleagues. The Attorney-General's argument centred around the issues of confidentiality and the question of "the public interest", *i.e.* disclosure should be restricted "if the public interest in concealment outweighs the public interest in a right to free publication".[48]

Decision. The Attorney-General argued further that Cabinet meetings are confidential and an injunction should be granted so as to prevent publication where the differing views of Ministers within Cabinet have been expressed, and any advice given by civil servants to Ministers on such occasions. The defendants argued that publication should only be prohibited where the issue of national security is involved. Lord Widgery C.J. when focusing his attention on the Attorney-General's "public interest" argument, stated that protection for joint Cabinet responsibility is essential in the short period, *e.g.* weeks or months,[49] but he questioned whether that protection should be sustained after a period of years.[50] There is no doubt that the convention of joint Cabinet responsibility exists and is confidential, and indeed necessary for the continuance of good government by present Ministers. But these relevant records from the diaries are some ten years old. Thus, for the Attorney-

General to succeed he must show, *inter alia*, (1) that by publishing there would be a breach of confidence; and (2) the public interest in concealment outweighed the public interest in publishing; and (3) that there are no other facets of the public interest contradictory to and more compelling than that relied upon. With regard to (1), it was decided that there exists a duty of confidentiality with regard to the differing views of Cabinet Ministers, and when it is in the public interest to do so, publication will be stifled. Although the convention of joint Cabinet responsibility remains, it does not mean that it will go on indefinitely, and there may come a time when minutes of Cabinet discussions should be available publicly. Whilst each case must be examined on its own particular facts, any investigation must include the harm which could be done to national security or whether the publication material is a live issue or the effect the publication might have on foreign relations, and finally, the public interest. In areas where the issue is somewhat hazy, "reliance must be placed on the good sense and good taste of the Minister or ex-minister concerned".[51] In this instance, would publication harm Cabinet discussions in future so that Ministers would fear that their views would be written about in some future publications? His Lordship thought not. Taking into account the age of the information and the changed circumstances since its writing (three general elections had since taken place), his Lordship refused the injunction and publication went ahead.

The *Spycatcher* Syndrome

5–040 Once the criminal process became too difficult to enforce successfully with any degree of regularity, the Government turned its hand to civil remedies against those who released unauthorised, confidential information to the general public. The main legal methods used were that of a permanent injunction plus accounting to the Crown for any profits made, as a result of publication. Such action was implemented by the Attorney-General in the now infamous case of the "Spycatcher" book by Peter Wright. The main issues in that case were whether an ex-member of the security services owed a lifelong duty of confidentiality to his former employees, and if so, whether in this instant case there was a breach of that duty, by the disclosure of confidential information written in the forthcoming publication of his book.

Introduction

5–041 Peter Maurice Wright was a former member of the Security Intelligence Services. After his retirement in 1976 he went to live in Australia. During his employment with MI5 he had access to some highly classified and confidential information. Between 1976 and 1985 he wrote his memoirs, detailing his own experiences as well as certain alleged unlawful activities carried on by MI5 during his time there, including phone tapping, illegal surveillance, threats to undermine the Government of the day, as well as suggesting that MI5 had been infiltrated by foreign agents and that the former head of the security services was working for the Soviets. In 1985 Wright's memoirs were due to be published in Australia under the main heading *Spycatcher*. A high degree of panic swept through Whitehall. It was not so much the thought of ex-employees of the security services writing their stories, but the thought of a former agent publishing highly confidential information abroad without first seeking the permission of the intelligence officials in Britain seemed particularly abhorrent. Had he made endeavours to publish the book in Britain there was a high probability that he would have been prosecuted under the Official Secrets Act 1989. Anyway, he was under an obligation to refer his manuscript to the security services first for inspection, prior to publication. From there it would have been passed onto the "D" Committee (now the "DA" Committee) for further vetting, where due to the nature of its contents, would undoubtedly have received a negative reception. The sequence of events which followed over the three years, 1985 to 1988, in both Australia and England can best be described as the "Spycatcher Syndrome", and the following chronological discussion is a somewhat brief explanation of those, to say the least, bizarre and unusual circumstances.

Spycatcher in Australia

September 10, 1985: **5–042**
The Attorney-General immediately sought an injunction from the Supreme Court of New South Wales to prevent publication on the grounds that the author owed a lifelong duty of confidentiality to the Crown. The Attorney-General based his arguments and submissions on the damage disclosure of confidential information would do to British national security, and that:

(a) disclosure would mean that friendly foreign nations would not trust the British security services to keep highly confidential and classified information secret; and

(b) co-operation between these nations would be seriously undermined as a result; and

(c) other members may seek to publish their memoirs of confidential information.[52] Undertakings were given by Wright and his publishers, Heinemann, not to release any of the material in the book pending trial.

November 17, 1986:
The trial began in New South Wales in front of Powell J.

March 13, 1987:
Attorney-General's action dismissed, but the previous undertakings given, pending trial, were extended until after the hearing of the appeal.

March 28, 29, 1987:
"Melbourne Age" and "Canberra Times" newspapers publish lengthy extracts from the book.

September 24, 1987:

Appeal dismissed by the New South Wales Court of Appeal.

October 13, 1987:
First publication of book, in Australia

June 2, 1988:
Again, the Attorney-General's appeal was dismissed, this time by the High Court of Australia.

Spycatcher in England

5–043 *June 22, 23, 1986:*
The *Observer* and *The Guardian* newspapers published articles concerning the forthcoming Australian trial and allegations mentioned in the, as yet, unpublished book.

June 27, 1986:
The Attorney-General applied for and was granted an *ex parte* interlocutory injunction against the *Observer* and *The Guardian*.

July 11, 1986:
At an *inter partes* hearing before Millett J., an injunction (hereinafter referred to as the "GO" injunctions) was granted restraining any future publication on any information regarding Mr Wright's work with the security services. However, the order contained three exceptions:

(a) quotations of attributions from past published works by another author, Chapman Pincher, and a TV programme broadcast by Granada,[53] was permitted;

(b) reporting on the trial in Australia was allowed, provided it was restricted to material disclosed in open court; and

(c) fair and accurate reporting from the debates in Parliament and hearings in any public court was also permitted.

July 25 1986:
The appeal by the newspapers against the "GO" injunctions were dismissed, although the Court of Appeal did vary slightly the conditions of the injunction. Thereafter, in *Attorney-General v. the Observer and The Guardian*[54] the appellant newspapers appealed on the grounds that:

(a) even if there is a breach of confidence by former members of the security services, that confidence is lost once the information is brought within the public domain; and further

(b) there can be no confidence in any wrongdoing by the security services; and finally

(c) the appellants ought not to be prevented from republishing those articles which were published prior to the Attorney-General's action.

The court held, that with regard to (c) if the original publications were unlawful (*i.e.* because of a breach of the Crown's obligation of confidence), then any further publication would mean profiting from an unlawful act, which would be unacceptable, and the same applies to other newspapers who wish to publish those articles. Concerning (b) the court said that it is in the public interest to know if the security services are breaking the law. They are subject like everybody else to the law and any matters of wrongdoing must be investigated. Therefore, the appellants argued that it was in the public interest that serious allegations of wrongdoing should be thoroughly examined.

Sir John Donaldson M.R. answered the above appeal by stating that with **5–044** regard to the issue of confidentiality, in some situations, "the weight of the public interest in the maintenance of the confidentiality will be small and the weight of the public interest in publication will be great," and therefore, "both the nature and circumstances of the confidentiality and the nature and confidentiality of the proposed publication have to be examined with considerable care."[55] Thus, it may be in the public interest to inform, for instance, the police or other relevant authority of a particular wrongdoing, but not in the public interest to publish it in a newspaper.[56] The Attorney-General argued that national security would be damaged if publication was allowed; friendly foreign countries might feel that the British intelligence service was not to be trusted to keep classified or confidential information secret. Also, if publication were allowed to go ahead, there would be the danger that other security members might wish to publish secrets which, whether intentional or not, could result in great damage being caused to national security.[57] Therefore, due to the high level of confidentially required for working in the security services, the court found that on the evidence available, that publication ought to be refused.

April 27, 1987:
The Independent newspaper published articles, describing in detail the various allegations in the still-as-yet unpublished book. That same day the London *Evening Standard* and the *Daily News* published extracts from *The Independent* article. Had the *Observer* or *The Guardian* published such articles they would have been in breach of the "GO" injunctions of July 25, 1986. Since *The Independent et al.*, were not parties to that previous injunction it would normally be assumed that they could not be liable under it. However, this was not necessarily so.

May 7, 1987:
The Attorney-General brought contempt of court proceedings against the *The Independent et al.*, for interfering with the administration of justice by

publishing the prohibited articles. Sir Nicolas Browne-Wilkinson V-C dismissed the Attorney-General's application on the grounds that *The Independent et al.* were not parties to the existing injunction.

July 12, 1987:
The Sunday Times published the first instalment of a serialisation of the book and agreed a figure of $150,000 with Mr Wright for the rights. In order to allay suspicion and to prevent an injunction against publication, the story was not printed in the first edition (government officials, it seems, receive delivery of the first edition) but in the later editions, by which time approximately 1.25 million copies had been printed and circulated.

July 13, 1987:
Contempt of court proceedings were brought by the Attorney-General against *The Sunday Times*. On the same day the book was published in the United States.

July 15, 1987:
Decision of Sir Nicolas Browne-Wilkinson V.-C. of May 7, 1987, reversed by the Court of Appeal (see above). *Att.-Gen. v. Newspaper Publishing plc.*[58]

July 22, 1987:
The "GO" injunctions are discharged by Sir Nicolas Browne-Wilkinson V.-C.

Chancery Division

5–045 Sir Nicolas Browne-Wilkinson, V.-C.:

On an application by *The Guardian* and the *Observer* to discharge the injunction of July 25, 1986, Sir Nicolas Browne-Wilkinson V.-C. decided that the injunctions should be discontinued. He stated in *Att.-Gen. v. Guardian Newspapers*[59] that the circumstances had dramatically changed since July 25, 1986. Apart from the printed allegations, extracts and the first instalment published by *The Sunday Times*, the book had already been published in the United States (some 50,000 copies had been sold in the first few days). Also, highly significant was the fact that the book was available to be purchased in the United Kingdom—no banning order had been applied for. Sir Nicolas decided that since the book was wholly within the public domain now, and no further damage could be done to the security services, there was no justification for enforcing the injunction for a further period. By way of a general observation, he said that "if the courts were to make orders manifestly incapable of achieving their avowed purpose, such as to prevent the dissemination of information which is already disseminated the law would to my mind indeed be an ass."[60]

July 24, 1987:

On appeal by the Attorney-General to the Court of Appeal, the decision was reversed and the injunction once again reinstated, with adjustments. *Att.-Gen. v. Guardian Newspapers Ltd.*[61]

Court of Appeal

Sir John Donaldson M.R.: **5–046**

Their Lordships Gibson L.J., Russell L.J. and especially Sir John Donaldson M.R. did not agree with the proposition put forward by Sir Nicolas Browne-Wilkinson V.-C., *i.e.* that once the information was out in the open, to continue with the injunction would be ridiculous. Their Lordships concentrated their arguments on the sanctity of keeping confidential information secret and concluded that the Attorney-General had an arguable case for permanent injunctions.[62] It was stated that whilst these publications had become public knowledge, they nevertheless had not lost their "seal of confidentiality". This is lost when the information becomes "public property". Public property, and by inference, the public domain only occurs when the information is revealed in open court.[63] A new proviso was added which read "This order shall not prevent the publication of a summary in very general terms of the allegations made by Mr Wright".[64] Accordingly, the injunction continued with modifications. As Gibson L.J. said, the injunction would not be futile "but . . . will do what the law sets out to do, namely to protect asserted rights as far as can fairly be achieved until, by trial, they are proved or disproved".[65]

July 30, 1987:
Appeal by the *Observer* and *The Guardian* to the House of Lords dismissed, by a majority (3:2) decision, *Att.-Gen. v. Guardian Newspapers*.[66] Their Lordships were for retaining the status quo, *i.e.* continuing the injunctions, until a full trial, (Lord Brandon, Lord Ackner, Lord Templeman, Lord Bridge and Lord Oliver dissenting).

House of Lords

Lord Brandon: **5–047**

Amongst the main issues (there were nine in total) discussed by Lord Brandon were, that since the publication of the book in the United States and elsewhere, had the Attorney-General's case deteriorated to a great extent? The newspapers argued that the contents of the book were public knowledge and any continuation of the injunction would be pointless as no further harm could reasonably be anticipated. His Lordship argued that if the memoirs had become public knowledge, and disclosure allowed, this would inevitably mean that Mr Wright would no longer be obligated under his duty of lifelong confidentiality; with the result that he would be free to return to England and publish the book there. This, his Lordship was not willing without further argument to accede to. With regard to "future damage", he was of the opinion that to discontinue the injunction would be to give the green light to other ex-members of the security services to publish secrets in breach of their duty of confidentiality, the consequences of which would, no doubt, undermine or damage the security services further. If the temporary injunctions were discharged now, there would be little point in proceeding to a full trial, since in the meantime further publications would be made, and the whole purpose of the trial would be otiose.

5–048 Lord Bridge (dissenting):

His Lordship was in, as he put it, "profound disagreement" with the majority. The main question was "whether there is any remaining interest of national security which those injunctions are capable of protecting and, if no, whether it is of sufficient weight to justify the massive encroachment on freedom of speech which those injunctions in present circumstances necessarily involves . . ."[67] He said that since the whole of the Wright allegations were public there was little point in maintaining the "GO" injunctions any longer, it was, as he described it, a "futile injunction". The damage, if any, had already been done. He was not overly impressed with the majority of their Lordships' decision to continue the injunctions, and still less approved of the extension of the injunction to include the preventing of reporting on the trial in Australia.

October 13, 1987:
The book went on sale in the Republic of Ireland.

October 27, 1987:
Proceedings by the Attorney-General commenced against *The Sunday Times* for the articles printed on July 12, 1987.

December 21, 1987:
The interlocutory injunctions against the *Observer* and *The Guardian* were discharged, *Att.-Gen. v. Guardian Newspapers (No. 2)*.[68]

Chancery Division

5–049 Scott J.:

Mr Justice Scott J. stated that certain allegations of iniquities are of such a high level of importance that it was in the public interest that they ought to be published. The relevant allegations here included that of the assassination attempt of president Nasser, the destabilising of the Wilson government, and the infiltration of Soviet spies within MI5. He said

> "the ability of the press freely to report allegations of scandal in government is one of the bulwarks of our democratic society . . . If the price that has to be

> paid is the exposure of the Government of the day to pressure or embarrassment when mischievous and false allegations are made, then in my opinion, that price must be paid".[69]

However, it is arguable that if certain sensitive publications resulted in panic and mayhem by the general public, then the releasing of specialised sensitive information should be restrained.

Scott J. found that the extracts printed in *The Sunday Times* were a mixture of issues some of which were in the public interest to be disclosed and others which he considered to be confidential and which needed to be protected from release, and therefore the Attorney-General was entitled to the injunctions granted on July 15, 1987 and to account for any profits made to the Crown as a result of the publication of that particular article. However, with regard to the present circumstances and in particular the fact that the information has already been released into the public domain, the necessity for a continued injunction was not warranted. Added to this was the fact that the contents of the book contained information which was (a) at least 12 years old and therefore mostly out of date; (b) trivial and insignificant; and (c) many of the allegations had previously been published in authorised works.[70] Accordingly, the granting of the injunctions were refused.

Regarding the "GO" injunctions, Scott J. looked at the relevant articles as a whole and concluded that what the publications contained was a "fair reporting" of the trial in Australia. Very little detail was given in these rather brief articles, compared with the later, more fully disclosed publications. Thus, under these circumstances, there was no breach of confidence.

February 10, 1988:
Appeal by the Attorney-General to the Court of Appeal against the decision of Scott J., dismissed, *Att.-Gen. v. Guardian Newspapers Ltd (No. 2)*.[71]

Court of Appeal

Sir John Donaldson M.R.: **5–050**

Whilst agreeing with much of what was said by Scott J. (see above), his Lordship did not see fit to agree with the further serialisation to be published by *The Sunday Times*. His reasons were that *The Sunday Times* by serialising the book had a contract with Mr Wright and were as he called it, "standing in the shoes of Mr. Wright", and likened it to being as if the book had been published here. As a result, such publications were to be prevented by that and any other newspaper. In this Sir John Donaldson M.R.'s thinking was in the minority.

Dillon L.J.: **5–051**

He agreed with the judgment of Justice Scott. With regard to balancing the public interest of confidentiality on the grounds of national security and the public interest of disclosure on the grounds of iniquity, his Lordship was of the opinion that iniquity does not automatically justify disclosure. The newspaper had a responsibility to consider where the source for that information originated, as well as

> "what ill-consequences to the national interest might follow from publication, whether by strengthening the nation's enemies . . . and whether any disclosure ought in the first place to be only to the appropriate security or police authorities rather than to the public at large."[72]

Thus, not every iniquity justifies publication. His Lordship seemed to wish to return to the law of breach of confidence already in existence.

October 13, 1988:
Appeal by the Attorney-General to the House of Lords against the decision of the Court of Appeal, dismissed, *Att.-Gen. v. Guardian Newspapers Ltd (No. 2)*.[73]

House of Lords

5–052 Lord Griffiths:
Whilst his Lordship dismissed the Attorney-General's appeal he was not prepared to sanction the future serialising of *The Sunday Times* (in agreement with Sir John Donaldson M.R.'s judgment in the Court of Appeal). His Lordship felt that *The Sunday Times* was so closely legally connected with Mr Wright's breach of duty that the same conditions should apply to *The Sunday Times* as it would to Mr Wright. Whilst Lord Goff had great sympathy with that view and that of Bingham L.J.,[74] he was not prepared to dismiss this part of the appeal and instead stated that, despite the past breach of confidence he was not prepared to prevent the continuing serialisation of the book.

5–053 Lord Keith of Kinkel:

What was perhaps more relevant in the instant judgment was his Lordship's statements regarding the duty of confidence owed to the Crown (as opposed to a private duty of confidence), which if breached may result in detrimental consequences to the interest of this country—

> "disclosure (of a public breach of confidence) may tend to harm the public interest by impeding the efficient attainment of proper governmental ends, and the revelations of defence or intelligence secrets certainly falls into that category."

Emphasis was put on the "harm" aspects, and if no harm was caused then despite the disclosure being in breach of confidence, it should nevertheless be permitted without the fear of ultimate legal action. In *Commonwealth of Australia v. John Fairfax and Sons Ltd*[75] Mason J. regarding "harm," stated that:

> "It is unacceptable in our democratic society that there should be a restraint on the publication of information relating to government when the only vice of that information is that it enables the public to discuss, review and criticise government action."

His Lordship pointed out that the damage, if indeed, there had been any, had already been done by the existing publications in the newspapers and the book itself, and was unlikely to cause any further damage to the public interest. Therefore, the injunction against the *Observer*, *The Guardian* and *The Sunday Times* would be refused. The publication of extracts from the book by *The Sunday Times* on July 12, 1987 was considered to be in breach of confidence. The newspaper was well aware of the confidential nature of the matter, since it had not been circulated to the public at this time. The defence that the allegations were previously published in the *Observer* and *The Guardian* did not justify future publications involving more specific information being revealed. The court said that mere allegations of wrongdoing, without more, did not amount to even a prima facie case against the security services. Thus, *The Sunday Times* was not entitled to disseminate more detailed extracts from the book and was to account to the Crown for all profits emanating from the published article but not future profits from any serialisation of the book.

Where it is the member or ex-member of the security services who wishes to disclose confidential information, the amount of damage required to be shown by the Crown may not be so detrimental as that needed against third parties before they will be prevented from publishing, since prima facie there is a lifelong duty of confidentiality between the past and present employees of the security services and their employers. Lord Keith said "the general public interest in the preservation of confidentiality, and in encouraging other Crown servants to preserve it, may suffice".[76] Thus, there may still be a breach by a former employee even though there was no harm done to the general public, but only limited damage to those working or who had worked for the security services. The issue may not be identical where third parties are involved. There, the balance lies in the public interest of disclosure, and indeed it may be their duty to do so. However, disclosure by third parties is subject to the amount of harm caused to the public interest by such revelations. If there is no damage then, it seems, freedom of speech takes precedent.

Lord Goff: **5–054**

His Lordship stated that the broader general principle of a duty of confidence comes into being when the confidante is aware that he is under an obligation not to reveal the information to someone else. He, however, said that the general principle had three limiting factors:

(1) the confidentiality principle only applies to confidential information: if no longer secret because the information has reached the public domain, then the principle no longer exists;

(2) the principle does not apply to information which is out of date, useless, or trivial;

(3) the principle may not apply where there is a public interest factor involved.

Whether the principle applied or not in this situation is a question of balancing between the public interest in maintaining confidence on the one hand, and on the other hand, a countervailing public interest supporting publication. There is a division between the secret information which it is in the public interest that the general public ought to be informed about, and those confidential matters that it is in the public interest to keep secret. Matters which involve serious criminal activities are *per se* publishable and should not be protected, and should be divulged to the public via the media or other means. Other matters, such as proved iniquities or wrongdoings, are not necessarily criminal but are to be treated like a hybrid, whereby it may, or may not be, in the public interest to disclose such behaviour. There may be other ways of highlighting the wrongdoings, *i.e.* by contacting the police or other relevant authorities, who hopefully would investigate the matter and take the appropriate action against the wrongdoers. Still further down the iniquities scale are wrongdoings which are merely alleged, as opposed to proven. The question then is should this type of behaviour be exposed to the general public? Lord Goff was of the opinion that the latter type should not be disclosed, presumably because of the danger that could flow from such revelations, especially where the alleged iniquities are unfounded. Further proof, he argued, was required before the confidante should be allowed to publish such matters, *i.e.* by further investigation and evidence from those in-the-know or other reliable sources.

Thus, where government confidential information is involved, it is not enough that the Crown designates a particular document as secret *per se*, but must go further and demonstrate that it is in the public interest that such information remain secret. The explanation Lord Goff gives for this reasoning is that it is in the public interest that "the workings of government should be open to scrutiny and criticism", but with exceptions. He felt that this was on all-fours with the European Convention on Human Rights, Art. 10, where the exceptions include those which are "necessary in the interest of national security and the preventing the disclosure of information received in confidence." Here, the author owed a lifelong duty of confidentiality to the security service. The question is whether there was a breach of that confidentiality by his disclosures of iniquities within the service. Publication of wrongdoing is, it would seem, a question of degree. If the wrongdoing was some minor iniquity, then the public interest in disclosure would not warrant it. If it is a serious wrongdoing but not highly criminal then it is difficult to state with any degree of certainty that the public interest should lean towards publication. All circumstances must be examined.

At this state of the proceedings, the forceful arguments by the Attorney-General included the issue that the availability of the contents of the book throughout the world should not by itself mean that the author's lifelong duty of confidence was at an end. This is so, since: (1) a person should not profit by his own wrongdoing; and (2) wrongdoing by Mr Wright cannot destroy his existing duty of confidentiality; and (3) third parties who were aware of Mr Wright's breach, are themselves in breach if they publish the contents of the book. Their Lordships, both in the Court of Appeal and the House of Lords, throughout these lengthy proceedings, were in agreement with regard to (2) above that the lifelong duty of confidentiality should remain. But Lord Goff himself put forward some powerful arguments why in some circumstances it should be abandoned.[77] Having cited examples to enforce the argument that once the subject matter of the obligation has been destroyed (in this case, the publication of confidential information), how can a confident still be restrained from disclosing information which is already public knowledge, and therefore no longer secret? The only remedy for the confider is one of damages, or restitution.[78] If otherwise, would it not lead to the bizarre situation that the confidant is "not even permitted to mention in public what is now common knowledge"?[79] In (3) above, if the obligation of confidence remains, then as Lord Goff argues, if those who know of the breach by the confidant repeat the information they must themselves be in breach of duty. But this could, he says, lead to absurd results, and some principle should be invoked to explain where "the buck" stops. Lord Goff made a very relevant observation when he said that perhaps Mr Wright's immunity from prosecution and any claims to restitution (the author living in Australia at this time) may have prompted the temptation to continue his lifelong duty of confidence, despite the destruction of the subject matter of that duty.[80] Had Mr Wright been in England, he would be accountable to any profits made to the Crown as well as damages resulting from any harm caused to the security services because of his disclosures. The injunctions were therefore not granted, and *The Sunday Times* was allowed to relaunch their serialisation of the book, but to account for profits from the article written in their newspaper on July 12, 1987.

Although it is very difficult to extract some precisely defined legal **5–055** principles from the events of the previous three years, the following is a very brief summary of what the courts decided to be the main points under civil law.

(1) Members and former members of the security services owe a lifelong duty of confidentiality to the Crown.

(2) Breach of that confidence to third parties, who are aware of the breach, puts those who receive such information under that same duty not to reveal or publish or make any disclosures, but only to the limited extent that publication would result in damage to the public interest.

(3) Whether to publish or not will depend on the balance between the public interest for confidential information to remain secret and the public interest of freedom of speech.

(4) It is for the Attorney-General to demonstrate that the confidential information was damaging to the public interest.

(5) Information which is now out of date, useless or innocuous will probably be allowed to be published.

(6) Confidential information which is now in the public domain, even if prior to publication it was considered damaging, will nevertheless now be permitted to be written about.

(7) Highly criminal activities by the security services are publishable. However, where iniquities are concerned, this will depend on whether disclosure is in the public interest or alternative methods such as reporting the wrongdoing to police or others in authority may be more appropriate in the public interest.

The case was taken to the European Court of Human Rights in *Observer and Guardian v U.K.*[81] The applicants complained to the Commission that the injunction contravened the right to freedom of expression guaranteed under Article 10. The Government argued that the interlocutory injunction was necessary to protect national security and for maintaining the authority of the judiciary. The Court found that there was a legitimate aim to be considered. For the period from July 11, 1986 to July 30, 1987, whilst the "GO" injunction was still in force, the Court considered that in the circumstances the measures taken by the national authorities were not disproportionate to the legitimate aim pursued. However, from the July 30, 1987 to October 13, 1988 (the "GO" injunction was still in force), the book had been published abroad, was sold world-wide and available in the United Kingdom. The Court decided that under these new circumstances, there were not sufficient reasons for the continuance of the "GO" injunction. As the Court said, even if the Attorney-General had won a permanent ban, in reality the issue was redundant; the confidentiality of the information had, by then, been destroyed. Further, even if the sole purpose of continuing the action by the Attorney-General was to dissuade other members or ex-members of the security services from divulging confidential matter, the Court said that these also were not sufficient reasons to continue with the interlocutory injunction, *i.e.* the measures taken by the national authorities were disproportionate to the legitimate aim pursued. Therefore, there was a violation of Article 10 from July 30, 1987 to October 13, 1988.

The problem of third party disclosure and the "harm" factor appeared once again, shortly after in the case of *Lord Advocate v. The Scotsman Publication Ltd.*[82]

Facts. Antony Cavendish was an ex-member of the British Intelligence Services (MI6) from 1948 until 1953. In 1987, he was refused permission from the Government to publish his memoirs entitled *Inside Intelligence*. Nevertheless, he went ahead and made 500 copies of the book, and at Christmas 1987, he sent 279 copies to various people. On December 27, 1987, *The Sunday Times* published an article about the book. The Attorney-General applied for and was granted an injunction restraining that newspaper from further publishing contents from the book or "any person having notice of this order." On January 5, 1988, *The Scotsman* newspaper published extracts. However, the newspaper refused to give any undertaking to the Lord Advocate to be likewise bound from printing any contents from the book. Thereafter, the Lord Advocate made a petition against the newspaper to interdict *The Scotsman* from disclosing, *inter alia*, any information gathered by Mr Cavendish during his period with MI6 or "any person having notice of said interlocutor". The interdict was not granted by the Lord Ordinary and thereupon, the Lord Advocate appealed to the House of Lords.

Decision. The appeal was based on similar grounds to those of the Attorney-General in *Spycatcher* on September 10, 1985, (see above), *i.e.* breach of the duty of lifelong confidentiality. The Government were in fact trying to put a "gagging" order on anyone who received the confidential information from Cavendish. It was conceded that there was no danger to national security if publication went ahead, *i.e.* a non-contents case. In examining the Lord Advocate's petition, Lord Keith of Kinkel pointed out that there could be no definite purpose in granting an interdict under such circumstances; quoting from his own speech given in the *Spycatcher* case,[83] he said that the emphasis in this case was on third parties having knowledge of the author's breach of confidence. The public interest balance lay in favour of disclosure and the newspapers should always be allowed freedom of speech, with a few exceptions,[84] including where disclosure would threaten the safety of the country in any way. Therefore, since the "damage" element was wholly redundant in this case, the appeal was dismissed and any third parties were entitled to print the contents of the book. Although the Official Secrets Acts 1989 was not in force at this time, Mr Cavendish would no doubt have been guilty under section 1(1) of that Act. However, under section 5 of the same act, it would have been up to the security services to prove the harm done, and since there was none, anticipatory or otherwise, Mr Cavendish would presumably not have been guilty under that section.

Throughout these whole breach of confidence proceedings it would be **5–056**
rather unfair and naive not to have some degree of sympathy with the position of the national security services. They were in the unfortunate position of being unable to confirm or deny accusations made by Mr Wright, Mr Cavendish or the press, or to acknowledge whether such statements were important or not, or indeed what actual damage, if any, would be caused by such revelations. If they were to do so, this would have the strange effect of disclosing secret information in order to rebut other secret information, and thus compromising the whole ethos of the security service itself.

Where the duty of confidentiality tack did not succeed, the Government tried another method of restraining publication, and that was via the argument that a member or former member of the security services owed a fiduciary duty to the Crown.

In *Attorney-General v. Blake*[85]:

Facts. The defendant was arrested and convicted on spying charges contrary to section 1(1)(c) of the Official Secrets Act 1911. Having worked for the Secret Intelligence Services from 1945, he began spying for the KGB in or about 1951 and from that time until his capture in 1961, he disclosed highly confidential and classified information. Although sentenced to 42 years imprisonment, he eventually escaped to Moscow, where in 1989 he wrote his memoirs, entitled *No Other Choice*. Part of the book related to his experiences as an SIS officer. The book was published in 1990 in the United Kingdom by Jonathan Cape Ltd without the security services' knowledge or permission. The Attorney-General sued on behalf of the Crown for all profits the defendant might receive from the sale of the book, on the grounds of a breach of duty owed to the Crown not to financially benefit from his former position as an employee of the SIS. There remained a balance of some £90,000 to be paid to the defendant plus all future royalties, which the Crown felt they were legally entitled to, as beneficial owners of the copyright. There were two main issues; (1) was the defendant in breach of his duties owed to the Crown and (2) if the answer was yes, would it necessarily mean that copyright and profits from the book now divested in the Crown?

Decision. The Attorney-General conceded that the contents of the book did not contain any classified or confidential material which would be of any danger to national security. Indeed, there was no breach of confidence. However, it was argued that there was a fiduciary duty owed by the defendant to the Crown, *i.e.* not to use his position as an ex-member of the SIS to benefit financially from the writing of his autobiography, detailing his treacherous activities in the SIS. Since *Spycatcher*, it had become well established that a member or former member of the Security Services owed a lifelong duty of confidentiality. However, that duty is restricted to information which is confidential or classified. In this case, no part of the book's revelations included material which was confidential. Therefore, the defendant had not committed any breach. It was stated by Sir Richard Scott, V.-C. in this case that, "the law would not impose a duty that represented an unreasonable restraint on the ability of an ex-member to earn his living by exploiting the experience and knowledge acquired during his years of service".[86] This was provided, of course, that the disclosures did not overstep the recognised bounds of damaging the intelligence service. Indeed, it would be the plaintiff, the court said, who was at fault by limiting the person's freedom of expression under Article 10 of the ECHR, unless one of the exceptions under that Article applied. Thus, since the answer to the first issue, regarding his duty to the Crown, was "no", the second issue did not arise, other than obiter.[87] Accordingly, the action was dismissed.

As an addendum to the main issue in the above case, the court found that the defendant was in breach of section 1(1) of the Official Secrets Act 1989, since under this section, there is no requirement that the information revealed must be secret or confidential; merely disclosing any such information is enough, but this was not argued by the Attorney-General. This case really concerned a somewhat unusual problem of restraint of trade. However, one of the distinguishing features of a restraint of trade is a pre-existing contractual relationship between the parties. In this case, there was a lack of such a contract. Here, there were no terms, express or implied which could constitute a duty on the part of the author to be obligated to the security services, other than the now recognised duty of keeping confidential information secret. Hence, there was no breach involved.

Unlike the American case of *Snepp and Co.*[88] where there was in existence a contract between an ex-member of the CIA and his employers which involved a clause stating that any published work by an ex-member who divulged confidential information was accountable for profits made from that material, unless prior approval for publication was given by the intelligence service. In that case there was a breach of contract and a constructive trust was formed whereby the U.S. Government was entitled to any profits accumulated from the sale of the book.

The *Blake* case then went to the House of Lords.

In a change from previous cases and from the decision of the Court of Appeal, the House of Lords imposed a duty to account for the profits from the book, based upon Blake's breach of the specific undertaking in his contract of employment not to disclose information acquired in office, whether in the form of a book or otherwise. Whilst he was not a fiduciary as such, since after widespread dissemination the information in question could no longer be regarded as confidential, he was in a very similar position and should not be permitted to profit from his wrongdoing. It is not entirely clear whether the duty of confidentiality thus expected of government employees is lifelong, but it is suggested that the speeches of the House of Lords can be read in that way. The *Shayler* cases have also shown the lack of predictability of equitable remedies in the maintenance of official secrecy. In *Steen v. Att.-Gen.*[88A]: **5–057**

Facts. The appellant was the former editor of *Punch* magazine and, together with its publishers, had been found to be in contempt of court (at common law) for publishing a column by David Shayler after injunctions had been issued against the latter to prohibit him form disclosing any information obtained during the course of his employment by the security services. Mr Steen had been warned in advance that the subject matter of a particular column article was viewed as likely to breach the injunction, but went ahead with publication, making a headline of the fact that it was "the story MI5 does not want you to read". The appellant contended that the purpose of the injunction had been to prevent publication of material which was likely to damage national security, and that it had not been demonstrated that the article could do so. Further, he argued that he had not had the necessary *mens rea* since he had not intended to publish material likely to injure national security, nor had he foreseen that the article could do so.

Decision. The Court of Appeal found:

(i) That there was no limitation of the material covered by the injunction: it covered all material obtained by Mr Shayler in the course of his security services employment.

(ii) The injunction thus covered material other than that concerned with national security.

(iii) There was no reason in the present case why the injunctions should protect narrower interests than those in *Spycatcher.*

(iv) Whilst re-publication of material which had already entered the public domain could not constitute contempt by a third party, publication of new material had happened in this case and violated the injunction since it disclosed material which *arguably posed a risk* of damaging national security. Hence the *actus reus* of contempt had been committed.

(v) However, Mr Steen lacked the necessary *mens rea* for contempt, since he had thought that the purpose of the injunction was only to prevent publication of material injurious to national security, and he had not intended to publish any such material. Thus his mistake meant that his appeal should be allowed. He could, however, have been guilty of aiding and abetting breach of the injunction, but this had not been argued by the Crown.

(vi) *Per* Lord Phillips M.R.:

> "This appeal demonstrates the limitations of the *Spycatcher* jurisdiction. It is not easy to draft an interlocutory injunction in terms that go no wider than is necessary to restrain the publication of material in respect of which the claimant has an arguable claim to confidentiality. It is, however, necessary to do this if the terms of the injunction are to equate with the purpose for which the injunction is ordered, namely the preservation of the confidentiality of the material in question. . .Third parties are not directly bound by the terms of such an injunction. If they are to be held liable for the contempt of interfering with the course of justice it must be demonstrated that the disclosure made by them defeated, in whole or in part, the court's purpose in granting the injunction and that they appreciated that it would do so. This will be particularly difficult to demonstrate if the court adopts the approach of ordering injunctions in wide terms, but delegating to the claimant the role of determining what is and is not to be restrained from publication".

5–058 But the *Shayler* case has also (so far) demonstrated the inflexibility of the Official Secrets Acts, even post-HRA, such that freedom of expression, necessity and public interest disclosure still cannot be argued as defences: in *R. v. Shayler*[88B]:

Facts. The defendant was charged (*inter alia*) with disclosure of security or intelligence documents without lawful authority, contrary to section 1(1) of the Official Secrets Act 1989, and pleaded not guilty. At a preparatory hearing the question was whether there was open to the defendant any defence based upon disclosure in the public interest or, alternatively, necessity. He argued that if no such defence was available to him, then there would be a breach of the Human Rights Act through failure to comply with Article 10. The Crown argued that there were no such defences under the Official Secrets Act 1989, and that they could not be implied.

Decision. No such defences were to be allowed. A defence of public interest disclosure had been specifically rejected in the White Paper, and an amendment to introduce such a defence to the Bill had been defeated. There was a good reason why present and former employees of the security services were regarded as intrinsically harmful to the public interest: such disclosures had an authority about them which meant that they were more credible, and they represented a betrayal of trust. Even if he had felt that he must tell someone what he believed to have been going on, the defendant did not have to make his disclosure to the whole world through the media. Whilst freedom of expression is of fundamental importance and the court must scrutinise any proposed limitation on that freedom, the fact that the defendant could have disclosed the information to a Crown servant under section 12 of the 1989 Act allowed him sufficient freedom. The fact that no damage needed to be proved where disclosure was by a security services member, in opposition to the position where the discloser had not been so employed, was justified because:

> "Disclosure by a member or former member of the Security Services reduces public confidence in the service's ability and willingness to carry out their essentially secret duties effectively and loyally. It betrays the trust shared between colleagues and, importantly, trust placed in the Services by informants and overseas agencies. It is the very fact of disclosure which is likely to cause damage rather than the particular nature of the document or information disclosed".

The lives of operatives could also be endangered. Thus it is likely that the U.K. would be in breach of its obligations under Articles 2 and 3 of the ECHR were they to permit a limited defence that disclosure was necessary to prevent injury or death. Further, should any defence be allowed, then a defendant would be able to raise issues which would require the Crown to reveal secret information in order to rebut "evidence", and again this could potentially be damaging to the national interest. Viewed as a whole, the restrictions on the defendant's freedom of expression were no more than was necessary to protect the legitimate aim of national security. Although it was arguable that a defence of duress by threats might be available to a charge under section 1 of the 1989 Act, for example if disclosure was forced by the placing of a gun to the head, there was no room for the common law to extend this to allow scope for a general defence of necessity.

It remains to be seen what will happen at Shayler's actual trial, although he does appear to have substantial public support and it is becoming increasingly difficult to convict in such cases; the case will be dealt with and commented upon on the Sweet and Maxwell website (see back cover for details) as soon as it becomes available.

R. v. Central Criminal Court, ex Parte Bright, Alton and Rusbridger,[88C]: **5–059**

Facts. David Shayler, a former MI5 employee, had made a number of allegations and revelations about the Security Services, most notably that there had been an unsuccessful assassination attempt on Colonel Gaddafi and that MI6 had been a part of the plot. Attempts to extradite Shayler from France to face charges under the Official Secrets Act 1989 failed.[89] After newspaper coverage of both Shayler's allegations and the Foreign Secretary's reply, *The Guardian* published an edited emailed letter from Shayler. *The Observer* then published an article by Bright which stated that Shayler had told *The Observer* the names of the agents who had been involved in the assassination plot. MI5 had seen a draft of the article before it was published but had not tried to stop it being published. Shayler next made further comments on his website including that Bright had a copy of his original letter to the Home Secretary.

Special Branch applied for special procedure production orders under PACE against Bright, the editor of *The Guardian* (Rusbridger) and the editor of *The Observer* (Alton). The officer seeking the orders stated that Bright was under investigation for an offence under section 5 of the 1989 Act and that he had reasonable grounds for belief that Bright had committed that offence. The material sought was stated to be related to the official secrecy offences believed to have been committed by Shayler and any other persons. The production orders were granted. The applicants applied to quash the orders, arguing *inter alia* that Bright's privilege against self-incrimination had been infringed.

Decision. The production orders were quashed, except that relating to the copy of the letter to the Home Secretary. If Bright were later prosecuted under the 1989 Act, then the relevance of Article 6 and the privilege against self-incrimination would be considered at that stage. In respect of the application against *The Guardian*, it did not appear that reasonable grounds for any relevant belief had been shown to exist; even if they had, then it was doubtful whether any useful and admissible evidence would have been obtained through the order, since Special Branch were attempting only to find Shayler's email address. Again, there had been insufficient explanation as to why documents were being sought from *The Observer*. But no damage to the proper functioning of the press would be done by upholding the production order re the copy of the letter to the Home Secretary, since it had not had any confidentiality attached to it.

***Per* Judge L.J.**:

> "The story of the Gaddafi bomb plot is either true or it is false, and unless there are compelling reasons of national security, the public is entitled to know the facts, and as the eyes and ears of the public, journalists are entitled to investigate and report the facts, as I hope they would, dispassionately and fairly, without prejudgment or selectivity."

But whether it is expressed as a result of the ECHR or (as the present judge preferred) as being the result of 250 years of domestic common law,

> "Inconvenient or embarrassing revelations, whether for the Security Services, or for public authorities, should not be suppressed. Legal proceedings directed towards the seizure of the working papers of an individual journalist, or the premises of the newspaper or television programme publishing his or her reports, or the threat of such proceedings, tends to inhibit discussion. When a genuine investigation into possible corrupt or reprehensible activities by a public authority is being investigated by the media, compelling evidence is normally needed to demonstrate that the public interest would be served by such proceedings".

Thus from the above, recent cases appear to show that the balance is tipping in favour of disclosure and of the public interest in press freedom and freedom of expression.

OFFICIAL SECRECY: THE DA NOTICE SYSTEM ("DEFENCE ADVISORY")

5–060 The methods of preventing or punishing disclosure of secret information which have been discussed so far in this chapter operate by way of civil or criminal law. DA Notices,[90] by contrast, are an extra-legal control upon disclosure by the media which operates entirely by goodwill and consent, albeit grudging consent and are more often than not adhered to for fear of the alternative consequences. The system is supervised by the Defence Press and Broadcasting Advisory Committee, which is made up of representatives from both government departments and broadcasting services. The Committee issues codes, or "notices" which state that information falling within certain defence categories (there are six categories in operation at present) should not be published. Restrictions apply to defence matters such as weapons, secret codes and installations, and the operations of the security and intelligence services. The notices, now known as "DA" notices are strictly legally unenforceable, lacking any legal sanctions, but a voluntary compliance is expected. Should editors and the like ignore such a notice, the Government may consider other means to prevent publication and to some extent, DA Notices overlap with the provisions of the Official Secrets Acts and the availability of civil remedies for breach of confidence; but there are also substantial discrepancies in the coverage of each.[91] It is likely that where a "DA" Notice has been issued on a particular subject it will be a relevant factor in the prosecution of a newspaper or broadcaster for an Official Secrets offence, particularly where it is being assessed whether damage has occurred or was likely as a result of the disclosure. However, even if permission is granted to disclose certain information which is considered by the Committee not to be detrimental to defence issues, that by itself will not necessarily mean that the publisher in question is exempt from prosecution under the Official Secrets Acts or under the civil law. For instance, in 1970 *The Sunday Telegraph* and others were prosecuted for publishing details of a "confidential" report regarding the supply of armaments to the Nigerian Government during their war with Biafra. The British Government had previously maintained that arms exports to Nigeria had remained at the same level as that prior to the conflict; in fact the report showed that some seventy per cent more weapons were being supplied. Despite the defence argument by the newspaper that they had been advised by the Secretary of the then "D" Committee that publication would not damage national security, and therefore disclosure was sanctioned (this was later disputed), the newspaper and others were eventually prosecuted under the then section 2 of the Official Secrets Act 1911. At trial there was evidence to show that by seeking permission prior to publication from the Foreign Office and the "D" Committee, the newspaper had acted in a responsible manner in wishing not to endanger national security. The jury eventually acquitted the defendants of all charges.[92] DA Notices in effect operate as an informal prior restraint upon the media and as such have received much criticism, but seem likely to endure for the conceivable future. In 1980[93] and again in 1992 the Defence Committee of the House of Commons conducted a review of the operation of DA Notices and gave the continuation of the system a guarded approval, although the media showed a split in views about the scheme's value.

Security and Intelligence Services

Until 1989 and 1994 respectively, the Security Service (MI5) and Secret Intelligence Service (MI6) had no statutory recognition, powers, complaints, or supervisory procedures. This situation seemed all the more ironic when compared with the huge amount of literature, mostly purporting to come from inside sources, about the "secret" services which was published prior to those dates. As the number of autobiographies and other accounts grew, it became a cause of concern that the secret services had an uncertain position constitutionally, and that some of their activities had no legal **5–061** justification. Works such as Peter Wright's *Spycatcher*, and the books of Nigel West caused concern and highlighted the lack of legal remedies for those whose rights had been infringed by the security services, in the purported defence of national security.

A brief description of the activities of the three main "secret" Government operations may be helpful. The Security Service is mainly concerned with counter-espionage, generally in Britain, and the bulk of its resources are expended on counter-terrorism. The Secret Intelligence Service is fairly self-explanatory; it is involved in the secret collection of information, and works closely with the Foreign Office. Most of its operations are overseas. GCHQ, the Government Communications Headquarters, is concerned with the interception and analysis of communications from other countries (whether "friend or foe"), from business and even from the ordinary individual. Each of these three services has now been placed on a statutory footing, with complaints and information procedures, and the Security Service has even been the subject of a mini book published by HMSO.[94]

The Security Services Act 1989 was the first statute to create more openness about the security services, albeit a limited change. It begins by acknowledging the existence of MI5 and listing its main functions.

Section 1:

> "(1) There shall continue to be a Security Service . . . under the authority of the Secretary of State.
> (2) The functions of the Service shall be the protection of national security and, in particular, its protection against threats from espionage, terrorism, and sabotage, from the activities of agents of foreign powers and from actions intended to overthrow or undermine parliamentary democracy by political, industrial or violent means.
> (3) It shall also be the function of the Service to safeguard the economic wellbeing of the United Kingdom against threats posed by the actions or intentions of persons outside the British Islands."

It has been argued that the definition of functions in section 1(2) is unacceptably broad[95] and could be used to justify surveillance of almost any person or group.

Section 2 confirms that the Security Service is under the control of a Director-General appointed by the Secretary of State. His responsibilities include: ensuring the efficiency of the Service; ensuring that the Service does not obtain information which is not necessary for the proper exercise of its functions; ensuring that the Service does not disclose any information except where its functions or the law require this; making an annual report on the Service's work to the Prime Minister and the Secretary of State. But section 2 does not make it clear exactly what role the Prime Minister and Secretary of State are to play in supervision of the Service, or whether they may give the Director-General orders.

Section 5 created a Tribunal for the purpose of investigation of complaints about the Service. The Regulation of Investigatory Powers Act 2000 unifies the rights to appeal under various statutes to one new Tribunal (see below). One problem which remains is that a person must know that he has been investigated, or at least suspect so, before he can make a complaint; if MI5 do their job well, then the person being investigated will have no such idea, and security service personnel are not permitted to "whistleblow", in spite of the existence of the Public Interest Disclosure Act 1998 (discussed below).

THE INTELLIGENCE SERVICES ACT 1994

The Intelligence Services Act 1994 performs a similar task in relation to the Secret Intelligence Service and GCHQ, but also goes into more detail about the authorisation of operations and the issuing of warrants. Section 1(1) states that there shall continue to be a Secret Intelligence Service, under the Secretary of State's authority, and that its main functions are: **5–062**

> "(a)to obtain and provide information relating to the actions or intentions of persons outside the British Islands; and (b) to perform other tasks relating to the actions or intentions of such persons."

This description is left vague, but some clarification is provided in section 1(2):

> "The functions of the Intelligence Service shall be exercisable only—
> (a) in the interests of national security, with particular reference to the defence and foreign policies of Her Majesty's Government in the United Kingdom; or
> (b) in the interests of the economic well-being of the United Kingdom; or
> (c) in support of the prevention or detection of serious crime."

The Intelligence Service is controlled by the Chief of the Intelligence Service (section 2). He is placed under a duty to ensure that the Intelligence Service only obtains information or discloses information "so far as necessary for the proper discharge of its functions" or as required by law (section 2(2)). He is to prevent the Intelligence Service from acting to further the interests of any one political party (section 2(2)(b)).

The continued existence of GCHQ is confirmed in section 3. Its functions are stated to be (section 3(1)):

> "(a) to monitor or interfere with electromagnetic, acoustic and other emissions and any equipment producing such emissions and to obtain and provide information derived from or related to such emissions or equipment and from encrypted material;
>
> (b) to provide advice and assistance about—
>
> (i) languages, including terminology used for technical matters, and
> (ii) cryptography . . .

to the armed forces, . . . to Her Majesty's Government . . ."

These functions are exercisable only in the following situations (section 3(2)):

"(a) in the interests of national security, with particular reference to the defence and foreign policies of Her Majesty's Government in the United Kingdom; or

(b) in the interests of the economic well-being of the United Kingdom in relation to the actions or intentions of persons outside the British Islands; or

(c) in support of the prevention or detection of serious crime."

GCHQ is again under the responsibility of a Director, with similar duties to those responsible for the other two services (section 4).

The issuing of warrants for entry of premises and interference with property or communications is covered by section 5. Any of the three services may apply to the Secretary of State for a warrant, which he may grant if he is satisfied that it is likely to be of substantial value in assisting any of their functions, and that no other method could reasonably be employed to achieve the necessary result (section 5(2)). Further powers and distinctions were created by RIPA 2000; see discussion of these new provisions in Chapter Eight.

Section 11 provides for the Intelligence and Security Committee which is charged with examining the expenditure, administration and policy of the three services; its nine members are drawn from both Houses of Parliament (excluding Ministers) an appointed by the Prime Minister after consultation with the Opposition Leader. The Committee is to make an annual report which is laid before Parliament. This Committee is intended as an independent overseer, to quell criticisms of the lack of any such body. Whether such measures, and indeed all these reforms and statutory declarations, will make any great difference to the accountability and operations of the security and intelligence services is a question for history.

Under section 65 of the Regulation of Investigatory Powers Act 2000 a new unified Tribunal is to be set up and will exercise jurisdiction over the hearing of complaints or proceedings in connection with various matters. As regards proceedings, the Tribunal will hear cases referring to actions which are incompatible with Convention rights (section 65(2)(a)), involving matters relating to the intelligence services, or any persons acting on their behalf (section 65(3)(a)–(d)); the investigatory powers under Part II or Chapter II of Part I; conduct involving the interception of communications via transmissions of a postal service or telecommunications system; or any entry or interference with property or wireless telegraphy (section 65(5)(a)–(f)). As regards complaints, an individual may complain to the Tribunal if he believes that he has been subject to conduct falling within section 65(5)(a)–(f)(see above) in relation to himself, his property, communications sent by or to him, or his use of any postal service, telecommunications service or system, and to have taken place in challengeable circumstances (section 65(4)(a) and (b)). Under 65(7) "challengeable circumstances" means if

(a) it takes place with the authority, or purported authority, of anything falling within subsection (8), *e.g.* authorisation or notice under Chapter II of Part I of RIPA; or authorisation under section 93 of the Police Act 1997; or notice under section 49 of RIPA; or

(b) the circumstances are that it would not have been appropriate for the conduct to take place without authority; but conduct does not take place in challengeable circumstances if it is authorised by, or under permission of a judicial authority.

Further, any individual may complain that he has not been able to adduce evidence as a result of section 17. Section 17 places certain limitations on the evidence which shall be disclosed for the purposes connected with legal proceedings involving intercepted communications or any related communications data (section 17(1)(a) and (b)).

In relation to section 65(2)(a), *i.e.* proceedings, the Tribunal "shall apply the same principles for making their determination in those proceedings as would be applied by a court on an application for judicial review" (section 67(2)). However, under 65(2)(b), *i.e.* complaint, the Tribunal is under a duty to fully investigate the complaint and/or authority and give their findings as if the complaint was an application for judicial review (section 67(3)) and may award compensation or other order as they think fit, including quashing, cancelling any authorisation or warrant or ordering the destruction of any records of information held (section 67(7)).

Freedom of Information Legislation

In summary, until 2000 the reforms to the criminal sanctions for disclosure **5–063**
of official secrets have made little difference to the overall system, which is still clearly characterised by an ethos of secrecy. Both criminal and civil sides to the issue assume that official information should remain secret or confidential, unless there is a strong reason in favour of disclosure; this was supported further by the non-legal compliance structures, whether DA Notices or the needless practice of requiring all civil servants to sign a copy of the provisions under the Official Secrets Acts (which has no legal implications at all).

It is against this background that arguments arose, and gained strength, in favour of specific legislation to create a system of freedom of information. Such legislation is a common feature of many countries with written constitutions, and the present Government made an election promise to introduce such legislation as a priority (although implementation of the legislation may take some time). The basic principle of freedom of information legislation is that of a reversal of the current secrecy ethos, with the result that it would be presumed that the public and the media should have free access to all government information, unless secrecy could be justified on public interest or other policy grounds, including of course national security.

In 1993 the White Paper on "Open Government"[96] was published by the then Government, following an inquiry which had sought to identify fields within government where excessive secrecy existed, and to suggest methods by which open government could be improved. The White Paper contained a suggested Code of Practice concerning government information in Annex A, which was intended to provide clarity as to which kinds of information should be available to the public, and which particular circumstances would justify the withholding of information from the public. In April 1994 a Code of Practice was brought into effect, based upon the proposals from the White Paper, and entitled "Code of Practice on Access to Government Information". The Code committed the Government to providing information to the public in a variety of situations:

(1) When major policies and decisions are announced, the Government will also "normally" disclose "the facts and analysis of facts which the Government considered relevant and important" in framing those decisions or policies.[97]

(2) The Government will reply to requests for information concerning "policies, actions and decisions" of government departments or of specified public authorities, by providing within approximately 20 days such information as is within the government's possession.[98] A charge may be made for the provision of such information[99] and the original documents concerned need not be provided.

(3) The Government will publish information which: explains the running of government departments; explains the reasons behind decisions to those persons who will be affected by them; and gives figures for costs, standards, targets, and results relating to public services.[1]

This appeared to be an impressive list of obligations to provide information, but there was also a long list of exemptions from those obligations. The exemptions include: the usual official secrecy categories of defence and the enforcement of law; the predictable categories of privacy, commercial confidentiality and individual confidentiality; immigration and nationality; the management of the economy and collection of tax; communications with the Royal Household; "the effective management and operations of the public service"; and, the broadest exemption, "information whose disclosure would harm the frankness and candour of internal discussion".

Thus there were in fact many important areas of government to which the obligations to provide information did not apply. Additionally, there was no special supervisory structure for the implementation of the Code of Practice; an individual who had a grievance had to take his complaint to the relevant government department first, then petition his Member of Parliament who should then approach the Parliamentary Ombudsman (the Parliamentary Commissioner for Adminstration) who would investigate the complaint and prepare a response.

In view of the above, the Code of Practice had a limited impact and did not create any legal right to information, nor did it have any effect upon the constraints imposed by the Official Secrets Acts and breach of confidence. It remains to be seen whether and to what extent the new Freedom of Information Act will form a radical departure from the present situation once it is brought into force, but it will at least create a right to know in limited circumstances.

FREEDOM OF INFORMATION AND THE RIGHT TO KNOW: THE FREEDOM OF INFORMATION ACT 2000

This statute, which is unlikely to come into force fully before 2005, in fact stems from a Labour manifesto commitment which spawned a White Paper *Your Right to Know* (Cm. 3818) in December 1997, two years of intense political and public debate, and then a Bill on November 18, 1999. A year later the Act was passed. Under its provisions a huge volume of information held by public authorities will become generally available, with resulting benefits for many categories of individual wishing to exercise their limited "right to know". Advantages over the previous Code of Practice on Access to Government Information include the following: **5–064**

- A statutory right of access to information is created for the first time in the U.K.;
- A far more comprehensive range of public authorities are covered by the new Act;
- The new Information Commissioner will be directly accessible to members of the public, whereas under the Code the intervention of a Member of Parliament was necessary;
- The right of access is to the original documents, or copies thereof, rather than to the information contained therein;
- The Public Records Act 1958 has been substantially amended to allow for access to documents governed by that scheme, subject to exceptions.

The Act represents a radical departure from the previous culture of secrecy, but critics argue that the limitations of the Act will prove more important than the rights which it creates. Further, it may cause an unexpected backlash in that companies may become unwilling to provide so much information to public authorities as they have previously provided, due to fear that the information might be disclosed; only if the company can provide convincing reasons as to why release of the information would be at least likely to prejudice their commercial interests, and even then the public authority holding the information would be permitted to disclose it if it believes that the public interest so requires. The Code of Practice seeks to prevent "gagging" clauses in public sector contracts, to minimise the potential for withholding of information on this basis.

The main changes which the Freedom of Information Act will introduce are as follows:

- A statutory right for a person to have communicated to him any information record which he can describe and which is held by a public authority, subject to a complex framework of exceptions and the payment of a small fee. All Government departments and bodies, regulators, the Greater London Authority, the NHS and educational authorities will be within the scope of the duty, with other bodies exercising a public function to be added by order of the Secretary of State;
- A Code of Practice on Access to Government Information, supervised by the new Information Commissioner, which will bring together the regimes for data protection and access to information, and will be supported by comprehensive advice and documentation for public authorities re. how they should act in order to comply with the new legislation and the corresponding duties and rights;
- Public authorities will fall under a duty to maintain "publication schemes" approved by the Information Commissioner and to publish information in accordance with such schemes. In other words, they must have a clear and accessible policy on publication which as far as possible makes information and documents available to the public. This is a major step towards accessibility and visibility in government activity, at least as far as non-controversial government functions are concerned;
- A right to appeal to the Information Commissioner, then to the Information Tribunal and eventually, on point of law, to a court;
- This will be supported by compulsory complaints procedures run by public authorities under which there will be appeal rights for those whose access to information is barred, and greater scrutiny of the decision whether or not to allow access in an individual case.
- Restructuring of previous information law, including the Data Protection Act 1998 (which will not be fully effective in any case until October 2001) and public records legislation.

EXCEPTIONS (subject to rulings by the Information Commissioner as to whether the information in question falls within the scope of an exception)—the following categories of information are exempt from the duty to disclose:

- Information provided in confidence: this largely preserves the position under the common law of confidentiality;
- Commercial interests: this is similar to the protection afforded by the previous Code of Practice on Access to Government Information; for example "trade secrets" are exempt from disclosure;
- Information, disclosure of which would be likely to prejudice relations between the Westminster parliament and the devolved authorities;
- Information relating to security services and bodies, where the exemption of the information is necessary to safeguard national security, or to uphold defence, the economy, international relations, law enforcement or health and safety;
- Information held for investigations into improper or illegal conduct, fitness or competence;
- Personal data covered by the Data Protection Act 1998, as amended;
- Information related to the formulation/development of government policy and ministerial communications (this exemption has been particularly controversial since it exempts the information as a class, without requiring evaluation of whether harm would be caused by disclosure);
- Environmental information, to be dealt with under a separate regime due to the UN Economic Commission Convention on Access to Information, Public Participation in Decision-making and Access to Justice in Environmental Matters.

Each Part of the statute will be examined in turn.

Part I: The Right of Access to Information Held by Public Authorities

Part I creates and explains the new right of access, including how to exercise it. The new right itself is to be found in section 1: **5–065**

"Section 1 General right of access to information held by public authorities.

(1) Any person making a request for information to a public authority is entitled—

(a) to be informed in writing by the public authority whether it holds information of the description specified in the request, and

(b) if that is the case, to have that information communicated to him.

(2) Subsection (1) has effect subject to the following provisions of this section and to the provisions of sections 2, 9, 12 and 14.

(3) Where a public authority—

(a) reasonably requires further information in order to identify and locate the information requested, and

(b) has informed the applicant of that requirement,

the authority is not obliged to comply with subsection (1) unless it is supplied with that further information.

(4) The information—

(a) in respect of which the applicant is to be informed under subsection (1)(a), or

(b) which is to be communicated under subsection (1)(b),

is the information in question held at the time when the request is received, except that account may be taken of any amendment or deletion made between that time and the time when the information is to be communicated under subsection (1)(b), being an amendment or deletion that would have been made regardless of the receipt of the request.

(5) A public authority is to be taken to have complied with subsection (1)(a) in relation to any information if it has communicated the information to the applicant in accordance with subsection (1)(b).

(6) In this Act, the duty of a public authority to comply with subsection (1)(a) is referred to as 'the duty to confirm or deny'."

As can be seen, section 1 itself limits the duty of public authorities to comply with requests for information, but further limitations are found in sections 2, 9, 12 and 14 of Part I, and in Part II. The Part I limitations are concerned with circumstances in which a public authority does not have to comply with a request; the Part II exceptions from the duty to provide information are related to the type and nature of the specific information requested.

Limitations

5–066 Section 1(3) delays a public authority's duty to comply with a request for information until sufficient details and description of the information requested have been provided by the applicant to enable the identification of the material requested. This does not mean that the applicant must be able to describe a particular document, merely to facilitate the retrieval of the requested information. Normally the information communicated to the applicant must be that held by the public authority at the time of receipt of the request, but section (4) allows account to be taken of amendments and deletions which would have occurred "in the normal course of events".

In section 2 the effect of the Part II exemptions is explained. Where an exemption is absolute (see below), there is no need to balance the public interest in disclosure of the information against the public interest served by the exemption.[2] But for all other exemptions this balancing exercise must be conducted. Section 2(1) states that a public authority is not under a duty even to confirm or deny that they are in possession of the requested information if either:

> "the information is given absolute exemption in Part II
>
> or
>
> in all the circumstances of the case, the public interest in maintaining the secrecy of the information outweighs the public interest in disclosing whether that authority holds the information."

Under section 2(2), the authority is similarly not under a duty to disclose the information if the information is subject to an absolute exemption in Part II or if, in all the circumstances of the case,, the public interest in maintaining the exemption outweighs the public interest in disclosing the information.

Public authority

There is no list of public authorities in the list due to the sheer length which it would have. Section 3(1) defines "public authority": **5–067**

> "(1) In this Act 'public authority' means—
>
> (a) subject to section 4(4), any body which, any other person who, or the holder of any office which—
>
> (i) is listed in Schedule 1, or
> (ii) is designated by order under section 5, or
>
> (b) a publicly-owned company as defined by section 6."

Schedule 1 uses generic descriptions of public authorities, including national and local government, and bodies related to the armed forces, education, the national health service, and the police.

Sections 4 and 5 allow the Secretary of State to extend the definition beyond those bodies by order, adding any body, office holder of person who appears to him to exercise functions of a public nature or provides services under a contract with a public authority where that authority's functions include the provision of that service. Section 6 defines a "publicly-owned company" as any company which is:

> "—wholly owned by the Crown
>
> or
>
> —wholly owned by any public authority which is listed in Schedule 1 except a government department or an authority which is listed only in respect of

certain information, and the company concerned is not related to the listed functions of the authority".

Information is "held" by a public authority:

"(2) For the purposes of this Act, information is held by a public authority if—

(a) it is held by the authority, otherwise than on behalf of another person, or
(b) it is held by another person on behalf of the authority."

Thus the fact that an authority is in bare possession of information will not trigger the duties to disclose, since holding information on behalf of another person or authority is not included. But geography does not matter: the physical position of the information is irrelevant, since information held elsewhere on behalf of a public authority does trigger the duty.

Requests for information

5–068 Any person or body regardless of nationality or residence may make a request for information, and there is no need to justify why the information is wanted. Only if a person has made vexatious or repeated requests (section 14) or the information requested is "personal information" (section 40(1))[3] will the identity of the person making the request be relevant to the authority. The conditions to be satisfied when making a request are found in section 8:

"Section 8 Request for information.

(1) In this Act any reference to a 'request for information' is a reference to such a request which—
 (a) is in writing,
 (b) states the name of the applicant and an address for correspondence, and
 (c) describes the information requested.
(2) For the purposes of subsection (1)(a), a request is to be treated as made in writing where the text of the request—
 (a) is transmitted by electronic means,
 (b) is received in legible form, and
 (c) is capable of being used for subsequent reference."

A fee may be payable (section 9) for processing a request, in which case it must be paid by the applicant within three months of the date of notification that a fee is payable. Disclosure of the information may be withheld until the fee is paid. The Secretary of State will be able to regulate the charging of fees and to provide an upper limit. If the applicant requires the information to be presented in a particular manner, *e.g.* by fax, then the additional costs of this method of delivery may also be charged. Section 12 exempts a public authority from the disclosure duty when the cost for so doing would exceed a limit set by the Secretary of State, but if the authority nevertheless chooses to disclose in such circumstances then an appropriate fee may be charged. This enables public authorities to disclose information where the volume of the documentation would otherwise make it extremely costly to provide, and to pass the costs on to the applicant.

On receiving a request for disclosure, a public authority must carry out its s.1 duty within 20 working days (section 10), subject to the provisions *re.* payment of fees. In circumstances where the balance of public interests between disclosure and withholding of information must be weighed, it is possible to exceed the 20-day deadline but in any case a decision must be reached on this issue "within a reasonable period". The applicant may request that the information should be provided in a particular form (section 11(1)) and the information must then be provided in that form so far as is reasonably practicable. If it is decided to reject such a request then the authority has a duty to provide reasons (section 11(3)). An authority has discretion to provide the information on tap or by other means when considered appropriate (section 11(4)), hence making provision for applicants with disabilities.

If a request is refused on the basis either that the information is exempt information or that there is an absolute exemption in the circumstances, then section 17(1) requires the authority to give the applicant notice of the argued exemption within 20 working days. If it is not possible to determine whether or not an exemption will apply within this period, then the notice must state so and must give an estimated date by which it is expected that the determination will have been made (section 17(2)). If under section 2 the balance of public interest re. exempt information is found to be either against disclosing whether the information is held or against disclosing the information itself, then again reasons for this decision must be provided (section 17(3)). In any of these situations, the notice must contain details of complaints and appeals procedures (section 17(7)).

PART II: EXEMPT INFORMATION

The following types or classes of information are exempt from the s.1 duty to disclose: **5–069 —072**

* Information accessible to the public by other means, *e.g.* already published (section 21)—this is an absolute exemption.

* Information intended for future publication, in circumstances where it is reasonable that the information should not be disclosed before publication, *e.g.* research projects (section 22). In some circumstances there is no duty to confirm or deny that such

information is held (section 22(2)), *i.e.* where to confirm or deny would itself disclose information which it is reasonable to withhold until the intended publication date. The mischief of this exception is to prevent the asking of "clever questions" in order to determine which measures are, for example, to be taken in the next Budget.

* Information directly or indirectly supplied by, or related to, bodies which deal with security matters (section 23(1)): this is not only an absolute exemption but also, under section 23(2), a certificate signed by a Minister is conclusive proof that the information fits this exemption (subject to an appeal to the Information Tribunal). There is no obligation to confirm or deny where to do so would itself disclose exempt information (section 23(5)).

* The national security class exemption under section 24 has caused concern. Any information not within the scope of section 23 is exempt whenever such an exemption is required in order to safeguard national security. Again, a Ministerial certificate is conclusive proof of exemption.

* Information the disclosure of which would, or would be likely to, prejudice the defence of the British Isles or of any colony, or the capability, effectiveness or security of the armed forces (section 26). The duty to confirm or deny does not arise where to do so would, or would be likely to, prejudice those defence interests (section 26(3)).

* Information which would, or would be likely to, prejudice relations between the U.K. and any other state, or international organisation, or to harm the interests of the U.K. abroad; or confidential information obtained from a state, an international organisation or international court (section 27), The duty to confirm or deny does not arise where to do so would, or would be likely to, prejudice those interests (section 27(4)).

* Information which would, or would be likely to, prejudice relations between any two U.K. administrations (section 28): again, the duty to confirm or deny does not arise where to do so would, or would be likely to, prejudice those interests (section 28(3)).

* Information the disclosure of which would, or would be likely to, prejudice the economic interests of the U.K. (section 29); again, the confirm/deny limitation applies.

* Information held by a public authority for the purposes of a criminal investigation or criminal proceedings conducted by that authority; this is a class exemption (section 30). Information

related to an authority's functions for the purposes of criminal investigations or proceedings is also exempted as a class if it was received from a confidential source (a.k.a. an informant). There is no obligation to confirm or deny the holding of any such exempt information, without any public interest balancing exercise having to be performed (section 30(3)).

* Information which would, or would be likely to, prejudice law enforcement interests (section 31).

Also exempted are the following, which are generally subject to the "likely to prejudice" test: **5–073**

- court records (section 32);
- audit functions (section 33);
- Parliamentary privilege (section 34);
- formulation of government policy (section 35)—this is an absolute exemption;
- prejudice to effective conduct of public affairs (section 36);
- communications with the Queen (section 37);
- health and safety (section 38);
- environmental information (section 39)—this is obtainable by other means;
- personal information (section 40)—access to this information is governed by the Data Protection Act 1998;
- information provided in confidence (section 41);
- legal professional privilege (section 42)—this is an absolute exemption;
- commercial interests (section 43)—trade secrets are an absolute exemption;
- information, the disclosure of which, would violate other laws or constitute contempt of court (section 44)—this is an absolute exemption.

Thus it is difficult to think of any information for which one or other of the exemptions would not be at least arguable. The fact that so many of the exemptions absolve the relevant public authority from the duty to confirm or deny the existence of the information does not facilitate the task of the information-seeker, nor does it create the appearance of a culture of openness.

The enforcement mechanisms of the 2000 Act have also come in for criticism. The Information Commissioner has powers to investigate complaints that public authorities have failed to comply with their duties under the Act (Part IV) and she can order the relevant public authority to carry out its duties. She may act of her own volition (s. 52) or in response to a complaint by an individual (s. 50). But, in a great departure from the original White Paper, the Information Commissioner's decisions are not final. If she orders a public authority to disclose information, that decision can be overridden under s. 53 by the executive issuing a certificate that the public authority's decision was correct. Further, Part V of the Act allows not only a complainant but also the public authority to appeal to the Information Tribunal (s. 57), and finally to the High Court on a point of law.

Full discussion of the effect of the Freedom of Information Act 2000 can only be made when it comes into force and it becomes apparent whether there is a general duty to disclose in practice, or whether the exemptions will be interpreted too widely to allow that to happen. Certainly, if the officials involved in administrating the Act wish to do so, they have sufficient tools and scope to be able to create a culture of openness, but they are not clearly obligated in that direction. More discussion of thc Freedom of Information Act 2000 will be available on the Sweet and Maxwell website after publication of this book.

Relevant ECHR Cases: The Definition of "National Security"

5–074 A number of relevant Strasbourg decisions will be found in the ECHR sections of other chapters of this book, principally those on privacy and obscenity.

For example, see *Leander v. Sweden*[4] and *Observer and Guardian v. U.K.*[5] (above). In *Vereniging Weekblad Bluf! v. The Netherlands*,[6] the ECHR stated[7] that:

> "National authorities must be able to take such measures [as seizure and destruction of periodicals and obtaining of injunctions restraining publication] solely in order to prevent punishable disclosure of a secret without taking criminal proceedings against the party concerned, provided that national law affords that party sufficient procedural safeguards".

Democratic societies may well need secret services and covert operations which can only be effective if their secrecy is maintained, and so national security restrictions upon freedom of expression may well be legitimate. However, since the information in question was clearly already in the public domain before the seizure and destruction of the offending issue of the periodical was ordered, the publisher's freedom of expression under Article

10 had been violated: it could not be argued that the interference with that freedom was "*necessary* in a democratic society", however legitimate the aim of maintaining national security might be. But the ECHR did not have any problem with the possibility of criminal prosecutions in the present case. Thus it is a delicate balancing act of competing rights which must be carried out here: in each situation it must be determined whether the specific facts require the restriction of freedom of expression on national security grounds, with special regard to the extent to which the information concerned is already in the public domain and whether the information is current or merely embarrassing historical revelations which need no suppression.

BRIEF OUTLINE AND GERMANE CASES

CHAPTER FIVE: OFFICIAL SECRECY AND FREEDOM OF INFORMATION

There are criminal sanctions for breach of official secrecy. **5–075**

*Official Secrets Act 1911 s.1: anti-espionage offences.
Chandler v. DPP [1964].

*OSA 1911 s.2: for comparison purposes only.
R. v. Ponting [1985]; *Secretary of State for Defence v. Guardian Newspapers* [1984].
*OSA 1920 s.1, s.7: extends scope of official secrecy offences to include retention of documents and acts preparatory to secrecy offences.
R. v. Bingham [1973].
S.9: powers of search and seizure.

*OSA 1989: creates 6 new categories or protected information, disclosure of which is a criminal offence.
s.1:
information concerning security and intelligence.
s.2:
defence.
s.3:
international relations.
s.4:
criminal investigations.
s.5:
interception of communications.
s.6:
confidential Government communications.

Damage requirement varies according to category.
Defences: *mens rea*; lawful authority.
In addition to the above criminal offences, official secrecy may also be maintained via civil law.
—Prior restraint and injunctions.
—Public breach of confidence
Att.-Gen. v. Jonathan Cape Ltd [1975]; (Spycatcher), *Lord Advocate v. The Scotsman Publication Ltd* [1990]; *Att.-Gen. v. Blake* [1996].
—DA Notices
Special rules for the security and intelligence services: Security Services Act 1989, Intelligence Services Act 1994.
Freedom of Information legislation: Freedom of Information Act 2000.

Endnotes

[1] *Att.-Gen. v. Guardian Newspapers (No. 2)* [1988] 3 All E.R. 545, at 852.
[2] *Chandler v. DPP* [1964] A.C. 763.
[3] *The Zamora* [1916] 2 A.C. 77.
[4] *Secretary of State for Defence v. Guardian Newspapers* [1984] 3 All E.R. 601.
[5] *The Zamora*.
[6] See *Burmah Oil Co Ltd v. Bank of England* [1980] A.C. 1090.
[7] *Conway v. Rimmer* [1968] A.C. 910.
[8] *Halford v. Sharples* [1992] 3 All E.R. 624.
[9] Official Secrets Act 1911, s. 1, below.
[10] Official Secrets Act 1989, below.
[11] Regulation of Investigatory Powers Act 2000, below.
[12] Education (No. 2) Act 1986, s. 44(1)(b).
[13–14] ss. 44 and 45 of the 1986 Act.
[15] For a fuller explanation of these terms see OSA 1911, s. 12.
[16] [1964] A.C. 763.
[17] *ibid.* at 790.
[18] OSA 1911, s. 3.
[19] *R. v. Parrott* (1913) 8 Cr.App.R. 186 *per* Phillimore J. at 192.
[20] *R. v. Bettaney* [1985] Crim.L.R. 104.
[21] *R. v. Fell* [1963] Crim.L.R. 207.
[22] [1964] A.C. 763.
[23] (1919) 83 J.P. 121.
[24] *Secretary of State for Defence v. Guardian Newspapers Ltd* [1984] 3 All E.R. 601.
[25] See *Official Secrets—The Use and Abuse of the Act*, David Hooper (Ed.) (Coronet Books, 1988).
[26] *ibid.* at 149.
[27] From A. Nicol, 1979, Crim.L.R. 284–291.
[28] [1985] see Crim.L.R. 318.
[29] *per* Lord Devlin and Lord Pearce in *Chandler v. DPP* [1964] A.C. 763.
[30] As amended by the Official Secrets Act 1939.
[31] This section includes "aids or abets and does any act preparatory . . . etc.". The word "and" is to be interpreted and read as "or" for the purposes of this section. See *R. v. Oakes* [1959] 2 All E.R. 92.
[32] [1973] 1 Q.B. 870.
[33] The 1939 Act amended s. 6 so that the consent of the Secretary of State is required before the police may summon a potential witness to be questioned about an offence under s. 1 of the 1911 Act, but after this procedure has been followed then failure to attend for such questioning, or failure to surrender information is an offence.
[34] See Ewing and Gearty, *Freedom under Thatcher*, for a full account of the case and further examples.
[35] Report, Cmnd 5104.
[36] Cmnd 408, 1988.
[37] Speech by Douglas Hurd, at that time the Home Secretary.
[38] Home Office Guidelines on Special Branch Work in Great Britain (1994) Paragraph 2 . . . "to assist the security service in carrying out its statutory duty under Security Services Act 1989 namely the protection of national security and, in particular, protection against threats from espionage, terrorism and sabotage . . .".
[39] Under the Official Secrets Act 1989 (Prescription) Order 1990 (S.I. 1990 No. 200). This list is not exhaustive and may be added to. Official Secrets Act 1989 (Prescription) (Amendment) Order 1993) S.I. 1993 No. 847 by adding to those who became Crown servants for the purposes of the Official Secrets Act 1989.
[40] Perhaps strangely, M.P.s who work within a Minister's private office are not included.
[41] See Official Secrets Act 1989 (Prescription) Order 1990.
[42] See full discussion of this new statute in Chapter 8, Privacy.
[43] Or a person who has been notified that he is subject to s. 1(1).
[44] "Lawful authority" is defined in s. 7(3) as a disclosure made to a Crown servant or it was officially permitted.
[45] Reform of section 2 of the Official Secrets Act 1911 CM 408, 1988.

[45A] [2001] E.W.C.A. Civ. 97.
[46] See for example *Argyll v. Argyll* [1967] Ch. 302 (information communicated between a married couple) and *Prince Albert v. Strange* (1849) 1 Mac & G. 25.
[47] [1975] 3 All E.R. 484.
[48] *ibid.* at 491.
[49] If made public, this would in effect result in abrogating the convention of joint cabinet responsibility. "Joint cabinet responsibility" exists "whereby any policy decision reached by the cabinet has to be supported by all members of the cabinet whether they approve of it or not" (at 490).
[50] Lord Widgery gave the example of Budget Day; to disclose the budget a day before would be a breach of confidence, but would be public knowledge thereafter (at 495).
[51] at 496.
[52] This was a part of the affidavit which Sir Robert Armstrong presented to the Australian court.
[53] Mr Wright had previously been interviewed in July 1984 on a TV programme called "World in Action" about national security.
[54] (1986) 136 N.L.J. 799.
[55] at 800.
[56] See *Francome v. Mirror Group Newspapers Ltd* [1984] 2 All E.R. 408; *Lion Laboratories v. Evans* [1985] Q.B. 528.
[57] *Att.-Gen. v. Guardian Newspapers* [1987] 1 W.L.R. 1248, at 1269 Sir Nicolas Browne-Wilkinson V.-C. said ". . . in weighing the harm to the public by the discouragement of future memoirs by future members of the security services, one has to bear in mind what to my mind is a very important factor, namely, that one should not restrain publication in the press unless it is unavoidable". Now also see HRA 1998, s. 12.
[58] [1988] 1 Ch. 33. (For full discussion of this case see below).
[59] [1987] 1 W.L.R. 1248.
[60] *ibid.* at 1269.
[61] [1987] 3 All E.R. 316, 333.
[62] Their Lordships were equally concerned that Mr Wright should not benefit financially from his revelations and breach of duty, thus discouraging ex-members of the security services from doing the same thing.
[63] at 337.
[64] *ibid.* at 339.
[65] at 341.
[66] [1987] 3 All E.R. 316, 343.
[67] *ibid.* at 345.
[68] [1990] 1 A.C. 109; [1988] 3 All E.R. 545.
[69] at 589.
[70] Chapman Pincher's "Trade is Treachery" and "Too Secrets too Long" as well as the Granada TV programme in 1984.
[71] [1988] 3 All E.R. 545, 594.
[72] at 619, 620.
[73] 3 All E.R. 545, 638.
[74] In the Court of Appeal his lordship said that "it is . . . to some extent anomalous that *The Sunday Times* should be free to do what Mr Wright and his Australian publishers could not", at 633.
[75] [1980] 147 C.L.R. 39; 32 A.L.R. 485.
[76] *Att.-Gen. v. Guardian Newspapers Ltd* [1990] 1 A.C. 109 at 256.
[77] Although he came down on the side of the majority, one feels he somewhat reluctantly agreed with his colleagues and put forward many examples and arguments which left this question still unresolved.
[78] *ibid.* at 662, 663.
[79] *ibid.* at 663.
[80] *ibid.* at 664.
[81] (1992) 14 E.H.R.R. 153.
[82] [1990] 1 A.C. 812.
[83] *Attorney-General v. Guardian Newspapers Ltd* [No. 2] 1990, 1 A.C. 109.
[84] Defamation and exceptions stated under Article 10 ECHR.
[85] [1996] 3 All E.R. 903.
[86] at 909.

[87] at 912.
[88] (1980) 444 U.S. 507.
[88A] CA, March 23, 2001.
[88B] Q.B.D. May 16, 2001.
[88C] [2001] E.M.L.R. 4, DC.
[89] He eventually came back voluntarily.
[90] It was first established in 1912 and was known merely as the "D" notice and was not publicly recognised until 1952. Since 1992 it became known as the "DA" notice.
[91] See Farrier, *Oxford Journal of Legal Studies* (Autumn 1990) for a detailed examination of the relationship between DA Notices and each of the potential legal actions.
[92] David Hopper See Official Secrets—The Use and Abuse of the Act, (Coronet Books, 1998); and Bailey Harris and Jones, *Civil Liberties—Cases and Materials* (4th ed., Butterworths), pp. 470–474.
[93] H.C. 773 (1979–80).
[94] MI5, the Security Service (1993).
[95] See *Leigh and Lustgarten* (1989) 52 M.L.R. 801.
[96] Cmnd 2290.
[97] para. 3.
[98] paras 3, 7.
[99] para. 7.
[1] para. 3.
[2] s. 2(3).
[3] If the applicant is himself the subject of the personal information then he will have a (limited) right of access to it—see Data Protection Act 1998, discussed in Chap. 8.
[4] [1987] 9 E.H.R.R. 433.
[5] [1991] 14 E.H.R.R. 153.
[6] [1995] 20 E.H.R.R. 189.
[7] *ibid*. at para 32.

CHAPTER 6

OBSCENITY, INDECENCY AND CENSORSHIP

INTRODUCTION

The law relating to obscenity and indecency is a source of much controversy **6–001** and an obvious candidate for reform, being derived piecemeal from some 20 different statutes and from the common law, and being greatly influenced by conflicting policy and by emotive arguments. In the current situation, clarity is lacking both in terms of the scope of the relevant legal prohibitions and in the principles upon which such prohibitions are based. Reforms have been advocated on many occasions, most forcefully by the Williams Committee in 1979,[1] but in contrast to the simplification which that Committee advocated, the law has in fact been further complicated by the introduction of successive statutory controls upon new categories of publications and behaviour. It is not merely a question of whether a defendant's behaviour is prohibited by either a statutory provision or the common law, but also of the form in which the defendant has expressed himself—conduct, written publications, film, broadcasting or live performance are governed separately by different legal provisions. In order to assess the current legal position concerning obscenity, indecency and related offences, it is necessary to look at the policy arguments both for and against such controls and offences, and also to examine the theoretical background within which these arguments exist.

Yet it is impossible to discuss indecency or obscenity offences without entering into the debate concerning morality and standards, both in private life and in the media. Restrictions upon the media on morality grounds have existed for almost as long as there has existed the means to print and distribute written material or pictures. To many, pornography is an attack against a variety of standards in society and its distribution should be prevented; but it has always been taken for granted that there should not be a complete ban upon either the distribution or the mere possession of all material which "right-thinking members of society" would consider to be offensive, immoral or pornographic. It should be noted that the legal regulations discussed in this chapter do not apply to pornography alone; what is obscene is a changing and diverse standard, as will be seen from the cases discussed below, and need not bear any relation to sex or sexuality.

6–002 The viewpoint of those who have attempted to justify the legal control of offensive material has tended to be based on a broad liberal theoretical tradition. Rather than proposing a total ban upon such material, discussion centres on methods of reconciling free speech with a limited regime of control of certain speech, and concludes that some offensive behaviour and speech must be tolerated in order to foster a free, open society in which the rights of all citizens are protected. Moral standards are unlikely to be the subject of general agreement in any modern society—one man's art is another man's pornography, what one man considers offensive may be comedy to another. Most societies consider that precise choices of morality are an individual's concern, not the State's. Thus the background to the debate concerning pornography and offensive material tends to be a liberal one which expects any restrictions imposed to be limited and targeted at particular categories of material, particularly if the sanctions to be imposed are criminal in nature and involve the threat of imprisonment. This can be seen, for example, in the report of the Williams Committee, to which a "harm principle" is intrinsic. Dating back at least as far as J.S. Mill,[2] such a principle argues that any law, but particularly criminal law, should only prevent individuals from exercising their freedom of choice in actions, beliefs and speech by limiting such behaviour in so far as it is necessary to impose limitations in order to uphold the rights of others, and that intervention by the State is necessary only where an individual's choice threatens to actually harm, rather than to merely annoy or inconvenience, others in society. It is the definition of "harm" which has been subject to debate: definitions range from verifiable physical injury to moral or ideological injury. The Williams Committee chose to avoid such complexities by arguing that the burden of proving that material risked harm, should be placed upon those who wish to interfere with the freedom of expression of others. It is on this basis that the Committee decided against banning all pornography, since they argued that its opponents had failed to establish that there is a verifiable link between viewing pornography in any form and any kind of harmful behaviour.

6–003 The Williams Committee made a series of recommendations which were not adopted but which would at least have simplified the law. It was recommended that written words should not be restricted at all, even if offensive, and that inoffensive illustrations accompanying offensive words should not be restricted. This is an extremely broad provision which would have contrasted strongly against restrictions imposed in many other countries, with the result that British pornography regulations would be more lax than those in, for example, the United States. A different attitude was taken to pictures, which were considered to be potentially far more harmful than text. The Committee proposed specific absolute criminal offences relating to dealing in child pornography or sadistic photographs. In addition, pictorial representations of violence, cruelty, sexual functions and nudity should be restricted in availability to persons over the age of 18, but only if it would otherwise be offensive to reasonable people. These restrictions were aimed at preventing children or the sensitive from being harmed by material which they were not freely choosing to experience. Thus the key term of "offensiveness" would be objectively defined and limited in its application to certain specified types of material.

However, after the Committee's Report was published in 1979, the new Conservative Government was among the many who attacked its conclusions. In particular, it was the proposed lack of restriction upon written material which came under attack—the proposed imposition of targeted restrictions of access to offensive material was better accepted, and this to a great extent is reflected in the present law. This targeted restriction of access to offensive or pornographic material has been criticised by both proponents and opponents of restrictions on freedom of expression, and the range of viewpoints represented within each category is wide.

Arguments in Favour of Controlling Behaviour

Almost without exception, written constitutions accept that there should be a limitation to the citizen's freedom of expression, based upon morality; Words, whether spoken or written, and even pictures can corrupt, deprave, shock or outrage the general public or sections of it, and may even cause others to commit acts of violence such as sexual offences. Lord Devlin argued in *The Enforcement of Morals*[3] that each society has a set of morals which are considered fundamental, and that an attack upon these morals justifies reprisal in exactly the same way as would armed insurrection or acts of physical violence. Thus pornography and other offensive or indecent material should be controlled since it represents an assault upon the values of a society. **6–004**

Others, particularly those arguing from a liberal perspective, state that although the harm principle should be applied, behaviour is only deserving of protection under the right of freedom of expression if it is of social utility; an individual's right to express himself via creating offensive or pornographic material is seen as of limited usefulness. For J.S. Mill, freedom of speech was a fundamental right since it enabled discovery of the truth by the debate of ideas. Pornography is not advanced as an "idea" or "truth" by many, and the risks engendered by its free availability may be seen as outweighing its social utility. It is difficult to argue that what is, for the most part, entertainment, is of higher value to society than the values which it is presumed to threaten.

The problem with both of the above viewpoints is the immense difficulty which has dogged those researchers who have attempted to prove that indecent or offensive material is in fact harmful. Although anecdotally and, to a limited extent, statistically, there is evidence that there is a link between pornography use and violent criminals; the link is neither conclusive nor uncontroversial and may in fact show nothing more than that many violent men who are in prison seek to use pornography, just as many non-violent men do. Some have argued a negative link, in other words that **6–005** pornography can serve as a non-violent outlet for urges which, if repressed, could erupt in violence.[4] But it is often argued in courtrooms that pornography has had a harmful effect on a defendant and is a cause of his anti-social behaviour; feminists argue that the harm caused is such a general feature of society that it is both taken for granted and incapable of empirical proof[5]; and some commentators claim to have demonstrated just such a proof of harm.[6] Thus there is evident confusion in this area, which does not help the development of clarity of principle.

Feminist approaches to a critique of obscenity and indecency laws tend to focus on a depiction of pornography as a method of degradation and control of women in society; crucially, pornography is seen not as merely the cause of violence but as violence against women in itself, presenting women as subjects, subservient, submissive, compliant and dominated by men. But feminism is a diverse discipline, encompassing a variety of viewpoints which come from various theoretical backgrounds and for our present purposes, it is only possible to outline some of the main arguments. One main group of feminist theorists see the term "pornography" as a method of concealing the reality of the degradation and abuse of women or children, as a legitimisation of male violence.[7] For Andrea Dworkin, pornography is a method of destroying "women's bodies and souls; rape, battery, incest and prostitution animate it; dehumanisation and sadism characterise it; it is a war on women . . . it is tyranny".[8] Pornography is also seen as presenting racist and homophobic stereotypes for its undiscriminating audience in the guise of the erotic.[9] For many feminists, there is no need to prove that pornography is harmful since this is self-evident; Edwards said [1997, p.99] "The consumption of pornography is harmful, the acts perpetrated on the victims within the pornography are harmful, the acts committed by those who ingest and reproduce the narrative in real life are harmful, as are the effects of the ubiquity of pornography on women's fear of sex crime, public safety and security". Thus pornography should at least be severely regulated in order to minimise its potential harmful effects upon society in general and individuals in particular.

Arguments Against Controlling Behaviour

6–006 Many authors have found it extremely difficult to provide any arguments in favour of the freedoms to create, publish and experience the obscene or pornographic, yet such arguments can in fact be drawn from a range of different perspectives. The exception is child pornography, which has few theoretical supporters and is far more difficult to justify from any perspective, given the implicit element of exploitation and the involved sexual offences.

As previously mentioned, arguments from liberalism aim to allow freedom of expression even of the distasteful or pornographic, so far as it does not harm or threaten society. But a more extreme version of this theme is sexual liberalism, which views pornography as simply being about sex, not power, depravity, or any other hidden symbolism. Sexual liberalism celebrates pornography as part of its belief that "sexual expression is inherently liberating and must be permitted to flourish unchecked, even where it entails the exploitation or brutalisation of others."[10] Legal restrictions are unjustifiable since pornography does not harm women or any other section of society—rather, it represents their freedom.

For some proponents of civil liberty, pornography is part and parcel of freedom from totalitarianism. For others, although pornography is harmful, that harm must be balanced against the greater harm to society which may flow from the suppression of ideas—censorship may only be justified where the balance of harm is in its favour. Some feminist perspectives argue against regulation of pornography or other obscene material on the arguably from the somewhat cynical or jaded basis that there is very little improvement which can be achieved in women's favour without first radically changing the very framework of society—since law is simply yet another tool of male domination, the law should not be used to restrict behaviour even if that behaviour is harmful. It is as if the regulation of pornography will legitimate it.[11] Other feminists oppose legal restrictions on pornography on the basis that popular culture is already full of the very same kinds of representations of women, children and other vulnerable groups that are visible in pornography, and thus regulation will both lack meaningful effect and focus on onc of the lesser forms of such representations. Yet another group is opposed to the use of the criminal law in this field, arguing instead that effective equality legislation is a far greater priority.[12]

Since pornography and other forms of obscenity by definition involve value judgments, it may be argued that certain works which have been published or created have such artistic or literary merit that there is a greater imperative towards allowing their expression than there is in their suppression. Such arguments have been made in cases discussed below, but rarely succeed.

Thus it can be seen that the issues concerning obscenity, indecency and pornography are complex and lack clarity of principle. Yet, even if legal regulation is to be imposed in this field, it remains to be considered what form such regulation should take.

THEORY AND CHOICE OF METHODS OF CONTROL

As previously discussed in relation to official secrecy, the regulation of any form of expression may take effect in a variety of different forms and at various stages in the creation or publication of the material which it is desired to regulate. The three main methods of regulation, which operates at different levels and have different effects, are as follows. **6–007**

(i) Censorship prior to publication

The most basic method of regulation of obscene material involves the imposition of a requirement that any material which is to be published or otherwise made available to the public must first pass the scrutiny of an **6–008** official censor. This form of regulation attracts the strongest disapproval or even condemnation since it acts as a prior restraint upon publication and thus prevents certain material from reaching an audience. There is also a possibility that a censor may exercise his discretion in an inappropriate manner, and so some form of appeal mechanism is desirable if such censorship is to be imposed. At the present time, this method of control applies in the United Kingdom to films or videos which are intended for distribution. The details of this regulation will be discussed below.

(ii) Use of the criminal law and its sanctions

6–009 Most of the criminal offences relevant to this topic operate as controls after publication of the obscene material has taken place. Thus it is possible to argue that the imposition of criminal liability is justifiable on the basis that the offences serve as a deterrent and a fair warning against publication of the prohibited types of material, and that those who seek to infringe the criminal law are deserving of punishment by criminal sanctions since they have exercised their freedom of action and knew the potential consequences. But the tenability of such arguments obviously depends upon the criminal law being fair, predictable and consistent, with appropriate sanctions for the harm caused by the defendant's actions. The focus of the criminal aspect of obscenity is therefore on the courts and the role of judges in applying and interpreting the relevant criminal offences. Judges and juries, applying legal principles and authorities, will have the final decision as to what is controlled by the criminal offences. It is this method of restriction which is the most frequent in the field of obscenity. Many of the offences have related powers of seizure or confiscation which serve to support the offences and may minimise potential harm which could otherwise flow from the commission of the original offence.

(iii) Regulating supply

6–010 The latest stage at which regulation is imposed is at the point of sale or supply of the material in question. The control may take the form of a requirement of licensing of premises which are to be used for the sale of particular types of publication, or a requirement that a notice of warning should be displayed prominently on such premises, or that certain categories of person should be excluded from entry into such premises. This method of regulation may be found in various statutes concerning pornography, which will be discussed below.

The Problems of Definitions

6–011 Before looking in detail at each of the criminal offences and other regulations which operate in the area of obscenity, it may be helpful to note that there are certain common terms within the offences which have technical and specialised definitions. The two most common terms used in the offences are obscenity and indecency. Indecency will be discussed below in the context of the offences to which it relates; an example of the technical definition given to obscenity can be seen in the following case.

Obscenity

Whether an article is obscene is judged not by the standards of the defendant, nor by the personal opinions of the judge or jury, but according to whether the article itself, viewed objectively, has a tendency to "deprave and corrupt". This test dates back to the common law which preceded the current statutory offences, where the leading case was *R. v. Hicklin*. **6–012**

Deprave and Corrupt

In *R. v. Hicklin*[13] the defendant sold (not for profit) some 2,000 copies of a pamphlet entitled *The Confessional Unmasked*, exposing certain practices of the Catholic Church including the depravity of the Romish Priesthood, the immorality of the confessional, and the questions put to women in the confession. His intention was not to corrupt or prejudice the public mind but to deter people from becoming Catholics. The court defined "obscenity" as "whether the tendency of the matter charged as obscenity is to deprave and corrupt those whose minds are open to such immoral influences, and into whose hands a publication of this sort may fall".[14] The pamphlet, the court said, was obscene. It was "the most filthy and disgusting and unnatural description it is possible to imagine".[15] Although the intention of the defendant was not to injure public morals by the publication of the obscene article, the natural consequences of such a publication would automatically have that effect, and it is no defence to say that that was not the purpose or motive in publication. **6–013**

The Obscene Publications Act 1959[16] and 1964; Criminal Offences Relating to Obscenity

Section 2 of the Obscene Publications Act 1959 creates an offence of publishing an obscene article. The offence is triable either way, with a maximum penalty of three years' imprisonment. The three elements of the offence are: publication; obscenity; and "article", each of which will be examined separately. **6–014**

Publication is defined extremely broadly in section 1(3) as follows:

> ". . . a person publishes an article who—
>
> (a) distributes, circulates, sells, lets on hire, gives, or lends it, or who offers it for sale or for letting for hire; or
>
> (b) in the case of an article containing or embodying matter to be looked at or a record, shows, plays or projects it, or, where the matter is data stored electronically, transmits that data".

Since the 1959 Act was enacted, techniques for data storage and retrieval have become far more sophisticated, with the result that new methods of "publication" have had to be considered by the courts in order to decide whether they fall within the ambit of the offence.

The Internet is clearly covered by the fortunate wording of section 1(3) which was amended by the Criminal Justice and Public Order Act 1994 to include the reference to data stored electronically, but in 1959 few commentators would have been able to foresee the invention of videos, floppy disks or hard drives. Cases have largely absorbed new technology within the statutory meaning of publication, but there is still a residual area of uncertainty as to whether, for example, each individual involved in the process of "publishing" material on a website will commit the offence. In *Dash*[17] it was held that pornographic images stored on computer disks are "published" within the meaning of the section 2 offence. The court in *Fellows*[18] held that any image created or stored electronically could fall within the section 2 offence, and that when a person accessed the stored data then it was "shown, played or projected" to him.

6–015 An article as broadly defined by section 1(2) includes "any description of article containing or embodying any material to be read or looked at or both, any sound record, and any film or other record of a picture or pictures". It is clear that the article must be designed for viewing or reading, rather than for use. In *Conegate v. Commissioners for Customs and Excise*,[19] inflatable sex dolls were held not to fit within the definition of "articles" since they were intended for use rather than for visual inspection by the buyer.

Images stored on computer disks fall within the definition of "articles" since they are treated as if they were photographs; downloading pornography from bulletin boards on the Internet will therefore potentially be an offence.[20]

For the section 2 offence, the article which is published must be obscene. The definition given to "obscene" according to section 1(1) is as follows:

> ". . . an article shall be deemed to be obscene if its effect or (where the article comprises two or more distinct items) the effect of any one of the items is, if taken as a whole, such as to tend to 'deprave and corrupt' persons who are likely having regard to all relevant circumstances, to read, see or hear the matter contained or embodied in it."

Thus, the effect of the article is crucial in determining whether it is obscene. Obscenity is neither to be judged by the defendant's own subjective standards, nor by the purely objective standards of a reasonable man. It is the potential effect of the article upon its likely audience which is to be assessed. The "deprave and corrupt" test is derived from the common law, as seen in *Hicklin* (above) and the Act does not provide any statutory definition or amendment to the term. The "deprave and corrupt" test has caused a great deal of difficulty for courts entrusted with the task of its interpretation.

Meaning of the Words "Deprave and Corrupt"

The Preamble of the 1959 Act states "an Act to amend the law relating to the publication of obscene matter, to provide for the protection of literature, and to strengthen the law concerning pornography". Whether the Act has accomplished this can be stated with a resounding "no". The first case to come before the courts soon after its enforcement was that of *R. v. Penguin Books Ltd.*[21] This prosecution involved the publication of D.H. Lawrence's *Lady Chatterley's Lover.* Copies of the book were voluntarily handed over to the police by the publishers. The defence argued *inter alia* that the book was not obscene as described by section 1(1), *i.e.* not likely to deprave or corrupt others. The court defined "depravity" as meaning "to make morally bad, to pervert, to debase or corrupt morally". To "corrupt" meant "to render morally unsound or rotten, to destroy the moral purity or chastity, to pervert or ruin a good quality, to debase, to defile". Merely to be shocked or disgusted by its contents was not enough.[22] The jury returned after three hours deliberation with a verdict of not guilty. Within the first three months of the unexpurgated version going on sale, over one million copies of the book were sold. The DPP, in bringing this prosecution only succeeded, as is all too common nowadays, in increasing the sale of the book out of all proportion to what ordinarily would be expected under normal conditions. **6–016**

In deciding whether an article tends to deprave and corrupt, courts have failed to provide a clear explanation of the effects which the article must be shown to have on its potential audience. It is not necessary to show that physical harm would be caused to the reader in terms of distress or shock, and indeed such effects are irrelevant; but effects such as the encouragement of sexual fantasy, immorality or illegal conduct would be sufficient. An article will tend to deprave and corrupt if it causes the likely audience to stray from the general moral standards of society prevalent at the time and in the particular context of the article in question. It will therefore be important to show that the article was persuasive or coercive in tone or nature, since an explicit article cannot tend to deprave and corrupt if its overall tone is one of disapproval of the offensive behaviour which it portrays. Further, simply leading the public into immoral activities is not enough. Breaching some of society's moral standards will not be related to depravity and corruption, *e.g.* a text explaining how to commit corporate fraud may result in criminal liability for incitement of offences, but is unlikely to be considered obscene for this reason.[23]

Under section (1):

> "an article shall be deemed to be obscene if its effect or (where the article comprises two or more distinct items) the effect of any one of its items is, if taken as a whole, such as to tend to deprave and corrupt persons who are likely, having regard to all relevant circumstances, to read, see or hear the matter contained or embodied in it."

6–017 In *R. v. Clayton and Halsey*,[24] two undercover police officers purchased some obscene photographs from the defendants' shop. The defendants were charged with publishing obscene articles under section 2(1) of the OPA 1959. They were convicted and appealed on a point of law, *i.e.* whether it was necessary that the article tend to corrupt and deprave any individual or whether it must tend to deprave and corrupt the particular person who purchased the articles. The court held that the effect of the article must be considered in relation to the particular recipient, in this case the police officers. In evidence, these officers said that, as part of their work, they had seen thousands of similar photographs and were not affected by them. As a result, the appeal was allowed.

Under section 1(3) the word "publishes" has a very broad meaning and apart from its ordinary definition[25] includes the handing over to any person of an obscene article. Thus, merely having it in one's possession, without transferring the material onto someone else, would not constitute an offence under this particular Act. However, now under section 1 of the OPA 1964 all that is required under that section, is for a person to "have" an obscene article for publication for gain for the offence to be made out.

The Obscene Publications Act 1964

6–018 The 1964 Act amended section 2 of the 1959 Act to include an additional offence, that of having possession of an obscene article with a view to publication for gain. According to section 1(2), an article is possessed for gain if, with a view to publication, a person has the article in his ownership, possession or control. Under section 2(1), any person who whether for gain or not publishes an obscene article or who has an obscene article for publication for gain shall be liable under this section. For the purposes of any proceedings for an offence under section 2, a person shall be deemed to have an article for publication for gain if with a view to such publication he has the article in his ownership, possession or control (Obscene Publications Act 1964, s.1(2)).

Thus, for this offence, no publication of the article need actually be made, but the future publication which is expected must be "for gain" to some person, who need not be the person who possesses the article. No definition is given of "gain"; presumably money will be the most usual type of gain envisaged, but other forms of profit are not excluded, so the offence might well apply where a group of people intend to swap obscene videotapes amongst themselves without any payment being involved. This offence was added in order to deal with two situations in particular. First, where a charge under section 2(1) of the 1959 Act is inappropriate since the article has not yet even been offered for sale, but has merely been displayed, for example in a shop window.[26] Secondly, where a publication was made to a person who was unlikely to be depraved or corrupted by the article. An example of the latter can be seen in *Clayton and Halsey*[27] (see above).

In OPA 1964, section 1(3)(b):

> "... the question whether the article is obscene shall be determined by reference to such publication for gain of the article as in the circumstances it may reasonably be inferred he had in contemplation and to any further publication that could reasonably be expected to follow from it, but not to any other publication."

Once the proceedings have been issued regarding "having" as distinct from "publishing", it is up to the prosecution to prove that any consequence of publication involved some gain, financial or otherwise. Further, it must be shown that the defendant contemplated passing on the article to persons who were going to be depraved and corrupted by the article. If such persons were not going to be so, no offence is committed, *e.g.* to a friend, or selling the articles to police officers, for instance, who were familiar with such material and unlikely to pass it on.[28] However, under section 1(3)(b), if it can be shown that a further publication could reasonably be expected to follow, whereby those recipients came within the class of persons likely to be depraved and corrupted, then the offence is proved. Thus in *R. v. O'Sullivan*,[29] the defendant had in his control articles with a view to selling or offering them for sale to sex shops. Once this had proved to be reasonably contemplated, it was then up to the jury to decide whether, on reasonable grounds, these articles would eventually be published to the general public, *i.e.* sold or offered for sale, hired, etc., and whether a significant number of persons would be likely to be depraved and corrupted by the relevant articles. Therefore, section 1(1) of the OPA 1959 and section 1 of the OPA 1964 must be read in conjunction with each other where the articles have not as yet been published, but only where there is intention of publishing the article for gain.[30]

Significant proportion

Who must be depraved and corrupted by the article in question? The **6–019** answer is that the effect of the article upon every member of the likely audience must be considered, but it is only necessary for the prosecution to show that the article would tend to deprave and corrupt a significant proportion of that likely audience. Exactly what constitutes a significant proportion of the likely audience is a question of fact to be decided by the jury (or magistrates), but it is clear that the "number" need not be a majority.[31]

The question was further discussed in *DPP v. Whyte*[32]:

Facts. The defendant and his wife, who were booksellers, were charged with having obscene books for publication for gain contrary to section 2(1) of the OPA 1959. The titles of the books included *Sexus Defectus*, *Giving it Away*, *Dear Cissy* and a magazine entitled *Dingle Dangle No. 3*. Regular customers of the bookshop were mostly men of middle age and upwards, although a minority were middle aged women and young people of both sexes. Whenever possible, the defendants did try to prevent those under 18 years of age from either entering the shop or going to the particular section where the "adult only" books were on show. The question for the court at first instance was (1) who were the "likely" persons to read or view the relevant material, and (2) did the articles have a tendency to corrupt and deprave a significant proportion of such persons? In answer to (1) the likely persons were middle aged and older men. Regarding (2), the justices described these regular customers as "inadequate, pathetic, dirty minded men seeking cheap thrills, addicts to this type of material whose morals were already in a state of depravity and corruption." They were not convinced that the books would deprave and corrupt a significant proportion of those men since the latter were unlikely to be further depraved and corrupted by the contents of these books. Accordingly, the defendants were acquitted. The prosecutor appealed. The Divisional Court dismissed the prosecutor's appeal. Thereupon, the DPP appealed on a point of law of general public importance, *i.e.* whether on the facts found and on the inferences drawn the justices were bound to convict.

Decision. Lord Wilberforce stated that "the Act is not merely concerned with the once for all corruption of the wholly innocent; it equally protects the less innocent from further corruption, the addict from feeding or increasing his addiction".[33] He argued that if one cannot corrupt a person who is already corrupted, then that assumes that the article in question is an obscene article, and if the justices are correct, and it cannot corrupt, since these likely readers are already depraved and corrupted by these articles, then the case is proved, albeit by a somewhat circular argument. Lord Cross was of similar mind and said that these corruptable persons were, by purchasing these books, being maintained in a state of depravity and corruption. Continuing that depravity takes time and the degree of corruption becomes deeper the more such persons visit these bookshops and purchase these obscene materials. Lord Salmon, dissenting, stated that there was no evidence that these "dirty old men" were not corrupted prior to being customers of the respondents, nor that they deteriorated further from reading or looking at more obscene material. The justices' decision (which he somewhat questioned) was on a finding of fact. He thought there was no point of law which could alter that decision and therefore he dismissed the appeal. However, by an overall majority of 3:2 the appeal was allowed.

This decision has some interesting implications. First, it treats pornography as having a "drip, drip" effect which leads to a state of addiction. Secondly, it seems to imply that a person may become "born again" as a person free from sexual addiction. As has been stated, it is whether an article tends to deprave and corrupt its likely audience which must be considered by the court in order to determine whether the article in question is obscene. It is thus necessary to consider how courts define the likely audience of an article; who are the likely persons upon whom the effect of the article is to be assessed?

"likely persons"

6–020 "An article cannot be considered obscene by itself, it can only be so in relation to its likely readers."[34] As was stated in *R. v. Calder*, "likely persons" cannot mean only one person, or necessarily a majority of persons or even the average recipient of the material, or only the most likely, but must include all other likely persons, whatever their age, sex, education, characteristics, etc. Persons which may be excluded are a negligible number (but which cannot be determined) and those unlikely to be involved. In *DPP v. Whyte*, not only middle aged men but any others who were likely to purchase material from the bookshop were to be included. Thus, unless it can be proved that only one class of individuals were involved, all other classes of likely persons must be taken into account. It may be the case that if only one likely class is considered out of many the significant proportion may be negligible. Other classes by themselves may constitute a negligible number, but added together may amount to a significant proportion for the purposes of a successful prosecution.

If the amount of persons who purchase the book is more than merely negligible then, provided there are some other likely persons involved in the purchases, the offence is made out. However, this is not a general rule and will vary according to, as his Lordship said, "the different character" of the particular book.[35] Lord Pearson, when discussing the "likely readers"[36] to be corrupted by obscene material gave the example that a serious medical book which was unlikely to be made available to persons not within the medical fraternity would not be considered to be obscene since its readership would be unlikely to be corrupted by its contents. However, there seems to be no reason why those who read such books would not themselves also be depraved and corrupted by the information therein contained. But, no doubt it would fail "the significant proportion" test. Lord Pearson also put forward the proposition that a potential criminal might sell a pornographic book knowing that only a small number out of the total will be corrupted by it. Does this mean that he may avoid prosecution in this case? His Lordship thought not. To reiterate, as stated in *O'Sullivan*[37] (as affirmed on appeal):

> "It is not necessary . . . to prove that anyone was depraved and corrupted by reading or seeing the article . . . The expression 'deprave and corrupt' is directed to the effect on the mind, to those who might be exposed to the material . . . The fact that the article in question is sold in premises frequented only by persons who are already depraved and who go there for the purpose of feeding their depravity, is not in itself sufficient to negative obscenity . . . it may or may not be your experience, and this is entirely a matter for you, that reading and viewing pornographic magazines and video recordings is not necessarily confined to the purchasers of these articles. They may be shown to others as a stimulus and spur to inducing a particular frame of mind, or inviting them to adopt a course of conduct similar to that kind illustrated by the material."

The defence of the aversion effect

A publication which causes the reader or viewer to feel revulsion, horror or **6–021**
disgust may not constitute obscene material if the result is that the recipient of this information is so revolted that it has the opposite effect and wholly

discourages that person from participating in those activities and therefore is unlikely to be depraved and corrupted. Thus, in: *R. v. Calder and Boyars Ltd*[38]:

Facts. The defendants were charged with (1) having an obscene article, namely a book entitled, Last Exit to Brooklyn and (2) publishing that same book contrary to section 2(1) of the OPA 1959. The book concerned the depraved and degrading way of life in Brooklyn. The defendendant argued that although it was shocking, horrific and outrageous, it did not encourage its readers to drug-taking, homosexuality or violence as depicted. Instead, its contents had the reverse reaction of one of revulsion and pity for that particular way of life. The defendants were nevertheless convicted.

Decision. The defendants appealed on the grounds that:

(1) the judge failed in his summing up to direct the jury adequately on the meaning of the word "obscene";

(2) the judge gave no proper direction to the jury on the section 4 "public good" defence (see page 260 *et seq.*, public good defence below); and

(3) the judge did not mention the defence of aversion on the issue of obscenity to the jury. In (1) above, Lord Salmon L.J. discussed how the jury should have been directed regarding the meaning of the word "likely persons" in section 1(1). He rejected that it necessarily meant all persons, or one person, or "the majority of persons or the average reader" who read the book. If the test for obscenity was governed purely by such persons, how could a defence for the public good in section 4 ever be successful. The proper direction was whether the article depraved and corrupted a significant proportion of those persons likely to read it, and it was for the jury to decide this question. Just what constitutes a significant proportion is a matter for the jury.[39] In (3) above, the judge at first instance did not put the defendant's argument on obscenity to the jury, *i.e.* that apart from a small minority "a minute lunatic fringe" of readers, the book's description of the degradation of living in Brooklyn would wholly discourage readers from emulating those individuals in the book, through revulsion, disgust and horror at such activities as drug-taking, violence, and homosexuality. Since this defence was not put to the jury, such an omission seriously prejudiced the defendants case and accordingly, the appeal was allowed.

6–022 In *R. v. Anderson*[40]:

Facts. The defendants were publishers of a magazine called "*Oz No. 28 School Kids Issue*". They were charged with, *inter alia*, publishing an obscene magazine and having obscene magazines for publication for gain contrary to section 2 of the OPA 1959. The contents of the particular magazine contained articles and pictures detailing items of a sexually explicit nature, including lesbianism, oral sex, and drugs. There were also some tame but nevertheless serious articles about school education in general. Some 20 days out of the full 27–day trial were taken up with expert opinion on whether or not the magazine itself was obscene. The judge in his summing up directed the jury that "obscene" meant its ordinary dictionary meaning of "repulsive, filthy, lewd and loathsome", and when deciding the issue the jury should consider these expressions. At trial the defendants argued, that although the illustrations were lewd and unpleasant, their effect would instead lead to repulsion and disgust and would discourage its readers from participating in such activities. Expert evidence was given by a psychiatrist to support this contention. The judge, however, failed to direct the jury adequately on this issue. The three defendants were convicted and imprisoned for periods of nine months and upwards each.

Decision. The grounds of appeal were (1) the judge misdirected the jury on the meaning of "obscene", and (2) the judge erred in not putting to the jury the aversive argument submitted by the defendant. Lord Widgery C.J. stated that expert evidence was not permitted to show whether or not the article was obscene, that remained solely for the jury to decide. Although it was wrongly admitted in this case, it did not damage the defendant's arguments. However, regarding (1), he said that including the words "lewd", filthy, etc., into the formula of obscenity, broadened the existing statutory definition of obscenity, *i.e.* to deprave and corrupt. There was a grave danger that the jury might consider such words as lewd, etc., in the same context as "obscene", which is not the same in its legal sense. Lord Widgery considered that the failure by the judge not to mention the aversion effect arguments adequately, together with the wide, incorrect meaning given to obscenity, amounted to "a very substantial and serious misdirection". Accordingly, on these specific charges, the appeal was allowed.

The public good defence section 4

The framers of the Obscene Publications Act 1959 were conscious of the **6–023** need to avoid censorship or banning of works which are truly of artistic merit—great literature may be explicit, and its creators are therefore exempted from criminal liability under section 2, and also from the forfeiture provisions under section 3 (discussed below). The main method by which the 1959 Act creates this exemption is the "public good" defence found in section 4 of the Act. This defence in effect justifies the publication of some obscene articles on the basis that the right to freedom of expression of some ideas outweighs arguments in favour of suppressing obscene speech.

Section 4(1) provides that the defence exists where:

> "publication of the article is justified as being for the public good on the ground that it is in the interests of science, literature, art or learning, or of other objects of general concern."

Thus it is not the article itself which must be shown to be for the public good, but the publication of the article. A court must balance the obscenity contained in the article against any of the listed merits which the article may contain. Under section 4 of this Act, the defendant has a defence if he can prove that publication of the article in question was justified as being for the public good on the ground that it was in the interest of science, literature, art or learning or of other objects of general concern. Under section 4, if the material contained in books and magazines did not deprave or corrupt its likely recipients, then that is the end of the matter. But if the court does deem the material to be obscene, then the defendant can argue that under the circumstances the publication was justified for the public good on the grounds that it is in the interest of those categories set out in section 4(1). Merely, because something is *per se* literary, it does not follow that the courts will sanction publication, it must further be shown that it was for the public good. In *R. v. Penguin*, the proper direction to the jury should have been that "if it was obscene, then if the defendant had established on a balance of probabilities that the merits of the book were so high that they outbalanced the obscenity so that the publication was for the public good, the jury should acquit."[41] Thus, the burden of proof upon the defendant is that of a balance of probabilities as opposed to that of beyond reasonable doubt. Under section 4(2) expert evidence is admissible as to the merits of the material but should be restricted to the literary issues involved and not the ethical issues which are outside the literary ambit of the respective material.[42] In *Attorney-General's Reference (No. 3 of 1977)*[43] the question of what is the meaning of "learning" in section 4(1) was discussed and whether the relevant article can be shown to have merit in the field of sex education or teaching about sexual matters. It was decided that "learning" meant "the product of scholarship.. . something whose inherent excellence is gained by the work of the scholar". Regarding the words "objects of general concern, Lord Wilberforce said in *DPP v. Jordan* that the words mean "fall within the same area and cannot fall in the total different area of effect on (in this instance) sexual behaviour and attitudes . . .".[44]

6–024 In *DPP v. Jordan*[45]:

Facts. The defendant owned a bookshop where she sold obscene material including films, books and magazines contrary to section 2(1) of the OPA 1959, as amended by section 1(1) of the OPA 1964. She was charged with 37 counts of possession of obscene articles for gain. The material was described as "hard pornography", detailing graphic sexual practises including perversion, brutality, group sex, fetishes, etc. She was convicted and appealed to the Court of Appeal. Her appeal was dismissed and the case eventually went to the House of Lords.

Decision. The appeal was based on the section 4 public good defence. The appellant submitted that the judge erred in law in not allowing expert evidence to be admitted to support the defence that pornographic material was psychologically beneficial to persons with certain sexual tendencies and may divert them from anti-social activities. The appellant argued that the words "objects of general concern", for the public good included the psychological health of the community. In this instance, the expert evidence to be given would say that all pornographic material had some psychotherapeutic value for certain individuals, including deviants, and therefore would act as an aid for those persons and prevent them from committing future anti-social or criminal behaviour. However, their Lordships held that the expert evidence had been rightfully rejected on the grounds that the psychological sexual benefit for a minority of people did not come within the framework of "objects of general concern". "Objects of general concern" should relate back to the "intellectual or aesthetic values"[46] of those or similar categories specified in section 4(1). In this case, the sexual benefits to those individuals was unrelated to the words of section 4.

The interests of a specific group of individuals are irrelevant, *i.e.* its effects on these persons are not pertinent when considering a defence under section 4. What is relevant is the wider issues of intellectual pursuit, the intrinsic value and merit of the particular article. Further, if an expert cannot find merits other than the obscenity itself, then section 4 cannot be used as a defence. There must be some other characteristics in the obscene article which outbalances its obscenity, *i.e.* some literary, artistic, scientific or other merit which must be found to be for the public good.

Where a person fails to introduce expert evidence into the proceedings **6–025**
under section 1, he may then, hope to get a second bite of the cherry and try to admit such evidence via a section 4 defence. But the elements are fundamentally different. Section 1 deals with depravity and corruption and with its effects on likely persons whilst, section 4 deals with the public good and the merits of the material as a part of literature.[47]

The jury must be given guidance in the summing up by the judge on the public good defence. The defence is only relevant once the jury consider the article obscene in the legal sense under the Act. They should be informed that:

> "(they) must consider on the one hand, the number of readers they believe would tend to be depraved and corrupted by the book, the strength of the tendency to deprave and corrupt, and the nature of the depravity and corruption; on the other hand, they should assess the strength of the literary, sociological or ethical merit which they consider the book to possess. They should then weigh up all these factors and decide whether on balance the publication is proved to be justified as being for the public good".[48]

One of the inherent problems of such a direction is one of consistency. In one part of the country, for instance, a jury may well consider an article as for the public good, whereas in another area the jury may find that the balance lies in the relevant article being obscene and accordingly a successful prosecution would result. Such inconsistencies lead to uncertainty in the law and confidence by the public in the legal system being eroded. Since moral values are at stake, the jury's task goes far beyond the mere finding of fact, in that they have to determine the question of obscenity from their own subjective viewpoint.

Normally, the courts will not permit the defendant to argue that the relevant article is not obscene because there are other similar articles in circulation which have not been made the subject matter of any prosecution, or in fact deemed obscene. However, where the public good defence is raised, it was stated in *R. v. Penguin* that in order for the jury to properly consider the merits of the relevant article, it was necessary that the jury be allowed to compare the defendant's book to similar books in that particular area of literature in order to reach a just and fair decision.

Expert Evidence

Under section 4(2) of this Act, expert evidence is admissible as to the **6–026**
literary, artistic, scientific or other merits of an article in order to establish or to negative the said ground. But the orthodox line of authority holds that

expert evidence is not admissible when it is the issue of obscenity which is being determined.[49] However, in some cases courts seem to have been willing to allow such evidence in circumstances where it should have been inadmissible; this shows the complexity of the issues and legal arguments involved in an obscenity trial, which may even sidetrack a court from the principles which it is supposed to be applying.

In *R. v. Skirving*[50]:

Facts. The defendants were charged under section 2(1) of the OPA 1959 for having 11 obscene articles entitled "Attention Coke Lovers—Freebasing, the Greatest Thing since Sex" for publication for gain. The book contained instructions and methods for taking cocaine to get the optimum effect, including, injection, snorting and smoking. Expert evidence was admissible which related to the medical effect of taking drugs. The judge allowed the evidence on the grounds that the effects of such drugs was not within the experience or knowledge of ordinary jurors. They were convicted and appealed.

Decision. The main grounds for the appeal were: (1) the judge was wrong to admit expert evidence on the effect of taking drugs, including cocaine; (2) in allowing the expert evidence, the defendants were prejudiced since the jury would put undue weight on the question of whether the cocaine tended to deprave and corrupt and not give enough attention as to whether the book itself tended to deprave and corrupt. The court said that the expert evidence was rightly admitted. The purpose of the evidence was to explain the nature of the drugs and their likely effects. This was necessary since such knowledge was not within the ordinary juror's expertise. The contents of the books were not experiences which the ordinary person would come into contact with during their normal every day life. It was necessary in order for the jury to determine the extent, if any, of the book's ability to deprave and corrupt for the effects on its likely readers to be explained to the jury. The court felt that without such evidence it would have been difficult to come to a fair decision. Lord Lane quoted from Lord Mansfield in *Folker v. Chadd*[51]

> ". . . The fact that an expert witness has impressive scientific qualifications does not by that fact alone make his opinion on matters of public nature and behaviour within the limits of normality any more helpful than that of the jurors themselves; but there is a danger that they may think it does."

The appeal was dismissed.

6–027 It has been argued by R. Stone—successfully, it is submitted—that the expert evidence in *Skirving* was irrelevant, because the evidence given concerned the effects of taking cocaine which was not the issue of the case. The relevant issue was whether the book itself was obscene, *i.e.* whether it would deprave and corrupt its likely readers. The jury in deciding that question did not lack the necessary experience to decide that point and required no guidance from experts in that area to make up its own mind. Allowing such evidence would tend only to confuse the jury on what it was they were deciding. Indeed, that was one of the grounds of appeal submitted by the defendants in that case.[52]

Whether to admit expert evidence in future cases will depend on the nature of the article. There is the danger that expert opinion given in these instances may influence the jury beyond its intention. Lord Lane said that drugs were not the same as sexual behaviour, which is within the experience of ordinary people. But with respect, there are many categories of sexual activities some of which are so abnormal and deviant (see below *R. v. Jordan*) that it may be necessary to introduce expert evidence to explain its likely effect on the persons who may seek to indulge in such activities. On the other hand, the smoking of cannabis, for instance, has become so commonplace, though even a drug, would it be really necessary to introduce expert evidence on its effects? Whether to admit or reject such evidence would be the unenviable decision for the judge to make.

In *DPP v. A and BC Chewing Gum Ltd*[53] the defendants were sellers of packets of bubble gum. Inside these packets were cards which showed violent war scenes. The main market for this gum was targeted towards young people, especially children. Expert evidence was allowed to show how these children would likely be affected by these cards. Lord Parker[54] stated that "as a general rule, a longstanding rule at common law, evidence is inadmissible if it is on the very issue the court has to determine". The main questions were, what sort of effect would those cards have on young people and children, what would it lead them to do? Since the effect was outside the knowledge of the ordinary jurors, evidence was permitted by a psychiatrist with the relevant expertise in this area, to adduce from the cards themselves what their effect on a child would be. However, the evidence must not be extended to ask whether these cards would tend to deprave and corrupt the young—that is for the justices or jury to decide. In *DPP v. Jordan*[55] it was stated that it was for the jury alone to decide whether the article would deprave or corrupt. Lord Wilberforce said that "(the jury) cannot be told by psychologists or anyone else what the effect of the material on normal minds may be".[56] If it were otherwise, what would be the point of swearing in a jury to decide something what has already been decided. **6–028**

Other Available Defences

The 1959 Act also provides a further defence which is typical of those available to strict liability in criminal offences, and takes the form of a denial of knowledge of the nature of the material published. Under section 2(5), a defendant will escape liability for the publication of an obscene article if he can prove that: (i) he had not examined the article; and (ii) he did not have any "reasonable cause to suspect" that the article was obscene. This defence will obviously be more useful to those who distribute articles produced by other people than to those who create the articles in the first place, since an originator of an article will have extreme difficulty in proving that he is ignorant of its obscene nature. Under section 2(5) of the 1959 Act, if the defendant can prove that he was not aware or had no reasonable cause to suspect that it was obscene material, then he will be acquitted. This particular defence is especially relevant to retailers or **6–029** wholesalers who deal in many different types of books, magazines and videos. Subsection 5 states that the defendant must prove "that he did not examine the article" in question, but even a cursory look may be sufficient to put the defendant on notice that obscene material may be contained in that particular article. Even if proof is accepted that no examination was made, but that nevertheless the defendant had reasonable cause to suspect that the material was obscene, then he may still be convicted. For example, a regular supplier of "soft-porn" convinces his retailer to buy a new magazine on the market for his more "discerning customers" which has a highly sexual provocative title, the retailer ought reasonably to suspect that there is a probability the article may contain potentially obscene material. A similar defence exists[57] for the offence of possession of an obscene article with a view to publication for gain, contrary to section 2 as amended by the 1964 Obscene Publications Act.

Forfeiture procedure

6–030 Where criminal proceedings have not been issued,[58] the police may instead take legal action against the obscene articles themselves, by way of forfeiture. This is achieved by the issue of a warrant under section 3 of the OPA 1959. Under section 3 of this Act, once the police have reasonable grounds for suspecting that a person has obscene articles on his premises[59] for publication for gain, they may apply to the local magistrate for a warrant to enter and search such premises, and seize the obscene articles. Under section 3(2), a legally issued warrant also permits the police to seize any documents relating to the trade or business carried on at those premises. The warrant must be precise on the issue of what exactly is the purpose of the search. If an information is too general, then the granting of the warrant should be refused. Thus, in *Darbo v. DPP*,[60] where the warrant stated "any other material of a sexual explicit nature, also any material relating to the running of the business", was held to be too imprecise, since the words "sexually explicit nature" could include material which was less than obscene. As a result, the warrant was invalid. Under section 3(3), any articles seized must be given over to the magistrate who issued the warrant in order to decide whether the articles should be forfeited or not. Normally, a summons will be issued to the occupier of the relevant premises, to appear before the court and show cause why any or all of the articles should not be forfeited. Indeed, under section 3(4), all interested persons are allowed to go before the court and give reasons why the articles should not be forfeited. These "interested persons" include authors, general publishers, suppliers, purchasers or controllers of the articles. Once cause has been rejected, or not given at all, then the magistrate will issue an order for the obscene articles to be destroyed. Otherwise, the articles should be released back to the relevant persons. It is not necessary for the magistrate to sift through each and every article in order to determine which ones constitute obscene material.[61]

Thus, in *R. v. Snaresbrook Crown Court ex parte Commissioner of Police of the Metropolis*[62]: **6–031**

Facts. The police were issued with warrants to search and seize obscene material from various premises in East London under section 3 of the OPA 1959. The relevant magistrates court issued under section 3(3) a summons in respect of 152,263 magazines, 2,864 books, 447 films and 197 videos. Further, under section 3(3), the possessors of the material gave evidence as to why it should not be forfeited. The court ordered approximately 70 per cent of the material to be forfeited. The possessors appealed against the decision. The respondents (the police) and the appellants (the companies) were requested by Judge Stable Q.C. from the Snaresbrook Crown Court to divide the material into three classes and take samples from each, from the most innocent to the most obscene.

Decision. The applicant (the police) submitted that: (1) viewing or reading only samples of materials and judging the whole by these samples was wrong in law; (2) the incorrect criteria were operated under section 363. It was not up to the police to take samples and make judgments as to what material in their opinion amounted to, or did not amount to, obscenity. It was stated that to examine each and every article in order to decide the obscenity question was, as Watkins L.J. said, a burden of "awesome proportions" on a judge. Thus, the judge, he said, was entitled to ask for samples to be taken to "enable him fairly to adjudicate upon the question in relation to all articles seized of whether or not the allegation of obscenity was made out".[64] However, the samples must be (a) properly representative of the whole and (b) a full explanation of the method in which the sampling was carried out must be given to the appellants. Once that has been achieved, it is unlikely that a higher court will overturn the issue on the question of fairness as a result of the judge's decision.

Summary of Obscenity

The basic requirements for obscenity of an article are that it must, if: **6–032**

(a) taken as a whole
(b) tend to deprave and corrupt
(c) a significant proportion
(d) of likely persons.[65]

Thus, in (a), particular passages may be obscene ("purple passages"), but that may not suffice, if the article, taken as a whole, does not fulfil the necessary requirements. However, if the article is made up of separate and distinct items, *e.g.* a magazine, then, each item may be considered separately, and if at least one is obscene then the whole article will be obscene (*R. v. Penguin*). In (b), the words were defined in *R. v. Hicklin*. In (c), the words are indefinable—can mean less than 50 per cent but more than a negligible number of persons (*DPP v. Whyte*). In (d), the words refer to the class of persons likely to read, see or hear the relevant article, taking into account age, gender, characteristics, etc. The following points should be noted:

(1) The obscene article need not be limited to sexual matters. (*John Calder v. Powell*).

(2) The intention of the owner, author or publisher is irrelevant. The only intention required is that of publishing. (*R. v. Hicklin*).

(3) It is effect of the obscene article on the mind of the person that is important, not whether the person takes some positive active step in fulfilling, for example, his fantasies.

(4) It is for the jury or magistrates to decide whether or not the particular article is obscene.

(5) Expert evidence is normally not admissible as to the effects of the article. However, expert opinion is permissible where (a) the defence of public good is concerned, but only on the issue of merit; (b) where juries do not have experience on the relevant issues (*A and BC Chewing Gum*).

Other Offences of Obscenity: Theatres Act 1968

6–033 Obscenity offences do not only cover written or other visual material. The Theatres Act 1968 relates to live performances of plays and ballets, and replaces the previous system of prior restraint, whereby the Lord Chamberlain had to be provided with a copy of the script for any such performance in advance and had a power to censor or veto any future performance of the work.[66] Such censorship proved an effective method of control of the theatre, but was highly controversial by the 1950s when British theatre was becoming more experimental and dealing with issues of social concern which might offend the more conservative members of the community. Pre-censorship could prevent the performance of works which have since become somewhat "consensus" and are now regarded as classics rather than as threats to the very fabric of society.[67] As a more practical point, the requirement of provision of a script for approval in advance of the performance obviously ruled out such now commonplace and popular types of performance as improvisation or extended monologues where the performer is left to flesh out and deviate from an outline script. For these and other reasons, the Joint Committee on Censorship of the Theatre recommended that the pre-censorship system should cease and be replaced by criminal offences and sanctions parallel to those covering printed articles.[68]

The offence under section 2 of the 1968 Act is committed by any person who presents or directs an obscene performance of a play.[69] A "play" is defined widely to include (section 18):

> "(a) any dramatic piece, whether involving improvisation or not, which is given wholly or in part by one or more persons actually present and performing and in which the whole or a major proportion of what is done by the persons performing, whether by way of speech, singing or acting, involves the playing of a role; and
> (b) any ballet given wholly or in part by one or more persons actually present and performing . . ."

The actors or performers are not liable for the offence, which is targeted rather at those who direct or arrange the relevant performance. Obscenity is defined in section 2(1): **6–034**

> "a performance of a play shall be deemed to be obscene if, taken as a whole, its effect was such as to tend to deprave and corrupt persons who were likely, having regard to all the circumstances, to attend it."

Thus the definition of obscenity in this context is the same as that used in the Obscene Publications Act 1959. It should be noted that it is the performance as a whole, not merely the script, which must be adjudged obscene in its context.

Section 3 provides for a defence of public good which is similar to that under the Obscene Publications Act 1959. The defence is made out if "the giving of the performance in question was justified as being for the public good on the ground that it was in the interests of drama, opera, ballet or any other art, or of literature or learning" (section 3(1)). Expert evidence is admissible in order to prove or to disprove the public good defence (section 3(2)). Common law indecency and conspiracy offences cannot be charged in relation to plays: section 2(4).

There have in fact been very few prosecutions commenced under section 2, partly because the consent of the Attorney-General is required (section 8). Controls on theatrical productions tend to come from practical rather than from legal sources, for example the need to keep those who fund a production happy, to ensure a consistent and appreciative audience, to secure favourable reviews. For other legal controls on the theatre, see the discussion of the Public Order Act 1986, section 20 below, which relates to threatening or insulting behaviour in a play which may stir up racial hatred.

Public Order Act 1986

Section 20 of the 1986 Act returns us to the topic of public performances of plays, but deals with a different mischief from the Theatres Act 1968; offensive words or behaviour which are likely to stir up racial hatred. Although this topic could be dealt with under various chapter headings, it is covered here for the sake of completeness. The offence in section 20(1) is as follows: **6–035**

> "If a public performance of a play is given which involves the use of threatening, abusive, or insulting words or behaviour, any person who presents or directs the performance is guilty of an offence if—
>
> (a) he intends thereby to stir up racial hatred, or
> (b) having regard to all the circumstances (and, in particular, taking the performance as a whole) racial hatred is likely to be stirred up thereby."

A person presenting or directing such a performance will have a defence if he can prove that he neither knew nor had any reason to suspect any one of the following (section 20(2)):

(a) that the performance would involve the use of the offending words or behaviour (for example, where a performer makes an unexpected outburst on stage); or

(b) that the offending words or behaviour were threatening, abusive or insulting (for example where a performer makes a "hidden" threat which will only be understood by the victim); or

(c) that the circumstances in which the performance would be given would be such that racial hatred would be likely to be stirred up (for example where a large proportion of the audience is made up of racists who are looking for a fight).

"Play" and "performance" have the same meanings as in the Theatres Act 1968, and the exemptions in the latter statute relating to performances for the purpose of rehearsal, recording or broadcast apply here too. The section 20 offence has parallels both with that under the Theatres Act 1968, and with those relating to harassment elsewhere in the Public Order Act 1986 and in the Protection from Harassment Act 1997. "Threatening, abusive or insulting" have the same meanings as used elsewhere in the Public Order Act 1986, discussed in an earlier chapter.

Indecency: Introduction

6–036 The Obscene Publications Acts are by no means the only source of censorship of publications or control of behaviour which is considered offensive. There are a number of statutory criminal offences under a variety of statutes which deal with offensive material, and there is also a residual bracket of offences at common law. Each of these offences will be discussed separately, but many of them employ a common central concept, "indecency", which will be discussed first. Whilst most of the cases on this topic do involve pornography or sexual behaviour, it should be remembered that, like obscenity, indecency does not have to relate to sex or sexuality; both obscenity and indecency involve breaking the moral standards of society in any manner.

What is indecency? Lord Reid in *Knuller v. DPP*[70] said "apart from statutory offences of application, (discussed below) there appears to be neither precedent nor authority of any kind of punishing the publication of written or printed matter on the ground that it is indecent as distinct from being obscene". Indecency reflects what the general public view as being against the moral standards of present-day living, *i.e.* anything which is construed as highly offensive, shocking, revolting, disgusting or outraging.[71]

6–037 In *R. v. Stanley*[72]:

Facts. The defendant was a film-maker who sold films to a mail order company. In answer to an advertisement, the company sent a film brochure to a 14 year old boy.

The defendant and the company were charged with, *inter alia*, sending two packets, namely brochures, through the post containing an indecent and obscene article, contrary to section 11(1)(b) of the Post Office Act 1953. Section 11(1) of the Post Office Act 1953 states that "a person shall not send . . . a postal package which . . . (b) encloses any indecent or obscene, print, painting, photograph, book, . . . film, (etc . . .)". The jury acquitted the defendants on the obscene aspect of the indictment but convicted him on the grounds that the brochures (and films, which were the subject of other charges) where indecent. The defendant appealed.

Decision. He appealed on the grounds, *inter alia*, that the words "obscene or indecent" as phrased had the same meaning, and once the jury acquitted him of not having material which was obscene, taking the words conjunctively, should also have acquitted him completely on that count. Lord Parker C.J. said that "the words 'indecent or obscene' convey one idea, namely, offending against the recognised standards of propriety, indecent being at the lower end of the scale and obscene at the upper end of the scale".[73] The court held that he was charged conjunctively although he could have been charged in the alternative, and added that "an indecent article is not necessarily obscene, whereas, an obscene article almost certainly must be indecent".[74] Accordingly, the appeal was dismissed.

Indecent Language and Behaviour

Indecent language may cause offence and revulsion to the average, decent **6–038**
person. However, whether the language can be categorised as legally indecent will depend on all the circumstances in which the offensive words were spoken, including the occasion, and in some instances what the intention of the speaker was. Thus, in *Wiggins v. Field*,[75] the defendant during a poetry recital spoke the offending words as part of a poem entitled "America: Go fuck yourself with your atom bomb". He was charged with using indecent language, contrary to a bylaw enacted under section 23 of the Municipal Corporation Act 1882. He was acquitted. On appeal by the prosecutor, it was decided that in the context of which the words were said, *i.e.* a serious poem by a well-known poet, and without any intent to be offensive, the language was not considered indecent. Although in other circumstances, said by someone else, the same words could be construed as indecent whether intentional or not.

However, in *Abrahams v. Cavey*,[76] the words, "Oh, you hypocrites, how can you use the words of God to justify your policies?" (the speaker was protesting against British support for American policy on Vietnam), whilst if said in a private house or on a public street would probably not constitute an indecent remark, spoken in a church, in front of politicians, and resulting in interrupting the service, the magistrates decided would offend against the recognised standards of propriety and the defendants were convicted of indecent behaviour.[77] Thus, foul language is not necessary for there to be a conviction for indecent behaviour. What is more important is where and in what circumstances the remark is made. Merely because the words are insulting does not necessarily mean that they are also indecent. Calling someone a "bastard", may be insulting but would not be considered to be by the ordinary person, by today's standards at least, indecent language.[78]

Indecency is a concept which is also found elsewhere in criminal law, for example, in the offences of indecent assault contrary to sections 14 and 15 of the Sexual Offences Act 1956, and case law on these offences may be helpful in formulating a definition of indecency for the purposes of the offences to be discussed in the remainder of this chapter. In indecent assault, indecency is clearly an objective concept; the test is whether "right-minded persons" would consider the defendant's actions to be "offensive to contemporary standards of modesty and privacy".[79] An action or article will either be objectively indecent, objectively decent, or ambiguous (capable of being regarded as either indecent or decent). The defendant's motive or secret enjoyment cannot render indecent that which is objectively decent; but if the action or article is ambiguous, then the defendant's motive will be relevant in determining whether the circumstances are indecent.[80]

Each of the specific statutory provisions creating indecency offences will now be examined in turn.

Post Office Act 1953

6–039 The offences created by the Post Office Acts 1953 relate to the sending of obscene material by post. It is an offence under section 11 of the Act to send, attempt to send, or to procure to be sent, a packet which contains any indecent or obscene article. "Obscene" in this context is given its normal dictionary meaning, not the special meaning used in the Obscene Publications Acts; thus it is not necessary for the prosecution to prove that the article would tend to deprave and corrupt any person. It is also unnecessary to show that the packet either did have, or would have had, any effect upon the actual recipient. "Procuring" an article to be sent includes ordering such an article by mail order or, presumably, via the Internet or telephone, so that in some circumstances the recipient of the obscene or indecent article will be liable in addition to the person who sent it.

Section 11(1)(c) creates a further offence of sending a postal packet, the outside of which is grossly offensive, indecent or obscene.

Under the Post Office Act 1953, the test of indecency is objective and the personal qualities of the recipient, *i.e.* age, gender, etc., and its effect on that person are immaterial. It is not a defence to say that the material was sent only to persons who would not find it indecent.[81] The test of objectivity would no doubt refer to the ordinary decent person, whose level of morality is that of the present-day standard of the average individual. It was stated in *Shaw v. DPP*,[82] by Lord Morris that:

> "even if accepted public standards may to some extent vary from generation to generation, current standards are in the keeping of juries, who can be trusted to maintain the corporate good sense of the community and to discern attacks upon values that must be preserved."

What is relevant is whether the material itself which is sent is of an indecent nature.[83] Thus, presumably it would be an offence to send oneself an indecent book, video, etc. through the post. Further, it is up to the jury to decide this matter without the aid of expert opinion on whether the material is indecent or not.[84]

Unsolicited Goods and Services Act 1971: Introduction

The Unsolicited Goods and Services Act 1971 deals with a particular mischief, that of material sent through the postal system or delivered otherwise to a person without the recipient having requested the material. It used to be a common sales ploy for publishers of books or producers of goods to send undemanded items to individuals, together with an invoice demanding payment before a particular date. This arrangement is not, and never has been, enforceable in contract law due to the principle that silence cannot form acceptance of a contract.[85] Since most people who received such goods were ignorant of the rules of contract law and in fact did not return them to the sender, instead paying the "debt", this could be a successful and profitable method of getting rid of goods which had proved difficult to sell in a more legitimate manner. The main aim of the legislation was to stop this practice, and so a statutory declaration was made in the Act to the effect that unsolicited goods will become the property of the recipient unless the sender himself makes arrangements for the return of the goods within a reasonable time. However, the Act was also seen as an opportunity to create a criminal offence which is far more relevant to our present discussion. Section 4 of the Act deals with the sending of unsolicited material which is sexually explicit. **6–040**

It is an offence under section 4 for a person to send, or to cause to be sent, unsolicited material which describes or illustrates human sexual techniques. The material sent may take the form of a book, a magazine, a leaflet, or material which advertises some other publication.

This Act was enacted for the protection of persons receiving unsolicited publications. Under section 4(1), it is an offence to send advertising material which is unsolicited and which describes or illustrates human sexual techniques. Under this section it is still an offence, even if the advertising material sent does not specifically deal with the description or illustration of human sexual techniques, provided the actual material, *i.e.* book, magazine, etc., that is being advertised does contain such descriptions or illustrations.[86] This particular interpretation of the section was considered to be the mischief of the legislation. Presumably, the mischief being that young children would see the human sexual techniques, or parents would regard such unsolicited mail as indecent either for themselves or young children, or it was against such mail-shots to be exhibited publicly. If the main reasons were for hiding such pictures or descriptions from young persons, then the defendants in *DPP v. Uhse* suffered unfairly, since the advertising material did not describe graphically or otherwise any sexual techniques. Only those who ordered a copy of the material would see the descriptions and that would be legal, unless the material itself was considered obscene.

Children and Young Persons (Harmful Publications) Act 1955

6–041 This little used statute was passed for a very precise reason which was soon superseded by the Obscene Publications Act 1959. The 1955 Act deals with publications aimed at children which contain explicit violence, crime, or horror. Generally speaking the offence was directed at preventing the publication and distribution of "horror comics".[87] It would now also cover the growing field of "graphic novels" aimed at a young audience, which do contain some words but the storyline is primarily conveyed by means of detailed illustrations. It is an offence under section 1 of the Act to publish an article which portrays the commission of a crime; or shows acts of violence or cruelty; or shows incidents of a "horrible or repulsive" nature. The published article must additionally be shown to be likely to corrupt a child or young person who might have access to it.

Protection of Children Act 1978: Introduction

6–042

> "When child pornography is considered it is much more difficult to sustain the arguments of freedom, choice and privacy and much more difficult to ignore the harm. The public policy concern and legal emphasis moves from protecting the rights of the consumer to a concern with the rights of the child within the pornography and the right of all children to security and protection . . .".[88]

Very few people have ever argued persuasively in favour of the liberalisation of the law relating to child pornography—freedom of expression in this manner is vastly outweighed by the need to protect the vulnerable. The harm principle discussed above is employed here, with the result that the test used in offences of obscenity involving children relates not to the effect of the material upon its audience but to the nature of the material itself. It will be of no avail for a producer of child pornography to claim that his work would only be available to those who are already "depraved and corrupted"; all that matters for the main offences in this area is that he has in fact produced, possessed, or published indecent images of a child.

The perceived threat involved in child pornography and fears that it was increasing were the prime reasons behind the introduction of the Protection of Children Act 1978. Originally the offences under the Act related to photographs and films, but they were extended by the Criminal Justice and Public Order Act 1994 to include video cassettes, and electronically stored images such as those held on computer disk or CD-ROM. References in the Act to photographs now include by implication the other methods of storage of images, as well as the negatives of any such photograph (section 7). It is an offence to:

(1) take, or permit to be taken, an indecent photograph of a child under the age of 16;

(2) show or distribute such a photograph;
(3) have in one's possession such a photograph with a view to its distribution or showing;
(4) possess such a photograph without a view to distribution or showing (although there is a statutory defence to this charge if the defendant can show a legitimate reason for possessing the photograph, or if he has not seen it and had no reason to suspect that it was indecent, or if he received the photograph as unsolicited goods and had not retained it for an unreasonable time—section 160, Criminal Justice Act 1988);
(5) publish an advertisement for such a photograph.

Search, seizure and forfeiture provisions parallel to those under the Obscene Publications Acts in sections 4 and 5 of the 1978 Act were introduced out of concern that organised paedophile rings were creating and distributing material which involved the exploitation of children.

The maximum penalty for an offence under the Protection of Children Act 1978 is three years' imprisonment on indictment, or six months' imprisonment, or a fine on summary conviction. The penalty for an offence under section 160 of the Criminal Justice Act 1988 is a fine. These penalties may seem low in comparison to the nature of the offence. If the nature of the photographs merits a higher sentence, then a prosecution may be possible under the Obscene Publications Act, provided that the "deprave and corrupt" test is met. However, prosecutors and the police prefer to proceed against those involved in child pornography by means of the Protection of Children Act in order to label the offender as a paedophile and thus enable his control, by shame, stigma and the new Register.

In *R. v. Graham-Kerr*[89]: **6–043**

Facts. The defendant took two photographs of a seven year old boy in the changing room of a swimming baths, without the knowledge or permission of the boy's parents. The parents, who were naturists, were at the swimming baths, but were not present when the incident took place. The defendant was charged with taking indecent photographs contrary to section 1(1) of the Protection of Children Act 1978. Though objected to by the defence, the judge allowed evidence of (a) the surrounding circumstances in which the photos were taken, and (b) the defendant's motives in taking the pictures,[90] *i.e.* he obtained sexual gratification from what he did. The judge directed the jury that whether the photos were indecent or not is a question of fact, and they should "apply the standard of decency which ordinary right thinking members of the public would set".[91]

Decision. He appealed on the grounds that the judge erred in allowing evidence under (a) and (b) above. He submitted that the only relevant question was whether the photos themselves were indecent. The Court of Appeal said that there must be proof that he intended to take the photos (here, there was no argument) and whether the photos were indecent. The judge was wrong to admit the evidence of (a) and (b) above, since the relevancy of the surrounding circumstances and the appellant's state of mind would only be valid where, for instance, the appellant claimed that the photos were taken accidentally, which was not the case here. If the evidence of (a) and (b) above had been excluded, the jury may not have found the photos (especially photo no. 2) to be indecent. Therefore, the appeal was allowed and the conviction quashed.

Interestingly enough, in the above case, since there were no actual photos or negatives (the film had not been developed yet), the defendant submitted that there could be no offence under section 1(1) of this Act. However, for whatever reasons, the defence did not pursue this line of argument.

6–044 Surrounding circumstances may be taken into account where the age of the child is a relevant factor. By section 7(3) "photographs . . . shall, if they show children and are indecent, be treated for all purposes of this Act as indecent photographs of children" (a child is a person under the age of 16 (section 2(3)). In *R. v. Owen*,[92] the defendant took some photographs of a 14 year-old girl, some of which were considered to be in provocative poses. The issue for the Court of Appeal was whether the jury should only consider whether the photos themselves were indecent or whether they could also take into account the age of the child. The court held that the age factor was a material issue. The word "indecent" in section 1(1) refers to the phrase "photograph of a child", and not to the words "to take or permit to be taken". Thus, since the jury are entitled to know the age of the child, they are further entitled to take that into account when considering whether the photograph was indecent.[93]

The offences under the 1978 Act, as amended, have a relatively narrow application; only indecent photographs or films are caught. Thus no specific offences relating to indecent writing about children were created; since there is great reluctance to prosecute the written word under the Obscene Publications Acts, those who deal in written child pornography have a free rein. A second problem, until recently, concerned "pseudo-photographs". A pseudo-photograph is a picture which appears to be a photograph, but has been created or manipulated in some other manner. It has been possible to doctor photographs since the invention of photography, for example by means of painting the negative to alter the image or to add detail, or by creating a composite image made from two or more pictures superimposed; but modern technology enables the creation of sophisticated images which may fool even experts into believing that the scene depicted actually existed and was photographed. Thus child pornography may be created without the involvement of any child; a child's face may be superimposed upon a photograph of an adult's body; expressions, actions and positions may be altered; an indecent image of a non-existent child may be created. Although there is no justification of criminalisation of such images on the basis of protection of children (since no child is actually exploited in the creation of the picture), we may revert to morality as a justification, as it may be argued that the existence of pornographic images of children is contrary to the public good, regardless of whether such images are real or otherwise created.

Pseudo-photographs were not expressly included within the definition of "photograph" for the offences under the Protection of Children Act 1978. Judicial creativity was not employed in this instance, not because judges were reluctant to construe the statute to include pseudo-photographs, but because the Crown Prosecution Service considered itself unable to bring a prosecution under the 1978 Act in such a situation, and so judges were not given an opportunity to debate the issue.[94] If a pseudo-photograph fits the definition of "obscene" under the Obscene Publications Acts (see discussion above) then prosecution under those offences is of course possible, but this would not apply to all the pictures under consideration here. **6–045**

The Criminal Justice and Public Order Act 1994 introduced amendments to the Protection of Children Act 1978 in order to deal with the problem of pseudo-photographs. Section 84(3) adds a new section 7(7) to the 1978 Act, which reads:

> " 'Pseudo-photograph' means an image, whether made by computer-graphics or otherwise howsoever, which appears to be a photograph".

Section 1(1)(a) of the 1978 Act is amended by sections 84(2)(a)(i) and (ii) of the 1994 Act so that it is now an offence for a person to "take, or permit to be taken, or to make any indecent photograph or pseudo-photograph of a child". The meaning of the word "making" of an indecent photograph was confirmed in the case of *R. v. Bowden*[94A] in which the defendant was charged with and convicted of making indecent photographs from the Internet. His defence was that he was merely in possession of these photographs, and nothing more. The Court of Appeal (Otton L.J.) stated that downloading and/or the printing or storing of computer data of indecent material constituted "making" indecent photographs. The word was to be given its natural and ordinary meaning, *i.e.* to cause to exist: to produce by action, to bring about (taken from the Concise Oxford English Dictionary). The definition also applied to negatives, copies of photographs and data stored on computer disk.

The offences under sections 1(1)(b), (c) and (d) were similarly amended to include pseudo-photographs as well as traditional photographs. Section 84(3) of the 1994 Act expands the definition of photograph in section 7(4) of the 1978 Act to include: "data stored on a computer disc (sic) or by other electronic means which is capable of conversion into a photograph", so that computer technology is encompassed. In *Fellows*[95] images stored electronically after being downloaded from the Internet were held to fall within the scope of the offences under the 1978 Act.

The new section 7(8) of the 1978 Act provides for liability where the pseudo-photographic picture does not in fact depict a child under 16 "where the predominant impression conveyed is that the person shown is a child notwithstanding that some of the physical characteristics shown are those of an adult". Thus it is now an offence to create, possess, or distribute an indecent pseudo-photograph of a person over the age of 16 if the person concerned appears to be under 16; but if it is a true photograph, there is no liability for any such activities if the person photographed is in fact over the age of 16. This is a difficult situation to justify. In spite of the amendments, there is still a gap in the legislation as far as explicit cartoon-style images are concerned.

Indecent Displays (Control) Act 1981

6–046 This Act controls the display of indecent material, such as pornographic magazines or sex aids, in shops, windows and any other place accessible or visible to the public. The Williams Committee had expressed concern about the availability of pornographic magazines in ordinary shops such as newsagents, and the Act was introduced by means of a Private Member's Bill shortly afterwards.

The offence under section 1(1) involves public display of any indecent matter; both "the person making the display and any person causing or permitting the display to be made shall be guilty".

Public Display

6–047 A "public display" involves "any matter which is displayed in or so as to be visible from any public place" (section 1(2)). A "public place" is "any place to which the public have or are permitted to have access (whether on payment or otherwise) while the matter is displayed", unless payment has been made in order to view the displayed matter, or the displayed matter is within a shop which has at its entrance an adequate warning notice (section 1(3)). The exemptions in section 1(3) only apply where persons under the age of 18 are denied access to the premises while the display exists. Displays in art galleries, museums, forming part of a performance of a play (within the meaning of the Theatres Act 1968), or included in a film exhibition (as defined and regulated by the Cinemas Act 1985), are also excluded from liability (section 1(4)).

Indecent matter

6–048 "Matter" is defined in section 1(5) to encompass "anything capable of being displayed, except that it does not include an actual human body or any part thereof"; flashers are therefore not liable, but the display of a photograph of the same naked person in the same window would be an offence. No specific definition of "indecent" is given by the statute; whether any given display is indecent will be determined according to the standards of the common law discussed above, in terms of "offensiveness" or "shock and disgust". However, any part of the matter which is not exposed to view may not be taken into account when judging the display for indecency; and the juxtaposition of different items may be a factor in indecency (section 1(5)). The offence relates to the display alone, and is unrelated to whether the matter may be legally possessed, sold or so on. There is no public good defence.

If a shop displaying indecent matter is to escape liability by means of a warning notice, such a notice must be displayed in a position such that it must be passed by every person gaining access to the premises; "the notice must be so situated that no one could reasonably gain access to the shop or part of the shop in question without being aware of the notice and it must be easily legible by any person gaining such access" (section 1(6)(d)). The warning notice must read exactly as follows:

> "WARNING: Persons passing beyond this notice will find material on display which they may consider indecent. No admittance to persons under 18 years of age".

The practical effect of the Act has been less than was expected. Sex shops of course display the statutory notice and take care with what may be visible in their windows, but the original concern of the Williams Committee remains unanswered since ordinary newsagents almost without exception continue to display "soft" pornographic magazines within the view, if not the easy reach, of children and of others who might not wish to be exposed to them. The unofficial method of self-regulation used by newsagents and other shops is to place any potentially indecent material on the highest shelves, but there is no special significance to such a practice. The Act has also been used for some unintended prosecutions, including the wearing of jokey explicit t-shirts.

Local Government (Miscellaneous Provisions) Act 1982: Licensing of "Sex Establishments"

This Act introduced a further method of regulating the sex shop and sexual entertainment industries. The previous method of regulation had centred upon an enterprising use of local authorities' planning powers and regulations, but proved inadequate by the 1980s to deal with the rising number of sex shops which had become concentrated in particular geographical areas, for example Soho, and which were perceived as an undesirable development. Since no specific planning regulations related to sex shops, there was no authority on which to prevent such shops from opening next door to primary schools, nor to limit the number of such establishments in one area. Planning law could have been amended to achieve the desired regulation of sex establishments, but this was not done. Instead, a specific licensing scheme for "sex establishments" was created by the 1982 Local Government (Miscellaneous Provisions) Act. **6–049**

Section 2 of the Act allows local authorities (*i.e.* councils and boroughs) to adopt by resolution the provisions of Schedule 3 to the Act, and thus to set up a licensing scheme for sex establishments. Schedule 3 creates a criminal offence of failure to obtain a licence where one is required; that is "no person shall knowingly . . . use any premises, vehicle, vessel or stall as a sex establishment except under and in accordance with the terms of a licence" granted by the local authority (paragraph 6(1)). A "sex establishment" may be either a "sex cinema" or a "sex shop". A "sex cinema" is a place used "to a significant degree" for the exhibition of moving pictures which are concerned primarily with, or are intended to encourage, sexual activity or acts of force or restraint related to sexual activity; or which are concerned primarily with genital organs or bodily functions. Sex cinemas are now generally dealt with according to the more expansive licensing provisions of the Cinemas Act 1985 (below), but the 1982 Act remains important as far as sex shops are concerned. A "sex shop" is a place of which the business "consists to a significant degree of selling, hiring, exchanging, lending, displaying or demonstrating 'sex articles' or other things intended for use in connection with, or for the purpose of stimulating or encouraging (i) sexual activity; or (ii) acts of force or restraint which are associated with sexual activity". There is a highly complex definition of "sex article" in paragraphs 4(3) and 4(4) of Schedule 3:

(a) anything made for use in connection with, or for the purpose of stimulating or encouraging (i) sexual activity or (ii) acts of force or restraint associated with sexual activity; or

(b) any article containing or embodying matter to be read or looked at, or any recording of sound or vision, which is concerned primarily with the portrayal of, or primarily deals with or relates to, or is intended to stimulate or encourage, sexual activity or acts of force or restraint associated with sexual activity, or is concerned primarily with the portrayal of, or primarily deals with or relates to, genital organs, or urinary or excretory functions.

6–050 This long and complicated definition will cover almost anything even remotely related to sex, as well as obvious items such as pornographic magazines and videos, vibrators, handcuffs and condoms. Condoms and other birth control devices are given a specific exemption from the licensing requirement on policy grounds (paragraph 6(2)). The definition's cumbersome nature is a result of its attempt to describe every article to be regulated, rather than to formulate a definition on the usual basis of the effect of the matter upon its audience; obscenity and indecency are not the tests here.

An establishment will only be a sex shop if, as stated above, it deals "to a significant degree" in sex articles or the other material listed. The term "significant degree" has caused problems for the courts and has been the subject of much debate. Some local authorities which have adopted the licensing scheme originally attempted to treat a shop as a sex shop, and therefore as requiring a licence, if it had on display for sale any more than a specific number of sex articles. This policy was challenged in the courts in the case of *Lambeth London Council v. Grewal*.[96] The defendant owned a general grocery and newsagents store where the magazines on display included between 16 and 20 different sex magazines. When council officials visited the shop, they warned the owner that he would be charged with operating an unlicensed sex shop if he displayed more than five sex articles. He was so charged, but the divisional court held that he was not guilty since no absolute limit could be placed by a local authority upon the number of sex articles which may be displayed in unlicensed premises; the shop must be shown to deal "to a significant degree" in sex articles if it is to require a licence. The court did not give any easy test for "significant degree", but stated that:

> "the ratio between the sexual and other aspects of the business will always be material. So will the absolute quantity of sales . . . the court will no doubt find it appropriate to consider the character of the remainder of the business. The nature of the display can be a relevant factor, and the nature of the articles themselves will also be material, since the definition . . . covers a wide spectrum of offensiveness. It would be wrong to say in law that any single factor is decisive".[97]

On the facts, less than 1.5 per cent of the shop's business was made up of the sale of the magazines in question, and so these sex articles in no way satisfied the "significant degree" requirement. Thus, a local authority cannot impose sex article quotas, but must operate its licensing system according to the proportion of an establishment's business which is related to sex articles.

Once classified as a sex shop, an establishment may nevertheless be **6–051** denied the licence which it would require in order to operate legally. A licence may be denied on a variety of grounds, which are found in paragraph 12 of Schedule 3. A licence must not be given to a person under the age of 18, or to a person or company outside the United Kingdom. There are also discretionary grounds for refusal of a licence, including the applicant's unsuitability, the number of other sex shops in the area, the character of the locality, and the nature of the other buildings in the area. A local authority is expressly permitted to decide that the suitable number of sex establishments for a particular locality is zero. Even if a licence is granted, it is almost always subject to conditions relating to such matters as opening hours, the external appearance of the premises, the visibility of the inside of the shop from the street, and so on. Licences may be varied or revoked, but a grievance and appeal procedure does exist (paragraph 27). Holding a licence does not provide any exemption from criminal liability for other offences, and the police often search licensed sex shops for obscene publications. Local authorities may charge a fee for the application for and granting of a licence, but the 1982 Act does not stipulate any maximum for such a fee, with the result that some local authorities currently charge thousands of pounds for the service. Licences are subject to annual review and renewal, thus providing an easy opportunity for supervision of the establishments.

Once licensing was introduced, many local authorities seized the opportunity to adopt the licensing scheme and to regulate strictly the number of sex establishments within their boundaries; notably, Soho has been all but emptied of sex shops. But this is by no means a general tendency, since the attitudes of local authorities to sex shops vary greatly. It should be noted in any case that the 1982 Act represents only a minor infraction of freedom of expression since it does no more than limit the availability of sex articles; any person wishing to buy such articles remains at liberty to do so, and any person wishing to sell such articles must simply follow the correct procedure in a sympathetic location. Neither category of person is in danger of committing any criminal offence if they follow the legal procedure.

The Customs Consolidation Act 1876 and Customs and Excise Act 1979; Controls on Imports: Introduction

6–052 In contrast to several other European states, the United Kingdom has a restrictive approach to pornography and tends to criminalise the distribution, production and even sometimes the possession of such material. Yet, in the modern world, it is becoming increasingly difficult to police the trade in obscene or indecent material, both due to new technology such as the Internet and to the fundamental principle of free movement of goods within the European Community. Fear that more "liberal" European states will be the source of an influx of hardcore pornography into the United Kingdom has caused feverish political debate, and it is true that the fear is to some extent justified. Measures to restrict the importation of pornography are not a new idea, but it is only comparatively recently that the statutory controls have been challenged on the basis that they conflict with the United Kingdom's obligations as a Member State of the E.C. It has been argued that the import restrictions operate as a type of discrimination in favour of United Kingdom products and against overseas competition; home-grown pornography is thought to be in some way preferable.

A further problem has been the working relationship between these import restrictions and the Obscene Publications Act 1959; this will be discussed below.

Section 42 of the 1876 Act prohibits the importation or otherwise bringing into the United Kingdom of the following items:

> "Indecent or obscene prints, paintings, photographs, books, cards, lithographic and other engravings, or any other indecent or obscene articles."

Section 49 of the 1979 Act states that:

> "where . . . any goods are imported, landed or unloaded contrary to any prohibition or restriction . . . under or by virtue of any enactment . . . those goods shall . . . be liable to forfeiture."

Importation of obscene or indecent material

This particular area of law concerns the free movement of goods within the European Community, and in this instance, obscene or indecent articles, and whether there exists any restrictions or prohibitions on such goods being prevented from being imported from one State to another. The consequences of importing pornographic articles are laid out under section 42 of the Customs Consolidation Act 1876 and the Customs and Excise Management Act 1979, *i.e.* such obscene or indecent articles, if found to be so, will be confiscated and destroyed upon entry to the United Kingdom and the importers guilty of an offence. Under section 72 of the Criminal Justice and Police Act 2001, the importation of indecent or obscene articles is now categorised as a serious arrestable offence under Part I of Schedule 5 to PACE and the Police and Criminal Evidence (Northern Ireland) Order 1989: thus giving Customs and Excise officers further powers to deal with investigations of this type. **6–053**

What articles are prohibited for the purposes of section 42? In *Derrick v. Customs and Excise Commissioners*,[98] the question arose whether a roll of film came within section 42. In that case, the defendants were importers of films and magazines of a sexually explicit theme, depicting acts of buggery and young naked girls (between the ages of five and 14) in different sexual positions with a man. The defendant tried to argue that cinematograph film was not *eiusdem generis* with the classification set out in section 42, nor would such film come under the phrase "or any other or indecent or obscene articles" since it was not possible to decide whether the film could properly be adjudged indecent or obscene simply by inspecting the film in its raw state, without first using some mechanism to project it. This, they argued, was in contrast with all the other types cited in section 42 which could immediately have been decided upon as obscene or indecent or neither. This was rejected, the section applies to any articles which are indecent or obscene or alternatively, the relevant film is a "photograph", since it comes within the definition of what a film is.

In *DPP v. Henn and Darby*[99]: **6–054**

Facts. The defendants were convicted of, *inter alia*, fraudulently evading the prohibition on the importation of indecent or obscene articles contrary to section 42 of the CCA 1876 and section 304 of the Customs and Excise Act 1952. (Henn was also charged and convicted of having obscene articles for gain contrary to section 2(1) of the OPA 1959 and 1964.)

Decision. The defendants appealed on the grounds that Article 30 of the EEC Treaty invalidated section 42 of the CCA 1876. Article 30 broadly specifies that restriction on imports (subject to Article 36) shall be prohibited between Member States. Article 36 states that prohibition on imports shall only be justified on the grounds of public morality, public policy, the protection of health and life of humans, etc., but such restrictions shall not constitute a means of arbitrary discrimination or a disguised restriction on trade between Member States. The appellants submitted that the prohibition of the items in question, while already available in Member States, was contrary to Articles 30 and 36. The Court of Appeal dismissed their appeal on the grounds that there existed no problem on the relevant issue of interpretation in these circumstances, *i.e.* the relevant obscene or indecent material was prohibited from importation under Article 36 as being either against public morality or on public policy grounds. After several unsuccessful requests by the appellants that a preliminary ruling should be given by the European Court of Justice on the issue of interpretation of the Articles, the House of Lords finally acceded to that request.

As a result of the following ruling by the ECJ, the House of Lords dismissed the appeal. The ECJ stated, *inter alia*, that a Member State prohibiting the importation of pornographic articles under section 42 of the CCA 1876 constituted a breach of Article 30. However, a Member State may prohibit the importation of obscene or indecent material as defined by its own domestic laws. In this instance, the material was found to be obscene under the OPA 1959 and 1964 and also under the CCA 1876. Further, if the grounds for refusing importation is justifiably based on public morality, then that would not be considered a means of arbitrary discrimination or a disguised restriction of trade contrary to Article 36, since there was an absence of "lawful trade" in these articles in the country of importation, *i.e.* these materials could not be manufactured or sold in the United Kingdom, subject to a few limited exceptions.

6–055 Although a Member State can prohibit importation of obscene or indecent articles on the grounds of "public morality", will that proposition still hold true where the importing country itself lawfully produces, manufactures or sells these goods on the domestic market without fear of prosecution? In *Conegate v. Customs and Excise Commissioners*[1] the defendant imported from Germany a consignment of life-size inflatable rubber dolls for sale in the United Kingdom, contrary to section 42 of the CCA 1876. Upon entry, the consignment was seized on the grounds that they were prohibited under section 42 and forfeited under the Customs and Management Act 1979. Conegate appealed, *inter alia*, on the grounds that the actions of the customs officers were not within Article 30 or 36 of the EEC treaty. Hodgson J. put forward six questions for the ECJ to find on a preliminary ruling. One of the important questions was, can there be a general ban on specific obscene or indecent articles, when those articles are themselves freely available on the domestic market, subject only to a number of provisos, *e.g.* a total prohibition of sending such articles through the post; certain restriction regarding their public display; licenses to sell such articles to persons of 18 years of age or older. Before such articles can be legally prohibited, must there be an absolute ban on their manufacture or sales within the importing country?

The first question, however, is can obscene and indecent articles be justified on the grounds of public morality under Article 36? It was already decided in *R. v. Henn* (see above) that:

> "it is for the Member States themselves to lay down their own standards of public morality and to legislate accordingly, even if in the result, legislation of

> one Member State is more restrictive than that adopted by other Member States, since attitudes vary from place to place, and indeed, from time to time".[2]

In the ECJ ruling, they stated that:

> "To have one rule for imports and a different one for the sale of domestically manufactured goods, which between them exclude imports from other Member States but permit the sale of domestic products is, in my view, insufficient to establish the justification of a prohibition on imports within the meaning of Article 36".[3]

Since there was no overall ban in the United Kingdom prohibiting the sale or manufacture of these goods, *i.e.* lawful trade existed, save some provisos which applied only to certain parts of the United Kingdom, there was therefore no justification for refusal to allow these articles to be imported.

The next important question is, if the imported articles are considered **6–056** obscene under section 42 of the CCA 1876, may the importers nevertheless put forward a public "good" defence under section 4 of the OPA 1959? In *R. v. Bow Street Magistrate's Court ex parte Noncyp Ltd*,[4] the applicants who were the owners of a bookshop called "Gay's the Word", wished to import a number of books for sale, with such titles as *Men Loving Men*, *Men in Erotic Art*, etc. The respondents (officers of H.M. Customs ad Excise) seized the books under section 42 of the CCA 1876 and brought condemnation proceedings for forfeiture on the grounds that the books were obscene. Further, whilst the obscene definition in section 1 of the OPA 1959 is to deprave and corrupt, under the CCA 1876 the meaning is wider, *i.e.* repulsive, filthy, lewd, loathsome. Under section 4 of the OPA 1959, there is, of course, the possibility of a "public good defence" available to anyone prosecuted under the Act. However, the applicants were not permitted to use that defence, either at the Bow Street Magistrate's Court, or on appeal to the Queen's Bench Divisional Court. They then appealed to the Court of Appeal. The applicants argued that without the admission of a section 4 defence, it would be impossible to state with any certainty that there was "no lawful trade" in the United Kingdom with regard to these books. This argument was rejected by the Court of Appeal. It was held that since there existed no lawful business dealings of such goods at all in the United Kingdom, section 42 of the CAA 1876 was solely applicable, and there was no need to refer to the OPA 1959, neither for the definition of "obscenity", nor for a possible defence under section 4. The court decided that once an article was considered as obscene under the OPA 1959, this alone made its trade in the United Kingdom unlawful. Even if a public good defence under section 4 was granted, it would still remain the fact that the article was obscene. The section 4 defence only prevents a person from criminal prosecution under section 1, it does not delete the obscenity of an article. Therefore, the possibility of a public good defence was entirely irrelevant to a consideration of section 42 of the CCA 1876, all the more as this Act did not provide such a defence itself.

6–057 However, as far as the definition of "obscenity" is concerned, section 1 of the OPA 1959 becomes relevant as soon as goods similar to those forfeited goods do exist in the United Kingdom. Only then does the possibility of the forfeiture constituting a contravention against Articles 30 and 36 EEC Treaty arises. In order to establish whether the forfeiture would be an arbitrary discrimination or a disguised trade restriction against goods coming from the EEC as opposed to domestic goods, under Article 36, the situation within the United Kingdom market has to be analysed, *i.e.* it becomes necessary to find out whether such goods are considered to be "obscene" under the OPA 1959 in the United Kingdom. However, since the definition of "obscene" is much wider under the CCA than the OPA (see above), goods can be banned from importation as obscene much easier. This might result in a situation where a product is prohibited from importation under the CCA 1876, whereas a similar domestic product would not necessarily fulfil the requirements of "obscene" under the OPA 1959 and would therefore not be banned from trade in the United Kingdom. In order to avoid such a situation, which would clearly be contrary to the principle of free movement of goods within the E.C., it seems that customs officers have made it a practice only to seize material which appears to fall under the OPA 1959 definition of obscene, *i.e.* material which is prone to "deprave and corrupt". Therefore customs officials should take into account as part of their duties both the CCA 1876 and the OPA 1959 when deciding whether to forfeit any articles as obscene.

Common Law Offences Relating to Obscenity, Indecency and Morality

6–058 It comes as a surprise to many that the statutory offences discussed so far are not the full extent of the law relating to obscenity and indecency; the common law remains an important, if highly controversial, source of regulation of this area. The two main common law offences which need to be considered in this context are corrupting public morals and outraging public decency. The related offences of blasphemy, indecent exhibition, indecent exposure and keeping a disorderly house will also be discussed. Two statutory offences are also relevant here: conspiracy to corrupt public morals and conspiracy to outrage public decency.

Corrupting Public Morals: Introduction

6–059 It has long been a subject of debate and obscurity whether there is a common law offence of corrupting public morals and, if such an offence does exist, what must be proved for a conviction. When the Criminal Law Act 1977 was drafted, great care had to be taken since it was not known whether either of the "offences" of corrupting public morals or outraging public decency did in fact exist. The uncertainty in this respect has caused the courts great problems of definition, analysis and application to the facts.

In *Shaw* (below) the House of Lords upheld the appellant's conviction for the offence of conspiracy to corrupt public morals without addressing the issue of whether a common law offence of corrupting public morals does exist; the Court of Appeal had previously held that it did. By analogy with the reasoning used in recent cases such as *Gibson*,[5] *May*[6] and *Rowley*,[7] (which all concern outraging public decency) it is likely that there is a common law offence of corrupting public morals. Unfortunately, it remains far from clear what the elements of the offence are. In *Knuller v. DPP*,[8] Lord Simon believed that corrupting public morals involved far more than merely leading people astray morally; rather it suggested "conduct which a jury might find to be destructive to the very fabric of society". To Lord Reid, the offence involved depraving people. Adding to the confusion, Lords Reid and Diplock did not accept that there was any such offence as corrupting public morals, but the remainder of the court were open to its existence.

Corrupting public morals is rarely charged, so why is it important to the **6–060** present discussion to decide whether such an offence exists? The answer is that there is an inchoate offence (an "incomplete" offence in that the offender has not yet achieved his ultimate aim) of conspiracy to corrupt public morals. It is well accepted that this offence does exist, but the test which must be applied for any type of criminal conspiracy depends upon whether what the defendant(s) has agreed to do would in itself involve a criminal offence if it were carried out. There are both statutory conspiracies and common law conspiracies, but almost all conspiracies are now statutory. A statutory conspiracy is, put simply, an agreement between two or more people to carry out a course of conduct which, if completed, would constitute a criminal offence (whether that resulting criminal offence would be statutory or common law) (section 1 of the Criminal Law Act 1977, as amended). Common law conspiracies are treated differently: section 5 provides—

> "(1) Subject to the following provisions of this section, the offence of conspiracy at common law is hereby abolished . . .
> (2) Subsection (1) shall not affect the offence of conspiracy at common law if and in so far as it may be committed by entering into an agreement to engage in conduct which—
>
> (a) tends to corrupt public morals or outrages public decency; but
> (b) would not amount to or involve the commission of an offence if carried out by a single person otherwise than in pursuance of an agreement."

Thus, if there is an offence of corrupting public morals, then the offence of conspiracy to corrupt public morals must be a statutory conspiracy; conspiracy to corrupt public morals will no longer exist as a common law offence. But if there is no such offence as corrupting public morals, then a conspiracy to corrupt public morals must be a common law offence. The same arguments apply regarding outraging public decency and conspiracy to outrage public decency (below). This situation is unnecessarily and unintentionally complex, and in desperate need of reform. The Law Commission recommended that common law conspiracies to corrupt public morals or to outrage public decency should be abolished, as should all common law offences relating to decency and morality, but these recommendations have not attracted much support (Law Com. No. 76).

6–061 In *Shaw v. DPP*,[9] the defendant published a booklet entitled "Ladies' Directory", paid for by prostitutes advertising in the booklet in order to entice customers for sexual intercourse and perverted sexual practices. The booklet (28 pages) included the women's names, addresses and photographs. The defendant was charged with, *inter alia*, (1) conspiracy to corrupt public morals and (2) publishing an obscene article contrary to section 2 of the OPA 1959.[10] The defendant was convicted and appealed.

The main grounds for appeal were that there was no known offence in existence in law of conspiracy to corrupt public morals.[11] Lord Simonds stated that whilst he agreed that it was not up to judges to make new criminal offences, he argued that "there remains in the court of law a residual power to enforce the supreme and fundamental purpose of the law, to conserve not only the safety and order, but also the moral welfare of the State and that it is the duty to guard it against attacks which may be the more insidious because they are novel and unprepared for.[12] He also stated that if such an offence did not exist, the courts would have failed in their duty as "servants and guardians of the common law".[13] However, Lord Reid dissented on the issue of whether such an offence exists. He was in favour of letting Parliament legislate for the introduction of new offences if required, and was of the opinion that only if the "conspiracy" was part of a criminal offence would an offence existed. But, if the conspiracy consists of a part of immoral behaviour (what he refers to as "the extension of public mischief")[14] then, he thought, it was for Parliament to intervene and legislate against such conduct. Thus, he thought that by making conspiracy to corrupt public morals an offence, the court was making a conduct punishable, where there was no existing precedent for doing so.[15] Nevertheless, the majority did conclude that, having considered many early decisions, that the offence of conspiracy to corrupt public morals does exist; the question of its provenance remains unresolved.

The *mens rea* (mental element) which must be established for the offence of corrupting public morals (assuming that such an offence does remain) is unclear; but the *mens rea* for a conspiracy to corrupt public morals is intention to carry out the planned, prohibited conduct.

Outraging Public Decency: Introduction

6–062 When compared to corrupting public morals, the existence of the common law offence of outraging public decency seems remarkably settled; yet the problems from the discussion above apply also to this offence.

It is now generally accepted that there is a common law offence of outraging public decency, although its boundaries and requirements remain somewhat imprecise. In *Mayling*[16] the Court of Appeal held that the offence did exist, but were vague as to its definition. In *Knuller* (below) the House of Lords was divided as to the existence of the offence; Lords Reid and Diplock thought that there was no such offence, but Lords Kilbrandon, Simon and Morris held that such an offence did exist at common law (and hence a conspiracy to outrage public decency would also be an offence). Lord Simon explained the offence of outraging public decency as follows:

> ". . . the substantive offence . . . must be committed in public, in the sense that the circumstances must be such that the alleged outrageously indecent matter could have been seen by more than one person, even though in fact no more than one did see it. If it is capable of being seen by one person only, no offence is committed . . . I do not think that it would necessarily negative the offence that the act or exhibit is superficially hid from view, if the public is expressly or impliedly invited to penetrate the cover. Thus, the public touting for an outrageously indecent exhibition in private would not escape . . . Another obvious example is an outrageously indecent exhibit with a cover entitled 'Lift in order to see' . . . This sort of instance could be applied to a book or a newspaper . . . The conduct must at least in some way be so projected as to have an impact in public".

From this we can extract requirements that: it must be possible that more than one person could be outraged; indecency seems to be involved, but it is not clear whether this is used as a synonym for "outrageous"; the act or exhibition concerned must occur in public. Lord Simon himself made it clear that he considered that "outraging public decency":

> "goes considerably beyond offending the susceptibilities of, or even shocking, reasonable people. Moreover the offence is, in my view, concerned with recognised minimum standards of decency, which are likely to vary from time to time . . ."

Several recent cases have afforded the courts an opportunity to confirm that there is an offence of outraging public decency.[17] This means that a conspiracy to outrage public decency will be a statutory conspiracy and so will use the definition and test from section 1 of the Criminal Law Act 1977 (see above). Thus there is no longer any common law offence of conspiracy to outrage public decency.

It should not be thought that merely because Parliament legislates for a prior criminal offence to become lawful, *e.g.* Sexual Offences Act 1967, making homosexual acts legal in private, the courts then will sanction all behaviour and activities to do with that lawful Act; the courts may still find various practices within that lawfulness to be against public morals and standards and bring charges against those persons who conspire to corrupt public morals and/or outrage public decency.

6–063 In *Knuller v. DPP*[18]:

Facts. The defendants were publishers of a magazine called "International Times" (circulation approximately 38,000 copies). Adverts in the magazine were placed by homosexuals, mostly, in order to induce other like persons to take part in various homosexual activities. The defendants were charged and convicted under two counts: (1) conspiracy to corrupt public morals and (2) conspiracy to outrage public decency. The defendants appealed on the grounds that neither offence existed at common law.[19]

Decision. The appellants argued that *Shaw v. DPP* was wrongly decided and should be overturned or, at least, distinguished from the present case, in favour of the appellants. They further argued with regard to count (2) that it did not apply in this case because (a) it had never before been used in cases concerning books or newspapers and should not be used here, and (b) since the adverts were placed inside the magazine, there was no "public" aspect involved in this case. Lord Reid, who was still reluctant to accept the existence of the offence of conspiracy to corrupt public morals[20] nevertheless said that "(it) really means to corrupt the morals of such members of the public as may be influenced by the matter published by the accused".[21] "Corrupt", he said, means more than, as the judge directed the jury in *Shaw v. DPP*, to "lead morally astray". It possesses a much stronger sense than that and means to "debauch, deprave or corrupt". He said that even though the Sexual Offences Act 1967 made homosexual practices in private legal, it may nevertheless still have a corrupting influence, especially by assisting and influencing others to indulge in such practices. But, he continued, the law would not intervene if such people wished to corrupt themselves in these instances. Ultimately, it is for the jury to decide whether or not the magazine corrupted in these circumstances. Thus, he would not overturn the jury's decision under count (1) and accordingly he dismissed that particular appeal. Lord Simon stated that it was now settled that conspiracy to corrupt public morals was part of English criminal law. It is not for judges to declare as a matter of law whether or not male homosexualism corrupts public morals; it is a matter of fact to be decided by the jury[22] and "the words 'corrupt public morals' suggest conduct which a jury might find to be destructive of the very fabric of society".[23]

Regarding count (2), conspiracy to outrage public decency, Lord Reid said it meant "that ordinary decent-minded people who are not likely to become corrupted or depraved will be outraged or utterly disgusted by what they read".[24] He was of the opinion that apart from a few statutory exceptions, no law existed whereby persons could be punished for publishing material merely because it was indecent (as opposed to obscene). The three existing indecent common law offences (a) indecent exposure of the person, (b) keeping a disorderly house and (c) exposure or exhibition in public of indecent things or acts, have nothing in common with the instant published matter. Could, therefore (apart from the three recognised examples above), such an offence exist so that it is more than merely indecent, *i.e.* something more than shocking, repulsive, filthy or loathsome, which outrages a decent person, but is less than obscene? Lord Reid thought that if such an offence does exist, its effect would be retrograde, in that the old law of a few "purple passages" in a book might again give rise to a possible prosecution in the future.[25] He therefore quashed count (2). Lord Simon, on the other hand said that if there are new circumstances, however novel, and they clearly fell within the offence then that, by itself, should not prevent the accused from being charged. Lord Morris said that even if the magazine and the adverts were sent only to those who were already homosexuals, the offence would still be committed, since those people could still be recorrupted under these offences.[26]

It is again not clear precisely what the required mental state (*mens rea*) is **6–064**
for the offence of outraging public decency. It is most likely that this is an offence of strict liability in the sense that it must be proved only that the defendant was aware of the nature of his act; it is not necessary to prove that he intended to outrage public decency or knew that this might occur. But, for the offence of conspiracy to outrage public decency, the mental state which must be established in the defendant is that of intention to carry out the agreement which would result in the outraged public decency.

What is common to both the above offences (conspiracy to corrupt public morals and conspiracy to outrage public decency from adverts placed in magazines) is the word "public", although they have different meanings according to in which offence the word is being applied. Regarding conspiracy to corrupt public morals, the word "public" refers to what was written in the magazine, not that the immoral act must be performed in some public area, unlike the common law of indecency where, *inter alia*, exposing oneself in a public place or exhibiting some obscene article constitutes an offence. In *Knuller v. DPP*, Lord Simon said "public" in this respect amounts to "certain fundamental rules regarded as essential social control which yet lack the force of law",[27] *i.e.* it refers to persons in society. In conspiracy to outrage public decency, "public" refers to the place in which the offence was committed. The reason being that ordinary, decent people should be able to go about their everyday business without being subjected to mental torment by those whose conduct falls below the acceptable level of normal human behaviour. In that case, the appellant argued that the offence of conspiracy to outrage public decency, which they admitted existed, was not sustained here since the adverts objected to were placed on the inside pages of the magazine, there being nothing objectionable on the front cover. But, despite this, Lord Morris said that even if the front cover is innocent and in good taste, if the contents inside outrage public decency then the offence is made out. However, Lord Simon preferred that there should be something written or shown on the outside to indicate that such adverts existed inside the magazine.

Directing the jury on the issues of conspiracy to outrage public decency

It is important that the judge must specifically direct the jury on a number **6–065**
of important issues should a similar case to *Knuller v. DPP* arise again. They should be directed that:

(a) They must be satisfied that the adverts themselves were lewd, disgusting and offensive, and that there was agreement between two or more persons to outrage public decency;

(b) Times change, and what may have offended them in the past, may not necessarily do so nowadays;

(c) Despite there being nothing objectionable from looking at the outside of the magazine, the offence may still be committed if the contents on the inside outrage public decency;

(d) Outraging public decency goes beyond shocking, and offending the susceptibilities of reasonable people. Outrage like "corrupt" is a very strong word;

(e) Where appropriate, the jury should be reminded that they live in a plural society, with a tradition of tolerance towards minorities, and that this atmosphere of toleration is itself part of public decency.[28]

Section 2(4) of the OPA 1959

6–066 Under section 2(4), "a person publishing an obscene article shall not be proceeded against for an offence at common law consisting of the publication of any matter contained or embodied in the article where it is the essence of the offence that the matter is obscene".

Referring back to the previous discussion, it again becomes important to consider in this context whether conspiracy to corrupt public morals remains an offence at common law; if it is now a statutory offence under the Criminal Law Act 1977, section 1, then there is no conflict with section 2(4) of the 1959 Act.

The mischief behind the words of section 2(4), is that where the offence is considered obscene under section 1(1), it is preferable that the defendant be given the opportunity to have a defence under section 4 of the OPA 1959 as if obscene charges were allowed at common law, it would permit the prosecution to bring charges knowing that a defence under section 4 would not be admissible.[29] As against this, under the common law the prosecution would have to show intent which might prove to be difficult, as distinct from the OPA where the only intent required is that of publishing. Moreover, the offence must still be relevant to the OPA 1959 and 1964 in that if the material did not concern publication, but merely an agreement to corrupt public morals[30] then the OPA would still not be the correct mode of prosecution, and the common law may be the only manner by which a prosecution may be brought, or alternatively, no prosecution at all.

The question arises as to why, when conspiracy to corrupt public morals is such a high level obscenity offence and should therefore be prosecuted under the OPA (because of the section 2(4) provision), it is to be brought under the common law? One answer is that conspiracy consists of two or more persons acting in agreement with each other to corrupt public morals. It is the agreement itself which is the *actus reus* of the offence. Thus, although the publication, *e.g.* adverts, on their face would not tend to corrupt or deprave its likely readers, nevertheless, those persons who answered the particular adverts may be corrupted into doing certain perverted sexual practices, by getting in touch with the advertisers, *e.g.* the prostitutes, as in *Shaw v. DPP*. Whereas, if a prosecution were to be instigated under the OPA, then the *actus reus* of the offence must be the publication.[31] The publication itself must tend to corrupt its likely readers. But, if the publication does not use words which provoke the necessary reaction under the OPA, then the prosecution will fail. What is important is the corruption which lies behind the words in the advert. If, for example, a newspaper has a "lonely hearts" column, whereby advertisers place innocent adverts for seeking partners or companionship, no problem arises. However, if the newspaper editor and advertisers are aware that the adverts are phrased in such a way so as to suggest highly obscene immoral conduct for those persons who reply to those adverts, then the court may well deem such adverts to constitute a conspiracy to corrupt public morals.

The Common Law Offence of Indecency

There is a small, but relatively important, group of residual common law offences related to indecency in "public" (in the sense of more than one person being involved, or the defendant being within a potential public gaze). These offences are perhaps best viewed as specific aspects of the "bracket" offence of outraging public decency, but have developed separately to a sufficient extent that they merit separate examination. In *Knuller*, the majority of the House of Lords believed that the three offences in this category which had been recognised in earlier case law were specific examples of a much broader, general common law offence of outraging public decency. The three categories, whether they are separate offences or examples of the same offence, are: indecent exhibition, indecent exposure, and keeping a disorderly house. **6–067**

Lord Reid in *Shaw v. DPP*,[32] said:

> "I think that they (the case authorities) establish that it is an indictable offence to say or do or exhibit anything in public which outrage public decency, whether or not it also tends to deprave and corrupt those who see or hear it".

"Indecent act" means some activity which is so lewd, disgusting or obscene that it constitutes an outrage on public decency.[33] As part of the offence of outraging public decency, the prosecution must prove that an indecent act has been committed in public, in the sense that more than one person must have been able to see it. "Public" refers to more than one person, but if there is only one observer and there was the possibility of others who were in the vicinity seeing the indecent act, then that will suffice for this offence to be made out.[34] The offence is not restricted to public areas alone, but may include private areas which can be viewed by the public, *e.g.* a private garden which passers-by may see into without any difficulty. However, inside a private house, to which the public do not have access, creates no offence of outraging public decency,[35] but if, for instance, the windows were open or the curtains pulled back and the public could clearly see into the house, then it is suggested an offence of outraging public decency may be committed, if the indecent act was projected, whether intentionally or not, to those persons on the outside.[36]

6–068 It is not necessary for the prosecution to prove that those who witnessed the incident were actually disgusted, revolted or annoyed. It is for the jury to decide whether the act complained of, in fact, was designed to have that effect. In *R. v. Mayerling*,[37] the defendant was convicted of committing indecent acts in a public lavatory with another person. The incident acts were witnessed by two police officers. It was said on behalf of the defendant, on appeal, that the police constables would not be disgusted or annoyed by such acts, and therefore, as in *R. v. Clayton and Halsey*,[38] the appeal ought to be allowed. However, the court decided that it was not necessary for the observers to be disgusted or annoyed—that was to be inferred. The court distinguished *R. v. Clayton and Halsey*, since in that case, the issue was one of whether the photographs depraved or corrupted those police officers who viewed them; in the particular circumstances they did not. Here, however, there was no reason why the police constables could not be disgusted or annoyed at the sight of the indecent activities committed by the appellants. Therefore, the appeal was dismissed.

(1) Indecent exhibitions: Introduction

6–069 In the words of Lord Reid in the case of Shaw (above), "it is an indictable offence to say or do or exhibit anything in public which outrages public decency, whether or not it also tends to corrupt and deprave those who see or hear it". These words were approved by the Court of Appeal in *Gibson and Sylveire* (below), which denied that an indecent exhibition was in essence an obscenity offence. Those who are charged on the basis of an indecent exhibition cannot claim a defence of public good based upon any artistic merit which the exhibition may possess. It should also be remembered that, as illustrated in the *Gibson* case, indecency does not necessarily have anything to do with sex. The viewing of art exhibitions or other public displays may come within the bounds of outraging public decency if those persons who view such displays are so appalled and abhorred by what they see that it results in undermining the normal standards of propriety.

6–070 In *R. v. Gibson, R. v. Sylveire*[39]:

Facts. The defendant, S, was in charge of an art gallery called "Young Unknowns' Gallery" in East London. As part of an art exhibition, the defendant, G, created a sculpture for display entitled *Human Earrings*, consisting of a freeze-dried human foetus, of some three months gestation, attached to the earlobe of a model's head. The earrings were hanging by a ring which was indented into the skull of the foetus. The defendants were convicted of outraging public decency. They appealed.

Decision. The appellants argued that the prosecution were prevented from bringing a common law charge, by section 2(4) of the OPA 1959. Lord Lane stated that, if "obscene" under the OPA 1959 had the wider definition, *i.e.* to include revulsion, disgust or outrage,[40] then either the prosecution should have been brought under the OPA, or not at all. However, it was stated that the only true meaning which can be given to an obscene article is its narrower definition in section 1(1), *i.e.* to deprave and corrupt, and only that meaning applies to section 2(4). Therefore, since the sculpture did not deprave or corrupt those who saw it, but only revulsion and disgust followed, then there was no error in bringing the prosecution under the common law. The appellants further argued that it was for the prosecution to prove that they intended to outrage public decency or were aware of the risk that such an outrage would ensue. The court held that there was no need for intention to outrage public decency. All that was required was that there was an intention to do the act, in this case, exhibit. The court accepted the prosecution argument that

> "the object of the common law offence is to protect the public from suffering feelings of outrage by such exhibition. Thus, if a defendant intentionally does an act which in fact outrages public decency, the public will suffer outrage whatever the defendant's state of mind may be".[41]

The appeal was accordingly dismissed.

Since the *mens rea* (mental state) required for offences against public decency has caused some confusion, a comparison between this and other similar offences may be helpful. Criminal law has a basic presumption that every offence requires proof of a prohibited mental state, such as intention or recklessness, in the defendant at the time of committing the offence. But there is in fact a large category of criminal offences of "strict liability", for which neither intention nor recklessness need be proven. Most strict liability offences are created by statutes, and it was thought that the common law did not contain any strict liability offences, but there are now notable exceptions to any such argument.[42] Whether a defendant is charged with an obscenity offence under section 1(1) of the Obscene Publications Act 1959 or with an offence of outraging public decency at common law will in fact make no difference in relation to the mental state which must be established by the prosecution; both offences are now offences of strict liability. If section 1(1) of the 1959 Act is charged, the only mental state which must be proved is that the defendant published the obscene article voluntarily; it is of no avail to him to argue that he did not intend to deprave or corrupt anybody or that he had no idea that this could be the consequence of his actions. If the charge is outraging public decency, it need only be shown that the defendant knew the nature of his actions; it will be similarly useless to him to protest that he neither intended to outrage public decency nor foresaw that this could be the result of what he had done voluntarily. Thus the remaining practical differences between the statutory offence and the common law offence are: first, that the section 2(4) artistic merit defence will only apply if the statutory offence is charged; and secondly, that the test for obscenity under section 1(1) is far more stringent (and thus harder to establish) than the indecency test for the common law offence. It is reasons such as these which lead to criticism of 6–071 the strict liability nature of the common law offence, since the combination of lack of available defences and an easily satisfied test for outraging public decency makes it easy enough to convict of this offence. There does not appear to be any pressing need for the presumption of *mens rea* to be overturned and strict liability to be imposed in this situation.

It should be remembered that both of the conspiracy offences discussed in this chapter (conspiracy to corrupt public morals and conspiracy to outrage public decency) do require proof of a mental state in the defendant; for both offences it must be established by the prosecution that the defendant intended to bring about the prohibited result which was involved in his plan. Thus a conspiracy charge is more difficult to prove than a completed offence.

(2) Indecent Exposure: Introduction

6–072 An indecent act, whether or not sexual, may constitute an offence against public decency at common law.[43] Indecent exposure of the defendant's own body is by far the most common example of the offence of outraging public decency. The exposure of the body must occur in public, but courts have consistently interpreted this to mean that the exposure must take place in a location which at least two persons could have seen, regardless of the number who actually witnessed it.[44] It need not be shown that anyone was annoyed or disgusted by the exposure,[45] merely that the exposure "in public" was indecent according to the established standards of society in general. In *Lunderbech*,[46] the defendant was observed masturbating in a children's playground by two police officers, who were not proved to have been outraged by this. The court held that where, as here, an act is plainly indecent, the jury are entitled to convict although it has not been established that the witnesses were in fact disgusted or annoyed. It is no use for the defendant to argue that he did not intend to annoy or outrage anyone, since the only state of mind which must be established against him is that he exposed himself voluntarily.

6–073 In *R. v. May*[47]:

Facts. The defendant, who was a school teacher, handed a letter to a pupil, S, in a classroom, which was written by the defendant. The letter stated that because of former indecent acts committed by the defendant, he, the defendant, had to be punished. S was instructed to order the defendant to perform certain indecent acts including telling the defendant to "fuck the desk", *i.e.* to simulate sexual intercourse on top of the desk. The defendant duly obeyed. S, on other similar occasions, along with another pupil, W, and without any prompting from the defendant, would use their own initiative and order the defendant to perform various sexual things on himself. The defendant was charged and convicted of, *inter alia*, outraging public decency.

Decision. The main ground of appeal was that for the commission of the offence the indecent act in question had to be seen by at least one other person, other than those taking part in the indecent activity. Since it was argued that S and W were participants and not merely observers, the offence was not made out. The court rejected this argument. They said that the appellant had acted alone, despite the fact that the boys collaborated in giving their own orders, sometimes without prompting from the appellant. The only contribution the boys made to the whole situation was merely to be there. The court decided that this did not make them accomplices or participants throughout this whole series of events.

(3) Keeping a disorderly house

What is the offence of keeping a disorderly house? It does not mean that a person should clean and vacuum the house regularly and if not, is liable to be prosecuted. The essence of this common law offence is that of using a place for immoral purposes. In legal terms, it was stated to mean the following, as set out in *R. v. Quinn*,[48] **6–074**

> "A disorderly house is a house conducted contrary to law and good order in that matters are performed or exhibited of such a character that their performance or exhibition in a place of common resort (a) amounts to an outrage of public decency, (b) tends to deprave or corrupt, or (c) is otherwise calculated to injure the public interest so as to call for condemnation and punishment."[49]

The court in that case said that this definition was restricted to performances or exhibitions which were indecent and that (a), (b) and (c) above were not mutually exclusive, and indeed, in some circumstances all three may overlap. The word "disorderly" was, in *R. v. Berg*[50] given its ordinary dictionary definition (Webster's dictionary), *i.e.* not regulated by the restraints of morality: unchaste, of bad repute, as a disorderly house. There must also exist the element of "open house", *i.e.* providing the general public with such sexual services that by their very nature constitute an outrage to public decency or "is otherwise calculated to injure the public interest to such an extent as to call for condemnation and punishment".[51]

In *R. v. Tan*,[52] the defendants argued against the charge of keeping a disorderly house, because what took place (the activities involved bondage, perversions, whipping, chaining, etc.) was with the full consent and wishes between the client and prostitute. This was rejected by the court. Parker L.J. said that though, for instance, a striptease act may not be criminal, even that may still exceed the law and become unacceptable and thus unlawful.[53] It is for the jury to set the standard on what is and what is not acceptable.[54] Because the offence is so wide in character and certainty, the judge must explain to the jury that in order to convict they must be satisfied that there was sufficient evidence of an open house.

In *Moores v. DPP*[55]: **6–075**

Facts. The defendant was the licensee of a pub. A male exotic dancer gave two performances on a particular evening. The second performance involved audience participation, whereby a woman from the audience rubbed oil on the dancer's penis which was covered behind a towel. The act also involved the dancer leaning over a woman in the "full monty". No complaints were made. The defendant was charged with keeping a disorderly house. He was convicted and appealed.

Decision. The defendant argued that in order to be guilty of this offence, he had to, *inter alia*, (1) use the premises persistently and, (2) have knowledge of the indecent act. With regard to (1), the court admitted that although there was no authority directly on this particular issue, nevertheless, what authority there was found favour with the appellant's arguments on this point.[56] Prior to this, there had never been a conviction of this offence where there had only been "one isolated incident".[57] Bingham L.J. said that "a house does not acquire the legal character of disorderliness because disorder occurs there on one occasion any more than a house becomes a . . . brothel because it is used for purposes of prostitution by more than one woman on a single occasion".[58] The court also accepted that knowledge was necessary in these circumstances. Accordingly, the appeal was allowed.

(4) Blasphemy

6–076 Blasphemy (or, more accurately, blasphemous libel) is a common law offence which dates back to the seventeenth century and was originally a crime against the State, an act of deep subversion.[59] It began as a method of protecting the Anglican faith from criticism and attack, particularly by atheists, regardless of the motive behind the defendant's words or acts. By the late nineteenth century, judges had refined the definition of the offence so that it became permissible to criticise the Christian faith, provided that the language used evidenced neither disrespect nor obscenity. In fact, blasphemy attracts far more attention and criticism as an offence than is merited by the number of prosecutions mounted—charges have been rare indeed in the twentieth century, with only one prosecution between 1922 and 1978, the now notorious case of *Whitehouse v. Lemon and Gay News*.[60] Early cases involved proof of no more than, for example, a denial of the truth of any tenet of Christianity,[61] but it appears that remarks made earnestly and inoffensively were not prosecuted. Lord Sumner stated in the House of Lords case of *Bowman v. Secular Society*[62] that the reasons why blasphemers are criminally punishable are:

> ". . . their manner, their violence, or ribaldry, or, more fully stated, for their tendency to endanger the peace then and there, to deprave public morality generally, to shake the fabric of society and to be a cause of civil strife".

If such a test were applied seriously, then it would be almost impossible to sustain a prosecution for blasphemy in the modern world since such extreme effects as thus enumerated by Lord Sumner would be almost impossible to achieve nowadays. Unfortunately for the defendants in the *Lemon and Gay News* case, the House of Lords employed a test which makes conviction far easier. "Endangering the peace" and "shaking the fabric of society" are no longer requirements.

In *Whitehouse v. Lemon and Gay News*[63]: **6–077**

Facts. The defendants were the editor and publisher of a newspaper which had published a poem, *The Love that Dares to Speak its Name* by James Kirkup, an acclaimed poet. In the words of Lord Diplock, the poem claims:

> "to describe in explicit detail acts of sodomy and fellatio with the body of Christ immediately after his death and to ascribe to Him during his lifetime promiscuous homosexual practices . . .".

Mary Whitehouse commenced a private prosecution against the defendants for blasphemous libel, and both defendants were convicted. The editor received a nine months suspended prison sentence, which was quashed by the Court of Appeal. Both defendants were fined, and the Court of Appeal upheld the fines. The defendants appealed to the House of Lords.

Decision. The House of Lords dismissed the appeal, by a majority decision of 3:2. The majority of the court held that there was no need to prove that the defendants intended to offend or shock Christians; the offence is one of strict liability, for which the only mental element which need be established is that the defendant intended to "publish" the words (whether in writing or speech).

Smith and Hogan[64] state from *Lemon* that "a publication is blasphemous if it is couched in indecent or offensive terms likely to shock and outrage the feelings of the general body of Christian believers in the community." The most obvious point of attack against blasphemy as it stands is that it is discriminatory, protecting only Christianity. An attempt was made recently to challenge this aspect of the offence, arguing that it should be available to defend any established religion.

In *R. v. Chief Metropolitan Magistrate, ex parte Choudhury*[65]:

Facts. A group of Muslims applied to the Divisional Court to challenge the decision of the chief magistrate, who had refused to issue a summons for blasphemous libel against Salman Rushdie, the author of *The Satanic Verses*, and its publishers. The Chief Magistrate's grounds for his refusal were that the religion of Islam was not protected by the law of blasphemous libel.

Decision. The court held that the law of blasphemy applies only to attacks on Christianity, and so the Chief Magistrate's refusal was correct. To allow a prosecution in this case would have been judicial legislation, in other words the court would have been usurping the legislative function which can only be exercised by Parliament. Since extremely complex matters of public policy would be involved in deciding on whether there should be any extension of the religions protected by blasphemy, and to which religions it should be extended, the court refused to engage in speculation as to any reform which should be made.

The plaintiffs attempted to bring a case based upon Articles 9 and 14 of the ECHR, but failed on the basis that Article 9 may not be used to create a positive obligation upon states to protect religious sensibilities.

Comparisons between *Lemon* and *Choudhury* are unfavourable and point strongly in favour of reform. The majority of the Law Commissions' Report on Offences Against Religion and Public Worship,[66] thought that the drafting difficulties involved in deciding the scope of protection of a widened blasphemy offence would be insurmountable, and so recommended the abolition of the existing, unfair and flawed offence. In 1994 the House of Lords tabled an amendment to a bill by which this abolition would have been achieved, but the then Government opposed the amendment so strongly that it was withdrawn. Abolition would not create any great problems since existing public order offences would plug the gap fairly efficiently, particularly if supported by the enactment of a new statutory offence of inciting religious hatred, as recommended by some reformers (including the minority of the Law Commission). Apart from these few high-profile cases, the offence of blasphemy has not been successful as a method of restraining objectionable "speech". An illustration of the problems invoked can be seen in relation to two films, *The Last Temptation of Christ* and *Monty Python's Life of Brian*, both of which are arguably blasphemous and are definitely capable of offending some Christians. The publishers of the latter sought legal advice from various well-qualified sources, but the experts were unable to agree as to whether the film script would endanger the publishers with criminal liability; the film went ahead uncensored and no prosecution was forthcoming. The former film caused media sensation and public outcry, with demands that a prosecution should be commenced against the film's distributors, but no such prosecutions were brought; sanctions took another form instead, that of bans imposed by some local councils so that cinemas in many areas were unable to show the film.

1. Film and Video

6–078 *Censorship of the media (excluding obscenity and indecency offences)*[67]

The discussion so far in this chapter has centred upon written, printed or spoken words in the context of liability for obscenity and indecency offences, but it must be recognised that the broadcast media and the film and video industries have an ever-increasing impact in modern life. Although film, video and broadcasting are subject to the criminal offences discussed above, there are additional measures of regulation which apply to these fields as a recognition of the effect which they may have upon their audiences.

Film and videos are regulated by a system of censorship which is broadly similar for both media, and is largely implemented by the BBFC—the British Board of Film Classification, together with local authorities. This regulation has in fact been in existence in some form since 1909,[68] but recent changes have greatly strengthened the control which may be exercised by the authorities. The Cinemas Act 1985 makes local authorities responsible for the licensing of premises in which films are to be shown to the public. Section 1 states:

"(1). . . no premises shall be used for a film exhibition unless they are licensed for the purpose . . .

(2) A licensing authority may grant a licence under this section to such a person as they think fit to use any premises specified in the licence for the purpose of film exhibitions on such terms and conditions and subject to such restrictions as (the licensing authority) . . . may determine.

(3) . . . it shall be the duty of a licensing authority in granting a licence under this section as regards any premises,—

(a) to impose conditions or restrictions prohibiting the admission of children to film exhibitions involving the showing of works designated, by the authority or by such other body as may be specified in the licence, as works unsuitable for children; and

(b) to consider what (if any) conditions or restrictions should be imposed as to the admission of children to other film exhibitions . . ."

Section 2 provides that:

"(1). . . no premises shall be used, except with the consent of the licensing authority, for a film exhibition organised wholly or mainly as an exhibition for children.

(2). . . a licensing authority may, without prejudice to any conditions or restrictions imposed by them on the granting of a licence, impose special conditions or restrictions on the granting of a consent under this section."

Thus local authorities have a duty to impose conditions which prohibit the admission of children to film exhibitions which are "unsuitable"; local authorities also have a power to impose conditions which relate to the admission of adults.

A "film exhibition" is an exhibition of moving pictures, but excludes **6–079** broadcasting. If a person is refused a licence, he may appeal to the Crown Court (section 16). Sections 5 and 6 provide exceptions to the licensing requirement for film exhibitions which are not made for profit and to which the general public are not admitted; thus non-profitmaking film clubs and home-made films are exempt. The duty to issue or withhold licences (as appropriate) and the power to impose conditions on licensed cinemas have been used in practice as a censorship tool. There are model licensing conditions which are drafted by the Home Office and which have been implemented by most local authorities, which include the following[69]:

"(1) no film, other than a current newsreel, shall be exhibited unless it has received a certificate of the British Board of Film Classification or is the subject of the licensing authority's permission;

. . .

(3) no film shall be exhibited if the licensing authority gives notice in writing prohibiting its exhibition on the ground that it 'would offend against good taste or decency or would be likely to encourage or incite to crime or to lead to disorder or to be offensive to public feeling'."

In London, there are further conditions in cinema licences, prohibiting the exhibition of any film which is likely to have any of the following effects:

(i) encouragement or incitement of crime;

(ii) leading to disorder;

(iii) stirring up racial, ethnic or sexual hatred;

(iv) promoting the sexual humiliation or degradation of, or violence towards, women;

(v) being such as to tend to deprave and corrupt persons who are likely to see it;

(vi) containing a grossly indecent performance which outrages the standards of public decency.

6–080 Thus the licensing system, as it is operated, is a censorship system rather than a formality. Films are granted certificates which permit them to be shown to persons above a particular age, based upon the content of the film and its subject matter. In fact, local authorities have long delegated most of their licensing responsibilities to the BBFC. In 1912 the film industry responded to local authorities' censorship powers by setting up the British Board of Film Censors (later renamed the British Board of Film Classification). The BBFC was intended to be an independent and objective body which would advise local authorities as to whether or not any particular film should be granted a certificate and, if so, which type. The BBFC has no statutory or other official power in relation to films, but in practice local authorities almost always delegate their powers to the BBFC. The BBFC will decide the minimum age of children who may be admitted to a film, and may deny a certificate altogether to particular films, or insist that cuts should be made before a certificate would be granted. The validity of the BBFC's exercise of censorship powers was challenged in *Mills v. LCC*,[70] but the court held that it is permissible for a local authority to delegate its powers to the BBFC, provided that the local authority retains for itself the final decision (at least in theory). Local authorities do sometimes overrule the BBFC's decision; for example in 1997 the film *Crash*, which links car crashes with sex, was banned by several local authorities in spite of the BBFC's decision to grant a certificate to that film.

The BBFC uses the following classification system for both films and videos:

— U (Universal): suitable for all persons, including children,

— Uc (Universal, particularly suitable for young children): applies only to videos,

— PG (Parental Guidance): some scenes may be unsuitable for very young children; may contain some non-sexual nudity, mild violence,

— 12: passed for viewing only by persons aged 12 or above; may include implications of sex within a relationship, some swearing, limited violence,

— 15: passed for viewing only by persons aged 15 or above; may include non-sexual nudity, even full frontal; brief sex; use of soft drugs; violence and horror,

— 18: passed for viewing only by persons aged 18 or above; may include controversial religious or sexual topics, full nudity, simulated sex, use of hard drugs, any expletives, graphic violence. But sadism, or the glamorisation of weapons or drugs, will not normally be permitted within this classification,

— R18 (restricted 18): passed for restricted distribution only through cinemas or sex shops with a special licence and to which no persons under the age of 18 have access. May contain graphic consensual sex as far as the law allows; pornographic language will not be censored.

If a film (or video) offends against the provisions of the criminal law, then it will be denied a certificate altogether, unless the BBFC considers that cuts can be made which will remove the offensive material. For example, the erotic video *Visions of Ecstasy* was denied a certificate on the ground that it might be blasphemous in its depiction of Saint Teresa in sexual activity with the crucified body of Christ.[71] When the BBFC refuses to grant a certificate to a film, or grants a certificate with a higher age restriction than was hoped for, the distributors of the film may approach local authorities one by one and so perhaps gain local certificates. Most of the cuts which the BBFC orders to be made to films relate to sexual violence, excessive or glorified violence, obscenity and similar topics, but the BBFC does not fetter its discretion by using any system of precedent. The fate of each film is decided on the merits of the film, with due attention being paid to the context and treatment of any controversial subject matter which it may contain.

While local authorities have no duty to censor films for adults, but merely **6–081** for children, it is clear that they may so act. In *R. v. Greater London Council, ex parte Blackburn*,[72] it was decided that, if a local authority does censor films for adults (whether it exercises such a power itself or affirms decisions made by the BBFC) then it must not allow the exhibition of any film which constitutes an Obscene Publications Act offence, or indeed any other criminal offence such as the indecency offences discussed earlier in this chapter. Obviously, videos were not included within the licensing requirements of the Cinematograph Act 1909, but their wide availability since the 1980s and, in particular, the growth of the home-viewing rental and retail video industries led to pressure for regulation. Concern ran especially high in relation to "video-nasties"; films containing horror, violence or explicit sex, and often all three. Until 1984, the only controls which operated on the provision of videos for the home market was obscenity law, both statutory and common law, and these offences may still be charged, but the Video Recordings Act 1984 introduced a system of censorship of videos prior to their release and distribution. The pressure towards censorship was increased by various campaign groups, who relied upon research findings which purported to show that children who were exposed to violent videos were likely to become violent, and that over a third of children under the age of seven were likely to have seen at least one video-nasty in their own home. These research studies have since been hotly disputed and the methodology has been shown to be flawed.[73]

The Video Recordings Act 1984 introduced a comprehensive system of video classification and censorship under which, in contrast to the situation concerning films, the BBFC is given statutory powers and duties. Sections 9–11 of the 1984 Act create criminal offences:

(i) Supplying/offering to supply a video recording of an unclassified work.

(ii) Possessing a video recording of an unclassified work for the purposes of supply.

(iii) Supplying a video recording in breach of its classification.

Supply need not be for gain, and includes hire, sale, exchange and loan. A recording is unclassified if no certificate has been issued for it by the BBFC. The classifications used are those listed above (U, PG, etc) with the exception that the "12" classification does not apply to videos.

6–082 There are, however, certain types of video which do not have to comply with the classification requirements of the 1984 Act: "exempted works" and "exempted supplies". An "exempted work" is one which, when viewed as a whole, is intended to "inform, educate or instruct", or is concerned with "sport, religion or music", or is a "videogame" (section 2(1)). But any of these works will not be exempt if it depicts "to any significant extent":

> ". . . human sexual activity or acts of force or restraint associated with such activity; mutilation or torture of, or other acts of gross violence towards, humans or animals; human genital organs or human urinary or excretory functions".

Section 89 of the Criminal Justice and Public Order Act 1994 extended the list of factors which will prevent a work from being exempt from classification, to include: "Techniques likely to be useful in the commission of offences" and; "criminal activity which is likely to any significant extent to stimulate or encourage the commission of offences", (*e.g.* videos on home bomb-making or the best methods of growing cannabis). Every video which is not exempted must be submitted to the BBFC for approval and classification before it is first distributed. When making its considerations, the BBFC is under a duty to have special regard to the likelihood of the video being viewed in the home (section 4); this requirement stems from concerns that videos are accessible to children in their own homes and that particular scenes can be replayed repeatedly, freeze-framed and held on screen for a prolonged time. Some of these concerns may have been overplayed,[74] but the statute does require the BBFC to recognise that a film which is shown at the cinema may not be suitable for home viewing except by a more restricted audience. It is in fact relatively common for a film which is, for example, a "15" at the cinema to be required to be cut before it can receive the same classification on video, or even to be granted an "18" on video release. Some distributors deliberately target audiences of different ages for the cinema and video releases of the same film, in effect releasing two different versions of the film which will be differently censored. "Exempted supplies" are: supplies other than for reward and not in the course or furtherance of business, (*e.g.* gifts), and supplies to participants of recordings of events, (*e.g.* a video of a wedding distributed to guests). There is a right of appeal against a decision by the BBFC to the Video Appeals Committee.

The Video Recordings Act 1993 added a general defence to the offences under the 1984 Act:

> (a) "that the commission of the offence was due to the act of default of a person other than the accused; and
> (b) that the accused took all reasonable precautions and exercised all due diligence to avoid the commission of the offence by any person under his control."

In 1994, the Newson Report was published in the wake of the public concern over the murder of James Bulger and the trial of his young killers. Much had been made in the media of a claimed link between exposure to video violence and the killings, and the Newson Report purported to prove this link and provide general evidence that violent videos cause an increase in violence in society. Although many academics criticised the report and attacked its methodology and claims, the Government was sufficiently affected to include within the Criminal Justice and Public Order Act 1994 the following provision. Under section 90 of the 1994 Act the BBFC must have "special regard" in exercising its functions under the 1984 Act to:

> "any harm that may be caused to potential viewers or, through their behaviour, to society the manner in which the work deals with—(a) criminal behaviour, (b) illegal drugs, (c) violent behaviour or incidents, (d) horrific behaviour or incidents, or (e) human sexual activity".

So, the BBFC is required to look not only at what the video contains but also the potential effects of viewing that material on its likely viewers. The question is not so much whether the video is obscene/indecent, but whether it could be harmful; thus videos are treated differently from other media as far as censorship is concerned.

The 1994 Act also increased the penalties for the offences under the 1984 Act to include prison terms of up to two years.

2. Broadcasting

6–083 In contrast to the distributors and producers of videos, broadcasters are subject to very little official censorship, relying instead upon an officially-sanctioned and longstanding system of self-regulation, supported by independent complaints and supervisory bodies. In fact, until 1990, television and radio were not even subject to the offences under the Obscene Publications Act 1959. Section 162 of the Broadcasting Act 1990 changed that, but the practical effect of the change is likely to be small since little is broadcast which would contravene the "deprave and corrupt" test under the 1959 Act. Explicit sex and violence are broadcast, but subject to a framework of rules and censorship which makes complaints relatively infrequent. Indeed, more complaints concern swearing than sex.

The Broadcasting Act 1990 created the Independent Television Commission[75] which is responsible for the licensing and regulation of all television services, terrestrial and satellite, except for those run by the BBC. In addition to many other functions, the ITC is under a duty to (section 6):

> ". . . do all that they can to secure that every licensed service complies with the following requirements, namely—
>
> (a) that nothing is included in its programmes which offends against good taste or decency or is likely to encourage or incite to crime or to lead to .disorder or to be offensive to public feeling;
>
> (d) that due responsibility is exercised with respect to the content of any of its programmes which are religious programmes, and that in particular any such programmes do not involve—
>
> (i) any improper exploitation of any susceptibilities of those watching the programmes, or
>
> (ii) any abusive treatment of the religious views and beliefs of those belonging to a particular religion or religious denomination".

There is a duty in section 7 to draw up and implement a Code of Practice relating to the showing of violence, for which special regard must be given to the likelihood of children watching at particular times. In 1991 the ITC published the first such Code, which was updated in 1993, and implements a "watershed" under which Family Viewing programming prevails until 9 p.m., with progressively more sex and violence being shown after that time until 5.30 a.m. But the Code recognises that it is impossible to exclude violence from broadcasting, since even news reports may legitimately include scenes of violence. The emphasis is placed upon responsible treatment and correct timeslots. The ITC, unlike its predecessor, is not a censor and is not expected to ban programmes before their intended broadcast.

The Broadcasting Act 1996 gives statutory duties to the Broadcasting Standards Commission, an independent body to which appointments are made by the Home Secretary. The BSC is placed under a duty to create and implement a Code of Guidance for broadcasters which deals with matters of decency, with particular attention to the depiction of sex and violence (section 108). The BSC is under a further duty to deal with complaints about indecency, sex or violence in broadcasts, and may have a hearing to enable it to reach a decision (sections 110 and 116). In spite of complex requirements as to notification of any hearing, procedure and publication of results, the BSC is easy to criticise as being "toothless" since its only sanction is that of forcing the broadcaster against whom the complaint was made to make a publication of its findings. The BBC is also placed under similar duties by the terms of its Royal Charter and by its Licence, including duties in relation to taste, decency, depiction of sex, violence and crime and avoidance of causing offence to the public.

RELEVANT ECHR CASES: ARTICLES 9 AND 10, FREEDOM OF RELIGION AND FREEDOM OF EXPRESSION

ARTICLE 9: RIGHT TO FREEDOM OF THOUGHT, CONSCIENCE AND RELIGION 6–084

1 Everyone has the right to freedom of thought, conscience and religion; this right includes freedom to change his religion or beliefs and freedom, either alone or in community with others and in public or private, to manifest his religion or belief, in worship, teaching, practice or observance.

2 Freedom to manifest one's religion or beliefs shall be subject only to such limitations as are prescribed by law and are necessary in a democratic society in the interests of public safety, for the protection of public order, health or morals, or for the protection of the rights and freedoms of others.

The words "thought", "conscience", "religion" and "belief" conjure up many different meanings according to their particular application and the circumstances in which they are used.

One of the hallmarks of any democratic society is the respect for another's religion or beliefs such that those persons wishing to follow their faith or convictions should not be interfered with by that State's authorities. Article 9(1) principally concerns the right of an individual not only the freedom to belong to a faith or possess different beliefs (which includes persons such as agnostics, atheists, pacifists,[76] sceptics etc.) but also to "manifest" that religion or belief via the means of worship, teaching, practice and observance.

The word "belief" encapsulates so many different ideas and categories (including the overlap with religion and thought and conscience) that it is doubtful whether its meaning can be pigeonholed into some particular class or other. A broad interpretation of the word may include various philosophies which are recognised in a democratic society. For example in *Arrowsmith v. United Kingdom*,[77] "pacifism" was recognised as a legitimate belief since it was, the Commission said, in its own right a philosophy and fell within the bounds of "thought and conscience" and was therefore protected by Article 9.[78] However, the manifestation of a person's belief may be somewhat restricted through the means of teaching, worship, observance and practice. Thus in *Arrowsmith*, the applicant, a pacifist, was convicted under the Incitement to Disaffection Act 1934, for distributing leaflets inciting those British soldiers who were about to do a tour of duty in Northern Ireland to desert. The question for the Commission was whether the applicant's action constituted a "practice" of her pacifist beliefs. The Commission said that the term "practice" "does not cover each act which is motivated or influenced by a religion or belief."[79] Having examined the content of the leaflet the Commission were of the opinion that the applicant was not attempting to advance pacifist ideals by promoting wholly non-violent policies but was solely trying to dissuade soldiers from serving in Northern Ireland and to desert. This "practice" was not considered to be a manifestation of her pacifist beliefs since the leaflets themselves did nothing to further the principles of pacifism itself and therefore fell outside the protection of Article 9(1).

Whilst the right to the freedom of thought and conscience are absolute, and not liable to State interference, the manifestation of religion or beliefs are restricted to the exceptions set out in Article 9(2). One of the main problems when dealing with expressing one's own beliefs is whether a contracting State's existing legislation which actually prohibits deliberate indoctrination in order to persuade others to convert is contrary to the Convention and especially "for the protection of the rights and freedoms of others" under Article 9(2).

In *Kokkinakis v. Greece*[80]:

Facts. The applicant, who was a Jehovah's Witness, was accused of attempting to proselytise a Christian Orthodox woman by undermining her beliefs. He was convicted under section 4 of the Act which define proselytism as:

> ". . . any direct or indirect attempt to intrude on the religious beliefs of a person of a different religious persuasion, with the aim of undermining those beliefs, either by any kind of inducement or promise of an inducement or moral support or material assistance, or by fraudulent means or by taking advantage of his inexperience, trust, need, low intellect or naivety".

The applicant complained to the Commission that his conviction violated his rights under, *inter alia*, Article 9 and that by not allowing him to "manifest" his religious beliefs was contrary to Article 9. He further argued that this denial was "incompatible with the spirit of tolerance which should exist in a democratic society".[81]

Opinion of the Commission. The main question was whether the applicant was legally prevented from propagating his beliefs under the exceptions in Article 9(2).

The Commission were of the opinion that the law was sufficiently precise to properly regard the Act as "prescribed by law". The purpose was for the protection of the rights of others—in this case the safeguarding of the Greek Orthodox woman's freedom of religion, and thus in this instance was a legitimate aim. The final question was whether it was "necessary in a democratic society". The respondent Government argued that the applicant took advantage of the woman's inexperience and feebleness, by her first agreeing to allow him to enter her home and then, by devious means, attempted to undermine her beliefs.[82] Although a Contracting State is given a wide margin of appreciation in these matters, the Commission felt that the inoffensive words and opinions used by the applicant could not have, in themselves, taken advantage of the woman nor undermined her existing religious beliefs. There was no satisfactory evidence that the woman was in fact inexperienced or feeble-minded. The Commission was of the opinion that the applicant's conviction in the circumstances was unjustified as representing such a pressing social need that the conviction was necessary for the protection of the religious beliefs of its citizens. Accordingly the exception in Article 9(2) was not justified for state interference as being of necessity under the circumstances.

Findings of the Court. Was the authority's interference justified by any of the exceptions in Article 9(2)? The main problem for the court was weighing up, on the one hand, the protection of the rights of others, and on the other hand, the behaviour of the applicant. The court distinguished between "bearing Christian witness" (true evangelism—an essential mission and a responsibility of every Christian and every Church), and "improper proselytism" (which includes offering material or social advantages in order to gain new members; exerting improper pressure on people in distress or need; using violence or brainwashing).[83] However, the court said that the authorities had not shown precisely what improper methods the applicant had used; merely citing section 4 of the Act without more, was not enough. Therefore his conviction could not be regarded as justified within the context of a pressing social need such that it was necessary for the protection of the rights and freedoms of others within Article 9(2). Accordingly, by a majority of six votes to three the Court found that there had been a breach of Article 9.

In a partly dissenting judgment Judge Pettiti said that "improper proselytism" was connected with freedom of religion in that it is the right of an agnostic philosopher to express his beliefs to try to share them and even to try to convert others. But he did accept that even here there were limits to persuasion, in that force or manipulative behaviour, brainwashing and other like techniques should not be permitted in order to convert others.[84] He further stated that:

> "The domain of spiritual, religious or philosophical beliefs belongs to the intimate sphere of beliefs and the right to express them. It is dangerous to allow the existence of a repressive system with no protections for the citizens and one has seen the hazards created by authoritarian regimes declaring freedom of religion in their Constitution whilst restricting it by instituting criminal offences on parasitism, subversiveness or proselytism".[85]

Article 10: Right to Freedom of Expression

1 Everyone has the right to freedom of expression. This right shall include freedom to hold opinions and to receive and impart information and ideas without interference by public authority **6–086**

and regardless of frontiers. This Article shall not prevent States from requiring the licensing of broadcasting, television or cinema enterprises.

2 The exercise of these freedoms, since it carries with it duties and responsibilities, may be subject to such formalities, conditions, restrictions or penalties as are prescribed by law and are necessary in a democratic society, in the interests of national security, territorial integrity or public safety, for the prevention of disorder or crime, for the protection of health or morals, for the protection of the reputation or rights of others, for preventing the disclosure of information received in confidence, or for maintaining the authority and impartiality of the judiciary.

It was stated in *Handyside v. United Kingdom*[86] that:

> "Freedom of expression, as secured in paragraph 1 of Article 10, constitutes one of the essential foundations of a democratic society and one of the basic conditions for its progress and for each individual's self-fulfilment. Subject to paragraph 2, it is applicable not only to 'information' or 'ideas' that are favourably received or regarded as inoffensive or as a matter of indifference, but also to those that offend, shock or disturb. Such are the demands of that pluralism, tolerance and broadmindedness without which there is no democratic society".[87]

From the above quotation it can be observed that the freedom of expression generally entitles an individual to communicate different types of information without fear of intervention by the national authorities. The information itself may include counselling and advice. In *Open Door Counselling and Dublin Well Women v. Ireland*,[88] a case which involved two organisations passing out information to pregnant women who wished to have abortions abroad, the court held that, even though the national authorities were to be given a wide margin of appreciation on the question of morals in their own country, such an interference (in this instance via an injunction) was a violation of Article 10. However, an individual does not have the right *per se* to receive information, *e.g.* personal records, which are confidential, from a public authority.[89]

Throughput of the information itself may take many forms including literature, films, artistic expression, publications, journalistic writings, programmes transmitted by the media and the like (all of which will be discussed below). Because of the wide interpretation given to the freedom of expression many cases which have come before the Commission and court have tended to overlap with other Articles, especially Articles 9, 11 and 14. However, this freedom is not unfettered and is subject to the exceptions set out in Article 10(2) provided, as in Articles 8, 9, and 11 any such interference is prescribed by law and necessary in a democratic society.

"Prescribed by law"

In Article 8(2) similar words appear, *i.e.* "in accordance with the law", and for the purposes of interpretation "prescribed by law" ought to be construed in like manner. In the case of *The Sunday Times v. United Kingdom*,[90] the court said that the meaning of the words "prescribed by law" must be interpreted "in a way that reconciles them as far as possible and is most appropriate in order to realise the aim and achieve the object of the treaty".[91] The word "law" applies to common law as well as to statute law. Further, the law in question must be clear, certain and consistent. In the above case, the Attorney-General was granted an injunction preventing the newspaper from publishing an article which would be detrimental to a possible litigant, *i.e.* by pressurising Distillers into making a more reasonable settlement (the "pressure principle,") or alternatively had the effect of prejudging the matter (the "prejudgment principle"). Since the injunction was an interference by a public authority, one of the main issues before the Commission was whether the contempt of court law came within Article 10(2) as justifying a restriction prescribed by law. The applicant contended that since the law was so vague and uncertain, it could not properly be regarded as "prescribed by law". The court said that the expression required the following two conditions: (i) the individual must have an adequate indication of the relevant law; (ii) the law must be formulated with sufficient precision that he must be able to reasonably foresee the consequences. The court decided that the domestic law was sufficiently precise and not "so new" so as to constitute the expression "prescribed by law". The next issue was whether it was a legitimate aim under Article 10(2); namely, "maintaining the authority and impartiality of the judiciary."[92] After considering the House of Lords' decision that Distillers (the possible litigant) were entitled to be protected by the courts from the "prejudices of prejudgment," the court said that the applicants were able to foresee, to a degree that was reasonable in the circumstances, a risk that publication of the draft article might fall foul of the principle.[93] Therefore they decided that there was a legitimate aim to be safeguarded. 6–087

As part of the "quality" of the domestic legal rules, the "prescribed by law" requirement implies a pre-existing law, and not "new law" which was created during the relevant domestic proceedings. Thus, in *Gay News Ltd and Lemon v. United Kingdom*,[94] the applicants were convicted under a private prosecution, of blasphemous libel for the publication of a poem entitled *The Love that Dares to Speak its Name*, describing acts of sodomy and fellatio with the body of Christ after His death. The applicants complained to the Commission that there was an unjustified interference with their freedom of expression as laid down in Article 10, and in particular that the action taken by the authorities was not justified as "prescribed by law" under Article 10(2), on the basis that the offence was not sufficiently certain or clear and extended the existing common law in this area. The main question to be decided under this offence was the issue of whether "*mens rea*" was required. This was clarified by the House of Lords (by a 3:2 majority), as being an offence of strict liability. Thus, there was no making of "new law" by the courts, merely an "acceptable clarification" of existing law. As a consequence, the court found that the Government had abided with the "prescribed by law" requirement. The next issue was whether the restriction or penalty suffered by the applicant was justified as being for a legitimate purpose; in this case "the protection of the rights of others" in Article 10(2). Since the whole purpose of the offence of blasphemous libel is "to protect the rights of citizens not to be offended in their religious (Christian) feelings by publications",[95] there was a legitimate aim to be safeguarded and therefore no violation of Article 10.

"Necessary in a democratic society"

6–088 The concept of "necessity" implies that "the interference corresponds to a pressing social need and, in particular, that it is proportionate to the legitimate aim pursued".[96] In *Handyside v. United Kingdom*,[97] the applicant published a book entitled *The Little Red Schoolbook* in the United Kingdom, after it was published in a number of other European countries without any legal complications. The book included chapters on "Learning, Education, Pupils and Thc Systcm". The chapter on "Pupils" concerned issues of sex and in particular, the relevant sections dealt with masturbation, orgasms, intercourse and pornography. In the United Kingdom, however, a prosecution against the applicant was brought under the Obscene Publications Act 1959 and 1964. He was found guilty and fined and copies of the book were forfeited and destroyed. The applicant complained to the Commission that, *inter alia*, his right to freedom of expression had been violated under Article 10. The applicant conceded that the interference was "prescribed by law", and further that the issues were legitimate and came within the "protection of morals" exception under Article 10(2). The main issue was whether the action taken by the authorities was "necessary in a democratic society". The safeguarding of moral standards differ between Contracting States, and it is recognised that the various individual countries are best able to judge the moral requirements of their own citizens ("margin of appreciation"), *i.e.* the action taken by the domestic law, "through 'restriction' or 'penalty' is reconcilable with freedom of expression as protected by Article 10".[98] The book's market was primarily aimed at children under 18 years of age, and the passages concerning sex encouraged young persons to commit questionable and even harmful sexual practices as well as other indecent acts. The court considered that the domestic courts were entitled to believe that the book would have "pernicious effects on the morals of many of the children and adolescents who would read it".[99] Thus the Government did have a legitimate aim to protect those morals.[99A] The applicant argued with regard to the word "necessity", that the measures taken by the authorities were disproportionate to the "pressing social need", especially since there were no prosecutions in Northern Ireland, Isle of Man, Channel Islands, and no convictions in Scotland. The court said that those places may have justifiable reasons why they did not do so (that is not the court's concern and besides, the domestic authorities are not under any compulsion to prosecute). Also, merely because other Contracting States permitted circulation of the book did not mean that the English convictions were incorrect. The court considered that each individual state is entitled to deal with their own safeguarding of morals, according to the circumstances pertaining to their own existing conditions, as they saw fit (a revised edition was afterwards circulated without any hindrance from the authorities).

In *The Sunday Times v. United Kingdom* (see above) despite the word "necessary" not possessing such a confined meaning as "indispensable" or even wide meanings as "desirable", "useful", or "ordinary", it does imply the existence of a pressing social need,[1] and despite the margin of appreciation given to Member States, the court has the "last word" on whether the respondent Government's interference was justified as being necessary within Article 10(2).[2] The court said that the "pressure principle" would have added very little to the already publicly debated arguments. The words "trial by newspaper" and the authority of the judiciary are, to a certain extent, intermingled in that if the article were published and the public were able to form an opinion prior to the court's findings, this may result in loss of respect and confidence in the court within the meaning of the legitimate aim. However, the court found that, although the proposed article was somewhat biased, nevertheless, the view of both sides were given, such that whatever decision was finally taken the authority of the judiciary would not be impaired. The freedom of expression included being informed of the facts, and in this case those facts were of public interest. Thus, the court said that "Those facts did not cease to be of public interest merely because they formed the background of pending litigation. By bringing to light certain facts, the article might have served as a break on speculative and unenlightened discussion".[3] Therefore, the court held that "the interference complained of did not correspond to a social need sufficiently pressing to outweigh the public interest in freedom of expression within the meaning of the Convention".[4] (by 11 votes to 9).

In the area of freedom of expression, the media play a vital role in the dissemination of information and opinion, but even they have certain obligations and responsibilities and must acknowledge that there are certain boundaries of expression which must not be crossed. Nevertheless, the Commission and court recognise that those who wish to impart information to the public should be given a wide degree of latitude before that right of expression is taken away under Article 10(2). In *De Haes and Gijsels v. Belgium*,[5] the applicants published a number of detailed articles in which they vehemently criticised, made personal attacks on and alleged bias against certain Court of Appeal judges over a custody judgment they had made. Three of the judges brought defamation actions against the applicants. The applicants complained to the Commission that although the infringement came under one of the legitimate aims; namely, the protection of the reputation or rights of others, the interference was not necessary in a democratic society under Article 10(2). The court did not doubt that it was in the public interest that the public should be aware of the custody battle going on and the decision of the court. They said that freedom of expression is not limited to publishing wholly innocent information which is inoffensive or indifferent, but may also include robust criticism that some may find objectionable, provided those statements do not overstep the bounds, such that interference is justified under the "legitimate aims" in Article 10(2). Here, opinions were given, which were based on fact, and thus were regarded by the court as permissible. The comments were in keeping with the overall tone of the events that had taken place. Therefore, there had been a violation of Article 10.

In *Lingens v. Austria*,[6] the applicant, a journalist, published two articles accusing the retiring Chancellor of being a Nazi sympathiser for political reasons, and stated that another politician, the leader of the Austria Liberal Party, who had served with the SS infantry, should resign from Parliament. The then Chancellor brought a defamation action against the applicant. He was convicted and complained to the Commission that there had been a violation of Article 10. Since it was conceded by the applicant that the interference was prescribed by law and involved a legitimate aim, *i.e.* for the protection of the reputation or rights of others, the remaining issue was, was the action taken by the authorities necessary in a democratic society? In reaching a decision, the court must not only consider the "proportionality principle", but also whether the reasons adduced by the Austrian courts to justify it are "relevant and sufficient". The court emphasised that political debate should not be stifled, and disagreed with the Vienna Court of Appeal that the purpose of a newspaper was merely to "impart information", without more, and then leave the reader to form his own opinions. It is within the bounds of freedom of expression for journalists to give their own opinions and make criticisms on political matters. In this sphere, the court regarded "the limits of acceptable criticism are accordingly wider as regards a politician as such than as regards a private individual".[7] Of course, politicians have the right to be protected even when on official public business, but as the court stated "in such cases the requirements of such protection have to be weighed in relation to the interests of open discussion of political issues".[8] Although, generally the articles were well balanced and in the public interest, the emotive words used (immoral, undignified, basest opportunism) were likely to injure the Chancellor's reputation. Nevertheless, the surrounding events which led to the article had to be considered, *i.e.* the aftermath of an election, and the harsh words used were not out of context in the circumstances. Also, the court found that the above expressions formed part of a "value judgment" (a distinction which the Vienna Court of Appeal did not make) and were not ones of fact; but his value judgments were based on undisputed facts and were made in good faith.[9] The applicant had the right to disclose publicly those opinions and ideas and therefore there was an interference with this freedom which was, the court decided, disproportionate to the legitimate aim pursued.

The principles set out in *Lingens v. Austria* (above), with regard to newspaper reporting, will equally apply, if not more so, to the media in general, *e.g.* television, film and radio. Thus, in *Jersild v. Denmark*,[10] the applicant, a broadcaster, was convicted of aiding and abetting a group of extremists called the "Greenjackets", by allowing the latter to spout racist remarks against immigrants and ethnic minorities in general, on a documentary TV programme. The applicant complained to the Commission of a violation of Article 10. The court in that case when evaluating whether the infringement was justified or not considered the case as a whole and specifically whether; **6–089**

(1) The reasons given by the national authorities to justify the infringement were relevant and sufficient; and
(2) The measures taken were appropriate to the legitimate aim pursued.
(3) The national authorities applied standards which were in conformity with the principles embodied in Article 10; and
(4) They based themselves on an acceptable assessment of the relevant facts. In this "assessment", regard will be had to
   (a) the manner in which the programme was prepared;
   (b) its contents;
   (c) the context in which it was broadcast;
   (d) the purpose of the programme, and
   (e) whether, from an objective point of view, the programme had as its purpose the propagation of racist views and ideas.[11]

The Government argued that the convictions were justified "for the protection of the reputation or rights of others". There was little doubt that the programme was a serious documentary about the problems of racism in that country. In 4(e) above, the court considered that the intention of the programme was not to promote racist ideas as such, but to expose the "Greenjackets" themselves and their violent and anti-social attitudes towards others. The court stated that interviewers should not be prevented from extracting from their interviewees statements which may be distasteful but are nevertheless matters of general public concern, "unless there were particularly strong reasons for doing so".[12] Although the remarks probably offended ethnic groups in general, taking into account the non-racist purpose of the programme, and the counter-balancing arguments contained in the programme, the court was not satisfied that the national authorities were justified in their interference with the applicant's programme. Therefore, there was a violation of Article 10.

Although freedom of expression extends to journalists shocking and even offending members of society in their writings, the press still have obligations and responsibilities towards the public which they must adhere to. For example, verbal abuse for its own sake and done with *mala fides* may constitute a justifiable interference by the national authorities. However, it will depend in which context the words were made and all the surrounding circumstances. For instance, in *Oberschlick v. Austria*,[13] the applicant, a journalist, referred to the leader of the Austrian Freedom Party, Mr Haider, as an idiot in a journal article, for making a provocative speech which glorified the achievements of the Nazi army during the Second World War. Mr Haider brought a successful private prosecution for libel and insult against the applicant. The applicant argued before the Commission that this was an interference under Article 10. The court stated that although the use of the word "idiot" was controversial it was said within the context of the speech made by Mr Haider. Since it was in conjunction with a political matter, and was merely an opinion, it was not considered by the court to be "disproportionate to the indignation knowingly aroused by Mr Haider".[14] Therefore, there had been a violation of Article 10.

Although the domestic law is given a wide degree of flexibility under Article 10, nevertheless the court is entitled to review that law and determine whether that applicant has been properly protected against a jury awarding excessive sums and be convinced that there are adequate guidelines in place by which a jury can properly determine the amount of damages to award. Thus, in *Tolstoy Miloslavsky v. United Kingdom*,[15] at the conclusion of a libel action, damages were awarded by the jury against the applicant for £1.5 million. The applicant complained to the Commission that, *inter alia*, the order for damages violated his right to freedom of expression under Article 10, namely, for the protection of reputation or rights of others. He argued specifically that the award of damages was of such magnitude that it could not be regarded as being prescribed by law, *i.e.* under the existing law it was not reasonable for the applicant or his legal advisers to foresee that such a high sum would be awarded. The court said that a high degree of flexibility (margin of appreciation) must be given to domestic law when considering an award of libel damages due to the individual circumstances of each case, and which falls within the law despite the "lack of specific guidelines in the legal rules".[16] Although the jury were given a certain amount of latitude concerning the sum to be awarded, this was subject to certain conditions which should be considered by them, *e.g.* vindication of the plaintiff's reputation, the seriousness of the libel itself, mental suffering, the absence of an apology, etc.[17] The court also considered that the amount may be lowered or set aside altogether if the assessment of damages were thought to be so illogical that it was unsustainable.[18] Therefore, the "prescribed by law" requirement was established. The key issue was whether the award was disproportionate to the legitimate aim pursued. The Government argued that due to the exceptional seriousness of the defamation itself, the amount awarded under such circumstances was reasonable. The court said that "under the Convention, an award of damages for defamation must bear a reasonable relationship of proportionality to the injury to reputation suffered".[19] The court was not convinced that there were adequate guidelines in place by which a jury could properly determine the amount of damages to award. Taking into account the enormity of the sum "in conjunction with the lack of adequate and effective safeguards at the relevant time against a disproportionately large award", the court ruled that there was a violation of Article 10. However, where the insult is against a person who holds religious beliefs, the national authorities may be given a wide margin of appreciation to deal with the offensive statements. This is subject to the freedom of expression that persons should accept constructive criticism and discussion on such matters in a democratic society.

In *Otto-Preminger Institute v. Austria*[20] the applicant organisation operated a cinema and wished to show a film titled *Council in Heaven*, about a nineteenth century trial on blasphemy, depicting in caricature form, God, Jesus Christ and the Virgin Mary, and portrayed Christ as mentally defective and denouncing Catholic morality. Prior to the showing, the film was seized and eventually forfeited. The applicants maintained before the Commission that such action was contrary to the freedom of expression and violated Article 10. The Government argued that the measures taken by them were aimed at the protection of the rights of others, namely religious beliefs, and the prevention of disorder. The main issue was whether the measures taken were necessary in a democratic society. The court said that freedom of expression encapsulates duties and responsibilities, which include, in this instance, with regard to religious beliefs, refraining from making gratuitously offensive remarks to others. Although general constructive criticism and public discussion on religious matters are permissible in a democratic society, it is difficult to be more explicit where the dividing lines should be drawn such that the debate becomes unacceptable and ought to be prohibited. Therefore, there must be a margin of appreciation left to the contracting state to decide at what stage expression becomes undesirable, with the general proviso that the domestic law must go "hand in hand with Convention supervision the scope of which will vary according to the circumstances".[21] The Government argued that the vast majority of the people in this area were catholic (87 per cent), and the steps taken were necessary so as to prevent public disorder. The applicant association said the films were restricted to over 17 year-olds and were shown late at night and would only interest people concerned with progressive culture. The court said that there were two conflicting freedoms in dispute, namely the freedom of expression versus the freedom of religion. In this regard, the individual state must be allowed a wide margin of appreciation in assessing the situation. The domestic courts did not regard the film as possessing any artistic merit nor contain any constructive public comment on religious matters, but instead considered it to be an abusive attack on the Roman Catholic religion. The court recognised that by seizing the film, the **6–090** authorities prevented possible public disorder and people's religious beliefs being verbally reviled. Since the national authorities were better placed to assess the situation, the court considered that they could not be regarded as having overstepped the margin of appreciation in this respect and therefore there was no breach of Article 10.

In this age of "investigative journalism", there is little doubt that informants play a very important role in providing the press with information which may involve matters of general public concern. In order for the media, in general, to fulfil the role of "public watchdog", one of the areas vital to the freedom of expression is the safeguarding of a sources identity from being revealed. Without this protection, sources would be reluctant to come forward for fear of some form of reprisals. Indeed, this basic protection from disclosure has now been recognised internationally by the introduction of legislation to this affect in various countries.[22] The court in *Goodwin v. United Kingdom*[23] respected this secrecy to the point of saying that "limitation on the confidentiality of journalistic sources call for the most careful scrutiny by the court"[24] and that the margin of appreciation normally allowed by contracting states is "circumscribed by the interests of democratic society in ensuring and maintaining a free press".[25]

The above case concerned the refusal by a journalist from revealing a sources identity under section 10 of the Contempt of Court Act 1981.[26] The applicant complained to the Commission that the court order requiring him to disclose the identity of his source was a violation of Article 10. The court declared that the action taken against the applicant was in accordance with the "prescribed by law" requirement and further that there was a relevant legitimate aim to be pursued, namely, protecting the reputation or rights of others. The main issue was whether the measures taken by the authorities were "necessary in a democratic society". The court said that the freedom from disclosure ought to be protected unless it is justified by an overriding requirement in the public interest.[27] In the domestic courts, the disclosure order was granted on the grounds of the harm it would do the plaintiff company, *e.g.* loss of jobs, damage to credit worthiness, possible bankruptcy, etc., if the source was not identified. The court recognised as relevant that if not stopped, the source could publish further confidential information to the detriment of the business, and since the source was unknown, no legal proceedings could be issued against that person. However, press freedom should not be interfered with, unless in extreme public interest circumstances, and the balance lay in favour of the interest of a democratic society in securing a free press.[28] In this instance, the balance lay in the public interest of retaining the sources identity which outweighed the interests of the possible damage to the business. Thus, there was no "overriding requirement" in the public interest under Article 10(2). The court regarded that the main issue was the prevention of the confidential information being published in the journal. This had already been achieved by the granting of an injunction prohibiting all publication. Since this averted the main danger, the disclosure order, which the court saw as having a very similar affect as the injunction (in itself an arguable issue) regarded the additional restriction as insufficient to constitute a lawful interference under Article 10(2). Thus, the measures taken (the disclosure order) were not proportionate to the legitimate aim pursued and therefore was a violation of Article 10 (eleven votes to seven).

Reasons for the interference by the national authorities must be both relevant and sufficient. A legitimate aim may be relevant but not sufficient; the latter being much more difficult to show.[29] In *Observer and Guardian v. United Kingdom*,[30] the Attorney-General wished to obtain a permanent injunction against the applicant newspapers from publishing confidential information relating to the security services. An interlocutory injunction was granted so as to restrain the newspapers from publishing any further articles on the subject matter (the "GO" injunction). To refuse the interlocutory application, and thus permitting publication of confidential information prior to the trial for the permanent ban on such material, would be like "shutting the barn door after the horse had bolted", *i.e.* all the confidential information would be by then in the public domain. The applicants complained to the Commission that the injunction contravened the right to freedom of expression guaranteed under Article 10. The Government argued that the interlocutory injunction was necessary to protect national security and for maintaining the authority of the judiciary. The court found that there was a legitimate aim to be considered. For the period from July 11, 1986 to July 30, 1987, whilst the "GO" injunction was still in force, the court considered that in the circumstances the measures taken by the national authorities were not disproportionate to the legitimate aim pursued. However, from July 30, 1987 to October 13, 1988 (the "GO" injunction was still in force), the book had been published abroad, was sold world-wide and available in the United Kingdom. The court decided that under these new circumstances, there were not sufficient reasons for the continuance of the GO injunction. As the court said, even if the Attorney-General had won a permanent ban, in reality the issue was redundant; the confidentiality of the information had, by then, been destroyed. Further, even if the sole purpose of continuing the action by the Attorney-General was to dissuade other members or ex-members of the security services from divulging confidential matter, the court said that these also were not sufficient reasons to continue with the interlocutory injunction, *i.e.* the measures taken by the national authorities were disproportionate to the legitimate aim pursued. Therefore, there was a violation of Article 10 from July 30, 1987 to October 13, 1988. **6–091**

Brief Outline and Germane Cases

Chapter Six: Obscenity, Indecency and Censorship

Definitions of obscenity: "deprave and corrupt" test. **6–092**
R. v. Hicklin [1868].

Criminal offences of obscenity.

6–093 *Obscene Publications Act 1959 s.2: publishing an obscene article; s.1(3).

Fellows [1997], *Conegate v. Commissioners for Customs and Excise* [1987]; *R. v. Penguin Books Ltd* [1961]; *R. v. Clayton and Halsey* [1963].

*OPA 1964 s.1(2): amends 1959 Acts s.2 to include additional offence of possession of an obscene article with a view to publication for gain.

Significant proportion rule: *DPP v. Whyte* [1972].

*OPA 1959 2.(4): defence of public good/artistic literary or scientific merit. *DPP v. Jordan* [1997]; *R. V. Skirving* [1985].

Forfeiture procedure: s.3 OPA 1959, *R. v. Snaresbrook Crown Ct, ex p. Commissioner of Police for the Metropolis* [1984].

Other offences of obscenity: see text for list of relevant statutes.

Criminal offences of indecency

6–094 Definition of indecency: *Knuller v. DPP* [1973]; *R. v. Stanley* 1965].

*Post Office Act 1953 s.11: sending indecent material by post.

*Unsolicited Goods and Services Act 1971 s.4: sending sexually explicit material by post.

Child-protection offences: Children and Young Persons (Harmful Publications) Act 1955; Protection of Children Act 1978—indecent photographs of children under 16; *R. v. Graham-Kerr* [1988].

*Indecent Displays (Control) Act 1981 s.1(1): offence of public display of indecent matter.

Other statutory indecency offences: see text.

Controls on imports.

Common law offences of obscenity, indecency and immorality:

— corrupting public morals.

— outraging public decency.

— blasphemy.

— indecent exhibition.

— keeping a disorderly house.

Shaw v. DPP [1962]; *Knuller v. DPP* [1972], s.2(4) OPA 1959; *R. v. Gibson and Sylveire* [1990]; *R. v. May* [1990]; *Moore v. DPP* [1992]; *Whitehouse v. Lemon and Gay News* [1979]; *R. v. Chief Metropolitan Magistrate, ex p. Choudhury* [1991].

Censorship of film and video

*Cinemas Act 1985 s.1: local authorities are responsible for licensing premises to be used for the showing of films to the public. S.2; local authority must impose conditions which prohibit admission of children to films which are unsuitable. BBFC: role and powers. **6–095**

*Video Recordings Act 1984 ss.9–11: criminal offences of supply or possession of unclassified videos.

*Broadcasting Act 1990, 1996.

Endnotes

[1] Report of the Committee on Obscenity and Film Censorship.
[2] *On Liberty*, (1859).
[3] (1965).
[4] See Howitt and Cumberpatch, *Pornography: Impacts and Influences* (1990).
[5] see Edwards, *Sex and Gender in the Legal Process* (Blackstone, 1996).
[6] see the United States' Attorney-General's Commission Report on Pornography and Prostitution (1986).
[7] See Edwards, *Sex and Gender in the Legal Process* (Blackstone, 1996), Chap. 3.
[8] *Pornography, Men Possessing Women* (1989).
[9] See for example Hernton, *Sex and Racism* (1970).
[10] Leidholdt, *The Sexual Liberals and the Attack on Feminism*, (1990) p.ix.
[11] See MacKinnon, *Towards a Feminist Theory of the State*, (1989) p. 238.
[12] See Itzin, *Pornography* (1992).
[13] (1868) L.R. 3 Q.B. 360.
[14] *ibid. per* Cockburn C.J. at 371.
[15] *ibid.* at 371.
[16] The Act only applies to England and Wales.
[17] (1993) 15 Cr.App.R. (S.) 76.
[18] [1997] 2 All E.R. 548.
[19] [1987] Q.B. 254.
[20] Sharples, *Daily Mail*, March 26, 1994.
[21] [1961] Crim.L.R. 176.
[22] See *R. v. Martin Secker Warburg* [1954] 1 W.L.R. 1138 and especially Stable J.'s charming philosophical direction to the jury.
[23] See Lord Reid in *Knuller* [1973] A.C. 435 at 456; it is possible to "lead persons morally astray without depraving and corrupting them".
[24] [1963] 1 Q.B. 163; [1962] 3 All E.R. 500.
[25] Distributes, circulates, sells, lets or hire; or offering the article for such purposes.
[26] As in *Mella v. Monahan* [1961] Crim.L.R. 175: an "invitation to treat" cannot be a publication within the meaning of the s.2(1) offence.
[27] [1963] 1 Q.B. 163.
[28] *R. v. Clayton and Halsey* [1962] 1 Q.B. 163.
[29] (1994) 144 New L.J. 635.
[30] *Attorney General's Reference (No. 2 of 1975)* [1976] 1 W.L.R. 710.
[31] *R. v. Calder and Boyars* [1969] 1 Q.B. 151.
[32] [1972] 3 All E.R. 12.
[33] *ibid.* at 19.
[34] *per* Lord Wilberforce in *DPP v. Whyte* [1972] A.C. 849 at 860.
[35] [1972] 3 All E.R. 12 at 21 where he discusses the "tragic and pathetic" nature of the book, *Last Exit to Brooklyn*, rather than its pornographic elements in *R. v. Calder and Boyars Ltd* [1969] 1 Q.B. 151.
[36] Lord Pearson said that "likely customers" does not necessarily mean "the regular customers", but may include even first-time buyers—at 22.
[37] [1995] 1 Cr.App.R. 455 at 464.
[38] [1969] 1 Q.B. 151.
[39] *ibid.* at 168.
[40] [1971] 3 All E.R. 1152.
[41] Crim.L.R. 177.
[42] See commentary *R. v. Penguin* (1961) Crim.L.R. 177.
[43] [1978] 1 W.L.R. 1123.
[44] [1977] A.C. 699 at 719.
[45] [1977] A.C. 699.
[46] *ibid. per* Lord Wilberforce at 718.
[47] *ibid.* at 725 *per* Lord Kilbrandon.
[48] See *R. v. Calder and Boyars* above *per* Salmon L.J. at 172.
[49] *Calder and Boyars* [1969] 1 Q.B. 151; *DPP v. Jordan* [1977] A.C. 699.
[50] [1985] 1 Q.B. 819.
[51] (1783) 3 Doug K.B. 157.

[52] R. Stone, "The Problems Persist", [1986] Crim.L.R. 139.
[53] [1968] 1 Q.B. 159.
[54] *ibid.* at 163 and 164.
[55] [1976] 3 All E.R. 775.
[56] At page 717.
[57] In s.1(3)(a) of the Obscene Publications Act 1964.
[58] "The jailing of persons connected with pornography has had no deterrent effect and have served only to waste taxpayers money on keeping in prison persons who are no danger to the public. Severe fines and suspended sentences would be a more sensible and more civilised alternative", Geoffrey Robertson and Andrew Nicol, *Media Law* (3rd ed., Penguin Books), p. 135.
[59] "Premises" under s.3(1) includes any stall or vehicle stated.
[60] [1992] Crim.L.R. 56.
[61] See *R. v. Snaresbrook Crown Court ex parte Commissioner for the Metropolis* (1984) 79 Cr.App.R. 184.
[62] (1984) 79 Cr.App.R. 184.
[63] *Olympia v. Hollis* [1974] 1 All E.R. 108.
[64] See *R. v. Snaresbrook* at 190.
[65] s.1(1) OPA 1959.
[66] Theatres Act 1843.
[67] *e.g.* the plays of Joe Orton or Harold Pinter.
[68] HMSO 1967.
[69] The performance may be in public or in private, but not in a private house on a "domestic occasion"—s.7(1). Rehearsals and performances given in order to enable a broadcast or film or record to be made are also exempted—s.7(2).
[70] [1973] A.C. 435 at 458.
[71] *Knuller v. DPP* (1972) 56 Cr.App.R. 633 at 643.
[72] [1965] 1 All E.R. 1035; 2 Q.B. 327.
[73] 2 Q.B. 372 at 333.
[74] *ibid.* at 334.
[75] (1968) 112 S.J. 656.
[76] [1967] 3 All E.R. 179.
[77] See Ecclesiastical Courts Jurisdiction Act 1860.
[78] *Lees v. Parr* [1967] Crim.L.R. 481.
[79] *Court* [1988] 2 All E.R. 221.
[80] *George* [1956] Crim.L.R. 52.
[81] *R. v. Straker* [1965] Crim.L.R. 239.
[82] (1961) 45 Cr.App.R. 113 at 177.
[83] *Kosmos Publications Ltd v. DPP* [1975] Crim.L.R. 345.
[84] *R. v. Stamford* (1972) 56 Cr.App.R. 398.
[85] See *Felthouse v. Brindley* [1862] 11 C.B.N.S. 869.
[86] *DPP v. Beate Uhse (U.K.) Ltd* [1974] 2 W.L.R. 50.
[87] See Barker, *A Haunt of Fears* (Pluto, 1984) for a full description of the events which led to the drafting of the legislation.
[88] Edwards, *Sex and Gender in the Legal Process* (1996).
[89] [1988] 1 W.L.R. 1098.
[90] Following *R. v. Court* [1988] 2 W.L.R. 1071.
[91] *R. v. Stamford* [1972] 2 Q.B. 391 the words "recognised standards of propriety" were used.
[92] (1988) 86 Cr.App.R. 291.
[93] *per* Stocker L.J. at 296.
[94] See Home Affairs Committee, *Computer Pornography*, p. vii where the CPS stated that it was unable to prosecute in a particular situation because the case related to pseudo-photographs.
[94A] *The Times*, November 19, 1999.
[95] [1997] 2 All E.R. 548.
[96] (1985) 82 Cr.App.R. 301.
[97] *per* Mustill L.J. at 307.
[98] [1972] 1 All E.R. 994.
[99] [1981] A.C. 850.
[1] [1986] 2 All E.R. 688.
[2] *ibid.* at 691 and 692.

[3] *ibid.* at 692.
[4] [1989] 3 W.L.R. 467.
[5] [1990] 2 Q.B. 619.
[6] (1989) 91 Cr.App.R. 157.
[7] [1991] 4 All E.R. 649.
[8] (1972) 56 Cr.App.R. 633.
[9] [1962] A.C. 220.
[10] He was also charged and convicted with living on the earnings of prostitution under s.30 of the Sexual Offences Act 1959.
[11] The appellant also appealed on the grounds that s.2(4) OPA 1959 excluded such a prosecution at common law.
[12] At page 267. But see *Knuller v. DPP* (1972) 56 Cr.App.R. 633 at 643 where Lord Reid disagreed with using the law in this manner to widening existing offences.
[13] At page 267.
[14] "public mischief" is the criminal counterpart of public policy, and the criminal law ought to be even more hesitant than the civil law in founding on it some new aspect. See page 267.
[15] At 276.
[16] [1963] 2 Q.B. 717.
[17] See *Gibson* [1990] 2 Q.B. 619; *Lunderbech* [1991] Crim.L.R. 784; *Rowley* [1991] 4 All E.R. 649.
[18] (1972) 56 Cr.App.R. 633.
[19] This case must now be read in the light of the Criminal Law Act 1977, ss. 1 and 5, dealt with above.
[20] See *Shaw v. DPP* above for his dissenting judgment.
[21] (1972) 56 Cr.App.R. 633 at 641.
[22] *ibid.* at 692.
[23] *ibid.* at 692.
[24] *ibid.* at 642.
[25] In 1928 Radcliffe Hall's, *The Well of Loneliness* (a book about lesbianism) the words "and that night they were not divided" were considered obscene.
[26] See also *DPP v. Whyte* [1972] A.C. 849 above.
[27] at 698 of *Knuller v. DPP*, see above.
[28] *ibid.*
[29] *ibid.* at 640, *per* Lord Reid quoting from Hansard, vol. 695, col. 1212 (who dissented in *Shaw v. DPP*) ". . . that a conspiracy to corrupt public morals would not be charged so as to circumvent the statutory defence in s.4" (Solicitor General). However, where a s.4 defence is not relevant, it seems that the door has not been fully closed and an obscenity charge may still, theoretically, be instigated under the OPA 1959 or 1964.
[30] See *Shaw v. DPP* [1962] A.C. 220 *per* Lord Tucker at 290.
[31] *ibid.*
[32] *ibid.* at 281.
[33] *R. v. Mayling* [1963] 2 Q.B. 717 at 726.
[34] *ibid.* at 724, Ashworth J. quoting from *R. v. Farrell* [1862] 9 Cox C.C. 446; *R. v. May* (1990) 91 Cr.App.R. 157 at 159.
[35] *R. v. Walker* (1996) 1 Cr.App.R. 111.
[36] *Smith v. Hughes* [1960] 2 All E.R. 859 The balcony of a house for soliciting men passing by in the street, was considered to be a "public place" under s.1(1) of the Street Offences Act 1959.
[37] [1963] 2 Q.B. 717.
[38] [1962] 3 All E.R. 500.
[39] [1990] 3 W.L.R. 595.
[40] *ibid.* at 598.
[41] *ibid.* at 602; [1991] 1 All E.R. 439 at 445.
[42] For example the offence of blasphemy, below.
[43] There is also a statutory offence of indecent exposure under the Vagrancy Act 1824, s.4, which is only applicable where a man exposes himself to a woman and intends thereby to insult her. The offence may be committed even in the man's own bedroom. Since it is clear that only one woman need witness the exposure, most "flashers" are charged with the statutory offence.
[44] *Thallman* (1863): D was on a roof of a building which could only be seen from the windows of other houses, yet was convicted.

[45] *Mayling* [1963] 2 Q.B. 717.
[46] [1991] Crim.L.R. 784.
[47] (1990) 91 Cr.App.R. 157.
[48] [1962] 2 Q.B. 245.
[49] *ibid.* at 255.
[50] (1927) 20 Cr.App.R. 38.
[51] *ibid.* at 1062, 1063.
[52] [1983] 1 Q.B. 1053.
[53] *R. v. Goldstein* [1971] Crim.L.R. 300.
[54] *R. v. Tan and others* [1983] 1 Q.B. 1053 at 1061.
[55] [1992] Q.B. 125.
[56] In *Marks v. Benjamin* [1839] 5 M.W. 565 although under a statutory offence (Disorderly House Act 1751), it was stated, that there must be something like an habitual keeping of the house.
[57] In *R. v. Brady and Ram* (1963) 47 Cr.App.R. 196 where evidence was admitted of prior occasions when the indecent act was performed, despite not being included in the present indictment.
[58] *Moores v. DPP* above at 132.
[59] See G. Robertson, *Freedom, the Individual and the Law*, pp. 248–254 (7th ed., 1993) for a more detailed treatment of the history of and issues involved in this offence.
[60] [1978] A.C. 617.
[61] *Taylor* (1676) 1 Vent 293.
[62] [1917] A.C. 406.
[63] [1979] A.C. 617.
[64] p. 724.
[65] [1991] 1 Q.B. 429.
[66] No.145, 1985.
[67] For a detailed examination of all aspects of censorship of the media see G. Robertson, *Freedom, the Individual and the Law*, Chap. 6.
[68] The Cinematograph Act 1909 was intended as a method of ensuring safety.
[69] See Bailey, Harris and Jones, p. 324.
[70] [1925] 1 K.B. 213.
[71] The ECHR has upheld the BBFC's opinion on this point in *Wingrove v. U.K.* (1997) 24 E.H.R.R. 1; the BBFC had refused a certificate to the film "International Guerrillas" on the basis of its clearly libellous depiction of the author Salman Rushdie. Although the Appeal Committee of the BBFC allowed a certificate on ground that Salman Rushdie himself had no wish to prosecute and that no criminal proceedings were likely to ensue, the ECHR agreed with the BBFC that a certificate should not be given to a film or video which infringe criminal law.
[72] [1976] 1 W.L.R. 550.
[73] see "Ill Effects" [1996] for more detailed coverage.
[74] See Robertson and Nichol, *Media Law*, (1992).
[75] Which replaced the similar Independent Broadcasting Authority.
[76] See *Arrowsmith v. U.K.* [1981] 3 E.H.R.R. 218.
[77] *ibid.*
[78] *ibid.* at para. 69.
[79] *ibid.* at para. 71.
[80] [1994] 17 E.H.R.R. 397.
[81] *ibid.* at para. 54.
[82] *ibid.* at para. 69.
[83] *ibid.* at para. 48.
[84] *ibid.* at 426.
[85] *ibid.* at 428.
[86] [1979] 1 E.H.R.R. 737.
[87] *ibid.* at para. 50 and see *The Sunday Times v. U.K.* (No. 2) [1992] 14 E.H.R.R. 229 at para. 50.
[88] [1992] 15 E.H.R.R. 244.
[89] See *Gaskin v. U.K.* [1990] 12 E.H.R.R. 36.
[90] [1979] 2 E.H.R.R. 245.
[91] *ibid.* at para. 48.
[92] ". . . the proper forum for the ascertainment of legal rights and obligations and the settlement of disputes relative thereto; . . .", *ibid.* at para. 55.

93 *ibid.* at para. 52. The "prejudgment principle".
94 [1983] 5 E.H.R.R. 123.
95 *ibid.* at para. 11.
96 *Gillow v. U.K.* (1986) 11 E.H.R.R. 325, at para. 55.
97 [1979] 1 E.H.R.R. 737.
98 *ibid.* at para. 49.
99 *ibid.* at para. 52.
99A A similar decision was given in the later case of *Muller and Others v. Switzerland* (1988) 13 E.H.R.R. 212.
1 see The *Sunday Times v. U.K.* [1979] 2 E.H.R.R. 245, above, at para. 59.
2 "Even a Contracting State so acting remains subject to the Court's control as regards the compatibility of its conduct with the engagements it has undertaken under the Convention". [1979] 2 E.H.R.R. 245 para. 66.
3 *ibid.* at para. 66.
4 *ibid.* at para. 67–68.
5 [1998] 25 E.H.R.R. 1.
6 [1986] 8 E.H.R.R. 407.
7 *ibid.* at para. 42.
8 *ibid.*
9 ". . . the existence of fact can be demonstrated, whereas the truth of value judgments is not susceptible to proof": (1986) 8 E.H.R.R. 407 at para. 46.
10 [1994] 19 E.H.R.R. 1.
11 *ibid.* at para. 31.
12 *ibid.* at para. 35.
13 [1998] 25 E.H.R.R. 357.
14 *ibid.* at para. 34.
15 [1995] 20 E.H.R.R. 442.
16 *ibid.* at para. 41.
17 *ibid.* at para. 42.
18 ". . . if it was so unreasonable that it could not have been made by sensible people but must have been arrived at capriciously, unconscionably or irrationally"—*ibid.* at para. 38.
19 *ibid.* at para. 49.
20 [1995] 19 E.H.R.R. 34.
21 *ibid.* at para. 50.
22 See *Goodwin v. U.K.* [1996] 22 E.H.R.R. 123.
23 *ibid.*
24 *ibid.* at para. 40.
25 para. 40.
26 See *X Ltd. v. Morgan-Grampian Ltd* (1991) 1 A.C.1. for full facts and domestic court decision.
27 [1996] 22 E.H.R.R. 123 at para 39.
28 *ibid.* at para. 45.
29 See *The Sunday Times v. U.K. (No. 2)* [1992] 14 E.H.R.R. 229 at paras 53–54.
30 [1992] 14 E.H.R.R. 153.

Chapter 7

CONTEMPT OF COURT

Introduction

In order for any legal system to be maintained and to flourish, rules must be enforced to protect the status, authority, integrity and fairness of the courts. A citizen's right to a fair trial depends upon the existence of mechanisms which operate in various ways: to protect the courts, judges, and juries from verbal or physical attack; to prevent the disclosure or publication of material, truthful or otherwise, which might prejudice a court case or otherwise harm the parties; to allow criminal and civil cases to proceed through court in the manner prescribed by law; to protect the reputations of the legal system, its components and its personnel from being brought into disrepute. It is in the public interest that these mechanisms should exist. Therefore there exist criminal and civil offences of contempt of court which attempt to support such legitimate interests as the administration of justice, the right to privacy and the right to a fair trial, and the sanctions of imprisonment or fines serve as a deterrent. **7–001**

But this is not as simple a situation as it may first appear to be; counterposed to such arguments stand equally powerful rights in favour of allowing some of the activities which the law of contempt of court seeks to prevent. Few would of course argue persuasively that there is any fundamental right of a citizen to intimidate witnesses, to threaten a judge or to reveal salacious and irrelevant details about the life of a defendant before his trial, for example; but the right to freedom of expression and the public interest in favour of free access to information, particularly where danger to the public may be concerned, are a different matter. Much of the content of any newspaper, or of any television or radio news broadcast, involves discussion of or comment upon matters and events which either do involve a court case or may do so in the near future. The media assert a right to report court cases and to comment upon issues of public concern, which may involve discussion of events which in time might lead to a prosecution; should the media be prevented from discussion of any crime or criminal trial in case something prejudicial to the defendant might be revealed, or does the public interest outweigh the private interests of the person accused or under suspicion? Although there is a real and unfortunate danger of "trial by media" which will be seen in the discussion of some of the cases in this chapter, it is an equal affront to civil liberties if information is kept out of the public domain when it concerns issues of true public concern and threat. So, as will be seen, freedom of expression, the public interest and the protection of the proper administration of justice sit in an uneasy balance when the law relating to contempt of court is examined.

What is Contempt of Court?

7–002 Contempt of court is not a single offence, but a broad category of offences drawn from both criminal and (to a lesser extent) civil law.[1] Its roots come from the common law and spread deeply into history, but important amendments were made by the Contempt of Court Act 1981. Contempt has its own rules and procedures which are unlike those of any other branch of law. It is not entirely clear to what extent the 1981 Act has affected the preceding common law offences, and indeed some key elements of the common law offences lack satisfactory and clear definitions in case law. The range of behaviour which may constitute contempt of court is vast, and will be discussed below. Thus it can be seen that this is a highly unusual and difficult "offence".

Civil and Criminal Contempt

7–003 Put simply, civil contempt of court is committed by breaching orders of the court or undertakings made to the court, for example by breaking the terms of an injunction which has been obtained in a civil court. Civil contempt is punishable by imprisonment or a fine in just the same way as is a criminal contempt; what differs is the rationale of such punishment. Civil contempt is punished in order to create or compel compliance with the court order concerned; what use would there be in having such important civil tools and remedies as injunctions if defendants were able to ignore them? Thus if, for example, an injunction has been obtained to prevent publication of material on the ground of official secrecy, it will be a civil contempt to publish that material in breach of the injunction. Criminal contempt of court is a broad category of offences concerning interference with the administration of justice. The most common categories of criminal contempt of court will be discussed in detail below, but random examples of behaviour which may constitute the offence include: publishing the previous convictions of a defendant during his trial; standing up in a civil or criminal court and making abusive comments about the judge; threatening a witness; refusing to give evidence once on the witness stand.

The rationale for punishment looks to the nature of the behaviour carried out by the defendant as well as to its actual or potential effects; criminal contempts are punishable because the conduct involved poses a serious threat to the administration of justice and is reprehensible. A deterrent effect may also be sought when contempt of court is alleged; the defendant may avoid or reduce his punishment by apologising, and others may be dissuaded from similar conduct if they are shown that even imprisonment may result.[2] Criminal contempt of court will be the basis of most of the discussion in this chapter, since it has greater civil liberties implications.

Where there has been a breach of civil contempt, it is generally up to the injured party to bring proceedings before the court; whereas regards criminal contempt, it is for the Attorney-General to bring the appropriate action, and the burden of proof in both categories is beyond reasonable doubt. However, there are many circumstances where a judge also possesses the power to take immediate action against any person for interfering with the due processes of law.

Arguments For and Against the Existence of the Offence

Many of the arguments advanced in the preceding chapters on freedom of expression, official secrecy and obscenity are again relevant to the present topic, which also raises issues of privacy and freedom of information. There are few criminal offences which encompass debate of such wide-ranging and contradictory freedoms; thus contempt of court merits some examination in terms of the countervailing pressures exerted by these aspects of civil liberties. **7–004**

As discussed in earlier chapters, freedom of expression extends to embrace arguments of freedom of information. A free press, and by implication free media of all descriptions, are seen as indicators of democracy; a healthy society will encourage a healthy degree of debate about all matters, including those related to the state and to politics, unless secrecy can be justified on some other basis of an overwhelming need for secrecy in order to serve the public interest in some other manner. The judiciary and indeed the entire justice system, both civil and criminal, are organs of the state; thus the public should be granted access to information about every aspect of the administration of justice, with exceptions only on the basis of a greater public interest that a particular piece of information should remain secret. As an abstraction of this principle, justice itself should be open to scrutiny: courtrooms should be open to the public; debate should be encouraged about the operation of justice; justice should be visible. Trials should only be closed if, again, a higher public interest in favour of secrecy can be proven in a particular case, for example if a child is involved and is considered to need protection from public attention or some other more immediate threat. Freedom of expression itself extends to allow freedom to criticise; justice and its officials should be strong enough to stand criticism and banter, since it is by responding to attack that laws and procedures may be refined, strengthened and improved. But against these arguments stand others with an equally strong pedigree.

In relation to the conduct of the media, in particular to the publication of information about suspects and trials, the existence of criminal offences of contempt may be justified by reference to confidentiality, privacy or administration of justice in terms of the provision of a fair trial. Much as it may be in the public interest to publish, for example, a newspaper report linking together the facts that a particular person is now on trial for rape and that a man with the same name has been acquitted three times previously of similar offences due to lack of forensic evidence, it is possible that such a report could influence members of the jury at the current trial towards conviction. Even if the defendant is in fact guilty as charged, he is entitled to be judged on the legal evidence as presented by the prosecution to the jury, and not on the allegations made by the media. The principle that a defendant is presumed innocent until proved guilty cannot be upheld unless the media and others are to be subjected to some legal restrictions. Privacy and confidentiality become involved in the debate where, for example, the law considers an individual or a section of society to be particularly vulnerable and deserving of protection from public display; thus it is contempt of court to publish or otherwise identify the names of victims of sexual offences in most circumstances, or of children charged with criminal offences. The privacy and confidentiality arguments are felt to be so persuasive in such cases that they have been enforced by statute. Even outside such categories, it is difficult to justify salacious gossip in terms of the public interest; although the public may indeed be interested in shocking details of the lives of those involved in a current court case, a distinction must be drawn between "that which interests the public" and "that which is in the public interest". Where contempt is committed by a private individual unconnected with any publication, for example by attacking a judge or by disrupting court proceedings, recourse must be made simply to arguments in favour of the due administration of justice. The legal system may appear strong enough to survive small blows and outbursts from the public, and it may be understandable if a defendant or victim loses his temper in court or is unwilling to give evidence, yet such occurrences have a cumulative effect upon the workability of the justice system and also send undesirable messages to wider society. Many judges have been criticised for imposing sentences of imprisonment upon those whose conduct consisted of, using recent examples, refusing to give a verdict whilst sitting on a jury panel or refusing to give evidence against an allegedly violent former partner, but such conduct will generally cause a trial to collapse and may result in a guilty defendant walking free. A finding of criminal contempt of court provides an opportunity for the person who has interfered with the administration of justice to reconsider his behaviour and, if appropriate, to remedy it via an apology. It is only in rare circumstances that a prison sentence of more than one week will be served.

Contempt of Court at Common Law—History and Principles

7–005 The precise origins of common law contempt of court are somewhat mysterious and disputed, but it has clearly existed as a defined set of principles since at least the early eighteenth century. Street[3] argues that it is considerably older. The generalities of common law contempt have changed little with time—in *The St. James Evening Post*,[4] Lord Hardwicke L.C. stated that:

> "Nothing is more incumbent upon courts of justice, than to preserve their proceedings from being misrepresented; . . . nor is there any thing of more pernicious consequence, than to prejudice the minds of the public against persons concerned as parties in causes, before the cause is finally heard . . . There cannot be any thing of greater consequences, than to keep the streams of justice clear and pure, that parties may proceed with safety both to themselves and their characters".

Whatever the origins of the offence, its scope has been refined and modified by successive cases and statutes over the last two centuries, with the result that there are at least five sub-categories of common law contempt:

(i) Contempt in the face of the court,

(ii) Scandalising the court,

(iii) Prejudicing or impeding civil or criminal court proceedings,

(iv) Interfering with the course of justice,

(v) Prejudging the merits of a case.

These will be discussed separately below, since they continue to exist, subject to the alterations imposed by the Contempt of Court Act 1981. However, the common law prior to 1981 was subject to certain recurrent criticisms, leading to the establishment of the Phillimore Committee on Contempt of Court, which published its findings in 1974.[5] The Contempt of Court Act 1981 was introduced partly as a response to the recommendations of the Phillimore Committee, but the resulting changes in the law have arguably served little purpose other than to complicate an already complex area of law.

The Phillimore Committee on Contempt of Court

The Phillimore Committee was formed in order to consider reforms to the **7–006**
offences of contempt of court. It found the common law in this area to be ill-defined in scope, which was unjustifiable since the penalty which may be imposed is one of imprisonment. The Committee is mindful of the need to draft contempt offences carefully in order to preserve freedom of expression to its maximum justifiable extent. Since contempt at common law is a summary offence, the Committee was concerned that it lacks the usual safeguards thought appropriate for any other criminal trial with such a potentially high sentence of imprisonment. Common law contempt was a strict liability offence; in other words, it was not necessary to establish any

prohibited state of mind in the defendant. All that had to be shown was that the defendant's conduct interfered with the course of justice in one of the recognised manners; it did not have to be established that the defendant intended this to happen, nor even that he foresaw that it might happen. The Committee strongly disapproved of the strict liability nature of common law contempt, and so recommended that:

(i) A criminal offence of conduct intended to pervert the course of justice should be used instead of contempt proceedings, unless there were urgent reasons in a particular case why contempt should be charged.

(ii) Strict liability contempt should continue to be an offence, but should only apply to publications which create a risk of serious prejudice to the course of justice.

(iii) The time-frame within which contempt of court could be charged should be narrowed considerably from the old *sub judice* rule to a test based upon whether there were any "active" court proceedings.

(iv) "Scandalising the court" which was one of the methods of committing common law contempt, should no longer form a contempt of court but should be redrafted as a separate criminal offence.

(v) "Contempt in the face of the court" should be a substantive criminal offence, and should only be charged as contempt of court if the defendant's safeguards in court were first strengthened.

(vi) The distinctions between civil and criminal contempt of court should be removed.

The Government did not accept all of the Phillimore Committee's recommendations, but some of them were introduced by the Contempt of Court Act 1981. But two issues in particular merit discussion at this stage. First, in what circumstances will interference with court proceedings constitute contempt, and what form must such interference take? Secondly, what is the scope of the offence of "scandalising the court"?

Interfering with Court Proceedings

7–007 The power to punish in these circumstances, when the offender has not been given the opportunity of a trial, is a heavy responsibility for a judge and should only be exercised with the utmost care and attention and not be abused. Lord Denning refers to it as "necessary power":

> "It is given so as to maintain the dignity and authority of the judge and to ensure a fair trial. It is to be exercised by the judge of his own motion only

> when it is urgent and imperative to act immediately, so as to maintain the authority of the court—to prevent disorder—to enable witnesses to be free from fear—and jurors from being improperly influenced and the like".[6] The heading of this section commonly refers to conduct by persons "in the face of the court".

This expression falls into two main categories—"direct and indirect". "Direct" generally concerns instances which occur inside the court room and therefore are likely to be perceived by the judge. "Indirect" is where the contempt takes place outside the court and the judge is unlikely to see or hear the person commit the offensive conduct.

"Direct" interferences

"In the face of the court" here, normally means that the offender does an act which the judge is fully aware of which results in the court proceedings being disrupted, interfered with, delayed, etc. such that the judge has no option but to bring the offender before the court, and if the offensive conduct warrants it, to fine and/or to sentence him to immediate imprisonment or indeed by other action which would remedy the contempt.[7] Typical examples of the type of contempt conduct here includes the following: shouting,[8] severe disruptions,[9] refusing to answer questions in court, wolf-whistles,[10] protesting in court,[11] disobeying the judge, throwing objects at the judge, threatening persons in court, witnesses refusing to testify,[12] jurors refusing to reach verdict, etc. Such is the sanctity of the court room that very little leeway is granted to those who show disrespect towards the proceedings. The proper, uninterrupted proceedings in a court of law take precedent over any unauthorised disruption, however justified and principled that disturbance may be. Thus, in *Morris v. Crown Office*,[13] Welsh students interrupted proceedings in court by shouting, singing and distributing leaflets in aid of promoting the equality of the Welsh language which they felt was being diminished in importance as opposed to English. Eleven of the students were sentenced to three months imprisonment each. They appealed. Whilst the court had great sympathy with their protest, it was declared that a court of law was not the place to vent such views. Such behaviour was untenable and although the severity of the contempt warranted the sentences, the appeal was allowed to the extent that they were released (having served seven days) and bound over to keep the peace. Salmon L.J. said that if similar circumstances occurred again, even six months imprisonment would not be regarded as excessive.[14] **7–008**

The guidelines for a judge to determine what specific action he should take regarding a contempt of court, in these circumstances, were set out in *R. v. Hill*,[15] where the offender shouted from the public gallery that the judge was biased and a racist. She was arrested and after hearing arguments by counsel was sentenced to seven days. On appeal, the Court of Appeal stated that the authority of the court must be upheld and all necessary steps must be taken to achieve this. These included:

(1) the judge ordering the offender to be arrested and detained;
(2) allowing the offender the opportunity to apologise;
(3) allowing counsel to give advice;
(4) granting an adjournment, if necessary;
(5) listening to counsel's submissions;
(6) fining or sentencing the offender, if warranted.

In *R. v. Moran*,[16] the contemner refused to give evidence against a co-accused on a charge of burglary (after having made a statement implicating the other person). The judge asked him to reconsider his actions. The contemner refused. The judge then sentenced him to six months' imprisonment. Shortly after, the contemner changed his mind and took the oath, but refused to give any direct evidence against the co-accused. The judge thereupon gave him another six months for perjury. On appeal, Lawton L.J. said that:

(1) the judge should reflect upon the best action to take provided the matter is not one of urgency, expediency and necessity;
(2) if time allows, whether the contemner should seek legal advice, but if action is necessary immediately which required sentencing to be passed, then there is no right to legal advice, and
(3) the contemner should have the opportunity to apologise.

Here, the judge acted too rashly, without considering the points (1) to (3) above and therefore the appeal was allowed.

"Indirect" interference

7–009 Any person who physically attacks, bribes, threatens, pressurises or frightens a juror or witness, or indeed anyone who is in any way connected with on-going official court business may be deemed to be interfering with the proper course of justice, thereby committing a contempt of court. In such cases as this, severe sentences may be passed down, especially if a trial has to be either postponed or discontinued because of the contempt. In *R. v. Giscombe*,[17] G, after having given evidence in a robbery trial returned each day as a spectator to court and sat in the public gallery. On one occasion, he shouted to a police officer witness that he was a liar. At the end of a particular day's hearing, G went up to a juror and asked him questions. As a result of this, the whole jury were discharged and a new trial had to take place. He was sentenced to four months' imprisonment. The court described such severe sentences as a punishment and a necessary deterrent in view of the gravity of the offence. In the above case, there was no direct threat to the juror and the severity of the sentence will be determined by what was said and done to the witness or juror.[18] Further, it makes no difference whether, for instance, a witness has already given evidence. Thus, in *Moore v. Clerk of Assize, Bristol*,[19] the witness was threatened by the offender after she gave evidence. Lord Denning M.R. said that the "court will always preserve the freedom and integrity of witnesses and not allow them to be intimidated in any way either before the trial, pending it, or after it".[20] The same will apply to court officials in the execution of their duty. Thus, in *Re de Court*,[21] C spat into the face of the Chancery Clerk of the Lists because the latter had refused to grant him a date for his case to be heard. C was well known for his practice of trying to bring cases which were found to be completely unjustified and ridiculous. However, it was difficult in this case to establish whether C had acted with the *mens rea* required for contempt of court. Medical evidence had been brought forward that C was not responsible for his actions. It was further argued that C had not interfered with the court itself, but with purely administrative matters of the court and that he could therefore not be held in contempt. Despite the medical evidence, the Vice Chancellor was, however, convinced that C had known exactly what he was doing when he spat at the court official and that he also had done so deliberately. C's action was clearly a physical attack on a court official in the execution of his official duties and therefore constituted contempt of court. Taking into account the special circumstances of the case and C's disturbed personality, the judge refrained from passing the usual fine or sentence of imprisonment and instead decided to ban him from entering any civil court premises in future and from pursuing any future court cases except under very stringent conditions.

In *Att.-Gen. v. Butterworth*,[22] a witness who gave evidence was afterwards victimised by a trade union to which he was a member and honorary treasurer and soon after was relieved of his appointments. It seemed that some of the members wanted to punish the witness for giving evidence. Lord Denning M.R. found this type of action to be reprehensible, unacceptable and would wholly discourage witnesses from testifying for fear of retribution being taken against them once the trial or hearing was over. He said that "victimisation is as great an interference with justice when it is done after a witness gets home as before he gets there".[23] Lord Denning's statements seems to be in accordance with the headnote of *R. v. Giscombe* (see above). However, Donovan L.J. said that "the question is whether the respondent's action was calculated so as to interfere, and this involves a consideration not of their state of mind on this particular point, but of the inherent nature of their act",[24] *i.e.* it was not necessary to prove an intention to interfere with the administration of justice, it will suffice if what the respondent did in this case was inherently likely to interfere with the course of justice. The course of justice interfered with here was that it should not deter other witnesses from giving evidence in any future proceedings should the occasion arise. As with witnesses, jurors equally receive the same protection. Thus, any interference with jurors through intimidation, threats, etc., will constitute an obstruction with the administration of justice. In *Att.-Gen. v. Judd*,[25] a jury member was harassed by a man whom she, as part of a jury, unanimously convicted. He tried to persuade her to write to the judge saying that she had made a mistake. She immediately went to the police.

A contempt of court which occurs outside the court room, even in the street,[26] need not necessarily appertain to a particular case or court. Thus in *Balogh v. Crown* Court[27]:

Facts. B, was employed as a solicitor's clerk to attend a pornography trial in court. After a while, he found the trial boring and decided to introduce a certain levity into the proceedings by releasing "laughing gas" through the ventilation system into the court. He first stole a half cylinder of nitrous-oxide. He then decided to place the cylinder on the roof where the ventilating ducts operated from. Access to these ducts could only be obtained from the next door court (court 1). However, before he could fully carry out the plan, he was arrested. He was charged with theft and detained. He admitted contempt of court. The judge in court 1 sentenced him to six months' imprisonment for contempt of court. On being removed from the court, B said, "You are a humourless automaton, why don't you self-destruct?" He subsequently appealed to the Court of Appeal.

Decision. The Court of Appeal stated that the Crown Court, being a superior court, is permitted to act of its own motion in punishing summarily an offender for contempt, provided, in all the circumstances, it was necessary, urgent and imperative[28] to take such action immediately. Otherwise, it was for the Attorney-General to take the necessary steps under Order RSC 52.[29] They said that (1) since the offender was already in custody on a charge of theft, there was no real urgency about the matter and (2) the offence itself had not been more than merely preparatory despite having the necessary criminal intention, but, that by itself, was not sufficient. Accordingly, the appeal was allowed.

Scandalising the Court

7–010 It has never been the policy in this country that any person who constructively criticises the law should be punished. However, that is not to say that a person has *carte blanche* to say or write anything he or she wishes about the courts and its administrators. Whilst the courts themselves put great emphasis on the freedom of speech, nevertheless, there have always existed laws which prevent publications that have the effect of ridiculing and undermining the authority of the courts. Whilst the freedom of speech should be protected at all costs, the judges are in the unenviable position of not being able to reply to verbal attacks made on them through publications in the media, except perhaps through the courts themselves. Such attacks are commonly referred to as "scandalising the court". In *R. v. Gray*,[30] it was stated that "scandalising the court" meant ". . . an act done or writing published calculated to obstruct to interfere with the due course of justice or the lawful process of the courts",[31] but, (he continued) "Judges and courts are also open to criticism if reasonable argument or expostulation is offered against any judicial act as contrary to law or the public good, no court could or would treat that as contempt of court". But no person could write or say anything if it amounts to, as Lord Russell C.J. said ". . . (a) personal; scurrilous abuse of a judge as a judge".[32] However, criticism, if not of a personal nature, is acceptable, if the object is to emphasise any defects in the law itself, and not the judge who applied it. In *R. v. Editor of the New Statesman, ex parte DPP*[33] the *New Statesman* published an article about a libel action, the verdict of which they considered to be "a substantial miscarriage of justice". The trial was presided over by Mr Justice Avory. The article concluded that individuals who have such opinions as Dr Stopes (the losing defendant in a libel action) "cannot apparently hope for a fair hearing in a court presided over by Mr Justice Avory—and there are a many Avorys". The court said the reason why it was a contempt of court was not to spare the feelings of a particular judge, but instead it is in the public interest that judges maintain the respect, independence, confidence and impartiality by not belittling their reputation and authority. Such remarks may have a detrimental effect on the carrying out of their judicial responsibilities as judges. In the above case, there was no ambiguity in the words written in the article; the words clearly meant that no person would get a fair hearing from the judge, *i.e.* "by lowering his authority it, (*i.e.* the article) interfered with the performance of his judicial duties".[34] However, in *R. v. Commissioner of Police of the Metropolis ex parte Blackburn (No. 2)*,[35] Mr Quintin Hogg, Q.C. wrote an article in *Punch Magazine* criticising a previous decision of, incorrectly, the Court of Appeal (it should have been a decision of the Queen's Bench Division). He referred to the judgment as an example of "blindness" by the judges; the Gaming Act 1960 was unrealistic, unworkable and contradictory and an erroneous decision of the Court of Appeal, and suggested that the police should disregard such a nonsensical law. B, the applicant, moved that the Court of Appeal should treat such remarks as contempt of court as their writing had the effect of ridiculing or lowering the authority of the court. The Court of Appeal said that Mr Hogg was entitled to make all the criticism he so wished. Salmon L.J. said "it is the unalienable right of everyone to comment fairly upon any matter of public importance . . . providing it keeps within the limits of reasonable courtesy and good faith".[36]

It is, up to now, unsettled whether the contemner must intend to undermine the authority of the judge or court, or whether it can be inferred from the writings that, provided there was an intention to publish and there was a scurrilous attack showing bias, that in itself, satisfied the contempt. Past domestic and Privy Council cases provide no clear answer. This is partly due to the fact that the issues have not been discussed fully in previous cases, at least not satisfactorily. In "Scandalising the Courts",[37] it was suggested that "the mischief aimed at is the shaking of the public confidence in the judges and system of justice, and such damage may be incurred by an unpremeditated torrent of abuse in the heat of the moment". Salmon L.J. in *Blackburn* said that he accepted that Mr Hogg acted in good faith and had no intention of committing the contempt, but he did not elaborate further. It is possible to speculate that some degree of intention is required, albeit such that if the attack on the judiciary is so vicious, it can be assumed that the contemner must have been aware of the likely damage his words would do to the authority of the administration of justice. If done in good faith, it may well provide a defence to negative any intention. Any criticism should be in good faith and without malice. Indeed, the article may even misrepresent the law, but if not done intentionally, then there is no contempt of court. In *Ambard v. Att.-Gen. for Trinidad and Tobago*[38]:

Facts. The Attorney-General issued a notice of motion against the appellant to show cause why he published an article (calculated to interfere with the due course of justice) which contained statements tending to bring the authority and administration of the law into disrepute and disregard. The article in question, compared and criticised two disparaging jail sentences by two different judges for two similar crimes (one sentence lenient while the other severe). The judge found the publisher in contempt of court for the criticism.

Decision. On appeal to the Privy Council, their Lordships found that no such interpretation could be given to the article in question. They said, *inter alia*, that "provided that members of the public abstain from imputing improper motives to those taking part in the administration of justice"[39] and act in good faith, they are immune from prosecution. "Justice is not a cloistered virtue: she must be allowed to suffer the scrutiny and respectful, even though outspoken, comments of ordinary men".[40] As a consequence, the appeal was allowed.

In the last hundred years or so, there have been remarkably few English cases in this area—not because of the lack of personal remarks made about judges, but because judges have either ignored the issues or the particular article has had such little effect on their decisions that to publicise their distaste would have done more damage than good. Nowadays, by stating, for instance, that "the law is an ass", whilst not, by itself, to be regarded as constructive criticism, nevertheless would not generally be considered to be a contempt of court.

FREEDOM TO PUBLISH VERSUS A FAIR TRIAL

STATUTORY CONTEMPT OF COURT: THE CONTEMPT OF COURT ACT 1981: INTRODUCTION

7–011 The Contempt of Court Act 1981 was introduced partly as a voluntary measure to liberalise and tidy the law of contempt of court, but also partly as a necessary response to the European Court on Human Rights' finding in *The Sunday Times* case[41] that English contempt law was in breach of Article 10 of the ECHR since the restriction on the freedom of expression which it imposed was not justified by any countervailing legitimate aim, and was not necessary in a democratic state as a means of ensuring the authority or impartiality of the judiciary. The 1981 Act was intended as a rationalisation and improvement of the law of contempt, but has only been partially successful. For some people, particularly the media and others who claim to act in the public interest, the statutory version of contempt of court is less likely to result in a conviction. But the 1981 Act did not abolish common law contempt of court, which persists in a modified form; thus contempt of court is now a confused and confusing offence.

The main effect of the 1981 Act is the following:

(a) The common law offences of contempt of court still exist, but may only be charged where it can be proven that the defendant intended to prejudice the administration of justice. Thus a *mens rea* requirement has been added to the common law.

(b) There is a new statutory offence of contempt, which is strict liability like the old common law, but is only committed by publication of something which creates a substantial risk that the course of justice will be seriously impeded or prejudiced. If no "publication" is involved, then only a common law contempt may be charged, and thus intention will have to be established.

(c) a new defence of "public interest" was introduced, but it only applies to the statutory, strict liability publication offence.

What is a Court?

Before moving on to examine the changes introduced by the Contempt of Court Act 1981, there is a basic issue which must be addressed. In order to delineate the operation of contempt of court, it is necessary to decide what is meant by "court". Over the centuries, the number of bodies and persons exercising judicial or quasi-judicial functions has greatly increased, with the result that this is not such a simple question as it may at first appear to be. Alongside the traditional civil and criminal courts there are many tribunals which fulfil specialist roles and have legal recognition and enforceable sanctions. Yet these tribunals do not have the legal title of "court". Should it be possible to commit contempt of court in respect of proceedings in a tribunal? If the justifications for the existence of offences of contempt of court are examined, it becomes apparent that such justifications apply just as strongly where proceedings take place in front of a tribunal as they do in formal courtroom proceedings, and this approach to a large extent is mirrored by the law. At common law there was some disagreement as to what differentiated a court from any other body. In *Att.-Gen. v. BBC*,[42] the House of Lords had to decide on this issue, but did not formulate a unanimous test. The BBC planned to screen a television programme about the Plymouth Brethren, a religious group. The programme contained an argument that the Brethren were not eligible for exemption from rates (local property taxation).[43] The Attorney-General sought an injunction to prevent the broadcast on the basis that it would prejudice proceedings at a local valuation court which was to decide upon that very issue. The BBC 7–012 argued in defence that the local valuation court was not a "court" for the purposes of contempt. The House of Lords held that the local valuation court was not a "court" as regards contempt because its role within the rates system as purely administrative rather than judicial. The majority of the House thought that the label attached to a body was not significant, so that whether Parliament had called a body a "court" was inconclusive: for the purposes of contempt, a body is a "court" if its activities are primarily judicial in function.

The Contempt of Court Act 1981 took a similar approach: section 19 gives the definition of "court" as including "any tribunal or body exercising the judicial power of the state". But the Act does not give further guidance as to which bodies satisfy this test. Thus it is left to the courts to decide whether each of the relevant bodies does exercise judicial power. In *Pickering v. Liverpool Daily Post and Echo Newspapers plc*[44] the plaintiff was attempting to prevent publication of details of a mental health tribunal which would decide on the issue of whether he himself was fit for release from a mental hospital. His argument was that any such publicity might influence the tribunal against him and prevent a fair trial, thus creating a contempt of court. The Court of Appeal had held that a mental health tribunal was a court for the purposes of contempt, and the House of Lords agreed. The House of Lords found that a mental health tribunal deals with matters which affect the liberty of individuals, and that its function is judicial: Lord Farquharson listed the following reasons for this decision;

> ". . . (such) tribunals[45] are independent of the state; they do not exercise a purely administrative function; they are required to act judicially and make their findings on the basis of the evidence submitted to them; they can administer an oath to the witnesses called before them; they have . . . the power to release, conditionally or otherwise, patients detained under the Mental Health Acts . . . Decisions of such consequence affecting the release from detention of patients who are subject to hospital orders made by the criminal courts of the country come within the description of 'any tribunal . . . exercising the judicial power of the state'".

So, the publications in question could potentially have been a contempt of court, but on the facts it was held that they were not and so the injunction was denied.

In the recent case of *General Medical Council v. BBC*,[46] the Court of Appeal held that the professional conduct committee of the GMC was not a "court" for the purposes of contempt. Even though its purpose was judicial; its procedures clearly followed that of a court and was incorporated by statute, it was not part of the judicial system of the State. Instead, its function was exercising "the self-regulatory power and duty of the medical profession to monitor and maintain standards of professional conduct".[47] Industrial tribunals have since been held to be courts for the purposes of contempt[48]; it is therefore submitted that most tribunals will be treated in the same way, and that only tribunals which are purely administrative in function will not. The measures introduced by the 1981 Act will now be examined and, where appropriate, the interplay between the statutory and common law offences will be discussed.

Sections 1 and 2: Strict Liability Contempt of Court

Section 1—The Strict Liability Rule

"Strict liability" is given its usual meaning in criminal law, albeit somewhat oddly and ambiguously phrased, by section 1, which states that the strict liability offence in section 2(2) has the result that ". . . conduct may be treated as a contempt of court as tending to interfere with the course of justice in particular legal proceedings regardless of intent to do so". It is submitted that section 1 should be interpreted as meaning that, regardless of whether intention (or indeed recklessness) can be established against the defendant, he may be guilty of contempt of court under the publication offence in section 2(2). However, it is no longer possible to convict a defendant of any type of common law contempt without proving intention to impede or prejudice the administration of justice. The expression "tending to interfere" suggests that behaviour may still amount to contempt, despite no actual interference having occurred, where some interference is inclined to result some time in the future. The words "particular legal proceedings", mean the present court proceedings in question. Therefore, it would seem that any contempt which does not have an affect on that specific trial or later trials relating to those accused, will not come under the umbrella of the Contempt of Court Act ("CCA"), but may still be actionable as contempt under the common law (see CCA 1981, s. 6). Thus, behaviour which, for instance, interferes with the due process of justice generally, other than the proceedings themselves, will not necessarily come within the Act, *e.g.* interfering with witnesses who have given evidence and the trial is now over. It is accepted generally that the words "regardless of intent" refer to whether the conduct was intentional or not, and not merely to behaviour devoid of intent. **7–013**

Section 2—Restrictions of the Strict Liability Rule

Section 2(2) provides that strict liability contempt of court only applies to: **7–014**
"a publication which creates a substantial risk that the course of justice in the proceedings in question will be seriously impeded or prejudiced". In *Megrahi v. Times Newspapers Ltd*,[48A] the petitioners were two Libyan nationals charged with the murders of 270 passengers on board a plane which exploded over Lockerbie in 1988. They were committed for trial on April 14, 1999: the trial to take place in the Netherlands in front of three High Court Judges of the High Court of Justiciary (HCJ). On May 23, 1999, *The Sunday Times* published an article entitled "Official: Gadaffi's Bomb Plot", directly implicating the Libyan leader as the person who

ordered the bombing, and also making references to the accused. The petitioners applied to the HCJ for the publishers, editor and journalist to be held in contempt under sections 1 and 2(2) of the Contempt of Court Act 1981. They argued that since they could opt for jury trial in Scotland (with the consent of the Lord Advocate) the article would no doubt influence potential jurors, although there no evidence that they would elect this mode of trial. Further, that the publishers and others be prevented from publishing any future articles relating to the proceedings which were likely to impede the administration of justice. Lord Justice-Clerk Cullen, when considering the boundaries of the administration of justice, reiterated the words of Lord Diplock in *Att.-Gen. v. Times Newspapers Ltd*[48B] to the effect that the due administration of justice requires:

(i) unhindered access to the courts;

(ii) an unbiased tribunal, and;

(iii) no usurpation by any other person of the function of that court.

He said that he was not convinced that the contents of the article (references to the case were merely incidental) fell foul of section 2(2) and that on the facts there was no undermining of public confidence in the administration of justice. It was seriously doubted that the judges would be influenced by such publications, even if the articles concerned the case itself, although he would not "exclude absolutely the risk of influence on this score".[48C] The petition was eventually dismissed. However, as to future publications, Lord Justice-Clerk Cullen said that publishers should be aware of the danger and risk of undermining the presumption of innocence by conveying the guilt of the accused prior to a court of law deciding the issue.

A "publication" includes "any speech, writing, programme included in a broadcast service[49] or other communication in whatever form, which is addressed to the public at large or any section of the public" (section 2(1)). The proceedings in question must be "active" at the time of the publication (section 2(3)); Schedule 1 defines "active proceedings" to include all procedural stages from arrest, or issue of an arrest warrant or summons, until conviction, acquittal, expiry of a warrant or a discontinuance in relation to criminal proceedings. Civil proceedings are active once a hearing is arranged or begins, and remain active until the conclusion or abandonment of the action. This gets rid of one of the major criticisms of the previous common law, namely that there was a lack of certainty as to when the law of contempt would operate. The common law test covered all situations where proceedings were *sub judice*, which was often used as a synonym for "proceedings being pending or imminent", but at common law it was clear that no formalities need yet have taken place towards the commencement of civil or criminal proceedings before a contempt could be committed. The case of *Savundranayagan and Walker*[50] had caused an outcry from the Press which resulted in the Phillimore Committee recommending that a new test should be introduced, and it is to provide this new, more certain test that section 2(3) restricts the strict liability rule to "active proceedings".

Substantial Risk of Seriously Impeding or Prejudicing Proceedings

To "impede" means to hinder or obstruct. To "prejudice" something or someone is to say or do that which is detrimental or injurious to the interest of that thing or person.[51] In *Att.-Gen. v. English*,[52] the House of Lords (Lord Diplock) said that the word "substantial" described the degree of risk required, and "seriously" meant the degree of impediment or prejudice to the course of justice. But, if the risk is only considered remote, that is not sufficient. Thus, if a verdict is completely inconsistent with the evidence or the trial has to be abandoned due to the publication, then, no doubt such an interference created a substantial risk of seriously prejudicing those particular legal proceedings.[53] However, in order to impede, it is not always necessary that the trial itself should be abandoned. Merely a delay may constitute the relevant impediment such that a contempt is thereby established. In *Att.-Gen. v. BBC*,[54] during a trial for the illegal importation of drugs, the BBC had broadcast a current affairs programme in which they reported, wholly inaccurately as it turned out, the day's events of the trial. The following day, it transpired that four of the jurors saw the programme. The Attorney-General argued that due to these errors, a juror might easily be influenced, by the content in the programme and not consider properly the evidence before the court. The judge, however, did not discharge the jury. Instead, he said that of overriding importance in concluding whether a substantial risk was created was the scale and relation of the material complained of to the significant issue of the trial. Using an objective test, and on the facts, a contempt was proved. Despite the trial continuing, there was nevertheless a real risk that the trial would have to be postponed and also the added risk that should the defendants be found guilty, the failure to discharge the jury could be good grounds for appeal against conviction. The risk factor may also be determined by the width of the publication in question.[55] Width of the risk is dependent upon the people who read, see or hear the statement. For example, in *Blackburn v. BBC*,[56] a radio interview from BBC Plymouth with an area frequency limited to the south and south west of England did not constitute a "real risk" of prejudicing pending criminal proceedings in London as it was highly unlikely that a potential juror at any trial in London, at some future time, would recall the interview in question. The risk factor would, of course, be much more real if the interview was transmitted throughout the whole country. Once it is established that there is a substantial risk, then the next question is, does it seriously impede or prejudice the trial? This is to be decided by the actual content of the publication and how far away in time is the trial to take place. In *Att.-Gen. v. News Group Newspapers* Ltd[57]: **7–015**

Facts.
March 11 and April, 1984:
The *Mail on Sunday* published articles about the cricketer Ian Botham alleging that whilst on a cricketing tour of New Zealand he smoked marijuana and supplied cocaine to others.
March 13 and April 9, 1984:
Mr Botham began a libel action against the *Mail on Sunday* and Associated Newspapers Group Plc.
April 6, 1986:
The *News of the World* published an article concerning Mr Botham's activities whilst on a cricketing tour of the West Indies, with the heading, "He snorted drugs on pitch. Botham cocaine and sex scandal.", and informed Botham's solicitor that they intended to publish further details concerning his New Zealand tour in 1984, alleging that he took drugs and indulged in various sexual activities.
March 1987:
Trial date, at the earliest.
The Attorney-General was granted an injunction preventing News Group Newspapers from publishing those articles. He appealed.

Decision. The appellants argued *inter alia* that:

(1) The question of whether publication should be permitted or not, lies in balancing freedom of expression against the parties' rights to a fair trial without external impediments or prejudice, *i.e.* the relevant publication.
(2) The freedom of expression should take priority where the trial does not take place for some three months in the future.
(3) The publication in question would not cause any "substantial risk of serious prejudice" to any future trial.

Under section 2(2), Lord Donaldson said that the words "substantial risk" and "seriously impede or prejudice" connote a double test. The word "substantial" here does not mean enormous or extremely large, but it must be more than merely *de minimus* or very small—some risk of interference will be sufficient. In this case, the trial was some ten months away, "by which time many wickets will have fallen, not to mention much water having flowed under many bridges, all of which would blunt any impact of the publication".[58]
Therefore, the appeal was allowed and the injunction discharged.

In the above case, it was expounded by the Master of the Rolls that juries are inclined to direct themselves to the evidence produced in court as opposed to what they see or hear in the media. Whilst it is accepted that this may be the case generally, especially the further away the trial is from the possible contemptuous publication, nevertheless, the more famous or infamous the person is or the more important the item, time alone may not erase the potentially prejudiced details already published; or indeed, alleviate the emotion a juror may feel as though he had read or seen the article the previous day of the trial. In many cases, the publicity given to a situation can never really be obliterated or even minimised from a potential juror's mind, no matter how long the period is between the time of knowing certain facts and the time of the trial. It is never an easy decision for the court to make. As Parker L.J. said in *A.-G. v. News Group Newspapers Ltd*[59]; "Each case must be decided on its own facts and a publication relatively close to trial may escape whereas another much further from trial will not do so by reason of the impact of its contents on the reader, listener or viewer, as the case may be". *In Att.-Gen. v. ITN*[60] (see below), Leggatt L.J. said "When the long odds against the potential juror reading any of the publications is multiplied by the long odds against any reader remembering it, the risk of prejudice is, in my judgment remote".[61] In *Att.-Gen. v. MGN*[62];

Facts. *January, 1994:*
Libel action by Miss G. Taylforth and Mr Knight against *The Sun* newspaper regarding a certain incident which took place on the A1 motorway.
May, 1989—March 1995:
T and K given abundant media publicity concerning their volatile relationship and K's previous criminal record.
April 7, 1995:
K charged with grievously bodily harm against T and another man.
April 18, 19, 22 and May 12, 13, 1995:
Articles published about the above incident.
Trial set down for October 16, 1995:
K successfully appealed for the trial to be set back because of all the media pre-trial publicity.
The Att.-Gen. applied for orders against the relevant newspapers for contempt of court under section 2(2) and section 1 of the Contempt of Court Act 1981 (no intentional contempt was alleged at common law). The issue again was one of fair trial versus freedom of speech.

Decision. The court laid down certain factors which must be applied under section 2:

(1) Each case must be considered on its own particular facts.

(2) The number of publications should be considered. The more publications, the greater the risk and therefore the likelihood of contempt.[63]

(3) There must be "some" risk involved which impedes a fair trial.

(4) The "substantial" risk must "seriously" impede or prejudice the proceedings.

The court in considering whether (4) applied will take into account;

(a) the likelihood of a prospective juror seeing or hearing the publication including, for example, how wide is the area and how many copies of the relevant publication have been distributed;

(b) its likely affect on the public at large; and

(c) the residual impact of the publication on a notional juror at the time of the trial,[64] taking into account the length of time between publication, the likely date of trial, the ability of the jury to dissociate themselves from the pre-trial publicity and concentrate solely on the evidence introduced at trial and finally, the likely affect of the judge's directions to the jury.

Regarding the published articles of the various newspapers of April and May with large emotive headlines like "Knight beat me to a pulp" and including statements such as "pounding my head with a hard edged weapon, an iron bar" (in fact no weapon was used), the court found that the articles did not reach the required degree of substantial risk that the proceedings would be seriously impeded or prejudiced. Thus, although examining each publication separately, no individual newspaper was guilty of contempt, the court did not find fault with the judge's staying proceedings on the grounds that the totality of the recent publications created prejudice against a fair trial.[65]

In *Att.-Gen. v. Times Newspapers* Ltd[66]:

Facts. A man called Michael Fagan broke into Buckingham Palace on two separate occasions. As a result of these break-ins he was charged on June 7 and July 9 with burglary. During this period, he was also charged with a assaulting his stepson and taking a motor vehicle without the owner's consent.
July 13:
The Sun and *The Daily Star* published articles about the charges, and Fagan's solicitor informed ITV that his client admitted to entering the palace on both occasions.
July 14, 15 and 18:
Newspapers including *The Sun* and *The Sunday Times* published stories surrounding the charges against Fagan. Fagan's solicitor asked the Att.-Gen. to take proceedings against *The Sunday Times* for contempt as the articles prejudiced a fair trial.
July 25:
The Sunday Times and *The Mail on Sunday* published articles about security at the Palace and Fagan's activities. The Attorney-General took action against these newspapers.
October 5:
Fagan was found guilty on an earlier unrelated charge of taking a motor vehicle without the owner's consent and sent to a mental hospital (he was released in January 1983).

Decision. Application against *The Sun* newspaper.
The published articles suggested that Fagan was a habitual drug user, a liar and had taken cigars from the Palace. The issue was whether under section 2, the reports especially regarding the drug issue, would create a substantial risk of seriously prejudicing a fair trial on a charge of burglary. The court thought not. The court declared that a jury was to be credited with more independence of mind that was sometimes suggested and would not be swayed by such reports, and considered the bad character contents to be too far removed as to not constitute having the required substantial risk on any forthcoming trial. As a result the application against that particular newspaper was dismissed.

Application against *The Daily Star*
Although the report by this particular newspaper was very similar to those of *The Sun*, the present article contained an admission by the accused that he had stolen some wine. Such a confession related directly to the instant charge of burglary and even taking into account the "independence of mind" of the jury, there was a real risk that at trial, it would be very difficult for the jury to extricate that confession from their minds, no matter how properly a judge directed a jury to deal only with the admissible evidence in court. Thus, in this instance, the court declared that the contempt had been established.

Application against *The Sunday Times*
The newspaper published inaccurate and mistaken articles surrounding the circumstances of the assault, *i.e.* that Fagan had stabbed his stepson; in fact, no such event had taken place. At any future trial, the differences between the facts presented at trial and those "facts" reported in the newspaper would no doubt cause some

consternation in a juror's mind. The court stated that the inaccuracy by itself did not constitute a contempt, but where in this case the article was reported on the front page and repeated in later articles on the same topic, this resulted in a substantial risk of prejudicing the accused's trial by jury. Also, further articles were published which were inconsistent with the facts. For instance, (1) it was reported that the motor vehicle charge had been dropped, when in fact, it had not. (2) The stepson's injuries had not been inflicted by Fagan, but had occurred sometime earlier. Such incorrect statements by the newspapers would invariably damage the prosecution case against F. As the court said, the jury "would have listened to the opening speech for the prosecution with incredulity and could not fail to have been adversely influenced towards the prosecution". Therefore, the articles amounted to contempt.

Although normally publishing a defendant's previous convictions would, assuming all other proper conditions applied, amount to a contempt,[67] the court must still evaluate all the circumstances surrounding the particular case in order to reach a fair and proper decision. When a trial is in progress, any reporting must, in general, be limited to the admissible evidence therein, save trivia or innocuous information which has no bearing on those proceedings. Once that line has been crossed, the substantial risk factor becomes relevant and may lead to contempt. Thus in *Att.-Gen. v. ITN*[68]: **7–016**

Facts. Two men, M and O, were arrested for the murder and attempted murder of two police officers. The following evening, a ITN news broadcast stated that one of the arrested men, M, was a convicted IRA terrorist and had, in 1981, escaped from a Belfast prison whilst serving a life sentence for killing an SAS officer. A photograph of M was then shown, and suggested that both suspects would be questioned about other terrorist activities. The next day, *The Daily Mail* published an article headed "IRA prison fugitive held for PC murder" reiterating what was said on ITN the previous evening. Other newspapers including *Today* and *The Daily Express* covered the same story in similar words. In London (where the trial was most likely to be held), some 4,000 copies in all would have been sold. The Attorney-General applied for contempt proceedings against ITN and the newspapers on the grounds that the crime story was covered by the whole media, such was the public interest in this particular area, and despite the lapse of time before the trial (anticipated to be in nine months' time), a juror would still be able to recall the important details of those publications.

Decision. Leggatt L.J. said that it was "wholly unlikely" that M's previous murder conviction would be given openly at trial and thus, if a juror had remembered that fact from a prior publication, that would certainly seriously prejudice a fair trial. Therefore, the issue was whether there was a substantial risk of that occurring. Regarding the ITN news broadcast, the court stated that what was relevant was the nature of the broadcast and publication. Having considered the report itself and the old photograph, the fact that the broadcast itself was very short and that ITV by its very nature ephemeral, together with the frequency of the reported IRA atrocities, the court considered that the trial in nine months hence made the particular broadcast less memorable to the point where it obviated the required substantial risk necessary for contempt. Regarding the newspaper publications, Leggatt L.J. said that the relatively small amount of the particular editions sold and their limited distribution coupled with the lapse of time, made anyone who read the articles sufficiently unlikely to remember the relevant details such that it would be prejudicial to any future proceedings.

Articles written in newspapers or statements made on television or radio, even taken out of context and not, for instance, meant to be taken seriously, may nevertheless, still amount to contempt if their effect is such that there is a substantial risk of seriously prejudicing an existing or pending trial. In *Att.-Gen. v. BBC*,[69] six months before the already well-publicised Maxwell brothers trial on charges of defrauding *The Mirror* pensioners out of hundreds of millions of pounds, the BBC had broadcast a programme on a Friday night called "Have I Got News for You", a satirical light-hearted current affairs quiz programme (it was generally repeated the following night). The words spoken on that programme were perceived as showing the Maxwell brothers to be guilty of the charges against them. This was despite the fact that:

(1) the comments were not to be treated as serious,

(2) the statements were brief,

(3) they did not concern the forthcoming case itself, and

(4) the trial was some six months away.

Nevertheless, the court regarded the words as "a readily memorable encouragement to viewers to regard the Maxwell brother as guilty". The BBC and the programme producers were each fined £10,000. It is suggested that no reasonable juror could possibly treat the comments made as anything but in the manner in which they were spoken, *i.e.* humorous, satirical, etc. A juror surely would possess the "independence of mind" to regard those comments, even if remembered six months later, as not to be taken seriously. It is regrettable that the freedom of speech should be gagged in this manner, when all that was uttered was merely to be construed as a joke. How such comments could create a real risk of seriously prejudicing a trial six months into the future should seriously be questioned.

Section 4—Postponement of court proceedings reporting

7–017 Section 4(2) provided that, in relation to legal proceedings held in public;

> ". . . the court may, where it appears to be necessary for avoiding a substantial risk of prejudicing to the administration of justice in those proceedings, or in any other proceedings pending or imminent, order that the publication of any report of the proceedings, or any part of the proceedings, be postponed for such a period as the court thinks necessary for that purpose".

Thus, although section 4(2) serves to protect contemporaneous reports of legal proceedings from contempt charges, section 4(2) gives courts a power to postpone (but not to prevent altogether) the publication of such reports where there is a pressing reason of justice to do so.

Once there is a conflict between a fair trial and open justice, a section 4(2) postponement order should only be invoked as a last resort. Thus, before a postponement order may be issued, a number of requirements must be adhered to in section 4(2):

(1) There must be a substantial risk to the administration of justice;

(2) it must appear to be necessary for avoiding that risk that a postponement order should be made, and if so,

(3) the court has a discretion whether or not to make such an order[70];

(4) the order must relate directly to the proceedings in question, not to reports which are peripheral or unconnected to the present case.

It is generally accepted that the words in (1) above, *i.e.* substantial risk, have the same meaning as in section 2(2), *i.e.* a risk which is not too remote[71]; more than merely minimal; not insubstantial. It is difficult to discover a more exact or helping meaning in previous authorities other than the descriptions given above. Once it has been established that there has been a substantial risk, only then is it required to consider in (2) above the words "appear to be necessary" in order to avoid the risk in question. But it does not automatically follow from that merely because it is necessary to avoid the risk a postponement order must be imposed. The judge involved should consider what other action, other than to gag the Press, would alleviate the risk so that a fair trial would ensure. In *Re Central Independent Television*,[72] the judge decided that the jury, having sat through a fraud and corruption trial lasting six weeks, were entitled to relax and watch TV during their overnight stay at an hotel to consider their verdict. He ordered that all reporting of the trial was to be postponed until after the verdict. The media appealed on the grounds that the judge erred in law in that the order was not necessary to avoid any substantial risk (if indeed there was one). The court held that the more efficient and better remedy was merely to order that the jury members do not watch or listen to the radio or TV. Since there was a proper alternative to a section 4(2) order, it should have been applied and therefore the appeal was successful. In *MGN Pension Trustees v. Bank of America*,[73] it was successfully argued by the applicants in that case that the application of the word "necessary" should only be adopted in limited circumstances in order to:

(1) ensure that an order is made only if it is needed in the practical sense that the prejudice cannot be avoided save by an order;

(2) to be sure that an order, if made, would be likely to cause the prejudice to be avoided; and

(3) the order is to be no wider in its ambit that is needed to avoid the predicated risk.[74] In section 4(2), the words "the court may . . .

order", a postponement order provides that the judge has a discretionary power to make such an order and should only be applied where (1), (2) and (3) above are satisfied. It is also interesting to note that the word "seriously" in connection with the word "prejudice" is omitted in section 4(2) whilst included in section 2(2). In *MGN*, it was suggested by Lindsay J. that there need only be a "slight or trivial prejudice" as opposed to serious, in order for section 4(2) to be invoked.[75] Where an order is imposed under section 4(2), there are very specific requirements in order to give it a legal effect. The order must include in writing:

(i) its precise scope;
(ii) the time at which it shall cease to have effect, and
(iii) the specific purpose of making the order.[76]

The adage "justice must not only be done but must be seen to be done" is especially prevalent where the media reporting of trials is concerned. In *R. v. Beck ex parte Daily Telegraph plc*,[77] the three accused werc charged under the first indictment with offences (34 in total) relating to the physical and mental abuse of children under their protection and care. There were also two other indictments laid against the defendants involving some 40 other counts. At the request of one of the defendant's counsel, a judge ordered the postponement of all reporting of the first trial. *The Daily Telegraph* along with three other newspapers appealed against this decision. It was recognised that in order for the postponement order to be upheld, there must not only be a substantial risk that the reporting of the trial would lead to prejudicing the administration of justice, but also that it was necessary to make such an order so as to avoid that risk.[78] The appellants argued that merely because there were going to be three separate trials, this in itself, did not warrant the introduction of a postponement order. The judge failed to consider this. They further argued on more general grounds that:

(1) the trial was of public interest concern,

(2) there was in this case the requirement of "open justice",

(3) was there other means of obviating the risk of prejudice?

(4) the judge failed to hear arguments from the newspapers on the reasons why such an order should not be granted, and

(5) the judge did not state the reasons behind his decision.

The court said that a judge when considering whether to issue a postponement order has to "enter into balancing act of the considerations which support the need for a fair trial by an unprejudiced jury on the one hand

and the requirement of open justice and a legitimate public interest and concern in these matters on the other".[79] Such considerations in this case included, if reporting was allowed, whether there would be a strong feeling of outrage and horror of the events which took place amongst the public, and thus, jurors. In the above case there was a substantial risk that the due process of justice would be hindered. However, taking into account the gravity of the charges, the general public interest concerned in the matter of a public authority allegedly involved in such mistreatment of children over a long period of time, and the ignored complaints by those children, the court felt on balance that the public ought to be properly informed of those wrongs. In this instance, the "necessary" factor did not reach the required level for the order to be made. As a consequence, the appeal was allowed and the postponement order discharged.

It is generally only the parties to the actual proceedings who may apply for a postponement order or make argument against one being imposed. But a judge is also empowered to listen to representations made by the media on the question of why it is in the public interest that the relevant proceedings ought to be discussed in the public domain. Such arguments centre around the issues of a lack of a substantial risk of any injustice resulting by such reporting and that it is not necessary for such an order to be made. In *R. v. Clerkenwell Magistrates' Court ex parte Telegraph plc*[80] on appeal by the applicant newspapers (four in all) against a refusal by a magistrate to hear arguments against a postponement order, the court held that a court has a discretionary power to hear and take into account when requested to do so, representations by the media when considering the operation under section 4(2). Further, when under section 4(2) there are reporting restrictions, it is not necessarily the case that the whole proceedings are prohibited from being made public. The postponement order may limit reporting to various procedures or issues within the trial itself such that a substantial risk of injustice may be averted. For instance, in *ex parte Telegraph* and other appeals,[81] there was to be three separate trials involving eleven defendants on the illegal importation of the drug, ecstasy. A number of the defendants (four in total) requested that reporting restrictions be invoked under section 4(2) until the conclusion of the trials. The media applicants objected to the broad terms of the order and argued limiting the order to the identity of those defendants only. The judge compromised and issued an order prohibiting:

(1) evidence and rulings given on the *voir dire*;
(2) identification of the relevant accused;
(3) identification of the principle prosecution witness V, an accomplice of a defendant;
(4) counsel's closing arguments and summing up.

The appellants appealed against this decision under section 159(1)(a) of the Criminal Justice Act 1988.[82] As to (3) above, a number of the defendants argued on full reporting restrictions because if otherwise, a potential prejudice was bound to occur if they were found guilty at the first trial of extending into subsequent trials, because the prosecution witness's testimony would add an unfair credibility about it beyond that which was unduly influential. There was full agreement between the parties that (2) above should be postponed. The court said that there did not exist a substantial risk of the prosecution witness's identity became known, since at the later trials, the judge could properly and adequately direct the jury on the importance of considering only the admissible evidence and not be influenced by the reporting on the former first trial. The court regarded V's evidence as only creating a "slight potential for prejudice" from any published reports. The court accepted the applicant's submission that since V's evidence was so crucial that "any prohibition of the contemptor means reporting (under section 4(1)) of material likely to identify him and his role in the case would make it almost impossible to report".[83] Accordingly, the judge's order was varied so that only the reporting of the identity of the defendants was postponed.

Sections 3, 4 and 5: Defences

7–018 The potential harshness of the strict liability contempt offence in section 2(2)) is mitigated by the creation of four specific defences which are not available at common law. These defences are:

> Section 3(1)) innocent publication; a person is not guilty of strict liability contempt if he publishes the material and at the time of publication "(having taken all reasonable care) he does not know and has no reason to suspect that relevant proceedings are active". For example, this section would give a defence to a newspaper editor who publishes an article about a suspected criminal after proceedings have been discontinued, but the person in question has been arrested without the editor's knowledge prior to the publication.
>
> Section 3(2) innocent distribution; a person is not guilty of strict liability contempt if he is the distributor of a publication which contains contemptuous matter and "at the time of distribution (having taken all reasonable care) he does not know that it contains any such matter and has no reason to suspect that it is likely to do so". As is typical of defences to strict liability offences in criminal law, the burden of proof for either a section 3(1) or a section 3(2) defence will lie upon the defendant.
>
> Section 4(1) provides that, as a general rule, a person is not guilty of contempt of court under the strict liability rule in respect of a fair and accurate report of legal proceedings held in public, published contemporaneously and in good faith. Thus reports for

local newspapers who attend court and report on cases will not be liable for the section 2(2) offence if what they publish was written in good faith and is a report of events in the court room. But the defence will not operate if publication is delayed; for example, it will still be a section 2(2) contempt to publish the report of an earlier rape conviction when the same man is, two years later, on trial for a similar offence.

Section 5—Discussion of matters of general public interest

The most significant defence under the 1981 Act is provided by section 5; the "good faith" or "public interest" defence: **7–019**

> "A publication made as or as part of a discussion in good faith of public affairs or other matters of general public interest is not to be treated as a contempt of court under the strict liability rule if the risk of impediment or prejudice to legal proceedings is merely incidental to the discussion".

This defence operates differently from the others which apply to the strict liability defence. As regards the section 5 defence, it is the prosecution who bear the burden of proof. The defendant need only raise the section 5 defence, and then the prosecution must establish beyond reasonable doubt that: the publication was not made in good faith; the publication did not concern either current affairs or "other matters of general public interest"; and that the risk of impediment or prejudice to legal proceedings was not "merely incidental" to the discussion. Contempt of court in this area does not exist solely to protect those parties involved in any possible litigation, but on a wider interpretation, whether it is in the public interest that all citizens should be safeguarded against anything said or written which has the consequences of undermining the authority of any present or future judicial proceedings in the public's eyes.

Meaning of "good faith"

The normal meaning of "good faith" refers to something done or said or written with honesty, sincerity and without malice. In order to discover whether a publication has in fact been made in good faith, it is necessary not only to look at the content of the particular article, broadcast, etc., but also to investigate into the reasons behind the publication itself. Most publications made in good faith on matters of public concern are generally biased in some manner, whether it be for a political party, contentious moral issues, causes or reforms, or other controversial matters of public concern. Provided the publications possess integrity, honesty and sincerity and have no negative underhanded motives, the Attorney-General would find it difficult to prove that the publication warranted the title *mala fides*. One instance where a publication could be construed as made in bad faith is when the publisher uses the media to pursue a personal grudge or settle **7–020** an "old score" or by trying to persuade a party from exercising their legal rights. An example of the former would be in the case of *Re Lonrho*,[84] where the proprietor of *The Observer* newspaper used his own power to wage a campaign against the owners of Harrods, alleging fraud and deceit, although in that case contempt was not proven. Another example was in *R. v. Hislop*[85] where the editor was found guilty of, *inter alia*, common law contempt in that the *Private Eye* magazine intended to persuade Mrs Sutcliffe, the party to a libel action against the magazine, from continuing that action by publishing derogatory reports about her. The Court of Appeal gave short shrift to the issue of good faith under section 5 by stating that "the respondent's intention negatived the existence of good faith".[86]

Thus, any proven intention to interfere with the administration of justice under the common law will presumably destroy the defence of good faith under section 5. However, it will not necessarily have the same outcome if a party is found guilty under the strict liability rule in the Contempt of Court Act 1981. Another instance of *mala fides* may arise where the media doggedly persist in a cause which, although they have no legal interest in, use their influence to badger a particular group or person unjustifiably. For example, in *Att.-Gen. v. Times Newspapers Publishing plc*,[87] (the "*Thalidomide case*") would the Attorney-General have been able to nullify the issue of good faith against the newspaper had the case been tried after the enactment of the Contempt of Court Act 1981?

Subject-matter "merely incidental to the discussion"

7–021 The rationale behind section 5 is to allow matters of public interest to be discussed openly in spite of the fact that there may be legal proceedings in progress at the time of publication. It was stated in *Att.-Gen. v. English*,[88] that the purpose of the words "merely incidental to the discussion" is to:

> ". . . strike a sensible balance between two important and often competing principles; on the one hand, the maintenance of unimpeded and unprejudicial justice to every litigant and defendant, and on the other hand the preservation of the freedom of discussion of matter of general public interest. Thus, section 5 provides in effect that bona fide discussion of matter of public interest need not be silenced if, as a mere incident of such discussion, a substantial risk of serious prejudice to particular litigant or defendant may arise".

The actual meaning of the phrase "merely incidental to the discussion" was stated by Lord Diplock in *Att.-Gen. v. English*[89] as "no more than an incidental consequence of expounding its main theme".[90] This, unfortunately, was not elaborated upon, and to what precise degree and circumstances do the words "merely incidental" refer, remain uncertain. As was expressed in *Att.-Gen. v. TVS Television*,[91] it can only be ascertained by considering the whole publication and how closely it relates to the legal proceedings in question. The greater the risk of prejudice to those proceedings, the less likely that the publication can be regarded as being merely incidental to the discussion, despite it being made in good faith and of general public interest.[92]

Section 5 is not intertwined with section 2(2) as may appear. They must be considered separately. But, if the court finds that there exists no real risk of seriously prejudicing existing proceedings under section 2(2), then section 5 does not have to be considered at all.[93] It is only when the Attorney-General has proved that there is the requisite risk must he further show that it was not merely incidental to the discussion but had overstepped that mark, assuming, of course, section 5 applied in the first instance. Hence, it is best not to consider section 5 as some form of defence since the burden of proof remains throughout on the Attorney-General. The main authority in this area is *Att.-Gen. v. English*[94]:

Facts. Dr Arthur, a paediatrician, was being tried for the murder of a Down's Syndrome baby, by starvation. During the third day of the trial, a journalist published an article in the *Daily Mail* an article entitled "The vision of life that wins my vote", in which the writer stressed his support for an independent pro-life candidate in a parliamentary by-election, Mrs Carr, herself handicapped through having no arms. The journalist wrote that "Today, the chances of such a baby surviving (referring to Mrs Carr) would be very small indeed. Someone would surely recommend letting her die of starvation, or otherwise disposing of her". He went on to emphasise the broader issues concerning the right to life including such moral questions as "Are human beings to be culled like livestock?". No mention was made in the article of the ongoing trial. The Attorney-General applied for an order against the editor and the proprietors of the newspaper for contempt. The Divisional Court held that had the article refrained from including the emotive pro-life words, as stated in the facts above, the whole moral message and purpose of the publication would still have remained intact and decided that the relevant assertions were "wholly expendable by the respondents without damaging the vigour and clarity of the vision of life sought to be portrayed".[95] Therefore, the particular words used not only constituted the required risk under section 2(2), but also the assertions did not come within the bounds of a discussion of general public concern. As a result, the contempt was established. The newspaper appealed. (As an addendum, Dr Arthur was eventually acquitted of all charges).

Decision. The House of Lords agreed with the Divisional Court that on the facts, the contents of the published article in question amounted to a contempt under section 2(2). On the main issue of section 5, it was agreed by all parties concerned that the respondents acted in good faith. Indeed, the journalist involved apparently was unaware that the trial was in progress. Previously, in the Divisional Court, it was stated that it was for the respondents to prove the requirements set out in section 5, *i.e.* good faith, general public interest and that the risk was merely incidental to the discussion.[96] However, in the House of Lords, Lord Diplock disagreed and said that it was up to the Attorney-General not only to prove section 2(2), but also to prove beyond reasonable doubt the requirements of section 5, *i.e.* by showing that the risk was more than merely incidental to the discussion. He said that not mentioning the comments concerning the death of new-born babies by starvation or otherwise, would, in fact, amount to disregarding the whole of Mrs Carr's election campaign, and stated that:

> "the test is not whether an article could have been written as effectively without these passages or whether some other phraseology might have been

> substituted for them that could have reduced the risk of prejudicing Dr Arthur's fair trial; but it is whether the risk created by the words actually chosen by the author was 'merely incidental to the discussion' ".[97]

Had the newspaper been restrained from publishing this article, Mrs Carr's whole election campaign would have been pointless since she would have been prevented from receiving any kind of publicity regarding the pro-life issues and further, the general public concern on this important theme would have been stifled from the time of Dr Arthur's being charged until his acquittal some nine months later.[98] The whole purpose of section 5 would be defeated if it was used in this way. As a result, the appeal was allowed.

Mere publication of facts which may otherwise have not come to the attention of a juror, do not automatically constitute a real risk of prejudicing the particular legal proceedings. Each case must be considered on its own facts, and the content of each publication and surrounding circumstances must be thoroughly examined. Further, the necessary risk must be a practical risk and not a theoretical risk.[99] Thus, the court, for instance, must consider from a pragmatic point of view, whether a juror would be so unduly influenced by the publication in question, that there was a real risk of insufficient weight being given by that juror to the evidence in court. In *Att.-Gen. v. Guardian Newspapers*,[1] the newspaper published an article criticising judges for being too eager to ban reports of white collar fraud trials, "for the sake of a few titbits which might affect the trial". The article gave mention of an ongoing trial where the defendant might also be, sometime in the future, prosecuted for offences in the Isle of Man. The trial had to be abandoned as a result of the article. The Attorney-General brought proceedings against the newspaper for contempt. However, it was held that "the practical risk of the publication engendering bias in juror of ordinary good sense was, insignificant".[1] Thus, not only was the required risk purely minimal, and therefore not contempt, but it was also held obiter that if section 5 were to be considered, the risk would only have been "merely incidental to the discussion". In *Att.-Gen. v. Times Newspapers Ltd*[2] an article in *The Mail on Sunday* strongly intimated of a homosexual affair between the Queen's resident police officer and the accused and described the latter as a "rootless neurotic with no visible means of support". Such a description tended towards the question of the accused's honesty and came within the ambit of section 2(2). However, the newspaper did have justifiable reasons under section 5 to invalidate the contempt if it could be shown that the article was merely incidental to the main public interest discussion of Her Majesty's welfare. Since the main object of the article was to highlight the inefficiency of the security procedures, the "neurotic" comments were construed as merely peripheral to the main public interest argument and therefore not likely to prejudice a jury's thinking. However, in the same case, *The Sunday Times* article discussed in great depth the accused's domestic problems alongside the general debate of the Queen's safety, and thus, could not be interpreted as being "merely incidental" to the overall general public discussion, and therefore the newspaper was guilty of contempt of court.

Section 6—Contempt of Court at Common Law

Section 6 of the 1981 Act states that: **7–022**

> "Nothing in the foregoing provisions of this Act—
>
> (a) prejudices any defence available at common law to a charge of contempt of court under the strict liability rule;
> (b) implies that any publication is punishable as contempt of court under the rule which would not be so punishable apart from those provisions;
> (c) restricts liability for contempt of court in respect of conduct intended to impede or prejudice the administration of justice".

Thus, section 6(a) allows the common law defences to continue to apply after the Act. Section 6(b) makes it clear that the Act does not extend the ambit of strict liability contempt of court but limits it scope to publications; and section 6(c) allows common law contempt of court to continue to exist in all situations where it can be established that the defendant's conduct was "intended to impede or prejudice the administration of justice". In relation specifically to the latter, it should be noted that the effect of section 6(c) is to amend the common law offences of contempt by introducing a new element of *mens rea*—he intention stated above. So, a distinction must be drawn between cases before and after the 1981 Act where the contempt charged is a common law offence. Prior to the introduction of the Contempt of Court Act 1981, the test for contempt of court at common law was one of strict liability, *i.e.* it was irrelevant to liability whether the contemner either intended or foresaw that his conduct would interfere with the course of justice. What was required was that his conduct did in fact so interfere in one of the prohibited manners. But cases did not always deal with this issue consistently: sometimes courts seemed to require intention or recklessness to be proved; and sometimes lack of intention was treated as a mitigation of sentence.

For instance, in *R. v. Bolam ex parte Haigh*,[3] *The Daily Mirror* published an article about Haigh, who was in custody on a charge of murder, describing him as a vampire and that he had committed other murders besides the one he was now being charged with. The court stated that such writings amounted to that of a "scandalous and wicked character", and "pandering to sensationalism" for the purpose of increasing its newspaper's circulation. Due to the seriousness of the offence and the reasons behind it, the editor was imprisoned for three months and the proprietors fined £10,000. In *R. v. Evening Standard ex parte Att.-Gen.*[4] K was on trial for the murder of his wife. A journalist attending the trial mistakenly reported back to the *Evening Standard* that a witness, D, had given evidence that K had asked her to marry him. That report was inaccurate. Nevertheless, that same evening, the newspaper innocently published that wrong evidence. K was later acquitted. The Attorney-General took proceedings against the newspaper, the editor and the journalist for contempt. Normally, such prejudicial, incorrect revelations would incur a severe penalty. However, the court found that:

(1) there was no intention to publish incorrect statements (nevertheless, intention is not required and is only relevant as a mitigating factor a lessen the seriousness of the offence)[5]:

(2) it made no different to the contempt whether K was found guilty or not;

(3) the editors and the proprietors were vicariously liable for the misrepresentations of the journalist.

Since the editor had no reason to doubt the journalist's version of events, and the reporting was an honest mistake, no fines were imposed on those persons, but the proprietors were fined £1,000 as it was considered to be a very serious error.

In *R. v. Thomson Newspapers Ltd ex parte Att.-Gen.*,[6] M was charged with stirring up racial hatred contrary to section 6(1) of the Race Relations Act 1965. Prior to the trial, *The Sunday Times* published an article and photographs of M, the contents of which included that M was "a brothel keeper, procurer, and property racketeer and muddled thinker". Such a description of the accused's bad character was a serious matter for the court since the article was likely to prejudice the fair trial of M which was pending. The Attorney-General sought contempt of court against the printers (Thomson), publishers (*The Sunday Times*) and editor. The court held that even though there was no doubt that this was a serious contempt, publication was not done intentionally to prejudice the fairness of the trial itself. Further, even though the newspaper had taken steps to avoid the possibility of contempt, the fact that there was a likelihood of prejudicing the trial was sufficient, and the publishers were fined £5,000. The editor escaped any penalty as the court decided that he had "not acted recklessly or turned a blind eye".[7] Also, in *R. v. Evening Standard*,[8] H was charged with theft from a bank. On the same day that an identification parade as due to taken place, the *Evening Standard* published an article and photographs of H with the headline "Hain, He's no Bank Robber". Thus, the photograph, comments about the identification parade and the headline, constituted a contempt of court in that the article was likely to prejudice a fair trial.

Such an error should not have occurred had the correct procedures been implemented. When deciding on the particular action to be taken, the court should take into account:

(i) the nature of the contempt;
(ii) the circumstances, *i.e.* intention, recklessness, mistake, etc.;
(iii) the circulation of the newspaper; and
(iv) the effect on the due process of justice.

Such is the importance of identification parades that any interference which could ultimately taint the fairness of the particular procedure is likely to prejudice a fair trial. Here, it was quite possible for potential witnesses to have seen the front page of the *Evening Standard*. Accordingly, the newspaper was fined £1,000. The enactment of the Contempt of Court Act 1981 was brought about as a direct consequence of the following case and as a result of the eventual findings under Article 10 of the European Court of Human Rights. Thus in *Att.-Gen. v. Times Newspapers Publishing plc*[9]:

Facts. Between 1958 and 1961, Distillers Company (Biochemicals) Ltd produced and sold under licence in the United Kingdom a sedative drug for pregnant women, which included an ingredient called "thalidomide". As a result of taking this drug, many women gave birth to children who suffered severe physical abnormalities. Between 1962 and 1966, some 70 writs were issued against Distillers, claiming damages for negligence in the manufacture and marketing of this product. In 1968, 62 of these action were settled out of court, with the proviso that no future action would be taken against Distillers. By 1971, some 389 further cases were pending against Distillers. In September of that same year, Distillers proposed setting up a trust fund for the children, but not all the parents agreed. By September 1972, a further settlement, involving a £3.25 million trust fund was in negotiation. Between 1967 and 1971, there had been some media coverage of the tragedy. On September 24, 1972, *The Sunday Times* published an article entitled "Our Thalidomide Children: A Cause for National Shame", criticising the proposals of Distillers as "grotesquely out of proportion to the injuries suffered", and urging Distillers (assets £421 million) to make a more generous offer. The Attorney-General took no action for contempt of court despite a request from Distillers that he do so. *The Sunday Times* proposed to write further articles, but they first sent a copy of a future article to the Attorney-General for his inspection. On October 12, 1972, the Attorney-General applied for an injunction and on November 17, an injunction was granted by the Divisional Court against *The Sunday Times* preventing publication of the future article. This injunction was discharged by the Court of Appeal The Attorney-General appealed to the House of Lords. The Attorney-General argued that it was a contempt of court for any newspaper to comment on a pending legal proceedings in any way which is likely to prejudice the fair trial of the action. This can occur by:

(1) the contents of the respective article bringing pressure on one of the parties so as to dissuade that party from continuing the claim;
(2) pressurising that party into making a settlement which he might not otherwise have done; or;
(3) influence him in some way over his conduct in the action.[10]

Decision. Lord Reid said that the whole issue in this case concerned public policy, and in particular a balancing of interests which may conflict: "Freedom of speech should not be limited to any greater extent than is necessary but it cannot be allowed where there would be real prejudice to the administration of justice".[11] The present appeal concerned only the proposed article to be published in *The Sunday*

Times. He was of the opinion that merely persuading a party from continuing with a claim is not a contempt of court. Thus, using influence which was "fair and temperate criticism" in order to dissuade a person from pursuing their claim falls within the scope of freedom of speech which newspapers are entitled to exercise. There was very little doubt that one of the purposes of that article was to put pressure on Distillers to offer more money but that by itself did not constitute a contempt of court. However, the issue of whether Distillers were negligent or not, had been written about, and if that were allowed to continue, views expressed may be governed by emotions and prejudice, without necessarily all the relevant evidence being put before the public, and thus could result in unfair and biased speculation and may amount to "trial by the media".[12] He said this could not be in the public interest and was "intrinsically objectionable". Such debate which could cause so much harm in prejudging the parties involved was not acceptable and should be avoided at all cost.[13] One of the Court of Appeal's arguments in discharging the injunction was based on that action being "dormant". Lord Reid disagreed. He said that settlement negotiations had been continuing the whole time, with no side prolonging the process unduly; thus, it could not be said that negotiations were inactive.

7–023 Lord Diplock said that there were certain requirement for the due administration of justice:

(1) There must be no obstacles preventing a person having access to the courts to hear their disputes.

(2) The decision of the court must be impartial and based solely upon admissible evidence.

(3) There must be no usurpation by any other person of the function of that court, *i.e.* trial by media.

Finally, he said "conduct which is calculated to prejudice any of these three requirements or to undermine the public confidence that they will be observed is contempt of court".[14] Thus, the proposed newspaper article by intimating that Distiller's negligence was the cause of the tragedy could result in the possible pre-judgment of the case by discussing in some detail its merits or facts, prior to any action being possibly considered in a court of law. This amounted to a contempt of court under the (3) requirement above. However, overall discussion on a topic which is of public interest is not to be prohibited at the expense of freedom of speech. As Lord Diplock said,

> ". . . if the arousing of public opinion by this kind of discussion has the indirect effect of bringing pressure to bear on a particular litigant to abandon or settle a pending action, this must be borne because of the greater public interest in upholding freedom of discussion on matters of general public concern".[15]

Lord Cross stated that the Attorney-General's arguments for contempt of court were based on law which was too broad in its declaration. To persuade a possible litigant not to proceed with a claim by such illegal means as threats, or by abuse, was a contempt of court, but not if the persuasion of another party was by fair and temperate words. Thus, the article already written on September 24 was generally accepted as not constituting a contempt of court. However, any future publication where the content was similar to that in the "appealed article" would amount to a contempt.

In *Att.-Gen. v. Newspaper Publishing plc*[16]:

Facts. The Attorney-General was granted an injunction against *The Guardian* and *The Observer* newspapers ("GO" injunctions) to prevent them from publishing any further details from the manuscript or book of Peter Wright, *i.e. Spycatcher*. On April 27, 1987, *The Independent* along with the *London Evening Standard* and *London Daily News* published detailed extracts from the book. The Attorney-General took proceedings against *The Independent, et al.*, alleging that the publications "intended or calculated to impede, obstruct or prejudice the administration of justice" by thwarting the "GO" injunctions already in place and therefore the newspapers were in contempt of court. At first instance, before Sir Nicolas Browne-Wilkinson V.-C., the question raised was, could an already existing injunction against the publication of an article be used to prevent others who had knowledge of the injunction, constitute a criminal contempt in that it interfered with the due process of justice? He decided it could not, on the general legal principles that a third party who was not subject to an order of the court cannot be bound by it. Thus, since *The Independent, et al.*, were neither parties to the previous action, nor subject to the injunctions, despite having knowledge of the injunctions, were not guilty of a contempt of court. The Attorney-General appealed.

Decision. The Attorney-General appealed on the grounds that *The Independent, et al.*, publications interfered with the administration of justice in that any future legal action to be taken against *The Guardian* and *The Observer*, may well now be impeded, obstructed or prejudiced.[17] Thus, the issue was not disobeying a court order, *i.e.* civil contempt, but one of obstructing the due process of justice, *i.e.* criminal contempt. Lord Donaldson said that the appeal was about ". . . the right of private citizens and public authorities to seek and obtain the protection of the courts for confidential information (not solely or necessarily official secrets) which they claim to be their property.[18] If the publications were allowed and therefore no longer confidential, what would be the point of any future trial? It would be otiose. It was this interference which the Attorney-General submitted to be the contempt. Confidential information, because of its very nature, once divulged, cannot become secret again. Once the whole question came within the common law and not the Contempt of Court Act 1981,[19] the issues of *actus reus* and *mens rea* were raised. The *actus reus* in this case consisted of the newspapers:

(1) publishing the actual confidential material;

(2) being aware of the already existing injunction against other newspapers; and

(3) the disclosure of which would destroy the subject matter of the article in whole or part.[20]

It was said that there was no doubt that *The Independent* interfered with the due process of justice, but that was not enough; did the publishers possess the necessary intent? Lord Donaldson thought, following the Phillimore Committee's[21] recommendation that what is required for contempt is for the act to be "specifically intended to impede or prejudice the administration of justice. Such intent need not be expressly avowed or admitted, but can be inferred from all the circumstances, including the foreseeability of the consequences of the conduct".[22] Lloyd L.G. when considering "intent" said that:

> ". . . intent may exist, even though there is no desire to interfere with the course of justice. Nor need it be the sole intent. It may be inferred, even though there is no overt proof. The more obvious the interference with the course of justice, the more readily will the requisite intent be inferred".[23]

The publication resulted in the unsustainability of the status quo, pending trial. Therefore, the court decided that the publication could amount to a criminal contempt and allowed the appeal, remitting the issue to the High Court.

In *Att.-Gen. v. Newspaper Publishing plc*,[24] the court once again considered the issues of the *actus reus* and *mens rea*. Under section 6(c) of the Contempt of Court Act 1981, it was up to the Attorney-General to prove beyond reasonable doubt that the publication (*actus reus*) in question by the respondents intended to impede or prejudice the due process of justice. It was enough if in all circumstances, it could be inferred that the requisite interference took place, despite the newspapers' intention not to obstruct the proper course of justice, if it was virtually certain that it would do so. The newspapers, *The Independent*, *The Sunday Times* and *News on Sunday* were each fined £50,000 for contempt.[25] The appeal against the fines only was later allowed on the grounds that despite having taken proper legal advice, the law in this area up to this time remained uncertain, and further, since the publication had no detrimental effect on the *The Guardian and The Observer* trial, the fines would not be sustained.[26] Nevertheless, the criminal contempt appeal itself was dismissed on the grounds that what the newspapers published was a direct impediment to the due administration of justice, not as against the "GO" injunctions but as a result of the destruction of the confidential subject matter itself.

7–024 It is common nowadays for the press to use its power to heighten public awareness of various good causes of national concern. However, it is quite another matter to use this power to intentionally influence public opinion against an individual in a situation in which the newspaper has a direct personal and financial involvement and against whom they are likely to bring legal proceedings in the foreseeable future. Any derogatory publication against a future defendant under these circumstances may constitute a contempt. Thus in *Att.-Gen. v. News Group Newspapers Ltd*[27]:

Facts. Newspaper reports were published regarding the alleged rape of an eight year old girl by a doctor B. However, police investigations showed that there was insufficient evidence to bring a prosecution against the doctor. *The Sun* newspaper in agreement with the child's mother decided to finance a private prosecution. The following day, *The Sun* newspaper published an article in which they strongly intimated that doctor B was guilty of rape under the headline "Doc groped me, says girl". The Attorney-General applied for contempt of court proceedings against the newspaper on the grounds that their conduct tended and was calculated to interfere with the prejudice any future trial in that there was a real risk of the legal system being impeded as a result of what was written in the published articles.

Decision. It was argued by the respondents that there was no legal action forthcoming or anticipated against Dr B and therefore no proceedings were imminent or pending. With regard to intention, the court declared that what was required was specific intent as set out in *Att.-Gen. v. Newspaper Publications* (see above). However, intention can be inferred from all the circumstances of the case including, but not solely, the articles, the financial agreement and the surrounding conduct of the respondents. The court decided that the editor must have foreseen that by the emotive language used in the articles, accompanied by the financial aid, the inference must be that *The Sun* wished to influence a jury decision at trial to reach a guilty verdict.

It remains unclear precisely what was meant by the requirement of "intention" for common law contempt under section 6(c). From the discussion so far, it can be seen that the following are the possibilities:

(i) Intention is to be given its strict meaning of purpose; the result of this would be that the prosecution would have to establish that the defendant acted as he did in order to interfere with the administration of justice deliberately. This is generally known as direct intention, and is always sufficient where intention is the *mens rea* for a criminal offence, or;

(ii) Intention may also be indirect; whilst the defendant may not wish to bring about the prohibited result, and may indeed even hope that it does not occur, he will indirectly intend it if he knows that it will occur as a result of his actions, barring miracles. Indirect intention is currently also always sufficient for conviction of a criminal offence which requires proof of intention, or;

(iii) In some circumstances, a court may be permitted to infer intention; that is, despite lack of proof that the defendant did in fact possess either direct or indirect intention, a court may decide from looking at all the circumstances that he must have intended the prohibited result because the defendant foresaw the prohibited result to be a virtually certain consequence of his conduct, and went ahead to cause that result. Cases make it clear that this situation is not a type of intention, but merely a question of evidence—an additional method of proving that intention did in fact exist.[28] It is still uncertain whether intention may be inferred in this manner for the purpose of establishing common law contempt of court.

Some cases appear to require direct intention to be proved, but others allow intention not be inferred. As a matter of general principle, the courts frown upon intention being inferred in relation to any offence other than murder. For reasons of simplicity in the already complex law of contempt and of consistency within the criminal law, it is submitted that only direct and indirect intention should suffice.[29] However, where an injunction has been issued by the court, the Court of Appeal stated in *P v. P (Contempt of Court: Mental capacity)*[29A] that "it was not necessary to show a wilful intention to disobey a court but merely a wilful and deliberate intention to do a prohibited act knowing the consequences".

"Pending" or "Imminent" Proceedings

7–025 Throughout the discussion of the 1981 Act, reference has been made to the requirement that legal proceedings must be "active" before a contempt can be committed. However under the common law, proceedings need only be either "pending or imminent". Unfortunately, the definitions of these two terms lack clarity. "Pending" generally refers to the time when the suspect is, at least, arrested, if not actually charged. The word pending possesses the characteristics of definiteness and immediacy. In the last hundred years, the goal posts have been considerably moved when it comes to deciding whether proceedings have been pending or not. At one time, it meant that anything published would be a contempt once a date had been set down for trial. Then, the test became anything which was said immediately before the proposed date of trial, but after being charged.[30] On the other hand, "imminent" refers to a very high probability that an arrest will be made, for example, the suspect cannot be found, but if found he will be arrested[31]; or even before when police are questioning a suspect. Imminent also may refer to a time period, *i.e.* the longer it takes to make an arrest the less imminent it becomes, and thus, as a consequence, publication may not harm any future trial.[32] The respondents in *Att.-Gen. v. News Group Newspapers Ltd*,[33] where a newspaper article strongly suggested that a doctor had raped an eight year old girl, argued that proceedings were neither pending or imminent. Although the Attorney-General conceded that the proceedings were not pending, they nevertheless said that they were imminent. The Attorney-General submitted that "proceedings are imminent when there is a likelihood or a real risk that they will be instituted in the near future and when there is a real risk, that the kind of publication as here would interfere with the course of justice".[34] Here, due to the respondent's financial and exclusive agreement and no doubt to the prospective increase in circulation of their newspaper, they wished wholeheartedly the trial to go ahead, despite the chances that the trial might not proceed if counsel gave advice against progressing any further with the case. The court took it upon itself to widen the already uncertain, meaning of imminent. Indeed, Walkin L.J. said that "contempt is not necessarily confined to those proceedings which are pending or imminent".[35] Here, due to the exceptional circumstances, the court was not willing to allow such press freedom to overlap and infringe on the due administration of justice, by carrying on their own crusade without properly taking into account the damage which would result by their "trial by newspaper" articles. The application was allowed and a fine of £175,000 was imposed on the newspaper.

Sadly, what can be gleaned from the judgment in the above case is only that the word "imminent" has a chameleon–type use, which changes in meaning according to the circumstances. To give the word some certainty, it means where a prosecution is virtually certain to be commenced and particularly where it is to be commenced in the near future, it is proper to describe such proceedings as imminent. However, "in the near future" will depend on the circumstances of the case, which inevitably leads us back to uncertainty. Thus in *Att.-Gen. v. Sport Newspapers Ltd*[36]:

Facts. A 15 year old girl had gone missing from a small village in Wales, and there was evidence to suggest that she might have been kidnapped. Two days later, E, who had a criminal record, which included rape, absconded from a nearby village, in suspicious circumstances. The police urgently wanted to interview him. On three separate occasions the police warned the media not to publish E's previous convictions lest it prejudiced any future legal proceedings and emphasised that irresponsible reporting might "jeopardise the safe return of the girl". Although media attention was focused on E, no newspaper published his previous convictions. However, two days after the police warnings, *The Sport* newspaper printed an article with the headline "Anna; man on run is vicious rapist", with a photograph of E under which was written "Sex monster". The story's main headline was "Evans was given 10 years for rape", and described details relating to his previous rape conviction. Two days later, a warrant was issued for the arrest of Evans. He was eventually arrested in France and extradited. The girl's dead body was found some two weeks later. The Attorney-General issued proceedings for contempt of court against the owner and editor of *The Sport* as well as the writer of the article on the grounds that (1) publication of the material complained of created a real risk of prejudice to the due administration of justice; and (2) that the alleged contemner published the material with the specific intent to causing such risk.[37] The issue before the court was whether contempt at common law necessarily includes the actual arrest of the suspect, or at least the issue of a warrant against the suspect, or indeed, must proceedings have been initiated at all? Is it enough that proceedings are "imminent" or "pending", or is a contempt possible even before these factors have taken place?

Decision. Bingham L.J. having thoroughly examined the previous law concluded that "a publication made with the intention of prejudicing proceedings which, although not in existence, are imminent may be contemptuous and punishable as such if they give rise to the required risk"[38] set out in (1) above. His reasons included that contempt is there to safeguard the interests of the defendant, so that he receives a fair and unbiased trial without prejudice. Such prejudice does not necessarily suddenly come into existence when proceedings begin but may commence at an earlier period, but they must at least be imminent. With reference to (2) above, *i.e.* intention, the editor of *The Sport* gave his reasons for publishing. He gave evidence that he thought that the public ought to be informed that such a dangerous person was at large and publicity might aid a capture sooner. He also believed that proceedings must be instigated before a contempt could be committed and that E's arrest would not be forthcoming in the foreseeable future. Bingham L.J. concluded on this issue that (agreeing with the decision in *Att.-Gen. v. Newsgroup Newspaper Ltd*[39] if the risk and intention referred to in (1) and (2) above are established, contempt may be committed even though proceedings are neither in existence nor imminent.[40] This statement seems to extend the boundaries even further, by suggesting that there may be contempt even where proceedings are not imminent, by looking not at what in fact occurred, *i.e.* the issue of the warrant, but what the respondent believed was likely to occur. Here, the publisher believed that an arrest warrant was not imminent, despite the fact that it was, and therefore there was no contempt. In the light of such evidence regarding the editor's beliefs, Bingham L.J. decided that the Attorney-General had not proved beyond reasonable grounds that the editor intended to prejudice any future trial and refused the application. Hodgson J. agreed with the decision of Bingham C.J. However, he was not prepared to concede that a real risk existed which would impede any forthcoming trial. He preferred instead to restrict contempt to "pending" proceedings only, *i.e.* a narrower interpretation, and he was not prepared to accept the decision in *Att.-Gen. v. Newsgroup Newspapers* as correct.

In *R. v. Savundranayagan and Walker*,[41] the appellant S appealed against his conviction on fraud charges on the grounds that there was a real risk that a jury had been prejudiced against him as a result of a pre-trial interview he gave on TV to David Frost, and the reports in the newspapers the following day. The court took the view that "none should imagine that he is safe from committal for contempt of court, if knowing or having good reason to believe that criminal proceedings are imminent, he chooses to publish matters calculated to prejudice a fair trial".[42] The court said that it was obvious, even prior to the interview, he was going to be arrested and charged with fraud, and that he himself, must also have realised this fact. Since the trial was some eleven months later and the jury having been properly directed on only to take into account the evidence before the court, they were unlikely to be influenced by the TV interview or subsequent reporting. The appeal was accordingly dismissed.

The mischief behind the word "contempt" is to punish those who deliberately and wantonly interfere with the due process of justice and should, it is suggested, not be limited to whether proceedings have begun or not but only as to where proceedings will or will not take place sometime in the future. Time is only relevant here to the extent of damage likely to be caused. No doubt, the longer it takes before the case comes to court, the weaker the resulting damage will be. Yet this is not true in all cases, and the passing of time in some instances will not necessarily diminish substantially the affect a particular report may have on an individual. Contempt of court proceedings may be brought under the common law and under the strict inability rule; they are not mutually exclusive. Thus in *Att.-Gen. v. Hislop*[43]:

Facts. In January 1987, Mrs Sutcliffe, wife of the convicted murderer Peter ("The Yorkshire Ripper") brought a libel action against the satirical magazine *Private Eye* in respect of articles written by them in February 1983. Three months prior to the action being heard, *Private Eye* again published two damaging articles about Mrs Sutcliffe, alleging:

(1) that she provided a false alibi for her husband's activities;

(2) that she knew her husband was a murderer; and
(3) that she was defrauding the Department of Social Security.

As a result, the Attorney-General brought contempt proceedings against the editor, Ian Hislop and the publishers by alleging:

(a) that the articles in question intended to put pressure on Mrs Sutcliffe to forego her libel action against them;
(b) the intention of the article was to prejudice the jurors' thinking against Mrs Sutcliffe in the forthcoming trial; and
(c) that there was a real risk that a fair trial would be prejudiced.

The application was unsuccessful on the grounds that the relevant articles would not unduly influence a juror's decision nor would the articles prejudice the firmness of the future libel proceedings. The Attorney-General appealed to the Court of Appeal.

Decision. The first question to be addressed was whether in (a) above, the respondents intended to unfairly dissuade Mrs Sutcliffe from continuing her libel action. Parker L.J. referred to the decision in *Att. Gen. v. Times Newspapers Ltd*[44] and stated that had the article amounted to no more than "fair and temperate" criticism to persuade a party from exercising her legal rights to bring the libel action, then that by itself, would not constitute contempt.
However, these particular articles went beyond that and consisted of "plain abuse, threats and misrepresentations", which had no connection with the libel action and thus constituted a common law contempt that the articles themselves would interfere with the administration of justice. With regard with (b) above, *i.e.* prejudicing potential jurors who saw the damaging articles or were told about their contents, the court held that, even though it was accepted that the respondents did not intend to prejudice jurors, notwithstanding that;

(i) it was likely that a juror would recall the damaging remarks made;
(ii) the trial was only some three months away;
(iii) the circulation of the magazine (209,000 copies sold approximately, with a readership of at least twice that) showed that there was more than merely a remote chance of a potential juror reading the disparaging articles and that there was a substantial risk that the trial itself would be prejudiced under the Contempt of Court Act 1981.

As a result, the Attorney-General's appeal was allowed and the respondents were fined £10,000 each.

Section 8—Jury deliberations

The sanctity of the jury room has long been held to be the cornerstone of **7–026**
the whole jury system. In Britain, it has always been understood that deliberations between members of the jury were sacrosanct and ought not to be discussed outside those legal confines; unlike some other countries, where jurors are allowed to discuss publicly the events which occurred earlier on in the jury room. The reasoning behind this was stated in *Att.-Gen. v. New Statesman*,[45] as being (a) that the finality of the jury's verdict was not to be undermined in any way, else public confidence would be diminished in the general correctness and proprietary of such verdicts and

not (b) to affect adversely the attitude of future jurors and the equality of their deliberations.[46] If discussion about the jury's deliberations were allowed to be made public, then jurors in the future may be hesitant to freely give their opinions in the jury room since afterwards they may be pressurised into giving their reasons on why they reached such a decision. Further, no doubt the convicted criminal might also take offence upon how the verdict was reached, and potential jurors might feel inhibited to express their true opinions for fear of reprisals, and thereby subjecting the whole jury system to an unpredictable future. Further, it was stated in *R. v. Lewis*[46A] that it was still the case that allegations of dissent during jury deliberations were still immune from investigation.[46B] Section 8 of the 1981 Act is entitled "Confidentiality of jury's deliberations" and provides that:

(1) "Subject to subsection (2) below, it is a contempt of court to obtain, disclose or solicit any particulars of statements made, opinions expressed, arguments advanced or votes cast by members of a jury in the course of their deliberations in any legal proceedings.

(2) This section does not apply to any disclosure of any particulars—

 (a) in the proceedings in question for the purpose of enabling the jury to arrive at their verdict, or in connection with the delivery of that verdict; or
 (b) in evidence in any subsequent proceedings for an offence alleged to have been committed in relation to the jury in the first mentioned proceedings, or to the publication of any particulars so disclosed."

Section 8(2)(a) exists to give assistance by the judge to the jury where they may have difficulties and problems relating to giving a verdict, *e.g.* on legal issues or evidential difficulties, majority verdict question and the like.

In *R. v. Mickleburgh*,[47] the appellant was convicted of, inter alia, handling stolen goods, after the jury had deliberated for some four hours. He appealed against his conviction on the grounds of a material irregularity. It was alleged by the foreman of the jury that the court usher had made certain comments to the jury regarding the appellant's testimony including that it should only take them (the jury) between 40 and 50 minutes to return a verdict; the implication being that the defendant was guilty. The question for the court was whether there was a risk that such comments would prejudice the jury's thinking. It is established law that it is strictly forbidden for any person, including court officials to give opinions or discuss the case with jurors. In this instance, even if the statements were in fact true, which was highly contestable, it was doubted whether the jury's deliberations would have been prejudiced by those comments. Thus, the appeal was dismissed.[48] In *Att.-Gen. v. Associated Newspapers Ltd*,[49] the word "disclose" in section 8(1) was discussed in detail. *The Mail on Sunday* had published an article detailing the account of three jurors during their deliberation period in a fraud trial, including their opinions of the evidence, and various discussions amongst themselves that went on in the jury room. The newspaper received this information, not by directly questioning the jurors involved, but via transcripts made by other persons, supposedly for research purposes, who had contacted and interviewed the jurors concerned. The Attorney-General brought contempt proceedings against the publisher, editor and journalist of the newspaper under section 8(a) on the grounds that it was a contempt to disclose any discussion at all which went on within the confines of the jury room. The respondents argued that the word "disclosure" was to be given a narrow meaning under the Act, *i.e.* "It applied only to conduct of a member of the jury in revealing particulars of its deliberation to a third party and not the further disclosure by that third party of detail already revealed".[50] The justification for this narrow interpretation, argued the respondents, was that the Act itself was introduced mainly as a consequence of the *Sunday Times v. U.K.*,[51] so that the law in this area conformed with the freedom of expression under Article 10 European Convention on Human Rights, suggesting that a narrow interpretation would be consistent with the Convention. The court did not accept that the freedom of expression was unnecessarily restrained. The Act solely restricted "secrecy" to what went on inside the jury room. The court considered that the "free, uninhibited and unfettered discussion by the jury in the course of their deliberations is essential to the proper administration of a system of justice which includes trial by jury".[52] Further, it was argued that if the meaning was too broad, so that disclosure under any circumstances would be illegal, then such secrecy would severely inhibit any research undertaken to evaluate and improve the jury system itself. The court having thoroughly examined the background which led to the enactment of section 8 generally, concluded that disclosure was not to be given its narrow and restricted meaning. It was to encompass all revelations made of discussions in the jury room by a juror to any other person outside who in turn may pass on that information to the media, and who may ultimately disseminate those findings to the general public. Once such confidential information reached the public domain, those responsible for the disclosure are guilty of contempt. Section 8 is unambiguous in its interpretation and application, *i.e.* to prevent jury deliberations from becoming public in the interests of justice.

Although deliberations in the jury room cannot be interfered with from external influences, including the court itself, nevertheless, discussion of the case in question by jurors may be open to scrutiny, where these discussions take place outside the confines of the jury room, for instance, in the corridors of the court, or inside the courts itself, or in a hotel in which the jury are staying overnight prior to returning to the jury room to consider their verdict. Thus, in *R. v. Young*,[53] a much publicised case, involving the jury's verdict in a murder trial which was influenced by a ouija board, used by four jurors in a hotel room on the night prior to rendering their verdict.

Via the ouija board, the jurors asked and received answers from the murdered victims including the words "Steven Young done it". The appellant, Young, was subsequently convicted of a double murder. The appellant appealed on the grounds of a material irregularity arguing that the jury's verdict was not solely based on the evidence given in court. One of the questions for the court was whether once the jury retired to consider their verdict, and had to stay overnight in a hotel, could their conduct during that period be considered to be "in the course of their deliberations", so that the court was not allowed to question the jury's behaviour where it related to the case in question? Since the judge should inform the jury that they should not deliberate during their overnight stay, it should not be considered to be part of their "retirement period". The court concluded that they could question the activities which went on at the hotel only, but not what transpired in the jury room later. They considered that what occurred in the hotel had to be considered as more than merely a light-hearted game and as a result was a material irregularity. The question was, did the jurors present believe the ouija and was there a risk that they might be influenced by the answers given by the ouija? The court answered in the affirmative and allowed the appeal whilst at the same time ordering a retrial.

Section 9—Tape recorders in court

7–027 Section 9 makes it a contempt of court to bring a tape recorder or other instrument for recording sound into court for use, or to use it in court, except with the leave of the court.[54] It is also contempt to publish any such recording "by playing it in the hearing of the public or any section of the public", or to dispose of any such recording with a view to such publication.[55] If leave is given to use a tape recorder in court, conditions may be attached by the court granting leave; breach of any such condition is contempt.[56] There is a power given to the court to confiscate any tape recorder brought into court without permission and any recording made by it; both may be sold or otherwise disposed of by the court as it thinks fit.[57] Tape recordings to be used in the production of official transcripts of court proceedings are of course exempted from the preceding requirements.[58] Thus, contrary to popular belief, a tape recorder may, with the permission of the judge, be brought into court. A Practice Direction[59] states that the court has a discretion to merit, when requested, the use of a tape recorder and the extent of that use during proceedings. When deciding to grant the application, the particular judge should take into account the following;

(a) whether there is a reasonable need for the recording to be made;
(b) be aware of the possibility that the recording may be given to witnesses who were excluded from the proceedings in court[60];
(c) be conscious of the possibility that the use of the tape recorder might disturb or interfere with the proceedings through being noisy or merely off-putting to those persons present.

Sections 10 and 11 on "disclosure of sources of information" and "prohibiting publication outside the court" respectively, will be dealt with later in the chapter on Privacy.

Section 12—Contempt in Magistrates' Court

Where magistrates' courts are concerned, the Act gives more detail about specific offences of contempt, which are as follows: **7–028**

Section 12(1)(a) wilfully insulting a justice, witness or officer of the court, or any solicitor or counsel, having business before the court, during their attendance at court or journey to or from the court; or;

Section 12(1)(b) wilfully interrupting the proceedings of the court, or otherwise misbehaving in court.

Where any of these contempts occurs, there is a power of detention and a sentence of up to one month's imprisonment or a fine (section 12(2)). For instance in *Re Hooker*,[61] the defendant, an experienced freelance court reporter, took with her into court a tape recorder to record the proceedings in question. After the commencement of those proceedings, the tape recorder was confiscated. She was eventually fined £500 and appealed. The court stated that the word "wilfully" in section 12(1)(b) included "some element of defiance, or at least conduct such as the court could not reasonably be expected to tolerate, had to be postulated".[62] Since the appellant's behaviour did not include either of the above requirements, the appeal was allowed. The court said that the situation was handled in a "wholly unsatisfactory manner". Despite being an experienced court reporter, the court said that they accepted she thought her behaviour was innocuous and said that her conduct did not interfere with the proceedings and that she had regretted what she had done. The "heavy-handed" attitude of the judge in that case, had contributed to the appeal being allowed because he immediately proceeded with contempt proceedings without first considering the other available options, *i.e.* investigating the matter thoroughly beforehand. However, in defence of the judge the law report itself does not adequately explain why such a person with her experience brought the tape recorder into court in the first place, without leave of the judge. Also in *Bodden v. MPC*[63] where a witness's testimony was unable to be heard in court due to protestors outside in the street using a loudhailer which interfered with the proceedings, the court held that the interruption was "wilful" when the defendant does an act with the intention of disrupting court proceedings or is aware of the risk but never the less continues with the act.

Section 14—Penalties for contempt

The maximum penalties for contempt of court by a superior court,[64] **7–029** whether at common law or under the strict liability rule, is a fixed term of imprisonment of up to two years (section 14(1)) or a fine; in the case of an inferior court a maximum term of imprisonment of one month or a limited fine. This is a change from the previous common law rule which allowed indefinite imprisonment and was an obvious problem in terms of civil liberties.

Brief Outline and Germane Cases

Chapter Seven: Contempt of Court

7–030 Contempt is a broad category of offences, both at common law and under statute. General issues: interfering with court proceedings; scandalising the court; what is a court.

*Contempt of Court Act 1981 s.1: strict liability contempt of court; only applies where there is a publication which creates a substantial risk of impeding or prejudicing the course of justice (s.2(2)). Proceedings must be active.
Att.-Gen. v. News Group Newspapers Ltd [1987]; *Att.-Gen. v. MGN* [1997]; *Att.-Gen. v. Times Newspapers* [1983]; *Att.-Gen. v. ITN* [1995].
S.4: postponements of reporting of court proceedings.
Defences to strict liability contempt: ss.3, 4 and 5; *Att.-Gen. v. English* [1982].

*CCA 1981 s.6: contempt of court still exists as an offence at common law, but it must be shown that the defendant's conduct was intended to impede or prejudice the course of justice. *Att.-Gen. v. Newspaper Publishing plc* [1988]; *Att.-Gen. v. News Group Newspapers* Ltd [1988].
Proceedings need only be pending or imminent: *Att.-Gen. v. Sport Newspapers Ltd* [1992]; *Att.-Gen. v. Hislop* [1991].

*CCA 1981 s.8: confidentiality of jury deliberations.

*CCA 1981 s.9: use of tape recorders in court.

*CCA 1981 s.10: protection journalists' sources.

*CCA 1981 s.12: contempt in magistrates court.

Endnotes

[1] It was stated in *Att.-Gen. v. Newspaper Publishing plc* [1988] that there are basically two types of contempt; civil contempt—which deals with "conduct which involves a breach, or assisting in the breach, of a court order; and criminal contempt is any other conduct which involves an interference with the due administration of justice . . .".
[2] See Arlidge and Eady, *Law of Contempt*, or N. Lowe, *Borrie and Lowe's Law of Contempt* for in-depth discussion of the issues and history of the offences.
[3] *Freedom, the Individual and the Law* (1982).
[4] [1742] 2 Atk 469.
[5] Cmnd 5794, 1974.
[6] *Balogh v. Crown Court* [1974] 3 All E.R. 283 at 288.
[7] See *Re de Court*, *The Times*, November 28, 1997, below.
[8] *R. v. Hill* [1986] Crim.L.R. 457.
[9] *R. v. Aquarius* [1974] Crim.L.R. 373; *R. v. Logan* [1974] Crim.L.R. 609.
[10] *R. v. Powell* (1994) 98 Cr.App.R. 224, where the offender gave a loud wolf-whistle to an attractive juror and was sentenced initially to 14 days imprisonment, reduced to one day on appeal.
[11] *Morris v. Crown Office* [1970] 2 Q.B. 114.
[12] *R. v. Montgomery* [1995] 2 All E.R. 28; *R. v. K.* (1984) 78 Cr.App.R. 82.
[13] [1970] 2 Q.B. 114.
[14] *ibid.* at 130.
[15] [1986] Crim.L.R. 457.
[16] (1985) 81 Cr.App.R. 53.
[17] (1984) 79 Cr.App.R. 79.
[18] *R. v. Goult* (1983) 76 Cr.App.R. 140. A sentence of 18 months was given for frightening a juror—reduced to nine months on appeal.
[19] [1972] 1 All E.R. 58.
[20] *ibid.* at 59.
[21] *The Times*, November 28, 1997.
[22] [1963] 1 Q.B. 696.
[23] *ibid.* at 721.
[24] *ibid.* at 725.
[25] [1995] C.O.D. 15.
[26] See *Bodden v. Metropolitan Police Commissioners* [1990] 2 Q.B. 397.
[27] [1974] 3 All E.R. 283.
[28] Defined in *R. v. Tamworth, exp. Walsh* [1994] C.O.D. 227.
[29] Under s.4(8) Court's Act 1971, the Crown Court has the jurisdiction with "the like powers, rights, privileges and authority as the High Court".
[30] [1900] 2 Q.B. 36.
[31] *ibid.* at 40.
[32] *ibid.*
[33] [1928] 44 T.L.R. 301.
[34] *ibid.* at 303.
[35] [1968] 2 Q.B. 150.
[36] *ibid.* at 155.
[37] Clive Walker, (1985) P.L. p. 359, 369.
[38] [1936] A.C. 322.
[39] *ibid.* at 335.
[40] *ibid.*
[41] [1979] E.H.R.R. 245.
[42] [1981] A.C. 303.
[43] The exemption under s.39 of the General Rate Act 1967 applies to places of public religious worship.
[44] [1991] 1 All E.R. 622.
[45] However, Parole Boards are not considered to be a "court" as they are subject to and under the authority of the Secretary of State.
[46] *The Times*, June 11, 1998.
[47] *per* Robert Walker L.J.
[48] Divisional Court in *Peach Grey and Co. v. Summers* [1995] 2 All E.R. 513.

[48A] (2000) J.C. 22.
[48B] (1974) A.C. 273 at 309.
[48C] (2000) J.C. 22 at 33.
[49] Added by the Broadcasting Act 1990, Sched. 20.
[50] [1968] 1 W.L.R. 1761: see discussion below.
[51] See *Att.-Gen. v. BBC*, *The Independent*, January 3, 1992.
[52] [1982] 2 All E.R. 903.
[53] *ibid.* at 919.
[54] *The Independent*, January 3, 1992.
[55] *ibid.* at 15.
[56] *The Times*, December 15, 1976.
[57] [1987] 1 Q.B. 1.
[58] *ibid.* at 16, *per* Sir John Donaldson M.R.
[59] [1987] 1 Q.B. 1 at 18.
[60] [1995] 2 All E.R. 370.
[61] *ibid.* at 383.
[62] [1997] 1 All E.R. 456.
[63] See *Att.-Gen. v. ITN* [1995] 2 All E.R. 370 at 381.
[64] 1 All E.R. 456 at 466.
[65] *ibid.* at 446.
[66] *The Times*, February 12, 1983.
[67] See *Att.-Gen. v. Associated Newspapers Ltd*, *The Independent*, November 6, 1997.
[68] [1995] 2 All E.R. 370.
[69] *The Times*, July 26, 1996.
[70] *MGN Pension Trustees v. Bank of America National Trust* [1995] 2 All E.R. 355 at 361.
[71] *Att.-Gen. v. English* [1982] 2 All E.R. 903 at 919.
[72] [1991] 1 W.L.R. 4.
[73] [1995] 2 All E.R. 355.
[74] *ibid.* at 362.
[75] *ibid.*
[76] Practice Direction (Contempt: Reporting Restrictions) [1982] 1 W.L.R. 1475.
[77] [1993] 2 All E.R. 177.
[78] *ibid.* at 180.
[79] *ibid.* at 181.
[80] *ibid.* at 183.
[81] *ibid.* at 971.
[82] "A person aggrieved may appeal to the Court of Appeal, if that court grants leave, against (a) an order under s.4 . . . of the Contempt of Court Act 1981 made in relation to a trial on indictment . . .".
[83] [1993] 2 All E.R. at 979.
[84] [1990] 2 A.C. 154.
[85] [1991] 1 All E.R. 911.
[86] *ibid.* at 924.
[87] [1974] A.C. 273.
[88] [1982] 2 All E.R. 903 at 911.
[89] *ibid.* at 903.
[90] *ibid.* at 920.
[91] *The Times*, July 7, 1989.
[92] The uncertainty is further compounded by Lloyd L.J. in *Att.-Gen. v. TVS* who advocated the idea of deciding by "first impression" and whether it is related closely enough to the particular trial to be considered more than merely incidental. This was later endorsed by Mann L.J. in *Att.-Gen. v. Guardian Newspapers Ltd (No. 3)* [1992] 3 All E.R. at 45, although he omitted the word "first". The words "first impression" were presumably taken from the transcript of the trial of *Att.-Gen. v. TVS*, since it is not mentioned in the Law Report of July 7.
[93] See *Att.-Gen. v. Guardian Newspapers (No. 3)* [1992] 38 All E.R. (see below).
[94] [1982] 2 All E.R. 903.
[95] *ibid.* at 911.
[96] *ibid.* at 912, Watkins L.J. in the Queen's Bench Divisional Court attempted to define the word "discussion". He said it meant "the airing of views and the propounding and debating of principles and arguments; not the making of accusations". This was rejected by Lord Diplock as being too limited an interpretation.

[97] *ibid.* at 920. Lord Diplock compared the above case with that of *Att.-Gen. v. Times Newspaper* [1973] 3 All E.R. 54. However, here neither Dr Arthur's name nor the trial were expressly stated in the article.
[98] *Att.-Gen. v. English* [1982] 2 All E.R. 903.
[99] see *Att.-Gen. v. Guardian Newspapers (No. 3)* [1992] 3 All E.R. 38 at 835.
[1] *ibid.*
[1] *ibid.* at 45.
[2] *The Times*, February, 12, 1983.
[3] (1949) 93 S.J. 220.
[4] [1954] 1 All E.R. 1026.
[5] See *R. v. Odhams Press Ltd* [1957] 1 Q.B. 73.
[6] [1968] 1 W.L.R. 1.
[7] *ibid.* at 6.
[8] *The Times*, November 3, 1976.
[9] [1974] A.C. 23.
[10] Based on the judgment of Buckley J. in *Vine Products Ltd v. Green* [1966] Ch. 484 at 495, 496. Recited at 295.
[11] at page 294.
[12] Lord Morris at 304 advocated that the Courts "owe it to the parties to protect them either from the prejudices of prejudgment or from the necessity of having themselves to participate in the flurries of pre-trial publicity".
[13] Lord Morris took a more direct approach to the issue of "blame" and said that the projected article went too far in that anyone who reads it, would decide that there was "a considerable case against Distillers".
[14] [1974] A.C. 23 at 309.
[15] *ibid.* at 313.
[16] [1988] 1 Ch. 33.
[17] The Att.-Gen. here was not acting in his capacity as a minister of the government, but as the guardian of the public interest in the due administration of justice.
[18] [1988] 1 Ch. 33 at 361.
[19] proceedings were not "active" within the Contempt of Court Act 1981.
[20] *per* Lloyd L.J.
[21] [1974] Cmnd 5794.
[22] [1988] 1 Ch. 33 at 374, 375.
[23] *ibid.* at 838.
[24] *The Independent*, May 9, 1989.
[25] The Att.-Gen. did not press for fines against the *Evening Standard* or *London Daily News*.
[26] *Att.-Gen v. Newspaper Publishing plc*, *The Independent*, February 28, 1990.
[27] [1988] 2 All E.R. 906.
[28] *Nedrick* [1986], *Walker and Hayles* [1990].
[29] See Borrie and Lowe, *Contempt of Court* (3rd ed., 1996), pp. 410 to 411 and 423 to 426.
[29A] *The Times*, July 21, 1999.
[30] *R. v. Parke* [1903] 2 K.B. 432.
[31] See *James v. Robinson* (1963) 109 C.L.R. 593.
[32] *R. v. Savundranayagan and Walker* [1968] 3 All E.R. 439.
[33] [1988] 2 All E.R. 906.
[34] *ibid.* at 919.
[35] *ibid.* at 920.
[36] [1992] 1 All E.R. 503.
[37] *ibid.* at 508.
[38] *ibid.* at 515.
[39] [1988] 2 All E.R. 906.
[40] [1992] 1 All E.R. 503 at 515, 516.
[41] [1968] 3 All E.R. 439.
[42] *ibid.* at 441.
[43] [1991] 1 All E.R. 911.
[44] [1974] A.C. 283.
[45] [1981] 1 Q.B. 1.
[46] *ibid.* at 6.
[46A] *The Times*, April 26, 2000.
[46B] See also *R. v. Millward* (1999) 1 Cr.App.Rep. 61.

[47] (1995) 1 Cr.App.R. 297.
[48] See *R. v. McCluskey* (1994) 78 Cr.App.R. 216, where a mobile telephone was used by a juror to make a business call in the jury room. Despite it being an irregularity, it did not go to the root of the case and therefore, the appeal was dismissed.
[49] [1993] 2 All E.R. 535.
[50] *ibid.* at 538.
[51] [1979] 2 E.H.R.R. 245.
[52] *Att.-Gen. v. Associated Newspapers Ltd* [1993] 2 All E.R. 535 at 543.
[53] [1995] 2 W.L.R. 430.
[54] s.9(1)(a).
[55] s.9(1)(b).
[56] s.9(1)(c), 9(2).
[57] s.9(3).
[58] s.9(4).
[59] (1982) 74 Cr.App.R. 73.
[60] Even if permission is granted, under s.9(1)(b) it is prohibited to publish a recording of the court proceedings or to play it the public or a section of the public.
[61] [1993] C.O.D. 190.
[62] *ibid.* at 191.
[63] [1990] 2 Q.B. 397.
[64] Under s.14(4A) a county court is now considered to be a "superior" court for the purposes of contempt offences.

CHAPTER 8

PRIVACY

INTRODUCTION

We live in complex times. The enthusiasm for sexual liberation and openness continues, yet the media revel in revealing each new sexual scandal. An individual's privacy is highly prized and sometimes legally protected, but scrutiny and vetting of any person who enters the public eye is often considered to be freely entered into by that person, whether or not his "celebrity" status is chosen by him. The law protecting a person's private life is every bit as complex as the policy reasons why such protection must be limited. The United Kingdom has signed treaties and conventions requiring the protection of an individual's privacy, but there is still no clear law or right with that name in domestic law. The United Kingdom is a party to various international treaties and other instruments related to human rights which recognises the existence of a right to privacy. Both the Universal Declaration of Human Rights[1] and the International Covenant on Civil and Political Rights[2] state that: **8–001**

> "No one shall be subjected to arbitrary or unlawful interference with his privacy, family, home or correspondence, nor to unlawful attacks on his honour and reputation . . . Everyone has the right to the protection of the law against such interference or attacks".

Thus, in international law, the United Kingdom is under an obligation to protect the privacy of its citizens, albeit an obligation which lacks an effective enforcement procedure and is limited to protection against "arbitrary or unlawful" interference. As has been seen in Chapter 2, the United Kingdom is also bound to uphold a citizen's right to "respect for his private and family life, his home and his correspondence" under the European Convention on Human Rights, a fact which has been heightened by the incorporation of the Convention into domestic law under the Human Rights Act 1998 and the subsequent "test cases" on privacy.[3] But the law of England and Wales still does not contain any single enshrined right to privacy: no statute creates any such general right, and the common law and equity only allow a limited recognition of privacy rights in specific situations. It can be stated that, although England and Wales do not recognise a single legal right to privacy, "privacy rights" do receive increasing protection by the law, but that protection is patchy, incomplete and hidden within a large number of disparate laws. There is no single "right to privacy", but rather a bundle of privacy-type laws which imply that some kind of right to privacy must exist. This chapter will examine the main protections for privacy at statute and common law and the effect of the Human Rights Act 1998, but first it may be helpful to discuss what is meant by the word "privacy" itself.

Intro

WHAT IS PRIVACY?

8–002 A society which permits individuals to choose how they are to lead their lives is one which will recognise the choice of privacy. This encompasses not only seclusion from neighbours or the avoidance of publicity but freedom from unwarranted interference by the state[4]:

> "In its most basic form, privacy is simply a condition, the state of seclusion, anonymity and secrecy . . . It is a state which can be lost, whether through the choice of the person in that state or through the action of another person . . . It is also an interest, to which people accord value: people have a need for privacy. When that interest is defeated, that is not just a loss, but an invasion or infringement of privacy. The question is, to what extent is it a legal right, so that infringements should be actionable at law?"[5]

Privacy may be regarded as a basic right of every human being, but there is surprisingly little consistency between the definitions which are used by authors, judges and reformers. For Stone[6] the right to privacy is narrowly drawn as: "The right to prevent, or to be compensated for, the unauthorised acquisition or publication of secret personal information". This definition limits the scope of privacy to a right to control the use of information about oneself; its ambit is the protection of reputation, the prevention of snooping and the regulation of chequebook journalism. It recognises a private realm relating to every individual which should not be invaded, but limits this realm to "secret personal information". But others regard the scope of privacy as being far wider. For the Calcutt Committee it was[7]: "The right of the individual to be protected against intrusion into his personal life or affairs, or those of his family, by direct physical means or by publication of information." The Calcutt definition treats physical intrusions such as breaking into a person's home or stalking as invasions of privacy rights rather than excluding criminal offences from the scope of privacy. It is submitted that Stone's definition is too narrow; why should it be an invasion of privacy to rifle through a person's private papers in order to obtain information, but no such invasion to rifle through the same papers in order to steal valuables? The two acts may be different when perceived from the perspective of the actor, but from the victim's point of view there may be no difference in their effect.

Other definitions go much further, regarding privacy as involving not only control over personal information and physical invasion, but also a "right to be left alone". For Westin[8]:

> "Privacy is the claim of individuals, groups or institutions to determine for themselves when, how and to what extent information about them is communicated to others . . . privacy is the voluntary and temporary withdrawal of a person from the general society through physical or psychological means . . ."

Every person wants, and needs, a private life, regardless of whether a **8–003**
particular person may be generally in the public eye. Evidence gathered by the Younger Committee[9] indicated that the public were most concerned about invasions of privacy in the forms of unwanted media publicity or exposure; misuse of personal information by bodies which hold personal records such as banks, employers, credit rating agencies, colleges and doctors; invasions of the home and home life by the media, private detectives, nosy neighbours, "doorsteppers" and the like; and problems in the commercial world such as industrial espionage. But a right to privacy will by its nature conflict with freedom of information and other competing liberties.

An individual's legitimate desire to define and maintain a private sphere in his life may come into battle with the public interest in a number of ways. The State needs information about its citizens in order to facilitate some of its functions; the National Health Service would be hindered if medical records could not be maintained, for example. In other respects, privacy may be a cloak for iniquity; if a company's finances are to be inspected for irregularity for the purpose of consumer protection, then secrecy cannot prevail. The police and other investigators cannot perform many of their functions without invading privacy, and the regulation of a great range of fields, from public safety to planning permission, requires data to be collected and held. The methods of defence of individual privacy against the claims of the state that such privacy must be secondary to the maintenance of the public interest in such matters as national security and the prevention of crime have been considered briefly in the chapters on police powers and official secrecy, and will be discussed in greater depth in this chapter. On another level, freedom of expression makes inroads into privacy, whether it is media investigation and reporting or private speech which is concerned. There is a public interest in the fair and accurate reporting of many items which involve a person's private life or details, as can be seen in recent "sleaze" reports. Equally, an individual cannot be prevented from truthful, non-malicious discussion of another's private details if freedom of speech is to have any value.

This conflict of rights has resulted in a field of privacy which can be defined both positively and negatively. All the possible definitions raised above are negative in the sense that they relate to freedom from invasion of a private field; they differ only in the breadth to which that field is drawn.

So, privacy may be seen as a right to prevent the collection of information about oneself and to prevent others from entering our private domain. But there is also a positive aspect to privacy, which is based in personal autonomy. If a person is to exercise his rights as a citizen freely there are certain preconditions which must be fulfilled. He must be able to make free choices about his private life, his body, his family, his home, his sexuality and sex life, for example. This view of privacy is more radical and controversial than that taken by courts in the United Kingdom at the present time, as will be clear from the cases discussed later in this chapter. But many other jurisdictions have taken the positive definition of the right to privacy as a constitutional principle: in France, for example, privacy laws have been passed, and in the United States, a comprehensive privacy right has been developed by the courts and academics.

Protection of Privacy: a Comparison

8–004 There is, perhaps surprisingly, no express constitutional guarantee of the right to privacy in the United States Constitution. However, a broad-ranging species of privacy has come to be guaranteed in the United States by means of a liberal interpretation of the Constitution by courts and academics. It is generally argued that the key stage in the development of the right was the publication of an article, Warren and Brandeis, "The Right to Privacy",[10] where it was claimed that the existing common law and equitable rights of property and confidentiality, although limited in their scope, were rooted in a more basic principle of the protection of privacy.[11] After a few years, United States courts began to recognise that there existed a tort of interference with privacy, and thus the common law was employed to protect such interests as the right to a private life, the right to a reputation, human dignity and the right to a person's own image. Each of these rights came to be developed to a wider extent than did the comparable rights in English law. But the process did not stop there: privacy has become subject to constitutional protection via a complicated series of implications. The First Amendment, which guarantees freedom of religious belief, of worship and of assembly, has been interpreted to include right to personal autonomy. The Fourth Amendment, which provides "The right of the people to be secure in their persons, houses, papers, and effects, against unreasonable searches and seizures . . ." is seen as a recognition of a more general privacy right. In effect, privacy is treated as if it were among the specific rights listed in the Constitution. In *Griswold v. Connecticut*[12] it was argued[13] that the narrow privacy rights seen in the First, Third, Fourth, Fifth and Ninth Amendments were part of a much greater right, but it has never been entirely clear just how far this general right extends or where it applies. There is a basic objection to judicial law-making in the United States, just as there is in the United Kingdom, although judicial creativity is obvious in both jurisdictions. Certain applications of privacy have been particularly controversial, giving rise to potent arguments that reform of the Constitution is the only method by which the rights which it protects should be extended in order to keep pace with changes in society. However, it is now clear that the United States not only has a right to privacy within its laws, but also that this right is regarded as constitutional and is enforced in a positive rather than negative interpretation. Privacy is seen as including not only protection from unwarranted invasions of a person's life but also such rights as freedom of parental choice in education,[14] the right of a woman to choose what happens to her own body in terms of the decision whether to have an abortion,[15] the right to use contraception[16] and other such aspects of personal autonomy. Each of the privacy rights has been the subject of heated debate in terms of policy and politics, particularly where abortion is concerned, but the concept of privacy has emerged from the battle largely unscathed. Refusal to extend its scope to include freedom of sexual choice has been based in fear that this would encourage homosexuality, but campaigns for change remain.

This brief explanation shows that it is possible for a legal system based on common law to develop a general right to privacy. Why then has this not occurred in England and Wales?

Historical Reasons for a Lack of Privacy Law

One of the most basic reasons why there is no domestic privacy law in England and Wales is the lack of a written constitution within which to interpret such a right. If all rights are enumerated in one series of documents then it is easier to extend their scope by analogy and implication, whereas when rights are drawn from a variety of differing sources it is more difficult to argue that a "new" right is fundamental and already exists. But much of the reason behind the lack of a guarantee of privacy comes from the historical development of the limited related rights which do exist. English law has for a long time been far more concerned to protect property rights and physical rights than social rights. Thus much of the current law which does in fact protect the privacy of the individual exists in theory to assert rights of that person's land or other property interests. **8–005**

But this need not have been the case, there was an alternative route which English legal history could have taken. In Chapter 3, the concept of "keeping the King's Peace" and, hence, breach of the peace, was discussed. "Peace" has long been held in high esteem, and was protected by each and every citizen, by the courts, by watchmen or by gangs of hoodlums, depending on the circumstances and the perspective from which history is viewed. According to Feldman[17]:

> "The idea that a person's home and family life were to be free from violent intrusions was powerful. The king's peace eventually developed to cover the whole country, but its roots were in the idea of personal, rather than national, security. The peace of the king was, originally, the peace of the householder writ large . . . The peace of the commoner's homestead mirrored the original,

Good intro

localized, peace of the king. It gave a right of compensation for those brawling within the homestead. It was not simply related to property rights, and could have developed into a legally protected sphere of personal freedom from interference and oversight, which is the essence of a right to privacy. However, it took another turn, no doubt influenced by prevailing economic forms and structures. It became associated at common law with the idea of real property".

8–006 By the eighteenth century, the common law was both preoccupied with the protection of property rights and reluctant to allow the creation of new types of right or interest. Equity stepped in to create novel rights and remedies, including breach of confidence and injunctions to prevent such breach. It is ironic that the American law of privacy took its root argument from English common law and equitable principles, and yet English law felt itself unable to do the same.[18] In combination with a written constitution, arguments that the common law recognised a right to privacy succeeded in the United States, but English courts did not follow the lead. In spite of repeated calls for reform throughout the twentieth century, there is no legal protection for privacy as such. The protection is given to various other related rights such as copyright, enjoyment of land, freedom from harassment and confidentiality. Most of the consultative bodies instructed to consider the introduction of a tort of invasion of privacy have decided against such a change. Each potential privacy law in turn has failed, and the Government has recently confirmed that there is no plan to introduce a privacy law in the future. The limited protection drawn from the bundle of existing legal actions is backed by media self-regulation, with legal restrictions upon the press kept in the background as a threat rather than as a probability. It is too early to assess the impact which Article 8 of the ECHR will have post-incorporation. Early indications are that privacy-related law will continue to develop incrementally and within the scope of the pre-existing domestic law, and so the process will be one of amendment of those legal rights and actions which do invade individual privacy unacceptably, rather than the creation of a new freestanding right.

Thus it remains the case that, at the present time, the law does not recognise any pure right to privacy, although there are in existence certain piecemeal laws which protect to some degree a person's right not to be interfered with either physically or by mental torment. These laws will be discussed below.

Trespass to the Land

8–007 The old adage that an "Englishman's home is his castle" may well become his hassle if others, without an express or implied authority, unjustifiably interfere with that person's property rights. It is accepted, as a general proposition, that a person has a right in law to the full enjoyment and use of his land without disruption or interference from another person, and also to protect that right from anything which encroaches onto his land from adjoining property, unless legislation or lawful authority forbids such action. Nowadays, many cases go through the courts which involve neighbour disputes over such problems as overhanging branches or bushes, or loss of light. Even where no actual harm, damage or inconvenience is caused as a result of the infringement, an action in trespass may still exist. Further, an action in nuisance may also coincide if a disruption is caused through damage, noise, excessively loud music, obnoxious smells, fumes, etc., emanating from an adjoining property. The definition of civil trespass, put simply, is: entry onto the land of another without lawful justification or licence. The entry must be physical, and so trespass is not committed by those who snoop or spy without such an entry onto the premises. The person who alleges that another has committed trespass against him must have been in possession of the land at the relevant time; thus a non-resident landlord will have no action but his tenant may. Many persons have lawful justification for entry into the premises of another, for example emergency services, police effecting an arrest, any person carrying out a court order; and in addition a landowner may grant either an express or an implied licence to a person to enter his land.

It seems that no trespass will be committed, in the absence of damage, by merely flying over private property without the express or implied permission of the owner of that property. However, it was stated in *Bernstein v. Skyview and General Ltd,*[19] that "it may be a sound and practical rule to regard any incursion into the airspace at a height which may interfere with the ordinary use of the land as a trespass rather than a nuisance".[20] In the above case, the plaintiff alleged that the defendant, a photographer, took aerial photographs of his house whilst flying aircraft across his land, and thus was guilty of trespass. The defendant argued the old maxim that "*Cujus est solum ejus est usque ad coelum, et ad inferos*" (whoever has the soil, also owns the heavens above and to the centre beneath) was not applicable in this age of space travel. The court said that the balance is best struck "in our present society by restricting the rights of an owner in the airspace above his land to such height as is necessary for the ordinary use and enjoyment of his land and the structures upon it, and declaring that above that height he has no greater rights in the airspace than any other member of the public".[21] The plaintiff argued that it was the taking of the photograph, which might ultimately be used for terrorist purposes, which was in contention. The court said that merely taking a photograph for innocent purposes and in the absence of any interference, was not illegal. Therefore, the plaintiff's action was dismissed. The court went on to state, *obiter*, that persistently taking aerial photographs would be regarded as harassment and a "monstrous invasion of privacy, and would constitute an actionable nuisance".[22] **8–008**

One of the questions which concerns a person's enjoyment of his own land is whether outsiders can by their actions interfere with that person's property while they remain on a highway. Can a trespass exist in those circumstances? The intention and purpose of the use of the highway is germane as to whether a person could be said to be a reasonable user of the highway. Generally, an individual may only legally use the highway for the purpose of "passing and repassing", but even that may constitute an unreasonable use, according to what the object is of that particular use. For example, in *Hickman v. Maisey*,[23] the defendant, a racing-tout, continued walking up and down a small area of highway (the sub-soil of which belonged to the plaintiff and which crossed the plaintiff's land) for approximately one and a half hours in order to spy on horses being trained on adjoining land. In that case, the intention and object of the defendant was relevant to the reasonableness of the use of that highway. The court held that a business purpose was not a proper use of the highway, in this instance, and constituted a trespass. Here, there was an interference with the owner's use of the land by spying and taking notes of the activities going on there. If this had been allowed to continue unabated, the consequences would have resulted in a devaluation of the land as a private area for training horses.[24]

8–009 However, a person's property is nevertheless invaded every day by persons who have either an express or implied licence to enter for lawful purposes. Such implied licencees include postmen, leaflet-droppers, electric or gas meter readers, canvassers,[25] etc. but are generally restricted to only go as far as the front door. That licence may be revoked at any time at the will of the occupier or owner. However, that person must be given a reasonable time to leave the property and return to the public highway. What amounts to a reasonable time, before he becomes a trespasser, will depend on all the circumstances of the particular case. Thus, in *Robson v. Hallett*[26] a constable acting in the execution of his duty was assaulted in a house, into which the owner had previously granted him permission to enter, but then shortly after revoked that licence. Upon being told to leave, he was immediately attacked without being given a reasonable time to quit that property. Further, officers who had been waiting outside had an implied licence to enter the garden of that property to assist their fellow officer, and therefore were also not trespassers. In any event, once a breach of the peace was in progress, they were entitled to go onto the property and prevent its continuance.

A withdrawal of an implied licence should be clearly stated, either in writing or orally. Thus, in *Snook v. Mannon*,[27] police noted the defendant driving erratically. When the defendant stopped in the driveway of his home, the police requested him to be breathalysed. He told the police to "fuck off". He was eventually convicted of drink-driving and appealed on the grounds that his vulgar language meant that the police should leave his property and therefore any arrest made after that was illegal. The court held that it depended on all the circumstances whether the words used actually meant a withdrawal of the implied licence. In this case, the vulgar language was merely seen as abusive and nothing more, and therefore the police officers were not to be considered as trespassers.[28]

NUISANCE

Private Nuisance

> "Private nuisance, giving rise to a civil action at the suit of an aggrieved individual, has on occasions been very widely defined to cover virtually any unreasonable interference with that individual's enjoyment of the land which he occupies. But an action for private nuisance is normally brought for some physical invasion of the plaintiff's land by some deleterious subject-matter—such as noise, smell, water or electricity—in circumstances which would not amount to trespass to land. It is much more doubtful if it would ever cover an activity which had no physical effects on the plaintiff's land, although it detracts from the plaintiff's enjoyment of that land. Thus spying on one's neighbour is probably not in itself a private nuisance although watching and besetting a man's house with a view to compelling him to pursue (or not to pursue) a particular course of conduct has been said to be a nuisance at common law. With regard to the latter type of conduct, however, it must be admitted that it is concerned with a situation very different from the typical case in which complaint is made of an invasion of privacy . . . As a remedy for invasions of privacy private nuisance has the same basic disadvantages as the action for trespass to land, namely that it can only be brought by the person who is from a legal point of view the 'occupier' of the land, enjoyment of which is affected by the nuisance".[29] **8–010**

The above quote represents the traditional boundaries of the action of nuisance. Nuisance is, put simply, a tort which is committed by unreasonable interference with a person's quiet enjoyment of his land. The owner or occupier of land is entitled to benefit from it without external influences reducing that benefit; thus smoke from a neighbour's chimney or excessive noise by a neighbour are within the scope of the tort of nuisance. But until recently, courts were of the opinion that nuisance could not be used as a tool for the protection of privacy; it is only in the last few years that a series of ground-breaking cases have extended the scope of nuisance to cover harassing which does not appear to be connected with the invasion of property rights. It is therefore arguable that nuisance is becoming a far more effective weapon against breaches of privacy, but only within the sphere of physical intrusions into the life of another. A distinction must be drawn between private nuisance, which concerns unwarranted interferences with enjoyment of land, and public nuisance, which concerns unwarranted interference with, or damage to, members of the public in the exercise of their rights as citizens. Recent developments in both types of action have extended the protection of privacy by the common law. Later in this chapter, statutory "nuisance" offences will be discussed.

Private nuisance seems to have moved away from the restriction that the unwarranted interference should relate to the enjoyment of land. It now appears that private nuisance may be committed by surveillance of a person, or by persistent harassment. It has also been argued that a separate tort of harassment does exist at common law, but views as to this are divided.[30]

In *Khorasandijan v. Bush*[31]:

8–011 **Facts.** The plaintiff and defendant were formerly friends, but the plaintiff had attempted to break off the friendship and the defendant was unhappy about this situation. The defendant began a course of conduct against the plaintiff which included threats of violence, actual physical violence and harassment by means of repeated abusive telephone calls to the house at which the 18 year old plaintiff lived with her parents. The plaintiff brought a civil case against the defendant, and was successful in obtaining an injunction to prevent him from "using violence to, harassing, pestering or communicating" with her. The defendant appealed against the award of the injunction on the basis that there was no tort of "harassing, pestering or communicating with" a person, and thus no injunction should have been granted to prevent what was lawful behaviour. He argued that nuisance was inapplicable since the plaintiff was merely a licensee in her parents' house and not the landowner.

Decision. The Court of Appeal dismissed the appellant's claim and held that an action for either privacy or nuisance of the tort of harassment could be supported on such facts. Dillin L.J. stated that:

> "To my mind, it is ridiculous if in this present age the law is that the making of deliberately harassing and pestering telephone calls to a person is only actionable in the civil courts if the recipient of the calls happens to have the freehold or a leasehold proprietary interest in the premises in which he or she has received the calls . . . If the wife of the owner is entitled to sue in respect of harassing telephone calls, then I do not see why that should not also apply to a child living at home with her parents."

He continued to state that, although damage is a necessary element of tort of private nuisance:

> "So far as the harassing telephone calls are concerned, however, the inconvenience and annoyance to the occupier caused by such calls, and the interference thereby with the ordinary and reasonable use of the property are sufficient damage. The harassment is the persistent making of the unwanted telephone calls, even apart from their content; if the content is itself as here threatening and objectionable, the harassment is the greater."

The injunction was justified as to each of its elements (violence, harassment, pestering and communication) since each of these actions would potentially constitute a tort of assault, nuisance or harassment. As regards the telephone calls, he said: "Telephone harassment is, in my judgement, . . . an actionable interference with (the plaintiff's) ordinary and reasonable use of property where she is lawfully present".

8–012 In *Burris v. Azadani*[32] it appeared for a while that courts were becoming more enthusiastic towards the idea of a separate "tort of harassment". However, later cases, principally the House of Lords decision in *Hunter v. Canary Wharf*,[33] have not upheld any such right where the claimant does not have an identifiable proprietary right or right of occupation of the land in question. Thus the potential of private nuisance to develop into a freestanding privacy right related to the home and to harassment has been significantly diminished. Commentators have argued that this situation is justified by policy considerations and that the resulting "gap" in privacy protection is filled by the criminal law under the Protection from Harassment Act 1997 and comparable case law however, the deficiencies of that legislation have been discussed elsewhere in this chapter. It may be noted at this stage that some of the notable uses of the 1997 Act to restrain harassment have been in cases where the defendants were animal rights protesters who claimed that they were exercising other rights such as freedom of expression and the right to demonstrate: see *Huntingdon Life Sciences v. Curtin*[34] and *DPP v. Moseley*.[35]

Public Nuisance

Intriguing developments have taken place in case law in recent years towards recognition of one particular privacy right. This right appears under the guise of the criminal offence of public nuisance, and runs parallel to other recent developments of the criminal law in relation to stalking behaviour (see *Ireland* [1996] below). Public nuisance is in fact both a crime and a tort, unlike private nuisance which is merely a tort. Thus public nuisance has a wider and more persuasive range of available remedies than does its close relation, including imprisonment. It is with the criminal offence that we are concerned here. Public nuisance is a crime on policy reasons: **8–013**

> ". . . a public nuisance is a nuisance which is so widespread in its range or so indiscriminate in its effect that it would not be reasonable to expect one person to take proceedings on his own responsibility to put a stop to it, but that it should be taken on the responsibility of the community at large".[36]

It should be noted that the requirements for a public nuisance differ in some important respects from those for private nuisance. Public nuisance will provide a remedy for persons who do not have any interest in the land upon which it occurs, and will give damages for personal injury and economic loss, whereas in private nuisance damages are generally for detriment to the land. The definition of public nuisance was considered by Romer L.J. in *Att.-Gen. v. P.Y.A. Quarries Ltd*[37] to be ". . . any nuisance is 'public' which materially affected the reasonable comfort and convenience of a class of her Majesty's subjects . . .".

Thus it must be shown that the defendant's behaviour was a nuisance to either a large number of people or a section of the public at large. If any particular person can show that he was affected to a greater degree than were the rest of the public by the nuisance in question, then he may sue for the tort of public nuisance and receive damages to compensate for his special loss; this option is in addition to a criminal prosecution. The most relevant application of public nuisance in terms of privacy came in the case of *R. v. Johnson*[38]: **8–014**

Facts. The defendant had made a large number of telephone calls, some obscene and some silent, to at least 13 different women in one geographical region between

1988 and 1994. He was charged with public nuisance, convicted and sentenced to community service and a fine. He appealed to the Court of Appeal on the basis that each telephone call was a single, isolated act towards one individual and so might have constituted private nuisance, but that it was incorrect to pool all these separate incidents and regard them as cumulatively constituting a public nuisance.

Decision. The Court of Appeal dismissed the appellant's appeal, accepting that his conduct was such as to constitute a public nuisance and that the conduct should be viewed as a whole rather than as unconnected incidents. The court held that:

(i) it was clear that the conduct in question did constitute a nuisance; it was therefore only necessary to decide whether it was public or private in nature.
(ii) when regarding the telephone calls as a course of conduct, their cumulative effect upon all the recipients should be evaluated.
(iii) this conduct was such that it "materially affected the reasonable comfort and convenience of a class of her Majesty's subjects" and therefore was a nuisance of a sufficiently widespread or indiscriminate nature that public nuisance was the correct charge.

It is interesting to compare this decision with those of the Court of Appeal in *R. v. Ireland* and *R. v. Constanza*, where criminal assault convictions were upheld for similar harassment behaviour. But for the fact that only one victim was involved in each of those cases, the rationale and policy behind the three cases seems remarkably similar. It is submitted that there is already the basis for protection of privacy in the criminal law when these cases are considered together with the Protection from Harassment Act 1997. It is simply a matter of recognising that a privacy right does exist as a result of these disparate provisions. Perhaps it is time for academic praxis along the lines of that which sparked the constitutional protection of privacy in the United States.

Breach of Copyright

8–015 The maker of a film, the taker of a photograph, or the writer of a letter, book or diary owns the copyright in that work, unless he has agreed otherwise. Thus copyright may protect privacy if, for example, private photographs or papers are taken without the owner's consent; publication may be prevented by means of an injunction and, if publication does take place, then damages will be available. Section 11 of the Copyright, Designs and Patents Act 1988 provides that the copyright in a "work" initially belongs to its "author", unless the work was created by an employee who was acting in the course of his employment. The law does not require any formality at all before copyright is created; the act of taking a photograph or writing a diary is enough. One problem is that copyright will only be of any use in privacy situations if the person whose privacy has been invaded owns the copyright to the work in question; there is no redress if, for example, a photographer takes a person's photograph without permission and publishes it, since it is the photographer and not the victim who will own the copyright to the picture. Section 85 of the 1988 Act deals with the situation where a photograph or film has been commissioned by a person other than the photographer/film-maker, but only in non-commercial transactions: although the taker of the photograph or maker of the film will own the copyright, a person who "for private and domestic purposes commissions the taking of a photograph or the making of a film has . . . the right" to prevent any of the following from occurring:

(i) copies of the work being issued to the public,

(ii) the work being exhibited or shown to the public, or;

(iii) the work being broadcast or included in a cable programme service.

Section 87 allows these rights to be waived, by contract or otherwise. Thus, in very limited circumstances, a right to privacy is enforced by this branch of law; for example, a couple who commission a wedding video will be able to prevent it from being broadcast or distributed, unless they have failed to read some small print granting a waiver.

In *The Lady Anne Tennant v. Associated Newspapers Group Ltd*,[39] two **8–016** photographs of Princess Margaret and two of a Mr Llewellyn at a fancy dress party, taken by the plaintiff, had been sold to and published by the *Daily Mail*, via a person called Waters, who had originally come into possession of the photos through the plaintiff's son. The plaintiff claimed, *inter alia*, that the defendants had infringed their copyright under the then Copyright Act 1956. The defendants argued that they believed that the copyright in the photos lay with Mr Waters and did not know of the plaintiff's claim to the photographs. Mr Waters had signed a document that if called upon he would be able to prove his copyright entitlement in the photographs of Princess Margaret—no mention was made of the Llewellyn photographs. The court held that there was no written evidence that he had copyright in the particular photos. Further, since Mr Water's document stated that the photos had been taken by Lady Anne Tennant, it would have been reasonable and prudent for the defendants to investigate Mr Water's claim of ownership of the copyright. The judge did not accept that the defendants had reasonable grounds for believing that the photos did not infringe the copyright laws and gave summary judgment for the plaintiff.

In *Williams v. Settle*,[40] the plaintiff, W, hired a professional photographer, S, to take photos of his wedding. Two years later, W's father-in-law was murdered. Shortly after that, W's wife gave birth. S sold photographs, in particular a wedding photograph to a newspaper for £15, which were eventually published in the *Daily Express* and *Daily Mail*. The court severely admonished both the defendant (for infringement of W's copyright) and the two newspapers "as principle villains and S's scandalous conduct and in total disregard not only for the legal rights of the plaintiff regarding copyright, but of his feelings and his sense of family dignity and pride. It was an intrusion into his life deeper and graver than an intrusion into a man's property".[41] Heavy punitive damages were awarded against the defendant for knowingly causing distress to the plaintiff.

DEFAMATION

8–017 Defamation is a group of torts which seek to protect a person's reputation from unwarranted attack, and at first glance these may appear to thereby protect privacy. But there are several reasons why practice defamation is of little use to those whose privacy has been invaded. First, a range of defences operate to restrict the liability to untrue statements and those where the maker does not believe in the statement's truth, whereas any right to privacy would surely apply equally where the information in question is true. Secondly, protecting a person's reputation from damage is not the same as protecting his privacy; the revelation of private facts about a person may be embarrassing or damaging to that person without causing any harm to his reputation in the eyes of others. Thirdly, an action for defamation, whether oral (slander) or published (libel) is costly and attracts no legal aid; it has become a matter of common belief that only the reputations of the rich and powerful are protected by defamation laws. Although it is not within the scope of this book to give detailed consideration to the laws of libel and slander, some general observations may be useful.

The basic requirements of slander are: a defamatory statement which either relates to the plaintiff or might be considered to do so, and which causes damage in the sense of loss to the plaintiff. A statement is defamatory if it either harms the plaintiff's reputation, or risks such harm.

For libel, there is no need to prove that the plaintiff suffered any loss as a result of damage to his reputation, but it must additionally be shown that the statement has been published or communicated in some relatively permanent form such as broadcasting.

For either kind of action, the defences available will include:

(i) justification/truth—if the defendant can show that his statement was substantially true;

(ii) fair comment—this applies if the defendant was merely expressing a truly-held opinion on a matter of public interest and was not expressing "malice" (which means lack of belief in the truth of the statement);

(iii) unintentional defamation—sections 2–4 of the Defamation Act 1996 allow a defamer to make an "offer of amends" if he defamed the victim unintentionally; a public apology can be offered and any rejection of this offer may operate as a defence to future defamation proceedings;

(iv) innocent dissemination—those who innocently spread another's defamatory statements are given a possible defence by section 1 of the 1996 Act—absolute and qualified privilege if the statement in question was made in any of the situations considered below.

Absolute privilege

Sometimes, a defamatory statement is not actionable simply because of the venue in which it was made. Absolute privilege means that no action for defamation may be commenced at all if the statement was made in one of the qualifying arenas. Parliamentary proceedings and court proceedings are given absolute privilege; communications between solicitor and client receive the same protection if they concern litigation; and so do statements made by Ministers of the Crown in the course of their official duties, regardless of whether they are in Parliament at the time. Thus any of these situations gives the speaker freedom to invade the privacy of any person by means of defamatory statements, safe from legal action. It is only in very extreme cases of deliberate abuse of the privilege that contempt proceedings might apply. The justification for the existence of absolute privilege is that fear of legal action should not be allowed to paralyse those whose roles in government or the legal system are pivotal and rely upon the ability to speak freely. Whether such justifications stand up to close scrutiny is a complex question which falls outside the bounds of this book. **8–018**

Qualified privilege

In addition to the absolutely protected speech categories above, there are further situations in which a qualified privilege will apply. The privilege is "qualified" because it is vulnerable and its protection will be lost if the plaintiff can show that the statement in question was made for an improper purpose or without a belief in its truth. This type of privilege exists in recognition of the public interest in favour of speech in certain situations. Qualified privilege may apply **8–019**

— where the statement is made by a person who is under a duty to make it, whether that duty arises from law, morality or the public interest; the person to whom it is communicated must have a recognised interest in receiving it. The reverse situation is also protected (*i.e.* where the person making the statement has an interest which requires protection and the recipient owes a duty)
— where the maker and the recipient of the statement share a common interest in the information (*e.g.* where a bank manager writes to others in the same field to warn them of a new type of fraud)
— where the person making the statement is acting to defend himself or his own property
— where the statement is a communication of a grievance to the authority which should deal with it, such as a constituent's letter to his Member of Parliament

— newspaper or broadcast reports of official proceedings such as the Annual General Meeting of a public company or local authority proceedings.

The House of Lords has recently examined the defence of qualified privilege in *Reynolds v. Times Newspapers Ltd, Ruddock and Witherow*.[42]

8–020 **Facts.** The claimant was the former Prime Minister of Ireland. The reasons behind his information were of public interest in the United Kingdom since he had been involved in the Northern Ireland peace process. Following his resignation, *The Sunday Times* published an article which intimated that he had misled political colleagues by suppressing information. After court action for defamation the claimant was awarded damages of one penny, and the judge ruled that the article was not subject to a defence of qualified privilege. Both sides appealed. The Court of Appeal found that misdirections by the trial judge had denied the claimant a fair trial, and further held that the defendant could not rely on the defence of qualified privilege at the retrial. The Court of Appeal stated that, when determining whether an occasion was privileged, a court must consider the nature, status and source of the material published and the circumstances of the publication. These issues were treated separately from the traditional questions of whether there had been a duty to publish the material and an interest in receiving the material. On appeal to the House of Lords, the defendants argued that publication of political material should be privileged, regardless of the factors which the Court of Appeal had taken into account.

Decision. The House of Lords found that it was essential for parliamentary democracy that there should be freedom to disseminate and receive information on political matters. Since section 12 of the Human Rights Act would soon be in force, courts should have particular regard for the right to freedom of expression, and the common law must be developed in accordance with Article 10. The democratic importance of a free press was an especially significant factor in weighing the balance between the protection of reputation and freedom of expression. *Per* Lord Steyn:

> "The starting point is now the right of freedom of expression, a right based on a constitutional or higher legal order foundation. Exceptions to freedom of expression must be justified as being necessary in a democracy. In other words, freedom of expression is the rule and regulation of speech is the exception requiring justification. The existence and width of any exception can only be justified if it is underpinned by a pressing social need. These are fundamental principles governing the balance to be struck between freedom of expression and defamation."

8–021 The approach of the European Court of Human Rights in cases such as *De Haes and Gijsels v. Belgium*[43] and *Lingens v. Austria*[44] was considered, and found to treat each case separately on its own particular facts rather than by category. Further, these cases draw a distinction between statements of fact and statements of opinion, and were found to give a high level of importance to speech about political matters.

The existing common law approach in defamation cases was in accordance with the ECHR rights, and "political information" should not be developed into a separate category, publication of which would always attract qualified privilege, since this would give inadequate protection to reputation. But the Court of Appeal's new test was incorrect and the previous, traditional test should remain. Section 12 of the Human Rights Act 1998 appears to focus on whether it is in the public interest to publish the particular material in question rather than on the category of information to which the material belongs, and hence categorising the material is neither necessary nor wise, and information of political interest is to be subject to the same test as all other material. Thus in all cases involving publication of matters of serious public concern, the following (illustrative) issues should be considered: the seriousness of the allegation; the nature of the information; the source of the information; the steps taken to verify it; the urgency of the matter; whether comment was sought from the claimant and whether the publication contained his side of the story; and the tone and circumstances of the publication. In the present case, (Lords Steyn and Hope dissenting) the article was not one which should be protected by privilege in the public interest.

Ian Loveland[45] criticises the House of Lords decision in *Reynolds* in **8–022**
comparison with the approaches to libel law taken by other jurisdictions. Although recognising the case as a step towards greater protection of freedom of political expression in domestic law, he regards the decision, particularly the speech of Lord Nicholls, as being too founded on the pre-existing common law and as failing to give sufficient priority to freedom of expression. Thus, although he views the result in that case as correct, he is disappointed that the opportunity to re-evaluate freedom of expression and to free it from its traditional common law role was missed. Further, in the light of the statements by the European Court of Human Rights in cases such as *Lingens v. Austria*, *Oberschlick v. Austria* and *De Haes and Gijsels v. Belgium* that freedom of political opinion and debate is at the very core of a democratic society and that the acceptable level of criticism of a politician is greater than that of an ordinary citizen, perhaps too much protection is being given to the reputations of those who are in the public eye.

One action which has stronger potential as a protection of privacy is that of malicious falsehood, which is in theory more accessible to the ordinary citizen than is the law of defamation for the simple reason that legal aid is available for an action based in malicious falsehood. Yet this is still a highly difficult claim to prove, and there have in fact been only six successful actions for malicious falsehood this century, not all of which were related to claims or privacy. The elements of this tort are otherwise very similar to those of an action for defamation—untrue statement, "malice" (in the sense of lack of a belief in the truth of the statement), damage to reputation—but it must further be shown that there was a consequential loss which arose from the defendant's actions.

Malicious Falsehood

An action in defamation primarily concerns the issue of seriously under- **8–023**
mining the reputation of the person against whom untruthful words are written or spoken (libel or slander). Malicious falsehood, or injurious

falsehood[46] as it is sometimes called, involves false statements made which do not necessarily damage a person's reputation but are published maliciously and as a consequence the person has suffered pecuniary damage. Generally, malicious falsehood actions concern untrue business statements made, for instance, a statement that a person's business has gone into liquidation would amount to malicious falsehood if done maliciously, was untrue and there was a likelihood that actual damage would be caused as a result.[47] It is for the plaintiff to prove that the statements themselves were untrue and were made maliciously in bad faith and as a result the plaintiff suffered financial damage. Unlike defamation actions, where a defendant has an absolute right to be heard by a jury, no such right exists in malicious falsehood actions, although the court does have a discretion, under certain circumstances, to order a jury trial. Further, legal aid is available for an action of malicious falsehood but not for defamation. Thus, in *Joyce v. Sengupta*[48] the plaintiff who worked for Princess Anne, was accused by the defendant, a journalist with the *Today* newspaper of publishing an article entitled "Royal Maid Stole Letters", of stealing confidential letters from her employer and handing them over to a national newspaper. The article also stated that the plaintiff was about to be dismissed, was prohibited from entering the Princess Royal's rooms which contained confidential matter as well as a statement that the police thought she was guilty. The plaintiff brought an action against the journalist and newspaper for malicious falsehood alleging that the various statements written about her were untrue. The judge at first instance struck out the action as an abuse of process. The plaintiff appealed. The Court of Appeal declared that there was an action to be tried and in particular commented about the police statement which was not investigated or verified by the defendants. The court said

> "This showed a calculated, reckless indifference to the truth or falsity of the allegations. Malice is to be inferred from the grossness and falsity of the assertions and the cavalier way they were published".[49]

As a result, the appeal was allowed and the judge's initial order was discharged. The plaintiff was in reality forced to bring this action under malicious falsehood since she could not afford to pay the potentially substantial legal costs involved had she lost.

The practice of using malicious falsehood as a cause of action is quite restrictive as can be seen from the above discussion. However, it was used to great effect, when all else failed, for an injunction application.

8–024 In the case of *Kaye v. Robertson*[50]:

Facts. The plaintiff, an actor called Gordon Kaye, star of the television comedy series, "Allo, Allo", was seriously injured in a road accident. Whilst recuperating in a private hospital room, a reporter and photographer from the *Sunday Sport*, unbeknownst to the hospital authorities, made their way to the plaintiff's room.

Despite a notice prohibiting visitors, save for a few special persons, the reporter and photographer managed to interview and photograph the plaintiff, who was in no real fit state to be questioned. Indeed, shortly after, the plaintiff could not recall what had previously occurred. The actor's agent, on the plaintiff's behalf, was granted an injunction which restrained the newspaper from publishing the proposed article and photographs. They appealed.

Decision. The court rejected the plaintiff's claim for an interim injunction on libel grounds. Such an injunction should be granted sparingly, and then only where a jury would inevitably find that the interview was libellous, which was not necessarily the case here. However, regarding the claim for malicious falsehood, the court said that any reasonable jury would find that what the defendant said in the original draft article was false. Further, the court stated that the plaintiff was not fully *compus mentus* and incapable of giving proper consent to an interview, and the defendants ought to have been aware of this, and thus the "malice" requirement was established. Finally, the plaintiff's near-death accident was extremely newsworthy and thus worth, in financial terms, a substantial amount. No doubt certain newspapers would pay highly for an exclusive interview after he had sufficiently recovered. The *Sport's* publication would seriously damage and devalue the potential prospect of a "first" by another newspaper, and therefore the respondent would suffer financial damage as a result. The court granted an injunction, but only to the limited extent that the appellants did not imply that the respondent agreed to be interviewed or photographed.

It was said in the above case by Bingham L.J. that:

> "if ever a person has a right to be let alone by strangers with no public interests to pursue, it must surely be when he lies in hospital recovering from brain surgery and in no more than partial command of his faculties. It is the invasion of his privacy which underlies the plaintiff's complaint. Yet it alone, however gross does not entitle him to relief in English law".[51]

Thus, the court showed their true sympathy with the plaintiff's predicament, yet were unable to give assistance via any pure right of privacy action. It is not obvious why an action of trespass to the land was not submitted by the plaintiff's in the above case as it would seem that all the ingredients for such an action would have been fulfilled and a full injunction granted on that basis alone.[52]

BREACH OF CONFIDENCE

Whilst breach of privacy claims are not generally recognised at law, many litigants turn to its closet relative, breach of confidence, as a means of preventing public exposure on matters they would prefer to remain private. Thus, the public dissemination of confidential information may amount to a breach, and as such, the injured party has a right to take legal proceedings against any person who breaks that confidence. It was stated in *Att.-Gen. v. Guardian Newspapers (No. 2)*[53] that a claim for breach of confidence: **8–025**

> "can arise out of a contract whereby one party ('the confident') undertakes that he will maintain the confidentiality of information directly or indirectly made available to him by the other party ('the confider') or acquired by him

> in a situation, *e.g.* his employment, created by the confider. But it can also arise as a necessary or traditional incident of a relationship between the confident and the confider, *e.g.* priest and penitent's lawyer and client; doctor and patient; husband and wife".

That does not represent an exhaustive list and case law continues to expand into other categories which will be discussed below. There may exist, under certain circumstances, a duty of confidence between the police and a suspect. In *Hellewell v. Chief Constable of Derbyshire*[54] the police were obliged to fingerprint and photograph a suspect charged with theft. Due to a spate of thefts in the area, copies of the photographs were supplied to certain businesses, as a deterrent against further crime being committed. In a civil claim by the suspect, *inter alia*, for breach of confidence, the court held that it was in the public interest to prevent and detect crime such that it was permissible for the photographs be circulated to the relevant businesses, but with the proviso that those photographs must be limited to be seen only by persons likely to be affected, *e.g.* staff and owners of businesses, but must not be displayed to the public at large. Consequently, the plaintiff's claim was dismissed.

At first sight, it may appear that breach of privacy and breach of confidence contain the same ingredients. Although there may be some overlap, in certain circumstances, between the two, there are fundamental differences which, in the case of breach of confidence, the courts are prepared to recognise as actionable at law. Whilst, at present, the courts do not grant relief for pure breach of privacy claims.

The difference between a breach of privacy and a breach of confidence was stated in Consultation Paper, Lord Chancellor's Department (July 1993): *Infringement of Privilege*, to be that "the issue of breach of confidence cases is disclosure, while the issue of breach of privacy cases is publicity.[55] A common example regarding invasion of privacy nowadays would be where a journalist publishes an article concerning a prominent M.P. who is having an extra-marital affair with his secretary. Despite being an invasion of privacy, unless untrue or on other grounds such as criminal or national security, the M.P. would probably be unable to prevent publication of this story. Another example may involve a photographer taking pictures of a famous person, and provided no trespass or other illegal conduct was involved, then publication would usually be permitted. In *Creation Records v. News Group Newspapers*,[56] the court decided that taking photographs of a private location used for the purposes of a future "Oasis" record album cover, where the photographer was aware that the taking of pictures was strictly prohibited, may well constitute an action for breach of confidence.

8–026 There are a number of ingredients which go to make up the term "confidential information".[57] They are as follows:

(i) It must wholly refer to information which is not in the public domain;

(ii) The information must have been entrusted to an individual or a limited number of persons;

(iii) The information must be private in nature;

(iv) Unauthorised disclosure of such information is strictly forbidden to the general public or a section of it. It is a question of degree[58]:

(v) Only the confider is permitted to bring legal proceedings.[59]

An early example of the working of this law was considered in *Prince Albert v. Strange*,[60] where Her Majesty, Queen Victoria, and Prince Albert had made various etchings of the Royal family and friends. Copper plates were sent to the printers to make impressions of these etchings for their own private use; a few copies were also sent to friends. One of the printer's employees, it seems, made some other copies for himself, which he eventually handed over to the defendant, Strange, who published them in a catalogue entitled "A Descriptive Catalogue of the Royal Victoria and Albert Gallery of Etchings", to be sold to the public. The plaintiff was granted an injunction prohibiting publication of the catalogue on the grounds that since the defendant, having improperly obtained these impressions, had no right to the property which was for private use only. The plaintiff was entitled to protect these drawings against any future publication in the absence of the plaintiff's consent or licence to do otherwise. Also, it would seem that the employee responsible for conveying these prints to the defendant was in breach of trust and breach of confidence and it was correct for equity to intervene under these circumstances and grant the injunction.

Breaches of Confidence in Business Dealings

For years, the type of relationship which existed between the confider and **8–027**
the confident played an important part in deciding whether an obligation of confidentiality existed. The closer the relationship, the more likely it was that the law would protect and preserve that confidentiality. This is especially prevalent in business negotiations where there is a high probability that any unauthorised disclosure would result in serious financial loss to the injured party.[61] In *Schering Chemicals v. Falkman*,[62] Shaw L.J. said:

> "the communication in a commercial context of information which at the time is regarded by the giver and recognised by the recipient as confidential, and the nature of which has a material connection with the commercial interests of the party confiding that information, imposes on the recipient a fiduciary obligation to maintain that confidence thereafter unless the giver consents to relax it."[63]

Although Lord Denning M.R. (dissenting) was more inclined against solely relying on the "business relationship" and emphasised that in breach of confidence cases an injunction should not be granted unless it can be justified on moral or social grounds.[64] In *Coco v. Clark*,[65] which again concerned business negotiations, Megarry J. used the "reasonable man" test to decide in what circumstances the recipient of confidential information should realise that such information was not meant to be made public. He said, as between business men, in a business type environment, with some eventual specific purpose, it would be difficult for a recipient to prove that the information he received was not meant to be confidential.[66] Thus, in business dealings, it may be inferred, given the close proximity of the parties involved, that confidentiality was intended.

Protection of Confidential Information Within Marriage

8–028 Personal information discussed within marriage has generally always been regarded by the courts as confidential and not for the public gaze, unless the spouses have done something to attract publicity. In *Argyll v. Argyll*,[67] the plaintiff, the Duchess of Argyll, applied for an injunction against her ex-husband, the Duke of Argyll and the editor and proprietors of the *People* newspaper against further publications of articles (two had already been published) in respect of secrets which referred to her private life and behaviour during her marriage, and which were communicated by her in confidence to her then husband. The question for the court was whether breach of confidence actions were restricted to contractual agreements and property rights. Having examined principally the decisions of *Prince Albert v. Strange*[68] and *Pollard v. Photographic Company*,[69] the court granted the injunction and emphasised the sanctity of marriage, by putting it on an even higher plain than a mere contract or legal status and stating that "The confidential nature of the relationship is of its very essence and so obviously and necessarily implicit in it that there is no need for it to be expressed".[70] Thus, even in the absence of established law, the court used its equitable discretion to direct the parties to retain confidential knowledge gained prior to their marriage break-up. The court also based its ruling on public policy grounds in that the maintenance of confidential information within marriage exists in order not to harm the very foundation of that institution and the courts will protect that from being undermined. The *Argyll* case was about "washing dirty linen in public". The Duchess did not wish to make public the very intimate details of their private lives, although their marriage had received a certain amount of publicity prior to this action.

However, where the life of a married couple is an "open book", through various publications and publicity, the court may be hesitant in granting an injunction to one party in order to prevent the other party exposing their already-highlighted private life. Such was the situation in *Lennon v. News Group Newspapers*[71] where John Lennon's first wife, Cynthia, decided to write a series of articles about herself and John. An application made by him to prevent publication on the grounds of breach of confidence, was dismissed. There was already in existence an abundance of published articles by both parties commenting on the most private and intimate details of their married life. There was, in reality, no breach of confidence since their lives were already in the public eye. Although the nature of the relationship was still important, what was more important was the publicity already surrounding that relationship.

Before confidential information can be elevated to the status where the court will recognise that disclosure of that information may amount to a legal action, it was stated in *Saltman v. Campbell Company Ltd*,[72] that three main conditions must be fulfilled:

(1) The information itself must have the necessary quality of confidence about it;

(2) That information must have been imparted in circumstances importing an obligation of confidence;

(3) There must be an unauthorised use of that information to the detriment of the party communicating it.[73]

(1) What type of information should be protected?

With the advent of more and more cases coming before the courts on breach of confidence grounds what does or does not constitute information is fast becoming somewhat blurred. Information which consists of mere gossip, trivia, tittle-tattle,[74] frivolity or innocuous material would not generally possess the "necessary quality" to come within the required criteria as the type of information which ought to be protected.[75] Added to the preceding list may be, on public policy grounds, information which concerns obscene or gross immoral behaviour. The problem is, of course, to determine what constitutes those offensive words. In *Stephens v. Avery*,[76] the plaintiff, S, informed the first defendant, A, that she had had a lesbian affair with a woman called T, who had recently been killed by T's husband. A disclosed this information to a newspaper which published the story. S brought an action for breach of confidence alleging that she had told A the information in confidence. A denied this. The defendant applied to have the action struck out as disclosing no reasonable cause of action. One of the main questions for the court was whether the information, *i.e.* the affair between S and T, amounted to confidential matter such that disclosure by A constituted a legal breach. The defendant argued, *inter alia*, that conduct of a grossly immoral nature should not be given the protection of the court. However, the court said that since there was no general recognisable accepted moral code, it would be wrong for a judge to put forward his own subjective standard on the issue. Accordingly, the judge found that there was a triable issue in this case. **8–029**

It is now established that normal sexual relations between two people possess the necessary quality such as to be actionable, if disclosed. This was based on the supposition stated in the above case of *Stephens v. Avery* that couples in general regard their own sex lives as not for public discussion.[77] This applied even if the parties involved are not married or do not have any recognised fiduciary relationship, but are merely friends, since it is not necessarily the relationship between the parties which is paramount, but the disclosure of that information. The principle regarding sexual behaviour in *Stephens v. Avery* was followed in *Barrymore (Michael) v. News Group Newspapers Ltd*,[78] where the plaintiff applied for an injunction against the *Sun* newspaper for an article published regarding his homosexual relationship with another man. In a claim for breach of confidence, the court said that by one of the parties handing over a "kiss and tell" story to the newspaper, that in itself, could amount to a breach of confidence. But, by merely stating that a relationship existed but not going into the details of that relationship, that disclosure alone would not constitute a legal breach of confidence in this case, since the plaintiff himself had already publicly professed to being homosexual. However, the article in question commented upon in-depth the plaintiff's relationship with his wife, which, the court said, "cross the line into breach of confidence". Accordingly, the injunction was granted.

(2) Obligation of confidence

8–030 The circumstances which decide whether confidentiality must be maintained are difficult to define with any real precision. As has already been discussed, in marriage normally it is not necessary to expressly state "keep it a secret"; it can be implied. It would seem that, in some circumstances, putting a tag on what type of relationship is involved before the issue of confidentiality arises may be of only minor importance. For instance, in *Stephens v. Avery*, Sir Nicholas Brown-Wilkinson V.-C. said that "the basis of equitable intervention to protect confidentiality is that it is unconscionable for a person who has received information on the basis that it is confidential subsequently to reveal that information.[79] It is not necessarily the relationship which is of the utmost importance, but the acceptance of the information. Although, where, the relationship is "purely business" in nature, that fact alone may imply that all discussions were to be treated as private and not to be disclosed.

(3) Detriment suffered by unauthorised use

8–031 Normally, the confider would suffer either financial damage or emotional distress or phychological pressure from any disclosure of confidential information, and provided the information possesses the necessary quality, the court will protect the injured party. However, it may be the case that no direct actual damage is caused by the disclosure. For example, A tells B that he looks after a famous person C who suffers from some life threatening disease. If this information is made public by B, people would probably applaud A's work, and therefore, no direct detrimental harm would be suffered by A. However, indirectly, it might cause harm to the relationship between himself and C, who may feel he has been betrayed by this revelation. Indeed, C may be entitled to sue A for breach of confidence. In *X (Health Authority) v. Y*,[80] Rose J. stated that "detriment in the use of information is not a necessary precondition to injunctive relief".[81] However, if detriment can be established, it is evidence towards retaining the confidentiality of the information. In the above case, information about two doctors with AIDS was about to be published and the health authority was granted an injunction against disclosure. The court said that there was a direct correlation between the use of the information and the detriment suffered by the plaintiffs through the leak of that information to the press, in breach of contract and breach of confidence by the informant(s).

Other Relationships

In *Woodward v. Hutchins*,[82] the *Daily Mirror* published various articles about **8–032** the plaintiff (alias Tom Jones, the singer). These articles were written by the defendant who had previously been in the employment of the plaintiff, as press agent. The articles referred to the plaintiff's antics on various occasions and were not complementary. He referred to the plaintiff as a "super-stud", wrote about his affair with Miss World and how he got "high" in a jumbo jet. Further articles were to be written about the singer and so the plaintiff applied for and was granted an injunction restraining the second defendants (the *Daily Mirror*) from disclosing any further confidential information about his private life on the grounds of breach of confidence. The defendants appealed. Lord Denning M.R. said that part of the job of a press agent included through publicity-making the public see his client in a very positive light so as to enhance his image and reputation. If what they presented to the public was a distortion of the truth, then the public ought to be allowed to read the true facts. He should be expected to take "the rough with the smooth". The court said "in these cases of confidential information, it is a question of balancing the public interest in maintaining the confidence against the public interest in knowing the truth".[83] Here, the balance lay in writing the truth—the public should not be mislead. The injunction was discharged. Lord Denning also said that the reported incidents had taken place in circumstances where there were members of the public present. What occurred could not be regarded as confidential since it was already in the public domain, *e.g.* the jumbo jet flight incident took place in front of other passengers.

No doubt, it is in the public interest that the media should not only report the news but also be allowed to practice "investigative journalism" into wrong-doings without unnecessary hindrance from the courts. Whether the confidential obligation involves withholding information which concerns some iniquity mixed in with some personal data, then no matter whether the obligation to secrecy was express or implied, the law will generally not protect such confidences. In *Khashoggi v. Smith*,[84] the defendant, the former housemaid of the plaintiff, entered into negotiations with the *Daily Mirror* regarding the publication of an article about a possible offence allegedly committed by, and other personal information about, the plaintiff, a woman of some notoriety. Since, it seemed, the plaintiff "courted publicity", "she ran the risk of the whole story and the whole truth being made public". Accordingly, the injunction against publication on the grounds of breach of confidence was refused.

Consent to disclose confidential information may only be given by the confider, provided, of course, that person possesses the true ownership in the particular information. In the recent case of *Secretary of State for the Home Department v. BBC*[85] (Ch. D.) (unreported) the plaintiff applied for an injunction to suppress the broadcasting of a television programme concerning certain interviews with high security prisoners. The interviewer, J, a psychiatrist, videotaped these conversations which, due to the special professional relationship, could only be made public with the consent of the interviewees, which he subsequently received. The plaintiff argued that the tapes were the property of the Crown and were confidential, and that publication would have a negative effect on the welfare of the prisoners and harm the public interest. This was rejected by the court which declared that, on the evidence, the tapes were the property of J, who had received permission from the prisoners to disclose them publicly. Further, it had not been established that the screening of the defendant's programme would damage the public interest. Therefore, the injunction was refused.

Defences

8–033 Where the media decide to publish information, certain defences exist which may exempt them from any form of liability. For instance, where:

(i) consent is given to reveal the otherwise confidential information;

(ii) The information itself is stale such that it no longer contains any real value to the confider[86];

(iii) the information is already in the public domain as in *Lennon v. News Group Newspapers*;

(iv) the information involved some form of "iniquity" as in *Woodward v. Hutchins* or *Khashoggi v. Smith*;

(v) lawful authority; and

(vi) the information is to be treated as a matter of "public interest".

The most used defence by the newspapers when publishing controversial material is that it is in the "public interest". The exact meaning of those words are wide, uncertain and imprecise.

Public interest

Confidential information is not to be treated as always having the property of privacy such that, in the absence of consent or authority, it can never be made public. There are certain instances whereby it is in the public interest that the confidential information be made known and circulated publicly. It is this balance between retaining the secrecy of confidential information and when it is in the public interest to reveal that confidence that has created the dichotomy in this area of the law. 8–034

In *Lion Laboratories v. Evans*[87]:

Facts. The plaintiffs were manufacturers of the Lion Intoximeter 3000, a device used by the police for breath testing suspected drink-drivers in order to measure the amount of alcohol taken. The first and second defendants, two ex-employees, contacted the third and fourth defendants (the editor and owners of the *Daily Express* newspaper) with confidential documents taken from the plaintiffs. The newspaper published an article headed "Exposed: The Great 'Breath Test' Scandal", alleging that the device had certain defects and gave faulty readings, such that many drivers may have been wrongly convicted. The plaintiffs applied for and were granted an injunction, *inter alia*, restraining the newspaper from disclosing any of the confidential information in the documents, being the property of the plaintiffs. The defendants appealed.

Decision. All parties conceded that the documents in question were confidential, and taken without authority, and publication of those documents would be in breach of confidence. However, the defendants argued that it was in the public interest that the material be published. There were two competing public interests involved here: (1) the public interest of companies and the like to retain the secrecy of confidential information. That confidentiality should be maintained unless there is some justifiable reason existing which overshadows the continuance of privacy. (2) There are certain matters which not only are the public entitled to be informed about, but also, under certain circumstances, the media have a responsibility to report, "even if the information has been unlawfully obtained in flagrant breach of confidence and irrespective of the motive of the informer".[88] The court said that such was the seriousness of the allegations, concerning as it did the lives and freedom of so many motorists (although there was no evidence of anyone being wrongly convicted) that it was in the public interest that the relevant documents be allowed to be published. The court also considered that there had previously been publicity detailing the inaccuracy of the device, but no libel claims were issued by the plaintiffs on those occasions. Damage, if there was any, had already been done, and any further damage by publication could be adequately compensated at trial. Accordingly, the injunction was discharged.

To give some further guidance in deciding whether publication should be allowed to proceed, Stephenson L.J. in *Lion Laboratories v. Evans* divided public interest into a number of categories for examination: 8–035

(1) What is interesting to the public is not necessarily in the public interest.[89] The subject-matter of the information must truly be an issue of public concern and not merely a story bound up in sensationalism to titillate the reader or viewer.

(2) Whether the media has some ulterior or private reason which outweighs the public interest, *e.g.* to increase circulation or viewing figures.[90] However, where the subject matter of the publication is a matter for genuine public concern, the circulation factor may be peripheral to the main argument of putting legitimate pressure on those parties trying to prevent publication to thoroughly investigate the particular story alleged by the media.

(3) Whether there are other avenues for disclosing confidential information other than the media, which may be more beneficial, e.g. police, local council, or the relevant responsible authority[91] or organisation. For instance, in the *X v. Y* case of the AIDS doctors (see facts below) the better course might have been for the employees to consult the British Medical Association in order that they take the necessary action.

(4) Whether or not some "iniquity" is involved is not the deciding factor, *i.e.* some form of anti-social behaviour, serious misdeeds, grave misconduct, criminal activity, etc. On the other hand, merely because there has been no recognisable misconduct by the plaintiff, on that ground alone it does not automatically mean that the public interest remains in keeping the confidential information from the public view. Prior to *Lion Laboratories v. Evans*, it seemed that a public interest defence alone, without some form of accompanying iniquity did not amount to the confidential information in question being allowed to be published. In *Lion Laboratories v. Evans*, no misconduct was involved, but that, by itself, did not mean that the confidential information would be protected from the public.

8–036 In *X (Health Authority) v. Y*[92]:

Facts. Information from hospital records was sold by one or more employees to the defendant newspapers implicating two doctors who despite suffering from AIDS were still in practice. The defendants published an article to the effect that doctors with the AIDS virus were continuing to treat patients. The defendants intended in their follow-up article to name the doctors in question. The plaintiffs, a health authority, applied for an injunction, *inter alia*, restraining the defendants from naming those doctors. It was admitted by both sides that there had been a breach of contract and confidence.

Decision. The defendants later on, amended their defence by agreeing to omit the names of the doctors or the hospital concerned, but still wished to write that two unnamed doctors continued to practise in the United Kingdom despite having AIDS. One of the main questions for the court was whether it was justified in the public interest that confidential information of this type be disclosed publicly. The courts declared that in this case, the public interest in confidentiality took precedent over the public interest in publication on the grounds that:

(1) Hospital records of AIDS patients should remain confidential in order to protect those patients from fear of "disloyal employees" who may wish to

disclose those records to the newspapers. All patients should feel secure that their files will not be revealed;

(2) No iniquity by the plaintiff was proved;

(3) Since there was already in existence open public discussion and various publications on the AIDS topic, denying the publication in this instance would be of "minimal significance";

(4) It was apparent that the plaintiffs would not be adequately compensated in damages if the publication were to go ahead and the plaintiffs were successful at trial.

Breach of Confidence, Freedom of Expression, the Human Rights Act 1998 and Recent Cases—the Development of a New Right to Privacy?

A number of interesting cases occurred around October 2, 2000, when the Human Rights Act 1998 came into force in England and Wales. Some of the cases appear to be straightforward breach of confidence cases into which a little "human rights language" has been inserted, but others appear to create, or at least be open to, new privacy-related rights. Put together, these cases are intriguing in that they appear to show that domestic courts are sometimes going beyond the existing language and scope of the pre-existing privacy-related rights and, further, that privacy is to be protected on some occasions even when there is a public interest argument for disclosure. It is thus becoming increasingly possible to argue that a new privacy right is being developed by the courts; the desirability of such a development in the face of governmental refusal to introduce such a right via statute must be questioned. Courts have also begun to comment on the "correct" approach to interpretation of section 12 of the Human Rights Act 1998. It remains to be seen whether these promising indications of openness to rethinking privacy rights will bear further fruit, but several areas will be examined here. 8–037

Secret filming

In *R v. Broadcasting Standards Commission, ex parte BBC*[93]: 8–038

Facts. Dixons complained to the Broadcasting Standards Commission that the BBC had infringed its privacy by undertaking secret filming of transactions at Dixons stores. The filming was for "Watchdog", which was investigating whether Dixons were selling second-hand goods as new. An undercover journalist was sent into Dixons stores to buy goods while being secretly filmed on a number of occasions, but no improper sales were uncovered and the film was never used. The Broadcasting Standards Commission upheld Dixons' complaint. The BBC brought proceedings to overturn the ruling, arguing, *inter alia*, that a company could not have any legal privacy rights; and that secret filming in a public place of non-intimate matters could not infringe a person's right to privacy. The judge found in favour of the BBC on these two issues. The BSC appealed.

Decision. The Court of Appeal referred to section 111(1) of the Broadcasting Act 1996, under which a complaint of infringement of privacy could be made by any "person whose privacy was infringed (s.130(1))", including a company. A company could definitely have private aspects which merited protection, and in order to determine whether any intrusion into this private sphere had occurred and was unwarranted, it was necessary to refer to Article 8 of the ECHR. But the BSC Code of conduct was approved by the Court of Appeal, with Lord Woolf stating that since its protection of privacy was stronger than that provided by the ECHR, courts should not use the ECHR to lower the protection of human rights in this context. *Per* Lord Woolf:

> "What constitutes an infringement of privacy or bad taste or a failure to conform to proper standards of decency is very much a matter of personal judgment. This is not an area on which the courts are well equipped to adjudicate. In relation to privacy, both the literature and the jurisprudence shows an understandable reluctance to propose a comprehensive definition. As Mr Beloff submitted, we are here in an area involving open textured concepts. An interference with privacy is not even like the elephant, of which it can be said it is at least easy to recognise if not define. The meaning of privacy can be influenced by the context in which it appears."

Further, Article 8 is concerned with respect for private and family life, which is not identical to the "privacy" protected by the BSC Code.

It was reasonable for Dixons to object to the secret filming of its employees, and in response the BSC had properly performed its task of setting the standards of acceptable conduct in broadcasting. Courts should be extremely reluctant to interfere with such standards, and the BSC's decision was well within its remit. Thus the appeal was allowed and the BSC's decision was restored.

This case is an important indicator of the potential for development of domestic law in response to the incorporation of Article 8. The Court of Appeal regarded that Article as providing superior protection to that available under the pre-existing domestic law and so argued that courts should now apply Article 8 when possible. Further, the present case has gone one step ahead of the European Court of Human Rights by finding that companies have a right to respect for their privacy, albeit within the Broadcasting Act 1996 so far.

It also appears that a privacy right may be claimed in respect of activities carried out in public, with the result that any covert filming may be an invasion of privacy. The case also gives some important indicators of how courts are to interpret the ECHR rights and case law. It will be interesting to see whether and to what extent future courts give companies human rights as they synthesise domestic law and the Convention rights, since the European Court of Human Rights has resisted all attempts so far towards giving companies substantive rights under the Convention.

Right to secret identity

8–039 In *Venables and Thompson v. Newsgroup and others*[94]:

Facts. The applicants were the killers of toddler Jamie Bulger. Now adults and due to be released from prison on licence with new identities, they sought injunctions to prevent the publication of any information which would identify them by their appearance, names and future whereabouts. The injunctions would bind the world, not just the media.

Decision. The injunctions were granted. The court accepted that it had a positive obligation under the Human Rights Act and the ECHR to uphold the applicants' right to respect for their private life, freedom from torture or inhuman or degrading treatment or punishment, and right to life. All three of those Convention rights were under threat if freedom of expression were not restricted in the present case. Thus, although there is a strong public interest in freedom of expression and journalistic freedom, the right to confidentiality of the applicants was more important on the facts. There was a very great possibility that vigilantes would physically attack the applicants if their whereabouts and identities could be established, and some newspapers might be involved in campaigns against the applicants. These risks were too great to be prevented by the Press Code or by individual editors. So, although it was recognised that the scope and application of the injunctions involved an extension of the previous law of confidence, Articles 2, 3 and 8 required this extension to be made. There had been huge and intense media attention about the applicants since their arrest, and almost all of the coverage had expressed great moral outrage. There were no signs that either the intensity or the type of coverage were likely to change. *Per* Butler-Sloss:

> "Under the umbrella of confidentiality there will be information which may require a special quality of protection. In the present case the reason for advancing that special quality is that, if the information was published, the publication would be likely to lead to grave and possibly fatal consequences. In my judgment, the court does have the jurisdiction, in exceptional cases, to extend the protection of confidentiality of information, even to impose restrictions on the Press, where not to do so would be likely to lead to serious physical injury, or to the death, of the person seeking that confidentiality, and there is no other way to protect the applicants other than by seeking relief from the court".

It was clearly an important factor that Articles 2 and 3 might otherwise be breached, since the judge stated that she was not certain whether a threatened breach of Article 8 would justify the restriction on freedom of expression on its own.

The court was faced with a potentially difficult balancing exercise here, since both the right to life and freedom of expression had recognition within domestic law before the Human Rights Act came into force. But since the facts were so extreme, the balance was easily weighed. It remains to be seen whether this ruling will be applied in more common circumstances; it seems unlikely that "ordinary" or even gangland criminals would be entitled to life-long anonymity, particularly in the light of public interest arguments in favour of publication in many such cases. However the case is notable for the degree to which it extends the law of confidence, even on the very unusual facts.

A privacy right for celebrities?

In *Douglas and Others v. Hello! Ltd*[95]: 8–040

Facts. The first two claimants, Michael Douglas and Catherine Zeta-Jones, had granted the third claimant, *OK*! magazine, exclusive rights to publish photographs of their wedding. But shortly after the wedding it became apparent that the defendants, a rival magazine, had gained possession of a number of unauthorised photographs of the wedding and were planning to publish them in an imminent edition. It was not known who had taken the photographs. The claimants sought and gained an interim injunction restraining the defendants from publishing the photographs. On appeal the defendants claimed that if the injunction were upheld then they would suffer damage as a result of being unable to produce an issue of their magazine for which the photographs were intended.

Decision. The Court found that English law does recognise an individual's right to personal privacy as reflected in both the equitable doctrine of breach of confidence and Article 8 of the ECHR. However, this right must be balanced against freedom of expression, which will often prevail. Section 12 of the Human Rights Act 1998 states:

> "(1) This section applies if a court is considering whether to grant any relief which, if granted, might affect the exercise of the Convention right to freedom of expression . . .
> (3) No such relief is to be granted so as to restrain publication before trial unless the court is satisfied that the applicant is likely to establish that publication should not be allowed.
> (4) The Court must have particular regard to the importance of the Convention right to freedom of expression and, where the proceedings relate to material which the respondent claims, or which appears to the court, to be journalistic, literary or artistic material . . . to . . . (b) any relevant privacy code."

Unwarranted intrusion into private lives could be redressed by the doctrine of breach of confidence. Following *Attorney-General v. Guardian Newspapers (No. 2)* [1990] 1 A.C. 109, it was no longer necessary to show a pre-existing confidential relationship between the parties in order to sue for breach of confidence. But further, courts were now required to give effect to the right of respect for private life under Article 8, albeit balanced against freedom of expression under section 12(3) of the Human Rights Act 1998. The Court found that section 12(3) did not seek to give priority to freedom of expression over all other rights, but merely to ensure that publication would only be prevented by injunction where the applicant was likely to succeed in the final case; this is a simple application of the general test of "balance of convenience" for interim injunctions under *American Cyanamid v. Ethicon* [1975] A.C. 396.

On the present facts, the claimants did have an actionable right of privacy which was now somewhat different form the commercial and employment situations in which breach of confidence had developed; however, there are degrees of privacy, as recognised in *Dudgeon v. U.K.* [1981] 4 E.H.R.R. 149, and the greater the intimacy of the situation, the greater the justification for any interference must be. By making their wedding into a publicity-ridden event, the first two claimants had swung the balance away from favouring respect for their private life and towards publication. Granting an interim injunction restraining publication before trial would be permissible where it concerned a truly private occasion. Thus, although the judges thought that the claimants had a privacy-related right which had been infringed, they agreed that the balance of convenience was against granting the injunction. Thus the claimants' rights would have to be vindicated at the full trial in damages, if at all.

This case sent waves of panic through the media, with some commentators fearing that domestic courts were heading towards privacy laws as strict as those of France. It was the first case, probably with many more to follow, in which a celebrity argued privacy rights under the Convention. It appears that domestic courts are at least open to a substantial strengthening of privacy law in the United Kingdom.

The meaning of section 12 of the HRA?

It appears that the courts are taking a restrictive approach to section 12 of the Human Rights Act 1998. In *Imutran v. Uncaged Campaigns and Lyons*[96] the Court of Appeal found that there was no real difference between section 12 and the pre-existing legal test under *Cyanamid* for when to restrain publication of an argued breach of confidentiality. In addition, section 12(4)'s balancing exercise between confidentiality and freedom of expression did not indicate a different result from that which would have occurred before its introduction. On the facts, there was a stronger argument in favour of confidentiality than there was in favour of either freedom of expression under Article 10 or section 12 of the Human Rights Act 1998. Thus a research laboratory's right to maintain confidentiality of its documents prevailed over freedom of expression and the public's right to know about animal experimentation **8–041**

Public Interest Disclosure Act 1998

Introduction

Radical changes have taken place in respect of "whistleblowing", *i.e.* the legal permissibility of, and protection for, drawing attention to unfair or illegal practices carried out by employers or public authorities. Until recently most large and/or well-advised companies would routinely use "gagging" clauses in contracts with employees and contractors, which understandably led to concern about the lack of public accountability of such companies for their decisions and actions. The Nolan Committee on Standards in Public Life[97] proposed the protection of whistleblowing employees of public bodies, in view of the very weak protection which the common law and statutory employment law had provided in this respect. The duties of employees (including fidelity, loyalty, and most importantly in the current context, confidentiality) meant that disclosures were rarely justified and so dismissal for whistleblowing was almost always outside the scope of scrutiny for either wrongful or unfair dismissal. Employees wishing to make a public interest disclosure thus faced losing their employment and future prospects, with little potential for legal redress. Further, employers were often successful in bringing actions in such circumstances for breach **8–042** of confidence, the threat of which must have dissuaded many a public-minded potential discloser from "rocking the boat". Government employees further had to fear action against them for criminal offences under the Official Secrets Acts, with unpredictable consequences (see the discussion of *Ponting* in Chapter 5.

The Public Interest Disclosure Act 1998 was a far-reaching reform of this situation, providing employment protection for whistleblowers within its scope and so reworking principles of both employment law and breach of confidence within its area of application. Perhaps unfortunately, Government employees still have to fear the Official Secrets Acts, but recent cases such as the *Blake*, *Shayler* and *Tomlinson* affairs show that the likelihood of success under that legislation appears to be diminishing.[98] Future Human Rights Act–based cases may also affect the delicate balance in both official secrecy cases and the remaining common law of breach of confidence (see *Ex parte Rusbridger, Alton and Bright*[99]).

8–043 Where disclosure is made by an employee, the former decision as to whether the disclosure has been made "in the public interest" has been replaced by the new criteria under the Public Interest Disclosure Act 1998. The Act aims to protect the employment rights of whistleblowers so that they cannot be harassed or dismissed for voicing reasonable concerns. This is a great step towards the bringing of concerns to light and the Act has been referred to as being among the strongest legislation protecting whistleblowers in the world.[1] However the Act creates a complex set of requirements before a worker may seek its protection; further, it excludes certain types of employees and does not cover certain disclosures. There is still no guarantee that an employer (or any other person) will take any action at all after a protected disclosure.

The Act, which has been in force since July 1999, protects qualifying employees by introducing amendments to the Employment Rights Act 1996. However, there is a strict list of requirements which must be satisfied: a worker (section 43K) must have made a qualifying disclosure (section 43B) to their employer (section 43C(1)(a)), or to another prescribed person (section 43E and 43F) or (in very limited circumstances) to an external person (section 43G and 43H); he then has a right not to be subjected to any detriment (section 47B).

Worker (section 43K of the Employment Rights Act 1996)

8–044 The Act uses a wide definition of worker. It is not limited to "employee", but is extended by section 43K to include any other person who:

"(a) works or worked for a person in circumstances in which—

(i) he is or was introduced or supplied to do that work by a third person, and

(ii) the terms on which he is or was engaged to do the work are or were in practice substantially determined not by him but by the person for whom he works or worked, by the third person or by both of them."

or

"(b) contracts or contracted with a person, for the purposes of that person's business, for the execution of work to be done in a place not under the control or management of that person . . ."

or

(c) provided medical, dental, ophthalmic or pharmaceutical services for a Health Authority;

or

(d) was on work experience or training other than that provided by an employer or by a educational establishment on a course run by that establishment.

Qualifying disclosure (section 43B of the Employment Rights Act 1996)

A qualifying disclosure is made where the worker reasonably believes that the information disclosed indicates that one or more of the following have occurred: **8–045**

a criminal offence;

non-compliance with a legal obligation;

a miscarriage of justice;

a threat to the health or safety of a person;

environmental damage;

or the deliberate concealing of any of these.

Disclosure to an employer (section 43C(1)(a) of the Employment Rights Act 1996)

Such disclosures will qualify the worker for employment protection so long as they are made in good faith. It remains to be seen how this will be interpreted, especially since many disclosing workers will have a real or apparent grudge as at least part of their arguable motivation for the disclosure. **8–046**

Disclosure to a prescribed person (sections 43D, 43E and 43F of the Employment Rights Act 1996)

Section 43D allows a worker to make a qualifying disclosure in the course of obtaining legal advice, regardless of whether he shows good faith. Under section 43E disclosure may be made to a Minister of the Crown, so long as **8–047** he acts in good faith. But the most powerful weapon a whistleblowing worker has is section 43F, which allows him to disclose the information concerned to any person prescribed by an order of the Secretary of State. The worker must reasonably believe that the information he discloses is substantially true; but, significantly, does not have to act in good faith.

Non-prescribed disclosure (sections 43G and 43H of the Employment Relations Act 1996)

8–048 If disclosure is made to any other person than those discussed so far, including the police or the media, then the highly complex requirements of section 43G are the worker's only chance of employment protection. Section 43G requires all of the following to be established:

- the disclosure was not made "for gain";
- it was reasonable in all the circumstances to make the disclosure;
- the disclosure was made in good faith;
- the worker reasonably believed that the information revealed was substantially true.

AND one of the following from section 43G(2), either:

a) the worker reasonably believed when he made the disclosure that he would be "subjected to a detriment if he had disclosed instead to his employer or to a prescribed person"; or
b) where there is no relevant prescribed person and the worker reasonably believed that disclosure to the employer could result in the evidence being concealed or destroyed;
c) in the past the worker has disclosed, to the employer or to a prescribed person, "substantially the same information".

But if the disclosure relates to what potentially could be a very serious or urgent situation, then section 43H allows a worker to make a qualifying disclosure to any person if:

- he acts in good faith; and
- it is reasonable in all the circumstances to make the disclosure; and
- he reasonably believes the information he discloses to be substantially true; and
- he does not disclose for personal gain; and
- the disclosure relates to an "exceptionally serious" breach.

It should be noted that, whenever disclosure is made to a non-prescribed person, then there will be a crucial issue, that of the identity of the person to whom the disclosure was made. It is submitted that disclosure to the police is far more likely to be "reasonable" than that to the media, for example.

Telephone Tapping

It is now established law that the only person permitted to proceed with an action for breach of confidence is the person who conveyed the original confidential information. The defendant in any such action is the recipient and/or any third party who reveals that information, and was aware that it was confidential. However, where confidential information is transferred through a means of communication whereby others, not meant or entitled to receive that communique, overhears or eavesdrops on that conversation, then the question arises whether those "uninvited" parties are under an obligation to retain the privacy of that communication. Such was the problem which arose in *Malone v. Commissioner of Police of the Metropolis (No. 2)*[2] where during the plaintiff's trial for handling stolen property, a policeman's notebook indicated that the plaintiff's telephone had been tapped, with the authority of the Secretary of State. The plaintiff brought a claim against the police based on property rights, right of privacy and breach of confidence. Megarry V.-C. stated that conveying confidential information via the telephone brings with it the inherit risk, which the speaker must be aware of, that there is a possibility of his conversation being overheard and includes those who deliberately tap into that phone call. In such a case, there is no responsibility on the interceptor to maintain a confidence on what was said. If, on the other hand, the "unknown overhearer" does have some duty of confidentiality, are there exceptions whereby the listener is free to divulge what he has heard? The answer lies in the conversation itself and whether the contents reveal some iniquitous conduct. If yes, then probably no duty of confidence arises. However, if there is only a suspicion of some criminal activity, then the question arises as to "whether there is just cause or excuse for tapping and for the use made of the material obtained by the trapping."[3] Provided all the legal requirements are adhered to for the interception, then the "just cause or excuse" principle is acceptable in order to assist in the prevention and detection of some crime which may have taken or is about to take place. Accordingly, the claim was dismissed. 8–049

Lord Denning in *Fraser v. Evans*[4] said that iniquity was "merely an instance of just cause or excuse for breaking confidence."[5] Thus, it may not necessarily be the case that only misconduct, criminal of fraudulent behaviour will entitle some form of legal surreptitious interception or allow the breaking of the obligation of confidentiality. The words "just cause or excuse" encompass much wider reasons to allow the courts to revoke the duty of confidentiality; examples include misleading the public,[6] price fixing,[7] manufacturing faults,[8] etc. Megarry V.-C. in *Malone v. CPM* gave further examples of such instances, which included private conversations between two passengers on a bus or train who ran the risk of being overheard by other passengers; private conversations of neighbours; confidential information transmitted over an internal office system runs the risk of some third party listening in on the conversation.[9] His conclusion was that he did not see any reason why anyone who overheard some secret in this way should be liable to legal proceedings if he uses or divulges what the has heard. Megarry V.-C. was unhappy with the common law, as it stood, in the area of telephone tapping and advocated legislation in this area which was brought into force under the Interception of Communications Act 1985 and is now part of the Regulation of Investigatory Powers Act 2000 (see below). The follow-on question is what is the position whereby a private individual or company decides to "bug" a person's telephone in order to publish the findings. Will the consequences remain the same as in *Malone* above? Does the speaker on a telephone accept the same risk that his conversation will be overheard by, for instance, crossed lines or unintentional interference or indeed authorised police phone tapping, as when some person deliberately eavesdrops by planting a "bug" into the telephone system? In *Francome v. Mirror Group Newspapers*[10]:

Facts. An unnamed source bugged the home telephone of the plaintiff, a champion jockey, and then offered the contents of the taped conversations to the defendants for publication. On discovering the existence of these tapes, the plaintiff brought an action against the defendants claiming, *inter alia*, damages for breach of confidence, and an injunction against the defendant publishing the contents. The judge granted the injunction and the defendants appealed.

Decision. The plaintiff argued that the telephone conversations in question were confidential. Further, since the information on the tapes was gained through criminal means (*i.e.* contrary to section 5 of the Wireless Telegraphy Act 1949), divulging what was said on the tapes would be illegal. The defendants denied any involvement in the actual bugging and therefore, they said, they could not be held liable for any criminal offence or breach of confidence. They further argued that they were entitled to publish the conversation on iniquity grounds in that what was stated on the tapes alleged that the plaintiff was in breach of behaviour which was either anti-social or involved some form of criminal activity, and therefore there should be no prevention from publication. The court expounded the virtues of the media, but said that sometimes "they confuse the public interest with their own interest". Further, the court could not see what public interest would be served by publishing the contents of the tapes which would not equally be served by giving them to the police or to the jockey club. Wider publication would only serve the interest of the *Daily Mirror*.[11] At this interlocutory stage, the court could not delve into issues of the defendants' claim of iniquity and public interest, since these involved questions of law and fact. However, if the defendants were permitted to publish, the damage done to the plaintiff might be irreparable and not be able to be fully compensated when the issues at trial were determined, whether the defendants were found liable or not, *i.e.* the damage having already been done. Therefore, part of the appeal was allowed but the injunction against publication remained, but only to the extent that the defendants were not permitted to use the contents of the tapes for their article. They could mention the findings of their investigation, and if sued for libel could produce the tapes as evidence to back up their story.

However, it is arguable that if there is serious misconduct, *e.g.* fixing of races, horse-doping, jockeys betting on races themselves (which is illegal), which would affect a significant section of the public, then there is a legitimate public interest such that the general public ought to be informed about these activities and not confine it to "in-house" authorities.

Conclusion

Nowadays, "sex scandal" stories about the rich and famous appear regularly **8–050** in our newspapers. Usually, these stories concern some adulterous affair which at the time, was not public knowledge. The vast majority of these stories would come under the umbrella as "interesting to the public" as opposed to "the public interest". If such disclosures were always considered to be in breach of confidence, then no doubt certain tabloid newspapers would be filled with a lot of blank pages. However, it is not unreasonable to assume that there is an implied, if not express obligation on the part of at least one of the parties involved to keep the affair secret. Both parties are generally aware of the problems of "going public" with the relationship. Nevertheless, the stories continue and the newspapers encourage such revelations. Unless breach of confidence principles are more properly attuned to modern day moral codes (whatever they are), it is likely that the uncertainty which prevails in this area will only lead to further doubt and confusion.

DATA PROTECTION ACT 1984

This Act was an attempt to regulate the ever-increasing number of **8–051** companies and other bodies which store information about individuals in an electronic form. It also serves a freedom of information aim. The advent of computerised information storage, transmission and retrieval systems highlighted the potential privacy problems related to the growth in "files" being kept on members of the public for diverse reasons by a huge variety of organisations, but it may seem strange to regulate computerised data but not files kept on paper. However, computers make it far easier to store large amounts of information and to collate information from different sources, and may make errors more likely to occur simply because of the increased capacity and options for data collection. When information could only be kept in folders piled up in storerooms, it was unlikely that a complete picture of a person's life or finances could be collected in one place. Now, computers are in constant communication with each other and the potential exists for comprehensive and detailed files to be kept about any person who drives a car, applies for jobs or credit, seeks medical treatment, or attends an educational facility, for example. One small error in one stored piece of information may be replicated at speed and stored in many other computers, causing damage or distress to the individual concerned. Credit ratings, C.V.s and criminal records all depend to some extent upon the accuracy and confidentiality of information stored electronically.

The Data Protection Act 1984 creates a series of obligations which attach to "data users", *i.e.* those who store information about others ("data subjects") electronically; any information which relates to a living person is labelled "personal data".[12] All data users were required to register as such with the Data Protection Registrar (now the Information Commissioner, see below). A data user must only use his data for the purpose for which it was collected, and must keep it up to date.[13] If a data subject finds that information kept about him is inaccurate, then he has a right to have it corrected or erased.[14] In order that a data subject may enforce this right, section 21 allows any person to ask a data user whether there is data stored about him, and a correct answer must be given. If data is held about the enquirer, then a copy of it must be provided to him. Otherwise, all stored data must be kept secure. If a data subject finds that inaccurate information is still held about him after he has requested that it should be amended or deleted, then he may obtain a court order to carry out his wishes (section 24). (Section 24) and a court may award compensation for any loss or damage which results from inaccurate data. A data user will have a defence against the award of compensation if it can show that the inaccurate material was supplied by a careless or malicious third party.

8–052 Schedule 1 also provides a series of "data protection principles" with which data users must comply, including the following:

(i) personal data may only be held for one or more specified lawful purposes;

(ii) information contained impersonal data must be obtained and processed fairly and lawfully;

(iii) personal data held for any purpose or purposes must not be used or disclosed in any manner incompatible with those purposes.

The operation of the Act was overseen by the Data Protection Registrar, who had powers of investigation, registration and supervision of data users. Criminal offences provide the necessary force behind these powers. However, criticism has fallen on the level of funding given to the Registrar and on the opportunities which exist for evading the principles of the Act. It was also of concern that unauthorised persons could obtain access to computer data relatively easily; computer hackers have caused havoc to certain databases in the past. The Computer Misuse Act 1990 was a response to this phenomenon, and creates criminal offences related to unauthorised access to information held electronically. Motive is irrelevant to such an offence. It is expected that the level of successful hacking incidents will fall due to this and other related measures; it is now just as risky to commit the "clean burglary" of the hacker as it is to break into an office and make off with files stored on paper.

But what about information which is held by traditional methods, in manual rather than computer form? Since the mid–1980s, rights of access to manually stored information have been gradually increased in response to campaigns for freedom of information. The Access to Personal Files Act 1987 allowed access to "accessible" information collected after the Act came into force, but does nothing to prevent secret files from being kept. A series of specific regulations followed, in response to ECHR cases. The Access to Personal Files Regulations 1989 obliged social services departments to give personal information to individuals about whom it has been collected, unless it would be possible to identify an unwilling source of the information. The Access to Medical Reports Act 1988 creates limited rights of access to medical records by, for example, insurance companies, thus protecting personal medical records in all other circumstances. Even the individual about whom medical records are kept does not have an automatic right of access to them, since there may be clinical reasons for hiding information from a patient.[15] Since November 1, 1991, the Access to Health Records Act 1990 has lessened the duality of the situation relating to medical records: it attempts to create a right of access to manual health records which is parallel to the right to computer health records under the Data Protection Act 1984. But the 1990 Act only applies to new records, not to those made before it came into force, and disclosure may be denied if it would result in serious physical or mental harm to the patient. Thus patients whose records are held on paper still have less rights to access and correct the information held about them than do those whose records happen to be held on computer. Now, the Data Protection Act 1998 is ending the slow process of coming into force, and so all records and documents, whether electronic or paper, will be subject to the data protection principles and the new Information Comissioner has stronger powers and a clearer mandate.

Data Protection Act 1998: an Overview

It is not possible within the confines of this book to do more than summarise and comment upon the main principles of the new regime for data protection: extra material will be available via the website once the Act is fully operational in late 2001, and as determinations of the Information Commissioner become available. **8–053**

The 1998 Act is by far the widest data protection legislation which has ever been attempted in the U.K., and goes far beyond its 1984 predecessor. It was created mainly in order to implement the E.C. Data Protection Directive 95/46 and Directive 97/66, which relates to privacy in telecommunications and the processing of personal data. The 1998 Act applies not only to computerised records but also to files held on paper. It seems comprehensive, but has already been amended by the Freedom of Information Act 2000, reflecting the difficult balance between access to information and confidentiality of personal information. In the latter respect, the 1998

Act is arguably the closest statute in the U.K. to a privacy law. One of its signal achievements will be in the field of employment: individuals will have access to paper files held on them by a variety of agencies and public authorities for the first time (excluding, unfortunately, personnel files), and such records will no longer be accessible to third parties without the consent of the individual to whom they relate.

The main thrust of the 1998 Act is to create an almost all-encompassing right of access to, and correction or destruction of, personal data by the person to whom it relates, the "data subject", regardless of the form and format in which the data is held. Personal data is any data which relates to a living person, who can be identified from the data itself or in combination with other information. Exemptions do exist for national security, crime, law enforcement, tax and the like. Persons and organisations holding personal data in any form ("data controllers") are now under a duty to notify the Information Commissioner of their operations and to conform with registration procedures. Failure to do so is a criminal offence. Data subjects will be able to apply for compensation if the Act's principles are breached, and will have power to prevent the processing of data which is likely to cause substantial damage or distress. The definition of "data controller" under the 1998 Act is much broader than that of its predecessor, and covers almost any activity involving data, including organising, retrieving, disclosing, transmitting, destroying, obtaining and recording. Data controllers have to adhere to the *data protection principles* in relation to all personal data in their control.

Data Protection Principles

8–054 The data protection principles are:

(1) All personal data must be processed fairly, lawfully, and only where one of the Schedule 2 conditions exists, *e.g.*: the data subject has given his consent to the processing; the processing is necessary for the performance of a contract by the data subject; the data controller is following his own legitimate interests. But where the data is sensitive personal data (Schedule 3), the data subject must have given express consent to the processing, which must in addition be necessary for one of the listed purposes, such as medical records. Specific duties are placed on data controllers in relation to sensitive data in employment and in relation to the protection of the rights of third parties.

(2) Personal data may only be obtained for one of the specified lawful purposes and may only be processed in accordance with those purposes.

(3) Personal data must not be irrelevant or excessive in relation to the purpose for which it is held

(4) Personal data must be accurate and kept up-to-date.

(5) It shall not be kept for any longer than is necessary for its purpose (but note that the Criminal Justice and Police Act 2001 has enabled police forces to keep data indefinitely for crime-control purposes: see Chapter 3).

(6) Personal data must be processed in accordance with, and subject to, the rights of the data subjects. The rights of data subjects under the Act include:

— s. 7(1)(a), the right to be informed on request (and after paying a fee) whether a data controller is processing any personal information of which he is the subject, and then to be informed of the type of information concerned, the purposes for which it is being processed, and its potential recipients;

— s. 8(2), the right to receive the information which constitutes the personal data;

— s. 10, the right to give notice to a data controller to cease processing of personal data where the processing is likely to cause substantial damage or substantial distress to the data subject;

— s.11, the right to prevent or terminate processing carried out for the purpose of direct marketing;

— s. 12, the right in effect to "rebut" decisions taken on the basis of processed personal data, *e.g.* credit scoring, work performance, psychometric testing in the workplace;

— the right to compensation where damage is caused by a data controller's breach of any of the Act's requirements;

— the right to complain to the Information Commissioner regarding a breach of any of the Data Protection Principles.

(7) Measures must be taken against unauthorised or unlawful processing of, or damage to, personal data

(8) Personal data shall not be transferred outside the EEA unless the recipient country guarantees an equivalent level of respect for and protection of the rights of the data subject.

There are, however, a number of complex exceptions to the Data Protection Principles and the consequent rights of the data subject, under Part IV of the Act and Schedule 7. Each needs detailed analysis on the facts of an individual case, but a basic guide is appropriate here:

— There is a broad national security exception, and a certificate given by a Crown Minister is conclusive evidence that the data concerned requires exemption on national security grounds.

— Data processed for: the prevention or detection of crime; the apprehension or prosecution of offenders; tax-related purposes; is exempt from most of the provisions of the Act.

— There are exemptions concerning health, education and social work purposes in section 30.

— Section 31 exempts certain regulators, particularly in finance and banking.

— Journalistic, literary and artistic purposes may be exempted where the data controller reasonably believes that publication would be in the public interest; this exemption aims to uphold freedom of speech and prevent use of the Act to obtain prior restraint of publication.

— Private processing by an individual for their personal, family or household purposes is exempt.

— Confidential references are generally exempt.

Enforcement

8–055 Where the Information Commissioner is satisfied that a data controller has contravened any of the Data Protection Principles, she may serve upon him an *enforcement notice* (s. 40(1)), requiring him to take, or refrain from taking, action within a specified period, and may require destruction or rectification of data. A conciliatory approach is to be taken where possible, although the Commissioner may apply for search and seizure warrants where necessary. If a matter of "substantial public importance" is involved, the Information Commissioner is able to give assistance to a party to actual or prospective legal proceedings. Appeal lies to the Information Tribunal, and then to the High Court on point of law. The Act also contains a number of criminal offences related to unauthorised processing and disclosure.

Interception of Communications Act 1985

8–056 Before the Interception of Communications Act 1985, tampering with or intercepting the communications of another person was not subject to a clear set of rules and procedures in the United Kingdom. Tampering with another's mail was, and remains, a criminal offence under the Post Office Act 1953, section 58, and also a tort; it could only be carried out with express authority from a senior Post Office official. Section 58(1) exempted from criminal liability any interference with a postal packet where a warrant was issued in the name of the Secretary of State who in practice delegated his power to the Post Office along with a series of non-binding guidelines as to the circumstances under which warrants should be granted. Since the monitoring, tapping or recording of telephone calls required no such express authority and did not seem to have any particular procedure, it fell into the Secretary of State to also create guidelines for these interceptions. After the Malone case, and as a direct response to the ruling in that case by the ECHR, the 1985 Act was introduced. It took the form of an additional framework of safeguards in relation to telephone tapping, and so does not prevent an aggrieved victim from using existing remedies such as those for trespass or breach of confidence if relevant. The 1985 Act legitimised telephone tapping: safeguards were introduced in the form of mandatory procedures for authorisation, but authorisation was possible only by the Secretary of State. However, the Act has now been superseded by the Regulation of Investigatory Powers Act 2000. It is hoped that the latter statute will create less infringements of privacy, but this will not necessarily be the case since many of its provisions are open to criticism, and some of the criticisms of the 1985 Act are still applicable to its successor.

The main points of criticism which were raised concerning the operation of the 1985 Act included the following. First, it did not apply to communications made by cordless or mobile telephones, since they are not part of the "public telecommunications system", in theory at least, interception of such communications is no offence. Of course, the practical difficulties involved in providing that such communications have been intercepted are immense due to the ease with which the interception can be carried out—equipment for picking up conversations made by a "wireless" methods is cheap and widely available, and detection is extremely unlikely. The privacy of mobile phone users is likely to be ensured far more effectively by means of sophisticated encryption techniques than by a regulatory framework which would be easy to evade. Secondly, there was no requirement that a person whose communications have been intercepted according to a warrant should be notified that the interception has taken place. Such a requirement would enable those who believe an interception has taken place to obtain an answer, and the requirement could of course be made subject to an exception for the protection of national security. The issuing of warrants was monitored in general by a Commissioner, but this provided no direct rights for an aggrieved individual whose privacy of communication has been, or may have been, invaded. Such a person has recourse only to an action for breach of confidence or trespass. Thirdly, the Act did not apply to "bugging" to other surveillance devices, and thus an opportunity to create consistency in this complex and confused area of law was missed.

Regulation of Investigatory Powers Act 2000

Modern detection and prevention of crime demands modern methods of **8–057**
investigation and up-to-date technology. Nowadays, a vital ingredient in many investigatory operations is the ability to gather information via

secretive and surreptitious means such as surveillance, eavesdropping, listening and monitoring devices, interception of information and so forth. Such methods generally involve covert operations where the target is not informed and unaware of any such investigation taking place. Since such methods involve interference with an individual's right to privacy, it is incumbent upon state authorities carrying out such activities to do so in a lawful manner in accordance with domestic law and to take account of the European Convention on Human Rights, especially Articles 6 and 8. In the past, the lack of legislation and sufficient control over various state authorities, such as the police and intelligent services, has led the United Kingdom being put in the invidious position of literally "being taken to court" over their intrusive methods of gathering incriminating evidence against individuals via telephone-tapping, bugging and the like. The turning point came in the case of *Malone (John) v. U.K.*,[16] which persuaded the government to introduce legislation, the Interception of Communication Act 1985, controlling the use of surveillance techniques within certain perimeters, and thus providing an individual with some limited degree of protection against state interference. Since then, legislation has been introduced in a piecemeal-type fashion to cover other areas of authorised secret intrusions, *e.g.* the Data Protection Acts 1984 and 1998, the Police Act 1997 and the Intelligence Services Act 1994. However, those existing laws did not prevent other cases coming before the European Court of Human Rights, including *Halford v. U.K.*[17] and *Hewitt and Harman v. U.K.*,[18] and showed that the existing laws were inadequate and limiting and did not provide sufficient safeguards against possible abuse by the state. Since the introduction of the Human Rights Act 1998 and the case of *Khan* the government has attempted to pre-empt future problems which may lead to individuals going to Strasbourg to enforce their rights under the Convention, by passing the Regulation of Investigatory Powers Act 2000.

The Regulation of Investigatory Powers Act 2000[19] (RIPA) was introduced to deal with:

> "the interception of communications, the acquisition and disclosure of data relating to communications, the carrying out of surveillance, the use of covert human intelligence sources and the acquisition of the means by which electronic data protected by encryption or passwords may be decrypted or accessed",[20–21]

and to establish a special tribunal to hear complaints by persons against, *inter alia*, possible abuses by state authorities under the Act.

Unlawful and authorised interception

8–058 Part I of the Act refers to the unlawful and authorised interception of specific types of communication carried out by public authorities. Section 1(1) states that "It shall be an offence for a person intentionally and without lawful authority to intercept, at any place in the United Kingdom, any communication in the course of its transmission by means of—(a) a public postal service; or (b) a public telecommunication system." Under section 1(2) such interception by a person with respect to a private communication system (*e.g.* mobile phone businesses, e-mails, pagers and the like) shall be a criminal offence, unless the interception comes within section 1(6)(a) or (b), *i.e.* the interceptor is a person with a right to control the operation or the use of the system; or he has the express or implied consent of such a person to make the interception. Interception of a communication in the course of its transmission takes place where the person modifies or interferes with the system or monitors transmissions via the system or wireless telegraphy (section 2(2)). Under section 1(3) a civil action may be taken by the sender or recipient against any person who does not possess the lawful authority to intercept communications in the course of transmissions.

Lawful authority may only be authorised by means of sections 3 or 4, or by warrant under section 5, or in relation to any stored communication, any statutory power for the purpose of obtaining or taking possession of such information (section 1(5)(a)–(c)). Under section 3 lawful authority is approved where (i) the interceptor has reasonable grounds for believing that the sender and recipient of the communication have consented to the interception (section 3(1)(a) and (b)); (ii) the interceptor has been given consent by the sender and surveillance has been authorised under Part II (section 3(2)(a) and (b)); (iii) the interception involves a postal or telecommunications service and is connected with the functions of those services (section 3(3)(a) and (b)); (iv) the interception of the transmission takes place via wireless telegraphy, and with the authority of a designated person under the Wireless Telegraphy Act 1949 for limited purposes, *e.g.* the issuing of licences under the Act or preventing interference with wireless telegraphy (section 3(4) and (5)). Lawful authority may also be granted to the interceptor, under certain circumstances, for purposes relating to obtaining information of communications against persons reasonably believed to be outside the United Kingdom (section 4(1)(a)–(e)). Section 4 also lawfully permits interceptions which constitute a legitimate business practice, as well as interceptions relating to prisons, high security psychiatric hospitals and state hospitals (section 4(2)–(6)).

Thus, under sections 3 and 4 interference by the state authorities is lawful in the absence of any judicial authorisation (*e.g.* a warrant) or supervision. As it stands, the lack of any judicial body to oversee that there are no abuses by the authorities of their powers in this respect may well be incompatible with ECHR law, and especially the "in accordance with the law" requirement under Article 8, unless the procedures for obtaining lawful authority are such that sufficient safeguards are in place to ensure against possible misuse by those authorised to intercept.[22]

Apart from the above, under all other circumstances, an interception warrant must be issued by the Secretary of State, before the conduct is considered lawful (section 5(1)). However, under section 5(2), prior to any warrant being issued, the Secretary of State must be satisfied that two main requirements are met. Firstly, the warrant must be necessary. The meaning of the word "necessary" is restricted to certain legitimate aims, including, in the interests of national security, for the preventing or detecting serious crime and for safeguarding the economic well-being of the United Kingdom (section 5(3)). Secondly, the action authorised must be proportionate to what is sought to be achieved by the granting of such a warrant. In other words, the action taken by the interceptor must not be so disproportionate that other methods would not have equally achieved the same or even better results, or that the action to be taken was of such minor importance, when balanced against possible violations of Articles 6 and 8, even when coming within the provisions of section 5(3).

Applications for warrants

8–059 Section 6 sets out of those persons who may legitimately apply for a warrant. They include, the Director-General of the Security Services, the Chief of the Secret Intelligence Services, the Commissioner of Police of the Metropolis and the chief constable of various police forces.[23] The technical requirements for an interception are provided by sections 7–9 and includes thc warrant stating the purpose, name of person or premises under investigation, the equipment to be used; identifying and describing the communications to be intercepted and the various duration period and renewal conditions to be applied.

Upon the issue of a warrant, section 12 provides that the Secretary of State may, by notice, order persons providing public postal services or public telecommunications services to comply with certain obligations as may be required of them, including providing operating assistance for a certain period as is deemed reasonable by the Secretary of State (sections 12(2) and (8)). Under section 13 a Technical Advisory Board (TAB) is to be established for referrals made by the subject of the order. The TAB will consider the technical requirements and financial consequences involved and report their findings to that person and the Secretary of State, who may then withdraw, modify of leave the notice unchanged (section 12(6)(a)–(c)). Where a person does provide assistance relating to postal or telecommunications services, that person shall be entitled to a fair contribution towards the costs incurred (section 14(1)).

Part II of the Act, *i.e.* sections 26 to 48, deals with surveillance and the use of covert human intelligence sources. Under these circumstances high level authorisation or warrants are not generally required for such operations. Section 26 does not deal with all types of surveillance, such as bugging or entering property or a vehicle for the purpose of placing surveillance equipment in order to gather information; those types of investigations are covered by other legislation, *e.g.* the Police Act 1997, the Intelligence Services Act 1994 and so forth. Section 26 is concerned with three specific areas of surveillance known as (i) directed surveillance; (ii) intrusive surveillance; and (iii) the conduct and use of human intelligence sources, *e.g.* informants and undercover personnel irrespective of whether or not they are employed within a particular state force or service.

Directed Surveillance

Directed surveillance is covert[24] surveillance which is "undertaken (a) for the purposes of a specific investigation or a specific operation; (b) in such a manner as is likely to result in the obtaining of private information[25] about a person; and (c) otherwise than by way of an immediate response to events or circumstances the nature of which is such that it would not be reasonably practicable for an authorisation under this Part to be sought for the carrying out of the surveillance" (section 26(2)). Directed surveillance also includes using equipment for providing information regarding the whereabouts of a vehicle, or events taking place on residential premises, but not used on the premises or in the vehicle itself. However, if the device is such that it consistently provides information of the same quality and detail as might be expected to be obtained from a device actually present on the premises or in the vehicle, then such surveillance is considered to be intrusive (section 26(4) and (5)).[26] **8–060**

Intrusive Surveillance

Intrusive surveillance is covert surveillance which "is carried out on any residential premises or in any private vehicle; and involves the presence of an individual on the premises or in the vehicle or is carried out by means of a surveillance device" (section 26(3)). Surveillance specifically carried out from outside any premises for the purpose of detecting a television receiver does not come within the meaning of directed or intrusive surveillance (section 26(6)). **8–061**

Covert Human Intelligence Sources

The meaning of a "covert human intelligence source" is set out in section 26(8)(a)–(c) and is where there exists a relationship for the purpose of obtaining information or providing access to any information to another person, or as a result of that relationship he covertly discloses information obtained. The remaining sections *i.e.* 27–48 of Part II concern the circumstances surrounding the lawful authorisation of surveillance and the use of human intelligence sources, including persons entitled to grant such authorisations; the rules relating to granting authorisations; their duration, extension, modification and renewals periods. **8–062**

Authorisation for directed surveillance and the use of human intelligence sources.

8–063 Of vital importance to any surveillance operation are the persons who ultimately make the decision on whether or not to grant authorisation. Under section 30 in relation to directed surveillance and human intelligence sources, the persons designated to make such decisions are "individuals holding such offices, ranks or positions with relevant public authorities as are prescribed for the purposes of this subsection by an order under this section" (section 30(1)). Those public authorities include the police and customs, the army, the intelligence and security services and any others designated by the Secretary of State.[27] However, prior to any authorisation being granted, the grantor must be satisfied that the authorisation was necessary and the surveillance proportionate for the particular purpose pursued. With regard to directed surveillance, under section 28(3) authorisation will only be granted where it is considered necessary certain specified grounds, including in the interests of national security; for the purpose of preventing or detecting crime or preventing disorder; in the interests of public safety; for the purpose of protecting public health; for the purpose of collecting or assessing various taxes; or for any other purpose set out in an order by the Secretary of State (section 28(3)(a)–(g)) and approved by both Houses of Parliament (section 28(5)). The authorisation conditions for directed surveillance are similar to those for covert intelligence sources under section 29, save principally that in the latter case the relevant investigating authority has certain obligations towards the source, including day-to-day responsibility for his security, welfare and supervision, maintaining a record of the sources activities and protecting the identity of the source from unnecessary disclosure (section 29(5)).

Authorisation for intrusive surveillance

8–064 The granting of authorisation for intrusive surveillance is more stringent than for directed surveillance or the use of human intelligence sources. Under section 32(1) only the Secretary of State and senior authorising officers have the power to grant authorisation for the carrying out of intrusive surveillance. "Senior authorising officers" includes chief constables of every police force in England and Wales, but outside London; the Commissioner of Police for the City of London; the Provost Marshal of the Royal Navy or Air Force Police; The Director General of the National Criminal Intelligence Service and so forth.[28] However, with regard to other state authorities, such as the intelligence services, the Ministry of Defence and Her Majesty's forces, intrusive surveillance authorisation (or in some cases the issuing of a warrant)[29] may only be granted by the Secretary of State and then only if in the interest of national security or for preventing or detecting serious crime (section 41)). As with directed surveillance and the use of sources the "necessary" and "proportionate" factors are also a requirement here before authorisation will be granted (section 32(2)). However, the "necessary" grounds are confined to, in the interests of national security or the economic well-being of the country, or for the purpose of preventing or detecting serious crime (section 32(3)). Where the operation involves a combination of directed surveillance or the use of covert sources and intrusive surveillance, then authorisation must be granted by the Secretary of State.

Police and Customs Authorisations

The Act also divides those state authorities which may apply for surveillance authorisation into two wide groups—"police and customs authorisations", which includes the National Criminal Intelligence Service, the National Crime Squad and Customs and Excise (sections 33–40) and "other authorisations" (sections 41–42). With regard to police and customs applications, the appropriate senior authorising officer designated to be so under sections 28 or 29 has the power to grant or refuse authorisation. Where the application concerns section 32, *i.e.* intrusive surveillance, and the matter is urgent, and it is not reasonably practicable in these circumstances to seek authorisation by a senior authorising officer or his designated deputy, then the authorisation may be considered by a person entitled to act on behalf of a designated person (section 34(1)–(3), *e.g.* a person holding the rank of assistant chief constable of a police force, or a person entitled to act for the Director General of the National Crime Squad if he is designated to do so by the Director General in an urgent case and so forth.[30] In the case of intrusive surveillance, where authorisation has been granted, cancelled or renewed to the police or customs by a person, that person must give written notice to a Surveillance Commissioner that he done so (section 35), who in turn will scrutinise the authorisation and decide whether or not to approve the authorisation. A Surveillance Commissioner shall only give his approval if he is satisfied that there are reasonable grounds for believing that the authorisation was necessary and proportionate to the legitimate aim pursued. If not, then he may quash, cancel or refuse to renew the authorisation (section 37(2)) and may order the destruction of any records, if not required for pending criminal or civil proceedings (section 37(5) and (7)). Any person with the power to grant authorisation may appeal against an order for intrusive surveillance by a Surveillance Commissioner to the Chief Surveillance Commissioner (section 38). The Chief Surveillance Commissioner will allow the appeal if he satisfied that (i) the "necessary" and "proportionate" requirements set out in section 32(a) and (b) have been met; and (ii) that the case was one of urgency (section 38(4)). Instead of quashing or cancelling the authorisation, the Chief Surveillance Commissioner may decide to modify the Surveillance Commissioner's order that he deems more appropriate in the circumstances (section 38(5)). **8–065**

Other Authorisations

8–066 Under sections 41 and 42, the granting of intrusive surveillance authorisations in this category refer to state authorities of a more specialised nature, for instance, the intelligence services, made up of the Secret Intelligence Service, GCHQ and the Security Service; officials of the Ministry of Defence and members of Her Majesty's forces[31]: or a public authority specifically designated by order of the Secretary of State, approved by Parliament. Intrusive surveillance authorisation may only be granted by the Secretary of State and then only on the grounds of national security and for the prevention or detection of serious crime (41(1) and (3)). Under section 42(1) any application for authorisation made by a member of the intelligence services must be granted by means of the issue of a warrant by the Secretary of State.[32] A single warrant may incorporate both an authorisation for intrusive surveillance and an intelligence services warrant (section 42(2).

The Grant, Renewal and Duration of Authorisation

8–067 Section 43 deals with the regulations concerning the granting, renewal and duration of authorisations. Authorisation granted by those entitled to do so under urgent conditions shall cease after 72 hours (section 43(3)(a)). All other authorisations where the use of covert intelligent sources are involved may last up to 12 months (section 43(3)(b)). In all other circumstances (excluding section 44) the period will last for no more than three months. However, renewal may be granted prior to the cessation period. Where renewal concerns the use of a human intelligent source a review of the matters and duties undertaken by the source must be examined (section 43(6) and (7)). Under section 43 (8) the Secretary of State may order that authorisation period be cut short than originally granted.

The Tribunal

8–068 Under section 65 a tribunal is to be set up and exercises jurisdiction over the hearing of complaints or proceedings in connection with various matters. As regards proceedings, the tribunal will hear actions which are incompatible with Convention rights (section 65(2)(a)), involving matters relating to the intelligence services, or any persons acting on their behalf (section 65(3)(a)-(d); the investigatory powers under Part II or Chapter II of Part I; conduct involving the interception of communications via transmissions of a postal service or telecommunications system; or any entry or interference with property or wireless telegraphy (section 65(5)(a)-(f)). As regards complaints, an individual may complain to the tribunal if he believes that he has been subject to conduct falling within section 65(5)(a)-(f) (see above) in relation to himself, his property, communications sent by or to him, or his use of the any postal service, telecommunications service or system, and to have taken place in challengeable circumstances (section 65(4)(a) and (b)). Under section 65(7) "challengeable circumstances" means if (a) it takes place with the authority, or purported authority, of anything falling within subsection (8), *e.g.* authorisation or notice under Chapter II of Part I of RIPA or authorisation under section 93 of the Police Act 1997 or notice under section 49 of RIPA; or (b) the circumstances are that it would not have been appropriate for the conduct to take place without it; but conduct does not take place in challengeable circumstances if it is authorised by, or permission of a judicial authority. Further, any individual may complain that he has not been able to adduce evidence as a result of section 17. Section 17 places certain limitations on the evidence which shall be disclosed for the purposes connected with legal proceedings involving intercepted communications or any related communications data (section 17(1)(a) and (b)).

In relation to section 65(2)(a), *i.e.* proceedings, the tribunal shall apply the same principles for making their determination in those proceedings as would be applied by a court on an application for judicial review (section 67(2)). However, under section 65(2)(b), *i.e.* complaint, the tribunal is under a duty to fully investigate the complaint and/or authority and give their findings as if the complaint was an application for judicial review (section 67(3)) and may award compensation or other order as they think fit, including quashing, cancelling any authorisation or warrant or ordering the destruction of any records of information held (section 67(7)).

Comment

From the above brief description of the Act it can be observed that the main features of the legislation concern authorisation of interception and surveillance. The Act attempts to eliminate malpractice, misuse and mistake by those in authority who decide to investigate individuals in circumstances which would normally be considered an invasion of privacy. However, it would be wrong to assume that the Act applies to all surveillance methods. There are already in existence many forms of intrusive devices which directly interfere with an individual's privacy and which are not covered by the Act, nor do such interfering methods require high-level authority or warrants. A typical example of this form of intrusion is the now very widely used and ever-present CCTV, in continual use 24 hours a day throughout the country, monitoring and recording our every movement—well nearly! Indeed the public is so used to the cameras' existence that they have become oblivious to their existence. The introduction of the RIP does little to alleviate an already overbearing problem and if not properly controlled may even exacerbate it. There are a number of worrying aspects regarding the Act which may make it fall foul of the Convention, in particular of Articles 6 and 8. For example, it is now possible for authorisation to be granted under sections 3 and 4 without any judicial control. Unless there are sufficient safeguards in place, such **8–069** authorisation may constitute arbitrary interference by the authorities. Also, the surveillance method themselves may lack proper legal foundation. For example, although intrusive surveillance powers may be granted by chief constables in restricted areas such as national security and prevention of serious crime (s. 32(3)), and then only where it is necessary and proportionate, consideration must also be given as to whether the interference was necessary in a democratic society. This last particular hurdle may prove difficult to overcome.

One problem is of course that since the target person is unlikely to discover the presence of any surveillance device, it is unlikely that anyone will discover whether there was a breach of the provisions of the Act. Even if a person does become aware of a surveillance operation against him, his only means of redress in domestic law is via the forthcoming creation of a tribunal. Whether the detailed provisions of the Act for the establishing of such a tribunal constitute it as being impartial and unbiased is arguable. There is no appeal from the tribunal (s. 69(9)): it is restricted to only those persons who are secretly targeted; the complainant has only one year to inform the tribunal, unless the tribunal itself decides, in the interests of equity, to permit proceedings after that period (s. 67(5)). It is foreseeable that it many cases the target will only discover the existence of the surveillance long after the operation has been concluded.

As yet it is too early to determine whether the Act and its operation will in practice be reasonable measures to combat serious crime and protect the country's security interests, or whether the Act possesses serious flaws which ought to be remedied. Whilst it is no doubt necessary to have the ability to investigate in secrecy where serious crime is concerned, this form of activity must be counterbalanced by the rights of the individual to go peaceably about his private business without the fear of unreasonable and unnecessary state intrusion. Further decisions of the European Court of Human Rights along the lines of *Khan* are possible and potentially hugely politically embarrassing in light of the track record of U.K. surveillance law in Strasbourg (discussed elsewhere in this chapter).

Police Act 1997

8–070 This statute may, on first glance, appear to do little more than to restate PACE powers of entry, search and seizure and to extend the procedures for authorization of telephone tapping and surveillance which already existed under the Interception of Communications Act 1985; however it has been the source of much controversy and it remains uncertain whether the 1997 Act will survive challenges on the basis of the ECHR. As discussed above, the lack of statutory police powers of tapping, bugging and surveillance had been pointed out and criticized by the European Commission on Human Rights in the case of *Malone v. U.K.*,[33] with the result that the Interception of Communications Act 1985 was passed in order to place existing Home Office surveillance guidelines for the granting of warrants on a statutory basis. But the 1985 Act, although stating broad grounds for such warrants to be requested, requires the Home Secretary's signature on any warrant unless the situation is one of urgency, and also allows the authorisation of surveillance only where the suspect is believed to be involved in, for example, such conduct as serious crime, breaches of national security or endangering the nation's economic health. The Conservative Government felt that these procedures limited police operations too greatly, and so in Spring 1997 the then Home Secretary, Michael Howard, announced the Bill which would later become the Police Act 1997. The Bill attracted a great deal of negative publicity and comment; this was largely due to its initial lack of any requirement that surveillance warrants granted under its authority should be subject to independent supervision. Indeed, the aim of the introduction of the Bill was to avoid any such supervisory body and so to allow the police to act spontaneously and with speed whenever bugging was believed to be necessary. Obviously, an outcry erupted from sources as diverse as Liberty, the Law Society and the Catholic Church; the Bill did not originally provide sanctity of conversations between solicitor and client or in the confessional. The U.K. would have been striding away from most other European countries in this respect by having no requirement of judicial authority for surveillance warrants. As a result of the outcry, a compromise was reached and the Act was amended to require that a judge should be appointed as an independent commissioner with the role of supervising and checking the grant of some warrants, although this safeguard applies only where certain categories of crime are suspected (section 91).

In order for a warrant (or "bugging order", as they are more commonly known) to be granted under the 1997 Act, authorisation must first be sought from the Chief Officer of Police (section 93(5)) unless this is not practicable in the circumstances, in which case it may be granted by an Assistant Chief Constable of the force who seek the warrant (section 94). Authorisation should normally be in writing but may be oral if required urgently (section 95). The police must, after receiving authorisation, immediately inform the commissioner, who may quash the authorisation and require the destruction of any records relating to any search which was carried out before the authorisation was overturned, unless the records are required as evidence in either civil or criminal court proceedings which are pending. It is the latter exeception which remains the greatest cause of concern from a civil liberties perspective; a groundless search and surveillance operation may result in the admission to court of evidence obtained illegally. However, if the search or bugging is to be of a private residence, a hotel room or offices, or if the information which is hoped to be obtained via the warrant is confidential, personal, or journalistic material, or may be subject to legal privilege, then the commissioner must be consulted before the police may obtain authorisation for the warrant (section 97). Once authorisation is obtained by any of these means, it lasts for three months if the authorisation was written but only 72 hours if it was provided orally. Renewal is however possible for a further period of three months.

Protection From Harassment

8–071 There are a number of specific statutory offences which relate to privacy interests, which will now be considered.

i) Stalking

8–072 Stalking has become a high-profile type of behaviour in the 1990s' media, yet the criminal law was until recently widely considered to be weak in its prevention and punishment of persistent harassment. Unsuccessful attempts were made to criminalise stalking by means of Private Members Bill in the mid-1990s, but lack of Government support put an end to such moves. A Stalking Bill was introduced in 1996 after a consultation process and considerable pressure towards legislation, and the eventual result was the Protection From Harassment Act 1997. The 1997 Act created two new criminal offences of repeated harassment, and introduced a new form of injunction to restrain such behaviour. But before the 1997 Act was even conceived, it had become apparent that the existing criminal law was not as inept at criminalising stalking behaviour as it had been believed. In a series of important cases, the Court of Appeal and later the House of Lords used judicial creativity to expand pre-existing criminal offences to encompass stalking. Thus there is now duplication of scope of protection against harassment in the criminal law, since the 1997 Act and the "creative" case law co-exist uneasily. Each has its shortcomings, as will be seen in the discussion which follows.

We shall look at the case law first, since it is chronologically earlier than the statutory law.

In *R. v. Burstow* 95[34]:

Facts. The defendant had formed an obsession with his victim, and continued to harass her even after he had been imprisoned for burgling her house. His actions included sending her abusive letters, making silent telephone calls, stealing clothes from her washing line, scattering condoms in her garden and bugging her house. The victim suffered from severe depression and psychological damage as a result of his actions. The defendant was charged with inflicting grievous bodily harm contrary to section 20 of the Offences Against the Person Act 1861. Depression is classified as a type of grievous bodily harm. The defendant appealed against his conviction, on the basis that he had not directly caused the victim's injuries by assaulting her.

Decision. The House of Lords upheld the defendant's conviction, and held that:

(1) No direct physical contact is necessary for conviction under section 20 or related offences;
(2) Psychiatric injury may be GBH.

Thus, if the defendant's actions cause the victim so much distress that she develops an ascertainable and medically proveable condition, liability may exist under the ordinary criminal law.

In *R. v. Ireland*[35]: 8–073

Facts. The defendant made a long series of silent telephone calls to his victims, who suffered serious psychological damage as a result. He was convicted of assault occasioning actual bodily harm contrary to section 47 of the Offences Against the Person Act 1861, and appealed on the basis that he could not be convicted of an offence involving "assault" in circumstances where there was no immediacy of danger; one of the elements of assault is that the victim must be caused to fear that unlawful violence would be inflicted upon her. On the facts, the defendant was at some distance from the victim and so argued that any threat implied from the telephone calls was not immediate.

Decision. The defendant's conviction was upheld by the Court of Appeal, whose reasoning was later approved by the House of Lords. Threats, whether express or implied from silence, made by telephone are sufficiently immediate for the purposes of conviction of any assault offence, even though the defendant may be remote. It is of course possible that he could inflict violence upon the victim by use of an agent on the scene.

Thus it is now possible to convict a harasser or stalker of any of a wide range of ordinary criminal offences based on assault, battery and the causing of physical injury. It can therefore be queried whether the Protection from Harassment Act 1997 was necessary.

Criticisms of the case law

Much was made at the consultation stage of the Stalking Bill of the 8–074
difficulty in proving *mens rea* in order to convict a stalker of any kind of assault, and this may be a problem in some cases. But, when viewed from another perspective, it is equally arguable that *mens rea* should have to be proved in such cases; if a stalker truly does not realise that he is causing distress to other people and is psychologically damaging others, then surely it is preferable to refer him for mental health treatment rather than to convict him of any criminal offence. At the Consultation Paper stage of the 1997 Act, there were worrying confusions between the words "intention" and *mens rea*—it appeared that no distinction was being drawn between the two—when in fact relevant assault offences require proof only that the defendant foresaw a risk of some harm to the victim in his conduct. Thus the offences under the 1997 Act were drafted to make conviction easier than under the existing criminal law, and place the rights of the alleged victim above those of the alleged stalker, as will be seen below.

The Protection From Harassment Act 1997

The more serious of the two criminal offences created by the 1997 Act is: 8–075

> Section 4(1) "A person whose course of conduct causes another to fear, on at least two occasions, that violence will be used against him is guilty of an offence if he knows or ought to know that is course of conduct will cause the other so to fear on each of these occasions".

This offence is punishable by up to five years' imprisonment, or a fine, or both.

The offence is objective in the sense that it does not matter whether the defendant knew that his actions caused the victim to fear violence, as long as a "reasonable person in possession of the same information would think the course of conduct would cause the other so to fear" on each occasion (section 4(2)). Section 4(3) provides specific defences to the section 4 offence where the defendant can show that:

"(a) his course of conduct was pursued for the purpose of preventing or detecting crime,

(b) his course of conduct was pursued under any enactment or rule of law or to comply with any condition or requirement imposed by any person under any enactment; or

(c) the pursuit of his conduct was reasonable for the protection of himself or another or for the protection of his or another's property."

So, police and other law enforcement agencies, and ordinary citizens asserting self-defence, will have defences to the more serious offence. The less serious offence is to be found in sections 1 and 2:

> Section 1(1) "A person must not pursue a course of conduct—
>
> (a) which amounts to harassment of another; and
> (b) which he knows or ought to know amounts to harassment of another.
>
> (2) For the purposes of this section, the person whose course of conduct is in question ought to know that it amounts to harassment of another if a reasonable person in possession of the same information would think the course of conduct amounted to harassment of the other".

Thus this offence is again assessed objectively. "Harassment" includes alarm and distress (section 792)). The maximum sentence for a section 2 offence is six months' imprisonment, or a fine, or both. The defences available to a section 2 charge differ slightly from those of the more serious offence, and are as follows: (Section 3(1)) It is not harassment if the person committing the course of conduct can show:

"(a) that it was pursued for the purpose of preventing or detecting crime;

(b) that it was pursued under any enactment or rule of law or to comply with any condition or requirement imposed by any person under any enactment; or

(c) that in the particular circumstances the pursuit of the course of conduct was reasonable."

The last defence opens an opportunity for the media, particularly "doorsteppers", to argue that their harassment of a victim was reasonable in the circumstances due to the public interest in the particular story and to their pursuit of a lawful career. This may remove much of the potential privacy protection of the section 2 offence.

In addition to these criminal offences, section 3 recognises a civil remedy for harassment as defined in section 1. Damages may be awarded for the victim's suffering and for any financial loss; and a victim of an actual or apprehended offence under either section 2 or section 4 may also obtain an injunction to prevent any further such offences (section 5). Breach of this injunction is a criminal offence in itself and is punishable by up to five years' imprisonment, a fine, or both.

Criticism of the 1997 Act

Some of the main objections to the 1997 Act will now be summarised. First, **8–076** the offences take much of their wording from public order offences, but operate in the same field as substantive criminal law assault offences. There is a possibility of greatly different sentences being imposed for identical behaviour if one case is dealt with under the 1997 Act and another under the prior criminal law. The sentences under the Act are much higher then those incomparable offences, and there is the potential of a prison sentence being imposed upon a defendant who has not been shown to have caused any actual harm to the victim, but merely appears likely to do so. There is no requirement for any *mens rea* to be proved in the defendant because the tests used are objective, and so a stalker with mental health problems (as is often the case) may be unfairly convicted. Although the 1997 Act draws heavily on offences under the Public Order Act 1986 and the Criminal Justice and Public Order Act 1994, those offences have lesser sentences unless *mens rea* can be shown. The new injunctions under the 1997 have potentially far-reaching implications since they may be open to challenge for breach of the ECHR; in common with the "neighbour nuisance" penalties and injunctions to be enacted by the Crime and Disorder Act 1998, the injunctions impose criminal sanctions for civil actions and so infringe civil liberties. The defences to the 1997 Act exclude from conviction many of those who in fact cause the most harassment (including journalists and doorsteppers) and this may not be justifiable. Finally, the overall result of the legislation is a situation of confusion and excessive plurality of remedies and actions which lack consistency of principle, sentencing or procedure.

Under section 44 of the Criminal Justice and Police Act 2001, section 7 of the Protection from Harassment Act 1977 Act has been amended to provide for "collective harassment", such that conduct by one person shall also be taken to be the conduct by another, if aided, abetted, counselled or procured by that other. Further, the knowledge and purpose of that other's conduct relates to what was contemplated or reasonably foreseeable at the time of their involvement (section 44(1)(a) and (b): now section 3A of the 1977 Act).

Protection from Journalists Revealing Sources—Section 10 Contempt of Court Act 1981

8–077 There is little doubt that information given by an informant to a journalist represents an important supply of valuable material to aid the investigation into matters of public concern, which might otherwise remain hidden: "The law and the courts have long recognised that there is public interest in newspapers being able to obtain and publish information which in some circumstances overrides the public interest in confidentiality".

Prior to the enactment of section 10 Contempt of Court Act 1981, a journalist's confidential sources were generally treated no differently in the eyes of the law from any other person who refused under oath to answer questions regarding the name of a "source". However, section 10 states:

> "No court may require a person to disclose, nor is any person guilty of contempt of court for refusing to disclose, the source of information contained in a publication for which he is responsible, unless it be established to the satisfaction of the court that disclosure is necessary in the interest of justice or national security or for the prevention of disorder or crime".

The section is restricted to "publications" as defined in section 2(1). However, it is not necessary for the publication to have already taken place, it is enough if the article is due to be published shortly. A court order under this section is not confined, as it may first appear, to only ordering the identity of the source, but includes disclosure of all information, written documents, tapes, photographs, etc., which might lead to the discovery of the name of the informant.[36] The burden of proof lies with the party seeking identification. However, before the court will make an order to that effect, the naming of the person must be relevant to the issues in the actual legal proceedings.

The meaning of section 10 is that journalist's sources ought to be protected from revealing their "insider" information to the court, but there are four exceptions to this which will be examined below.

The meaning of the word "necessary"

8–078 Whether a judge deems disclosure necessary is a question of fact, based on the seriousness of the damaged caused to the party who suffers from its dissemination. Evidence must show why, on a balance of probabilities, it is necessary for the court to order disclosure; it is not enough that it is merely convenient or suitable; it must be "really needed".[37] In *Re an Inquiry under the Company Securities (Insider Dealing) Act 1985*,[37A] it was stated that "necessity is a relative concept and the damage of need before an act or measure can be said to be necessary, although not clear, is a question which is to be answered without reference to some objective standards, must in the end, be and remain a matter of judgement". Lord Bridge in *X Ltd v. Morgan-Grampian Ltd*,[38] said that where the above statement pertains to national security or prevention of crime, being so serious, then the necessity of disclosure "follows almost automatically". However, even here, although disclosure would almost certainly be ordered in the case of national security, Lord Griffith in *Re an Inquiry, etc.* left the door somewhat ajar when he said that a judge still might refuse a disclosure order if, regarding the prevention of crime, the crime was of a "trivial nature", or the journalist's life is threatened or in serious danger through divulging the informant's name.[39]

The meaning of "in the interest of justice"

This exception, in relation to the qualified immunity of disclosure of a source, centres around the damage done to the party whose information has been divulged. The injured party is entitled to protect himself from "serious legal wrongs", *i.e.* the unauthorised revealing of confidential information, by ordering the journalist to reveal the identity of the informant. Lord Bridge in *X. Ltd v. Morgan-Grampian Ltd*,[40] gave the example of a disloyal employee who reveals information to an outsider. If the employer suffers "grave damage" as a consequence, it would be in the interest of justice that he be able to identify the employee, in order to dismiss him, despite no legal action being taken against that employee. It is a question of balance in that the judge should only order disclosure if the activity is of "such preponderating importance" that it takes precedence over the general rule of non-disclosure. It is a question of fact, taking into account such material considerations as: **8–079**

(1) Whether his very livelihood depends on it. However, if only a minor inconvenience, then probably no disclosure would be warranted.

(2) The nature of the information; thus, the greater the legitimate public interest in the information revealed, generally the greater will be the importance of protecting the source.

(3) How did the informant acquire the information?

    (a) If acquired legally, then there is a greater likelihood that the source's identity will be protected.
    (b) If taken without authority, then the likelihood would be in favour of disclosure being ordered.[41]

In 3(b) above, no matter how the information was acquired, if there was a legitimate public interest in revealing an iniquity by the source, then the argument for disclosure of his identity is undermined, unless the crime was of such minor importance that the balance may still lie in disclosure. The above criteria was applied in the case of *X Ltd v. Morgan-Grampian Ltd*[42]:

Facts. The plaintiffs (two companies) wished to re-finance their business through prospective lenders. They prepared a confidential document setting out their business proposals. A copy of the document was left unattended in their office. That copy reached G, a journalist, through an informant. The informant was interviewed by G, who made notes of the conversation which was later to be used in an article published in *The Engineer* journal. The plaintiffs applied for an injunction restraining publication and also sought an order for the disclosure of G's notes in the interests of justice in order that the plaintiffs could possibly identify the source. The order was granted but G refused to hand over the notes and was found to be in contempt of court. The defendant appealed.

Decision in the Court of Appeal. Lord Donaldson referred to whether or not the court should order disclosure as a "balancing exercise", *i.e.* "balance" between the public interest in maintaining the secrecy of the source's identity or whether disclosure is necessary in the interests of justice:

> "In achieving the balance, the court will no doubt take account of the degree of confidentiality which attached to the information, the seriousness of the consequences of any actual or further apprehended breach of that confidentiality in terms of the doorway through which he has passed, (i.e. one of the four exceptions) and, without prejudice to other factors which may be relevant in particular cases, the degree of true public interest in what is or may be disclosed in terms of the revelation of 'iniquity' and so on",[43]

always, of course, bearing in mind that the general rule is that of against revealing the identity of the source. The exceptions in this case were in the interest of justice and prevention of crime. The court considered the re-finance document of such importance because of the potential jeopardy to people's jobs, the company's international reputation and the possible liquidation of the company itself, that the administration of justice is better served by ordering G to identify his source. Here, the public interest lay in ordering disclosure but in some similar situation, the public interest might result in protecting the informant's name, if, for instance, some serious misconduct prejudicial to the interest of the company was perpetrated by its directors. No such iniquity was involved in this case. Further, no legitimate pubic interest was concerned here such that the public interest lay in confidentiality. The more important the source's disclosure, such that it will have a detrimental effect on the company, the more likely the court is to order disclosure. The court ordered that G hand over the notes in a sealed envelope to the court, to be either opened if G lost his appeal or to be returned to him if the appeal was allowed. This he refused to comply with. Thereupon, the defendants appealed to the House of Lords.

Decision in the House of Lords. The House of Lords found that the plaintiff's business was likely to suffer very serious financial damage, as well as the strong possibility of many of the employees losing their jobs, if disclosure of the informants name was withheld. By the theft of the document, the argument for protecting the source's identity was seriously undermined and not "counterbalanced by any legitimate interest which publication of the information was calculated to serve".[44] Accordingly, the appeal was dismissed.

Prevention of crime

8–080 In *Re an Inquiry under the Company Securities (Insider Dealings) Act 1985*,[45] the respondent, a journalist, published two articles regarding the future take-over of various companies and insider-dealing. Inspectors were appointed by the Secretary of State for Trade and Industry to discover who informed the journalist of these activities. The inspectors could not be more specific on who or what precise deals were involved. On a narrow interpretation of the words "prevention of crime", the evidence was rather scant in that the inspectors could not point directly to any particular deals which the source informed the journalists about. On a broad interpretation of the words, the inspectors were trying to prevent widespread insider dealing through leaks received from various governmental departments. The journalist's information regarding his informant was vital to the inspectors' investigation. It was doubted whether even disclosing that source would completely stifle future insider-dealing. Nevertheless, the name of the informant was considered necessary to prosecute the person(s) involved and to prevent crime in general in this area, or at least assist in diminishing and discouraging future criminal activities. The journalist continually refused to reveal his source and was fined £20,000.

National Security

One of the reasons why disclosure is more likely to be ordered, under the **8–081** exception of national security, is the fear that future leaks may endanger the security of the nation and therefore it is of the utmost importance that the informant be exposed. For instance, in *Secretary of State for Defence v. Ltd*,[46] a civil servant leaked some documents to *The Guardian* concerning the deployment of nuclear missiles at Greenham Common. The Secretary of State wanted the documents themselves, not for their intrinsic value, but as a means of discovering the name of the informer. The main question for the court was whether the disclosure was necessary in the interests of national security. Despite one of the stolen copied documents having the classification "Secret", there was nothing in it to suggest that its unauthorised disclosure would imperil national security. Nevertheless, there was a fear that if the "insider" source could not be identified, future information might be leaked which could damage national security. Further, foreign allies might be very hesitant in trusting Britain with any highly classified information if there remained an undiscovered "mole" within British intelligence. By a three to two majority, the appeal was dismissed. The majority held that where a document is classified, *e.g.* "top secret", "confidential", "secret," etc., and related closely to the defences of this country, then despite not specifically mentioning the words "national security", it may still come within the meaning of those words and therefore constitute a possible deception to a journalist's liberty to protect his sources.[47] Lord Fraser (minority) stated that the evidential requirement had not been met by the Crown. He said that the court must be satisfied that disclosure is "necessary", *e.g.* that inquiries had already been made by the proper authorities as to the identification of the informant, but not evidence was submitted to that fact.[48] Nor, it seems, was the matter considered urgent, in order to prevent further interests being disclosed. But no evidence was adduced of this. Indeed, the opposite was the case. Some 12 days had elapsed between publication and the request for handling over the documents. Thus, in the absence of proper evidence and without diluting the word "necessary", he disagreed with the majority of their Lordships.

8–082 In *Ashworth Hospital Authority v. MGN Ltd*[49]:

Facts. A hospital employee, in breach of confidence and in breach of contract, supplied certain medical information held on a database about the convicted murderer, Ian Brady, to an intermediary. The intermediary passed the information onto a journalist with *The Mirror* newspaper, who published various extracts from it. The hospital applied for a court order requiring, *inter alia*, the defendants to deliver up all the data and extracts in their possession, to stop further publication and to disclose the names of the informants under section 10 of the Contempt of Court Act 1981. Rougier J. granted the order on the grounds that the unauthorised disclosure created a highly detrimental impact on the security and morale of the staff, and that there was a risk of further disclosures if the particular employee was not identified.

Decision. The defendants appealed, *inter alia*, on the grounds that the order was in violation of Article 10 of the ECHR. Since this case was brought after the Human Rights Act 1998 came into force, the court of Appeal went on to consider whether section 10 of the Contempt of Court Act 1981 was compatible with Article 10 of the ECHR, under sections 2 and 3 of the Human Rights Act 1998. The court had also to consider whether the order to reveal the source was "necessary in a democratic society", when considering the legitimate aims specified in Article 10. The court stated that "the approach to the interpretation of section 10 should, in so far as possible: (1) equate the specific purposes for which disclosure of sources is permitted under section 10 with legitimate aims under Article 10; (2) apply the same test of necessity to that applied by the European Court when considering Article 10" (at para. 78). It was noted by Lord Phillips M.R. that the hospital could argue in its claim for disclosure of the source that "in the interests of justice", as far as this case was concerned, meant 'for the protection of health, the protection of rights of others and preventing the disclosure of information received in confidence (at para. 84).

The court then turned their attention to the "necessary" requirement and in particular considered the "pressing social need" and "proportionate" corresponding elements in deciding whether in the interests of justice the public interest in disclosure outweighed the public interest in protecting the identity of the journalist' sources. When considering this aspect of the proceedings, the court referred to a number of hitherto U.K. and ECHR decided cases, and stated that in this case, "until the source is identified and dismissed, there must be a significant risk that his or her venality will lead to the sale of further confidential information" (at para. 93). The court readily accepted that the decisions of the European Court demonstrated that the freedom of the press has in the past carried greater weight in Strasbourg than it has in the courts of this country (at para. 97). Nevertheless, the Master of the Rolls concluded that:

"the disclosure of confidential medical records to the press is misconduct which is not merely of concern to the individual establishment in which it

> occurs. It is an attack on an area of confidentiality which should be safeguarded in any democratic society. The protection of patient information is of vital concern to the National Health Service and, I suspect, to Health Services throughout Europe. This is an exceptional case. If the order made by Rougier J. discourages press sources from disclosing similar information in the future, this will be no bad thing" (at para. 99).

Accordingly, the appeal was dismissed.

There is no doubt that the press should not have unqualified freedom from publishing information acquired through an employee or intermediary source. *Ashworth* is testament to the situation that any publication of medical information received in breach of confidence will not be tolerated by the courts, unless the information contains some wrong-doing on the part of the public authorities, and not merely for monetary gain. The negative effect of this for the future may be that where a state authority does commit some infraction it is less likely to be discovered if there is the ever-present fear that the informant's identity will be ultimately revealed. Further, in the absence of theft or other criminal activity, the courts may be more reluctant to order disclosure of a source where the informant is an employee of a business as distinct from a public authority. As a consequence, where a company suffers grave damage as a result of the publication, then in the interests of justice, the domestic courts are more likely to order disclosure of a source's name than the European Court of Human Rights.[50] **8–083**

Contempt of Court Act Section 11—Exceptions to "Open Court" Proceedings

Court proceedings in general, should be open to members of the public and the press. The purpose behind open justice is that the public ought to be encouraged to take an interest, as well as an understanding and appreciation of the legal proceedings in practice. Hopefully, society as a whole would benefit from such comprehension, as well as acting as a deterrent to those thinking of indulging in any criminal activity. Therefore, all relevant information, the names an addresses of witnesses, as well as defendants, should normally be known in open court. However, there are rare instances where the entire proceedings are held *in camera*. There are also statutory exceptions to "open court" proceedings. For instance, section 4 of the Sexual Offences (Amendment) Act 1976 states that the name, address or photo of the victim of a rape offence shall not be published. Other types of information which may be repressed on a judge's order include, the withholding of a witness's name and/or address; matters involving national security; written messages of details for the court's eyes only; protecting the privacy of children,[51] etc. **8–084**

In *R. v. Central Independent Television plc*[52]:

Facts. The father of S, a five year old child, had been convicted of indecency involving four young boys. Central TV was about to broadcast a programme which included the father, a paedophile. His estranged wife, R, sought an injunction against the showing of the programme on the grounds that people would recognise the father and, if not obscured, would associated him with R, and consequently with S, who would suffer serious harm as a result of the identification. The judge ordered that if the programme was to go ahead, the face of the father must be blocked out. The respondents refused. The judge granted the injunction (originally the TV company agreed not to broadcast R's and S's names or addresses or the fact that the father had a family). The respondents appealed.

Decision. Although the court held that there are statutory laws which protect information and identification involving children in court proceedings (section 12(1)(a) of the Administration of Justice Act 1960), it is the proceedings themselves which are to be protected. If any information relates wholly to the child and not the proceedings, that will not necessarily be protected, since no privacy exists for child or adult alike. But protection may be given to cases where the court itself has already been entrusted with a legal responsibility in the care and upbringing towards the child,[53] *e.g.* where a child has been made a ward of court. In this case, the father's conviction was not a relevant factor to the care and upbringing of the child. If the opposite was the position, Hoffman L.J. said, "it would be exercised to restrain the identification of any convicted criminal who has young children".[54] This was not a situation where the interest of privacy of the child was to be balanced against the freedom of the press, since no right to privacy exists.[55] The Appeal was allowed, permitting the full report to be transmitted.

8–085 Under section 11:

> In any case where a court (having a power to do so) allows a name or other matter to be withheld from the pubic in proceedings before the court, the court may give such directions prohibiting the publication of that name or matter in connection with the proceedings as appear to the court to be necessary for the purpose for which it was so withheld.

The whole purpose of section 11 is based on the exceptions to the "open justice" principles. Where the court possesses a power to make such orders which derogate from the normal open court principles, it should only do so if it appears that the due administration of justice will seriously suffer or be unworkable unless some form of action is taken to avert this. This will depend on the damage likely to be done; a fact to be determined by the court after having taken account of all the material circumstances of the particular case. Prior to the Contempt of Court Act, the common law dealt quite effectively within this area and still remains relevant to those decisions taken today. For instance, in *Att.-Gen. v. Leveller Magazine Ltd*[56]:

Facts. During committal proceedings at a Magistrates' Court against two journalists for offences under the Official Secret Act, the prosecution called a witness "Colonel B"; his true identity to be kept secret on the grounds of national security. His real name was initially only divulged to the court, the defendants and their counsel. He gave evidence that his appointment to his present army unit was published in the *Wire Magazine*. Subsequently, through reading the magazine, his true identity was published elsewhere by some journalists. The Attorney General brought proceedings for contempt of court against the defendants, alleging that the magistrates had expressly prohibited Colonel B's identity being exposed. This was denied by the clerk of the court and the hearing went ahead on that basis. The defendants were found to be in contempt and appealed.

Decision. Lord Diplock said:

> ". . . where a court in the exercise of its inherent power to control the conduct of proceedings before it departs in any way from the general rule, (*i.e.* open justice), the departure is justified to the extent and to no more than the extent that the court reasonably believes it to be necessary in order to serve the ends of justice".[57]

However, a court could decide that they will deviate from open justice where it is necessary in the interests of the due administration of justice to do so, *e.g.* by expressly prohibiting a witness's name to be published. Any person who knows of the decision and who tries to frustrate a direction of the court by, for instance, publishing that name, is in contempt of court, as interfering with the administration of justice.[58] Here, no such direction was given and therefore the appeal was allowed.

However, even where no direction is given for the press, for instance, to withhold publication, there may still be contempt if they know that by publishing the name it would probably interfere with the administration of justice. There are certain rudimentary and obvious situations where, in the absence of any direction, it could be inferred, without too much difficulty, that a person knew that to publish would be obstructing the administration of justice, and therefore be in contempt. The direction or order by the court must be clear and precise. Any ambiguity may make the direction by the judge unenforceable. For example if the judge merely "requests" that a journalist refrain from publishing the proceedings, it would appear that if the publication went ahead, the parties responsible would not be in contempt of court, at least not on those grounds.[59]

In Camera Proceedings

It is one matter giving a court the inherent power to prohibit the identity of **8–086**
a defendant's name or address being published, it is, however, quite a big step to grant the court the power to authorise them to allow a trial to be held *in camera*. If such were the norm, the principles of open justice and the freedom to report the proceedings would be greatly undermined in any democratic society. In *R. v. Malvern Justices, ex parte Evans*,[60] the defendant, a woman, pleaded guilty on a drunk-driving charge and requested that her plea in mitigation be held *in camera*; her reasons being that she was very distraught and embarrassed in having to reveal, in public, very personal details about her failed marriage and private medical history. The magistrates acceded to her request and members of the public, which included a journalist, were ordered to leave. The sentence was later given in open court. The journalist and the publishers of the newspaper sought judicial review on the grounds that the magistrates had erred in law, arguing that, there were not legitimate exceptional grounds for departing from the open

court principles and no reasonable tribunal in the circumstance would have agreed to the defendant's request. The question for the court was whether the magistrates had the power to sit *in camera*. Watkin L.J. cited Viscount Reading C.J. In *R. v. Governor of Lewes Prison, ex parte Doyle*[61] who stated that:

> ". . . where the administration of justice would be rendered impracticable by the presence of the public, whether because of the case could not be effectively tried or the parties entitled to justice would be reasonably deterred from seeking it at the hand of the court, the court has the power to exclude the public".[62]

Therefore, the application was dismissed. However, mere inconvenience or embarrassment is not enough to produce an *in camera* order, there must be such forceful reasons that no other course exists. Such occasions would be quite exceptional. Indeed, in the above case, Watkin L.J. said, he questioned the magistrates' decision in that case, whose reasons, he said, seemed "wholly unsustainable and out of accord with principles".[63] Further, any application for an order that the trial be held *in camera* must itself be made *in camera*, otherwise, the whole purpose would be redundant since the disclosures would be heard by all those in open court.[64]

Withholding the Name or Address of the Defendant

8–087 There are instances where the court will permit the writing down of names, addresses and other details which will only be disclosed to the judge, the prosecution, the defendant and his counsel. But, the power should not be used simply to protect privacy or avoid embarrassment.[65] In *R. v. Evesham J.J., ex parte McDonagh*,[66] the defendant, a former M.P., was convicted of driving his car without a proper MOT certificate. He applied for an order requesting that his address not be divulged in court, since he feared being harassed by his former wife, against whom he had an injunction preventing her from molesting him. The order was granted. In the Divisional Court, it was decided that this issue did not concern the due administration of justice but rather that the magistrates felt sympathy for the defendant's predicament. It was stated that "section 11 was not enacted for the benefit of the comfort and feelings of defendants".[67] Therefore, the open court principles should be maintained and his address disclosed to the court.

Withholding the Name of a Witness

8–088 The withholding of a person's name and address has been extended to witnesses appearing in court. For instance, in *R. v. Central Criminal Court, ex parte Crook*,[68] where the court allowed the principal witness, who was also the victim, in a case involving kidnapping and unlawful sexual intercourse, to withhold her name and address in court and not to have them published outside the court. The applicant sought judicial review. This was rejected on non-jurisdictional grounds, but it was said obiter, that such non-disclosure practice should be strictly limited and that, "It was part of the essential nature of British criminal justice that cases should be tried in public and that consideration must outweigh the individual interests of particular persons" (*per* Lord Justice Stephen). However, it is arguable that, on public policy grounds, witnesses should be treated differently from defendants. If some anonymity were not given to witnesses, then indirectly the administration of justice may be seriously interfered with, since potential witnesses would be reluctant to come forward and testify for fear of some form of retribution or harassment following the publication of those personal details.[69]

Although it has long been the practice that witnesses should reveal their addresses in open court, there does not seem to be a fundamental or purposeful reason why this should be so, unless the address is relevant to the actual proceedings or there is some doubt as to the witness's abode, or another reason which makes the address material to that person's evidence.[70]

Protection is already given to witnesses in blackmail cases, where the very nature of the offence is that the witness, usually the victim, requires anonymity. If subsequently that witness realises that his identity will be revealed, he may decide to recant and not give evidence. This, of course, will affect future trials of this nature and frustrate the police and prevent criminals from being brought to trial. In *R. v. Socialist Worker, ex parte Att.-Gen.*,[71] a judge ordered that two prosecution witnesses in a blackmail trial, only be referred to as X and Y. During the trial, the *Socialist Worker* newspaper published the real names of X and Y. As a result, the Attorney-General made an application for contempt of court against the publishers. The respondents were found guilty on the grounds that the publication itself was made "in defiance of the judge's direction" and was a "blatant affront to the authority of the court". The respondents argued that there was no express prohibition from writing their names in the press. But, the court said, that was not the main issue. The main contention was that there was a total disregard for the administration of justice, in that by publishing the witnesses' names, it made the directions given by the judge at the trial meaningless, and was detrimental to future blackmail witnesses by making such people fear of giving evidence in future trials, if the court would not protect their identity and prevent publication.

Defendant Should be Able to Confront his Accuser

For justice to be seen to be done, the defendant is entitled to see a witness, **8–089**
especially his accuser, giving evidence against him. Notwithstanding that, there may exist exceptional circumstances whereby a prosecution witness's full identity should be withheld. For instance, the courts may adopt a method of screening in order to protect a witness, usually the victim, when giving evidence, from having to directly confront the defendant, though the

defendant may see the witness via a video monitor. A judge should consider very carefully the following factors before using his discretion:

(1) Was there a real likelihood that if the witness gave evidence either he or his family would suffer harm?

(2) The evidence must be sufficiently relevant and important to make it unfair to make the Crown proceed without it.

(3) The court must be satisfied that there could be no undue prejudice to the accused.

(4) The court should balance the need for protection of the evidence against unfairness, presumably to the accused.

(5) The Crown must satisfy the court that the credit worthiness of the witness has been fully investigated.[72]

Privacy and the Press

8–090 Sixty years ago, the only remedy available to the general public against press intrusion into an individual's private life was by an already existing legal redress, assuming there was one, through the courts—a long and expensive procedure. Since no right of privacy exits in this country, the media were left to their own judgement and devices to decide whether it was in the public interest that the public had a right to know certain private details about some individual. Such was the press industry's pre-occupation with the freedom of speech, that it was in their own interest that legal restraints through legislation should be avoided at all cost. On the other hand, the standard of press reporting was felt by the public and politicians alike to be deteriorating and some form of action needed to be taken. A Royal Commission of the Press was set up to investigate into the problem, and reported in 1949 with its recommendations. As a result, the General Council of the Press was established in 1953, made up wholly of press membership (26 in total), to curb irresponsible journalism and introduce a code to bind the press's behaviour; but it was, in reality, ineffectual. A second Royal Commission in 1962 recommended introducing legislation to deal with the ever-mounting problem. The press took this threat very seriously, but were given one last chance at self-regulation with the establishment of the Press Council in 1964. But this particular organisation also, initially at least, proved inadequate, due partly to not commanding the respect of the press industry itself.

In 1972 the Younger Committee was set up in order to examine the progress of the Press Council and made various proposals to improve its overall effectiveness. In 1976 the Press Council published the "Press Council Declaration of Principle on Privacy" to "uphold the right of individuals to be protected against unwarranted intrusion into their private lives or affairs". The main theme running throughout the declaration was the justification of publication into the private lives of individuals, provided it is for legitimate public interest. The words "public interest" were not precisely defined except that it was "not only prurient or morbid curiosity" and that intrusion was justified "when the circumstances relating to the private life of an individual accompanying a public position may be likely to affect the performance of his duties or public confidence in him or his office". The findings of a third Royal Commission in 1977 were that the Press Council did not adequately satisfy the purpose for which it was established and recommended improvements under the threat, once again, of a statutory Press Council being enacted. The Press Council was made up of 18 lay members, 18 press representatives and an independent chairperson. It was independent and self regulatory. Improvements were made to the composition of its membership and complaints procedure, and a Complaints Committee was introduced to adjudicate over grievances with the public (in the absence of legal representation). However, the response to complaints by the public were ineffective, unsatisfactory to say the least, and often too little, too late. The procedure was slow and beaurocratic, and since compensation could not be awarded, many cases were either abandoned, delayed or left the aggrieved wholly frustrated.

The lethargy, or worse, partisan, adjudications of the Press Council led in 1990 to the Report of the Committee on Privacy and Related Matters ("Calcutt Report") to investigate into the declining press standards regarding the intrusion and protection of privacy and to improve recourse against the press. The report recommended that "the press should be given one final chance to prove that voluntary self-regulation can be made to work" (para. 14.38). They recommended that the present Press Council be disbanded and a new self-regulatory body to take its place to be called the "Press Complains Commission". This new body was to "publish, monitor and implement a comprehensive code of practice for the guidance of both the press and the public (para. 15.7). The report made various recommendations which included:

(1) An effective means of redress for complains against the press (para. 15.3).

(2) To consider complaints relating to unfair treatment by the press. These should be widely published (para. 15.4).

(3) Publish a code of practice for the guidance of both the press and public (para. 15.7).

(4) A "hot-line" to be introduced to prevent improper reports about an individual, prior to publication (para. 15.11).

(5) The composition of the commission to consist of 12 members and 1 chairperson, with subcommittees.

(6) The PCC must be adequately self-financed by the press industry themselves.

The Report further recommended that the following "physical intrusions" to constitute criminal offences:

(a) Entering private property or placing a surveillance device on private property, without consent, with intent to obtain personal information, for publication.

(b) Taking photographs of individuals on private property, for publication, with intent that the individual shall be identifiable (para. 6.33).

But there would be certain public interest defences to (a) and (b) above, if the act was done for the purpose of:

(i) preventing, detecting or exposing the commission of any crime, or other serious anti-social conduct; or

(ii) for the protection of health and safety; or

(iii) under any lawful authority (para. 6.35).

8–091 In January 1991, the Press Complaints Commission was established. In 1993 Sir David Calcutt published the "Review of Press Self-regulation" which examined the intervening progress of the newly formed PCC, as well as considering better protection from physical intrusion, and the possibility of a new statutory tort of infringement of privacy (para. 1.7). The conclusion of the Review was a scathing attack on the PCC for its lack of effectiveness and partisan attitude when dealing with matters between the press and the public. The Review said that the PCC was not an independent body (as it should be) and did not command the confidence of the public. Apparently, their "last chance" had evaporated. The Review now recommended, with modification, the criminal offences stated in the first Report, but added the defences that publication should be for (a) the purpose of preventing the public from being mislead by some public statement or action of the individual concerned or (b) for the purpose of informing the public about matters directly affecting the discharge of any public function of the individual concerned. The Review said the time had come for a statutory press tribunal (wholly independent of government, so that it would not be the "mouth-piece" of the Government) to be set up, which would be able to impose heavy finds for breaches of the code of practice and award compensation to proven aggrieved parties. The Review also proposed laws to "fill in the gaps" of the already existing legislation in place, *i.e.* the Interception of Communications Act 1985. Further, a new tort of infringement of privacy was also recommended. Sir David Calcutt concluded that the recommendations were "not designed to suppress free speech, or to stultify a vibrant and dynamic press. They are designed principally to ensure that privacy, which all agree should be protected, is protected from unjustifiable intrusion and protected by a body in which the public as well as the press has confidence" (para. 8.7).

The Review, from a press point of view, was not received with great enthusiasm; in fact it was condemned by the press industry as unwelcome and unworkable (although many politicians considered many of the proposals worthy of further debate); their criticisms ranged from draconian, impracticable, to unrealistic and a complete mish-mash. Peter Preston, editor of *The Guardian* and then member of the PCC said that the recommendations were "like wearing 15 overcoats in case it rains". The Review did not result in any change in the law, but provided the necessary "jolt" to the existing complacency, and between 1993 until now there have been a number of positive changes. Some would argue not enough and that the only true way forward was through legislation. However, with the incorporation of the European Convention into our domestic law, the need for changes at this time may not be so great. At present, any remedy for breach of privacy must go through the PCC and this will now be discussed below in detail.

The Press Complaints Commission

The PCC at present consists of seven members of newspapers (six editor and one chairperson and editor in chief of Associated Newspapers) and also nine lay members from various other professions and a chairperson, Lord Wakeham. At the very heart of the PCC is the Code of Practice, which continues to be updated. **8–092**

The Codes of Practice

In the booklet setting out the present Code of Practice clauses, it states that "The Code is the cornerstone of the system of self-regulation to which the industry has made a binding commitment". The press industry recognise that there is a limitation on what and how events can be reported when the issues involve intruding into individuals' private lives. In previous Codes of Practice, the word "should" appears when describing the various responsibilities attributed to the press; this has now been substituted by the word "must"—no doubt introduced in order to emphasise the necessity of complying with the relevant clause. Sadly, the Code is rather scarce in defining its terms (exception: "private places" in clause 3). The Code includes the following clauses: **8–093**

Accuracy

Newspapers must make sure that the published articles themselves are not being inaccurate, misleading or distorted; and if so, those responsible must apologise and promptly correct the mistake (clause 1). The degree of **8–094** inaccuracy is important; if only minor, then probably no breach, unless it changes the whole or substantial meaning of the article. A common complaint in this area is where a journalist questions an interviewee and there are conflicting statements about what was actually said.

Opportunity to reply

8–095 A fair opportunity to reply to inaccuracies must be given to individuals or organisations when reasonably called for (clause 2). This clause only refers to "inaccuracies" (excluding misleading or distorting). There is also no indication as to what "when reasonably called for" means.

Privacy

8–096 The Code accepts that everyone is entitled to respect for his or her private family life, home, health and correspondence. Using long-lens photography to take pictures of people in private places without their consent is unacceptable. "Private places" include public or private property where there is a reasonable expectation of privacy (clause 3).

It may not be an invasion of privacy where, for instance, the press publish a story about a well-known personality or politician having an extra-marital affair when that person gives the impression of having a happy marriage. Misleading the public in this way, the press would argue, entitles them to publish the truth.

Harassment

8–097 "Journalists and photographers must neither obtain, nor seek to obtain information or pictures through intimidation, harassment or persistent pursuit". Persistently telephoning, questioning and pursuing individuals is strictly prohibited, when requested to desist; and also to leave an individual's property when asked (clause 4). For the first time the words "persistent pursuit" have been included. This phrase was no doubt introduced as a result of the untimely death of the Princess of Wales.

Intrusion into grief or shock

8–098 "In cases involving grief or shock, enquiries must be carried out and approaches made with sympathy and discretion" (exception to this being the reporting of judicial proceedings) (clause 5). So, it seems that provided the press offer "sympathy and discretion" that does not exclude them from pursuing their story at a funeral or church or at an horrific accident, where people may be suffering from some form of psychological trauma.

Children in sex cases

The press must not, even where the law does not prohibit it, identify children under the age of 16 who are involved in cases concerning sexual offences, whether as victims or as witnesses (clause 7). **8–099**

Listening devices

"Journalists must not obtain or publish material obtained by using clandestine listening devices or by intercepting private telephone conversations" (clause 8). Thus, it would seem that information gathered by a similar means, as in the *Francome* case, would still not be publishable unless a public interest factor could be determined. **8–100**

Hospitals

The press must obtain permission before making enquiries or entering non-public areas in hospitals or similar institutions (clause 9). This was introduced as a result of the *Kaye v. Robertson* case and a complaint against the press was upheld when the press intruded into the privacy of Countess Spencer whilst she was recuperating at a private clinic (see below). **8–101**

Innocent relatives or friends

"The press must avoid identifying relatives or friends of persons convicted or accused of crime without their consent" (clause 10). **8–102**

Misrepresentation

Journalists must not generally obtain information or pictures through misrepresentation or subterfuge (clause 11). **8–103**

There are at present 16 clauses in force. The others are headed; Victims of Sexual Assault (clause 12); Discrimination (clause 13); Financial Journalism (clause 14); Confidential Sources (clause 15); and Payment for Articles (clause 16).

The Code makes it clear that issues concerning, taste, decency and the like, are matters which are to be considered outside the confines of their responsibility, and therefore not the subject of complaint. Thus, where a sequence of photographs were published showing a boy committing suicide, by jumping off a bridge, the Commission, after receiving a complaint by the boy's father said that they have "never sought to adjudicate on matters of taste and offensiveness". Despite the fact that the family suffered distress and anguish as a result, the Commission did not deem the press as intrusive given the highly public location in which the event took place and the public interest involved.[73]

Public Interest Defence

8–104 Because of the impossibility of a clear definition of "public interest",[74] the newspapers have tended to rely on this defence to justify publication. Lord Wakeham himself admitted that "over-use of the public interest defence in the Code could undermine effective self-regulation", and public confidence in the PCC would be weakened by the unwarranted intrusion into the private lives of individuals "backed up by the flimsiest of public interest defences". At present, clauses 3, 4, 6, 8, 9, 10, 11, and 16 of the Code are subject to the "public interest" factor. The Code states that the defence of public interest is available to include such situations as:

(1) Detecting or exposing crime or a serious misdemeanour.

(2) Protecting public health and safety.

(3) Preventing the public from being mislead by some statement or action by an individual or organisation.

(4) In any case where the public interest is invoked, the PCC will require a full explanation by the editor demonstrating how the public interest was served.

(5) Where children are involved there must be "an exceptional public interest" which outweighs the principles concerns of the child. The inclusion of this particular defence suggests that the Royal children ought to have some protection from interference into their private lives. How this will operate in reality will have to be judged from future reports, once the furore of the Princess of Wales' death has abated.

Guidance for Editors when Considering Questions of Public Interests[75]

8–105 Lord Wakeham outlined seven "tests" that the PCC will investigate when questioning editors in cases where the defence of public interest as used:

(1) Is there a genuine public interest involved in invading someone's privacy as defined by clause 18 of the Code—detecting or exposing crime; protecting public health; preventing the public from being mislead—or is this simply a story which interests the public, public welfare or public prurience?

(2) If there is indeed a genuine public interest, have you considered whether there are ways to disclose it which minimise the invasion into the private life of the individual concerned?

(3) If you are using photographs as part of the story, which will have to (or have already been) obtained by clandestine means and therefore compound the invasion of privacy, does the public

interest require their automatic publication or are they simply illustrative?

(4) If there is a genuine public interest which cannot be exposed in any other way than intrusion, have you considered whether there is any way to minimise the impact on the innocent and vulnerable relatives of the individual concerned, and in particular the children?

(5) If you are intending to run a story about someone connected or related to a person in the pubic eye in order to illustrate a story about that public figure, are you satisfied that the connection is not to remote and that there is a genuine public interest in mentioning that connection?

(6) Where you are preparing to publish a story seeking to contrast what a public figure has said or done in the past with his or her current statement or behaviour, have you satisfied yourself that it is fair to make such a comparison and that the original statement or behaviour was recent enough to justify publication in the public interest?

(7) If you are intending to run a story about the private life of an individual where there used to be a public interest, have you applied each of these questions afresh in case such a defence no longer exists?

Complaints Investigated

In 1995, there were 2,487 complaints against various newspapers; 2,004 **8 106**
were held not to be legitimate for reasons including: no case to prove under the codes (1,026); delays; that matters concerning taste, decency and the subject-matter were considered to be outside the ambit of the codes (988). Out of the remaining 483 cases, 420 were resolved or not pursued, 28 were upheld after adjudication, whilst 34 were dismissed. Thus, just over one per cent of complains were regarded by the PCC as justifiable and warranted criticism. It is interesting to note that in 1995 there were only 122 investigated complains against the daily newspapers (including tabloid and broadsheet). Throughout the whole year, *The Sun* received 15 complains whilst *The Daily Sport* received one and *The Daily Star*, five.[76]

In 1996, the PCC received 3,023 complains, an increase of 20 per cent from 1995, and double the amount since its inception in 1991. The PCC put the increase down to the public being made more aware of the existence of the organisation itself. Of these complaints, some 54.5 per cent concerned accuracy; just under 15 per cent concerned issues of privacy (up from 13.2 per cent the previous year). Some 10 per cent (306) complaints concerned the *Euro '96* football championship. The fourth highest categorign complaint, out of a list of 18, was related to discrimination—6.8 per cent[77–78] (down from 7.8 per cent in 1995).

In 1997, a total of 2473 complains were made, of which 1871 were not investigated for the following reasons; outside remit (complaint involved matters of taste, advertising material, decency, etc.), delay; fell outside the Code, third party complaints; 520 were resolved prior to adjudication. Of those complaints that actually went forward for adjudication (82 in total), 33 were upheld, whilst 49 were rejected.[79]

How to Make a Complaint

8–107 The complaint procedure is relatively straightforward. Indeed, the PCC, have issued a "Complainants' Charter" to further assist aggrieved parties. Anyone (individual or organisation) who has a complaint should first write to the editor in question stating their grievance. If they do not receive a reply after a reasonable time, usually after seven days, or the reply is unsatisfactory, then they should write or contact the Commission within one month of publication (although later complaints may be admitted in certain circumstances). The complainant will receive an acknowledgment within five working days and an up-to-date progress report at intervals, no longer than 15 days apart. Providing the complaint comes within the Code, then the relevant editor will investigate the problem, and if found to be in breach, will publish an apology and/or a correction. If, for whatever reason, a solution in these grounds is neither acceptable, nor possible, then the Commission itself will adjudicate on the matter and reach a decision to either uphold the complaint or dismiss it. If upheld, a report will be published detailing their findings. The following example illustrates the workings of the Commission;

Example of a Complaint Proceeding[80]

8–108 In 1995 the *News of the World* published an article with the headline "Di's Sister in Booze and Bulimia Clinic". The article discussed in detail Countess Spencer's (now ex-wife of the Earl Spencer) psychological problems and showed a photograph of her walking in the private grounds of the clinic, taken with a long range camera from outside the property, without her consent. Earl Spencer issued a complaint on the grounds of breach of privacy (now clause 3); intrusion into privacy in private place without permission, *i.e.* a hospital (now clause 9); and harassment (now clause 4). He stated that under these circumstances, there could be no public interest defence. He said that if anybody needed privacy and freedom from harassment it was a person suffering from psychological disorders.

The editor of the *News of the World* in his defence argued that the Earl courted publicity in return for payment and publicity, and thus waved his and his family's right for privacy. He further argued that since she allegedly, in previous other publications, admitted to having eating disorder problems, she herself had put her illness into the public domain.

Adjudication

The Commission decided that the publication of a photograph of the Countess in a private clinic with a telephoto lens was serious breach of the Code and constituted an intrusion into her private life within clause 3. On whether a public interest defence as made out, the Commission stated that despite the Earl seeking publicity in the past, this did not necessarily mean that "every aspect of the private affairs of his wife is a matter which the press has a right to put into the public domain". Even prior comment published in previous articles did not mean that the Countess "had opened her illness to public scrutiny or that there is a public interest justification for the articles and photographs printed". Accordingly, the complaint was upheld. Mr Rupert Murdoch, the publisher, issued a statement: "I have no hesitation in making public this remonstration and I have reminded Mr Morgan (the editor) forcefully of his responsibility to the Code . . .". Later, the editor issued a statement unreservedly accepting responsibility for the breach and apologised for the article and photograph. However, merely making enquiries about the health of the Countess at the clinic, and after having been refused information departed, and did not thereafter publish anything relating to the Countess, was not, in that instance, a breach of the Code.[81] **8–109—112**

Article 8: Right to Respect of Privacy

> 1 Everyone has the right to respect for his private and family life, his home and his correspondence. **8–113**
> 2 There shall be no interference by a public authority with the exercise of this right except such as in accordance with the law and is necessary in a democratic society in the interests of national security, public safety or the economic well-being of the country, for the prevention of disorder or crime, for the protection of health or morals, or for the protection of the rights and freedom of others.

The ECHR treats privacy in a very different manner from that of United Kingdom law. Both the scope of the rights protected and the nature of the protection granted differ from our domestic law but the exceptions to Article 8 are so wide that in fact incorporation of the Convention may do little to strengthen privacy law in the United Kingdom. It should be noted that Article 8 requires "respect for" a person's private life, etc., rather than granting an absolute right to a private life or indeed to a home in which to live. Before embarking on the interpretation of this particular Article and the relevant case law, it is especially important that the following steps be considered in order to decide whether a violation of Article 8 has been shown:

(1) Does the complaint fall within the rights protected by Article 8?

(2) Is there an infringement of these rights? If yes, then;
(3) Under Article 8(2), is this infringement justified, *i.e.* in accordance with the law? If yes, then;
(4) Is the infringement within the legitimate aims stated in Article 8(2), *i.e.* national security, prevention of disorder or crime, etc.? If yes, then;
(5) Were the measures taken by the public authorities "necessary in a democratic society"; the word "necessary" meaning a "pressing social need" which was proportionate to the legitimate aim pursued. If yes, then;
(6) The infringement is justified.

A number of expressions or terms consistently occur throughout the relevant case law of Articles 8, 9, 10 and 11 and it is best to refer to them now, and give a general explanation as to their meaning, so that when cited they will be used in abbreviated form. Thus, for instance, the expression under Article 8(2).

"In accordance with the law"

8–114 This expression is stated in Article 8(2). A similar expression "prescribed by law" is stated in Articles 5, 9, 10 and 11. In order to eliminate interference by the arbitrariness of public authorities, an individual's right under the above Articles (and others) is protected by the Convention, in that the interference must be"lawful". The "law" in the above expressions may be either under the common law or statute law. The whole phrase "in accordance with the law" implies "that there must be a measure of legal protection in domestic law against arbitrary interference by public authorities with the rights safeguarded by paragraph".[82] Thus member countries must provide national laws which are sufficiently precise so that individuals can foresee, with a certain degree of reasonableness, the consequences of their conduct, in order that an individual's rights may be properly safeguarded from any arbitrary interference by the national authorities.[83–84] The interpretation of the whole expression suggests two main requirements:

> "First, the law must be adequately accessible: The citizen must be able to have an indication that is adequate in the circumstances of the legal rules applicable to a given case. Secondly, a norm cannot be regarded as a 'law' unless it is formulated with sufficient precision to enable the citizen to regulate his conduct; he must be able—if need be with appropriate advice—to foresee, to a degree that is reasonable in the circumstances, the consequences which a given action may entail: . . . Those consequences need not be foreseeable with absolute certainty: . . .".[85]

For instance, undercover operations involving national security, terrorism and serious crime in general, carry with them the inherent danger of being abused if allowed to be conducted without proper legal supervision. In this, the Government is given some leeway, but there must be sufficient safeguards incorporated into the law to minimize the risk of any abuse.

In *Malone v. U.K.*,[88] the applicant complained to the Commission that his telephone conversation had been intercepted by the police and that his telephone had been "tapped" and "metered" (a meter check printer was used to record all the numbers dialled on his particular telephone), and therefore such interference by a public authority contravened the applicant's protection of his right to respect for his private life under Article 8. Since the Government admitted the actual interception, the main issue for the court was whether what the Government did was "in accordance with the law" and "necessary in a democratic society" under Article 8(2). The words "in accordance with the law" are to be given the same meaning as "prescribed by law" or "provided for by law" in other Articles under the Convention and the term "law" includes both common law and legislation.[89] It would defeat the whole purpose of secret surveillance if the suspect could reasonably foresee that he was being spied upon. Nevertheless, the court said that "the law must be sufficiently clear in its terms to give citizens an adequate indication as to the circumstances in which and conditions on which public authorities are empowered to resort to this secret and potentially dangerous interference with the right to respect for private life and correspondence".[90] Because of its secrecy element, the court said that:

> ". . . the law must indicate the scope of any such discretion conferred on the competent authorities and the manner of its exercise with sufficient clarity, having regard to the legitimate aim of the measure in question, to give the individual adequate protection against arbitrary interference".[91]

They found that the "obscurity and uncertainty" of the law in this area did not even afford an individual the basic legal protection required. Thus, the interception was not "in accordance with the law".[92] This case restricted the ambit of communication interception by the police. As a consequence of this case, the Interception of Communications Act 1985 was introduced to provide individuals with appropriate protection by setting out in statute the circumstances and the conditions by which public authorities would be allowed to carry out their undercover surveillance operations. Unfortunately, the 1985 Act provided little redress for an aggrieved individual; it focused rather upon creating a statutory scheme for the authorisation of interception of communications by the police and security services.

Due to the uncertainty and weakness of the Act, it has been repealed and replaced by a more detailed regulatory framework. Its successor, the Regulation of Investigatory Powers Act 2000, goes little further towards this although it does provide access to a tribunal (see discussion above), even though it was a response in part to the finding that the previous regulations violated Articles 8 and 13. In *Khan v. U.K.*[93] the court found that covert surveillance of the applicant violated his right to respect for his private life under Article 8 since, at that time, there were no clearly defined privacy rights in English law and thus the surveillance could not be "in accordance with law". It was therefore unnecessary to consider whether the interference with the applicant's rights was "necessary in a democratic society".

In *Klass v. Germany*[93A]:

8–115 **Facts.** The applicants (five lawyers) complained that although under domestic legislation the authorities were empowered to open mail and inspect their contents and to use secret surveillance techniques under limited circumstances, the persons under investigation were (i) not always informed of such operations once they had ceased and (ii) had no remedy before the courts against the possible abuse of such measures. The specific legislation referred to by the applicants was the Restriction on the Secrecy of the Mail, Post and Telecommunications Act (1968) (known as the "G 10"). Accordingly, the applicants argued that the legislation lacked the adequate safeguards against possible abuse by the authorities and therefore constituted, *inter alia*, a breach of Article 8(2). Although the mere use of such surveillance techniques was, prima facie, an interference by the authorities with an individual's right to respect for his private and family life and his correspondence under Article 8(1), the question for the court to decide was whether such an interference was justified under Article 8(2). In this case, the Government argued that it was justified for all the exceptions mentioned in Article 8(2), and in particular in the interests of national security and for the prevention of disorder or crime.

Decision. One of the main questions to be considered by the court was whether the interference was necessary in a democratic society. Whilst accepting that legislation permitting surveillance may be necessary within limited circumstances, there must also be laws that protect individuals against abuse by the authorities in such situations. The court stated that there must be adequate and effective guarantees in place to deal with possible abuses:

> "(It) depends on all the circumstances of the case, such as the nature, scope and duration of the possible measures, the grounds required for ordering such measures, the authorities competent to permit, carry out and supervise the measures, and the kind of remedy provided by the national law" (at para. 50).

Under existing domestic law, prior to permission being given for any surveillance operation there must be facts indicating that certain criminal acts were being committed or planned and that such action was necessary because any other method would not prove successful or alternatively, any other means of investigation would be considerably more difficult (at para. 51). Further, according to the government, proper administrative procedures were in place to ensure that any surveillance application was "not ordered haphazardly, irregularly or without due and proper consideration" (at para. 51), *e.g.* permission may only be granted by the appropriate Minister, on application by the head of certain services, such as the Army Security Office or the Federal Intelligence Service. There also existed strict implementation measures for the surveillance including: a maximum period of three months before the application must be renewed; reviewing the surveillance; discontinuing the operation when no longer necessary; information obtained from the surveillance must not be used for any other purpose and all relevant documentation must be destroyed when no longer required (at para. 52). Whilst there was no judicial process available for deciding the legality of a surveillance order, there existed the Parliamentary Board and G 10 Commission to oversee proper compliance, which provided strict safeguards against abuse by the authorities. The applicants argued that this amounted to "a form of political control, inadequate in comparison with the principle of judicial control which ought to prevail", (at para. 54). Despite the court's preference for some form of judicial supervision, it stated that "the exclusion of judicial control does not exceed the limits of what may be deemed necessary in a democratic society" (at para. 56). The court concluded that in consideration of the strict safeguards and controls laid down, the relevant bodies were sufficiently independent and balanced (the Parliament Board included opposition members) to act in an objective manner.

The court also considered the question of whether or not the person under surveillance should be notified once the operation had terminated. The applicants maintained that he should always be so informed; thus permitting the individual concerned to take legal action against the relevant authorities where he considered the surveillance action not to be necessary in a democratic society. The court examined the practical ramifications where an individual was not subsequently notified of the surveillance. It noted that surveillance operations might last over long periods. Even after the investigation has ended, disclosing the operation may result in exposing the workings of, for instance, the intelligence services and their agents, and which may consequently prove detrimental to those services. Therefore, the lack of notification *per se* was not incompatible with Article 8(2). However, the court declared that (confirming a prior judgment of the Federal Constitutional Court) "the person concerned must be informed after the termination of the surveillance measures as soon as notification can be made without jeopardising the purpose of the restriction" (at para. 58). The court concluded that the interference which flowed from the respective legislation was necessary in a democratic society in the interests of national security and for the prevention of disorder or crime under Article 8(2) and, accordingly, was not in violation of Article 8.

In *Halford v. U.K.*[94] the applicant, an assistant chief constable, had been **8–116** consistently refused promotion. She brought proceedings against the Home Office and Merseyside Police Authority alleging sex discrimination. She alleged that a campaign was being waged against her, which included intercepting all her telephone calls. The Government conceded that there was "a reasonable likelihood" that her office business calls had been intercepted (but not her home telephone). That amounted to an interference by a public authority. Therefore, was such an interference justified under Article 8(2) with regard to the phrase "in accordance with the law"? Since interception by the police of calls on their own internal system was not covered by the Interception of Communications Act 1985 she was not afforded an adequate indication as to the circumstances and conditions in which the public authority were likely to intrude into her private life, and therefore a violation of Article 8 was established.

The question of whether the interference was in accordance with the law is to be measured against the "adequate accessibility and foreseeability" factors mentioned above but also by examination of the existing legal procedures in order that the individual is sufficiently protected against any arbitrary intervention by the State. Thus in *Leander v. Sweden*[95] the balance was between protecting its national security against the seriousness of the interference with the applicant's right to respect for his private life.[96] In that case, the applicant was temporarily employed as a technician with the Naval Museum (which was next to the naval base), but was not given a permanent post due to a "personnel control"[97] investigation carried out which allegedly showed him to be a security risk. The applicant was subsequently not permitted to challenge those accusations before a tribunal. He complained to the Commission that this constituted an attack on his reputation and therefore was in breach of Article 8. The police register, which was governed by the Personnel Control Ordinance ("PCO") legislation, contained information regarding his private life and since he was not given the opportunity to rebut these allegations, he argued that this constituted an interference with his right to respect for private life under Article 8(1). Applying in Article 8(2) the "in accordance with the law" principles set out in *Malone v. U.K.* above, the court found that the methods used with the accompanying safeguards within the PCO were sufficiently explicit and detailed such that the law would not be open to abuse or unfettered discretion, and indeed, gave the individual the required adequate indication when and in what circumstances this information might be released, Therefore, there was no breach of Article 8(1).

However, the mere compilation and the disclosure of private information may constitute *per se* an interference with an individual's right to respect for his private life under Article 8. It follows that secret surveillance activities for the purpose of gathering and storing (not necessarily releasing) on file information concerning a person's private life also may constitute an interference with that right.[98] In *Hewitt and Harman v. United Kingdom*,[99] the applicants alleged that M15 had been conducting secret surveillance operations for the purpose of compiling and storing information about them, to be retained by the Security Services. The Commission found on the evidence that such records existed and determined whether the interference could be justified under Article 8(2) by first examining whether the information was kept "in accordance with the law". The Commission reiterated the principles of the expression as set out in *The Sunday Times v. United Kingdom*[1] and *Malone v. U.K.* (see above), and stated that since the Security Services' activities and in particular their secret surveillance activities did not possess the force of law, nor was there "provided a framework which indicates with the requisite degree of certainty the scope and manner of the exercise of discretion by the authorities in the carrying out of secret surveillance activities,"[2] the interference was not "in accordance with the law" under Article 8(2). Therefore there had been a breach of Article 8.

It is for the domestic courts to review, interpret and apply their own laws. Any interference by the court into these matters is strictly limited. Thus, provided the domestic law reaches the necessary "quality" about it, including the practices and procedures being sufficiently precise and executed and provided that Article 8(2)applies then public authority interference is permitted. In *Chappell v. United Kingdom*,[3] the execution of an *Anton Piller* order was considered to possess the necessary quality so as to be justified under Article 8(2), despite the shortcomings in the procedure followed, provided they were not so serious so as to be disproportionate to the legitimate aim pursued.[4]

ARTICLE 8(2)

"Necessary in a democratic society"

An interference may only be justified where it is "necessary in a democratic society". The word "necessary" is to be equated with a pressing social need. Thus, the reasons why the authorities intervened against the individual's particular right was to safeguard some pressing social need. But in doing so, the state must not act disproportionately to the legitimate aim pursued, *i.e.* not to use a "sledgehammer to crack a nut". If the State does take measures which are disproportionate then it is in violation of the relevant Article.[5] **8–117**

"Legitimate aim"

This term refers to the exceptions listed in paragraph 2 of Articles 8, 9, 10 and 11, *e.g.* in Article 8(2) "for the protection of health or morals". Should the respondent state wish to justify their interference into an individual's rights stated in the above Articles, they must show that the domestic law used was justified for one or more of the exceptions stated in the list. Each relevant Article has its own exhaustive list, which, in many cases may overlap with the list in another Article. If the state cannot show that the relevant exception justified the interference, then there is a violation of the Article in question. **8–118**

"Margin of appreciation"

Margin of appreciation originates from the premise that "the machinery of protection established by the Convention is subsidiary to the national systems safeguarding human rights."[6] Further, between existing contracting states their respective domestic laws differ in many aspects to, at least, some degree. Hence, the Convention recognises that the individual state is in a far better position to judge what laws are best suited for its own citizens, and to deal with those who break those laws. Therefore, these States are given a margin of appreciation or a certain degree of flexibility when the court has to decide whether or not the measures taken by these States, (e.g. restrictions, penalties, conditions, etc.), were justified in infringing the rights of the individual, and whether it was "necessary in a democratic society" to do so. However, that margin of appreciation is not without its limitations and it is the court who has the last say, and, for example, where Article 10 is concerned "is empowered to give the final ruling on whether a restriction or penalty is reconcilable with freedom of expression as protected by Article 10.[7] **8–119**

ARTICLE 8(1) "PRIVATE LIFE"

> "The object of Article 8 is essentially that of protecting the individual from arbitrary interference by the public authorities. It does not merely compel the State to abstain from such interference; in addition to this primarily negative **8–120**

undertaking there may be positive obligations inherent in an effective respect for private or family life".[8]

For example, in *X and Y v. The Netherlands*,[9] a 16-year-old mentally-handicapped girl was raped in a privately-run nursing home. At that time, Dutch law only permitted the victim to make a criminal complaint. Since the girl was unable to do so, her father attempted to file the complaint on her behalf, but was prevented from doing so under the domestic law. The court said, "This is a case where fundamental values and essential aspects of private life are at stake. Effective deterrence is indispensable in this area and it can be achieved only by criminal law provision."[10] Since the law in this case was wholly inappropriate to the situation which existed, there was a violation of Article 8.

"Private life" includes sexual life and where existing legislation affects the victims' life, there may well be a violation of Article 8. In this type of situation, the individual is in a dilemma; if he continues his normal sexual practices, he may face breaking the existing law; if he refrains from breaking the law by not indulging in those sexual acts, the well-being of his personal life is being interfered with.[11] In *X v. United Kingdom*,[12] the applicant was sentenced to a total of two years and six months on buggery offences against two 18-year-old males. The main ground of complaint was whether the existing law (Sexual Offences Act 1956 and 1976) which forbade homosexual activity with persons below the age of 21,[13] amounted to an interference with his right to respect for private life. Regarding whether the age of consent was "necessary in a democratic society", the Commission said that a comparison with other European countries was not the test, "but the reasonable and objective nature of the arguments adduced in favour of the actual age limit chosen",[14] and this is "to be examined on its own merits and in the context of the society for which it is considered appropriate".[15] The Government argued that it was necessary "to protect young men from influences and pressures of an undesirable kind"[16] and stated that young men involved in homosexual relationships would be subject to substantial pressures which could be harmful to their psychological development.[17] The Commission accepted that interference could be justified if it would be for the protection of health and morals or of the rights of others. The Commission took into account the recommendations by the Wolfenden Committee which were eventually accepted by Parliament, and the detailed examination by Parliament on this sensitive topic, as well as the views of the respondent government, and formed the opinion that the age of consent of 21 years was not unbalanced. Therefore there was interference which was necessary in a democratic society for the protection of the rights of others. But even the Commission questioned the paradox that it was lawful to vote at 18 (heterosexual activities are lawful from the age of 16) and enter into other legal transactions, *e.g.* contracts, but not indulge in homosexual behaviour.

In *Dudgeon v. United Kingdom*,[18] the applicant, a homosexual, was questioned (but not charged) by the police in connection with various gross indecency offences between consenting males in Northern Ireland, under section 61 and section 62 of the Offences Against the Persons Act 1861 and the Criminal Law Amendment Act 1885. He complained to the Commission that this caused him hardship, fear and distress and interfered with his right to respect for his own private life. Laws in Northern Ireland at that time (but not the remainder of the United Kingdom) prohibited homosexual acts between consenting males over 21 years of age, but criminal prosecutions were very rare in this area, although theoretically still enforceable. The Government argued that such laws were justified under Article 8(2) as being for the "protection of morals" or "the protection of the rights and freedoms of others," and this became the main issue to be decided before the court. The court said that when dealing with the moral interests of the immature the above two phrases in Article 8(2) should be considered as one, for the purposes of evaluation. Whilst it was accepted as a general rule that society needs some guidance when attempting to preserve some form of moral standards, the question for the court was whether the existing laws could be considered "necessary" and usually the particular country is best placed to decide what laws are best suited to cope with that "pressing social need", hence the latitude given to domestic laws in this area. Nevertheless, the court is entitled to evaluate those laws, if called upon. The Government argued that there was strong opposition in Northern Ireland against any reform of the status quo. In particular, the Government said that Northern Ireland society was said to be "more conservative and to place greater emphasis on religious matters . . ."[19] and argued that the "moral climate in Northern Ireland in sexual matters is one of the matters which the national authorities may legitimately take into account in exercising their discretion".[20] The court had to consider under Article 8(2) whether the legislation in force was proportionate to the legitimate aim pursued. They said with regard to males over 21 years of age, that nowadays, homosexual practices had been recognised throughout Europe and it was unacceptable to consider that such behaviour, under the category of a "pressing social need", should still be considered illegal. Under the "proportionality principle" the court said that:

> ". . . such justifications as there are for retaining the law in force unamended are outweighed by the detrimental affects which the very existence of the legislative provisions in question can have on the life of a person of homosexual orientation like the applicant".[21]

Therefore the existing law was disproportionate to the legitimate aim pursued.[22]

In *Adt v. United Kingdom*[23]: **8–121**

Facts. The applicant's house was searched by police and a number of items were seized, including video tapes which showed him engaging in sexual acts with four other men. He was charged with gross indecency on the basis of one of the tapes.

The sexual acts depicted were consensual, non-violent and took place in the applicant's home. The tapes had not been shown to anyone other than the participants. The applicant was convicted and the tapes were seized and destroyed. He did not appeal against conviction after legal advice that he had no prospect of success. He alleged that his conviction for gross indecency was a violation of Article 8(m) both on the general basis that the criminal law prohibited consensual homosexual activity in a private place if it involved more than two participants, and also because that law had resulted in his conviction. The Government responded that there had been no interference with the applicant's right to respect for his private life since the sexual activity concerned was not within the definition of "private life" under Article 8.

Decision. The court found that there had been an interference with the applicant's right to respect for his private life in both ways he had alleged. The interference was in accordance with the law and had the legitimate aims of protecting morals and protecting the rights and freedoms of others. Thus the key issue was whether the law and its use in the applicant's conviction were necessary in a democratic society. Whilst it is possible that State interference with some sexual activities will be justified, this did not apply in the present case since the sexual activity was carried out in private without any intention to publicise it. As held in *Dudgeon*, the margin of appreciation is very narrow in cases which involve intimate aspects of private life. There were insufficient reasons both for the existence of the legislation which criminalised private homosexual acts and for the conviction of the applicant, which was disproportionate. Hence there was a violation of Article 8. The court did not find it necessary to consider the applicant's additional allegation that the law in question violated Article 14 in combination with Article 8 by criminalising homosexual male activity only.

In *Sutherland v United Kingdom*, the issue of ages of consent was finally resolved when the case was struck off the list; the Sexual Offences (Amendment) Act 2000 came into force on January 8, 2001 and reduced the age of consent for gay men to 16.

In *Lustig-Prean and Beckett v. U.K., Smith and Grady v. U.K.*:

Facts. The applicants were all homosexual member of the armed forces. The Ministry of Defence at that time banned homosexuals from the armed forces, ostensibly on grounds including their "effect on the forces' fighting power and discipline". After investigations into their sexuality, each of the applicants was discharged form the services due to their homosexuality, and the Court of Appeal rejected their applications for judicial review. The applicants alleged that the investigations and their subsequent treatment violated Articles 8, 14, 3, 10 and 13.

Decision. The court found violations of Articles 8 and 13. The investigations carried out by the Ministry of Defence and the subsequent discharges of the applicants were very serious interferences with their right to respect for their private lives. There was no moral or capacity-based justification for the Ministry of Defence's policy against homosexuals serving in the armed forces. No convincing reasons had been given for the discharge of the applicants and, further, the investigations into their sexuality were coercive, continued after the applicants had stated that they were homosexual, and were not justified by medical, security or disciplinary reasons.

Article 8(1): "Home"

8–122 The right to respect for one's private life from arbitrary intervention also extends to public authority interferences which affect an individual's home, including problems relating to some forms of nuisances,[26] various types of search or seizure of property from within a person's house[27] and the general right, if not absolute, to live how one pleases. In *Miailhe v France*[28]:

Facts. The applicants complained that their home, from which they conducted business, was searched and documents seized (some 15,000 documents) by customs officials, in violation of Article 8. The relevant search and seizures were carried out under Articles 64 and 454 of the Customs Code, as part of an investigation into illegal financial dealings with other countries. The charges were eventually dropped as a result of changes in the law.

Decision. The Government argued that the interference was justified under Article 8(2), as being in the interest of the economic well-being of the country and for the prevention of crime. The applicants contended that the seizure of some 15,000 documents (made up of both personal and business papers) was not justified. They submitted that Article 64 of the Customs Code contravened Article 66 of the 1958 Constitution which made search and seizures subject to judicial authorisation. Further, they argued that prior to the change in the law, "there were no curbs on custom powers or safeguards against abuse by custom officers" (at para. 34) and thus their actions were not necessary in a democratic society, as required. The Government responded that the customs' actions were necessary since this was the only means at the disposal of the authorities to properly investigate illegal financial dealings with other countries. They further stated that safeguards existed to protect the applicants' rights in such circumstances, *e.g.* rigorous judicial supervision; the presence of a police officer during the search; only certain ranked officers were authorised to establish offences and so forth. Such safeguards ensured that there was a proper balance between the requirements of law enforcement and the protection of the rights of the individual (para. 35). The court, confirming previous case-law, stated that "the exceptions under Article 8(2) are to be interpreted narrowly and the need for them in a given case must be convincingly established" (para. 36). The court rejected the Government's arguments that there existed adequate and effective measures to protect the individual against abuse. They stated that:

> ". . . in the absence of any requirement of a judicial warrant the restrictions and conditions provided for by law, which was emphasised by the government, appear to lax and full of loopholes for the interferences in the applicants' right to have been strictly proportionate to the legitimate aim pursued" (para. 38).

Accordingly, they found there to be a violation of Article 8.

In *Buckley v. United Kingdom*,[29] the applicant lived in a caravan on land which she acquired from her sister. She applied retrospectively for planning permission to have three caravans occupying the land. She was refused permission on the grounds that:

(a) the caravans could be accommodated on other sites;

(b) the caravans being there, would take away from the rural beauty of the surrounding countryside; and

(c) the access to the land was not wide enough for two vehicles to pass.

She was served with an enforcement notice requiring her to remove the caravans from the land. She refused and was fined. The applicant complained to the Commission that she was prevented from living in a caravan on her own land and living the traditional lifestyle of a gypsy. The Commission stated that the interpretation of "home" is independent of whatever the domestic law classifies the word to mean. What amounts to a "home" will depend upon the factual circumstances of each individual case, *i.e.* the existence of sufficient and continuous links. The court, following *Gillow v. United Kingdom*,[30] found that the applicant came within the meaning of the word "home" which included:

(i) buying the land in order to set up residence there;
(ii) living there continuously; and that
(iii) this was her only home.[31]

Thus the removal order in respect of her right to her home amounted to an interference by a public authority under Article 8(1). The next issue was weighing up the pros and cons of the interest of the individual against the community as a whole (the "proportionality principle"). The court accepted the Government's argument that the planning provisions were aimed at:

> ". . . furthering highway safety and the preservation of the environment and public health. The legitimate aims pursued were therefore public safety, the economic well-being of the country, the protection of health, and the protection of the rights of others".[32]

Was what the public authorities had done disproportionate in order to achieve their legitimate aims? The applicant could have applied for an official caravan site nearby, but she continually refused. The word "necessity" implies that the interference corresponds to a pressing social need and that it is proportionate to the aim or aims pursued. In assessing the proportionality, regard must be had to whether a fair balance had been struck between the demands of the general interest of the community and the requirements of the protection of the individual's fundamental rights. ("The proportionality principle").[33] Further, in determining whether an interference is justified the court will take into account that a margin of appreciation is left to the contracting state, which are in principle in a better position to make an initial assessment of the necessity of a given interference.[34] The scope of this flexibility will depend on "the nature of the Convention right in issue, its importance for the individual and the nature of the activities concerned". In this instance, the court felt that issues such as planning policies were best left to be decided by the individual State authorities. However, when evaluating the respect for the applicant's home, the scope of this flexibility will have to be considered, and this will include the protection afforded by the authorities to the applicant. The applicant had been offered an alternative caravan site, but she rejected this option. Her caravan could not have been hidden enough so as to sufficiently reduce the damage done to the scenic beauty of the countryside. The applicant was fined a small amount and had not been, up until then, evicted. Thus, the court found that the authorities had behaved in a responsible and reasonable manner and were justified under the circumstances to interfere with the applicant's right to respect for her home. Therefore, there was no violation of Article 8(2).

In *Chapman, Beard, Costner, Lee and Smith v. United Kingdom*,[35] the applicants were all gypsies who were refused planning permission by local authorities to live in caravans on land which the applicants themselves owned. They argued, *inter alia*, that the refusal was a violation of Article 8 and Article 14. The court found that there were no violations on the facts since the actions taken against the applicants were in accordance with the law and had the legitimate aim of protecting the environmental rights of others. Further, the margin of appreciation which applies to planning decisions is a wide one, and the rights of society outweighed the personal interests of the applicants. There is no right under Article 8 to be given a home, and in any case each applicant had alternative living options.

Nowadays, more and more businesses tend to run their commercial **8–123** affairs, or at least a fair percentage of their business, from their personal residence. Alternatively, certain private transactions go on in the workplace, such that it might not realistically go under the name "business". The court in the following case recognised this overlap and gave a wider definition to the meaning of "home", so that it includes both business and an individual's personal abode. In *Niemietz v. Germany*,[36] the applicant, who was a lawyer, had his offices searched by the police under a warrant which stated that they were looking for documents which would reveal the true identity of a person who was under criminal investigation for insulting behaviour towards the court. They found no relevant documents during the search. The Federal Constitutional Court found that the warrant had been properly issued, and accordingly dismissed the applicant's appeal for an unlawful search. The applicant complained to the Commission that, *inter alia*, the search was a violation of his right to respect for his home and correspondence, under Article 8. The Government argued that "home" did not include the applicant's business premises or his professional life. The court considered that "private life" was not limited to only an individual's personal life (what they referred to as the "inner circle"), and excluded all else. "Respect for private life must also comprise to a certain degree the right to establish and develop relationships with other human beings".[37] Thus, in business life an individual may develop close links with others which make it difficult to decide whether those people form exclusively part of the "inner circle", or purely business ties. This highly potential overlap becomes somewhat nebulous when considering a more precise meaning of "private life". Thus, on these grounds alone, the court rejected the Government's argument that Article 8 could not apply to searches against business premises. The question then arose was whether the interference was justified under Article 8(2). The search was justified as being "necessary", *i.e.* threats against a judge. However, since the warrant included any document the search itself was disproportionate to the specific aim pursued, due to the damage which could result from a lawyer's confidential files being searched indiscriminately. Accordingly, there was a violation of Article 8.

Every person has a limited right to information about the basic elements which make up his past life, *e.g.* his identity, childhood years. This is especially pertinent where a person from an early age has been taken into an orphanage or care home. A refusal by the authorities to permit access to personal history records may sometimes not be justified, and be considered as an interference with his right to respect for private life under Article 8(1).[38] In *Gaskin v. United Kingdom*,[39] the applicant, who had been in care until he was 18, wished to see his case records for future legal proceedings for ill-treatment by the local authority. The local authority refused access on the grounds that disclosure would be contrary to the public interest.[40] On appeal to the Court of Appeal, it was decided that these records were private and confidential[41] and in the public interest ought not to be disclosed. The applicant complained to the Commission that the refusal of full access to those records was in breach of his right to respect for his private and family life within Article 8(1). The Government argued, in front of the Commission, that those records could not be construed as relating to the applicant's private life, or alternatively, before the court, that there was no intrusion established into his right to respect for private life. In certain circumstances, there may be a positive obligation on the local authorities to release those records in the public interest; in this instance, in order for the applicant to learn more fully his past personal details. The Government stated that the records could be inspected if individual contributors gave their permission (some contributors did in fact give the required permission for access—19 out of 46). The court pointed out that the confidentiality of the writers of these documents ought to be protected, in the public interest, unless waived. However, there was no procedural system where one of the writers was not available for his consent or improperly refused consent.[42] Since no independent authority decided "whether access has to be granted in cases where a contributor fails to answer or withholds consent", the applicant was put at a disadvantage *vis-à-vis* the local authority and therefore there had been a violation of Article 8.

Article 8(1) Family Life

8–124 The issue of "arbitrary interference by the public authorities" is especially prevalent regarding family matters. The court acknowledges the positive role the family plays in any democratic society and is prepared to recognise and develop such a unit in situations which may be in contravention to a Member State's domestic legal position. For instance, the question of illegitimacy has, thankfully, lost its stigma in recent times when it comes to the entitlement of recognition under the law. Under Article 8, the right to respect for family life includes illegitimate as well as legitimate children for the purposes of a "family". An important part of that right is that the

Contracting State should, through its laws, have a "respect", and acknowledge the existence of an illegitimate child, with all the advantages that family life has to offer. Where domestic laws exist to constrain or hamper that illegitimate child's right, there may be a violation of Article 8 if such recognition is not forthcoming. The child must not be prevented in any way from attaining a normal life within the family environment. For instance, in *Marckx v. Belgium*,[43] an unmarried mother was compelled by deed to be the legal guardian of her own baby some one year after the birth of her child. The child would not be recognised by domestic law as part of her family until she signed. Further, by recognising her baby in this manner, she was restricted to bequeathing to her her entire property. If she refused to sign, then in law the "family" did not come into being. Neither did an illegitimate child form part of the grandparents' family as far as inheritance rights on intestacy were concerned. Illegitimate children under the age of 21, who wished to marry, had to receive their guardians' consent, as opposed to the grandparents' consent in normal cases. In this situation, the law should have protected the child so as to provide an easy integration into the family and society as a whole. The court said that the present law with regard to respect for family life, as it stood, "thwarts and impedes the normal development of such life".[44] Therefore, there was a violation of Article 8.

"Respect" for a family life implies an obligation on the State to act in a manner calculated to allow family ties to develop normally. In *Johnston v. Ireland*,[45] because of the no-divorce laws existing in Ireland at that time, the applicant, a man who was still married, began cohabiting with a woman who gave birth to a daughter who was illegitimate. The "respect" in this case was that the daughter ought to be placed legally and socially in a position akin to that of a legitimate child. In this instance, the mother had the sole guardianship of the child, although the father could have applied to have access to that child, but not as guardian jointly with the mother. Even if the couple eventually married (they had been together for 15 years), this would not have made the child legitimate. There was no existing judicial procedure then whereby these inequalities could be rectified re. respecting the natural family ties. Since there were considerable differences between this applicant, the child, and legitimate children, there was a violation of Article 8. The law in Ireland has since changed to bring the court's recommendations in line with giving illegitimate children equal recognition within the family.

Interference with family life may occur where some members are prohibited from entering into or remaining in a country in which the rest of the family are presently resident. Each Contracting State has the right to control immigration and apply their own domestic law for these purposes. The court will not interfere with these laws, otherwise than requesting the respective countries to abide by their obligations and requirements under the Convention.[46] In *Abdulaziz Cabales and Balkandali v. United Kingdom*,[47] the applicants were lawfully resident in the United Kingdom. Their husbands were refused permission to enter the country and to permanently live with them, under the then immigration rules. They complained to the Commission of *inter alia*, violations of Article 8. The court regarded the applicants as coming within the meaning of "family life", *i.e.* which includes, taking separately, the existence of a family, a lawful marriage, and cohabitation. The applicants argued that "respect for family life", included the right to live permanently in the United Kingdom and that living without their husbands was inconsistent with this principle.[48] The word "respect" has wide and varied meaning according to the practices followed in each Contracting State. Accordingly, the court permits "a wide margin of appreciation in determining the steps to be taken to ensure compliance with the Convention with due regard to the needs and resources of the community and of individuals".[49] In this instance, the court would not interfere against the ruling of a domestic court for refusing the husband's permanent settlement in the United Kingdom. Indeed, there were no reasons or obstacles why they could not settle in their husbands' country (or their own, since the women were not born in the United Kingdom). Therefore, there was no violation of Article 8. However, when Article 8 was taken in conjunction with Article 14, the Court found a violation on the grounds of discrimination, not of race or birth, but of sex.

8–125 Art. 8 may also be used in custody and access cases, but not always with any prospect of success. In *Glaser v. United Kingdom European*[50]:

Facts. The applicant was born in India and lived in South Africa before moving to the U.K. with his wife and three children. When he and his wife began divorce proceedings, he was originally allowed contact with his children, in his wife's presence, but after unproven allegations that he had sexually abused the children she would not allow him access. The applicant obtained an order for supervised access but his ex-wife would not always let him see the children as arranged. Psychiatric reports showed that the children were distressed and scared of the applicant and that he had been unreasonably harsh in his treatment of them; they all wished to live with their mother and did not wish to see their father. Contact was increased after a series of contact orders were granted and for a time the applicant's ex-wife complied, but she then moved to Scotland with the children and denied all access.

The applicant brought a case to the High Court but attempts to trace the children were unsuccessful. He then had them made wards of court and obtained an injunction prohibiting the mother from removing them from the jurisdiction without leave of the court. The police and DSS were involved in attempts to trace the mother, eventually successfully, but she refused to disclose her address or negotiate. The Child Support Agency then disclosed the address to the High Court, but the mother and children had moved again. Further court action allowed the applicant to send letters to the children but not to be given their address. He then began proceedings for the English contact order to be enforced in Scotland.

The applicant withdrew the application when, he believed, it became clear that he would not succeed. He the tried again, but the Scottish court had reports prepared into the sexual abuse allegations and reinvestigated the matters already decided by the English court. Contact was granted but again the mother refused to allow it. Yet more court action followed and finally the applicant was allowed contact with his children after almost seven years. Since the relevant domestic law is clear that the rights of the parents should only be interfered with when this is required by the interests of the child, and that it is almost always in the best interests of a child to have contact with both parents, the applicant alleged violations of Articles 8 and 6 in that the domestic authorities had failed to effectively enforce his right to contact with his children (Article 8) and had subjected him to unreasonable delay in his legal proceedings, failed to provide legal aid and treated him unfairly at trial (Article 6).

Decision. The court stated that its role in parental disputes over custody was not to substitute itself for the domestic authorities but to review the decisions made by those authorities with regard to the margin of appreciation. There was an effective and simple procedure by which the applicant could enforce his rights and the primary obstacle to this was the actions of the mother. The court accepted that:

> ". . . the applicant faced significant difficulties in enforcing his rights to contact, which involved courts in two jurisdictions, but would note that these flowed inevitably form the unilateral actions of the mother, and her determination to avoid complying with the court order".

Thus the authorities had taken reasonable steps to locate the family and to deal with the applicant's requests for enforcement of contact orders, and had not delayed unduly. Coercive steps such as imprisoning the mother for contempt of court were not found to have been required. Thus there was no breach of Article 8 since the authorities had not failed to protect the applicant's right to respect for his family life. Further, the delay in the proceedings did not violate Article 6 (1) since: the proceedings were very complex; the courts examined and dealt with each of the applicant's claims within a reasonable time of him bringing them; and part of the delay was due to the applicant's own actions. The applicant's remaining Article 6 arguments were also rejected, and the court found that his allegation of violation of Article 9 by the courts' attitude to his Catholic beliefs was unsubstantiated.

There is a great deal of overlap between the right to respect for family life under Article 8 and the right to found a family under Article 12. Yet some cases will fail to satisfy the tests for a finding of a violation of either Article, since neither Article creates an absolute right. Although in general prisoners have the same human rights as any other persons, including the right to respect for their private life as seen in *Golder v. U.K.* and *Silver v. U.K.*, some rights are inevitably restricted under a sentence of imprisonment. The domestic rule is that a prisoner, once convicted, retains all rights which were not expressly or impliedly removed as a result of his lawful detention in custody.[51] Thus in *R v. Secretary of State for The Home Department, ex parte Mellor*[52]: **8–126**

Facts. The applicant was a prisoner serving a life sentence for murder and unlikely to be released before 2006, when he would be 35. He had married a former prison officer whilst in prison, and she would be 31 at his likely release date. They were both very keen to have a child. He requested to be allowed to found a family citing Article 12, and stated that since there were no guarantees that he would ever be released he would like to do so by artificial insemination. This would involve him visiting a hospital to give a sperm sample. There were no medical or legal reasons why the treatment should not go ahead. But in November 1998 the Home Secretary refused the request, citing both concerns about the stability of the couple's relationship and the fact that the only reason why artificial insemination was required was the husband's imprisonment.

The Home Secretary's policy was to refuse all artificial insemination requests unless there were truly exceptional circumstances. The Prison Service criteria therefore refused insemination unless it was medically necessary and conception would not be possible after the prisoner's release. Even if these factors did exist, there were many other policy reasons to be satisfied before insemination would be allowed. Mr Mellor therefore sought judicial review of the decision, arguing:

1. His right to have a child by artificial insemination had not been expressly taken away by statute, nor had it been removed by necessary implication; thus he must still be allowed to enjoy that right.
2. The Secretary of State's refusal was unjustified and based on irrelevant factors; any decision to have a child was for the couple alone to make. He should have concerned himself only with matters affecting prison security, order and discipline.
3. The refusal also effectively prevented Mrs Mellor from exercising her own right to found a family.

Decision. Forbes J. found that Article 8 does not give a fundamental right to a prisoner to provide sperm for the artificial insemination of his wife and, even if he did have such a right, it would be part of the right to marry and found a family under Article 12. In *Hamer v. U.K.*[53] the Commission stated that Article 12 does not mean that at all times it must be made possible for a person to procreate: "It would seem that the situation of a lawfully convicted person detained in prison in which the applicant finds himself falls under his own responsibility, and that his right to found a family has not otherwise been infringed". Thus in the present case the refusal of conjugal visits for prisoners is justified, and so is the refusal of conception by other means:

> "In reality, what Mr Mellor seeks is to be granted the privilege or benefit of being afforded access to artificial insemination services because an inevitable consequence of his lawful detention in custody is that he is unable to cohabit with his wife and he cannot enjoy any conjugal visits from her, therefore making it impossible for his wife to conceive a child by the usual natural means".

The Home Secretary's policy was not irrational and was one which he was entitled to make, given the various public interest considerations involved. Thus the application was refused.

Article 8(1) Correspondence

8–127 Correspondence nowadays is not restricted merely to letters and written communications but extends to telephones (see below), wire services, e-mail and the like, and in general any interference with private communications by the public authorities is to be considered a violation of Article 8. However, correspondence between prisoners and outsiders has led to that right being questioned. For instance in *Golder v. United Kingdom*[54] the court considered whether the preventing of writing to a solicitor with a view to taking a libel action against a prison officer was a violation of Article 8(1) and especially whether the interference was justified for "the prevention of disorder or crime". The court held that the applicant had a right to consult a solicitor and that it was not up to Home Secretary to consider the legal prospects for any possible future proceedings—that is the court's domain. Therefore, by refusing the free flow of correspondence on this matter, interference could not be justified as being "necessary in a democratic society", and therefore, there had been a violation of Article 8.

In *Campbell v. United Kingdom*[55]:

Facts. The applicant was convicted of murder in Scotland and sentenced to life imprisonment there (recommended to serve no less than 20 years). In respect of possible future legal proceedings against the Secretary of State for Scotland, for various claims suffered by the applicant whilst in prison, and complaints to the Commission, the applicant wished to write to his solicitor without his correspondence being interfered with. The Deputy Governor of the Prison gave him an assurance that only matters concerning his ECHR complaint would not be tampered with, but that all other mail would be scrutinised, under the then Prisons (Scotland) Act 1952. The Government admitted that some ECHR mail had been opened. The applicant complained to the Commission that such interference with his correspondence by the prison authorities was a breach of Article 8.

Opinion of the Commission. The Commission cited *Silver v. United Kingdom*,[56] that a prisoner has the same rights with regard to the free flow of correspondence as any ordinary person, unless it can be justified under Article 8(2) and that any interference in principle amounts to a violation of Article 8. The opening of the correspondence was found to be "in accordance with the law" under the then section 35 of the Prisons (Scotland) Act 1952. Although legal professional privilege should be protected, letters which contain matter which is confidential between lawyer and client may be opened in circumstances where there is a reasonable suspicion that the privileged channel of communication is being abused.[57] The expression "necessary in a democratic society" has the meaning that the interference must correspond to a "pressing social need" and be proportionate to the legitimate aim pursued. In such cases, the opening of letters may be justified for the prevention of disorder and crime.[58] In this instance, no such accusations were made by the Government. Therefore (by 11 votes to one) there was a violation of Article 8 regarding his possible future proceedings against the Secretary of State for Scotland. The Commission also formed the opinion that general correspondence between a solicitor and his client, because of the professional status of solicitors, did not reach the required exemption of a "pressing social need" and this amounted to a breach of Article 8(2). In a partly dissenting opinion, Mr H.G. Schermers distinguished between incoming and outgoing mail. He said incoming mail should always be opened, (to ensure that no drugs had been enclosed) but if verified that it is from the prisoner's lawyer, then it should not be read. All other incoming mail, since it probably does not contain confidential information, should be read. But in general, outgoing mail should not be opened since it may contain detrimental accusations against prison officers themselves.

Finding of the Court. Having found that the interference was "in accordance with the law" and that there was a legitimate aim involved, *i.e.* the correspondence did not contain material which was detrimental to prison order and security or related to crime, the court then went on to consider whether it was necessary in a democratic society, *i.e.* corresponded to a pressing social need and that it was proportionate to the legitimate aim pursued. The court said that letters between solicitor and client are generally privileged but could be opened, but not read, where there are reasonable grounds to suspect that some illicit object or substance was enclosed. The letter may be read in circumstances where "the authorities have reasonable cause to believe that the privilege is being abused in that the contents of the letter endanger prison security or the safety of others or are otherwise of a criminal nature",[59] and provides sufficient safeguards against the possibility of abuse. Therefore, there was a violation of Article 8(2).

In a partly dissenting judgement, Judge Morenilla stated that since the applicant was considered to be a dangerous man (a Category A prisoner for over two years), there was a necessity to open his mail in the prisoner's presence to ensure that no illegal material was enclosed which would imperil the safety and security of the prison.

Brief Outline and Germane Cases

8–128 It should be borne in mind that there will soon be new case law regarding in the relationship between the protection of privacy in United Kingdom law and the rights under the ECHR, but at present the protection given to privacy rights by United Kingdom law is patchy and comes from many disparate sources.

Trespass

A person's right to use and enjoyment of his land.
Bernstein v. Skyview and General Ltd [1978]; *Snook v. Mannon* [1982].

Public Nuisance
Criminal offence and also a tort.
Att.-Gen. v. PYA Quarries [1957]; *R. v. Johnson* [1996].

Private Nuisance

Breach of copyright
Copyright, Designs and Patents Act 1988 ss.11, 85, 87.

The Lady Anne Tennant v. Associated Newspapers Group Ltd [1979]; *Williams v. Settle* [1960].

Defamation
Malicious falsehood
Kaye v. Robertson [1991].

Breach of confidence
Att.-Gen. v. Guardian Newspapers (No. 2) [1990].

Requirements:
Creation Records v. News Group Newspapers [1997]; *Prince Albert v. Strange* [1849].
Argyll v. Argyll [1965]; *Stephens v. Avery* [1988]; *Barrymore v. News Group Newspapers* [1997].

Defences:
Lion Laboratories v. Evans [1984]; *X v. Y* [1988].

Telephone tapping:
Malone v. Commissioner of Police of the Metropolis (No. 2) [1979]; *Francome v. Mirror Group Newspapers* [1984].

Protection of journalistic sources: s.10 CCA 1981.

Data Protection Act 1984.

Interception of Communications Act 1985.

Protection From Harassment Act 1997.
Burstow [1996]; *Ireland* [1997].
Malicious Communications Act 1985.

Privacy and the Press.

Press Complaints Commission—role and powers; Codes of Conduct.

Police Act 1997.

Endnotes

[1] Article 2.
[2] Article 17.
[3] Article 8.
[4] "Infringement of privacy", Consultation Paper, July 1993, para. 3.7.
[5] *ibid.*, para. 3.12.
[6] *Textbook on Civil Liberties*, (Blackstone Press, 1997), p. 338.
[7] Report on the Committee on Privacy and Related Matters, Cmnd 1102, 1990.
[8] *Privacy and Freedom*, p. 7 (1970).
[9] Report on the Committee on Privacy, Cmnd 5012, 1972.
[10] 4 Harv. L.R. 193–220.
[11] See Feldman, *Civil Liberties and Human Rights in England and Wales*, Chap. 8 for a more detailed discussion on U.S. privacy law and surrounding issues.
[12] (1965) 381 U.S. 479.
[13] By Douglas J.; the remainder of the supreme court took a somewhat narrower approach.
[14] See *Meyer v. Nebraska* (1923) 262 U.S. 390.
[15] *Roe v. Wade* (1973) 410 U.S. 113.
[16] *Griswold v. Connecticut*.
[17] Feldman, *Civil Liberties and Human Rights in England and Wales*, (Oxford University Press), pp. 381–82. Grateful acknowledgment is made to the author and publisher for their permission to quote from this work.
[18] See the Warren and Brandeis article, cited above.
[19] [1978] 1 Q.B. 479.
[20] *ibid.* at 486.
[21] *ibid.* at 488.
[22] *ibid.* at 489.
[23] [1900] 1 Q.B. 752.
[24] The trainer could not have sued for trespass—only the owner of the land. See *Kaye v. Robertson* below where there might have been a successful action in trespass had the hospital authorities decided to take action against the press intruders.
[25] *Dunster v. Abbott* [1954] 1 W.L.R. 58.
[26] [1967] 2 Q.B. 939.
[27] [1982] Crim.L.R. 601.
[28] Prior refusal to enter the grounds of a property may be strong evidence to suggest that any future entry will not constitute an implied permission to be there.
[29] Younger Committee Report, app. 1, para. 18.
[30] See *Patel v. Patel* [1988] 2 F.L.R. 179 and *Khorasandijan v. Bush* [1993] Q.B. 727.
[31] [1993] Q.B. 727, C.A.
[32] [1995] 1 W.L.R. 1372.
[33] [1997] A.C. 655.
[34] *The Times*, December 11, 1997.
[35] *The Times*, June 23, 1999.
[36] Lord Denning in *Att.-Gen. v. P.Y.A. Quarries* [1957] 2 Q.B. 169.
[37] [1957] 2 Q.B. 169.
[38] [1996] Crim.L.R. 504.
[39] [1979] 5 F.S.R. 298.
[40] [1960] 1 W.L.R. 1072.
[41] *ibid.* at 1082.
[42] [1999] 3 W.L.R. 1010.
[43] [1997] 25 E.H.R.R. 1.
[44] [1986] 8 E.H.R.R. 407.
[45] In "A New Legal Landscape? Libel Law and Freedom of Political Expression in the United Kingdom", E.H.R.L.R. 5 [2000] 476–492.
[46] Also called "trade libel".
[47] See *Radcliffe v. Evans* [1892] 2 Q.B. 524.
[48] [1993] 1 W.L.R. 337.
[49] *ibid.* at 340.
[50] [1991] F.S.R. 62.
[51] *ibid.* at 70.

[52] This was supported by P. Prescott in *Kaye v. Robertson—A Reply* (1991) 54 M.L.R. 451–546. The only real pertinent question being whether Mr Kaye would in law be allowed to bring the action, and if not whether the hospital would take it upon themselves to sue for trespass.
[53] [1990] 1 A.C. 109 at 176 and 177 and see *Att.-Gen. v. Guardian Newspapers Ltd* [1988] 3 All E.R. 545 at 659.
[54] [1995] 4 All E.R. 473.
[55] At para. 4.5.
[56] *The Times*, April 29, 1997.
[57] "Confidential communication" is defined in the Oxford English Dictionary, Second Edition, Vol. 3 as "a communication made between parties who stand in a confidential relation to each other, and therefore privileged in law"; entrusted with secrets.
[58] See *Stephens v. Avery* below.
[59] See *Fraser v. Evans* [1968] 3 W.L.R. 1172. In (v), any legal action for breach of confidence may only be instigated by the confider, unlike proceedings against some form of breach of privacy where generally the person who publishes the particular details stands in no pre-existing relationship with his "victim", but nevertheless, a claim may be brought under one of the other recognised protection laws, such as trespass, defamation, Copyright and Patents Act 1988, etc.
[60] [1849] De Gex and Smales' Report, Vol. II 1848–1849, page 652.
[61] It was stated that in *British Steel Corporation v. Granada Television Ltd* [1981] that there is "a very strong public interest in preserving confidentiality within any organisation, in order that it can operate efficiently, and also be free from suspicion that it is harbouring disloyal employees."
[62] [1981] 2 All E.R. 321.
[63] *ibid.* at 337.
[64] *ibid.* at 334.
[65] [1969] R.P.C. 41.
[66] *ibid.* at 48.
[67] [1965] 2 W.L.R. 790.
[68] [1849] De Gex and Smales' Report, Vol II 1848–1849, at page 652.
[69] [1889] 40 Ch.D. 345.
[70] *ibid.* at 801.
[71] [1978] F.S.R. 573.
[72] [1948] R.P.C. 65.
[73] Adapted in *Coco v. Clark* [1969] R.P.C. 41.
[74] Stated by Megarry J. in *Coco v. Clark* above, when referring to the consideration under which the court might use its equitable discretion.
[75] Where commercial interests are involved, the confidential information must have some novelty or originality about it, even if, for instance, the product concerned, had to be made up from everyday materials available on the open market. See *Coco v. Clark* [1969] R.P.C. 41 at 47.
[76] [1988] 1 Ch. 449.
[77] *ibid.* at 454.
[78] [1997] F.S.R 600.
[79] *Stephens v. Avery* [1988] 1 Ch 449 at 456.
[80] [1988] 2 All E.R. 648.
[81] *ibid.* at 656.
[82] [1977] 1 W.L.R. 760.
[83] *ibid.* at 764.
[84] (1980) 124 N.L.J. 149.
[85] (1997) Ch.D. (unreported).
[86] See *Att.-Gen. v. Jonathan Cape Ltd* [1976] Q.B. 752.
[87] [1984] 3 W.L.R. 539.
[88] *Lion Laboratories v. Evans* [1984] 3 W.L.R. 539 at 546.
[89] *British Steel Corporation v. Granada Television Ltd* [1981] A.C. 1096 at 1168 where it was said that the public are interested in many private matters which are no real concern of theirs and which the public have no pressing need to know.
[90] *Francome v. Mirror Group Newspapers* [1984] 1 W.L.R. 892 at 898.
[91] *ibid.*
[92] [1988] 2 All E.R. 648.
[93] [2000] 3 All E.R. 989.

[94] [2001] E.M.L.R. 10.
[95] *The Times*, January 16, 2001.
[96] [2001] 2 All E.R. 385.
[97] [1995] HMSO Cm. 2850.
[98] See Chap. 5, "Official Secrecy and Freedom of Information".
[99] [2001] E.M.L.R. 4.
[1] C. Camp, "Openness and Accountability in the Workplace" (1999) 149 N.L.J. 46.
[2] [1979] 2 All E.R. 620.
[3] *ibid.* at 646.
[4] [1969] 1 All E.R. 8.
[5] *ibid.* at 11.
[6] *Woodward v. Hutchins* [1977] 1 W.L.R. 760.
[7] *Initital Services Ltd v. Putterill* [1967] 3 All E.R. 145.
[8] *Lion Laboratories v. Evans* [1984] 3 W.L.R. 539.
[9] *Malone v. CPM*, see above, at 645.
[10] [1984] 2 All E.R. 408.
[11] *ibid.* at 413.
[12] ss. 4 and 5.
[13] s. 5 and Sched. 1.
[14] Sched. 1.
[15] For example it may be considered better that a terminally ill person should live his remaining days without the knowledge that he is about to die; although there are arguments against this, it does happen.
[16] (1994) 7 E.H.R.R. 14.
[17] (1997) 24 E.H.R.R. 523.
[18] (1992) 14 E.H.R.R. 657.
[19] Received Royal assert July 28, 2000.
[20–21] Scc preamble to Statute.
[22] See *Klass v. Germany*.
[23] For a complete list see section 6(2)(a)–(j).
[24] "Covert" means that surveillance is carried out in such a manner that the persons under surveillance are unaware of its existence (section 26(10)).
[25] "Private information" in relation to a person includes any information concerning his private or public life (section 26(9)).
[26] Directed surveillance also includes interception via a postal service or communication system where consent has been obtained by the sender or recipient (section 48(4)).
[27] For a full list see Sched. 1 of the Act.
[28] For a full list see s. 32(s).
[29] s. 44.
[30] For the complete list of those entitled to act on behalf of a senior authorising officer or designated deputy see s. 34(4).
[31] Her Majesty's forces exclude the Royal Navy Regulation Branch, the Royal Military Police and the Royal Air Force Police—these services come under the same category as other police forces.
[32] See also s. 5 of the Intelligence Services Act 1994.
[33] [1985] 7 E.H.R.R. 14.
[34] [1996].
[35] [1997] 1 All E.R. 112.
[36] See *Re an Inquiry under the Company Securities (Insider Dealing) Act 1985* [1988] A.C. 660 at 710 where it was stated that "it cannot, . . . be an essential characteristic of such information that the result to which it will lead should be predicated with precision before it is even known what the information is".
[37] *ibid.* at 704, *per* Lord Griffith: "necessary has meaning which lies somewhere between 'indispensable' on the one hand, and 'useful' or 'expedient' on the other . . .".
[37A] *ibid.* at 709.
[38] [1990] 2 W.L.R. 421.
[39] *ibid.* at 703.
[40] [1991] 1 A.C. 1 at 43.
[41] In "Protecting Journalists' Sources" by Stephanie Powers [1992] P.L. 61 it was stated that "In giving such emphasis to the manner in which information as obtained, the court is showing a preoccupation with breach of confidence and is not giving sufficient weight to the public interest in the free flow of information".

[42] [1991] 1 A.C. 1.
[43] [1990] 2 W.L.R. 421 at 438.
[44] *ibid.* at 45.
[45] [1988] A.C. 660.
[46] [1985] A.C. 339.
[47] *ibid.* at 354, *per* Lord Diplock.
[48] Lord Roskill (majority) disagreed and said that it was not necessary to prove that all other avenues had been tried. Such investigation takes time and might damage the grounds for an eventual application if it could have been made earlier.
[49] (2001) 1 W.L.R. 515.
[50] See *Goodwin v. U.K.* (1996) E.H.R.R. 123.
[51] See Children and Young Persons Act 1933, ss. 39(1) and 49(1).
[52] [1994] 3 W.L.R. 20.
[53] See *Re W* [1992] 1 W.L.R. 100.
[54] [1994] 3 W.L.R. 20 at 38.
[55] See John Gardiner, "Another Step Toward a Right of Privacy", N.L.J. (February 17, 1995), pp. 225–226.
[56] [1979] A.C. 440.
[57] *ibid.* at 450.
[58] *ibid.* at 452.
[59] See *R. v. Socialist Worker, ex p. Att.-Gen.* [1975] Q.B. 637.
[60] [1988] 1 Q.B. 540.
[61] [1917] 2 K.B. 254.
[62] *ibid.* at 271.
[63] *R. v. Malvern Justices, exp. Evans* [1988] 1 Q.B. 540 at 550.
[64] *R. v. Tower Bridge Magistrates' Court, ex p. Osbourne* (1989) 88 Cr. App. R. 28.
[65] *R. v. Westminster County Council, ex p. Castelli*, *The Times*, August 4, 1995.
[66] [1988] Q.B. 553.
[67] *ibid.* at 562.
[68] *The Times*, November 8, 1984.
[69] A similar point was made by Borrie and Lowe, *The Law of Contempt* by, (3rd ed.), pp. 302–303.
[70] But now see the Criminal Justice Consultative Council's Trial Issues Group's "Statement of National Standards of Witness Care in the Criminal Justice System" and approved by Lord Bingham C.J., where it was stated that it is not necessary for a witness to give their address. Also see 161 J.P. 351–353 for a full discussion on this issue.
[71] [1975] Q.B. 637.
[72] see *R. v. Taylor (Gary)* [1994] T.L.R. 484: in this case, the defendant could not directly see the witness, because she was behind a screen, but he could see her on a video monitor.
[73] PCC Report No. 4. October–December 1997, p. 6.
[74] The Code of practice literature in the booklet states that "the Code should not be interpreted so narrowly as to compromise its commitment to respect the rights of the individual, nor so broadly that it prevents publication in the public interest".
[75] Quoted from Lord Wakeham's speech on Privacy and Public Interest, hosted by the Michael Page City Executive Club in Pall Mall on November 21, 1996.
[76] Press Complaints Commission Annual Report 1995.
[77–78] PCC Annual Report 1996.
[79] Figures provided by PCC Reports [1997] Nos. 37–40 inclusive.
[80] PCC Report No. 29, March/April 1995, p. 6.
[81] *ibid.*, p. 10.
[82] *Malone v. U.K.* [1985] 7 E.H.R.R. 14 at para. 67.
[83–84] See *Margareta and Roger Andersson v. Sweden* [1992] 14 E.H.R.R. 615 at para. 75.
[85] *The Sunday Times v. U.K.* [1979–80] 2 E.H.R.R. 245 at para. 45.
[86] [1979] 2 E.H.R.R. 214.
[87] *ibid.* at para. 50.
[88] [1985] 7 E.H.R.R. 14.
[89] See *Huvig v. France* [1990] 12 E.H.R.R. 528 on the meaning of "law" at paras 27–28.
[90] *ibid.* at para. 67.
[91] *ibid.* at para. 68.
[92] *ibid.* at para. 79.
[93] App. No. 35394/97; judgement May 12, 2000.

[93A] (1978) 2 E.H.R.R. 214.
[94] 73/1996/692/884, *The Times*, July 3; [1997] 24 E.H.R.R. 523.
[95] [1987] 9 E.H.R.R. 433.
[96] *ibid.* at para. 59.
[97] "Personnel control" means "the obtaining of information from police registers in respect of persons holding or being considered for appointment to posts of importance for national security" (para. 24).
[98] *Klass v. Germany* [1979–1980] 2 E.H.R.R. 214.
[99] [1992] 14 E.H.R.R. 657.
[1] [1979–80] 2 E.H.R.R. 245.
[2] *ibid.* at para. 40.
[3] [1990] 12 E.H.R.R. 1.
[4] *ibid.* at para. 66.
[5] For a full discussion of "necessary in a domestic society" see Art. 10, p. 94.
[6] *Handyside v. U.K.* [1979–80] 1 E.H.R.R. 737 at para. 48.
[7] *ibid.* at para. 27.
[8] *X and Y v. The Netherlands* [1986] 8 E.H.R.R. 235 at para. 23.
[9] *ibid.*
[10] *ibid.* at para. 27.
[11] *Dudgeon v. U.K.* [1982] 4 E.H.R.R. 149 at para. 41.
[12] [1979–80] 3 E.H.R.R. 63.
[13] Now 18 years of age; but likely to be reduced to 16 in the near future in order to be consistent with the rule for heterosexual sex. See *Sutherland v. U.K.* [2001] 24 E.H.R.R. Ch.D. 220.
[14] [1979–80] 3 E.H.R.R. 63 at para. 147.
[15] *ibid.* at para. 148.
[16] *ibid.* at para. 149.
[17] *ibid.* at para. 154.
[18] [1982] 4 E.H.R.R. 149.
[19] *ibid.* at para. 56.
[20] *ibid.* at para. 57.
[21] *ibid.* at para. 60.
[22] For decisions involving transsexuals see *Rees v. U.K.* [1986] 9 E.H.R.R. 56 and *Cossey v. U.K.* [1991] 13 E.H.R.R. 622.
[23] App. No. 35765/97.
[24] [2001] App. No. 000251864/94.
[25] [1999] App. Nos 00031417/96, 00032377/96, 00033985/96, 0033986/96.
[26] See *Powell and Raynor v. U.K.* [1990] 12 E.H.R.R. 355.
[27] See *Niemietz v. Germany* [1993] 16 E.H.R.R. 97.
[28] (A/256–C): App. No. 1266/87, February 25, 1993.
[29] [1995] 19 E.H.R.R. CD 20, 2 P.L.R. 10.
[30] [1986] 11 E.H.R.R. 325.
[31] No proceedings had been taken against her under the Caravan Sites Act 1968 ("to provide adequate accommodation for gypsies"), nor the Criminal Justice and Public Order Act 1994 ("unauthorised campers").
[32] [1995] 2 P.L.R. 10 at 23.
[33] *ibid.* at para. 73.
[34] *ibid.*
[35] [2001] App. Nos 00027238/95, 00024882/94, 0024876/94, 00025289/94, 0025154/94.
[36] [1993] 16 E.H.R.R. 97.
[37] *ibid.* at para. 29.
[38] *Leander v. Sweden* [1987] 9 E.H.R.R. 433 at para. 48.
[39] [1990] 12 E.H.R.R. 36.
[40] The public interest in this case being "the efficient functioning of the child care system on the one hand, and the applicant's interest in having access to a coherent record of his personal history on the other": *ibid.* at para. 40.
[41] Boarding-Out of Children Regulations 1955—Reg. 10.
[42] [1990] 12 E.H.R.R. 36 at para. 49.
[43] [1979–80] 2 E.H.R.R. 330.
[44] *ibid.* at para. 14.
[45] [1987] 9 E.H.R.R. 203.

[46] Some protection is given to immigration problems under the Fourth Protocol, but as yet, the U.K. has not ratified this particular Article.
[47] [1985] 7 E.H.R.R. 471.
[48] *ibid.* at para. 66.
[49] *ibid.* at para. 67.
[50] ECHR, August 29, 2000.
[51] *Raymond v. Honey* [1983] 1 A.C.I.
[52] [2000] Q.B.D. July 31, 2000.
[53] (1982) 4 E.H.R.R. 139.
[54] [1979–80] 1 E.H.R.R. 524.
[55] [1993] 15 E.H.R.R. 137.
[56] [1983] 5 E.H.R.R. 347.
[57] *Campbell v. U.K.* [1993] 5 E.H.R.R. 137 at para. 55 and *Campbell and Fell v. U.K.* [1984] 7 E.H.R.R. 165 at paras 111–113.
[58] [1983] 5 E.H.R.R. 347 at para. 44.
[59] *ibid.* at para. 48.

CHAPTER 9

FREEDOM FROM DISCRIMINATION

1. Introduction

Discrimination is a fact and reality in society, albeit an unpleasant and undesirable one, but people are discriminated against on a regular basis for a huge variety of grounds. Yet discrimination itself is a lawful and to some extent a necessary element of the workings of any part of society: it would be impossible to recruit the best person for a job if all applicants had to be treated equally regardless of ability or qualifications, for example; each person is free to choose his own friends on any basis he wishes to adopt; and it would not be in anyone's best interests to require all manufacturers of children's clothing to also make clothes for adults. We expect our children to learn to differentiate between right and wrong, yet these are standards which change over time and between societies. In a perfect world, there would be equality of opportunity for all people, but in the real world different people have different abilities and resources. Poverty, upbringing, educational ability or performance and physical attractiveness all play discriminatory roles in a person's life, yet such factors are beyond the reach and control of discrimination legislation. **9–001**

Freedom of choice is a valued right of the individual; it is only when such freedom conflicts with the fundamental rights of others to fair treatment that it must be limited. There are certain types of discrimination where individual freedom of choice and behaviour is subordinated to a higher moral ideal, and so discrimination on grounds of sex, race and disability is in most regards unlawful. Other types of discrimination may soon be addressed by law, principally age discrimination. But there is another dimension to anti-discrimination law as it currently stands; even where the law does attack discrimination, it only does so in a limited number of fields which are considered particularly important, such as education, housing and employment. It is still perfectly legal to refuse to admit a person to your own home on the basis of race or sex, for example; it is impossible for the law to prevent a person from forming his own views on the basis of unjustifiable prejudice, so the law seeks only to prevent such prejudiced views from finding an outlet and does not make many inroads into the private views and behaviour of individuals.

The relativity of moral standards in society is reflected in the law. Thus anti-discrimination law is a complex and partial field within which reform is gradual and piecemeal. The historical development of the statutory legal framework and relevant case law for each of racial, sexual and disability discrimination will be examined separately, and possible reforms will also be addressed.

2. Racial Discrimination: Race Relations Act 1976: Introduction

9–002 The Race Relations Act 1976 was a modelled to a large extent upon the Sex Discrimination Act 1975, but was the third statute to prohibit discrimination on racial grounds. The need for a statutory ban on racial discrimination was evidenced throughout the 1950s and 1960s; increased immigration was met by intolerance, unfair treatment in employment and services, fear and rioting. The colour of a person's skin makes it easy to identify him for unfair treatment, and the common law rarely prevented discrimination or provided any remedy since it did not have any traditional basis on which to do so. The first legislative step was the Race Relations Act 1965, which provided only a limited prohibition on discrimination in particular fields; it created an offence of incitement to racial hatred, and outlawed discrimination in the provision of particular services, such as the granting of tenancies, and the use of dance halls and public houses. But it was a hesitant and narrow response to a large and widespread problem, and made no attempt to tackle such obvious problems as discrimination in employment. The Race Relations Board was placed in charge of a system of conciliation, with legal remedies available only when all else had failed. Criticism of both the scope of the Act and the enforcement procedure was almost immediate.[1] As a result, it was swiftly followed by the Race Relations Act 1968, which extended the scope of the statutory prohibition to cover racial discrimination in the fields of employment, housing, provision of goods or services, and advertisements. The 1968 Act also strengthened enforcement procedures by giving the Race Relations Board a power to bring cases to court, and set up a new body entrusted with the promotion of positive race relations—the Community Relations Commission. But this second statute was again short-lived. It had become obvious that racial discrimination remained rife by the early 1970s; although the extension of the scope of the law had largely removed the most obvious evidence of racial discrimination, such as job advertisements which stated that only white applicants need apply, it was still perfectly possible for an employer to achieve a discriminatory result by manipulating or evading the law. The White Paper which preceded the 1976 Race Relations Act stated that:

> ". . . the time has come for a determined effort by Government, by industry and unions, and by ordinary men and women, to ensure fair and equal treatment for all our people, regardless of their race, colour or national

origins. Racial discrimination, and the remediable disadvantages experienced by sections of the community because of their colour or ethnic origins are not only morally unacceptable, not only individual injustices for which there must be remedies, but also a form of economic and social waste which we as a society cannot afford . . .".[2]

"It is not possible to provide a quantifiable measure of the practical impact of the 1968 Act. Generally, the law has had an important declaratory effect and had given support to those who do not wish to discriminate but would otherwise feel compelled to do so by social pressure. It had also made crude, overt forms of racial discrimination much less common . . . And yet, . . . statutory bodies have forcefully drawn attention to the inability of the legislation to deal with widespread patterns of discrimination, especially in employment and housing, a lack of confidence among minority groups ineffectiveness of the law, and a lack of credibility in the efficacy of the work of the Race Relations Board and the Community Relations Commission themselves. The continuing unequal status of Britain's racial minorities and the extent of the disadvantage from which the suffer provide ample evidence of the inadequacy of existing policies".[3]

The 1976 Act repealed the earlier legislation and extended the fields in which discrimination on racial grounds is forbidden to include contact workers, clubs and partnerships. The definition of racial discrimination was also extended to include indirect discrimination and discrimination on the basis of nationality. The Act provides civil actions and remedies for unlawful discrimination, rather than criminalising it; the State is only incidentally involved in the resolution of disputes between individuals about discrimination. The aim of the law is no longer to achieve conciliation, but to provide legal remedies for discrimination and ultimately to investigate and act to prevent it. A new body was created to promote racial equality, investigate allegations and, to some extent, provide victim support—The Commission for Racial Equality. The role and functions of this body will be examined at a later stage in this chapter; first, it is necessary to look at the scope of the statutory prohibition of racial discrimination. All statutory references in the following discussion are to the Race Relations Act 1976, unless otherwise stated.

What is Racial Discrimination?

Section 1 of the 1976 Act provides that: **9–003**

"1(1) A person discriminates against another in any circumstances relevant for the purposes of any provision of this Act if—

(a) on racial grounds he treats that other less favourably than he treats or would treat other persons; or
(b) he applies to that other a requirement or condition which he applies or would apply equally to persons not of the same racial group as that other but—

(i) which is such that the proportion of persons of the same racial group as that other who can comply with it is considerably smaller than the proportion of persons not of that racial group who can comply with it; and

(ii) which he cannot show to be justifiable irrespective of the colour, race, nationality or ethnic or national origins of the person to whom it is applied; and

(iii) which it is to the detriment of that other because he cannot comply with it.

1(2) It is hereby declared that, for the purposes of this Act, segregating a person from other persons on racial grounds is treating him less favourably than they are treated."

This is taken further by section 2:

"(1) A person ('the discriminator') discriminates against another person ('the person victimised') in any circumstances relevant for the purposes of any provision of this Act if he treats the person victimised less favourably than in those circumstances he treats or would treat other persons, and does so by reason that the person victimised has—

(a) brought proceedings against the discriminator or any other person under this Act; or
(b) given evidence or information in connection with proceedings brought by any person against the discriminator or any other person under this Act; or
(c) otherwise done anything under or by reference to this Act in relation to the discriminator or any other person; or
(d) alleged that the discriminator or any other person has committed an act which . . . would amount to a contravention of this Act, or by reason that the discriminator knows that the person victimised intends to do any of those things, or suspects that the person victimised has done, or intends to do, any of them.

(2) Subsection (1) does not apply to treatment of a person by reason of any allegation made by him if the allegation was false and not made in good faith."

Thus there are three types of unlawful discrimination under the Act:

(1) Direct discrimination (treating a person less favourably on racial grounds).

(2) Indirect discrimination (applying a condition with which it is more difficult for persons of a racial group to comply).

(3) Victimisation.

Each of the types of discrimination will be looked at separately.

1. Direct discrimination: section 1(1)(a)

9–004 Direct discrimination is when a person is treated less favourably than another on the basis of his race; for example, if a person is denied housing or employment when a person of another race would have been accepted.

The reason why the lesser treatment is given is irrelevant; there is no need to establish that the discriminator was even aware that he was discriminating against the victim, simply that this actions had that effect. The discriminator will still be liable even if he acted out of a misguided desire to protect the victim from the actions or prejudices of others, for example because the victim would be the only black employee in a company where other employees were known to have racist beliefs. In *R. v. CRE, ex parte Westminster City Council*,[4] it was held that the victim had been treated less favourably on racial grounds when he was moved to another workplace because he had been the victim of discrimination by other employees. The question is simply whether, but for the victim's race, he would have been treated differently. The leading authority on this point is the sex discrimination case of *James v. Eastleigh Borough Council*,[5] where Lord Goff stated in the House of Lords:

> ". . . cases of direct discrimination under section 1(1)(a) can be considered by asking the simple question: would the complainant have received the same treatment from the defendant but for his or her sex?[6] This simple test . . . avoids, in most cases at least, complicated questions relating to concepts such as intention, motive, reason or purpose, and the danger of confusion arising from the misuse of those elusive terms".

But the victim's race need not be the only reason why he was treated less favourably; it need only be a substantial cause of the less favourable treatment. In *Owen & Briggs v. James*[7] it was held that it was irrelevant that there were other reasons why a black job applicant had been rejected, if race played an important part in the employer's decision. To decide whether the victim's treatment was "less favourable", it is necessary to compare like with like:

> ". . . in judging whether there has been discrimination you have to compare the treatment actually meted out with the treatment which would have been afforded to a man having all the same characteristics as the complainant except his race or his attitude to race. Only by excluding matters of race can you discover whether the differential treatment was on racial grounds".[8]

The use of racial stereotypes is discrimination; for example as in *Alexander v. Home Office*,[9] where a West Indian prisoner had applied to work in the prison kitchens but his request was turned down, and a report made about him stated that he had: "the anti-authoritarian arrogance that seems the be common in most coloured inmates". It was held that the complainant had been treated as part of a negative racial stereotype rather than as an individual. So, it is discriminatory to make assumptions about a person based upon a belief in stereotypical racial characteristics, but it would be lawful if a person were treated less favourably because of a characteristic which he himself does possess and which could be attributed to a particular race. This distinction is difficult to draw and may provide discriminators with a relatively easy excuse; *e.g.* "I rejected the applicant for the job because his English was poor, not because people of this racial/ nationality tend to have poor English".

Section 1(2) provides that segregation is to be regarded as less favourable treatment. It is the fact of segregation which is at issue here; even if the facilities provided for the segregated groups are identical, discrimination occurs. In *PEL Ltd v. Modgill*,[10] a factory shop had an entirely Asian workforce. There had previously been white employees, but gradually vacancies had been filled by word of mouth among the local Asian community. A complaint was made on the basis of segregation, but the Employment Appeal Tribunal held that there must be evidence of either a policy of segregation, or factual segregation due to an act of the employer. Mere failure to recruit workers of other racial groups was not, therefore, less favourable treatment. One difference between the legislation forbidding racial discrimination and that relating to sex discrimination is that, for racial discrimination to be proven, it is not necessary to show that the less favourable treatment was based upon the victim's race; it need only be shown that the less favourable treatment was given "on racial grounds".[11] In *Zarcynska v. Levy*,[12] the tribunal held that the complainant, a bar worker, had been unlawfully discriminated against when she was dismissed for refusing to follow an order that she was not to serve black customers. Thus the racial grounds in question related to a third party.[13]

9–005 *"On racial grounds": section 3* Where it is direct discrimination contrary to section 1(1)(a) which is alleged, it must be shown that the complainant was treated less favourably "on racial grounds". Section 3(1) provides a further definition of this term;

> "3(1) In this Act, unless the context otherwise requires—
> 'racial grounds' means any of the following grounds, namely colour, race, nationality or ethnic or national origins;
> 'racial grounds' means a group of persons defined by reference to colour, race, nationality or ethnic or national origins, and references to a person's racial group refer to any racial group into which he falls. (2) The fact that a racial group comprises two or more distinct racial groups does not prevent it from constituting a particular racial group for the purposes of this Act.
> . . .
> 20(4) A comparison of the case of a person of a particular racial group with that of a person not of that group under section 1(1) must be such that the relevant circumstances in the one case are not materially different, in the other."

Thus it is clear that "racial grounds" stretch beyond race; and also that a person may simultaneously be a member of several different racial groups, depending on whether the analysis is based upon nationality skin colour, ethnic origin, etc.

9–006 *"National origins"* The term "national origins" was also part of the 1968 Race Relations Act, and so the decision of the House of Lords in *Ealing London Borough Council v. Race Relations Board*[14] is still relevant. The facts concerned the council's refusal to place a Polish man on its waiting list for council housing because he was not a British subject, as the rules required at that time. The House of Lords held that the victim had not been discriminated against unlawfully here because there is a distinction to be drawn between "nationality" and "national origin". The discrimination in question was on the basis of nationality, which was not prohibited under the 1968 Act (but now would be, under its replacement.) According to Lord Cross (at p. 365);

> "There is no definition of 'national origins' in the Act and one must interpret the phrase as best one can. To me it suggests a connection subsisting at the time of birth between an individual and one or more groups of people who can be described as a 'nation'—whether or not they also constitute a sovereign state. The connection will normally arise because the parents or one of the parents of the individual in question are or is identified by descent with the nation in question, but it may also sometimes arise because the parents have made their home among the people in question . . . Of course, in most cases a man has only a single 'national origin' which coincides with his nationality at birth in the legal sense and again in most cases his nationality remains unchanged throughout his life. But 'national origins' and 'nationality' in the legal sense are two quite different conceptions and they may well not coincide . . ."

Each of the terms in section 3 is therefore to be given its natural or popular meaning rather than a specialised legal or technical meaning.

"Nationality" The term "nationality" as a basis of discrimination was added to the list by the 1976 Act. Section 78(1) states that nationality includes "citizenship". But some types of discrimination are permitted by the 1976 Act and other legislation, for example higher university fees for students from outside the European Union. **9–007**

"Ethnic origins" The definition of "ethnic origins" was discussed in the House of Lords case of *Mandla v. Dowell Lee*[15]: **9–008**

Facts. A Sikh boy was refused admission to a private school because the school rules would not have permitted him to wear the turban required by his religious beliefs. His father lodged a complaint with the Commission for Racial Equality, and legal proceedings were begun on the basis that the refusal to admit the boy to the school was, *inter alia*, indirect discrimination contrary to section 1(1)(b) and section 17(a) of the 1976 Act. The County Court and the Court of Appeal both rejected the claim on the ground that Sikhs were not a "racial group" within the meaning of section 3(1). The complainant appealed to the House of Lords.

Decision. The House of Lords unanimously decided that Sikhs were a "racial group" within section 3(1). Lord Fraser stated that, in answer to the question of whether Sikhs constitute a racial group:

> "It is not suggested that Sikhs are a group defined by reference to colour, race, nationality or national origins. In none of these respects are they distinguishable from many other groups, especially those living, like most Sikhs, in the

> Punjab. The argument turns entirely upon whether they are a group defined by 'ethnic origins' . . . I recognise that 'ethnic' conveys a flavour of race but it cannot, in my opinion, have been used in the Act of 1976 in a strictly racial or biological sense . . . the word 'ethnic' still retains a racial flavour but it is used nowadays in an extend sense to include other characteristics which may be commonly thought of as being associated with common racial origin".

He considered that there were seven characteristics which indicated that a group was a "racial group" on the basis of ethnic origins. The first two characteristics he considered to be essential:

> "(1) a long shared history, of which the group is conscious as distinguishing it from other groups, and the memory of which it keeps alive;
> (2) a cultural tradition of its own, including family and social customs and manners, often but not necessarily associated with religious observance."

The remaining five characteristics he considered to be non-essential, but relevant:

> "(3) either a common geographical origin, or descent from a small number of common ancestors;
> (4) a common language, not necessarily peculiar to the group;
> (5) a common literature peculiar to the group;
> (6) a common religion different from that of neighbouring groups or from the general community surrounding it;
> (7) being a minority or being an oppressed or a dominant group within a larger group, for example a conquered people (say, the inhabitants of England shortly after the Norman conquest) and their conquerors might both be ethnic groups".

Lord Templeman took a somewhat simpler approach to determination of whether Sikhs constituted an ethnic group, and decided that they did because they constitute a "separate and distinct community" derived from characteristics such as "group descent, a group of geographical origin and a group history".

It should be noted that discrimination on the basis of religion or of politics is not within the scope of the Act. Discrimination against Muslims will not constitute direct discrimination under the Act since Muslims are not a racial group but followers of a widespread world religion. The same will apply to Christians. But in *Seide v. Gillette Industries Ltd*,[16] the tribunal stated that discrimination against a Jewish man would fall under the 1976 Act if it was based not up on the complainant's religion but rather upon the fact that he was of Jewish ethnic origin. The decision in *Mandla v. Dowell Lee* (above) now confirms that this is the case; Jews are a racial group because they have shared cultural traditions and descent. The same approach was taken in the case of *Commission for Racial Equality v. Dutton*[17]:

Facts. The defendant ran a public house in Hackney and, having had previous disagreements with travellers living in caravans which were illegally parked, he displayed a sign in his pub which stated "No Travellers". The CRE received a complaint and brought proceedings on the ground that the sign was an unlawful advertisement displayed contrary to section 29. The County Court rejected this claim on the basis that gypsies were not a racial group, and the CRE appealed to the Court of Appeal.

Decision. The Court of Appeal followed the reasoning in *Mandla* and held that gypsies are a racial group when given a narrow definition, but "travellers" are not. Nicholls L.J. stated that the two possible meanings of "gypsies" are: first and correctly, "a member of a wandering race (by themselves called Romany), of Hindu origin, which first appeared in England about the beginning of the sixteenth century and was then believed to have come from Egypt"; and, secondly and more colloquially, " 'a person who habitually wanders or who has the habits of someone who does not stay for long time in one place': in short, a nomad". Thus, if the persons alleged to be victims of discrimination fall within the first, narrower definition then they will constitute a racial group by virtue of ethnic origin, applying the characteristics listed in *Mandla*:

> "On the evidence it is clear that such gypsies are a minority, with a long shared history and a common geographical origin. They are a people who originated in northern India. They migrated thence to Europe through Persia in medieval times. They have certain, albeit limited customs of their own regarding cooking and the manner of washing. They have a distinctive style of dressing, with heavy jewellery worn by the women . . . They also furnish their caravans in a distinctive manner. They have a language or dialect . . . They do not have a common religion, nor a peculiar, common literature of their own, but they have a repertoire of folk-tales and music passed on from one generation to the next".

But in the case of *Crown Suppliers v. Dawkins*,[18] the Employment Appeal Tribunal held that Rastafarians did not constitute a racial group; Neill L.J.[19] said that, although Rastafarians do share certain identifiable characteristics, such as a strong cultural tradition involving music, dress and so on, they do not have a separate identity as far as ethnic origins are concerned. It seems to have been an important factor in the decision that Rastafarians had only existed for around sixty years. In *Gwynedd County Council v. Jones*,[20] the tribunal held that language was also not a decisive factor alone in determining a group's existence by ethnic origins; thus the Welsh should not be divided into two ethnic groups (those who could speak Welsh and those who could not) on the sole basis of language.

2. Indirect discrimination: section 1(1)(b)

It is not enough to make direct discrimination unlawful, since the most effective types of discrimination are generally indirect. Indirect discrimination is viewed by some as the more serious type, since it has the potential to remain hidden within society and may appear to be unrelated to discrimination in any way. For example, a condition that job applicants should be of a particular faith or have attended a particular university may be far more difficult for persons of some ethnic backgrounds to comply with. Yet the person who creates the condition in question may have no idea that he is in fact operating a discriminatory system; it is often the case that the **9–009** implications of imposing the condition have not been considered fully. So, unlike direct discrimination, indirect discrimination is rarely fully deliberate. But indirect discrimination is also difficult to identify; it is a less common basis for cases being brought either to court or tribunal,[21] and forms the subject of relatively few CRE investigations. It is obviously far easier to spot and take action against acts of direct discrimination, such as job advertisements which include racial criteria, than indirectly discriminatory practices which may be termed "institutional racism".

The 1976 Act took its stance against indirect discrimination from U.S. law. In the White Paper[22] which preceded the Act it was argued that the extension of the law to make indirect discrimination unlawful was necessary:

> "One important weakness in the existing legislation is the narrowness of the definition of unlawful discrimination . . . it is sufficient for the law to deal with overt discrimination. It should also prohibit practices which are fair in a formal sense but discriminatory in their operation effect".

Section 1(1)(b) creates the following requirements before indirect discrimination may be established:

(1) the application of a requirement or condition;

(2) which is such that the proportion of persons from a particular racial group who can comply with it is considerably smaller;

(3) and which cannot be justified without reference to racial grounds;

(4) and result in detriment to the victim.

Thus there are four elements which require further elaboration: requirement or condition; proportion; lack of justification; and detriment.

9–010 *"Requirement or condition"* A "requirement or condition" must be mandatory, but need not appear in any written rules; it is enough that it constitutes the "normal practice". In *Perera v. Civil Service Commission (No. 2)*,[23] the Court of Appeal distinguished between (1) requirements and conditions, which must be complied with by, *e.g.* job applicants and (2) other factors which may be taken into account by the employer in making the decision. The complaint related to applications for the post of legal assistant in the Civil Service; it was necessary for applicants to be either barristers or solicitors, and so this was a "requirement or condition". But other factors which were taken into account when deciding whether to employ an applicant, such as ability in the English language and relevant work experience in the United Kingdom, were held not to be requirements or conditions since it was possible that an outstanding applicant could be appointed in spite of having poor English or lack of United Kingdom work experience. The case of *Perera* was criticised in later decisions such as *Meer v. London Borough of Tower Hamlets*,[24] on the basis that the interpretation made of "requirement or condition" was inconsistent with the policy behind the 1976 Act since the Act aimed to widen the prohibition of discrimination rather than to allow some forms of indirect discrimination to continue. However the test in *Perera* has recently been confirmed in *Bhudi v. IMI Refiners Ltd.*[25]

In the Second Review of the Race Relations Act 1976 by the CRE, published in 1992, the CRE proposed reform of the definition of indirect discrimination in the following respects: first, the words "requirement or condition" should be replaced by "practice, policy or situation"; secondly, the *Perera* test should be abandoned; and thirdly, the defence of justification (see below) should only apply where there was a situation of "necessity". Such reform would greatly widen the scope of the prohibition on indirect discrimination, and would aid complainants in establishing a case.

"Proportion is considerably smaller" It must be shown that the proportion **9–011**
of persons from the complainant's racial group who can satisfy the requirement or conditions "considerably smaller" than the proportion of persons from other groups who can fulfil the condition or requirement. This seemingly simple statement in fact involves several stages and issues. Two racial groups must be selected, the complainant's and the "comparison" group; the proportion of each who satisfy the requirement or condition must be calculated; there is a technical meaning for the words "can comply"; and it must be shown that the proportion of the complainant's racial group who satisfy the condition is "considerable smaller". Each of these stages has given rise to case law.

a) Selection of the groups: according to section 3(4) of the 1976 Act.

> "A comparison of the case of a person of a particular racial group with that of a person not of that group under section 1(1) must be such that the relevant circumstances in the one case are the same, or not materially different, in the other".

But the main problem here is in determining to which racial groups the complainant belongs. Any person may be described with reference to several criteria which may well each place him in a different racial group; he may be described as British, black, or of African descent, by reference to religion, and so on. The complainant will be left to decide for himself to which racial group he belongs, and will have to fight his case on that basis; if he selects the wrong option, then he may well lose. The court or tribunal will examine the two "pools" of persons who satisfy the requirement or condition concerned, and will carry out the comparison, but the compliant may be required to back up his claim with statistical evidence as to the size of the relevant pools. It is not always even possible to predict which racial groups the court will consider to constitute the two pools.

In *Orphanos v. Queen Mary College*[26]:

Facts. The complainant was a Greek Cypriot student who, on applying to the College, was required to pay tuition fees at the overseas student rate of £3,600. If he had been classified as being "ordinarily resident" in the E.C. for the previous three years then he would have been charged only £480. He argued that this was a "requirement" which constituted indirect discrimination contrary to sections 1(1)(b) and 17 of the Race Relations Act 1976.

Decision. The House of Lords held that indirect racial discrimination had been established, but this was not sufficient to allow the complainant to succeed in obtaining restitution of the difference between the higher fee paid and the lower fee; the discrimination was found not to have been intentional, and so section 57(3) was not satisfied. In the speech by Lord Fraser, he stated that it was not enough for the complainant to show that he belonged to three racial groups (Cypriot, non-British and non-E.C.):

> "I agree that Mr Orphanos belongs to each of these groups, and that each of these is a 'racial group' as defined by section 3(1) as extended by section 3(2). But I do not agree that it makes no difference which of these groups I used for the comparison under section 1(1)(b)(i). The comparison must be between the case of a person of the same racial group as Mr Orphanos and the case of a person not of that racial group, but it must be such that 'the relevant circumstances in the one case are the same, or not materially different, in the other': see section 3(4). The 'relevant circumstances' in the present case are, in my view, that Mr Orphanos wished to be admitted as a pupil at the college, so the comparison must be between persons of the same racial group as him who wished to be admitted as a pupil to the college, and persons not of that racial group who so wish".

He went on to delineate the two relevant pools as: non-British, non-E.C. nationals; and British or E.C. nationals. This avoided the problems evident in attempting to compare the relatively proportion of Greek Cypriot nationals and non-Greek Cypriot nationals who could comply with the condition. But it was not necessarily predictable that the pools would be chosen on that basis.

b) What does "can comply" mean?

9–012 The proportion of each of the two pools who "can comply" with the requirement or condition is to be calculated and compared. But is this phrase to be understood in terms of physical ability to comply, or practical ability to comply? There may be no physical, theoretical or legal reason why a particular racial group should be less able to fulfil the condition, but the factual reality of the situation may be that compliance is extremely difficult for members of that group, for any of a large number of reasons. Thus in *Mandla v. Dowell Lee* (above) it was physically and theoretically possible for a Sikh boy to wear the compulsory school uniform and so to comply with the conditions of attendance at the school, but putting on the school cap was impossible in practical terms without removing his turban and so breaking the tenets of his faith. The House of Lords used the second, wider interpretation of "can comply", defining it in the sense of practical ability to comply with the condition whilst upholding the racial group's religious and cultural traditions; thus indirect discrimination was established.

Also, in *Raval v. DHSS*,[27] the tribunal held that whether a racial group can comply with a condition is to be determined at the time of the event which forms the basis of the complaint; it is irrelevant that the complainant or other members of the same racial group could have taken steps which would allow them to comply with the condition at a later date. Thus a requirement that an applicant should have 'O' Level English could be indirect discrimination since less people of Asian origin could factually comply with it, even though they were free to take the examination at any time and so had the ability to comply with the requirement.

c) How is it to be determined whether the relevant proportion is "considerably smaller"?

The term "considerably smaller" lacks precision, and case law has not provided any agreed formula. The CRE reform proposals suggest that a 20 per cent difference would be a workable test, and Stone argues that a 10 per cent difference is sufficiently significant, although it is possible that in a specific case the court might regard a smaller difference as significant (or indeed a larger difference might not always be enough to prove a case, particularly where the actual numbers of people in the relevant pools are small). Since racial discrimination law does not have to comply with the Equal Treatment Directive, the useful test within Article 2 of the that Directive is unavailable here (see below in section on sex discrimination). It has even been argued that if the proportion of a racial group who can comply with the requirement or condition is zero, then there is no indirect discrimination since zero is not a proportion of the group.[28] Other cases have disagreed on the point,[29] and in most situations where none of a racial group can comply with a requirement or condition there will of course be a claim available for direct discrimination.

"Justification irrespective of racial grounds" If the indirect discriminator can show that the requirement or condition is justified for reasons other than race, then he will have a valid defence. There are certain situations particularly in relation to employment, where a requirement or condition may be important or even necessary for practical reasons, even though it may be indirectly discriminatory. For example, the wearing of hard-hats on building sites is justifiable on grounds of safety, in spite of the fact that this condition indirectly discriminates against Sikhs. But the cases have not always taken a consistent approach to the meaning of the word "justifiable". Originally, a strict approach was taken: in *Steel v. Union of Post Office Workers*,[30] Phillips J. thought that it was appropriate to "distinguish between a requirement or condition which is necessary and one which is merely convenient and for this purpose it is relevant to consider whether the employer can find some other and non-discriminatory method of achieving his object". So, he thought that a condition or requirement could only be justifiable if it was necessary. But in *Ojutiku v. Manpower Services Commission*,[31] Eveleigh J. stated the test simply as[32]: **9–013**

> ". . . it would be enough simply to ask myself: is it justifiable? But if I have to give some explanation of my understanding of that word, I would turn to a

dictionary definition which says 'adduce adequate grounds for'; and it seems to me that if a person produces reasons for doing something which would be acceptable to right-thinking people as sound and tolerable reasons for so doing, then he has justified his conduct".

But this test of "acceptability to right-thinking people" was quickly criticised,[33] and was replaced by the Court of Appeal in *Hampson v. Department of Education*[34] although the House of Lords reversed the decision made by the Court of Appeal, it did so on other grounds and did not deal with the issue of justification.

Hampson v. Department of Education

9–014 **Facts.** The complainant had qualified as a teacher in Hong Kong and taught there for eight years before completing further training and being promoted. After coming to the United Kingdom in 1984, she applied for qualified teacher status but her application was rejected for several reasons, including the ground that the training which she had undertaken in Hong Kong did not satisfy the condition, set by the Department of Education, of a three-year training course (her initial training had taken two years). She claimed that the condition amounted to indirect discrimination contrary to section 1(1)(b) and section 12 (see below).

Decision. The Court of Appeal accepted that the three-year training rule was a "requirement or condition" within section 1(1)(b) which was proportionately more difficult for the persons of the complainant's racial group (Hong Kong Chinese origin) to comply with. In considering whether the requirement was justifiable, Balcombe L.J. approved the test suggested by Stephenson L.J. in *Ojutiku v. Manpower Services Commission* which involved "rejecting justification by convenience and requiring the party applying the discriminator condition to prove it to be justifiable in all the circumstances on balancing its discriminatory effect against the discriminator's need for it". Balcombe L.J. continued by stating that:

> "In my judgement 'justifiable' requires an objective balance between the discriminatory effect of the condition and the reasonable needs of the party who applies the condition".

He further thought it desirable that the tests for justification in relation to racial discrimination, sex discrimination and under the E.C. Equal Treatment Directive should be made consistent with each other[35]; for this reason he approved the decision of the European Court of Justice in *Bilka-Kaufhaus GmbH v. Weber von Hartz*.[36]

The remainder of the Court of Appeal agreed with Balcombe L.J. as to the interpretation of the defence of justification. The case was referred to the House of Lords on the issue of a defence under section 41 (the argument was that the refusal to recognise the complainant's training was done with "lawful authority"). The Court of Appeal had found that the section 41 defence did apply; the House of Lords reversed this point and sent the case to an industrial tribunal for a new hearing.

Balcombe L.J.'s test for justification was approved by the House of Lords in *Webb v. EMO Air Cargo*.[37] Thus it is clear that the test is currently interpreted as objective; the reasonableness of the requirement or condition must be established by balancing the discriminatory effect against the need for the requirement or condition. But the application of this test does seem to vary from case to case, as is natural with a question of fact such as this test.

"Detriment" In order to prove indirect discrimination it is not enough that the complainant is able to demonstrate that he is unable to comply with a requirement or condition; he must also be able to demonstrate that he has suffered detriment due to that inability to comply. Put simply, detriment need not be a financial loss or similar; it is rather a requirement of proof that the complainant suffered some kind of ascertainable disadvantage.[38] So, if the complainant did not suffer at all as a result of the indirect discrimination, he will not succeed in a claim. For example, if there is an advertisement for a job which contains an unjustifiable indirectly discriminatory requirement, such as 20 years' residence in London, the complainant will not be able to bring an action if there is some other reason why he was rejected for the position, such as lack of essential educational qualifications. But this does not mean that the unjustifiable indirect discrimination will go unchecked; the Commission for Racial Equality may mount an investigation into possible discriminatory practices (see below). **9–015**

Section 28: discriminatory practices

> Section 28(1): "In this section discriminatory practices means the application of a requirement or condition which results in an act of discrimination which is unlawful . . . or which would be likely to result in such an act of discrimination if the persons to whom it is applied included persons of any particular racial group as regards which there has been no occasion for applying it". **9–016**
> Section 28(2): "A person acts in contravention of this section if and so long as—
>
> (a) he applies a discriminatory practice; or
> (b) he operates practices or other arrangements which in any circumstances would call for the application by him of a discriminatory practice".

In some situations, indirect discrimination may be so effective that there is no individual complainant who can bring an action; for example in the *Percy Ingles Bakeries Ltd case*,[39] there had been no applications for employment by black people to one bakery in three years, and so although it was highly likely that discrimination was occurring, no individual complainant could exist. In such situations section 28 allows the CRE to make a formal investigation and to issue a non-discrimination notice if it finds that "discriminatory practices" are being applied. But if direct discrimination is found to exist rather than indirect, then section 28 does not apply.

3. Victimisation: section 2

9–017 Any potential complainant about discrimination may legitimately fear reprisal or victimisation if he goes ahead with his complaint; such fears arise especially in relation to discrimination in employment, where the complainant may have to face the person against whom he has started action at work each day. Victimisation is therefore treated as a type of discrimination in itself, so that the complainant will have an extra claim if victimisation does occur. Section 2 of the Race Relations Act 1976 defines victimisation in terms of treating a person less favourably because he has, or it is suspected that he has, done one of the following:

(1) brought proceedings against the discriminator under the Act;

(2) given evidence or information in connection with any discrimination proceedings;

(3) "otherwise done anything under or by reference to the Act" to the discriminator;

(4) alleged that the discriminator has done something which would contravene the Act.

Thus victimisation by a third party is covered by the section, and whistleblowers are also protected from victimisation even if they have not suffered any direct or indirect discrimination themselves. But it must be shown that the action which is alleged to constitute victimisation of the complainant was done because of one of the four reasons above; if another reason for the victim's treatment exists, then a claim of victimisation will fail. In *Aziz v. Trinity Street Taxis*,[40] a taxi driver was fired by his company after he had made covert recordings of conversations relating to a potential action for racial discrimination. The Court of Appeal held that, although the complainant had been treated less favourably, this was due not to his involvement in the racial discrimination action but to the breach of trust represented by his making the tape-recordings in the first place. It was decided that the complainant would have been dismissed for his actions whatever their purpose had been; thus it was irrelevant that the recordings were made for the purpose of proving racial discrimination, since the result would have been the same if they had been made, for example, as part of a practical joke. The unfortunate consequence of cases such as *Aziz* is that the way is left relatively clear for discriminators to victimise complainants and then claim that the latter would have been treated in the same way regardless of the claim of racial discrimination.

4. The Scope of Racial Discrimination

9–018 Under the 1976 Act, a complainant who could establish that he had been treated less favourably on racial grounds did not automatically have a claim against the discriminator; in many fields and situations, such discrimination would be perfectly lawful. The law provided a remedy only if the discrimination related to one of the categories of unlawful discrimination set out in Parts II-IV of the 1976 Act, which were:

(1) education
(2) employment and recruitment
(3) goods, facilities and services
(4) housing
(5) clubs
(6) advertisements
(7) charities

It is still necessary to examine these categories under the 1976 Act, even though the Race Relations (Amendment) Act 2000 has created a general statutory duty on public authorities not to discriminate on racial grounds in the exercise of any of its public functions, since many discriminators will not fit the definition of "public authority"[41] in the 2000 Act. Each of these areas of unlawful discrimination will be examined separately.

Education. Section 17: Discrimination by bodies in charge of educational establishments.

Under section 17, it is unlawful for a "responsible body" to discriminate in relation to an educational establishment against a person— **9–019**

"(a) in the terms on which it offers to admit him to the establishment as a pupil; or
(b) by refusing or deliberately omitting to accept an application for his admission to the establishment as a pupil; or
(c) where he is a pupil of the establishment—

(i) in the way it affords him access to any benefits, facilities or services, or by refusing or deliberately omitting to afford him access to them; or
(ii) by excluding him from the establishment or subjecting him to any other detriment."

The bodies to which this section applies include almost every education establishment at any level or for any age group, whether state-run or private, from schools to universities and colleges. It applies to any kind of discrimination under the Act, whether direct, indirect or victimisation.

Section 18 makes it unlawful for a local education authority to do any act which amounts to racial discrimination in carrying out its functions.

Section 19(1) states that: "Without prejudice to its obligations to comply with any other provision of this Act, a body to whom this subsection applies shall be under a general duty to secure that facilities for education provided by it and any ancillary benefits or services, are provided without racial discrimination". Sections 18 and 19 apply only to "racial discrimination", and not to victimisation.

Unlawful discrimination in relation to education may occur in a wide variety of ways. It may relate to the decision whether or not to admit a student to an establishment; the conditions attached to admission; exclusion; benefits, facilities or services provided; or punishment. There is no duty on education authorities to ensure that there is a racial balance in a school within its area *R. v. Bradford Metropolitan Borough Council, ex p. Sikander Ali*.[42] The discrimination has sometimes arisen for positive motives; for example the London Borough of Ealing used to operate a policy under which Asian children from Southall were sent to schools with a preponderance of white pupils in other local areas, with the aim of improving their English.[43] Such policies were found not to be justifiable since they were against the results of educational research showing that such schemes were unlikely to work. The important educational discrimination case of *Mandla v. Dowell Lee* has been discussed above.

Employment and recruitment. Section 4

9–020 "(1) It is unlawful for a person, in relation to employment by him at an establishment in Great Britain, to discriminate against another—

(a) in the arrangements he makes for the purpose of determining who should be offered that employment; or
(b) in the terms on which he offers him that employment; or
(c) by refusing or deliberately omitting to offer him that employment.

(2) It is unlawful for a person, in the case of a person employed by him at an establishment in Great Britain, to discriminate against that employee—

(a) in the terms of employment which he affords him; or
(b) in the way he affords him access to opportunities for promotion, transfer or training, or to any other benefits, facilities or services, or by refusing or deliberately omitting to afford him access to them; or
(c) by dismissing him, or subjecting him to any other detriment."

Section 4 applies equally to an employer or to acts committed by the latter's other employees or his agents (section 32). In *De Souza v. The Automobile Association*,[44] it was held that section 32 makes an employer vicariously liable for discrimination committed by his employees if they were acting in the course of their employment. But merely being on duty or at work at the time of the discrimination does not mean that it was carried out "in the course of employment"; for example, in *Irving v. The Post Office*,[45] the Post Office was not vicariously liable for the racially abusive words written on an envelope by a postman, because he was in no way performing his duties at the time he wrote it. He happened to be at work at the time, but his employment was merely the setting for his act, rather than the act being part of his employment. But an employer has a defence under section 32(3) if he can establish that he took all reasonably practicable steps to prevent the employee from doing the discriminatory act or such acts in the course of his employment. In *Balgobin v. London Borough of Tower Hamlets*,[46] it was held that an employer had taken all "reasonably practicable steps" to prevent sexual harassment by employees where there was both a proper and adequate system of staff supervision and the employer had an explicit equal opportunities policy.

Employment-related discrimination may be unlawful in two different spheres; first, during the recruitment process[47]; and secondly, once a person is already in employment.

a) Discrimination in recruitment All stages of the recruitment process fall within the ambit of section 4. Section 4(1)(a) prohibits discrimination in the arrangements which are made in order to determine who should be offered employment, thus including interviews, the processing of application forms and so on. Both direct and indirect methods of discrimination are forbidden. Section 4(1)(b) deals with the terms on which the offer is made. Section 4(1)(c) prohibits an employer from refusing to offer a job to a person on racial grounds. But in many situations which theoretically breach section 4(1), it may be extremely difficult to prove that racial discrimination was involved in the victim's treatment, except where the applicant is clearly by far the best applicant for the job, or where the employer had made statements of which there is evidence. **9–021**

For example, in *Owen and Briggs v. James*[48]:

Facts. The complainant had applied for the job in question on two occasions. The first application resulted in an interview, after which she received a rejection. She then reapplied after seeing the post re-advertised and was interviewed again, the employer having failed to realise that this was the same applicant. She was again rejected for the post. At the tribunal, the employer claimed that there was no section 4(1) discrimination and that the reasons for the complainant's rejection were: first, that she had been unemployed for a period of three years; and secondly, that she had failed to declare that she had previously been interviewed for the same job.

Decision. The tribunal found that it is not necessary for race to be the sole reason why employment is refused under section 4(1)(c). The facts that the job had been offered to a white applicant with fewer qualifications than the complainant, and that the employer had made general racist comments to other applicants, were sufficient evidence of unlawful discrimination.

If there is provable discrimination, the scope of the ban is wide. There is no requirement in section 4(1)(a) or (b) that the discrimination should be deliberate; as long as there is discrimination in the way the recruitment arrangements operate, it does not matter that there was no discrimination in the way the arrangements were made. See *Brennan v. Dewhurst Ltd.*[49]

If recruitment is to be made by formal advertisement, then section 29 applies:

> "Section 29(1) it is unlawful to publish or cause to be published an advertisement which indicates, or might reasonably be understood as indicating, an intention by a person to do an act of discrimination, whether the doing of that act by him would be lawful or . . . unlawful."

As a result it is now unusual for an advertisement to contain statements which show clear intention to discriminate. But since many posts are filled by means other than formal advertisement, written application and interview, section 29 cannot prevent discrimination in situations such as where news of a vacancy is spread informally to friends and acquaintances. Informal "networking" may often result in the replication of existing attributes of a workforce, and so may perpetuate factual discrimination even if the employer does not intend this result.

Only the CRE may bring proceedings under section 29, either by investigating and then issuing a non-discrimination notice (section 58) or by taking court action, usually for an injunction. It should be noted that section 29 makes it unlawful to advertise a thing which it would be perfectly lawful to do, for example, where the employee would have the benefit of an exception or defence to the remainder of the Act. Section 29 does not only apply to advertisements in relation to employment; it will have equal impact if, for example, accommodation is advertised (see discussion of discrimination in relation to housing, below). The CRE Code of Practice for the elimination of racial discrimination and the promotion of equality of opportunity in employment recommends that employers should follow stringent procedures to ensure fairness at every stage of the recruitment process, and so aims somewhat higher than the legal requirements of the 1976 Act.

9–022 *b) Discrimination against employees* In relation to an existing employee, unlawful discrimination may relate to: terms of employment; access to opportunities and benefits; or dismissal and other detriments. Concerning terms of employment, there is a difference here between racial and sex discrimination, since there is no equivalent statute to the Equal Pay Act 1970; offering a person less pay on racial grounds would fall within section 4(2)(a) of the 1976 Act. Thus the relevant comparison for determining whether there has been differential treatment is whether a hypothetical person not of the complainant's racial group, would have been treated differently, whereas under the Equal Pay Act it is necessary to show that a particular real man is treated more favourably. All other contractual terms are included, thus in *Malik v. British Home Stores*[50] it was found by a tribunal to be discrimination where a company required its female employees to wear a skirt, since Muslim women are expected to cover their legs.

How is to be determined whether an employee was denied promotion or another benefit on racial grounds rather than for any other, legitimate, reason? In *West Midlands Passenger Transport Executive v. Singh*,[51] it was held that evidence that persons of a particular racial group are considerably more likely to fail to be promoted may show that there is a stereotyped assumption about that racial group in operation, whether such an assumption is conscious or unconscious. This recognises the difficulty in finding objective criteria by which to assess the suitability of a candidate for promotion, and looks instead to trends or tendencies in an employer's promotions record. But the problems and issues surrounding promotion are similar to those in relation to recruitment, as may be seen in *D'Silva v. Hambleton and Nurdin & Peacock Plc*[52]:

Facts. The complainant was a checkout assistant for a retail company owned by the defendant. She applied for a promotion to the company's cash office, where she had already done some relief work. The office had two shifts: the early shift, which was entirely staffed by white employees; and the late shift, which had black or Asian staff. The advertised position was for the early shift, and there were five applicants, four of whom (including the complainant) were Asian, and one of whom was white. The white applicant was appointed. No interviews had been held. On asking her manager, who had been responsible for the appointment, why she had been rejected, the complainant was told that it was due to lack of experience and ability, but the manager refused to put his reasons into writing. At a later date, five more reasons for her non-promotion were supplied. The complainant suffered depression as a result of her treatment and received psychiatric care.

Decision. The tribunal found that the complainant had been unlawfully racially discriminated against by her employer, all of whose reasons for the non-promotion were rejected. The tribunal criticised every stage of the company's procedure in relation to promotion, citing lack of safeguards against discrimination, failure to promote the most qualified candidate, the inconsistencies in the reasons given for the complainant's treatment and the appearance of a "cover up". The case was seen as a warning of the dangers which may be involved when an employer, such as the defendant, fails to follow the CRE Code of Practice, and the damages awarded (total £11,695) reflected both the severity of the discrimination and the medical problems which it caused.

"Detriment" in section 4(2)(c) has proved to be a difficult term to define, but it is clearly a question of fact whether a detriment has occurred. In *Barclays Bank v. Kapur*,[53] Bingham L.J. stated that "detriment" is capable of encompassing almost any discriminatory conduct by an employer. Harassment and bullying are detriments, unless applied equally to all racial groups. In *Burton and Rhule v. De Vere Hotels*,[54] the tribunal held that an employee suffers a detriment if his employer causes or permits a discriminatory act to occur, in circumstances where the employer had the ability to prevent its occurrence. The victims, who were Caribbean, were casual waitresses at a dinner party where the speaker made racist and sexist comments. Other diners responded in an equally offensive way. The tribunal stated that the management of the hotel should have had a "contingency plan", knowing the views and propensities of the speaker, to protect the victims from the discriminatory behaviour of the speaker and guests. Detriment has also been held to encompass many other types of treatment including demotion, transfers and the issuing of formal warnings. However, employers are given the benefit of specific exemptions from liability for racial discrimination, of which the most important is genuine occupational qualification.

9–023 *Genuine occupational qualification* In some jobs, a person of a particular racial background or group may be the most appropriate employee. The most obvious examples of this are dramatic roles where authenticity is sought, and the provision of personal services which by their nature are most effectively performed by a person of that racial group.

> "Section 5(1) In relation to racial discrimination—
>
> (a) section 4(1)(a) or (c) does not apply to any employment where being of a particular racial group is a genuine occupational qualification for the job; and
> (b) section 4(2)(b) does not apply to opportunities for promotion or transfer to, or training for, such employment.
>
> 5(2) Being of a particular racial group is a genuine occupational qualification for a job only where—
>
> (a) the job involves participation in a dramatic performance or other entertainment in a capacity for which a person of that racial group is required for reasons of authenticity; or
> (b) the job involves participation as an artist's or photographic model . . . for which a person of that racial group is required for reasons of authenticity; or
> (c) the job involves working in a place where food or drink is . . . provided to and consumed by members of the public . . . in a particular setting for which, in that job, a person of that racial group is required for reasons of authenticity; or
> (d) the holder of the job provides persons of that racial group with personal services promoting their welfare, and those services can most effectively be provided by a person of that racial group."

But it is not a genuine occupational qualification if there is a job vacancy and (section 5(4):

> ". . . the employer already has employees of that racial group in question—
>
> (a) who are capable of carrying out the duties . . . and;
> (b) whom it would be reasonable to employ on those duties; and
> (c) whose numbers are sufficient to meet the employer's likely requirements in respect of these duties without undue inconvenience."

The first three exceptions under section 5(2) require "reasons of authenticity". It is an issue of continuing sensitivity whether dramatic roles should necessarily be played only by persons of the racial or ethnic group of the character concerned, but section 5(2)(a) makes this possible. Section 5(2)(c) allows restaurants to employ staff of the nationality of the cuisine served. But, whichever of the section 5(2) exemptions is claimed, it is to be construed narrowly, since the word "only" is used in the statute.[55] The final exemption under section 5 "personal services", is the most complex. The word "personal" indicates that there should be close contact between the provider and the recipient of the service, and that the identity of both persons is important. It is unlikely that section 5(2)(d) would be satisfied where there is neither physical contact or face-to-face meetings involved. But the boundaries of the words "that racial group" in section 5(2)(d) are broad: where the services are to be provided to persons from a racial group defined by colour, (*e.g.* "black people", "ethnic minorities") then a tribunal may find that a person of that colour would most effectively provide those services, even though he may himself be of a different ethnic group from many or all of his clients.[56] When deciding whether a genuine occupational qualification exists, a tribunal must balance the competing needs of prevention of discrimination and aiding minorities in society, and to some extent the employer may be the best person to judge whether a person of that racial group is the best person for the position in question.[57]

Other exceptions There are other situations in which an employer will not be liable for discrimination. Employment in a private household is exempted from section 4(1) and (2), but victimisation may still give rise to a complaint. The reluctance to prevent people from discriminating in their own homes may perhaps come from understandable privacy reasons, but it is also equally arguable that employment is such an important and regulated area that the employee should not lose his rights due to the venue of his employment, and that in any case many laws already regulate how people behave in their own homes. Other exceptions include training where the skills learned are to be used outside Britain (section 6) and the employment of "seamen recruited abroad" (section 9). The latter exception allows the recruitment of overseas workers from poorer countries at lower wages than would have to be paid to an E.C. resident. **9–024**

Goods, facilities, services

"Section 20(1) It is unlawful for any person concerned with the provision (for payment or not) of goods, facilities or services to the public or a section of the public to discriminate against a person who seeks to obtain or use those goods, facilitics or scrviccs— **9–025**

(a) by refusing or deliberately omitting to provide him with any of them; or
(b) by refusing or deliberately omitting to provide him with goods, facilities or services of the like quality, in the like manner and on like terms as are normal . . . in relation to other members of the public . . ."

"Section 20(2) The following are examples of the facilities and services mentioned in subsection (1)—

(a) access to and use of any place which members of the public are permitted to enter;
(b) accommodation in a hotel, boarding house or other similar establishment;

(c) facilities by way of banking or insurance or for grants, loans, credit or finance;
(d) facilities for education;
(e) facilities for entertainment, recreation or refreshment;
(f) facilities for transport or travel;
(g) the services of any profession or trade, or any local or other public authority."

None of the words "goods, services or facilities" are given a statutory definition, save for the examples in section 20(2). But some further general observations are possible. Unlawful discrimination in this area could be committed by retailers, manufacturers, hotels, places of public entertainment or recreation (but not private clubs), members of the professions, pubs, banks, tradespeople and public transport providers, to name a few. Thus this provision is extremely broad, and is aimed at affecting a wide section of society; it is hoped that by making discrimination unlawful by those who deal with the public will have a more general effect upon society in general, and disseminate more positive attitudes through communities.

The most difficult application of this category of unlawful discrimination has been in relation to the provision of public sector facilities and services. Section 20(2) refers to "any local or other public authority"; to what extent does this include the actions of government? The courts have sometimes take a narrow approach. See the sex discrimination case of *R. v. Entry Clearance Officer, Bombay, ex p. Amin*,[58] but generally a distinction is drawn between when a local or public authority is exercising a "duty" (which will not be within section 20) and when it is performing a "service" within section 20. Thus in *Savjani v. IRC*,[59] it was thought that the Inland Revenue had two functions: the duty of collecting the correct amount of tax; and the service of providing information to the public. So the latter will fall within section 20. But the exercise of immigration-related powers by the Home Secretary is duty, not a service.[60] The CRE has argued[61] that section 20 should apply to all areas of governmental activity, including immigration, planning, the police and so no. Case law has slightly reduced the impact of the CRE's criticisms; for example, in *Farah v. Commissioner of Police for the Metropolis*[62] the Court of Appeal held that when a police officer is dealing with members of the public, his actions fall within section 20 and so he could be found to have discriminated unlawfully according to that section; but his employer (the Commissioner of Police) would not be vicariously liable. But now these situations would be caught by section 1 of the Race Relations (Amendment) Act 2000 and so the relevant public authorities would be guilty of unlawful discrimination in the exercise of their functions, subject of course to the new statute being interpreted in the manner in which it was intended to be.

A further issue related to vicarious liability for race discrimination has recently been determined by the House of Lords. In *Hallam v. Cheltenham Borough Council and Others*[63]:

Facts. The applicants, who were of Romany gipsy origin, hired council premises for a wedding reception. Local police were worried that because of this and of trouble at recent similar events, there might be trouble at the reception. They communicated their worries to the council, including some inaccurate information. The council responded by imposing conditions on the reception, including that it should be a ticket-only event. The applicants treated this as a repudiatory breach of contract and held the reception elsewhere. They then issued proceedings against the council for breach of contract, and against the council and three police officers for unlawful racial discrimination under the Race Relations Act 1976.

The council were found guilty of both charges, but the police officers were found to have done too little to be liable as accomplices to the discrimination under section 33(1). The judge also found that, although their conduct left much to be desired, the police officers did not have an overtly racist motive and had believed that they were acting in the public interest. The applicants challenged this decision in relation to two of the police officers, arguing that they had "knowingly" aided the council to commit the unlawful discrimination, and so should have been liable under section 33(1). The Court of Appeal found that the police officers had clearly aided the council in their discrimination (*per* Judge L.J.):

> "In my judgment the conclusion that the officers contributed to the decision made by the council to break their contractual arrangements with the plaintiffs is inescapable. It is true that they did not seek to urge, persuade or induce the council to do so, and equally true that it remained open to the council, notwithstanding the information from the police, to permit the wedding to go ahead in any event, or even subject to conditions which might have been suggested in such a way as to be acceptable to the plaintiffs. Nevertheless, although the process was not irreversible or inevitable, without the information provided by the officers and their assumption that information from such a source was accurate, the council would not have begun to lose confidence in or eventually to review their contractual arrangements. So, although ultimate responsibility for the decision rested with the council alone, and not the police officers, of itself that did not provide a sufficient justification for the conclusion that liability was not established".

However, the appeal was dismissed because it had not been shown that the police officers had had the required "knowledge" under section 33(1). The applicants appealed to the House of Lords.

Decision. The House of Lords broke down the issues into a series of questions. Firstly, what was the unlawful act committed by the council? The answer to that was: the decision to apply conditions to the applicants' use of the premises on the basis of their racial origin. Secondly, did the police officers aid the council to do the unlawful act? The original judge had decided that they did not, since they were merely "helpful" to the council, and the council could have reacted in a number of other possible ways to the information supplied. The House of Lords found that there were no grounds on which they could disturb this finding. This does not mean that the giving of information which another uses to perform an act of discrimination will never create liability under section 33(1), simply that the police officers would have had to have been found to have had greater involvement and knowledge in order to be liable on the present facts. *Per* Lord Millett:

> "In the present case the police provided information which helped the council to reach a decision what to do about the situation; but this is not the act which the statute makes unlawful. The information which the police provided did nothing to help the council to carry out their decision, whether to cancel the reservation of the Pump Room for the wedding reception or to impose conditions on entry. That was the act which the statute made unlawful, and in doing it the council neither needed nor obtained the aid of the police. The distinction may appear narrow and even technical, but it is neither. The man

> who helps another to make up his mind does not thereby and without more help the other to do that which he decides to do. He may advise, encourage, incite or induce him to do the act; but he does not aid him to do it."

Thus the appeal was dismissed.

Housing

9–026 "Section 21(1) It is unlawful for a person, in relation to premises in Great Britain of which he has power to dispose, to discriminate against another—

> (a) in the terms on which he offers him those premises; or
> (b) by refusing his application for those premises; or
> (c) in his treatment of him in relation to any list of persons in need of premises of that description.
>
> (2) It is unlawful for a person, in relation to premises managed by him, to discriminate against a person occupying the premises—
>
> (a) in the way he affords him access to any benefits or facilities, or by refusing or deliberately omitting to afford him access to them; or
> (b) by evicting him, or subjecting him to any other detriment."

Both existing tenants and home-seekers are protected by section 21. The main activities caught by the section are: "disposal of premises", whether in the private or public housing sector; access to benefits or facilities on the premises; the operation of social housing lists by local authorities; and eviction or other "disadvantage".

9–027 *Disposal of premises* This term includes not only the sale of premises, but also leasing or letting the creation of tenancies and the granting of licences. A public or private landlord is forbidden from discriminating in any of these respects, and so cannot discriminate in whether he offers the premises to a person, or on the terms of the offer. So the owner or manager of premises may not operate a "colour bar". But there are exceptions to this general rule. A private owner of premises who wishes to sell them without using the services of an estate agent and without advertising the sale will be able to discriminate lawfully, since he has the benefit of section 21(3):

> "Subsection (1) does not apply to a person who owns an estate or interest in the premises and wholly occupies them unless he uses the services of an estate agent for the purposes of the disposal of the premises, or publishes or causes to be published an advertisement in connection with the disposal."

Hence he may refuse to sell to a particular person or group on racial grounds, or may ask a higher price on that basis; section 21 seems to lack the aims seen in other parts of the legislation, which seek to change attitudes in society as well as to remove obvious discriminatory practices. Many of the most pernicious and objectionable racist attitudes and behaviour do not give rise to liability under current legislation.

A further exception to section 21 is the "small dwelling rule", which also applies to section 20 (above). A person who is letting accommodation, or allowing it to be assigned or sublet, does not discriminate unlawfully if the premises are small, shared and he or a relative is resident:

> "section 22(1) Sections 20(1) and 21(1) do not apply to the provision by a person of accommodation in any premises, or the disposal of premises by him, if—
>
> (a) that person or a near relative of his "the relevant occupier" resides, and intends to continue to reside, on the premises; and
>
> (b) there is on the premises, in addition to the accommodation occupied by the relevant occupier, accommodation (not being storage accommodation or means of access) shared by the relevant occupier with other persons residing on the premises who are not member so his household; and
>
> (c) the premises are small premises."

Premises are "small" when they satisfy the tests set out in section 22(2):

> "(a) in the case of premises comprising residential accommodation for one or more households . . . in addition to the accommodation occupied by the relevant occupier, there is not normally residential accommodation for more than two such households and only the relevant occupier and any member of his household reside in the accommodation occupied by him;
>
> (b) in the case of premises not falling within paragraph (a), there is not normally residential accommodation on the premises for more than six persons in addition to the relevant occupier and any members of his household."

These somewhat complicated provisions allow resident landlords in all but large buildings to discriminate, and arguably extend undesirably far; there is a great difference between discriminating in connection to who is to live in a spare room, and discriminating as a matter of course in connection to a stream of short-term tenants in a building of bedsits where there is a shared kitchen. It is arguable that the drafting of this exception should be tightened if it is to remain. At present, a resident landlord in small premises is at liberty to discriminate openly on racial grounds.

Clubs For many years, particularly while the legislation prior to the 1976 Act was in force, private clubs which discriminated on the basis of race were a source of difficulty in showing such discrimination to be unlawful. Attempts were made to bring complaints under the earlier equivalent to section 20 of the 1976 Act, but this involved the problem of showing that a private club offered its facilities or services to either the public in general or a section of the public. Prior to the enactment of the 1976 Act, the House of Lords held in the case of *Charter v. Race Relations Board*[64] that clubs with official rules and procedures for such matters as membership were not regulated by the 1968 Act because they did not offer their services to a section of the public. Only clubs which were not "genuine" were caught by the anti-discrimination legislation. As a result of this problem, the White Paper[65] which preceded the 1976 Act sought to overturn this rule on the **9–028** basis that the number of clubs and members' organisations in society is now huge, they provide a wide range of services and facilities, and so their impact is great enough that they should not be able to discriminate. But certain small, voluntary organisations were considered worthy of exemption, either because the are truly private in nature, or because they seek to help persons from a particular ethnic or national group rather than to disadvantage others.

Thus, in the 1976 Act:

> "Section 25(1) This section applies to any association of persons (however described, whether corporate or unincorporate, and whether or not its activities are carried on for profit) if—
>
> (a) it has twenty-five or more members; and
> (b) admission to membership is regulated by its constitution and is so conducted that the members do not constitute a section of the public within the meaning of section 20(1); and
> (c) (exception for trade unions, which are dealt with by section 11).

(2) It is unlawful for an association to which this section applies, in the case of a person who is not a member of the association, to discriminate against him—

> (a) in the terms on which it is prepared to admit him to membership; or
> (b) by refusing or deliberately omitting to accept his application for membership.

(3) It is unlawful for an association to which this section applies, in the case of a person who is a member or associate of the association, to discriminate against him—

> (a) in the way it affords him access to any benefits, facilities or services, or by refusing or deliberately omitting to afford him access to them;
> (b) in the case of a member, by depriving him of membership, or varying the terms on which he is a member; or
> (c) in the case of an associate, by depriving him of his rights as an associate, or varying those rights; or
> (d) in either case, by subjecting him to any other detriment."

Thus, for most clubs, it is now unlawful to discriminate on racial grounds in any of the following respects: in the decision whether to make an offer of membership; in the terms upon which a membership is offered; in all aspects of the treatment of existing members and associates, from access to facilities to alteration of terms of membership and withdrawal of membership.

But section 26 provides an exception if the main object of an association is "to enable the benefits of membership (whatever they may be) to be enjoyed by persons of a particular racial group defined otherwise that by colour". The "main object" of an association is to be defined by looking at "the essential character of the association" and "all relevant circumstances, including, in particular, the extent to which the affairs of the association are so conducted that the persons primarily enjoying the benefits of membership are of the racial group in question". Thus it is not unlawful to have a club which seeks to further religious, national or cultural interests, provided that it does not operate a colour bar. For example, an Irish Association, an Austrian Cultural Society or a Muslim Recreational Group will not be unlawful unless they restrict membership on the basis of colour, or alternatively are open to at least a section of the public and so are caught by section 20. It is indirect discrimination which has caused the greatest difficulty in relation to clubs, since nomination and membership rules may make it factually harder for persons of a racial group to gain membership. For example, many associations require new members to be nominated and "sponsored" by existing members; this requirement will, in a predominantly white association, often result in new nominees having a similar background and racial group to the existing membership. Non-discrimination notices have been issued by the CRE in relation to such procedures.

Charities Section 34 removes from the terms of any charitable trust any restriction based upon colour. Therefore a charity which conferred benefits upon, for example, "white university students" would be allowed to continue to exist, but the word "white" would be deleted from the class of persons entitled to benefit from the charity's funds or activities. But section 34 does not have this effect in relation to restrictions based on any other category of racial grounds. Any such charity is however likely to be void on other grounds, such as public policy, lack of certainty or capriciousness. **9–029**

Race Relations (Amendment) Act 2000: A Wider Ambit for Race Discrimination Law

The Race Relations (Amendment) Act 2000 was introduced in response to recommendations of the MacPherson Report and a review by the CRE, which proposed that the legislation should be expanded to cover all public services and to impose vicarious liability in respect of the police. In addition the new Act imposes a duty upon certain public authorities to promote equal opportunities and work towards the elimination of unlawful discrimination, and reduces the scope of the previous Act's national security exception. Each of these amendments will be explained and examined separately. **9–030**

1. Public authorities (section 1 of the 2000 Act)

Section 1 adds new sections 19B-F to Part III of the 1976 Act. Section 19B makes it unlawful for a public authority[66] to discriminate against a person on racial grounds in the execution of any of its public functions. However, there follows a list of express exemptions: the intelligence services, the Houses of Parliament and proceedings in Parliament (section 19B); judicial **9–031** and legislative actions (section 19C); acts done by a Minister or authorised official in relation to immigration or nationality functions where the discrimination is on grounds of nationality or ethnic or national origins (section 19D)[67]—it will however be unlawful under section 19B for such a Minister or official to discriminate on grounds of colour or race; or decisions to discontinue or not to institute criminal proceedings. This last exception is intended to prevent a person using the new legislation to uncover the reasons why the decision was made not to prosecute.

2. General statutory duty on public authorities to promote race equality

9–032 Under section 2 the former section 71 of the 1976 Act becomes section 71 and section 71A–E. Section 71(1) requires public authorities listed in Schedule 1A, when carrying out their functions, to have due regard to the need to eliminate unlawful discrimination and to promote equality of opportunity and good relations between persons of different racial groups. The Secretary of State may create specific duties upon some, or all public authorities to improve the performance of the general duty (section 71(2) and (3)). He must consult the CRE before doing so (section 71(4)). He may also add or remove bodies from the list of public authorities in Schedule 1A (section 71(5)). Section 71A is dealt with in the chapter on immigration law. Section 71B confers similar order-making powers on Scottish Ministers and provides that the Secretary of State shall make orders concerning Welsh authorities only with consent from the Welsh National Authority. The CRE may issue Codes of Practice giving guidance to public authorities on how to carry out their section 71 duties (section 71C). As usual a breach of Code is not actionable in itself but may be considered relevant by a court or tribunal. Further the CRE may issue compliance notices requiring a public authority to conform to its duties under any section 71(2) order (section 71D) and may ultimately seek a court order requiring a public authority to provide relevant information or to comply with a compliance notice (section 71E).

9–033 *Section 3: Crown and government appointments* Section 3 extends the protection of the 1976 Act under section 76 (government appointments) to all such appointments by inserting sections 76(3)–(11). Thus it is now unlawful for any Minster or government department to discriminate on racial grounds when recommending or approving an appointment to an office or position, or conferring an honour.

9–034 *Section 4: police liability* New sections 76A and B radically change police liability in relation to racial discrimination. Police authorities and police chiefs may no longer discriminate against constables; and police chiefs become vicariously liable for discriminatory acts committed by constables under his direction and control, subject to a defence if he took reasonable steps to prevent the act of discrimination. Compensation may also be paid out of the police fund.

Section 7: national security Under sections 42 and 69B of the 1976 Act, an act of racial discrimination was not unlawful if carried out for the purpose of national security, and if a Ministerial certificate was given stating that this was the case then the classification could not be challenged. But in *Tinnelly and McElduff v. U.K.*[68] the European Court of Human Rights found the power to issue such certificates to be a violation of Article 6(1). The Employment Rights Act 1999 removed the power in to issue certificates in employment- related cases, and section 7 of the 2000 Act does the same for non-employment related cases. Further, section 7 modifies the "national security" defence to discrimination, bringing it into line with the ECHR by adding a requirement that not only must the act in question be done in for the purpose (or legitimate aim) of safeguarding national security, it must also be justified by that same purpose. Section 8 provides for special procedures to be applied by courts when dealing with discrimination cases involving national security issues, including the exclusion of the claimant and his representative from court. **9–035**

5. *The Commission for Racial Equality*

Section 43 of the 1976 Act established the CRE, and delineated its powers: **9–036**

> "(1) There shall be a body of Commissioners named the Commission for Racial Equality . . . appointed by the Secretary of State . . . which shall have the following duties—
>
> (a) to work towards the elimination of discrimination;
> (b) to promote equality of opportunity, and good relations, between persons of different racial groups generally; and
> (c) to keep under review the working of this Act and, when they are so required by the Secretary of State or otherwise think it necessary, draw up and submit to the Secretary of State proposals for amending it."

The CRE may give financial or other assistance to other organisations working in the field of equal opportunities (section 44), or undertake or sponsor relevant research (section 45), issue Codes of Practice in relation to the promotion of equality of opportunities in employment or housing (section 47, as amended), assist individuals in pursuing complaints under the Act (section 66), or conduct formal investigations (section 48).

Thus the CRE has wide powers and influence in relation to the enforcement of the legislation and also has a more general promotional role in society. Some of these will now be examined in greater detail.

Formal investigations

Formal investigations may be undertaken in relation to an issue, a person or an organisation. The powers which may be used in such an investigation are contained in sections 48–50. Section 48 allows the Commission to **9–037** conduct formal investigations either when they think fit, or when required to do so by the Secretary of State, for any purpose connected with carrying out their duties under section 43. But section 49 lays down a series of procedural requirements for any formal investigation. The CRE must draw up terms of reference for the investigation, in consultation with the Secretary of State if the investigation is at his instigation (section 49(2)). The Commission must give notice that an investigation is being held (section 49(3)). Two types of formal investigation are possible: a named–person investigation or a general investigation. If named persons are to be investigated, then they are to be notified and given an opportunity to make representations (section 49(4)). The CRE may require persons to provide written information, to produce documents of to give "evidence" in person (section 50(1)). Thus its powers are very strong, and it may be for that reason that the courts have tended to interpret sections 48–50 in a narrow manner.

In *London Borough of Hillingdon v. CRE*[69]:

Facts. The CRE wished to formally investigate complaints that Hillingdon's housing policy discriminated on racial grounds. Among the evidence was that a white Rhodesian family had been given council accommodation but an Asian family had been refused accommodation and had been delivered to the Foreign Office. The House of Lords considered the grounds upon which the CRE could mount a formal investigation and the scope which an investigation could have.

Decision. The House of Lords held that, in relation to a named person investigation, the CRE could not begin the investigation unless it had reasonable grounds for belief that a named person had done an act which was unlawful, *i.e.* that discrimination had in fact taken place. "Fishing expeditions" are not permissible, and opposing views of the situation should be considered equally when determining whether such reasonable grounds exist. Lord Diplock stated that[70]:

> "To entitle the Commission to embark upon the full investigation it is enough that there should be material before the Commission sufficient to raise in the minds of reasonable men, possessed of the experience of covert racial discrimination that has been acquired by the Commission, a suspicion that there may have been acts by the person named of racial discrimination of the kind that it is proposed to investigate".

In *Commission for Racial Equality v. Prestige Group*,[71] Lord Diplock again stated the above passage and then seemed to qualify it slightly by continuing:

> ". . . and had at any rate some grounds for so suspecting albeit that the grounds upon which any such suspicion was based might, at that stage, be no more than tenuous because they had not yet been tested".[72]

So, if there is a particular area of activity which is causing the CRE concern, it cannot mount a named–person formal investigation as a test case unless it can show reasonable grounds for suspicion that that person has committed an unlawful act of discrimination. If such an investigation is to be made, it should take the form of a general investigation, which looks at an area of activity, (*e.g.* the employment of ethnic minorities in factories) rather than the actions of any one person or organisation. In relation to general investigations, there is no power to require evidence to be given by a person and no non-discrimination notice can be issued, although a separate named–person investigation may be launched if sufficient evidence is found to justify such a step. Whichever of the two types of investigation is commenced, it will culminate in a report and often recommendations. But in the case of a named–person investigation, if the CRE is satisfied that a person has committed, or is continuing to commit, an unlawful act then it may undertake legal proceedings (see below) or may issue a non- discrimination notice (section 58). However, no notice may be issued unless and until the named person has been warned that the Commission is considering so acting and has been given an opportunity to make oral or written representations, thus recognising that the CRE's powers in this respect are quasi-judicial and so the individual must be given access to the usual legal rights. A non- discrimination notice may: require a person not to commit acts of discrimination; require changes in practice; and require the person named to inform the Commission when such changes have taken place and the form in which they have been implemented. The named person has a right of appeal to an industrial tribunal if employment matters are concerned, or to a county court in other situations (section 59). But if there is no compliance with a non-discrimination notice, then the CRE has no further sanctions of its own to impose, and must approach the county court for the grant of an injunction if it wishes to proceed (section 62).

Providing assistance for individual complainants

Section 66 allows the CRE to assist an individual who wishes to start a complaint relating to allegations of racial discrimination. The Commission's discretion about when to so assist a complainant is broadly drafted; once a complainant has made an application to the CRE for assistance, the latter may (but does not have to) give its help if it "thinks fit to do so" on one of three grounds: **9–038**

section 66(1)

"(a) the case raises a question of principle; or
(b) it is unreasonable, having regard to the complexity of the case or the applicant's position in relation to the respondent or another person involved or any other matter, to expect the applicant to deal with the case unaided; or
(c) by reason of any other special circumstances."

Thus it is almost always possible for the CRE to involve itself in proceedings relating to any individual complaint where it so wishes. The types of assistance which may be given are also wide, ranging from giving or arranging advice or representation to attempting to settle the dispute.

Bringing proceedings in its own right

9–039 There are certain types of proceedings which only the Commission may commence, including: discriminatory advertisements (section 29); instructions to discriminate (section 30); and pressure to discriminate (section 31). Where one of these categories is concerned, the Commission will commence proceedings in an industrial tribunal if it is an employment case, or in the county court for other actions. The Commission may ask for various remedies, such as a declaration that there has been a breach of the Act (section 63(2)(a)); an injunction from a court to prevent further breaches (section 43(4)); or, if the Commission believes that a person who has already been found to have discriminated unlawfully is likely to do so persistently, then it may also apply to a county court for an injunction (section 62).

Enforcement by individuals

9–040 In spite of the important role and functions of the CRE, the main method of redress for breach of the Act is via an individual legal action. The means to be taken depend upon the subject-matter of the complaint. If the complaint is related to employment, then it must be brought to an industrial tribunal (section 54). If it concerns education, housing, goods facilities or services then it is to be brought before the county court (section 57), although most complaints relating to education must first be sent to the Secretary of State. There is a standard form questionnaire which is produced as an aid for the individual complainant, who may ask the defendant to answer on it questions concerning, for example, his reasons for his actions; any answers provided may be admitted in evidence, and failure to answer may stand against the defendant (section 65). If an individual complaint succeeds, then damages may be awarded for injury to feelings, suffering, any physical effects and so on, in addition to the usual range of civil remedies. Legal aid is available for court proceedings but not for tribunals.

3. Sexual Discrimination: Equal Pay Act 1970, Article 141 of the Treaty of Rome, and Sex Discrimination Act 1975

9–041 It is impossible to do justice to the volume and variety of legal principles involved in the prohibition of sex discrimination within the constraints imposed by the size and scope of this book. It is therefore recommended that students make use of one of the many excellent and detailed texts written specifically on the subject. However, the scope of the domestic law related to sex discrimination will be considered in this chapter, which will also highlight the main differences between the laws concerning racial discrimination and sex discrimination, and will look briefly at the impact of E.C. law on the domestic law.

Equal Pay Act 1970

This confusingly-named statute in fact came into force in 1975, in combination with the Sex Discrimination Act of that year. But the equal pay movement began long before this. The Trades Union Congress of 1888 passed a resolution in favour of equal pay for men and women, and the TUC continued to do so for the next 75 years, culminating in a call for legislation made at the 1963 TUC. In the meantime, the issue had been investigated by three Government Committees and three Royal Commissions, although their recommendation fell short of true pay equality; for example in 1916 the Atkin Committee,[73] thought that pay equality between men and women was justified only in situations where both sexes were employed in the same industry and to some extent shared duties. In jobs where there was a clear division between "men's work" and "women's work", pay should reflect this difference of skills, with the implication that women's work was of lesser value. The Atkin Committee also upheld the exclusion of women from certain occupations. Similar views were raised by the Asquith Commission,[74] which was however more divided in its recommendations. The Commission thought that equal pay should be adopted by the public sector, but not throughout employment. The majority believed that the differences between men's and women's pay largely reflected differences in ability and efficiency between the sexes, and argued that the imposition of equal pay as a general requirement would create widespread unemployment, particularly for women. But the minority regarded pay as being for work done, not for the attributes of the worker, and so stated that rates of pay should be set according to the value of the job, not the sex of the person performing it. The Government accepted the Commission's report but it was not implemented because other legislation was regarded as of greater importance in the years immediately after the Second World War. In the meantime there were extra-legal moves towards implementing equal pay in the Civil Service, which was completed by 1961. This defused the wider equal pay movement because it was civil servants who had supported it most strongly, but in 1961 the TUC changed its policy and began to argue in favour of a general principle of equal pay for work of equal value. By the time the Labour Government came to power in 1964, it was committed to introduce equal pay legislation, and eventually the Equal Pay Bill 1970 was introduced. A five-year grace period was allowed before its implementation so that employers and trade unions had time to change policy, rules and practice, and so there was a double legislative impact on sex discrimination in 1975, when the Sex Discrimination Act was also passed. **9–042**

Originally, the 1970 Equal Pay Act was relatively effective since it relied heavily on collective bargaining; section 3 gave a power to the Central Arbitration Committee to add protection of women to terms and collective bargaining agreements which applied only to men. This helped to get rid of many instances where a lower rate of pay applied only to women, who were paid even less than unskilled men. Since most people's wages were, and still are, determined by collective bargaining, the section 3 power was used widely by the Central Arbitration Committee not only to get rid of "women's rates" but to go beyond the legislation's aims by raising women's pay above that of unskilled men. Some employers were helpful in this respect and took equal opportunities on board, but others attempted to avoid the legislation by, for example, continuing to have a "women's rate" of pay but making it appear to be applicable to either sex although in fact no men were paid at that rate. But in 1979 a court decision stopped many of the CAC's positive practices by holding them to be *ultra vires*.[75] The end of the original equal pay framework was brought about by the EEC, which found that the United Kingdom had failed to fully implement the Equal Treatment Directive (see below).[76] Thus section 3 of the 1970 Act was repealed and replaced by the Sex Discrimination Act 1986, which makes void any discriminatory clauses in collective agreements and certain other sets of rules. This process was completed by the Trade Union Reform and Employment Rights Act 1993 which amended the 1986 Act in order to add a previously-lacking right to complain to an industrial tribunal, which may declare void and discriminatory provision in collective agreements, trade union rules, employers' rules and the rules of professional bodies.

The Equal Pay Act 1970, as amended, now provided that a woman's contract contains an implied "equality clause" where she is employed on "like work"; work formally rated as equivalent under the Job Evaluation Scheme, or "work of equal value" when assessed against a "comparable man". The equality clause means that any term of the woman's employment contract which is less favourable than the comparable man's will be amended to bring it into line with the corresponding term in the man's contract; and any beneficial term lacking from the woman's contract but present in the man's will be applied to her (section 1(2)). Both men and women are able to use section 1(2) in an action for equal pay. It is impossible to evade the provisions of the Equal Pay Act by contractual terms. However, there is a defence if the employer is able to prove that the difference in pay between the woman and the comparable man is due to a material factor other than the difference of sex. Because women continue to be paid less on average than men, the Equal Opportunities Commission issued a Code of Practice in March 1997 which aims to eliminate such discrimination.

Sex Discrimination Act 1975

9–043 The 1975 Act ("SDA") was the long-awaited result of decades of campaigning to ensure that women should be recognised as equal to men. It was passed at the height of the women's rights movement, after great changes in society's attitudes towards the role of women had arisen from such factors as women's employment in many traditionally male industries during the Second World War, the more general acceptance of feminism and the greater liberalism of the sixties. In one sense, women were the beneficiaries of the human rights movement—they were the only "minority" which was, and still is, in fact a majority. One of the factors which promoted change was the introduction of the American Civil Rights Act 1964, which prohibited sex discrimination at the same time as racial discrimination. It came to be realise that women were entitled to equal treatment to that given to men in many spheres, not merely in the narrow sense of equal pay. In the early 1970s two Private Members Bills relating to equal opportunities were attempted, and a Parliamentary Select Committee considered these amongst other evidence, deciding that there was a need for legislation in order to outlaw sex discrimination. In 1974 a White Paper titled *Equality for Women* was published by the new Labour Government,[77] and resulted in the 1975 Act. At almost the same time, the Equal Treatment Directive came into force in E.C. law (see below); the two legislative frameworks, domestic and E.C., differ only in detail but the 1976 Act is not a direct result of the Directive. The similarities in the two instruments' prohibition of discrimination however are great enough that the United Kingdom did not regard it to be necessary to pass further legislation in order to give effect to the Directive. The 1975 Act's main application is to employment-related discrimination, but is does extend beyond this into an almost identical anti-discrimination framework to that created by the Race Relations Act 1976, which was modelled upon it.

The main provisions of the 1976 Act will now be outlined, and comparison will be made where relevant to the corresponding provisions of the Race Relations Act (above).

Direct Discrimination

Section 1(1)(a) of the Sex Discrimination Act prohibits direct discrimina- **9–044**
tion in almost identical words to section 1(1)(a) of the Race Relations Act. A person unlawfully discriminates against a woman (which includes a man) if "on the grounds of her sex he treats her less favourably than he treats or would treat any man . . .". For example, to refuse to allow a woman to box professionally for reasons including alleged medical evidence that pre-menstrual tension makes women more likely to suffer injury from competitive boxing, has recently been found by an industrial tribunal to be unlawful discrimination. This case also illustrates that stereotypical assumptions made on the basis of sex are still current at the end of the twentieth century, and reminds the reader that although most sex discrimination cases relate to employment, the scope of the ban on discrimination is far wider that this extends to include housing, clubs, services and so on.

In *James v. Eastleigh Borough Council*[78]:

Facts. The local council allowed all pensioners to swim for free in its pools. The complainant was a 62 year old man who had to pay the usual fee for use of the services, whereas his 62 year old wife could use the pool without charge since the retirement age for women was lower (at the time 65 for men, 60 for women). The council did not intend to discriminate against men; its motives were positive. The case went to the House of Lords.

Decision. The House of Lords held that the statutory pensionable age is a factor which directly discriminates on the basis of sex. Thus any differentiation between men and women on the basis of pensionable age will share the same discriminatory effect, and will be unlawful. The overt basis for the differential treatment was sex, and so the discrimination was direct; it is irrelevant that there was no intention to discriminate. Lord Goff stated that the test is simply whether the person would have received different treatment "but for" his or her sex, and continued by saying that the use of such a straightforward test:

> ". . . avoids, in most cases at least, complicated questions relating to concepts such as intention, motive, reason, or purpose, and the danger of confusion resulting form the misuse of these elusive terms".

The statutory pensionable age for men and women has since been equalised at 65.

The application of sexual stereotypes which are unjustified will be direct discrimination; for example, to refuse to employ married mothers because they are thought to be less reliable,[79] or to refuse to employ young women for a job which involved lifting, on the basis that a "big strong lad" was needed rather than a "young lady".[80]

9–045 There are some differences between the sex and race discrimination legislation in relation to direct discrimination. Segregation is not a type of "less favourable treatment" on grounds of sex. Secondly, the less favourable treatment accorded to the victim must be on the basis of his or her own sex, not that of another person (section 1(1)(a)), unlike racial discrimination which may be related to the race of a third party.[81] Thirdly, there is an additional head of direct discrimination under the Sex Discrimination Act:

> "section 3(1) A person discriminates against a married person of either sex in any circumstances relevant for the provisions . . . if—
>
> (a) on the ground of his or her marital status he treats that person less favourably than he treats or would treat an unmarried person of the same sex;".

But the protection applies only to the married; it is perfectly lawful to treat a person less favourably on the basis that they are single. But it should be noted that the ECJ has construed the principle of equal treatment to extend to discrimination about transsexuals and other sexuality-based discrimination[82] and domestic cases have followed suit since they are required to do so by interpreting the Sex Discrimination Act in accordance with E.C. law.[83]

Indirect discrimination

9–046 Section 1(1)(b) of the SDA applies the same test for indirect discrimination as that in section 1(1)(b) of the RRA 1976. Thus it is indirect discrimination to apply to a woman any requirement or condition which would also be applied to a man, but with which a considerably smaller proportion of women can in fact comply. Section 3(1)(b) extends this to include marital status as a ground of indirect discrimination. As for racial discrimination, the requirement or condition must lack objective justification and must have caused the complainant detriment.

For sex discrimination, it is simple to determine the relevant groups for comparison under section 1(1)(b); they will be "men" and "women" in otherwise identical circumstances. Thus, in *R. v. Secretary of State for Education, ex parte Schaffter*,[84] each appropriate pool when comparing the proportions of men and women who could comply with an eligibility requirement for education grants[85] was a pool of all students with dependent children claiming grants, and not a pool of single lone parents. Since more than four times as many female lone parents were not eligible for grants, the condition was prima facie indirect discrimination.

Justification, detriment and victimisation (sections 4 SDA) are all defined in the same way as under the racial discrimination legislation.

The remainder of the SDA 1975 is almost identical to the provisions discussed above in relation to the RRA 1976. However, the "genuine occupational qualifications" for sex discrimination are different: section 7 of the SDA exempts situations where being of one sex is a "genuine occupational qualification for the job", that is; **9–047**

> Section 7(2)(a) reasons of physiology or authenticity, *e.g.* in dramatic performances;
>
> Section 7(2)(b) reasons of decency or privacy due to physical or visual contact being part of the job;
>
> > Section 7(2)(ba) where the post involves living or working in a private home and will include physical or social contact with a degree of intimacy;
>
> Section 7(2)(c) where the job comes with sleeping accommodation;
>
> Section 7(2)(d) where the job is at a single-sex establishment (*e.g.* a prison);
>
> Section 7(2)(e) the job provides personal welfare or educational services and can most effectively be performed by a person of that sex;
>
> Section 7(2)(h) where the job is one of a pair to be held by a married couple.

For reasons of space, the work of the Equal Opportunities Commission cannot be detailed here, but its powers are broadly similar to those of the CRE (SDA, s. 53 and Sched. 3).

It should be noted that divergence between the sex and race discrimination statutes is now increasing, since there is no sex-based equivalent to the Race Relations (Amendment) Act 2000.

The Impact of E.C. Law

9–048 A very brief discussion of relevant principles of E.C. law may be useful at this point. E.C. law's outlook on discrimination is narrow, focusing upon sex discrimination in relation to employment. But where it does apply, E.C. law will overrule domestic law in the case of any conflict. Questions of interpretation of E.C. law may be referred to the European Court of Justice by a United Kingdom court or tribunal. The ECJ has, in a series of landmark decision, held that United Kingdom law on sex discrimination does not comply with the relevant E.C. law and so the offending legislation has been amended. Students are recommended to consult one of the many excellent works on this topic for a far more detailed understanding of this area if required; space and subject constraints allow only the briefest enumeration of relevant principles here.

The most important aspects of the relevant E.C. law for the present discussion are as follows.

(i) The ECJ has recognised that the elimination of sex discrimination is a fundamental human right, and regards itself as under a duty to make sure that the right is upheld.[86]

(ii) Article 141 of the Treaty of Rome states that men and women should receive equal pay for equal work. This has been held by the ECJ to apply to indirect discrimination as well as to direct discrimination. In *Bilka-Kaufhaus GmbH v. Karin Weber von Hartz*,[87] the EJC held that a policy which is imposed regardless of sex but which in fact applies to more women than men in relation to pay will breach Article 141, unless the employer can show that the policy is truly justifiable on economic grounds.

(iii) The Equal Pay Directive (75/117) extends the effect of Article 119 to encompass a principle of equal pay for work of equal value.

(iv) The Equal Treatment Directive (76/207), as extended, aims to create equal treatment for men and women in access to employment, working conditions, pensions, self-employment and social security rules. Article 2 of the Directive states:

> ". . . the principle of equal treatment shall mean that there shall be no discrimination whatsoever on grounds of sex either directly or indirectly by reference in particular to marital or family status".

The prohibition of sex discrimination is applied to the following areas: decisions on selection and promotion of employees (Article 3); access to vocational training and guidance (Article 4); dismissal (Article 5); and victimisation (Article 7).

Although the Equal Treatment Directive is not substantially different form, and is in some respects narrower than, the Sex Discrimination Act 1975, it has given rise to some important decisions on such issues as retirement ages of men and women, for example *Marshall v. Southampton & South West Hampshire Water Authority*.[88]

(v) Other Directives, including the Pregnant Workers Directive and the Occupational Social Services Directive.

There is a difference in effect between the above E.C. provisions. Article 141 has both horizontal and vertical direct effect. "Direct effect" is the principle that a provision is enforceable in domestic courts without further legislation being required. "Vertical" direct effect allows reliance upon Article 141 in domestic courts for claims against the State; "horizontal" direct effect allows the Article to be relied upon in domestic courts for claims between individuals. But the Directives have only vertical direct effect (*Marshall v. Southampton*, above) and so cannot be relied upon when the dispute is between individuals. Thus whether E.C. law will be of use to a victim of sex discrimination will depend upon both the type of discrimination and the identity of the discriminator. But, in *Webb v. EMO Cargo United Kingdom Ltd*,[89] the House of Lords held that, although a Directive does not have direct effect upon an individual discriminator who is not an "emanation of the State", United Kingdom courts are under a duty to interpret domestic legislation on the same point as a Directive in accordance with the Directive, so long as this can be done without distorting the meaning of the United Kingdom legislation. So, if there is a possible interpretation of domestic legislation which is in accordance with a Directive, then it should be used. But if no such compatible interpretation is possible, then the domestic legislation should be the subject of court challenge.

4. Positive Discrimination on Grounds of Race or Sex

Although the main thrust of anti-discrimination law is prohibitory, both the **9–049** RRA and the SDA allow positive discrimination in certain, limited situations. There have been many campaigns to allow employers to take positive action to redress the balance in situations where a racial group or a sex is under-represented in a particular job. A recent and controversial example of this was seen in the drafting of women-only lists of candidates for "safe" constituencies at the 1997 General Election. Some see positive action as the only quick and effective method of combatting obvious structural inequality; others regard it as patronising (an expression of a belief that the persons in question cannot "make it" on their own merits), divisive and unlikely to create good relations between racial groups or the sexes. It has also been suggested that the genuine occupational qualifications in both statutes are used in an unjustifiable way to discourage applications by dominant groups for example by over-emphasising in a job advertisement the amount of services to be provided for the welfare of one sex or racial group. Whatever the view taken, the law allows positive discrimination only in circumstances of special needs or discriminatory training.

The special needs exemption applies only in the racial discrimination legislation. Section 35 of the Race Relations Act 1976 states that nothing in Parts II to IV of the Act shall render unlawful:

> "any act done in affording persons of a particular racial group access to facilities or services to meet the special needs of person of that group in regard to their education, training or welfare, or any ancillary benefits."

So, teaching in a particular language can be provided, or persons of one racial group may be given training in how to set up and run a small business, but the potential scope of section 35 is much wider and might encompass single-religion schools and facilities. In *Hughes v. London Borough of Hackney*,[90] it was stated by an industrial tribunal that section 35 cannot allow the provision of job opportunities.

Discriminatory training is allowed under both Acts in situations where there is under-representation of one sex or racial group in a particular field of employment, either nationally, locally or with a single employer. Training bodies (only RRA, s. 37), employers (RRA, s. 38, SDA, s. 48) or "any person" (only SDA, s. 47 as amended by Sex Discrimination Act 1986, s. 4) may make training available to the under-represented group, in order to encourage them to make use of such employment opportunities as do exist. But priority cannot be given to that group in interviews or applications, promotions or the allocation of work. Thus these provisions are limited to a promotional role rather than a combative one. The CRE Code of Practice encourages employers to use regular monitoring of their workforce in order to find instances of under-representation and to then target job advertisements in employment agencies, newspapers and careers' offices which are likely to be most accessible to that group.

5. Disability Discrimination: Disability Discrimination Act 1995

9–050 The Disability Discrimination Act 1995 ("DDA") was the result of a concerted campaign to extend the protection of anti-discrimination legislation. It has been criticised as a partial measure which reflects the compromise effected in order to allow it to be passed. Previous measures on the issue had been extremely limited. The Disabled Persons (Employment) Acts 1944 and 1958 set up a voluntary register of people with disabilities and obliged employers with 20 or more employees to fulfil a quota of three per cent of the workforce being people with disabilities, as well as establishing certain other limited duties. The quota no longer applies. Between 1982 and 1994 there were 17 attempts to reform the law in this area by introducing Bills, most of which had cross-party support, yet none of them became law. It was only in 1994 that the campaign reached such heights of popularity and publicity that legislation seemed inevitable, with disabled people mounting protests such as sit-ins on public transport to protest about lack of access. In 1994 the Government defeated the last of the attempts to legislate by Private Members Bill on this issue, and introduced a consultation document.[91] Six months later the Disability Discrimination Bill was introduced into Parliament and quickly passed, although its implementation was deferred until February 12, 1996. The new Act merely provided a framework for the law, which continues to be supplemented and updated by detailed regulations.

Although welcomed as a declaratory measure, the Act has been criticised for not going far enough. It also contains defences and exemptions which do not apply under sex or racial discrimination and which are difficult to justify objectively. The most contentious points are:

(i) The DDA 1995 only outlaws direct discrimination in relation to disability; indirect discrimination is not addressed.

(ii) The Act allows direct discrimination to be justified and so free from legal liability.

(iii) The DDA did not originally set up a Commission to enforce and uphold its provisions; the Government announced plans to redress this in 1997, which were carried out in 1999. The DDA's creation of the National Disability Council was denounced as meaningless and powerless in Parliamentary debate.[92] Hopefully the Disability Rights Commission will be more effective.

(iv) Exemptions exist under at least part of the Act for each of the police, armed forces, prison services, firms with less than 20 employees and education.

(v) The act uses a definition of "disability" which focuses upon "impairments" in the individual, and so both its language and understanding have been criticised for being out of date; it does not see beyond physical and mental "defects" to include wider problems which have just as disabling an effect of a person's treatment in society as does a mobility problem.

Political pressure is likely to give rise to further reforms, particularly in relation to the rising campaign for public transport providers to be required to make their transport accessible to disabled people.

The main aspects of the Act will now be considered.

"Disability"

9–051 Section 1(1) defines disability as: "a physical or mental impairment which has a substantial and long-term effect on his ability to carry out normal day-to-day activities."

Schedule 1 expands this by requiring that, if the complainant's mental disability arose from illness, then the illness must have medical recognition.[93] An illness has long-term effect if it lasts for more than a year.[94] Normal day-to-day activities are; movement; dexterity; co-ordination; continence; ability to carry or lift objects; speech, hearing, eyesight; memory, concentration, learning and understanding; and perception of the risk of physical danger.[95] Any person who was formerly registered disabled remains so classified until at least December 1999.[96]

"Discrimination"

9–052 As stated above, only direct discrimination is prohibited under the 1995 Act. The definition of discrimination is found in sections 5, 14, 20, and 24 of the Act, and has two elements:

— because of a reason related to the victim's disability, the discriminator treats a person less favourably than he treats or would treat others to whom the reason does not apply and;

— the discriminator is unable to show that his treatment of the victim is justified.

General points which can be noted about this definition are: in contrast with the SDA and RRA, positive discrimination is not unlawful under the Disability Discrimination Act; justification is possible for direct disability discrimination, but not under the other two statutes; but otherwise the definition here is very similar to those for direct discrimination under the other two statutes.

As with the other types of unlawful discrimination covered above, disability discrimination does not exist in a vacuum. It is not enough to show that there was direct discrimination against the victim; it must also relate to one of the headings below.

Employment

9–053 This is dealt with in Part II of the Act, which is the main body of the statute. Section 4 makes it unlawful for an employer to discriminate on grounds of disability in relation to any aspect of employment, from advertisements to interview, promotion and training. Employers must also take reasonable steps to address any disadvantages which a disabled employee might face, *e.g.* by providing wheelchair access, or an interpreter, or altering hours of work (section 6). But the provisions in relation to employment only apply to employers who have 20 or more employees (section 7), and there is a defence of justification (section 5).

Goods/facilities/services

Section 19 prohibits the refusal or deliberate failure to provide goods, facilities or services to a disabled person which would have been provided to the general public. Reasonable changes must be made to buildings or policies (section 21). But there is a defence of justification here, as well as in relation to employment, which is broadly drafted (section 20). **9–054**

Education

Disability discrimination in education is not actually made unlawful by the Act, which instead creates a duty incumbent upon further and higher education institutions to produce statements about the facilities which they make available to disabled students. **9–055**

Housing

Disability discrimination in relation to the disposal of premises or their management is unlawful under section 22, but there are exceptions for: small dwellings (section 23); owner occupiers who arrange private sales (section 22(2)); and justified discrimination (section 24). **9–056**

Public transport

The Act also contains the machinery by which regulations are being made concerning increasing access to public transport for disabled people. Although many cases have been brought under the Disability Discrimination Act 1995, it is only recently that appeal cases have established the correct procedure which a tribunal must use when deciding whether unlawful discrimination has occurred in a particular case. It has been held that there is a sequence of stages by which a claim of disability discrimination must be considered. **9–057**

In *Morse v. Wiltshire County Council*[97]:

Facts. The appellant had worked as a road worker for the respondent for approximately 34 years. He was injured in a road accident in 1986 after 23 years of employment. In 1996, the employer's financial circumstances necessitated a reduction of the workforce, and the appellant was among those selected for redundancy. It was a relevant factor to his selection that workers with valid driving licences were considered of higher priority to the company; the appellant, because of his disability, could not satisfy this criterion for selection. The respondent admitted that the appellant had a disability within the meaning of the Act, and that they had subjected him to a detriment by selecting him for redundancy for a reason related to his disability. They argued however, that the discrimination which the appellant suffered was not unlawful since it was "justified" within the meaning of section 5(3) of the Act.[98] Section 5(3) provides that discriminatory treatment ". . . is justified if, but only if, the reason for it is both material to the circumstances of the particular case and substantial". The appellant however argued that the Council had failed to discharge the duty which it owed under section 6 of the Act, which provides:

"(1) Where—
(a) any arrangements made by or on behalf of an employer, or;
(b) any physical feature of premises occupied by the employer, place the disabled person concerned at a substantial disadvantage in comparison with persons who are not disabled, it is the duty of the employer to take such steps as it is reasonable, in all the circumstances of the case, for him to have to take in order to prevent the arrangements or feature having that effect."

The original industrial tribunal dismissed the case and queried whether the Council had been under a section 6(1) duty in relation to Morse.

Decision. The Employment Appeal Tribunal found that the Council did owe the appellant a section 6(1) duty and thus must establish that its behaviour was justified if it was to escape a finding of unlawful discrimination. In order to test whether a justification did exist, the following sequence of steps should be taken by a tribunal.

(1) Did the employer owe a section 6(1) duty in relation to the employee? If so, then;
(2) Had the employer taken whatever steps were reasonable in all the circumstances in order to prevent the disabled person from being placed at a substantial disadvantage when compared against persons who were not disabled?
(3) Only if it was found that the employer had failed to comply with a section 6(1) duty should the tribunal consider whether the employer's behaviour was justified with reference to sections 5(2) and (4). Relevant factors would include the explanation which the employer advanced for the redundancy or other treatment, but whether the reasons were "material" and "substantial" were to be judged objectively.

It has been seen time and again in cases that the requirements of the statute can be highly complex, *e.g.* even though there is discrimination under section 5(2) and section 6, there will be no remedy for this unless the discrimination is also unlawful under section 4. Although the Secretary of State may issue Codes under section 53 with the aim of eliminating discrimination against disabled persons in employment and in fact did so in December 1996, section 53(4) provides that breach of any Code provision does not in itself give rise to a remedy, but any such breach may be taken into account by any court or tribunal when determining another issue. Again, even when all the requirements appear to be satisfied, it is uncertain whether a court will agree—in a recent case the Court of Appeal applied a low standard for the employer's duty;

9–058 In *Cave v. Goodwin*[99]:

Facts. The employee, Mr Cave, was required to attend a disciplinary hearing concerning an allegation of gross misconduct. He brought a case to a tribunal on the basis, *inter alia*, of disability discrimination. He had epilepsy and a learning disability and alleged that two factors had left him at a substantial disadvantage in the proceedings. Firstly, he had been suspended by letter, when his employers knew that he had difficulty reading. Secondly, the employer had only given him permission to be accompanied at the hearing by a colleague, not by a friend. The tribunal found that he had not been discriminated against, although he did have a relevant disability, since the effect of the situation on him was not severe in the circumstances. The contents of the letter had been explained to him by colleagues; and it was clear from the forthright and well-expressed manner in which he gave his evidence at the tribunal that the claimant's disability did not have such a severe effect upon him that he should be allowed a free choice as to who accompanied him to the disciplinary hearing.

The claimant then appealed to the Employment Appeal Tribunal, who found by majority that no sufficient comparison had been made under section 6(1) between the applicant's position and that of an able-bodied person in the same circumstances, and also that the applicant's request to have a non-employee accompany him to the hearing had not been properly considered by the employer or the tribunal. Since the employer had failed to make any adjustment for the applicant's disability, the EAT set aside the tribunal's decision and sent the case to a fresh tribunal. The employers appealed to the Court of Appeal

Decision. The original tribunal had not erred in law in relation to the suspension letter, although the employer's actions were certainly open to criticism. Again there was no error of law in relation to the choice of representative at the disciplinary hearing.The original tribunal had given full consideration to the facts and to the application of the relevant law. Although it had not made an express comparison between the effect of the employer's actions on Mr Cave and the effect which they would have had upon a non-disabled person, such a comparison was implicit in their reasoning. Since it is not the role of the EAT to question findings of fact but merely to deal with he application of law to those facts, the EAT's decision was set aside and the original tribunal's findings were reinstated.

Enforcement

The main method of enforcement is by individual complaint to an industrial **9–059**
tribunal for employment matters (section 8) or to the county court for other matters (section 25). Compensation is similarly assessed and awarded as for the other discrimination actions. In fact, the enforcement procedures under the 1995 Act are almost identical to those under the 1975 and 1976 Acts, above. The Government has recently established a Disability Rights Commission to perform a supervisory and enforcement function and to draft Codes of Practice.

In summary, it is to be hoped that the law forbidding disability discrimination will be strengthened and extended until it more closely resembles its racial and sex discrimination "cousins". A movement away from regulations and towards a more detailed statute would also be preferable since it would reduce the present confusion for the potential complainant, who currently has to investigate a series of regulation before he will know whether he has a claim. It is to be hoped also that the new supervisory body will have real powers and will enable change in society's attitudes.

9–060 The Convention's anti-discrimination provision is Article 14, which provides:

> "The enjoyment of the rights and freedoms set forth in this Convention is to be secured without discrimination on any grounds such as sex, race, colour, language, religion, political or other opinion, national or social origin, association with a national minority, property, birth or other status".

Several points must be made about this Article before the relevant cases are examined. Firstly, it does not create a free-standing absolute right to freedom from discrimination; it merely prohibits discrimination in relation to the other rights and freedoms under the Convention. Thus only discrimination which can be fitted within the Convention rights can be redressed under the Human Rights Act or in Strasbourg. However, it does not have to be shown that one of the other Articles has been violated: simply that the facts of the case fall within the *scope* of one of the other Articles. The approach is thus similar to that under Article 13. Secondly, once Article 14 is triggered, its scope is much broader than that under domestic or European anti-discrimination law: not only is the list of types of prohibited discrimination far wider than sex, race and disability, it is also merely illustrative, since discrimination *on any unjustified ground* in relation to the Convention rights and freedoms is prohibited. This factor is likely to lead to some interesting HRA challenges in domestic courts, since the U.K. has a number of statutes which employ discriminatory standards, and further there are differences between the relevant domestic statutes on race, sex and disability discrimination which may not stand up to scrutiny. Thirdly, there is no express mention of exceptions in Article 14 where discrimination is lawful, but the Strasbourg Court has consistently interpreted the Article such that discrimination is lawful only where it has an objective, reasonable and proportionate justification. The extent to which justification is possible at all depends upon the type of discrimination involved in the case: as will be seen, sex and race discrimination are rarely tolerated by the Strasbourg Court and so are extremely difficult to "justify". Fourthly, it has been a frustrating aspect of the Strasbourg case law that there are very few cases in which discrimination has been the basis of a violation: although Article 14 is very often argued, in most cases where an Article 14 violation might well have been found, the Strasbourg Court has found a violation of another Article and has simply stated that it was not necessary to consider the Article 14 issue. Thus somewhat paradoxically the best evaluation of Article 14's scope and limitations is found in cases where there was no other Convention argument, and these are often the weakest cases. In order to assist the reader, relevant ECHR cases have been divided into the familiar categories of sex discrimination, racial and religious discrimination, and "other".

6. SEX DISCRIMINATION

The general principles of the prohibition of sex discrimination under Article 14 are to be found in *Abdulaziz, Cabales and Balkandali v. United Kingdom*[1]: 9–061

Facts. The applicants, women born outside the U.K. who had legally settled in the U.K. and had been given the right to remain indefinitely, had each married after coming to the U.K. and sought permission for their husbands to enter or to remain in the U.K. Permission was refused in each case. The applicants claimed that U.K. immigration rules were discriminatory as to sex and race, and violated the right to respect for family life since the women were being deprived of their husbands. Mrs Balkandali also alleged discrimination on grounds of birth. All three applicants alleged violations of Articles 3 and 8.

The Commission was of the opinion that there had been a breach of Article 14 in conjunction with Article 8, and that the absence of effective domestic remedies was a violation of Article 13.

Decision. The ECHR rejected the Government's assertion that Article 8 had not been breached since the couples in question had never had a "family life" to be given respect. The ECHR decided that a "family life" started with a genuine, lawful marriage and so each of the applicants had sufficiently embarked upon "family life" to be protected by Article 8. However, the rights of the applicants to a family life had to be balanced against the State's right to control the entry of non-nationals into its territory via immigration law. There was no breach of Article 8, taken alone, since each applicant had the freedom to establish a family life in either her own or her husband's home country, and each applicant knew that it was unlikely that her husband would qualify for U.K residence. The ECHR went on to dismiss the allegations of discrimination on grounds of race or birth since there was no differential treatment on either of these grounds, but found that there was a violation of Article 14 taken together with Article 8 on grounds of sex. Under the 1980 Immigration Rules a husband settled in the U.K. had far more chance of obtaining permission for his wife to enter or to remain in the U.K. than did a wife in the same factual situation. The Government had argued that this differential treatment was objectively and reasonably justified because it had the aim of limiting "primary immigration" and there was a pressing social need to protect the domestic labour market in a time of mass unemployment. Since men were more likely to be seeking employment than were women, male immigration was though to be more dangerous to the labour market. The Government further argued that preventing immigration was a method of securing good race relations. The ECHR rejected all these arguments, stating that:

> "..the advancement of the equality of the sexes is today a major goal in the member states...This means that very weighty reasons would have to be advanced before a difference of treatment on the ground of sex could be regarded as compatible with the Convention".

The Government had failed to show any convincing reason of sufficient weight to justify the differential treatment. The ECHR also found a violation of Article 13 but rejected the applicants' claim for compensation.

In the case of *Schmidt v. Germany*,[2] it was found that sex discrimination will almost never be justified. Further, it is not permissible to make assumptions about women's roles and abilities. In *Schuler-Zgraggen v. Switzerland*[3]: 9–062

Facts. The applicant contracted a serious illness, which required her to give up work, and she was granted an invalidity pension. Some six years later she gave birth to a son. She was then given a medical in order to assess her ability to work, and the subsequent report stated that she was completely unfit for clerical work but 60–70 per cent fit for housework. Her pension was then cancelled on the ground that her family circumstances had radically changed due to the birth of her son, the improvement in her health and her ability to care for her son and her home. When she appealed she was denied access to her medical files. The domestic courts held that the applicant was not entitled to a pension since, even if she had been well enough to work, as a woman she was expected to give up her job once she became a mother and devote herself to housework. Further, if she really wanted to work, then the refusal to pay a pension could be the push she needed.

The applicant complained, firstly, that she had not received a fair trial as guaranteed by Article 6 due to the lack of access to her medical records and the fact that she had only ever been able to make representations in writing, not in person, and that the court's assumption that even if she had been well she would have given up work to be a mother was sex discrimination. The Commission stated that whether social security proceedings are within the ambit of Article 6(1) is a complex issue since they have public law features such as compulsory insurance and State assumption of responsibility for social protection, but also private law issues such as the economic nature of the right to a pension, and the links with employment law and insurance law, which are private in nature. The Commission decided by 10 votes to five that the lack of an oral hearing did not violate Article 6(1), but were so divided as to the reasoning behind this that no helpful summary is possible, although the common thread was that Article 6(1) did not apply to the law in question. The limitation of access to medical files was also not found to be a violation of Article 6(1) (13:2), with seven of the majority finding that there was no "civil right" to be determined and so Article 6(1) was not applicable, and the remainder finding that the applicant had sufficient access to her files by the time the case reached appeal stage. Lastly, the Commission found (9:6) that there had been no violation of Article 6 in conjunction with Article 14 by sex discrimination. Again, there were divisions among the Commission as to reasoning. Six of the majority argued that, since Article 6 did not apply due to the lack of a "civil right", Article 14 could not come into play. The remaining three of the majority regarded the applicant's claim of discrimination as relating to the substance of the domestic court's decision and not to the procedures followed, and so found that they had no jurisdiction to examine it.

Decision. The ECHR disagreed with the Commission's findings as to jurisdiction and whether social security proceedings involved determination of a "civil right" for the purposes of Article 6(1). Article 6(1) was held to be applicable since the applicant had suffered an interference with her income and so was claiming an individual economic right. But the ECHR went on to find that there had been no breach of Article 6(1), either by the lack of an oral hearing or by the refusal of prompt access to medical files. Since the issue is whether the proceedings, viewed as a whole, were fair, the fact that the applicant had been given access to her medical files in time to prepare her appeal was sufficient; and it would be impractical to expect that every social security appeal should involve an oral hearing.

But the ECHR did find that there had been a breach of Article 6(1) in conjunction with Article 14. The domestic courts had assumed that the applicant would have given up work when she became a mother if she had not been unwell. This assumption:

> ". . .cannot be regarded...as an incidental remark, clumsily drafted but of negligible effect. On the contrary, it constitutes the sole basis for the reasoning,

> thus being decisive, and introduces a difference of treatment based on the ground of sex only".

Since there was sex discrimination, this difference of treatment could be justified only by extremely persuasive reasons, and no such reasons had been shown to exist in the present case.

It is not only women who may benefit form Article 14, as will be seen **9–063**
from two illustrative cases. The issue in *Van Raalte v. Netherlands*[4] was sex discrimination in relation to State benefits. Domestic law exempted unmarried childless women over the age of 45 from having to pay contributions towards child benefit. There was no similar exemption for men. The applicant was an unmarried, childless, man over the age of 45 who argued that the exemption breached Article 1 of the First Protocol in conjunction with Article 14. The exemption was abolished by statute in 1989, and the applicant lost his domestic case for sex discrimination. The domestic courts held that the legislature had not intended to discriminate since the difference of treatment was based not on a difference in sex but on a difference in factual situation: women over 45 rarely procreate but men over 45 do. Thus the women exempted would almost certainly never claim child benefit. However, the principle had still been violated. The ECHR held unanimously that there had been a violation of Article 14 in conjunction with Article 1 of the First Protocol. There was clearly a difference of treatment based on sex. Thus it had to be determined whether there was objective and reasonable justification for the difference. The ECHR pointed out that a central feature of the child benefit scheme was that all citizens were required to contribute, regardless of their potential entitlement. Thus the exemption contradicted the scheme's policy. Since, *inter alia*, unmarried childless women over 45 may adopt, foster or become stepmothers and thus claim child benefit, there was no logic to the exemption. None of the reasons put forward by the Government could form an objective and reasonable justification, especially to the higher standard expected in cases of sex discrimination.

Again, men should be given paternity rights and benefits if such are available to women. But in practice most such cases have been found to be justified on the facts. In *Petrovic v. Austria*[5]:

Facts. The applicant was a married university student who also worked part time. His wife, a graduate, was a civil servant. After the birth of their child, the applicant took parental leave to care for the child whilst his wife returned to work. He claimed a benefit, parental leave payments, but was refused this on the ground that the benefit was payable only to mothers. Although the relevant legislation was later amended to allow payments to fathers who were primary carers, the change did not apply retrospectively to the applicant. He claimed sex discrimination in relation to his right to respect for private and family life, *i.e.* a breach of Article 14 in conjunction with Article 8. The Commission stated that the denial of the benefit in question was not in itself a breach of Article 8 since that Article does not oblige a state to give financial assistance to parents so that they can care for their children full time. However, the benefit exists in order to promote daily life and so its provision is a method by which the state performs its obligations under Article 8 to show respect for family life. Thus it was possible to argue a breach of Article 14 in conjunction with Article 8 here. The applicant was ineligible for the parental leave benefit simply because he was a man. There was therefore a difference of treatment on grounds of sex. Since sex equality is a major goal in modern society, such a difference of treatment will be justified only by very weighty reasons. There is no reason why fathers should be less able to care for a newborn child than mothers. If a state provides a scheme of parental leave payments, then they must be granted in a non-discriminatory manner. The lack of a common standard among Member States regarding social security schemes does not excuse any state's discrimination. No objective and reasonable justification had been demonstrated for the discrimination and hence (by a vote of 25:5) there was a violation of Article 14 in conjunction with Article 8.

Decision. However, the ECHR took a different view. The parental leave allowance fell within the scope of Article 8 since it was:

> ". . .intended to promote family life and necessarily affects the way in which the latter is organised as, in conjunction with parental leave, it enables one of the parents to stay at home to look after the children".

Hence Article 14 could come into play. The ECHR agreed that there was a difference of treatment on grounds of sex, that equality is a major goal and therefore that very weighty reasons are needed to justify such a difference of treatment. However, such benefits originally only applied to mothers in all Contracting States, and have gradually been extended to fathers as societies' views of parenthood have changed:

> "It therefore appears difficult to criticise the Austrian legislature for having introduced in a gradual manner, reflecting the evolution of society in that sphere, legislation which is, all things considered, very progressive in Europe".

Hence the difference in treatment was within the margin of appreciation and there was no violation of Article 14 in conjunction with Article 8 (7:2)

Judges Bernhardt and Spielmann however, gave a joint dissenting opinion in which they argued that Article 14 had been breached:

> "It is in reality the traditional distribution of family responsibilities between mothers and fathers that gave rise to the Austrian legislation under which only mothers were entitled to parental leave allowance. The discrimination against fathers perpetuates this traditional distribution of roles and can also have negative consequences for the mother; if she continues her professional activity and agrees that the father should stay at home, the family loses the parental leave allowance to which it would be entitled if she stayed at home. It is correct that States are under no obligation to pay any parental leave allowance, but if they do so, traditional practices and roles in family life alone do not justify a difference in treatment of men and women".

It is argued that this is the better view, especially in the light of recent legislative developments both in domestic and European law.

Discrimination on Grounds of Race, Nationality or Religion

9–064 The most famous case in this category relates to racial discrimination in immigration law. In *East-African Asians v. United Kingdom*[6]:

Facts. The 31 applicants had all sought leave to enter Britain or to remain there permanently, and leave had been denied. 25 of the applicants were citizens of the United Kingdom and its colonies, and the other six were British "protected persons", *i.e.* not British subjects. The Government argued that the refusal was neither degrading treatment under Article 3 nor discriminatory, since the U.K. is not a party to any Convention right to enter one's own country and the relevant legislation applied to all persons regardless of race. The applicants alleged a violation of Article 3 and of Article 14.

Decision. The Commission treated racial discrimination as a type of degrading treatment, and hence did not find it necessary to examine Article 14. Deportation of a person could be inhuman or degrading treatment in exceptional circumstances, whether that person is an alien or a citizen. The two groups of applicants were considered separately. The group of 25 citizens alleged that they had been promised free entry and that since their continued residence in East Africa was illegal, they were being rendered stateless and subject to intense hardship. The Commission found that the Commonwealth Immigrants Act 1968, which imposed immigration controls on most East African Asian citizens, was racially motivated, and applied to a racial group. The government had argued that the Act was intended to promote racial harmony, but the Commission rejected this claim and stated that the Act discriminated against East African Asians on grounds of race. The Commission also found that, although it had not been demonstrated that there had been any formal pledge of free entry for East African Asian citizens, the applicants had relied upon their belief in such a pledge and so had failed to obtain any other citizenship. These special circumstances strengthened the 25 citizens' case. The Government could have foreseen the hardship to be faced by the applicants before the 1968 Act was passed. The Commission found that:

> "...a special importance should be attached to discrimination based on race; that publicly to single out a group of persons for differential treatment on the basis of race might, in certain circumstances, constitute a special form of affront to human dignity; and that differential treatment of a group of persons on the basis of race might therefore be capable of constituting degrading treatment when differential treatment on some other ground would raise no such question".

Thus the racial discrimination amounting to degrading treatment violated Article 3 (6:3).

The second category, however, the six "protected persons", were treated differently. These applicants were not affected by the 1968 Act but regulated by earlier legislation. They were not British subjects and the relevant legislation did not distinguish between categories of British protected persons on any racial basis. Thus there was no racial discrimination and hence no degrading treatment in relation to the six applicants (unanimous).

A further argument of breach of Articles 8 and 14 was made in respect of three of the applicants, whose wives had already been granted permanent residence in Britain. The Government argued that the husbands and wives had separated voluntarily and that even where Article 8 does guarantee a right for a family to reside together in a particular place, that place is where the husband lawfully resides rather than the wife. The Commission rejected the Government's arguments: under the legislation a wife was entitled to join a U.K.-resident husband, and so the three applicants had been subject to discrimination on the ground of sex in relation to their family lives (7:2).

Cases have also found a violation of Article 6(1) where a trial court refused to take notice of juror's racist remark, for instance in *Remli v. France*,[7] and below, in *Gregory v United Kingdom*[8]: **9–065**

Facts. The applicant, who is black and a British citizen, was tried for robbery. During jury deliberations a note was passed to the judge by the jury which stated: "Jury showing racial overtones. One member to be excused". The judge consulted prosecution and defence counsel and it is unclear whether defence counsel asked for the jury to be discharged. The jury were recalled and the judge redirected them that (*inter alia*) "any thoughts or prejudices of one form or another, for or against anybody, must be put out of your minds... It is the evidence alone which decides the case...". The jury were unable to reach even a majority verdict so the judge again redirected them, and after a total of over five hours of jury deliberations the jury found the applicant guilty by 10:2 majority. He sought leave to appeal against his six-year prison sentence on the basis that the trial judge should have considered discharging at least one member of the jury on the basis of racial prejudice, but leave was refused. The Court of Appeal interpreted the note as meaning that:

> ". . .one member of the jury felt that there was a general overtone of racial comment which was unacceptable and not, as the applicant is suggesting, one member of the jury being so racially prejudiced as to be unable to give proper consideration to the matters before him".

Although the judge could have discharged any or all of the jury for bias, he would have needed evidence of actual bias which had a real danger of affecting the mind of the juror or jurors. The applicant alleged violations of Articles 6 and 14. The Commission's opinion was that neither provision had been violated.

Decision. Dealing first with the allegation that the applicant had been denied a fair trial, the ECHR stated that public confidence in the fairness of criminal proceedings is vital, and that impartiality of trials must be shown from both a subjective and an objective viewpoint. The trial judge's decision to redirect rather than discharge jurors had not been shown to be wrong, and the redirection was clear and forceful.

> "While the guarantee of a fair trial may in certain circumstances require a judge to discharge a jury it must also be acknowledged that this may not always be the only means to achieve that aim. In circumstances such as those in issue, other safeguards, including a carefully worded redirection to the jury, may be sufficient".

This case was distinguishable from the *Remli* case since the Gregory judge had taken sufficient steps towards guaranteeing the court's impartiality. Thus there was no violation of Article 6(1).

The applicant's second allegation was that the trial judge and appeal court had treated racial bias less seriously than they would have treated any other type of bias, citing cases where juries had been discharged for less serious allegations of bias. The ECHR however found that this allegation did not give rise to any separate issue under Article 14, and so there was no violation. However, Judge Foighel gave a dissenting opinion in favour of finding a breach of Article 6(1) by reason of discrimination. He argued that:

> ". . .the members of the jury are given no advance warning on how they are to address an unexpected occurrence of racism within the jury... it is of the utmost importance that remedies should be in place to enable a trial judge to ensure that the decision of the jury is not tainted with any objective suspicion of bias ...a speech from a judge—a redirection—cannot dispel racial prejudice within a jury, if such prejudice exists. The only safeguard which could have been offered by the trial judge in this case was to discharge part or the whole of the jury, or

at least to have conducted a more probing enquiry into the effect of the note on the jury's deliberations".

Article 14 has been employed to argue for a right to education in accordance with religious beliefs (*Valsamis v. Greece*[9]) and in a child's native language (*Belgian Linguistic case (No. 1)*[10] and *Belgian Linguistic case (No. 2)*[11]).

A further interesting line of cases has concerned religious discrimination. In *Kokkinakis v. Greece*[12]: **9–066**

Facts. The applicant, a Jehovah's Witness, had been arrested more than 60 times for proselytism, and had been imprisoned several times. The circumstances of the most recent case were that he and his wife were invited into a woman's home and began a discussion with her. Her husband called the police and the applicant and his wife were convicted of the criminal offence of proselytism. The applicant alleged breaches of Articles 7, 9 and 10 in relation to his criminal conviction.

Decision. The ECHR took the view that the focus of the applicant's case was the "logical and legal difficulty of drawing any even remotely clear dividing-line between proselytism and freedom to change one's religion and...to manifest it". What is the difference between proselytism and teaching or preaching? Freedom of thought, conscience and religion is an essential precondition for pluralism and so for democratic society. Whilst the legislation had the legitimate aim of protecting the rights and freedoms of others, the ECHR considered that the applicant's criminal conviction was not necessary in a democratic society since it was disproportionate to that aim. There is a difference between "bearing Christian witness" and "improper proselytism". The former is an essential task for every true Christian, according to the World Council of Churches: the latter is incompatible with other people's freedom of thought, involves improper pressure or means, and may stretch as far as brainwashing or violence. The domestic courts had not shown that the applicant had done any more than bear witness, and so there was a breach of Article 9.

The ECHR did not consider that there had been a breach of Article 7 and decided that it was unnecessary to discuss Article 10. Although the applicant had raised Article 14 as a late argument, the ECHR did not consider it necessary to discuss whether there had been discrimination on the ground of religion since a breach of Article 9 had been established.

Discrimination on Other Grounds in Relation to a Convention Right

A simple list can show the breadth of Article 14, although of course a violation is not always found. Many of the following cases are dealt with elsewhere in this book: **9–067**

* Discrimination on the basis of political opinion: *McLaughlin v. United Kingdom*[13]
* Discrimination on grounds of lifestyle: *Smith v. United Kingdom*[14]
* Discrimination against terrorist suspects *re.* the right to silence and access to a solicitor: *Murray v. United Kingdom*[15]
* Discrimination on grounds of wealth: *S and M v. United Kingdom*[16]

* Discrimination against prisoners in the provision on education: *X v. United Kingdom*[17]
* Discrimination in relation to illegitimacy; and the right to a name: *Stjerna v. Finland*[18]
* Discrimination about moral views: compulsory sex education in schools: *Kjeldsen, Busk Madsen and Pedersen v. Denmark*[19]
* Discrimination on ground on mental capacity: *X and Y v. The Netherlands*[20]
* Discrimination on ground of belief (pacifism): *Arrowsmith v. United Kingdom*[21]
* Discrimination on grounds of residence: *Darby v Sweden*[22]
* Disability discrimination: *Botta v. Italy*[23]

9–068 This last case deserves some examination, since it points out the difficulties which often occur in Article 14 cases, and shows that although Article 14 would have been stronger than domestic disability discrimination law on the facts, it is the first hurdle of applicability at which most cases fall.

Facts. The applicant, who is physically disabled, went to a seaside resort on holiday and found that there were no facilities for disabled access to the beach and sea, such as ramps and specially equipped washrooms and toilets. Italian law requires private beaches to facilitate the access of disabled people. The applicant was given permission to drive his vehicle onto a public beach which had no facilities, and the public prosecutor discontinued proceedings against the local authorities at the holiday resort for failing to enforce the relevant law. Mr Botta alleged violations of Articles 3, 5, 13 6(1) and 14. The Commission declared the application admissible in relation to Articles 3, 5, 8 and 14 only, but was of the opinion that none of these provisions had been violated.

Decision. Dealing first with the alleged violation of Article 8, the ECHR decided that "private life" includes a person's physical and psychological integrity. Since the applicant's claim was one of inaction by the State in securing respect for such aspects of his family life, a state has obligations to act positively in this way only where there is a "direct and immediate link between the measures sought by the applicant and the latter's private and/or family life". Mr Botta's claim of rights to access to a beach and the sea while on holiday concerned:

> ". . .interpersonal relations of such broad and indeterminate scope that there can be no conceivable direct link between the measures the State was urged to take in order to make good the omissions of the private bathing establishments and the applicant's private life".

Hence Article 8 did not apply, taken alone. Turning to Article 8 in conjunction with Article 14, the ECHR again rejected the claim. The applicant had argued that he had unjustifiably been treated less favourably than he would have been if he had not been disabled. Although the law promoted equality, in factual situations there was a difference of treatment affecting the applicant. But since Article 14 has no independent existence if the facts of a case do not fall within another Convention right, and Mr Botta had failed to show that any other right was applicable, Article 14 could not apply. Hence there could be no violation.

But let us end upon a positive note. Although in Chapter 1 the view of Article 14 was predominantly negative, it is a tool which could be used, post-HRA, to hugely expand the scope of domestic discrimination law and to remove the inconsistencies between the pre-existing race, sex and disability statutes. Without a margin of appreciation, such developments may be easier. At the very least, the state will be forced to justify existing legally-sanctioned discrimination.

Brief Outline and Germane Cases

Chapter Nine: Discrimination

1. Racial discrimination 9–069

*Race Relations Act 1976 s.1:

s.1(1)(a) direct discrimination on racial grounds-treating a person less favourably on racial grounds. *Owen & Briggs v. James* [1982]; *Alexander v. Home Office* [1988]; s.1(2); *Zarcynska v. Levy* [1978]. racial grounds includes national origins and ethnic origins: *Mandla v. Dowell Lee* [1983]; *CRE v. Dutton* [1989].

s.1(1)(b) indirect discrimination on racial grounds-detrimentally applying a requirement or condition, which is such that the proportion of a racial group who can comply with it is smaller, and which is not justified.
Perera v. Civil Service Commission (No. 2) [1983]; *Orphanos v. QMC* [1985], *Hampson v. Department of Education* [1990]; *Webb v. EMO Cargo* [1993], s.28.

s.2 victimisation.
Aziz v. Trinity Street Taxis [1988]

*RRA 1976 Parts II–IV: the law provides a remedy against discrimination only in the following fields:

- — education (ss.17–19); *R. v. Bradford Metropolitan Council ex p. Sikander Ali* [1993].
- — employment and recruitment (s.4); *Owen and Briggs v. James* [1982]; *D'Silva v. Hambleton and Nurdin & Peacock plc* [1997]; but "genuine occupational qualifications", s.5.
- — goods, facilities, services (s.20).

— housing (s.21).

— clubs (s.25, 26).

— charities (s.34).

Role and powers of Commission for Racial Equality; *London Borough of Hillingdon v. CRE* [1982].

2. Sexual Discrimination

Similar framework to racial discrimination legislation.

*Equal Pay Act 1970 s.1(2): equal pay for work of equal value.

*Sex Discrimination Act 1975 s.1:

5.1(1)(a) direct discrimination on grounds of sex.
James v. Eastleigh Borough Council [1990], s.3.

s.1(1)(b) indirect discrimination on grounds of sex.
s.3, *R. v. Shaffter* [1987], s.7.

Role and powers of EOC.

3. Impact of E.C. law.

— *Defrenne v. Sabena* [1979]
— Article 119 of EC Treaty
— Equal Pay Directive

4. Positive discrimination on grounds of race or sex.

5. Disability Discrimination.

Disability Discrimination Act 1995.

Endnotes

[1] See Street, Howe and Bindman, Report on Anti-Discrimination Legislation (1967).
[2] Para. 4.
[3] Paras 31, 33, Cmnd. 6234.
[4] [1985] I.C.R. 827.
[5] [1990] 2 A.C. 751.
[6] The test applies equally well to racial discrimination.
[7] [1982] I.R.L.R. 502.
[8] *per* Browne-Wilkinson J. in *Showboat Entertainment Centre v. Owens* [1984] I.R.L.R. 7.
[9] [1988] I.R.L.R. 190.
[10] [1980] I.R.L.R. 142.
[11] Whereas for sex discrimination the less favourable treatment must be shown to have been given to the victim "on the ground of her sex" (see discussion below).
[12] [1978] I.R.L.R. 532.
[13] See also *Showboat Entertainment Centre v. Owens* [1984] 1 W.L.R. 384.
[14] [1972] A.C. 342.
[15] [1983] 2 A.C. 548.
[16] [1980] I.R.L.R. 427.
[17] [1989] 1 All E.R. 306, Court of Appeal.
[18] [1991] I.R.L.R. 327.
[19] [1993] I.C.R. 517.
[20] [1986] I.C.R. 833.
[21] Perhaps because no compensation is payable in industrial tribunals for indirect discrimination unless it can be shown that the condition was applied with the intention of treating the victim less favourably.
[22] Cmnd. 6234, p. 8.
[23] [1983] I.C.R. 428.
[24] [1988] I.R.L.R. 399.
[25] [1994] I.R.L.R. 204.
[26] [1984] A.C. 761.
[27] [1985] I.C.R. 685.
[28] See *Wong v. GLC* (1980) EAT 524/79.
[29] See *Greencroft Social Club v. Mullen* [1985] I.C.R. 796.
[30] [1978] I.C.R. 181.
[31] [1982] I.C.R. 661.
[32] *ibid.* at 667.
[33] See Browne-Wilkinson J. in *Clarke v. Eley (IMI) Kynoch Ltd* [1983] I.C.R. 165.
[34] [1990] 2 All E.R. 25.
[35] See discussion later in this chapter.
[36] [1987] I.C.R. 110 (see below).
[37] [1993] I.R.L.R. 27.
[38] See *BL Cars Ltd v. Brown* [1983] I.C.R. 143.
[39] F. Invest. Rep. 1983.
[40] [1988] I.R.L.R. 204.
[41] Which is that from s.6 of the Human Rights Act 1998.
[42] *The Times*, October 21, 1993.
[43] See *Race Relations Board v. London Borough Council of Ealing (No. 2)* [1978] 1 W.L.R. 112.
[44] [1986] I.R.L.R. 103.
[45] [1987] I.R.L.R. 289.
[46] [1987] I.R.L.R. 401.
[47] There is some overlap here with the category of "advertisements", which will be discussed below.
[48] [1982] I.R.L.R. 502.
[49] [1983] I.R.L.R. 357.
[50] (1980) COIT 987/12.
[51] [1988] I.R.L.R. 186.
[52] [1997] 1 CL 254.
[53] [1989] I.R.L.R. 387.
[54] [1996] I.R.L.R. 996.

[55] *London Borough of Lambeth v. CRE* [1989] I.R.L.R. 379.
[56] *London Borough of Lambeth v. CRE* [1990] I.R.L.R. 230.
[57] See *Tottenham Green Under Fives Centre v. Marshall* [1989] I.R.L.R. 126.
[58] [1983] 2 A.C. 818.
[59] [1981] Q.B. 458.
[60] See the sex discrimination case of *R. v. Immigration Appeal Tribunal, ex p. Kassam* [1980] 2 All E.R. 330.
[61] Review of the Race Relations Act 1976, (1992).
[62] [1997] 1 All E.R. 289.
[63] HL, March 22, 2001.
[64] [1973] A.C. 868.
[65] Cmnd. 6234.
[66] Using the definition of "public authority" in s.6 of the Human Right Act 1998.
[67] Since some discrimination is required between different nationalities, for example, when determining whether an applicant is entitled to enter or remain in the U.K., or qualifies as a refugee under the UN Convention: see Chap. 11 for full discussion of how the 2000 Act reforms immigration policy and rules.
[68] [1999] 27 E.H.R.R. 249.
[66] Using the definition of "public authority" in s.6 of the Human Right Act 1998.
[69] [1982] 3 W.L.R. 159.
[70] *ibid.* at 791.
[71] [1984] 1 W.L.R. 335.
[72] *ibid.* at 481.
[73] *Report of the War Cabinet Committee on the Employment of Women in Industry*, (1916) Cmnd. 135.
[74] *Royal Commission on Equal Pay*, (1946) Cmnd. 6937.
[75] *R. v. CA.C. ex p. Hymac* [1979] I.R.L.R. 481.
[76] *EEC Commission v. United Kingdom* [1982] I.C.R. 578.
[77] The departing Conservative Government had taken steps towards legislation on the subject, including the publication of a consultation document, and draft legislation was being prepared.
[78] [1990] I.R.L.R. 288.
[79] *Hurley v. Mustoe* [1981] I.C.R. 490.
[80] *Cockroft v. Restus Ltd* Industrial Tribunal 12420/89.
[81] See *Zarcynska v. Levy* [1979] 1 All E.R. 814; waitress sacked for insisting on serving black customers when employer had banned this, was the victim of direct discrimination.
[82] *e.g. P v. S and Cornwall CC* [1996] I.R.L.R. 347.
[83] See *R. v. C* [1997] EAT June 27.
[84] [1987] I.R.L.R. 53.
[85] Lone parents who had never married did not receive a hardship grant, whereas those who had been married were eligible.
[86] *Defrenne v. SABENA (No. 3)* (Case 149/77) [1979] E.C.R. 1365.
[87] [1986] I.R.L.R. 317.
[88] Case 152/84 [1986] I.R.L.R. 140.
[89] [1993] I.R.L.R. 27.
[90] Unreported, COIT February 6, 1986.
[91] *A Consultation on Government Measures to Tackle Discrimination against Disabled People*, (Department of Social Security, 1994).
[92] *Hensard*, May 22, 1995.
[93] Para. 1(1).
[94] Para. 2(1).
[95] Para. 4(1).
[96] Para. 7.
[97] *The Times*, May 11, 1998.
[98] As stated above, the 1995 Act allows a defence of justification even where the alleged discrimination is direct: s. 5(1).
[99] CA, March 14, 2001.
[1] [1985] 7 E.H.R.R. 471.
[2] 20 E.H.R.R. 205.
[3] 16 E.H.R.R. 405.
[4] 24 E.H.R.R. 503.

[5] E.C.H.R. February 28, 1998: App. No. 20458/92.
[6] 3 E.H.R.R. 76: Judgement of December 14, 1973.
[7] 22 E.H.R.R. 283: App No 16839/90, April 26, 1996.
[8] E.C.H.R. October 21, 1996.
[9] (1996) 24 E.H.R.R. 294.
[10] 1 E.H.R.R. 241.
[11] 1 E.H.R.R. 252.
[12] (1993) 17 E.H.R.R. 397: Series A No. 260-A.
[13] 18 E.H.R.R.C.D. 85.
[14] *ibid.*
[15] 22 E.H.R.R. 29.
[16] 18 E.H.R.R.C.D. 172.
[17] 4 E.H.R.R. 252.
[18] 24 E.H.R.R. 195.
[19] (1976) 1 E.H.R.R. 711.
[20] Series A No 91 E.C.H.R., February 27, 1985.
[21] [1978] 3 E.II.R.R. 218.
[22] 13 E.H.R.R. 774 Series A No. 187.
[23] E.C.H.R. February 24, 1998.

CHAPTER 10

EMERGENCY POWERS: THE PREVENTION OF TERRORISM

"We have been set the difficult task of maintaining a double perspective; for, while there are policies which contribute to the maintenance of order at the expense of individual freedom, the maintenance without restriction of that freedom may involve a heavy toll in death and destruction. Some of those who have given evidence to us have argued that such features of the present emergency provisions as the use of the Army in aid of civil power, detention without trial, arrest on suspicion and trial without jury are so inherently objectionable that they must be abolished on the grounds that they constitute a basic violation of human rights. We are unable to accept this argument. While the liberty of the subject is a human right to be preserved under all possible conditions, it is not, and cannot be, an absolute right, because one man may use his liberty to take away the liberty of another, and must be restricted from doing so . . . The suspension of normal legal safeguards for the liberty of the subject may sometimes be essential, in a society faced by terrorism, to counter greater evils. But if continued for any period of time it exacts a social cost from the community; and the price may have to be paid over several generations".[1] **10–001**

The State reserves for itself in narrowly-defined situations of emergency, the power to use greater force than is its usual approach. When there is perceived to be an immediate threat to the nation's safety, sanctity or continued well-being from any of a variety of sources, then the State may use its reserved emergency powers in order to alleviate the situation and deal effectively with the danger. But it must be recognised that the use of emergency powers of any kind may cause hardship to individuals whose usual rights are suspended. Emergency powers exist in Britain in both general and specific form. General emergency powers may be defined as those which allow the State to deal with any emergency which may arise, be it a strike, war, a nuclear energy leak or a serious flood. Specific emergency powers may be defined as those which allow the State to use greater force than is generally available to it, and to suspend the rights of certain individuals, but only in relation to a particular threat, such as the continuing situation concerning the status of Northern Ireland and the violence which has resulted. This chapter will focus upon the specific powers which have their source in anti-terrorism legislation and apply only where a person is suspected of involvement in terrorist activities; but there are also a range of situations of public emergency in which the state has additional general powers to act outside its normal framework of capabilities. The most obvious example is where there is a war or the threat of war, but emergencies may also occur in peacetime. The Emergency Powers Act 1920 (amended in 1964) allows the Government to make a proclamation of a state of emergency in peacetime where it appears that there is likely to be an emergency which threatens:

> ". . . by interfering with the supply and distribution of food, water, fuel or light, or with the means of locomotion, to deprive the community, or any substantial portion of the community, of the essentials of life". (Section 1(1))

A proclamation of a state of emergency may last for up to a month, which is renewable, and allows regulations to be made by the Government in order to deal with the threatening situation. Proclamations have been made to deal with major strikes, most notably in the 1970s, but there have also been some situations where the Government could have used the Act but chose not to do so, for example the Miners' Strike of 1984–5. Reasons for this may be due to political pressure or public disapproval, but it may simply be that the Government has not needed to use these powers since it has at its disposal a range of other powers under legislation concerning essential services and utilities.[2] The remainder of this chapter will discuss the specific emergency legislation which targets terrorism. Since 1974, there has been a dual system in operation in Britain in relation to many of the rights of suspects which have been examined in previous chapters: the PACE rules, the normal immigration rules and the normal relevant common law rules apply to any ordinary individual who may be suspected of involvement in a crime, and he is therefore entitled to those safeguards; but where a person is suspected of terrorism, then a separate set of rules and procedures operates, with a resulting lower standard of safeguards for the suspect's rights. This chapter will look at the history of the emergency powers legislation and highlight the differences between that legislation and the treatment of an "ordinary" suspect. Recent developments in this field have expanded the definition of terrorism and the scope of the special provisions which relate to terrorist suspects; these, and the uncertain future of Northern Ireland, will also be examined.

History

10–002 The legislation concerning the situation in Northern Ireland is merely a symptom of a long-standing territorial dispute. Since 1800 there have in fact been a long list of Acts which created special powers in relation to the control of life in Ireland. Such legislation allowed a diverse range of action, including the creation of a specialist anti-terrorist unit, the suspension of habeas corpus, special arrest, search and detention powers and the limitation of the right to silence in relation to terrorism. There were several Acts in the twentieth century governing police powers in Northern Ireland, but it was the Prevention of Terrorism Act 1974 which consolidated and concentrated special police powers in relation to terrorist suspects. The Act was passed in the immediate context of the Birmingham pub bombings of November 1974, when 21 people were killed and over 180 injured, which created a widespread anti-Irish feeling and public and media demands for greater action to be taken against the IRA in particular, and other paramilitary organisations in general. There were even attacks on random Irish people in the street. Six suspects, who became known as the Birmingham Six, were quickly arrested and convicted (and their convictions quashed sixteen years later). The Prevention of Terrorism (Temporary Provisions) Bill was already partly drafted, and the Government introduced it to Parliament within days of the bombings. But its major provisions were not new, and it drew upon the Northern Ireland (Emergency Provisions) Act 1973 and the Prevention of Violence (Temporary Provisions) Act 1939. The Bill was passed within a day and without opposition. It received Royal Assent after 48 hours. Its major provisions will be examined below, but in general the 1974 Act gave the police extended arrest, search and detention powers and created the ability to control movement of persons between Britain and Northern Ireland. The Secretary of State was granted a power to issue exclusion orders which ban a person from residence in the United Kingdom. The IRA and other paramilitary organisations were made illegal and it became an offence to support them.

Although intended to be a temporary measure, most of the 1974 Act and the Prevention of Terrorism (Temporary Provisions) Act 1989 are still law, and now enshrined in permanent form in the Terrorism Act 2000. The 1974 Act was aimed only at fighting political violence connected to Northern Ireland, but it was extended in 1984 to encompass "international terrorism", though over 96 per cent of cases under the 1989 Act related to Northern Ireland.[3] Further, almost all PTA detainees were eventually released without charge, and so doubt can be raised whether the volume of arrests and detentions under the Acts is justifiable. The Northern Ireland terrorism legislation has been reviewed several times, and was renewed annually. It was amended in 1976. The Shackleton,[4] Jellicoe[5] and Colville Reports[6] each started from the premise that emergency powers continued to be necessary in relation to Northern Ireland and so, although each recommended specific reforms and questioned the extent of existing powers, none of these Commissions challenged the continued existence of the "temporary" provisions. The Jellicoe Report resulted in the 1976 version of the Act being replaced by the Prevention of Terrorism Act 1984, which was again replaced by the Prevention of Terrorism Act 1989 after the Colville Report. The 1989 Act was re-enacted and amended by the Prevention of Terrorism (Additional Powers) Act 1996. The 1989 Act will be discussed below. However, as will be seen, recent developments in relation to the Government and policing of Northern Ireland have brought the anti-terrorism legislation under scrutiny, and it seemed for a time that it would be repealed without replacement, but in fact it has been replaced by a new, broader and permanent Terrorism Act 2000, which will be explained and discussed in detail below.

Until recently there was also further emergency powers legislation in force for Northern Ireland. The Northern Ireland (Emergency Provisions) Act 1996 re-enacted and amended the Northern Ireland (Emergency Provisions) Act 1991; a new statute was again passed in 1998 and was the last in a continual line of statutes which have granted special powers for dealing with serious offences. There was a great deal of overlap between the powers given to police under this statute and the Prevention of Terrorism Act. The present Government committed itself in the British-Irish Agreement reached on Good Friday 1998 to repeal the Northern Ireland (Emergency Provisions) legislation, and began to move towards this almost immediately by passing the 1998 version of the Act, which partially repealed its predecessor. The NIA applied only in Northern Ireland, but most of its provisions have been adopted in the Terrorism Act 2000 and their application extended to cover not only Irish terrorism but also domestic and international terrorism. Whilst this could be seen as a positive step towards a cohesive anti-terrorist strategy, this situation fits uneasily against the Government's Good Friday commitment to "repeal" those very provisions which still exist in a remarkably similar form.

The Peace Process

10–003 Although detailed discussion of the legal, political and constitutional implications of the British-Irish Agreement (assuming an endorsement by referendum) is beyond the scope of this book, it should be noted that the focus of anti-terrorism legislation is shifting. The Northern Ireland peace process has resulted in a new role for anti-terrorism law in the field of the prevention and investigation of terrorism generally and internationally, rather than being limited almost entirely in its use to the investigation of cases relating to Northern Ireland. The Government, having conducted a review of anti-terrorism legislation worldwide repealed the PTA in 2000 (see below), thus ending the rightly-criticised process of continual renewal of the "temporary" legislation year after year, decade after decade. It was hoped that many of the criticisms of the PTA from a civil liberties and human rights perspective would vanish when the new Act is introduced, and that the removal of the power to make exclusion orders in 1998 was a stage towards that end. The extent to which previous optimism on this front was deserved will be examined in this chapter, but it may be noted at this stage that many of the criticisms of the previous temporary legislation may still be made of its permanent replacement which, further, has its own human rights flaws. Until the Terrorism Act 2000 has been in force for a sufficient amount of time to generate its own body of case law, it cannot be fully evaluated, but some key issues will be highlighted below. It may be that some sections of the new Act are incompatible under the Human Rights Act 1998.

The Prevention of Terrorism Acts—the historical background to the Terrorism Act 2000

Until 2000 the main statute in relation to the prevention of terrorism remained the Prevention of Terrorism (Temporary Provisions) Act 1989, but was amended many times in recent years. The discussion of the statutes will, for ease of study, follow the same headings as those used previously in the chapter on PACE. Thus stop and search, entry search and seizure, arrest, detention, questioning and so on will be examined separately. **10–004**

1. Stop and Search

The Prevention of Terrorism Acts contained several powers for police to stop and search persons or vehicles, and these powers operated differently from those available under PACE. The Prevention of Terrorism (Temporary Provisions) Act 1989, as amended by section 81 of the Criminal Justice and Public Order Act 1994 and by the Prevention of Terrorism (Additional Powers) Act 1996, contained the following stop and search powers. **10–005**

Section 13A: stop and search of vehicles and passengers. Under section 13A, a police officer of the rank of Commander or Assistant Chief Constable could authorise stop and search powers to operate in a specified geographical area for a period of up to 28 days "if expedient to do so in order to prevent acts of terrorism". The authorisation could be extended for further periods of 28 days. Section 13A(3) gave a constable in uniform the power: **10–006**

> "(a) to stop any vehicle;
> (b) to search any vehicle, its driver or any passenger, for articles of a kind which could be used for a purpose connected with the commission, preparation or instigation of acts of terrorism . . ."

(Section 13(3)(c) was repealed by the 1996 Act, below).

It should be noted that, once authorisation was in place, the section 13A powers were much wider than the corresponding powers available under PACE section 1 or section 4. Section 13A was one of very few stop and search powers which did not require the constable exercising the power to have reasonable grounds for suspicion that articles of the prohibited type were being carried. Indeed, no grounds whatsoever were necessary, since section 13A(4) stated that a constable exercising section 13A powers could stop and search any vehicle or person "and make any search he thinks fit whether or not he has any grounds for suspecting that the vehicle or person is carrying articles" which could be used for purposes related to terrorism.

Section 13B: search of pedestrians. Section 1 of the Prevention of Terrorism (Additional Powers) Act 1996 repealed section 13A(3)(c) of the 1989 Act, which had previously allowed an authorised constable to stop a **10–007** pedestrian and search "any thing carried by him for articles which could be used for a purpose connected with the commission, preparation or instigation of acts of terrorism", and inserted a new section 13B. In contrast to section 13A(3)(c), section 13B allowed the pedestrian himself to be searched, rather than being limited to a power to search packages and parcels.

Section 13B allowed the search of a person, and of anything which he may be carrying. Authorisation was required from a Commander or Assistant Chief Constable, but could be given orally initially and then confirmed in writing as soon as was reasonably practicable. Authorisation again lasted for up to 28 days and was renewable. There were two safeguards which applied to section 13B searches of pedestrians: first, the Secretary of State had to be informed as soon as was reasonably practicable that such searches had been authorised in the area concerned, and could cancel or limit authorisations; and secondly, searches by constables which were carried out in public could only require a person to remove his "headgear, footwear, outer coat, jacket or gloves". The same limitations were also inserted into section 13A, making the safeguards for section 13 more comparable to those for PACE searches. Again, there was no requirement for reasonable grounds for suspicion that the person to be searched had on his person any article concerned with terrorism.[7]

All powers of stop and search under the Prevention of Terrorism Acts had to be exercised in compliance with PACE Code of Practice A, discussed in Chapter 3. A pedestrian who was stopped and/or searched had an additional right to receive a written statement of this, on application within 12 months (section 13B(10)).

Criminal Justice and Public Order Act 1994, s. 60.

10–008 A more limited power of stop and search was created by section 60 of the 1994 Act, under which a Superintendent could give written authorisation for stop and search powers in a particular locality to exist for up to 24 hours, if he reasonably believed that incidents involving serious violence might occur in that locality. Once authorisation had been given, it could be extended for another six hours if the authorising officer believed that this would be expedient because of offences which had occurred or were reasonably suspected to have occurred within the scope of the authorisation (section 60(3)). The section 60(4) power allowed a uniformed constable to stop and search any pedestrian for offensive weapons or dangerous instruments. Section 60 also allowed a constable to stop a vehicle and search both the vehicle and its passengers for such items. No reasonable suspicion requirement was attached to section 60; thus, in common with section 13A and B of the 1989 Act (above) searches could be speculative, random, or part of a systematic programme of searching all persons in a particular location. There was a power to seize any item which the constable reasonably suspected to be an offensive weapon, or which was a dangerous instrument, found during a search (section 60(6)). Section 2 of

PACE and Code A did apply, and so there were safeguards for the manner of the search, and for the suspect's right to be given information before he was searched.

2. Entry, Search and Seizure

Even though PACE powers of entry and search without warrant, which have been discussed above are generally sufficient to enable their use in terrorism investigations, there were additional powers under the temporary anti-terrorism legislation. **10–009**

a) Emergency searches without warrant. Schedule 7 of the 1989 Prevention of Terrorism (Temporary Provisions) Act, as amended by section 2 of the 1996 Act. Schedule 7, paragraph 7(1) gave power to an officer of at least the rank of Superintendent to authorise in writing a search of premises if he had reasonable grounds for belief that "the case is one of great emergency and that in the interests of the state immediate action is necessary". The State's interests were not defined. **10–010**

b) Search warrants and production orders. Schedule 7, paragraph 2 of the 1989 Act also allowed a search warrant to be granted in relation to terrorism offences. However, it should be noted that the grounds for obtaining a search warrant under paragraph 2 contrasted markedly against those under PACE; the police did not need to be satisfied that the suspect has committed any particular offence, and so might merely have suspicion that he is involved in terrorism in some imprecise manner. The police could apply to a justice of the peace for a warrant to search premises, and the justice must then be satisfied of the existence of the following criteria: **10–011**

(i) that an investigation was underway which concerns terrorism;

(ii) that there were reasonable grounds for belief that on the premises in question there would be found to be material which was likely to be of substantial value to the investigation;

(iii) that gaining entry to the premises by obtaining the consent of the occupier was impracticable;

(iv) that immediate entry was necessary.

Generally, the material must not be excluded, special procedure or legally privileged material, but a production order for excluded or special procedure material could be granted by a circuit judge in exceptional circumstances. In *R. v. Crown Court, ex p. Salinger*,[8] a series of guidelines were stated for the obtaining of such search warrants from the crown court:

(1) A supporting written statement of evidence should be submitted with the application, in which the nature of the information on

which it is based should generally be explained, although "very secret" sources and information need not be stated.

(2) The officer making the application may be required to give evidence to the court in person.

(3) Before he could grant the production order, a judge had to be satisfied that the following criteria exist: an investigation related to terrorism was in progress; there were reasonable grounds for belief that the material in question would be of substantial value to the investigation; and that there was a "public interest" reason for the order to be issued.

(4) The person against whom such an order was to be enforced was entitled to be given as much information about the circumstances and reasons for the order as could be given without raising a danger of compromising security.

(5) In other respects, the procedure was very similar to that under PACE; for example, if an order is not complied with, then a search warrant could be issued (PTA 1989, para. 5).

In relation to production orders, there was a further exception to the right to silence where terrorism investigations were concerned. Once material had been obtained via a production order or search warrant, it was open to a circuit judge to order a person concerned with that material to explain its significance, save where he was protected by legal professional privilege. But any such explanation could not be used against that person in criminal proceedings unless he had given evidence which conflicted with his explanation or was being prosecuted for making a false statement (paragraph 6(4) of Schedule 7)).

In *DPP v. Channel Four Television*,[9] it was held that a defendant who refuses to produce material for which an order has been issued will be in contempt of court. There is no defence of protection of confidential sources. In this case it was argued that production of the material might risk the lives of sources close to terrorist organisations, but the court rejected this as a ground for withholding the information.

Section 2 of the 1996 Act amended Schedule 7 of the 1989 Act by inserting paragraph 2A, which allowed an application by the police to a justice of the peace for the grant of a warrant to search either particular non-residential premises or a list of such premises. Thus, if the premises to be searched were not a person's home, it was much easier for the police to obtain a warrant to gain entry. The new paragraph 2A of Schedule 7 of the 1989 Act was comparable to the power under section 8 of PACE, except that section 8 requires, *inter alia*, reasonable grounds for suspicion that a serious arrestable offence has been committed. An officer of the rank of Superintendent or above could apply to a justice of the peace for a warrant under paragraph 2A and, if it was granted, it had to be carried out within

24 hours of its issue. But if there was a "great emergency", which was again left undefined, then the Superintendent himself could authorise a search of non-residential premises and even journalistic material, excluded material and special procedure material could be searched for and seized.[10]

c) Cordons and parking prohibitions and restrictions. Section 5 of the 1996 Act inserted sections 16C and D into the 1989 Act. Under section 16C, the police had a power to impose a police *cordon*, whereas section 16D allowed the police to impose *parking restrictions and prohibitions*. These powers were passed in reaction to the City of London bombing campaign. **10–012**

Cordons should be authorised by a Superintendent but if it was an urgent situation, then authorisation could be given by an officer of lower rank. An oral authorisation was possible, but had to be confirmed in writing as soon as was reasonably practicable. If a constable gave authorisation, this had to be confirmed or cancelled by a Superintendent (Schedule 6A). A police cordon could be imposed if it was "expedient to do so in connection with an investigation into the commission, preparation or instigation of an act of terrorism" (*e.g.* searching for explosives or evidence). Cordons could exist for up to 14 days, and Schedule 6A also allowed the police to carry out related functions, including moving or removing any vehicle, and ordering individuals to leave or move vehicles. Schedule 6A, paragraph 7 of the PTA gave a power of search where a cordon had been authorised and set up. This power required written authority from at least a Superintendent who had reasonable grounds for belief that there was material on the premises which would be of substantial value to the investigation, and which was not excluded material, special procedure material or subject to legal privilege. Once authorised, a constable could enter and search the specified premises within the cordon and could seize any such items found.

Parking prohibitions or restrictions could only be authorised in order to prevent acts of terrorism; thus the police might prevent parking in front of Government buildings if it was feared that they could be a target for car bombs. Authorisation had to come from a Commander of the Metropolitan Police or an Assistant Chief Constable elsewhere. There was an offence under section 16D(7) of breaching a parking prohibition or restriction.

d) Powers to search goods. Section 3 of the 1996 Act amended Schedule 5 of the 1989 Act by inserting section 4A. The new section provided a power to search goods and baggage, even if it was unaccompanied; **10–013**

> Schedule 5, section 4A(1), "For the purpose of determining whether they are or have been involved in the commission, preparation or instigation of acts of terrorism . . . an examining officer may search any goods which have arrived in or are about to leave Great Britain or Northern Ireland."

Anything found in such a search could be detained for examination for up to seven days (section 4A(6)). If the searcher believed that something found might be needed as evidence in criminal proceedings, then he "may detain it until he is satisfied that it will not be so needed." (section 4A(7)). The new power was thus very wide. Items found during such a search might be detained even if they were totally unconnected with terrorism, for example drugs.

3. Arrest

10–014 The Prevention of Terrorism legislation itself created many arrestable offences and so the PACE provisions for arrest were often used, but there was an additional arrest power provided by section 14 of the Prevention of Terrorism Act 1989.

> Section 14 "(1) Subject to subsection (2) below, a constable may arrest without warrant a person whom he has reasonable grounds for suspecting to be
>
> (a) a person guilty of an offence under section 2, 8, 9, 10, or 11 . . .;
> (b) a person who is or has been concerned in the commission, preparation or instigation of acts of terrorism to which this section applies; or
> (c) a person subject to an exclusion order.
> (2) The acts of terrorism to which this section applies are—"
> (a) acts of terrorism connected with the affairs of Northern Ireland; and
> (b) acts of terrorism of any other description except acts connected solely with the affairs of the United Kingdom, or any part of the United Kingdom other than Northern Ireland."

It was necessary to draw a distinction between 14(1)(a) and 14(1)(b). Section 14(1)(a) merely made certain of the specific PTA offences arrestable; the only practical difference here from arrest under section 24 of PACE was in relation to the maximum length of detention after arrest, which will be explained later in this chapter. But section 14(1)(b) created a far wider arrest power: although the constable had to have reasonable grounds for his suspicion, he need only have had a suspicion that the arrestee was related to acts of terrorism in one of the stated manners, and so his suspicion need not have been that any particular offence had been committed. This meant that a suspect could be, and generally was, arrested under section 14(1)(b) for the purpose of questioning him and furthering a general investigation, rather than in order to charge him with any offence. As will be stated below, a suspect may still be detained without charge for up to seven days on the basis of a reasonable suspicion that he is, for example, in contact with a terrorist organisation. His detention may be used as a means of extracting information about terrorism rather than in order to collect evidence on which to charge him with an offence; over 90 per cent of PTA arrestees were released without charge, and there is no reason to believe that matters will be any different under the Terrorism Act 2000.

What is terrorism? Many of the PTA provisions, and indeed several other statutes, involved this term. The main definition was given in section 20 of the 1989 Act as the "use of violence for political ends", which included "the use of violence for the purpose of putting the public, or any section of the public in fear". This definition was arguably wider than is necessary and included behaviour which most people would not regard as terrorist. If students demonstrating against the introduction of tuition fees get into a scuffle with police or security guards, are their actions terrorist? It is not argued here that they would be subject to arrest and detention on that basis, but the definition of terrorism could have been refined. As will be seen below, the definition of terrorism under the 2000 Act is even broader and potentially encompasses religious organisations and animal rights activists, amongst others.

The test under section 14 was considered in the case of *O'Hara v. Chief Constable of the Royal Ulster Constabulary*,[11] where the House of Lords held that the test had two stages: first, the arresting officer must have formed in his own mind a suspicion that the arrestee was concerned in acts of terrorism in one of the manners stated in section 124; and secondly, that a reasonable man would have reached the same conclusion on the evidence available. Since the arresting officer had attended a briefing at which information had been given to him and upon which he had acted, in circumstances where a reasonable man would also have formed the same suspicion concerning the arrestee, the arrest was lawful.

Additional powers related to arrest. On or after a terrorist suspect's arrest, **10–015** the PTA provided a number of related powers which could be used in order to gather evidence. A search warrant could be granted for the purpose of finding and arresting a suspect; a suspect could be stopped and searched in circumstances where there were section 14 grounds for his arrest; and, after arrest, the arrestee could be searched for evidence. Under section 15 of the 1989 Act;

> "(1) If a justice of the peace is satisfied that there are reasonable grounds for suspecting that a person whom a constable believes to be liable to arrest under section 14(1)(b) . . . is to be found on any premises he may grant a search warrant authorising any constable to enter those premises for the purpose of searching for and arresting that person . . .
> (3) In any circumstances in which a constable had power under section 14 to arrest a person, he might also, for the purpose of ascertaining whether he had in his possession any document or other article which could constitute evidence that he was a person liable to arrest, stop that person and search him.
> (4) Where a constable had arrested a person under that section (section 14) for any reason other than the commission of a criminal offence, he, or any other constable, could search him for the purpose of ascertaining whether he had in his possession any document or other article which could constitute evidence that he was a person liable to arrest."

Sections 15(10)–(14) applied the PACE safeguards and provisions re taking of fingerprints and the obtaining of intimate and non-intimate samples. Thus a person arrested on suspicion of involvement in terrorism might be subjected to broadly the same procedures and with similar safeguards to a person arrested under PACE.

4. Detention

10–016 It has been seen elsewhere in this book that the United Kingdom has been held to be in breach of its ECHR obligations in relation to the detention of terrorist suspects under the PTA. It is principally the extended length of detention without charge possible under the PTA which caused civil liberties concerns. A terrorist suspect could, and still may, be detained for a total of up to seven days without charge and without the benefit of the normal PACE detention reviews and procedures. Further, the authorisation of extensions of detention beyond the initial 48-hour period did not come under the scrutiny of the courts, unlike the corresponding PACE provisions.

10–017 *Initial detention after arrest.* The grounds for authorisation of detention after a section 14 arrest were to be found in Schedule 3, paragraph 3(3)(a): a reviewing officer had to be satisfied that further detention without charge was necessary for the purpose of preserving or obtaining evidence which: related to an offence under section 2, 8, 9, 10 or 11 of the Act; or which showed that the detainee had been concerned in the commission, preparation or instigation of acts of terrorism. Paragraph 3(3)(b) also required that the reviewing officer must be satisfied that the investigation was being carried out diligently and expeditiously. After each review, he must record its outcome (paragraph 8); and before he made any further review decision, he must give the detainee, and any legal representative he may have, a chance to speak (paragraph 6). So, for the first 48 hours after arrest, a person arrested under the PTA 1989 was to be treated in a very similar way to a person arrested under PACE. It was only after the initial 48 hours' detention that large differences emerged, since at that point the Home Secretary had a power to authorise detention for up to an extra five days without any apparent requirement of grounds and with no necessary review of detention during that time.

10–018 *Extended detention.* Section 14(4) of the 1989 Act provided: "Subject to subsection (5) below, a person arrested under this section shall not be detained . . . for more than forty-eight hours after his arrest."

But section 14(5) stated that:

> "The Secretary of State may, in any particular case, extend the period of forty-eight hours . . . by a period or periods specified by him, but any such further period or periods shall not exceed five days in all and if an application for such an extension is made the person detained shall as soon as is practicable be given written notice of that fact and of the time when that application was made."

10–019 Rights to have someone informed of detention and to receive legal advice Where a person was detained under the anti-terrorism provisions of the PTA 1989, his PACE rights to have someone informed that he is being held in custody and to have access to legal advice were subject to two extra powers of delay, in addition to those already existing under PACE. The detainee's access to either right could have been delayed if the officer concerned had reasonable grounds for belief that the prompt exercise of the right would have either of the following consequences, (section 56(11) and section 58(13)):

> "(a) lead to interference with the gathering of information about the commission, preparation or instigation of acts of terrorism; or
> (b) by alerting any person, make it more difficult
> (I) to prevent any act of terrorism; or
> (II) to secure the apprehension, prosecution or conviction of any person in connection with the commission, preparation or instigation of an act of terrorism."

Any delay in access to either right had to be authorised by at least a superintendent, and could not extend beyond 48 hours (section 56(11)(b) and section 58(13)(a)).

There was no right to receive private access to a solicitor. Section 58(14) provided that an independent uniformed Inspector could attend during a detainee's legal access if this is authorised by a Commander or Assistant Chief Constable. The authorising officer had to have reasonable grounds for belief that, unless supervision occurred, either (a) or (b) above would take place. It is however arguably preferable that a detainee should be granted this supervised access to legal advice rather than being denied it altogether via a "delay" of access which lasts for the entire period of his detention.

Access to a solicitor was also not available as of right when a terrorist suspect was being interviewed. In *R. v. Chief Constable of the Royal Ulster Constabulary ex p. Begley*,[12] the House of Lords held that, whilst there is an established common law and statutory right for a suspect to consult a solicitor outside the interview room, there is no recognised right to have a solicitor present in the interview itself when being questioned under the terrorism provisions; its omission from the relevant legislation was seen as a manifestation of the deliberate will of Parliament and so the House of Lords considered itself unable to create any such right. However, successive legislative changes ensured that a terrorist suspect did have some further safeguards during interview. He became entitled to silent video recording and to audio tape recording of the interview.[13]

The temporary legislation came in for its share of criticism over the **10–020**
years, even though very strong public interest reasons were argued in its favour. But even in the cases where courts were most critical of the legal provisions and their enforcement, there was always a tension between the very real need to combat terrorism and the human rigths of terrorist suspects. Compare the following two quotes from the House of Lords in *ex parte Kebilene*[14]:

> "On its face section 16A of the Act of 1989 enables a person to be found guilty of a very serious offence merely on reasonable grounds of suspicion. It

> may be highly inconvenient that this should not be permissible, an inconvenience brought out by the list of broadly comparable provisions to be given by my noble and learned friend Lord Hope of Craighead, but at best it is doubtful whether Article 6(2) [of the ECHR] can be watered down to an extent that would leave section 16A unscathed" (*per* Lord Cooke).

and

> "Then there is the nature of the threat which terrorism poses to a free and democratic society. It seeks to achieve its ends by violence and intimidation. It is often indiscriminate in its effects, and sophisticated methods are used to avoid detection both before and after the event. Society has a strong interest in preventing acts of terrorism before they are perpetrated—to spare the lives of innocent people and to avoid the massive damage and dislocation to ordinary life which may follow from explosions which destroy or damage property. Section 16A is designed to achieve that end" (*per* Lord Hope).

THE TERRORISM ACT 2000: OLD LAW IN NEW BOTTLES?

BACKGROUND

10–021 After Lord Lloyd of Berwick's Inquiry into legislation against terrorism was published in December 1996, an official response was needed . . .

In December 1998 the government published a consultation document, *Legislation against terrorism*.[15]

OVERVIEW

10–022 The Terrorism Act 2000 received Royal Assent on July 20, 2000 and was brought into force in February 2001. The new Act extends and reforms the existing structure of anti-terrorism legislation,[16] whilst converting it from temporary to permanent in nature. This it achieved by repealing the previous legislation and re-enacting the bulk of it, with substantial amendments. The Emergency Powers legislation was due to expire on August 24, 2000 and the consultation document for the 2000 Act had suggested that it should be allowed to lapse without renewal. However the new Act reflects the Government's view that the security situation in Northern Ireland is not yet ready for such a change, and thus Part VII of the Act creates fresh temporary legislation for Northern Ireland, subject to annual review and with a maximum duration of five years.

Apart from these measures, the Act extends to any terrorism: domestic, Irish or international, thus creating a standard definition of terrorism with a uniform framework of regulation, and ironing out inconsistency in rules and their application. This change will enable the United Kingdom to ratify the UN Convention for the Suppression of Terrorist Bombings and the UN Convention for the Suppression of the Financing of Terrorism. However these gains have been achieved by dramatically extending the scope of the terrorist offences and related police powers.

The Act is broadly structured as follows: **10–023**

Part I—definition of terrorism and transitional measures until the Act is fully in force.

Part II—proscribed organisations and related offences.

Part III—offences related to, and forfeiture of, terrorist property.

Part IV—powers to investigate terrorism, including cordons and property searches.

Part V—police powers of stop and search, arrest and detention.

Part VI—offences related to terrorist organisations and terrorist purposes.

Part VII—police, army and security powers for Northern Ireland.

Part VIII—definitions and co-operation provisions.

Part I: Definition of Terrorism and the Transitional Measures

Section 1: definition of terrorism

Section 20 of the Prevention of Terrorism (Temporary Provisions) Act 1989 **10–024** defined terrorism as: "the use of violence for political ends", and included "any use of violence for the purpose of putting the public or any section of the public in fear". This limited definition was only applicable to use of violence in connection with Northern Ireland, whether domestic or on an international scale. The Consultation document which preceded the 2000 Act proposed that the time was right for a wider definition which would be able to cover terrorism of all forms, whether motivated by politics, religion, or ideology. It should also cover some non-violent acts such as interfering with the water and power supplies, since such acts may risk life and health. Both domestic and international terrorism should be encompassed by a single regulatory framework. Another change to be made was that violent acts committed for their own sake, such as assassinations, should be encompasses by the new definition, regardless of whether there was an ulterior aim of influencing government or intimidating members of the public.

Thus in the Terrorism Act 2000, "terrorism" is defined as:

> "(1) In this Act 'terrorism' means the use or threat of action where—
>
> (a) the action falls within subsection (2),
> (b) the use or threat is designed to influence the government or to intimidate the public or a section of the public, and

(c) the use or threat is made for the purpose of advancing a political, religious or ideological cause.

(2) Action falls within this subsection if it—

(a) involves serious violence against a person,
(b) involves serious damage to property,
(c) endangers a person's life, other than that of the person committing the action,
(d) creates a serious risk to the health or safety of the public or a section of the public, or
(e) is designed seriously to interfere with or seriously to disrupt an electronic system.

(3) The use of threat of action falling within subsection (2) which involves the use of firearms or explosives is terrorism whether or not subsection (1)(b) is satisfied.

(4) In this section—

(a) "action" includes action outside the United Kingdom,
(b) a reference to any person or to property is a reference to any person, or to property, wherever situated,
(c) a reference to the public includes a reference to the public of a country other than the United Kingdom, and
(d) "the government" means the government of the United Kingdom, of a Part of the United Kingdom or of a country other than the United Kingdom.

(5) In this Act a reference to action taken for the purposes of terrorism includes a reference to action taken for the benefit of a proscribed organisation."

Section 2: transitional provisions

10–025 Section 2(1) repealed the Prevention of Terrorism (Temporary Provisions) Act 1989 and the Northern Ireland (Emergency Provisions) Act 1996. However, some provisions of the EPA were preserved[17] until the coming into force of Part VIII of the 2000 Act, which relates to Northern Ireland.

PART II: PROSCRIBED ORGANISATIONS

10–026 The main body of this part of the 2000 Act re-enacts the proscription provisions from Part I of the PTA and sections 30 and 31 of the EPA. However, there are some differences.

Formerly, proscription applied only to organisations which were involved or concerned in Irish terrorism, but now there is an ability to proscribe any organisation involved in domestic, Irish or international terrorism. The previous system differentiated between proscription for Great Britain and proscription for Northern Ireland; in future there will be one system throughout the whole of the United Kingdom. Also, a decision to proscribe an organisation is now challengeable by appeal to the Secretary of State and then, if appeal is unsuccessful, by further appeal to the Proscribed

Organisations Appeal Commission (POAC). This is an improvement at least on the prior method of appeal via judicial review, the inadequacy of which was highlighted by the fact that no proscribed organisation had ever done so.

Section 3: proscription

"(1) For the purposes of this Act an organisation is proscribed if— **10–027**

(a) it is listed in Schedule 2, or
(b) it operates under the same name as an organisation listed in that Schedule.

(2) Subsection (1)(b) shall not apply in relation to an organisation listed in Schedule 2 if its entry is the subject of a note in that Schedule.

(3) The Secretary of State may by order—

(a) add an organisation to Schedule 2;

(b) remove an organisation from that Schedule;

(c) amend that Schedule in some other way.

(4) The Secretary of State may exercise his power under subsection (3)(a) in respect of an organisation only if he believes that it is concerned in terrorism.
(5) For the purposes of subsection (4) an organisation is concerned in terrorism if it—

(a) commits or participates in acts of terrorism,
(b) prepares for terrorism,
(c) promotes or encourages terrorism, or
(d) is otherwise concerned in terrorism."

The list of organisations which were proscribed under the PTA and EPA is preserved by section 3 in Schedule 2. Proscription now applies throughout the United Kingdom, and the explanatory notes to the 2000 Act remark that the Government is now considering whether to add to the list organisations which are concerned in international terrorism. However, the 2000 Act is an extension of proscription *per se* since some of the organisations in the Schedule 2 list were previously proscribed only in Northern Ireland and not in the United Kingdom.

Sections 4–6 deal with appeals against proscription and provide that an aggrieved organisation seeking deproscription must first approach the Secretary of State then, if he refuses to deproscribe, the remedy lies in an application to the POAC. Grounds for appeal under section 5 are:

"(1) There shall be a commission, to be known as the Proscribed Organisations Appeal Commission.
(2) Where an application under section 4 has been refused, the applicant may appeal to the Commission.
(3) The Commission shall allow an appeal against a refusal to deproscribe an organisation if it considers that the decision to refuse was flawed when considered in the light of the principles applicable on an application for judicial review.

(4) Where the Commission allows an appeal under this section by or in respect of an organisation, it may make an order under this subsection.
(5) Where an order is made under subsection (4) the Secretary of State shall as soon as is reasonably practicable—

(a) lay before Parliament, in accordance with section 123(4), the draft of an order under section 3(3)(b) removing the organisation from the list in Schedule 2, or
(b) make an order removing the organisation from the list in Schedule 2 in pursuance of section 123(5).

(6) Schedule 3 (constitution of the Commission and procedure) shall have effect."

Thus ECHR rights may form the basis, or part of the grounds for appeal. A further appeal then exists on question of law (section 6). deproscription of an organisation at any of these stages will allow a person convicted of a related offence to appeal against conviction and to seek compensation (sections 7 and 8). A person seeking deproscription has immunity from prosecution based on evidence collected for or presented at those proceedings (section 10); so, he may not on that basis be charged with, e.g. membership of a proscribed organisation.

Sections 11 and 12: offences of membership of, and support for, proscribed organisations

10–028 Section 11: "Membership.

(1) A person commits an offence if he belongs or professes to belong to a proscribed organisation.
(2) It is a defence for a person charged with an offence under subsection (1) to prove—

(a) that the organisation was not proscribed on the last (or only) occasion on which he became a member or began to profess to be a member, and
(b) that he has not taken part in the activities of the organisation at any time while it was proscribed.

(3) A person guilty of an offence under this section shall be liable—

(a) on conviction on indictment, to imprisonment for a term not exceeding ten years, to a fine or to both, or
(b) on summary conviction, to imprisonment for a term not exceeding six months, to a fine not exceeding the statutory maximum or to both.

(4) In subsection (2) "proscribed" means proscribed for the purposes of any of the following—

(a) this Act;
(b) the Northern Ireland (Emergency Provisions) Act 1996;
(c) the Northern Ireland (Emergency Provisions) Act 1991;
(d) the Prevention of Terrorism (Temporary Provisions) Act 1989;
(e) the Prevention of Terrorism (Temporary Provisions) Act 1984;

(f) the Northern Ireland (Emergency Provisions) Act 1978;
(g) the Prevention of Terrorism (Temporary Provisions) Act 1976;
(h) the Prevention of Terrorism (Temporary Provisions) Act 1974;
(i) the Northern Ireland (Emergency Provisions) Act 1973."

Section 12: "Support.

(1) A person commits an offence if—
(a) he invites support for a proscribed organisation, and
(b) the support is not, or is not restricted to, the provision of money or other property (within the meaning of section 15).

(2) A person commits an offence if he arranges, manages or assists in arranging or managing a meeting which he knows is—

(a) to support a proscribed organisation,

(b) to further the activities of a proscribed organisation, or

(c) to be addressed by a person who belongs or professes to belong to a proscribed organisation.

(3) A person commits an offence if he addresses a meeting and the purpose of his address is to encourage support for a proscribed organisation or to further its activities.

(4) Where a person is charged with an offence under subsection (2)(c) in respect of a private meeting it is a defence for him to prove that he had no reasonable cause to believe that the address mentioned in subsection (2)(c) would support a proscribed organisation or further its activities.

(5) In subsections (2) to (4)—

(a) "meeting" means a meeting of three or more persons, whether or not the public are admitted, and
(b) a meeting is private if the public are not admitted.

(6) A person guilty of an offence under this section shall be liable—

(a) on conviction on indictment, to imprisonment for a term not exceeding ten years, to a fine or to both, or
(b) on summary conviction, to imprisonment for a term not exceeding six months, to a fine not exceeding the statutory maximum or to both."

These offences are similar to their predecessors, section 30 EPA and section 2 PTA.

Section 13: uniforms

Under section 13 it is an offence to wear the uniform of a proscribed **10–029** organisation. This provision is the same in substance as its predecessors, section 3 of the PTA and section 31 of the EPA, but adopts the penalties from the PTA, thus reducing the former EPA offence to summary only[18] and the maximum prison sentence available to six months.[19]

It has been argued that this section would cover the wearing of a T-shirt with a religious slogan; it remains to be seen whether interpretations in practice and in case law will allow this potential to be realised.

Part III: Terrorist Property

In common with Part III of the PTA, this part of the Act deals with the **10–030** provision of assistance to terrorism in relation to property, such as money laundering but is broader than the PTA was in this respect. Reference to "terrorist finance" has now been replaced with "terrorist property", to underline that the offences are committed regardless of whether the property involved is money. "Terrorist property" includes both property to be used for terrorism and the proceeds of acts of terrorism, and all the resources of a proscribed organisation, even their grocery money (section 14). Again, the offences apply to all terrorism, domestic, Irish or international. There is also a new set of powers for police, immigration officers and customs officials to seize money at borders and to bring proceedings for its legal forfeiture (sections 24–31). These powers are modelled upon similar provisions under the Drug Trafficking Act 1994.

Sections 15, 16 and 17 preserve and expand section 9 and 10 of the PTA, which contained the offences of fundraising, using and possessing money, and entering into funding arrangements for a proscribed organisation. But the new offences replace "for a proscribed organisation" with "for terrorist purposes", and so have far greater scope.

Section 18 contains the offence of money laundering, which is the same as that under section 11 of the PTA, but of course applies to "laundering" of any property, not just of money. As before[20] banks and businesses are required to report any suspicion of the laundering of terrorist money or of the commission of any other offence under sections 15–18. But section 18 of the PTA, which required the reporting of suspicions which arose in home life, has not made an appearance in the 2000 Act after adverse comment from academics and Lord Lloyd. Sections 20 and 21 restate section 12 of the PTA, so that disclosure of information by businesses to the police has legal protection (section 20) and informants and persons unwittingly involved with terrorist property are able to escape prosecution under section 21. In order to do so they must inform the police as soon as reasonably practicable and must cease their involvement if requested to do so by the police.

The forfeiture provisions for terrorist property are found in sections 22 and 23 and broadly follow section 13 of the PTA, although the procedure had been widened to include the proceeds of a terrorist property offence even when those proceeds were never themselves intended for use in terrorism. This gets rid of a small but annoying loophole in the previous legislation and allows the twin forfeiture procedures under the Criminal Justice Act 1988 and the 2000 Act to work more smoothly together.

Part IV: Terrorist Investigations

10–031 In connection with "terrorist investigations", police are given extra powers broadly the same as those under the PTA. Sections 33–36 restate the cordoning powers which were created by the Prevention of Terrorism (Additional Powers) Act 1996 and formed section 16C and Schedule 6A of the PTA as amended. Thus an area may be cordoned for the purposes of a terrorist investigation, and it is an offence to breach a cordon. Section 37 activates Schedule 5 of the Act.

Schedule 5

Paragraphs 1–3 replace paragraphs 2 and 2A of the PTA with similar powers, allowing warrants to be issued to search either residential or non-residential premises and seize anything likely to be of substantial value to a terrorist investigation.[21] The seizure power is broader than its predecessor, however, which only allowed items relevant to the present investigation to be seized. As before, excluded and special procedure material are treated separately. Production orders are covered by paragraphs 5–10 (formerly paragraphs 3–4 of Schedule 7 of the PTA); search warrants in respect of excluded and special procedure material are covered by paragraphs 11 and 12 (formerly paragraphs 1–3 of Schedule 7 of the PTA). Explanation orders, which were found in paragraph 6 of Schedule 7 of the PTA, are now within paragraphs 13 and 14 of Schedule 5, but with one significant difference. Since a person's response to an explanation order is "information given under compulsion", it cannot normally be used in evidence against him as this would violate the privilege against self-incrimination or right to silence (see *Saunders v. U.K.*[22]) Under the PTA, there were two exceptional circumstances in which a response to an explanation order could nevertheless be used in evidence against him: **10–032**

(i) where the defendant is being tried for the offence of giving a false or misleading answer to the explanation order (which was paragraph 6 (3)(a) of the PTA); or
(ii) in a trial for any other offence, where in that trial the defendant made a statement which was inconsistent with his response to the explanation order (which was paragraph 6(3)(b) of the PTA).

For obvious human rights reasons related to the development of the right to silence and the privilege against self-incrimination, only the first of these exceptional circumstances has been maintained by the 2000 Act.

In relation to Northern Ireland only, paragraph 8 of Schedule 7 of the PTA provided that the Secretary of State could authorise police to search for, or to require the production of, material connected to the investigation of terrorist financing offences or of the offence of directing a terrorist organisation. Paragraphs 19–21 reinstates these powers, for Northern Ireland only, in a temporary form which hopefully will become redundant in the near future.

PART V: COUNTER-TERRORIST POWERS

The special police powers in respect of terrorist suspects have been retained: thus stopping, searching (sections 42 and 43) and arresting (section 41) terrorist suspects still have a separate regime from those dealt with under PACE. If the police reasonably suspect that a person is involved in terrorism, then they may arrest him, even though they fall far short of having the reasonable grounds for suspicion of the commission of a specific offence which would be required if he were a non-terrorist suspect. **10–033**

Under sections 44–47 the general effect of section 13A and 13B of the PTA is maintained: police may stop and search vehicles, persons within the vehicles, and pedestrians, subject to this being done for the purpose of prevention of terrorism. As under the PTA, authorisation is required before a particular area will be subject to these rules, and has an initial duration of 28 days. Renewal is possible. However one difference from the PTA is that unless an authorisation for vehicle stop and search powers in an area is confirmed by the Secretary of State within 48 hours of being granted, it becomes inoperative. Sections 48–52 allow parking restrictions to be applied, for a limited period and in a defined area, for the prevention of terrorism. Schedule 7, which is brought into effect by section 53, covers port and border controls.

Schedule 8 is concerned with the detention of terrorist suspects, and largely preserves the previous rules under the PTA. Paragraph 1 allows the Secretary of State to direct at which places a detainee should be held. Paragraphs 2–20 cover the treatment of detainees, including the taking of intimate and non-intimate samples, and refusal of access to a solicitor in limited circumstances. A Code of Practice on the now compulsory audio-recording of interviews at police stations is required by paragraph 3, with potential for the rules and Code to be extended to require video recording. Paragraphs 21–28 deal with reviews and extension of detention. Paragraph 29 allows an officer of at least the rank of superintendent to apply for a warrant of further detention when a terrorist suspect has been arrested under section 41. An application for extension must normally be made within 48 hours, or exceptionally within six hours of the expiry of that period (paragraph 30).The maximum period of detention from the time of arrest is seven days (paragraph 29). It therefore appears that little has been achieved by criticism of the rules concerning, and factual treatment of, detained terrorist suspects in the United Kingdom.

Part VI: Ancillary Offences

10–034 Part VI brings together a variety of other terrorism-related offences, some of which previously only applied to Northern Ireland, including: training persons with weapons (sections 54 and 55); directing a terrorist organisation, whether or not it has been proscribed (section 56); possession offences (sections 57 and 58); and inciting terrorism anywhere in the world (sections 59–61). The latter offence merits some attention, since its predecessor, the Criminal Justice (Terrorism and Conspiracy) Act 1998 contained offences of conspiring in the United Kingdom to commit criminal acts abroad, but now incitement of terrorist acts to be committed abroad is included. This is a step towards greater coherence between domestic and international anti-terrorism provisions. Sections 62–64 will further help to achieve this coherence, since they will bring United Kingdom law into line with its obligations under the UN Convention for the Suppression of Terrorist Bombings and the UN Convention for the Suppression of the Financing of Terrorism.

PART VII: SPECIFIC PROVISIONS FOR NORTHERN IRELAND

This part of the 2000 Act provides a detailed package of powers, offences and reforms relating only to the situation in Northern Ireland. It is outside the scope of the present discussion, and many of its provisions are intended to remain in force only temporarily. As has been demonstrated by all the anti-terrorist legislation prior to the 2000 Act, "temporary" provisions can be remarkably durable and resemble permanent ones, but it is best perhaps to end on a positive note and look forward to a situation in Northern Ireland where such specific regulations and powers are no longer necessary. **10–035**

Since, at the time of writing, there is no case law basis upon which to critique the new legislation, critical comment will be available on the website as soon as the main sections of the 2000 Act have been tested in court.

RELEVANT ECHR DECISIONS

A number of decisions of the European Court of Human Rights which concern terrorism and, in particular, the treatment of terrorist suspects, have been dealt with elsewhere in this book, such as in Chapters 2, 3 and 8. Particular attention should be paid to the following cases: **10–036 —038**

Murray v. U.K.[23]
Fox, Campbell and Hartley v. U.K. [24]
Brannigan and McBride v. U.K. [25]
Brogan v. U.K. [25]
Lawless v Ireland (No.3) [26]
Murray v. U.K. [27]
Ireland v. U.K. [28]

An updated list of relevant ECHR cases will be available on the website shortly after publication of this book.

BRIEF OUTLINE AND GERMANE CASES

CHAPTER TEN: EMERGENCY POWERS AND THE PREVENTION OF TERRORISM

I. Stop and Search

*Prevention of Terrorism (Temporary Provisions) Act 1989, s. 13A: stop and search of vehicles and passengers. **10–039**

*PTA 1989 s. 13B: search of pedestrians.

*CJPOA 1994 s.60: authorisation for stop and search in particular area.

2. Entry, search and seizure

10–040 *PTA 1989 Sched.7 para.7: emergency searches without warrant; search warrants and production orders.

R. v. Crown Court, ex p. Salinger [1993]; *DPP v. Channel Four Television* [1993].

*PTA 1989 ss.16C and 16D: police cordons and parking restrictions and prohibitions.
*PTA 1989 Sch.5 s.4A: power to search goods at ports or airports.

3. Arrest

10–041

*PTA 1989, s.14: arrest without warrant of persons suspected, on reasonable grounds, of involvement in terrorism.

O'Hara v. Chief Constable of the Royal Ulster Constabulary [1997].
Additional powers relating to arrest: s.15.

4. Detention

10–042 Initial detention after arrest: Sch. 3 para. 3(3)(a).

Extended detention: s.14(4).

Rights to have someone informed of detention and to receive legal advice.

R. v. Chief Constable of the Royal Ulster Constabulary, ex p. Begley [1997].
Right of silence.
Terrorism Act 2000.

Endnotes

[1] Gardiner Committee, *Report of a Committee to consider, in the context of civil liberties and human rights, measures to deal with terrorism in Northern Ireland*, Cmnd. 5487 (1975), paras 15, 17.
[2] *e.g.* the Electricity Act 1989 which allows the Secretary of State to "give such directions as appear to him" to be required to alleviate a civil emergency, defined as any "natural disaster or ther emergency which, in the opinion of the Secretary of State, is, or may be, likely to disrupt electricity supplies".
[3] See Hillyard, *Suspect Community: People's Experience of the Prevention of Terrorism Acts in Britain*, (Pluto, 1993), p. 5 onwards for statistics and much greater discussion.
[4] *Review of the Operation of the Prevention of Terrorism (Temporary Provisions) Acts 1974 and 1976*, Cmnd. 7324 (1978).
[5] (1983) *Review of the Operation of the Prevention of Terrorism (Temporary Provisions) Act 1976*, Cmnd. 8803 (1983).
[6] (1987) *Review of the Operation of the Prevention of Terrorism (Temporary Provisions) Act 1984*, Cm. 264 (1987).
[7] The PTA powers should only be used for anti-terrorist purposes, but there is an obvious potential for abuse since there is no need to prove that there were reasonable grounds for a search carried out under either s. 13A or s. 13B.
[8] [1993] 2 All E.R. 310.
[9] [1993] 2 All E.R. 517.
[10] Compare with PACE powers.
[11] *The Times*, December 13, 1996.
[12] [1997] 1 W.L.R. 1475.
[13] Northern Ireland (Emergency Provisions) Act 1998, s. 53A required the Secretary of State to make a Code of Practice in relation to this, and the Code was immediately passed by Statutory Order.
[14] [1999] 3 W.L.R. 972.
[15] Cm. 4178 (1998).
[16] The Prevention of Terrorism (Temporary Provisions) Act 1989, the Northern Ireland (Emergency Provisions) Act 1996 and the Criminal Justice (Terrorism and Conspiracy) Act 1998.
[17] By s. 2(2) and Sched. 1.
[18] From triable either way.
[19] From 12 months.
[20] Under PTA, s. 18.
[21] In urgent cases warrants and explanations may be issued by a police Superintendent, as long as he notifies the Secretary of State.
[22] [1996] 23 E.H.R.R. 313.
[23] [1994] 19 E.H.R.R. 193.
[24] [1990] 13 E.H.R.R. 157.
[25] [1994] 17 E.H.R.R. 539.
[25A] [1989] 11 E.H.R.R. 117.
[26] [1961] 1 E.H.R.R. 15.
[27] [1996] 22 E.H.R.R. 29.
[28] [1988] 2 E.H.R.R. 25.

CHAPTER 11

IMMIGRATION: EXTRADITION AND DEPORTATION

By Bruce Tattersall, Barrister, Visiting Lecturer in Law, School of African and Oriental Studies, University of London

INTRODUCTION

Liberal British tradition has always prided itself on having an "open door" policy regarding refugees; political asylum seekers and those who could demonstrate a claim British Citizenship. From Kossuth, through Marx to Lenin and Ho Chi Min, there appears to be a tradition of tolerance and forbearance in the British system to the extent of giving those who have fled questionable justice in other countries the benefit of the doubt. This has not always been a disinterested activity. Foreign governments change and with them so do ideologies, policies and trade. As one judge put it succinctly, "Today's Garibaldi may well form tomorrow's government".[1–2] Further, the economic boom of the late 1950s and 60s would not have been possible without the large-scale immigration of West Indians and Asians, which was actively encouraged by successive United Kingdom governments. These immigrants were largely full British passport holders with rights of residence in the United Kingdom. On arrival, they formed a large, significant, minority of the employees in the service industries from transport to the NHS. With them, however came racial prejudice and intolerance on a large scale, with all the profound difficulties of integration into British society that they implied. A similar process has occurred at the end of the twentieth century where distrust of "economic" migrants coincided with a very real need for skilled workers in such poorly paid but essential areas as nursing and teaching. **11–001**

For those who still hold to the myth of liberal, tolerant Britain, it may come as a surprise to learn that a British Citizen may not have a right of residence in the United Kingdom; that an alien has no right of political asylum and may even be sent back to the country from which he fled, and that from 1974 to 2000, the United Kingdom employed a form of internal exile, which was probably in breach of the European Convention on Human Rights, and the very kind of absolutism for which the old USSR was rightly condemned. In these areas, the growth of legislation, as opposed to common law, should be viewed against political, social and economic developments, changes and upheavals in the United Kingdom, Europe and elsewhere. It is notable that the stringency of immigration application procedures has varied proportionally to the number of possible immigrants and the decline in the areas of the British economy where they were perceived as having the most economic use. Politicians have also found pressure to restrict immigration, especially recently, of "economic" asylum seekers irresistible to the extent of so penalising asylum seekers as to attempt to deny them income and housing support, making Britain the last refuge of the most desperate. It is almost as if the choice for some is to die by violence in their native country or to starve on the streets, here. Further the impact of EU legislation has been already felt in the United Kingdom, especially the Schengen agreement that allowed free movement within most states on mainland Europe, but erected what purported to be stringent barriers to those trying to enter from outside. The Dublin Convention has at least simplified the vexed question of in which EC country an asylum seeker should make their application. Influxes of Albanians into Italy and Algerians into Spain have been hard to prevent. Once such illegal immigrants are within the Schengen area they are free to move within it and the United Kingdom Government has been afraid of their coming here. The 1993, 1996 and 1999 legislation dealing with asylum-seekers becomes intelligible in this light.

There are four discrete elements in Immigration law that deal with the rights of the individual to enter, remain and not to be removed from the United Kingdom; they are the negative aspects of that right, *viz.*:

1. Extradition.
2. Deportation.
3. Exclusion.
4. Asylum.

Extradition

11–002 Extradition is a creature of Statute, replacing the common law principle that alien fugitives should not be surrendered and the contradictory prerogative that the Crown has the right to expel whomsoever it wishes. Applying to both British citizens and aliens, it involves judicial; quasi-judicial and administrative procedures. As such, it is susceptible to the usual legal remedies of habeas corpus; appeal and judicial review. The principle is that if A commits an "extradition" crime in country B and flees to the United Kingdom, then B, under certain circumstances, has the right to demand the surrender of A to justice, irrespective of A's nationality.

This right is endorsed in a series of Extradition Acts of 1870; 1873; 1935 and 1989 as well as the Suppression of Terrorism Act of 1978 and the

Terrorism Act 2000. The law operates reciprocally, through treaties between the United Kingdom and other national governments, individually and collectively.[3] As we shall see, anyone who has an Extradition Notice served on them has a number of rights to appeal, especially if the crime is "political" in nature.

The prime intention of all the acts is to return "fugitive criminals" who are either accused or convicted of an "extradition" crime to the state claiming that extradition. The initial Act of 1870 was amended in 1873 and in 1935. All these Acts were consolidated in the 1989 Act. A special Act applies to the Irish Republic, The Backing of Warrants (Irish Republic) Act 1965. The 1978 Act is the definitive legislation but elements of the previous acts remain actively on the statute book; notably the list of crimes for which extradition is possible, which is, as amended, under Sch. 8 of the 1873 Act.

This was demonstrated in a recent case of *R. v. Secretary of State for the* **11–003** *Home Department, ex parte Gilmore and others*.[4-5] Gilmore appealed to the Queen's Bench Divisional Court for the quashing of an extradition order of the Home Secretary on the grounds that the crime of which he was accused in the USA was not an extradition offence. His crime corresponded to offences of conspiracy to commit offences under the Theft Act 1968. Counsel for the Home Secretary contended that offences of conspiracy had always been extradition crimes under the 1870/3 Acts. The court differed and followed Lord Lowry's decision in *Government of the USA v. Bowe*,[6] which stated "Where the description of a listed offence is specific . . . the offence of conspiracy or an attempt to commit these offences cannot be included in the list by implication". Counsel for the Home Secretary further submitted that the 1989 Act had freed the Anglo-American Treaty, brought into effect in 1976, from the restraints of the 1870 Act. This failed on the grounds that the procedures of that Act were preserved by the 1989 Act. Thus, the list in the 1870 Act could be limited but not extended. On this basis, the appeal was allowed and the extradition order quashed.

This decision indicates that the courts still take a principled line on what constitutes an extradition offence and will not add to the 1870 list or casually surrender an accused to a country demanding extradition, at least for mind crimes, rather than substantive offences.

This conspiracy exception seems to have been closed in some respects as demonstrated in the case of *R. v. Bow Street Magistrates Court*; *Adeniyi Momodu Allison, ex parte the Government of the USA*,[7] where the House of Lords allowed the appeal by the USA from the decision of the divisional court dismissing the application of the USA for Judicial Review of a magistrate's decision not to order the extradition of Mr Allison, under section 2 of the Computer Misuse Act 1990. The offences of which Allison was to be extradited were two of conspiring to obtain computer data to which he had no authority to access: in layman's terms "hacking". The Lords referred to *Gilmore*, but did not overrule it. They relied on the fact that the 1990 Act had made the conspiracy to access the material a crime and therefore it became an "extradition" offence under the Act. The 1976

Treaty was irelevant and the 1870 Act could have such crimes added to it by statute, as here. This leaves the law as to conspiracies and extradition somewhat unclear but the tendency does seem to be that conspiracies of a really serious nature as outlined in the Terrorism Act 2000[8] will tend towards being interpreted as "extradition" crimes.

The 1989 Act

11–004 This Act permits almost all countries in the world to extradite those accused or convicted of an "extradition" crime. An "extradition" crime is defined in section 2 as "conduct" in the territory of a foreign state; a designated Commonwealth country or a Colony and the Hong Kong Special Administrative Region[9] which, if the conduct had occurred in the United Kingdom would constitute an offence punishable with a term of 12 months' imprisonment or any greater punishment.[10] It is noticeable that the term used is "conduct", not "crime", which appears to allow fiscal offences or misdemeanours, which may not be criminal in the originating country but which are in the United Kingdom, to fall within the Act.[11]

For Commonwealth countries the ingredients of the conduct must be made out in order to establish that a fugitive offender is guilty of a corresponding United Kingdom offence for the purpose of establishing that conduct as a United Kingdom crime. It is insufficient to adduce evidence in support of the case, which a United Kingdom court would not be permitted to review and which it could not use to determine the corresponding criminal case in the United Kingdom.[12] This situation is well illustrated in the case of *Proulx v. The Governor of H.M. Prison (Brixton) and others; R. v. Bow Street Magistrates Court and others ex parte Proulx*[13] Here the appellant was seeking conjoined habeas corpus and Judicial Review against the decision for committal under section 9(8) of the Extradition Act 1989. The gravemen of the case was that the only evidence available was a confession by the appellant to an *agent provocateur* and that such evidence should be excluded under section 76 or section 78 of the Police and Criminal Evidence Act 1984 as either being inadmissible confession evidence or under the general discretion to exclude. The divisional court found that as long as the decision of the magistrate was that of a reasonable magistrate directing himself properly and in accordance with the law, any matters of fairness and admissibility were for the trial judge in the extraditing country to decide. In general the offence does not have to be particularly serious as along as a possible penalty is 12 months' imprisonment; no matter how large a fine, as the only penalty would bar extradition, neither does the offence need to be identical in all its elements to any United Kingdom offence.

It is also possible to be extradited for an extra-territorial offence committed outside a requesting country. This term is not defined in the Act, but refers to conduct seen by some foreign country as an offence committed outside its borders. Again in such circumstances, the same conditions as to a comparable United Kingdom crime apply.[14]

Extradition Powers of other Countries

The countries that have extradition agreements with the United Kingdom are defined fairly broadly; either they are foreign countries with which the United Kingdom has an extradition agreement or a Commonwealth state. An Order in Council must exist, for foreign countries under section 4 or under section 5 for Commonwealth States. Such an Order allows the provisions of Part III of the Act, which deals with the procedure to be adopted for extradition, to be implemented. A new feature of the 1989 law is found in section 3(3)(b) that of "special extradition arrangements" that apply in particular, individual cases, when no general agreement is extant. This procedure is implemented under section 15 under which the Secretary of State (usually the Home Secretary[15]) issues a certificate of "special extradition arrangements" that are individual and specific to a particular "person" and establish no general agreements with the requesting country. **11–005**

Extradition is further facilitated for those nations that do not have "general extradition arrangements" through section 22. Section 22(2) lists several International Conventions[16] which deem any state, which is a signatory, to have a similar status to those who do have such arrangements, permitting bi-lateral Orders in Council to be made for offences covered by those Conventions.

Restrictions

Extradition is a draconian measure and legislation has always recognised that there are certain classes of person to whom it should not be applied.[17] Section 6(1) gives the restrictions under which a person should not be returned to a requesting country or kept in custody for that purpose. Paragraphs (a)–(d) can be read separately or conjointly and it is for an "appropriate authority"[18] to decide which section (if any) applies. Para (a) is the most used category and applies if the offence is of a "political" character. No definition has been given of this in the Act or any previous ones. A working definition was effectively established in *Re Castioni*,[19] that for a person to avoid extradition, the "extradition" conduct should be incidental to acting in a political manner. Here Castioni, a political opponent of the Swiss government, shot and killed a member of the cantonal assembly in the course of an uprising. Such conduct was found to be incidental to the political purpose and his extradition was refused. **11–006**

The best, recent exegesis on the definition of "political" was given by Viscount Radcliffe in *R v. Governor of Brixton Prison, ex Parte Schtraks*[20]:

> "Generally speaking, the courts' reluctance to offer a definition has been due, I think to the realisation that it is virtually impossible to find one that does not cover too wide a range . . . In my opinion the idea that lies behind the phrase 'offence of a political character' is that the fugitive is at odds with the state that applies for his extradition on some issue connected with the political control or government of that country . . . the requesting state is

> after him for reasons other than the enforcement of the criminal law in its ordinary aspect".

The instant case concerns a grandfather's attempt to resist extradition for contempt of court in Israel for failure to return, under a court order, his grandson to his parents. The grandfather had abducted him in order to give him an Orthodox Jewish upbringing which he feared he would not receive in Israel. In a writ of habeas corpus the grandfather claimed *inter alia* that his offences were of a political character. On the evidence, the House of Lords refused his appeal on the grounds expressed by Viscount Radcliffe, above.

Despite the apparently wide defences given in *Castioni* and *Schtraks*, the restriction afforded by the "political" exemption is normally unavailable when a criminal act, especially an act of violence, is seen a being the primary activity in conduct which has a political component and is not political *per se*. This restriction has been further eroded by the Suppression of Terrorism Act 1978, combined with a consistent feeling in the courts that "not all refugees were worthy of compassion and support"[21] and that actions formerly seen as political had become "depoliticised".[22] Under the 1989 Act, which confirmed the Suppression of Terrorism Act,[23] a list of crimes was codified which should not be regarded as of a political character. These include: murder; manslaughter; rape; kidnapping; abduction; offences against the person; causing explosions likely to endanger human life or property; certain firearms offences; hijacking and attempts or conspiracy to commit any of the above. Genocide is also not regarded as an offence of a political character.[24] This section formalised and codified the development of judicial decisions since the 1870 Act, reflecting the work of The Law Commission on the subject.[25] It may be argued that the judicial reasoning applied in extradition cases is itself political. This is in the sense that the nature of the regime requesting extradition appears to be considered, as well as the character and actions of the person requesting not to be extradited. Such reasoning is evident in the two earliest cases where the judicial decisions appear to irreconcilable, on the facts.

11–007 In *Re Meunier*,[26] Meunier was a French anarchist who claimed that his bombing of a barracks, in which two bystanders were killed, was a political offence under the 1870 Act. Here in contrast to *Castioni*, where the person killed was a Swiss government representative, this offence was found not to be political on the esoteric and obscure grounds that, for an offence to be political:

> "there must be two or more parties in the State, each seeking to impose the Government of their own choice on each other".[27]

Consequently, the learned judge then found that, since M was an anarchist, he could not be seen to be a representative of any party intending to impose a government since "the party of anarchy is the enemy of all Governments".[28] Such a decision cannot be isolated from its time, when all

Europe considered itself under attack from many violent groups especially anarchists. It reflects that concern along with distinguishing *Castioni*, since in the instant case, it was innocent bystanders who were killed. Similar cases have usually be decided along the lines of *Meunier*, evidencing a distaste for the loss of the lives of innocent people uninvolved in the political struggle. Today, both cases would be judged extraditable under the 1989 Act.

Meunier can be contrasted with *R. v. Governor of Brixton Prison, ex parte Kolczynski*,[29] a decision made in the light of another menace, that of Communism. At the height of the Cold War, judges tended towards a sympathetic reception for those resisting extradition behind the Iron Curtain. Here, rebellious Polish trawlermen seized their boat on the high seas and brought it into Whitby, where they requested political asylum. The Polish government, relying upon an extradition treaty between the United Kingdom and Poland, demanded their return for an extradition crime—mutiny. Following the ratio in both *Castioni* and *Meunier*, there appears, on the evidence, no sign of two or more political parties disputing the governing of Poland. The court distinguished the above cases by arguing, that, since there was no effective opposition to the "police state"[30] then existing in Poland and that they should give a wider interpretation to the 1870 Act, especially since there was little doubt that the Polish government would regard the actions of the trawlermen as a political crime.

This verdict appears as the ultimate judicial interpretation of "political" crime. Both subsequent cases and the 1989 statute have so far curtailed the definition that it hardly seems to exist as a restriction, even in its truncated form.

The political exception was found to have a geographical component, **11–008**
that prevented its application, in *Cheng v. Governor of Pentonville Prison*.[31] Cheng, a Taiwanese, had attempted to assassinate the vice-premier of that country. The attempt took place in New York. Thus, it was the USA which applied for extradition, not Taiwan. The House of Lords found, by a majority decision, that the offence was not a political act against Taiwan, but a simple criminal act *vis-à-vis* the USA. Lord Simon, in a minority judgment, made an elegant defence of the concept of a political crime having an international status, irrespective of where it was committed, although he acknowledged that the law needed to be changed in the light of increasing international terrorism. Again, this case would fall under both the 1978 and 1989 Acts as a crime which would be defined as non-political. The legislators took Lord Simon's hint.

The most recent case which examined the definition of political according to the straitened definition of the 1989 Act was *T. v. The Secretary of State for the Home Department*.[32] T, an Algerian, had an ostensible political purpose in attempting to overthrow a despotic government, which had suborned the democratic process by declaring the results of general elections, which were unfavourable to itself, invalid. T, in protest, caused an explosion at Algiers airport, killing 10 people. Such a crime was not deemed to be political, under the test the court applied, that of being not sufficiently closely or directly linked to its purpose, presumably of bringing down the Algerian Government.

As has been seen above, the application of the Suppression of Terrorism Act has disallowed the claiming of political status for a large range of offences. However, the other restrictions as listed in the 1989 Act still apply. Section 6(1)(b) allows a defence that the offence was one under military law which has no equivalent under general criminal law. Section 6(1)(c) forbids extradition if the request is a pretext for prosecuting or punishing a person on account of race; religion; nationality or political opinions. In the latter case the person must have expressed some actual political opinions. It is not enough to be the centre of political controversy.[33] Section 6(1)(d) has a similar function to (c) in that the person, if returned would be prejudiced, at trial, for the same categories as (c). In such cases the court would need to find a reasonable chance; substantial grounds for thinking or a strong possibility that the person might be dealt with in these ways for the above reasons.[34]

11–009 Section 2 restricts the return of those found guilty *in absentia* when it is considered that to return such a person would not be in the interests of justice.

Section 3 applies to where *autrefois convict* and *autrefois acquit* would be possible defences; the doctrine of double jeopardy.

Section 4 allows for an extradited person to leave that country, where he is to be tried for an extradition crime, in order to avoid trial for any other offence he committed before previously leaving that country, except for further extradition offences. The court assumes that the extraditing government will honour such an obligation under this section and therefore there is no need to consider this when granting extradition.

11–010 In *Royal Government of Greece v. Governor of Brixton Prison*,[35] one Kotronis, a Greek national, claimed that the evidence of his purported conviction in Greece was not conclusive proof of that conviction and that it had been arrived at in disregard of the laws of natural justice. He stated that the conviction was a pretence to have him extradited for his political beliefs. He contended that he was a political opponent of the Greek Junta and would be detained in Greece on return, either after or in lieu of serving his sentence. The divisional court allowed his appeal and argued that, in exceptional circumstances and given the political state in Greece, it was possible for the court to look behind the certificate of conviction, and regard it as a nullity.[36] However, the House of Lords reversed the decision, taking the formalist view on the naive grounds enunciated by Lord Reid:

> "... so it would be a clear breach of faith on the part of the Greek Government, if he were detained in Greece, otherwise than for the purpose of serving his sentence, and it appears to me to be impossible for our country or for your Lordships, sitting judicially to assume that any foreign Government with which Her Majesty's Government has diplomatic relations may act in such a manner".[37]

This reluctance to bind other governments over undertakings that fugitive offenders would only be dealt with for the extradition offence was raised in *R. v. Governor of Brixton Prison ex parte Osman (no 3)*.[38] Osman applied for habeas corpus on the grounds that, if he were returned to Hong Kong for an extradition crime, on the assurance by the Hong Kong government that they would abide by section 6(4) of the Act, he would still be in prison in 1997 when Hong Kong was handed over to China and that China would not be bound to keep to the assurance. The Hong Kong government would be in no position to enforce the guarantee on China and since China had no extradition arrangements with any other country, he would be without protection. The court found, that as long as it could satisfy itself that the agreement to guarantee Osman special protection was valid as far as the then government of Hong Kong was concerned, it should not look beyond that to any possible changes in the political or legal situation, which might alter the agreement.

Such a decision may seem strange in the light of the certainty of political change in 1997 and the very obvious risks to the applicants afterwards. However the courts took the view that the status of prisoners after the handover was a political, not a judicial, matter and it should be left to the United Kingdom, Hong Kong and Chinese governments to negotiate on this.

Procedure

Part III of the Act sets out the procedure to be adopted in the course of extradition. The first step is an extradition request on behalf of the country asking for extradition. This document must itemise the particulars of the person they wish to extradite; the particulars of the offence; any warrant for arrest or certificate of conviction and sentence.[39] The Home Secretary will then issue an "authority to proceed" unless he finds such an authority illegal or outside the provisions of the Act. A warrant on this authority is normally issued by the chief metropolitan magistrate.[40] After arrest the person should be brought before the magistrate for committal. Under the 1989 Act there is no longer any need for the magistrate to consider whether there is a prima facie case against the person such as would justify committal in the United Kingdom. The Act is confusing in this respect since section 9(8)(a)–(b) requires the court of committal to hear representations in support of the extradition request. Such evidence needs to be sufficient to warrant trial in the United Kingdom had the extradition offence taken place here.[41] Section 9(8)(a) allows for any country which has an Order in Council giving effect to general extradition arrangements to circumvent this provision and to apply section 9(4)(b) which states there is no need to furnish the court of committal with the evidence required under section 9(8)(a). This is the standard formula which follows the European Convention on Extradition of 1957[42] and effectively bars a magistrate from examining the evidence. However, he may do so in the case of special extradition arrangements with a nation to which an Order in Council does not apply, or under one of the Conventions mentioned above. The **11–011** magistrate is further restricted in investigation in that he cannot examine whether the proceedings could amount to an abuse of process. He cannot request further evidence other than that submitted by the requesting country. In *Re Evans*[43–44] Lord Templeman made this clear:

> "The Act of 1989 does not make provision for evidence and in my opinion the magistrate sitting as the court of committal is not bound or entitled to admit evidence. Conduct does not have to be proved, a *prima facie* case need not be made out and possible defence are excluded".[45]

Further proceedings can be instigated by the requesting country, if committal is refused, on a point of law to the divisional court, thence to the House of Lords. The final say lies with the Home Secretary under section 12 who has discretion to refuse the order if the offence is trivial; by reason of the process of time; or if the application is in bad faith or not in the interests of justice and therefore unjust or oppressive to return the person.[46] The laws of the country which are seen as unjust and oppressive must be interpreted as they stand. Any undertaking given by the requesting country not to enforce them should be ignored.[47]

This seems to sit uneasily with the fact that, although under S12(2)b the Home Secretary will not return a person accused or convicted of a crime which carries the death penalty in the requesting country, if such a crime does not carry it here, it appears that an assurance that the death penalty will not be applied is sufficient for that person's return.[48]

Conclusion

11–012 The effectiveness of the law on extradition has been facilitated by the restrictions on the political exemption to near vanishing point under the conditions laid down in the two main Acts. The dismantling of the Iron Curtain has also tended to eliminate the political exception. Mutineers on a Polish ship would not, one suspects be treated so leniently today, as with *Kolczynski*. The internationalising of crime, especially banking fraud, drug dealing and international violence, have resulted in most stable countries having reciprocal rights for deportation, although it is noticeable that some states, such as Germany, still baulk at extraditing their own nationals.

Case Study: Former President Augusto Pinochet

11–013 In the Autumn of 1998, the former dictator of Chile (1973 to 1990), Augusto Pinochet, was visiting London for medical treatment when, on October 16, Spain issued an international warrant for his arrest for crimes against humanity and requested his extradition to Spain. Later the same day a stipendiary magistrate issued a provisional warrant under section 8(1) of the Act for Pinochet's arrest for an extradition crime, that of murdering Spanish citizens in Chile between 1973 and 1983. On his arrest Pinochet applied to the Secretary of State to exercise his powers under section 8(4) to cancel the warrant. This he chose not to do. Subsequently, there was a second international warrant accusing Pinochet of torture and conspiracy to torture between 1982 and 1993. Pinochet appealed for judicial review of the two warrants. The divisional court under Bingham L.C.J. found that there was nothing irregular in two warrants being issued but that the murder of Spanish citizens in Chile as opposed to Spain was not an extradition crime and that the first warrant was invalid. They also found that the Home Secretary was right not to interfere in questions of law; any interference by him would blur the legal and ministerial functions. However they supported Pinochet in one important respect, finding that he had immunity from prosecution as he had been Head of State at the time of the alleged offences.[49] On appeal by the Spanish Government and the Commissioner for the Metropolis the House of Lords found against Pinochet[50] on the narrow grounds that actions taken by a former Head of State would continue to enjoy immunity from prosecution for criminal acts undertaken in the exercise of his functions as Head of State. However international Law did not regard torture and the taking of hostages as acts of state and the definition of torture in section 134 (1) of the Criminal Justice Act 1988 placed such acts outside state immunity.

What happened next was as unexpected as it was unprecidented. It was revealed conveniently for Pinochet that Lord Hoffman was a director of Amnesty International Trust, a charity controlled by Amnesty International specifically charged with opposing torture. Given this, a successful challenge was made to a differently–constituted House of Lords[51] which allowed a re-hearing on the grounds of the appearance of possible bias on Lord Hoffman's part.[52]

This rehearing[53] before a bench of seven Law Lords found *inter alia* that torture committed outside the United Kingdom before September 29, 1988, the date of the Criminal Justice Act 1988, was not an extradition crime. Thus any charges of torture or conspiracy to torture against Pinochet were non-extraditable. However, any subsequent torture would be an extradition crime. In these circumstances, there was one charge of torture after the crucial date and that would be sufficient to allow the appeal. Pinochet was never extradited to Spain since the Home Secretary found that he was not mentally competent to stand trial despite sucessful attempts to have the medical reports upon which this decision was made disclosed.[54] Pinochet was subsequently returned to Chile where, much recovered, he received a hero's welcome.

Deportation

Unlike Extradition, Deportation is an administrative act, based on the **11–014** concept of citizenship and right of residence, at the disposal of the Secretary of State. There is no necessity for any criminal offence to have been committed by the person threatened with Deportation and there is no comparable legal process to extradition to be employed in its execution.

The only available remedy against a decision to deport lies in an appeal to an Immigration Adjudicator, habeas corpus and judicial review. A further, critical difference is that no British citizen may be deported.

Citizenship

11–015 Historically, any citizen of the British Empire and Commonwealth was a British citizen, with rights of entry, residence and employment in the United Kingdom. Waves of immigration in the 1950s and 60s of whites from the "old" Commonwealth; blacks from Africa and the Caribbean; Asians from India, Pakistan and East Africa; led to increasing racial tension. An awareness grew that restrictions would need to be placed upon those who previously had been accorded unrestricted rights of entry and residence. It was hoped that this would help prevent race relations becoming even worse. The principal Act defining citizenship and right of residence is the British Nationality Act 1981, which replaced the provisions of previous British Nationality Acts 1948 to 1965. Although most sections of the previous Acts were repealed by the 1981 Act, many of the provisions in that Act derived from the previous ones. The main provision of the Act regarding citizenship was to replace citizenship of the United Kingdom and colonies with three separate and discrete categories of citizenship, each invested with decreasing rights of abode and increasing higher risks of deportation defined by the 1971 Immigration Act, s.1(1).

They are:

1. British Citizen.
2. British Dependent Territories Citizen.
3. British Overseas Citizen.

Category 1 is the only one to have a right of abode in the United Kingdom expressed in the 1971 Act in terms which echo the British passport: "shall be free to live in, and to come and go to and from the United Kingdom without let or hindrance".[55] All other persons are deemed not to have the above rights but:

> ". . . they may live, work and settle in the United Kingdom by permission and subject to such regulations and control of their entry into, stay in and departure from the United Kingdom as is imposed by this Act".[56]

Under section 1(4) of the Act the Secretary of State has wide delegatory powers concerning how the practical application of the 1971 Act should be implemented. Any such rules are laid before Parliament which gives either House 40 days to disapprove. These rules are seen as "just as much a part of the Law of England as the Act itself".[57]

Section 2 of the 1971 Act defining the right of abode in the United Kingdom was substituted by the British Nationality Act 1981, s.39(2) but remains substantially in force. Essentially, only British Citizens and Commonwealth Citizens, who immediately before the commencement of the British Nationality Act were Commonwealth citizens (with the right of abode in the United Kingdom derived from section 2(1)(d) or section 2(2) of this Act as then in force and "has not ceased to be a Commonwealth citizen in the meanwhile")[58] have rights of abode. This is a closed group and not capable of extension.[59]

All other visitors have no rights of abode and fall under section 3 which enumerated the conditions under which they may stay in the United Kingdom.[60] The time of staying may be limited or may be indefinite and, if limited, it may be granted with additional conditions restricting employment or occupation and/or requiring the subject to register with the police. The crucial factor is who can be deported and on what grounds. They are set out in section 3(5) & (6). Under (5) "a person shall be liable to deportation from the United Kingdom . . . if, having only a limited leave to enter or remain, he does not observe a condition attached to the leave or remaining beyond the time limited by the leave; or (b) The Secretary of State deems his deportation to be conducive to the public good; or (c) if another person to whose family he belongs is or has been ordered to be deported.

Section 6 allows for the deportation of those over 17 years of age convicted **11–016**
of an offence punishable by imprisonment provided that, on conviction he is recommended for deportation by a competent court. Generally speaking, this court should give reasons, but the Court of Appeal may supply its own reasons, if the court of first instance does not.[60–61] Section (6) is drafted very widely leaving the Secretary of State with unfettered powers. Historically these powers have been used in a number of distinct sets of circumstances, although these precedents may not be the only cases in which the section might be invoked.

Firstly it has been implemented when, on conviction, a court has not recommended deportation. In such circumstances the Court of Appeal Guidelines given in *R. v. Nazari*[62] would, presumably, be applied. Consideration would be given to the seriousness of the offence; the effect on the offender's family and the political system of the country to which the offender would be deported.[63]

It was found in *R. v. Immigration Appeal Tribunal, ex parte Patel* that, if the immigration laws have been "avoided by a dishonest deception"[64] either to obtain leave to enter or remain, then the public good deportation may be effected. *Patel* also endorsed the marriage of convenience as grounds for a public good deportation.

People whose political views are seen as dangerous or repellent; whose religious beliefs are seen as harmful are among those who are likely to be deported. In 1996, Muhammad al-Masari, a Muslim fundamentalist hostile to the Saudi Arabian regime, was ordered to be deported to Dominica on what appear to be a combination of political and religious grounds. The easiest ground to invoke for a public good deportation is "for reasons of national security". All that is required is a statement from the Home Secretary to that effect. Such a decision is not susceptible to judicial review, unless bad faith or *ultra vires* acts can be demonstrated. The only redress is by appeal to the panel set up to advise the Home Secretary on prospective deportees. This was demonstrated in *R. v. Secretary of State for the Home Department, ex parte Hosenball*,[65] which was applied at the time of the 1991 Gulf War in *R. v. Secretary of State for the Home Department, ex parte Cheblak*.[66] Cheblak was a Lebanese academic lawyer who had worked for the Arab League in London and had been granted indeterminate leave to reside in the United Kingdom, where he had lived since 1979. His academic studies were mostly about Iraq, but seemed ostensibly innocent and as it proved were so. However the Home Secretary issued him with a deportation order. He appealed both on the grounds of habeas corpus and for leave to apply for judicial review. The Appeal court refused to grant a writ of habeas corpus on the grounds that such a writ would not apply since Cheblak was in legal custody according to Schedule 3 of the 1971 Immigration Act, para. 2(4) and that judicial review was not possible as the court could not look behind the Secretary of State's decision once he had invoked the magic formula of national security.

11–017 Such ministerial decisions have fallen foul of the ECHR in the past as in *R. v. Secretary of State for the Home Department, ex parte Chahal*.[67] Chahal was a Sikh militant who was served with a deportation order on the grounds of national security. Once more the Court of Appeal followed *Hosenball* and refused to look behind the Home Secretary's decision. However, in this case there was evidence of previous torture by the Indian authorities and the court took it upon itself to balance the national security grounds against the rights of the individual. Here, they came down on the side of the State and refused leave for judicial review of the minister's decision. In making this judgment, the Court of Appeal took into account that the Home Secretary had consulted the Indian government as to Chahal's future treatment after his deportation to that country.

> "Were he to be charged, the Secretary of State believes that Mr. Chahal would be subject to prosecution for alleged criminal activities not for his political beliefs of expressions. If Mr. Chahal was so charged the Secretary of State is satisfied that he would receive full protection by the Indian government from mistreatment while held in custody".[68]

Subsequently, the case went to the European Court of Human Rights[69] who found in Chahal's favour on the grounds of breaches of Articles 3, 5(4) and 13 of the European Convention of Human Rights. Under Article 3, forbidding torture, the court found that the conduct of a potential deportee was not material if substantial grounds could be shown that the detainee would be at risk of torture in the country to which it was proposed he should be sent. On the facts of the case they found that the Punjab police were a law unto themselves and that the torture of prisoners was a regular occurrence. Further they also pursued Sikh militants outside their home state into parts of India where they had no authority.

The court held under 5(4) of the Convention that although Chahal's detention was lawful there was no effective way that judicial review could be used to end such detention. To make judicial review effective, confidential material relevant to the security of the State may have to be unavoidably used and that some mechanism could be found to use such material in a manner which accommodated legitimate security concerns but also satisfied the need for individual procedural justice. The court made no suggestions how this might be done.

Similarly, under Article 13 of the Convention on the individual's right of **11–018** effective remedy, both judicial review and advisory panel procedures were found to be inadequate remedies for a complaint under Article 3 since it was impossible for a decision to be reviewed under Article 3 with reference solely to the risk to the applicant, without referring to national security considerations.

The above decisions in *Chahal* will impact upon domestic law now the European Convention is imbedded in the Constitution through the Human Rights Act 1998. It compels the domestic courts to abide by Articles 3 and 5(4) which may allow those who espouse violence still to remain in the United Kingdom. In domestic law the Special Immigration Appeals Commission Act 1997 will also apply.[70] It is also noticeable that Article 13 is not one of the articles of the Convention appended in Schedule I of the Human Rights Act, which are incorporated in the Constitution.

Threatened deportations such as *Chahal* seem at first sight to be indistinguishable from extradition, in that the deportee has very little say in to where he is to be returned, often being sent back to his native country where there is a real risk of his receiving inhuman treatment. In *Chahal*, the Court of Appeal considered that they would be at no real risk say in Bombay, but the ECHR found that the Punjabi police paid no attention to state boundaries and that they would, very likely pursue him outside the Punjab. Similarly in *R. v. Secretary of State for the Home Department, ex parte Robinson*,[70–71] the Court of Appeal approved the deportation of a Tamil back to Sri Lanka on the grounds that he would be safe from violence if he remained in Colombo.

The scope of Article 3 of the ECHR has been broadened by the case of **11–019** *D. v. United Kingdom*.[72] Here, the applicant, born in St. Kitts, arrived in the United Kingdom, and was found to be in possession of cocaine. He was refused entry to the United Kingdom and was prosecuted, and on being found guilty he was sentenced to six years' imprisonment. Whilst in prison he was diagnosed as suffering from AIDS. On release in 1996 he was placed in detention prior to his removal to St. Kitts. His physical condition was very poor and it was contended that his removal to St. Kitts would severely shorten his life expectancy and make him vulnerable to a whole range of infections, because of his being accustomed to a high standard of medical care which he would not receive in St. Kitts. The applicant requested that the Home Secretary should allow him to stay in the United Kingdom on compassionate grounds. On refusal by the Chief Immigration Officer, the applicant applied unsuccessfully for leave to apply for judicial review. The Court of Appeal further dismissed his application and he applied to the ECHR. This court found unanimously that the British Government had breached Article 3 of the ECHR on the grounds that the applicant's return to St. Kitts would expose him to conditions of acute mental and physical suffering to the extent that they would constitute inhuman treatment. Despite the *caveats* that this was an exceptional case this decision widens the application of Article 3 to include unintentional suffering not caused by the government of the country to which the applicant is to be deported. It remains to be seen what the full impact of this decision will be.

E.C. Citizens

11–020 E.C. citizens and citizens of the European Economic Area[73] are not British citizens and are, therefore, subject to deportation under section 3(5) of the 1971 Act. However, under E.C. law they have the right to free movement between member state for "economic" purposes—work or establishing business; tourism; medical treatment, etc.,[74] and cannot be deported unless there are "public policy, public security and public health grounds". The law in this respect is still in the process of rationalization, but it seems that a previous conviction of a criminal offence is not *per se* a reason for exclusion on public policy grounds. The public interest ground is pitched high and requires that:

> "previous criminal convictions are relevant only insofar as the circumstances which gave rise to them are evidence of personal conduct constituting a present threat to the requirements of public policy."[75] and there needs to be "a genuine sufficiently serious threat affecting one of the fundamental interests of society".[76]

The recent Court of Appeal case of *B. v. Secretary of State for the Home Department*[76A] indicates how high this ground is pitched. B was born in Sicily in 1955 but had moved to the United Kingdom with his parents when he was seven years old. He was never a British citizen although he married in the United Kingdom and had two children. In 1994 he was convicted of a number of acts of gross indecency and indecent assault on his daughter and was sentenced to five years' imprisonment. On release the Home Secretary issued a deportation order under section 3(5). The Court of Appeal, allowing his appeal citing both E.U. and domestic law, decided that such an action was disproportionate and that his continued residence in the United Kingdom was of real weight under E.C.H.R. Art. 8 allowing him a private family life, which he could not enjoy in Italy. If he were deported there, this would effectively be a form of exile due to his real ties to the United Kingdom and his lack of ties to Italy.

It may also be difficult for any country in the EEA to deport an EEA citizen from another country, unless some form of sanction is also taken against nationals of the former country for similar behaviour to that which makes that person liable to deportation. In *Adoni & Cournaille v. Belgian State*,[77] two French "waitresses" who appeared to have "undesirable morals" were issued with deportation notices from Belgium. Their deportation was not based upon any criminal activity, but purely by reason of their conduct, suspected prostitution. In this case the European Court found as above that such conduct would not give rise to repressive measures against Belgian citizens and therefore it should not give rise to such measures against nationals of other member states.

Appeals & Challenges

Part II of the 1971 Act establishes a system of appeal first to an adjudicator and then if dissatisfied with that determination, by either side to an Appeal Tribunal. The 1999 Act has varied these conditions but the principles remain the same. **11–021**

All those threatened with deportation are entitled to appeal in this way except:

1. Those recommended for deportation by a court which has found the deportee guilty of an offence. They are dealt with under the Immigration rules 1994; 373 under which an order to deport is stayed prior to a conventional appeal against conviction and sentence.
2. Those who are to be deported on public good or national security grounds who now have a right of appeal under the 1997 Act.

Thus, the cases which come before the appeal procedure are relatively simple, since both the criminal and the controversial are removed from its remit.

Habeas Corpus and Judicial Review

These remain as remedies as well as the above procedure under the 1971 and 1999 Acts. Habeas corpus is only available if the Home Secretary has acted *ultra vires* and when any detention is thus seen as unlawful. As noted in *Cheblak* above, detention under the blanket of national security is seen as lawful and therefore not liable to challenge on the grounds of habeas corpus. **11–022**

The most egregious case in which an application for habeas corpus was made is *R. v. Governor of Brixton Prison, ex parte Soblen*.[78] Soblen, a United States national, had been sentenced to life imprisonment in the USA for conspiracy to obtain and deliver defence secrets to the USSR. When released on appeal, he fled to Israel, whence he was forcibly deported to Athens and placed on a regular El Al flight to New York via London. Even before Soblen landed in London, the Home Secretary had instructed that he should be given notice of refusal to land in the United Kingdom on the grounds of Soblen's presence being undesirable and not in the public interest. On the aeroplane from Athens Soblen deliberately inflicted knife wounds on himself which necessitated his removal to hospital on his landing in London. Subsequently, El Al was instructed to remove Soblen to the USA, which it did not do. Almost contemporaneously, *The Times* reported that the United States Government has requested the United Kingdom Government to return Soblen to the USA. In 1963 conspiracy to commit espionage was not an extradition crime. A further deportation order was issued to Soblen and the Home Office announced in a press statement that it was the intention of the Home Secretary to deport Soblen to the USA. At this point, Soblen, now in Brixton Prison, made an application for habeas corpus on the grounds that the home Secretary's actions were *ultra vires* and that, particularly, the deportation order was a sham, being issued for the unlawful purpose of extraditing a political fugitive convicted of a non–extradition offence. The court of first instance dismissed the application and Soblen appealed to the Court of Appeal. In the interim, Soblen had expressed a desire to be deported to Czechoslovakia, which had indicated its willingness to accept him. The Court of Appeal found that there was no evidence of the Home Secretary having an ulterior motive in returning Soblen to the USA and that such a deportation was not at the request of the USA, for:

> "The evidence does not show that this is anything other than a genuine deportation. The United Kingdom Government were from the beginning for good reasons wishing and trying to procure removal of the applicant from the United Kingdom to the United States of America, being the country to which he belongs. The United Kingdom had good reasons, apart from any representations eventually made, or indeed made at any time, by the United States' Government".[79]

Further, the Home Secretary did not need to consider deporting Soblen to Czechoslovakia, having an unfettered discretion over where to send him. On these grounds, the Court of Appeal rejected and approved the deportation order. Soblen committed suicide before it could be carried out.

Soblen can be seen as the mirror image of *Kolczynski* occurring in the febrile atmosphere of the Cold War. However, it raises again, the general, unresolved, question that, if deportation is a "sham" and equivalent to "deportation by the back door" it may be possible to have the Home Secretary's decision judicially reviewed on the grounds of bad faith or *Wednesbury* unreasonableness. Once again, if the blanket of national security is invoked the courts will be reluctant to look behind it, as with *Hosenball*[80] above. the principle of which was applied in *Cheblak*:

> "When the public interest requires that information be kept confidential, it may outweigh even the public interest in the administration of justice".[81]

Conclusions

The legal nature of Immigration and Deportation has radically altered in the past three decades as a result of three separate, but related, social and economic trends which have had a profound effect on the law. The first was the continuing public opinion that the United Kingdom had accepted and was accepting too many immigrants, especially from the "new" Commonwealth and that they could not be readily assimilated into British society. It was suggested that such immigrants were not truly British on the grounds that they might cheer for the wrong country at a Cricket Test match. The second factor was the United Kingdom joining the European Union in 1972. This radically altered the statue of E.U. citizens, their rights of residence and employment in the United Kingdom according to the Treaty of Rome. The final factor, linked to the previous two, was the denial of residence rights to Commonwealth citizens, except under very restricted circumstances. **11–023**

From these three elements, most of the legal problems have arisen. Cases such as *Patel* are comprehensible given the desire to gain entry to a country where the deportees' relations live in comparative prosperity. The worst aspects of Deportation law are seen in its apparently arbitrary implementation in cases where the subject has committed no crime, yet is granted fewer rights than someone who has and is threatened with extradition. In cases such as *Hosenball*, *Cheblak*, *Chahal* and *Robinson* politics and international relations weigh heavily upon the disinterested judicial process. Although judges would deny the influence of any overt political pressure or a desire to placate powerful or friendly governments, in realpolitik it must be a factor. The new legislation in the 1997 Special Immigration Appeals Act has gone some way in combating this. The 1999 Act giving a unified single right of appeal for both asylum seekers and those threatened with deportation may be faster, but not necessarily fairer.[82]

Asylum

Nowhere has the dilemma of balancing an "open door" policy, with its risk of admitting bogus applicants, versus the restrictive policy, with its risk of deporting the legitimate applicant, been seen in a more striking light than in the area of political asylum. In recent years, the tendency has been towards a restrictive regime, reinforced by three particular acts, the Asylum and Immigration Appeals Act 1993, the Asylum and Immigration Act 1996 and the Immigration and Asylum Act 1999. The 1996 Act had three main objectives, in the words of the then Home Secretary, Michael Howard: **11–024**

> "... first to strengthen our asylum procedures so that bogus claims and appeals can be dealt with more quickly; secondly to combat immigration racketeering through stronger powers; and thirdly, to reduce economic incentives, which attract people to come to this country in breach of our immigration laws".[83]

These acts have differentiated asylum seekers from those merely seeking not to be deported. Although they have no longer have a separate appeal structure of "special adjudicators" and an appeal tribunal, they may be still be sent to a "safe" third country while their appeal is considered. There is a strong suspicion that much asylum law is motivated, not by the moral requirement to do justice, but the pecuniary need to save government money. This is demonstrated in the parts of the Acts which set out deliberately to deny asylum seekers financial support, especially sections 8, 9, 10 and 11 of the 1996 Act, which excludes most of them from taking up employment, receiving housing benefit or assistance, receiving child benefit or any social security benefits at all.[84] Sections 95 to 98 of the 1999 Act further reduce the lot of asylum seekers by introducing a voucher system. They no longer receive more than a small cash allowance—the rest is paid in vouchers which are only exchangable for necessities at specified shops. Further, asylum seekers can be dispersed over the United Kingdom against their will under section 101 of the 1999 Act. The intention behind this is to discourage "economic asylum seekers". Since any legitimate applicant will have an economic element in his request, for persecution often goes with poverty, this seems unduly harsh and these provisions have been challenged to a limited success in the courts. Section 9 of the 1996 Act cannot be implemented retrospectively for asylum seekers resident in the United Kingdom before the Act came into force.[85] On the other hand, asylum seekers are obliged to pay council tax, even if they are impecunious, since no express provision is made in the act to exclude them from paying.[86] It has also been decided that an asylum seeker can obtain employment pending his appeal against deportation when he is not in receipt of social service benefits on the grounds that without an income he would not have the funds to pursue his case.[87]

As stated above, there is no "right of asylum":

> ". . . although it is easy to assume that the appellant invokes a 'right of asylum' no such right exists. Neither under international nor English municipal law does a fugitive have any direct right to insist on being received by a country of refuge".[88]

The decision to permit asylum seekers to enter or stay is one of executive discretion mitigated by statute as to which country unsuccessful applicants may be returned.

11–025 All asylum claims are based on a ruling that to deport an asylum seeker would place the United Kingdom Government in breach of the Geneva Convention relating to the Status of Refugees of 1951 and the Protocol of that Convention.[89] To be classed as a refugee under the Convention, the asylum seeker must be a person who:

> ". . . owing to a well-founded fear of being persecuted for reasons of race, religion, nationality, membership of a particular social group or political opinion, is outside the country of his nationality and is unable or, owing to

> such fear, is unwilling to avail himself of that protection of that country; or who, not having a nationality and being outside the country of his former habitual residence as a result of such events, is unable or, owing to such fear, is unwilling to return to it".[90]

and about whom Article 1F of the Convention does not apply, covering those who have:

> "(a) Committed a crime against peace, a war crime, or a crime against humanity, as defined in the international instruments drawn up to make provision in respect of such crimes.
> (b) he has committed a serious non-political crime outside the country of refuge prior to his admission into that country as a refugee.
> (c) he has been guilty of acts contrary to the purposes and principles of the United Nations".[91]

The Case of *T. v. The Secretary of State for the Home Department* again gives us the latest House of Lords thinking on this Convention and its effect on domestic law. Here, there was no doubt that T had a well-founded fear of persecution if he was returned to Algeria. However, the House of Lords decided that his crime fell into the category of Article 1F and therefore, T was not a refugee according to the Convention. A further complication was that no other country apart from Algeria was willing to receive him upon deportation and therefore the authorities would have no option but to deport him there.

Fear of prosecution has to be within the parameters set by the convention and the applicant needs to demonstrate that he falls into a particular racial, religious, national, social or political group to be successful. It is not enough to be tortured when that appears to be the norm in one's home country. In *Ward v. The Secretary of State for the Home Department*,[92] the applicant had claimed in an earlier, unsuccessful, application for asylum, to have been tortured by the Peruvian police on suspicion of being a member of the Sendero Luminoso (the Shining Path) terrorist group. Her initial application was refused on the grounds that:

> "The Secretary of State considered that the problems you have faced, even if true, amounted to nothing more than the sort of *random difficulties faced by many thousands of people in Peru*".[93]

Thus it appears that if violence is endemic and arbitrary an appeal can fail. However, endemic and calculated violence does not imply that an applicant may succeed, either. Similar grounds have been used for the return of Tamils to Sri Lanka, as with *R. v. Secretary of State for the Home Department, ex parte Robinson* where, as stated above, the applicant was to be returned to Colombo. Although it was admitted that violence against Tamils was commonplace in the north of Sri Lanka, Lord Woolf M.R. was of the opinion that Colombo was "not found to be not safe".[94]

The definition of a "particular social group" has also been made in a **11–026**
highly restrictive sense. The Court of Appeal when faced with the Deportation of a midwife employed by the Algerian Ministry of Health, who

claimed that by giving her clients contraceptive advice, she was in danger of attack from Muslim Fundamentalists, sided with the Home Secretary against her. The grounds were that she was not a member of a "particular social group" liable to attack.[95] The court held that government employed mid wives, although they had a common employer; could not be such a group: "The expression 'particular social group' does not in my view cover a body linked only by the work they do".[96]

This exemption does, however apply to Pakistani women in real fear of the death penalty imposed for adultery by Shiria law. Two cases[97] decided together by the Court of Appeal showed the reluctance of the courts to define new areas of this category on the grounds that "solitary individuals" did not exhibit "cohesiveness, co-operation or interdependence"[98] which were seen as the prerequisites required to be defined as belonging to a particular social group. However the House of Lords reversed this judgment in a courageous decision[99]:

> "Domestic abuse of women and violence towards women is prevalent in Pakistan. That is also true of many other countries and by itself it does not give rise to a claim to refugee status. The distinctive feature of this case is that in Pakistan women are unprotected by the state: discrimination against women in Pakistan is partly tolerated by the state and partly sanctioned by the state". (*Per* Lord Steyn)

All appeal for asylum on the grounds of the 1951 Convention must be made to any of the adjudicators appointed by the Lord Chancellor. It used to be the case[1] that an asylum claimant could not be removed from the United Kingdom prior to the final decision of the Home Secretary. Section 2 of the 1996 Act removes this right in certain (and probably most) circumstances under which a person can be sent to a "safe third country" as long as the Home Secretary has certified that certain conditions have been satisfied.[2] The person must not be a national or citizen of the country to which he is to be sent; that there should be no threat to his life or his liberty in that country by reason of his race, religion, nationality, social group membership or political opinion and that the government of the safe third country would not send him to another country which would be unsafe. Since other such countries often have similar laws it is possible for a person in these circumstances to be further deported from that safe third country to another, and then to another, etc., in an unedifying version of pass the parcel. The procedure of expedited appeal applies even if the asylum seeker has made a claim for asylum prior to the 1996 Act coming into force.[3]

11–027 An appeal against such certification is available[4] on the grounds that the criteria set out in section 2(2) of the 1996 Act have not be complied with. This appeal takes precedent over any actual deportation decision and must be adjudged before any substantive appeal can be made. This further delays the uncertainty of the asylum seeker. Further, if the applicant is to be sent to an European Union country or one on a list designated by the Home Secretary[5] the appeal can only be made from that country to which the asylum seeker is sent.

Appeals have been made, particularly by those sent to France. Before the 1996 Act special adjudicators had often held that France was not a safe third country on the grounds that asylum seekers, especially Algerians, might not have a proper opportunity to have their claims determined in accordance with French law and the 1951 convention. This was the claim made in *R. v. Secretary of State for the Home Department, ex parte Canbolat*.[6] Canbolat was a Turkish Kurd who arrived in Britain from France and sought asylum on the grounds that she feared persecution in Turkey. The Home Secretary issued a deportation certificate following section 2(2) of the AIA 1996, authorising her return to France as a safe third country. After an unsuccessful attempt for leave for judicial review, the Court of Appeal found that before the Secretary of State should send an asylum seeker to a safe third country, he should satisfy himself that there was no real risk to the applicant in being sent there as long as his decision was reasonable. In this case it was, because normally the French immigration courts functioned fairly and:

> "The unpredictability of human behaviour or the remote possibility of changes in administrative law or procedures which there is no reason to anticipate would not be a real risk".[7]

On these grounds the application was refused.

However, the House of Lords took a principled stand in *R. v. Secretary of State for* the *Home Department, ex parte Adan & others*[8] where they found that if safe third countries restrict the interprtation of the Convention in such a way as "persecution" only covered conduct attributable to a state, then asylum seekers threatened with violence from non-State bodies should not be sent there.

Substantive asylum appeals have to be made to an adjudicator who **11–028**
decides on the merits of each individual case. There is an appeal from the adjudicator's decision to the Immigration Appeal Tribunal except for claims "without foundation". These are enumerated in paragraph 5 of Schedule 2 of the 1993 Act, as amended in section 1 of the 1996 Act. The intention behind this emendation was to extend the special appeals procedure to expedite claims for asylum under the "fast track procedure" eliminating the appeal to the tribunal. Under this system asylum seekers from countries which are under section 5(2) "designated in an order made by the Secretary of State by statutory instrument as a country or territory in which, it appears to him that there is in general no serious risk of persecution"[9] are susceptible to the "fast track" procedure. This list was based on those countries "who generate significant number of claims in the United Kingdom, and that a very high proportion of claims prove to be unfounded".[10]

In addition, the absence of a country from the list does not imply a lack of safety; it merely demonstrates that this is a country which does not feature largely in United Kingdom asylum applications and therefore the

Government has not taken a view one way or the other. This seems to suggest that a bogus applicant from a country not on the list will have a better chance of asylum than a legitimate one from a country on the list. Others who are denied an appeal to the Immigration Appeal Tribunal are those who have a fear of persecution, which may be irrelevant, unfounded or outdated; are recommended for deportation after conviction of a crime; those who base their claim on fraud or whose claims are frivolous or vexatious.[11]

Despite all the repressive and hasty actions embodied in this fast track procedure it has not markedly accelerated the rate at which cases are dealt with, neither has it shortened the ordeal of those waiting for decisions, often in unpleasant custodial conditions. In addition there is a risk of confrontation with E.C. law, as with *Chahal*, and the Human Rights Bill will undoubtedly have an impact. However, cases which have reached the European Court of Human Rights have often been decided in a similar way to domestic courts. Concern over illegal immigrants and bogus asylum seekers is a factor all over Europe and the courts appear to be in consensus in this area. In *Rehmat Khan v. United Kingdom*,[12] the European Court took a robust view rejecting the applicant's appeal on the grounds that there was an "absence of any further grounds for believing the applicant was under a continued threat"[13] especially as his political party, the PPP, was now in power in Pakistan. The ECHR made no observation as to the risk if he was the supporter of another and appears to have made its decision on similar grounds to *Canbolat*, above and the 1996 Act.

11–029 The House of Lords came to a similar decision in *Adan v. Secretary of State for the Home Department*,[14] where they decided that an applicant for asylum needed to demonstrate a current fear of persecution; a past or historical fear being insufficient, and that the dangers to life inherent in a civil war did not amount to persecution. In this case, the applicant had fled from Somalia in June 1988 at which time he had a well-founded fear of persecution from the then government. He arrived in the United Kingdom with his family in October 1990, was refused asylum, but all were granted exceptional leave to stay. Mr Adan wished to have his status confirmed as an asylum seeker because there were certain benefits to this status which were not available for those who had merely exceptional leave to remain. The Lords allowed the Home Secretary's appeal on the above grounds indicating that the Government of Somalia had changed and therefore the applicant had no current fear of persecution. They observed that the wording of Article 1A of the Convention is always couched in the present tense. Further they found that the Convention was not drafted in a manner to allow those fleeing from civil war to fall under the Convention. It was submitted that everyone involved in a civil war was subject to the ordinary risks of that conflict and therefore, a person who was at no greater risk than any other should not be able to claim the protection of the Convention. Such a decision requires a nice judgment as to when the persecution of a minority becomes a civil war rather than putting down a rebellion and when does a persecuted group become a faction in such a war, as well as some historical crystal ball gazing. If one government is superseded by another, then it is not beyond the bounds of possibility that it, too, may be superseded. It is debatable whether the courts should become involved in such metaphysical speculation. One is left with the strong suspicion that such conclusions are giving legal disguise to public policy.

Since *Re M*,[15] it has been possible to find a minister in contempt of court in his official capacity, for removing a person from the United Kingdom against the instructions of the Court. In this case, M a Zairian, came to the United Kingdom in 1990 seeking political asylum. His request was rejected by the Home Secretary and in March 1991 his application for Judicial Review on that decision was refused. On May 1, 1991, the day he was to be removed back to Zaire, he made two applications; one to the Court of Appeal and after this was unsuccessful a second one to the High Court with new legal representatives on what were claimed to be fresh grounds. The High Court judge indicated he wished the applicant's deportation to be postponed prior to the consideration of the new case. Home Office officials sent M back to Zaire that night, in apparent ignorance of the judge's instructions. On hearing this, the judge made an *ex parte* order requiring the Home Secretary to return M safely to the United Kingdom. The Home Secretary, claiming Crown Immunity, canceled M's return. Subsequently the Court of Appeal found the Home Secretary personally guilty of contempt. The House of Lords endorsed the contempt ruling but in the Home Secretary's official capacity. Thus, even the Home Secretary is bound by the timetable and conditions set by the courts. He must, if required, have an asylum seeker returned to the United Kingdom for consideration of his case. How practical such a requirement might be is open to question. A persecuted person returned to the country of his persecution is hardly likely to be returned safely from it on the request of the Home Secretary. If that person is killed or imprisoned or tortured on his return, he and the United Kingdom government have the bleak consolation that his request for asylum was legitimate, rather like the suspected witch who drowned in the ducking stool.

The impact of *Chahal* was such that one of the first Acts of the new Labour Government, the Special Immigration Appeals Act 1997, for which *Chahal* "provides the basis for the Bill",[16] was specifically drafted to take away the decision making process over national security asylum and deportation cases from the three advisers and put them on a firmer, fairer basis. The new Special Immigration Appeals Commission (SIAC) has replaced the Appeals Tribunal for appeals against the decisions of an adjudicator in sections 13, 14 and 15 of the 1971 Immigration Act.[17] These cover refusal of leave to enter the United Kingdom; variation or refusal to vary limited leave to stay and application of a deportation order, except, in all cases in which these actions are executed "in the public good". This Act has made the grounds of deportation by virtue of national security susceptible to review by the new Commission.[18] Such a commission will hopefully obviate such errors of fact as were misinterpreted in *Cheblak*. The SIAC will also adjudicate on EEA citizens' appeals.[19]

11–030 For asylum seekers the new procedure will be applied instead of the special adjudicator procedure, except for those who fall under paragraph 6 of Schedule 2 of the Immigration and Asylum Act 1993. This again refers to those whose exclusion, departure or deportation is in the interests of national security.[20] The SIAC, on allowing an appeal, will give directions as it thinks fit to effect its decision and such a decision will be binding on the Secretary of State or any other official.[21] This is a radical departure as it removes the final decision from the Secretary of State and presumably from the political arena. The SIAC's decision is appealable on a question of law, with leave of the SIAC, or if such leave is withheld, that of the Court of Appeal.[22]

The procedure may examine the reasons for a previous decision without giving the appellant full particulars[23] but it will make provisions to receive a summary of the evidence taken in his absence.[24] A person may also be appointed to represent the appellant where he and his legal representative are excluded.[25]

These provisions go some way to addressing the concerns of the European Court of Human Rights to a fair trial as expressed in *Chahal*, but the independence of the Commission is still open to serious doubt.

Comments and Conclusions on Asylum

11–031 The laws and rules covering asylum have become more restrictive in recent years. Successive United Kingdom governments, keen to be seen to be "tough" on terrorism and international crime, are also embarrassed by Tamil Asylum seekers taking their clothes off outside the Law Courts and Pakistanis threatening to starve themselves to death. The long waiting lists for appeals and the poor quality of the accommodation in which some asylum applicants are detained for long periods have exacerbated the problem. Rather than let more applicants into the United Kingdom, governments have simplified and expedited the process of deportation. Potential asylum seekers, such as Romanian Gypsies, have been shown videos of how bad the lot of asylum seekers is in the United Kingdom, with the hope of dissuading them from coming here. This approach has been part of a concerted European effort, which has had a measure of success. According to the latest Eurostat Asylum Report for 1995 the numbers of asylum seekers in the E.U., Norway and Switzerland numbered some 290,000 compared with some 325,000 in 1994, a decrease of some 11 per cent. There were fewer from Yugoslavia but the numbers of those from Turkey, Iraq and Pakistan showed an increase.

The Republic of Ireland and Northern Ireland

11–032 The relationship between the United Kingdom[26] and the Republic of Ireland has always been close, with movement between the two unrestricted by any passport or immigration controls. This is reflected in specific legislation which eases the extradition of those charged or convicted of crimes in the Republic which has reciprocal legislation for the return to the Republic of those charged or convicted of crimes in the United Kingdom.[27] The positive effects of this legislation have often been marred by the often strained relationship between the two countries over the problems in Northern Ireland. These are exacerbated by the derogation of the Province from some of the articles of the European Convention on Human Rights and the past application of Exclusion Orders, which could expel British Citizens from the mainland of the United Kingdom and Northern Ireland. The main legislation for extradition to the Republic is the Backing of Warrants (Republic of Ireland) Act 1965.[28] Under this Act, if a warrant issued by a court in the Republic, which carries with it a summarily prison sentence of six months or is an indictable offence, is endorsed in the United Kingdom by a magistrate after a hearing at which the police state on oath that the subject of the warrant is in the magistrate's area, then the magistrate merely endorses the warrant. It can then be executed as if it were a warrant issued by the magistrate for an offence under his jurisdiction.[29] There is no authority to look behind the warrant but the usual safeguards are included, such as that no order will be made if it appears that the elements of the offence on the warrant do not correspond to any offence in the United Kingdom.[30] Section 2(2)(a) allows for a "political" defence which, to be effective, must be shown to the satisfaction of the justices. However, the Suppression of Terrorism Act 1978 and other legislation mentioned above disposes of most of such claims. If a magistrate fails to make an order, then a crown court may make an order for a statement of case by the magistrate for the opinion of the High Court. On the other hand, the accused may make an application for a writ of habeas corpus, but cannot adduce any new evidence on at least the political point.[31]

Exclusion Orders

There are two Acts which used to enforce Exclusion Orders. They are the **11–033** Prevention of Terrorism Act 1974 and the substantive act with the same title of 1989.[32] They were the result of continued attempts to try to solve the violent unrest in Northern Ireland by sending those who may sympathise or promote such policies, but against whom no criminal acts are found, back to Northern Ireland or the Republic. There were three types of Exclusion Order which applied to "acts of Terrorism connected with the affairs of Northern Ireland".[33] In all cases they applied for three years but could be extended.

1. Exclusion order from the United Kingdom.[34] This was the most severe and could not be employed against British Citizens. It could be served on anyone whom the Secretary of State was satisfied had been "concerned in the commission, preparation or instigation of acts of terrorism",[35] and was attempting to enter the

United Kingdom with those purposes. If the person was normally resident in the United Kingdom, the "the Secretary of State shall have regard to the question whether the person's connection with any country or territory outside the United Kingdom is such as to make it appropriate that such an order should be made".[36] In the context, this is a coded way of saying that such a person would be sent to the Republic.

2. Exclusion from Northern Ireland. This section 6 allowed any person to be excluded from Northern Ireland. The conditions for exclusion were similar to those for the United Kingdom[37] and the Act seemed largely drafted to deport citizens of the Republic and Northern Ireland Republicans, with British Citizenship, back to the Republic. In this situation a British Citizen who "is at the time ordinarily resident in Northern Ireland and has been ordinarily resident in Northern Ireland throughout the last three years"[38] or was excluded from Great Britain, could not have an order made against him.
3. Exclusion from Great Britain. Section 5 allowed any person, for reasons as with sections 6 and 7 above to be excluded from Great Britain. Once more as with section 7 above there is a provision for "connection with any country or territory" which implies that British citizens may be sent to Northern Ireland or the Republic. Once more there is a three-year residency provision—also, anyone excluded from Northern Ireland could not be sent there.

Unlike deportation, the family of someone subject to an Exclusion Order could not be excluded.

Once any of the above orders are made the procedure outlined in Schedule 2 of the Act was enforced. Section 1 defined the period of the order; three years, which may be extended after its end or terminated by the Secretary of State at any time. Anyone about to have an exclusion order against them was entitled to notice under section 2 of the above and has the right to make representations. He was allowed seven days in which objections may be made to the order; or if he was outside the relevant territory of exclusion or he had voluntarily left it within seven days, he had 14 days to appeal. Such representations were made to a suitable person nominated by the Secretary of State and he could request a personal interview with that adviser.[39] If the person was in Great Britain then that interview must be granted, if outside "if it is reasonably practical"[40] in an appropriate country—Northern Ireland, the Republic or Great Britain depending on from which country the person was to be excluded.

The person may be kept in custody pending the decision of the Secretary of State,[41] the making of which decision "shall take into account everything which appears to him to be relevant",[42] in particular the advice of the adviser, representations of the applicant and the Schedule 2 interview.

However, as with Deportation, the Secretary of State could take into account other matters without telling the adviser or the applicant what they are. The Secretary of State was under no obligation to give reasons which makes any challenge practically impossible. Thus, judicial review was effectively prevented and would be usually blocked by the usual national security claim which prevents the necessity for the Secretary of State having to give reasons.[43]

One case in this area, that of *R. v. Gallagher*,[44] in which the applicant sought reasons for his exclusion, none being given, along with the name of his adviser, who was not identified—was sent by the Court of Appeal to the European Court of Justice. The substance of this was a request for a finding on Article 9(1) of Directive 64/221 of the EEC, dated February 25, 1964, which states that foreign nationals should not be expelled from a member country before "a competent authority has given its opinion" and that, although the competent authority may be appointed by the Secretary of State it had to have "absolute independence". The ECJ found that the article had to be applied although, despite this, the identity of that authority need not be known to the applicant or the court.[45] **11–034**

In *R. v. Secretary of State for the Home Department, ex parte Adams*,[46] it was held that the Home Secretary's decision to enforce an Exclusion Order was judicially reviewable under "the most exceptional circumstances".[47] In this case, Gerry Adams, the leader of Sinn Fein, had been invited by Tony Benn to speak at Westminster in the Grand Committee Room of the House of Commons. This was a green and red flag to many a Tory bull. Subsequently the Home Secretary made an Exclusion Order under section 5(a). Adams mounted a challenge, stating that the order and the refusal to revoke it were unlawful, constituting an act for an improper purpose and unreasonable and unlawful under E.C. law in breach of Article 8(a)(1)(b) of the E.C. Treaty, concerning the rights of individuals to know the reasons for executive decisions. The court found that the purpose of the Exclusion Order was, in part, to save the Government potential political embarrassment, but it had no means of knowing the other reasons because the national security issue raised by the Government prevented it looking behind the Order. The Court appeared to be saying that merely to save governmental embarrassment would be unlawful, but here there were other stronger reasons for the Home Secretary's actions and the court would have to accept their bona fides. They referred the E.C. aspect to the ECJ for a ruling on the applicant's right to know reasons.

Conclusions and Comments on Exclusion

These Orders rose out of the fact that the tripartite relationship of London, Belfast and Dublin was *sui generis*. Extradition was always possible to the Republic but not to Northern Ireland, and Deportation was not possible given the reciprocal rights of the citizens of the two countries. Therefore, Exclusion was seen as the only pragmatic way of isolating those who were **11–035** seen as the perpetrators and supporters of violence and unrest. The major concern for civil libertarians is that there was no need for any criminal charge in either of the three territories, for an Order to be enforced. Indeed, if a crime had been committed, then extradition or simple, straightforward arrest would apply. Thus, this draconian measure, which would divide families and put a strain on Anglo-Irish relations, is seen as an arbitrary administrative act incapable of thorough legal monitoring or correction. Governments defended the orders arguing that they need a quasi-deportation law on the grounds of national security and public interest. They rebutted their failure to attempt to pursue any criminal conviction by claiming that the most dangerous terrorists are those against whom nothing criminal can be proved or against whom the evidence they have would be inadmissible in court. Such a reluctance to expose their information to forensic examination may lie in the sources of their intelligence: the intelligence agencies, special branch and informers. All governments would be naturally reluctant to expose these to the light of day. Still, given the above there is a strong prima facie case that the Orders could have been challenged successfully in the ECJ or the ECHR. The new Labour Government promised an early review of the system, so on October 30, 1997, the then Home Secretary, Jack Straw, announced to the House of Commons that, having in mind the opinion of Viscount Colville, who in his report called Exclusion Orders "draconian", he was revoking all 12 remaining orders still extant. He continued that he was "minded" to let them lapse when the legislation again came before the House in 1998.[48] Remembering that what a minister has in mind he can just as easily put out of mind, it remains to be seen if this promise is fulfilled. Although there had been no Orders made subsequent to this statement, there was a suspicion that unless or until a peaceful solution to Ulster is arrived at, this unfortunate form of internal exile may continue. This is what effectively happened in the Terrorism Act 2000, when the orders finally lapsed. If the power-sharing agreement in Northern Ireland collapses we may yet see the reintroduction of similar orders. For this reason and for the very authoritarian nature of these orders they are of more than historical interest and are included here.

Conclusions

11–036 The law in this chapter is a field on which contending elements of national and individual interests, international alliances and trade, national security, public good, politics and morality meet. Not only is domestic law involved but that of the United Nations, the E.C. and other countries, as well as International Conventions. Given these it is hardly surprising that the law here often is less than Olympian and has to descend to the *agora*. A recent case, much reported in the press in 1996 but not legally noted, that of the Saudi dissident and Muslim fundamentalist, Dr Muhammad al-Masari, may serve as a useful example to illustrate this febrile mix.

Masari had long held contrary views to the ruling clan in Saudi Arabia, often resorting to robust personal insults towards King Faud and other members of his family whilst inciting revolution against them. After being detained and tortured he fled to Britain in 1994, where he continued his attack by way of faxes sent to Saudi Arabia. He also founded an organisation of fellow dissidents: The Committee for the Defence of Legitimate Rights. The British Government was under considerable diplomatic pressure to silence him and if possible to return him to Saudi Arabia. The King had directly raised the issue with the Foreign Secretary on his visit to Saudi Arabia in 1995, at a time when negotiations for the sale of British arms to that country had reached a delicate position. Saudi Arabia was in the previous year, 1994, one of Britain's biggest customers for armaments, buying in that year some £1.5 billion of British goods. Thus, some important sections of the United Kingdom economy were heavily dependent on Saudi goodwill.

Fearing the displeasure of an ally and also, legitimately distrusting Dr al-Masari, the Home Secretary issued him with deportation papers on January 4, 1996, with the intention of deporting him to the Caribbean island of Dominica, which he designated as a "safe haven" for the good, fax-sending doctor. The Prime Minister of Dominica had personally stated that Dr al-Masari would be accepted there. Coincidentally, the United Kingdom Government had just announced a large increase in its overseas aid to Dominica. Dominica was chosen since al-Masari had previously been successful in establishing that the Yemen was not a safe haven for him to be sent to and the United Kingdom government was at a loss as to his destination. Dominica seemed the ideal solution, except for al-Masari who had never heard of it before, and the inhabitants of the island who threatened a general strike if al-Masari had the temerity to land there. On appeal, al-Masari won on the grounds that the Home Secretary had not considered the effective safety of Dominica and he was granted a four-year stay. Much fear was expressed that this would be economically disastrous for British companies. Some indeed, let forth howls of complaint and threats of redundancies; MPs of all shades fumed and fretted and many balance sheets and annual reports of companies trading with Saudi Arabia found the good doctor a convenient scapegoat for lowered profits and sales. In deep and sincere gratitude for his being allowed to remain, Dr al-Masari issued a condemnation of Jews and the state of Israel to the effect that the Jews should be eliminated and Israel obliterated. This tirade was voiced in such extreme terms that the CPS considered prosecution under the Race Relations Act. His opinions were, ironically, hardly different from those held by the Saudi regime he wished to supersede. He appeared on *Have I Got News for You*, was dismissed as leader of his Committee and sank into obscurity. The Saudi Government said they would take no retaliatory action against the United Kingdom or British companies and trade and diplomacy went back to normal.

11–037 In this case the law showed a commendably disinterested concern for someone who was not a particularly deserving cause but who had legal rights to free speech, since none of his diatribes were against English law. Judge Pearl showed formidable strength of purpose against the then Home Secretary and went as far as he could to show his displeasure at Michael Howard's pusillanimous actions. If such a stand had led to disastrous consequences to British firms would it have been seen as so principled? These are questions of economic and ethics but they are ones that have sometimes to be answered one way or the other. Does the loss of British jobs weigh more heavily than the right of some dissident bigot to send faxes against a corrupt regime which happens to be our ally or is free speech such a principle that it is absolute? Many commentators stated that they would be happy to see al-Masari remain but to keep silent. The courts rightly rebutted this on the grounds that although free speech was not an absolute right of asylum seekers, it would be illegal and unenforceable to compel his silence.

Fortunately, few cases have the complexity and publicity of *al-Masari* but almost all have this mixture of Politics law and morality. The *al-Masari* case affected the format of the Terrorism Act 2000. Under this terrorism is defined very widely in sections 1 and 2 and the first list of proscribed organisations which came into force on March 29, 2001 demonstrated the wide net the Act casts.[49] How much membership of such organisations will lead to accelerated extradition or deportation remains to be seen.

EXTRADITION

11–038 Extradition has seen such a narrowing of the political exemption as to have become almost automatic, if a case can be made. Even here, as in *Gilmore*, the courts take a principled line as far as the 1873 list of extradition crimes is concerned. A universal determination to take drastic action against terrorism has further strengthened extradition procedures to the extent that almost no challenge is allowed on the substance of any charge. It can be argued that returning people to countries with no right of habeas corpus and little prospect of a foreseeable trial should require at least some form of examination by the magistrate on some points such as alibi evidence. The Home Secretary has the final word and may prevent extradition on the unjust or oppressive grounds.[50] Similarly the courts are naturally reluctant to look behind any conditions to which the receiving country will bind itself, its bona fides are usually accepted since there is little the judiciary can do to see they are obeyed. However there are cases where such judicial impotence is either cowardice or naiveté and there is an argument for taking a strong judicial line as in the Hong Kong cases of *Osman* and *Lee*, mentioned above. The claim that the fate of such persons is a "political" matter, rather than one for judicial consideration, is disingenuous.

DEPORTATION

This area of law has been codified, in recent years, by Acts of Parliament with the intention of making the United Kingdom inhospitable to those who have no right of residence here. There is little doubt that the recent decades have seen a drastic increase in illegal and spurious immigrants. They have caused a miserable backlog in the courts exacerbated by the basic problem that in immigration law, unlike other areas, the appellant wishes to delay the legal process, not accelerate it, in order to stay here as long as possible. The appeal process has been seen as, to a degree, unsatisfactory by the courts through its covert application by means of a purely administrative procedure against which any appeal is difficult. The Special Immigration Appeals Act 1997 and the Immigration and Asylum Act 1999 can be perceived as measures to regularise and formalise the process, outside the political arena. Further, the implications of *D. v. the United Kingdom* have not yet become apparent. Previously Article 3 of the ECHR has only been applied to those who would be exposed to risk of deliberate violence, imprisonment, torture or death. *D.* has extended its ambit to include those whose health is threatened by the lack of facilities the deportee had enjoyed in the United Kingdom in the country to which he is to be deported. The incorporation of the ECHR into British legal systems will in general lead to convergence in such areas. **11–039**

The most questionable area lies in the wide scope of Deportation which can make it seem indistinguishable from Extradition. *Robinson* and *Ward* are recent examples of this dangerous trend where the courts appear to have a largely complacent attitude seemingly incompatible with the political violence in the native countries to which the deportees are to be returned. Another factor in the operation of Immigration law which has gone almost unobserved is that under Article 6 of the Race Relations (Amendment) Act 2000 an accusation of racial discrimination cannot be brought against the Immigration authorities in challenging a refusal for residence of asylum. The effect of this has already been seen in the accelerated methods adopted towards Kosovan Albanians and Kurds whereby their ethnicity has been a potent factor in refusal of asylum and a quick deportation.

The EEA

The stature of EEA citizens in the United Kingdom is such that it appears almost impossible to effectively deport them under Community laws, demonstrated in cases such as *Bouchereau*. The only effective method of deportation for non-criminal behaviour may lie in taking some form of sanction against United Kingdom citizens for similar activities to which the United Kingdom government may wish to deport an EEA national. The concept of full European citizenship marches inexorably along with that of the common currency. The burgundy passport of all EU citizens is a pointer towards this future. **11–040**

Asylum

11–041 It is in the application of the new Asylum laws, the full impact of which is not yet apparent, that the full severity of them has been manifested. As is seen in *Chahal* and *Cheblak*, there is wide scope for injustice and unwise popularist action by Home Secretaries. This may be mitigated by the legislation in the Special Immigration Appeals Act 1997. There is no doubt that not all requests for asylum are legitimate. It is, after all, a method of obviating normal deportation criteria by claiming a particular status as an individual persecuted for political, social or racial reasons, and thus requires the closest scrutiny. However the very exceptional nature of legitimate asylum seekers, and the manner of their escape—often without papers or with forged ones, frequently weighs against them, for in this respect it is hard to effectively differentiate the legitimate from the bogus. The "fast track" procedure does not assist this subtle judgment since it gives even less time and opportunity for a thorough investigation, especially if the applicant is sent out of the United Kingdom, whilst a decision is made. There is a strong suspicion that this part of the 1996 and 1999 Acts have more to do with administrative convenience allied to the hope that the turbulent applicant will desist, than any sense of natural justice, a suspicion borne out by ECHR rulings.

The existence of the "White List" as part of the expedition of deportation procedures also endangers those applicants from countries on it. The list seems arbitrary and demand-related—the more asylum-seekers come from any given country, the more likely that most will be "unfounded" given the nature of the process and, therefore the stronger the likelihood of that country remaining on it. The list seems particularly unresponsive to institutional change. That formulated in 1995 is still current, and one could question the presence of India and Pakistan on it, given *Chahal*, *Shah* and *Islam*.[51] It is noteworthy that no countries have been added, either. This may show a commendable reluctance to expose citizens of other countries that could be added to this peculiar manoeuvre. The final aspect of asylum law is the discouragement of "economic" asylum seekers. As indicated above, all asylum seekers have an economic element in their application. Most immigrants *are* looking for a better life. However government policy, as with Romanian, Czech and Slovak gypsies trying to cross the Channel, seems to be, first, to publicise in their native countries how hard conditions are in the United Kingdom; no money, no housing, terrible weather; and second to carry out these threats if they are admitted through the clauses of the 1999 Act denying state benefits.[52]

Successive Governments have killed the myth of Liberal Britain and the perception of these islands now must be to many of a mean-spirited, uncharitable, uncaring country on the edge of Europe which will not have its complacent comfort endangered by the very kind of people who were so often accepted here in the past, the poor, but enterprising all in the name of fiscal prudence, efficiency and a purblind nationalism. The early twenty-first century is not a good time to be a fleeing political dissident, a poor asylum seeker or a threat to United Kingdom trade. Public opinion and governments are set against them. The law deals with them with all the humanity it can muster, for that one can be thankful but not optimistic.

Brief Outline and Germane Cases

Cases and Statutes cited. **11–042**

Extradition

Extradition Acts: 1870; 1873; 1935; 1989. **11–043**
Suppression of Terrorism Act 1978.

Definition of Extradition Cases.

R. v. Secretary of State for the Home Department, ex parte Gilmore and others.

Times Law Reports, July 4, 1997.

Government of the USA v. Bowe [1990] 1 A.C. 500.

Restrictions on Extradition.

a) "Political" restrictions.

Re Castioni [1890] 1 Q.B. 149.

R. v. Governor of Brixton Prison, ex Parte Schtraks [1964] A.C. 556.

Re Meunier [1894] 2QB 415.

R. v. Governor of Brixton Prison, ex parte Kolczynski [1955] 1 Q.B. 547.

Cheng v. Governor of Pentonville Prison [1973] A.C. 931, HL.

T. v. The Secretary of State for the Home Department [1996] 2 All E.R. 865, HL.

b) Previous non-extradition offences.

Royal Government of Greece v. Governor of Brixton Prison [1971] A.C. 250, HL.

R. v. Governor of Brixton Prison, ex parte Osman (no. 3) [1992] 1 All E.R. 122.

R. v. Governor of Pentonville Prison, ex parte Lee [1993] 3 All E.R. 504.

R. v. Governor of Belmarsh Prison [1995] 3 All E.R. 634.

c) Procedure for extradition.

Re Evans [1994] 1 W.L.R. 1006, HL.

DEPORTATION

11–044 a) Acts.

British Nationality Acts 1948; 1965; 1981.

Immigration Act 1971.

b) Deportation after criminal conviction.

R. v. Nazari [1980] 3 All E.R. 880.

c) Deportation after deception.

R. v. Immigration Appeal Tribunal, ex parte Patel [1988] 2 W.L.R. 1165.

d) Public Good & National Security.

R. v. Immigration Appeal Tribunal, ex parte al-Masari, unreported.

R. v. Secretary of State for the Home Department, ex parte Hosenball [1977] 1 W.L.R. 766, CA.

R. v. Secretary of State for the Home Department, ex parte Cheblak [1991] 2 All E.R. 219.

R. v. Secretary of State for the Home Department, ex parte Chahal [1995] 1 W.L.R. 526, CA.

e) Relative safety in other parts of deportee's native country.

R. v. Secretary of State for the Home Department, ex parte Chahal [1995] 1 W.L.R. 526, CA.

R. v. Secretary of State for the Home Department, ex parte Robinson [1997] 3 W.L.R. 1162; [1997] 4 All E.R. 210.

f) Deportation and the European Court of Human Rights.

R. v. Secretary of State for the Home Department, ex parte Chahal [1995] 1 W.L.R. 526, CA.

D. v. United Kingdom [1997] E.H.R.L.R. 534.

g) Rights of citizens of E.C. and EEA.

R. v. Bouchereau 2 E.C.R. [1977] 1999.

Adoni & Cournaille v. Belgian State (1982) 2 E.C.R. 1665.

h) Appeal under Habeas Corpus.

R. v. Governor of Brixton Prison, ex parte Soblen [1963] 2 Q.B. 243.

i) Deportation as "disguised" extradition.

R. v. Governor of Brixton Prison, ex parte Soblen [1963] 2 Q.B. 243.

R. v. Secretary of State for the Home Department, ex parte Chahal [1995] 1 W.L.R. 526, CA.

R. v. Secretary of State for the Home Department, ex parte Robinson [1997] 3 W.L.R. 1162; [1997] 4 All E.R. 210.

ASYLUM

a) Acts. **11–045**

Immigration and Asylum Act 1999

Asylum and Immigration Appeals Act 1993

Asylum and Immigration Act 1996

Special Immigration Appeals Act 1997

Geneva Convention on the Status of Refugees 1951

b) General principles.

T. v. The Secretary of State for the Home Department [1996] 2 All E.R. 865, HL.

R. v. Secretary of State for the Home Department, ex parte Robinson [1997] 3 W.L.R. 1162; [1997] 4 All E.R. 210.

c) Membership of threatened group under Convention.

Ward v. The Secretary of State for the Home Department [1997] Imm. A.R. 236.

Ouanes v. Secretary of State for the Home Department [1998] 1 W.L.R. 218, CA.

R. v. Immigration Appeals Tribunal, ex parte Shah & Islam v. Secretary of State for the Home Department [1998] 1 W.L.R. 74, CA.

d) Sent to "safe" country.

R. v. Secretary of State for the Home Department, ex parte Canbolat [1997] 1 W.L.R. 1569, CA.

e) Changed circumstances in deportee's native country.

Rehmat Khan v. United Kingdom [1997] E.H.R.L.R. Issue 2.

f) Appeals & minister in contempt.

Re M [1993] 3 W.L.R. 433, HL.

Ireland

11–046 a) Acts

Backing of Warrants (Republic of Ireland) Act 1965.

Prevention of Terrorism Act 1989 (1974).

b) Conditions for Warrant.

Re Nobbs [1978] 1 W.L.R. 1303.

c) Exclusion Orders

i) no need to give reasons.
R. v. Secretary of State for the Home Department, ex parte Stitt, The Times, February 3, 1987.
R. v. Gallagher, The Times, February 16, 1994.

ii) and Judicial Review.
R. v. Secretary of State for the Home Department, ex parte Adams [1995] All E.R. (E.C.) 177 Q.B.

Endnotes

[1–2] *per* Lord Diplock in *R. v. Governor of Pentonville Prison, ex p. Cheng* [1973] A.C. 931, HL at 946.
[3] "Extradition is a bond of mutual confidence in the administration of justice by the courts of both nations. It proceeds on the assumption that impartial justice will be done to the party surrendered". Report of the Royal Commission on Extradition, 1878.
[4–5] (1998) 1 All E.R. 264: (1998) 2 W.L.R. 618.
[6] [1990] 1 A.C. 500 at 521.
[7] [1999] 1 W.L.R. 33, HL.
[8] s. 64.
[9] s. 1 (2A) as added from July 1, 1997.
[10] s. 2(1)(a).
[11] There are, as yet, no recorded cases.
[12] *Government of Canada v. Aranson* [1989] 3 W.L.R., HL 436; [1989] 2 All E.R. 1025.
[13] [2000] 1 All E.R. Q.B.D.
[14] Such a crime may become more common if European countries decide to extradite those found guilty under their legislation of sex crimes in S.E. Asia.
[15] In Scotland and Northern Ireland it can be the corresponding Secretary of State.
[16] The list is to be found in *Halsbury's Statutes* (4th ed.), Vol. 17 587–8.
[17] *e.g.* it is the only method by which a British citizen can be forcibly removed from the U.K.
[18] Defined as the Secretary of State; Court of committal; High Court; High Court of Judiciary on application for habeas corpus or for review of order of committal.
[19] [1890] 1 Q.B. 149.
[20] [1964] A.C. 556 at 589, 591.
[21] *per* Lord Mustill in *T. v. The Secretary of State for the Home Department* [1996] 2 All E.R., HL 865 at 875–6.
[22] *ibid.*
[23] s. 24(1)a of the Suppression of Terrorism Act 1978.
[24] s. 23 *ibid.*
[25] Lord Mustill's speech in *T* (above) gives a closely-argued summary of the development of extradition law. See para. 11–024.
[26] [1894] 2 Q.B. 415.
[27] *ibid.* at 419, *per* Cave J.
[28] *ibid.*
[29] [1955] 1 Q.B. 547.
[30] *per* Lord Goddard at 551.
[31] [1973] A.C. 931, HL.
[32] [1996] 2 All E.R. 865, HL: *T* was a case of asylum seeking; but in its facts it is indistinguishable from extradition.
[33] *R. v. Governor of Pentonville Prison, ex p. Taja* [1971] 2 Q.B. 274, *per* Lord Parker CJ at 289C.
[34] These criteria were established in *R. v. Governor of Pentonville Prison, ex p. Fernandez* [1971] 2 All E.R. 24; [1971] 1 W.L.R. 459: affirmed in *Fernandez v. Government of Singapore* [1971] 2 All E.R. 691; 1 W.L.R. 987, HL.
[35] [1971] A.C. 250, HL.
[36] *ibid., per* Waller J.
[37] *ibid., per* Lord Reid at 278–9.
[38] [1992] 1 All E.R. 122; confirmed in *R. v. Governor of Pentonville Prison, ex p. Lee* [1993] 3 All E.R. 504 & *R. v. Governor of Belmarsh Prison* [1995] 3 All E.R. 634.
[39] s. 7(2)(b).
[40] s. 8(1)(a).
[41] The test to be applied is whether, if the evidence adduced stood alone at the trial, a reasonable jury, properly directed, could accept it and find a verdict of guilty.
[42] 5 *European Year Book* 563.
[43–44] [1994] 1 W.L.R. 1006, HL.
[45] *ibid.* at 1013.
[46] s. 12(2)(a).
[47] *Armah v. Government of Ghana* [1966] 3 All E.R. 177, HL.
[48] *Soering v. U.K.* (1989) 11 E.H.R.R. 439.

[49] By virtue of the State Immunity Act 1978; the Vienna Convention on Diplomatic Relations and Sched. 1 to the Diplomatic Privileges Act.
[50] [1998] 3 W.L.R. 1456: (Lords Slynn, Lloyd, Nicholls, Steyn & Hoffmann).
[51] [1999] 2 W.L.R. 272 (Lords Browne-Wilkinson, Goff, Nolan, Hope and Hutton).
[52] This decision seems disingenuous. What would have happened if Lord Hoffman had been a director of a charity *in favour* of torture?
[53] [1999] 2 W.L.R. 827 (Lords Browne-Wilkinson, Goff, Hope, Hutton, Saville, Millett and Phillips).
[54] *R. v. Secretary of State for the Home Department, ex p. Amnesty International* Lawtel 31/1/2000: reversed in *R. v. Secretary of State for the Home Department, ex p. Amnesty International* Lawtel 15/2/00.
[55] s. 1(1).
[56] s. 1(2).
[57] *per* Roskill L.J. in *R. v. Chief Immigration Officer Heathrow Airport, ex p. Salamat Bibi* [1976] 3 All E.R. 843: 1 W.L.R. 979, CA at 895.
[58] s. 2(1)i & ii.
[59] The position of citizens of what are now to be called British Overseas Territories is currently (April 2001) under consideration after the publication of a White Paper *Partnership for Progress* and it is possible that they will be given, along with citizens of Gibraltar and the Falkland Islands, the right of abode in the United Kingdom. The total number of such citizens is some 130,000.
[60–61] *R. v. Hikmet Bozat* [1997] 1 Cr. App. R., CA: s. 271.
[62] [1980] 3 All E.R. 880.
[63] *ibid., per* Lawton L.J. at 885 g-h: "It is for the Home Secretary to decide in each case whether an offender's return to his country of origin would have consequences which would make his compulsory return unduly harsh".
[64] [1988] 2 W.L.R. 1165, HL at 1171, *per* Lord Bridge of Harwich.
[65] [1977] 1 W.L.R. 766, CA.
[66] [1991] 2 All E.R. 219.
[67] [1995] 1 W.L.R. 526, CA.
[68] *ibid.* Letter from the Home Secretary quoted by Nolan L.J. at 537–8.
[69] ECHR Reports (1996) Vol. 22, p. 1831.
[70–71] [1997] 3 W.L.R. 1162; [1997] 4 All E.R. 210.
[72] [1997] E.H.R.L.R. 534.
[73] The EEA comprises all the E.C. states plus Norway and Liechtenstein.
[74] The first two under the Treaty of Rome Arts 48–51:52–58. The other two under the Arts to "provide or receive services": 59–66.
[75] *R. v. Bouchereau* 2 [1977] E.C.R. 1999 at 2015 (2).
[76] *ibid.* at 2015 (3).
[76A] (2000) Imm.A.R. 478; I.L.R. June 26, 2000.
[77] (1982) 2 E.C.R. 1665.
[78] [1963] 2 Q.B. 243.
[79] *ibid., per* Pearson L.J. at 313.
[80] [1977] 1 W.L.R. 766, CA.
[81] *ibid., per* Denning M.R. 782 at H.
[82] Under ss. 74–78 of the 1999 Act.
[83] H.C. Official Report, Vol. 268, ser. 6, col. 699 (December 11, 1995).
[84] If an applicant for asylum is successful, he may claim retrospectively for these by s. 11(2) of the 1996 Act.
[85] *R. v. Hackney LBC, ex parte K, The Times*, November 17, 1997.
[87] *R. v. Hackney LBC, ex parte Adebiri, The Times*, November 5, 1997.
[88] *R. v. Secretary of State for the Home Department, ex p. Jammeh* (1998) 10 Admin. L.R. Q.B.D. 1, *per* Lord Mustill in *T. v. The Secretary of State for the Home Department* [1996] 2 All E.R. 865 at 868.
[89] As stated in the Asylum and Immigration Appeals Act 1993, ss. 1&2.
[90] Convention Art 1A(2) C.M.D. 9171 (1954).
[91] Convention Art. 1F.
[92] [1997] Imm. A.R. 236.
[93] *ibid.* at 238; author's italics.
[94] [1997] 3 W.L.R. 1162, CA.
[95] *Ouanes v. Secretary of State for the Home Department* [1998] 1 W.L.R. 218, CA.

[96] *ibid.*, *per* Pill L.J. at 224.
[97] *R. v. Immigration Appeals Tribunal, ex p. Shah & Islam v. Secretary of State for the Home Department* [1998] 1 W.L.R. 74, CA.
[98] *ibid.*, *per* Staughton L.J. at 93 D.
[99] [1999] 2 W.L.R. 1015.
[1] Under s. 6 of the 1993 Act.
[2] Under s. 2(2) (a)-(c) of the 1996 Act.
[3] *R. v. Secretary of State for the Home Department, ex p. Chowdry, The Times*, March 3, 1998.
[4] Under s. 3 of the 1996 Act.
[5] In addition to all E.U. states the list currently comprises Canada, Norway, Switzerland, USA: S.I. 1996 No. 2671 October 19, 1996, updated November 27, 2000.
[6] [1997] 1 W.L.R. 1569, CA.
[7] *ibid.*, *per* Woolf M.R. at 577 H.
[8] [2001] 2 W.L.R. 143.
[9] Currently Bulgaria, Cyprus, Ghana, India, Pakistan, Poland, Romania. SI 1996 No. 2671.
[10] *per* Michael Howard, Home Secretary: H.C. Official Report, Vol. 268, ser. 6, col. 703 (December 11, 1995).
[11] s. 5(4) of the 1996 Act.
[12] [1997] E.H.R.L.R. Issue 2.
[13] *ibid.*
[14] *The Times*, April 6, 1998.
[15] [1993] 3 W.L.R. 433, HL.
[16] *per* Mike O'Brien, Minister of State for the Home Department, on introducing second Commons reading: H.C. Official Report 1764, vol. 299 col. 1054 (October 30, 1997).
[17] s. 2 of the Special Immigration Appeals Act 1997 (SIACA).
[18] The composition of the Commission, to be appointed by the Lord Chancellor, has not yet been decided, but ministers see it composed of a judge, an immigration officer and someone with security experience.
[19] SIACA, s. 2(c).
[20] *ibid.*, s. 2(1)(g).
[21] *ibid.*, s. 4(2).
[22] *ibid.*, s. 7(1)(2).
[23] *ibid.*, s. 5(3)(a).
[24] *ibid.*, s. 5(3)(d).
[25] *ibid.*, s. 6(1).
[26] Correctly the United Kingdom of Great Britain and Northern Ireland.
[27] "As is well known, the provisions for extradition between this country and the Republic of Ireland are much more simple and domesticated than the extradition proceedings which apply in the rest of the Commonwealth, or even the rest of the world. For current purposes Ireland is almost treated as part of England and vice versa for the purposes of extradition", *Per* Widgery C.J. in *Re Nobbs* [1978] 1 W.L.R. Q.B. at 1303 H.
[28] The corresponding Act in the Republic is the Extradition Act 1965.
[29] Backing of Warrants (Republic of Ireland) Act, s. 1(1).
[30] *ibid.*, s. 2(2).
[31] *Re Nobbs*, above.
[32] These ceased to have effect *per* the Terrorism Act 2000, s. 2.
[33] s. 4(2) of the Prevention of Terrorism Act 1989.
[34] *ibid.*, s. 7.
[35] *ibid.*, s. 7(1)(a).
[36] *ibid.*, s. 7(3).
[37] *ibid.*, s. 6(1)(a)(b).
[38] *ibid.*, s. 4(a); it is for the applicant to prove this; *vide* Sched. 2, para. 9(1) of the Act.
[39] *ibid.*, Sched. 2, para. 4(2)(a)(b).
[40] *ibid.*, Sched. 2, para. 4(1)(a)(b).
[41] *ibid.*, Sched. 2, para. 5A(1).
[42] *ibid.*, Sched. 2, para. 4(5).
[43] See *R. v. Secretary of State for the Home Department, ex p. Stitt, The Times* February 3, 1987.
[44] *The Times*, February 16, 1994.
[45] Case C–175/94 *R. v. Secretary of State for the Home Office, ex p. Gallagher*. 1 E.H.R.L.R. 1996 37–44.
[46] [1995] All E.R. (E.C.) 177, Q.B.

[47] *ibid.*, *per* Steyn L.J. at 185 e.
[48] H.C. Official Report No. 1764, Vol. 299, col. 1028–9 (October 30, 1997).
[49] S.I. 2001 No. 1261.
[50] These rarely used powers were taken by the Home Secretary over the request by Germany for the extradition of Rosin Macalisky over her disputed part in an IRA raid on a British base in Germany. There was strong alibi evidence but the magistrate could not consider it. Macalisky was pregnant and subsequently gave birth in custody and was found to be mentally ill. It was on the latter ground that the Home Secretary refused extradition.
[51] Pakistan has now been omitted by the House of Lords in *R. v. Secretary of State for the Home Department, ex p. Javed* I.L.R. July 16, 2001.
[52] One unforeseen consequence of this action is to throw the cost of their support upon local authorities who lack the finances and facilities to do so effectively. This is despite the authority under the Act to disperse asylum seekers.

INDEX

All references are to paragraph numbers